SPACE LAW

A Treatise

Third Edition

Francis Lyall and Paul B. Larsen

Routledge
Taylor & Francis Group

LONDON AND NEW YORK

Designed cover image: StephanieFrey/Getty Images ®

Third edition published 2025
by Routledge
4 Park Square, Milton Park, Abingdon, Oxon, OX14 4RN

and by Routledge
605 Third Avenue, New York, NY 10158

Routledge is an imprint of the Taylor & Francis Group, an informa business

© 2025 Francis Lyall and Paul B. Larsen

First edition published by Ashgate 2009
Second edition published by Routledge 2018

British Library Cataloguing-in-Publication Data
A catalogue record for this book is available from the British Library

ISBN: 978-1-032-69837-3 (hbk)
ISBN: 978-1-032-80339-5 (pbk)
ISBN: 978-1-003-49650-2 (ebk)

DOI: 10.4324/9781003496502

Typeset in Galliard
by Apex CoVantage, LLC

SPACE LAW

As space continues to attract substantial public and private investment and has become ever more active, the third edition of this book has been updated to cover recent developments. This includes the legal bases of UN Resolution 76/3, the Space3030 Agenda, which envisages 'space as a driver of sustainable development' and sets out an extensive programme for the future. The work also takes account of adaptations and augmentations to basic space treaties. It examines the increasing commercialisation of space in areas such as space tourism and space mining, for which four states have already adopted relevant legislation. The impact of new technologies such as satellite constellations and micro-satellites are also scrutinised. At a time when space tourism is available to those who can afford it and when the moon will shortly be revisited with a prospect of permanent bases, this third edition provides a firm base for the next generation of space lawyers. As with previous editions, the work draws from governmental, international organisational and other authoritative sources as well as the relevant literature in the field. The book will be an essential and comprehensive resource for students, academics and researchers as well as space agencies, governments and space-active companies. It will also be of value to technical operatives and managers who need to know the legal context within which they work.

Francis Lyall is Emeritus Professor of Public Law, University of Aberdeen, Scotland, UK. He is also Honorary Director of the International Institute of Space Law and a member of the International Academy of Astronautics.

Paul B. Larsen is formerly of the Southern Methodist University and the US Department of Transportation and a professor of space law (adjunct) at Georgetown University Law Center, Washington, DC, USA.

For our progeny, Astrid, Heidi, Fiona Elisabeth, Gillian Ann, Francis James, Samuel James, Rachel Alice, Abigail Heather and Susanna Grace – who may yet travel into space.

CONTENTS

PREFACE

Like its predecessors, this book is the outcome of the many years of our interest in space law. We met in the Space Law class run by the regrettably late Ivan Vlasic at the Institute of Air and Space Law at McGill University in 1963–1964. Ivan's enthusiasm infected us. Our paths diverged, but friendship continued. FL went into academic law, largely at the University of Aberdeen, Scotland. PBL went on from the McGill Institute to the Institute of Air and Space Law at Cologne University, and then to Yale University and the Southern Methodist University, Texas. He later entered the legal department of the US Federal Department of Transportation, combining that with a teaching appointment at the Georgetown Law Center, both in Washington DC. Our careers over these 60 years are coterminous with the development of space, and its companion, space law.

Writing for this book has been intriguing. We seek to present the bulk of space law as it stands early in the third decade of the 2000s, although neither of us would necessarily defend every word, phrase or opinion; the views of collaborators can diverge. Any book treatment of such a diverse subject is more akin to a fresco than to an etching. Etchings can do things that are impossible to achieve in a mural of c. 300,000 words. We are trying to present a view of space law as a whole; detail may vanish, but we have indicated where further information and contrary views may be found. Some material cited is of historical interest now but is included because we believe that to understand the law as it is, you have to know how we got to where we are.

We have one major advantage over our predecessors: the Internet. Much documentary material on the history of space together with current legislation and governmental, inter-governmental and agency practice is now available electronically. Many journal articles are now accessible without the need to travel to specialised libraries. Lexis, Westlaw and HeinOnLine contain vast quantities of legal material, and we thank our respective educational establishments as subscribers to these electronic services. Indeed, having come close to developing cranial hernias, we might complain about the volume of material now thus accessible. Much has happened since our edition of 2018, let alone that of 2009.

Since we intend this volume to be a research tool as well as a treatise, we have cited copiously, although recognising that citations may be the barnacles of the written word.

Apart from that caveat, we would particularly recommend the annual *Proceedings of the International Institute of Space Law*, the *Annals of Air and Space Law*, the *Journal of Space Law*, *Air and Space Law*, the *Journal of Air Law and Commerce* and the *German Journal of Air and Space Law* (ZLW). The three volumes of the *Cologne Commentary on Space Law* form a new major source for which its contributors are also to be profoundly thanked, and many other non-space-specialist journals occasionally carry important contributions.

Not all that has been read has been footnoted; that would have rendered merely a list. We apologise for the omission of articles and data that others may consider more suitable than those we have included. Time has converted some cited material to history – note the publication dates – and some is of variable quality. However, as we hope that this tome will be used as a teaching instrument, we believe that students should learn themselves to evaluate sources. Many articles cited contain more data on space law than the particular point or area for which we refer to them. Much repeat material is available elsewhere to inform the readership of a particular non-specialist journal. Finally, we recognise that there are elements missing from our research and citations, in particular from French, German, Spanish, Italian and Russian sources. This is partly because of our linguistic limitations and partly because the material has not been available to us. Even so, once one starts to search, there is a vast quantity of articles on and discussions of space law.

We have provided URLs for many Internet sites, but users should appreciate that these may not always work; data can be archived or re-classified, and sites cease to exist. We can do nothing about that, but we encourage the e-competent to seek alternative locations for the data. As a result of fatigue, we expect that some citations may be erroneous, and we would appreciate notification for their correction. Although there can be problems with Wikipedia, we suggest that, with due caution, readers may pursue some further information within the confines of that intriguing development in the arena of *soi-disant* knowledge. Its technical articles appear to be sound.

At pp. 177–178, towards the end of his treatment of the literature in his seminal *Space Law* (London: Stevens, 1965), C.W. Jenks suggested that in the wake of McDougal, Lasswell and Vlasic's monumental treatise *Law and Public Order in Space* (New Haven and London: Yale UP, 1963), later authors would find themselves constrained by developments and the decisions that would made subsequent to that work. The 'purely speculative phase' of space law had already passed, and a beginning was made to the task of establishing the rule of law in space. Notwithstanding, Jenks felt that there

> still remains unanswered the fundamental question of chaos or control posed by Jessup and Taubenfeld in their *Controls for Outer Space and the Antarctic Analogy* (New York: Columbia UP, 1959) whether space would become an arena for power struggles similar to those for territory, or whether by 'taking time by the forelock' a radical solution for the problem of control of space would be evolved.

In our view, radical solutions have indeed emerged, although perhaps not always as Jenks expected.

Basic principles of equal access to space, of freedom of its exploration and use, of a prohibition of national sovereignty, and of the lawfulness of only peaceful uses of space, have been developed and applied in a variety of circumstances. Jenks would be intrigued by what we describe in this text. Writers now have indeed 'an authoritative point of departure to guide and discipline' their work. The law is there. Space affects us all. Thankfully, there are the rules and regulations which we have endeavoured to review. Not all is perfect. Developments continue. In places, we have suggested their improvement.

We have tried to state the law and take account of technical developments and proposals in broad through 1 August 2023, although on occasion, it was possible to include later data and developments. However, we acknowledge gaps in our reading and recollection of material. The field will not remain still, but we hope that these pages will provide a reliable platform for others to launch their own investigations.

Over the years and during the writing of this book, many have helped us, unravelling histories and providing materials and insights. Some have done so under condition of anonymity, and it would therefore be invidious to list others. Accordingly, we here simply record our thanks for many helpers. However, we do expressly thank our wives, Heather and Judith, for their encouragement and their much patience.

Francis Lyall
Paul B. Larsen

ABBREVIATIONS AND ACRONYMS (EXCLUDING OBVIOUS ABBREVIATED REFERENCES)

AASL	*Annals of Air and Space Law* (McGill University)
AJIL	*American Journal of International Law*
ATS	Australian Treaty Series
Bevans	C.I. Bevans, *Treaties and Other International Agreements of the USA*, 13 vols. 1968–1978
BYIL	*British Yearbook of International Law*
CFR	Code of Federal Regulations (US)
Cheng	Bin Cheng, *Studies in International Space Law* (Oxford: Clarendon Press, 1997).
Christol	C.Q. Christol, *The Modern International Law of Outer Space* (New York and Oxford: Pergamon Press, 1982).
CNES	The French Centre Nationale d'Etudes spatiales (www.cnes.fr)
CoCoSL I	*Cologne Commentary on Space Law*, Vol. 1 (Cologne: Carl Heymanns Verlag, 2009), S. Hobe, B. Schmidt-Tedd, K-U. Schrögl, eds. (G.M. Goh, asst. ed.).
CoCoSL II	*Cologne Commentary on Space Law*, Vol. II (Cologne: Carl Heymanns Verlag, 2013), S. Hobe, B. Schmidt-Tedd, K-U. Schrögl, eds. (P. Stubbe, asst. ed.).
CoCoSL III	*Cologne Commentary on Space Law*, Vol. III (Cologne: Carl Heymanns Verlag, 2015), S. Hobe, B. Schmidt-Tedd, K-U. Schrögl, eds. (P. Stubbe., asst. ed.).
CS	ITU Constitution. Immediate reference is to CS articles. Additional numbers in brackets refer to the now customary paragraph numbering.
CTS	C. Parry, ed. *The Consolidated Treaty Series, 1648–1918*, 231 vols. (New York: Oceana).
CV	ITU Convention. Immediate reference is to CV articles. Additional numbers in brackets refer to the now customary paragraph numbering.

ECSL	European Centre for Space Law (www.esa.int/About_Us/ ECSL_European_Centre_for_Space_Law)
ESA	European Space Agency (www.esa.int/ESA)
GEO	geosynchronous orbit
Gorove	S. Gorove, *Developments in Space Law: Issues and Policies* (Dordrecht: Nijhoff, 1991).
GSO	geostationary orbit
Hague Recueil	Hague Academy of International Law, *Recueil du Cours*, cited by vol. no. and year/vol.
HEO	highly elliptical orbit
Hudson	M.O. Hudson, *International Legislation*, 9 vols. (New York: Carnegie Endowment, 1931–1950).
IAF	International Astronautical Federation (www.iafastro.com)
ICJ	International Court of Justice (www.icj-cij.org/homepage/index.php)
IISL	International Institute of Space Law (www.iafastro-iisl.com)
ILC	International Law Commission (legal.un.org/ilc/)
ILM	International Legal Materials, American Society of International Law
ITU	International Telecommunication Union (www.itu.int)
J. Sp. L.	*Journal of Space Law* (University of Mississippi)
JBIS	*Journal of the British Interplanetary Society*
LEO	low Earth orbit
Legal Problems	*Legal Problems of Space Exploration – A Symposium*, US Senate, 87th Cong. 1st Sess., S. Doc. No. 26, USGPO, 1961.
Lyall	F. Lyall, *Law and Space Telecommunications* (Aldershot UK: Dartmouth; Brookfield VT: Gower, 1989).
Lyall/Larsen	F. Lyall and P.B. Larsen, *Space Law* in *The Library of Essays in International Law* (Aldershot and Burlington, VT: Ashgate, 2007).
Lyall ITU	F. Lyall. *The International Telecommunication Union and the Universal Postal Union* (Farnham: Ashgate, 2011).
Manual I–IV	*Manual on Space Law*, 4 vols., N. Jasentuliyana and R.S.K. Lee, eds. (Dobbs Ferry, NY: Oceana, 1979–1981).
Marboe	I. Marboe, ed., *Soft Law in Outer Space: The Function of Non-binding Norms in International Space Law* (Vienna: Böhlau Verlag, 2012).
MEO	Medium Earth Orbit
NASA	National Aeronautics and Space Administration (US) (www.nasa.gov)
OOSA	UN Office for Outer Space Affairs, Vienna (www.oosa.org)
PCIJ	Permanent Court of International Justice (1922–1946).
PP	ITU Plenipotentiary Conference, now designated by year held: e.g. PP-22 denotes the Plenipotentiary Conference, Bucharest, 2022.
Proc.	IISL *Proceedings of the Annual Colloquium of the International Institute of Space Law*, cited by year and volume number.
RIAA	Reports of International Arbitral Awards (UN: Geneva)
RR	ITU Radio Regulations

UKSA	United Kingdom Space Agency (www.gov.uk/government/ organisations/uk-space-agency)
UKMS	UK Miscellaneous Series cited by year, number and Command Paper number. Treaties in the Misc. series have not been ratified by the UK.
UKTS	United Kingdom Treaty Series, cited by year, number and Command Paper number. Successive series have different abbreviations.
USC	United States Code – consolidates federal congressional legislation.
ZLW	Zeitschrift für Luft und Weltraumrecht (Institute of Air and Space Law, Cologne University)

MAJOR SPACE TREATIES

OST Treaty on Principles Governing the Activities of States in the
     Exploration and Use of Outer Space Including the Moon and
     Other Celestial Bodies, UNGA Res. 2222 (XXI); (1968) 610
     UNTS 205; (1968) UKTS 10, Cmnd. 3519; 18 UST 2410,
     TIAS 6347; 6 ILM 386; 61 AJIL 644: in force 10 October 1967.

ARRA Agreement on the Rescue of Astronauts, the Return of
     Astronauts and the Return of Objects Launched into Outer
     Space, 22 April 1968; UNGA Res. 2345 (XXII); 672 UNTS
     119; 1969 UKTS 56, Cmnd. 3997; 19 UST 7570, TIAS 6559; 7
     ILM 151; (1969) 63 AJIL 382: in force 3 December 1968.

Liability Convention on International Liability for Damage Caused by
     Space Objects, 29 March 1972; UNGA Res. 2777 (XXVI); 961
     UNTS 187; (1974) UKTS 16, Cmnd 5551; 24 UST 2389, TIAS
     7762; (1971) 10 ILM 965; (1971) 66 AJIL 702: in force 1
     September 1972.

Registration Convention on the Registration of Objects Launched into Outer
     Space, 14 January 1975; UNGA Res. 3235 (XXIX); 1023 UNTS
     15; (1978) UKTS 70, Cmnd 7271; TIAS 8480; (1975) 14 ILM
     43; (1979) 18 ILM 891: in force 15 September 1976.

MA   Agreement Governing the Activities of States on the Moon and
     Other Celestial Bodies, UN Doc. A/34/664. Nov. 1979, 5
     December 1979; UN Doc. A/34/20, Annex 2; UN Doc. A/
     RES/34/68; 1363 UNTS 3; (1979) 18 ILM 1434: in force 11 July 1984.

ITU *Collection of the basic texts of the International Telecommunication
     Union adopted by the Plenipotentiary Conference* (Geneva: ITU, 2015).

UN Charter Charter of the United Nations and Statute of the International
     Court of Justice, I UNTS XVI; (US) 59 Stat, 1031, TS 993;
     (1946) UKTS 67, Cmnd. 7015; 9 Hudson 327; 3 Bevans 1153;
     (1945) 39 AJIL Supp. 190.

1

INTRODUCTION

Actors, History and Fora

Introduction

Sputnik I, launched on 4 October 1957, took the attention of the world. In his non-fiction book *Danse Macabre* (1981), the U.S. horror writer Stephen King writes of the interruption of the showing of a film in small-town New England. The cinema manager told the audience what had happened, and the screening was abandoned. People went out in a fruitless attempt to try to see the satellite.[1] Since then, space has transformed modern life. Four decades after Sputnik I, the Preamble of the 'Space Millennium: Vienna Declaration on Space and Human Development' (1999) recognised

> that significant changes have occurred in the structure and content of world space activity, as reflected in the increasing number of participants in space activities at all levels and the growing contribution of the private sector to the promotion and implementation of space activities.[2]

Two decades on, much has been accomplished, but more will be done.[3] On 26 October 2021, the UN General Assembly adopted Resolution 76/3, The Space3030 Agenda: Space as a Driver of Sustainable Development, which after summarising what has been done sets out an extensive programme for the future.

Satellites route data, email and other communications to fixed and mobile instruments, and provide multi-channel TV direct to homes and hotels. Global positioning systems help

---

1 Sputnik I was 58 cm (25 inches) in diameter and weighed 83.6 kg (184.3 lbs). A. Siddiqi, *Sputnik and the Soviet Space Challenge* (Gainesville: Florida UP, 2003) and '*Sputnik* 50 Years Later: New Evidence on Its Origins' (2008) 63 *Acta Astronautica* 529–539.

2 'Space Millennium: Vienna Declaration on Space and Human Development': Third United Nations Conference on the Exploration and Peaceful Uses of Outer Space, Vienna, 30 July 1999: www.unoosa.org/pdf/reports/unispace/viennadeclE.pdf. Cf. the UN Millennium Declaration, UNGA Res. 55/2, 2000. S.M. Pekkanen, 'Governing the New Race' (2019) 113 *AJIL Unbound* 92–97.

3 T. Masson-Zwaan, 'New States in Space' (2019) 113 *AJIL Unbound* 98–102. We also note that space mining is lurking on the threshold; see Chapter 7 The Moon, Asteroids and Other Celestial Bodies.

DOI: 10.4324/9781003496502-1

navigation, allowing us to know the exact locations of aircraft, ships and motor vehicles, or ourselves. With small devices and satellite signals, we roam the countryside in relative safety.[4]

Remote sensing has many benefits. Weather is monitored and increasingly accurate predictions made. Typhoons, cyclones, tornadoes and hurricanes are known, often days in advance. Ocean health and climatic events such as El Niño and its cognate La Niña are observed and better understood. We monitor fisheries, land use, farming, deforestation, vegetation coverage and aridity.

Animal and bird migration patterns are discovered. Potential disasters, volcanic and otherwise, are becoming predictable. Satellite technology informs and aids our reaction to dire events. Space has allowed major developments in understanding the universe. The major planets have all been scrutinised (although some only briefly). We have been to the moon and are going back. Robotic rovers explore Mars. Space telescopes have shown something of the beauty and complexity of our universe and given astronomers much to work with. Theories have been developed, tested, modified and sometimes abandoned. Space tourism is imminent. There may be residential space stations and settlement on, first, the moon, and thereafter?

All this has involved law, and appropriate law has had to be developed.

What Is Space Law?

The world order is set by the Charter of the United Nations.[5] All space treaties refer to it as they elaborate principles and rules.

What is 'space law'? Where does it sit within the architecture of international law? At its broadest, space law comprises all the law that may govern or apply to outer space and activities in or relating to it. A central core exists, but the term should be considered a label attaching to a bucket that contains many different types of rules and regulations rather than as denoting a conceptually coherent single form of law. It differs from 'the law of contract' or 'the law of tort(s)/delict' where 'the law' elaborates a series of concepts within a single phylum.

'Space law' is akin to 'family law' or 'environmental law', where different laws are denoted by what they deal with rather than deriving from the rational development of a single legal concept. 'Space law' is the Law of Space. Space law is also unusual in that despite all the arguments as to where space 'is', the location of space 'out there' remains indeterminate.[6] Terrestrially, space law can range from an insurance contract for a particular space launch to the broad principles that govern how states, and the entities they authorise, act in outer space. Space law can therefore sometimes be the application of existing domestic laws such as contracts to a new field of activity. Sometimes it is a formal international treaty. Space law is particulate law, developed to deal with the practical problems of the use and exploration of outer space. Some of it is *lex exceptionalis*, departing from normal rules.

---

4 Use a compass and map as well. Relying only on GPS on a mobile phone can get you lost.
5 The Charter of the United Nations, I UNTS XVI; (US) 59 Stat. 1031, USTS 993; 1946 UKTS 67, Cmd. 7015; 1945 Can TS 7; 9 Hudson 327; 3 Bevans 1153; 1 Peaslee 1288; 39 AJIL Supp 190; www.un.org/en/charter-united-nations/; https://treaties.un.org/doc/publication/ctc/uncharter.pdf.
6 See *infra* Chapter 6 Of Boundaries and Orbits.

Space law is recent law. The developments in technology of the last one hundred sixty years have required the law to respond.[7] More properly, 'law never seeks to regulate technology, but rather aims to place order in the competing human interests that result from that technology'.[8] Regulation has had to be invented, adopted and implemented, and appropriate procedures developed. The process has not always kept the law up to date with technological development in general, and, as will be seen elsewhere in this book, this flaw remains.[9] Because technical advances have blurred state boundaries and in practice eroded many sovereign competences, international agreement has often become essential.[10] Space is an area in which it has become necessary to deal with technology on a global basis. Although most take it for granted and do not comprehend the technicalities involved, the opening of space has had immense effects.

Origins

Space law is a modern field of regulation, but although its birthdate might be thought to be 1957 with that launch of Sputnik I, its origins lie much further back. Once Sputnik showed access to space to be practicable, earlier speculations, suggestions and discussions had to be converted into actual rules and practices.

As the nineteenth century made way for the twentieth, international aviation, at first by un-powered balloon and then by dirigible (notably the Zeppelin), drew the attention of lawyers, academic and otherwise, as well as of government and the military. Among the

---

7 We select one hundred sixty years as dating from the establishment of the International Telegraph Union in 1865; see Chapter 8 Radio and the International Telecommunication Union.

8 M. Bourbonniere, 'National-Security Law in Outer Space: The Interface of Exploration and Security' (2005) 70 *J. Air L. & Comm.* 3–62 at 3.

9 F. Lyall, *Technology, Sovereignty and International Law* (Abingdon: Routledge, 2022); P.V.M. Rao, ed., *50 Years of Space: A Global Perspective* (Hyderabad: Universities Press, 2007). Cf. the concept of 'cultural lag' – that the pace of change in technologies exceeds the ability of society to cope with it: W.F. Ogburn, *Social Change, with Respect to Culture and Original Nature* (Chicago University Press, 1964). (Ogburn's insight drew our attention via S.M. Jackson, 'Cultural Lag and the International Law of Remote Sensing' (1997–1998) 23 *Brook. J. Int. L.* 853–885) [Lyall/Larsen 469–501].

10 M. Lachs, 'The Development and General Trends of International Law in Our Time' (1980-IV) 169 *Hague Recueil*; *The Law of Outer Space: An Experience in Contemporary Law-Making* (Leiden: Sijthoff, 1972, Nijhoff, 2010) and 'Thoughts on Science, Technology and World Law' (1992) 86 *AJIL* 673–699 [Lyall/Larsen 3–29]; L.B. Sohn, 'The Impact of Technological Changes on International Law' (1973) 30 *Wash. Lee L. Rev.* 1–18; M. Bourquin, 'Pouvoir scientifique et droit internationale' (1947-I) 70 *Hague Recueil* 331; M.W. Mouton, 'The Impact of Science on International Law' (1966-III) 119 *Hague Recueil* 183–260; A.E. Gottleib, 'The Impact of Technology on the Development of Contemporary International Law' (1981-I) 170 *Hague Recueil* 115–329; J.L. Charney, 'Technology and International Negotiations' (1982) 76 *AJIL* 78–118; P.F. Cowhey, 'The International Telecommunications Regime: The Political Roots of Regimes for High Technology' (1990) 44 *Int. Org.* 169–199; J.W. Dellapenna, 'Law in a Shrinking World: The Interaction of Science and Technology with International Law' (2000) 88 *Ky. L.J.* 809–884; C.B. Picker, 'A View from 40,000 Feet: International Law and the Invisible Hand of Technology' (2001) 23 *Cardozo L. Rev.* 149–219; I. Brownlie, 'International Law in the Context of the Changing World Order', in N. Jasentuliyana, ed., *Perspectives on International Law: Essays in Honour of Judge Manfred Lachs* (Dordrecht: Nijhoff, 1995) 49–61; C.W. Jenks, 'International Law and Activities in Space' (1956) 5 *Int. Law Quart.* 99–114; his 'The New Science and the Law of Nations' (1968) 17 *ICLQ* 327–345; and his 'Orthodoxy and Innovation in the Law of Nations' (1971) 57 *Proc. Brit. Academy* 215–235. Cf. C.W. Jenks, *Space Law* (London: Stevens; New York: Praeger, 1965), *The Common Law of Mankind* (London: Stevens, 1958) and *A New World of Law? A Study of the Creative Imagination in International Law* (London: Longmans, 1969).

suggestions to facilitate and regulate air traffic was for a series of zones above the territory of a state analogous to the law of the sea – a 'territorial' zone with freedom of flight above it – but these musings were about air space, not space as we now know it.[11] Thanks to the First World War, the eventual outcome was the affirmation in Art. 1 of the Paris Convention of 1919 of the 'complete and exclusive sovereignty' of a state over its superjacent air space.[12]

This principle, which quickly attained the status of dogma, was reaffirmed in Chicago in 1944.[13] Some, however, began to contemplate higher things. What rules might apply or should be adopted to deal with activities in space?[14]

Discussion of outer space as a region requiring specialised rules of law took on an immediacy after the Second World War,[15] but the first harbingers were much earlier.[16] In 1910, Emile Laude noted a need for law beyond that for 'locomotion' in the layer of 'breathable air'.[17] Beyond 'breathable air' were layers of 'unbreathable gas' and 'ether'. Laude also noted potential problems in the ownership and use of the Hertzian (radio) waves[18] and conflated the need for new law for the gaseous layers and those for the Hertzian waves under the name of the 'law of space'.

However, it was not until 1926 that 'space law' was mentioned as a separate legal category. In the course of a paper mainly on aviation, V.A. Zarzar of the Soviet Air

11 For more detail, see Chapter 6 Air Space.
12 Convention on the Regulation of Aerial Navigation, Paris, 1919, 11 LNTS 173; 1922 UKTS 2, Cmnd 1609; 1 Hudson 359; 13 Martens (3d) 61; (1923) 17 AJIL Supp. 195. Cf. 'Draft International Convention on Aerial Navigation', Paris 1910, Appendix to the Report of the (UK) Civil Aerial Transport Committee, 1918 UKSP Vol. V, 17, Cmnd 9218: www.bopcris.ac.uk/imgall/ref8301_1_1.html.
13 Convention on International Civil Aviation, Chicago (1944) 15 UNTS 295; 9 Hudson 168; 61 Stat. 1180, TIAS 1591; 3 Bevans 944; (1953) UKTS 8, Cmnd 8742; (1945) 39 AJIL Supp 111; ICAO Doc. 7300/9, 2006.
14 S. Hobe, ed., *Pioneers of Space Law* (Leiden: Nijhoff, 2013) reviews the contributions of A. Meyer, E. Pepin, J.C. Cooper, E.A. Korovin, V. Mandl, A.G. Haley, G. Göedhuis, E.M. Galloway, R. Quadri, C.W. Jenks and M. Lachs.
15 Many pre-Sputnik articles are printed or cited in *Legal Problems of Space Exploration – A Symposium*, US Senate, 87th Cong. 1st Sess., S. Doc. no. 26, 1961 (*Legal Problems Symposium*). There was a first edition – *Space Law – A Symposium*, US Senate, 85th Cong. 2nd Sess., 1959 – which we have not seen. Jenks, *Space Law*, supra n. 10, 97, notes that the first edition contains some material which is not in the second, but the second includes materials not in the first. For a categorised listing of articles on different problems, see *'The Law of Outer Space' Report to the National Aeronautics and Space Administration*, Project Reporters, N. de B. Katzenbach and L. Lipson (Washington: American Bar Foundation, 1960) (*Legal Problems Symposium*, 779–983). See also M. Smirnoff, 'The Legal Status of Celestial Bodies' (1961–1962) 28 *J. Air L. & Comm.* 385–404 for summaries of many articles not only in legal journals down to their dates; M.M. Binzer, 'Law for Outer Space' (1960) 46 *Women Lawyers J.* 12–20. Cf. for post-Sputnik scientific speculation *The Next Ten Years in Space, 1959–1969*, Staff Report, House Select Committee on Astronautics and Space Exploration, H. Doc. 115, 86th Cong. 1st Sess. (USGPO, 1959).
16 What follows relies on Jenks, *Space Law*, supra n. 10, 97–179, S.E. Doyle, *Origins of International Space Law and the International Institute of Space Law of the International Astronautical Federation* (San Diego: Univelt, 2002) and Doyle's 'Concepts of Space Law before Sputnik' (1997) 40 *Proc. IISL* 3–13. We also acknowledge with thanks as yet unpublished material that Dr Doyle made available to us. See also H.D. Hazeltine, *The Law of the Air* (London: Hodder & Stoughton, 1911) 1–53.
17 Revue International de Locomotion Aérienne, 1910, noted by Jenks, *Space Law*, supra n. 10, 97.
18 As to the 'use' of Hertzian waves, Laude's questioning seems strange since there had already been the Berlin Preliminary Conference on Wireless Telegraphy of 1906 and the subsequent Convention on Radio-telegraphy of 1909. See *infra* Chapter 8, and F. Lyall *International Communications: The International Telecommunication Union and the Universal Postal Union* (Farnham and Burlington: Ashgate, 2011) 44–56.

Ministry gave as his view that there was an upper limit to state sovereignty over air space and that a separate legal regime would be required to deal with the arena beyond this 'upper zone' in which international travel by high-altitude flight and interplanetary communication would be free from control by subjacent states.[19] In 1929, Walter Schönborn of Kiel University stated the upward limit of the sovereignty of a state as the boundary of the atmosphere.[20] In 1928, Herman Potočnik of Slovenia, writing under the alias Hermann Noordung, published *The Problem of Space Travel: The Rocket Motor*. In it he discussed the establishment of a space station in geostationary orbit for use for Earth observation for civil and military purposes, but he was concerned with technicalities, not legalities.[21]

Vladimir Mandl of Pilsen, Czechoslovakia, wrote about the rocket experimenters of the 1920s.[22] In 1932, he turned his attention to rules for space, albeit in short compass.[23] In what is the first published survey of the topic, Mandl conceived of 'space law' as distinct and different from the law of the sea and the air, although he was willing to use some of their concepts as analogues through which solutions to the problems of space might be found.

In a section titled 'The Future', Mandl suggested that state sovereignty should be restricted in its vertical dimension and that there should be freedom in the area above and beyond state sovereignty. Presciently, he also suggested that air law was not suitable for dealing with spacecraft, that – subject only to mitigation by contributory negligence – astronauts should be liable for damage they caused, that spacecraft launched under the sovereignty of a state should when in outer space remain subject to the sovereignty of that state, that the commander of a spacecraft should have authority over its crew and that the

19 Doyle, *Origins, supra* n. 16, at 1–4, discussing and quoting extracts from V.A. Zarzar, 'Public International Air Law', in *Problems of Air Law, A Symposium* (in Russian) (Moscow, 1927): trans. Leo Kanner Associates, NASA TM-76913, June 1982. The Doyle quotation is from a translation by B. Lehenbauer of 1988.

20 W. Shönborn, 'La nature juridique de territoire' (1929) 30 *Hague Recueil* 81–189 at 158.

21 K. Grunfeld and S. Hobe, 'Hermann Potočnik Noordung – A Great Pioneer of Space Law' (2022) 71 *ZLW* 401–416. The original publisher misdated the book as 1929. See *infra* Chapter 6 n. 126. E. Stuhlinger et al., eds., *The Problem of Space Travel* (NASA History Series, NASA SP-4026, 1999): www.hq.nasa.gov/office/pao/History/SP-4026/contents.html. For the modern origin of the use of the geostationary orbit, see Clarke *infra* n. 33, and Chapter 10, n. 11.

22 Doyle, *Origins, supra* n. 16, 5–9. W. Ley, *Rockets, Men and Missiles in Space* (New York: Signet, 1969); V. Kopal, 'Vladimir Mandl: Founding Writer on Space Law', in F.C. Durant III and G.S. James, eds., *First Steps Towards Space* (Washington: Smithsonian Press, 1974) 87–90 (not seen).

23 V. Mandl, *Das Weltraum-Recht: Ein Problem der Raumfahrt* [The Law of Outer Space: A Problem of Spaceflight] (Berlin: Mannheim; Leipzig: Bensheimer, 1932), 48 pp. (not seen). See S.E. Doyle, *Pioneers of Space Law: Vladimir Mandl (1899–1941)* (IISL, 2023) for a biography and translation. See also V. Kopal and M. Hoffmann, 'Vladimir Mandl', in Hobe, *supra* n. 14, 57–69; V. Kopal, 'Vladimir Mandl – Founder of Space Law' (1968) 11 *Proc. IISL* 357–361, 'The Question of Defining Outer Space' (1980) 8 *J. Sp. L.*, 154–173 at 154 and 'The Evolution of the Doctrine of Space Law', in N. Jasentuliyana, ed., *Space Law: Development and Scope* (Westport and London: Praeger, 1992) 17–32, at 18–19; D.F. Dolan, 'Vladimir Mandl; The Founding Father of Space Law' (2022) 7 *Jus Gentium; J. Int. Leg. Hist.* 85–98. See also G. Reintanz, 'Vladimir Mandl – the Father of Space Law' (1968) 11 *Proc. IISL* 362–365, who quotes a letter by Mandl reviewing his career. Mandl could not find a publisher willing to take on the book and paid for an edition of 500 copies himself. Only 18 copies were sold in 1932 and 7 in 1933. He gave the rest away. Mandl also wrote about parachutes, patented a design for a high-altitude rocket and wrote a technical treatment of *The Problem of Interstellar Traffic* in 1932. An advocate of technocracy, he published *Technocracy – Economic System of the Future* in Prague in 1934 and *Essays of a European Technocrat* in Los Angeles in 1936. He died of tuberculosis in 1941.

link between an individual and the territorial state of his nationality might change as new communities beyond the Earth developed.[24]

In 1933, Y.A. Korovin presented a paper on the 'Conquest of the Stratosphere and International Law' at a Leningrad air law conference.[25] He rehearsed the pre-First World War arguments in favour of state sovereignty over air space and acknowledged that some had argued for a 'free zone' above and beyond state sovereignty. However, on grounds of safety and military security, Korovin came down in favour of unlimited state sovereignty.[26]

Science was making advances. Modern rocketry begins with the experiments of Konstantin Tsiolkovski, Robert H. Goddard, Hermann Oberth and others in the early years of the twentieth century.[27] Societies were established to discuss and foster space matters.[28] The German Rocket Society (the VfR – *Verein für Raumschiffahrt*) was founded in 1927 and what is now the American Institute of Aeronautics and Astronautics in 1932.[29] The British Interplanetary Society, established in 1933, started to publish its Journal in 1934. By the later 1930s, rocketry had made sufficient progress for military interests to be aroused, and a blanket of secrecy was cast over experiments.[30] Then, the German use of the V-2 in the later months of the Second World War revealed the progress that their scientists had made and the potential inherent in such devices.

There is nothing like war for producing progress in technology. At the end of the Second World War, both East and West scrambled to augment their science personnel by expediting the immigration of relevant German scientists, apparently without regard to questions of war crimes, and the stage was set.[31] At first, the military aspects of rocket science had precedence, with ballistic and inter-continental missiles being developed. However, the technology was also capable of peaceful use.

The International Geophysical Year of 1957 was to introduce satellites for the scientific exploration of the Earth.[32] Of the more immediate benefits to be brought by space, Arthur

---

24 See Kopal and Reintanz, both *supra* n. 23, and Kopal, *supra* n. 21, quoted in Doyle, *Origins, supra* n. 16, at 8.
25 E. Korovin, 'La Conquéte de la Stratosphere et le Droit International' (1934) 41 *Rev. Gen. de Droit Int. Pub.*, 675–686. See G.P. Zhukov, V.S. Vereshchetin and A.Y. Kaputsin, 'Evgeny Alexandrivich Korovin', in Hobe, *supra* n. 14, 49–55.
26 Doyle, *Origins, supra* n. 16, 12–14.
27 W. Ley, *Rockets, Missiles and Space Travel* (New York: Viking Press, 1958); W. von Braun and F.I. Ordway, *History of Rocket and Space Travel*, 4th ed. (New York: Crowell, 1972); D.A. Clary, *Rocket Man: Robert H. Goddard and the Birth of the Space Age* (Hyperion, 2003); B.V. Rauschenbach, *Hermann Oberth: The Father of Space Flight 1894–1989* (Fine Art, 1994). For Tsiolkovski see Wikipedia.
28 Doyle cites F.H. Winter, *Prelude to the Space Age – the Rocket Societies 1924–1940* (Washington: Smithsonian Institute, 1983) and A.G. Haley, *Rocketry and Space Exploration* (New York: Van Nostrand, 1958). See also previous note.
29 T.D. Crouch, *Rocketeers and Gentlemen Engineers: A History of the American Institute of Aeronautics and Astronautics . . . And What Came Before* (Washington: AIAA, 2006).
30 On 10 October 1939, the British Interplanetary Society (BIS) circulated a note to all its members to 'cease activities'. The Society resumed in 1945. See BIS Chronology: www.bis-spaceflight.com.
31 G. DeGroot, *Dark Side of the Moon* (London: Jonathan Cape, 2006) 12–28; W.A. McDougall, '. . . *the Heavens and the Earth: A Political History of the Space Age* (New York: Basic Books, 1985); P.M. Sterns and L.I. Tennen, 'Ethics and the Conquest of Space: From Peenemunde to Mars and Beyond' (2007) 50 *Proc. IISL* 456–467 at 464–467; J.I. Gabrynowicz, 'Space Law: Its Cold War Origins and Challenges in the Era of Globalization' (2004) 37 *Suffolk U. L. Rev.* 1041–1066.
32 An intriguing discussion is R.D. Launius, 'An Unintended Consequence of the zn: Eisenhower, Sputnik, the Founding of NASA' (2010) 67 *Acta Astronautica* 254–263.

C. Clarke's prescient suggestion in 1945 of using the geostationary orbit for communication satellites is perhaps the most famous.[33] It was also Clarke, however, whom Doyle identifies as the first post-War author to articulate the need for an upper limit on state sovereignty in the interests of the development of space science,[34] as he did in a 1946 lecture that was triggered by the statement of US General H. Arnold that the design of a true spaceship was 'all but practicable today'.[35]

Clarke also observed that action would be needed to forestall extraterrestrial imperialism and consequent conflict. Doyle further notes that various other concepts relevant to space activities also began to appear in the 1940s. That the moon is 'the common heritage of mankind' was stated by one of the Council of the British Interplanetary Society in 1949.[36] However, the idea that an area or region might be set aside under international control for peaceful scientific purposes only emerged in relation to Antarctica.[37]

Space Law Institutions and Fora After the Second World War

After the War, a variety of international associations and bodies ranging from academe to government became important fora for the expression of views and suggestions as to what law should govern in matters of outer space. Articles began to be written,[38] and in due course there were books.[39]

The International Astronautical Federation, the International Academy of Astronautics and the International Institute of Space Law

The founding of the International Astronautical Federation (IAF) in 1950 was an important development.[40] Although few papers at its early congresses were directed to questions

33 A.C. Clarke, 'Extra-terrestrial Relays: Can Rocket Stations Give World-Wide Radio Coverage?' (October 1945) *Wireless World* 303–308. Clarke foresaw such stations being manned and using vacuum tubes, the transistor lying unperceived in the future.
34 A.C. Clarke, 'The Challenge of the Spaceship: Astronautics and Its Impact on Human Society' (1946–1947) 6 JBIS 66–67, quoted by Doyle, *Origins, supra* n. 16, at 15–17. Doyle's view is that Clarke based his thoughts on reason and not on familiarity with the work of Mandl.
35 Third Report of the Commanding General of the Army Air Forces to the Secretary of War (Washington: US Army Air Forces, 1945), cited by Doyle, Origins, *supra* n. 16, at 15.
36 R.A. Smith, 'Correspondence: Man and His Mark' (1949) 8 JBIS 131–132, quoted *in extenso* by Doyle, *Origins, supra* n. 16, 18–19. Doyle at 19–20 also quotes a French pamphlet, *L'Astronautique* (Paris: Presses Universitaires de France, 1949), in which one Lionel Laming wrote that 'the conquest of space may mean that all the solar system, not only the Earth, deserves to be considered as the heritage of mankind'.
37 'Discussion asked on Territorial Problems of Antarctica', *US Department of State Bulletin*, 5 Sept. 1948, 301, quoted by Doyle, *Origins, supra* n. 16, 17–18.
38 See *supra* n. 15.
39 E.g. P.C. Jessup and H.J. Taubenfeld, *Controls for Outer Space and the Antarctic Analogy* (New York: Columbia UP; Oxford: Oxford UP, 1959); J.G. Verplaetse, *International Law in Vertical Space* (New York: Rothman, 1960); C. Chaumont, *Le Droit de l'Espace* (Paris: Presses Universitaire de Paris, 1960); A.G. Haley, *Space Law and Government* (New York: Appleton-Century-Crofts, 1963); G. Gal, *Space Law* (Leiden: Sijthoff, 1969); S.H. Lay and H.J. Taubenfeld, *The Law Relating to the Activities of Man in Space* (Chicago University Press, 1970).
40 See www.iafastro.com/. For an outline and discussion of the creation of the IAF and its eight conferences as of 1957, with special reference to their legal content, see Doyle, *Origins, supra* n. 16, 22–79; cf. A.G. Haley, *supra* n. 39, 343–370. See also R.D. Crane, 'Background of the International Institute of Space Law' (1961) 4 *Proc. IISL* 153–170; C.Q. Christol, 'Influence of the International Institute of Space Law and the

of law,[41] the IAF provided and provides a major forum for discussing the exploration and use of space and for disseminating information both at its meetings and through the series *Acta Astronautica* and the *Proceedings of the International Institute of Space Law*.

In 1960, the IAF established the International Academy of Astronautics (IAA), membership in which is prized by individuals active in all forms of space activities. Like the academies of classical times, it brings together individuals to exchange ideas and experience and thereby contribute to the advancement of space and astronautics. Every year, conferences are organised on major space activities and problems.

The IAA has four sections: basic science, engineering sciences, life sciences and social sciences, law falling within the last of these. Membership is through election by the existing members, and full members are elected for life. Corresponding members are elected for five years but may be considered for election as full members after two years.[42]

The Eighth IAF International Congress on Astronautics was held in October 1957, four days after the launch of Sputnik I. It elected as IAF President Andrew G. Haley, a US lawyer who had for some years been active within the IAF and in promoting 'space law'.[43] It was therefore not surprising that the Congress also decided to establish a special IAF committee under the chairmanship of John Cobb Cooper to 'define the respective areas of jurisdiction for air and space law'.[44]

A year later, in 1958, a Colloquium on Space Law attracted to The Hague forty-four participants from ten countries. This resolved that a Permanent Legal Committee should be established within the IAF open to jurists of associations affiliated with the IAF to study problems of space law which might be included in an international convention. The IAF Congress accepted this later in 1958.[45] At a London Colloquium in 1959, the name of the committee was changed to the International Institute of Space Law (IISL), and its constitution and bylaws were accepted by the Bureau of the IAF at the Eleventh IAF Congress, Stockholm 1960.[46]

International Law Association on the Development of Space Law' (1993) 42 *ZLW* 430–441 and data on the IAF in *Legal Problems, supra* n. 38, xvi–xxi.

41 Stuttgart, 1952 paper by A. Meyer; Innsbruck 1954 by A. Cocca; Rome 1956 by A. Cocca and by E. Pepin; Barcelona, 1957 by A.G. Haley and by E. Pepin.

42 V. Kopal, 'Evolution of the Statutes and Membership of the International Academy of Astronautics' (1985) 28 *Proc. IISL* 52–60 and 'The Contribution of the International Astronautical Federation to International Cooperation in Outer Space and the Development of Its Constitution' (1993) 36 *Proc. IISL* 48–68; F. von der Dunk, 'Report on Relevant Work of the International Institute of Space Law', in K.-H. Böckstiegel, ed., *Project 2001, Legal Framework for the Commercial Use of Space* (Cologne: Carl Heymanns Verlag, 2002), 35–36. See also H. Moulin, ed., *IAF: The First 50 Years* (Paris: IAF, 2001).

43 A.D. Haley, *Space Law and Government* (New York: Appleton-Century-Crofts, 1963; IISL website, 2023). S.E. Doyle, 'Andrew G. Haley', in Hobe, *supra* n. 14, 71–96; S.E. Doyle. 'Space Law and Government – 50 Years Later' (2013) 39 *J. Sp. L.* 1–22; S. Freeland, 'A Natural System of Law – Andrew Haley and the International Regulation of Outer Space' (2013) 39 *J. Sp. L.* 77–98. When Haley ceased to be president of the IAF and reverted to being its general counsel, he set up eleven working groups to consider various matters space law would have to deal with. See A.G. Haley and W. Heinrich Prince of Hanover, 'Foreword' (1959) 2 *Proc IISL* iii–vii.

44 See *infra* n. 59 for Cooper and the McGill Institute of Air and Space Law.

45 See M.S. Smirnoff, 'The Role of the IAF in the Elaboration of Norms of Future Space Law' (1959) 2 *Proc. IISL* 147–155 at 150–152 for a draft Space Law Convention.

46 E. Pepin, *International Institute of Space Law – A Brief History* (New York: AIAA, 1982); S.E. Doyle, *Origins of International Space Law and the International Institute of Space Law of the International Astronautical Federation* (San Diego: Univelt, 2002) 80–93. Alex Meyer criticised the use of the nomenclature of an

The IISL, with institutional and individual members, holds annual colloquia during the IAF congresses.[47] Occasional regional colloquia are also organised. The annual international Manfred Lachs Moot Court Competition, named for the former president of the Institute, is open to students.[48] Regional rounds are organised, and the winners take part in the world final. This, held as part of the annual colloquium, is judged by three judges of the International Court of Justice. In cooperation with the European Centre for Space Law (ECSL), the IISL presents a workshop/symposium at the annual meeting of the COPUOS (Committee on the Peaceful Uses of Outer Space) Legal Subcommittee and has official status as an observer at COPUOS sessions.[49]

Academic and Similar Institutions

Teaching is important in spreading knowledge on space law and for its development.[50] To help spread the word, the UN Office of Outer Space Affairs (UN OOSA) published a curriculum setting out the major areas that should be covered.[51] In most instances, the first space law courses emerged as an adjunct to aviation law, and aviation remains the major thrust of the endeavours of most of the specialised institutes that offer space law. However, and unsurprisingly given the numbers of states and enterprises now active in space, a goodly number of universities and other academic institutions around the world now offer lectures and occasional courses in space law or include brief coverage as part of a general course on Public International Law.[52]

Chronologically, the Institute of Air and Space Law at the University of Cologne is the oldest specialised institute, albeit with a hiccup.[53] Begun in 1925 as the Institute of Air Law in Köningsberg (Kaliningrad), it moved to Leipzig in 1929 and to Berlin in 1940, where its Library was bombed.[54] In 1950, the institute reopened in Cologne under Professor Alex Meyer and thereafter has gone from strength to strength.[55] The institute offers

---

'institute' with 'directors': 'Space Law and Government: Considerations on the Book with the Same Title by Andrew G. Haley' (1964) 13 *ZLW* 4–43 at 42–43.

47 S. Hobe, ed., *The International Institute of Space Law: Six Decades of Space Law and Its Development(s) (1960–2020)* (IISL, 2020).

48 IISL, *Manfred Lachs Space Law Moot Court Competition: The First 25 Years* (The Hague: Eleven Publishing, 2016).

49 For COPUOS, see *infra* n. 90.

50 On the importance of teaching, see M. Lachs, 'Teachings and Teaching on International Law' (1976-III) 151 *Hague Recueil* 161–252; G. Lafferranderie, 'Faut-il toujours enseigner le droit de l'espace?' (2006) 55 *ZLW* 517–540.

51 *Education Curriculum on Space Law* ST/SPACE/6 (Vienna: UN OOSA, 2014): www.unoosa.org/oosa/en/ourwork/spacelaw/space-law-curriculum.html. On OOSA, see *infra* n. 82.

52 OOSA publishes a self-notifying list of institutions teaching space law: www.unoosa.org/documents/pdf/spacelaw/eddir/EducationOpportunitiesinSpaceLaw2020.pdf.

53 H. Bittlinger, *History of the Institute of Air and Space Law of the University of Cologne* (Cologne: IASL, 2005); H. Bittlinger, M. Benkö and S. Hobe, *Institute of Air and Space Law, University of Cologne, 1925–2015* (Cologne: IASL, 2015); K.-H. Böckstiegel, 'Report and Reflections on the Teaching of Space Law at the Institute of Air and Space Law at Cologne University' (1986) 29 *Proc. IISL* 208–211. For current data, see www.ilwr.jura.uni-koeln.de/8366.html?&no_cache=1&L=1.

54 Its then director, R. Scheichler, suspected of belonging to a resistance group following the 1944 plot to assassinate Hitler, was executed in 1945.

55 S. Hobe, 'Alex Meyer', in Hobe, *supra* n. 14, 4–18.

taught courses and postgraduate supervision as well as organising symposia and colloquia.[56] Instrumental in the compilation of the magnificent *Cologne Commentary on Space
Law* (2009–2015), it publishes the *Zeitschrift für Luftrecht und Weltraumrecht* retaining
the numbering of, but replacing, the *Zeitschrift für Luftrecht* (1952–1959) and the earlier
Archives of Air Law (1931–1943).

The first Dutch doctoral thesis on air law was published in 1910.[57] It largely drew on
analogies from the law of the sea. In 1938, formal studies in air law began at Leiden University with the appointment of Daniel Göedhuis. A chair was established in 1947. The
remit of the appointment was extended to space law in 1961.[58] Retiring in 1977, Professor
Göedhuis was succeeded by Henri Wassenberg, on whose initiative the Leiden Institute
of Air and Space Law was established in 1986. It offers taught courses and postgraduate supervision. Leiden also organises symposia and colloquia, with some concentration
on European aspects of space law. Also in Europe, the International Space University –
founded in 1987 – is located in Strasbourg, France (www.isunet.edu/). Providing graduate-
level courses in a two-month summer session and a master's programme. its courses
encompass science, technical, engineering, business and policy aspects of space with a view
to training space professionals.

In 1951, McGill University in Montreal established an Institute of International Air
Law under the directorship of John Cobb Cooper, a well-known aviation lawyer who
had contributed significantly to discussions on space law.[59] The institute was renamed the
Institute of Air and Space Law (IASL) in 1957, and many of its graduates (including the
authors of this book) have been active in space law.[60] Apart from teaching and postgraduate research supervision, the IASL organises symposia and colloquia and since 1976 has
annually published *Annals of Air and Space Law*. The *McGill Manual on International
Law Applicable to Military Uses of Outer Space* has begun to be issued.

In the US, the Space Policy Institute at the Elliot School of International Affairs of
George Washington University, Washington, DC, functions mostly in the area that its
title indicates. However, policy is a significant factor in the development of space law,
and its products are influential, particularly in US developments.[61] Also in Washington
DC, Georgetown University Law Center offers courses and research supervision in space
law. The University of Mississippi School of Law, active in space law for many years,
offers an LL.M. The late Professor Stephen Gorove established its *Journal of Space Law*
in 1973, publishing articles and data on current developments.[62] The College of Law
at the Lincoln Campus of the University of Nebraska offers an LL.M. program in space
and telecommunications law, and a number of other US universities now have courses
on space law.

---

56 E.g. *Project 2001* directed by Professor K.-H. Böckstiegel, continued by *Project 2001 Plus* under Professor S.
   Hobe.
57 *De Luchtvaart in het Volkenrecht* ('Aerial Navigation According to the Law of Nations') by Johanna (Jenny)
   Francina Lycklama à Nijeholt, 1910.
58 P. van Fenema and T. Masson-Zwaan, 'Daniel Goedhuis', in Hobe, *supra* n.14, 99–125.
59 R.S. Jakhu and M. Ancona, 'John Cobb Cooper', in Hobe, *supra* n. 14, 35–47, and *supra* at n. 44 for his
   involvement in the IISL.
60 *The Institute of Air and Space Law, 1951–1976* (Montreal: McGill University, 1976).
61 See www.gwu.edu/~elliott/researchcenters/spi.html. ESPI (*infra* n. 68) and the Elliot School cooperate:
   www.gwu.edu/~spi/
62 See https://olemiss.edu; https://law.olemiss.edu/academics-programs/llm/

The study of space law has developed elsewhere, sometimes through institutes similar to those above and sometimes through local cooperation between academic and practising lawyers. For example, in France the University of Paris XI runs courses in space law, and telecommunications and space law are part of the curriculum in Toulouse. In Spain, the University of Jaen provides teaching in space law and organises colloquia.

In South America, the University of Salvador in Buenos Aires established a chair of air and space law in 1960, and a National Institute of Air and Space Law in 1962. Now some fifty Argentine universities offer space law within programmes on public international law. Space law is studied on similar bases in Brazil, Chile, Mexico and Uruguay. National and international conferences and symposia are also held.[63]

In India, unsurprisingly given its emergence as active in space, many universities offer courses or classes in space law. In Japan, several universities teach space law, and JAXA, the Japan Aerospace Exploration Agency, created in 1993 by the amalgamation of three agencies, is supportive of these efforts.[64] Space law is now available at several Chinese universities. It is also now taught at the Moscow State Institute of International Law and at the Institute of International Law of the People's Friendship University.[65]

In 1990, under the leadership of Dr G. Lafferranderie, then the legal advisor to the European Space Agency (ESA), ECSL was created.[66] Its members are academics and practitioners in the field. ECSL holds symposia, colloquia and workshops, and its website provides much documentation as well as links to other space law sites.[67] Since 1992, the ECSL has run an annual a two-week course on space law and policy at different locations throughout Europe for students from European universities. It also holds an annual one-day practitioners' forum at which experts and practitioners review problems and developments in a particular area of space law. The ECSL organises the European regional round of the IISL Manfred Lachs Moot Court competition. It has permanent observer status at the annual meeting of the COPUOS Legal Subcommittee and cooperates with the IISL in presenting a symposium prior to that meeting.

The European Space Policy Institute (ESPI) was established in Vienna in 2005 by decision of the ESA Council. Working both through staff and an 'Academic Network', it conducts studies and provides reports on mid- to long-term issues of space policy intended to assist relevant decision-makers. It also publishes a series of studies in space policy.[68]

Apart from the use of space law as examples in other courses,[69] The Hague Academy of International Law has included space law as a specific topic in its annual courses on a

---

63 See the Latin-American Association for Air and Space Law: www.alada.org/ and the Latin-American Institute for Air, Space and Commercial Aviation Law: https://uia.org/

64 M. Ogsawara and J. Greer, eds., *Japan in Space* (The Hague: Eleven Publishing, 2021); S. Aoki, 'National Space Laws of Japan: Today and Tomorrow' (2014): www.unoosa.org/documents/pdf/spacelaw/activities/2014/pres10E.pdf.

65 G.P. Zhukov, 'Teaching of the International Space Law in Russia', in A.Y. Kapustin and G.P. Zhukov, eds., *The Contemporary Problems of International Space Law* (Moscow: Peoples' Friendship University, 2008) 524–528.

66 G. Lafferranderie, 'The European Centre for Space Law', in K.-H. Böckstiegel, ed., *Project 2001, Legal Framework for the Commercial Use of Space* (Cologne: Carl Heymanns Verlag, 2002) 47–50.

67 See www.esa.int/About_Us/ECSL_-_European_Centre_for_Space_Law

68 See www.espi.or.at/. Reports may be downloaded from the ESPI website.

69 For example, J.E.S. Fawcett, 'General Course' (1971-III) 113 *Hague Recueil* 468–472, 553–557; A.E. Gottlieb, 'The Impact of Technology on the Development of Contemporary International Law' (1981-I) 170 *Hague Recueil* 115–329, particularly at 223 ff.

number of occasions.[70] In 1998, the Study Session of The Hague Academy was devoted to international telecommunications.[71]

A number of other legal bodies, societies and associations either have given intermittent attention to questions of space law or have sections that deal with such matters. Founded in Brussels in 1873, the International Law Association is a nongovernmental organisation. Membership is voluntary. Working through branches and international committees, the ILA studies and helps clarify international law. It has consultative status with a number of UN specialised agencies and other organisations.

Through its Space Law Committee, the ILA has produced a number of reports on space law ranging from consideration of the space law treaties to the commercial use of space.[72] Similarly an Outer Space Committee of the International Bar Association has debated an increasing number of practical, legal, commercial and regulatory issues arising from the development of space businesses.[73] The American Society of International Law has occasionally devoted a meeting to space law and its *American Journal of International Law* has carried a number of articles on space law, as may its *AJIL Unbound* series.

Within the United Nations

Within the UN system, various divisions and agencies deal with space as part of their responsibilities.[74] To fully enumerate these would be otiose, but as will be seen elsewhere in this book, the International Telecommunication Union (ITU) (radio) and the World Meteorological Organisation (remote sensing) are obvious examples. Others such as the International Civil Aviation Organisation (ICAO), the International Maritime Organisation, the World Intellectual Property Organisation and the United Nations Education, Scientific and Cultural Organisation (UNESCO) all have 'space' interests.

---

70 The principal space law considerations at sessions of The Hague Academy of International Law are R. Quadri, 'Droit International Cosmique' (1959-III) 98 *Hague Recueil* 505–599; D. Göedhuis, 'Conflicts of Law and Divergences in the Legal Regimes of Air Space and Outer Space' (1963-II) 109 *Hague Recueil* 256–346; M. Lachs, 'The International Law of Outer Space' (1964-III) 113 *Hague Recueil* 1–114; G.P. Zhukov, 'Tendances Contemporaines du Developpement du Droit Spatial International' (1978-III) 161 *Hague Recueil* 229–328; N.M. Matte, 'Aerospace Law: Telecommunication Satellites' (1980-I) 166 *Hague Recueil* 119–249; M.G. Marcoff, 'Sources de Droit International de L'Espace' (1980-III) 168 *Hague Recueil* 9–122; I.H.Ph. Diedericks-Verschoor, 'Similarities with and Differences between Air and Space Law Primarily in the Field of Private International Law' (1981-III) 172 *Hague Recueil* 317–423; D. Göedhuis, 'The Problems of the Frontiers of Outer Space and Air Law' (1982-I) 174 *Hague Recueil* 367–407; S. Gorove, 'International Space Law in Perspective – Some Major Issues, Trends and Perspectives' (1983-III) 181 *Hague Recueil* 349–409.
71 The Hague Academy of International Law Research Session, 1998: Topic, Space Telecommunications, L. Rapp, Franco-phone Director, F. Lyall, Anglo-phone Director. See *Legal Implications of Global Telecommunications*, Hague Academy of International Law, 1998 (Dordrecht: Nijhoff, 1999).
72 M. Williams, 'The Role of the International Law Association in the Development of the Law of Space', in K.-H. Böckstiegel, ed., *Project 2001, Legal Framework for the Commercial Use of Space* (Cologne: Carl Heymanns Verlag, 2002) 37–45; Christol, *supra* n. 40. The ILA website is www.ila-hq.org/. For reports, see www.ila-hq.org/en/committees/.
73 See www.ibanet.org/
74 M. Benkö and M. De Graaff, *Space Law in the United Nations* (Dordrecht: Nijhoff, 1985); V. Kopal, 'Evolution of the Main Principles of Space Law in the Institutional Framework of the United Nations' (1984) 12 *J. Sp. L.* 12–25; J. Simsarian, 'Outer Space Cooperation in the United Nations' (1963) 57 *AJIL* 854–867. Cf. 'Coordination of space-related activities within the United Nations system: directions and anticipated results for the period 2020–2021: Report of the Secretary-General' A/AC.105/1210 and previous reports.

The United Nations Programme on Space Applications assists nations in using space technology for economic, social and cultural development. There is also a UN interagency coordination group, the Interagency Meeting on Outer Space Affairs, part of the responsibilities of UN OOSA.[75] Major matters may also be referred to the UN Administrative Committee on Coordination, which, for example, accepted the ITU suggestion of the holding of the World Summit on the Information Society of 2003–2006.[76]

The UN has held three World Conferences on the Exploration and Peaceful Uses of Outer Space, with technical fora and associate workshops. These were directed at the development of space activities, encouraging the spread of space technology and highlighting the benefits of space applications, particularly for the developing countries. UNISPACE I was held in 1968,[77] UNISPACE II in 1982.[78] In 1999, UNISPACE III adopted a major declaration of aims and priorities[79] and UNISPACE+50 in 2018.[80] Their outcomes can be seen elsewhere in this book, for example in the emphasis on sustainability.[81] Recently, with Space3030, the UN set out its hopes for the future.

The United Nations Office for Outer Space Affairs[82]

UN OOSA is located in Vienna.[83] The central UN Secretariat met the technical needs of the COPUOS when it was first set up,[84] and the function later passed to a specialised Outer Space Affairs Division, transmuting into an Office for Outer Space Affairs within the Department for Political Affairs in 1992. Relocated to Vienna in 1993, the office expanded to *inter alia* include servicing the COPUOS Legal Subcommittee, previously a task of the Legal Secretariat in New York. Since then, it has developed a major role in furthering knowledge and practice in space activities and law.

75 For OOSA, see *infra* n. 82. See 'International Cooperation in the Peaceful Uses of Outer Space: Activities of Member States', A/AC.105/1248 with adds. Cf. Reports A/AC.105/842 (2005), A/AC.105/1114 (2016). A/AC.105/1238, with adds.
76 See documents at www.itu.int/net/wsis/including *WSIS Outcome Documents* and the WSIS Forum Documents. See also WSIS in Chapter 8.
77 Seventy-eight UN member states, nine specialised agencies and four other international organisations attended.
78 N. Jasentuliyana and R. Chipman, *International Space Programmes and Policies: Proceedings of the Second United Nations Conference on the Peaceful Uses of Outer Space (UNISPACE), Vienna Austria, August 1982* (Amsterdam and New York: North Holland, 1984). The Background Papers are A/CONF.101/BP/1–4.
79 Third United Nations Conference on the Exploration and the Peaceful Uses of Outer Space: The Space Millennium: Vienna Declaration on Space and Human Development, Vienna, 30 July 1999: www.unoosa.org/pdf/reports/unispace/viennadeclE.pdf. Cf. *The Space Millennium: Selected Priorities for Space Activities in the 21st Century: An Initiative to Encourage the Engagement of Non-Government Entities: Working with Governments in the Promotion and Implementation of Selected Recommendations Resulting from UNISPACE-III* (Washington: AIAA, 2000). See also UNISPACE III+5: A/59/174.
80 Cf. www.unoosa.org/oosa/en/ourwork/unispaceplus50/index.html. Four pillars for the development of a nation in relation to space were identified: space economy, space society, space accessibility and space diplomacy.
81 See 'Fiftieth anniversary of the first United Nations Conference on the Exploration and Peaceful Uses of Outer Space: space as a driver of sustainable development', UNGA 73/6, adopted without vote, 26 October 2018.
82 Reference point, *supra* nn. 51, 75. The OOSA website is www.unoosa.org/.
83 M. Othman, 'United Nations Office for Outer Space Affairs', in K.-H. Böckstiegel, ed., *Project 2001, Legal Framework for the Commercial Use of Space* (Cologne: Carl Heymanns Verlag, 2002) 27–33.
84 For COPUOS, see *infra* n. 90.

Headed by a director, UN OOSA is now the main node for space affairs within the UN.[85] It has four sections, Executive Secretariat; Committee, Policy and Legal Affairs; Space Applications and UN-SPIDER.[86] It maintains the Register of Space Objects on behalf of the Secretary General and makes available other space data and documentation. It provides information on space (factual and theoretical, including law which is both) to the UN system, to UN member states, to space-active entities, to academe and to individual researchers. It is very active in disseminating knowledge of the benefits of space and its regulation.[87]

UN OOSA maintains a directory of educational opportunities in space law and can provide fellowships for individuals attending seminars. From the later 1990s, and particularly since UNISPACE III, OOSA both itself and in partnership with other agencies, governments and academic institutions has organised conferences and training programmes to spread expertise and knowledge as to space law and space applications.[88] For instance, in 2014, following consultation with educators and space law experts, UN OOSA published a model Education Curriculum on Space Law to encourage teaching.[89] OOSA could do more but is constrained by finances.

The Committee on the Peaceful Uses of Outer Space[90]

COPUOS was created as an eighteen-member Ad Hoc Committee of the General Assembly by UNGA Res. 1348 (XIII), 'Question of the Peaceful Use of Outer Space', 13 December 1958.[91] Made permanent one year later by Part A of UNGA Res. 1472 (XIV) of 12 December 1959, its membership was increased to twenty-four.[92] That the Assembly saw fit to entrust such matters to a specially denominated committee and not simply to add 'space' to the remit of an existing main Committee of the Assembly indicates that the

85 See www.unoosa.org/oosa/en/aboutus/structure.html
86 For UN-SPIDER, see Chapter 12 Remote Sensing.
87 See UN OOSA annual reports and www.unoosa.org/oosa/en/aboutus/index.html.
88 Cf. UN OOSA Space Law for New Space Actors project: www.unoosa.org/oosa/en/ourwork/spacelaw/capacitybuilding/advisory-services/index.html.
89 See *supra* n. 51.
90 Reference point, *supra* n. 49. M. Friel and C.D. Johnson, *The COPUOS Briefing Book* (Secure World Foundation, 2023): https://swfound.org/media/207570/copuos-briefing-book_-digital-1.pdf.
91 The members were Argentina, Australia, Belgium, Brazil, Canada, Czechoslovakia, France, India, Iran, Italy, Japan, Mexico, Poland, Sweden, the United Arab Republic (Egypt and Syria 1958–1961), the UK, US and USSR. However, Czechoslovakia, Poland and the USSR declined to participate. E. Galloway, 'The United Nations Committee on the Peaceful Uses of Outer Space: Accomplishments and Implications for Legal Problems' (1959) 2 *Proc. IISL* 30–41 at 31.
     See also Cheng, 150–211; P.C. Jessup and H.J. Taubenfeld, 'The Ad Hoc Committee on the Peaceful Uses of Outer Space' (1959) 53 *AJIL* 877–881; P.G. Dembling and D.M. Arons, 'Space Law and the United Nations: The Work of the Legal Subcommittee of the United Nations Committee on the Peaceful Uses of Outer Space' (1966) 32 *J. Air L. & Comm.* 329–386; V. Kopal *supra* n. 74 and 'The Work of the Committee on the Peaceful Uses of Outer Space', in K.-H. Böckstiegel, ed., *Project 2001, Legal Framework for the Commercial Use of Space* (Cologne: Carl Heymanns Verlag, 2002) 17–26; S. Marchisio, 'The Evolutionary Stages of the United Nations Committee on the Peaceful Uses of Outer Space (COPUOS)' (2005) 31 *J. Sp. L.* 219–242. Cf. M. Benkö and Kai-Uwe Schrögl, *International Space Law in the Making: Current Issues in the UN Committee on the Peaceful Uses of Outer Space* (Paris: Editions Frontiéres, 1993).
92 Albania, Argentina, Australia, Austria, Belgium, Brazil, Bulgaria, Canada, Czechoslovakia, France, Hungary, India, Iran, Italy, Japan, Lebanon, Mexico, Poland, Romania, Sweden, the United Arab Republic, the UK, the USA and the USSR.

Assembly recognised the peculiar problems involved in the space *materiél*. It also indicated that here was a new area of activity – a tabula rasa – calling for new thinking and new procedures. Certainly as a result, COPUOS has been significantly involved in the development of space law.[93]

Ad hoc COPUOS began with eighteen members,[94] but as of 2022, membership is one hundred two.[95] This is supposed to equitably represent the interests of the developed and developing countries and to provide geographic world coverage. Through COPUOS, therefore, over 50% of the UN membership is potentially involved in the development of space law. It is arguable that enlargement has democratised the development of international law in that more states participate in the discussions and decisions through which progress is made. During the process, they can articulate their interests and, to an extent, secure them.[96]

But in fact, this size is unwieldy.[97] As we will describe, and subject to the reservations we express, the result may be a lowering of the standard of any eventual text as the urge to reflect all the voices and interests may reduce the product to the lowest common denominator.[98] Deficiencies and defects in the expertise (and interest or commitment) of some delegations have led to a slowing in the rate of productive work.[99]

COPUOS works through the main Committee and two subcommittees, Scientific and Technical and Legal, the latter normally being responsible for the initial drafts in legal matters.[100] Each sub-committee reports to the main Committee, which reports annually to the

---

93 N. Jasentuliyana, *International Space Law and the United Nations* (The Hague: Kluwer, 1999) 23–32. Para 11 of the COPUOS Report to the 2007 General Assembly (A/62/20) noted, 'the instrumental role it had played in constructing the legal regime governing outer space activity for peaceful purposes, which was an entirely new branch of international law, and in providing a unique platform at the global level for enhancing international cooperation for the benefit of all countries, in particular in the area of using space applications for sustainable development'. The wide-ranging content of successive reports (A/71/20) shows how COPUOS continues to play that role.

94 Listed *supra* n. 91.

95 Successive membership is catalogued at www.unoosa.org/oosa/en/ourwork/copuos/members/evolution. html. But note *infra* n. 108.

96 Successive UNGA COPUOS reports relate the views expressed by delegations at meetings of the two Sub-Committees and the main Committee: see annually A/[GA meeting number]/20. Views can be diverse and, sometimes, given the history of space law, wild and/or ill-informed.

97 COPUOS is one of the largest UN committees.

98 Cf. G. Hafner, 'Certain Issues of the Work of the Sixth Committee of the Fifty-Sixth General Assembly' (2003) 97 *AJIL* 147–162 at 148–150, on the enlargement of UNCITRAL.

99 S. Neil Hosenball, former Legal Adviser to NASA and a participant in the early years of COPUOS, told one of us that a major reason for the early success of the Committee was that although the Cold War was then in full swing, the delegates were a small knowledgeable group who knew and respected each another and were friends. In addition, they were of sufficient standing that they knew their home governments would support what they worked out. Problems could therefore be chewed over informally and solutions arrived at without posturing or polemic. Over the years, that advantage may have dissipated, Cf. the development of space cooperation between the USA and USSR during this time, particularly the Dryden-Blagonravov Agreement of 1962 (1963) 2 *ILM* 195–198: E.C. and L.N. Ezell, *The Partnership: A History of the Apollo-Soyuz Space Project*, NASA History Series SP-4209, 1978: www.hq.nasa.gov/pao/History/SP-4209/toc. htm.

100 P.G. Dembling and D.M. Arons, 'Space Law and the United Nations: The Work of the Legal Subcommittee of the United Nations Committee on the Peaceful Uses of Outer Space' (1966) 32 *J. Air L. & Comm.* 329–386; S. Marchisio, 'The Evolutionary Stages of the Legal Subcommittee of the UN COPUOS' (2005) 31 *J. Sp. L.* 219–242; K.-U. Schrögl, 'Is UNCOPUOS Fit for the Future: Reflections at the Occasion of the 50th Session of Its Legal Committee' (2011) 60 *ZLW* 93–102.

UN General Assembly (UNGA) which every year adopts a corresponding resolution. Particular resolutions as to 'principles' which states may/should/ought to obey are therefore determined by, and have weight related to, the care with which they have been formulated.

COPUOS and its subcommittees normally proceed by consensus.[101] The one instance (so far) in which it did not produced UNGA Res. 37/92, the Direct Broadcasting Resolution of 1982. The Resolution was approved by majority vote both in COPUOS and in the General Assembly.[102]

However, since almost all the states whose practice it might affect either abstained or voted against, it is generally reckoned that this resolution is without significant effect.[103] The resultant realisation (or confirmation) that a GA Resolution is not legislation, and that, although adopted by a majority vote, it can be rendered ineffective by contrary voting, seems to have strengthened the practice of consensus within COPUOS. However, what does consensus mean, and what is its effect?

Consensus is a form of agreement reached without a vote, but one which does not necessarily imply unanimity among the parties.[104] Abstention from the discussion of a point or absence of dissent does not mean assent; an individualistic or idiosyncratic interpretation of particular language may therefore be passed over un-noticed by, or even concealed

---

101 L.B. Sohn, 'Introduction: United Nations Decision-Making: Confrontation or Consensus?' (1974) 15 *Harv. J. Int. L.* 438–445, cf. his 'Sources of International Law' (1995–1996) 25 *Ga. J. Int. & Comp. L.* 399 at 405; E. Galloway, 'Consensus Decision-making by the United Nations Committee on the Peaceful Uses of Outer Space' (1979) 7 *J. Sp. L.* 3–13. As to consensus in the early days in COPUOS, note the comment by the Chairman: 'Consensus is certainly a very painstaking process, it requires great patience and mutual understanding, particularly in an atmosphere of tension and distrust. However, while taxing the patience of delegates it turned out to be effective', M. Lachs, 'The Treaty on the Principles of the Law of Outer Space 1961–1992' (1992) 39 *Neth. Int. L. Rev.* 291–302 at 293. Cf. Sohn, *supra* n. 10, at 6–10. A less enthusiastic view was expressed by F.B. Shick, 'Space Law and Communication Satellites' (1963) 16 *West. Pol. Quart.* 14–33 at 17–19. See also S.N. Hosenball, 'The United Nations Committee on the Peaceful Uses of Outer Space: Past Accomplishments and Future Challenges' (1979) 7 *J. Sp. L.*, 95–113; Dembling and Arons, *supra* n. 100; M. Benkö, G. Gruber and K.-U. Schrögl, 'The UN COPUOS: Adoption of Principles Relating to the Use of Nuclear Power Sources in Outer Space' (1993) 42 *ZLW* 35–64 at 35–49; C.Q. Christol, 'The Use of a Nuclear Power Source: Nuclear Power Sources in Outer Space' (1981) 30 *ZLW* 47–71; V. Kopal, 'The Use of Nuclear Power Sources in Space: A New Set of UN Principles?' (1991) 19 *J. Sp. L.* 103–122. See also M. Benkö and G. Gruber, 'The UN COPUOS: Adoption of Principles on the Remote Sensing of Earth from Space' (1987) 36 *ZLW* 17–46.

As to 'consensus' generally, see F. Lyall, 'The Role of Consensus in the ITU', in M. Hofmann, ed., *Dispute Settlement in the Area of Space Communication* (Baden-Baden: Nomos, 2015) 33–42; B. Busan, 'Negotiating by Consensus: Developments in Technique at the United Nations Conference on the Law of the Sea' (1981) 75 *AJIL* 324–348; A. D'Amato, 'On Consensus' (1970) 8 *Can. YBIL* 104–122; A.E. Gotleib, 'The Impact of Technology on the Development of Contemporary International Law' (1981-I) 170 *Hague Recueil* 115–329 at 141–146; C.W. Jenks, 'Unanimity, the Veto, Weighted Voting, Special and Simple Majorities and Consensus as Modes of Decision in International Organizations', in *Cambridge Essays in International Law: Essays in Honour of Lord McNair* (London: Stevens, 1965), 48–63 at 55–62. As to consensus in a different area of law, see R. Rosenstock, 'The Declaration of Principles of International Law Concerning Friendly Relations: A Survey' (1971) 65 *AJIL* 713–736.

102 'Principles Governing the Use by States of Artificial Earth Satellites for International Direct Television Broadcasting', *UNGA* 37/92, 1982; analysed CoCoSL III, 1–79. Because consensus had not been achieved within COPUOS, the draft Resolution was not presented to the Assembly by COPUOS but was moved by group of non-aligned states: see Chapter 10 at n. 106.

103 Cf. C.Q. Christol, 'Prospects for an International Regime for Direct Television Broadcasting' (1985) 34 *ICLQ* 149–158; CoCoSL III, 79, para 210.

104 See materials cited in nn. 99 and 101, *supra*.

from, other parties. That said, within COPUOS, a proposed text, whether it be of a draft treaty, resolution or other formal statement, is negotiated and revised until all are willing to accept it and allow it to go forward as the mind of the (Sub-)Committee.

The advantages of consensus are that it facilitates compromise, and in the case of treaties, parties may be more likely to ratify provisions in whose drafting they have participated. While the space-competent nations obviously tend greatly to influence matters in COPUOS, other states play a part in the process. Indeed, some are influential through acting as mediators between divergent positions.[105] More importantly, consensus means that the space-competent nations will not get what they want from COPUOS without the consent of the space-incompetent, while the latter will not get their interests represented and articulated without the consent of the space-competent.

On the other hand, consensus may result in ambiguity, permitting or masking divergent views as to the exact meaning of a phrase, a provision or even a text. Not all participants have equal command of the language being used and may misunderstand or mistake meaning.[106] What are basically rhetorical flourishes can be included to accommodate personalities, and prolonged negotiations can dilute 'the resulting legal product into a catalogue of platitudes'.[107]

Further, as time goes by and more space activities are initiated, compromise between divergent interests becomes difficult: precision collides with vagueness. More and more states are active in space, and with the spread of commercialisation and private enterprise, some want precise language, while others seek to fudge. Other points can be made. Not all members of COPUOS attend.[108] Some send representatives who lack expertise and standing, often lower-ranked diplomats in the local embassy (usually Vienna), for whom space questions are not a priority.[109] Some read statements prepared and sent from home, do not participate usefully in discussion and debate and cannot assent to text without instructions from home, even when 'home' may not be that well informed on the matter at issue in any case. It also has to be said that, unfortunately, such problems are not confined to the non-space-competent nations. Although attendance at COPUOS subcommittees may be better, and some may consider that the Main Committee will just accept what a subcommittee recommends that has contributed, it has to be said that an absence ratio of c. 15–20% is a bad symptom.

---

105 Thus, Austria was important in the arrival at the text of the 'Principles Relating to the Remote Sensing of the Earth from Outer Space', 3 December 1986; UNGA Res. 41/65, as to which see Chapter 12 n. 45 ff.

106 For example, in English the basic meaning of 'to exploit' is 'to make use of'. Some fix on its secondary meaning, which is 'to enrich oneself at the expense of others'. Cf. discussions of Art. XI of the Moon Agreement in Chapter 7.

107 Per R.G. Steinhard, 'Outer Space', in O. Schachter and C.C. Joyner, eds., *United Nations Legal Order* (ASIL, Grotius: Cambridge UP, 1995), vol. 2, 753–787, at 759. Cf. D. Tan, 'Towards a New Regime for the Protection of Outer Space as the "Province of All Mankind"' (2000) 25 *Yale J. Int. L.* 145–194 at 165–166.

108 Chapter I E para 8 of the 2022 COPUOS Report (A/77/20) lists the attendance of 84 of 100 state members at the full committee meetings of 2022. In 2020, attendance was 76 out of 95, and COVID-19 intervened in 2020; in 2019, attendance was 79 out of 92. The absence of members is not good for any committee. However, the Committee always allows input from a number of non-members, which may broaden its thinking. Observers from other bodies are also present, no doubt interacting informally with the delegates.

109 Cf. N. Jasentuliyana, 'Lawmaking in the United Nations', in N. Jasentuliyana, ed., *Space Law – Development and Scope* (Westport and London: Praeger, 1992) 33–44 at 35–36.

Despite all this, COPUOS has been valuable in the development of space law. It has developed principles and the treaties establishing many of the ground rules for the exploration and use of space. However, as space law matures and as what is required tends more and more to be private and domestic law solutions for particular problems, it may be that COPUOS will take a back seat and that substantial developments will be found elsewhere.[110] New springs may break out among the sources of law to deal with new space law problems. We hope COPUOS will cope.[111]

Other Fora

Space law is contributed to in other ways. First, national legislation is increasing. International obligations have had to be accommodated within domestic law, and there, national interests are protected. This body of space-related domestic laws is not entirely self-consistent, and their vagaries affect general space law.[112]

Second is the contribution of international institutions and agencies that engage in or are otherwise involved in space at both the policy- and law-making levels; policy necessarily works out in law. Obviously at its simplest level, the agents include the foreign offices, state departments or their equivalent and government departments that supervise or control technical matters. Precisely how this works depends on the constitutional arrangements of each state: in the US, space is dealt with by entities such as NASA and the Department of Defense, while individual states also enact relevant local laws.[113]

In China, space policy is set by the State Council and complied with by the relevant departments of government.[114] The Indian Space Research Organisation operates under the Indian government.[115] In Russia, much takes place through the Russian State Space Corporation, Roscomsos (www.roscosmos.ru/). In a variety of instances, however, governments and national agencies have come together cooperatively to engage in space activities with consequent effects on space law. Of these, one obvious example is the ESA, which we consider later in this chapter. Again, various national agencies have come together to establish more or less formal international fora to discuss matters of common concern and arrive at compatible procedures and ways of doing things. Such include the Consultative Committee for Space Data Systems (https://public.ccsds.org), the International

---

110 Cf. F. von der Dunk, 'The Undeniably Necessary Cradle – Out of Principle and Ultimately Out of Sense' [Note the italicised capitals] in G. Lafferranderie and D. Crowther, eds., *Outlook on Space Law over the Next 30 Years* (The Hague: Kluwer, 1997) 401–414. *Per contra*: the Working Paper by COPUOS Chairman, 'Future Role and Activities of the Committee on the Peaceful Uses of Outer Space' A/AC.105/L.268, 10 May 2007: www.unoosa.org/pdf/limited/l/AC105_L268E.pdf, which does foresee in effect the contracting out of some matters. Cf. the recognition by COPUOS of the role of the IADC in debris: see Chapter 9.
111 Cf. K-U. Schrogl, 'Is UNCOPUOS Fit for the Future' (2011) 60 *ZLW* 93–102.
112 See UNGA 68/74, 2013, 'Recommendations on national legislation relevant to the peaceful exploration and use of outer space': CoCoSL III 483–603. A. Froehlich and V. Seffinga eds., *National Space Legislation: A Comparative and Evaluative Analysis* (Vienna: Springer, 2018); R.S. Jakhu, *National Regulation of Space Activities* (Vienna: Springer, 2010). See also the UN OOSA compilation of national space legislation: www.unoosa.org/oosa/en/ourwork/spacelaw/nationalspacelaw.html.
113 For US space policy, see Chapter 15 sv. United States. See also S. Mirmina and C. Schenewerk, *International Space Law and Space Laws of the United States* (Cheltenham: Edward Elgar Publishing, 2022) Part III, 86–249.
114 Y. Zhao, *National Space Law in China* (Leiden: Brill, 2015).
115 www.isro.gov.in

Committee on Global Navigation Satellite Systems[116] and the Inter-Agency Space Debris Coordination Committee (www.iadc-home.org.).

Within Europe, many states have set up a space-related government department or agency. In Italy, the Italian Space Agency (www.asi.it) promotes and coordinates space activities, as does the Dutch agency the Netherlands Institute for Space Research (www. sron.nl). In Spain, the Instituto National de Technico Aeroespacial (www.inta.es) acts as the national space agency. The Danish National Space Center (www.space.dtu.dk) is a research centre within the Ministry of Science, Innovation and Technology.

The French Centre Nationale d'Études Spatiales (CNES; https://cnes.fr) was founded in 1961 and plays a coordinating role in space matters.[117] Its powers are extensive, including implementing policy and executing space programmes in collaboration with academic and industrial partners, which may include military and defence programmes. Under a contract with ESA, the CNES's Launch Directorate leads on all matters relating to Ariane launchers and Arianespace, including supervising production, marketing and actual launch. CNES also interacts with ESA as a main channel of French interest in that body.

The German Aerospace Centre (www.dlr.de) is the major entity involved in space activities at the governmental level. Acting under a board of directors, it is basically both a space research centre and Germany's Space Agency. Historically, the West German Deutsche Forschungs-und Versuchsanstalt für Luft-und Raumfahrt was formed in 1969 from three related organisations to act as a testing and research institute. It was renamed the Deutsche Forschungsanstalt für Luft-und Raumfahrt (DLR) in 1989. Following the reunion of East and West Germany, a new single space agency named DARA (Deutsche Agentur fur Raumfahrtangelegenheiten) GmbH brought together the operational space interests of both former governments. Working through four technical directorates and several advisory committees, DARA both formed and executed German space policy, including the overall German space programme. A further reorganisation in 1997 brought together DARA and DLR under the latter's title. DLR now conducts research, encourages industry and administers the German space budget as well as interacting with other national space agencies and industries. It is also active in aerospace matters.

UK responsibilities for space used to be dispersed among many government departments. The British National Space Centre (BNSC), established in 1985, sought to coordinate UK space efforts, with policy aimed at developing commercially attractive activities. BNSC was reorganised in 2005, but the policy aim remained achieving clear scientific and commercial objectives rather than developing technology as an end in itself.[118] That has changed.

On 1 April 2010, the United Kingdom Space Agency (UKSA), an executive agency sponsored by the Department for Business, Innovation and Skills, replaced BNSC.[119] UKSA is now responsible for all strategic decisions on the UK civil space programme and cooperates with other departments including the Ministry of Defence, the Foreign and Commonwealth Office and the Civil Aviation Authority (CAA). In 2014, a national space

---

116 See www.unoosa.org/oosa/en/ourwork/icg/icg.html and *infra* Chapter 11.
117 Loi Française no. 61–1382 du 19 Décembre 1961 (1) Instituant un Centre National D'Études Spatiales.
118 Cf. *UK Space Strategy: 2003–2006 and beyond* (BNSC, 2003); *UK Space Strategy: 2008–2012 and beyond* (BNSC, 2008).
119 www.gov.uk/government/organisations/uk-space-agency

security policy was published.[120] UK space legislation was reorganised in 2018, and the current national space security document was published in 2021.[121]

Although technically a UK space licence is granted by a Secretary of State, in fact, UKSA now deals with licensing UK space activities outside of the UK under the 1986 Outer Space Act for activities outside of the UK, while the CAA deals with domestic activities under the 2018 Space Industry Act.[122] The other main UK government department of direct relevance for space is the Office of Communications (Ofcom; www.ofcom.org.uk) established by the Office of Communications Act 2002, with functions and powers set out in the Communications Act 2003. Ofcom deals with all questions of radio – essential virtually all space activities – and is the notifying administrative agency to the ITU for UK frequency assignments.[123]

The European Space Agency

All the European agencies and states cooperate in the programmes of the ESA, with which the Canadian Space Agency has a cooperation agreement.[124] The ESA is a major actor in space exploration and use.[125] It also participates in forming space law through the internal procedures that it has evolved, through the negotiation of international agreements (e.g. the Space Station agreements[126]) and through its implementation of international space practices. As its title indicates, it is an international organisation.

Immediately after the Second World War, some European states had separate programmes in rocketry and other technologies. Thus UK efforts to develop in rocketry produced the Blue Streak and Black Knight programmes, which were not particularly

---

120 National Space Security Policy, 2014, UKSA/13.1292: www.gov.uk/government/uploads/system/uploads/attachment_data/file/307648/National_Space_Security_Policy.pdf.
121 National Space Strategy (UK Gov. September 2021): https://assets.publishing.service.gov.uk/government/uploads/system/uploads/attachment_data/file/1034313/national-space-strategy.pdf. See also Chapter 15, The Military Use of Outer Space.
122 F. Lyall, 'United Kingdom Space Law' (2022) *ZLW* 216–223.
123 On radio matters, see Chapter 11 Global Navigation Satellite Systems.
124 The Canada–European Space Agency: Agreement on Cooperation (1979) 18 *ILM* 332–336, was renewed and extended, most recently by Can. TS 2019/27: www.treaty-accord.gc.ca/text-texte.aspx?lcid=1033&id=105577&t=637952712985556211. A number of other 'Arrangements' exist for Canadian/ESA cooperation in specific programmes, beginning with the Arrangement for Cooperation in the Conduct of Remote-Sensing Programs between the Canada Centre for Remote Sensing and the European Space Agency, 1977 (1978) 17 *ILM* 107–109. The current list comprises Can. T.S. 2012/26 as to Telecommunications Systems, 2012/27 as to Earth Observation, 2012/28 as to the space exploration programme 'Aurora', 2012/29 as to the Life and Physical Sciences and Applications in Space, 2012/30 as to Global Monitoring for Environment and Security, 2012/31 as to General Support Technology and 2012/32 as to Transportation and Human Exploration Preparatory Activities.
125 J. Wheeler, 'Europe' (2023) 4 *The Space Law Review*: https://thelawreviews.co.uk/title/the-space-law-review/europe; M. Ferrazzani and A. Soucek, 'Experiences from and Prospects for the ESA Convention' (2015) 64 *ZLW* 288–309; G. Lafferranderie, *European Space Agency* (The Hague: Kluwer, 2005); K. Madders, *A New Force at a New Frontier* (Cambridge: Cambridge UP, 1997); *The Implementation of the ESA Convention – Lessons from the Past*, ECSL, ed. (Dordrecht: Nijhoff, 1994); S. Hobe et al., eds., 'Legal Aspects of the Future Institutional Relationship between the European Union and the European Space Agency', Proceedings of a Workshop, Project 2001, Brussels 5–6 December 2002 (Cologne: Cologne Institute, 2003). See also *infra* n. 135.
126 See Chapter 4 Space Stations.

successful.[127] By the late 1950s, it was clear that cooperation within Europe was necessary to match the financial, technical and intellectual resources of the USSR and US.[128] Europe did not want to be left behind.

Therefore, in the early 1960s, Europe was instrumental in the creation of INTELSAT as an international endeavour, protecting its nascent space industries,[129] but steps had already been taken to bring European space activities together. In 1960, the Council of Europe[130] recommended creating a European agency to promote the peaceful uses of outer space and to develop and build a space vehicle.[131] To that end, a European Preparatory Commission on Space Research (COPERS) was set up in 1960.[132]

COPERS discussed whether a single European agency should bring forward all European space efforts but decided that launches should be dealt with by a separate organisation, in part because not all European states were as interested in launches as in space technology. Therefore, in 1962, the Convention for the Establishing of a European Organisation for the Development and Construction of Space Vehicle Launchers (ELDO) was adopted,[133] followed by a Convention for the Establishment of a European Space Research Organisation (ESRO), with slightly different parties.[134] However, the ESRO experience was not happy. In due course it was appreciated that having two European 'space' organisations was not useful, so in 1975 ESRO and ELDO were fused to form the ESA by the Convention for the Establishment of a European Space Agency,[135] the new organisation working informally for some years before the Convention actually came into force. Beyond the initial members, accession depends on all existing members agreeing (Art. XXII).[136] A member state can denounce the Convention, although its financial dues

---

127 C.N. Hill, *A Vertical Empire: The History of the UK Rocket and Space Programme, 1950–1971* (London: World Scientific Publishing, 2001); C.H. Martin, *De Havilland Blue Streak* (London: BIS, 2002, 2015).

128 Mid-wifed by UNESCO, the European Organisation for Nuclear Research at Geneva is another example of such cooperation. See https://home.cern/about.

129 See Chapter 10 Satellite Communications.

130 Council of Europe, www.coe.int/en/web/portal/home. A.H. Robertson, *The Council of Europe* (London: Sweet and Maxwell, 1956); *Forty Years of Cultural Cooperation at the Council of Europe, 1954–94* (Brussels: Council of Europe, 1997).

131 Council of Europe Recommendation 251, 24 September 1960.

132 Agreement setting up a Preparatory Commission to study the possibilities of European Collaboration in the Field of Space Research, 1961 UKTS 60, Cmnd. 1425; 10 *Eur. YB.* 111–115, extended by First Protocol, 1962–3 Cmnd. 2091; Second Protocol, 1962–3, Cmnd. 2122; Third Protocol, 1963–4, Cmnd. 2173; Fourth Protocol, 1963–4, Cmnd. 2350.

133 Convention for the Establishing of a European Organisation for the Development and Construction of Space Vehicle Launchers, 1962, 507 UNTS 177; 1964 UKTS 30, Cmnd 2391; 1964 ATS 6. The initial parties were Australia, Belgium, France, West Germany, Italy, The Netherlands and the UK. Australia was a member so that its launch facilities at Woomera could be used (cf. Chapter 11, n. 31).

134 Convention for the Establishment of a European Space Research Organisation, 14 June 1962, 528 UNTS 33; 1964 UKTS 56, Cmnd 2489; 10 *Eur. YB.* 115; 1965 4 ILM 306–320. Initially there were eleven parties: Belgium, Denmark, France, West Germany, Ireland, Italy, The Netherlands, Spain, Sweden, Switzerland and the UK. Ferrazzani and Souček, *supra* n. 125, at 291 n. 10, note that Ireland was the only founding member not a member of ESRO and ELDO, the prior organisations.

135 Convention for the Establishment of a European Space Agency, 1297 UNTS 161, 187; 1981 UKTS 30, Cmnd 8200; 1975 14 ILM 855–908, text at 864–908; 23 *Eur. YB.* 825. M.G. Bourely, 'Le nouveau cadre de la coopération spatiale européene: L'Agence spatiale européene' (1975) 29 *Rev. fr. de droit aérien* 233–67; R.F. von Preushen, 'The European Space Agency' (1978) 27 *ICLQ* 46–60. See also n. 125 *supra*.

136 The initial membership is listed *supra* n. 134. As of 2022, ESA has twenty-two member states and a number of associate members: www.iafastro.org/membership/all-members/european-space-agency-esa.

remain exigible for the period until the denunciation takes effect (Art. XIV). ESA may be dissolved by agreement of its members, and it 'shall be dissolved' if its membership drops to less than five (Art. XXV).

The purpose of ESA is to promote European space research, technology and applications (Art. II). This involves cooperation and internationalisation between national space programmes. To that end, members are obliged to notify ESA of their plans for civil space activity and to cooperate with other members within the agency's framework, although not to the exclusion of cooperation with non-ESA members (Annex IV).

ESA itself has operational competence (Art. V). With respect to ESA activities themselves, due regard is given to distributing procurement and other contracts, establishments, facilities, etc. to reflect contribution to ESA activities (Arts VII and VIII and Annex V). Collaboration with space and other agencies is legislatively allowed and in practice encouraged (Art. XIV). The exchange of information and data between the Agency and all member states is to be facilitated (Art. III), as is the exchange of personnel (Art. IV). Technical data and inventions that are the property of the Agency are disclosed to all members and may be used by them free of charge (Art. III.4).

The ESA structure comprises the Council and a Directorate under a Director General (Art. X). The Council is composed of all members, meeting as required at either delegate or minister level (Art. XI.1–2).[137] It adopts policy and approves activities and budgets (Art. XI). ESA activities divide into mandatory activities in which all parties take part and optional activities where a member state may formally declare itself non-participant (Art. V).[138] The Director General is appointed for a defined term by a two-thirds majority of the Council and may be removed.

Assisted by technical and other staff, the Director General is the chief executive officer of the Agency as well as its legal representative[139] and is responsible for implementing Council programmes and running the various ESA establishments (Art. XII). The responsibilities of the Director General and staff are exclusively international, and they neither seek nor receive instructions from states or agencies other than ESA. States undertake not to seek to influence staff in the discharge of their duties (Art. XII.4). ESA and its mandatory programmes are financed by its members in three-yearly tranches in accordance with a scale relating to national income for the previous three years, although no member is required to pay more than 25% of the total (Arts. I.3, XIII and Annex II). Optional programmes are financed similarly by their participant members (Art. XIII and Annex III). There is provision for dispute settlement by arbitration (Art. XVII).

Although other European collaborative agencies pursue their own space interests,[140] ESA is the main European intergovernmental organisation engaged in space activities.[141]

---

html#:~:text=ESA%20has%2022%20Member%20States%3A%20Austria%2C%20Belgium%2C%20 the,Kingdom.%20Latvia%2C%20Lithuania%20and%20Slovenia%20are%20Associate%20Members.

137 An ESA member that fails in its obligations may have its membership terminated by a two-thirds vote of all member states (Art. XVIII). However, its liability for any unpaid dues or contributions remains (Art. XXIV).
138 A member non-participant in an optional activity has no vote in decisions as to that activity (Art. XI.6.a). A member in arrears on its contributions loses its vote until the default is remedied (Art. XI.6.b).
139 ESA has legal personality (Art. XV), and its staff have international status (Annex I). A Headquarters Agreement with France has been concluded (Art. I.4 and Annex I).
140 K. Suzuki, *Policy Logics and Institutions of European Space Collaboration* (Aldershot: Ashgate, 2003).
141 For current activities, see the ESA portal: www.esa.int/esaCP/index.html.

However, European space policy is affected and now to a degree determined by the European Union.[142] The original European Economic Community (EEC) was primarily a commercially oriented institution. The expanded EU now serves many more purposes, and EU members are space oriented.[143] However, as the EEC does not itself engage in space activities, we have decided to deal with the EU's space aspect separately in Chapter 14 along with other state implementations of space law and policy.

European Union

In 2003, a White Paper on European Space Policy was published,[144] and a framework agreement was drafted between the then European Community and the ESA; it entered into force in 2004 as the first step towards a formal EU stance on space that involved creating a Space Council.[145] These steps were followed by a council resolution on space policy of 2007 aimed at the better coordination of space activities between the ESA, the EU and their member states.[146] The process continued through the amendment of the EU basic documents by the Lisbon Treaty of 2009 to include space competence as an EU function.[147] Subsequent developments have general and commercial aspects, so we will consider them in the discussion of the European Union in Chapter 14.

In 2016, a Space Strategy for Europe was adopted, and matters are being taken forward; we await developments. Much will depend on whether, or how far, the EU institutions and the EU member states positively interact within the specific space interests of the latter.[148] We must also note that since our previous edition, the UK has withdrawn from the European Union.[149]

142 There are many weighty volumes on the EU.
143 Cf. I. Marboe, 'European Union as a New Actor in Outer Space', CoCoSL III 601–602; L.J. Smith and I. Baumann, eds., *Contracting for Space: Contract Practice in the European Space Sector* (Farnham: Ashgate, 2011).
144 *Space: A New European Frontier for an Expanding Union: An Action Plan for Implementing the European Space Policy*, European Commission COM (2003) 673; cf. European Commission, Green Paper, European Space Policy, COM (2003) 17: http://esamultimedia.esa.int/docs/space-green-paper_en.pdf. See also Chapter 14, Europe and the European Union.
145 Consultation on 'Common Guidelines' for the signing of the Framework Agreement between EC and ESA, EU Council, RECH 152, 12858/03. The Space Council members comprise all EU and ESA Member and Cooperating States.
146 N. Peter, 'The EU's Emergent Space Diplomacy' (2007) 23 *Space Policy* 97–107. Information archived to February 2015: http://ec.europa.eu/enterprise/space/index_en.html. Annual conferences are held on European space policy. See also the European Space Policy Institute (*supra* at n. 68).
147 Treaty of Lisbon amending [the EU Treaties], 2702 UNTS 3; 2010 UKTS 7, Cm 7901; 2007 EC Scr. 13, Cm 7294. See *Consolidated Texts of the EU Treaties as Amended by the Treaty of Lisbon*, UKSP Cm 7310, Art. 189: www.gov.uk/government/uploads/system/uploads/attachment_data/file/228848/7310.pdf and *A Comparative Table of the Current EC and EU Treaties as Amended by the Treaty of Lisbon*, Cm 7311: www.gov.uk/government/uploads/system/uploads/attachment_data/file/228835/7311.pdf. Cf. I. Marboe, 'European Union as a New Actor in Outer Space', CoCoSL III 601–602.
148 'Space Strategy for Europe', Communication from the Commission: https://eur-lex.europa.eu/legal-content/EN/TXT/PDF/?uri=CELEX:52016DC0705&from=EN. See also 'A new Space Strategy for Europe': https://ec.europa.eu/commission/presscorner/detail/en/AC_16_3888. F. Mazurelle, J. Wouters and W. Thiebaut, 'The Evolution of European Space Governance: Policy, Legal and Institutional Implications' (2009) 6 *Int. Org. L. Rev.* 155–189; F.G. von der Dunk, 'The EU Space Competence as Per the Treaty of Lisbon: Sea Change or Empty Shell?' (2011) 54 *Proc. IISL* 382–392.
149 UK withdrawal from the EU may financially affect what the EU can afford to do. It has detached the UK from the EU regulations and procedures in relation to space. It will have no effect on UK membership of

United States

The views and practices of the US heavily influence and interact with space law, although the rise of other major space-competent states means that influence may wane. US space policy is set by the President and has obvious implications for space law.[150] President Kennedy's setting of the goal of getting to the moon and back by the end of the 1960s was, of course, a major impetus to technical development.[151] Since then, various presidential and congressional commissions have influenced space policy and therefore law.[152]

Within the US government, responsibilities at the federal level depend on the nature and impact of the space technology involved.[153] Treaties go through the appropriate procedures of negotiation, ratification and implementation and usually involve the State Department. Naturally, the Defense Department and the military authorities are heavily engaged in space matters.[154] Additionally, in that most satellites require radio for their

---

ESA, though ESA may be financially affected indirectly by the effect of Brexit on the EU. In addition, the UK may find that its companies have difficulty attracting procurement contracts for Copernicus and other programmes where EU requirements are relevant.

150 For progression, see Chapter 15 United States. At the time of this writing, President Biden has not changed the US policy statement of 2020 (Trump): 'National Space Policy of the United States, 2020' (https://trumpwhitehouse.archives.gov/wp-content/uploads/2020/12/National-Space-Policy.pdf). See also 'National Space Policy of the United States of America, 2010' (Obama): https://obamawhitehouse.archives.gov/sites/default/files/national_space_policy_6-28-10.pdf; G.S. Robinson, 'The 2010 United States National Space Policy' (2010) 59 *ZLW* 534–550: 'US National Space Policy 2006' (Bush) (unclassified): https://obamawhitehouse.archives.gov/sites/default/files/microsites/ostp/national-space-policy-2006.pdf, summarised at (2007) 101 *AJIL* 204. G.S. Robinson, 'The U.S. National Space Policy: Pushing the Limits of Space Treaties?' (2007) 56 *ZLW* 45–49, with declassified text at 49–57; 'US Space Policy 1996': www.fas.org/spp/military/docops/national/nstc-8.htm, or http://history.nasa.gov/appf2.pdf. A tabular comparison of the 1996 and 2006 policy documents is at www.stimson.org/?SN=WS200610101122. Cf. T. Barnett, 'United States National Space Policy: 2006 & 2010' (2011) 23 *Fla. J. Int. L.* 277–291. For the Carter Policy of 1978, see W.D. Reed and R.W. Norris, 'Military Use of the Space Shuttle' (1980) 13 *Akron L. Rev.* 665–88 at 673–674.

　　Resolving issues as to US national space policy is the remit of the National Science and Technology Council. Cf. N.C. Goldman, *Space Policy: An Introduction* (Ames: Iowa State UP, 1992); R. Cargill Hall, 'The Origins of US Space Policy: Eisenhower, Open Skies and Freedom of Space', in J.M. Logsdon, et al., eds., *Exploring the Unknown: Selected Documents in the History of the US Civil Space Program* (NASA SP-4407, 1995) 213–229.

151 President J.F. Kennedy, *Special Message to Congress on Urgent National Needs*, 25 May 1961, *Public Papers of the President: John F. Kennedy* (US GPO, 1961) 403–405, or his Address at Rice University on 12 September 1962: www.jfklibrary.org/Historical+Resources/Archives/Reference+Desk/Speeches/JFK/003POF03SpaceEffort09121962.htm. It has to be said that going to the moon in the 1960s had been foreseen as possible by various scientists – see Staff Report, H. Doc. 115, 1959 (*supra* n. 15) at 3–5, with accompanying testimonies. However, see G. DeGroot, *Dark Side of the Moon* (London: Jonathan Cape, 2006) as to the background and arguable futility of the first endeavour.

152 For instance, see *A Journey to Inspire: Report of the Presidential Commission on Implementation of United States Space Exploration Policy* (the Aldridge Commission) 2004 (USGPO 2004: ISBN 0-16-073075-9): www.hq.nasa.gov/office/pao/History/aldridge_commission_report_june2004.pdf; the *Report of the Commission on the Future of the United State Aerospace Industry*, 2002 (USGPO, 2002): www.hq.nasa.gov/office/pao/History/AeroCommissionFinalReport.pdf; and the *Report of the Advisory Committee On the Future of the U.S. Space Program* (the Augustine Commission) 1990 (USGPO, 1991): www.hq.nasa.gov/office/pao/History/augustine/racfup1.htm.

153 The various US space policy documents, *supra* n. 150, give an indication of the many departments involved.

154 D.R. Terrill, Jr., *The Air Force Role in Developing International Outer Space Law* (Maxwell AFB, AL: Air UP, 1999; UP of the Pacific, 2004): http://aupress.maxwell.af.mil/Books/Terrill/terrill.pdf; H.C. Dethloff, *Suddenly, Tomorrow Came: A History of the Johnson Space Center 1957–1990* (The NASA History Series:

functioning, the US Federal Communications Commission (FCC) is active both in licensing and in international negotiations such as the various ITU conferences.[155] Licensing space activities is mainly the responsibility of the Federal Aviation Administration, part of the Department of Transportation.[156] The commerce, environmental and transportation agencies have other obvious space interests.[157] However, the US agency with which 'space' is most clearly associated in the public mind is the National Aeronautics and Space Administration, NASA.[158] The extensive citation of NASA materials in our later pages demonstrates its importance.

NASA SP-4307, 1993); A.J. Dunar and S.P. Waring, *Power to Explore – History of Marshall Space Flight Center 1960–1990* (Washington: USGPO, 2000).

155 See the FCC website: www.fcc.gov. The FCC operates under the Communications Act 1934 as amended. Cf. M.D. Paglin, ed., *A Legislative History of the Communications Act of 1934* (New York: Oxford UP, 1989).

156 For FAA history, see www.faa.gov/about/history/brief%5Fhistory/. An example of FAA regulation that may be relevant (or imitated) worldwide is the various provisions in 14 CFR §§ 401, 415, 435, 440 and 460 that were amended to implement 'Human Space Flight Requirements for Crew and Space Flight Participants: Final Rule' (2006) 71 *Fed. Reg.* 75616–75645. See *infra* Chapter 5.

157 See also Chapter 15, United States.

158 J.C. Cooper, 'Memorandum on the "National Aeronautics and Space Act of 1958"' (1958) 25 *J. Air L. & Comm.* 247–252 (text of Act at 253–64); S.N. Hosenball, 'NASA and the Practice of Space Law' (1985) 13 *J. Sp. L.* 1–7. The original Act and its current incarnation are respectively available at https://history.nasa.gov/spaceact.html and www.nasa.gov/offices/ogc/about/space_act1.html. Cf. *Legislative Origins of the National Aeronautics and Space Act of 1958* (NASA History Series, Monographs in Aerospace History no. 8, 1998): https://history.nasa.gov/45thann/images/legorgns.pdf; R. Handberg, *Reinventing NASA: Human Spaceflight, Bureaucracy, and Politics* (Westport: Praeger, 2003). See https://history.nasa.gov for an extensive list of other materials.

2

SOURCES OF SPACE LAW

Space law has many varied constituents. It has elements of both public and private international law, and it manifests within national legal systems as they cope with the problems of space within their jurisdictions and as they implement relevant international law. In addition, there is now a large body of hybrid public/private arrangements and other relationships – some trans-border – between space-active entities. In this, space law is not unique; international law is coping with similar interactions in many different circumstances.[1] The sources of the 'space law' we will consider are, however, a prime example. We treat of these elements *seriatim* in general before taking up particular issues in the chapters that follow.

Sources

A source of law is where you look while determining the law on a particular matter. Within a national legal system the basic sources are legislation, its interpretation and the concepts developed in and by common law where the constitution permits that to happen. As Lord Diplock said in a different connection, law 'is a maze and not a motorway'.[2] The discussion and process of legislation during its enactment, in the explanations by judges of their decisions based on that legislation or on common law, in its implementation by government, and the comments and debate of publicists of one type or another, all help to clarify the law, indicate its desirable development and identify *lacunae* and other problems. The international legal system is similar.[3]

---

1 E.B. Weiss, 'The Rise or the Fall of International Law?' (2000–2001) 69 *Fordham L. Rev.* 346–372.
2 Per J. Diplock, *Morris* v *C.W. Martin and Sons Ltd*, [1966] 1 QB 716 at 730, [1965] 2 All ER 755 at 784.
3 G. Fitzmaurice, 'The Law and Procedure of the International Court of Justice, 1954–9. General Principles and Sources of International Law' [1959] 35 BYIL 183–231; C. Parry, *The Sources and Evidences of International Law* (Manchester: Manchester UP, 1965); H. Thirlway, *The Sources of International Law*, 2nd ed. (Oxford: Oxford UP, 2019); L.B. Sohn, 'Sources of International Law' (1995–1996) 25 *Ga. J. Int. & Comp. L.* 399–406; G.M. Danilenko, *Law – Making in the International Community* (Dordrecht: Nijhoff, 1992); V.D. Degan, *Sources of International Law* (Leiden: Brill, 1997); R.Y. Jennings, 'The Internal Judicial Practice of the International Court of Justice' (1988) *BYIL* 31–47; M. Mendelson, 'The International Court of Justice and the Sources of International Law', in V. Lowe and M. Fitzmaurice, *Fifty Years of the International Court*

DOI: 10.4324/9781003496502-2

The literature on space law, both national and international, is considerable, if of variable quality. Books are appearing, and many collections of chapters by various hands usefully focus on particular areas. Some early material remains foundational; some is obsolete.[4] Some journalism, and even law review or colloquia articles, is not always well-founded in fact or science.

Some writers, vociferous in their conclusions, appear to lack knowledge of legal principle or existing law. Some contributions are simple propaganda and amount to 'result-oriented jurisprudence'. The reference to publicists in Art. 38.1.d of the Statute of the International Court of Justice is to the 'teachings of the most highly qualified publicists', a three-word restriction which it is well to recall.[5] The core of well-considered, well-sourced, cogent writing is surrounded by a penumbra of inadequate and faulty material, but which is of itself a testimony to the vitality of the space effort. The problem to be faced is the disciplining of unthinking entrepreneurial enthusiasm by cogent law.

Another problem of space law literature is that analysis is not always well-executed. While it is true that much law is a matter of rights and duties, a broader analysis of legal relations can reveal hidden depths and divergences. Issues often are not as simple as they can seem if we only speak of 'rights' and 'duties'. Here the insights of W.N. Hohfeld are helpful.[6] Legal relationships do consist *inter alia* of rights and duties, but these are not straightforward opposites.

The simplistic assertion of a 'right', which is then taken to imply a 'duty', may mask a complexity of relationships. Fundamentally, all legal relationships are bilateral and should be analysed as such. In a given relationship, one side has four possibilities: a 'right or claim', a 'privilege or liberty', a 'power' or an 'immunity'. A 'right' is matched by 'no right' on the other side, 'privilege' by 'duty', 'power' by 'disability' and 'immunity' by 'liability'. For Hohfeld, these four relationships are jural opposites. There are also jural correlatives, each being present if the other exists: 'right' and 'duty', 'privilege' and 'no right', 'power' and 'liability' and 'immunity' and 'disability'. Such analysis can be useful in analysing what we are usually content to lump together as the rights and duties of 'space law'.

of Justice: Essays in Honour of Sir Robert Jennings (Cambridge: Cambridge UP, 1996) 63–89 (Part II of this book contains six articles on the sources of international law). See also *infra* n. 31. Contrast F. Pollock, 'The Sources of International Law' (1902) 18 *L.Q.R.* 418–429 or (1902) 2 *Col. L. Rev.* 511–524.

4 *'The Law of Outer Space': Report to the National Aeronautics and Space Administration*, Project Reporters, N. de B. Katzenbach and L. Lipson (Washington: American Bar Foundation, 1960) (*Legal Problems Symposium*, 779–983); S.H. Lay and H.J. Taubenfeld, *The Law Relating to Activities of Man in Space: An American Bar Foundation Study* (Chicago University Press, 1970); M.S. McDougal, H.J. Lasswell and I.A. Vlasic, *Law and Public Order in Space* (New Haven: Yale UP, 1963), A.G. Haley, *Space Law and Government* (New York: Appleton-Century-Crofts, 1963); C.W. Jenks, *Space Law* (London: Stevens; New York: Praeger, 1965); A.S. Primadov, *International Space Law* (Moscow: Progress Publishers, 1976).

5 Cf. M. Peil, 'Scholarly Writings as a Source of Law: A Survey of the Use of Doctrine by the International Court of Justice' (2012) 1 *Cam. J. Int. & Comp. L.* 136–161.

6 W.N. Hohfeld, 'Some Fundamental Legal Conceptions as Applied in Judicial Reasoning' (1913–1914) 23 *Yale L.J.* 16; 'Fundamental Legal Conceptions as Applied in Judicial Reasoning (1916–1917) 26 *Yale L.J.* 710; cf. his 'Faulty Analysis in Easement and License Cases' (1917–18) 27 *Yale L.J.* 66: W.N. Hohfeld, *Fundamental Legal Conceptions as Applied in Judicial Reasoning*, W.W. Cook, ed. (New Haven: Yale UP, 1964) or D. Campbell and P. Thomas, eds. (Aldershot: Ashgate, 2001). See also P. Schlag, 'How to Do Things with Hohfeld' (2015) 78 *Law & Cont. Probs.* 185–234; W.W. Cook, 'Hohfeld's Contributions to the Science of Law' (1919) 28 *Yale L.J.* 721; A. Kocourek, *Jural Relations* (Indianapolis: Bobbs-Merril, 1928, 1973). For Hohfeld in space law, see K.A. Baca, 'Property Rights in Outer Space' (1993) 58 *J. Air Law & Comm.* 1041–1085 at 1048 ff.

Domestic Space Law

Much practical space law develops within the varied legal systems of the world, particularly those of space-active states.[7] This has three main aspects: the response of the legal system through the setting up of new structures and procedures to deal with space, the application of existing rules of the domestic legal system to space matériel and the implementation of international agreements within the state. As much of the space effort is privatised and commercial entrepreneurs have become involved, the response of municipal/domestic law is of increasing importance.

One obvious area of municipal law that may be involved in dealing with questions of space is contracts. A contract contains the rights and obligations agreed between the parties, subject to any constraints imposed by the governing legal system on grounds of public policy. But the 'law of contract' is not a universal: national systems differ in detail. Similarly, other areas of law such as tort (delict), and the procedures for the settlement of legal dispute can have application to space.

Such areas of law already have a settled array of concepts. However, developing fields of application such as space might require new ideas or the modification of known concepts.[8] Then, what is agreed on in those contracts, determined by courts in response to delict/tort, necessary legislation and other emergent practices, results in new concepts and fresh analyses of known rights, duties and remedies. These come to be the governing law of the field.

For instance, the maritime law of today was largely the creation of English merchants and shippers and their lawyers as they coped with the spread of the English merchant fleet. English courts were willing to take jurisdiction in disputes arising from maritime contracts and disputes irrespective of the locality of their origin.[9] To some degree, US law plays a similar role in the development of general world space law.[10] For instance, the notion of

---

7 A. Froehlich and V. Seffinga, eds., *National Space Legislation: A Comparative and Evaluative Analysis* (Vienna: Springer, 2018); R.S. Jakhu, *National Regulation of Space Activities* (Dordrecht: Springer, 2010); I. Marboe, 'National Space Law', in F. von der Dunk with F. Tronchetti, eds., *Handbook of Space Law* (Cheltenham: Edward Elgar, 2015) 127–204. See also 'Recommendations on National Legislation Relevant to the Peaceful Exploration and Use of Outer Space' UNGA Res. 68/74, 2013; CoCoSL III 483–603. See also International Law Association, 'Draft Model Law for National Space Legislation and Explanatory Notes' (2012) 75 *Int. L. Ass'n Rep.* 307–314; S. Hobe, 'The ILA Model Law for National Space Legislation' (2013) 62 *ZLW* 81–96.

  UN OOSA has a listing of national space legislation, sometimes with relevant links: www.unoosa.org/oosa/en/ourwork/spacelaw/nationalspacelaw/index.html. Much US domestic space law is in Title 51 of the US Code (www.archives.gov/federal-register/cfr; the OOSA US entry shows space law elsewhere in the Code).

8 Cf. L.J. Smith and I. Baumann, eds., *Contracting for Space* (Farnham: Ashgate, 2011).

9 London courts still hear maritime cases which have no connection with the UK other than that the contract involved specifies English law as its governing law because over the years, the English courts became recognised as expert in a complex field. The concepts they worked out that defined rights and duties in maritime commerce are known and trusted.

10 F. Lyall, 'Space Law: What Law or Which Law?' (1992) 34 *Proc. IISL* 240–243. Cf. S. Eigenbrodt, 'Out to Launch: Private Remedies for Outer Space Claims' (1989) 55 *J. Air L. & Comm.* 185–222; P.L. Meredith and G.S. Robinson, *Space Law: A Case Study for the Practitioner. Implementing a Telecommunications Satellite Business Concept* (Dordrecht: Martinus Nijhoff, 1992). Despite developments since its publication, and although written from a US point of view, the Meredith book provides good insight into the complexity of space business and the various legal obstacles involved. For US cases to its date, see S. Gorove, *Cases on Space Law: Texts, Comments and References* (Oxford: University of Mississippi: *J. Sp. Law*, 1996) and 'The Growth of Space Law through the Cases' (1996) 24 *J. Sp. Law* 1–21. Cf. C.Q. Christol, 'Persistence Pays Off:

'cross-waivers' in procurement and launch contracts is an intriguing development originating in the US.[11] Again, the hearings, procedures, requirements and orders of the US Federal Communications Commission make law for those that require its approval, not only for US nationals.[12] However, the point must also be made that in questions of private law, there is no general 'US law'. Instead there are the laws of the several US states, which may differ in detail.[13]

That said, the precise meaning of particular contractual terms when applied to space is being worked out in the domestic courts of various countries, not only the US. The space insurance business is refining ideas as to when risk passes, what constitutes a mission failure and the like. Below the official levels of law and the determination of disputes, concepts are honed and polished as differences are settled between parties without recourse to judicial or arbitral procedures, but with a consequent effect on the language of later agreements.[14] The problem for an academic lawyer/author such as the writers is that many space contracts, disputes and settlements are subject to commercial confidentiality and cannot be examined by independent observers. Those framing and agreeing space-relevant contracts and settling all sorts of space disputes may be developing concepts and particular 'space' meanings for familiar terms we are at present unaware of.

The private international rules of a legal system are also important for those working in space law. Well-drawn contracts should contain a clause agreeing that the governing legal system will govern the interpretation of the contract and the forum for the settlement of any dispute. Those advising on space law may therefore have to be aware of or take

---

The Case of Hughes Aircraft Company v. U.S.A., 1979–1999' (1999) 42 *Proc. IISL* 199–207; B.L. Smith, 'Recent Developments in Patents for Outer Space' (1999) 42 *Proc. IISL* 190–198; S. Eigenbrodt, 'Out to Launch: Private Remedies for Outer Space Claims' (1989) 55 *J. Air L & Comm.* 185–222; R. Trinder, 'Recent Developments in Space Law Litigation' (1991) 5 *Georgetown J. Law &Tech.* 45–62. See also the cases listed at: www.esa.int/SPECIALS/ECSL/SEMT9MMKPZD_0.html.

11 P.B. Larsen, 'Cross-Waivers of Liability' (1992) 35 *Proc. IISL* 91–96; P.L. Meredith, 'Risk Allocation Provisions in Commercial Launch Contracts' (1991) 34 *Proc. IISL* 264–273; M. Schaefer, 'The Need for Federal Preemption and International Negotiations Regarding Liability Caps and Waivers of Liability in the U.S. Commercial Space Industry' (2015) 33 *Berkeley J. Int. L.* 223–273. Cf. G. Carminati, 'French National Space Legislation: A Brief Parcours of a Long History' (2014) 36 *Houston J. Int. L.* 1–18 at 15.

   Cross-waivers can operate on an interstate basis as well. See Chapter 4 Space Stations and cf. the 'Agreement between the USA and Japan concerning Cross-Waiver of Liability for Cooperation in the Exploration and Use of Space for Peaceful Purposes, Exchange of Notes' (1995): www.jaxa.jp/library/space_law/chapter_4/4-2-2-12_e.html.

12 Lyall, *supra* n. 10. S. Ospina, 'International Satellite Telecommunications: An Assessment of their Past and Future', in K.-H. Böckstiegel, ed., *'Project 2001' – Legal Framework for the Commercial Use of Outer Space* (Cologne: Carl Heymanns, 2002) 283–303, at 301.

13 But note the US Uniform Commercial Code, discussed more fully in Chapter 13. See J.J. White and R.S. Summers, *Uniform Commercial Code* (St Paul: West Publishing, 1989); *The Portable Universal Commercial Code*, 2nd ed. (Washington: American Bar Association, 1997).

14 In 'Spacecraft Failure-related Litigation in the United States: Many Failures but Few Suits' (1996) 38 *Proc. IISL* 22–25, P.L. Meredith summarises instances through the date of its writing. She shows that often at the end of a dispute, settlement leads to the 'law' not being fully argued to a final determination. For instance, one celebrated case, *Martin Marietta v. INTELSAT* (1991) 763 F. Supp. 1327 (1993) 991 F. 2d. 94, is actually unsatisfactory because it was settled between the parties and has left on the law reports puzzling (and in the opinion of some, erroneous) views as to the concept of gross negligence and how it should affect a contractual dispute. Cf. R. Sadowski, 'Insuring Commercial Space Travel' (2012) *ZLW* 79–94 at 90; K.B. Watson, 'Have the Courts Grounded the Space Law Industry? Reciprocal Waivers and the Commercial Space Launch Act' (1998) 39 *Jurimetrics* 45–58. See *supra* n. 11, and the next paragraph.

informed advice as to the particular law of many different jurisdictions. The important case, *Martin Marietta* v. *INTELSAT* (1991) 763 F. Supp. 1327; (1993) 991 F. 2d 94, was decided under the law of Maryland.[15] The SPOT contract for the supply of remote-sensing data made it subject to the jurisdiction of the Commercial Court of Toulouse, France. How many are familiar with the detail of the laws of Maryland or of French commercial law?

Attempts to harmonise the law are therefore important, not only in the field of space law. The efforts of UNCITRAL, the WTO and the European Union towards harmonisation can affect the development of space law. In 2001, the International Institute for the Unification of Private Law produced the Convention on International Interests in Mobile Equipment. Its Protocol on Space Assets, adopted in 2012, may be a significant step forward in financing space endeavours.[16] Other space-relevant 'harmonisation' occurs almost without being noticed. For instance, the European Union adopts its own space policy.[17] The rules and procedures of the International Telecommunication Union (ITU) as to the allocation of radio frequencies, the registration of assigned frequencies and orbits, the work of coordination to avoid harmful interference, the standard setting, and the regular meetings of its study groups, conferences and assemblies make all else possible as they are implemented within states.[18] The informal cooperation and effective harmonisation brought about through other agencies are also important.

The implementation of an international agreement within a particular state's domestic law is governed by the constitutional law of that state. As a general proposition, in international law a state may not plead defects or particularities of its constitutional machinery to avoid international obligation. Whether a duly ratified treaty or other international agreement forms part of the law of a state differs from country to country; some require the participation of the legislature, in whole or in part. For example, Art. II.2 of the US Constitution requires the 'advice and consent' of two thirds of the Senate for the ratification of an international treaty, but a duly ratified treaty is then part of US law.[19]

---

15 Cf. *supra* nn. 10 and 14. The 991 F. 2d 94 opinion is a later amended version of 978 F. 2d 140.

16 Convention on International Interests in Mobile Equipment, Cape Town, 2001: 2037 UNTS 341; 2014 UK Misc. Ser. 1, Cm 8786; US Sen. T. Doc. 108–110. The Space Assets Protocol of 2012 is not yet in force. See 'The Space Protocol, 2012', in Chapter 14.

17 See http://ec.europa.eu/growth/sectors/space/index_en.htm

18 See Chapter 8.

19 In US law, an international treaty is a major international agreement. An executive agreement (which outsiders might also classify as a treaty) can be made by the President, duly authorised by an existing treaty or statute to obligate the USA. It binds without the requirement of Senate consent. However, note the question of whether a treaty is self-executing within the US use of the concept. In *Medellin* v *Texas* (2008) 552 US 491, 128 S. Ct 1346, 170 L. Ed. 2d 190, the US Supreme Court held that the federal executive could not intervene in a state matter even if US international obligations were involved through the ICJ decision in *Avena and Other Mexican Nationals (Mexico v. USA)* 2004 ICJ Rep. 12. Fifty-one Mexicans had been convicted and sentenced in the USA, but they or their consuls had not been informed as required under the Vienna Convention on Consular Relations, 1963 (569 UNTS 261). President Bush issued a memorandum to the effect that state courts should give effect to the ICJ decision, but a majority in the Supreme Court considered that the ICJ Statute was not self-executing and the US President lacked the power to give the treaty internal effect, that power residing with Congress. In June 2008, Mexico asked the ICJ for an interpretation of the 2004 Judgment and requested Provisional Measures. The measures, announced on 16 July, included that any execution should not proceed until the request was dealt with. Medellin was executed on 5 August 2008, the day that further appeals to the US Supreme Court for a writ of habeas corpus and a stay of execution were rejected (171 L. Ed. 2d 833). On 19 January 2009, interpreting its 2004 Judgment, the

In the UK, ratifying a treaty is a matter for the Crown alone, acting on the advice of ministers. A treaty duly ratified by the UK which has come into force invokes the international obligation of the UK, but as a matter of internal law, the ratification of an international agreement does not of itself change UK law.[20] That requires legislative procedures.[21]

The development of national space legislation in various countries is to be welcomed. The golden age of the space treaties, 1967–1979, is now well past. Many new legal issues have since emerged, but a resurgence of general space treaty-making seems unlikely.[22] However, a number of UNGA resolutions have been adopted following their negotiation in COPUOS.[23]

Following UNISPACE III in 1999, OOSA arranged workshops to educate individual countries, governments and legislators on space matters and encouraged the adoption of

---

ICJ found the USA in breach of its international obligations (2009 ICJ 3). Cf. 'Agora: *Medellín*' [2008] 102 *AJIL* 529–72. Other US states complied with the Presidential Memorandum. In another case, Aguilera, the matter was overtaken by a grant of clemency by the Governor of Oklahoma, reducing a death sentence to life imprisonment. Cf. *Case concerning the Vienna Convention on Consular Relations (Paraguay v. US)* 1998 ICJ Rep. 248 (Provisional Measures) (the Breard case: discontinued 1998 ICJ Rep. 426); *Breard v. Greene* 523 US 371; 118 S. Ct. 1352; 140 L. Ed. 2d 529 (Breard was executed in Virginia the same day his case was dismissed); the *LaGrand Case (Germany v. USA)* (2001) ICJ Rep. 466 and *Federal Republic of Germany et al. v. US et al.* (1999) 526 US 111; 119 S. Ct. 1016; 143 L. Ed. 2d 192 (LaGrand was executed in Arizona on the same day his case was dismissed by the US Supreme Court). Note: on 5 April 2005 the USA withdrew from an Optional Protocol that gives the ICJ jurisdiction in applying the Vienna Convention on Diplomatic Relations and the Vienna Convention on Consular Relations. The US considered that it was not appropriate that an international court should be able to reverse a decision of the criminal justice system of a country. Cf. *Leal Garcia v Texas* (2011) 564 US 940; (2012) ILM 49–53, where the Supreme Court (Justices Breyer, Ginsburg, Kagan and Sotomayor dissenting) refused a stay of execution to see whether Congress would enact domestic legislation on such matters. Leal Garcia was subsequently executed.

J. Quigly, 'The United States' Withdrawal from International Court of Justice Jurisdiction in Consular Cases: Reasons and Consequences' (2009) 19 *Duke J. Comp. & Int. L.* 263–305; M. Surdokas, 'International Law for American Courts: Why the "American Law for American Courts" Movement is a Violation of the United States Constitution and Universal Human Rights' (2013–2014) 2 *U. Balt. J. Int. L.* 103–126; C. Smith, 'At the Intersection of National Interests and International Law: Why American Interests Should Assume the Right of Way' (2013–2014) 2 *U. Balt. J. Int. L.* 191–220; D.P. Stewart, 'Introductory Note to the US Supreme Court: Garcia v. Texas' (2012) 51 *ILM* 44–48; S. Babcock, 'The Limits of International Law: Efforts to Enforce Rulings of the International Court of Justice in U.S. Death Penalty Cases' (2012) 62 *Syracuse L. Rev.* 183–198; J.R. Broughton, 'Federalism, Harm and the Politics of Leal Garcia v. Texas' (2012) 62 *Syracuse L. Rev.* 199–208; D. Sloss, 'Legislating Human Rights: The Case for Federal Legislation to Facilitate Domestic Judicial Application of International Human Rights Treaties' (2012) 35 *Fordham Int. L.J.* 445–487.

20 With the exception of a treaty of peace, which has immediate internal effect in the UK. See F. Lyall, *British Law* (Baden-Baden: Nomos, 2004) 78–79, 104. Cf. *R. (on the application of Miller and another) v. Secretary of State for Exiting the European Union* [2017] UKSC 5.

21 F. Lyall, 'United Kingdom Space Law' (2022) 71 *ZLW* 215–223.

22 Bullet point 7 of Sec. 2 of the 2006 Bush revision of US National Space Policy stated that the USA would 'oppose the development of new legal regimes or other restrictions that seek to prohibit or limit US access to or use of space' (2007) XXXII AASL 475–486: http://fas.org/irp/offdocs/nspd/space.pdf. The Obama Space Policy of 2010 does not contain such an expression: https://obamawhitehouse.archives.gov/sites/default/files/national_space_policy_6-28-10.pdf. Bullet point 6 of the Principles section of the Trump Space Policy of 2020 states the US 'will seek to deter, counter and defeat threats . . . hostile to the national interests of the United States and its allies': https://trumpwhitehouse.archives.gov/wp-content/uploads/2020/12/National-Space-Policy.pdf. That said, a space treaty that lacks US acceptance would have limited relevance. Cf. R. Byerly, ed., *Space Policy Reconsidered* (Boulder: Westview, 1989). On the Obama Space Policy see T. Barnet, 'United States National Space Policy, 2006 & 2010' (2011) 23 *Fla. J. Int. L.* 277–291.

23 CoCoSL III, *passim.* See references elsewhere throughout this book.

national space legislation. Since our last edition, this informative and educative undertaking has been continued and diversified to encompass other UN bodies, to much benefit. Now better informed, countries lacking national legislation have come to understand that states that have relevant national provisions exert more influence than they do over the launch and space services markets. They therefore have been motivated to adopt their own national legislation, as the OOSA National Space Law Collection tabulates.[24] The increasing private commercial uses of outer space are thus becoming regulated in detail by national provisions.

We hope that these newly engaged states not only implement both multilateral and bilateral international law but specifically institute laws so that what is provided is consistent with other international laws. Such domestic legislation can regulate more intensively and extensively than do the space law treaties. Space law in general can therefore be rendered more certain by the intelligent adoption of appropriate national provisions.[25]

Memoranda of Understanding (MOUs)

In recent decades, a practice has arisen whereby parties, whether states, state agencies, companies or individuals, do not conclude formal contracts but rather enter into memoranda of understanding (MOUs). As a matter of law, there is no generally agreed-on definition of an MOU; a web search for 'memorandum of understanding' can produce a large number of hits. Some are examples and some are attempts to define the terms. However, the definitions are varied and even contradictory.

An MOU is more formal than a 'gentleman's agreement' but less than a contract. It may, but need not, precede a contract. It is certainly a record (but not necessarily an exhaustive one) of what the parties intend. In a mutual enterprise, the MOU is often what the parties set down as their respective commitments and expectations. It may include financial provisions, but the obligations enunciated cannot be founded on as a matter of law. In itself it can be a form of 'soft law'.[26] However, irrespective of how analysts choose to anatomise it and suggest its phylogeny, the MOU has become an integral tool in the elaboration of rights and duties, privileges and immunities, in international space activities.

MOUs were extensively used between parties during the construction and use of the International Space Station.[27] They were also used for the introduction and operation of Global Mobile Personal Communications by Satellite (GMPCS). Signatories to the arrangement implementing the GMPCS MOU of 2003 now accept systems registered with the ITU and allow their operation within their territories.[28] So MOUs do not fit

---

24 See UN OOSA, 'National Space Law Collection' supra n. 7.

25 Cf. UNGA Res. 68/74 of 11 December 2013, 'Resolution on national legislation relevant to the peaceful exploration and use of outer space'. On which see CoCoSL III, 483–603; T.C. Brisibe, 'An Introduction to the UN COPUOS Recommendations on National Legislation Relevant to the Peaceful Exploration and Use of Outer Space' (2013) 62 *ZLW* 728–739. See also C. Brunner and E. Walter, eds., *National Space Law: Development in Europe – Challenges for Small Countries* (Vienna: Böhlau, 2008) (in German); R. Jakhu, ed., *National Legislation of Space Activities* (Dordrecht: Springer, 2010); F.G. von der Dunk, ed., *National Space Legislation in Europe* (Leiden: Brill, 2011).

26 *Infra* 'Soft Law'.

27 See Chapter 4 Space Stations.

28 Global Mobile Personal Communications by Satellite, Arrangements of 2003. See ITU Doc. 11, 7 June 2003: www.itu.int/osg/gmpcs/. International coordination and arrangements are also arrived at in COPUOS

neatly within the traditional analyses of 'law', but they are important in space activities. Their major problem comes when parties take different views as to the extent to which a MOU binds.[29]

Working Arrangements, Informal Standards, Recommendations, Resolutions and Procedures

The outputs of a number of less formal structures and arrangements have relevance for space activities, and hence indirectly, for space law. One such is the Consultative Committee for Space Data Systems (CCSDS), established in 1982 (http://public.ccsds.org). Bringing together the major space agencies for mutual support, CCSDS develops agreed-upon space data-handling systems, sets standards for inter-operability and contributes to reducing both development costs and time. Intellectual property notwithstanding, the wheel does not have to be constantly re-invented. An International Space Exploration Coordination Group of space agencies (www.globalspaceexploration.org) founded in 2007 meets regularly to discuss matters of common interest in the exploration of space and, as the name implies, coordinate their vision for, and activities in space.

Separately the Interagency Operations Advisory Group (www.ioag.org), established in 2000, meets quarterly. Its eight members at present comprise ESA, NASA and the Canadian, French, German, Italian, Japanese and UK space agencies, with the Australian, Chinese, South Korean, Russian, South African and UAE equivalents having observer status. Its remit includes *inter alia* the coordination of space communications policy, high-level procedures, technical interfaces, matters related to interoperability and space communications.

Another body, the Space Frequency Coordination Group (SFCG) (www.sfcgonline. org) formed in 1980, has a much broader membership representing the radio frequency managers of thirty-three space agencies and eleven observers; it provides a forum for discussing matters of mutual interest, particularly in the management and effective use of space-radio frequencies. The SFCG publishes its resolutions and recommendations on its website. These are not legally binding and depend on their voluntary acceptance and implementation by space agencies. Finally, another important field is covered by the Inter-Agency Space Debris Coordination Committee (IADC) (www.iadc-online.org) which, created in 1981, works to mitigate space debris. The IADC work was the basis of the UN Guidelines approved in 2007, but compliance remains a matter for individual space agencies and is not formal international law.[30]

---

committees and subcommittees such as the International Committee on GNSS and the GNSS Service Committee; see P.B. Larsen, 'International Regulation of Global Navigation Satellite Systems' (2015) 80 *J. Air L. & Com.* 365–422. See also Chapter 12.

29 M. Bourely, 'The Legal Hazards of Transatlantic Cooperation in Space' (1990) *Space Policy*, 323–331, discussing differences between the ESA and the USA. In the US, executive agreements have a status similar to that of treaties. Cf. M. Forteau, 'Non-legally Binding International Agreements' Annex I to Report of the ILC, A/77/10, 2022, 351–362.

30 On 22 December 2007, UNGA Res. 62/217 approved the COPUOS endorsement in its Report (A/61/20) of voluntary guidelines for the mitigation of space debris adopted by the Inter-Agency Space Debris Coordination Committee. See CoCoSL III, 605–652, and *infra* Chapter 9, Environmental Regulation – 'Space Debris'. Cf. S. Hobe and J.H. Mey, 'UN Space Debris Mitigation Guidelines' (2009) 58 *ZLW* 388–402; F. Tronchetti, 'The Problem of Space Debris: What Can Lawyers Do About It' (2015) 64 *ZLW* 332–352.

Within the scientific community, the work of many bodies has relevance for space law. Thus the Committee on Space Research (COSPAR) (www.cosparhq.cnes.fr) was established in 1958 in the wake of Sputnik I by the International Council for Science. Governed by its Charter, the highest organ of COSPAR is its Council, on which representatives of national scientific institutions and international scientific unions serve. COSPAR has an extensive publications programme, arranges meetings and colloquia, advises the UN and other international bodies, and is a major forum for the presentation of the results of space research. The remit of the International Astronautical Federation has been outlined in Chapter 1. The search for extraterrestrial intelligence is dealt with in Chapter 16.

Finally in this section is the legally ambiguous status of the ITU resolutions and recommendations. These, considered more fully in Chapter 8, can vary in bindingness, ranging from binding through strongly recommendatory to suggested.

Public International Space Law

Public international space law is part of ordinary public international law and shares in its sources.[31] Unlike many other areas of international law, space law has had to respond quickly to rapid technical developments.[32] Whether it has always accomplished that task satisfactorily is a question, particularly now as to whether the multilateral space treaties were framed in terms able to encompass later developments.

When those treaties were being adopted, only states, and effectively only two states, were capable of engaging in space activities. Now many states are independently space competent and others are buying launch and other services. Many international organisations and commercial companies now are space active and others have ambitions. The sources of space law and their applicability to what is actually happening in practice are

---

For the 2022 position see the Inter-Agency Space Debris Mitigation Guidelines, IADC–02–01, Revision 1, September 2007, and the IADC Protection Manual, IADC-04-03, Version 7.0, September 2014, and Key Definitions, April 2013, etc. available through www.iadc-online.org/index.cgi?item=docs_pub.

31 H. Thirlway, 1. *The Sources of International Law*, 2nd ed. (Oxford: Oxford UP, 2019), and 2. 'The Sources of International Law', in M.D. Evans, ed., *International Law* (Oxford: Oxford UP, 2014) 91–117. C. Parry, *The Sources and Evidences of International Law* (Manchester: Manchester UP, 1965); L.B. Sohn, 'Sources of International Law' (1995–1996) 25 *Ga. J. Int. & Comp. L.* 399–406; I. Brownlie, *Principles of Public International Law*, 6th ed. (Oxford: Oxford UP, 2003) (new ed. pending) 3–29; R. Jennings and A. Watts, *Oppenheim's International Law*, 9th ed. (London: Longman, 1992) Vol. 1, 22–25, all together with the materials they cite. See also *supra* n. 3.

32 F. Lyall, *Technology, Sovereignty and International Law* (Abingdon: Routledge, 2022); M. Lachs, *The Development and General Trends of International Law in Our Time*, Vol. 169 (Hague: Receuil, 1980–IV); and his 'Thoughts on Science, Technology and World Law' (1992) 86 *AJIL* 673–699 [Lyall/Larsen 3–29]; O. Schachter, 'Scientific Advances and International Law Making' (1967) 55 *Cal. L. Rev.* 423–430; J.L. Charney, 'Technology and International Negotiations' (1982) *AJIL* 78–118; A.E. Gottleib, 'The Impact of Technology on the Development of Contemporary International Law' (1981–I) 170 *Hague Recueil* 115–329; B. Beebe, 'Law's Empire and the Final Frontier: Legalizing the Future in the Early Corpus Juris Spatialis' (1998) 108 *Yale L.J.* 1737–1774; J.W. Dellapenna, 'Law in a Shrinking World: The Interaction of Science and Technology with International Law' (2000) 88 *Ky. L.J.* 809–884; C.B. Picker, 'A View from 40,000 Feet: International Law and the Invisible Hand of Technology' (2001) 23 *Cardozo L. Rev.* 149–219; C.W. Jenks, 'International Law and Activities in Space' (1956) 5 *Int. Law Quart.* 99–114; *Space Law* (London: Stevens, 1965); 'The New Science and the Law of Nations' (1968) 17 *ICLQ* 327–345; 'Orthodoxy and Innovation in the Law of Nations' (1971) 57 *Proc. Brit. Academy* 215–235; and *The Common Law of Mankind* (London: Stevens, 1958).

therefore crucial as the use of space increases. If their applicability is defective, the law will have to change.

Carried through virtually verbatim from its predecessor,[33] Art. 38.1 of the Statute of the International Court of Justice lists sources to which the Court is to look in determining a case.[34]

The Court, whose function is to decide in accordance with international law such disputes as are submitted to it, shall apply:

a. international conventions, whether general or particular, establishing rules expressly recognized by the contesting states;
b. international custom, as evidence of a general practice accepted as law;
c. the general principles of law recognized by civilized nations;
d. subject to the provisions of Article 59, judicial decisions and the teachings of the most highly qualified publicists of the various nations, as subsidiary means for the determination of rules of law.

(Art. 38.1)

Whether that list is closed or whether it may be added to has been a matter of controversy over the decades, but there seems to be an increasing acceptance that the 'sources of international law' may (or should) include elements not there enumerated.[35] Space law is an area in which that may be true.

As far as the subsidiary means referred to in Art. 38.1.d are concerned, a large body of space literature has emerged over the decades. Much of that is composed of discussions of international law, some from the most highly qualified publicists from the various nations. As for 'judicial' decisions, we have a number of decisions by domestic tribunals.[36] So far, we have no decisions on space law by the International Court itself,[37] or published by international arbiters.[38]

---

33 Cf. Art. 38.1 of the Statute for the Permanent Court of International Justice of the League of Nations 1921 6 *LNTS* 391–413. That Statute was authorised by Art. 14 of the Covenant of the League of Nations, 1919, 1919 UKTS 4, Cmd. 153; 1920 ATS 1; M.O. Hudson, *International Legislation* (Washington: Carnegie Endowment, 1931) Vol. I, 1–17. In the ICJ text, the one change from the PCIJ text was the addition (at the suggestion of Chile) of the phrase 'whose function is to decide in accordance with international law such disputes as are submitted to it'. See paras 10 and 14 of a Memorandum by the Secretariat of the ILC, A/CN.4/691, fully cited *infra* n. 50.

34 Note that this sentence says 'list sources'. It does not say 'lists the sources'. Cf. R.S. Jakhu, S. Freeland and K.-W. Chen, 'The Sources of International Space Law: Revisited' (2018) 67 *ZLW* 606–667.

35 See *supra* nn. 3 and 31. L.B. Sohn, ' "Generally Accepted" International Rules' (1986) 61 *Wash. L. Rev.* 1073–1080; M. Lachs, *The Law of Outer Space: An Experience in Contemporary Law-Making* (Leiden: Sijthoff, 1972; reissued 2010).

36 Cf. materials in Gorove, *supra* n. 10. The decisions of NASA, the US Federal Aviation Administration and the US Federal Communications Commission should also be borne in mind.

37 The ICJ could be required to decide on questions of 'space law'.

38 Arbitrations on space disputes have occurred but are not publicly available for reasons of commercial secrecy; this may change. In 2011, the Permanent Court of Arbitration adopted Optional Rules for the Arbitration of Disputes Relating to Outer Space Activities of 2011: https://pca-cpa.org/wp-content/uploads/sites/175/2016/01/Permanent-Court-of-Arbitration-Optional-Rules-for-Arbitration-of-Disputes-Relating-to-Outer-Space-Activities.pdf. See F. Pocar, 'An Introduction to the PCA's Optional Rules for Arbitration of Disputes Relating to Outer Space Activities' (2012) 38 *J, Sp. L.*171–185; Rules at 187–210; S. Hobe, 'The Permanent

General principles of law is a category too indefinite clearly to connect with the detail of space law.[39] Treaty and custom, however, are very relevant. There is also the question of the legal weight or significance of the various UN declarations and resolutions on principles on matters of space law, to which we will turn after dealing with custom.

Space Treaties

Treaties are the major source of international law, as they show the willingness of states ratifying them to be bound by the obligations they contain, to exercise the rights and privileges which they state and implicitly to allow other parties to exercise their correlative or equivalent rights and privileges. The best-known space law treaties are those adopted through the mechanisms of the United Nations: the Treaty on Principles Governing the Activities of States in the Exploration and Use of Outer Space Including the Moon and Other Celestial Bodies, 27 January 1967;[40] the Agreement on the Rescue of Astronauts, the Return of Astronauts and the Return of Objects Launched into Outer Space, 22 April 1968;[41] the Convention on International Liability for Damage Caused by Space Objects, 29 March 1972;[42] the Convention on the Registration of Objects Launched into Outer Space, 12 November 1974;[43] and the Agreement Governing the Activities of States on the Moon and other Celestial Bodies of 5 December 1979.[44] Of these, the Outer Space Treaty of 1967 (OST) is generally accepted as foundational, containing in part at least principles of a generality that have passed into customary law.[45] We will deal with the detail of these treaties in later chapters. Suffice it here to note that as of 1 January 2022, one hundred eighty-four states had signed or ratified one or more of the various treaties that are specifically relevant for space law.[46]

The UN space treaties are the outcomes of compromise, argument and debate. They were birthed through COPUOS, the UN Committee on the Peaceful Uses of Outer

---

Court of Arbitration Adopts Optional Rules for the Arbitration of Disputes Relating to Outer Space Activities' (2012) 61 *ZLW* 1–25.

39 W. Friedmann, 'The Uses of "General Principles" in the Development of International Law' (1963) 57 *AJIL* 279–299; E. Voyiakis, 'Do General Principles Fill "Gaps" in International Law?' (2009) 14 *Austrian Rev. Int. & Eur. L.* 239–256. See also C.C. Jalloh, 'Subsidiary means for the determination of rules of international law' Annex to Report of the ILC, A/76/10, 2021, 210–229.

40 610 UNTS 205; 1968 UKTS 10, Cmnd 3519; 18 UST 2410, TIAS 6347; (1967) 6 ILM 386; [1967] 61 AJIL 644.

41 672 UNTS 119; 1969 UKTS 56, Cmnd 3997; 19 UST 7570, TIAS 6559; (1968) 7 ILM 151; [1969] 63 AJIL 382.

42 961 UNTS 187; 1974 UKTS 16, Cmnd 5551; 24 UST 2389, TIAS 7762; (1971) 10 ILM 965; [1971] 66 AJIL 702.

43 1023 UNTS 15; 1978 UKTS 70, Cmnd 7271; 28 UST 695, TIAS 8480; (1975) 14 ILM 43.

44 1363 UNTS 3; (1979) 18 ILM 1434; UN Doc. A/34/664, Nov. 1979; UN Doc. A/34/20, Annex 2; UN Doc. A/RES/34/68.

45 We discuss the question of custom deriving from treaty in Chapter 3 while dealing with the OST. On the tenth anniversary of the OST in 1977, the UNGA confirmed the importance of the Treaty and expressed itself convinced that it had 'played a positive role in the implementation of the purposes and principles of the Charter of the United Nations and the progressive development of the law of outer space' (UNGA Res. 32/195).

46 Both the IISL and OOSA publish an annual report on the status of the space treaties, including details of signatures and ratifications. See https://iislweb.space/2001-standing-committee-report/ or the annual *Proc. IISL* and www.unoosa.org/oosa/en/ourwork/spacelaw/treaties/status/index.html.

Space, a body which usually proceeds on the basis of consensus.[47] As a result, some of their language is not transparent and does not for easily determining the rights and privileges, duties and obligations they contain. Further, the treaties were adopted when only states and state agencies were exploring outer space.

Now, many commercial space enterprises are engaged in a whole gamut of space activities, including space telecommunications, direct broadcast satellites and privately owned remote-sensing services. Would-be entrepreneurs clamour for property rights on the moon and other celestial bodies. Private launch services are willing to meet the demands of entrepreneurs. Commercial space ports are planned in various places world-wide. Some businesses are even offering space tourism.[48] Such was not in contemplation when the space treaties were formulated.

The UN space treaties are not the sum total of relevant treaty rights and obligations for space law. Many other treaties and international agreements will be referred to in the following pages. It is well, however, to here point to the instruments and outputs of the ITU, particularly the Radio Regulations, as fundamental for all active uses of space.[49] Other treaties are more limited in their effect on space activities, but, as treaties, if relevant they are the first source to look to in determining a question of space law.

Custom

'International custom as evidence of a general practice accepted as law' (ICJ Statute Art. 38.1.b) is the other major formal source of international space law.[50] Custom is traditionally thought of as requiring both state practice and the *opinio iuris sive necessitatis*. The practice need not be wholly uniform, but it must be undertaken in the belief it is binding and required by law as opposed to being merely convenient or mutually beneficial.[51] In the assessment whether an alleged custom exists, recourse may be had to accounts of state practice in digests of international law,[52] the internal memoranda and legal opinions of governments insofar as they are available, official statements of governmental attitudes

---

47 COPUOS and consensus are discussed in Chapter 1.
48 See Chapter 5.
49 The ITU is dealt with in Chapter 8.
50 Custom is considered in the texts cited *supra* n. 31, but see also materials in A. Perreau-Saussine and J. B. Murphy, eds., *The Nature of Customary Law* (Cambridge: Cambridge UP, 2007) Part B, 149–335. Cf. from the Secretariat of the ILC: 'Identification of customary international law. The role of decisions of national courts in the case law of international courts and tribunals of a universal character for the purpose of the determination of customary international law. Memorandum by the Secretariat', ILC 68th Sess. 2016, A/CN.4/691. Cf. also the International Law Association report on the 'Formation of Customary (General) International Law' (2000): www.ila-hq.org/en/committees/index.cfm/cid/30); M.P. Scharf, 'Seizing the "Grotian Moment": Accelerated Formation of Customary International Law in Times of Fundamental Change' (2010) 43 *Cornell Int. L.J.* 439–469; J. Long and Wu Xie, 'The Concept of Long – Term Sustainability of Outer Space Activities as an Emerging Source of International Law' (2021) 45 *J. Sp. L.* 46–110. See 'Identification of customary international law', Chapter V, ILC Report A/73/10, 2018, 117–118 and associated documents. In 2019, by UNGA Res. 73/203, the Assembly approved the ILC conclusions on identifying customary international law. See also our discussion of custom and the OST in Chapter 3 *infra*.
51 But see *infra* n. 57.
52 Cf. M.M. Whiteman, *Digest of International Law* (US State Department, 1962–1973). Accounts of US practice in international law are published in the *AJIL*. The *BYIL* covers UK practice.

and positions by persons qualified to speak for government,[53] and compilations such as the working drafts and discussions of the International Law Commission[54] and, in our area, the *travaux preparatoires* of the space agreements.[55]

Recourse may also be had on occasion to treaties, for it is possible for a treaty established in appropriate terms to form customary international law. This is different from specific treaty provisions, which articulate existing customs. We will discuss this more fully in the next chapter in relation to the Outer Space Treaty itself.

In the arena of space law, it is interesting to see how often the accounts of UN debates and the proceedings of COPUOS and its constituent subcommittees are quoted as indicating practice and *opinio iuris*.[56] But how far these accounts are really just advocacy and how far reportage is obscure. The fact is that space materiél is in flux. Coming to an opinion as to the ambit and application of international custom in relation to space remains difficult.[57] The phenomenon of soft law does not help.[58] There has not been an appropriate case or international arbitration by a highly qualified arbiter that could dissolve many uncertainties as to customary international space law. Many are willing to express their views (including the authors), but judicial clarity would be welcome.[59]

UN Resolutions

Space has a further potential source of law, the UNGA, which as a community of nations has to date promulgated five Declarations of Principles in space matters as well as several Recommendations. What is their standing and effect?

---

53 For example, by state delegations at meetings of COPUOS. It is said that the autobiographies of statesmen may be helpful, *sed quaere*. See also n. 56 *infra*.

54 Annually the ILC produces two volumes of material on matters on its agenda.

55 UN OOSA has made available the *travaux* of the five space treaties: www.unoosa.org/oosa/en/ourwork/spacelaw/treaties/travaux-preparatoires.html.

56 Unedited transcripts of COPUOS meetings are available from OOSA: e.g. www.unoosa.org/oosa/documents-and-resolutions/search.jspx?view=documents&f=oosaDocument.series_s1%3ACOPUOS\%2FT#COPUOS_T566. See also *supra* n. 55.

57 The difficulty is not helped by debate as to the nature of 'custom' in modern international law. See B.D. Lepard, *Customary International Law: A New Theory with Practical Applications* (Cambridge: Cambridge UP, 2011). Cf. also J.L. Goldsmith and E.A. Posner, 'A Theory of Customary International Law' (1999) 66 *U. Chi. L. Rev.* 1113–1171; their 'Understanding the Resemblance Between Modern and Traditional Customary International Law' (2000) 40 *Va. J. Int. L.* 639–672; and their 'Further Thoughts on Customary International Law' (2001–2002) 23 *Mich. J. Int. L.* 191–200, responding to M.A. Chinen, 'Game Theory and Customary International Law: A Response to Professors Goldsmith and Posner' (2001) 23 *Mich. J. Int. L.* 143–190. Cf. E. Voyiakis, 'Customary International Law and the Place of Normative Considerations' (2010) 55 *Am. J. Jurisp.* 163–299; C.A. Bradley and M. Gulati, 'Withdrawing from International Custom' (2010–2011) 120 *Yale L.J.* 202–275; M. Hakimi, 'Making Sense of Customary International Law' (2020) 118 *Mich. L. Rev.* 1487–1538; W.A. Smith, 'Using the Artemis Accords to Build Customary International Law: Vision for U.S.-Centric Good Governance Regime in Outer Space' (2021) 86 *J. Air L. & Comm.* 661–700; H.O. Frandsen, 'Customary International Law as a Vessel for Global Accord: The Case of Customary Rules-of-the-Road for Governing the Orbital Highways of Earth' (2022) 87 *J. Air L. & Comm.* 705–757. See also *infra* Chapter 3, sv. 'Elements of the Outer Space Treaty as Customary Law'.

58 S. Freeland and Y. Zhao, 'Rules of the "Space Road:" How Soft Law Principles Interact with Customary International Law for the Regulation of Space Activities' (2020) 44 *J. Sp. L.* 405–432; Freeland articles *infra* n. 95; P. Martinez, 'The Role of Soft Law in Promoting the Sustainability and Security of Space Activities' (2020) 44 *J. Sp. L.* 522–564. Cf. A.D. Pershing, 'Interpreting the Outer Space Treaty's Non-Appropriation Principle: Customary International Law from 1967 to Today' (2019) 44 *Yale J. Int. L.* 149–178; L.C. Byrd, 'Soft Law in Space: A Legal Framework for Extraterrestrial Mining' (2022) 71 *Emory L. J.* 801–840.

59 That said, we appreciate the views expressed in books, articles and lectures by such ICJ Judges Manfred Lachs, Vladen Vereshchetin, and Abdul Koroma.

The role of UNGA resolutions in public international law is controversial.[60] Certainly they are not legislative instruments that make law, although they may reflect customary law or contribute towards its development. That said, a number of UN Declarations contain interesting and valuable statements that purport to be statements of international law. One notable example is the Universal Declaration of Human Rights of 1948.[61] Another is the 1970 Declaration on Principles of International Law concerning Friendly Relations and Cooperation among States in accordance with the Charter of the United Nations.[62]

However much one would want to see these statements complied with, it has to be recognised that in practice their authority is limited, and their prescriptions are often ignored or remain controversial. Consider also the chequered history of such as UNGA Res. 1803 (XVII) on Permanent Sovereignty over Natural Resources of 1962, and its successor, the Charter of Economic Rights and Duties of States of 1974 (UNGA Res. 3281 (XXIX)). Some see a binding element in a repeated sequence of General Assembly affirmations, but there is a contrary argument that repeated exhortations are simply indicators that the desired practice is not occurring.[63] The ICJ did not take the opportunity to express a view

60 Generally, see O. Schachter, 'United Nations Law' (1994) 88 *AJIL* 1–23; F.B. Sloan, 'The Binding Force of a "Recommendation" of the General Assembly of the United Nations' (1948) 25 *BYIL* 1–33, B. Sloan, 'General Assembly Resolutions Revisited (Forty Years Later)' (1987) 58 *BYIL* 39–130; D.H. Johnson, 'The Effect of Resolutions of the General Assembly of the United Nations' (1955) 32 *BYIL* 97; C.C. Joyner, 'UN General Assembly Resolutions and International Law: Rethinking the Contemporary Dynamics of Norm-Creation' (1981) 11 *Cal. W. Int. L.J.* 445–78; R. Rosenstock, 'The Declaration of Principles of International Law Concerning Friendly Relations: A Survey' (1971) 65 *AJIL* 713–36 at 714–5; H.H. Almond, Jr., 'General Principles of Law-Their Role in the Development of the Law of Outer Space' (1986) 57 *U. Colo. L. Rev.* 871–83; L.F.E. Goldie, 'A Note on Some Diverse Meanings of "The Common Heritage of Mankind"' (1983) 10 *Syracuse J. Int. L. & Com.* 69–112 at 69–91; G. Arangio-Ruiz, 'The Normative Role of the General Assembly of the United Nations and the Declaration of Principles of Friendly Relations' (1972–III) 137 *Hague Recueil* 419–572; J. Castaneda, 'Valeur juridique des resolutions des Nations Unies' (1970 I) 129 *Hague Recueil* 205–332; also his *The Legal Effect of UN Resolutions* (New York: Columbia UP, 1969). Cf. P.C. Szasz, 'General Law-making Processes', in O. Schachter and C.C. Joyner, eds., *United Nations Legal Order* (ASIL: Grotius Publications, 1995), Vol. 1, 35–108; I. Brownlie, *Principles of Public International Law*, 7th ed. (Oxford: Oxford UP, 2008), 15; Thirlway 1, *supra* n. 31, 79–81. See also the International Law Association report on the 'Formation of Customary (General) International Law' (2000), *supra* n. 50, Part V, and Commentary Sections 28–32; and Scharf, *supra* n. 50, at 445–453. See also Lauterpacht, *infra* n. 61.

As to the making of the space declarations and resolutions, see their entries in CoCoSL III. In N. Jasentuliyana, ed., *Space Law: Development and Scope* (New York: Praeger, 1992) see N. Jasentuliyana, 'The Lawmaking Process in the United Nations' 33–44, and V. Kopal, 'Evolution of the Doctrine of Space Law' 17–32; V. Kopal, 'The Role of United Nations Declarations of Principle in the Progressive Development of Space Law' (1988) 16 *J. Sp. L.* 5–20; V. Kopal, 'Origins of Space Law and the Role of the United Nations', in C. Brunner and A. Soucek, *Outer Space in Society, Politics and Law* (Vienna: Springer, 2011) 221–233; F. Pocar, 'The Normative Role of COPUOS', in G. Lafferranderie, ed., *Outlook on Space Law over the Next Thirty Years* (The Hague: Kluwer, 1997) 415–421.

61 Universal Declaration of Human Rights, UNGA Res. 217 (III), 8 December 1948. H. Lauterpacht, 'The Universal Declaration of Human Rights' (1948) 25 *BYIL* 354–381, where the author, citing various views and statements by those involved in its formulation, analyses the legal standing and other weight of Declaration.

62 Declaration on Principles of International Law Concerning Friendly Relations and Cooperation Among States in accordance with the Charter of the United Nations, UNGA Res. 2625/XXV (1970); A/8082: (1970) 9 ILM 1292. Cf. Rosenstock, *supra* n. 60; Arangio-Ruiz, *supra* n. 60. The Declaration was later declared by the ICJ to be declaratory of customary international law: see n. 68 *infra*, second para.

63 S.A. Bleicher, 'The Legal Significance of Re-Citation of General Assembly Resolutions' (1969) 63 *AJIL* 444–478; Arangio-Ruiz, *supra* n. 60 at 476–477 ('the doctrine of repeated shouting') and 482–486.

in the Nicaragua Case of 1986,[64] although as we will see matters were different a decade later.

Notwithstanding the equivocal position of a good many General Assembly resolutions, the space resolutions (or certain of their elements) may in effect be treated as sources of space law either in the future, or, as we are inclined to argue, even now.[65] Every year, the UNGA adopts a Resolution on the annual COPUOS report. Normally, that has limited relevance in the formation of law other than encouraging the Committee in its work, but there are five Resolutions in which the Assembly has adopted a Declaration of Principles on space matters; with one exception, these were adopted without vote and hence are of the highest form of UNGA Resolution: the Declaration of Legal Principles Governing the Activities of States in the Exploration and Use of Outer Space, UNGA Res. 1962 (XVIII) of 1963 ((1964) 3 ILM 157); the Principles Relating to the Remote Sensing of the Earth from Outer Space, UNGA Res. 41/65 of 1986 ((1986) 25 ILM 1331), the Principles Relevant to the Use of Nuclear Power Sources in Outer Space, UNGA Res. 47/68 of 1992; the Declaration on International Cooperation in the Exploration and Use of Outer Space for the Benefit and in the Interest of All States, Taking into Particular Account the Needs of Developing Countries, UNGA Res. 51/122 of 1996. The 1982 Resolution as to Principles Governing the Use by States of Artificial Earth Satellites for International Direct Television Broadcasting, UNGA Res. 37/92 stands alone as a space-relevant Resolution adopted by a majority vote of the Assembly.[66]

---

64 Thirlway 2, *supra* n. 31, at 100 notes that in *Military and Paramilitary Activities in and against Nicaragua (Nicaragua v. United States of America) Merits, Judgement,* 1986 ICJ Rep. 14, the ICJ made reference to General Assembly Resolutions but chose not to characterise these as a source of law, holding the following at para 184: 'The mere fact that States declare their recognition of certain rules is not sufficient for the Court to consider these as part of customary international law and as applicable as such to these States'. While UNGA resolutions might indicate *opinio iuris,* there was no evidence of actual state practice. Thirlway 1, *supra* n. 31, at 79, also notes a similar approach in the Advisory Opinion on the *Legality of the Threat or Use of Nuclear Weapons,* 1996 ICJ 226 at para 73. Had the Court considered General Assembly resolutions a creative source of law independent of custom, it could have taken those opportunities. However, cf. *infra* n. 68: UNGA resolutions do sometimes have a role to play in ICJ decision-making.

65 See n. 60 and A. Terekhov, 'U.N. General Assembly Resolutions and Outer Space Law' (1997) 40 *Proc. IISL* 87–107; C.Q. Christol, 'The United Nations and the Development of International Law-Unanimous Resolutions of the General Assembly Dealing with Outer Space' (1965) 23 *Proc. Inst. of World Affairs,* reprinted in his *Space Law-Past, Present and Future* (Deventer: Kluwer, 1991), 311–328; J.G. Sauveplanne, 'Freedom and Sovereignty in Air and Outer Space' (1965) 12 *Neth. Int. L. Rev.* 242 at 234; D. Göedhuis, 'Reflections on the Evolution of Space Law' (1966) 13 *Neth. Int. L. Rev.* 109–49 at 112–122; famously, B. Cheng, 'United Nations Resolutions on Outer Space: "Instant" International Customary Law?' (1965) 5 *Ind. J. Int. Law* 23, rep. Cheng 125–49; S.M. Schwebel, 'The Effect of Resolutions of the U.N. General Assembly on Customary International Law' (1979) 73 *Proc. ASIL* 301–309; R.R. Baxter, 'Treaties and Custom' (1970–I) 129 *Hague Receuil* 27–105, discussing UNGA Resolutions at 69–74; M.D. Öberg, 'The Legal Effect of Resolutions of the UN Security Council and General Assembly in the Jurisprudence of the ICJ' (2006) 16 *EJIL* 879–906 and cf. his 'The Legal Effects of United Nations Resolutions in the Kosovo Advisory Opinion' (2011) 105 *AJIL* 81–90. See also comments in 1963 I YBILC (Meeting 685 – A/CN.4/685) in discussions as to *ius cogens*: S. Rosenne at 74 (para 12) (UNGA resolutions were not *ius cogens* but could have some effect in forming law); Ago at 75 (para 24) (agrees with Rosenne as to UNGA resolutions); de Luna at 75 (para 25) (UNGA resolutions not a source of international law and hence could not be the source of peremptory rules), G. Tunkin at 76 (para 30) (rejecting the Rosenne view), Yaseen at 76 (para 32) (UNGA resolutions not direct source of law but have an undoubted effect on the international legal order), Bartoš at 77 (para 36) (in general, resolutions have no binding formal authority, except those as to the running of the UN itself). See also *infra* n. 106.

66 See *infra* at n. 71.

Perhaps of lower status though still important are the more recent advisory or horta-
tory UNGA Resolutions. These do not set out formal UN principles but do indicate
desirable lines of conduct. Through 2022, they are UNGA Res. 59/115, 2004, on the
concept of the launching state; 2006 UNGA Res. 62/101, 2006, on registration of space
objects; UNGA Res. 68/74, 2013, which makes recommendations on national legislation
and others. On these lines, we also note the Assembly's 2007 endorsement of the *Space
Debris Mitigation Guidelines of the Committee on the Peaceful Uses of Outer Space* (UNGA
Res. 62/217, paras 26).[67] More recently, UNGA Res. 74/82, 2019, para 2, welcomes
the *Guidelines for the Long-term Sustainability of Outer Space Activities* (2019 COPUOS
Report A/74/20, Annexes I and II).

Account must also be taken of other General Assembly Resolutions that antedate the
adoption of the space law treaties, notably International Cooperation in the Peaceful
Uses of Outer Space, UNGA Res.1721 (XVI) of 20 December 1961, and the same titled
UNGA Res.1802 (XVII) of 19 December 1962. It seems to us that this sequence of reso-
lutions could fall into those of the 'normative character' referred to by the ICJ in the 1996
Advisory Opinion on the Legality of the Threat or Use of Nuclear Weapons. At para 70, the
ICJ stated,

The Court notes that General Assembly resolutions, even if they are not binding, may
sometimes have a normative value. They can, in certain circumstances, provide evidence
important for establishing the existence of a rule or the emergence of an *opinio juris*.
To establish whether this is true of a given General Assembly resolution it is necessary
to look at its content and also the conditions of its adoption; it is also necessary to see
whether an *opinio iuris* exists as to its normative character. Or a series of resolutions may
show the gradual emergence of the *opinio iuris* necessary for a new rule.[68]

---

67 On all of these, see CoCoSL III and references to them where relevant elsewhere in this book.
68 *Legality of the Threat or Use by a State of Nuclear Weapons in Armed Conflict*, Advisory Opinion, 1996 ICJ
Rep. 226 at para 70; (1996) 35 ILM 809. Cf. Thirlway, *supra* n. 65. Contrast this with the view the ICJ
took in the Nicaragua case, *supra* n. 64. Note also a statement by Dean Rusk, the then US Secretary of State
appearing in 1962 before the US Senate Foreign Relations in connection with the then pending communications satellite legislation. Speaking of UNGA Res. 1721 (XVI) he said, 'Although the resolution "commends"
the principles to member states, the United States takes the position that these principles are presently the
law: the unanimous action of the General Assembly in adopting the resolution as action by the governments
of the world assembled, confirms this view' (1962) *Dept. of State Bull.* 318; (1963) 57 *AJIL* 127–128 at 127.
   In *Case Concerning Armed Activities on the Territory of the Congo (Democratic Republic of the Congo v.
Uganda)*, 2005 ICJ Rep. 1 at 56 (para 162), the Court cited UNGA Res. 3341 (XXIX) of 14 December 1974, on the definition of aggression, and UNGA Res. 2625 (XXV) of 24 October 1970, on friendly
relations between states, as being declaratory of customary international law. At para 244, the ICJ also commented that the permanent sovereignty of a state over its natural resources is expressed in UNGA Res. 1803
(XVII) 14 December 1962, UNGA 3201 (S – VI) 1 May 1974 and UNGA Res. 3281 (XXIX) 12 December 1974. In its Advisory Opinion on the *Western Sahara*, 1975 ICJ Rep. 12, paras 54–59, the ICJ cited the
1970 UN Declaration on Friendly Relations and various UNGA resolutions specifically on Western Sahara
as being of value in the development of international law on such matters. UNGA Res. 25/2625 was also
referred to in paras 87–88 of the Advisory Opinion on *The Legal Consequences of the Construction of a Wall
in the Occupied Palestinian Territory*, 2004 ICJ 136, as reflecting customary law prohibiting the acquisition
of territory by use of force. See also observations by the Court in the South-West Africa Advisory Opinion,
*Legal Consequences for States of the Continued Presence of South Africa in Namibia (South – West Africa)
Notwithstanding Security Council Resolution 276 (1970)*, 1971 ICJ 16. Cf. S.M. Schwebel, 'The Effect of
Resolutions of the UN General Assembly on Customary International Law' (1979) 73 *Proc. ASIL* 301–309.

Even should the reader be disinclined to accept the normative character of the space resolutions, it is nonetheless clear that, as Boyle and Chinkin put it, the space-competent states
may safely 'proceed on the assumption that there would be no opposition to activities
conducted in conformity with the principles endorsed by the resolution'.[69]

The space resolutions fall into two groups, those prior to and those after the 1967
Outer Space Treaty. The Preambles of those prior to the OST show a development. For
instance, Resolution 1721 of 1961 'Commends [certain principles] to States for their
guidance in the exploration and use of outer space'. Resolution 1802 of 1962 'believes'
that states should act in conformity with international law in the exploration and use of
outer space and stresses the 'necessity of the progressive development of international law
pertaining to the elaboration of basic legal principles governing the activities of States'
while using and exploring space.

The famous Space Principles Resolution, UNGA Res. 1962 of 1963, is less tentative.[70]
It '[s]olemnly declares' that states 'should be guided' by the principles it contains in their
exploration and use of outer space. The sequence of these resolutions therefore shows a
progression from 'commending' to 'declaring' and 'should be guided'. However, after the
1967 Treaty, the UN space resolutions simply adopt the principles which state or com-
mend COPUOS decisions.

This change in language shows that the UNGA at least considers that it is moving
within a defined area of competence, a matter important when considering the Resolutions
that were adopted without vote. Only the 1982 Resolution on Direct Broadcast Principles
(UNGA Res. 37/92) was adopted by a majority vote, but most of the states that would
be affected by its requirements abstained or voted against it and consequently were categorised as 'persistent objectors'.[71] Many therefore consider the 1982 Resolution to be
without substantive effect, although others believe that some of its elements have value.
However, that the Direct Broadcast Resolution was effectively torpedoed strengthens the
weight attaching to space resolutions adopted without vote when considering them as
evidence as to the emergence of international custom.

The UNGA resolutions adopted prior to the OST have particular common elements
that carry forward into the Treaty. All indicate that the exploration and use of space is to
be governed by international law.[72] Resolutions 1721/1961 and 1962/1963 indicate that
outer space and celestial bodies are free for use by all states,[73] that national appropriation

69 Boyle and Chinkin, *supra* n. 65, at 227; V. Lowe, *International Law* (Oxford: Oxford UP, 2007) 41–2
    accepts the UN space resolutions as formative of law; cf. R.J. Lee, 'Reconciling International Space Law
    with the Commercial Realities of the Twenty-First Century' (2000) 4 *Sing. J. Int. & Comp. L.* 194–251 at
    204–205.

70 For a US view of the negotiation of the Space Principles Resolution of 1963, see *Soviet Space Programs, 1962–
    1965: Organization, Plans, Goals, and International Implications*, Staff Report, Committee on Aeronautical
    and Space Sciences, US Senate, 89th Cong. 2d Sess, December 30, 1966, at 498–509. Since the first edition
    of this book was published, UN OOSA has made available on-line the *travaux préparatoires* of the 1963
    Resolution: www.unoosa.org/oosa/en/ourwork/spacelaw/treaties/travaux-preparatoires/declaration-of-
    legal-principles.html.

71 V. Kopal, 'The Role of United Nations Declarations of Principles in the Progressive Development of Space
    Law' (1988) 16 *J. Sp. Law* 5–20. See CoCoSL III 1–79 on the Direct Broadcasting Resolution and *infra*
    Chapter 10. For the 'persistent objector', see Chapter 3 at n. 81.

72 UNGA Res. 1721/1961, Part A, para 1(a): UNGA Res. 1802/1962, Preamble second para 'Believing';
    UNGA Res. 1962/1963, para 4. Cf. OST, Art. III.

73 UNGA Res. 1721/1961, Part A para 1(b); UNGA Res. 1962/1963, para 2. Cf. OST, Art. I, para 2.

is barred both for outer space and in respect of celestial bodies[74] and that space is to be used for peaceful purposes.[75] Resolution 1721/1961 speaks in its preamble of a belief that 'the exploration and use of outer space should be only for the betterment of mankind and to the benefit of States irrespective of the stage of their economic or scientific development'.

The Preamble of the 1963 Resolution using the same formulation also believes and then 'solemn[ly] declar[es]' that states 'should be' so guided, providing in its very first numbered paragraph that the 'exploration and use of outer space shall be carried on for the benefit and in the interests of all mankind'.[76] Article I para 1 of the OST re-formulates the language of these preambles and that of para 1 of the 1963 Resolution as a legal obligation, the fulfilment of which was to cause dissatisfaction, discussion and a further UNGA Declaration in 1996.[77] Lastly, UNGA Res. 1802/1962 Part I para 3 asked COPUOS to expedite its work on such matters as the basic legal principles that should apply in space, liability for accidents and on rescue and return of astronauts and 'other legal problems'.

Principles as to liability for accidents are dealt with in general terms in para 8 of the 1963 Resolution, with rescue and return appearing in para 9. Importantly, para 5 of that resolution articulates the principle that states are responsible for national activities, including the activities of nationals, and for seeing that such activities comply with international law.[78] All these points were later to appear in the OST, but it would seem they had already been consented to at least in skeletal form by the UN's members.

The UNGA space resolutions adopted subsequent to the OST are of a different character. They are either elaborations of ideas found in the Treaty, or they apply its generalities in particular instances. It would be otiose to go through them *seriatim* other than to make that statement, but one example may be given. The major part of Principle II of the Remote Sensing Principles of 1986 repeats verbatim the requirement of OST Art. II that outer space exploration and use be carried out for the benefit and in the interests of all countries, irrespective of their degree of economic or scientific development.[79]

Otherwise, it suffices to observe that the UNGA, greatly increased in size since 1967, has adopted six formal space resolutions without vote, relating to Remote Sensing (1986, UNGA Res. 41/65), Nuclear Power Sources in Space (1992, UNGA Res. 47/68), Benefit (1997, UNGA Res. 51/122), the Concept of the Launching State (2004, UNGA Res. 59/115), Registering Space Objects (2007, UNGA Res. 62/101) and National

---

74 UNGA Res. 1721/1961, Part A para 1(b); UNGA Res. 1962/1963, para 3. Cf. OST, Art. III.
75 UNGA Res. 1721/1961, Title and Part A, first preambular para 'Recognising' and implication from second, 'Believing'; UNGA Res. 1962/1963, preambular para 'Recalling'. Cf. OST, Art. IV.
76 Emphasis has been added in the preceding sentences to bring out the progress shown by the successive language of 'belief', 'should be' and 'shall'.
77 See the Declaration on International Cooperation in the Exploration and Use of Outer Space for the Benefit and in the Interest of All States, Taking into Particular Account the Needs of Developing Countries, UNGA Res. 51/122, 1996.
78 Such responsibility may also be inferred from the general notions of state responsibility in international law, but here our point is that the principles of responsibility and duty of supervision are set out in both the 1963 Resolution on Principles and the Outer Space Treaty.
79 Principles Relating to the Remote Sensing of the Earth from Outer Space, 3 December 1986; UNGA Res. 41/65. See Chapter 12 Remote Sensing.

Legislation (2013, UNGA Res. 68/74). These (and although it is basically ineffective, even the Direct Broadcasting Resolution of 1981 (UNGA Res. 37/92)) show that the generality of states are willing to lay out principles and rules under which the exploration and use of space should be conducted, and municipal space affairs be arranged.[80] The evidence so far at least is that space-competent states do generally comply with the broad principles expressed in these resolutions and operate within the framework of the general rules of the OST: freedom of access and use, the application of international law, peaceful uses and a ban on territorial claims in space.

It is perverse to ignore these statements by the UN General Assembly and pretend that they are entirely without legal effect. While we would not go so far as to classify them as 'instant customary international law',[81] and with the exception of the 1982 Direct Broadcast Principles, the history of compliance with the UN space resolutions has swiftly elevated each at least into the category of soft law.[82] In fact, as time has gone on, the softness has tended to dissipate: the Remote Sensing Principles date to 1986 and the Nuclear Power Principles to 1992, and since then, states whose activities and practice fall within their compass have been acting within their recommendations. More uncertainty may attach to the effects of the Space Benefits Declaration of 1997, but we note with interest the activity within the ITU directed towards the spread of the benefits of space.[83]

Writing in 1969 of the 1963 Principles Declaration, C.W. Jenks said,

> The cautious will, of course, continue to warn us not to read into the approval of the Declaration by the General Assembly more than is really there, but how much is there depends primarily on how much we wish to be there. When governments make it clear in the deliberations of the General Assembly that they regard a declaration about to be adopted as a statement of international law as it is accepted by the members of the United Nations, it is altogether unseemly for responsible scholars to dismiss it as a statement of intention which has not created any new obligations incumbent on Members of the United Nations.[84]

---

80 The UN resolutions to date are dealt with in CoCoSL III, *passim*.

81 The term comes from the title to Bin Cheng, 'United Nations Resolutions on Outer Space: "Instant" International Customary Law?' (1965) 5 *Indian J. Int. L.* 23 (rep. Cheng, 125–149). In fairness, Cheng does not argue true 'instant' for all UN resolutions, although he indicates that some resolutions that were appropriately worded and adopted unanimously or without vote may show a new emergent *opinio iuris*. However, the arresting title of his article has stuck, perhaps too easily, in the minds of many. Cf. Arangio-Ruiz, *supra* n. 60, at 452–460, 471–486; L.B. Sohn, 'The Law of the Sea: Customary International Law Developments' (1984–1985) 34 *Am. U. L. Rev.* 271–280. In 'The Development of International Law and the Peaceful Uses of Outer Space' (2011) 54 *Proc IISL* 3 at 16, ICJ Judge A.G. Koroma quotes G.J.H. Van Hoof, *Rethinking the Sources of International Law* 1983 at 86, that 'customary law and instantaneousness are irreconcilable' and Weil (cited *supra* n. 92) at 435 to the effect that instant custom is 'no mere acceleration of the custom-formation process, but a veritable revolution in the theory of custom'.
    See also discussion in our Chapter 3 of the possibility of a transition from treaty law to custom.

82 See *infra* at n. 88.

83 See Chapter 8, particularly The Telecommunication Development Sector (ITU-D), and ITU involvement in the World Summit on the Information Society. See also Chapter 10.

84 C.W. Jenks, *A New World of Law? A Study of the Creative Imagination in International Law* (London: Longmans, 1969) 210. However, as Arangio-Ruiz (*supra* n. 60) at 476–479 points out, the practice of states in accordance with a statement is necessary for there to be customary law. See also discussion of custom in Chapter 3.

Manfred Lachs, the president of the International Court of Justice, noting the statements made by delegations during the adoption of the 1963 Principles, wrote similarly:

> Thus, by expressing their will to be bound by the provisions of the document in question, they consented to be bound, and there is no reason why they should not be held to it. For their intention seems to have been clear, the question of form, therefore, ceased to be of the essence.[85]

Decades on from these words, and given the intervening history of compliance with the UN space declarations, the point seems clear.

Maybe some would require a judicial statement for final validation of the matter, and in that case, they may have to wait. Some may prefer to see the space declarations as non-binding instruments similar to a 'Highway Code', where reasons for non-compliance have to be extremely cogent. For others, the development of space law through UN declarations is a clear new source of international law, as may be seen in, for instance, the Space Benefits Declaration or the Remote Sensing Principles as laying down general law.[86] We cannot agree with such a broad approach even to the space resolutions. What can be said is that certain fundamentals contained in and reiterated in successive space resolutions and complied with by states, particularly those whose conduct and practice is most clearly affected, are materials from which custom is formed.[87]

Soft Law[88]

Finally, for completeness, we must say something specifically about soft law.[89] Having developed relatively recently, it is a strange curiosity. As we will shortly discuss, discussion and criticism of soft law usually centre on its alleged failure in precisely the element that 'law' would require: enforceability. However, we suggest a different approach: soft law should be considered a subdivision of the concept of legality, compliance with its prescriptions (if that is not too strong a term to use) giving assurance that what is done (or not done) lies within the parameters of legality. After all, all law has an element of softness in its actual application. To quote from a field rather different from international law,

> The concept of legality requires that the law should be stated in reasonably clear terms. It is important to recognize, however, that absolute certainty is impossible. Every legal concept and every legal rule will inevitably be surrounded by a penumbra of uncertainty.

---

85 M. Lachs, *The Law of Outer Space: An Experience in Contemporary Law-Making* (Leiden: Sijthoff, 1972, 2010), 127–128. (D. Goedhuis, 'Influence of the Conquest of Outer Space on National Sovereignty: Some Observations' (1978) 6 *J. Sp. Law* 37–46 at 40 quotes p. 138 from the differently paged first publication). Attention should also be given to the statement of the then US Secretary of State in 1962, *supra* n. 65.

86 See *infra* Chapter 12.

87 V. Lowe, *International Law* (*supra* n. 68) at 41–42 accepts the UN space resolutions as formative of law.

88 Reference point n. 82 *supra*.

89 Of course there is also the debate whether international law is law or 'law properly so called'. See G.L. Williams, 'International Law and the Controversy Concerning the Word "Law"' (1945) 22 *BYIL* 146–163, who wrote at 163: 'The only intelligent way to deal with a verbal question like that concerning the definition of the word "law" is to give up thinking and arguing about it. By no other means can the controversy be brought to an end.'

In part this is due to the inherent uncertainty of the language in which legal concepts are expressed. More specifically, and perhaps more importantly, legal rules and concepts do not exist in an abstract world of pure ideas; they exist in order to be applied to particular factual situations in the real world, and in the course of that application the concepts or rules may develop to a greater or lesser degree. It is obviously impossible to predict every possible factual situation to which a concept or rule might apply, and thus it is impossible to predict how the concept or rule might be applied in any possible case; some degree of uncertainty is inevitable. The most that can be hoped for is a degree of reasonable clarity.[90]

This feature of the law was also recognized by the European Court of Human Rights in *Sunday Times* v *United Kingdom* (1979–80) 2 EHRR 245, at paragraph 49:

[A] norm cannot be regarded as a 'law' unless it is formulated with sufficient precision to enable the citizen to regulate his conduct: he must be able – if need be with appropriate advice – to foresee, to a degree that is reasonable in the circumstances, the consequences which a given action may entail. Those consequences may not be foreseeable with absolute certainty: experience shows this to be unattainable. Again, whilst certainty is highly desirable, it may bring in its train excessive rigidity and the law must be able to keep pace with changing circumstances. Accordingly, many laws are inevitably couched in terms which, to a greater or lesser extent, are vague and whose interpretation and application are questions of practice.

Soft law shares many of the characteristics just mentioned, but of course, the enforcement of its principles through formal process is lacking. There may be mechanisms and procedures to both develop and articulate its content and review failures in compliance with it, but it cannot be formally enforced. The expression 'soft law' can invest practice with a patina of probity that is misleading as to its legal weight.

That said, however, the term is in common currency and is used to embrace a variety of things ranging from regularised individual practices to informal agreements to more formal guidelines adopted by official bodies. As such, it denotes a disparate rag-bag, but we seem to be stuck with it as a general and fairly useful term. Perhaps it is best thought of as an agglomeration of elements that seek to attract and persuade to action or to refrain from action, but without coercion or other overt pressure.[91] Soft law develops a culture in which some practices are accepted as normal and encouraged while others are not and are thereby discouraged.

---

90 Per Lord Drummond Young in *Ross* v *Lord Advocate* (2016) CSIH 12 at paras 71–72. The case was an appeal against the refusal of the Lord Advocate to issue specific guidance on when someone assisting another to commit suicide would be prosecuted in Scotland. The appeal failed.

91 Cf. J.S. Nye, *Soft Power: The Means to Success in World Politics* (New York: Public Affairs, 2005) his *The Powers to Lead: Soft, Hard and Smart* (New York: Oxford UP, 2008), 'Get Smart: Combining Hard and Soft Power' (2009) 88 *For. Aff.* 160–163, and cf. 'US Power and Strategy After Iraq' (2003) 82 *For. Aff.* 60–73. We note that in discussing the call in UNGA Res. 1721 B (XVI) to voluntarily inform the UN Secretary General of their launch of objects into space, data which he would enter into a publicly available register, CoCoSL II at 239 suggests that the resolution falls into the category of soft law.

Some find the classification soft power or soft law to be an error, even anathema.[92] Others take a different view.[93] While it is true that there is occasionally a muddle in its use, it is present in various fields of law general.[94] For many, it represents a major category of activity in the formation of some new international law.[95] It is found in international environmental law.[96] It is certainly present in space law.[97]

The law of science is directed at explaining phenomena and allows for predicting the consequences of particular sets of circumstances. The law of lawyers also allows prediction but differs in that by legislation or other modes of law-making, consequences can be changed. In space law, soft law can be the gestation-period of law and legal principle – occasionally aborted[98] but often successful. And when it works well, it produces regularity of practice and reliability, a common understanding of the concepts and a mutual acceptance leading to trust.

While 'soft law' remains soft, it does have disadvantages; by definition it is not binding, which makes lawyers uneasy. Its content is dependent on compliance rather than enforcement. Different participants may interpret it differently, leading to a lack of consistency or uniformity of practice.[99] On the other hand, the soft law approach can be useful.[100]

92 P. Weil, 'Towards Relative Normativity in International Law?' (1983) 77 *AJIL* 413–442; K. Raustiala, 'Form and Substance in International Agreements' (2005) 99 *AJIL* 581–614; L. Blutmann, 'In the Trap of a Legal Metaphor: International Soft Law' (2010) 59 *ICLQ* 605–626.

93 B. Sheppard, 'Norm Supercompliance and the Status of Soft Law' (2014) 62 *Buffalo L. Rev.* 787–879. Cf. J.L. Goldsmith and E.A. Posner, 'International Agreements: A Rational Choice Approach' (2003–2004) 44 *Va. J. Int. L.* 113–143.

94 A. di Robilant, 'Genealogies of Soft Law' (2006) 54 *Am. J. Comp. L.* 499–554; cf. J.E. Gerson and E.A. Posner, 'Soft Law: Lessons from Congressional Practice' (2008–2009) 61 *Stan. L. Rev.* 573–628.

95 R.R. Baxter, 'International Law in "Her Infinite Variety"' (1980) 29 *ICLQ* 549–566; S. Freeland, 'The Role of "Soft Law" in Public International Law and Its Relevance to the International Regulation of Outer Space', in Marboe (*infra* n. 97) 9–30; S. Freeland, 'For Better or for Worse? The Use of "Soft Law" within the International Legal Regulation of Outer Space' (2011) XXXVI *AASL* 409–445; P.B. Larsen, 'GNSS Soft Law Standards Are Developing in the United Nations' (2014) 57 *Proc. IISL* 273–284; A. Boyle, 'Soft Law in International Law-Making', in Evans (*supra* n. 31), 118–136; F. Francioni, 'International "Soft Law": A Contemporary Assessment', in Lowe and Fitzmaurice (*supra* n. 3) 167–180. Cf. T.M. Franck, 'Legitimacy in the International System' (1988) 82 *AJIL* 705–759; K.W. Abbot and D. Snidal, 'Hard and Soft Law in International Governance' (2000) 54 *Int. Org.* 421–456. Sohn, *supra* n. 3, points out that advisers to government search many sources: to us, the accumulation of these appear best explained as soft law.

96 N.E. Clark, 'Gauging the Effectiveness of Soft Law in Theory and Practice: A Case Study of the International Charter on Space and Major Disasters' (2018) 43 *Air & Sp. L.* 77–112. Cf. *infra* Chapter 9.

97 I. Marboe, ed., *Soft Law in Outer Space: The Function of Non-Binding Norms in International Space Law* (Vienna: Böhlau Verlag, 2012); F. Tronchetti, 'Soft Law', in C. Brunner and A. Soucek, *Outer Space in Society, Politics and Law* (Vienna: Springer, 2011), 619–637; B. Wessel, 'The Rule of Law in Outer Space: The Effects of Treaties and Nonbinding Agreements on International Space Law' (2012) 35 *Hastings Int. & Comp. L. Rev.*, 289–322; G.M. Goh, 'Softly, Softly Catchee Monkey: Informalism and the Quiet Development of International Space Law' (2009) 87 *Neb. L. Rev.* 725–746; P.J. Blount, 'Renovating Space: The Future of International Space Law' (2012) 40 *Denv. J. Int. L. & Pol.* 515–532; Hobe and Mey, *supra* n. 30; Freeland and Zhao, *supra* n. 58.

98 As in the case of the Direct Broadcast Principles of 1982, UNGS Res. 37/92; CoCoSL III, 1–80. See Chapter 6 Direct Satellite Broadcasting. Cf. also Lyons *infra* n. 99.

99 The UN/IADC guidelines on the mitigation of space debris (*supra* n. 30) are leading space agencies to a uniform approach to such matters. But cf. G.T. Lyons III, 'New Habits and Hard Law: Putting Old Soft Law "Sanctions" and the Space Debris Epidemic Out to Pasture' (2014) 40 *J. Sp. L.* 453–479. Would clearer enforceable rules be better – or achievable?

100 See citations *supra* nn. 93–95.

Ex natura, it is a flexible process that allows for its content to be adapted to new requirements and changing technologies in a way that treaty finds difficult.[101] Eventually in some
areas it could birth international custom.[102]

Again it is quite clear that while treaty making is a matter for states (which may not
always be as well informed as might be desirable), soft law can allow non-state entities, and
particularly those whom it may directly affect, to take part in its formation.[103] While this
can result in special pleading and self-interest, it is nonetheless desirable that in areas of
technical knowledge and swift advance, knowledgeable participants are welcomed.[104] To
be effective, space law has to be made by those who understand the technologies and technicalities that it is to regulate. Soft space law provides a framework for engaging in space
activities which supplements the hard law of the treaties and other formal international
agreements. It is generally reliable, flexible and effective. Doctrinaire concepts of 'law' that
would exclude it from consideration do a disservice.[105] Certainly one can anatomise in
order to understand, but one thereby ends up with a corpse. Space law, whether in formal
hard law or less formal soft law, is a vibrant field.

We conclude that the regularisation of space activities through the self-regulation of
participants in accordance with soft law is the concept at work.[106] In this chapter, we have
covered some of the fora and practices through which soft space law is developing. The
UN space resolutions are other examples, and yet other examples will be found scattered
throughout this book.

---

101 In Chapter 4, we suggest that although the treaties on rescue and return, on liability and on registration
contain provisions for their revision, to re-consider these would be to open a can of worms. As we note,
practice is in fact modifying the way the Registration Convention works. Perhaps this is soft law at work.

102 Cf. J.M. Beard, ' "Soft Law" as an Impediment to the Regulation of Space Activities with Military Implications: A View from the US Congress' (2014) 57 *Proc. IISL* 699–717. Beard noted that some US Congress members viewed the Draft EU Code of Conduct for outer space activities (ICOC) as an illegitimate,
unconstitutional and potentially back-door device intended to create an unsanctioned but legally binding
mechanism for arms control, binding the US through its principles becoming international custom. We
discuss the ICOC in Chapter 15 c. n. 200.

103 The Associate Member category in the ITU is a formal example of non-state participation in the formation
of international law through the elaboration of practices and requirements via the various ITU study groups:
see Chapter 8.

104 Lyall, *supra* n. 32, 202–203.

105 Cf. W. Twining, 'General Jurisprudence' (2007) 15 *U. Miami Int. & Comp. L. Rev.* 1–60 at 32–52.

106 Cf. O. Schachter, 'The Twilight Existence of Nonbinding International Agreements' (1977) 71 *AJIL*
296–304; M. Ferrazzani, 'Soft Law in Space Activities', in G. Lafferranderie, ed., *Outlook on Space Law
over the Next Thirty Years* (The Hague: Kluwer, 1997) 429–447; G. Danilenko, *Lawmaking in the International Community* (Dordrecht: Martinus Nijhoff, 1993) 203–210: A. Boyle and C. Chinkin, *The Making
of International Law* (Oxford: Oxford UP, 2007) 'Soft Law' at 211–229; C. Chinkin, 'The Challenge of
Soft Law: Development and Change in International Law' (1989) 38 *ICLQ* 850–866; D. Tan, 'Towards a
New Regime for the Protection of Outer Space as the "Province of all Mankind" ' (2000) 25 *Yale J. Int. L.*
145–194 at 179–184. See also *supra* n. 65.

3

THE OUTER SPACE TREATY, 1967

The Treaty on Principles Governing the Activities of States in the Exploration Use of Outer Space, including the Moon and Other Celestial Bodies (OST) adopted by the General Assembly of the United Nations on 19 December 1966, and opened for signature on 27 January 1967, entered into force on 10 October 1967.[1] By that date, it had been signed by ninety-three states and ratified by sixteen, a total of one hundred nine out of a then UN membership of one hundred twenty-three, about 88%. As of 2023, it has been ratified by one hundred thirteen states and signed by another twenty-three,[2] a total of one hundred twenty-eight out of a UN membership of one hundred ninety-three, about 66%.

In its annual Resolutions on the Reports of the Committee on the Peaceful Uses of Outer Space (COPUOS), the UN General Assembly regularly exhorts states to sign and ratify the OST and the other space treaties. It is therefore disappointing that the number of states committed either by ratification or signature to this fundamental statement of principles on the exploration and use of space has increased by only nineteen in fifty-five years, a small number given the increase of seventy in UN membership. The proportion of parties or signatories to over-all UN membership is an element to be borne in mind when assessing the importance of the OST. However, it is equally important that arguably no state likely to enter space itself – as opposed to buying service from another – is a non-party.

---

1 Treaty on Principles Governing the Activities of States in the Exploration and Use of Outer Space Including the Moon and Other Celestial Bodies, London, Moscow and Washington, 27 January 1967, 610 UNTS 205; 1968 UKTS 10, Cmnd. 3519; 18 UST 2410, TIAS 6347; (1967) 6 ILM 386; [1967] 61 AJIL 644. For an exhaustive/ting analysis see S. Hobe, B. Schmidt-Tedd, K.-U. Schrögl, eds. (G.M. Goh, asst. ed.) *Cologne Commentary on Space Law*, Vol. I (Cologne: Carl Heymanns Verlag, 2009) (CoCoSL I). See also P.G. Dembling, 'Principles Governing the Activities of States in the Exploration Use of Outer Space, Including the Moon and Other Celestial Bodies' I Manual, 1–51; Cheng, 215–264; Christol, 12–58; and *infra* n. 12.
2 For the IISL and UNOOSA annual reports on the status of the space treaties, including detail of signatures and ratifications, see: https://iislweb.space/2001-standing-committee-report/ (or the annual *Proc. IISL*) and www.unoosa.org/oosa/en/ourwork/spacelaw/treaties/status/index.html.

DOI: 10.4324/9781003496502-3

Some speak of the Outer Space Treaty as 'the Magna Carta of Space'. That sobriquet may betray an ignorance of the detail and history of the Magna Carta of 1215.[3] However, it has become part of the parlance of modern space law, and the OST is certainly 'one of the key developments in the entire realm of international law'.[4] Even though it can be argued that some of the principles it enunciates were already part of international custom, their incorporation in a treaty confirmed their status as between the parties. Further, as we will argue, some principles of the OST may now properly be said to have become customary, and hence binding on all states.

It was important that space activities be the subject of rules, but what these were had to be agreed internationally. It had to be clear whether or not claims to sovereignty in space could be made. Responsibility had to be established for the 'ownership' of space activities at the state level and for the supervision of non-state actors. Liability in the case of damage or devastation had to be established. Astronauts should be rescued. Space objects should be 'returned to sender' or at least 'returnable to sender'. Custom and practice would have taken too long to produce rules of sufficient detail to cope with such matters. The UN space resolutions were insufficient. Something closer to legislation was required.

The OST provides a solid foundation for the development of much of space law. It translates into treaty obligations the basic ideas expressed in those earlier UN space resolutions, and in particular in the Principles Declaration of 1963.[5] The advantage of treaty form is that it removes, or at least substantially diminishes, uncertainty. In the 1960s, there was doubt (which may remain[6]) as to the authority of UN resolutions. League of Nations resolutions had often not been effective, and it had always been made clear that these were without legal force.[7] Incorporating the ideas of the 1963 Declaration and the other space resolutions into a treaty removed doubt.[8]

Another major impetus towards the production of the OST was the likelihood that, following President Kennedy's famous challenge,[9] man would reach the moon in the near

3 Magna Carta provided for rights for the Church, for nobles and for 'free men' (not a large class in 1215), including trial by a jury of one's peers but only if one was 'free'. Most of the text comprises minor provisions. Forgotten for centuries thereafter, its 'fundamental' ideas became influential only some four hundred years later during struggles between Crown and Parliament when it provided a slogan rather than law. A. Arlidge and I. Judge, *Magna Carta Uncovered* (Oxford: Hart, 2014). Cf. British Library: www.bl.uk/treasures/magnacarta/magna.html.

4 A.E. Gotlieb, 'The Impact of Technology on the Development of Contemporary International Law' (1981-I) 170 *Hague Recueil* 115–329 at 311 n. 484. See also D. Göedhuis, 'An Evaluation of the Leading Principles of the Treaty on Outer Space of 27th January 1967' (1968) 15 *Neth. Int. L. Rev.* 17–41; M. Lachs, 'The Treaty on Principles of the Law of Outer Space, 1961–1992' (1992) 39 *Neth. Int. L. Rev.* 291–302.

5 'International Cooperation in the Peaceful Uses of Outer Space', UNGA Res. 1721 (XVI), 20 December 1961; 'International Cooperation in the Peaceful Uses of Outer Space', UNGA Res. 1802 (XVII) 19 December 1962; 'Declaration of Legal Principles Governing the Activities of States in the Exploration and Use of Outer Space', UNGA Res. 1962 (XVIII) 1963, (1964) 3 ILM 157. UN OOSA has made available on-line the *travaux preparatoires* of the 1963 Principles Resolution: www.unoosa.org/oosa/en/ourwork/spacelaw/treaties/travaux-preparatoires/declaration-of-legal-principles.html.

6 See the discussion as to the legal weight or relevance of General Assembly Resolutions in Chapter 2.

7 Some of its declarations were later mirrored by UN General Assembly Resolutions, the 'Universal Declaration of Human Rights', 1948, UNGA Res. 217 (III).

8 J.F. McMahon, 'Legal Aspects of Outer Space: Recent Developments' (1965–66) BYIL 417–432 at 417–419.

9 President Kennedy: 'I believe that this nation should commit itself to achieving the goal, before this decade is out, of landing a man on the Moon and returning him safely to Earth' in 'Special Message on Urgent National Needs to a Joint Session of the US Congress' on 25 May 1961. *Public Papers of the Presidents: John F. Kennedy* (US GPO, 1961), 403–405.

future.[10] A formal legal regime to deal with space was more than desirable. Several hundred satellites had already been launched,[11] a number of lunar probes had been launched and the American Gemini programme was already practising techniques of docking and spacewalk that would be required for a moon landing. Space law had to advance and advance quickly.

Although it builds on the space resolutions that had been argued through in the period 1960–1963, negotiation of the treaty took time.[12] As with the resolutions, much seems to have depended on the personal relationships of the principal negotiators involved, relationships which allowed political posturing to be elided in the general interest.

It is a truism that lawyers prefer to adapt known agreements and law rather than invent something entirely new. One obvious potential model for outer space was the Antarctic Treaty of 1959, relating as it does to activities in a similarly inhospitable location.[13] That treaty, entered into by twelve parties in the wake of the success of the scientific exploration of Antarctica during the International Geophysical Year of 1957, froze the seven territorial sector claims made by Argentina, Australia, Chile, France, New Zealand, Norway and the UK (Art. IV.1).[14]

No acts or activities during its currency were to afford any basis for territorial claims (Art. IV.2). Antarctica was to be open for further scientific exploration (Art. II) but only for peaceful purposes (Art. I). Cooperation and the exchange of personnel and information were provided for (Art. III). Nuclear explosions and the deposit of nuclear waste were prohibited (Art. V). Bases might be established anywhere in Antarctica,[15] and the inspection of bases by other parties to confirm compliance with the treaty provisions was allowed (Art. VII).[16] This agreement as to activities in inhospitable territory provided suitable analogues for the discussions as to a legal regime for outer space.[17]

---

10 While proposing what a space treaty ought to contain, President L.B. Johnson indicated that it was important to ensure that 'our astronauts and those of other countries can freely conduct scientific investigations of the Moon' (1966) 54 *Department of State Bulletin*, 900, 7 May 1966.

11 D.F.S. Portree and J.P. Loftus, Jr., 'Orbital Debris: A Chronology', NASA/TP-1999-208856 1999: https://ntrs.nasa.gov/api/citations/19990041784/downloads/19990041784.pdf.

12 UN OOSA has put the OST *travaux preparatoires* on-line: www.unoosa.org/oosa/en/ourwork/spacelaw/treaties/travaux-preparatoires/outerspacetreaty.html. P.B. Larsen, 'A Sample of Space Law Opinion' (1966) 27 *Ohio State L.J.* 462–478, surveys opinion among leading space law experts immediately prior to the OST.
    P.G. Dembling and D.M. Arons – 1. 'The Evolution of the Outer Space Treaty' (1967) 33 *J. Air L. & Comm.* 419–456 [Lyall/Larsen 151–188] (cf. P.G. Dembling, 'Principles Governing the Activities of States in the Exploration Use of Outer Space, Including the Moon and Other Celestial Bodies', I Manual, 1–51); – 2. their 'Space Law and the United Nations: The Work of the Legal Sub-Committee of the United Nations' Committee on the Peaceful Uses of Outer Space' (1966) 32 *J. Air L. & Comm.* 329–386, continued in – 3. their 'The United Nations Celestial Bodies Convention' (1966) 32 *J. Air L. & Comm.* 535–550; J.F. McMahon, 'Legal Aspects of Outer Space' (1962) 38 *BYIL* 339–399; H.G. Darwin, 'The Outer Space Treaty' (1967) 41 *BYIL* 278; I.A. Vlasic, 'The Space Treaty: A Preliminary Evaluation' (1967) 55 *Cal. L. Rev.* 507–520; B. Cheng, 'Le Traité de 1967 sur l'espace' (1968) *J. de Droit Int.* 532; cf. B. Cheng, 'The 1967 Outer Space Treaty: Thirtieth Anniversary' (1998) 23 *Air & Sp. L.* 156–165. Both Cheng and Christol (*supra* n. 1) cite extensively.

13 The Antarctic Treaty 1959, 402 UNTS 71; 12 UST 795, TIAS 4780; 1960 UKTS 71, Cmnd. 1535; [1960] 54 AJIL 477; (1980) 19 ILM 860–2: www.bas.ac.uk/about/antarctica/the-antarctic-treaty/the-antarctic-treaty-1959/.

14 The other original parties to the Antarctic Treaty were Belgium, Japan, South Africa, USA and USSR. See now the Scientific Committee on Antarctic Research: www.scar.org/antarctic-treaty-system.

15 For the purposes of the treaty Antarctica is the area south of 60° south (Art. VI).

16 On the Antarctic Treaty System see C.G. Joyner and S. K. Chopra, eds., *The Antarctic Legal Regime* (Dordrecht and Boston: Nijhoff, 1988); C.G. Joyner, 'Challenges to the Antarctic Treaty: Looking Back to See Ahead' (2008) 6 *NZ YBIL* 25–62; *Antarctic Treaty System: An Assessment* (National Research Council, National Academies Press, 1986). See also www.bas.ac.uk/.

17 P. Jessup and H.J. Taubenfeld, *Controls for Outer Space and the Antarctic Analogy* (New York: Columbia UP, 1959); H.J. Taubenfeld, 'The Antarctic and Outer Space', in Joyner and Chopra (*supra* n. 16) at 269 ff. See

Another international instrument affording some guidance during the negotiation and drafting of the OST was the Nuclear Test Ban Treaty of 1963,[18] which had entered into force just before the UNGA adopted the 1963 Space Principles Resolution.[19] As its full title indicates, the Nuclear Test Ban Treaty bans nuclear weapon testing *inter alia* in space. Article I speaks simply of the banning of nuclear weapon tests 'in the atmosphere, beyond its limits, including outer space', but the treaty lacks specificity as to where outer space might be. Nonetheless, it provided straw to help make the bricks of the OST. States were already thinking along such lines.

Apart from international agreements, many other materials were germane to the discussions. The US and the USSR produced many suggestions and draft agreements.[20] Specific proposals had been brought forward to COPUOS and its Legal Subcommittee, and, as noted earlier, the UN General Assembly itself had adopted three important resolutions regarding space.[21] All such was grist for the mill. It was also important to have the concurrence of as many countries as possible for the sake of universality of the treaty: a space treaty of limited membership would have been less than useful.

In the UN of 1967, most members did not have space-faring capability, but they were the vast majority of the Assembly. They therefore had a bargaining lever: a universally acceptable treaty would not be adopted without their concurrence. Essentially, these states wanted to preserve their future options for when they became actors in space. In principle, they wanted future rights to use outer space equal to the rights of the then current space powers. They therefore sought and got the principle of equality in the use of outer space that is enshrined particularly in the language of Art. I.[22]

The result was a treaty of seventeen articles adopted by acclamation.[23] It is the base on which the exploration and use of outer space takes place in accordance with legal norms.[24] More particularly, while some of its provisions required (and may still require) elaboration, focus and crystallisation in later agreements, future developments have a good foundation in the 1967 treaty. Certain of its provisions are fundamental.

The Treaty[25]

The OST is a universal treaty, open to all states (Art. XIV.1). At the time of its adoption, only two states were active in space, the USA and the USSR. These, along with the UK,

---

also O.J. Lissitsyn, 'The American Position on Outer Space and Antarctica' (1959) 53 *AJIL* 126–131. Cf. J.E. Faria, 'Draft to an International Covenant for Outer Space – The Treaty of Antarctica as a Prototype' (1960) 3 *Proc. IISL* 122–127.

18 Treaty Banning Nuclear Weapon Tests in the Atmosphere, in Outer Space, and Under Water, Moscow, 1963: 480 UNTS 43; 1964 UKTS 3, Cmnd. 2245; 14 UST 1313, TIAS 5433; 1964 2 ILM 883, text at 889–891.

19 Declaration of Legal Principles Governing the Activities of States in the Exploration and Use of Outer Space, UNGA Res. 1962 (XVIII) of 1963: 1964 3 ILM 157.

20 See the OST *travaux preparatoires* and the other materials cited *supra* n. 12, particularly those of Dembling and Arons.

21 See previous note and *supra* n. 5.

22 On the objectives of developing countries see N. Jasentuliyana, 'Article 1 of the Outer Space Treaty Revisited' (1989) 17 *J. Sp. L.* 129–144. For an analysis of Art. I see S. Hobe, *CoCoSL I*, 25–43.

23 See materials cited *supra* n. 12; J.F. McMahon, 'Legal Aspects of Outer Space: Recent Developments' (1965) 41 *BYIL* 417–439 [Lyall/Larsen 189–202]; H.G. Darwin, 'The Outer Space Treaty' (1967) 41 *BYIL* 278; Cheng, 215–264; Christol, 12–58.

24 The OST is the sole subject of CoCoSL I. We do not cite the detail of its analysis of the treaty.

25 Citation *supra* n. 1.

are its depositaries (Art. XIV.2).[26] Ratification by them along with any other two states was made necessary for its coming into force to ensure that the principal space actors were bound by its terms (Art. XIV.3).[27] Other states are bound as from the date of deposit of their ratifications (Art. XIV.4). The treaty applies to the space activities of individual states, to those of their national entities (Art. VI), to joint state activities and to the activities of international organisations of which a state party to the treaty may be a member (Art. XIII).

Any party may propose amendment of the OST (Art. XV). Any amendment comes into force for accepting parties when they form a majority and thereafter for other states on the date that they accept it (Art. XV). We consider that amendments are undesirable unless all parties accept them simultaneously. As a general proposition, space law would not be well served were divergent versions of the OST to be the law as between a variety of parties. The treaty sets out principles. Their integrity should be preserved, but they must be interpreted flexibly.[28] Parties may withdraw from the OST on one year's notice (Art. XVI). While we hope that no party withdraws from the OST, we believe we can argue that in any case, a withdrawal would not remove a party from those obligations in the OST which have now passed into customary law.

The OST Preamble narrates a variety of concerns as lying behind the decision to agree on the treaty. These include the general common interest in space and in its use for peaceful purposes[29] and belief that that space use should benefit all as well as in the need for mutual understanding and cooperation. In the latter connection, we observe that references to cooperation, consultation and due regard for the interests of other states recur throughout the text (Arts. I para 3, X, XI). Cooperation has, however, proved patchy and encouraged by economic and financial considerations rather than the aspirations expressed in the OST. Even so such considerations are not to be despised.

A welcome development was coherence in the general international approach to space endeavours, with coordinated rather than competitive space activities,[30] for instance the International Space Station.[31] However, we fear that competition, isolation, individuation

---

26 Having states as depositaries of the OST rather than the UN Secretary General allows non-UN members more easily to become parties to the OST. See Dembling and Arons 1, *supra* n. 12, at 454 and Manual I at 33–34.

27 Requiring only five ratifications to come into force is a feature of all five UN Space Treaties: OST Art. XIV.3; ARRA Art. 7.3; Liability Convention Art. XXIV.3; Registration Convention Art. VIII.3; Moon Agreement Art. 19. Only the OST (Art. XIV.2) and ARRA (Art. 7.3) required ratification of the UK, US and USSR.

28 Cf. A. Froehlich, ed., *A Fresh View on the Outer Space Treaty* (ESPI, Vienna: Springer, 2018); G.D. Kyriakopoulos and M. Manoli, eds., *The Space Treaties at Crossroads: Considerations de Lege Ferenda* (Vienna: Springer, 2019); R.S. Jakhu and S. Freeland, 'Vital Artery or Stent Needing Replacement: Global Space Governance System without the Outer Space Treaty' (2018) 61 *Proc. IISL* 505–520; W.A. Smith, 'Using the Artemis Accords to Build Customary International Law: A Vision for a US – Centric Good Governance Regime in Outer Space' (2021) 86 *J. Air L. & Comm.* 661–700. The Artemis Accords will bypass some of the constraints of the OST. See Chapter 7.

29 The OST Preamble notes the condemnation of propaganda likely to cause a threat to peace in UNGA Res. 110 (II), and states that the Parties consider it applies to space. See Chapter 11 – 'Direct Satellite Broadcasting'.

30 Cf. W.A. McDougall, '. . . *the Heavens and the Earth: A Political History of the Space Age* (New York: Basic Books, 1985); G. DeGroot, *Dark Side of the Moon* (London: Jonathan Cape, 2006); J.I. Gabrynowicz, 'Space Law: Its Cold War Origins and Challenges in the Era of Globalization' (2004) 37 *Suffolk U. L. Rev.* 1041–1066.

31 See Chapter 4 – 'Space Stations'.

and the urge to 'win' is increasing.[32] On the other hand, cooperative institutions have been established.

The Consultative Committee for Space Data Systems (CCSDS), set up in 1982 to establish standards for space data and its handling, has contributed greatly to interoperability and has meant that common problems have been given common solutions open to all.[33] *The Global Exploration Strategy: Framework for Coordination* (2007) provided for establishing a formal, voluntary and non-binding international coordination mechanism in which common interests are discussed.[34] This augured well for collaboration and cooperation as space activities develop, although we suspect that national pride could restrict the current efficacy of the mechanism.

After the Preamble, the OST text launches into its catalogue of principles, most of which were foreshadowed in the UNGA Resolution of 1963.[35] We consider that certain of these, particularly Arts. I–III, have now the status of customary as well as of treaty law, and we will elaborate that point at the end of this chapter. The fundamental principles are that international law applies in outer space, that there is freedom in the exploration and use of space and that there is no national sovereignty in space or over celestial bodies; some might add that space is to benefit all. How precisely space can or may benefit all is a matter of contention, and we will come to that, but other matters are clearer. It is interesting to note that the fundamental principles can be expressed tersely, just as fundamental particles are themselves small.

The first fundamental is the place of law. The role or rule of international law in space is a basic principle now contained in Art. I, para 2 and Art. III. This is nothing new. '[I]nternational law including the Charter of the United Nations applies to outer space and celestial bodies' was commended to states for their guidance in the exploration and use of outer space by the General Assembly on 20 December 1961,[36] and that the 'activities of states in the exploration use of outer space shall be carried on in accordance with international law' was part of para 4 of the 1963 Declaration on Space Principles.[37] Its para 2 also speaks of space exploration and use being carried out in accordance with international law. In short, space is not lawless: it is not somewhere where one is free of legal constraint or principle.

---

32 Competition for natural resources in space is with us (see Chapter 7). Space now clearly figures in state considerations of commercial development, security and defence, including the establishment of specialised military forces (see Chapter 15).

33 See http://public.ccsds.org. Current Charter: https://public.ccsds.org/about/charter.aspx. In 2022, CCSDS had eleven member agencies, thirty-two observer agencies and one hundred thirty associates. Through its structures and working groups, space communications experts have produced much useful work.

34 The Strategy was adopted in 2007 by fourteen space agencies: ASI (Italy), BNSC (UK), CNES (France), CNSA (China), CSA (Canada), CSIRO (Australia), DLR (Germany), ESA (European Space Agency), ISRO (India), JAXA (Japan), KARI (Republic of Korea), NASA (USA), NSAU (Ukraine) and Roscosmos (Russia). See www.nasa.gov/pdf/296751main_GES_framework.pdf; www.homepages.ucl.ac.uk/~ucfbiac/Case%20for%20Space_files/GES.pdf; www.lpi.usra.edu/meetings/leagilewg2008/presentations/oct28pm/Baltuck4079.pdf. Cf. *A Journey to Inspire: Report of the Presidential Commission on Implementation of United States Space Exploration Policy* (the Aldridge Commission) 2004 (USGPO, 2004): www.hq.nasa.gov/office/pao/History/aldridge_commission_report_june2004.pdf.

35 Declaration of Legal Principles Governing the Activities of States in the Exploration and Use of Outer Space, UNGA Res. 1962 (XVIII) of 1963: 1964 3 ILM 157.

36 Part A, para 1.a, 'International Cooperation in the Peaceful Uses of Outer Space', UNGA Res. 1721 (XVI), 20 December 1961.

37 *Supra* n. 5.

The second fundamental is enshrined as OST Art. I para 2: outer space and celestial bodies are free for exploration and use by all states. This was foreshadowed in the prior UN resolutions, appearing in Part A 1.b of UNGA Res. 1721 (XVI), 1961, and para 2 of the 1963 Declaration on Space Principles, UNGA Res. 1962 (XVIII).[38] The treaty article adds that the exploration and use of outer space is to be 'without discrimination of any kind, on a basis of equality' and that 'there shall be free access to all areas of celestial bodies'. It is important to note the way in which these rights are formulated in Art. I.

These are rights of all states, not just rights mutually recognised by the parties to the OST and restricted to them. In this, there are echoes of Art. I of the Paris and Chicago Conventions, which 'recognise' that every state has rights in the air space above its territory.[39] Every state/country may explore and use outer space.

The third fundamental is that there is no national appropriation of space or of celestial bodies, that outer space and celestial bodies are not subject to national appropriation appeared originally in Part A, para 1.b of UNGA Res. 1721 (XVI).[40] The notion is elaborated in para 3 of the 1963 Space Principles Declaration, where it is added that national appropriation cannot occur 'by claim of sovereignty, by means of use or occupation or by any other means'.[41] That language was brought over *seriatim* into OST Art. II.

Non-lawyer readers should note that the term 'occupation' as used here is a technical term of international law. Occupation involves both 'being there' and the intention to act as sovereign in relation to the occupied location,[42] and that intention is excluded by the

---

38 *Supra* n. 5.

39 Convention on the Regulation of Aerial Navigation, Paris, 13 October 1919, 11 LNTS 173; 1922 UKTS 2, Cmnd. 1609; 1 Hudson 359; 13 Martens (3d) 61; (1923) 17 AJIL Supp. 195; Convention on International Civil Aviation, Chicago, 7 December 1944 (1944) 15 UNTS 295; 61 Stat. 1180, TIAS 1591; 1953 UKTS 8, Cmnd. 8742; 9 Hudson 168; 3 Bevans 944; (1945) 39 AJIL Supp 111.

40 In September 1960 speaking to the UNGA President Eisenhower suggested that celestial bodies would not be subject to national appropriation by any claims of sovereignty: D.D. Eisenhower, 'Address before the Fifteenth General Assembly of the United Nations, 22 September 1960'; Public Papers of the Presidents of the United States, Eisenhower 1960–61, Doc. 302, 707–720, § v at 714; *Legal Problems* at 1009; Univ. of Michigan Digital Library: http://quod.lib.umich.edu/p/ppotpus/. Earlier, see O. Schachter, 'Who Owns the Universe?', *Colliers*, 22 March 1952, 36 and 70–71, rep. in C. Ryan, ed., *Across the Space Frontier* (London: Sidgwick and Jackson, 1952) 118 ff. Cf. Note: 'National Sovereignty of Outer Space' (1961) 74 *Harv. L. Rev.* 1154–1175. The setting aside of territory from claims of sovereignty may have begun with discussions early in the twentieth century as to Spitzbergen and the Svalbard archipelago, which gave rise to the 1910 proposal of T.W. Balch that 'East and West Antarctica' [areas not claimed in 1910] should 'become the common possessions of all of the family of nations': T.W. Balch, 'Arctic and Antarctic Regions and the Law of Nations' (1910) 4 *AJIL* 265–275 at 274–275; cf. J.B. Scott, 'Arctic Exploration and International Law' (1909) 3 *AJIL* 928–941 at 941. These notions, based on a belief in the impossibility of permanent settlement, were departed from, but in measure reappear with the Antarctic Treaty (*supra* n. 13). The Svalbard Treaty, 1920, 2 LNTS 7; 1924 UKTS 18, Cmd. 2092; 2 Bevans 269; (US) 43 Stat. 18–92, TS 686, recognised Spitzbergen and the rest of the archipelago as Norwegian, but provided for freedom of hunting and access to fishing grounds. See W. Østreng, *Politics in High Altitudes: The Svalbard Archipelago*, R.I. Christophersen, trans. (London: Hurst, 1977). Cf. M. Bourbonniere and R.J. Lee, 'Legality of the Deployment of Conventional Weapons in Earth Orbit: Balancing Space Law and the Law of Armed Conflict' (2007) 18 *Eur. J. Int. L.* 873–901 at 900–901.

41 We note the curiosity that the end of Art. 11 of the Venezuelan Constitution states that: 'The Republic has rights in outer space and in those areas which are or may be the Common Property of Humanity, on such terms, to such extent and subject to such conditions as may be determined by public international agreements and by the national legislation'. What does this mean as a matter of international law?

42 See M. Huber, Arbitrator, *Island of Palmas Arbitration* (1928) 2 *RIAA* 831–71 [1928] 22 *AJIL* 867–920: R.Y. Jennings and A. Watts, eds., *Oppenheim's International Law*, 9th ed., Vol. I, 'Peace' (London: Longman,

terms of Art. II.[43] A base on a celestial body, or an orbital position – including a geostationary location or a position at a Lagrange point – may be 'there', but its location is not amenable to or open for a claim of sovereignty to be made.[44]

Despite the exclusion of claims of sovereignty by OST Art. II, in 1976, a Bogotá conference adopted a declaration[45] in which its signatories – Colombia, Ecuador, Indonesia, the Congo, Kenya, Uganda and Zaire (then the Democratic Republic of the Congo) – asserted that geostationary orbit (GSO) is a scarce natural resource which is not part of outer space, and each claimed rights in relation to that portion of the GSO above its territory.[46] Suffice it here to say that, as is clear from statements within it, the trigger for the declaration was the increasing use of GSO slots, the failure of attempts by the equatorial states to be recognised as having a special interest in them and a fear they would thereby miss out on some of the benefits of space.[47] While the episode serves to show the dissatisfaction of some countries as to their access to and benefit from space activities, in practice, the Bogotá Declaration claims appear dead.[48]

Potential dissatisfaction felt by developing countries as to the distribution of benefit from space activities leads us back to OST Art. I. That the exploration and use of outer space should be 'only for the betterment of mankind and to the benefit of states irrespective of the stage their economic or scientific development' appeared in the preambular paragraph 'Believing' in both UNGA Res. 1721 of 1961 and the 1963 Declaration of Space Principles. In the 1963 Declaration, para 1 further declares that 'exploration and

---

1996), Part 2, 686–696 (§§ 250–257); I. Brownlie, *Principles of Public International Law*, 6th ed. (Oxford: Oxford UP 2003) 124–125 and 133–138.

43 As discussed in Chapter 7, *c.* n. 36, 'Sovereignty and Title to Immoveables', the prohibition of national appropriation excludes sovereign appropriation by private individuals and entities. An individual may make a claim, but this is ineffective of itself. A sovereign 'title', valid against third parties, depends on it being recognised by a national legal system. The occasionally alleged 'expansion' of OST Art. II by Art. 11.3 of the Moon Agreement follows MA Art. 11.2, which restates OST Art. II for the Moon and the other subjects of the MA. MA Art. 11.3 is a clarification (for entrepreneurs and politicians?) and not innovative. That said it is open to states to recognise as valid claims of ownership of materials procured in space. See US Code Title 51, Ch. 513, § 51303 as to rights given by the US Space Resource Exploration and Utilization Act of 2015, and the IISL Board of Directors 'Position Paper on Space Resource Mining', December 2015: https://iisl. space/iisl-position-paper-on-space-resource-mining/; and the end of n. 44 *infra*. See further discussion of space mining in Chapter 7.

44 Cf. the US statute 'Implantation of the United States Flag on the Moon or Planets' (PL 91–119, 18th November, 1969, 83 Stat. 202) which provides: 'The flag of the United States, and no other flag, shall be implanted or otherwise placed on the surface of the Moon, or on the surface of any planet, by the members of the crew of any spacecraft making a lunar or planetary landing as a part of a mission under the Apollo program or as a part of a mission under any subsequent program, the funds for which are provided entirely by the Government of the United States. This act is intended as symbolic gesture of national pride in achievement and is not to be construed as a declaration of national appropriation by claim of sovereignty'. Similarly s. 403 of the U.S. Space Resource Exploration and Utilization Act of 2015, Pub. L. 114–90, states: 'It is the sense of Congress that by the enactment of this Act, the United States does not thereby assert sovereignty or sovereign or exclusive rights or jurisdiction over, or the ownership of, any celestial body.' See US Code Title 51, Ch. 513, § 51303 as to rights given under that legislation.

45 The Declaration of the First Meeting of the Equatorial States, Bogotá, 1976 (1978) 6 *J. Sp. Law* 193–196; Manual, 2: 383. See also Chapter 6 The Bogotá Declaration.

46 An application of the 'lighthouse' principle? See Chapter 4.

47 Christol, 463–533 with its notes traces the debate down to its date.

48 See also Chapter 6 on the boundary question as well as the geostationary orbit and Chapter 8 on the ITU.

use of outer space shall be carried on for the benefits and the interests of all mankind'. The language is consolidated in the first paragraph of Article 1 of the OST:

> The exploration and use of outer space including the Moon and other celestial bodies shall be carried out for the benefit and in the interests of all countries irrespective of their degree of economic or scientific development and shall be the province of mankind.

Here, the insistence of the previous space resolutions that all countries benefit has had added to it the notion of outer space as being 'the province of all mankind'. This latter phrase is difficult to interpret as a matter of law, although rhetorically, it adds a little gloss to the freedom of exploration and use to be found in para 2 of Art. I.[49]

The implications of the requirement that the 'exploration and use shall be carried out for the benefit and in the interests of all countries irrespective of their degree of economic or scientific development' are extending as time goes on. It has to be said that the high expectations the requirement raises, and indeed the statements in Resolutions 1721 and 1962, seem in the early years not to have been met to the satisfaction of the non-space-active countries. The Bogotá Declaration is but one example. The question was, and maybe still is, whether the benefit must be shared in a practical sense, perhaps including technology transfer,[50] or whether the requirement is met simply by the activities being beneficial in a generalised way, which might even encompass merely being non-harmful.[51]

Dissatisfaction with the flow-through of benefit to the non-space-active states was expressed at the Second United Nations Conference on the Exploration and Peaceful Uses of Outer Space (UNISPACE II) in 1982. In due course, the matter was placed on the agenda of COPUOS, and its product became UNGA Res. 51/122, adopted without vote on 13 December 1996 as the 'Declaration on international cooperation in the exploration in use of outer space for the benefit and in the interests of all states taking into particular account the needs of developing countries'.[52]

Paragraph 1 of the 1996 Declaration took up the language of OST Art. I and makes an interesting addition to it. The second sentence of the Declaration states that the international cooperation which it calls for 'shall be carried out for the benefit and the interests of all states irrespective of their degree of economic, social or scientific and technological development and shall be the province of all mankind', thus far the words of the OST. However, the Declaration para 1 then adds a sentence: 'Particular account should be taken of the needs of developing countries'. The Declaration exhorts space-active states to cooperate with developing countries, particularly those with 'incipient space programmes'

49 But see E. Fasan, 'The Meaning of "Mankind" in Space Legal Language' (1974) 2 *J. Sp. L.* 125–131.
50 N. Jasentuliyana, *International Space Law in the United Nations* (The Hague: Kluwer, 1999) 169–186, an update of the article cited *infra* n. 52.
51 S. Gorove, 'Implications of International Space Law for Private Enterprise' (1982) 7 *AASL* 319 at 321; Bourbonniere and Lee, *supra* n. 40, at 885.
52 The Declaration is analysed by S. Hobe, F. Tronchetti, V. Mani and H. Zhao, CoCoSL III, 299–362. Cf. N. Jasentuliyana, 'Article 1 of the Outer Space Treaty Revisited' (1989) 17 *J. Sp. L.* 129–144; M. Benkö and K.-U. Schrögl, 'History and Impact of the 1996 UN Declaration on "Space Benefits"' (1997) 13 *Space Policy* 139–143; R. Jakhu, 'Legal Issues Relating to the Global Public Interest in Outer Space' (2006) 32 *J. Sp. L.*, 31–110; E. Carpanelli and B. Cohen, 'A Legal Assessment of the 1996 Declaration on Space Benefits on the Occasion of its Fifteenth Anniversary' (2012) 38 *J. Sp. L.* 1–38.

(para 3), in the most effective manner possible, including through cooperative ventures whether governmental or non, commercial or non, global and multilateral, regional or bilateral (para 4).

Such cooperation should be aimed at promoting outer space and science and technology together with its applications, developing appropriate capabilities and interested states and facilitating the exchange of expertise and technology (para 5). Organisations and agencies dealing with development aid should consider how they may develop the potential of space in their programmes (para 6). In all this, however, it is recognised that the emphasis must be on cooperation, and that states cannot be *required* to engage in space activities to their detriment.

Cooperation is to be 'on an equitable and mutually acceptable basis'. The terms of any contract for such a venture are to be fair and reasonable and in full compliance with 'legitimate rights and interests of the parties concerned as for example the intellectual property rights' (para 2). The facilitation of exchange of expertise and technology is to be 'on a mutually acceptable basis' (para 5). Such qualifying phrases could limit attainment of the aspirations of the sentences containing them.

The terms and thrust of the Space Benefits Declaration together with comparable language in the Remote Sensing Principles of 1986,[53] and in parts of the ITU Constitution and Convention and other ITU documents,[54] reflect an insistent demand from the developing countries. The underlying stratum of thought is similar to the concept of the 'common heritage of mankind', a concept considerably developed in recent decades, particularly since its application in Part XI of the Law of Sea Convention of 1982.[55] The International Sea-Bed Authority implements a regime for the exploitation of the deep sea beyond national jurisdiction. The concept is similarly to be found in the Moon Agreement of 1979, Art. 11 of which binds parties to that agreement to establish a regime for the exploitation of the resources of the moon and their equitable distribution to all once such exploitation becomes feasible.[56]

Others have sought to interpret the Antarctic Treaty of 1959 as in effect making Antarctica part of the common heritage of mankind.[57] It has to be said that in the latter case, doing so is to read back into history concepts that were not present when the Antarctic Treaty was being negotiated. Similarly, it is inappropriate to interpret OST Art. I as implying at that stage the existence of the notion of a regime of 'common heritage'.

Certainly the concept of common heritage as it appears to be developing does have elements that are present in the OST. There is the setting aside of outer space from national sovereignty (OST Art. II). There is the language of benefit and interests in OST Art. I para

---

53 'Principles Relating to the Remote Sensing of the Earth from Outer Space', 3 December 1986; UNGA Res. 41/65 (1986) 25 ILM 1331. CoCoSL III, 81–188. See Chapter 13.

54 See Chapter 8.

55 UN Convention on the Law of the Sea, 1982, 1833 UNTS 3; 1999 UKTS 81, Cmnd. 4524; (1982) 21 ILM 1261–354: Part XI. The Deep Seabed, as revised by the Agreement to Implement Part IX of the Law of the Sea Convention, UNGA Res. 48/263 1999 UKTS 82, Cmnd. 4524; (1994) 33 ILM 1309. Cf. Lyall, *supra* n. 4, 27–32.

56 Agreement Governing the Activities of States on the Moon and other Celestial Bodies, 1363 UNTS 3; (1979) 18 ILM 1434, text adopted without vote, UNGA Res. 34/68. See *infra* Chapter 7.

57 The Antarctic Treaty 1959, *supra* n. 13, set aside Antarctica for peaceful and scientific purposes only, and froze the pre-existing territorial claims for its duration.

1, together with its reference to the exploration and use of outer space being the 'province of all mankind'. However common heritage requires that there be a formal international regime established for supervising the exploitation of the resources of the common heritage, as is the case with Part XI of the 1982 Law of the Sea Convention, and such is simply not present in the OST.

More accurately, it was not in the minds of the negotiators and drafters of the OST that there should be such a common controlling regime as is implied in the later concepts of common heritage. In 1967, it was evident that states were going to explore and use outer space. Although some consideration was called for regarding the interests of others, and all states should benefit 'irrespective of their degree of economic or scientific development', the establishment of a binding and directory common heritage regime was simply not in contemplation.[58]

So much for the language of Art. 1 para 1, and the Space Benefits Declaration. However, in addition to the legalese, we note that notwithstanding the legal position, the developing countries have indeed seen significant benefit from the use of space by the space-competent. Other chapters in this book deal with the regulation of radio including for space activities (Chapter 8), satellite telecommunications, direct broadcasting (Chapter 10), global positioning (Chapter 11) and remote sensing (Chapter 12). In all these areas, benefit has come to all states that wish to have it. Communications have been revolutionised,[59] education has come through satellite broadcasting and sensing from space has helped deal with the exploitation of natural resources and dangers from natural disasters. While it is true that commercial considerations have entered in, it is also the case that competition has benefited states willing to exploit it.

We now move on to consider the remaining articles of the OST. Article IV obliges states not to put nuclear weapons or weapons of mass destruction into space, whether in orbit or otherwise stationed in space, or on the moon or other celestial bodies.[60] The moon and other celestial bodies are to be used exclusively for peaceful purposes. Military bases, exercises and the testing of weapons are forbidden. Notwithstanding, military personnel may take part in scientific exploration, and the use of military equipment for scientific purposes is permitted.[61] Such generalities require further elaboration, as in the Moon Agreement of 1979, albeit that agreement has not been a success.[62]

Repeating the substance of para 9 of the 1963 Declaration of Principles,[63] OST Art. V requires that astronauts (undefined) be regarded as 'envoys of mankind in outer space', be given all possible assistance when in an emergency or distress – by other astronauts when they are active in outer space – and in appropriate cases be returned to the state of registry

---

58 Cf. the discussion of the Moon Agreement in the US Congress Report, *Agreement Governing the Activities of States on the Moon and Other Celestial Bodies,* Committee on Commerce, Science, and Transportation (US) 96th Cong. 2d Sess. (Committee Print 1980) and *infra* Chapter 7 Common Heritage.

59 Telecommunications has enabled the Internet, with incalculable effects.

60 Cf. the Nuclear Test Ban Treaty, 1963, *supra* n. 18. S. Hobe, 'The Meaning of "Peaceful Purposes" in Article IV of the Outer Space Treaty' (2015) XL *AASL* 9–24.

61 See Chapter 15 on military activities in space.

62 Agreement Governing the Activities of States on the Moon and other Celestial Bodies, 5 December 1979; 1363 UNTS 3; (1979) 18 ILM 1434, adopted without vote UNGA Res. 34/68. See CoCoSL II, 325–426 and *infra* Chapter 7.

63 *Supra* n. 5.

of their space vehicle along with it.[64] These matters were elaborated on in the Agreement on the Rescue of Astronauts, the Return of Astronauts and the Return of Objects Launched into Outer Space (ARRA), adopted one year after the OST.[65]

Articles VI and VII are partially innovative and go together.[66] In general, international law, a state is responsible only for acts attributable directly to it or indirectly through the acts of its officials acting in an official capacity. Ordinarily a state is not responsible *simpliciter* for the activities of its nationals.[67] That said, in the *Trail Smelter Arbitration* of 1935, the court held that a state could be held liable if it permitted the use of its territory by private individuals in a way which caused damage to another state.[68]

OST Art. VI clearly lays international responsibility for national activities in outer space on a state party. This includes activities conducted by nongovernmental bodies as well as those by state organs. The activities of nongovernmental bodies must be authorised by the state of their nationality and be subjected to its continuing supervision.[69] This sounds well, and in many instances no doubt works satisfactorily. However, questions must now be raised, as private enterprise is active in space. Businesses may incorporate and exercise their activities in states that may lack the expertise, personnel or knowledge to properly discharge their responsibilities under Art. VI.[70] The space activities of an international organisation must also comply with provisions of the OST. Here, the duty is laid on both the organisation and the OST parties that are its members (Art. VI *ad fin*).

Article VII then takes these matters further, providing for liability for damage caused by space activities. *Trail Smelter* depended partly on the long-standing failure of Canada to curb the activities of the smelter at Trail, a continuing nuisance.[71] Space is different: any damage is likely to occur swiftly and may be catastrophic. Space activities are inherently dangerous, so it is right that they should be properly supervised, and that liability should follow in the event of damage.[72]

However, should liability attach to the actor, as is normal, or also to the authoriser/supervisor? The decision arrived at in the OST is that in space activities, the authoriser/supervisor should indeed also be liable. Article VII therefore provides that a state is liable for damage caused to another state through its own space activities and of those subject to its jurisdiction, licensing and supervision.

The extension of state responsibility and liability to damage caused by its non-state entities is unusual. It remains an important innovation in international law, although the

64 As to 'state of registry' see *infra* at n. 77 and *infra* Chapter 4.
65 Agreement on the Rescue of Astronauts, the Return of Astronauts and the Return of Objects Launched into Outer Space, 22 April 1968; 672 UNTS 119; 1969 UKTS 56, Cmnd. 3997; 19 UST 7570, TIAS 6559; 7 ILM 151; [1969] 63 AJIL 382. See CoCoSL II, 1–82 and *infra* Chapters 4 and 5. As of 2023 ARRA had ninety-nine parties and twenty-two signatories. The OST had one hundred thirteen parties and twenty-three signatories.
66 B. Cheng, 'Article VI of the 1967 Space Treaty Revisited: "International Responsibility", "National Activities", and "The Appropriate State"' (1998) 26 *J. Sp. L.* 7–32.
67 A state is not liable for an accident caused by the careless driving of a private citizen national.
68 *Trail Smelter Arbitrations* (*US* v *Canada*) (1938 and 1941) 3 RIAA 1905–1982.
69 UNGA Res. 68/74 makes 'Recommendations on national legislation relevant to the peaceful exploration and use of outer space'.
70 See *infra* at n. 77.
71 *Supra* n. 68.
72 In Common Law jurisdictions the case of *Rylands* v *Fletcher*, [1868] AC 1, involving the bursting of a reservoir is famous as establishing the 'doctrine of dangerous things'.

provision of Art. VII was further refined in the 1972 Liability Convention.[73] That Convention, of course, only binds its parties, and it has fewer ratifications than the OST.[74] There is therefore a quadruple regime for liability for space activities: that of the OST for its parties, that of the Liability Convention for its parties, one under 'normal' international law should anyone care to try that avenue and finally, in appropriate instances, there might be recourse to a remedy under national law.

Repeating the terms of para 7 of the 1963 Declaration of Space Principles,[75] OST Art. VIII provides that in relation to objects carried on their registries, states retain jurisdiction and control over objects launched as well as over any personnel on board. A space object cannot be abandoned to become *res nullius*; it remains the property of its state of registry.[76] When the OST was drafted, a state 'registry' was an unidentified institution.[77] Para 1 of Part B of UNGA Res. 1721 (XVI) had called on states through the UN Secretary General to inform COPUOS of launches so that they might be registered, and para 2 requested him to maintain a public registry of these notifications.[78] However, at that stage there was no formal requirement that states should establish their own registries.

The matter is made somewhat clearer (at least for its parties) by the 1976 Registration Convention.[79] The final sentence of OST Art. VIII provides for returning to a state of registry space objects found outside of the territory of that state. As we will see in Chapter 4, the duty as to return of objects was clarified in ARRA the year after the OST.[80] Curiously, however, although the first sentence of OST Art. VIII holds that a state of registry retains jurisdiction over a space object 'and over any personnel thereof', there is no reference in its final sentence to the position as to the return or rescue of astronauts, a matter ARRA clearly takes up, its title relegating the return of objects to last place.

Given the subsequent development of space activities, major questions must be asked of Arts. VI, VII and VIII. Simply put, the language is insufficiently clear. As Bin Cheng pointed out, a number of terms in Art. VI do not carry the clarity of meaning that might

---

73 Convention on International Liability for Damage Caused by Space Objects, 1972; 961 UNTS 187; 1974 UKTS 16, Cmnd. 5551; 24 UST 2389, TIAS 7762; (1971) 10 ILM 965; [1971] 66 AJIL 702. See CoCoSL II, 83–226, and *infra* Chapter 4.

74 As of 2023 the Liability Convention had ninety-eight parties and nineteen signatories (contrast ARRA, *supra* n. 65). The OST had eleven hundred thirteen parties and twenty-three signatories.

75 *Supra* n. 5.

76 A small plaque beside the replica of the Viking I Mars Lander in the Smithsonian Air and Space Museum in Washington, DC, affirms the US property right in the Lander located on Mars, NASA having transferred its ownership to the Smithsonian. In a sale of Russian space memorabilia at Sotheby's New York on 11 December 1993, the Lunokhod-1 lunar rover located on the Mare Imbrium (the Sea of Rains) was sold for US$60,000 (estimate US$5000). The object was stated to be 'resting on the surface of the Moon'. Sotheby's and the consignor of the object for the sale undertook no obligation to deliver possession. Only the current title rights of the owner were sold, without assurance as to the claims of others, including possible salvagers. See P.D. Nesgos, UN COPUOS Symposium on Commercial Activities in Space, March 1994 (1994) 37 *Proc. IISL* 305–314 at 305–316; Sotheby's Auction Catalogue, 'Russian Space History', December 1993; D.H.R. Spennemann, 'The Ethics of Treading on Neil Armstrong's Footprints' (2004) 20 *Space Policy* 279–290.

77 Reference point, *supra* n. 64.

78 *Supra* n. 5.

79 Convention on the Registration of Objects Launched into Outer Space, 1975; 1023 UNTS 15; 1978 UKTS 70, Cmnd. 7271; TIAS 8480; (1975) 14 ILM 43. See CoCoSL II, 227–324, and *infra* Chapter 4. As of 1 January 2022 the Convention had seventy-five ratifications and three signatories. The OST had one hundred thirteen parties and twenty-three signatories.

80 See *supra* n. 65.

be thought to be desirable.[81] Article VI imposes duties as to licensing and supervision. Liability is the concern of Art. VII. Jurisdiction and control exercised by a state of registry is a major element of Art. VIII and applies to both the space object and its personnel. Even if one interprets such language as inclusively as possible, because a number of states are involved in the duties enumerated, there is the opportunity for evasion on the argument that something is someone else's responsibility.

Further, even if the system does *ex facie* work, it must be asked whether all states that enter upon or license space activities are competent to discharge their responsibilities.[82] Have they the trained personnel, knowledge of the science and skills to properly evaluate applications for licences, scrutinise reports and confirm that all is well? And should there be a disaster, have they the funds to meet a claim for damages?

'Flags of convenience' are a well-known problem which was alleviated, but not yet solved, by the 1984 UN Convention on the Law of the Sea and the 1986 UN Convention on Conditions for the Registration of Ships.[83] Private enterprise already seeks out tax havens from which to conduct its space business. The matter of the corporate 'veil' may therefore be relevant. Entrepreneurs engaged in a space activity may conceal their identities behind shell companies to avoid being the target of required supervision by their real home states under OST Arts. VI and VIII, or the home state, the *siège social*, might impose more stringent legal rules for operating an enterprise. The ratio in the *Barcelona Traction* case could be an obstacle.[84] 'Lifting the veil' should be considered at least in relation to space businesses.[85]

Articles IX, X and XI are mainly directed at the conduct of space activities; cooperation and mutual assistance are called for in all three. Under Art. IX, the harmful contamination of the moon and other celestial bodies is to be avoided, as are adverse changes to Earth's environment. Appropriate avoidance measures are to be taken.[86] States are also to consult other states whose activities might be subjected to 'potentially harmfully interference' by an activity or experiment it intends to pursue. This consultation is engaged in either of a

---

81 Cheng, *supra* n. 66.

82 Some 'small states' see licensing space activities as a potential method of generating income. F. Lyall, 'Small States, Entrepreneurial States and Space' (2006) 49 *Proc. IISL* 382–390 and 'Expanding Global Communications Services' Sess. III, *Proceedings of the Workshop on Space Law in the Twenty-first Century*, UNISPACE III Technical Forum, 63–80 at 69–71. As discussed in Chapter 8, the Tonga/Tongasat problem occurred when Tonga notified some 30 GSO orbital positions to the ITU, and thereafter leased those successfully registered to foreign entrepreneurs. In 2001 the micro-state of Niue (pop. 1200) proposed to launch its own satellite to GSO, financed by foreign capital, to be built, launched and operated by foreign companies but with Niue to take 35% of any revenue. The proposal failed. Luxembourg has legislated to allow it to license asteroid mining.

83 On 'flags of convenience' in space see materials, *supra* n. 82, and discussion in Chapter 4 at n. 76. Cf. the UN Convention on the Law of the Sea, Montego Bay, 1984, 1833 UNTS 3; 1999 UKTS 81, Cmnd. 4524; (1982) 21 ILM 1261; Convention on Conditions for the Registration of Ships (1987) 26 ILM 1232 (2022, not in force). Some national legislation has, to some extent, helped through setting standards of ship-worthiness and employment protection for shipping entering national waters.

84 *Barcelona Traction, Light and Power Co. Limited* (New Application, 1962) *(Belgium v. Spain)* (1962–1970) (Second Phase) 1970 ICJ 3. Belgium and the Belgian owners of a Canadian company were held to have no standing to sue.

85 See Chapter 4, towards the end of the discussion of the Registration Convention.

86 See Chapter 10.

state's own volition (*ex proprie motu*) or at the request of a state that fears such interference with its activities.

Art. X mandates that a state engaging in space activities 'consider on a basis of equality' any request by another state to observe the flight of space objects it launches. Under Art. XI, states are required to inform the UN Secretary General, the public and the scientific community 'to the greatest extent feasible and practicable' of the 'nature, conduct, location and results' of their space activities. The UN Secretary General is to disseminate such information immediately and effectively and now does so through OOSA. Certainly a little – but not much – information has been published in compliance with Art. XI on the nature of things we cannot know the impacts of the tests of feasibility and practicability.[87]

Although other articles have an application to activities on the moon and other celestial bodies (particular the contamination and harmful interference provisions of Arts IX), OST Art. XII is *sui generis*. Doubtlessly derived from Art. VII of the Antarctic Treaty,[88] it provides for all 'stations, installations, equipment and space vehicles on the moon and other celestial bodies' to be open to representatives of other parties 'on a basis of reciprocity'. Reasonable notice is to be given to allow consultations, to allow maximum safety precautions to be taken and to avoid interference with the normal operations of the facility to be visited.[89] We will return to the moon and other celestial bodies in Chapter 7.

Elements of the Outer Space Treaty as Customary Law

Are there now some rules of customary international law specifically applicable to space? Despite some modern discussions of the nature of custom,[90] we think that there are, and that in their development, the OST in particular has played a significant role. It is important that there be such customary law. To bring this out, we base the following questions on principles enunciated in the OST.[91]

---

87 Thus the US notified missions carrying radioactive materials e.g. Cassini (A/AC/105/677 with Add.1), New Horizons (A/AC.105/864), Mars Mission 2011 (A/AC.105/1012) and the Mars mission 2020 (A/AC.105/1233) devices covered under the Nuclear Power Principles Resolution (as to which see *infra* Chapters 4 s.v. Liability and 10 s.v. 'Contamination' and 'Near Earth Environment'). China notified that the Chang'e 4 would carry radioactive isotopes (A/AC.105/1207), and the re-entry of the Tiangong-2 space laboratory (A/AC.105/1201). Cf. Notes by Russia and China in relation to a Mars launch that failed (A/AC.105/647, 648, 658 and 669). The UN OOSA list of Art. XI notifications is at www.unoosa.org/oosa/en/treatyimplementation/ost-art-xi/index.html.

88 See the Antarctic Treaty, *supra* nn. 13 and ff.

89 Concerns would include the requirement for oxygen and other essential provisions, together with the capacity of an installation. We note that, in the film *2001: A Space Odyssey* (1968), Russian access to US 'Moon Base Clavius' is refused on (spurious) health grounds. Cf. in Chapter 5, a discussion of safety and 'worst case' problems affecting astronauts.

90 Cf. Chapter 2, n. 50ff.

91 We acknowledge that the other space treaties and the UN space resolutions have also played a role in the emergence of custom in space. Cf. I. Marboe, ed., *Soft Law in Outer Space: The Function of Non-binding Norms in International Space Law* (Vienna: Böhlau Verlag, 2012); V.S. Vereshchetin and G.M. Danilenko, 'Custom as a Source of International Law of Outer Space' (1985) 13 *J. Sp. L.* 22–35; V. Vecchio, 'Customary International Law in the Outer Space Treaty: Space Law as Laboratory for the Evolution of Public International Law' (2017) 66 *ZLW* 491–502; B. Wessel, 'The Rule of Law in Outer Space: The Effects of Treaties and Nonbinding Agreements on International Space Law' (2012) 35 *Hastings Int. & Comp. L. Rev.*, 289–322; C.L. Carr and G.L. Scott, 'Multilateral Treaties and the Environment: A Case Study in the Formation

What is the relevance of the OST for those states that are not parties to it? What if a party to the treaty, availing itself of the provisions of Art. XVI, were to withdraw from the treaty upon the expiry of one year's notice of denunciation? What if a signatory were to delete its signature?[92] What if a party were to propose an amendment of the treaty that would conflict with certain elements of it?[93]

Putting this the other way round, have any elements of the treaty passed into customary law with the effect that they cannot be controverted by subsequent agreement or unilateral action? Have any of its obligations become principles of law *erga omnes* or even *ius cogens*? Are there principles of space law which cannot now be escaped from?

We would argue that certain elements of the OST have indeed passed into or now reflect customary international law. At a minimum, international law applies in outer space (Art. III); outer space, including the moon and other celestial bodies, is not subject to national appropriation by any means (Art. II); outer space is free for exploration and use by all (Art. I), but such exploration and use is to be for the benefit of all (Art. I); states are responsible for national activities and the activities of their nationals in outer space; states are under a duty to authorise and a continuing duty to supervise such activities (Art. VI) and states are liable for damage caused to other states by such activities (Art. VII).

These principles cannot be evaded if customary international law has formed on those matters. As stated in Art. 43 of the 1969 Vienna Convention on the Law of Treaties,[94]

---

of Customary International Law' (1999) 27 *Denv. J. Int. L. and Pol.* 313–335; W.A. Smith, 'Using the Artemis Accords to Build Customary International Law: Vision for U.S.-Centric Good Governance Regime in Outer Space' (2021) 86 *J. Air L. & Comm.* 661–700, and the discussion of 'Soft Law' and of 'Custom' in Chapter 2 *supra* following n. 50.

92 A signatory to a treaty, but which has not yet ratified, must abstain from acts which would contradict the object and purpose of the Treaty, Art. 18, Vienna Convention on the Law of Treaties of 1969 (*infra* n. 94), which articulates the customary law on the matter. Cf. the withdrawal of the US signature of the Rome Statute of the International Criminal Court: 'International Criminal Court: Letter to UN Secretary General Kofi Annan', US Department of State press release, May 6, 2002: available at: www.state.gov./r/pa/prs/ps/202/9968pf.htm. On 15 November 2016 Russia also withdrew its signature of the Rome Statute of the International Criminal Court.

Cf. also the withdrawal of the US from the compulsory jurisdiction of the ICJ in the light of its decision to take jurisdiction in the Nicaragua case (*US Dept of State Bulletin*, 18 January 1985); the withdrawal of the US from the Anti-Ballistic Missile Treaty of 1972, effective 13 June 2002; the US withdrawal from the Protocol giving the ICJ jurisdiction in relation to the Vienna Convention on Consular Relations in the light of the ICJ decision in *Avena and Other Mexican Nationals (Mexico v. US)* 2004 ICJ Rep. 12, which involved breach of the Convention and possible death penalties (March 2005) (see Chapter 2, n. 19); and the withdrawal of France from optional clause of the ICJ (1959) 8 *ICLQ* 735.

93 This is indicated as a possibility in later passages of the Bogota Declaration (*supra* at n. 45).

94 Vienna Convention on the Law of Treaties, 1969, 1155 UNTS 331; 1980 UKTS 58, Cmnd. 7964; 8 ILM 679; [1960] 63 AJIL 875–903. Although some states (including the US) have not ratified the Convention, it is believed that its statements as to these principles of international law and the interpretation of treaties articulate customary international law and are not simply provisions applicable only as between its parties. Thus the ICJ has on occasion cited the Convention as expressing or codifying principles of customary international law and has become more relaxed in so doing. Cf. the references to the Convention in the Judgment on the *Application of the Convention on the Prevention and Punishment of the Crime of Genocide (Croatia v. Serbia)*, 2015 ICJ Rep. 3 at paras 95, 99 and 138, and in the *Case Concerning Maritime Dispute (Peru v Chile)*, 2014 ICJ Rep. 3 at 57 paras 57 and 58, and cases there cited. Earlier, just after the Convention came into force see the Advisory Opinion on the *Legal Consequences for States of the Continued Presence of South Africa in Namibia (South West Africa) Notwithstanding Security Council Resolution 276 (1970)* (the 'Namibia Case'), 1971 ICJ Rep. 16 at 47, para 94, the *Fisheries Jurisdiction Case (UK v Iceland) Jurisdiction of the Court*, 1973 ICJ Rep. 3 at 18 para 36, together with the *Gabčíkovo-Nagymaros Project (Hungary v*

which encapsulates the relevant general international law, where a treaty ceases or where a state withdraws from a treaty, this does 'not in any way impair the duty of any State to fulfil any obligation contained in the treaty to which it would be subject under international law independently of the treaty'.[95] Further, the existence of treaty provisions does not preclude a third state from becoming bound by a rule otherwise expressed in a treaty if that rule has become recognised as a rule of customary international law.[96]

These questions are not the speculations of academe, without further or real relevance. There are non-signatories to the OST which could afford to independently establish launching facilities and buy in technical expertise in order to venture into outer space. There are non-party countries that might be willing to lease territory for the construction of a space port and otherwise grant facilities through which entrepreneurs, hiding behind shell companies, might engage in space activities. Are such beyond the reach of the law, or would they be caught by the major elements of space law as we know it?

The years have seen considerable debate about the relationship between treaty and custom.[97] Certainly it is possible that a treaty can put into formal words the content of

Slovakia) 1997 ICJ Rep. 7 at 38 para 46, and cases there cited. Cf. also the reference as to the Convention and the interpretation of treaties in the *Beagle Channel Arbitration (Argentina/Chile)*, 52 ILR 93 at para 15. As to US views of the Convention see E. Criddle, 'The Vienna Convention on the Law of Treaties in U.S. Treaty Interpretation' (2004) 44 *Virg. J. Int. L.* 431–500. The US State Department notes that the US had signed the Convention but that the Senate has not given its consent. Notwithstanding, the US considers that many of the Convention provisions 'constitute customary international law on the law of treaties' (whatever that form of words means): www.state.gov/s/l/treaty/faqs/70139.htm.

95 R.R. Baxter was of the view that withdrawal can have an effect in modifying custom, since: 'If enough states cease to be parties and go into the "opposition" customary international law will be changed thereby' ('Treaties and Custom' (1970-I) 129 *Hague Receuil* 27–105 at 98). We would hope that there would not be such a withdrawal from the OST, at least by those whom its provisions most affect. Cf. Art. 5 of the Vienna Convention on the Succession of States in respect of Treaties, Vienna, 23 August 1978, 1946 UNTS 4; (1980) BPP Misc. 1, Cmnd. 7760; (1978) 17 ILM 1488; (1978) 72 AJIL 971; Final Act A/CONF. 80/32 (in force 6 Nov. 1996) to the same effect. As to the elaboration of the Convention by the International Law Commission, see Sir Arthur Watts, *The International Law Commission 1949–1998: Vol. 2: The Treaties* (Oxford: Oxford UP, 1999) Part II, 609–826.

96 Vienna Convention, *supra* n. 94, Art. 38.

97 For example: R.R. Baxter – 1, 'Multilateral Treaties as Evidence of Customary International Law' (1967–8) 30 *BYIL* 275–300; and – 2, his 'Treaties and Custom' (1970-I) 129 *Hague Receuil* 27–105; M. Akehurst, 'Custom as a Source of International Law' (1974–5) 47 *BYIL* 1–54; A. D'Amato, 'Manifest Intent and the Generation by Treaty of Customary Rules of International Law' (1970) 64 *AJIL* 892–902; A. D'Amato, *The Concept of Custom in International Law* (Ithaca: Cornell UP, 1971); T. Meron, 'The Geneva Conventions as Customary Law' (1987) 81 *AJIL* 348–370; M.E. Villiger, *Customary International Law and Treaties* (Amsterdam: Nijhoff, 1985), Chapter 5, 'Generation of New Customary International Law', 183–205; B. Cheng, 'The Contribution of Air and Space Law to the Development of International Law' (1986) 39 *Curr. Leg. Prob.* 181–210 (Cheng, 671–697); I. Brownlie, 'General Course on International Law' (1995) 255 *Hague Receuil* 9–227 at 36–50; and his *Principles of Public International Law*, 6th ed. (Oxford: Oxford UP, 2003), 12–14; J.I. Charney, 'The Persistent Objector Rule and the Development of Customary International Law' (1985) 56 *BYIL* 1–24; J.I. Charney, 'International Agreements and the Development of Customary International Law' (1986) 61 *Wash. L.R.* 971–996; L.B. Sohn, 'The Law of the Sea: Customary International Law Developments' (1984–1985) 34 *Am. U.L.R.* 271–280; L.B. Sohn, 'Generally Accepted International Rules' (1986) 61 *Wash. L.R.* 1073–1080; V. Kopal, 'Evolution of the Doctrine of Space Law', in N. Jasentuliyana, ed., *Space Law: Development and Scope* (New York: Praeger, 1992) 17–32; T. L. Stein, 'The Approach of the Different Drummer: The Principle of the Persistent Objector in International Law' (1985) 26 *Harv. Int. L.J.* 457–482; A. Terekhov, 'U.N. General Assembly Resolutions and Outer Space Law' (1997) 40 *Proc. IISL* 87–107 [Lyall/Larsen 101–11]; C.L. Carr and G.L. Scott, 'Multilateral Treaties and the Formation of Customary International Law' (1997) 25 *Denv. J. Int. L. & Pol.* 71–94.

law that already exists as customary international law. Article 1 of the Paris Convention on Aerial Navigation, 1919,[98] in which the High Contracting Parties 'recognise that every Power has complete and exclusive sovereignty over the air space above its territory', is an example.[99] Major portions of the 1982 UN Convention on the Law of the Sea[100] and of the 1969 Vienna Convention on the Law of Treaties[101] also fall into that category.

There is the further possibility that a treaty can help 'make' international custom by articulating propositions that are or become binding on states which are neither parties to nor signatories of the treaty. This is also not purely a matter of academic discussion or theory. It has figured in argument before the ICJ, as well as being discussed in various of its judgements, and, as noted above, is set out in Art. 38 of the 1969 Vienna Convention on the Law of Treaties.[102]

The leading discussion by the International Court of the creation of custom through treaty remains the *North Sea Continental Shelf Cases* of 1969.[103] There, the argument of Denmark and The Netherlands was that the equidistance rule for division of the

98 Convention on the Regulation of Aerial Navigation, Paris, 1919, 11 LNTS 173; 1922 UKTS 2, Cmnd. 1609; 1 *Hudson Int. Leg.* 359; [1923] 17 AJIL Supp. 195.

99 The wording of Art. 1 indicates that state sovereignty was a general principle for all states not only to the Parties to the 1919 Paris Convention. Before the First World War there had been no such general agreement. See J.C. Cooper, 'The International Air Navigation Conference, 1910' (1952) 19 *J. Air L. & Comm.* 127–143, rep. J.C. Cooper, *Explorations in Aerospace Law, Selected Essays* (I.A. Vlasic, ed.) (Montreal: McGill UP, 1968) 105–124, and his 'State Sovereignty in Space, 1910–1914' at 126–136. But cf. *infra* Chapter 4: did the 1919 treaty not create customary law?

100 UN Convention on the Law of the Sea, 1982, 1833 UNTS 3; (1982) 21 ILM 1261–354, as amended by the 'Agreement to Implement Part XI of the Law of the Sea Convention', UNGA Res. 48/263; (1994) 33 ILM 1309; 1999 UKTS 81, Cmnd. 4524 (Treaty) and 1999 UKTS 82, Cmnd. 4525 (Part IX Amendment); see conveniently, *The Law of the Sea, United Nations Convention on the Law of the Sea* (New York: UN, 1997).

101 *Supra*, n. 92.

102 *Supra*, at n. 96.

103 *North Sea Continental Shelf Cases*, 1969 ICJ Rep. 1, Cf. Baxter – 2, *supra* n. 97, at 61–69 on that Case, and 57–74 generally on 'Multilateral Treaties as Constitutive of New Customary Law'. Discussions on lines similar to what follows, although not directed towards space law as such, are: H.W.A. Thirlway, 'The Sources of International Law', in M.D. Evans, ed., *International Law* (Oxford: Oxford UP, 2003) 117–144 at 134–136; and his, 'The Law and Procedure of the International Court of Justice 1960–1989 (Part Two)' (1990) 61 *BYIL* 1–134 at 97–98 dealing with 'Growth of a Customary Rule Subsequently to a Convention'; Sir Robert Jennings and Sir Arthur Watts, eds., *Oppenheim's International Law*, 9th ed., Vol. I, 'Peace' (London: Longman, 1996) Part 1, 25–31 (§ 10) on 'Custom' and 31–6 (§ 11) on 'Treaties and Custom'; A. Cassesse, *International Law* (Oxford: Oxford UP, 2001) at 120 and referring back to 63–64, considers space law as an area in which customary international law has been formed *inter alia* by the relevant UN Resolutions and the Outer Space Treaty. Curiously Cassese also cites the Moon Agreement of 1979 as formative of custom, but its lack of success militates against that since it does not meet the ICJ requirements to which we are coming. Cf. G.M. Danilenko, *Law-Making in the International Community* (Dordrecht: Martinus Nijhoff, 1993) 203–210; H.W.A. Thirlway, *International Customary Law and Codification* (The Hague: Kluwer, 1972) particularly 'International Law through the United Nations', 61–79; Scott and Carr, *supra* n. 97 *ad fin.*

In its Advisory Opinion on the *Legality of the Threat or Use of Nuclear Weapons*, Advisory Opinion, 1996 1 ICJ Rep. at 256–257 (paras 75–80) (1996) 35 *ILM* 869, the Court states that the Hague and Geneva treaties on the Law of Armed Conflict (LOAC) are now part of customary international law. At para 219 of its Judgement in the *Case Concerning Armed Activities on the Territory of the Congo (Democratic Republic of the Congo v. Uganda)*, 2005 ICJ Rep. 1 (2006) 45 ILM 277, the Court refers to certain of the Hague Regulations annexed to Convention IV on the Rules and Customs of War of 1907 (36 Stat. 2277, TS 539,

continental shelf articulated in Art. 6 of the 1958 Geneva Convention on the Continental Shelf had passed into custom and therefore bound Germany even though Germany was not a party to the Convention. Although declining to so hold in that particular instance, the Court, together with some of the judges who filed separate or dissenting opinions, was clear that a suitably drawn treaty can indeed form the basis of a rule of general international law. Paragraph 71 of the Judgement (and the first sentence of para 72) indicates that the relevant provisions of such a treaty must be of a fundamentally norm-creating character, or at least have that potential. Where that is the case, then according to para 71, under such a rule,

> while only conventional or contractual in its origin has since passed into the general *corpus* of international law and is accepted as such by the *opinio juris*, so as to have become binding even for countries which have never, and do not, become parties to the Convention. There is no doubt that this process is a perfectly possible one and does from time to time occur: it constitutes indeed one of the recognised methods by which new rules of customary international law may be formed.

However, para 71 concludes with this warning: '[a]t the same time this result is not likely to be regarded as having been attained'.

According to the 1969 Judgement, various elements must be considered for any conventional rule to attain customary status. These include the lapse of time between the coming into force of the relevant treaty and the point at which international customary law is alleged to have appeared,[104] whether non-party states have objected to the treaty rule being sought to be categorised as custom[105] and the numbers and nature of the states party to the treaty. Here, the 1969 Judgement is immensely helpful when considering the concepts of the OST. Paragraph 73 begins,

> With respect to the other elements usually regarded as necessary before a conventional rule can be considered to have become a general rule of international law, it might be that, even without the passage of any considerable period of time, a very wide-spread and representative participation in the convention might suffice of itself, provided it included that of States whose interests were specially affected.

In the instance of the North Sea Continental Shelf, the Court noted that the ratifications to the 1958 Convention were not considerable for a number of states to which

---

1 Bevans 631) on bombardment and pillage and on the duties of an occupying power as having become or articulating customary law.

104 *North Sea Continental Shelf Cases*, 1969 ICJ Rep. 3, para 74. In the *Case* the periods of time involved were held to be too short. The date of the Judgement was only ten years after the Continental Shelf Treaty had been signed and just five years since it had come into force. The ICJ actions had been brought only three years after the Treaty came into force for its parties, and less than one year had elapsed between its coming into force and the breakdown of negotiations between the parties to the case.

105 J.I. Charney, 'The Persistent Objector Rule and the Development of Customary International Law' (1985) 66 *BYIL* 1–24; T.L. Stein, 'The Approach of the Different Drummer: The Principle of the Persistent Objector in International Law' (1985) 26 *Harv. Int. L.J.* 457–482.

participation was not open or to which the matter was of no interest by reason of their being landlocked. However,

> [t]hat non-ratification may sometimes be due to factors other than active disapproval of the convention concerned can hardly constitute a basis on which positive acceptance of its principles can be implied: the reasons are speculative, but the facts remain.

As to the matter of time, para 74 of the Judgement *ad med.* observes:

> Although the passage of only a short period of time is not necessarily, or not of itself, a bar to the formation of a rule of customary international law on the basis of what was originally a purely conventional rule, an indispensable requirement would be that within the period in question, short though it might be, State practice, including that of States whose interests are specially affected should have been both extensive and virtually uniform in the sense of the provision invoked; – and should moreover have occurred in such a way as to show a general recognition that a rule of law or legal obligation is involved.

The time between the conclusion of a treaty and some of its principles becoming customary law can therefore be short. It is again indicated that those states most affected by such a potential customary rule should demonstrably comply with it if it is to be considered as a rule of law, as opposed to a mere practice.

That leaves the question whether state parties to a treaty containing a 'general norm-creating' provision are obeying the treaty or a new rule of customary law. The last sentence just quoted from the 1969 Judgement does not help us. Obviously there is recognition of a rule or legal obligation, but is that a 'general recognition'?

Here, reference to dissenting opinions in the 1969 case can help. Considering the creation of custom in Part III of his Judgement, Judge Lachs agreed with the Court majority that a treaty provision can indeed form the basis of a general rule binding on non-parties.[106] He also indicated that ordinarily, a long period of time may well be required for the establishing of a new rule of customary as opposed to treaty law but that, as he went on,

> the great acceleration of social and economic change, combined with that of science and technology, have confronted law with a serious challenge: one it must meet, lest it lag even farther behind events than it has been wont to do.

Then, very germane to the argument as to space law and the OST, Judge Lachs cited the freedom of access to space above air space as a clear example of the way in which a rule of customary international law can swiftly develop.[107]

---

106 *North Sea Continental Shelf Cases*, 1969 ICJ Rep., 3, Diss. Op. Lachs, 219–240 at 225–232.

107 Cf. Sir Gerald Fitzmaurice, 'A new rule of customary law based on the practice of States can in fact emerge very quickly, and even almost suddenly if new circumstances have arisen that imperatively call for legal regulation – though the time factor is never wholly irrelevant' – 'The Law and Procedure of the International Court of Justice, 1951–54: General Principles and Sources of Law' (1953) 30 *BYIL* 1–70 at 31. That Sir Gerald made this throwaway but intriguing comment while actually discussing Historic Rights does not diminish its potential application to space law.

In his dissent, Judge Sorenson took a similar line. At pp. 233–234 of the ICJ report, he took up the question of the length of time needed to create custom and noted that the Court had previously held that only a short time might be required, based only upon recent state practice. He stated,

> This is particularly important in view of the extremely dynamic process of evolution which the international community is engaged in at the present stage of history. Whether the mainspring of this evolution is to be found in the development of ideas, in social and economic factors, or in new technology, it is characteristic of our time that new problems and circumstances incessantly arise and imperatively call for legal regulation. In situations of this nature, a convention adopted as part of the combined process of codification and progressive development of international law may well constitute, or come to constitute, the decisive evidence of generally accepted new rules of international law. The fact that it does not purport to be simply declaratory of existing customary law is immaterial in this context. The convention may serve as an authoritative guide for the practice of States faced with the relevant new legal problems, and its provisions thus become the nucleus round which a new set of generally recognised legal rules may crystallize. The word 'custom', with its traditional time connotation, may not even be an adequate expression for the purpose of describing this particular source of law.[108]

Judge Sorenson was writing of the 1958 Continental Shelf Convention, a treaty that had been elaborated through the procedures of the International Law Commission (ILC), a body which acts on the basis of years of gathering and sifting state practice, and by the need to consolidate and codify existing law. The OST was developed through COPUOS, a rather different body with, perhaps, not the complex legal background or expertise of the ILC. However, COPUOS does operate (in the main) by consensus,[109] and it certainly did so in developing the OST.[110]

The whole process from the establishing of COPUOS to the final text of the OST took less than a decade. COPUOS was entering into a new area of law with only some General Assembly Resolutions and the work of a very few academic studies to help guide. Nonetheless, what Judges Lachs and Sorenson wrote can apply to elements of the OST. They meet the criteria set out by the Court itself and by other separate opinions in the North Sea Continental Shelf Cases of 1969.

What of scholarly discussions of the point? Amongst commentators, L.B. Sohn suggested that in the case of the later 1982 Law of the Sea Convention, new norms of customary international law might well be readily developed through the negotiation of general international treaties.[111] This view was attacked by J.I. Charney as perhaps an unduly liberal attitude and fraught with the difficulty that the Law of the Sea negotiations certainly did

---

108 As to this last sentence, cf. M. Mendelson, 'The Subjective Element in Customary International Law' (1995) 66 *BYIL* 177–208.

109 See Chapter 2, 'COPUOS'.

110 The *travaux préparatoires* of the OST are available at: www.unoosa.org/oosa/en/ourwork/spacelaw/treaties/ travaux-preparatoires/outerspacetreaty.html.

111 L.B. Sohn, 'The Law of the Sea: Customary International Law Developments' (1984–5) 34 *Am. U. L. Rev.* 271–280. Cf. P. Weil, 'Towards Relative Normativity in International Law?' (1983) 77 *AJIL* 413–442.

not necessarily clearly appear in the *travaux preparatoires*.[112] While not wholly discounting the possibility that custom could be so developed, Charney preferred to stick with international custom established by the traditional means, advising caution when considering any suggestion that a rule of custom has been established arising out of a treaty provision. We might agree with that approach in general, but the principles of space law enshrined in the OST may well be examples of precisely such an occurrence.[113]

What should not be counter-argued is that the Outer Space Treaty was merely the traditional 'package deal'. Although the text was arrived at by consensus within COPUOS and is clearly based upon the General Assembly space resolutions, the OST was not a codification and consolidation of already existent concepts of law adopted by a general conference where the overall package is the result of compromise of existing interests by the states party to it. In codification/consolidation, an existing rule of customary law may be articulated in treaty form, but other rules agreed by the conference are based on 'bargain', their terms being formed to reflect compromise rather than *opinio juris*. Such treaties do not readily form custom.

By contrast, the 1967 Treaty was, as Lachs might have said, the intelligent foreseeing of the need for legally regulating a new set of problems and was a major attempt to lay down ground rules for the future worked out by a group of experts and then submitted to the General Assembly for its action. There may have been an element of compromise of interest in some of its terms, but the fundamental principles of space law were considered largely prospectively in the absence of existing rules, albeit with the harbingers of the General Assembly resolutions.[114]

Acceptance of the OST is excellent.[115] As of 2023, one hundred thirteen states out of a UN membership of one hundred ninety-three had ratified the OST. The ratifying states include at present all the space-competent and space-active states.[116] By far, the vast majority of the states whose interests are affected are parties to it. In addition, twenty-three

---

112 J.I. Charney, 'International Agreements and the Development of Customary International Law' (1986) 61 *Wash. L. Rev.* 971–996 at 991–996. At n. 88 Charney notes that much of the negotiation of the Law of the Sea Treaty took place 'off the record'. The COPUOS negotiations of the OST were comparable, as to which see *supra* n. 110.

113 Cf. V.S. Vereschetin and G.M. Danilenko, 'Custom as a Source of International Law of Outer Space' (1985) 13 *J. Sp. Law* 22–35 [Lyall/Larsen 113–26]. M.S. McDougal, 'The Emerging Customary Law of Space' (1963–1964) 58 *Nw. U. L. Rev.* 618–642; cf. H.H. Almond, Jr., 'General Principles of Law – Their Role in the Development of the Law of Outer Space' (1986) 57 *U. Colo. L. Rev.* 871–883. Treaty morphing into custom may be seen elsewhere: C.L. Carr and G.L. Scott, 'Multilateral Treaties and the Formation of Customary International Law' (1996) 25 *Denv. J. Int. L. & Pol.* 71–94, and their 'Multilateral Treaties and the Environment: A Case Study in the Formation of Customary International Law' (1998–1999) 27 *Denv. J. Int. L. & Pol.* 313–335. However, cf. L.F.E. Goldie, 'A Note on Some Diverse Meanings of "The Common Heritage of Mankind"' (1983) 10 *Syr. J. Int. L. & Com.* 69–112, Kelly, *infra* n. 114 and Bradley and Gulati, *infra* n. 131. See also ILC, 'Identification of Customary International Law' (2016) *II YBILC* 59–82; 'Draft Conclusions on the Identification of Customary International Law' (2018) *II YBILC* 901–113.

114 See H. Thirlway, 'The Law and Procedure of the International Court of Justice 1960–1989 (Part Two)' (1990) 61 *BYIL* 1–134 at 98–102 discussing 'the significance of conventions: voting, participation and the "package deal"' together with materials there cited. J.P. Kelly, 'The Twilight of Customary International Law' (1999–2000) 40 *Va. J. Int'l L.* 449–543 broadly argues that the traditional concept of 'custom' is now inadequate, and that treaty agreement on the basis of full discussion is preferable. However, the broad principles of the OST would seem to lie precisely within such a notion.

115 *Supra* at n. 2.

116 It may interest some that the Democratic Republic of Korea ratified the OST in 2007.

signatory states are bound by their signatures not to act contrary to the basic thrust of the Treaty.[117] State practice is extensive and appears to be virtually uniform; there is freedom of access to space, no objections to over-flight by satellites, no territorial claims (by states at least) to the moon or other celestial bodies and no military use of space (at least in the aggressive meaning of 'military use').[118]

As for the matter of lapse of time, the OST has been in force since 1967 – well over half a century by the time these pages are published – and was well ratified from its early days; lastly, there has been no formal objection to the OST. In this instance, no persistent objector argument can really stand.[119] Perhaps some of the emergent nations might include it among the 'international law' that existed before they did and hence were not involved in its making,[120] but the argument is stronger that the OST forms part of the corpus of the legal system in which they have come into being.

Further support for the proposition that elements of the OST have passed into customary international law can be found from various UNGA resolutions adopted after the OST that deal with space.[121] Indeed the space resolutions (or some of them) may in the future in effect be treated as sources of law in themselves.[122] However, we are content here for

---

117 See Art. 18 of the Vienna Convention on the Law of Treaties and *supra* n. 92.

118 Cf. 'The Space Millennium: Vienna Declaration on Space and Human Development' adopted by the Plenary Meeting of the Third United Nations Conference on the Exploration and Peaceful Uses of Outer Space, Vienna, 30 July 1999 (A/CONF.184/6 30 July 1999), the Preamble of which *inter alia* recognises 'that active support for space activities is expressed in the observance by States and by international organisations of the provisions of the outer space treaties'. Other paragraphs refer to other particular aspects of space law. The text is available at www.unoosa.org/pdf/reports/unispace/viennadeclE.pdf.

119 The signatories of the Bogota Declaration (*supra* n. 45) took the view that OST Art. II did not apply to the geostationary orbit, but even they conceded that satellites in other orbits were travelling in outer space. This is not a substantial objection to the non-sovereignty principle of OST Art. II.

120 This point is made in the Bogota Declaration (*supra* n. 45).

121 See Chapter 2 – 'UN Resolutions', Marboe, *supra* n. 91, and CoCoSL III, *passim*.

122 See previous note and: A. Terekhov, 'U.N. General Assembly Resolutions and Outer Space Law' (1997) 40 *Proc. IISL* 87–107 [Lyall/Larsen 101–11]; C.Q. Christol, 'The United Nations and the Development of International Law – Unanimous Resolutions of the General Assembly Dealing with Outer Space' (1965) 23 *Proc. Inst. of World Affairs*, reprinted in his *Space Law – Past, Present and Future* (Deventer: Kluwer, 1991), 311–328; J. Castaneda, 'Valeur juridique des resolutions des Nations Unies' (1970-I) 129 *Hague Recueil* 205–332; and his *The Legal Effect of UN Resolutions* (New York: Columbia UP, 1969); famously, B. Cheng, 'United Nations Resolutions on Outer Space: 'Instant' International Customary Law?' (1965) 5 *Ind. J. Int. Law* 23 (rep. Cheng 125–149); S.M. Schwebel, 'The Effect of Resolutions of the U.N. General Assembly on Customary International Law' (1979) 73 *Proc. ASIL* 301–309; L.B. Sohn, 'The Impact of Technological Changes on International Law' (1973) 30 *Wash. & Lee L. Rev.* 1–18 at 6–10. H. Thirlway, 'The Sources of International Law', in M.D. Evans, ed., *International Law* (Oxford: Oxford UP, 2003) 117–144 at 141 notes that in the Nicaragua Case, *Military and Paramilitary Activities in and against Nicaragua (Nicaragua v. United States of America) Merits, Judgement*, 1986 ICJ Rep. 14, the International Court made some reference to General Assembly Resolutions, but chose not to characterise these as a source of law, holding at para 184: 'The mere fact that States declare their recognition of certain rules is not sufficient for the Court to consider these as part of customary international law and as applicable as such to these States'. Thirlway comments that had the Court considered General Assembly Resolutions as a creative source of law independent of custom it would have taken that opportunity in the Nicaragua Case. Cf. the whole concept of 'soft law': O. Schachter, 'The Twilight Existence of Nonbinding International Agreements' (1977) 71 *AJIL* 296–304; M. Ferrazzani, 'Soft Law in Space Activities', in G. Lafferranderie, ed., *Outlook on Space Law over the Next Thirty Years* (The Hague: Kluwer, 1997) 429–447, Marboe, and our discussion of 'soft law' *supra* Chapter 2.

present purposes to cite them only as buttressing the argument as to developing a customary nature for certain provisions of the OST. The combination of the OST principles and their resonance with UN resolutions, most of which had been adopted without vote is a significant mass establishing the customary status of those principles.[123]

Again, measures adopted after the OST provide evidence of the customary nature of certain of its elements. The argument is the same as that for the post-OST UN resolutions: the space treaties proceed on the basis that outer space requires regulation within the general framework of law established by the OST. Take, for example, the revised International Satellite Organisation Agreement (ITSO), and the revised International Mobile Satellite Organisation Agreement.[124] There are also the various cooperation agreements and MOUs relating to space activities. These all proceed on the basis of the general principles of space law. Practice under such agreements and understandings conforms to the statements as to principle contained in the OST. Both practice and *opinio juris* are present since the various parties clearly recognise that compliance with these principles is the way to proceed and they act accordingly.

Of course, for these arguments, much depends on what one understands by a rule of customary international law and how its existence is to be seen.[125] Obviously the matter could be closed were the International Court formally to state in a contentious case that particular elements of the OST do have customary status and are therefore binding on all states whether or not they are parties to the treaty. Short of that, we point to various official statements made at the time the General Assembly adopted the OST.[126]

We point to the affirmations of the UN resolutions prior to the Treaty. We point to the virtually unanimous adoption without vote of some of the post-OST resolutions. Equally, and perhaps more importantly, we look to what states have done – and not done – to state practice. After all, to quote the exact terms of Art. 38.1.b of its statute, the International Court of Justice is to apply 'international custom, as evidence of a general practice accepted as law'.

The general practice is fundamental, but the statute provides no guidance indicating how it is to be identified as accepted. Practice is the whole basis of custom. In the article already referred to, Sir Gerald Fitzmaurice, then legal adviser to the UK Foreign Office and himself later a distinguished judge of the International Court, commented on the dissenting opinion of Judge Read in the *Anglo-Norwegian Fisheries Case* of 1951. Read had said, 'Customary international law is the generalisation of the practice of States' and had gone

123 B. Wessel, 'The Rule of Law in Outer Space: The Effects of Treaties and Nonbinding Agreements on International Space Law' (2012) 35 *Hastings Int. Comp. L. Rev.* 289–322.
124 See Chapter 10: www.itso.int, and www.imso.org.
125 A difference of approach is often discernible between commentators whose legal background is a code-based legal system, and those from common law systems, just as there is between legal positivists and those that allow a greater role to 'natural law'. The former tend to want to see equality between practice and formally expressed *opinio juris*, while the others are more content to rely on the observation of practice and can deduce *opinio* from silence.
126 These statements, as well as others made when the other UN Space Treaties were adopted, can conveniently be found in the *Commemorative Edition of United Nations Treaties and Principles on Outer Space Published on the Occasion of the Third United Nations Conference on the Exploration and Peaceful Uses of Outer Space (UNISPACE III)*, A/CONF.84/BP/15.

on to suggest that the essential element of custom was state practice rather than formal declarations and the like.[127] Fitzmaurice observed,

> While this point of view must probably not be pressed so far as to rule out the probative value, and the contribution to the formation of usage and custom, of State professions in their various forms (legislation, declarations, diplomatic statements &c.), it is believed to be a sound principle that, in the long run it is only the actions of States that build up practice, just as it is only practice ('constant and uniform', as the Court has said) that constitutes a usage or custom, and builds up eventually a rule of customary international law.[128]

Sir Gerald was writing of an international custom developing, as it were, independently: we are considering custom begotten by treaty. When one puts state practice in relation to space alongside the UN space resolutions, the OST and the other space agreements, the MOUs, the working arrangements, etc., it is difficult to conclude other than that the fundamental principles of the OST are indeed now custom, and as such bind all states.

All that said, we note recent discussion as to whether a state can withdraw from a rule of international custom.[129] Were that possible, it could obviously affect our argument. However, we would counter-argue that even if the concept of international custom comes to be modified to allow such a withdrawal, it could occur only by the emergence of a contrary custom in the practice of a number of states.[130] That has not happened and is unlikely to happen in respect of the fundamental principles of the OST.[131]

The argument can be taken one step further. There is no evidence of any persistent objector to the OST principles, let alone the emergence of contrary practice on the part of a group of states.[132] Indeed, there is considerable strength in the argument of Carl Q. Christol that the fundamental principles of the OST now come into the category of *ius cogens*, principles of law that cannot be receded from, any attempt to legislate to the contrary being void.[133]

127 *Fisheries Case (United Kingdom v. Norway)*, 1951 ICJ Rep. 1, Dissenting Opinion of Judge J.E. Read, 186 at 191.
128 G. Fitzmaurice, 'The Law and Procedure of the International Court of Justice, 1951–54: General Principles and Sources of Law' (1953) 30 *BYIL* 1–70 at 68.
129 The basic argument is that it is anomalous that a state can withdraw from a treaty but not from a custom. Cf. Bradley and Gulati, *infra* n. 131; C.L. Lim and O. Elias, 'Withdrawing from Custom and the Paradox of Consensualism in International Law' (2010) 21 *Duke J. Comp. & Int. Law Quart.* 143–156.
130 In Scots Law a contrary practice can displace a rule of the common law, but for that there must be overt practice: cf. *Brown v Magistrates of Edinburgh*, 1931 SLT 456.
131 Thus, citing the example of outer space, C.A. Bradley and M. Gulati were of the view that states cannot withdraw from customary rules as to global commons: see their 'Withdrawing from International Custom' (2010) 120 *Yale L.J.* 202–275 at 212. Cf. their 'Customary International Law and Withdrawal Rights in an Age of Treaties' (2010) 21 *Duke J. Comp & Int. Law Quart.* 1–30. The whole Fall 2010 Part of the Journal contains a symposium on withdrawal from international custom. The general argument is interesting but seems of little relevance for the customary law of space.
132 In any event the 'persistent objector' does not destroy the general principle of customary law objected to. It merely means that that objector is not bound by it. Cf. J.L. Trachtman, 'Persistent Objectors, Cooperation, and the Utility of Customary International Law' (2010) 21 *Duke J. Comp & Int. Law Quart.* 221–233 together with materials *supra* nn. 97, 105 and 119.
133 C.Q. Christol, 'Judge Manfred Lachs and the Principle of Jus Cogens' (1994) 22 *J. Sp. Law* 33–45.

Non-signatories to or withdrawers from the OST cannot avoid its fundamental obligations, and buccaneering entrepreneurs cannot dodge its provisions by sophisticated devices, shell companies and appropriate contracts. Suggestions that they can are misleading fantasies, but it is important for the future of space exploration and use as well as of space law that these chimeras be clearly seen to be such. Bluntly, we consider that there is no lawful method by which the broad principles of the public international law of space can be circumvented. It is true that new agreements and arrangements are being worked out for aspects of the commercial and private exploitation of space,[134] but the major states' rights and duties that comprise the framework of space law in its public international aspect are clear both under the OST and now under customary international law.

---

134 B. Cheng, 'The Commercial Development of Space: The Need for New Treaties' (1991) 19 *J. Sp. L.* 17–44 (rep. Cheng, 641–670); B. Beck, 'The Next, Small, Step for Mankind: Fixing the Inadequacies of the International Space Law Treaty Regime to Accommodate the Modern Space Flight Industry' (2009) 19 *Alb. L.J. Sci. & Tech.* 1–38 and materials cited *supra* n. 28. Cf. the U.S. Space Resource Exploration and Utilization Act of 2015, Pub. L. 114–90, *supra* n. 44, and our discussion of space mining, *infra* Chapter 7.

4

SPACE OBJECTS

Control, Registration, Return and Liability – Treaties and Practice

Introduction

Three UN treaties, the Agreement on the Rescue and Return of Astronauts (ARRA) of 1968, the Liability Convention of 1972 and the Registration Convention of 1975, expanded the provisions of the Outer Space Treaty of 1967, affording for their parties a degree of precision to the rights and duties, responsibilities and constraints it sets out. Now decades old, and maybe capable of improvement, they remain the sources for major issues of space law and have not been subject to amendment.[1]

This chapter deals with space objects, reserving most questions of persons for separate treatment in Chapter 5. ARRA figures only in its technical provision for space objects. The Moon Agreement of 1979 and celestial bodies are covered in Chapter 7.

The formation of space law brought together different and sometimes divergent legal traditions of the world to cope speedily with new problems in a way that the formulations of earlier international law did not.[2] Older international law often emerged over decades and more or less within a fairly coherent set of legal traditions and expectations. Space law has developed in a world where many legal systems, methods of argument and debate and divergent interests have melded to cope with rapidly evolving technologies.[3]

We take the material in the order of control, registration, the return of space objects and liability for damage before turning to the space stations and finishing with questions

---

1 Contrast the ITU treaties which have been subject to change as the ITU has, within its specialised area, grappled with such matters as the use of radio in space. See *infra* Chapter 8.
2 To repeat citations from Chapter 1, see M. Lachs, 'Thoughts on Science, Technology and World Law' (1992) 86 *AJIL* 673–699; C.W. Jenks, 'International Law and Activities in Space' (1956) 5 *ICLQ* 99–114, 'The New Science and the Law of Nations' (1968) 17 *ICLQ* 327–345. See also the argument towards the end of Chapter 3 that elements of the OST are customary law.
3 Again cf. the materials of n. 2 *supra*, F. Lyall, *Technology, Sovereignty and International Law* (Abingdon: Routledge, 2022); A.E. Gottleib, 'The Impact of Technology on the Development of Contemporary International Law' (1981-I) 170 *Hague Recueil* 115; J.L. Charney, 'Technology and International Negotiations' (1982) *AJIL* 78–118; J.A. Bosco, 'International Law regarding Outer Space: An Overview' (1990) 55 *J. Air L. & Comm.* 609–652.

DOI: 10.4324/9781003496502-4

of intellectual property raised by inventions on such bodies. The basic treaties that involve the relevant content of the OST were the 1975 Registration Convention,[4] ARRA of 1968 and the Liability Convention of 1972. This chronoclastic order allows a better appreciation of the overall structure of law composed by these treaties. The literature tends to consider them individually; the ratifications of these treaties vary both in number and in parties, and the original commentators dealt with each as they were adopted or tended to write about each in isolation. That has some advantages. Nonetheless it is desirable to see the complete picture.

It is vital that this overall structure of law can be described. Space activities are dangerous, subject to possibly catastrophic failures and potentially devastating to uninvolved others. While an accident on launch may be confined to the territory of a launching state, in many instances, another state may also be affected. It was therefore important that space activities be the subject of rules and of an inter-connecting set of agreements more precise than the broad principles of the OST. How responsibility should be established for supervision, for ownership at the state level, and for liability in the case of damage or devastation, needed clarification. Those who license space activities should have sufficiently accurate knowledge to avoid difficulties. The connection between an occurrence and its author must be clear. Astronauts should be rescued. Space objects should be returned to sender or at least returnable to sender.

The three treaties covered in this chapter have now been in force for many years. Both the Registration and Liability Conventions have a provision calling for consideration of its revision on the UN General Assembly agenda ten years after it came into force.[5] In both instances, technically, the Assembly did consider whether to review but did not go on to call for the revision of either.[6] That could indicate that these treaties are satisfactory as they are, that there is indifference as to their contemporary suitability or simply that other matters have taken the attention of the international community.

An alternative, however, could be that to review them would be to open the proverbial 'can of worms'. It is unlikely that anything approaching unanimity or consensus would be arrived at were these matters to be re-negotiated today. Instead, there has been an increased use of UN resolutions and other arrangements as to practice that has deflected criticism of inadequacies in the formal treaty provisions or occasionally supplied clearer content for looser treaty requirements. Thus we see UNGA Res. 62/101 of 2007 on the registration of space objects,[7] and the 2013 UNGA Res. 68/74 on national legislation.[8]

---

4 As will be seen *infra* at n. 17, apart from the provisions of the Registration Convention, it remains competent to register in terms of UNGA 1721 (XVI) c.

5 Registration Convention, Art. X; Liability Convention, Art. XXVI.

6 There does not appear to have been much discussion of an actual review of either: see Question of the review of the Convention on International Liability for Damage Caused by Space Objects, UNGA Res. 37/91, 1982 and Question of the review of the Convention on the Registration of Objects launched into Outer Space, UNGA Res. 41/66, 1986. Both conclude with an exhortation to states to ratify or accede to the Convention.

7 Recommendations on enhancing the practice of states and intergovernmental organisations in registering space objects, 2007, UNGA Res. 62/101. K.-U. Schrogl and N. Hedman, 'The UNGA General Assembly Resolution 62/101 of 17 December 2007 on Recommendations on Enhancing the Practice of States and Intergovernmental Organisations in Registering Space Objects' (2008) 34 *J. Sp. L.* 141–162; CoCoSL III 401–481.

8 Recommendations on National Legislation Relevant to the Peaceful Exploration and Use of Outer Space, 11 December 2013, UNGA Res. 68/74; CoCoSL III 483–603.

We will also note the 1992 UNGA Res. 47/68 on Nuclear Power Sources[9] and the Space Debris Mitigation Guidelines of 2007.[10] These interact with liability and the use of space, although they will also figure in our consideration of the space environment in Chapter 9.

The number of ratifications and signatures of the three treaties varies. To some extent, that falsifies our attempt to consider them as a quasi-bundle, but even granted that limited point, compliance with and implementation of the package is the way forward for space law. When dealing with the COPUOS annual reports, the General Assembly regularly recommends that all states sign and ratify the UN space treaties, although that exhortation has not had much immediate effect. However, as more states have begun space activities in recent years, signature, ratification and compliance with treaties has reassuringly increased.[11]

Responsibility, Control and Jurisdiction

The fundamental principles regarding responsibility for space activities, the control to be exercised over them and jurisdiction in such matters are contained in OST Arts VI and VIII. Under Art. VI, a state bears international responsibility for its own activities and for those of its nationals in outer space. The activities of nongovernmental entities are to be duly authorised and to be subject to continuing supervision by the appropriate state.

Responsibility for the activities of an international organisation is to be borne by that organisation and the state parties to the OST that are its members. A state party to the OST on whose registry an object is launched into space retains jurisdiction and control over the object and any personnel (OST Art. VIII). Appropriate registration is therefore important, and the simple reference to a registry in Art. VIII has been extended by the Registration Convention.

Ownership of a space object is not affected by its launch into space (OST Art. VIII). Similarly, the ownership of a space object constructed elsewhere than on Earth is unaffected by that origin (OST Art. VIII). There is no suggestion that a state or other entity can divest itself of obligations in relation to space objects by abandonment. In short, we believe that a state cannot cease to be responsible for or avoid any correlative duties by abandoning a space object. A sunken state ship is only instance in international law where a state can abandon something for which it has responsibility.[12]

Some might argue that under the international law of treaties, such provision applies only to parties to the OST. It is difficult to accept such a suggestion, although, particularly

---

9 Principles Relevant to the Use of Nuclear Power Sources in Outer Space, 14 December 1992, UNGA Res. 47/68; (1993) 32 ILM 921–926 (with Introductory note by C.Q. Christol, 917–920); CoCoSL III 189–297.

10 Space Debris Mitigation Deadlines of the Committee on the Peaceful Uses of Outer Space, endorsed in 2007 by UNGA Res. 62/217; CoCoSL III 605–657.

11 An annual IISL Committee Report contains a table of alterations in the signatures and ratifications from 1999. See the annual *Proc IISL* or https://iislweb.space/2001-standing-committee-report/. UN OOSA provides a table of current signatures and ratifications: www.unoosa.org/oosa/en/ourwork/spacelaw/treaties/status/index.html.

12 In theory, territory may be formally abandoned. Abandonment of territory may also be inferred. As to the abandonment of sunken warships and other state vessels, see D.J. Bederman, 'Rethinking the Legal Status of Sunken Warships' (2000) 31 *Ocean Dev. & Int. L.* 97–125; S. Drumgoole, 'The International Agreement for the Protection of the *Titanic*: Problems and Prospects' (2006) 37 *Ocean Dev. & Int. L.* 1–31.

in relationship to space debris, an owner may be difficult to find. The generality of the rules on the use of space would be needlessly compromised were a state able to avoid its obligations by abandoning a space object.[13]

Registration

The concept of an official register maintained for various purposes is old. In most countries, information as to the ownership of immoveable property is compiled on an official register.[14] Many types of mobile property are similarly dealt with. Vehicles are registered (licensed), as are ships[15] and aeroplanes.[16] It was therefore not surprising that in Part B of UNGA Res. 1721 (XVI) of 20 December 1961, the General Assembly called on states to 'furnish information promptly' to the UN 'for the registration of launchings' and requested that the Secretary General maintain a public registry of the information received. This procedure remains available.[17] Two years later, paras 7 and 9 of the 1963 Declaration on Space Principles, UNGA Res. 1962 (XVIII), referred to a state as having a registry of 'objects launched into outer space' and to the 'state of registry' of a 'space vehicle'. However, it took a further thirteen years for the idea of registration of space objects fully to emerge in treaty form with the data to be registered fully set out.[18] In the meantime, OST Art. VII had, without further explanation, provided that a 'State Party to the Treaty on whose registry an object launched into outer space is carried' retains jurisdiction and control over it and its personnel.

---

13 See also Chapter 9.
14 The general public land title registries in Scotland go back to 1617, replacing a less formal but public system that for most parts of the country dated from the thirteenth century. Entry in the Scottish land register gives a title valid against all comers. Curiously, land registries are not public in all states.
15 Cf. Art. 5 of the Convention on the High Seas, Geneva, 29 April 1958, 450 UNTS 82; 1963 UKTS 5, Cmnd. 1929; 13 UST 2312, TIAS 5200; [1958] AJIL 842; and Art. 91 of the UN Convention on the Law of the Sea, Montego Bay, 10 December 1982, 1833 UNTS 3; 1999 UKTS 81, Cmnd. 4524; (1982) 21 ILM 1261; US Tr. Doc. 103–39. Note: Convention on Conditions for the Registration of Ships, 7 February 1986, UN Doc. TD/RS/CONF/19/Add. 1; (1987) 26 ILM 1229 at 1236–1250 (not yet in force: see *infra* n. 74).
16 Cf. formerly Art. 6 and Annex A, Convention on the Regulation of Aerial Navigation, Paris, 13 October 1919, 11 LNTS 173; 1922 UKTS 2, Cmnd. 1609; 1 Hudson 359; 13 Martens (3d) 61; [1923] 17 *AJIL* Supp. 195: Arts 17–21 and Convention on International Civil Aviation, Chicago, 7 December 1944 (1944) 15 UNTS 295; 61 Stat. 1180, TIAS 1591; (1953) UKTS 8, Cmnd. 8742; 9 Hudson 168; 3 Bevans 944; [1945] 39 *AJIL* Supp 111; ICAO Doc. 7300/9, and 'Aircraft Nationality and Registration Marks', Annex 7 to the ICAO Convention.
17 Information supplied is published by UN OOSA in the A/AC.105/INF series, available through the OOSA website: www.unoosa.org., e.g. www.unoosa.org/oosa/en/spaceobjectregister/submissions/malaysia.html.
    Notifications under the Res. 1721 B procedure are also on the general list: www.unoosa.org/oosa/en/SORegister/index.html. A defect of the Res. 1721 procedure is that it does not require the detail that the Convention does, although some states notifying under it do provide additional information.
18 The first suggestion of international and national registries for spacecraft appears in Arts 6 and 7 of the suggested Project of an International Convention on Space Law, in M.S. Smirnoff, 'The Role of the IAF in the Elaboration of Norms of Future Space Law' (1959) 2 *Proc. IISL* 147–155 at 150–152. See also 'Historical Background and Context', CoCoSL II, 234–238; C. Dalfen, 'Towards an International Convention on the Registration of Space Objects: The Gestation Process' (1971) 9 *Can. YBIL* 252–268; and materials cited *infra* n. 23.

The registration of space objects is now commonly addressed under the 1975 Registration Convention.[19] When an object is launched into space, it should be entered in the register maintained by the UN Office for Outer Space Affairs (OOSA), which now consolidates the information provided to the UN under UN Res. 1721 (XVI) 1961,[20] and in the register maintained by the state of launching as defined in the Registration Convention (Art. I).[21] Internationally, the UN's is the more important register, allowing the clear identification of at least one of the states involved in the launch of a space object. It does have other purposes, but entry in that register is important for grounding responsibility, for ownership, for the exercise of control and in the worst case, for liability.

That said, we would note that not all launches and/or space objects are so registered. Some space-active states are not parties to the Convention. Some have not yet established a national registry. In some instances where two or more states are involved in space launches, they have not agreed *inter se* on which should act to register the objects involved. Again, some private activities, often including cube-sats, are not nationally registered. We hope such instances will diminish.[22]

The Convention on Registration of Objects Launched into Outer Space, adopted by UNGA Res. 3235 (XXIX) on 12 November 1974, opened for signature on 14 January 1975 and entered into force on 15 September 1976.[23] As at 1 January 2023, it had been ratified by seventy-five states, rather better than the fifty-one of our first edition.[24] As noted, the General Assembly regularly recommends that all states sign and ratify the UN space treaties, but progress in this case seems slow, especially now that many states are procuring launches of their own satellites. Four international organisations, ESA, EUMETSAT, EUTELSAT and INTERSPUTNIK, have accepted its rights and obligations.

As its full title indicates, the Registration Convention mandates entering objects launched into outer space in a formal official registry maintained by a relevant state.[25] It also provides for the maintenance of a central world register by the UN Secretary General with open public access to it (Art. III). These national and international registries create means and procedures to assist in identifying space objects in addition to any other means of identification that may exist. This mandatory system therefore allows space objects to be

---

19 Citation *infra* n. 23.
20 Outlined *supra* n. 17.
21 Submissions are listed at www.unoosa.org/oosa/en/spaceobjectregister/submissions/states-organisations. html and www.unoosa.org/oosa/en/SORegister/index.html. See Di Pippo, *infra* n. 46, significantly updating the 'Practice of States and International Organizations in Registering Space Objects: Background Paper by the Secretariat' (COPUOS), A/AC105/C.2/L.255 + Corr. 1 and 2 (2005).
22 Cf. Di Pippo, *infra* n. 46.
23 Convention on the Registration of Objects Launched into Outer Space, 14 January 1975; 1023 UNTS 15; 1978 UKTS 70, Cmnd. 7271; TIAS 8480; (1975) 14 ILM 43–48. For analysis, see CoCoSL II 227–324. The *travaux préparatoires* are available at www.unoosa.org/oosa/en/ourwork/spacelaw/treaties/travaux-preparatoires/rescue-agreement.html.
  Discussions include A.A. Cocca, 'Convention on Registration of Objects Launched into Outer Space', I Manual 173–193; Christol 213–245; Cheng 286–356 updating I Manual 83–172. Cf. F. von der Dunk, 'Beyond *What? Beyond Earth Orbit?* . . . ! The Applicability of the Registration Convention to Private Commercial Manned *Sub-Orbital* Spaceflight' (2013) 43 *Cal. West Int. L.J.* 269–349.
24 Source *supra* n. 11. As of mid-2023, a further three states had signed but not yet ratified the Registration Convention: Burundi, Iran and Singapore.
25 Notifications are listed in www.unoosa.org/oosa/en/spaceobjectregister/national-registries/index.html.

identified both to plan launches and – equally (or more) importantly – as a means by which space objects that have caused damage may be traced to their launching state.[26] Registration also establishes a link between a space object (including any personnel aboard) and a particular state for the purposes of jurisdiction, control and the return of space objects set out in OST Art. VIII and in ARRA, to which we are coming.

Article I of the Registration Convention defines its terms. 'Launching state' means (1) a state that launches or (2) procures the launching of a space object or (3) a state from whose territory or (4) from whose facility a space object is launched (Art. I(a)). Whether this is entirely satisfactory under modern conditions is a question. The term 'space object' is defined to include the component parts of a space object as well as its launch vehicles and parts thereof (Art. I(b)). The last phrase is important because implicates debris as included under the Convention.[27] The term 'state of registry' means a launching state on whose registry a space object is carried in accordance with Art. I(c).

Under Article II, it is the duty of a launching state to maintain a registry of the space objects it has launched into Earth orbit or beyond[28] and to notify the UN Secretary General of its establishment (Art. II.1).[29] It has to be said, however, that states have not always acted timeously.[30] Under Art. II.2, where two or more launching states are involved with the space object, they are to determine which is to register the object.[31] This could be important in two circumstances.

First, OST Art. V para 1 requires the return of astronauts to the state of registry of their space vehicle.[32] Second, under OST Art. VIII, the state party to the OST that has registered the object launched into outer space 'retains jurisdiction and control over such object, and over any personnel thereof, while in outer space or celestial body'. However, Art. II.2 of the Registration Convention acknowledges that other agreements may be concluded among launching states as to jurisdiction and control over a space object and over any personnel thereof.[33] The arrangements for the International Space Station (ISS) is an obvious example. Article 5.1 of the 1998 Intergovernmental Agreement on the

---

26 Technically, the Convention applies only to its parties, but should a non-party state suffer damage from or by a space object, its procedures would allow it to identify which states might have caused the damage. Cf. Art. XXI of the Liability Convention 1972 discussed below.

27 A number of notifications relate to debris from satellite launches and deployments. See, for example, notifications by the US by Notes Verbale of 1977 (ST/SG/SER.E/5) and 2004 (ST/SG/SER.E/449). The UN OOSA Online Index does not contain notifications that are only about debris.

28 See *supra* n. 18. Note that the duty to register emerges '[w]hen a space object is launched into earth orbit or beyond' (Art. II.1). Prospective registration or the registration of a failed launch does not happen. An entry in the registry is deleted when the object is no longer in Earth orbit (Art. IV.3).

29 As of July 2023, forty-four notifications of registries (inc. ESA and EUMETSAT) are listed: www.unoosa. org/oosa/en/spaceobjectregister/national-registries/index.html. Our second edition noted twenty-seven.

30 Contrast the UN OOSA listing of national legislation, including some states that have not yet, or have only partially, acted: www.unoosa.org/oosa/en/ourwork/spacelaw/nationalspacelaw.html. Curiously, the UK, which has maintained a registry since 1974 (now under the Outer Space Act 1986, c. 38, s. 7) formally notified the UN only on 24 June 2015: ST/SG/SER.E/INF/32, 30 July 2015.

31 Cf. Art. 10 of the Framework Agreement between the Government of the United States of America and the Government of the French Republic for Cooperative Activities in the Exploration and Use of Outer Space for Peaceful Purposes, 2007 (2006) 32 *J. Sp. L.* 447–463, under which agreement will be reached as to which party will register each object to be launched under the Agreement.

32 As discussed in more detail later, curiously ARRA requires the return of objects or astronauts to the relevant launching state.

33 Cf, the UK Supplementary Register, *infra* n. 35.

International Space Station provides that each Partner in the enterprise is to register the flight elements that it provides, the European Space Agency being the agent for the European Partner in this matter.[34]

The actual content of a domestic space register and the conditions under which it is maintained and kept up-to-date is a matter for the state maintaining that particular registry (Art. II.3). The UN Secretary General maintains a separate register to which there is full and open access (Art. III.1 and 2).

States are required as soon as practicable to send to the Secretary General specified information as to a space object which they have registered (Art. IV.1). In practice, this requirement may set minima for the content of a state registry since at least that information is likely to be included amongst the data it holds.[35] The basic information to be sent to the UN registry comprises (a) the name of the launching state or states; (b) an appropriate designator of the space object or its registration number; (c) the date and territory or location of the launch; (d) the basic orbital parameters including (i) the nodal period,[36] (ii) the inclination,[37] (iii) the apogee,[38] and (iv) the perigee[39] of the orbit and (e) the general function of the object. In addition, since a major purpose of the Registration Convention is to identify space objects, Art. V provides that when a space object launched into Earth orbit or beyond is marked with a designator or registration number or both,

---

34 For the space stations, see *infra* following n. 186.
35 Cf. the information entered in the UK registry as of May 2021:
    https://assets.publishing.service.gov.uk/government/uploads/system/uploads/attachment_data/file/988206/UK_Registry_of_Space_Objects_May_2021.pdf. The UK also maintains a Supplementary Registry of Outer Space Objects. These are objects which the UK has licensed but either the UK is not the launching state or it has been agreed that another state would put it on its register: https://assets.publishing.service.gov.uk/government/uploads/system/uploads/attachment_data/file/925089/UK_Supplementary_Registry_of_Space_Objects_-_October_2020.pdf.
    Some national registries record a great deal. For example, under Art. 5 of its National Decree no. 125/95, Establishment of the National Registry of Objects Launched into Outer Space, Argentina registers (1) if the object has been launched jointly with one or more other launching states, the international conventions concluded with that state or states; (2) an appropriate designator of the space object; (3) anticipated date and territory or location of launch; (4) anticipated basic orbital parameters including (a) nodal period, (b) inclination, (c) apogee and (d) perigee; (5) anticipated general function of the space object; (6) name and address of the owners and/or operators of the space object; (7) the firms participating in the construction of the space object and of its launch vehicle; (8) the launch service provider; (9) the insurances arranged; (10) the party responsible for exercising control over the space object; (11) the location and characteristics of the satellite tracking, telemetry and command station and of the master or tracking station, if applicable; (12) on-board transmission power and frequencies of the space station; (13) the mass of the space object; (14) the anticipated useful life of the space object; (15) precautions taken with regard to non-pollution of outer space, including celestial bodies, in particular whether mechanisms have been provided for placement in a transfer orbit at the end of the useful life of the space object; (16) anticipated date of disintegration, recovery or loss of contact with the space object; and (17) identifying mark located on non-disintegrable parts. Under Art. 6, when the mission of a registered space object is complete, or at the end of its useful life, or it is disabled by accident or otherwise such that it is unfit for further use, that information is also recorded in the register (Source: unofficial translation in *National Legislation and Policy: Selected Texts*, compiled for the UN/Nigeria Workshop on Space Law, November 2005). Art. 4 of the Smirnoff suggested Project of 1959, *supra* n. 18, called for data only on the spacecraft, location and exact time of flight, its duration and its aim.
36 How long the object takes to complete one orbit.
37 The angle between the plane of the orbit and the plane of the ecliptic stated in degrees, 90° being a polar orbit.
38 The high point of the orbit.
39 The low point of the orbit.

the state of registry is to notify the Secretary General of this datum when submitting the basic information required under Art. IV.1.[40] It is also open to a notifying state to provide additional information should it so wish (Art. IV.2).[41] Correlative to the duty to enter a launch in the register, a state is required to notify the Secretary General 'to the greatest extent feasible and as soon as practicable' of space objects that the Secretary General has already been notified of that are no longer in Earth orbit (Art. VI.3).[42]

The UN Register of Objects Launched into Outer Space, established on 16 November 1976, is maintained by OOSA.[43] Notifications are contained in the ST/SG/SER.E series. OOSA has also developed a practice of including in the Register (with appropriate colour coding and square bracketing) data on space objects that have not been formally entered in it but of which it is aware.[44] In addition, as noted above, it is still competent for a state to notify citing Part B of UN Res. 1721 (XVI).[45] Notifications under this procedure are recorded in the A/AC.105/INF series in a practice that antedates the Registration Convention.[46]

UN OOSA therefore in effect maintains two registers, the Convention Register and a Resolution listing, which complement each other but need not contain the same data. OOSA itself mitigates the problem by displaying entries on the two together on its website.[47] The disparity can be partially resolved if states re-submit data already reported under UN Res. 1721 (XVI) for the purposes of the Registration Convention, but practice has been patchy. Indeed it is possible for the same object to appear on both the 1721 Resolution and the Convention listings, its launch being on the former and a change in status

40 COSPAR, the Committee on Space Research, provides a COSPAR ID which consists of the year of launch and its number within that year. For COSPAR, see Chapter 9, n. 52. Art. 6 of the 1959 Project of an International Convention – Space Law would have required clear nationality markings on spacecraft: *supra* n. 18.
41 Thus, ESA provides data on the radio frequency plan being used by space objects it documents. For ESA, 'Space Object Registration by the European Space Agency: Current Policy and Practice', COPUOS Legal Subctee 54th Sess., April 2015, A/AC.105/C.22015/CRP.18; www.unoosa.org/pdf/limited/c2/AC105_C2_2015_CRP18E.pdf and generally 'ESA Space Object Registration Policy', 28 March 2014, CoCoSL III 473–475, and the relevant entries in the ST/SG/SER.E/INF series on the UNOOSA website. Cf. n. 35 *supra*.
42 E.g. Note Verbale of 18 February 2004 from The Netherlands that a former INTELSAT and later New Skies satellite is no longer in geostationary orbit: A/AC.105/824. Notwithstanding Art. IV.3, the UN Register still carries data on non-Earth-orbiting space probes such as Pioneers 10 and 11: see A/AC.105/INF.255 and 275.
43 See www.unoosa.org/oosa/spaceobjectregister/index.html. Cf. the OOSA Annual Report for 2021, Chapter 9, 82–85, Space Objects Registration.
44 According to its website, UN OOSA gets its unofficial information from the media, from official press releases and from COSPAR. Amateur publications also publish satellite data. For an example, see *infra* n. 65.
45 As noted *supra* n. 17, para 1 of UNGA 1721 (XVI) called on states to provide launch information to COPUOS through the UN Secretary General so that launchings could be publicly registered. Para 2 asked the Secretary General to maintain such a public registry.
46 The IISL-ECSL Symposium for the COPUOS Legal Subcommittee, April 2016, was told that as of 1 April 2016, UN OOSA had issued 428 documents under UNGA 1721B (XVI) registering nearly 6000 objects: S. Di Pippo, 'Registration of Space Objects with the Secretary-General': www.unoosa.org/documents/pdf/copuos/lsc/2016/symp-03.pdf. See also S. Di Pippo, 'Registration of Space Objects with the United Nations Secretary-General' (2016) 63 *ZLW* 364–374, together with data in papers by W. Ailor, *infra* n. 97.
47 As of 1 April 2016, UN OOSA reckoned that between the two Registers, 92% of all functional space objects have been registered, amounting to 6722 objects since 1961: Di Pippo, *supra* n. 46. However, in 2022, the Register website indicated that 88% of space objects had been registered.

being on the latter. One cannot help feeling that a single Register providing the same data for all launches and objects in space would be an improvement.[48] That said it seems that, aided by an official form, compliance with the Convention is improving.[49]

While one function of the international Register is the provision of information that states may use in planning their own launch activities, also important is the identification of a space object that has caused damage, but the information published might be insufficient for identification in a particular case.[50] Article VI of the Convention therefore provides that where the information thus publicly available has not enabled a state party to identify a space object which has caused it damage, or which may be of a hazardous or deleterious nature, other parties, including those with monitoring and tracking facilities, have a duty to respond 'to the greatest extent feasible' to a request for assistance by either the affected state party or the UN Secretary General.

The state requesting help is also to the greatest extent feasible to provide information as to the time, nature and circumstances of the events giving rise to the request. Such data would permit calculations to work out the probable launch site for the space object concerned. Assistance is not necessarily free but is to be provided under 'equitable and reasonable conditions'. Arrangements for assistance are 'the subject of agreement between the parties concerned'. So far there have been no instances of the use of Art. XI.

Mutatis mutandis, the references to states in the Registration Convention are deemed to be apply to an intergovernmental organisation conducting space activities if the organisation declares its acceptance of the rights and obligations of the Convention and provided also that a majority of state members of the organisation are state parties to the Convention and to the OST (Art. VII.1). State members of any such organisation that are party to the Convention are to take all appropriate steps to ensure that the organisation makes such a declaration (Art. VII. 2). Naturally, intergovernmental organisations added to the Convention are excluded from signing or ratifying the Convention, propose amendments to it or withdraw from it (Arts. VII–XII) because such powers are matters for states alone (Art. VII.1). As of 2023, only four intergovernmental organisations had accepted the Convention, ESA, EUMETSAT, EUTELSAT and INTERSPUTNIK.[51]

Any state party can propose amendments to the Registration Convention. These enter into force for those accepting them when a majority of the state parties accept the proposal. Thereafter, each remaining state party is bound by an amendment when it accepts it (Art. IX). Fortunately no amendments have been proposed so far. It would be awkward were the Convention to exist in many forms because amendments had resulted in various states being bound by different versions of the text and its amendments.

Withdrawal from the Convention is an option, becoming effective one year after notice is given to the Depositary, the UN Secretary General (Art. XI). So far, no state has done

---

48 Cf. 'Practice of States and International Organizations in Registering Space Objects: Background Paper by the Secretariat' (COPUOS). A/AC105/C.2/L.255 + Corr. 1 and 2 (2005). Cf. Di Pippo, *supra* n. 46.

49 UNOOSA Registration Information Submission Form: www.unoosa.org/oosa/en/spaceobjectregister/resources/index.html; CoCoSL III, 476–481. Cf. *infra* n. 55.

50 Cf. L. Perek, 'The 1976 Registration Convention' (1998) 47 *ZLW* 351–360 and 'Basic Problems in Space Traffic' (2003) 46 *Proc. IISL* 322–331.

51 Cf. 'Space Object Registration by the European Space Agency: Current Policy and Practice', COPUOS Legal Subcommittee 2015, A/AC.105/C.22015/CRP.18; www.unoosa.org/pdf/limited/c2/AC105_C2_2015_CRP18E.pdf. EUTELSAT has withdrawn from the system.

so, and that is good. Ten years after the Convention entered into force in 1976, the possibility of its revision was duly included in the UNGA agenda (Art. X), but this timetabled review was not proceeded with.[52] It remains that revision of the Convention may be considered at the request of one third of its state parties and passed the concurrence of a majority of the parties. In that case, a review conference would be convened which would take into account any relevant technological developments including in the identification of space objects (Art. X).

Were a single general Space Convention ever adopted,[53] the content of the duties under the Registration Convention should certainly be improved as part of that codification. There is, however, an argument that in practice, many of its defects or problems have been or could be mitigated or solved by changes in the registration procedures and by developing national laws rather than revising the Registration Convention.[54] Indeed, a major step has been through states nationally complying with the recommendations of UNGA Res. 62/101, 2007.[55] These, addressing some of the criticisms earlier in this chapter, are directed towards the harmonisation of state registration practice.[56]

For instance, the orbital data provided could be more precise.[57] Thus, operative para 2(a) of UNGA Res. 62/101 recommends that states notify, where appropriate, any international designator approved by the Committee on Space Research, use coordinated universal time (UTC) as the time reference for the launch; utilise kilometres, minutes and degrees as the standard units for basic orbital parameters and provide any other useful data in addition to information about the general functionality of the object. Paragraph 2(b) then suggests that additional information could also be provided about any geostationary orbit location if appropriate, any change in operational status (including when a space object is no longer functional[58]), the approximate date of decay or re-entry if states can provide accurate information and the date and physical conditions of the moving of a space object to a disposal orbit. The sub-para then recommends that states provide web links to official information on space objects that they notify. Such developments will also be aided as states increasingly conform to the recommendations of UNGA Res. 68/74 regarding the content of national space legislation.[59] Certainly the existence of the OOSA Registration Information Submission Form

---

52 'Question of the review of the Convention on the Registration of Objects launched into Outer Space', UNGA Res. 41/66, 1986. The Secretary General was asked to prepare for the COPUOS Legal Subcommittee a report on the past application of the Convention (para 5).

53 See Chapter 17.

54 Cf. K-U. Hörl and J. Hermida, 'Change of Ownership, Change of Registry? Which Objects to Register, What Data to Furnish, When and Until When?' (2003) 46 *Proc. IISL* 454–463, [Lyall/Larsen 263–272].

55 'Recommendations on enhancing the practice of states and international intergovernmental organisations in registering space objects', UNGA Res. 62/101, 2007: CoCoSL III, 401–481. These were based on App. III to the Report of the COPUOS Legal Subcommittee on its 46th Sess. March/April 2007 and the conclusions of a Working Group on the Practice of States and International Organisations in Registering Space Objects – A/AC.105/891. For effects of Res. 62/101, see *supra* n. 51 and the UN OOSA model registration form, *supra* n. 49.

56 Note the Preamble to UNGA Res. 62/101 statement that nothing in the Conclusions of the Working Group or the Resolution itself 'constitutes an authoritative interpretation of or a proposed amendment to the Registration Convention'.

57 See Hörl and Hermida, *supra* n. 54. Cf. Finch, *infra* n. 70.

58 Some states already provide such data: cf. the UN OOSA ST/SG/SER.E series. Cf data on the re-entry of Tiangong-2, A/AC.105/1201, July 2019.

59 'Recommendations on National Legislation Relevant to the Peaceful Exploration and Use of Outer Space', 11 December 2013, UNGA Res. 68/74. For detailed commentary, see CoCoSL III 483–603. Cf. T.C.

encourages bureaucrats responsible for such matters to provide more information than they might otherwise consider necessary.[60]

With the development of commercialisation and private enterprise in space, a problem emerged which the framers of the Registration Convention did not contemplate.[61] Could a launching state that carried a space object on its registry transfer its responsibilities? This had implications both for international trade and commerce in space assets and for the rights and duties of states.[62] As a matter of practice, transfers between registries do occur.[63] AsiaSat 1 and 2 and Apstar-I and IA were transferred from the UK registry to China as part of the transfer of Hong Kong to China.[64] This created no difficulties as China was the territorial launch site, but the transfer of INTELSAT satellites to Dutch company New Skies NV was a different matter.

Following that transfer, the OOSA registry displayed information about the satellites in square brackets and highlighted them in green, indicating that the data is known to OOSA but has not been officially provided under the Registration Convention.[65] A Dutch Note to OOSA on 29 July 2003 referred to this and specifically disavowed The Netherlands as being subject to the Registration Convention, the Liability Convention or ARRA for these satellites but accepting that The Netherlands is, as the national state of New Skies NV, responsible for their operation under OST Art. VI and exercising jurisdiction and control under OST Art. VII.[66] This made clear a problem with the utility in modern commercial activities of the concept of launching state or launching authority in ARRA and the Liability and Registration Conventions: there is the possibility of logical anomalies.

Brisibe, 'An Introduction to United Nations COPUOS Recommendations on National Legislation Relevant to the Peaceful Exploration and Use of Outer Space' (2013) 62 *ZLW* 728–739. See also the ILA, 'Draft Model Law for National Space Legislation and Explanatory Notes' (2012) 75 *Int. L. Ass'n Rep* 307–314; S. Hobe, 'The ILA Model Law for National Space Legislation' (2013) 62 *ZLW* 81–96.

60 See *supra* n. 49.

61 K-H. Böckstiegel, 'The Term "Launching State" in International Space Law' (1994) 36 *Proc IISL* 80–83; K.-U. Schrögl and C. Davies, 'A New Look at the "Launching State": The Results of the UNCOPUOS Legal Subcommittee Working Group "Review of the Concept of the 'Launching State'"2000–2002' (2002) 44 *Proc. IISL* 286–301; M. Hofmann and A. Loukakis, eds., *Ownership of Satellites* (Baden-Baden: Nomos, 2017), Part III, including F.G. von der Dunk, 'Transfer of Ownership in Orbit: from Fiction to Problem' at 29–43.

62 M. Gerhard, 'Transfer of Operation and Control with Respect to Space Objects – Problems of Responsibility and Liability of States' (2002) 51 *ZLW* 571–581. See also Chapter 13.

63 For the UK, see Section 11 of the 'Procedures for the Management of Satellite Filings' March 2019: www.ofcom.org.uk/__data/assets/pdf_file/0022/140926/new-procedures-1.pdf.

64 See the entries for AsiaSat 1 (1990–030A) and AsiaSat 2 (1995–064A) in the UNOOSA Registry, together with UK Note Verbale of 27 March 1998: ST/STG/SER.E/333, and related Note Verbale by China, ST/STG/SER.E/334, both covering all four satellites.

65 Reference point *supra* n. 44. Similar problems will exist under the Cape Town Space Protocol if a satellite operator defaults on a security interest and a foreign financing agent with a registered security seeks repossession; see P.B. Larsen, 'Berlin Space Protocol: Update' (2015) 64 *ZLW* 361–395. Cf. *infra* Chapter 13.

66 Note Verbale of 29 July 2003 from The Netherlands: A/AC105/806 as to satellites 2002-019A and 2002–057A; www.unoosa.org/pdf/reports/ac105/AC105_806E.pdf. Cf. Note Verbale of 18 February 2004 from The Netherlands: A/AC.105/824 on the removal of 1988–040A from geostationary orbit; www.unoosa.org/pdf/reports/ac105/AC105_824E.pdf. See also the UN OOSA Registry data on these objects. The Netherlands is party to OST, ARRA and the Liability and Registration Conventions.
    In a Note Verbale of 22 October 2013 (ST/SG/SER.E/690), the UK provided data on Quetzat-1 but stated that the UK had only authorised the launch and a Luxembourg company, SES, was its operator: www.unoosa.org/documents/pdf/ser690E.pdf. The Note also requested that the UK be removed as the state of registry for SES-1.

The national state of the owner of a satellite should carry the satellite in a domestic register and show up as such in the OOSA register. However, through commercial agreements and financial transactions, ownership of a satellite, or its transponders, may lie with national entities from several states.[67] The recommendations of UNGA Res. 62/101 as to registration practice have helped.[68] Its operative para 4 accepts that changes in registry happen and suggests that following the change in supervision of a space object in orbit, the state of registry, in cooperation with the appropriate state under OST Art. VI, should notify OOSA of any additional information, such as the date of change in supervision, the identity of the new owner or operator and any change of orbital position or function of the space object.[69]

Some problems remain. The central registry at OOSA should be more swiftly informed of the required data; a brief scan of the OOSA registry shows that many states report late. Some report every six months (which is scarcely timeous), and others even later. Indeed, were the Convention to be revised, one improvement would be a proper time-table within which notifications to OOSA should be made.[70] Again, it would be useful to strengthen the identification of a space object under Art. V by requiring that all large detachable solid parts of space objects have identifiers, designators or an adequate registration number stamped or otherwise contained, embossed or engraved on them and not only on one or two places on an object as is the current practice.[71] Such could assist the return of a found object, as well as any claim for damages.

The Convention requires that only one of potentially several launching states is to enter a space object in its domestic register and give the requisite data to the central world registry.[72] This leaves open the possibility that the connection between the state of registry and the actual owner/operator of a space object may be weak. Because OST Art. VII links the jurisdiction and control over space objects (as well as their return if lost) to the state of registry, the selection of the state of registry could be important.

---

67 Perhaps the owner of the largest portion by physical size or mass night be considered the 'appropriate' owner whose home state should act, and, in the event of equality, the home states of the owners should agree which state will act, on the model of Art. II. 2 of the Registration Convention.

68 *Supra* n. 55. See also *infra* n. 72.

69 This would appear to homologate the actions of the UK and The Netherlands, *supra* nn. 64 and 66.

70 E.R. Finch, Jr., in 'Heavenly Junk II: Recent Developments in Space Debris' (1994) 8 *Air & Sp. Lawyer* (No. 4) 8–10 at 9, proposed a limit of two hours within which a report of a launch of a nuclear power source would have to be made to the UN Secretary General and a further limit of twenty-four hours for the reporting of other satellite launches.

71 Cf. Art. 17. 1 of the Russian Federation Law on Space Activities, 1993: 'Space objects of the Russian Federation shall . . . have markings certifying their appurtenance to the Russian Federation'. The Law is translated in *Project 2001: Workshop on Legal Framework for Privatising Space Activities*, Vienna, 1999 (Cologne: International of Air and Space Law, 2000) 249–60, and *Project 2001 Workshop on Legal Framework for Commercial Launch and Associated Services*, Bremen, 2000 (Cologne: International of Air and Space Law, 2001) 313–324.

72 Operative para 3 of the UNGA Res. 62/101 recommendations on registration practice suggests that intergovernmental organisations should work out which state member should register, that states that are launcher states by virtue of the use of their territory or facilities should coordinate agreement as to the launcher for Convention purposes and that in joint launches, each space object should be separately registered. Further, launch service providers should encourage clients to ensure that relevant states register space objects.

The international community has encountered difficulties with the registry system in international shipping and the concept of the 'flag of convenience'.[73] A genuine link between a state and a space object is desirable. Such would forestall commercial entrepreneurs seeking to avoid the rigours of legal requirements as to supervision and liability through setting up shell companies in less space-competent countries.[74] Tracing back through such arrangements to the real owners would be possible. Today, we do this routinely to deal with terrorism, organised and trans-national crime, money-laundering and tax evasion. The corporate veil should be disregarded where buccaneering entrepreneurs, seeking to avoid the supervision which their real home state might well exercise, try to find a less rigorous 'home' for the licensing and supervision of their activities. In space, the highest standards should be required in the interests of all. States meeting such standards ought to be encouraged to establish space registries,[75] but those incapable of fully discharging their international obligations of supervision and control should refrain from acting as states of registry, and any attempts to do so should not be given recognition. Flags of convenience in space should be unlawful.[76]

A related set of questions arises from the concept of launching state in the Registration Convention. Article I provides two categories of association with a given enterprise that can constitute a state as a launching state, the one entrepreneurial, launching or procuring the launch, and the other territorial: launch from state territory or facility.[77] This may have been satisfactory when the Convention was young, and for many purposes it remains adequate. However, launches today can be very complex. Sea Launch was but one example.[78]

---

73 Cf. F. Lyall, 'Expanding Global Communications Services', Sess. III, *Proceedings of the Workshop on Space Law in the Twenty-first Century*, UNISPACE III Technical Forum, 63–80 at 69–71; F.G. Von der Dunk, 'Towards "Flags of Convenience" in Space' (2012) 55 *Proc. IISL* 811–836; A. Taghdiri, 'Flags of Convenience and the Commercial Space Flight Industry: The Inadequacy of Current International Law to Address the Opportune Registration of Space Vehicles in Flag States' (2013) 19 *B.U. J. Sci. & Tech. L.* 405–432; cf. Ro, *infra* n. 211, at 217–221, 'Part D: Avoiding Patent Liability by Using Flags of Convenience'. Aviation has had similar problems.

74 There is an argument that at least in such areas, the ratio from *Barcelona Traction, Light and Power Co, Limited (New Application: 1962) (Belgium v. Spain)* (1962–1970) (Second Phase) 1970 ICJ 3 (1970) 9 ILM 227 should be departed from. Cf. F. Lyall, 'Small States, Entrepreneurial States and Space' (2006) 49 *Proc. IISL* 382–390; L. Perek, 'Strengthening the Registration Convention' (1985) 28 *Proc. IISL* 187; B. Cheng, 'The Commercial Development of Space: the Need for New Treaties' (1991) 19 *J. Sp. L.* 17–44) (rep. Cheng, 641–670). The UN Convention on Conditions for the Registration of Ships, Geneva, 1986 (1987) 26 ILM 1229–1250, is not yet in force. Under its Art. 19, forty ratifications are required, but so far it has only fifteen.
   Some states not themselves space-competent have deliberately sought to attract space businesses. Cf. the use of small states by telecommunication enterprises as their states of registry or as their domiciles. See Chapter 8.

75 Cf. UNGA Res. 'Application of the concept of "Launching State"', UNGA 59/115, 10 December 2004; CoCoSL III, 362–400.

76 Even under the existing rules, it would be useful were those states currently maintaining registries of space objects to comply more diligently and accurately with their Registration Convention duties.

77 See also the arrangements for Baikonour: M. Bjornerud, 'Baikonour Continues: The New Lease Agreement between Russia and Kazakhstan' (2004) 30 *J. Sp. L.* 13–36.

78 A. Kerrest, 'Launching Spacecraft from the Sea and the Outer Space Treaty: The Sea Launch Project' (1998) 23 *Air and Sp. Law* 16–21 [Lyall/Larsen 333–8], and his 'The Launch of Spacecraft from the Sea', in G. Lafferranderie and D. Crowther, eds., *Outlook on Space Law over the Next 30 Years* (The Hague: Kluwer, 1997) 217–233; J.J. Lee, 'Legal Analysis of Sea Launch License: National Security and Environmental Concerns' (2008) 24 *Sp. Pol.* 104–112.
   Note: Sea Launch is currently inactive following the Russian intervention in the Ukraine in 2014.

In that particular instance, the published arrangements between the partner–entrepreneurs made their activities subject to US law,[79] but other partnership arrangements may be more obscure – perhaps deliberately. Today, one launch may put the satellites of a diversity of national owners into orbit.

Again, when is a state a procuring state? If a subcontractor provides a part for a mechanism within a satellite, is its national state thereby a procuring state? In instances of complex entrepreneurial arrangements, and/or of multi-national involvement in a launch object, the possibility arises (as indicated above) for a state of registry to be selected so as to choose a regime whose competence is not up to the proper exercise of the jurisdiction and control of OST Art. VIII.

Finally we must come to the question of whether the Registration Convention remains useful without substantial revision even with implementation of the recommendations of UNGA Res. 62/101 of 2007. In the light of our comments so far, the answer must be equivocal.[80] First, the Convention remains in many ways unproven. It has not yet been used to determine whether a particular object that has caused damage is traceable to a particular state.[81] Second, it is clear that not all launches are registered in accordance with its terms, though this may improve.[82] Third, some notifications are not made as timeously as is desirable.

The latter criticisms mean that the UN Register is not a reliable source of data for those planning launches. The Master International Frequency Register maintained by the ITU might be more helpful, although it does not contain data on debris or other space objects which are not radio stations.[83] Unsurprisingly therefore, informal arrangements now exist under which some at least of the potential launching states notify each other of some impending launches and exchange data on the related space objects. While one objective of these arrangements is the avoidance of false alarms as to a nuclear attack, another effect is that states can plan their activities in possession of relatively up-to-date data.[84]

The future may lie along those informal mutual lines rather than the cumbersome procedures of registration with the UN. If not, the Registration Convention should be

---

79 The Agreement between the Government of the United States of America and the Government of Ukraine regarding International Trade in Commercial Launch Services, 1995, *US State Dept Bull.* 96–51; 1996 WL 195515; (1996) 24 *J. Sp. L.* 187–189 (expired 2001).

80 L. Perek, 'The 1976 Registration Convention' (1998) 47 *ZLW* 351–360; M. Bourely, 'Is It Necessary to Re-Negotiate the Convention on Registration?' (1988) 30 *Proc. IISL* 227–233; Y. Zhao, 'Revising the 1975 Registration Convention: Time for Revision?' (2004) 11 *Aust. Int. L.J.* 106–127; Cheng, *supra* n. 74; A.J. Young, *Law and Policy in the Space Stations Era* (Dordrecht: Nijhoff, 1989) 271–291.

81 Insofar as we understand the matter, objects found and returned to their owners have so far been identified by information contained in or impressed on the object, not by the use of the Convention to calculate their probable origin.

82 Some military satellites are not registered. Other space objects have not been registered through the relevant authority neglecting so to do. In 2016, UN OOSA reckoned some 92% of registrable objects had been registered. See *supra* n. 47 and Di Pippo, *supra* n. 46.

83 See Chapter 8.

84 S.C. Larrimore, 'International Space Launch Notifications and Data Exchange' (2007) 23 *Space Policy* 172–179; cf. R. Cargill Hall, 'Comments on Traffic Control of Space Vehicles' (1965) 31 *J. Air L. & Comm.* 327–342. See also 'The Hague International Code of Conduct against Ballistic Missile Proliferation', 2002 (HCOC): www.hcoc.at/. State subscribers to the Code notify each other in advance of launches into outer space or test flights, giving detail of the planned launch notification window, the launch area and the planned direction of the launch (Art. 4.a.iii).

amended, or administrative practice developed to supplement it. The central registration of intended launches coupled with the timely notification of actual launches would also be useful. Of course, this raises the spectre of the 'phantom satellite' that plagued the ITU procedures,[85] so the principle of first come, first served should not be available in such an arrangement.

The Return of Space Objects (ARRA)

The aphorism 'what goes up must come down' is not necessarily true for space objects. However, most objects launched into low Earth orbit (LEO) are likely to return to Earth in the course of time thanks to gravity.[86] Some may be brought back deliberately, as in the deorbiting of Sky-Lab and Mir or the planned return of spacecraft. But a launch may be unsuccessful, and a space object may become lost either on Earth or in space. This section, therefore, considers the legal provision for the return of space objects. Of course, a space-craft might have personnel on-board. Were we dealing with the space treaties *seriatim*, we would treat ARRA, the Agreement on Rescue and Return, as a whole. Much of ARRA is about the rescue and return of astronauts, but the topic of astronauts deserves the separate consideration we will give it in Chapter 5. Of course, the circumstances of a rescue may well involve a spacecraft: that is, a space object. Again even if a rescue is unsuccessful, it may result in the space object being found. And certainly it is true that every so often a space object is found on Earth.

ARRA, adopted on 19 December 1967 as UNGA Res. 2345 (XXII), opened for sig-nature on 22 April 1968 and entered into force on 3 December 1968,[87] only some fifteen months after the OST, because of the imminent increase in the activities of astronauts, the uncertainty of space technology and therefore the potential need for their rescue. How-ever, what to do about lost and/or found space objects was a natural correlative. Initially

---

85 F. Lyall, 'Paralysis by Phantom: Problems of the ITU Filing Procedures' (1997) 39 *Proc IISL* 187–193. Tightening the requirements of notification under the ITU procedures has diminished the problem. See Chapter 8.

86 The useful life of many LEO satellite is about five years. Most re-enter the atmosphere within ten years. The US FCC Second Report and Order (IB Docket Nos. 22–271 and 18–313), 'In the Matter of Space Innova-tion; Mitigation of Orbital Debris in the New Space Age', adopted 6 October 2022, will *require* the deorbit-ing of satellites which the FCC licenses from LEO (at or below 2000km) by no later than five years from the end of mission. The life of small satellites is c. six to ten months, and that of micro-satellites can be as low as weeks. See Chapter 6 Orbits and Chapter 9 Small Satellites and *infra* at n. 30 regarding the debris problem.

87 Agreement on the Rescue of Astronauts, the Return of Astronauts and the Return of Objects Launched into Outer Space, 22 April 1968; 672 UNTS 119; 1969 UKTS 56, Cmnd. 3997; 19 UST 7570, TIAS 6559; (1968) 7 ILM 151–154; [1969] 63 AJIL 382.

V. Kopal, 'The 1968 Rescue Agreement – History of Negotiations and Their Outcome', in G. Laffer-randerie and S. Marchisio, eds., *The Astronauts and ARRA – Lessons Learned* (European Centre for Space Law, 2011) 109–121, and his 'The Agreement on Rescue of Astronauts and Return of Space Objects', in E. McWhinney and M.A. Bradley, eds., *New Frontiers in Space Law* (Leyden: Sijthoff, 1969) 193–210; P.G. Dembling and D.M. Arons, 'The Treaty on Rescue and Return of Astronauts and Space Objects' (1967–1968) 9 *William and Mary L. Rev.* 630–663; R. Cargill Hall, 'Rescue and Return of Astronauts on Earth and in Outer Space' [1969] 63 *AJIL* 197–210; P.H. Houben, 'Agreement on the Rescue of Astronauts, the Return of Space Objects' (1968) 15 *Neth. Int. L. Rev.* 121–32; R.S.K. Lee, 'Agreement on the Rescue of Astronauts, the Return of Astronauts and the Return of Objects Launched into Outer Space' 1 Manual 53; B. Cheng, 'The 1968 Astronauts Agreement or How Not to Make a Treaty' (1969) 23 *Y.B. Int. Aff.* 185–208 (rep. Cheng 265–285); Christol 152–212.

it was thought that liability for damage should also be covered in the same instrument, but as it became clear that that topic would require protracted negotiations, liability was side-lined, and rescue and return was dealt with as a priority.[88]

ARRA, designed to 'develop and give further concrete expression' to particular duties imposed by the OST (Preamble), is open to all states (Art. 7.1). Participation by the US and the USSR, the two states that were then space-competent, was essential. Like the OST, it required five ratifications, including by the UK, the US and the USSR (also its depositories (Art. 7. 2)) to come into force (Art. 7. 3).

Accession to ARRA is immediate on the deposit of appropriate notice with the depositaries (Art. 7. 4). Amendments may be proposed by any state party, an amendment entering into force for state parties accepting the amendment when accepted by a majority of the state parties and thereafter for each remaining state party when it accepts that amendment (Art. 8). Withdrawal takes effect one year after written notification to the depositaries (Art. 9). Unlike the Registration Convention, ARRA has no provision as to review, and, though there have been suggestions that it should be reconsidered, no formal steps have been taken.[89] As of 1 January 2023 ARRA had been ratified by ninety-nine states, a further twenty-two signatories having not yet ratified it.[90] So far, three intergovernmental organisations have accepted the Convention: ESA, EUMETSAT and INTERSPUTNIK.[91]

ARRA distinguishes between duties owed by its parties to the personnel of a spacecraft and those in relation to a space object. The latter includes but is not necessarily confined to a spacecraft (i.e. a space object capable of carrying an astronaut) and encompasses also 'component parts' of an object (Arts. 5 and 6). ARRA uses the term 'launching authority', a more concise and restricted formulation than the 'launching state' found in the Liability and Registration Conventions.

Under ARRA Art. 6, the launching authority is the state responsible for the launching of an object, or in appropriate cases the intergovernmental organisation concerned in the launch, provided that the organisation has accepted ARRA's rights or obligations and that a majority of its member states are parties to ARRA and to the OST.[92] ARRA therefore is not in harmony with the Liability or Registration Conventions. The phrase 'the state responsible for launching' (Art. 6) is highly ambiguous. The later definitions of launching state in the Liability and Registration Conventions represent an advance, particularly the former, whose Art. 1 (b) provides that ' "launching" includes attempted launching' – obviously a circumstance where accident is likely.

---

88 Dembling and Arons, *supra* n. 87 at 631 and 'Space Law and the United Nations: The Work of the Legal Subcommittee of the United Nations Committee on the Peaceful Uses of Outer Space' (1966) 32 *J. Air L. & Comm.* 329–386 detail the work of the first four sessions of the COPUOS Legal Subcommittee, which considered rescue and return. Houben, *supra* n. 87, at 121–2 credits the USSR with taking the initiative and notes a willingness to compromise based on its potential need for the rescue of its astronauts in parts of the globe to which it did not have ready access.

89 S. Marchisio, 'Reviewing the Astronauts Convention: The Role of COPUOS', in Lafferranderie and Marchisio, eds., *supra* n. 87, 141–163.

90 See *supra* n. 11.

91 Cf. 'Space Object Registration by the European Space Agency: Current Policy and Practice', COPUOS Legal Subcommittee 2015, A/AC.105/C.22015/CRP.18; www.unoosa.org/pdf/limited/c2/AC105_C2_2015_CRP18E.pdf. EUTELSAT has withdrawn from the system.

92 See also the problem of the space object transferred post-launch from an owner in one state to an owner in another, *supra* at n. 66 and *infra* at n. 113.

ARRA Art. 1 deals with the initial dissemination of information about an incident. A contracting party receiving information or discovering that the personnel of a spacecraft have had an accident, are experiencing conditions of distress or have made an emergency or unintended landing has two duties. It must notify the launching authority of the spacecraft, or if it cannot immediately identify that authority, it is publicly to announce what has happened (Art. 1(a)). It is also to notify the UN Secretary General, who should disseminate the information without delay (Art. 1(b)). These duties apply to an ARRA party whether the incident occurs in territory under its jurisdiction, on the high seas or in a location not under the jurisdiction of any state. Articles 2 and 3 specify duties as to search and rescue that are relevant here as coping with a rescue may involve dealing with a space object.

When the personnel of a spacecraft land in its territory, an ARRA party is to take 'all possible steps to rescue them and render any necessary assistance' (Art. 2). The authority that launched the spacecraft and the UN Secretary General are to be informed of the steps it has taken and how they are proceeding. Rescue operations are directed and controlled by the contracting party, which is to 'act in close and continuing consultation' with the launching authority.

The launching authority has no right to intervene, but its cooperation is required if its assistance would contribute substantially to the operation. However, it is not clear who determines whether assistance by the launching authority would facilitate the rescue. The thrust of Art. 2 is therefore that it is for the rescuing state, not the launching state, to deal with the matter, the launching authority having to be invited if it is to participate. It is up to the finding state to decide whether to ask for help by the launching state.[93] This could be important where the physical spacecraft might be of acute interest to the rescuing authority.

Article 3 is different. It applies should the personnel of a spacecraft 'have alighted' on the high seas or anywhere not under the jurisdiction of any state. Under these circumstances, any contracting party 'in a position' to extend assistance is to do so 'if necessary' to ensure a speedy rescue. There is no division of primary and secondary responsibility similar to that between the territorial state and the launching authority in Art. 2.

As in Art. 2, state parties performing a rescue are to inform the launching authority and the UN Secretary General of progress. However, the Art. 3 duty applies only to contracting states 'which are in a position to' extend assistance if assistance 'is necessary'. In determining the extent of this duty, account is therefore taken of the location where the astronauts have alighted. As we will see in Chapter 5, this has varied implications.

A landing on the high seas may not require assistance from states other than the launching authority; the strength of the duty is limited by a state being in a position to assist and the state's assistance being necessary. As Dembling and Arons note,[94] because the duty is not that 'all possible' steps are to be taken, Art. 3 would not require states to endanger lives by engaging in a rescue effort or to divert shipping from other essential operations.

---

93 Cf. statements by the USA quoted by Dembling and Arons, *supra* n. 87 at 648 nn. 61 and 62, that should the territorial party and the launching authority not agree, ultimately 'the territorial party would of course have the final say in the matter'.
94 Dembling and Arons, *supra* n. 87 at 651.

However, as they also note, the fact that persons are in difficulty on the high seas might well bring the matter into the legal obligations as to safety of life and assistance at sea.[95]

Article 3 speaks of 'alighting' not only on the high seas but also to 'any other place not under the jurisdiction of any state'. There are not many parts of the surface of the Earth that are not under the jurisdiction of any state, but in the view of some, Antarctica (or parts of it) is one. The US does not recognise any of the varied claims to areas of the Antarctic, and some Antarctic claims overlap. We hope that were the landing in an area of competing claims all the relevant parties would cooperate and not argue where the duty lay and that in other cases, matters would be clear.

The search for a spacecraft may or may not produce living personnel, but it could result in discovery of a space object or its parts. Space objects and their component parts are the subject of both OST Art. VIII and ARRA Art. 5. Under OST Art. VIII, jurisdiction and control of a space object is retained by the state it is registered with;[96] its ownership is unaffected by being in outer space, by being on a celestial body or by its return to Earth. Space objects, or their parts, found beyond the territory of the state of registry are to be returned to that state, which may be asked first to provide identifying data. These obligations are further explicated in ARRA.

Under ARRA Art. 5, when a contracting party receives information or discovers that a space object or its component parts has returned to Earth in its territory, it is to notify the launching authority and the UN Secretary General (Art. 5.1);[97] the same applies if the object is discovered on the high seas or any other place not under the jurisdiction of a state. If the object is in the territory of an ARRA party, there is no obligation to act; the party decides whether recovery is practicable. Should the launching state request recovery, it is for the ARRA party to determine what is practicable and it may ask for the assistance of the launching authority. The launching authority has no power to intervene other than to make the request for the recovery (Art. 5. 2).

Objects found beyond the territorial limits of the launching authority are to be returned to or held at the disposal of the representatives of the launching authority (Art. 5. 3). If asked, the launching authority is required to provide identifying data prior to the return of the object or parts concerned. In all cases, the expenses of recovery and return are to be borne by the launching authority (Art. 5.5). Finally, and extraordinarily, if the object or its

---

95 Dembling and Arons, *supra* n. 87 at 650, the International Convention on the Safety of Life at Sea, London, 1914, 219 CTS 177, 1914 108 BFSP 283; the International Convention on the Safety of Life at Sea (SOLAS), 1184 UNTS 2; (1980) UKTS 46, Cmnd. 7874; 32 UST 47, TIAS 9700; (1975) 14 ILM 963; Art. 98 of the UN Convention on the Law of the Sea, Montego Bay, 1982, 1833 UNTS 3; 1999 UKTS 82, Cmnd. 4525; (1982) 21 ILM 1261; US Tr. Doc. 103–39. F. Lyall, *Technology, Sovereignty and International Law* (Abingdon: Routledge, 2022) 54–56.

96 See *supra* Registration.

97 For practice, see C. Elizey, 'Request and Return; A Look at the Retrieval of United States Commercial Space Launch Objects That Return to Earth' (2021) 45 *J. Sp. L.* 201–238. For listings of objects reported, see www.unoosa.org/oosa/en/treatyimplementation/arra-art-v/unlfd.html. Cf. Á.F. dos Santos, 'Analysis of the Legal Instrument signed between Brazil and the United States of America regarding the Return of a Space Object' (2010) 53 *Proc. IISL* 227–233. An early example is the 1991 notification by Argentina in relation to the re-entry of the Salyut space station and the attached COSMOS-1686 part landing in Argentina; see A/46/92. In 2000, South Africa reported the discovery of three objects, probably the remains of a US Delta launcher: A/AC.105/740. In October 2012, the UK advised of the discovery of part of a payload faring that washed up on a beach in Bermuda, which it appears was from a US Atlas V rocket (A/AC.105/1040).

parts have hazardous or deleterious elements, the ARRA party finding it may (not must) notify the launching authority. If it does, the authority then has a duty under the direction and control of the ARRA party to take effective steps 'to eliminate possible danger or harm' (Art. 5. 4).[98]

These are interesting provisions, but they do not clearly deal with all space objects that may be found. There are spent robotic probes on the moon, as well as the landing modules of the Apollo series of landings and debris from various impact tests. There are active and spent probes on Mars and the remains of unsuccessful landings. In such instances, the application of ARRA may have to interact with the calls for the creation of 'heritage' sites on the moon or Mars should these proposals be accepted by the international community.[99]

In space itself, there are defunct satellites and all sorts of remote orbiting debris.[100] While Art. 5 largely predicates action on the request of the launching authority, and, of course, ownership is unaffected,[101] there may be a case in the future for requiring the removal of some space objects at the expense of their launching authority. However, this takes us into the question of the space environment, which we consider in Chapter 9. In the meantime, we note that satellites have been retrieved from space.[102]

In February 1984, during the tenth Shuttle mission (Challenger: STS-41-B), the privately financed Palapa B 2 and Westar VI satellites were placed in transition orbits prior to ultimate location in geostationary orbit. However, their kick-motors failed, and the satellites remained in orbits some 600 miles/1000 km up. A limited command facility remained, and they were lowered to some 200 miles/300 km in November 1984. The

---

98 Prior to discovering the Cosmos 954 debris, *infra* n. 168, Canada asked the USSR about the fuel on the satellite. Then in notifying the USSR of discovering the debris on its territory, Canada referred to ARRA. See (1979) 18 ILM 899 at 910–914. In due course, a formal claim for compensation under the Liability Convention was made. The USSR was not asked in terms of ARRA Art. 5.5 to 'take effective steps' to eliminate the danger, perhaps because Canada (and the US) hoped to learn much from the debris. In the 1991 Salyut/COSMOS-1686 instance (*supra* n. 97), no potentially harmful substances were involved.

99 We discuss such proposals in Chapter 7.

100 We consider it unlikely that ARRA will be invoked any time soon in respect to such as Pioneers I and II, New Horizons or Rosetta and Philae.

101 OST Art. VIII. A small plaque beside the replica of the Viking I Mars lander in the Smithsonian Air and Space Museum in Washington, DC, affirms the US property right in the lander located on Mars, NASA having transferred its ownership to the Smithsonian: www.nasm.si.edu/exhibitions/GAL100/viking.html. On 11 December 1993, at Sotheby's New York as part of a sale of Russian space memorabilia, the Lunokhod-1 lunar rover, (launched 10 November, landed 17 November 1970 on the Mare Imbrium Sea of Rains) was sold for US$66,500 (estimate US$5000). The location of the object was stated as 'resting on the surface of the Moon'. Neither Sotheby's nor the consignor of the object for the sale undertook obligations to deliver possession. Only the current title rights of the owner were sold, without assurance as to the claims of others, including possible salvagers. See P.D. Nesgos, 'UN COPUOS Symposium on Commercial Activities in Space, March 1994' (1994) 37 *Proc. IISL* 305–314 at 305–306. See also Sotheby's Auction Catalogue 'Russian Space History' December 1993: http://news.bbc.co.uk/1/shared/spl/hi/pop_ups/06/sci_nat_enl_1164637269/html/1.stm.

102 What follows deals with the retrieval of a satellite from orbit and its return to Earth. It should be noted that on occasion, a satellite in an initial erroneous orbit can be redirected, including in one case by the use of a trans-lunar orbit (Hughes 601HP/Asiasat 3 in 1998): see E. Belbruno, ed., *New Trends in Astrodynamics & Applications: An International Conference* (New York: Annals of the New York Academy of Sciences, 2005) 1065. A similar effort was not carried through in the case of Arabsat 4A in 2006, and it was deorbited on 24 March 2006: www.msnbc.msn.com/id/11999597/. In 2014, the fifth and sixth satellites for the Galileo system entered wrong orbits and were appropriately redirected in 2015: http://esamultimedia.esa.int/docs/galileo/Galileo_Sav_flyer_j15_low-res.pdf.

fourteenth Shuttle mission (Discovery: STS-51-A) was able to capture both and returned them to Earth.[103] This retrieval and return involved both private and state actors, a mixture not contemplated by the space treaties. Appropriate contracts between NASA and the owners/insurers had to be worked out for the task. Insurers paid the costs, and both satellites were refurbished and later re-launched, this time successfully.[104]

Liability

Gravity ensures that a satellite in low Earth orbit and parts of its launch vehicle will at some point re-enter the atmosphere. A space object eligible for return, as we have just considered, may have caused damage in coming to rest where it is found. Accidents during launch were frequent early on and remain possible. It is therefore not surprising that questions of damage were present in discussions of a legal regime for space.[105] When what became ARRA was first proposed, 'liability' was intended to be part of the text.[106] However, it was soon realised that that was a question more difficult than aid to astronauts or the return of space objects, so the topic was left for later, more protracted, negotiation. Of course, the facts of space activities have a bearing on the law of space, but it should not be thought that in the absence of specific provisions there was no applicable law. Ordinary international law might, and could still, be invoked,[107] as, in an appropriate instance, might national law.[108]

General Principles of Liability

International law as to the liability of a state for damage caused to another state has a long history. Cases such as the Trail Smelter arbitration,[109] the Corfu Channel case[110] and the

---

103 Space Shuttle Mission STS-51A, NASA Press Kit April 1995 (Release no. 84–149): www.jsc.nasa.gov/history/shuttle_pk/pk/Flight_014_STS-51A_Press_Kit.pdf. Palapa B-2 was actually caught and guided into the shuttle bay by hand! Cf. 'The Shuttle at Work', in H.C. Delhoff, *Suddenly, Tomorrow Came, A History of the Johnson Space Center* (NASA History Office, 1993) 285–305: www.jsc.nasa.gov/history/suddenly_tomorrow/suddenly.htm) for servicing missions to scientific satellites and retrieval of experiments. The long-duration exposure facility spacecraft was put into orbit by the Space Shuttle Challenger in April 1984. Approximately the size of a single-deck bus, it had neither fuel nor engines. On 9 January 1990, Space Shuttle Colombia retrieved it and landed it on 20 January 1990.

104 See Smith and S.M. Lopatkiewicz, 'Satellite Recovery: A Lawyer's Perspective' (1985) 2 *Air & Sp. Lawyer* 1, summarised in R.M. Jarvis, 'The Space Shuttle Challenger and the Future Law of Outer Space Rescues' (1986) 29 *Int. L.* 591–621 at 608–609. In the Arabsat 4A instance, *supra* n. 102, an element of the decision to de-orbit was the willingness of the insurers to declare a total loss.

105 M.S. McDougal, 'Artificial Satellites: A Modest Proposal' (1957) 51 *AJIL* 74–77.

106 P.G. Dembling and D.M. Arons, 'Space Law and the United Nations: The Work of the Legal Subcommittee of the United Nations Committee on the Peaceful Uses of Outer Space' (1966) 32 *J. Air L. & Comm.* 329–386.

107 We will see *infra* that Art. XII. 2 of the Liability Convention contemplates the possibility of an action for damages being pursued under domestic law or another international agreement beyond the Convention provisions.

108 S. Eigenbrodt, 'Out to Launch: Private Remedies for Outer Space Claims' (1989) 55 *J. Air L. & Comm.* 185–222.

109 *Trail Smelter Arbitration* (US v Canada) (1938–41) 3 RIAA 1905; [1939] 33 AJIL 182; [1941] 35 AJIL 684.

110 The *Corfu Channel* Case (UK v Albania), 1949 ICJ Rep. 1.

Chorzow Factory case[111] establish that a state can become internationally liable for damage caused to another state and that the obligation requires that reparation be made. The work of the International Law Commission (ILC) on state responsibility has presented a useful succinct statement of the law that we may expect increasingly to be referred to as persuasive, if not authoritative.[112] The ILC documents cover the normal principles of international law in such matters. The question is whether and how these are to be found within space law. There are several elements: the general liability for space matters under the OST, its provision as to damage and the more specific Liability Convention.

Liability Under the Outer Space Treaty

OST Art. I para 2 indicates that outer space is to be used 'in accordance with international law', and Art. III reiterates that states party to the OST are to carry on their space activities 'in accordance with international law'. From these alone, it may be deduced that the ordinary rules of international law as to compensation for damage caused by one state to another state apply in a space-related incident. The ordinary thrust of international law as to damage would not change even if what was involved was damage in space or damage done by a space object.

OST Art. VI provides further clarity. States party to the OST bear 'international responsibility for national activities in outer space . . . whether such activities are carried on by governmental agencies or by nongovernmental entities, and for ensuring that national activities are carried out in accordance with the provisions' of the Treaty. Further, the activities of nongovernmental entities in outer space 'shall require authorisation and continuing supervision by the appropriate state party to the treaty'. The effect of these requirements is that a state cannot wash its hands of the results of the activities of its nationals. It has authorised and supervises them. If, therefore, the activities cause damage, a nexus is constituted between them and the home state sufficient to impute liability on the part of the state.[113]

Another plank in the OST liability regime is Art. VIII. As noted elsewhere, this introduces without further explanation the concept of a registry of space objects maintained by individual states. A state with which an object launched into outer space is carried retains jurisdiction and control over the object and over any personnel on the object while it is in outer space or on a celestial body. Simply put, this means that a state cannot get out of its international obligations through the abandonment of the object.

---

111 The *Chorzow Factory Case (Merits)* (Germany v. Poland) 1928 PCIJ 4, Ser. A, No. 13.

112 'Responsibility of States for Internationally Wrongful Acts' ILC, 2001 (A/56/10) (http://untreaty.un.org/ilc/texts/instruments/english/draft%20articles/9_6_2001.pdf) and the draft on 'International liability for injurious consequences arising out of acts not prohibited by international law': 'Prevention of Transboundary Harm from Hazardous Activities' ILC, 2001 (A/56/10): http://untreaty.un.org/ilc/texts/instruments/english/draft%20articles/9_7_2001.pdf. See also B.A. Hurwitz, *infra* n. 115, 146–203 for a discussion of the earlier ILC deliberations.

113 The failure of a state to authorise would not allow it to escape liability. Cf. the ILC Draft Articles on State Responsibility, *supra* n. 112. However, note the problem of the post-launch transfer of a satellite's ownership from an owner in one state to an owner in another, *supra* at n. 66. The Netherlands has indicated its view that such a transfer imposes duties as to operation on the state of the new owner under OST Art. VI and jurisdiction and control duties under OST Art. VII but not under ARRA, the Liability Convention or the Registration Convention, although The Netherlands is party to all three.

Many provisions of the OST therefore are usable for dealing with liability for damage caused by space activities. However, it had been obvious from an early stage in the development of the Treaty that more specific provision was needed. Responding to a COPUOS report (UNGA Doc. A/5181), the General Assembly of 1962 referred to various proposals annexed to the report and specifically requested that the Committee 'continue urgently its work on liability for space vehicle accidents'[114] The following year, liability for damage was included in the 1963 Declaration of Legal Principles (UNGA Res. 1962 (XVIII) para 8, stating that a state launching or procuring the launch of an object into outer space, together with a state from whose territory or facility the object is launched, 'is internationally liable for damage done to a foreign state or to its natural or juridical persons in air space, or in outer space.' OST Art. VII mirrors the language of the 1963 Principles on liability. Parties that launch or procure the launch of an object into space, or from whose territory or facilities a launch takes place, are internationally liable for damage done to another state party or to its natural or juridical persons on the Earth, in air space or in outer space.

The OST therefore provides for a regime of liability for damage caused by a space object, fixes the responsibility to authorise and supervise space activities, requires compliance with duties as to control and supervision and shuts the door on avoidance of liability. However, the Treaty is imprecise as to the nature of the liability for damage, as it was perhaps entitled to be, given that in the 1960s, the ILC was only in the middle of its discussions of state responsibility.

That said, it was something of a relief – not to say a necessity – that the OST provisions surrounding liability for damage have been further elaborated. The Registration Convention of 1974 (considered above) gave clarity to a system under which states responsible for space objects may be traced. The Liability Convention elaborates a state's liabilities and how compensation for damage may be recovered.

The Liability Convention

The Convention on International Liability for Damage caused by Space Objects was adopted by the UNGA on 29 November 1971.[115] Opened for signature on 29 March 1972, it entered into force on 1 September. Its depositaries are the UK, the then USSR and the US (Art. XXIV. 2). As of 1 January 2023, the Convention had ninety-eight state parties, together with a further nineteen signatories.[116] Whether it should be revised was to be put

---

114 International Cooperation in the Peaceful Uses of Outer Space. UNGA Res. 1802 (XVII), Sec. 1. 3.
115 Convention on International Liability for Damage Caused by Space Objects, 29 March 1972; 961 UNTS 187; 1974 UKTS 16, Cmnd. 5551; 24 UST 2389, TIAS 7762; (1971) 10 ILM 965–972; [1971] 66 AJIL 702. See (US) Senate Committee on Foreign Relations, *Convention on International Liability for Damage Caused by Space Objects*, S. Exec. Rpt. 38, and (US) Senate Committee on Aeronautical and Space Sciences, *Report on the Convention on International Liability for Damage Caused by Space Objects: Analysis and Background Data* (Comm. Print), both 92d Cong. 2d Sess.; B.A. Hurwitz, *State Liability for Outer Space Activities in Accordance with the 1972 Convention on International Liability for Damage Caused by Space Objects* (Dordrecht: Kluwer, 1992); P.G. Dembling, 'A Liability Treaty for Outer Space Activities' (1970) 19 *Am. U. L. Rev.* 33–47; W.F. Foster, 'The Convention on International Liability for Damage Caused by Space Objects' (1972) *Can. YBIL* 137–185; C.Q. Christol, 'International Liability for Damage Caused by Space Objects' (1980) 74 *AJIL* 346–371; E.F. Hennessey, 'Liability for Damage Caused by the Accidental Operation of a Strategic Defense Initiative System' (1988) 22 *Cornell Int. L.J.* 317–337.
116 See *supra* n. 11. As to membership by international organisations, see *infra* at n. 119.

on the provisional UNGA ten years after it entered into force. Alternatively, after five years and at the request of one third of its parties and with the consent of a majority, a conference could have been held for the purpose. (Art. XXVI). Neither of these options has so far been pursued.

Amendments to the Convention can be proposed by any party (Art. XXV). Amendments enter into force for each state party accepting them upon their acceptance by a majority of states party to the Convention, and thereafter for each remaining state party on the date the party accepts it (Art. XXV). As we have indicated in relation to other international space agreements, we hope that the universality or commonality of the Liability Convention amongst its parties is not compromised by this amending process. Withdrawal from the Convention becomes effective one year after notice being given to the depositary governments (Art. XXVII). So far, no party has withdrawn.

The Liability Convention does not affect other international agreements that its parties may have entered (Art. XXIII.1). Further, the Convention is not envisaged as being necessarily the absolute last word on such matters. Article XXIII. 2 declares that no provision of the Convention is to prevent states from 'concluding international agreements reaffirming, supplementing or extending its provisions'.[117]

The Liability Convention can apply to entities other than states. Its provisions also apply to any international intergovernmental organisation conducting space activities that declares acceptance of the Convention rights and obligations if a majority of its members are parties to the convention and the OST (Art. XXII.1).[118] Parties to the Convention that are members of such a space-active organisation are supposed to take steps to ensure that the organisation does make such a declaration (Art. XXII. 2). Under 2023 ESA, EUMETSAT, EUTELSAT and INTERSPUTNIK had done so.[119] Of them, in 1977, ESA established principles for the apportionment of liability among its members and the Agency itself.[120]

The Preamble notes that 'notwithstanding the precautionary measures to be taken by state and international intergovernmental involved in the launching of space objects, damage may on occasion be caused by such objects'. It then recognises 'the need to elaborate effective international rules and procedures concerning liability for such damage and to ensure that in particular the prompt payment . . . of a full and equitable measure of compensation to victims of such damage'. The Convention was therefore intended to strengthen 'international cooperation in the field of the exploration and use of outer space for peaceful purposes'.

Article 1 of the Convention defines terms. Under Art. 1(a), 'damage' means 'loss of life, personal injury or other impairment of health; or loss of or damage to property of States or of persons, natural or juridical, or property of international intergovernmental organisations'.[121] Liability attaches to a launching state which, repeating OST Art. VI, is defined

---

117 Note Sundahl, *infra* n. 128.

118 Reference point *infra* n. 138.

119 See *supra* n. 11.

120 Resolution of the Council of the European Space Agency on the Agency's Legal Liability, ESA/C/XXII/Res. 5, 13 December 1977; (2005) XXX AASL Part II, 265–270.

121 There are questions as to what constitutes damage to property: does it include indirect damage such as loss of profits? Some legal systems do not recognise indirect damage, considering that category too speculative. See Hurwitz, *supra* n. 115, 12–20, and cf. Art. 30 of the Russian Federation Law on Space Activities, *supra*

in Art. I(c) as a state which launches or procures the launching of a space object and any state from whose territory or facility a space object is launched.[122] To avoid doubt, Art. I(b) provides that launching includes attempted launching.[123] Finally, for clarity, Art. I(d) states that the term 'space object' 'includes component parts of a space object as well as its launch vehicle and parts thereof'. It is commonly accepted that 'parts thereof' includes debris caused by the break-up of a launch vehicle.[124]

Articles II and III elaborate the concept of liability for the purposes of the Convention. In so doing, they depart from the generalised notion of liability expressed in OST Art. VII and differentiate between two categories of liability, absolute and fault-based. Article II provides that a launching state is 'absolutely liable' to pay compensation for damage caused by its space object on the surface of the Earth or to aircraft in flight.[125] It therefore appears to have adopted the principle found in many legal systems that the creator of a situation where there is the possibility of acute and catastrophic danger is liable without proof of fault to pay compensation if that danger eventuates: the doctrine of 'dangerous things'.[126]

---

n. 71, under which the Federation guarantees full compensation for 'direct damage inflicted as a result of accidents in carrying out space activity in accordance with legislation of the Russian Federation'.

122 See again the problem of the post-launch transfer of a satellite's ownership from an owner in one state to an owner in another, *supra* at nn. 66 and 113. See also the UK notifications of October 2013, *supra* n. 66, and of March 2015 of a change of supervision of the Skynet network, ST/SG/SER.E/743: www.unoosa.org/res/osoindex/data/documents/gb/st/stsgser_e743_html/ser743E.pdf.

123 When does an attempt to launch begin: when the launch vehicle is on the launch pad at testing, is ready to go, at ignition or at lift-off? Cf. Hurwitz, *supra* n. 115, 20–21. For practical purposes, this could be agreed on between parties as part of an insurance contract.

124 Thus, in Note Verbale of 16 April 2004 giving UN OOSA information for January and February 2004, the USA included 'objects not previously reported' but which had been identified since the previous US report. These objects, for which orbital characteristics had already been given, comprised 'spent boosters, spent manoeuvring stages, shrouds and other non-functional objects' from a Delta 1 launch on 8 July 1977, a Delta 1 launch on 10 March 1977, a Seasat 1 launch on 27 June 1978 and a NOAA 7 launch on 23 June 1981. See OOSA/COPUOS ST/SG/Ser.E/449.

125 Absolute liability in international law is otherwise found in relation to damage from aircraft (Convention on Damage caused by Foreign Aircraft to Third Parties on the Surface, Rome, 1952: 310 UNTS 182; 1953 UK Misc. Ser. 7, Cmd. 8886) and in a number of treaties in connection with nuclear incidents, many of which are not in force: Convention on Third Party Liability in the Field of Nuclear Energy of 1960, as amended by the Additional Protocol of 1964; 956 UNTS 264; 1968 UKTS 69, Cmnd. 1211 and the Protocol of 16th November 1982: www.nea.fr/html/law/nlparis_conv.html; International Convention on Civil Liability for Nuclear Damage, Vienna, 1963, 1063 UNTS 2651964 UK Misc. Ser. 9, Cmnd. 2333 (1963) 2 ILM 727. Cf. Convention on the Liability of the Operators of Nuclear Ships, Brussels, 1962, [1963] 57 AJIL 268–278 (not yet in force). See also the University of Oregon International Environmental Agreements Database Project at ica.uoregon.edu.

See also Dembling, *supra* n. 115; G. Arangio-Ruiz, 'Third Party Liability of the Operators of Nuclear Ships' (1962–III) 107 *Hague Receuil*, 601 ff; and *The 1997 Vienna Convention on Civil Liability for Nuclear Damage and the 1977 Convention on Supplementary Compensation for Nuclear Damage – Explanatory Texts* (Vienna: IAEA, 2007): http://www-pub.iaea.org/MTCD/publications/PDF/Pub1279_web.pdf.

126 Now largely departed from in its most simple form, the doctrine of dangerous things has long roots in domestic laws, the famous English case of *Rylands v. Fletcher* (1868) LR 3 HL 330 being but one example. Cf. French Civil Code, Arts 1382–1386; German Civil Code, Arts 618, 823, 836–838; Roscoe Pound, *An Introduction to the Philosophy of Law* (New Haven: Yale UP, 1922) 163 ff. In para 22 of its Claim regarding Cosmos 954, Canada stated that absolute liability attaching to activities involving a high degree of risk is a general principle of international law. See *infra* n. 169 and text following.

Article III provides that where damage is caused elsewhere than on the surface of Earth by a space object to the space object of another launching state or to persons or property on-board, the launching state is liable only if the damage is due to its fault or the fault of persons for whom it is responsible.[127] That means, of course, that in-orbit accidents caused by orbital debris may well never be satisfactorily dealt with. The idea of sharing these risks among those engaged in space activities makes logical sense, although it seems not to appeal to actual participants.[128]

Article IV deals with the specific instance of damage caused to a third state by the collision of two space objects belonging to other states. If damage is so caused elsewhere than on the surface of Earth to a third state or its natural juridical persons, the first two states are jointly and severally liable to the third state (Art. IV.1). In the event that the damage is caused to the third state on the surface of Earth or to an aircraft in flight, the liability of the launching states is absolute (Art. IV.1(a)). Where the damage to the third state does not occur on the surface of Earth, the liability of the first two states is based on fault, that being the fault of either of the first two states or the fault of persons for whom either of them is responsible (Art. IV.1(b)).

Where there is joint and several liability under Art. IV.1 the damaged state may seek the entire compensation from all or any of the launching states involved (Art. IV.2). Additionally, the burden of compensation is apportioned between the states that are jointly and severally liable in proportion to the extent to which they were at fault (Art. IV.2). This means that if the space object of State A by its fault collides with a space object of State B and sends it into the space object of State C, State C can claim compensation from State A or State B or from both. As between State A and State B, State A would in due course have to reimburse State B for any compensation that it has paid. If the extent of the fault of the joint and several liable states cannot be established, the burden of the compensation is apportioned equally between them (Art. IV.2).

Where two or more states jointly launch a space object, they are jointly and severally liable for any damage caused (Art. V.1). While the precise nature of that liability is controlled by Arts. II and III of the Convention, Art. V.3 makes it clear that what might be termed a passive participant, a state whose territory or facility is the launch location, is included among the states liable for all the consequent events, although that is already provided for by Art. I(c).[129]

In the case of a joint launch, a state that suffers damage may seek the entire compensation from all or from any of the jointly and severally liable states at its option (Art. V.2). If a launching state pays compensation, it is entitled to claim proportionate indemnification from the other launching states involved (Art. V.2). Article V.2 further envisages that

127 H.A. Baker, 'Liability for Damage Caused in Outer Space by Space Refuse' (1988) 13 *AASL* 183–225. Cf. the operation of the International Oil Pollution Compensation Funds, www.iopcfund.org/. The collision of Iridium 33 and Cosmos 2251 in February 2009 intrigues. The Cosmos satellite was derelict, but the Iridium one still had propellant. Could it have avoided the collision? Was it negligent not so to do? See *infra* n. 184.

128 M.J. Sundahl, 'Unidentified Orbital Debris: The Case for a Market-Share Liability Regime' (2000) 24 *Hastings Int. & Comp. L. Rev.* 125–154; B.A. Hurwitz, 'An International Compensation Fund for Damage Caused by Space Objects' (1991) 34 *Proc. IISL* 201–204.

129 Cf. Agreement between the French Government and ESA Concerning the Guiana Space Centre, selected provisions (2005) XXX AASL Part II, 253–256.

the participants in a joint launch may agree among themselves the apportionment of any potential financial obligations they may incur through liability arising from the launch.[130]

A launching state may be exonerated from the absolute liability of Art. II, damage to the surface of the Earth or to aircraft in flight where it is established that the claimant state or its natural or juridical persons caused the damage wholly or partially deliberately or by gross negligence (Art. VI.1). One might envisage such exoneration applying where it is shown that the claimant state had negligently or deliberately aggravated the damage, for example by interfering with a nuclear device on a crashed space object. No exoneration is granted where the damage has resulted from activities of the launching state which are not themselves in accordance with international law (Art. VI.2).[131]

The Liability Convention does not apply to damage caused by a launching state to its own nationals (Art. VII(a)).[132] Nor does it apply to foreign nationals while they are taking part in the operation of the space object from launch until descent or while they are in the immediate vicinity of a planned launch or recovery area if the launching state had invited them into that area (Art. VII(b)). The exclusion of foreign nationals may be explained by the brocard *volenti non fit iniuria*. Nonetheless, one would assume (or at least hope) that in appropriate circumstances, the launching state would either insure these foreign nationals or be willing as an act of grace to provide full compensation for any damage done to them.

A state suffering damage by a space object, or whose natural or juridical person has so suffered, may claim compensation from a launching state (Art. VIII.1). The process starts with the sending of an appropriate diplomatic note to the launching state involved (Art. IX). Should there not be diplomatic relations between the damaged state and the launching state, the claim may be submitted through a third state or through the UN Secretary General provided that both the claimant state and the launching state are UN members (Art. IX). So far, only one such claim has been made: the Cosmos 954 incident.[133]

The procedures for presenting a claim under the Convention diverge in two major ways from the general rules of international law as to state responsibility. First, presenting a launching state with a claim for compensation under the Convention does not require the prior exhaustion of local remedies (Art. XI.1). It remains competent for local remedies to be pursued – that is not excluded by this provision of the Convention. However, it is not appropriate or acceptable to simultaneously pursue a claim under the Convention and seek compensation through the remedies of the launching state itself (Art. XI.2).[134]

---

130 E.g. 'Exchange of Notes between the Government of the United Kingdom of Great Britain and Northern Ireland and the Government of the People's Republic of China concerning Liability for Damage during the Launch Stage of the Apstar-1, Apstar-2, and Apstar-2 Satellites', Peking, 28 June 1994, 1995 UKTS 7, Cmnd. 2737 and the similar agreement for the Launch Stage of the Apstar-IA and Apstar-IIR Satellites, Peking, 5 and 6 February 1996, 1996 UKTS Cm 3274; Memorandum of Agreement on Liability for Satellite Launches between the Government of the United States of America and the Government of the People's Republic of China', 1989 (2005) XXX AASL Part II, 259–260. See also the 1977 ESA Council Resolution on the liability of that Agency, *supra* n. 120.

131 Cf. D.S. Rudesill, 'Precision War and Responsibility: Transformational Military Technology and the Duty of Care under the Laws of War' (2007) 32 *Yale J. Int. L.* 517–545.

132 Reference point, *infra* nn. 135 and 136. Thus it did not apply to ground damage in the US from the break-up of the Shuttle Columbia on re-entry in 2003.

133 See *infra* n. 168 and following text.

134 Eigenbrodt, *supra* n. 108.

Second, the Convention departs from the ordinary rule regarding the nationality of claims. Normally, a state can claim for damage to its national, and if it does not do so, that ends the matter. However, under the Convention, should the state of nationality not present a claim, another state may claim for damage sustained in its territory by any natural or juridical person (Art. VIII.2). It therefore is possible for State B to present a claim on behalf of a State A national, provided that the State A national suffered damage in State B's territory and that State A's national was neither a national of the launching state nor engaged in operating the space object (Art. VII).[135] Further, should neither the state of nationality nor the state where the damage occurred present a claim, then the state of permanent residence of the damaged person or entity may claim (Art. VIII.3), again subject to the qualification that the injury is not to a national of the launching state or to someone operating the space object (Art. VII).[136] The Rule of Nationality of Claims is therefore comprehensively breached, though not to the extent of allowing any state to set up as an international claims agency or broker.

Time limits for the presentation of claims are laid down in Art. X. Under Art. X.1, a claim for compensation is to be presented not later than one year after the occurrence of the damage or the identification of the launching state which is liable. If, however, a state did not know of the damage, or was not able to identify the relevant launching state, it may present a claim within one year following the date on which it learns of the damage or identifies the launching state (Art. X.2). This period is not, however, unlimited; it expires one year following the date on which a state could reasonably have been expected to have learned of the facts through the exercise of due diligence (Art. X.2). While a claimant state must not delay presenting a claim until the full extent of the damage is known, it can revise a claim and submit additional documentation once the full extent of damage becomes known (Art. X.3).

Any compensation payable for damage under the Convention is assessed in accordance with the ordinary rules of international law. It is intended to return the damaged person, state or international organisation – as far as is monetarily possible – to the position that would have existed had the damage not occurred (Art. XII).[137] Monetary compensation is paid in the currency of the claimant state or, at its option, in the currency of the state from which the compensation is due, unless the claimant and liable states agree otherwise (Art. XII).

If an international intergovernmental organisation is liable under the Convention, that liability is joint and several with that of its members which are separately party to the Convention (Art. XXII.3).[138] However, any claim for compensation from the organisation must first be presented to the organisation and only if the organisation has not paid compensation within six months may a claimant state invoke the liability of members of the organisation that are parties to the Convention (Art. XXII.3(a) and (b)). Where an organisation which has declared its acceptance of the rights and duties under the Convention is a claimant, that claim is presented to the launching state by any state member of the organisation which is also a state party to the Convention (Art. XXII.4).

---

135 Cf. text at n.132 *supra*.
136 Cf. text at n. 132 *supra*.
137 Cf. the *Chorzow Factory Case (Jurisdiction)* (Germany v. Poland), 1927 PCIJ 4, Ser. A, No. 9.
138 International organisations may accept rights and duties under the Convention; see *supra* text at n. 118.

It is to be hoped that questions of compensation for damage by a space object would be settled without major difficulty through diplomatic channels. This happened in the case of Cosmos 954.[139] If, however, settlement has not occurred within one year from the date from which the claimant state submits its documented claim to the launching state or states, either party may request the establishment of a Claims Commission (Art. XIV). A Claims Commission is composed of three members, one appointed by the claimant state and one appointed by the launching state; if there is more than one launching state involved, they can together appoint only one member (Art. XVII). The third member, the chairman, is chosen by the parties jointly (Art. XV.1).

Parties appoint their members within two months of the request to establish the Commission (Art. XV.1). If the chairman is not agreed within four months to the request for a Commission, either party may request that the UN Secretary General appoint a chairman within a further two months (Art. XV.2). A party to a procedure under the Claims Commission system cannot stall others by refusing to make its appointment. If one of the parties does not make its appointment within the stipulated period, at the request of the other party, the chairman constitutes a single member Claims Commission (Art. XIV.1). A vacancy arising during the currency of a Commission is filled by the same procedure as for the original appointment of the person concerned (Art. XVI.2). The Commission determines its own procedure (Art. XVI.3) and where it sits (Art. XVI.4). The expenses of the Commission are borne equally by the parties unless the Commission decides otherwise (Art. XX).

The Claims Commission decides the merits of the claim and determines the amount of any compensation (Art. XVIII). Unless the Commission has only a single member, Commission decisions are taken by a majority vote (Art. XVI.5): the view taken by the Chairman may therefore be crucial. In making its determination, the Commission is to give due regard to international law and principles of justice and equity, restoring the damaged person or state as far as may be to the position that would have existed had the damage not occurred (Art. XIX.1, referring to Art. XII).

The decision or award of the Commission is given as promptly as possible and, unless the Commission finds it necessary to delay, is to be given no later than one year from the date of its establishment (Art. XIX.3). The decision or award is to be made public and also delivered to the parties and the UN Secretary General (Art. XIX.4). The Commission must state the reasons for its decision or award (Art. XIX.2). Unfortunately the decision or award of a Claims Commission is not necessarily binding on the parties. It is final and binding if the parties have so agreed, but if not, it is only 'final and recommendatory' (Art. XIX. 2). Although the parties are to consider a recommendation in good faith (Art. XIX.2), we would have preferred the outcome of a Claims Commission proceeding to be binding and therefore more certain to conclude the matter. However, we believe that an international practice is developing that states abide by recommendatory international arbitral decisions.[140]

Penultimately, we note that Art. XXI of the Liability Convention makes special provision for the catastrophic if a space object causes damage presenting a 'large scale danger to human life' or 'seriously interfering with the living conditions of the population or the

---

139 See *infra* at n. 168.
140 P.B. Larsen, 'The US–Italy Air Transport Arbitration: Problems of Treaty Interpretation and Enforcement' (1967) 61 *AJIL* 496–520.

functioning of vital centres'.[141] In such an event, all states party to the Convention (and in particular launching states) are to examine giving appropriate and rapid assistance to any state which has so suffered. This does not affect the rights or obligations of the states that are party to the Convention.

If appropriate, the catastrophe provision should be read along with the 'Principles Relevant to the Use of Nuclear Power Sources in Outer Space' (UNGA Res. 47/68, 1992).[142] Under its Pr. 5.1 and 2, the launching state of a space object with a nuclear power source that becomes aware that the object is malfunctioning and there is a risk that radioactive materials will return to Earth is required 'in timely fashion' to inform potentially affected states and the UN Secretary General[143] of the system parameters of the object[144] and the radiological risk involved.[145] Information is to be provided as soon as possible, updated as required and with increasing frequency as re-entry approaches so that affected states may plan for potential problems (Pr. 5.2).[146]

In such cases, Pr.7.1 requires all states having space monitoring and tracking facilities to help track the object, resulting in a greater degree of clarity as to which state(s) may be directly affected. After re-entry, under Pr. 7.2, the launching state is to offer any affected state the assistance necessary to eliminate actual and possible harmful effects. This includes identifying the location of debris and its retrieval and associated clean-up.[147] Last, we express the hope that the ethos of Art. XXI of the Liability Convention and the correlative nuclear power principles will inform the reaction of states to potential threats and actual damage caused by things other than space objects.[148]

Compensation for Damage, Liability Caps and Insurance

The compensation for damage under both OST Art. VII and, where relevant, the Liability Convention, is determined as a matter of international law and imposed on the launching state or states.[149] The liability of the state is always easily dealt with, but if the state

141 See *infra*, Practice.
142 As to which see CoCoSL III 189–297 and *infra* Chapter 9 Contamination and Near Earth Environment.
143 For the purpose of the Nuclear Power Principles, and without affecting their Pr. 9 as to liability and compensation, the launching state is the state having jurisdiction and control at the relevant point in time (Pr. 2.1). Cf. Note Verbale by The Netherlands relative to certain satellites transferred from INTELSAT to New Skies NV, *supra* n. 66.
144 The name of the launching state and an address for further information; the international designation; the date and territory or location of launch; information required for best prediction of orbital lifetime, trajectory and impact region; general function of spacecraft.
145 The type of nuclear power source (radioisotropic or reactor), the probable physical form, amount and radiological characteristics of fuel and contaminated materials likely to reach the ground.
146 Occasionally, reports of incoming objects are carried in the media. Cf. *infra* at n. 174 on the BeppoSax re-entry. Technically, the Principles did not apply, as that satellite was not nuclear powered, but reports as to its probable fate were issued with increasing frequency.
147 Cf. the provisions of ARRA, *supra*.
148 See Chapter 9 Planetary Defence.
149 It has been suggested that as many space activities are now conducted by private enterprise, the Liability Convention should be amended to permit damages being sought directly from these companies: A.P. Reinert, 'Updating the Liability Regime in Outer Space: Why Spacefaring Companies Should Be Internationally Liable for Their Space Objects' (2020) 62 *William & Mary L.R.* 324–356; A. Caley, 'Liability in International Law and the Ramifications on Commercial Space Launches and Space Tourism' (2014) *Loy. L.A. Int. & Comp. L. Rev.* 233–262.

has been involved through activities that it has licensed, it may seek indemnification from the perpetrator(s). In licensing commercial activities, many countries therefore require applicants to have an insurance policy covering in whole or in part the compensation for which the state might be liable if the activity causes damage.[150] However, to encourage enterprise, it is increasingly common for states to cap the amount for which they will seek indemnification. The levels set for the cap vary. We here outline two examples.[151]

In the US, 51 USC §50914(a) lays down general requirements for the licensing of US commercial space launch activities.[152] Under Sec. 50914.(a)(1) and (4), liability insurance must be obtained or financial responsibility shown in amounts to compensate for damage caused, but the sums involved vary. First, Sec. 50914.(a)(2).(3).B recognises that there may be a limit to the willingness of the insurance industry to accept risk. Accordingly, the insured amount may be limited to the maximum liability insurance available on the world market at reasonable cost.

Further, under 51 USC §§ 50914(a).(3), the maximum insurable amount for the total claims relating to one launch or re-entry is capped at US$500 million for claims by third parties for death, bodily injury or property damage or loss resulting from an activity carried out under the licence and at US$100 million for damage or loss to government property. However, under Sec. 50914(a).(2), after consultation with NASA, the US Air Force and others, the US Secretary of Transportation may set different requirements.[153] The purpose of these variable and total limits is to ensure that commercial space activities are not deterred by an inability to fully off-set, either by insurance or otherwise, any US international liability for damage consequent on the licensed activity.

In the UK, an amended Outer Space Act 1986, c. 38, now deals with space activities undertaken elsewhere than in the UK, while the Space Industry Act 2018, c. 18, covers activities on mainland UK.[154] Both have provision for a liability cap, the levels of which is set by the Department of Transport.[155] Under both Acts, space activities must normally be licensed. Under the 1986 Act requirements, a licensee must indemnify the UK government against any claims that arise from activities defined in s. 1 and incur UK state liability under the Liability Convention (s. 10). A licensee must therefore obtain insurance from the public insurance market (s. 5(2)(f)). The licence may set a limit to the liability of the licensee (s. 10(1A)), in which case the UK government will meet any excess above that limit.

However, an activity subject to the 1986 Act may be exempted from UK licensing requirements where the UK government has an arrangement with another state that secures compliance with its international obligations (ss. 3(2)(b) and 3(3)). Under the 2018 Space Industry Act, space activities require an operator's licence (s. 3) unless the UK

---

150 UN OOSA maintains links to and data on national space laws at www.unoosa.org/oosa/en/SpaceLaw/national/index.html.

151 Another example is Australia, as discussed in Chapter 14.

152 US Code, Title 51 – Transportation; Subtitle IX – Commercial Space Transportation; Chapter 701 – Commercial Space Launch Activities. See www.faa.gov/licenses_certificates/commercial_space_transportation/.

153 M. Schaefer, 'The Need for Federal Preemption and International Negotiations Regarding Liability Caps and Waivers of Liability in the US Commercial Space Industry' (2015) 33 *Berkeley. J. Int. L.* 223–273; M. Tse, '"One Giant Leap [Backwards] for Mankind": Limited Liability in Private Commercial Spaceflight' (2013) 79 *Brook. L. Rev.* 291–320.

154 See *infra* Chapter 14.

155 'Guidance: Commercial spaceflight: launch liabilities and insurance' (Department of Transport, 2021). Currently, the cap for standard operations is £60m, but other considerations may increase the requirement in a particular case.

has arrangements with another country to secure compliance with its international obligations (s. 4.1) or licensing is unnecessary (s. 4.2). Liability for injury or damage by space-flight activity caused within the UK or to aircraft in flight is absolute, and compensation is recoverable from the operator (s. 34(2)). An operator causing damage must indemnify the UK against any claim against it (s. 36).

The Act provides that the licence may specify a limit to the licensee's liability (s. 12.2), particularly when carrying out activities exempted by regulation (s. 4.4(e)–(f)). Under the Space Industry Regulations, 2021 SI 792, the operator licence must specify a limit for liability (Reg. 220(1)). However, no limit is available where the licensee has been grossly negligent or committed wilful misconduct in the performance of its obligations or other requirements (Reg. 220(3)).

There is a numerically small but important insurance market that covers what may be termed industrial space losses. Launchers may explode or be destroyed by ground command, and satellites may fail to be put into correct orbit or wholly or partially fail to operate. The intricacies of this area of commerce, law and practice lie beyond the scope of this book. Suffice it to say that there are many intriguing cases, most of which are dealt with by negotiation or arbitration, the terms and findings of which are not usually generally available.[156]

Sometimes where there was no insurance, there have been interesting cases on contract.[157] On occasion, insurers have taken over ownership of a failed satellite and following settlement have arranged for its recovery, refurbishment and later sale.[158] Insurance premiums are based on perceived risks, the history of a launcher, the satellite manufacturer and other relevant considerations.[159] Insuring the first launch of a new launcher can be difficult, and prohibitively expensive if not impossible.

Practice

It is convenient to sketch some occurrences.[160] So far, no major disasters have occurred despite the re-entry of many space objects and large chunks of space debris. Most end up in the oceans or on land without causing actionable damage.[161] These may be classified as potential instances of surface damage. Damage in space could be different since Art. III of the Convention would require proof of fault to ground a claim. There have been occurrences in space which might have raised questions of liability, but so far no official claims have been made.[162]

---

156 As we noted in Chapter 2, contracts including insurance contracts, practice, compromise and agreement are working out concepts suitable for the space business. Unfortunately, commercial confidentiality (secrecy) usually means that this developing area is not available for public scrutiny or to interested academics.

157 Thus we have *Martin Marietta v. INTELSAT* (1991) 763 F. Supp. 1327; (1993) 991 F. 2d. 94, and cf. S. Gorove, *Cases on Space Law: Texts, Comments and References* (Oxford: University of Mississippi: *J. Sp. Law*, 1996).

158 See *supra* n. 104.

159 K. Malinowska, 'Risk Assessment in Insuring Space Endeavours: A Legal Approach' (2017) 42 *Air and Sp. L.* 329–348.

160 O.A. Volynskaya, 'Landmark Space-Related Accidents and the Progress of Space Law' (2013) 62 *ZLW* 220–236.

161 See BeppoSax, *infra* at n. 174. Many space station supply shuttles end up in the Pacific.

162 Perhaps the developments in lunar activities require a new approach to liability in that sphere. See E. Morozova and A. Laurenava, 'To the Moon and Back: On the Way to a Well-Balanced Liability Framework for Lunar and Cislunar Activities' (2021) 45 *J. Sp. L.* 176–200.

The Liability Convention has twice been activated in respect of surface damage, the circumstance under which Art. II imposes absolute liability. Parts of Skylab landed on 11 July 1979 east of Perth, Australia, in desert, causing no damage.[163] NASA advertised for claims but received none relevant in terms of the Convention.[164]

More serious was the disintegration of Cosmos 954 over northern Canada in January 1978.[165] Cosmos 954, launched by the USSR on 18 September 1977, was a radar surveillance satellite. Subsequent to malfunction, it crashed in the Northwest Territories of Canada on 24 January 1978, scattering debris including radioactive materials over 124,000 km² south of the Great Slave Lake and spilling over into northern Alberta and Saskatchewan. Operation Morning Light, mounted by Canada and the US, lasted until October 1978 and resulted in an estimated recovery of about 0.1% of the satellite's nuclear power source.[166] When it became clear that the satellite would come to earth, Canada asked the USSR about its composition and possible hazardous elements but apparently got no response. Canada informed the UN Secretary General of the discovery of the satellite debris.[167]

On 23 January 1979 the Government of Canada presented a claim to the USSR for CAN\$6,041,174.70 for the damage caused by the crash and on 15 March 1979 provided further documentation in support of its claims. The Canadian claim was presented under both the Liability Convention and general international law.[168] The USSR disclaimed liability, and the matter was settled in 1981.[169] Some have argued that this was not an instance of the Liability Convention at work, but the Canadian claim was expressly made *inter alia* under the Convention, and the Convention does contemplate settlement through diplomatic negotiations (Arts. IX and XIV).[170]

---

163 Cf. US House of Representatives, Committee on Science and Technology, Subcommittee on Space Science and Applications, *NASA Skylab Re-entry, Hearing June 4, 1979* (Washington: GPO, 1979).

164 NASA had publicised that Skylab was on a re-entry course and apparently received some claims for compensation for nervous shock and worry from persons in the Indian sub-continent apprehensive that it would land on them, but no state pursued the matter. We also understand that the US did not request return of the debris. Wikipedia states that the Shire of Esperance, West Australia, fined NASA US\$400 for littering. The fine was later paid by a US radio station. Cf. C.W.D. Thompson and C.E. Benson, 'The De-Orbit of Skylab' Chapter 19 of *Living and Working in Space: A History of Skylab*, NASA-SP-4208, 1983; S. Freeland, 'There's a Satellite in My Backyard! – MIR and the Convention on International Liability for Damage Caused by Space Objects' (2001) 24 *U.N.S.W. L. J.* 462–484. See also M.E. Howell, 'Mir Space station': www.space.com/news/spacestation/esperance_mir_010320.html.

165 Elizey, *supra* n. 97, refers to Cosmos 954 throughout; Hurwitz, *supra* n. 115, 113–140.

166 See https://science.gc.ca/eic/site/063.nsf/eng/97309.html; C.G. Weiss, 'The Life and Death of Cosmos 954': www.cia.gov/readingroom/docs/CIA-RDP85B01152R000200260006-4.pdf; L. Heaps, *Operation Morning Light* (New York: Ballantine, 1979).

167 See A/AC.105/214 and 214/corr.1 of 8 February 1978, A/AC.105/217 of 6 March 1978 and A/AC.105/236 of 22 December 1978.

168 'Canada: Claim against the USSR for Damage caused by Soviet Cosmos 954' (1979) 18 ILM 899–930.

169 'Canada – Union of Soviet Socialist Republics: Protocol and Settlement of Canada's Claim for Damages Caused by Cosmos 954, Moscow, 2 April 1981': (1981) 20 ILM 689; (2005) XXX Part II, AASL 261–263.

170 There has been much discussion of Cosmos 954. See *inter alia* P.G. Dembling, 'Cosmos 954 and the Space Treaties' (1978) 6 *J. Sp. L.* 129–136; E. Galloway, 'Nuclear Powered Satellites the USSR Cosmos 954 and the Canadian Claim' (1979) 12 *Akron L.R.* 401–415; B. Schwartz and M.L. Berlin, 'After the Fall: An Analysis of Canadian Legal Claims for Damage Caused by Cosmos 954' (1982) 27 *McGill L.J.* 676–720; J.A. Burke, 'Convention on International Liability for Damage Caused by Space Objects: Definition and Determination of Damages after the Cosmos 954 Incident' (1984–1985) 8 *Fordham Int. L.J.* 255–285; A.F. Cohen, 'Cosmos 954 and the International Law of Satellite Accidents' (1984–5) 10 *Yale J. Int. L.*

Many other re-entries have subsequently taken place.[171] Obviously it is better if large objects deorbit under as much control as possible.[172] On 7 February 1991, the USSR Salyut 7/Cosmos 1686 Space Station re-entered the Earth's atmosphere after nine years' service. Weighing 36,700 kg, it posed a threat that part of it might land on a populated centre. The Soviet controllers attempted to tumble the object to bring it down in the Atlantic Ocean. However, this was unsuccessful, and Salyut 7 re-entered over Argentina, scattering debris over the town of Capitan Bermudas near Buenos Aires. Parts landed in the town, although there were no injuries or serious damage.

On 23 March 2001, the Russian space station Mir was successfully deorbited following braking burns by its engines. Although the debris did not land exactly within the predicted track, it caused no damage on its re-entry.[173] Soon after that, on 4 June 2001, NASA successfully deorbited the 14,000 kg Compton Gamma Ray Observatory into the South Pacific.

Uncontrolled re-entries are more worrying, and there was considerable concern as to the re-entry of the BeppoSax satellite in 2003 from a near circular equatorial orbit. Launched in 1996 as part of a joint Italian–Dutch programme (A/AC.105/INF400), the satellite was in a roughly circular LEO equatorial orbit ranging between plus and minus 3.95°.[174] Fuel-less, its re-entry could not be controlled. Some forty fragments –a total mass of 650 kg – were likely to reach ground level. At risk were shipping; aircraft and portions of equatorial South America, Africa and the Far East. Thirty-one countries and territories were warned of the impending re-entry.

The satellite did not contain fissionable elements, so the Nuclear Power Principles did not apply. Nevertheless, the operators issued with increasing frequency reports as to the possible re-entry and impact points. During the whole process, Italy provided regular status reports on the satellite. BeppoSax splashed into the Pacific south of Hawaii and northwest of the Galapagos Islands at approximately 22.06 UTC on 29 April 2003. Finally, as

---

78–91; M.S. Straubel, 'Space Borne Nuclear Sources – the Status of their Regulation' (1986) 20 *Valparaiso U.L. Rev.* 187–218; E.G. Lee and D.W. Sproule, 'Liability for Damage Caused by Space Debris: The Cosmos 954 Claim' (1988) 26 *Can. YBIL* 273–279; D. Goren, 'Nuclear Accidents in Space and on Earth: An Analysis of International Law Governing the Cosmos-954 and Chernobyl Accidents' (1993) 5 *Geo. Int. Env. L. Rev.* 855–95; Volynskaya, *supra* n. 160, at 220–227; C.B. Picker, 'A View from 40,000 Feet: International Law and the Invisible Hand of Technology' (2001) 23 *Cardozo L. Rev.* 149–219 at 178. Cf. Elizey, *supra* n. 97.

171 The German satellite Rosat (2.5 tonnes) landed in the Bay of Bengal in October 2011. Had it stayed in orbit 10 minutes longer, it would have hit Beijing. However, see the calculation of probability of damage in BeppoSax data discussed later. See also R.P. Patera and W.H. Ailor, 'The Realities of Entry Disposal' (1998) 99 *Adv. in Ast. Sc.* 1059–1071. NORAD, the joint US–Canadian North American Aerospace Defense Command, regularly asks planes to report sighting re-entrant debris. Sometimes pilots report debris burning below them. NORAD was established in 1958, see www.norad.mil. Many instances are noted in L. Punnakanta, 'Space Torts: Applying Nuisance and Negligence to Orbital Debris' (2012–2013) 86 *S. Cal. L. Rev.* 163–98.

172 Even if a re-entrant object is under some degree of control, much depends on the precise angle(s) at which the object (including debris) hits the denser atmosphere layers and the surface it presents to them. It is much like skimming a stone across water – unpredictable within some parameters. A cinematic representation is towards the end of *Moonraker* (1979), when Bond destroys (eventually) globular glass vessels containing deadly gas released from Hugo Drax's space station. Bond's pursuit vessel and the gas containers skip across the upper levels of the atmosphere.

173 See *infra* n. 191.

174 For the Italian/Dutch project, see http://heasarc.gsfc.nasa.gov/docs/sax/saxgof.html and https://heasarc.gsfc.nasa.gov/docs/sax/sax.html. A special Italian website was built to supply information to potentially affected states that were requesting local information. (A.AC.105/803).

to surface damage, the disintegration during re-entry of the Space Shuttle Columbia in 2003 scattered hundreds of pieces of debris over the southern US. This being entirely US territory, the Liability Convention did not apply. Apart from questions of actual surface damage, we here note the interesting questions of whether a state should be under a duty to seek to avoid a potential terrestrial impact by its re-entrant object[175] and whether a state may without liability destroy the space object of another state which threatens either itself or a third state.[176] The former instance has occurred, but without that element of duty. The latter is open for discussion.

Different considerations may apply in what might be termed a space-to-space incident since Art. III of the Liability Convention allows claims for damage based only on fault. Obviously this might involve the direct act of a state, but any redeployment of a satellite could result in collision and damage. Further, a government authorising space activities normally requires a licensee to comply with any instructions it may give,[177] and any damaging result is attributable to the instructing state. But is that arguable when an event occurs involving two licensed objects? We note the 2019/2020 exchange between China and the US that centred on the Chinese space station and the Starlink system.[178]

Of known incidents of direct state action, several are of interest, all of which involve a state destroying its own property. On 11 January 2007, China destroyed an obsolete weather satellite at some 865 km/575 miles into space, releasing a cloud of debris that has remained in orbit with the potential of collision with other space objects.[179] In Project Burnt Frost, on 20 February 2008, the US destroyed its failing satellite US-193 at a height of 110 miles to dissipate its hydrazine propellant and increase the chances that little debris would reach the surface of Earth.[180] Had they not done this, there was a high probability that the propellant container would impact the surface with consequent danger to property and human life. In confirming its action, the USA also intimated its readiness to aid any state affected by the remains of US-193.

On 27 March 2019, as part of Mission Shakti, India destroyed an obsolete satellite and caused a debris cloud.[181] On 15 November 2021, Russia destroyed its Kosmos 1408, resulting in astronauts in the ISS having to seek shelter lest the Station be hit by debris.[182] In all these incidents, it is clear that the destruction of the satellite was the deliberate intention of the state that launched the missile. Therefore, in all the incidents, it could have been argued that fault was present if damage were caused by the debris clouds.[183]

---

175 Controlled re-entries always attempt either to cause the break-up and destruction of a re-entrant at high altitude or to guide the object(s) into the oceans.

176 See *infra* n. 180.

177 Cf. (UK) Outer Space Act 1986, ss. 5.(e), 8.1–2 and 10.2(b)).

178 See A/AC.105/1262 and A/AC.105/1265.

179 S. Aoki, 'Space Arms Control: The Challenges and Alternatives' (2009) 52 *Jap. YBIL* 191–230 at 210–211; K.K. Nair, 'China's ASAT Test: A Demonstrated Need for Legal Reform' (2007) 33 *J. Sp. L.* 191–194; F. Walsh, 'Forging a Diplomatic Shield for American Satellites: The Case for Re-evaluating the 2006 National Space Policy in Light of a Chinese Satellite System' (2007) 72 *J. Air L. & Comm.* 759–799.

180 J. Oppenheim, 'Danger at 700,000 Feet: Why the United States Needs to Develop a Kinetic Anti-Satellite Missile Technology Test-Ban Treaty' (2012–2013) 38 *Brooklyn J. Int. L.* 761–796. See Wikipedia 'US-183' and materials *supra* n. 179.

181 See www.bbc.co.uk/news/world-asia-india-47729568. Wikipedia, 'Mission Shakti'. The satellite's orbit was well below that of the ISS.

182 See www.bbc.co.uk/news/science-environment-59307862. Wikipedia, 'Kosmos 1408'.

183 These are instances of ASATs. See Chapter 16 The Military Use of Outer Space.

One space incident that might have involved the Liability Convention is the collision between Iridium 33 and Cosmos 2251 at 788 km/485 m on 10/11 February 2009.[184] Here, there was some argument that the Iridium satellite did have some on-board propellant and the Cosmos did not and that the collision might have been avoided because its probability had been observed by US tracking services. However, no official complaint was made within the one-year period required by Art. X of the Liability Convention.

Finally under Practice, we note the importance of the mitigation of space debris and the steps that are being taken towards that desideratum. Recommendations of the Inter-Agency Space Debris Coordination Committee were the basis of the mitigation guidelines approved in 2007.[185] Compliance therewith remains a matter for individual space agencies and is not formal international law.

Space Stations

There is no international definition of a space station, but they are generally understood to be space objects that are left in space having been constructed as long-term dwellings or research laboratories to be occupied by a crew ferried as required.[186] As a matter of international law, this presents no problems when the space station constructed by a state and is used solely by its nationals. When the station is a cooperative venture between states, or the crew is of nationals of different countries, more formal arrangements are necessary. Registration, control, jurisdiction and any liabilities have to be arranged.[187]

Several space stations have been established and operated for a number of years, but as of 2023, only two, the Tiangong Space Station (TSS) (Tiangong–3) and the International Space Station (ISS), remained in orbit. In 2022, perhaps as a consequence of the Ukraine imbroglio, Russia announced that it would cease participation in the ISS in 2024 but more recently extended that to 2028 and may construct its own space station. Previous space stations were Salyut 7, Skylab, Mir, Tiangong-1 and Tiangong-2. The modular

---

184 Volynskaya, *supra* n. 160, at 229–231; H.H. Hertzfeld and B. Basely-Walker, 'Legal Note on Space Accidents' (2010) 59 *ZLW* 230–240; F.G. von der Dunk, 'A Sleeping Beauty Awakens: the 1968 Rescue Agreement after Forty Years' (2008) 34 *J. Sp. L.* 411–434; his 'Too-Close Encounters of the Third-Party Kind: Will the Liability Convention Stand the Test of the Cosmos 2251-Iridium 33 Collision' (2009) 52 *Proc. IISL* 199–209; M. Meija-Kaiser, 'Collision Course: 2009 Iridium-Cosmos Crash' (2009) 52 *Proc. IISL* 274–284; L. Bressack, 'Addressing the Problem of Orbital Pollution: Defining a Standard of Care to Hold Polluters Accountable' (2010) 43 *Geo. Wash. L. Rev.* 741–780.

185 UNGA Res. 62/217, 2007, approved the COPUOS endorsement of the IADC voluntary guidelines for the mitigation of space debris. See CoCoSL III, 605–652, and *infra* Chapter 9 Space Debris. Cf. S. Hobe and J.H. Mey, 'UN Space Debris Mitigation Guidelines' (2009) 58 *ZLW* 388–402; F. Tronchetti, 'The Problem of Space Debris: What Can Lawyers Do About It' (2015) 64 *ZLW* 332–352.

See now the Inter-Agency Space Debris Coordination Committee *IADC Protection Manual*, IADC-04–03, Version 7.1, 2018: www.iadc-home.org/documents_public/view/page/6/id/81#u; IADC Space Debris Mitigation Guidelines, IADC-02–01, Rev. 3. 2021: www.iadc-home.org/documents_public/view/id/172#u; and 'Support to the IADC Space Debris Mitigation Guidelines' IADC-04-08 Rev, 5.8, 2021: www.iadc-home.org/documents_public/view/id/173#u.

186 We distinguish the single-module spacecraft that were in the Salyut series. Cf. the space station agreements, *infra* nn. 195, 198 and 199.

187 C.Q. Christol, 'Space Stations Political, Practical and Legal Considerations' (1984) 7 *Hast. Int. & Comp. L. Rev.* 521–542.

Salyut 7 was the last in the Salyut series. Occupied intermittently between May 1982 and June 1986, it was deorbited in 1991.[188]

Skylab, launched on 14 May 1973 and was deorbited on 11 July 1979.[189] Being an exclusively US project, and its re-entry having caused no damage, Skylab is of limited legal interest.[190] Mir, a modular space station, was occupied continuously by successive missions for nearly ten years.[191] Its first components were launched on 19 February 1986 and subsequently added to by the Soyuz programme. In its first years, Mir was entirely Russian, but in 1993, partly for financial reasons, the US and USSR agreed to cooperate in the Mir programme as a precursor to the ISS. Mir was deorbited on 23 March 2001. No legal problems ensued.[192]

Uninvolved in the ISS,[193] the Tiangong series is part of China's increased space activities. Tiangong-1 ('Heavenly Palace') was launched on 29 September 2011 and Tiangong-2 on 15 September 2016. Both were deorbited without incident. Construction of the TSS began with the launch of its core module, Tianhe ('Harmony of the Heavens') on 29 April 2021 to orbit between 340 km/210 m and 450 km/280 m and at an inclination of 41.47°. Its assembly continues. The TSS is permanently crewed and operational. As a solely Chinese undertaking, it presents no immediate international legal problems.

Begun in 1998 and completed in 2010, the ISS is in orbit at c. 400 km/250 m elevation and an inclination of 51.6°. The plan is that it will be deorbited in 2031, with a splash down of unburnt fragments at Point Nemo, southeast of Hawaii, the furthest point from any land. Alternatively, it could be disassembled in space and at least some parts used in the construction of another space station.[194]

The ISS is the result of many discussions, agreements and reconsiderations.[195] In 1984, the US proposed constructing Space Station Freedom, a multipurpose space facility in which others might participate, but this did not proceed.[196] However, in 1988, Canada,

---

188 See text following n. 171 *supra*. G.S. Ivanovich, *Salyut – The First Space Station: Triumph and Tragedy* (Berlin: Springer Praxis, 2008).

189 See *supra* n. 163.

190 See *supra* nn. 163, 164; L.F. Belew, ed., *Skylab, Our First Space Station*, NASA History Series SP-400: (NASA, 1977): http://history.nasa.gov/SP-400/sp400.htm; W.D. Compton, *Living and Working in Space: A History of Skylab*, NASA History Series SP-4208 (NASA, 1983) which includes as its Chapter 19 C.W.D. Thompson and C.E. Benson, 'The De-Orbit of Skylab': http://history.nasa.gov/SP-4208/sp4208.htm.

191 The word *mir* can mean either 'peace' or 'world'. D.M. Harland, *The MIR Space Station: A Precursor to Space Colonization* (New York: John Wiley, 1997); D.M. Harland, *The Story of Space Station Mir* (Berlin: Springer Praxis, 2005); NASA History website, *History of Shuttle-MIR*: http://spaceflight1.nasa.gov/history/shuttle-mir/; www.space.com/19650-mir-space-station.html. F. Lyall, 'Mir Matters' (2000) *Scots Law Times* 76–79.

192 The actual Mir splash-down was some hundreds of miles from the predicted area, disappointing those on-board two chartered aircraft who had hoped to see the re-entry. The 'controlled re-entry' of a space object is not as predictable in its outcome as one might think or hope. See also *supra* n. 172.

193 At one stage, it appeared possible that China would join in, but this prospect receded: Y. Zhao, 'Legal Issues of China's Possible Participation in the International Space Station: Comparing to the Russian Experience' (2013) 6 *J. East Asia and Int. L.* 155–174.

194 International Space Station Transition Report pursuant to Section 303(c)(2) of the NASA Transition Authorization Act of 2017 (P.L. 115–10) (NASA, January 2022).

195 J. Logsdon, *Together in Orbit: The Origins of International Cooperation on the Space Station*, NASA Monographs in Aerospace History no. 11, 1998: http://history.nasa.gov/monograph11.pdf; C. Morgan, *Shuttle-Mir: The United States and Russia Share History's Highest Stage* (SP-2001–4225). NASA, Lyndon B. Johnson Space Center, 2001: http://history.nasa.gov/SP-4225/toc/toc-level1.htm. See also http://spaceflight1.nasa.gov/history/shuttle-mir/. For an ISS bibliography, see www.hq.nasa.gov/office/hqlibrary/pathfinders/iss.htm.

196 President R. Reagan, 'State of the Union Address', US Congress, 24 January 1984: http://reagan2020.us/speeches/state_of_the_union_1984.asp.

ESA, Japan and the US agreed to cooperate in building such a station;[197] before the 1988 agreement was implemented, however, various major design changes were made, and Russia was added to the enterprise. Accordingly, a new agreement was adopted.[198]

The legal basis of the ISS is a 1998 intergovernmental agreement (IGA).[199] Various memoranda of understanding (MOUs) between the participants deal with details on sections of the ISS and its construction.[200] The result is a complex of legal and sublegal arrangements that we lack the space to detail.[201]

197 Agreement Among the Government of the United States of America, Governments of Member States of the European Space Agency, the Government of Japan, and the Government of Canada on Cooperation in the Detailed Design, Development, Operation, and Utilization of the Permanently Manned Civil Space Station, Washington, DC, 29 September 1988; 1989 UK Misc. Ser. 9, Cmnd. 705; US Dept of State 92–65; (1988) 37 ZLW 341. Various Memoranda of Understanding were entered into on its basis between NASA and the other participants. See Moenter, *infra* n. 201, at 1044–1049; E. Sadeh, 'Technical, Organizational and Political Dynamics of the International Space Station Program' (2004) 20 *Space Policy* 171–188.

   Note: within ESA, the ISS is an optional programme in which not all ESA members participate. The UK did not join until 2011.

   For the development of the 1988 arrangements, see N. Goldman, *American Space Law* (1st ed. Ames: Iowa State Press, 1988; 2nd ed. San Diego: Univelt, 1996); D.D. Smith, *Space Stations: International Law and Policy* (Boulder: Westview Press, 1979); A.J. Young, *Law and Policy in the Space Stations' Era* (Dordrecht: Nijhoff, 1989); Logsdon, *supra* n. 195; *Civilian Space Programs and the U.S. Future in Space* (US Cong. Office of Technology Assessment, OTA-STI-241, 1984): http://govinfo.library.unt.edu/ota/Ota_4/DATA/1984/8406.PDF; *Space Stations and the Law: Selected Legal Issues – Background Paper* (US Cong. Office of Technology Assessment, OTA-BP-ISC-41, 1986): http://govinfo.library.unt.edu/ota/Ota_3/DATA/1986/8627.PDF; E. Galloway, 'The Space Station: United States Proposal and Implementation' (1986) 14 *J. Sp. L.* 14–39; H. DeSaussure, 'The Impact of Manned Space Stations on the Law of Outer Space' (1984) 21 *San Diego L. Rev.* 985–1014; and his 'Tort Jurisdiction over the New International Space Station' (1989) 32 *Proc. IISL* 404; M. McCord, 'Responding to the Space Station Agreement: The Extension of US Law into Space' (1989) 77 *Geo. L.J.* 1933–58; H. Shin, '"Oh, I Have Slipped the Surly Bonds of Earth": Multinational Space Stations and Choice of Law' (1990) *Cal. L. Rev.* 1375–1414; S.R. Malpass, 'Legal Aspects of the United States/International Space Station' (1991) 14 *Houst. J. Int. L.* 183–202; A.D. Watson and W.G. Schmidt, 'Legal Issues Surrounding the International Space Station' (1996–1997) 7 *U.S. A.F. Acad. J. Legal Stud.* 159–176; D.C. Stewart, 'Resolution of Legal Issues Confronting the International Space Station Project: A Step Forward in the Development of Space Law' (1989) 29 *Va. J. Int'l L.* 745–762.

198 L.F.H. Cline and G. Gibbs, 'Re-negotiation of the International Space Station Agreements – 1993–1997' (2003) 53 *Acta Astronautica* 917–925. See also *infra* n. 201.

199 Agreement among the Government of Canada, Governments of the Member States of the European Space Agency, the Government of Japan, the Government of the Russian Federation, and the Government of the United States of America Concerning Cooperation on the Civil International Space Station: Washington, DC, 29 January 1998, TIAS 12927, in force 27 March 2001: www.state.gov/wp-content/uploads/2019/02/12927-Multilateral-Space-Space-Station-1.29.1998.pdf; (2005) 30 AASL-II, 201–225. Excerpted F.G. von der Dunk and M.M.T.A. Brus, *The International Space Station: Commercial Utilisation from a European Perspective* (Leiden: Nijhoff, 2007), Annex 5, 227–241. The ISS is an ESA optional programme which the UK did not contribute to or participate in until 2012.

200 The legal effect of MOUs is considered *supra* Chapter 2. The following are the ISS MOUs:

   1. Canada: www.nasa.gov/mission_pages/station/structure/elements/nasa_csa.html
   2. Japan: www.nasa.gov/mission_pages/station/structure/elements/nasa_japan.html
   3. ESA: www.nasa.gov/mission_pages/station/structure/elements/nasa_esa.html
   4. Russia: www.nasa.gov/mission_pages/station/structure/elements/nasa_rsa.html

   Cf. On prior cooperation, see 'Space Station: Memorandum of Understanding Between the United States of America and the European Space Agency', Washington, DC and Paris, 11 and 18 March 1997, TIAS 12844. Cf. also R. Veldhuyzen and E. Grifoni, 'No Exchange of Funds – the ESA Barter Agreements for the International Space Station' (1999) 99 *ESA Bulletin*: www.csa.int/csapub/bulletin/bullet99/veld99.pdf.

201 F.G. von der Dunk and M.M.T.A. Brus, *The International Space Station: Commercial Utilisation from a European Perspective* (Leiden: Nijhoff, 2007); S. Mirmina and C. Schenewerk, *International Space Law and*

The IGA is an agreement between partner states, each providing elements specified in Annexes (Art. 1). Withdrawal requires one year's notice, and provision is made for terms and conditions of a withdrawal to be agreed (Art. 28).[202] Article 11 and the associated MOUs deal with the crew. The human component of ISS operation is, of course, crucial, but here we sketch the law relating to the hardware and postpone crew matters until Chapter 5 Astronauts.

The ISS is developed, operated and used in accordance with international law, including the OST, ARRA and the Liability and Registration Conventions (Art. 2.1).[203] The IGA is not to be interpreted as modifying rights and duties under the space treaties other than IGA Art. 16 (cross-waivers of liability) (Art. 2.2.a) or rights and obligations in the exploration and use of outer space through activities unrelated to the ISS (Art. 2.2.b). Further, nothing in the IGA can constitute the basis of a claim to national appropriation over outer space or any portion of it (Art. 2.2.c).

Under Art. 4, the state parties' space agencies are cooperating agencies, and each retains ownership of the elements and equipment, which each state contributes to the ISS (Art. 6). Each partner registers the elements which it supplies as space objects and retains jurisdiction and control over the objects (Art. 5). Transfer of ownership of the ISS elements or equipment does not affect the rights and obligations under the IGA (Art. 6.3). Any transfer requires prior notification to the partners, and transfer to a non-partner or an entity under the jurisdiction of a non-partner must have the consent of all the partners (Art. 6.4).

Partners are responsible for the management, design, development and operation of the elements they supply but are required to consult and act cooperatively in appropriate areas (Arts. 7–10).[204] All partners have user rights which relate to their input and are entitled to select their users, but each can exchange or barter rights with other partners (Art. 9). Of course, access to the ISS has to be agreed on so that the ISS can sustain its occupants for a sufficient period but not overstretch the accommodation.

Transport is provided by those with that capability on a reimbursable but equal fee basis (Art. 12).[205] Data and goods are to be exchanged as required (Art. 19) and appropriate customs arrangements made (Art. 18). Funding is on the basis of an equitable sharing of common systems costs, with each partner paying for its specific responsibilities for modules (Art. 15). However, funding remains a problem.[206] Importantly, Art. 16 covers a complex set of arrangements for the cross-waiver of liabilities between partners and contractors.

Space Laws of the United States (Cheltenham: Edward Elgar, 2022) 65–73; A. Farand, 'Space Station Cooperation: Legal Arrangements', in G. Lafferranderie and D. Crowther, eds., *Outlook on Space Law over the Next 30 Years* (The Hague: Kluwer, 1997) 125–160; R. Moenter, 'The International Space Station: Legal Framework and Current Status' (1999) 64 *J. Air L. & Comm.* 1033–1056; L.L. Manzione, 'Multinational Investment in the Space Station: An Outer Space Model for International Cooperation' (2002) 18 *Am. U. Int'l L. Rev.* 507–536. Brazil and others have entered into related cooperation agreements.

202 Russia will withdraw in 2028.

203 Cf. C.M. Petras, ' "Space Force Alpha": Military Use of the International Space Station and the Concept of "Peaceful Purposes" ' (2002) 53 *Air F. L. Rev.* 135–181.

204 Management arrangements deal with various matters. A. Gorbiel, 'Orbiting Inhabited Space Stations: Selected International Legal Aspects' (1984) 7 *Hastings Int. & Comp. L. Rev.* 509–520 (pre-IGA).

205 After the NASA STS Shuttle programme ended in 2011, astronauts and supplies were ferried by Russia. However, since 2020, the US company SpaceX has also taken cargo and personnel to the ISS.

206 L.L. Manzione, 'Multinational Investment in the Space Station: An Outer Space Model for International Cooperation?' (2002) 18 *Am. U. Int. L. Rev.* 507–534. Cf. P.M. Figlola et al., 'US Space Programs:

Intellectual Property

Intellectual property is involved in two separate ways in relation to space. One is the intellectual property that is generated in order that space is used. The other is the intellectual property in discoveries made in space on such vehicles as the ISS.

Patent law is inherently territorial. In general, national patent law applies only within the territory of the national state concerned. Patent laws vary greatly from state to state. For example, for decades, the US awarded patents to the first person to invent, whereas most other countries awarded a patent to the first person to file for that patent. That has changed since the first edition of this treatise,[207] but the situation still exists elsewhere. The World Intellectual Property Organisation (WIPO) is striving to create international uniformity,[208] but national patent practices are so ingrained in domestic commerce that changes are slow to arrive.

Many patent questions have arisen from inventions and applications made and developed for the purposes of space activities.[209] Specific provision is made in some of the documents of international organisations as to the sharing and availability to their members of intellectual property created for the purpose of the organisation.[210] In other instances, intellectual property claims have been used as part of the commercial struggle between companies.

Different questions may arise as to inventions made in space.[211] Ordinarily, the location where an invention is made will affect where and when it is patentable. When an invention is made in space, where it is made could become a matter of dispute. The US has specific

---

Military, Civil and Commercial' (CRS Issue Brief for Congress, no. IB 92011, Congressional Research Service, Library of Congress, 2006) at 2–3: www.fas.org/sgp/crs/space/IB92011.pdf.

207 35 USC § 105 deals with inventions in outer space: see *infra* n. 212.

208 www.wipo.int/portal/index.html.en. 'Intellectual Property and Space Activities: Issues Paper prepared by the International Bureau', April 1994: www.wipo.int/export/sites/www/patent-law/en/developments/pdf/ip_space.pdf. Cf. OECD, *The Space Economy at a Glance* (OECD, 2007).

209 E.g. *Hughes Aircraft v. US* (1996) 86 F. 3d 1566; 1996 US App. LEXIS 14848; 39 USPQ 2D (BNA) 1065 (1998) 140 F. 3d 1470; 1998 US App. LEXIS 6857; 46 USPQ 2D (BNA) 1285, cert denied 1 March 1999, 525 US 1177; 119 S. Ct. 1112; 143 L. Ed. 2d 108; 1999 US LEXIS 1545 and *Boeing v. US* (2005) 69 Fed. Cl. 397; 2005 US Claims LEXIS 398; 80 USPQ 2D (BNA) 1108; Cf. C.Q. Christol, 'Persistence Pays Off: The Case of Hughes Aircraft Company v. USA, 1979–1999' (1999) 42 *Proc. IISL* 199–207; B.L. Smith, 'Recent Developments in Patents for Outer Space' (1999) 42 *Proc. IISL* 190–198.

210 Cf. the INTELSAT Definitive Arrangements: F. Lyall, *Law and Space Telecommunications* (Aldershot: Dartmouth; Brookfield, VT: Gower, 1989) 129–141. Cf. Art. 9 and Annex 1 of the USA/UK 'Agreement for Cooperation in Research and Development of Weapons Detection and Protection-Related Technologies', Washington, 3 July 2002 (UK) Cmnd. 6584.

211 L. Malmen, 'Exploitation of Space and Patent Law: How the Current Legal System Ineffectively Protects Private Companies in the Commercial Space Industry' (2021) 20 *Santa Clara J. Int, L* 80–101; Y. Zhao, 'Intellectual Property Protection in Outer Space: Reconciling Territoriality of Intellectual Property with Non-Territoriality in Outer Space' (2017) 7 *Queen Mary J. Intell. Prop.* 137–155; A. Trimarchi, 'International Space Station – A Focus on Intellectual Property Rights Main Emphasis on the ESA Perspective' (2016) 65 *ZLW* 533–550; W.C. Pannell, 'Pirate Battles in Outer Space: Preventing Patent Infringement on the 8th Sea' (2016) 46 *U. Mem. L. Rev.* 733–760; E.I. Winston, 'Patent Boundaries' (2014–2015) 87 *Temp. L. Rev.* 501–546, at 526–537; A.M. Balsano and J. Wheeler, 'The IGA and ESA: Protecting Intellectual Property Rights in the Context of ISS Activities', in von der Dunk and Brus, *supra* n. 201; L.B. Malagar and M.A. Magdoza-Malagar, 'International Law of Outer Space and the Protection of Intellectual Property Rights' (1999) 17 *Boston U. Int. L.J.* 311–366; T.U. Ro et al., 'Patent Infringement the Outer Space in Light of 35 U.S.C. Sec. 105: Following the White Rabbit Down the Rabbit Loophole' (2010) 17 *Bost. U. J. Sc. Tech.* 202–231; T.D. Guyenne, ed., *Proceedings of the Workshop on Intellectual Property Rights and Space*

legislation as to inventions in space, making the test of US patentability for an invention made in space depend on whether it is made 'under the jurisdiction or control' of the US. Chapter 10, §105(a) of the US patent legislation (35 USC §§ 101–105) therefore provides that inventions 'made, used or sold in outer space on a space object or component thereof under the jurisdiction of the United States shall be considered to be made, used or sold within the United States' unless governed otherwise by an international agreement to which the US is party.[212] This was first added to US patent law by the Patents in Space Act 1990[213] and was intended to encourage private commercial participation in space activities.[214] It was also part of the terrestrial US attempt to have patents registered in the US and therefore made available to US commerce before they are registered elsewhere.[215] Not all have seen this as a welcome development.[216] Unlike the US, most states have not extended their patent laws to inventions in outer space. A legal vacuum may therefore exist for inventors from those states that have not enacted appropriate legislation.

Inventions onboard the ISS are governed specially and separately by Art. 21 of the ISS Agreement.[217] Article 21.2 provides that

for the purposes of intellectual property, an activity occurring in or on a Space Station flight element shall be deemed to have occurred only in the territory of the Partner

---

Activities – A World-Wide Perspective, Paris 1994 (ESA SP-378); S. Mosteshar, ed., *Intellectual Property and Invention in Outer Space: Liability and Intellectual Property Rights* (Dordrecht: Nijhoff, 1995).

212 35 USC § 105, 'Inventions in outer space'. B. Parrish, 'Commercializing Space: Intellectual Property Concerns with Space Act Agreements' (2013) *J. Air L. and Comm.* 651–688. Inventions made in US national space efforts may be claimed by the US (51 USC 20135). As to invention on the current ISS, see *infra* at n. 217.

213 The Patents in Space Act 1990, Pub. L. 101–580, Sec. 1(a), Nov. 15, 1990, 104 Stat. 2863). G.H. Reynolds, 'The Patents in Space Act' (1990) 3 *Harv. J.L. & Tech.* 13–30; G. Lafferanderie, 'The United States Proposed Patent in Space Legislation: An International Perspective' (1990) 18 *J. Sp. L.* 1–10; D.L. Burk, 'Protection of Trade Secrets in Outer Space Activity: A Study in Federal Preemption' (1993) 23 *Seton Hall L. Rev.* 560–640; Ty S. Twibell, 'Space Law: Legal Restraints on Commercialisation and Development of Outer Space' (1997) 65 *UMKC L.R.* 589–642; J.H. Shoemaker, 'The Patents in Space Act: Jedi Mind Trick or Real Protection for American Inventors on the International Space Station?' (1999) 6 *J. Intell. Prop. L.* 395–424.

214 G.J. Mossinghoff, 'Intellectual Property Rights in Space Ventures' (1985) 12 *J. Sp. L.* 136–162; F. Kosmo, 'The Commercialisation of Space: A Regulatory Scheme That Promotes Commercial Ventures and International Responsibility' (1988) 61 *S. Cal. L. Rev.* 1055–1090; J.F. Kohler, 'Space Pharmaceuticals: Will the United States Fumble Another High Technology Industry' (1992) 58 *J. Air L. & Com.* 511–554; A.M. Balsano, 'Space Technology and International Cooperation – the Role of Intellectual Property' (1995) 20 *Air & Sp. Law* 177–188 [Lyall/Larsen 503–14]; A.M. Balsano and A. de Clercq, 'The Community Patent and Space – Related Inventions' (2004) 30 *J. Sp. L.* 1–11; L.L. Risely, 'An Examination of the Need to Amend Space Law to Protect the Private Explorer in Outer Space' (1999) 26 *West. St. Univ. L. Rev.* 47–70; J.A. Jiru, 'Star Wars and Space Malls: When the Paint Chips Off a Treaty's Golden Handcuffs' (2000) 42 *S. Tex. L. Rev.* 155–182 at 166–75; A.A. Hutcheson, 'Dollars and Sense: Why the International Space Station Is a Better Investment than Deep Space Exploration for NASA in a Post-Columbia World' (2004) *J.L. Tech. & Pol.* 295–320.

215 US Code Title 35 consolidates US patent legislation, while Title 37 of the Code of Federal Regulations deals with patents, trademarks and copyright.

216 T. Smith, 'A Phantom Menace – Patents and the Communal Status of Space' (2003) 34 *Victoria U. Wellington L. Rev.* 545–570; cf. D.P. Homiller, 'From *Deep South* to the Great White North: The Extraterritorial Reach of United States Patent Law after *Research in Motion*' (2005) *Duke L. & Tech. L. Rev.* 0017: www.law.duke.edu/journals/dltr/articles/2005dltr0017.html.

217 *Supra* n. 199. Art. 21 is complex. We here indicate only its international law elements. As to the ESA view, see www.esa.int/About_Us/Law_at_ESA/Intellectual_Property_Rights/Patents_and_space-related_inventions. See also articles by Trimarchi, Pannell and Winston, *supra* n. 211.

State of that element's registry, except that for ESA-registered elements any European Partner State may deem the activity to have occurred within its territory.[218]

Article 21.1 defines 'intellectual property' as having the same meaning as in Art. 2 of the Convention Establishing the World Intellectual Property Organization, 1967.[219] Article 21 therefore means that the patentability of inventions or discoveries on board the ISS depends upon in which module the invention occurs.[220] It should also be noted that 35 USC §105.b indicates that the USA may enter into agreements under which inventions in the other ISS modules would also be registrable in the USA.

A problem of the current situation is that the arrangements under the ISS Agreement pertain only to the ISS; any patent activity deriving from invention elsewhere in space is not covered. There is a danger that national divergences will emerge as states enact their own legislation. It would be useful if there were an international treaty specifically on intellectual property generated in space, all space-competent states became parties to the treaty and they each implement it in their national patent laws.[221] A general and uniform system of patent protection for inventions made in outer space would give investors confidence in outer space research and encourage such activities. Ultimately, 'space' could be incorporated into the worldwide uniform patent regime towards which WIPO is working.

218 The second sentence of Art. 21.2 states that that provision is not affected by the participation of an ESA partner state or its cooperating agency in an activity 'in or on' the flight element belonging to another partner's space station element.

219 Convention Establishing the World Intellectual Property Organization, Stockholm, 1967, 828 UNTS 5, 21 UST 1749, TIAS 6932, 1970 UKTS 52, Cmnd. 4408. Omitting the literary and artistic elements, the definition of intellectual property found in Art. 2 (viii) includes inventions in all fields of human endeavour, scientific discoveries, industrial designs and all other rights resulting from activity in the industrial, scientific or industrial fields.

220 The first sentence of IGA Art. 21.1 provides that 'Subject to the provisions of this Article, for purposes of intellectual property law, an activity occurring in or on a Space Station flight element shall be deemed to have occurred only in the territory of the Partner State of that element's registry, except that for ESA-registered elements any European Partner State may deem the activity to have occurred within its territory'. The second sentence states that that is not affected by the participation of an ESA partner state or cooperating agency.

221 H. van Traa-Engelman, 'The Need for a Uniform System Protecting Intellectual Property Rights in Outer Space' (2008) 51 *Proc. IISL* 38–43; Malagar, Ro, Pannell, and Winston, all *supra* n. 211.

5

ASTRONAUTS

Our earlier editions dealt with the rights and duties of, and with respect to, 'astronauts'. In recent years, the concept has been put under strain by the emergence of the 'space tourist', a phenomenon that does not fit the traditional category. Not all on board a cruise liner are sailors, nor are passengers on aircraft pilots or stewards. We therefore consider the special requirements of space tourism towards the end of the chapter. First, we concentrate on the traditional professional astronaut.

Who Is an Astronaut?

Generally, law should be clear. As a statement of principles, the OST is commendable, but further elaboration has been needed, of which the definition of astronauts is but one example. OST Art. V calls for them to be regarded as envoys of mankind in outer space, for them to be given assistance if they land in another state's territory and sent home and for astronauts of one state to give all possible assistance to those of another, but it confines assistance to activities in space. It assumes that the meaning of the term 'astronaut' is pellucid.

What, or who, is an astronaut?[1] At one level, the question appears absurd: everyone knows what an astronaut is. To adopt a phrase from an English case, the term has an 'elephantine quality of being easy to recognise' – you cannot define it, but you know when you see it.[2] On those lines, and consonant with the normal principles of treaty interpretation, the ordinary meaning of the term would apply.[3] However, what is the 'ordinary

---

1 The Russian term is cosmonaut; the Chinese is *taikonaut.*
2 Per L.J. Lawton, speaking of 'fairness' in *Maxwell v. Department of Trade and Industry* [1974] Q.B. 523 at 539; [1974] 2 All ER 122 at 132.
3 Cf. Vienna Convention on the Law of Treaties, 22 May 1969, 1155 UNTS 331; (1980) BTS 58, Cmnd. 7964; (1969) 8 ILM 679; [1969] 63 AJIL 875. Terms are normally to be interpreted in accordance with their ordinary meaning in the light of the purpose of a treaty (Art. 31.1). However, a special meaning is to be 'given to a term if it is established that the parties so intended' (Art. 31.4).

DOI: 10.4324/9781003496502-5

meaning' of 'astronaut'? The word conjures the image of someone in a space suit, and that certainly was the case when the space treaties were elaborated. In fact, there is no formal definition of astronaut in international law.

In the development of space law, 'astronaut' first appears in the paragraph 'Stressing' in the Preamble to UNGA Res. 1802 (XVII), 1962, and in the third operative paragraph, in which COPUOS was asked to 'continue urgently' its work on principles of space law, including 'assistance to' and the 'return' of 'astronauts'.[4] Paragraph 9 of the 1963 'Principles' Resolution brought in the language of astronauts as 'envoys of mankind',[5] calling for them to be given aid when required and in appropriate cases for their return to the state of registry of their vehicle. On 19 December 1966, UNGA Res. 2222 (XXI) para 4(a) requested that COPUOS continue its work on 'an agreement on assistance to and return of astronauts and space vehicles'. OST Art. V took that into law. But still the term 'astronaut' remained undefined.

One might have expected a definition of astronaut to appear in the 1968 Agreement on the Rescue of Astronauts, Return of Astronauts and the Return of Objects Launched into Outer Space (ARRA),[6] but notwithstanding its formal title, and the paragraph 'Noting' in its Preamble, the operative text refers to 'the personnel of a spacecraft', not to 'astronauts'.[7] Thereafter, the Preambles to the Liability and Registration Conventions and the Moon Agreement refer to ARRA and do not further explicate the term 'astronaut'.

MA Art. 3.2 prohibits the use or threatened use of force in relation *inter alia* to the personnel of spacecraft, not to astronauts. However, MA Art. 10.1 provides one parameter for the definition of an astronaut, binding its parties to 'regard any person on the moon as an astronaut' within the terms of OST Art. V, and 'as part of the personnel of a spacecraft' for the purposes of ARRA. Yet surely one need not go as far as the moon clearly to acquire astronaut status.

---

4 UNGA Res. 1802 (XVII) para 4 referred to US and USSR proposals on the rescue and return of astronauts.
5 This strange expression appears in the 1963 Principles and OST Art. V para 1, but the full phrase, 'envoys of mankind in outer space', should not be truncated. The phrase may be dismissed as rhetoric and certainly does not import any terrestrial diplomatic status. Cf. Bin Cheng, ' "Space Objects", "Astronauts" and Related Expressions' (1992) 34 *Proc. IISL* 17–27; Cheng, 259, 460: *contra* R. Jakhu and R. Battacharya, 'Legal Aspects of Space Tourism' (2002) 45 *Proc. IISL*, 112–131 at 119; S. Hobe and J. Cloppenburg, 'Towards a New Aerospace Convention? – Selected Legal Issues of "Space Tourism" ' (2004) 47 *Proc. IISL* 377–385; J. Arnould, 'Does the Concept of "Envoys of Mankind" have a Future?', in G. Lafferranderie and S. Marchisio, eds., *The Astronauts and Rescue Agreement* (Paris: ECSL, 2011) 25–34. I.H.Ph. Diedericks-Verschoor, 'Search and Rescue in Space Law' (1977) 19 *Proc. IISL* 17, considered that the reference in the 1963 Principles and OST Art. V to astronauts as 'envoys of mankind' ruled out passive participants (passengers) on a commercial flight from the international obligations as to rescue and return.
6 Agreement on the Rescue of Astronauts, the Return of Astronauts and the Return of Objects Launched into Outer Space, 22 April 1968; 672 UNTS 119; 1969 UKTS 56, Cmnd. 3997; 19 UST 7570, TIAS 6559; (1968) 7 ILM 151–154; [1969] 63 AJIL 382.
7 F. Lyall, 'Who Is an Astronaut? The Inadequacy of Current International Law' (2010) 66 *Acta Astronautica* 1613–1617; S. Langston and S.J. Pell, 'What Is in a Name? Perceived Identity, Classification, Philosophy and Implied Duty of the "Astronaut" ' (2015) 115 *Acta Astronautica* 185–194. S. Gorove, 'Legal Problems of the rescue and return of astronauts' (1968–1969) 3 *Int. Lawyer* 898–902 at 898–9 considered that personnel could refer to both trained pilots of a spacecraft and mission specialists such as scientists or physicians but not to 'regular passengers' or to stowaways(!).

Any definition of astronaut for legal purposes would appear to require two or perhaps three elements, an element of training,[8] an element of altitude and perhaps an element of duration. There also is the matter of their selection.[9] As to training, initially all but one astronaut was a trained member of either military or civilian governmental space agencies.[10] Now, with the emergence of 'space tourists', an element of training has been introduced for the customers. Commercial up-and-down flights will involve both trained pilots and paying passengers who will not perform any operational function.[11] The training of passengers will be rudimentary, health checks being more significant. The US FAA rules for space tourists distinguish what is required of 'crew' and of 'space-flight participants'.[12] The UK has followed a similar route.[13]

Another element in defining astronaut status should be 'how high'?[14] In practice, for terrestrial altitude records, the Fédération Aéronautique Internationale accepts the Von

8 For training, see *infra* nn. 12, 104 and 109.
9 Lyall, *supra* n. 7. Cf. www.esa.int/esearch?q=astronaut+selection. As to selection for the ISS, see *infra* n. 61.
10 Christa McAuliffe, killed in the 1986 Challenger explosion, was a civilian schoolteacher, not a NASA or government employee, allowing her representatives to bring a claim, which was settled. All later US mission specialists have had to become government employees. R.M. Jarvis, 'The Space Shuttle Challenger and the Future Law of Outer Space Resources' (1986) 20 *Int. Lawyer*, 591–622; J.A. Beckman, 'Citizens Without a Forum: The Lack of an Appropriate and Consistent Remedy for United States Citizens Injured or Killed as a Result of Activity Above the Terrestrial Air Space' (1999) 22 *Boston Coll. Int. & Comp. L. Rev.* 249–278; H.A. Douglas, 'Death in Pursuit of Space Travel: An Analysis of Current Methods of Recovery for Families of Astronauts and the Need for Reform' (2004) 26 *Whittier L. Rev.* 333–357. J.R. Hansen, *First Man: The Life of Neil Armstrong* (London and New York: Simon and Schuster, 2005); A. Smith, *Moondust* (London: Bloomsbury, 2005).
11 Space tourism is discussed more specifically later in this chapter. Tourists have paid for a visit to the ISS, but that is different from what is now envisaged.
12 51 USC §50902 ss. 2 and 20, as revised by the Commercial Space Launch Amendments Act, 2004 (Public Law 108–429) and the US Commercial Space Launch Competitiveness Act, 2015, 114th Cong., H.R. 2262 (Public Law 114–90, 129 Stat. 712).
   The US Rules: US Federal Aviation Administration: 'Human Space Flight Requirements for Crew and Space Flight Participants: Final Rule' (2006) 71 Fed. Reg. no. 241, 75616–45; 14 CFR Parts 401, 415, 431, 435, 440 and 460 (as amended). Crew includes those who perform 'activities . . . directly relating to the launch, re-entry or other operation of or in a launch vehicle or re-entry vehicle that carries human beings'. Space flight participant 'means an individual who is not crew, carried aboard a launch vehicle or re-entry vehicle' (14 CFR § 401.5). A space flight participant is required to waive all claims and assume personal responsibility for participation in a flight (App. E to Part. 440; 2006) 71 Fed. Reg. 75642–3. Basically, the requirements for the crew of a tourist flight are rigorous, while those for the 'participants' are largely good health coupled with rudimentary training as to safety and escape procedures (14 CFR § 460.51 (2006) 71 Fed. Reg. 75645).
   As to what crew and space flight participants are to be informed about so they can give 'informed consent' (*infra* n. 47) and the waivers to be executed, see 14 CFR Part 460; (2006) 72 Fed. Reg. 75643–5, as they may be amended. See also FAA, 'Draft Guidelines for Commercial Suborbital Reusable Launch Vehicle Operations with Space Flight Participants', 11 February 2005: www.faa.gov/about/office_org/headquarters_offices/ast/licenses_permits/media/FD_Passenger_Guidelines_2-11-05.pdf. On suborbital flight see US FAA, 'Streamlined Launch and Reentry License Requirements' (2020) 85 *Fed. Reg.* 79566–79740 at 79696–79700. T.R. Hughes and E. Rosenberg, 'Space Travel (and Politics): The Evolution of the Commercial Space Launch Amendments Act of 2004,' (2005) 31 *J. Sp. L.* 1–79.
13 See *infra* at n. 108.
14 Cf. Chapter 6 as to the boundary question. T. Masson-Zwaan, 'Private Law Aspects of Suborbital Flights: Second and Third-Party Liability and Insurance' (2022) 87 *J. Air Law & Comm.* 423–443; V. Nase, 'Delimitation and the Suborbital Passenger: Time to End Prevarication' (2012) 77 *J. Air L. Comm.*, 747–767; S.M. Langston, 'Suborbital Flights: A Comparative Analysis of National and International Law' (2011) 37 *J. Sp. L.* 299–392.

Kármán Line at *c.* 100 km/62 miles (275,000 ft) as marking the space/air boundary. In 2004, Virgin Galactic performed two successful experimental flights that won the Ansari X-Prize as they both went higher than 100 km.[15] An orbital flight would clearly qualify whatever one thinks of the boundary question, but what of the suborbital flight?

The second sentence of OST Art. V.1 speaks of a 'space vehicle' involved in the landing of an astronaut. What does that mean? All high-altitude passenger conveyances are pressurised. When does a container become a vehicle: when it is sealed against loss of air? When might it become a space vehicle? In the US, any person going higher than 50 miles is awarded 'astronaut wings'.[16] Whether such straws in the wind contribute to a definition for legal purposes is unclear. The possibility of the 'space plane' skipping out of the denser atmosphere for a brief period is also to be considered – would/should its passengers be astronauts?[17] Lastly, the duration and extent of the flight should be taken into account, which, *ex natura*, would exclude some space tourists and passengers in suborbital flight.

Rescue and Return

Concern for the welfare of astronauts was early present. As noted, rescue and return was recognised as a topic that had to be tackled. Accordingly, Art. V.1 of the OST provided for a duty on state parties to give assistance to astronauts in an emergency, accident or distress when found in the territory of another state party or on the high seas. Article V.2 then extends that duty to outer space and on celestial bodies,[18] with Art. V.3 requiring the reporting of potential dangers to the life or health of astronauts. But these OST statements lacked detail. How could these duties be accomplished? The major expositions of obligations as to the welfare of astronauts are in ARRA and the Moon Agreement.

ARRA was adopted on 19 December 1967 as UNGA Res. 2345 (XXII)) and entered into force on 3 December 1968.[19] Its Preamble states that it is designed to 'develop and give further concrete expression' to the duties imposed on parties to the OST in its call

---

15 T.R. Hughes and E. Rosenberg, 'Space Travel (and Politics): The Evolution of the Commercial Space Launch Amendments Act of 2004,' (2005) 31 *J. Sp. L.* 1–79.

16 The US Army, Navy, Air Force, Marine Corps and Coast Guard each award their own badges. Civilian astronauts are awarded astronaut badges. Astronaut pins are awarded to all astronauts, silver on completion of training and gold following a space mission. Brian Binnie (1953–2022), pilot of SpaceShipOne, which flew in December 2004, was twice given astronaut wings by the US FAA. Binnie, an Aberdeen loon by upbringing, was awarded an LL.D. by the University of Aberdeen in 2007.

17 Cf. Chapter 6 at *c.* n. 72ff.

18 R. Cargill Hall, 'Rescue and Return of Astronauts on Earth and in Outer Space' [1969] 63 AJIL 197–210 at 205 suggests that the rescue obligation could include a duty to mount a rescue mission to an orbiting spacecraft from Earth. See *infra* as to ARRA Arts 2–4. J.W. Doolittle, 'Man in Space: The Rescue and Return of Downed Astronauts' (1967) 9 *USAF JAG Rev.* 4–7 at 7 considered OST Art. V unambiguous on the duty to rescue but thought that, where appropriate, costs may have to be negotiated.

19 Agreement on the Rescue of Astronauts, the Return of Astronauts and the Return of Objects Launched into Outer Space, 22 April 1968; 672 UNTS 119; 1969 UKTS 56, Cmnd. 3997; 19 UST 7570, TIAS 6559; (1968) 7 ILM 151; [1969] 63 AJIL 382.

P.G. Dembling and D.M. Arons, 'The Treaty on Rescue and Return of Astronauts and Space Objects' (1967–1968) 9 *William and Mary L. Rev.* 630–663 [Lyall/Larsen 203–36]; R. Cargill Hall, *supra* n. 18; P.H. Houben, 'Agreement on the Rescue of Astronauts, the Return of Space Objects' (1968) 15 *Neth. Int. L. Rev.* 121; R.S.K. Lee, Agreement on the Rescue of Astronauts, the Return of Astronauts and the Return of Objects Launched into Outer Space' 1 Manual 53; Cheng 265–85; Christol 152–212.

for rendering all possible assistance to astronauts in the event of accident, distress or emergency landing including assisting with their prompt and safe return. Yuri Gagarin had orbited the Earth in Vostok 1 back in 1961 and others had followed, but the impetus for ARRA, only one year after the OST, was an expected imminent increase in space activities, the likelihood of a moon landing, development accidents and two tragedies.[20]

The increasing number of astronauts and the dangers of space exploration indicated a need for rescue arrangements. Initially it was thought that liability for damage should also be dealt with in ARRA, but as it became clear that liability would require protracted negotiations, its consideration was deferred, and rescue and return was addressed as the priority.[21] That aid be given to those in danger or difficulty is not an innovation. It is both a moral requirement and one of law. Whether it is a duty in a municipal legal system, and its extent if any, does vary from state to state, but in international law, it has long roots.

Safety of life at sea is of major concern, and apart from treaty provision,[22] seamen have long treated rescue as a normal moral imperative; lifeboat services are provided in many maritime countries.[23] It is not surprising that astro-*nauts* (italics added) are provided for. In aviation, Art. 25 of the Chicago Convention[24] imposes on its parties a duty to assist aircraft in distress and to search for missing aircraft. That duty is elaborated in its Annex 12 on Search and Rescue (complemented by a three-part Manual, ICAO Doc. 6731), which

20 In 1967, three US astronauts – V. Grissom, E. White and R. Chaffee – died in a fire in the Apollo 1 capsule during training on 27 January, and the Russian V. Komarov died when his parachute failed on re-entry on 24 April. Later disasters have been the asphyxiation of the crew of Soyuz 11 during re-entry in June 1971 (Wikipedia, 'Soyuz 11'), the Challenger explosion of 1986 (see the *Report of the Presidential Commission on the Space Shuttle Challenger Accident* (the Rogers Commission Report, June 1986) and Implementations: https://history.nasa.gov/rogersrep/51lcover.htm and http://history.nasa.gov/sts51l.html. Cf. R. Feynman, *What Do You Care What Other People Think?* (New York: Norton, 1988)); cf. *Report of the Presidential Commission on the Space Shuttle Challenger Accident (USGPO, 1986)*: http://pirate.shu.edu/~mckenndo/pdfs/The%20Space%20Shuttle%20Challenger%20Disaster.pdf. As to the Columbia Shuttle breakup during re-entry on 1 February 2003, see the *Report of the Columbia Accident Investigation Board*: https://history.nasa.gov/columbia/CAIB.html, particularly www.nasa.gov/columbia/home/CAIB_Vol1.html, together with the *Columbia Crew Survival Investigation Report*, NASA/SP-2008–565: www.nasa.gov/pdf/298870main_SP-2008-565.pdf. There have also been near-misses. On 15 September 1967, Gemini 8 (Armstrong and Scott) had to be brought down in the Pacific instead of the intended Atlantic landing area because coping with an unexpected roll problem had almost exhausted the spacecraft thruster propellant. On 18 April 2008, the Russian Soyuz TMA-11 re-entry vehicle landed almost 260 miles short of its intended landing zone after a steeper than planned re-entry: www.space.com/missionlaunches/080419-expedition16-landing-day.html. Apparently, other re-entries have had similar problems.
21 Dembling and Arons (*supra* n. 19) at 631; cf. P.G. Dembling and D.M. Arons, 'Space Law and the United Nations: The Work of the Legal Subcommittee of the United Nations Committee on the Peaceful Uses of Outer Space' (1966) 32 *J. Air Law and Comm.* 329–386 for the early work on rescue and return by the COPUOS Legal Subcommittee during its first four sessions.
22 International Convention on the Safety of Life at Sea, London, 1914, 219 CTS 177, 1914 108 BFSP, 283; the International Convention on the Safety of Life at Sea (SOLAS), London 1 November 1974: 1184 UNTS 2; (1980) UKTS 46, Cmnd. 7874; 32 UST 47, TIAS 9700; (1975) 14 ILM 963; Art. 98 of the UN Convention on the Law of the Sea, Montego Bay, 10 December 1982, 1833 UNTS 3; 1999 UKTS 82, Cmnd. 4524; US Tr. Doc. 103–39; (1982) 21 ILM 1261; (1994) 33 ILM 1309. See also Chapter 11.
23 The UK Lifeboat service, the Royal National Lifeboat Institution, is manned by volunteers: www.rnli.org.uk/.
24 Convention on International Civil Aviation, Chicago, 7 December 1944 (1944) 15 UNTS 295; 61 Stat. 1180, TIAS 1591; (1953) UKTS 8, Cmnd. 8742; 9 Hudson 168; 3 Bevans 944; [1945] 39 AJIL Supp 111; ICAO Doc. 7300/9, 2006.

sets appropriate standards and recommended practices including that contracting states provide such for their territories and for proximate areas of the high seas.[25]

In compliance, many national air forces have search and rescue units. There is also the involvement of space in the operation of the COSPAR (Committee on Space Research)–SARSAT Satellite Search and Rescue System, which uses low Earth orbit (LEO) and geostationary orbit satellites as part of its infrastructure.[26] Lastly, we note the search-and-rescue duties undertaken by INMARSAT and other GDMSS service providers, supervised by the International Maritime Satellite Organisation.[27]

ARRA is open to all states (Art. 7.1) and as of 1 January 2023 had ninety-nine ratifying states and a further twenty-two signatories.[28] ARRA distinguishes the duties owed by contracting parties to the personnel of a spacecraft from those in relation to a space object. The latter category, which is not necessarily confined to a spacecraft (a space object capable of carrying an astronaut) (Arts. 5 and 6), was covered in Chapter 4.

ARRA Art. 1 deals with the initial dissemination of information about an incident. It imposes two duties. First, an ARRA party must immediately notify the relevant launching authority (defined in Art. 6, *infra*) if it receives information or discovers that the personnel of a spacecraft have suffered an accident, are experiencing conditions of distress or have made an emergency or unintended landing in territory under its jurisdiction or on the high seas or any other place not under the jurisdiction of any state. If the party cannot identify the launching authority or get in touch with it, it is immediately to make a public announcement by all appropriate means (Art. 1(a)).

Second, the ARRA party is to notify the UN Secretary General of the facts, and the Secretary General 'should' disseminate the information without delay (Art. I.b). The relevant 'launching authority' is the state responsible for the launch or the intergovernmental organisation concerned in the launch, in the latter case provided that the organisation has accepted rights or obligations provided for under ARRA and a majority of its member states are contracting parties of both ARRA and the OST (Art. 6). The 'state responsible for launching' is a very ambiguous phrase that could include a state which finances a launch but which has no actual connection with the technicalities of the launch. ARRA is therefore not congruent with the Registration or Liability Conventions in its definition of an important state involved in any occurrence that activates it.

ARRA Arts. 2–4 deal with personnel rescue and return. Curiously, while ARRA Art. 5.5 provides that the expense of recovering and returning a space object or its component parts is to be borne by the launching authority, Arts. 2–4 are silent as to the cost of rescue and return of astronauts, let alone of tourists carried aloft by private companies.[29]

Under Art. 2, when an ARRA party knows that the personnel of a spacecraft have landed in its territory due to accident, distress, emergency or unintended landing, it is

---

25 In 1993, ICAO and the International Maritime Organisation set up a joint working group to coordinate their responses to maritime aviation search and rescue.

26 For the COSPAS–SARSAT Satellite Search and Rescue System, see www.cospas-sarsat.int/.

27 As to which see *infra* Chapter 11.

28 See the IISL and UNOOSA annual reports on the status of the space treaties, including detail of signatures and ratifications: https://iislweb.space/2001-standing-committee-report/ (or the annual *Proc. IISL*) and www.unoosa.org/oosa/en/ourwork/spacelaw/treaties/status/index.html.

29 R.M. Jarvis, 'The Space Shuttle Challenger and the Future Law of Outer Space Rescues' (1986) 29 *Int. L.* 591–621 at 613–618. Cf. P.G. Dembling, 'Cosmos 954 and the Space Treaties' (1978) 6 *J. Sp. L.* 129; Doolittle, *supra* n. 18.

immediately to take 'all possible steps to rescue them and render any necessary assistance'. It is to inform both the launching authority and the UN Secretary General of these steps and how they are proceeding. An effect, if not a purpose, of these duties, is to achieve openness and publicity, making it much more difficult for a state to sequester the personnel of a foreign spacecraft for military or other reasons. The later requirement for the safe and prompt return to the representatives of the launching authority (Art. 4) ties in with that suggestion.[30]

In the Art. 2 case, where the rescuing state is acting on its own territory, the launching authority has no right to intervene but is required to cooperate if its assistance would help in a prompt rescue or contribute substantially to search and rescue operations. Actual operations are subject to the direction and control of the territorial party, which is to 'act in close and continuing consultation' with the launching authority (Art. 2). That said, the thrust of Art. 2 is that the affected contracting party, not the launching authority, deals with the situation. The launching authority has to be invited for it to participate. It is therefore for the territorial state to decide whether to ask for the help of the launching authority.[31]

The language of Art. 3 is different. Article 3 applies if the personnel of a spacecraft have 'alighted' on the high seas or anywhere else not under the jurisdiction of any state. Under these circumstances, any contracting state 'in a position to' assist is to act if assistance 'is necessary' to ensure a speedy rescue. There is no division of primary and secondary responsibility similar to that between the territorial state and the launching authority under Art. 2. The duty under Art. 3 is laid on all that are in a position to assist. Article 3, therefore, takes account of the location where the astronauts have landed. That has varied implications.

First, a landing on the high seas could, but does not necessarily, require the assistance of states other than the launching authority. For many years, the USA regularly retrieved its re-entrant astronauts from the Pacific. The involvement of other states is not necessary when the 'alighting' is in a specified drop zone policed by the launching authority. Were the 'alighting' not so arranged, another state might or might not be in a position to help. In that case the duty to assist is a duty to assist.

But unlike Art. 2, there is no Art. 3 duty to take 'all possible' steps to assist. Another state might not be 'in a position to' assist for geographic reasons or because its participation in a rescue would not be technically feasible. Not all states have facilities adequate for a sea rescue. And as Dembling and Arons note, because the duty is not expressed as requiring that all possible steps be taken, a state party would not be required by Art. 3 to endanger lives by engaging in a rescue effort or to divert its shipping from other essential operations.[32] However, as Dembling and Arons also note, the fact that persons are in difficulty on the high seas might bring the matter under the other international legal obligations as to safety of life and assistance at sea.[33]

30 The requirements of Arts. 2–4 may reflect the military background of the early space flights. G.C.M. Reijnen, *The United Nations Space Treaties Analysed* (Gif-sur-Yvette, France: Editions Frontiéres, 1992) 160.
31 Cf. US statements, quoted by Dembling and Arons, *supra* n. 19, at 648 nn. 61 and 62, that should the territorial party and the launching authority not agree, ultimately 'the territorial party would of course have the final say in the matter'.
32 Dembling and Arons, *supra* n. 19, at 651.
33 Dembling and Arons, *supra* n. 19, at 650, citing the Convention for the Unification of Certain Rules with Respect to Assistance and Salvage at Sea, Brussels, 1910, 212 CTS 217; 1913 UKTS 4, CD. 6677; 37 Stat. 1658, TS 576; 7 Martens (3d) 728; 1 Bevans 780: and the Convention on the High Seas, 1958, Geneva, 29

Second, Art. 3 speaks of 'alighting' not only on the high seas but also to 'any other place not under the jurisdiction of any state'. The high seas apart, few areas of the Earth are now not under the jurisdiction of any state, but in the view of some, Antarctica is one. Among others, the US does not recognise any of the varied claims to areas of the Antarctic, and some Antarctic claims overlap. We would hope that were the landing in an area of competing claims, all the relevant parties would cooperate and not argue where the duty lay and that in other cases matters would be clear.

Third, the other obvious place where astronauts might alight and face trouble is the moon or another celestial body. Few would be able to provide assistance under such circumstances, but were astronauts of another state in the vicinity, the question might arise. It might, however, result in an extraordinarily awkward matter: difficult decisions could hinge on the available volume of air supply.[34]

Finally, it should be noted that ARRA Arts. 2 and 3 deal with the instance where the endangered personnel have 'alighted' one way or another. At first sight, these articles therefore do not apply to what may come to be the most common instance where a rescue is needed: in-flight difficulties in orbit, including problems with the International Space Station (ISS), or a space hotel, or on longer missions such as Artemis. However, Dembling and Arons suggest that in these circumstances, the matter would be covered by the second sentence of Art. V of the OST: 'In carrying on activities in outer space and on celestial bodies, the astronauts of one State Party shall render all possible assistance to the astronauts of other States Parties'.[35]

Arguably this language may not require a launch in order to rescue, but that is a semantic point that we hope would be ignored were a rescue mission otherwise feasible.[36] We further note that ARRA Art. 1 speaks of a state receiving information that 'the personnel of a spacecraft have suffered accident or are experiencing conditions of distress . . . in any other place not under the jurisdiction of any State'.[37] However, the duty under Art. 1 is only to inform the launching authority and the UN Secretary General. It is not an obligation to rescue.[38]

When the personnel of a spacecraft have been found under any of the circumstances of Arts. 2–3, under Art. 4 they are to be safely and promptly returned to representatives of the launching authority. The obligation is unconditional. Apparently, there was discussion as to whether return could be refused on the basis that the personnel had committed a crime (e.g. spying) or had claimed asylum, but these points were considered unnecessary to pursue in the negotiation of the text. The obligation to return is clear.[39] The only gap in the provision is that the state having custody of the personnel might consider that the landing or alighting did not fall within the 'emergency or accident' terms of Arts. 1–3 but was in

---

April 1958, 450 UNTS 82; 1963 UKTS 5, Cmnd. 1929; 13 UST 2312, TIAS 5200; [1958] 52 AJIL 842. The relevant agreements are now those cited *supra* n. 22.

34 When teaching jurisprudence at Aberdeen, F.L. constructed a tutorial problem based on such factors. Within two weeks, Apollo 13 launched and had its problem. See also *infra* at n. 65 as to the perils of long-range missions.

35 Dembling and Arons, *supra* n. 19, at 649–650; cf. Jarvis, *supra* n. 29.

36 But note the difficulties that may attend a rescue: see 'Long range missions' *infra* at n. 65.

37 A spacecraft in orbit would be under the jurisdiction of its launching state (OST Art. VIII).

38 But cf. Cargill Hall, *supra* n. 18.

39 Cf. Doolittle, *supra* n. 18.

fact intentional.[40] Article 4 does not require that the personnel be returned to the territory of the launching authority, only to its representatives. Curiously, while the costs of returning a space object to its launching authority are payable by that authority (Art. 5.5), Arts. 2–3 do not provide for the reimbursement of expenses incurred in the rescue and return of personnel.

The other place where duties to assist astronauts are laid down is in the Moon Agreement, the provisions of which, it must be noted, extend to all celestial bodies within the solar system other than Earth unless a specific set of legal norms in relation to that other body is in force (MA Art. 1.1).[41] While the Agreement is not in force for the bulk of states, and its members do not include any state that currently engages in astronaut activities on its own account, its provisions do cast light on desirable conduct. For instance, MA Art. 10.1 requires state parties to take all practicable measures to safeguard life and health of persons on the moon and to offer shelter in their stations and installations to those in distress (Art. 10.2).

In the event of an emergency involving a threat to life, a state party may use the equipment, vehicles, installations, facilities or supplies of another state party (MA Art. 12.2). As with ARRA Arts. 2–4, however, there is no mention of costs. Finally, under MA Art. 13, a state party that learns of a crash or forced or other unintended landing on the moon of a space object or its component parts which it itself did not launch is to inform the appropriate launching state; realistically, however, no obligation to rescue is included in this provision.

Protection of Astronauts

One elementary part of the protection of astronauts is that their space vehicles should be safe, but there will always be risks in complex technologies. The national laws of launching states should ensure that risk is minimised, but there have been disasters, and there will be in the future.[42] The investigation of accidents is therefore important.[43]

The effect of space on the human frame remains a matter of acute interest. It is crucial that an astronaut be fit to meet the stresses and strains involved.[44] Osteoporosis and muscle deterioration remain problems. Naturally this involves and justifies monitoring and experiment.

The ethos and control of experimentation on humans is a matter of profound contention, *inter alia* for historical reasons. While there is no doubt that the results of the German experiments on inhabitants of the concentration camps were of major interest to scientists, the conduct of those experiments was an element of charges brought against those who conducted them. One result was the 'Nüremberg Code', first enunciated in the

---

40 Dembling and Arons, *supra* n. 19, at 652–653, noted the Austrian view that under these circumstances, the ARRA obligation would not overcome a local rule as to the grant of asylum.

41 The provisions of the Moon Agreement also apply to orbits round the moon and to trajectories to or around it (MA Art. 1.2); see also Chapter 7.

42 See *supra* n. 20. The 2007 Report of the NASA Aerospace Advisory Panel indicates concern about the safety elements of the planned Constellation Program. See Part II 'Pivotal Issues' 28–34; www.hq.nasa.gov/office/ocr/asap/documents/2007_ASAP_Annual_Report.pdf.

43 See Chapter 14 for information on the space laws of various states.

44 Cf. NASA Space Flight Human System Standard: Vol. 1, Revision A, 'Crew Health' (NASA-STD-3001): https://standards.nasa.gov/standard/nasa/nasa-std-3001-vol-1.

Judgement in the 'Doctors Trial' of 1947,[45] as subsequently amended by Declarations of the World Medical Association in 1964.[46]

This sets out ten conditions for appropriation human experimentation. They include the voluntary consent of the subject given on the basis of full information, that fruitful results should be obtained which are not procurable by other means, that unnecessary suffering be avoided and that no experiment be conducted where there is reason to believe that death or disabling injury will occur.[47] There are, of course, significant pressures upon would-be astronauts. Care is needed to ensure that the enthusiasms of astronauts, or their controllers, do not lead them to transgress these parameters. Astronauts might otherwise be invited to sign documents releasing their controllers and the manufacturers of their equipment from legal liability in the event that something goes wrong, but the terms of any such release should be narrow. There are degrees of negligence. No astronaut should be invited to sign his/her own death-warrant, nor should passengers.[48]

That said, there are other questions to which attention has to be paid. Space is a very dangerous environment,[49] but ARRA is largely of terrestrial application. OST Art. V.2 requires astronauts to give each other mutual aid when active in outer space and on celestial bodies. OST Art. V.3 requires parties immediately to inform other parties and the UN Secretary General of any phenomena in outer space that pose a threat to life or health of astronauts.[50] One such is radiation.[51]

---

45 *Trials of War Criminals before the Nüremberg Military Tribunals under Control Council Law No. 10*, Vol. 2 (Washington: USGPO, 1949) 181–182. The Code is available on many websites – Google 'Nuremberg Code'.

46 The Declaration of Helsinki (1964) of the World Medical Association on medical experiments on humans: www.wma.net/what-we-do/medical-ethics/declaration-of-helsinki/doh-jun1964/, as amended to 1989: www.wma.net/what-we-do/medical-ethics/declaration-of-helsinki/doh-sept1989/. By various Declarations adopted in Geneva in 1948, 1968, 1984, 1994, 2005 and 2006, the Association has amended the correlative Hippocratic Oath on the duties of a physician which doctors swear on their graduation. The current International Code of Medical Ethics adopted by the Association is at www.wma.net/policy/current-policies/?text=International+Code+of+Medical+Ethics&type=&year_from=1980&year_to=2022.

47 For the USA, NASA Policy Directives establish a complex system including minimal risk and the requirement of informed consent for human participants. See NASA NPD 7100.8G Protection of Human Research Subjects: https://nodis3.gsfc.nasa.gov/npg_img/N_PR_8900_001B_/N_PR_8900_001B_.pdf and related NASA Procedural Requirements which set out a structure for the approval of research projects. For the NASA Medical and Ethics Division, see: www.nasa.gov/offices/ochmo/divisions/medpolicy/index.html#.Yx4IxCHMK-8. On both the NPD and NPR documentation see https://nodis3.gsfc.nasa.gov/main_lib.cfm.

Part VI of the ISS Code of Crew Conduct (cited *infra* n. 61) provides that 'No research on human subjects shall be conducted which could, with reasonable foresight, be expected to jeopardize the life, health, physical integrity, or safety of the subject'. It goes on to require research procedures involving ISS crew to be approved by a multi-lateral review board.

48 Space tourists are considered *infra* at n. 93.

49 'Space Safety Report: Vulnerabilities and Risk Reduction in US Human Space Flight Programs' (Washington: George Washington U, 2005); J.N. Pelton, *Space Exploration and Astronaut Safety* (Reston: AIAA, 2006) and 'Improved Space Safety for Astronauts' (2005) 21 *Space Policy* 221–225; Cf. the Final Report of the International Space Station Independent Safety Task Force, 2007 (www.nasa.gov/pdf/170368main_IIST_%20 Final%20Report.pdf) for considerations of risk relevant not only for the ISS but also for extended missions.

50 Cf. MA Art. 5.3.

51 Perhaps a fertile astronaut should be given the opportunity (or right?) to freeze sperm or eggs so as to obviate possible sterility through radiation exposure. See 'NASA Space Flight Human System Standard: Vol. 1: Revision A, 'Crew Health' NASA-STD-3001, *supra* n. 44, Problems of radiation are included. See also *infra* n. 52.

Suitable provision must be made for protecting astronauts from the perils of radiation from any nuclear devices powering spacecraft or any base as well from solar and
cosmic radiation.[52] Solar and radiation threats increase massively beyond the shielding
of the Earth's magnetic field and the Van Allen belts.[53] Space suits do not wholly protect
against solar or cosmic radiation: astronauts return to the safety of the ISS if a solar storm
is detected while they are outside. Redesign and further invention continue, with various
institutions researching and developing appropriate technologies.[54]

Equally, spacecraft and any lunar or Mars base would require appropriate and lasting
shielding. While a spacecraft can be oriented to present a minimal target to solar radiation,
a base cannot. Apart from radiation, there is also the possibility of meteorite impact. The
topography of the moon and Mars, as well as the proven meteoric collisions with space
probes and other spacecraft, show the dangers. Again, suitable design and shielding materials will be required.

Medical facilities and suitable arrangements are also important. Evacuation to terrestrial
accommodation may be feasible in LEO, but not from the moon or Mars or long-range
journeys. In both a spacecraft and a celestial base, physical illness must be able to be coped
with, as must accident and mental trauma.[55] What would on Earth be debility or an illness

---

52 US National Research Council et al., *Managing Space Radiation Risk in the New Era of Space Exploration*
(Washington: National Academies Press, 2008); US National Research Council et al., *Radiation Hazards
to Crews of Interplanetary Missions: Biological Issues and Research Strategies* (Washington: National Academies Press, 1996); US National Research Council, Report of a Workshop, *Space Radiation Hazards for
the Vision of Space Exploration* (Washington: National Academies Press, 2006): www.nap.edu/catalog.
php?record_id=11760#toc; L. Lane et al., eds., *Workshop Report on Managing Solar Radiation* (2007)
NASA/CP-2007-214558: http://event.arc.nasa.gov/main/home/reports/SolarRadiationCP.pdf. T.A.
Parnell et al., *Report of the Materials Science Panel on Radiation Effects and Protection for Moon and Mars
Missions*: http://science.nasa.gov/newhome/headlines/space98pdf/cosmic.pdf. Cf. R.A. English et al.,
'Apollo Experience Report – Protection Against Radiation' (NASA, Technical Note D-7080, 1973: http://
history.nasa.gov/alsj/tnD7080RadProtect.pdf); R.K. Tripathi and J.E. Nealy, 'Mars Radiation Risk Assessment and Shielding Design for Long-Term Exposure to Ionizing Radiation' (2007 IEEEAC Paper 1291 –
NASA Technical Reports Server, Doc. Id. 20080013522: http://ntrs.nasa.gov/search.jsp?R=815626&id=2
&qs=N%3D4294967190); M. Hempsell and R. Moses, 'The Impact of Radiation Protection on the Design
of Space Habitats' (2008) 61 JBIS 146–153; J.W. Wilson et al., 'Issues in Deep Space Radiation Protection'
(2001) 49 *Acta Astronautica* 289–312. See also the discussion of the UNGA Nuclear Power Principles of
1992 in Chapter 10.
53 Solar radiation is linked to sun spots, which largely (but not entirely) follow a twenty-two-year cycle of
intensity. Cosmic radiation is unpredictable. Cf. www.spaceweather.com. The present ISS orbits below the
Van Allen belts, so astronauts are to a degree protected from solar radiation. Its crew take shelter in better-
protected areas when warned of solar flares. In 2015–2016, astronaut Scott Kelly spent a year in space.
Part of the mission was to calibrate the effect of solar radiation on him through a comparison with his twin
brother Mark, who had remained on Earth. See A. Witze, *Nature*, 26 January 2017, at www.nature.com/
news/astronaut-twin-study-hints-at-stress-of-space-travel-1.21380?dom=AOL&src=syn, and his Wikipedia
entry. For work on the protection of astronauts on a trip to Mars see www.nasa.gov/feature/goddard/real-
martians-how-to-protect-astronauts-from-space-radiation-on-mars. Cf. the NASA Space Radiation Working
Group: https://srag.jsc.nasa.gov/spaceradiation/how/how.cfm.
54 Cf. n. 52 *supra*. See the work of the Human Spaceflight Laboratory, University of North Dakota: https://
aero.und.edu/space/human-spaceflight-lab/. A new US space suit has been produced for the US return to
the Moon: cf. www.nasa.gov/mission_pages/constellation/main/spacesuit.html.
55 A.A. Cocca, 'Legal Aspects of Mental and Physical Workload of Astronauts' (1994) 37 *Proc. IISL* 213–221.
G.A. Landis, 'An all-woman crew to Mars: a radical proposal' (2000) 16 *Space Policy* 167–169, makes sense.
Since 1993, Australia and NASA have run a joint programme on the effects of isolation on human health. Its
results have relevance for extended space missions: *New Scientist*, 3 October 2008: http://space.newscientist.
com/article/dn14870-antarctic-bases-offer-lessons-for-space.html; www.msnbc.msn.com/id/27000348/.

of minor concern could be actively dangerous or even fatal in space.[56] Medical training, even at a rudimentary level, should be given to some personnel, if not all.

Tele-medicine could help, but the inescapable time delay on messaging is a limiting factor. On long-range missions, reserved provision for on-board hospitalisation is unlikely. In due course, a moon base might have specialised provision for medical facilities sufficient to cope with many occurrences. In short, medical facilities will be needed, but what is 'practicable' in the context of space?

Then there is the matter of criminal activity. What of theft, assault, rape or murder? The ISS arrangements provide for such matters.[57] Under the Intergovernmental Agreement (IGA),[58] parties retain criminal jurisdiction over their nationals on the ISS (Art. 22).[59]

Should misconduct of a national affect the life or health of the national of another party or damage the flight element (sc. Module or equipment) of another party, the national state of the alleged perpetrator is to consult the other party at its request as to their respective interests in a prosecution. The affected partner state may exercise criminal jurisdiction ninety days after the consultation (or other agreed period) if the national state of the perpetrator so agrees or fails to prosecute under its legal system. Extradition is possible (ISS IGA, Art. 22.3) and mutual assistance required (ISS IGA, Art. 22.4). Article 22, however, does not limit and is not limited by the ISS Code of Crew Conduct provided for under ISS IGA Arts 11.2 and 11.6 or the related Intergovernmental Memoranda of Understanding for its assembly.[60]

---

56 On Apollo 13, F.W. Haise was affected by a urinary tract infection. On other space missions, the common cold has caused problems.

57 Cf. A. Farand, 'Astronauts' Behaviour on Board the International Space Station: Regulatory Framework' Sec. 3, 'Criminal Jurisdiction', in *Legal and Ethical Framework for Astronauts in Space Sojourns* (UNESCO, 2005): http://portal.unesco.org/shs/en/file_download.php/785db0eec4e0cdfc43e1923624154cccFar and.pdf; J. Hermida, 'Crimes in Space: A Legal and Criminological Approach to Criminal Acts in Outer Space' (2006) XXXI AASL 405–423; H.P. Sinha, 'Criminal Jurisdiction on the International Space Station' (2004) 30 *J. Sp. L.* 85–127; T.A. de Roos, 'Disciplinary and Criminal Law in Space', in F.G. von der Dunk and M.M.T.A. Brus, eds., *The International Space Station* (Leiden: Martinus Nijhoff, 2006) 115–123. In 1999–2000 a 110-day mission experiment Sphinx-99 (Simulation of Flight of International Crew on Space Station) conducted on the ground in Russia failed partly due to an incompatibility of cultures: www.jamesoberg. com/04142000assualt_rus.html.

58 Agreement among the Government of Canada, Governments of the Member States of the European Space Agency, the Government of Japan, the Government of the Russian Federation and the Government of the United States of America Concerning Cooperation on the Civil International Space Station: Washington, DC, 29 January 1998, in force 27 March 2001; (2005) 30 AASL-II, 201–225; www.state.gov/wp-content/ uploads/2019/02/12927-Multilateral-Space-Space-Station-1.29.1998.pdf.

Excerpts from the IGA are in Annex 5 to F.G. von der Dunk and M.M.T.A. Brus, *The International Space Station: Commercial Utilisation from a European Perspective* (Leiden: Nijhoff, 2007), 227–241.

59 The question therefore may arise as to jurisdiction over a space tourist who is not a national of an ISS participant state. See G. Catalano Sgrosso, 'Legal Status, Rights and Obligations of the Crew in Space' (1998) 26 *J. Sp. L.* 163–186 and her 'Legal Status of the Crew in the International Space Station' (1999) 42 *Proc. IISL* 35–49.

60 See www.nasa.gov/mission_pages/station/structure/elements/partners_agreement. The 1998 MOUs are between NASA and the relevant authorities in:

1. Canada – www.nasa.gov/mission_pages/station/structure/elements/nasa_csa.html.
2. Japan – www.nasa.gov/mission_pages/station/structure/elements/nasa_japan.html.
3. ESA – www.nasa.gov/mission_pages/station/structure/elements/nasa_esa.html.
4. Russia – www.nasa.gov/mission_pages/station/structure/elements/nasa_rsa.html. S. Mirmina and C. Schenewerk, *International Space Law and Space Laws of the United States* (Cheltenham: Edward Elgar, 2022) 71–73.

The ISS Code of Crew Conduct broadly sets out what its title implies.[61] A party to the ISS IGA must approve the Code before providing an ISS crew member and is to ensure that that crew member observes the Code (ISS IGA Art. 11.2). The Code applies from the assignment of the crew member to a particular ISS visit to the end of the post-flight requirements. The Code ranges from a prohibition on taking materials on-board for private gain[62] to questions of harassment to the protection of intellectual property.[63] Disciplinary procedures are for the national state of an astronaut, although there is a commonality in the aims to be secured.

Another concern for astronauts is space debris, which can threaten life, particularly in LEO, where most current astronaut activity takes place. Space debris has been generally recognised as a major problem, albeit the efforts to diminish its impact remain recommendations and non-binding practices.[64] Debris may not constitute 'harmful interference' as such, but it is a potential menace, and it is necessary to prevent problems for all astronauts everywhere. A punctured space suit, spacecraft, capsule or moon base could spell disaster, raising questions for long-range missions. Suffice it here to note that collision avoidance manoeuvres are increasing in number for both manned and unmanned spacecraft.

Long-Range and Long-Duration Missions

Long-range and long-duration missions present particular problems.[65] Illnesses caused by psycho-social pressures or inherent personality instabilities may lead to diminished competence or reliability.[66] The environment of a spacecraft or of a moon or Mars base might aggravate any inherent tendencies to mental instability. Provision must be worked out in advance and implemented.[67]

Long-range missions include projects to set up manned bases on the moon or Mars or long-duration space flight and would also include projects such as a space hotel. We have

---

61 'International Space Station Crew-member Responsibilities' (US) 14 Code of Federal Regulations (CFR), §§ 1214.402–4. See 'Principles Regarding Processes and Criteria for Selection, Assignment, Training and Certification of ISS (Expedition and Visiting) Crew-members', ISS Participants Multilateral Crew Operations Panel, November 2001: www.spaceref.com/news/viewsr.html?pid=4578.
62 Presumably for later sale in the space souvenir market or for advertising purposes. Cf. US Astronaut rules, *supra* n. 61.
63 See outline in Farand, *supra* n. 57.
64 See UNGA Res. 62/217 approving the COPUOS endorsement of a set of voluntary guidelines for the mitigation of space debris. See CoCoSL III, 605–657, and *infra* Chapter 9 Debris. For the USA, see NASA: https://orbitaldebris.jsc.nasa.gov/library/usg_orbital_debris_mitigation_standard_practices_november_2019.pdf. Cf. the FCC requirements in first 'In the Matter of Mitigation of Orbital Debris', Second Report and Order; IB Docket no. 02–54, 19 FCC Rcd. 11567; June 2004, replaced by the US FCC Second Report and Order (IB Docket Nos. 22–271 and 18–313) 'In the Matter of Space Innovation; Mitigation of Orbital Debris in the New Space Age', adopted 6 October 2022, which will *require* the deorbiting of satellites that the FCC licenses from LEO (at or below 2000km) by no later than 5 years from the end of mission. See also NASA's 'Orbital Debris Quarterly News': http://orbitaldebris.jsc.nasa.gov/newsletter/newsletter.html.
65 Reference point nn. 34 and 36.
66 Cf. V.K. Parihar et al., 'Cosmic radiation exposure and persistent cognitive dysfunction' (2016) 6 *Sci. Rep.*, 34774: www.nature.com/articles/srep34774. See also *supra* n. 53 and note re Scott Kelly.
67 See *supra* n. 55.

outlined some medical considerations, but in relation to long-range missions, the 'unthinkable' must be thought about in advance.[68] Were an astronaut to die, decomposition onboard a space-ship would be unacceptable. It would be better to abandon the body to space,[69] although the loss of mass could affect the calculation of any later 'burns' for course corrections.[70]

Another possibility would be to put the body into a special bag, place it outside the spacecraft for a while and then retrieve it. The deep-frozen body could then readily be reduced to dust.[71] Burying a body on the moon or Mars could be considered as contrary to the international duty not to contaminate celestial bodies, although the disposal of human effluvia seems likely to occur.[72] But returning a body to Earth for burial from Earth or Mars is not likely to be practicable, let alone cost-effective, for many decades.[73]

68 During NASA's training of astronauts, contingency simulations include the possibilities of accident and death. See C. Hadfield, *An Astronaut's Guide to Life on Earth* (London: Macmillan, 2013) 58–61. The programme includes families.

69 Cf. David Bowman's release of the body of Frank Poole towards Jupiter in the film *2001: A Space Odyssey* (1968), the space burial of Mr Spock in *The Wrath of Kahn* (1982) and 'Space Oddity' (1969) by David Bowie. Two questions therefore arise: (1) under such circumstances, is a dead astronaut a space object, and (2) if so, should he/she be put on the UN Register? Apparently, some states have already registered shrouds in orbit 9: see Chapter 4, c. n. 124. In the event of total catastrophe, should a spacecraft be treated as the equivalent of a ship graveyard? Cf. the (UK) Protection of Military Remains Act, 1986, and sites designated thereunder. S. Drumgoole, 'Military Remains on and around the Coast of the United Kingdom: Statutory Mechanisms of Protection' (1996) 11 *Int. J. Mar. and Coastal Law*, 23–46. Cf. also the (US) Sunken Military Craft Act, 2004, Pub. L. No. 108–375, §§ 1401–1408, 118 Stat. 2094–98; D.J. Bederman, 'Congress Enacts Increased Protections for Sunken Military Craft' [2006] 100 AJIL 649–663. See also P. Hershey, 'Regulating Davy Jones: The Existing and Developing Law Governing the Interaction with and Potential Recovery of Human Remains at Underwater Cultural Heritage Sites' (2012) 27 *J. Env. L. and Litig.*, 363–400; J.R. Harris, 'The Protection of Sunken Warships as Gravesites at Sea' (2001) 7 *Ocean and Coastal L.J.* 75–130. See *infra* n. 72 as to disposal on the moon or another celestial body.

70 After the explosion in Apollo 13, dumping urine and other waste was prohibited so as not to alter the mass of the crippled vehicle. This allowed Ground Control to calculate the 'burn' necessary for the return trajectory to Earth.

71 Cf. D. Oberhaus, 'To Boldly Go Where No Body Has Gone Before': https://slate.com/technology/2015/04/death-in-space-the-ethics-of-dealing-with-astronauts-bodies.html.

72 States are 'to conduct exploration of' the Moon and other celestial bodies 'so as to avoid their harmful contamination' (OST Art. IX). Cf. MA Art. 7.1: 'In exploring and using the moon, States Parties shall take measure to prevent the disruption of the existing balance of its environment whether by introducing adverse changes in that environment, by its harmful contamination through the introduction of extra-environmental matter or otherwise'. Article 7.2 then speaks of radioactive materials, but biological contamination may be more to be avoided. One could have fun with the wording of part of MA Art. 8.2.b, which allows the 'placement' of personnel below its surface, and its Art. 11.3, which while prohibiting property rights on the moon also speaks of such placement below the surface. What of a burial ground? Would cremation be preferable? As for effluvia, the environs of the US base at the South Pole are not reassuring. Astronauts must avoid harming the moon environment: cf. P.B. Larsen, 'Application of the Precautionary Principle to the Moon' (2006) 71 *J. Air L. Comm.* 295–306. On Mars, perhaps a body could be used as fertiliser for the future colony, but interment without total incineration of earth bacteria would breach the rules as to planetary protection: see Chapter 9 c. n. 57.

73 Cf. C.D. Simak, *Cemetery World* (1972).

Other conditions of ultimate crisis may arise.[74] What if there were an air leak in a base, a space hotel or a spacecraft?[75] Help might be forthcoming from other astronauts,[76] but in most instances, such help would probably be impossible. On Earth, it is accepted that in submarine navigation, water- and air-tight doors may have to be sealed to preserve the submarine as a whole, any consequent loss of life notwithstanding. It must be clear that a similar rule would apply in the air-less conditions of space or an extra-terrestrial base. But what if the residual air is insufficient to preserve the lives of all the surviving personnel?[77] Such problems have occupied philosophers and terrestrial courts. On occasion, they have been occluded from civil or criminal proceedings.[78] As far as court consideration is concerned, one famous English case is *Regina v. Dudley and Stephens,* 14 Q.B.D. 273 (1884); [1881–85] All E.R. Rep. 61, where a cabin boy, Richard Parker, was killed (perhaps) and eaten (certainly) to preserve the life of others in a lifeboat after the 1884 sinking of the *Mignonette* off the Cape of Good Hope. A defence of necessity was not accepted, and the accused were convicted of murder and sentenced to death. This was speedily commuted to six months' imprisonment without hard labour.[79]

A leading US case is *United States v. Holmes,* 26 F. Cas. 360 (1842); (1842) 5 Wheat. 412, where a seaman was tried for manslaughter. He had ordered some to be thrown overboard from an overloaded lifeboat to prevent it sinking, thereby saving the remainder. Holmes was found guilty and sentenced to some months in prison and a fine. Both cases are notable for their discussions of matters on which different legal traditions arrived at divergent results.[80]

74 President Nixon had a statement prepared to use if the engine of the Lunar Excursion Module of Apollo 11 had failed to fire and the occupants (Armstrong and Aldrin) been stranded on the moon. See *inter alia* http://watergate.info/1969/07/20/an-undelivered-nixon-speech.html; http://watergate.info/nixon/moon-disaster-speech-1969.shtml; www.thesmokinggun.com/archive/apollo1.html; http://en.wikipedia.org/wiki/In_Event_of_Moon_Disaster#Contingency_television_address. Cf. W. Safire, 'Essay: Disaster Never Came': http://query.nytimes.com/gst/fullpage.html?res=9B0CE2D7103CF931A25754C0A 96F958260. Presumably subsequent presidents have had similar texts prepared.

75 What if there is an air leak in a space hotel and only some can be rescued? Cf. M.J. Sundahl, 'The Duty to Rescue Space Tourists and Return Private Spacecraft' (2009) 35 *J. Sp. L.* 163–200; F.G. von der Dunk, 'Passing the Buck to Rogers: International Liability Issues in Private Spaceflight' (2007) 86 *Neb. L. Rev.* 400–38 at 408–409 and 435–437; A. Caley, 'Liability in International Law and the Ramifications on Commercial Space Launches and Space Tourism' (2014) *Loy. L. A. Int. & Comp. L. Rev.* 233–262.

76 'the astronauts of one state Party shall render all possible assistance to the astronauts of another State Party' (OST Art.V.2); 'States Parties shall offer shelter in their stations, installations, vehicles and other facilities to persons in distress on the moon' (MA Art. 10.2). See also *supra* n. 18.

77 After the explosion on Apollo 13, the Lunar Excursion Module, designed for two people for two days, was used by three people for four days.

78 G.R. Stewart, *Ordeal by Hunger: The Story of the Donner Party* (New York: Houghton Mifflin, 1992); P.P. Read, *Alive: The Story of the Andes Survivors* (London: Secker and Warburg, 1974), rep. as *Alive: Sixteen Men, Seventy-two Days, and Insurmountable Odds* (London: Harper Perennial, 2005). Cf. the facts behind Théodore Géricault's painting 'The Raft of the Medusa' (1819), the Louvre, Paris.

79 A.W.B. Simpson, *Cannibalism and the Common Law* (Chicago University Press; London: Hambledon, 1984). Dudley emigrated to Sydney, Australia, and became a successful boat-builder and ship-chandler, dying in 1900. Stephens went back to sea and died in 1914. Given the offence charged, that hard labour was not imposed was unusual for the time. See also Hanson, *infra* n. 82. Cf. J.R. Kahns, 'The Application of the Death on the High Seas Act (DOHSA) to Commercial Space Flight Accidents' (2011) 37 *J. Sp. L.* 279–298.

80 See, famously, Lon Fuller, 'The Case of the Speluncean Explorers' (1949) 62 *Harv. L. Rev.* 616–654 and (1999) 112 *Harv. L. Rev.* 1851–1875. See also A. D'Amato, 'The Speluncean Explorers – Further Proceedings' (1979–1980) 32 *Stan. L. Rev.* 467–485; W.N. Eskridge, Jr, 'The Case of the Speluncean Explorers; Twentieth-Century Statutory Interpretation in a Nutshell' (1993) 61 *Geo. Wash. L. Rev.* 1731–1753; N.R.

How should such questions be treated in the context of space? Much depends on the gravity of what the defence of necessity seeks to excuse. Would not preserving many under the conditions of insufficient air be defensible?[81] In fact, at the time of *Dudley v. Stephens*, cannibalism did occur in similar circumstances: those in lifeboats would draw lots as to who should die, individuals voluntarily giving up their own lives to save others.[82] We applaud Captain Titus Oates, who left Robert Falcon Scott's party on its return from the South Pole in 1912 in the (apparent) belief that if he sacrificed himself, the others might survive to make it to the next food dump.[83] Circumstances may force similar decisions in space. Should suicide pills be an essential component of the medical kit? And therefore, crucially how should the person or persons to die be selected?[84] Should it be voluntary, or determined by ballot, by lot, by majority vote? Should it be the person least important for the mission,[85] or decided by the fiat of the mission commander or by Mission Control?[86] Before such questions arise, the law must be clear.

On a similar line of thought, consideration must be given to the possibility that an astronaut becomes deranged and/or murderous. An astronaut who becomes incapable of functioning as a member of the group is one thing, but circumstances are different if he or she becomes a danger to the others.[87] Should he or she become murderous or deluded

---

Cahn et al., 'The Case of the Speluncean Explorers: Contemporary Proceedings' [7 new Opinions] (1993) 61 *Geo. Wash. L. Rev.* 1754–1811; 'The Case of the Speluncean Explorers: A Fiftieth Anniversary Symposium' [6 new Opinions] (1999) 112 *Harv. L. Rev.* 1834–1923; J. Allan, 'A Post-Speluncean Dialogue' (1994) 44 *J. Leg. Educ.* 519–530; J. Allan, *The Speluncean Case* (London: Barry Rose, 1999); P. Suber, *The Case of the Speluncean Explorers: Nine New Opinions* (London: Routledge, 1998, 2002). Cf. A.M. Sanders, Jr, 'Newgarth Revisited: Mrs Robinson's Case' (1997–8) 49 *South Car. L. Rev.* 407–61; J.B. Ruhl, 'The Case of the Speluncean Polluters: Six Themes of Environmental Law, Policy and Ethics' (1997) 27 *Env. L.* 343–73; P.L. Caron and R. Gely, 'Affirmative Refraction: Grutter v. Bollinger through the Lens of the Case of the Speluncean Explorers' (2004) 21 *Const. Comment* 63–106.

From a philosophical perspective, cf. J.J. Thomson, 'The Trolley Problem' (1984–1985) 94 *Yale L.J.* 1395–415; E. Rakowski, 'Taking and Saving Lives' (1993) 93 *Col. L. Rev.* 1063–1156; T. Stacey, 'Acts, Omissions and the Necessity of Killing Innocents' (2001–2002) 29 *Am. J. Crim. L.* 481–520; T. Stelzig, 'Deontology, Governmental Action, and the Distributive Exemption: How the Trolley Problem shapes the Relationship between Rights and Policy' (1998) 146 *U. Penn. L. Rev.* 901–959; E.L. Uhlmann, D.A. Pizarro, D.H. Tannenbaum and P.H. Ditto, 'The motivated use of moral principles' (2009) 4 *Judgment and Decision Making*, 476–491, or www.sas.upenn.edu/~baron/journal/9616/jdm9616.html.

Similar questions also arise in triage decisions in medical practice and disaster management: J.G. Hodge Jr, 'Legal Triage during Public Health Emergencies and Disasters' (2006) 58 *Admin. L. Rev.* 627–644.

81 J.S. Mill, *Utilitarianism* (1863) (many eds). Cf. Tom Godwin, 'The Cold Equations' (1954: the sacrifice of one in the interests of the many or of the mission. Cf. John 11: 50.

82 N. Hanson, *The Custom of the Sea* (New York: Doubleday/Wiley, 2000).

83 M. Smith. *I Am Just Going Outside: Captain Oates–Antarctic Tragedy* (London: Spellmount/Tempus, 2006).

84 R. Balleste. 'The Ethics of Space Exploration: Harrowing Stories of Death, Survival, and the Unknown' (2022) 37 *Conn. J. Int. L.* 138–162 at 159–161.

85 Status as a fee-paying passenger or space tourist could prove crucial: operational crew are essential.

86 See *supra* n. 80, particularly Rakowski. Cf. A.C. Clarke, 'Transit of Earth' (1971), *Arthur C. Clarke: The Collected Stories* (London: Gollancz, 2000) 883–893.

87 The ISS Code of Crew Conduct does not specifically deal with the use of force to quell a problematic crew member. Farand (*supra* n. 57) at para 2.3.3.5 states that the negotiators of the Code felt the power of the commander to 'use reasonable and necessary means' to discharge his responsibilities would cover the matter but nonetheless included in the minutes of the meeting that finally approved the Code a statement that such 'means' could include proportional physical force or restraint if necessary for the safety of the crew member or of the ISS itself. Cf. Sinha *supra* n. 57, at 126–127.

and indifferent to general safety, summary execution may be prudent, but how should such a case be determined?[88]

It follows that before long-term missions are embarked on, clear decision-making processes should be identified to cope with worst cases as well as with behaviour of more limited concern. It is also necessary to establish appropriate codes of conduct; such should not be unduly precise but should leave room for the informed input of those administering it. At first, we may expect a maritime/military command structure, but that will not be suitable in larger communities.[89]

In the case of an extra-terrestrial base, whether on a celestial body or a space station with many occupants and a degree of permanence, it will be necessary in due course to provide some sort of 'constitution' as well as administrative and court procedures,[90] but such questions take us well beyond what we are prepared at present to discuss. Much is a question of policy other than law. Policy must dictate the answers to many questions relating to the safety of astronauts. The law must follow, incorporating where necessary decisions and determinations in legal form. In other matters law must provide procedures.

The worst-case scenarios require fuller consideration than they have had to date.[91] In this, the UNESCO Commission on the Ethics of Scientific Knowledge and Technology (COMEST) may play a role.[92] Its work on the ethics of outer space is thought-provoking.

---

88 It might be the mission commander who is the problem. Cf. H. Wouk, *The Caine Mutiny* (1951, many eds) and the later film (1954). Mental stability is a factor assessed in astronaut recruitment, but even the best test may fail. Cf. 'NASA Astronaut Health Care System Review Committee February–June, 2007: Report to the Administrator': www.nasa.gov/pdf/183113main_NASAhealthcareReport_0725FINAL.pdf. G.S. Robinson, 'Astronauts and a Unique Jurisprudence: A Treaty for Spacekind' (1984) 7 *Hastings Int. Comp. L. Rev.* 483–499 at 484–491 considers the possible effects of space on the physical and mental health of an astronaut. Present NASA procedures for space station emergencies are contained in the *International Space Station Integrated Medical Group (IMG) Medical Operations Book: All Expedition Flights*, Mission Operations Directorate, Operations Division, JSC-48511-E1, 24 August 2000: www.nasa.gov/centers/johnson/pdf/163533main_ISS_Med_CL.pdf. Relevant sections speak of restraining the individual, the use of tranquillising drugs and the possible removal of the person. Such procedures may not suffice on long-range missions where removal is not an option.

89 W. Erlank, 'Governance, Authority, and Chain of Command in Crewed Space Voyages: Some Thoughts' (2023) 48 *Air and Sp. L.* 165–182.

90 Cf. M.H. Ryan and I. Kutschera, 'Lunar-based Enterprise Infrastructure – Hidden Keys for Long-term Business Success' (2007) 23 *Space Policy* 44–52; 'Self-Government in Space', in G.S. Robinson and H.M. White, Jr, *Envoys of Mankind: A Declaration of First Principles for the Governance of Space Societies* (Washington: Smithsonian Press, 1986), 196–206, and 'A Convention for Space-kind: Treaty Governing the Social Order of Long-Duration or Permanent Inhabitants of Near or Deep Space', ibid. at 266–270; Robinson, *supra* n. 88, and G.S. Robinson, 'No Space Colonies: Creating a Space Civilization and the Need for a Defining Constitution' (2004) 34 *J. Sp. L.* 169–179; his 'Space Law for Human*kind*, Transhumans and Post-Humans' (2008) XXXIII AASL 287–324; his 'Transcending to a Space Constitution: The Next Three Steps Toward a Defining Constitution' (2006) 32 *J. Sp. L.* 147–175; T. Masson-Zwaan, 'New States in Space' (2019) 113 AJIL Unbound 98–102; D.N. Feofanov, 'Luna Law: The Libertarian Vision in Heinlein's The Moon is a Harsh Mistress' (1995–6) 63 *Tenn. L. Rev.* 71–141. Cf. A. Froehlich, ed., *Assessing a Mars Agreement Including Human Settlements* (Vienna: Springer, 2021). As a curiosity we note the existence of 'Asgardia': https://asgardia.space/en/. H. Alshamsi et al., 'Asgardia 2117: From Theoretical Science to a New Nation in Outer Space' (2018) 16 *Santa Clara J. Int. L.* 37–60. Cf. www.sciencealert.com/a-multinational-group-wants-you-to-join-asgardia-the-first-outer-space-nation-with-a-mission-to-defend-earth.

91 Cf. *supra* nn. 69–72 and text following n. 80. Balleste *supra* n. 84, at 160 notes the last sentence of Art. 6.1 of the International Covenant on Civil and Political Rights (999 UNTS 171) states: 'No one shall be arbitrarily deprived of his life'.

92 COMEST: https://en.unesco.org/themes/ethics-science-and-technology/comest. Cf. M. Couston, 'Spatioethique – Reflexions sur La Teneur Ethique du Droit Spatial', in A. Kerrest, ed., *L'Adaption du Droit de l'Espace ses Nouveau Défis – Liber Amicorum, Mélanges en l'honneur de Simone Courtieux* (Paris: Editions Pedone, 2007) 49–86 (also 2004 *Rev. Fr. de Dr. Aer. et Sp.*).

Space Tourism[93]

A space tourist is different from an astronaut. The tourist is the logical equivalent of the passenger on a plane or a cruise liner. The phrase 'space tourism' is unfortunate. The term 'private space flight' might be preferred by some, although it masks the distinction of crew and passenger.[94] However, the traditional expression prevails in journal articles and the media, so we use it. The topic has generated much interest.[95] Companies such as Virgin Galactic, Blue Origin and Space-X are ready to engage in the space tourism business.[96]

For space tourism, the basic question remains where is space? There is no international agreement.[97] Does a simple 'up-pause-and-down' flight qualify?[98] The assertions of the advertising industry and space tourism entrepreneurs do not have legal standing.[99] Where 'space' 'is' affects which law may be applicable. If a touristic activity involves entry to space, space law may apply. If it does not, it does not. The result may be that the legal requirements for the different types of 'space' tourism will vary.

---

93 Reference point n. 48 *supra*.
94 F.G. von der Dunk, 'Passing the Buck to Rogers: International Liability Issues in Private Spaceflight' (2007) 86 *Neb. L. Rev.* 400–438 at 402–403.
95 S. Freeland. (1) 'Up, Up and . . . Back: The Emergence of Space Tourism and its Impact on the International Law of Outer Space' (2005) 6 *Chic. J. Int. L.* 1–22; (2) 'Fly Me to the Moon: How will International Law Cope with Commercial Space Tourism?' (2010) 11 *Melb. J. Int. L.* 90–118; C.E. Parsons, 'Space Tourism: Regulating Passage to the Happiest Place Off Earth' ((2006) 9 *Chapman L. Rev.* 493–526; J.C. Easter, 'Spring Break 2023 – Sea of Tranquility: The Effect of Space Tourism on Outer Space Law and World Policy in the New Millennium' (2003) *Suffolk Transnat. L. Rev.* 349–83; S.H. Bromberg, 'Public Space Travel – 2005: A Legal Odyssey into the Current Regulatory Environment for United States Adventurers Pioneering the Space Frontier' (2005) 70 *J. Air Law & Comm.* 639–71; F. von der Dunk (1) 'Space for Tourism? Legal Aspects of Private Spaceflight for Tourist Purposes' (2006) 49 *Proc IISL* 18–28; (2) 'Passing the Buck to Rogers: International Liability Issues in Private Spaceflight' (2007) 86 *Neb. L. Rev.* 400–38; (3) 'Space Tourism, Private Spaceflight and the Law: Key Aspects' (2011) 27 *Sp. Pol.* 146–152; (4) 'The Regulation of Space Tourism', in E. Cohen and S. Spector eds., *Space Tourism: The Elusive Dream* (Bingley: Emerald Pub., 2019) 177–199, or https://digitalcommons.unl.edu/spacelaw/114/; T.R. Hughes and E. Rosenberg, 'Space Travel (and Politics): The Evolution of the Commercial Space Launch Amendments Act of 2004,' (2005) 31 *J. Sp. L.* 1–79; S. Hobe, 'Legal Aspects of Space Tourism' (2007) 86 *Neb. L. Rev.* 439–458; R.D. Launius and D.R. Jenkins, 'Is it finally time for Space Tourism' (2006) 4 *Astropolitics* 253–280; P.S. Dempsey, 'United States Space Law: Commercial Space Launches and Facilities' (2006) 49 *Proc. IISL* 69–78; S.H. Bromberg, 'Public Space Travel – 2005: A Legal Odyssey into the Current Regulatory Environment for United States Adventurers Pioneering the Space Frontier' (2005) 70 *J. Air Law & Comm.* 639–671; Zhao Yun, 'A Legal Regime for Space Tourism: Creating Legal Certainty in Outer Space' (2009) 74 *J. Air L. Com.* 959–982; T. Masson-Zwaan and R. Freeland, 'Between heaven and earth: The legal challenges of human space travel' (2010) 65 *Acta Astronautica* 1597–1607; R. Sadowski, 'Insuring Commercial Space Travel: Seeking Solutions to a Futuristic Problem' (2012) 61 ZLW 79–94; M. Tse, '"One Giant Leap [Backwards] for Mankind": Limited Liability in Private Commercial Spaceflight' (2013) 79 *Brook. L. Rev.* 291–320; C. Albert, 'Liability in International Law and the Ramifications on Commercial Space Launches and Space Tourism' (2014) 36 *Loy. L.A. Int & Comp. L. Rev.* 233–262; M. Benkö, A. Zickler and R. Gabriele, 'Space Tourism: Facts and Fiction' (2015) 64 ZLW 50–53; Ankit K. Padhy and Amit K. Padhy, 'Legal conundrums of space tourism' (2021) 184 *Acta Astronautica* 269–273; A-S. Martin and S. Freeland, 'A Round Trip to the Stars?: Considerations for the Regulation of Space Tourism' (2022) 47 *Air and Sp. L.* 261–284.
96 See https://virgingalactic.com; www.blueorigin.com; www.spacex.com.
97 See Chapter 6.
98 An inverted bungee jump?
99 The Virgin Galactic website speaks of 'astronaut passengers': www.virgingalactic.com.

General

Space tourism was not in the contemplation of those who drafted the OST.[100] However, it is certainly a lawful use of space in terms of OST Art. I paras 1–2, and as such, its benefit should be the province of all mankind – provided you can afford the fare. All the states that are likely soon to permit space tourism are party to the four basic space treaties: the OST, ARRA, and the Registration and Liability Conventions. Tourism involving landing on the moon would take several days and would bring into play the Moon Agreement as between its parties.[101]

Licensing

A state that authorises space tourism determines the terms on which it will license the activity. Obviously these terms should be reflective of any relevant international obligations. States are likely to have regard for the health and safety of participants. However, since participants will play different roles, and these may affect international legalities, it is necessary to consider that element separately.

Participation[102]

In space tourism, there is an obvious difference between the crew, who are trained to operate the vehicle, and the customers, who have not. Space tourist customers are there for an experience provided as a service by the crew. Does that matter in law? It would be strange if it did not: those merely along for the ride do not easily fit the category 'astronaut' discussed earlier.

National legislation has seen the problem. In the US, private space flight is allowed.[103] A distinction is made between crew and a space flight participant.[104] The crew includes those who perform 'activities . . . directly relating to the launch, re-entry or other operation of or in a launch vehicle or re-entry vehicle that carries human beings'. A space flight participant is 'an individual who is not crew, carried aboard a launch vehicle or re-entry vehicle'.[105] Crew are subject to the general US regulation of astronauts,[106] but particular provision is made for passengers, including the requirement of informed consent.[107]

---

100 We have not gone through the OST *travaux preparatoires* to confirm this point. See UN OOSA: www.unoosa.org/oosa/en/ourwork/spacelaw/treaties/travaux-preparatoires/outerspacetreaty.html.
101 A round trip to the moon without landing would take at least three days. Art. 10.1 of the Moon Agreement would provide tourists with ARRA protection for its parties.
102 Reference point *infra* n. 126.
103 51 USC §50902 ss. 2 and 20, as revised and 51 USC 50905.
104 See *supra* n. 12, and the provisions of the US Federal Aviation Administration: 'Human Space Flight Requirements for Crew and Space Flight Participants: Final Rule' (2006) 71 Fed. Reg. no. 241, 75616–45; 14 CFR Parts 401, 415, 431, 435, 440 and 460 (as amended).
105 14 CFR § 401.5. See Hughes and Rosenberg *supra* n. 95.
106 As to which see *supra* at n. 47.
107 51 USC 50905 ss. (5)(A)–(D). Cf. Florida Statutes, Title XXV, Chapter 331.501 'Spaceflight: informed consent': www.leg.state.fl.us/Statutes/index.cfm?App_mode=Display_Statute&Search_String=&URL=0300-0399/0331/Sections/0331.501.html and www.flsenate.gov/Session/Bill/2023/1318/Analyses/2023s01318.rc.PDF See also G. Catalano Sgrosso, *supra* n. 59; T. Knutson, 'What is "Informed Consent" for Spaceflight Participants in the Soon-to-Launch Space Tourism Industry?' (2007) 33 *J. Sp. L.* 105–122; S. Hobe and R. Popova, 'Legal aspects of human orbital and suborbital spaceflight: Some legal medical and ethical

In the UK, the Space Industry Act, 2018. c. 5 and related regulations take account of space tourism.[108] Under s. 9(9), 'taking part in spaceflight activities includes being carried in a spacecraft or carrier aircraft without being involved in the operation of it'. Section 17(1) prohibits the holder of a space flight licence from allowing an individual to take part 'in a prescribed role or capacity' in a spaceflight activity unless the individual has met criteria prescribed by regulation as to age and mental capacity. Section 18 and Schedule 2 provide for 'training regulations' to set requirements as to the training, qualifications and medical fitness of those taking part in space flight activities.[109] Training is the subject of Chapter 4 of the Space Industry Regulations (2021 SI 792). Under Reg. 69, a licensed operator must provide an approved training programme for crew (Reg. 69(1)(a)), and separately for 'individuals who participate in the licensed activities but do not perform a specified role or act in a specified capacity' (Reg. 69(1)(b)).[110]

Whether other states will adopt similar measures remains to be seen. However, such legislation provides a basis on which to consider the insurance of non-crew participants and perhaps some clarity as to informed consent and questions of waivers of liability. A simple waiver of liability no matter how comprehensively framed will not offset claims based on negligence, gross negligence or wilful misconduct in every jurisdiction of the world. Perhaps an analogue of the 1929 Warsaw Convention is required for commercial space-flight passengers.

Registration

Almost all space objects are registered in accordance with the Registration Convention. That is important. Astronauts are returned to the state of registry when they land in the territory of another state (OST Art. V.1). OST Art. VIII provides that the state of registry retains 'jurisdiction and control over such object, and over any personnel thereof' (OST Art. VIII). Neither 'astronaut' nor 'personnel' is defined with sufficient clarity for the purposes of space tourism.

Some space tourism may require registration. However, the duty to register in a national registry and with the UN arises only when 'a space object is launched into earth orbit or beyond' (Art. II.1). Unlike the Liability Convention and irrespective of national legislation, attempted or failed launches are not registrable internationally unless component parts of the object, or of its launch vehicle, made it into orbit (Art. II.1, with Art. I(b)); that is, space tourism,[111] and vertical or up-and-down tourism, does not involve registration.[112]

considerations' 7–8 (2017) *Reviews in Human Space Exploration* 1–5; G. Kluge et al., 'Commercial suborbital space tourism – proposal on passenger's medical selection' (2013) 92 *Acta Astronautica* 187–192.
108 Reference point n. 13 *supra*.
109 Under the UK Space Industry Act, 2018, s. 18(a) licensees must not permit unqualified individuals to take part in space flight activities. Sections 1.5.b and 61(2)(b) and 69(2)(b) bring the use of balloons for space tourism within the scope of the legislation. The upper limit for balloons is c. 50 km.
110 Cf. A. Simmonds, 'The UK Perspective on Informed Consent in Commercial Space Travel' (2020) 45 *J. Sp. L.* 367–390.
111 Suborbital flight is flight to high altitude but at a speed that does not involve sending the vehicle into orbit. Cf. ICAO Working Paper, C-WP/12436, 'Concept of Suborbital Flight', COPUOS, A/AC.105/C.2/2010/ CRP.9: www.unoosa.org/pdf/limited/c2/AC105_C2_2010_CRP09E.pdf. See also ICAO Legal Committee 36th Sess., Dec. 2015, 'Commercial Space Flights', LC/36-WP/3-2: www.icao.int/Meetings/ LC36/Working%20Papers/LC%2036%20-%20WP%203-2.en.pdf. Cf. P. van Fenema, 'Suborbital flights and ICAO' (2005) 30 *Air Sp. L.* 396–411.
112 Cf. F.G. von der Dunk. (1) 'Beyond *What?* Beyond *Earth Orbit?* . . ! The Applicability of the Registration Convention to Private Commercial Manned *Sub-Orbital* Spaceflight' (2013) 43 *Cal. West. Int. L. J.* 269–341, and materials *supra* n. 95.

While the OST uses 'astronaut' and 'personnel' as we have already described, the Registration Convention does not use the term astronaut but refers in general terms to OST Art. VIII. 'Personnel' is only used relating to how multiple launching states register under the Convention and that without prejudice to their separately agreeing as to the jurisdiction over the personnel of the object being registered (Art. II.2 *ad fin*).

Liability

Space tourism will involve disaster. In the case of suborbital tourism, such matters will be dealt with by national law, including where necessary rules of private international law.[113]

The 1972 Liability Convention defines damage as including 'loss of life, personal injury or other impairment of health' (Art. I(a)). It holds a launching state absolutely liable for damage caused by its space object to the surface of the earth or to aircraft in flight (Art. II), subject to exoneration if the claimant state or the persons it represents have been grossly negligent or intended the damage (Art. VI.1) but not if the launching state has contravened international law, the UN Charter or the OST (Art. VI.2). Elsewhere, liability requires proof of fault (Art. III). The Convention does not apply to damage caused to nationals of the launching state (Art. VIII(a)) or to foreign nationals participating in the operation from launch until descent (Art. VIII(b)).

In the ordinary case, no claim will arise with respect to nationals whether crew or customers, but what of foreign nationals who are customers of the service and not operationally involved? And what if it is one of these foreign customers who, interfering with the operation of the space object, causes the damage?[114] In the case where another customer is damaged, the home state of a damaged national could perhaps bring a claim. In the case of the national causing the damage, it would presumably be impossible to prove the negligence of the launching state. There appears to be no possibility that the home state of the interfering foreign national could incur liability.[115] Maybe it should. We therefore note that no provision of the Liability Convention prevents states from 'concluding international agreements reaffirming, supplementing or extending its provisions' (Art. XXIII.2). A protocol could usefully extend or clarify the terms of the Convention as they may apply to space tourism. In addition, the 'Warsaw' provisions in international air law should be considered a model at both the international and national levels. Capping liability would protect the embryonic space tourist industry from being wiped out by a single disaster.[116]

---

113 As to the capping of liability, see *infra* prior to n. 116.
114 Tourism to the ISS raises a question as to jurisdiction over a space tourist who is not a national of an ISS participant state. See G. Catalano Sgrosso, 'Legal Status, Rights and Obligations of the Crew in Space' (1998) 26 *J. Sp. L.* 163–186 and her 'Legal Status of the Crew in the International Space Station' (1999) 42 *Proc. IISL* 35–49.
115 Under ordinary international law, a state is not liable for the private activities of its nationals. As a customer, the national is acting in a private capacity.
116 Cf. Tse, *supra* n. 95. Note J.R. Kuhns, 'The Application of the Death on the High Seas Act (DOHSA) to Commercial Space Flight Accidents (2011) 37 *J. Sp. L.* 279–298 as to jurisdiction.

ARRA

Terrestrial ARRA

In the event of an accident or emergency, space tourists may require rescue. We will deal with rescue in space in the next section. Here we are concerned with terrestrial occurrences.

Despite including the term 'astronauts' in its title, the operative articles of ARRA deal with 'the personnel of a spacecraft'. It is possible to argue, as we did earlier, that in space tourism there is a difference between crew and customer. Others consider that in ARRA, personnel includes all on board a space object.[117] However, for the terrestrial purpose, there is no need to enter into otiose argument as to the duty to rescue. Crew and customers will be together, and it is not conceivable that rescuers would confine their services only to crew.[118] That said, it is arguable that rescued tourists need not be returned to the launching authority should they so wish (Art. IV).

ARRA in Space

Space tourists may become stranded in space. That might occur on a simple orbital flight, or, in the remoter future, were a space hotel in orbit or on the moon to suffer damage. It would be physically difficult to deal with such events, and it might well require difficult decisions to be made.[119] We restrict ourselves to sketching the legal issues.[120]

Apart from the possibility that the commercial entrepreneurs engaged in space tourism have their own plans for the rescue of clients,[121] other measures as to rescue or aid would be desirable. The ARRA provisions have limited relevance should there be an emergency.[122] ARRA does not *require* a rescue attempt to be mounted: that duty applies only when there has been a landing on Earth (Art. 2).

In space and on the moon, astronauts are required to assist each other (OST Art. V.2), but the question remains whether tourists are astronauts within the terms of the OST, especially given that Art. 10 of the Moon Agreement classifies all on the Moon as astronauts. In any event, the Moon Agreement has not been ratified by states likely to be licensing moon tourism, and as discussed in Chapter 7, the Agreement does not contemplate hotels.

---

117 Freeland, *supra* n. 95, (1) at 10; (2) at 103–104; cf. Hobe, *supra* n. 95, 454–458.
118 See also Sundahl, *infra* n. 121.
119 Cf. discussion following n. 69 *supra*; J.R. Kahns, 'The Application of the Death on the High Seas Act (DOHSA) to Commercial Space Flight Accidents' (2011) 37 *J. Sp. L.* 279–298. We expect an up-to-date version of the film *The Towering Inferno* (1974).
120 See also Chapter 7 The Moon, Asteroids and Other Celestial Bodies.
121 M.J. Sundahl, *supra* n. 75, recommended that companies providing space tourism should not only rely on state rescue obligations but should also have their own plan for rescue. R. Cargill Hall, *supra* n. 18, at 205 speculated as to a duty to rescue from an orbiting spacecraft.
122 R. Cargill Hall, *supra* n. 18, suggests that the ARRA obligations would include a duty to mount a rescue mission to an orbiting spacecraft from Earth. Cf. also M.J. Sundahl, 'Rescuing Space Tourists: A Humanitarian Duty and Business Need' (2007) 50 *Proc. IISL* 204–214; (2) *supra* n. 75; S. Wood, 'Applicability of Rescue and Return Obligations under the Outer Space Treaty and the Return and Rescue Agreement to "Astronauts" and "Personnel" Stranded in Outer Space' (2013) 56 *Proc. IISL* 107–125.

Environmental Considerations

Outer space is a dangerous environment. It is also fragile and unable to heal itself from the effects of human activities. The footsteps of the first astronauts on the Moon will remain visible for many years; there are no weather effects to erase the evidence of human visits. Before lunar tourism happens, we hope that adequate measures will have been taken to set aside and protect sites of historic significance.[123]

The lunar environment may be compared with that of Antarctica, which also remains in its original natural state, but it is precisely its pristine state that attracts tourists. Indeed, US President Eisenhower recognised the analogy when he introduced the Antarctic Treaty to the UN General Assembly as the model for an outer space treaty.[124] In prohibiting claims to sovereignty in outer space (Art. II), the OST protects the outer space environment from damage being done to its fragile natural state (Art IX). In Antarctica, this principle requires caution and the improved evaluation of environmental impact before engaging in activities. The principle applies similarly in outer space.[125]

Customer Care

We expect that space tourism will be rigorously regulated to secure the health and safety of customers. Informed consent will be integral to participation, as will the assessment of the mental and physical health of each tourist, not to mention the crew.[126]

Conclusion

Space tourism interacts with but is not limited to international space law. Orbital and beyond-orbital tourism are certainly subject to the international rules, albeit uneasily. The relevant language of the space treaties is unsatisfactory. A solution would be a protocol bringing together the concepts of 'astronaut', 'operational personnel', 'personnel' and 'persons on board' for the purposes of international law. Both ARRA Art. 8 and Arts. XXV and XXVI of the Liability Convention contemplate the amendment of their terms. A single protocol might be more suitable than dealing with them separately. National law will doubtless continue to consider the requirements imposed on crew and customers as separate matters.

In the immediate future, it is suborbital and vertical space tourism that are the most likely to develop, with regular flights being the intention of most enterprises providing the service. In both instances, questions of space traffic management emerge, and steps will be needed to interweave such activities with traditional aviation.[127]

---

123 See Chapter 7 following n. 66.
124 Dwight D. Eisenhower, Address to the UN General Assembly, S. Doc No 26, at 1009 (1st Sess. 1961), quoted extensively Chapter 16 n. 36.
125 P.B. Larsen, 'Application of the Precautionary Principle to the Moon' (2006) 72 *J. Air L. Comm.* 295–306 at 297. See also Chapter 7 on heritage sites.
126 For US and UK rules see text following n. 102 *supra*.
127 Cf. S.M. Mousavi Sameh, 'Suborbital Flight: Environmental Concerns and Regulatory Initiatives' (2016) 81 *J. Air L. Comm.* 65–94; R. Balleste, 'Worlds Apart: The Legal Challenges of Suborbital Flights in Outer Space (2017) 49 *N.Y.U. J. Int. L. & Pol.* 1033–1062. See also Chapters 6, 9 and 17 sv. Space Traffic Management.

6

OF BOUNDARIES AND ORBITS

In previous chapters, we discussed the actors in space law, its sources, the four treaties that prescribe much of its basic content and astronauts. We have yet to discuss celestial bodies including the moon, but first we need to look at two matters. One is a fundamental question of boundaries: when or where does space law apply? The other is the orbit and its use.

The Air/Space Boundary

One of the stranger things about space law is that the location of 'space' for legal purposes has not yet been definitively settled. Should the physicalities rule, or are other considerations relevant? Early discussions were trammelled by historic notions of air space, in which space as we now conceive of it was not in mind. Notwithstanding, they may still affect modern discussions. The 'boundary question' lurches on.[1]

There is no general international agreement as to any boundary between air space and outer space; the Outer Space Treaty and its companions are silent. The only formal general statement in international law is in the ITU Radio Regulations.[2] In the future, space and air space may well be delineated similar to the distinction we make between the high seas and other areas of the sea subject to national sovereignty,[3] but as we write, uncertainty

---

1 M. Benkö and E. Plescher, *Space Law: Reconsidering the Definition/Delimitation Question and the Passage of Spacecraft Through Foreign Airspace* (The Hague: Eleven Publishing, 2013); T. Gangale, *How High the Sky?: The Definition and Delimitation of Outer Space and Territorial Airspace in International Law* (Leiden: Brill Nijhoff, 2018).

2 RR 1.177 defines 'deep space' as 'Space at distances from the Earth equal to, or greater than, 2×10^6 km' (sc. 2,000,000 km/1,243,000 miles). The orbit of the moon varies between *c.* 363,000 km/225,000 miles and c. 406,000 km/252,300 miles. The ITU deep space is therefore some five times further than the moon. Cf. L. Perek, 'Deep Space at WARC ORB-88' (1989) 32 *Proc. IISL* 255–258. Where is 'shallow' space? Perek indicates that it might be suitable to fix on the lowest possible for a satellite to orbit the Earth.

3 The statement is loose, but it will serve. The older simple distinction between the high seas and national waters is now inadequate. The Law of the Sea now recognises a right of innocent passage through territorial waters together with state jurisdiction beyond territorial waters for particular purposes including the Exclusive

DOI: 10.4324/9781003496502-6

remains – not that space law exists, but as to the exact location of its application. Needless to say, there have been many suggestions.

A state exercises sovereignty in a three-dimensional quasi-cone. This comprises in the horizontal plane the land territory of a state together with its territorial sea should there be one. Historically, state sovereignty extends downwards in the vertical plane *usque ad inferos* – down to Hell. Upwards in the vertical plane, a state is sovereign over the air space above its land territory and territorial sea – *usque ad coelum* – up to Heaven.

Above the high seas beyond the territorial sea, the air space is not subject to the sovereignty of any state, although for civil aviation purposes, it may in part be subject by agreement to air traffic control and may include areas subject to military surveillance and sometimes control.[4]

Our interest is the air space above state territory.[5] Corresponding with the suggestions of early writers,[6] it is clear that the rules of outer space apply somewhere above state territory. OST Art. VI speaks of activities 'in' outer space and Art. I para 3 deals with freedom of scientific investigation 'in' outer space – so you can be 'in' the 'somewhere'. However, the boundary between air space and outer space is, as a matter of law, uncertain, although even in the earliest days commentators saw the need for recognising the two jurisdictions.[7]

The matter is obscured by the language used. 'Boundary', 'delineation', 'above', 'somewhere' (italics added), 'arena' or 'area' subject to sovereignty, space as 'beyond' air space – such formulations carry overtones, often hidden from their users. The language is metaphoric, drawing upon concepts of space and boundary appropriate to physical distinctions, the boundary line between domestic properties or between states being obvious referents.[8] The language predisposes to unconsciously prejudging the issue. Even a simple phrase

---

Economic Zone and the Continental Shelf. An integration of such questions for traffic control purposes might be one solution. See *infra* 'Space Traffic Management' (n. 104ff), and in Chapter 9.

4 In Air Defence Identification Zones (ADIZs), all aeroplanes are required to identify themselves and may be subject to direction. ADIZs are constituted mainly for aviation safety but may also have security aspects. Most ADIZs lie within national air spaces, but some apply over parts of the high seas. See ICAO *Aeronautical Information Services: Annex 15 to the Chicago Convention* (13th ed., ICAO, 2010) App I, ENR 5. S. Lee, 'Back to Air in Disarray?: Disparity in Practices and Interpretations on ADIZs Disrupting the Safety of Civil Aviation' (2022) 87 *J. Air Law & Comm.* 271–298; J. Su, 'The Practice of States on Air Defense Identification Zones: Geographical Scope, Object of Identification, and Identification Measures' (2019) 18 *Chinese J. Int. Law* 811–836; R. Abeyratne, 'In search of theoretical justification for air defence identification zones' (2012) 5 *J. Trans. Sec.* 87–94; P. A. Dutton, 'Caelum Liberum: Air Defense Identification Zones Outside Sovereign Airspace', [2009] 103 AJIL 691–709; A.S. Williams, 'The Interception of Civil Aircraft over the High Seas in the Global War on Terror' (2007) 59 *Air Force L. Rev.* 73–152; M. Bourbonniere and L. Haeck, 'Military Aircraft and International Law: Chicago Opus 3' (2001) 66 *J. Air L. Comm.* 885–978.

5 The Harp and Martlet high-altitude research projects run by Gerald Bull in the 1960s might have launched a satellite using a gun (cf. Jules Verne, *From the Earth to the Moon*, 1865). See J. Adams, *Bull's Eye: The Assassination and Life of Supergun Inventor Gerald Bull* (New York: Times Books, 1992); W. Lowther, *Arms and the Man: Dr. Gerald Bull, Iraq and the Supergun* (London: Macmillan, 1991); D. Grant, *Wilderness of Mirrors: The Life of Gerald Bull* (Toronto: Prentice Hall, 1991).

6 Cf. Chapter 1 at n. 6 ff.

7 For the views of commentators as to its date, see A.G. Haley, 'Space Law and Metalaw – Jurisdiction Defined?' (1957) 24 *J. Air L. Comm.* 286–303.

8 For example, the wall that marked the boundary between East and West Berlin or the man-made sand banks that demarcate Western Sahara and Morocco. River boundaries can be more fluid; see *Case concerning the Frontier Dispute (Benin v. Nigeria)* 2005 ICJ Rep. 90. Cf. the use in US constitutional law of Benjamin Franklin's throwaway remark about a 'wall of separation between Church and State' – e.g. *Everson v. Board of Education* (1947) 330 US 1, and subsequent cases.

such as 'space lies beyond air space' can foster an assumption that a physical distinction must be reflected in the legal differentiation – that 'space' is farther away than 'air space'. That is not necessarily true. We must therefore always test the language of discourse, not to eliminate metaphor and analogy[9] but at least to ensure that their overtones do not impede a proper appreciation of the matter under discussion.[10]

When questions of space law fully emerged, well-developed concepts of air law already existed. To employ another metaphor, space law had to enter a field that was already considerably occupied by the tangled growth and under-growth of air space sovereignty; indeed, the jurisdiction of states over their air space ante-dates any question of its upper limit.

However, historically, that 'jurisdiction' was simply the right to make and enforce rules as to the use of the air space coterminous with the state. Although the language in some legal writing before the development of aviation may be construed to have a bearing upon the modern question, it is specious to argue that these hyperbolic statements were intended to deal with questions of the use of air space by transit through or above it. A famous gloss by Accursius of Bologna is to the effect that *'cuius est solum eius est ab inferos usque ad coelum'*.[11]

However, the gloss and its variants were conceived in relation to property boundaries and incursions by tree branches, projecting balconies and oriel windows. The Romans and the mediaeval commentators had no concept of sovereignty over or of air space similar to the modern notions. Problems of sovereignty and the need for legal control came much later. But come they did. We therefore briefly summarise the development of state control over air space as it existed prior to space and then turn to the question of a boundary between air space and outer space.

Air Space

It took about one hundred forty years for the modern concept of air space to emerge within international law. Before that, the problems of over-flight were domestic, and their solutions lay within municipal law. Joseph and Étienne Montgolfier are generally

---

9 An impossible task, Wittgenstein notwithstanding: L. Wittgenstein, *Tractatus Logico-Philosophicus* (German ed. 1921: Eng. trans, 1921: many eds).
10 Cf. Glanville Williams, 'Language and the Law' (1945) 61 *Law Q. Rev.* I, 71–86; II, 179–195; III, 293–303; IV, 384–406; VI (1946) 62 *Law Q. Rev.* 387–406. See also C.K. Ogden and I.A. Richards, *The Meaning of Meaning*, 10th ed. (London: Routledge and Kegan Paul, 1949); H. Palmer, *Analogy* (London: Macmillan, 1971); P. Ricoeur, trans. R. Czerny, *The Rule of Metaphor* (London: Routledge and Kegan Paul, 1978); F. Lyall, 'Of Metaphors and Analogies', *Slave, Citizens, Sons: Legal Metaphors in the Epistles* (Grand Rapids: Academic Books, 1984) 183–189.
11 Coke, *On Littleton*, 4a (many eds); W. Blackstone, *Commentaries on the Laws of England*, 4 vols, 3rd ed., R.M. Kerr (London: John Murray, 1862), Book II 'Of the Rights of Things', 16 (18) quoting the *cuius est* brocard (*infra*); F. Lardone, 'Airspace Rights in Roman Law' (1931) 2 *Air L. Rev.* 455–467; J.C. Cooper, 'Roman Law and the Maxim "Cuius est solum" in International Air Law', in I.A. Vlasic, ed., *Explorations in Aerospace Law: Selected Essays by John Cobb Cooper* (Montreal: McGill UP, 1968) 54–102; W. Guldimann, 'Cuius est Solum, Eius est Usque ad Coelum' (1952) 1 ZLW 213–233; H.D. Klein, 'Cuius Est Solum, Eius Est . . . Quousque Tandem?' (1959) 26 *J. Air L. Comm.* 237–254; F. Lyall, 'The Maxim "*Cuius Est Solum*" in Scots Law' (1978) *Jur. Rev.* 147–169: B.V. York, 'International Air Law in the American Republics' (1932) 3 *J. Air L.* 411–445; C. Cahoon, 'Low Altitude Airspace; A Property Rights No-Man's Land' (1990) 56 *J. Air L. Comm.* 157–198.

accepted as having begun ballooning, bringing their hot air balloon to Paris in 1783 after experimenting in their hometown of Avignon. The first manned flight was made on 21 November 1783 by J.-F. Pilâtre de Rozier, who also became the first flight casualty when his balloon caught fire and crashed on 15 June 1785. Appreciating the dangers of uncontrolled descents of the new apparatus, one Lenoir, a Paris police lieutenant, prohibited balloon flights in the city without special permit from 23 April 1784.[12] In the same year, Ypres in Belgium adopted similar legislation, as did Namur, France, in 1785 and Hamburg, Germany, in 1786.[13]

The first international flight came in 1785 when Pierre Blanchard and John Jeffries flew from Dover to Calais, and in the next few years, ballooning took off, if we may use the expression. In the English case of *Pickering* v. *Rudd* (1815) 4 Camp. 218; 1 Stark 56, the court doubted *obiter* whether an action of trespass was competent in respect of the mere transit of a balloon over property. In France in 1819, the Count D'Angles, Police Prefect for the Department of the Seine, required balloons to be equipped with parachutes, and prohibited the performance of aeronautical experiments during harvest time.[14]

Naturally, military applications were developed. A French Aerostatic Corps was used for observation during the Battle of Fleurus between France and Austria in then-Netherlands on 26 June 1794. During the US Civil War (1861–1865), the North used tethered balloons to observe the landing of cannonades, particularly at the Petersburg trenches.[15] During the Siege of Paris in the Franco-Prussian War of 1870–1871, some bold souls made their escape by night by over-flying the German lines in 'free' balloons but were threatened that they would be treated as spies were they brought down.[16]

Later, 'dirigible balloons' developed by various inventors allowed a degree of controlled flight through carrying an engine able to power a suitable propeller and a suitable configuration within a frame confining the balloons. Of these, the 'Zeppelins', products of the German company founded by Graf von Zeppelin in 1898, are the most famous. In 1909, Prime Minister Clemenceau of France introduced duties on balloon imports from abroad.[17] However, by then, balloons and dirigibles were regularly crossing international boundaries, and governments were becoming concerned. In the meantime, academic

---

12 Cf. the earlier proclamation published by the French government on balloon ascents, signed by De Sauvigny Lenoir, 27 August 1783, telling the Paris population not to be afraid of balloon experiments starting from the Champs de Mars. Appendix C to E.C. Vivian, *A History of Aeronautics* (US: Indypublish.com, 2002) (available in Gutenberg).

13 *Shawcross & Beaumont on Air Law*, 2nd ed. (London: Butterworths 1951) 3, cited in P.H. Sand, G.M. Pratt and J.T. Lyon, *An Historical Survey of the Law of Flight* (Montreal: Institute of Air and Space Law, McGill University, 1961) 5; Lord Hope of Craighead, 'Some Thoughts on the Evolution of Air Law' (2005) *Jur. Rev.* 153–171; D.L. Rhoades, *Evolution of International Aviation: Phoenix Rising* (Aldershot: Avebury Aviation (Ashgate), 2006) 13–20; P.B. Larsen, J. Gillick and J. Sweeney, *Aviation Law: Cases, Laws and Related Sources*, 2nd ed. (Leiden: Brill/Nijhoff, 2012) 1–83; P.S. Dempsey, *Public International Air Law* (Montreal: McGill Univ., 2008) 14–40.

14 H.G. Hotchkiss, *Treatise on Aviation Law* (2nd ed., New York: Baker-Voorhuis, 1938) 4, cited by Sand, Pratt and Lyon, *supra* n. 13, 5.

15 The Union Army Balloon Corps was established in 1861–1863 as a civilian adjunct to the federal Army.

16 See Kuhn, *infra* n. 18 at 116–117.

17 As to both, see Sand, Pratt and Lyon, *supra* n. 13, 5.

writing had begun.[18] In 1901, Paul Fauchille had published 'Le domain aerien et le regime juridique des aérostats'.[19]

The development of the dirigible airship brought questions of air space jurisdiction into academic prominence. While sporadic and limited municipal regulation had earlier sufficed,[20] international uniformity in national rules was increasingly seen as desirable. Various suggestions were discussed, including, by analogy with the Law of the Sea, designating internal air space, a territorial air space and above it a 'High Seas of the Air' in which there would be freedom of navigation.[21] International cross-boundary flights became common, making it desirable, not to say necessary, to have international agreement as to whether a state had jurisdiction over its air space and, if so, what the nature of that jurisdiction might be. Could intruders be excluded or otherwise dealt with?[22]

In 1910, the French Government convened a Conference on the Regulation of Air Navigation.[23] Various proposals were made during the Conference, which, although it reflected a technical failure in that no treaty was adopted at its conclusion, did see the completion of a draft convention dealing with varied aspects of the subject including nationality of aircraft, registration, documentation of aircraft and of pilots, photographic and radio equipment, rules of the air and prohibited zones.[24]

---

18 S.E. Baldwin, 'The Law of the Airship' [1910] 4 AJIL 95–108; A.K. Kuhn. 'The Beginnings of an Aërial Law' [1910] 4 AJIL 109–132; B. Lee, 'Sovereignty of the Air', [1913] 7 AJIL 470–496; G.D. Valentine, 'The Air – A Realm of Law' (1910) 22 *Jur. Rev.* 16–27, 85–104, and his 'Sovereignty or Freedom in the Atmosphere' (1911) 23 *Jur. Rev.* 324–336. Among now almost forgotten authors in the latter article, Valentine names Meurer (1909), Henri-Couannier (1910), Loubeyre (1911), Bielenberg (1911) Catellani (1911), H.B. Leech (*The Jurisprudence of the Air*, 1910), J.F. Lycklama à Nijeholt (*Air Sovereignty*, 1910) and Hazeltine (*infra* n. 22). Sand, Pratt and Lyon, *supra* n. 13, name also Manduca (1891), Pampaloni (1892) and Wilhelm (1891), which we have not traced.

19 P. Fauchille, 'Le domaine aerien et le regime juridique des aérostats' (1901) 8 *Rev. Gen. de Droit Int. Pub.* 414 (also Paris: Dalloz, 1901); 'La Circulation Aérienne de les Droit de États en Temps de Paix' (1910) 1 *Rev. Jur. Int. de la Locomotion Aérienne* 9–16. See also his Report on the 'Projet de convention sur le regime des aérostats en temps de paix' to the 1910 Paris Session de L'Institut de Droit International, together with a draft convention (1910) 23 *Ann. L'Inst. de Droit Int.* 297–311, with response by M. Von Bar at 312–319.

20 In 1908, the Council of Kissimee City, Florida (now more famous as being next door to Orlando and Disneyland), enacted air traffic control regulation arrogating to itself control to a vertical limit of 20 miles, well above the then ballooning limit.

21 Cf. J.F. English, 'Air Freedom: The Second Battle of the Books' (1931) 2 *J. Air Law* 356–372; H.B. Jacobini, 'International Aviation Law: A Theoretical and Historical Survey' (1953) 2 *J. Pub. L.* 314–332; A. Mérignhac, 'Le Domaine aérien privé et public et les Droits de l'Aviation en temps de paix et de guerra' (1914) 21 *Rev. Gén. de Dr. Int. Pub.*, 205.

22 On the doctrinal development at this time, see H.D. Hazeltine, *The Law of the Air* (London: Hodder and Stoughton, 1911); W.M. Gibson, 'The Development of International Air Law to 1919' (1931) 5 *Temple L.Q.* 161–184, and *supra* n. 18.

23 A. Meyer & A.A. Benvenisti, *Le Code de l'Air* (German Report) (1910). 1 *Rev. Jur. Int. de la Locomotion Aérienne* 72–79, together with all the early volumes of the Revue. J.C. Cooper, 'The International Air Navigation Conference, Paris, 1910' (1952) 19 *J. Air L. & Comm.* 12, reprinted, Cooper, *Explorations, supra* n. 11, 104–124.

24 'Draft International Convention on Aerial Navigation', Paris 1910, Appendix to the Report of the Civil Aerial Transport Committee, 1918, 1918 UKSP Vol. V, 17, Cd. 9218 (not now readily available electronically), but see http://searcharchives.bl.uk/primo_library/libweb/action/display.do?tabs=detailsTab&ct=display&fn=search&doc=IAMS040-002291961&indx=1&recIds=IAMS040-002291961&recIdxs=0&elementId=0&renderMode=poppedOut&displayMode=full&frbrVersion=&dscnt=0&frbg=&scp.scps=scope%3A%28BL

However, for a variety of political and economic reasons, the Conference was unable to come to agreement on a final text.[25] Spurred by the varied positions revealed by the Paris Conference, the UK enacted the Aerial Navigation Act of 1911, its Preamble affirming the absolute right of the UK to the air space above its territory.[26] This position was strengthened in the Aerial Navigation Act of 1913, which under Sec. 2 authorised the Secretary of State, if necessary, to order the shooting down of intruders that failed to obey instructions.[27]

The First World War totally changed the attitude of states that had hankered after air space analogues to the concept of the high seas beyond territorial air space, or a general right of innocent passage through air space on the model of the Law of the Sea. The military potential of aviation had become very clear during the years of the War. Although the dirigible was to remain relevant for another fifteen years or so,[28] aircraft had been developed which could carry significant loads and that were faster, more versatile and improvable. Therefore, when the French convened a second conference on international air law, the matter required little discussion.

The first Article of the International Convention on Air Navigation, Paris, 1919,[29] recognised that 'every Power has complete and exclusive sovereignty over the air space above its territory'. Note the language: this was in effect the creation of an international custom by a treaty provision. It was not an agreement as to the law to be applied solely between the High Contracting Parties: the Parties 'recognised' a legal principle applicable to all states, including states that were not parties to the Convention and states which, having been on the losing side in the Great War, were not present at the Paris Conference.

Of course, the absolute rule of sovereignty had to be modified at least between the Parties to ease commerce, but the default position was sovereignty. Thus, the freedom of innocent passage of aircraft might be agreed on as between the High Contracting Parties,

---

%29&tab=local&dstmp=1440425403979&srt=rank&mode=Basic&&dum=true&vl%28freeText0%29=Rep orts%20of%20the%20Civil%20Aerial%20Transport%20Committee&vid=IAMS_VU2).

25 Crudely, in the UK view, overriding concerns of military security required the 'complete and absolute sovereignty' of the subjacent state. The then-current technology made long-distance access to the British Empire across other states improbable; for the UK, freedom of innocent passage was therefore irrelevant. German interests were different, however: Graf von Zeppelin had established dirigible technology, skills and factories in Germany. Germany was topographically ideal for a hub-and-spoke system of aerial routes within Europe. Germany therefore desired sovereignty subject to a right of innocent passage, as it would thereby dominate the new aviation business. Although with some security concerns, France sympathised with the idea of freedom of aerial navigation, subject to necessary safeguards achieved through 'prohibited zones'.

26 This had been the official UK position at Paris, although it is clear that as a result of the debate there, the UK negotiators were themselves willing to countenance a more limited right of sovereignty. Their wavering was rejected, particularly by the military establishment, when they returned to the UK.

27 J.C. Cooper, 'State Sovereignty in Space: 1910–1914', in *Beitrage zum internationalen Luftrecht: Festschrift fur Alex Meyer* (Dusseldorf, 1954) or Cooper, *Explorations, supra* n. 11, 125–136.

28 Catastrophes such as the destruction of the British 'R101' in 1930, of the US Navy dirigibles 'Akron' in 1933 and 'Macon' in 1933, and the German Hindenburg in 1937 saw the virtual end of the large airship as a commercial or military proposition. Interest in dirigibles renewed in the 1990s. In August 2016, the Airlander 10, a hybrid UK airship, affectionately known as 'The Flying Bum', made its maiden flight. See www.hybridairvehicles.com/.

29 Convention on the Regulation of Aerial Navigation, Paris, 13 October 1919, 11 LNTS 173; 1922 UKTS 2, Cmnd 1609; 1 Hudson 359; 13 Martens (3d) 61; (1923) 17 AJIL Supp. 195. J.C. Cooper, 'United States Participation in Drafting the Paris Convention, 1919' (1951) 18 *J. Air L. & Comm.* 266, reprinted, Cooper *Explorations, supra* n. 11, 137–155.

but its detail was to be a matter for negotiation between states and would remain subject to the agreement of over-flown states (Art. 2). Where innocent passage was conceded, states could impose conditions as to admission and as to routes (Art. 15), and prohibited zones could be created for military reasons (Art. 3). In short, although developments allowed for a greater freedom of international aerial navigation in the inter-war years, the base always remained one of state sovereignty over air space. Thereafter, in the inter-war period, other air law conventions proceeded on a similar basis.[30]

The principle of state sovereignty is maintained in the Convention on International Civil Aviation, Chicago, 1944, Art. 1, repeating virtually verbatim Art. 1 of the 1919 Paris Convention: 'every State has complete and exclusive sovereignty over the air space above its territory'.[31] Various countries have incorporated this concept in their constitutions or provided for it by legislation.[32] Indeed, almost every state has now ratified the Chicago Convention.

In its default position on sovereignty, the Chicago Convention is a classic case of a general international agreement articulating the customary international law recognised by the Paris Convention of 1919. Modern customary international law and the Chicago and other agreements on international civil aviation proceed on the basis that a state is sovereign over its air space. The evidence in the matter is brutal. In the ultimate a state is entitled to enforce its sovereignty, as an exercise of that sovereignty, shooting down an unauthorised intruder. Over the years a number of aeroplanes, both civil and military, have so been shot down.[33] While the International Civil Aviation Organisation (ICAO)

---

30 The Ibero-American Convention, Madrid, 1926, 45 Stat. 2409, 3 Hudson 2032, 2 Bevans 617; the Pan-American Convention on Commercial Aviation, Santiago, 1928, 129 LNTS 223; 40 Martens (3d) 379; 4 Hudson 2354; 47 Stat. 1901; TS 840; 2 Bevans 698; (1928) 22 AJIL Supp. 124. Cf. H.S. Le Roy, International Air Law Trends' (1945) 31 *Virg. L. Rev.* 448–456; D. Göedhuis. (1) 'Civil Aviation after the War' [1942] 36 AJIL 596–613; (2) 'Sovereignty and Freedom in the Air Space' (1955) 41 *Trans. Grot. Soc.* 137–152. See also Larsen and Dempsey, both *supra* n. 13.

31 Convention on International Civil Aviation, Chicago, 1944, 15 UNTS 295; 61 Stat. 1180, TIAS 1591; (1953) UKTS 8, Cmnd 8742; 9 Hudson 168; 3 Bevans 944; [1945] 39 AJIL Supp 111; ICAO Doc. 7300/9. See also the Protocol on the Authentic Trilingual Text, 1968 (adding French and Spanish), 740 UNTS 21; 19 UST 7693, TIAS 6605, and the Protocol on the Authentic Quadrilingual Text, Montreal, 1977 (adding Russian). Further amendments to the Convention adding Arabic and Chinese authentic texts have been agreed to but are not yet in force.

32 In the initial draft of the 'Space Flight Liability and Immunity Act 2007' proposed to add Art. 24 to the Virginia Code as Title 8.01, Sec. 8.01–227.8, the 'Definitions' clause would have defined 'suborbital' as meaning 'a distance at or above 62.5 miles from the Earth's mean sea level'. This did not survive to final enactment. See http://leg1.state.va.us/cgi-bin/legp504.exe?071+ful+HB3184 and http://leg1.state.va.us/cgi-bin/legp504.exe?071+ful+CHAP0893. In the New Mexico 'Gross Receipts and Compensating Tax Act, 2007', when dealing with deductibles from taxable receipts from space and space-port activities, Sec. 7-9-54-2.(3), 'space' is defined to mean 'any location beyond altitudes of sixty thousand feet above the earth's mean sea level': http://nxt.ella.net/NXT/gateway.dll?f=templates$fn=default.htm$vid=nm:all.

33 Cf. the facts of *Aerial Incident of July 27, 1955 (Preliminary Objections) Israel v. Bulgaria,* 1959 ICJ Rep 127; *Aerial Incident (Pakistan v. India)* Application, 10 August 1999, and Judgement 21 June 2000, 2000 ICJ Rep. 12 [cited for background facts: case dismissed for lack of jurisdiction]; 'Documents concerning the Korean Air Lines Incident' (1983) 22 ILM 1109ff; 'Interception of Civil Aircraft' (1983) 22 ILM 1185; J.T. Phelps II, 'Aerial Intrusions by Civil and Military Aircraft in Times of Peace', [1985] 107 *Mil. L. Rev.* 255–304; M. Kido, 'The Korean Airlines Incident on September 1, 1983, and some Measures following it' (1997) 62 *J. Air L. & Comm.* 1049–1070; B.E. Foont, 'Shooting down Civilian Aircraft: Is There an International Law' (2007) 72 *J. Air L. Com.* 695–726; Bourbonniere and Haeck, *supra* n. 4.

   Francis Gary Powers was shot down over Russia in 1960 while flying a US U-2 spy plane. In 1995, the balloon D-Caribbean was shot down during a balloon race. Flying from Switzerland, it had approached a

has added to the Chicago Convention an article which by international agreement would minimise the loss of life and secure that under all circumstances every effort is taken to preserve life in civil aviation,[34] the default position – the base from which the law operates – remains the right of a state to take measures to assert its sovereignty, if necessary by the most drastic means.

Outer Space

Although states are willing to enforce their sovereignty over 'their' air space, there is no formal record of any state objecting to being simply over-flown by the satellite of another state.[35] Some consider it premature to suggest that there is a rule of customary international law that a state may not object to such over-flight since there is no formal evidence that states think that no valid objection can be made as a matter of law, but continued state silence on the matter will lead inexorably to the dissipation of any inchoate right to object, if it has not already done so.[36] Certainly in the 1980s there was talk of military efforts, particularly in the US and the Soviet Union, to develop technology to remove 'hostile' satellites, but those preparations were actuated by military planning for security rather than upon doctrinal principle as to sovereignty.[37]

military aerodrome in Belarus and had not responded to warnings: http://flightsafety.org/ap/ap_july96.pdf; http://aviation-safety.net/wikibase/wiki.php?id=43102. In 1996, Cuba shot down a 'Brothers to the Rescue' plane that may have entered its air space without permission: see UN SC Res. 1067 (1996); 'Shoot-down of the Brothers to the Rescue Planes', Hearings before the Sub-Committee on Crime of the US House of Representatives Committee on the Judiciary, 106th Cong. 1st Sess., House Doc. 63–608, Ser 36. In November 2015, Turkey shot down a Russian warplane alleged to have intruded into Turkish airspace from Syria. In the 1990s and early 2000s, various attempts to circumnavigate the globe by balloon without landing ran into problems securing permission to enter the air space of certain countries. For example, attempts by Richard Branson and Steve Fossett were hampered or delayed by the requirement to get over-flight permission from various states. Cf. US concern over Chinese balloons in early 2023: www.nytimes.com/2023/02/08/us/politics/china-spy-balloons.html.

34 Chicago Convention, *supra* n. 31, Art. 3 *bis*, adopted by the 25th (Extraordinary) Session of the ICAO Assembly, in force 1 October 1998. This provision binds parties to the Convention, but not all states are parties. Some non-parties might consider – or be thought to consider – themselves not bound by such 'law' were they to be over-flown without prior permission.

35 For an immediate response to Sputnik, I see J.C. Cooper, 'The Russian Satellite – Legal and Political Problems' (1957) 24 *J. Air L. Com.* 379–383. Cooper noted that while the USSR was not then party to the Chicago Convention, it did forcefully assert its right to deny the entry of foreign aircraft into its air space.
   There is a rumour that President Eisenhower, knowing of the Russian plans for Sputnik, did not press for the USA to be first in space, as, if the USA did not complain of over-flight by Sputnik, it would establish freedom of space and the USSR would not able object to over-flight by US satellites: G. DeGroot, *Dark Side of the Moon* (London: Cape, 2007) 57; see also D.R. Terrill, Jr., *The Air Force Role in Developing International Outer Space Law* (Maxwell AFB, AL: Air UP, 1999; Univ. Press of the Pacific, 2004), Ch. 1: http://aupress.maxwell.af.mil/Books/Terrill/terrill.pdf; A.K. Lai, *The Cold War, the Space Race and the Law of Outer Space* (Abingdon: Routledge, 2021) 11–26. As to later argument about over-flight for remote sensing, see Chapter 10.

36 Cf. J.I. Charney, 'The Persistent Objector Rule and the Development of Customary International Law' (1985) 56 BYIL 1–24.

37 To be effective, intervention would have to occur earlier in an orbit than 'over' the intervening state. Cf. the destruction by China of one of its obsolete weather satellites on 11 January 2007. See K.K. Nair, 'China's ASAT Test: A Demonstrated Need for Legal Reform' (2007) 33 *J. Sp. L.* 191–194; F. Walsh, 'Forging a Diplomatic Shield for American Satellites: The Case for Re-evaluating the 2006 National Space Policy in Light of a Chinese Satellite System' (2007) 72 *J. Air L. & Comm.* 759–799; J. Oppenheim, 'Danger at 700,000

The Bush Space Policy Determination of 2006 spoke of dissuading or deterring other states from impeding US rights in space, and, if necessary, denying adversaries the use of space capabilities contrary to US national interests.[38] There was nothing similar in the Obama Space Policy,[39] but the Trump Space Policy of 2020 re-introduced such language.[40] It, however, reflects military considerations rather than a doctrinal position as to sovereignty and over-flight.

Might a state legitimately interfere with a satellite short of its destruction, for example, to re-orbit or deflect a satellite on a crash trajectory? As before, such intervention would probably have to be above another state. Self-defence or the avoidance of damage would be arguable, but that is different from intervention as a simple assertion of sovereignty.[41]

All that said, it is logical to differentiate air space and outer space. The cogency of that logic has increased significantly during the years of space exploration and use. Arms limitation agreements distinguish between weapon systems that are or are not located in space, but they do not themselves define space for their purposes. They appear to rely on a common understanding of what or where space 'begins'.[42] The needs of arms limitation agreements may therefore compel some resolution of the matter. However, a boundary between air space and outer space could be determined for the purposes of arms control without it necessarily being read through to rule on other questions of civil interest.

Put shortly, and military questions apart, we do not yet have a clear rule formally and precisely differentiating air space and outer space. Space-capable states have seen no reason potentially to restrict their abilities to use space by coming to agreement on its lower boundary. Non-space-faring states are in no position to exercise any pressure in the matter. So one of the questions, which we debated at McGill University Seminars back in 1963–1964 under the able guidance of Professor Ivan A. Vlasic, remains 'How High is Up?'

Outer Space/Air Space

A boundary between outer space and air space was thought necessary even as technology was making access to the higher levels of the atmosphere possible.[43] For instance,

---

Feet: Why the United States Needs to develop a Kinetic Anti-Satellite Missile Technology Test-Ban Treaty' (2013) 38 *Brooklyn J. Int. L.* 761–796.

38 *US National Space Policy*, 2006, Sec. 5 Principles, bullet point 5. Cf. *infra* Chapter 16, United States.

39 *US National Space Policy*, 2010: https://obamawhitehouse.archives.gov/sites/default/files/national_space_policy_6-28-10.pdf.

40 *US National Space Policy*, 2020: https://trumpwhitehouse.archives.gov/wp-content/uploads/2020/12/National-Space-Policy.pdf.

41 H. DeSaussure, 'An International Right to Re-Orbit Threatening Satellites' (1978) 21 *Proc IISL* 92–98; Best Applicant Memorial, Jessup Moot Court Competition 1980 (1980) *ASILS Int. L.J.* 149–167 at 152–4. On 21 February 2008, some 130 miles/247 km above the Pacific, a missile launched from the USS Ticonderoga destroyed an uncontrolled re-entering satellite, US-193, which carried a block of frozen hydrazine. The justification given was to avoid potential contamination on Earth. Cf. materials cited *supra* n. 37.

42 Treaty Banning Nuclear Weapon Tests in the Atmosphere, in Outer Space and Under Water, Moscow, 5 August 1963, in force 10 October 1963, 480 UNTS 43; 14 UST 1313, TIAS 5433; (1964) UKTS 3, Cmnd. 2245; (1963) 2 ILM 883; (1963) 57 AJIL 1026. Goodman (*infra* n. 48) argues that an agreed-on vertical boundary for state sovereignty is needed for the protection of space assets, particularly as society is increasingly reliant on space-borne assets.

43 J.C. Cooper, 'High Altitude Flight and National Sovereignty' (1951) 4 *Int. L.Q.* 411–418; Cf. J.C. Hogan, 'Space Law Bibliography' (1956) 23 *J. Air L. & Comm.* 317–325.

in 1956, the Fourth Session of the Fiftieth Annual Meeting of the American Society of International Law, nominally devoted to international air law, in effect discussed the vertical delimitation of air space, albeit not as a boundary as such.[44] COPUOS discussed it ad hoc during its first meetings, but to the surprise of many, its first Report took the view that no priority should be given to the question of delimitation and indeed that agreement would be premature.[45] Interestingly, that Report also noted that the lower boundary of space and the upper boundary of state jurisdiction need not coincide but might overlap – a view which still has resonance. Throughout the intervening years, COPUOS has had the boundary question on its agenda, but no agreement has been forthcoming.[46]

Over the years the question 'where, as a matter of law, does space begin' has produced many theories, suggestions and arguments. In the early days, military considerations played a role, but that element tended to drop from sight until recently.[47] The suggestions can be grouped. The basic division is between theories which concentrate on physical elements – the 'spatial' or 'spatialist' approach – and the idea that altitude is less important than the purpose or 'function' of the instrumentality involved – the 'functional' approach.[48]

44 'International Air Law' (1956) *Proc. ASIL* 84–115, with Discussion Paper by J.C. Cooper, 'Legal Problems of Upper Space' 85–93; Cooper, *Explorations, supra* n. 11, 269–297.

45 Cf. J.C. Cooper, 'Fundamental Questions of Outer Space Law' Cooper, *Explorations, supra* n. 11, 287–297 at 289 [Lyall/Larsen, 61–69 at 62]; P.B. Larsen, 'A Sample of Space Law Opinion' (1966) 27 *Ohio State L. J.* 462–479.

46 COPUOS Secretariat, 'Historical summary on the consideration of the question on the definition and delimitation of outer space', A/AC.105/769 (2002) and A/AC.105/769 Add.1 (2020); V. Kopal, 'The Question of Defining Outer Space' (1980) 8 *J. Sp. Law* 154–173 [Lyall/Larsen 129–48]; Christol 435–546. And see *infra* n. 48.

47 E.g. D.B. Craig, 'National Sovereignty at High Altitudes' (1957) 24 *J. Air L. & Comm.* 384–397; D.R. Reinhardt, The Vertical Limit of State Sovereignty (2007) 72 *J. Air. L. & Comm.* 65–140, and next note.

48 COPUOS Secretariat, Background paper, 'Question of the Definition and/or the Delimitation of Outer Space', A/AC.105/C.2/7 (1970) with A/AC.105/C.2/7/Add 1 (1977) identified some nine major categories of spatialist theories, with additional sub-categories. Most recently see the 2022 Legal Sub-Committee Report A/AC/105/1260, paras 52–77, and the COPUOS Report, 2022, A/77/20, paras 207–213.

See also J.F. McMahon, 'Legal Aspects of Outer Space' (1962) 38 BYIL 339–399 at 340–57; C. Voûte, 'Boundaries in Space', in B. Jasani, ed., *Peaceful and Non-Peaceful Uses of Outer Space* (London: Taylor & Francis, 1991) 19–35; R.F.A. Göedhart, *The Never Ending Dispute: Delimitation of Air Space and Outer Space* (Gif-sur-Yvette: Editions Frontiers, 1996); A.G. Haley, *Space Law and Government* (New York: Appleton Century Crofts, 1963), 75–117 (cf. his 'Survey of Legal Opinion on Extraterrestrial Jurisdiction' (1960) 3 *Proc. IISL* 37–92); M.S. McDougal, H.D. Lasswell and I.A. Vlasic, *Law and Public Order in Space* (New Haven and London: Yale UP, 1963) 321–349 (the index entry is to 'Boundaries between outer space and air-space (a comedy of errors)'); D. Göedhuis, 'The Problems of the Frontiers of Outer Space and Air Space', 174 *Hague Recueil* 1982-I, 371–407 (cf. his 'An Evaluation of the Leading Principles of the Treaty on Outer Space of 27th January 1967' (1968) 15 *Neth. Int. L. Rev.* 17–41 at 28–33, 'To Which Area do the Rules of the Treaty apply?'); J.G. Verplaetse, *International Law in Vertical Space* (South Hackensack: Rothman, 1960); 'Note: 'National Sovereignty of Outer Space' (1961) 74 *Harv. L. Rev.* 1154–1175; G. Oduntan, *Sovereignty and Jurisdiction in the Airspace and Outer Space* (Abingdon: Routledge, 2012); Cheng 5–9, and ''The Legal Regime of Airspace and Outer Space: The Boundary Problem' (1980) V AASL 323, rep. Cheng, 525; Christol, 435–536.

See also P. Jessup and H.J. Taubenfeld, *Controls for Outer Space and the Antarctic Analogy* (New York: Columbia UP, 1959) 265–82; H.J. Taubenfeld, 'A Regime for Outer Space' (1961) 56 *Nw. U. L. Rev.* 129–67, and 'Outer Space: The "Territorial" Limits of Nations' (1969–1970) 38 *Fordham L. Rev.* 1–22; S.B. Rosenfeld, 'Where Airspace Ends and Outer Space Begins' (1979) 7 *J. Sp. Law* 137–148; L. Perek, 'Scientific Criteria for the Delimitation of Outer Space' (1977) 5 *J. Sp. Law* 111–124; T.W. Goodman, 'To the End of the Earth: A Study of the Boundary between Earth and Space' (2010) 36 *J. Sp. L.* 87–114; Kopal, *supra* n. 46.

If there were no upward limit to the jurisdiction of a state above its territory, three problems would emerge.[49] First, there is the 'lighthouse' effect. Were the jurisdiction of a state to extend indefinitely in a cone projected vertically from the centre of the earth and bounded by the lateral limits of the state, bodies such as the moon and the planets, not to mention other galaxies, would occasionally and briefly come within that cone of 'illumination'. That is absurd.[50]

Second, unlimited upward sovereignty does not correspond with the realities of the use of space as they have developed. No country has formally given permission for over-flight by all or any satellite, but satellites zip around and pass over many states.[51] States are bound not to put weapons of mass destruction into orbit (OST Art. 4), but the inference is that no permission is required for orbiting other objects,[52] and that state jurisdiction has a vertical limit, because the 'complete and absolute sovereignty' of Art. 1 of the 1944 Chicago Convention means permission is required for transit through air space. Finally, OST Art. II states that there is no state sovereignty in space, which implies that an unlimited verticality of state sovereignty does not exist.[53] But is a determinate boundary necessary?[54]

The Spatialist Approach

Among spatialist theories and suggestions, one possibility is to consider 'effective control'.[55] Just as once upon a time the 'three-mile limit' was (inaccurately) described as being the distance to which a state could from its land territory control the sea off its coasts, an

49 M. Milde, 'Considerations on Legal Problems above State Territory' (1958) 5 *Rev. Cont. Law* 5–22, 'Conclusion' extracted *Legal Problems* 1102–1108; contradicted by J. Zourek, 'What is the Legal Status of the Universe' (C.T. Barek trans.) *Legal Problems* 1109–1117; G.V. Leopold and A.L. Scafuri, 'Orbital and Super-Orbital Space Flight Trajectories – Jurisdictional Touchstones for a United Nations Space Authority' (1959) 36 *U. Det. L J.* 515–534 (rep. *Legal Problems* 520–39); G.V. Leopold, 'Cosmic Surveillance by Spaceflight Momentum (1960) 6 *Wayne L Rev.* 311–339.

50 Cf. reaction to the re-classification of Pluto and the curious memorial presented to and adopted by the New Mexico House of Representatives in March 2007 that Pluto be considered a planet as it 'passes overhead through New Mexico's excellent night skies': New Mexico, 48th Legislature, First Session, 2007, House Joint Memorial 54: www.nmlegis.gov/sessions/07%20Regular/memorials/house/HJM054.html; see also www.nmlegis.gov/Sessions/09 Regular/final/HM040.pdf. See also Illinois General Assembly Senate Resolution SR0046 of 26 February 2009 that 'as Pluto passes overhead through Illinois' night skies, that it be reestablished with full planetary status': www.ilga.gov/legislation/96/SR/PDF/09600SR0046lv.pdf.

51 See also in Chapter 10 Space Objects in Orbit.

52 In 1959, E. Korovin argued that the then satellites were orbiting in accordance with permission contained in the arrangements for the International Geophysical Year, 'International Status of Cosmic Space' (1959) *Int. Aff.* (Moscow) 53–59, rep. *Legal Problems* 1062–1071 at 1065. That argument does not now hold.

53 This is also fatal to the claims of the Bogota Declaration, 1976, *infra* at n. 182.

54 Cf. S.N. Hosenball and J.S. Hofgard, 'Delimitation of Air Space and Outer Space: Is a Boundary Needed Now?' (1986) 57 *U. Colo. L. Rev.* 885–893. In 1958, Jacobini (*infra* n. 55) considered it premature to define a boundary but also reckoned that different instrumentalities (military or civilian) might require different boundaries.

55 S.M. Beresford, 'The Future of National Sovereignty' (1959) 2 *Proc. IISL* 5–10; H.T.P. Binet, 'Toward Solving the Space Sovereignty Problem' (1959) 2 *Proc. IISL* 11–16; H.B. Jacobini, 'Effective Control as Related to the Extension of Sovereignty in Space' (1958) 7 *J. Pub. L.* 97–119; J.M. Spaight, *Aircraft in War* (London: Macmillan, 1914), and *The Sky's the Limit: A Study of British Air Power* (London: Hodder, 1940), and *Air Power and War Rights* (London: Longman, 1st ed., 1924, 3rd ed. 1947). During the 1870 Siege of Paris the German authorities indicated that they would treat as a spy anyone in a balloon they had shot down: *supra* n. 16.

argument might be made that the sovereignty of a state should extend vertically as high as it is able to enforce that sovereignty. That argument has problems.

First, it would mean that the sovereignty of different states would extend to different heights depending on the quality of their munitions, a proposition not likely to be generally acceded to. Second, to set a boundary at the height to which the most potent state could exercise control would be nonsense for less able states. Third, anti-satellite tests by China, India, Russia and the US have destroyed satellites above minimum satellite orbital heights.[56] Last, because satellites in orbit travel at speeds in excess of 7 km a second,[57] the period that any satellite is above many states is extremely limited, and the opportunity to enforce or apply effective control is transitory.

If a boundary has to be recognised, some would want to rely on 'objective scientific determinants'. The problem with many of those is that they do not point to a particular height.[58] Even so, a considerable number of proposals for the demarcation of space and air space are based upon scientific criteria. One easily dismissed category is related to the gravity of Earth. Gravity-related positions such as the Lagrange points relative to the earth and the moon are significant in the use of space,[59] but these are inappropriate for setting a limit to air space.

Gravispheres have similar problems as the effect of Earth's gravity tapers off and are variable depending on the location of other gravity-possessing objects.[60] Any notion that a state should by sovereign right control any part of the gravisphere that might result in damage being done to it by a 'falling object' is clearly ridiculous. Re-entrant objects may pass over many states.

The varied layers of the atmosphere might be thought to be more useful in determining a space/air boundary. However, whichever atmospheric layer one selects, the fact is that these layers vary in altitude depending on atmospheric heating and cooling and the fluctuations in density depending on weather conditions and solar radiation.[61] Various altitudes/

---

56 See Chapter 9 The Near Earth Environment, para 2. G.T. Lyons III, 'New Habits and Hard Law: Putting Old Soft Law "Sanctions" and the Space Debris Epidemic out to Pasture' (2014) *J. Sp. L.* 453–479; J. Oppenheim, 'Danger at 700,000 feet: Why the United States needs to develop a kinetic anti-satellite missile technology test-ban treaty' (2013) 38 *Brook. J. Int. L.* 761–795 at 761–764, and cf. discussion of ASAT activities in Chapter 16.

57 This figure relates to a circular orbit. A satellite in elliptical orbit travels much faster when approaching its perigee.

58 McDougal, Lasswell and Vlasic, *supra* n. 48, at 338.

59 See *infra* – 'Lagrange Points'.

60 Göedhart, *supra* n. 48, 39–42. The major gravisphere boundary is where the gravity effect of the earth is greater than that of the sun. In fact, the centre of the earth is displaced some 1000 km towards the sun because of the sun's gravity. Further, the gravity field of Earth is not uniform because of mountains and deep ocean trenches; see results of the Gravity Recovery and Climate Experiment: https://earth.gsfc.nasa.gov/geo/missions/grace, and https://gracefo.jpl.nasa.gov/. While this is important for satellite orbits, it is without relevance for state sovereignty.

61 J.C. Hogan, 'Legal Terminology for the Upper Regions of the Atmosphere and for the Space beyond the Atmosphere' (1957) 51 AJIL 362–375; J.C. Cooper, 'The Problem of a Definition of "Air Space"' (1958) 1 *Proc IISL* 38–44. The principal layers are (roughly): the troposphere (sea level to *c.*10 km/8.6 nautical miles), the stratosphere (*c.* 10 km/8.6 nautical miles to *c.* 40–50 km/35–44 nautical miles), the mesosphere (*c.* 40–50 km/35–44 nautical miles to *c.* 80 km/70 nautical miles), the thermosphere (*c.* 80 km/70 nautical miles to *c.* 675 km/420 nautical miles) and the exosphere (*c.* 675 km/420 nautical miles to 10,000 km/6200 nautical miles). Air layers are thicker at the equator and shallower at the poles. The ozone layer, which protects life on Earth from ultra-violet radiation, lies within the stratosphere at heights varying between 20 and

heights vary in their effects on the human frame. At 15 km/9 miles, there is no oxygen; at 19 km/12 miles, fluids evaporate. At 45 km/27 miles, there is no protection from ultraviolet radiation, and at 50 km/31 miles, there is none against cosmic rays; at 200 km/125 miles, air resistance is negligible, although it is enough to slow a satellite.[62] Whether any of these can be used to indicate a boundary between air space and outer space is doubtful.[63]

However, we do note that the French text of the Outer Space Treaty refers in para 1 of its Preamble to 'l'espace extra-atmospherique'. That said, only twice is reference made to 'atmosphere' in relation to 'space' as a matter of international law. One comes in Art. I.1.a of the Nuclear Test Ban Treaty of 1963,[64] by which the Parties undertake 'to prohibit, to prevent, and not to carry out any nuclear weapon test explosion, or any other nuclear explosion, at any place under its jurisdiction or control: (a) in the atmosphere; beyond its limits, including outer space'. This is not very helpful, 'its limits' being uncertain.

The other reference is in the ITU Radio Regulations (RRs) and is more sensible. Intriguingly, in its very first consideration of the requirements of space radio in 1959, the ITU defined a space station as a transmitter located 'on an object that is beyond, or is intended to go beyond the major portion of the earth's atmosphere' (1959 RR 1.72).[65] RR 1.64 now defines a space station as being 'located on an object which is beyond, is intended to go beyond, or has been beyond the major portion of the Earth's atmosphere', and RR 1.178 currently defines a spacecraft as a 'man-made vehicle which is intended to go beyond the major portion of the Earth's atmosphere'. By contrast an 'Earth station' is located 'either on the Earth's surface or within the major portion of the Earth's atmosphere', thus including ground stations and aircraft (RR 1.63). Such terminology at least recognises some need for a definition of space, albeit that regarding whether a 'major portion' of the atmosphere relates to density or height is unresolved except by common sense.[66]

Other atmosphere-related possible boundaries concentrate on the 'instrumentality' of flight and look to the lifting characteristic of an aero-dynamic wing and the use of air-breathing engines, which is, of course, the matériel of the international civil aviation regulated under the Chicago Convention.[67] John Cobb Cooper, originally an aviation lawyer,

---

25 km (*c*. 10.5–13.5 nautical miles). Under the UK Space Industry Act, 2018, c. 5, s. 61(2), objects launched from the UK that go beyond the stratosphere are entered in the UK space register.

Note: Altitude is calculated in nautical miles, not statute miles; 1 nautical mile = 1.15 statute miles, or 1852 metres.

62 Orbiting at *c*. 350 km/190 nautical miles, the ISS is slightly slowed by residual atmosphere and is occasionally raised in orbit. Towards its end, Mir was significantly slowed by the upper fringes of the atmosphere, and one reason for its being de-orbited was the difficulty of regularly 'repairing' its orbit.

63 Göedhart, *supra* n. 48, Ch. 4, 35–38.

64 Treaty Banning Nuclear Weapon Tests in the Atmosphere, in Outer Space and Under Water, 1963, *supra* n. 42.

65 Reference point *infra* n. 89.

66 L. Perek pointed out that no matter the problems of the lawyers, for practical reasons, scientists know where space is. See n. 73 *infra*.

67 Cited *supra* n. 31. Annexes 6 and 8 to the Chicago Convention on the Operation of Aircraft, defines aircraft in terms of atmospheric flight: Art. 2 of a 'Project of an International Convention on Space Law' of 1959 stated, 'The outer space begins where the possibility to fly ceases for the propelled and jet planes deriving support in the atmosphere from reactions of the air': M.S. Smirnoff, 'The Role of the IAF in the Elaboration of Norms of Future Space Law' (1959) 2 *Proc. IISL* 147–155 at 151.

The space plane and vehicles for vertical space tourisms do not derive lift from the atmosphere for at least part of their flights. What law applies? Cf. S. Hobe and J. Cloppenburg, 'Towards a New Aerospace Convention: Selected Legal Issues of "Space Tourism"' (2004) 47 *Proc. IISL* 377–85; F. von der Dunk, 'Beyond

was in his later years of the view that national sovereignty should certainly extend to the height at which normal aircraft might operate but with an added belt above that. In his view, the 'normal' was some 20–25 miles,[68] but an additional 50 miles should be contemplated through which other states might have a 'right of passage' for launch and re-entry purposes.[69] Above some 100 km/62 miles (275,000 ft), an airplane cannot derive any lift from its wing but has to travel so fast that it exceeds escape velocity. This is the Von Kármán Line, named for the person who calculated its position, and was strongly urged by Andrew G. Haley as an upper limit of 'primary jurisdiction'.[70]

The Von Kármán Line is accepted by the Fédération Aéronautique Internationale as marking the space/air boundary for its purposes. However, although the Fédération does promulgate standards as well as keeping records, it is a nongovernmental body, and its views do not bind states.[71] In any event, the altitude of the Von Kármán Line is not constant but ultimately depends on air density.

It is possible to invert the question of a boundary based on atmospheric density and approach the matter from 'outside'. As a matter of fact, an orbit of a space object below some 200 km/110 nautical miles rapidly decays, and an elliptical orbit that descends below some 120 km/65 nautical miles is usually fatal.[72] Because of atmospheric drag, a satellite cannot ordinarily remain in orbit if it comes below some 90 km/48 nautical miles, which suggests a useful or effective boundary.[73] On those lines, the International Law Association suggested as early as 1968 that the term 'outer space' as used in the OST should be interpreted to include all space at or above the lowest perigee attained by 27 January 1967, the date when the OST came into force.[74]

What? Beyond Earth Orbit? . . .! The Applicability of the Registration Convention to Private Commercial Manned *Sub-Orbital* Spaceflight' (2013) 43 *Cal. West Int. L.J.* 269–349.

68 Modern commercial aviation flies at up to 47,000 ft (15 km/9.5 nautical miles) though usually at *c.* 32,000–42,000 ft. The Concorde flew at 60,000 ft (19 km/12 nautical miles). Spy planes can reach 100,000 ft (30 km/18.5 nautical miles).

69 Cooper at first suggested 300 miles as the upper limit of sovereignty; see his 'Legal Problems of Upper Space' 85–93; Cooper, *Explorations, supra* n. 11, 269–297. He later but reduced that to 20–25 miles with an additional 50 miles in the light of later, better scientific knowledge; see 'The Boundary Between Territorial Airspace and International Outer Space', Cooper, *Explorations, supra* n. 11, 229–304. Cf. his 'The Upper Airspace Boundary Question' (1963) 6 *Proc. IISL* 1–8, and 'Passage of Spacecraft through the Airspace', which curiously in HeinonLine is paged as (1963) 6 *Proc. IISL* 1–13. All this is analogous to early Fauchille ideas as to state jurisdiction in air space. In 1902, Fauchille was suggesting a territorial limit of 500 metres – which curiously may relate to the height of the Eiffel Tower (300 metres – the later communication masts add 24 metres): see *supra* n. 19.

70 A.G. Haley, *supra* n. 48, 77–79, 96–107; see also his 'Space Age Presents Immediate Legal Problems' (1958) 1 *Proc IISL* 5–27. But see T. Gangale, 'The Non Karman Line: An Urban Legend of the Space Age' (2017) 41 *J. Sp. L.* 151–178.

71 Founded in 1905, the Fédération Aéronautique Internationale is based in Paris; see www.fai.org/.

72 Some orbits are highly elliptical, with very low perigees and very high apogees. Such orbits can remain over areas of the Earth without being geostationary. LEOs are typically between some 400 and 1600 nautical miles (740–3000 km).

73 L. Perek, *supra* n. 48; cf. his 'Remarks on Scientific Criteria for the Definition of Outer Space' (1971) 19 *Proc. IISL* 191. Writing in 1977, Perek noted that in principle, a satellite could be constructed of sufficient durability to go below 60 miles and survive in orbit, but its mass-to-weight ratio would not be cost-effective and little advantage would be gained by a lower altitude. Nonetheless, it is believed that some military surveillance satellites can go lower than 60 miles and be boosted back to a safe altitude – cf. the L-Sat used during the 1981 Falklands War.

74 Report of the Fiftieth Conference of the International Law Association, Buenos Aires, 1968 (London, 1969) xxii and 157 ff, drawing on the prohibition in OST Art. IV of placing nuclear weapons 'in orbit around the earth'. The proposal was made specifically without prejudice to an even lower perigee being agreed on at a

The remaining suggestion for a space/air boundary defined in physical terms is that an arbitrary altitude should be selected. Thus in 1975, Italy proposed a boundary at 90 km/48 nautical miles based on the reasoning that it lay between the 60 km/32 nautical mile upper limit of any aeroplane flight and 120 km/65 nautical miles, then thought to be the lowest possible orbit. In 1976, and for similar reasons, Belgium proposed an arbitrary 100 km/55 nautical miles.[75] In 1979, the then-USSR proposed that the boundary between outer space and air space should be fixed 'by agreement among States at an altitude not exceeding 110 km [60 nautical miles] above sea level'; this to be confirmed by an appropriate treaty.[76] Such proposals make a sense given that a fixed altitude is clear and is not dependent on variable physical features such as atmospheric density or vehicle technology.[77]

Many of the physical elements impleaded by commentators point to an altitude of 100/110 km (55/60 nautical miles) as being a suitable frontier. Further, whether a space object was at such an altitude could readily and conclusively be established by radar. There are more than straws in the wind.

It is intriguing to find that when looking at potential radio requirements of future sub-orbital flight, the ITU World Radio Conference of 2015 (WRC-15) referred to 100 km, 'considering' that 'the boundary between the Earth's atmosphere and space is usually assumed to be 100 km above the Earth's surface.'[78] 'Usually assumed' is interesting phraseology. Again, an EU Regulation on the export of dual-use materials exempts from its application items launched to heights of 100 km and over.[79] Finally, in its model, the International Law Association left open the possibility that a national law could prescribe that activities at an altitude of 100 km be considered space activities.[80]

As yet, few formal limits are set in national legislation.[81] The UK Space Industry Act 2018 ss. 2(6), 61(2) and Schedules sets exceeding the stratosphere as requiring a launch licence, but without defining it spatially. In 2002, Australia modified its definitions of 'launch' and 'space object' in its Space Activities Act, 1998. A launch licence is now required only if the vehicle or payload is intended to reach more than 100 km above sea level.[82] In May 2016, Denmark enacted its own space legislation. It also defines 'outer

---

later date. Cf. Bin Cheng, 'International Responsibility and Liability for Launch Activities' (1995) 20 *Air Sp. L.* 297–320, Cheng, 598–619.

75 Italy – A/AC.105/PV.155, 11–12; Belgium – A/AC.105/C.1.76, 13, both quoted by G. Zhukov and Y. Kolosov (B. Belitzky trans.), *International Space Law* (New York: Praeger, 1984) 164.

76 USSR–COPUOS Working Paper, 'Approach to the Delimitation of Airspace and Outer Space', A/AC/105/C.2/L.121 (1979), Annex IV to A/AC.105/240; cf. its later paper A/AC/105/C.2/L.139, 4 April 1983. Zhukov and Kolosov, *supra* n. 75, 160–162. See also Kopal, *supra* n. 46, at 173.

77 Goodman, *supra* n. 48, at 94–95 and 112 endorsed 400,000 feet (c. 122 km) as a suitable height. This is the approximate re-entry level of manned space missions.

78 Cf. ITU Res. 772 (WRC–2019) *recognising*. WRC 2023 will further consider 'Stations on board sub-orbital vehicles'.

79 EU, Council Regulation 1334/2000, O.J. (L. 159) Annex.

80 International Law Association, 'Draft Model Law for National Space Legislation and Explanatory Notes' (2012) 75 *Int. L. Ass'n Rep*, 307–314 at 308.

81 The South African Space Affairs Act 1993, s.1 skates around this question by defining outer space as being above 'a height at which it is in practice possible to operate an object in orbit around the earth'. Many would think 100 km a neater phrasing.

82 (Australia) Space Activities Act 1998, Sec. 8 'Definitions' – 'launch' as amended by the Space Activities Amendment Act 2002. See also COPUOS Doc. 'National Legislation and Practice Relating to the Definition of Outer Space', A/AC.105/865/Add.1, 20 March 2006.

space' as being located more than 100 km above sea level.[83] The United Arab Emirates controls launching to or through an Identified Area defined as an 'area eighty kilometres or more above the average level of the sea level'.[84] Such moves may be symptomatic, and, while themselves not definitive of 'outer space', when taken along with those of the ITU and EU,[85] are perhaps indicators of a future general acceptance in practice of an agreed frontier. An agglomeration of unilateral definitions of the air/space boundary in national legislation and other regulation would, if reasonably uniform, eventually crystallise the law.[86]

The Functional Approach

The functional approach to an upper limit to the sovereign jurisdiction of a state is different from the spatialist. The 'functionalist' is less concerned with physical factors but stresses the purpose for which an instrumentality exists and for which it is being employed at the relevant time. The initial suggestions of a number of commentators[87] remain potent.[88]

The point is that there are two legal regimes with relevance for objects in transit above the surface of the Earth, air law and space law. A distinction can be made between them in that air law should apply to aviation and space law to activities directed towards the use of space. The difference between them would depend on the intention behind the activity involved. Thus, as we noted in describing their definitions of 'space station' and 'space craft', ITU RR1.64 and RR 1.178 include as one criterion 'intended to go beyond'.[89] If intention is a crucial determinant, space law would apply to a space launch which is

---

83 Vedtaget af Folketinget ved 3. behandling den 3. maj 2016: Forslag til Lov om aktiviteter i det ydre rum, [Law on the Activities in the Outer Space], s. 4.4. The Law is at www.ft.dk/RIpdf/samling/20151/lovforslag/L128/20151_L128_som_vedtaget.pdf

84 UAE Federal Law No. 12 of 2019 on the Regulation of the Space Sector: https://space.gov.ae/Documents/PublicationPDFFiles/SpaceSectorFederalLaw_EN.pdf.

85 For the ITU and EU, see *supra* nn. 78 and 79.

86 Regrettably, most states do not delimit air space or outer space. See A/AC.105/865 and Additions. We note that A/AC.105/865 Add. 27 of 21 February 2022 reports that Armenia now defines the outer space boundary at 100 km, and for Indonesia, space begins at approximately 100–110 km.

87 The first suggestion of the functional approach seems to be M. McDougal and L. Lipson, 'Perspectives for a Law of Outer Space' (1958) 52 AJIL 407–431 (cf. McDougal et al., *supra* n. 48, 352–355). See also Leopold and Scafuri, *supra* n. 49; R. Quadri, 'Droit international cosmique' 98 *Hague Recueil* 1959-III, 505–597; C. Chaumont, 'Les perspectives que doit adopter le droit de l'éspace' (1960) 7 *Rev. de droit cont.* 5; Cf. J.G. Sauveplanne, 'Freedom and Sovereignty in Air and Outer Space' (1965) 12 *Neth. Int. L. Rev.* 228–250 at 239ff; D. Göedhuis, 'The Question of Freedom of Innocent Passage of Space Vehicles of One State through the Space above the Territory of another State which is not Outer Space' (1959) 2 *Proc. IISL* 42–43 and 'The Influence of the Conquest of Outer Space on National Sovereignty: Some Observations' (1978) 6 *J. Sp. Law* 37–46; M.W. Mouton (G.M. Wilner, ed.) 'The Impact of Science on International Law' 119 *Hague Recueil* 1966-III, 183–257 at 201–2; B. Cheng, 'The Legal Regime of Airspace and Outer Space: The Boundary Problem. Functionalism *versus* Spatialism: The Major Premises' (1982) 19 *Ann. Chinese Soc Int. L.* 1–39, Cheng 441–456.

88 G. Gal, 'Space Treaty and Space Technology: Questions of Interpretation' (1972) 15 *Proc. IISL* 105, his *Space Law* (Leiden: Sijthoff, 1969) 105ff. and his 'Thirty Years of Functionalism' (1997) 40 *Proc. IISL* 125. Cf. para 86 of the 2015 Report of the COPUOS Legal Subcommittee, A/AC.105/1090. See also the views of states and ICAO on delimitation etc in A/AC.105/1112 and its Adds, recently Add 9, 2021.

89 These definitions have been in the Radio Regulations since 1959. On the RRs, see Chapter 8.

aborted without reaching orbit because it is a space activity, but air law was applied to the carriage of a space shuttle by a Boeing 747.[90] Of course, silly objections can be made; is the construction of a satellite not space-related and hence by this theory subject to 'space law'? Common sense can deal with such quibbles. However, more serious objections lie to hand.

First, there may be ambiguity and even dispute between states as to the classification of a particular activity. Second, it is not sensible entirely to omit the location of an activity from consideration and fix only on its intention. Given that there is international air law, some role must be left for the three-dimensional aspect of a space activity.[91] Third, we must have a solution to the boundary question that will survive future developments. Were a 'functional' classification to be determinative of the application of air or space law, which law would apply to the space plane?[92] It might, of course, be possible to agree different heights for different purposes, including for the application of particular treaties,[93] but that would be undesirably complex and difficult to apply.

A Boundary

If a boundary is to be agreed on, it would seem best to adopt an arbitrary height that does not seriously depart from physical possibilities. The lowest practicable perigee for orbital satellites appears to be approximately 100 km (62 miles).[94] That may vary a little depending on the speed of the satellite and the actual density of the atmosphere at the time. Notwithstanding such variations, settling on such a figure would remove the underlying question for the OST and other space treaties and agreements. If outer space is free for all to use (OST Art. I), it is indeed desirable to know where that arena is.[95]

Similarly, it is necessary to know where space 'is' if we are intelligently to regulate weapons or activities that act ground to space, space to ground, air to space, space to air and space to space. A boundary is also already assumed to exist in one space treaty. The distinction made in the Liability Convention between absolute liability for damage to the surface of the Earth or to aircraft in flight (Art. II) and fault-based liability for damage elsewhere (Art. III) implies a physical boundary. Finally, as we have also noted, national legislatures and international organisations seem increasingly to use 100 km as demarcating outer space, albeit informally.

---

90 When the Shuttle landed elsewhere than back at Cape Canaveral it was returned on a modified Boeing 747.

91 High-altitude platforms operate above the height normal aviation does.

92 The question is old: G.P. Sloup, 'The NASA Space Shuttle and Other Aerospace Vehicles: A Primer for Lawyers on Legal Characterisation' (1978) 8 *Cal. West Int. L.J.* 403–53; T.L. Masson-Zwaan, 'The Aerospace Plane; An Object at the Cross-roads of Air and Space Law', in T.L. Masson-Zwaan and P.M.J. Mendes de Leon, eds., *Air and Space Law: De Lege Ferenda – Essays in Honour of Henri A. Wassenbergh* (Dordrecht: Nijhoff, 1992) 247–61; Hobe and Cloppenburg, *supra* n. 67; Nase and Langston, both *infra* n. 100. Cf. whether a non-crew-member passenger in a spacecraft is an astronaut, Chapter 5, c. n. 5.

93 Voûte, *supra* n. 48, 22–23 and 34–35. Treaties relating to military uses of technology might adopt divergent altitudes as their zone of application. See Chapter 16.

94 See proposals outlined *supra* following n. 74, and Perek *supra* nn. 2, 48 and 73.

95 Cf. *supra* nn. 46 and 48 and text following n. 74

Transit

Solving one fundamental problem by adopting a 'physical' space/air boundary would raise another.[96] It is all very well to say that anything below a certain altitude above a state traverses the air space of that state, but so what? Space objects in low Earth orbit (LEO) travel in excess of 7.5 km/5 nautical miles a second. That is too fast for states other than those with extensive territories effectively to manifest sovereignty. However, the real problem comes not with the space object in orbit but with its entry to the lower atmospheric regions, where it might interact, not to say interfere, with terrestrial aviation. Assuming we are not discussing an occurrence that inflicts damage,[97] there is the problem of transit in launch or re-entry.[98]

If there is a limit to vertical state sovereignty, the possibility exists that on launch or re-entry, a spacecraft might enter the air space of another state. At present, most launchings are from locations such that 'space' (wherever that is) is reached either before the territory of the launcher state is left or the launch goes out over the high seas. This will not remain the position.[99] Again the re-entry of a satellite, and more importantly a manned spacecraft, may mean traversing a state other than a launcher state at a suborbital altitude. If only for safety reasons an accommodation between the subjacent state and the state having jurisdiction over the space object would be needed in matters of air traffic control.[100] The point was early recognised in proposals as to the demarcation of space and air space. Paragraph 2 of the David Davies Memorial Institute Draft Code of 1962 provided that

> [No] spacecraft launched from the territory of any State may at any stage of its flight enter the air space of another State without the consent of that State; provided that such consent shall not be withheld if prior notice has been given to that State of the intended flight and it has been shown to its satisfaction that the flight is solely for scientific and peaceful purposes and shall be so controlled as to obviate the danger to aircraft.[101]

A USSR proposal of 1979 also suggested that, notwithstanding an arbitrary boundary set at an upper limit of 100–110 km/60–62 miles, a space object should retain the right to over-fly the territory of other states to reach orbit or return to Earth.[102] In such a case, in

---

96 Benkö and Plescher, *supra* n. 1.
97 This point assumes the transit or entry to air space is controlled. Other circumstances might obtain. See *infra* as to space traffic management and Chapter 4 Liability.
98 Transit has a number of applications in international law. See E. Lauterpacht, 'Freedom of Transit in International Law' (1958–9) 44 *Trans. Grot. Soc.* 313–356.
99 Singapore and the United Arab Emirates are among those with plans to construct a spaceport. Most launches from Baikonur in Kazakhstan travel over Russia and are the subject of agreement between these states. See M. Bjornerud, 'Baikonur Continues: The New Lease Agreement between Russia and Kazakhstan' (2004) 30 *J. Sp. L.* 13–36 (with translation of the Lease 26–36).
100 V. Nase, 'Delimitation and the Suborbital Passenger: Time to End Prevarication' (2012) 77 *J. Air L. & Comm.* 747–767; S.M. Langston, 'Suborbital Flights: A Comparative Analysis of National and International Law' (2011) 37 *J. Sp. L.* 299–392.
101 David Davies Memorial Institute, 'Draft Code of Rules on the Exploration and Uses of Outer Space' (1963) 29 *J. Air L. & Comm.* 141–150.
102 See nn. 76 and 87. See also G. Zhukov and Y. Kolosov (trans. B. Belitzky), *International Space Law* (New York: Praeger, 1984) 160–171; D. Göedhuis, 'Reflections on the Evolution of Space Law' (1966) 13 *Neth. Int. L. Rev.* 109–149 at 122–142.

the lower parts of its trajectory, a spacecraft or other space object should be made subject to relevant air traffic control.[103] In the meantime, we note that domestic Russian legislation itself specifically provides for such matters.[104]

Space Traffic Management

Perhaps the whole concept of air space is now unhelpful. Sovereignty in the air space was really a functional rather than a territorial concept, a state controlling what is done in the air space rather than being 'sovereign' in the manner it is sovereign over its physical territory.[105] Air traffic control, air safety, pollution, etc. are what concern a state, not 'ownership'. Were we to get away from concepts of property in relation to sovereignty, concentrate more on the notion of jurisdiction for various purposes and think of the boundary question in those terms, the regime of aviation and of space could be assimilated, with air traffic regulation becoming applicable when a spacecraft is proceeding within the same spatial coordinates as 'normal' aircraft.[106] M.W. Mouton observed in 1966,

> The opening up of the third dimension for human activities, and in particular the first step in outer space, may make a revision of existing notions of law necessary. We may have to give up playing with analogies, such as the regimes of the high seas, territorial seas and contiguous zones, because the third dimension has its own and very different characteristics.[107]

Proposals have emerged for a unified system of control of aviation and space.[108] The fusion of terrestrial air traffic and space launch and re-entry traffic control has a certain attraction

---

103 A.D. Terekhov, 'Passage of Space Objects through Foreign Airspace: International Custom?' (1997) 25 *J. Sp. Law* 1–16 distinguishes re-entrant satellites which fall into air space by natural forces from operational space objects deliberately entering the air space of a state during take-off or landing. As to these last, he considers that customary law has not yet emerged. Cf. his 'Passage of Space Objects through Foreign Airspace' (1989) 32 *Proc. IISL* 50–55. See also J. Malenovský, 'To the Problem of the Right of Free Passage through the Airspace of Other States during the Post-Takeoff and Return Phases of Space Flight' (1982) 25 *Proc. IISL* 131–134; P.L. Meredith, 'The Legality of Launch Vehicle Passage through Foreign Airspace' (1985) 54 *Nordisk Tidsskrift Int. Ret.* 19–32; Hobe and Cloppenburg, *supra* n. 67.

104 'The space object of a foreign state can execute a single innocent flight through the air space of the Russian Federation with the purpose of inserting such an object into an orbit around the Earth or further in outer space, as well as with the purpose to return it to the Earth under the condition of advance notice of appropriate services of the Russian Federation about time, place, trajectory and other conditions of such flight', Art. 19.4, Russian Federation Law on Space Activity (translated) in *Project 2001: Workshop on Legal Framework for Privatising Space Activities*, Vienna, 1999 (Cologne: Inst. of Air and Space Law, 2000) 249–260 and *Project 2001 Workshop on Legal Framework for Commercial Launch and Associated Services*, Bremen, 2000 (Cologne: Inst. of Air and Space Law, 2001) 313–324.

105 Cf. Beresford, *supra* n. 55.

106 Cf. *supra* n. 87.

107 Mouton, *supra* n. 87 at 203. Cf. Sauvenplanne, *supra* n. 87; R. Cargill Hall, 'Comments on Traffic Control of Space Vehicles' (1965) 31 *J. Air L. & Comm.* 327–342; P.B. Larsen, Larsen, Minimum International Norms for Managing Space Traffic, Space Debris, and Near Earth Object Impacts (2018) 83 *J. Air L. & Comm.* 739–785; 'Space Traffic Management Standards' (2018) 83 *J. Air L. & Comm.* 359–390; and 'Outer Space Traffic Management, Space Situational Awareness Requires Transparency' (2008) 51 *Proc. IISL* 338–350.

108 R.S. Jakhu et al., *The Need for an Integrated Regulatory Regime for Aviation and Space* (Vienna: Springer, 2011); P.P. Fitzgerald, 'Inner Space: ICAO's New Frontier' (2014) 79 *J. Air L. Com.* 3–34; C.B. Halstead,

and could well be combined with a more general system of space traffic management. However, rather than seeking such a fusion with the current ICAO arrangements, a new Convention dedicated to such matters might well be preferable.[109] We discuss this possibility further in Chapter 9.

Orbits

Space law has to do with the use of space, most of which involves satellites in orbit, but what does 'orbit' mean?

When a satellite is in orbit, it is in motion around the centre of the earth, the earth itself rotating below it. Orbits are classified as LEO (c. 100–500 km/66–310 miles) taking some ninety+ minutes for each orbit, medium Earth orbit (MEO) (or intermediate circular orbit (ICO)) (c. 2000–35,000 km/1240–21,750 miles) taking two to twelve hours to complete an orbit and the geosynchronous or geostationary orbits (GSO) (c. 35,786 km/22,236 miles above the equator).

LEOs vary from the equatorial plane to polar orbits. They are roughly circular, their perigee and apogee (low and high points) being comparable. LEOs lie below the Van Allen radiation belts and hence are to a degree protected from solar radiation.[110] Satellites in LEO are used for sensing and for communications systems that are now increasingly configured in satellite constellations.[111]

MEO or ICO lies between 2000 and 35,000 km (1240–21,750 miles). Satellites in MEO take anything from two to twelve hours to complete an orbit. MEOs are used mainly

---

'Prometheus Unbound – Proposal for a New Legal Paradigm for Air Law and Space Law: Orbit Law' (2010) 36 *J. Sp. L.* 143–206; P.B. Larsen, 'Space Traffic Management – the Bin Cheng Model' (2020) 56 *J. Sp. L.* 519–521.
   Suborbital flight may involve both space and air space. Cf. ICAO Working Paper, C-WP/12436, 'Concept of Suborbital Flight', COPUOS, A/AC.105/C.2/2010/CRP.9: www.unoosa.org/pdf/limited/c2/AC105_C2_2010_CRP09E.pdf. See ICAO Legal Committee 36th Sess., Dec. 2015, 'Commercial Space Flights', LC/36-WP/3-2: www.icao.int/Meetings/LC36/Working%20Papers/LC%2036%20-%20WP%203-2.en.pdf. Cf. T. Masson-Zwaan, 'Private Law Aspects of Suborbital Flights: Second=and Third-Party Liability and Insurance' (2022) 87 *J. Air Law & Comm.* 423–443; V. Nase, 'Delimitation and the Suborbital Passenger: Time to End Prevarication' (2012) 77 *J. Air L. Com.* 747–767; R. Jakhu and R. Battacharya, 'Legal Aspects of Space Tourism' (2002) 45 *Proc. IISL* 112–131; R. Abeyratne, 'Space Tourism – Parallel Synergies Between Air and Space Law' (2004) 53 ZLW 184–202; P.B. Larsen, 'Outer Space Traffic Safety Standards' Proc. Sixth IAASS Conference – Safety is Not an Option, Montreal, Canada 21–23 May 2013 (ESA SP-715, Sept. 2013); Hobe and Cloppenburg, *supra* n. 67.
109 R. Abeyratne, 'Bringing a Commercial Space Transport Regulatory Regime under ICAO – is it Feasible?' (2013) 62 ZLW 387–397.
110 The ISS is in LEO. The average working life of an ordinary LEO satellite is five years. When it takes effect in 2024, the US FCC Second Report and Order (IB Docket Nos. 22–271 and 18–313) 'In the Matter of Space Innovation; Mitigation of Orbital Debris in the New Space Age', adopted 6 October 2022, will *require* the deorbiting of LEO satellites at or below 2000 km by no later than five years from the end of mission. The Order does not apply to satellites already in orbit. The previous Order *recommended* deorbiting within 25 years. M.B. Runnels, 'On Launching Environmental Law into Orbit in the Age of Satellite Constellations' (2023) 88 *J. Air L. & Comm.* 181–207.
111 The Iridium constellation has sixty-six satellites, with additional back-up spares already in orbit (www.iridium.com). Other LEO communications providers are Orbcomm, a twenty-nine-satellite constellation (www.orbcomm.com/), and Globalstar, a forty-satellite system (www.globalstar.com/). See Chapter 10, *c.* n. 206.

by global positioning satellite configurations, including the US GPS system,[112] though they are also used for some communications satellites.[113]

A 'parking orbit' or 'transfer orbit' may be a LEO or a MEO and is used temporarily after launch before a satellite or space probe is put on its final trajectory. A speciality of these orbits is the geostationary transfer orbit, an elliptical orbit with a LEO perigee and GSO apogee. Its name indicates its function. A 'graveyard' 'disposal' or 'junkyard' orbit is used for satellites which it would be too expensive or difficult to deorbit to Earth at the end of their useful life.[114] As noted in Chapter 9, defunct satellites with radioactive power sources on board are to be placed in a 'sufficiently high' orbit, normally beyond the GSO.[115] The ITU Radiocommunication Sector Recommendation S.1003–2 (12/10) on 'Environmental Protection of the Geostationary-satellite Orbit' requires that states ensure that at the end of their useful lifetime geostationary satellites be transferred to a 'supersynchronous graveyard orbit' that does not intersect with the GSO.[116] As the name implies, in GSO, a satellite remains each day in the same position relative to a point on Earth. Of these the best-known is an eastward circular orbit some 35,786 km/22,236 miles above the equator, which we discuss later.[117] It is largely used by communications, remote-sensing (mainly meteorological) and direct broadcasting satellites.[118]

In geosynchronous Earth orbit (GEO), a satellite keeps pace with the sidereal motion of the earth. A subset of the GEO is the highly elliptical earth orbit (HEO), which has a wide variation between apogee and perigee.[119] In apogee, satellites in HEOs can remain visible from a point on Earth for up to twelve hours and may be geosynchronous without being geostationary. Such orbital configurations are used *inter alia* by communication satellites (e.g. the Russian Moliyna series in the INTERSPUTNIK system). Satellites in GEO or HEO are geosynchronous without necessarily being geostationary – that is, their orbits match Earth's sidereal rotation with the effect that they return to the same place in the sky at the same time each day.[120]

Access to orbits used to not be a matter of contention because space was thought to be 'so large'. However, this is changing. Orbital positions that remain 'constant' with respect to Earth are of greater interest than others. Because GSO positions remain constant with respect to the surface of the earth, they are attractive for both scientific and commercial purposes. For science, several of the Lagrange points we will shortly come to

---

112 For the GPS system, see www.gps.gov/systems/gps/space/ and *infra* Chapter 11.

113 A satellite in a suitable MEO can provide communications facilities for the north and south polar areas as can a LEO configuration. A location in the GSO will not.

114 Cf. NASA Technical Standard, NASA-STD-8719.14C, 'Process for Limiting Orbital Debris' (2021): www.nasa.gov/sites/default/files/atoms/files/process_for_limiting_orbital_debris.pdf. Sections 4.6 ff deal with various methods of post-mission disposal. See also our discussion of small satellites *infra* Chapter 9.

115 Recommendation S.1003–2 (12/2010), 'Environmental Protection of the geostationary-satellite orbit': www.itu.int/dms_pubrec/itu-r/rec/s/R-REC-S.1003-2-201012-I!!PDF-E.pdf. This Recommendation was first adopted in 1993 as ITU-R S.1003 (04/93). See Chapter 9 c. n 117.

116 See Chapter 4, at *c*. n. 74.

117 See *infra* n. 123.

118 See Chapters 7 and 9. The GSO is also used for communications intercept monitoring satellites, e.g. the UK Skynet facility.

119 The apogee is the high point and the perigee the low point in the orbit. In its apogee phase, a satellite in HEO remains visible from a point on Earth for up to twelve hours.

120 ITU RR 1.188 '*geosynchronous satellite:* An Earth *satellite* whose period of revolution is equal to the period of rotation of the Earth about its axis'. Cf. 'Interputnik' in Chapter 10 and *infra* Chapter 11.

are important. Questions of access to Lagrange points or GSO slots will emerge as these become congested.

GSO, MEO and LEO, as well as orbits well out into inter-planetary space, are available on a first-come, first-served basis. The only control currently existing is exercised through the ITU procedures outlined below and in Chapter 8. In the future, proposals as to space traffic management should be implemented.[121] Some orbits are becoming congested, and the threat of the proliferation of debris from defunct satellites and other sources is real.[122]

The Geostationary Orbit

The GSO is a circular torus at c. 35,786 km/22,236 miles in equatorial plane.[123] While the GSO toroid is a variety of the geosynchronous orbit, it is not to be confused with that configuration.[124] Within the GSO, a satellite in eastward orbit remains apparently stationary relative to points on the surface of Earth, although for technical reasons, the orbital position will require occasional minor correction.[125]

First identified by Herman Potočnik (1892–1928),[126] the GSO was suggested by Arthur C. Clarke in 1945 as a suitable location for a telecommunications satellite system, and much modern international telecommunication and direct broadcasting remain dependent on satellites in GSO.[127] Satellites so located are also engaged in Earth observation, notably meteorology, and, it is understood, electronic and other surveillance.[128] The GSO is a very suitable satellite location for many purposes. However, as the earth is an oblate spheroid, not a sphere, signals from the GSO cannot be received north and south of 82°. Further, because the inhabitable parts of the Earth are not distributed evenly around the globe, positions in certain sections of the GSO are in high demand.[129] Until recently, communication systems using LEO satellites required ground stations to track individual satellites as they passed. Uninterrupted service required tracking accuracy maintained by at

---

121 See Chapter 9 Space Traffic Management at *c.* n. 97.

122 See Chapter 9 Space Debris at *c.* n. 99.

123 ITU RR 1.189: '*geostationary satellite*: A *geosynchronous satellite* whose circular and direct *orbit* lies in the plane of the Earth's equator, and which thus remains fixed relative to the Earth; by extension, a *geosynchronous satellite* which remains approximately fixed relative to the Earth'. See also ITU Report 'on the use of the geostationary orbit (GSO) and other orbits' A/AC.105/C.1/2022/CRP.18.

124 See *supra* at n. 119.

125 GSO satellites that run out of propellant before being relocated to a graveyard orbit tend to drift to positions 60°E or 60°W, the Lagrange positions on the GSO. Cf. R. Jehn and C. Hernandez, 'International Practices to Protect the Geostationary Ring' (2001) 1 *Space Debris*, 221–233; C. Hernandez and R. Jehn, 'Classification of Geostationary Objects' (2001) 1 *Space Debris*, 235–337; L. Perek, 'Space Debris at the United Nations' (2002) 2 *Space Debris*, 123–136.

126 Writing under the pseudonym 'Hermann Noordung', in 1928, Herman Potočnik published *The Problem of Space Travel – The Rocket Motor* (Berlin: Schmidt & Co., 1928), which envisaged a geostationary orbital space station from which Earth might be observed for civil and military purposes. He did not suggest its use for telecommunications. A version is at www.hq.nasa.gov/office/pao/History/SP-4026/contents.html. K. Grunfeld and S. Hobe, 'Hermann Potočnik Noordung – A Great Pioneer of Space Law' (2022) 71 ZLW 401–416.

127 A.C. Clarke, 'Extra-terrestrial Relays: Can Rocket Stations Give World-Wide Radio Coverage?' *Wireless World* (October 1945), 303–308. As to telecommunications from GSO see Chapter 10.

128 See Chapter 12 World Meteorological Organisation and EUMETSAT.

129 A. Kogan et al. 'Stagnating Orbits and Constellations for Communications Applications' (2004) 54 *Acta Astronautica* 281–294.

least two antennae dishes to catch each satellite in the configuration as it rose, with perhaps a third antenna to provide backup.

A geostationary system is much simpler since the terrestrial transmitting/receiving antenna points to a fixed location on the GSO.[130] It also avoids the problem of signal frequency variation caused by a LEO satellite approaching and then receding from the ground station.[131] However, the point may be blunted for modern constellations in LEO and wide-angle terrestrial receptors. These do not have quite the signal delay inherent in GSO systems.[132]

That particular arcs of the GSO are in demand has caused problems of access that were early recognised,[133] and over the years, many technical studies have investigated how satellites could be located closer to each other.[134] Were all satellites uniform in their design and purpose, minimum spacing could be readily achieved to ensure that they did not mutually degrade their signals and services. However, the matter is made difficult because satellite systems vary considerably in their technical characteristics. Polarisation of signals and directional antenna can help, but safe GSO satellite spacing is a complex question calculated for each system, and today has to be taken into account and invoked in both the initial location and any subsequent relocation of satellites.[135]

Lagrange Points

There are five astronomic Lagrange points. Joseph-Louis Lagrange, for whom they are named, was a French mathematician who, working on the 'three body problem' in 1772, discovered that the position of a third body of negligible mass will remain relatively static

---

130 See Chapter 10 'Direct Broadcasting'. Cf. A. Chayes and L. Chazen, 'Policy Problems in Direct Broadcasting from Satellites' (1970) 5 *Stan. J. Int. Stud.* 4–20; B.A. Hurwitz, 'The Labyrinth of International Telecommunications Law: Direct Broadcast Satellites' (1988) 35 *Neth. Int. L. Rev.* 145–180; Zhukov, *supra* n. 102, 127–136; A.S. Piradov, *International Space Law* (Moscow: Progress, 1976) 182–96. Cf. *In the Matter of Inquiry into the Development of Regulatory Policy in Regard to Direct Broadcast Satellites for the Period Following the 1983 Regional Administrative Radio Conference* (1982) 90 FCC 2d 676 and later developments. See also Georgetown Space Law Group, 'DBS under FCC and International Regulation' (1984) 37 *Vand. L. Rev.* 67–144; and P.B. Larsen et al. 'Direct Broadcast Satellites: National and International Regulation' (2004) 8 *Modern Legal Systems Cyclopedia*.

131 Cf. the sound of an approaching and then receding siren.

132 See *infra*, Constellations'.

133 M. Meija-Kaiser, *The Geostationary Ring* (Leiden: Brill, 2020); G.C.M. Reijnen and W. de Graaf, *The Pollution of Outer Space in Particular of the Geostationary Orbit* (Dordrecht: Nijhoff, 1989). K.G. Gibbons, 'Orbital Saturation: The Necessity for International Regulation of Geosynchronous Orbits' (1979) 9 *Cal. W. Int. L.J.* 139–156; C.R. Stevens, 'The Geostationary Orbit: The Need for an Integrated Policy' (1995) 23 *J. Sp. L.* 183–195; S. Cahill, 'Give Me My Space: Implications for Permitting National Appropriation of the Geostationary Orbit,' (2000) 19 *Wis. Int. L.J.* 231–248; J.C. Thompson, 'Space for Rent: The International Telecommunication Union, Space Law and Orbit/Spectrum Leasing' (1996) 62 *J. Air L. & Comm.* 279–311 [Lyall/Larsen 375–407].

134 Cf. COPUOS 'The Feasibility of Obtaining Closer Spacing of Satellites in the Geostationary Orbit', A/AC.105/340 (Rev. 1) 1985; (1985) 13 *J. Sp. L.* 76–101. Cf. P. Abdurrasyid, 'The Outer Space Treaty and the Geostationary Orbit' (1987) 12 AASL 131. The GSO remains on the COPUOS agenda: Report of the Committee on the Peaceful Uses of Outer Space, 2022, A/63/20, paras 179–180. See also the 2022 Report of the Legal Sub-Committee, A/AC.105/1258, paras 250–261 and the ITU Report, A/AC.105/C.1/2022/CRP.18.

135 Cf. ITU-R Recommendation S.1003–2 (12/2010), 'Environmental protection of the geostationary-satellite orbit', *supra* at n. 115.

relative to two other considerably larger bodies that themselves are in near-circular orbits. A number of Lagrange points in the solar system have been identified as various solar bodies are in appropriate mutual configuration. Sun–Earth Lagrange point L-1 lies between the earth and the sun and has been used by two scientific satellites, SOHO and ACE.[136] Sun–Earth Lagrange point L-2, one million miles beyond the earth and moon, is the location of various instruments including the James Webb Space Telescope launched in 2022 and ESA's Euclid launched in 2023.[137] L-2 has also been used as a staging point for explorations further out into the solar system. Lagrange point L-3, on the other side of the sun in the sun–Earth configuration, has no planned use at present. Sun–Earth Lagrange points L-4 and L-5 are 60° ahead and behind the earth in its orbit and are not at present of great interest. Points L-4 and L-5 in the moon–Earth configuration (sometimes known as the Trojan points) are 60° ahead and behind the moon in its orbit of the earth. Satellites located there, or in halo or Lissajous orbits round them, are relatively stable,[138] and could be of use either for scientific purposes or for Earth–moon telecommunications from parts of the moon not normally visible from the earth. Those Lagrange points that are practicably usable given present technology and in current plans are subject to the basic legal dogma of OST Art. II that outer space is not subject to national appropriation.[139] Since a satellite situated at any Lagrange point is useless without radio links, their use is dependent on ITU regulations and procedures, which we will outline later.[140]

Small Satellites and Large Constellations

Small satellites and large constellations are recent developments affecting the use of orbits. Small satellites can carry out many of the tasks performed by their expensive cousins, including remote sensing and tele-communication.[141] They are simple, specialised,

136 The NASA/ESA Solar and Heliospheric Observatory (SOHO) project has placed a sun observation satellite in halo orbit at sun–Earth L-1. (A halo orbit orbits the Li-1 point and requires occasional correction.) The NASA Advanced Composition Explorer (ACE) satellite is in a Lissajous orbit around the same point and is sampling the space environment around it. (A Lissajous orbit requires occasional correction but less than a halo orbit). See also the Stereo Mission: www.nasa.gov/mission_pages/stereo/main/index.html; and the Hinobe (Solar B) Missions: https://solarb.msfc.nasa.gov/. B.C. Bromley et al. have suggested that a cloud of lunar dust inserted into L-1 could help cool the Earth: 'Dust as a solar shield' PLOS Climate, February 2023: https://doi.org/10.1371/journal.pclm.0000133.

137 The Gaia Probe (three-dimensional star mapping) has been in Lissajous orbit at Moon–Earth L-2 since 2014. ESA's Euclid mission probe (dark energy and dark matter) was launched to L-2 in July 2023. Having been decommissioned, the no longer functional Wilkinson Microwave Anisotropy Probe (WMAP) (2001–2010) Planck Observatory (2009–2013) and the Herschel Space Observatory (2009–2013) remain there, presenting a problem for later use of the location.

138 'Relatively stable' – satellites in both locations require occasional correction through the use of on-board propellants. Eventually such will be exhausted, and the satellite will become uncontrollable. Obviously before that a satellite should be re-located to either a parking or a destruction orbit.

139 L.D. Roberts, 'The Law of the Commons: A Framework for the Efficient and Equitable Use of the Lagrange points' (1990) 6 *Conn. J. Int. L.* 151–172.

140 See also Chapter 8.

141 I. Marboe, ed. *Small Satellites: Regulatory Challenges and Changes* (Leiden: Brill, 2016); A. Froehlich, ed., *Legal Aspects Around Satellite Constellations* (Springer, 2021); I. Marboe and K. Traunmuller, 'Small Satellites and Small States: New Incentives for National Space Legislation' (2012) 38 *J. Sp. L.* 289–320; P.B. Larsen, 'Small Satellite Legal Problems' (2017) 82 *J. Air L. & Comm.* 275–310; 'Profit or Safety: Where

mass-produced, often active for only a short period and are disposable. They are cheap – usually using the same technology as smart-phones – making them suitable for scientific experiments of limited purpose and duration. Launch can be relatively inexpensive, using spare capacity on 'orthodox' launches obtained through brokers who agglomerate the needs of many separate projects.[142]

Small satellites come in a variety of forms.[143] Categories are mini-satellites (100–500 kg), micro-satellites (10–100 kg.), nano-satellites (1–10 kg.), pico-satellites (0.1–1 kg.) and femto-satellites (<0.1 kg).[144] The cubesat, a subcategory of the nano-satellite with a mass of up to 1.33 kg, is 10 cm. in all three dimensions.[145] Most cubesats are in LEO and have a very short life – only days in some cases – before re-entry and burn up.

Being space objects, small satellites fall within the scope of the normal requirements of the OST and other international space law. Perhaps in the future, ARRA and/or the Liability Convention may be activated through an occurrence involving one.[146] Licensing and supervision by an appropriate state,[147] and its compliance with ITU procedures, are

---

is Outer Space Headed?' [(2021) 86 *J. Air Law & Comm.* 531–584; C. Suwijak, and S. Li, 'An Overview of the Situation of Small Satellites According to the United Nations Space Treaties' (2022) 13 *Beijing Law Review*, 304–319. UN OOSA supervises the UN Basic Space Technology Initiative: www.unoosa.org/oosa/ourwork/psa/bsti/.

142 Cf. I. Baumann and O. Heinrich, 'Key Contractual Aspects in Hosted Payloads and Condominium Satellite Projects', in M. Hofmann and A. Loukakis eds., *Ownership of Satellites* (Baden-Baden: Nomos, 2017) 147–162; J.D. Rendleman, 'Brave New World of Hosted Payloads' (2013–4) 39 *J. Sp. L.* 129–180; M. Smith and S. Smith, 'Legal Issues Presented by Hosted Payloads' (2012) 55 *Proc. IISL* 495–508. See also *infra* n. 155.

143 For classification see ITU Radiocommunication Sector Report, 2014, ITU-R SA.2312–0, 'Characteristics, definitions and spectrum requirements of nanosatellites and picosatellites, as well as systems composed of such satellites': www.itu.int/pub/R-REP-SA.2312, or www.itu.int/dms_pub/itu-r/opb/rep/R-REP-SA.2312-2014-PDF-E.pdf. See also ITU Radiocommunication Sector Report, 2015, ITU – RSA2348–0, 'Current practice and procedures for notifying space networks currently applicable to nanosatellites and picosatellites': www.itu.int/en/ITU-R/space/Documents/R-REP-SA.2348-2015-PDF-E.pdf. Cf. NASA Technical Standards, *infra* n. 156, sec. 3.3.

144 ITU-R SA.2312–0, *supra* n. 143, Table 1. Mini-satellites use the GEO, MEO and LEO as well as HEO and have mission durations of five to ten years. The others use LEO or HEO and last from one to three years, except the femto variety, whose life is always less than twelve months. Many operate using technology akin to smart-phones.

145 The companion satellite monitoring the impact in the Double Asteroid Redirection Test (DART) (2022) was a cubesat, Italian-built and managed. See Chapter 9 n. 246.

146 All the states likely to launch small satellites are parties to ARRA and the Liability Convention. See Chapter 4.

147 In particular, remote-sensing satellites can require special licensing because of the military importance of the information being collected. See Chapter 12 Remote Sensing.

Alarmingly, the Dutch government was initially unwilling to require cubesats to be licensed, on the basis that lacking any propulsive or controlling element, a cubesat was inactive and hence not performing an activity in space. This has been corrected. The initial decision seems to an example of the occasional incomprehension of administrators and of others avoiding procedures they consider unnecessary. The 'activity' argument is spurious. It is as if a thrower has no responsibility for a dart once it has left the hand. See T.L. Masson-Zwaan, 'Registration of Small Satellites and the Case of the Netherlands', in Marboe, *supra* n. 141, 174–194 at 190–191, and in T.L. Masson-Swaan *Widening the Horizons of Outer Space Law* (Leiden: Leiden Law School, 2023) 179–197 at 194–195; N. Palkovitz and T. Masson-Zwaan, 'Operating under the Radar: Nano-Satellites, International Obligations and National Space Laws' (2012) 55 *Proc. IISL* 566–578; N. Palkovitz and T. Masson-Zwaan, 'Small but on the Radar: The Regulatory Evolution of Small Satellites in the Netherlands' (2015) 58 *Proc. IISL* 601–612.

important.[148] With the plethora of short-life small satellites, and communication services by way of constellations, ways will have to be sought to simplify and speed the administrative process. Certainly small satellites of long duration and higher orbits should be registered in accordance with the current rules including the required data. While it seems unnecessary to insist that each individual satellite go through a separate licensing process, the identification of particular satellites could be important, most obviously when damage has been caused.

ITU Considerations

Whatever their function, small satellites and constellations require being assigned particular radio frequencies and occupy locations in particular orbits.[149] As Art. 44.2 (196) of the ITU Constitution makes clear, frequencies and orbits are limited natural resources that are to be used rationally, efficiently and economically. As shown in Chapter 8, the ITU system seeks through various means to achieve that aim.

Article 5 of the Radio Regulations allocates specific spectrum bands to particular uses, and the procedures of the Radiocommunication Sector and the Master International Frequency Register (MIFR) provide a degree of security for the users of space. In addition, there are procedures for dealing with satellite networks. However, ITU procedures could be swamped by the numbers of notifications of assignment that may be imminent. Technically, the orbit and frequency assignment of every small satellite and every element of a constellation have to be separately dealt with. Potential interference with assignments already registered on the MIFR has to be checked, even where a notifying state has already achieved coordination with other states. How to cope has therefore been under active consideration for some years.[150]

Constellations

Constellations of small satellites providing broadband telecommunication services from low orbits are now with us. Requiring less signal strength, their nearness to receivers provides clear links, and successive over-lapping footprints avoid any need to track individual satellites. Enterprises such as Iridium and Space Exploration (SpaceX) have begun to launch constellations of satellites into lower orbits, and others are in the planning stage.[151] Constellations, presumably licensed by single states, could be registered both nationally and internationally in bulk with specific data being held separately.

---

148 When several satellites of different nationalities are together in a single launch, appropriate arrangements for their separate registration on different national registries and with UN OOSA will be needed unless states agree otherwise.

149 A. Matas et al., 'The ITU Radio Regulations Related to Small Satellites', in Marboe, *supra* n. 141, 236–264.

150 WRC Res. 32 (WRC–19) sets frequency assignment procedures for non-GSO networks and short-duration missions. See also RR Art. 9, sec. I.

151 Technically, the Iridium constellation of sixty-six satellites is not composed of small satellites. Each are 689 kg., above the definition of mini-satellite, *supra* n. 144. Nonetheless, it illustrates and is part of the 'constellation' problem. On Iridium, see Chapter 10 c. n. 262. The StarLink system is being deployed by Space-X. EUTELSAT and One-Web propose a mixed MEO/LEO constellation for 2028. Other commercial companies also have plans.

Debris and End-of-Mission Disposal

Multitudes of small satellites in LEO create a collision danger and risk space debris saturation triggering the Kessler syndrome.[152] Given their tininess, when inactive and probably uncontrollable, they could threaten other users of space. However, the problem of debris is not confined to the very small. Some small satellites, including those used in some constellations, could result in anything up to 500 kg. of errant metal.

When a small satellite has reached the end of its mission, the question of its disposal arises. On this, the Space Debris Mitigation Guidelines of 2007 are significant,[153] as are the international standards noted in Chapter 10.[154] Both the ESA and the US government presently require small satellites in LEO to make atmospheric re-entry by natural forces within twenty-five years after the completion of mission but no more than thirty years after launch, though the US FCC is changing its requirements.[155] For more detail as to possible implementation of regulation, the NASA technical standards on the limitation of orbital debris are persuasive.[156] These should be considered by other states when drafting their own regulations.[157]

In the NASA standards, much depends on where the satellite is situated at its end-of-mission, whether LEO, MEO, GSO or HEO. Complex requirements are set out for a variety of possibilities involving atmospheric re-entry, use of a storage orbit, or direct retrieval.[158] Atmospheric re-entry, of course, raises the possibility of damage falling within the parameters of the Liability Convention.[159] Whether that Convention could be applied were a collision to occur in space while a spent satellite is being moved to a storage orbit would, of course, depend upon proof of fault.

---

152   The Kessler Syndrome predicts a steady increase in debris as the cascade effect of collisions results in a closure of outer space. See Chapter 4, c. n. 173 ff, and Chapter 10 at n. 150. G. Karucalioglu, 'Impacts of New Satellite Launch Trends on Orbital Debris', *Space Safety Magazine*, June 2, 2016 (www.spacesafetymagazine. com/space-debris/impact-new-satellite-launch-trends-orbital-debris), estimates 'that from 2036 collisions [will] start to occur regularly', increasing space debris collisions and near-collisions. We note the 2021 exchange between China and the US arising from the potential collision of the Tiangong Space Station and a Starlink satellite: See A/AC.105/1262 and A/AC.105/1265.

153   See CoCoSL III, 625–629, with analysis 630–642. See also Chapter 9 c. n. 174.

154   Cf. International Standards ISO 24113:2011 (under review) on passage through LEO, and ISO 16164:2015 on post-mission disposal. See Chapter 9 c. n. 118.

155   The US FCC Second Report and Order (IB Docket Nos. 22–271 and 18–313) 'In the Matter of Space Innovation; Mitigation of Orbital Debris in the New Space Age', adopted 6 October 2022, will *require* the deorbiting of satellites from LEO (at or below 2000 km) by no later than five years from the end of mission. The previous order *recommended* deorbiting within twenty-five years. The new order will come into effect in 2024.

156   See NASA Technical Standard, NASA-STD-8719.14 as to the 'Process for Limiting Orbital Debris' (version of 2021): https://standards.nasa.gov/sites/default/files/standards/NASA/C/0/nasa-std-871914c.pdf, and the earlier Handbook: https://standards.nasa.gov/sites/default/files/standards/ NASA/Baseline/1/nasa-hdbk-871914_baseline_with_change_1.pdf. Cf. our discussion of debris in Chapter 10.

157   Cf. (UK) Ofcom, 'Procedures for the Management of Satellite Filings', March 2019, and 'Non-geostationary satellite systems: Licensing updates', and 'Annexes 1–6', and 'Non-geostationary satellite systems: Licensing Guidance' both December 2021.

158   NASA STD, *supra* n. 156, secs. 4.6–7. Atmospheric re-entry, whether caused by natural forces or triggered by deorbiting, is feasible for the lower orbits. See supra n. 155. In higher orbits a storage (or junkyard) orbit may be feasible. In the absence of the Shuttle, or similar vehicle, direct retrieval is not at present an option.

159   See Chapter 4.

Access to Orbit

Particularly in its second paragraph, OST Art. I provides for freedom of access to space, and we argued in Chapter 3 that that has become a principle of customary international law. In one sense, access to orbit is therefore available to any state that either possesses the appropriate technology or can afford to purchase a launch. The launch purchase option is, however, subject to the existing commitments and willingness of a launch provider and its licensing state.[160] In another sense, however, controls on access to space operate through the mechanisms and procedures of the ITU.[161] Without these, there is no point in launching a satellite.

When the use of space began, it was clear that the ITU had a major role to play in ensuring clear radio communication with and from a satellite. Well before any UN action, the 1959 ITU World Administrative Radio Conference (WARC-59) *inter alia* amended the ITU Radio Regulations to include definitions of an 'earth station', a 'space station', a 'space service' and an 'earth/space service'.[162] In 1963, an Extraordinary Administrative Radio Conference was devoted entirely to space matters.[163]

However, although the RRs were thereafter amended by successive radio conferences as to radio frequency allocations and associated procedures for space services, the ITU was not given formal jurisdiction in relation to the GSO and other orbits until the Minneapolis Plenipotentiary Conference of 1998.[164] Now, a state notifying the ITU Radiocommunication Bureau of a planned frequency assignment includes data as to the orbit the satellite is proposed to use.[165]

---

160 Cf. US National Space Policy of the United States, 2020: https://trumpwhitehouse.archives.gov/wp-content/uploads/2020/12/National-Space-Policy.pdf. Cf. also Secs 2 and 7 of 'US National Space Policy' (2006) (Bush): https://obamawhitehouse.archives.gov/sites/default/files/microsites/ostp/national-space-policy-2006.pdf, and contrast 'US National Space Policy 2010' (Obama): https://obamawhitehouse.archives.gov/sites/default/files/national_space_policy_6-28-10.pdf. See also Chapter 1, c. n. xxx103.

161 For the ITU and its procedures, see Chapter 8. Cf. J. Wilson, 'The International Telecommunication Union and the Geostationary Orbit' (1998) 23 AASL 241–270; A.M. Solana, 'The International Telecommunication Union and the Third World's Quest for Equitable Access to the Orbit/Spectrum Resource' (1984) 4 *Bost. Coll. Third World Rev.* 183–204. Cf. the 2008 problem encountered by Protostar-1 when it lost its initial sponsorship by Singapore and eventually was registered with the ITU via INTERSPUTNIK and Belarus. See ITU Circular Telegram CTITU 11S(SSD)O-2008003054 of 8 October 2008.

162 An earth station is located 'either on the Earth's surface or within the major portion of the Earth's atmosphere and intended for communication with one or more space stations; or with one or more stations of the same kind by means of one or more reflecting satellites or other objects in space' (RR 1.63). The contrast is with a terrestrial station, which is for terrestrial service (RR 1.62). The definitions of space station and earth/space service have now been clarified by a number of definitions of different satellite services incorporated into RR 1.19 ff on radio services (q.v.).

163 *Partial Revision of the Radio Regulations: Final Acts of the Extraordinary Administrative Radio Conference to Allocate Frequency Bands for Space Radio Purposes*, Geneva, 1963, 15 UST 887, TIAS 5603; (1964) 3 ILM 91–106.

164 ITU Constitution Art. 1.2.a and b (10–12), Art. 12.1.1 (78), Art. 44.2 (196). The ITU Convention Arts 11.2.a (151 and 12.2.4.a (177) set out duties under which the Radiocommunication Sector helps secure the equitable, effective and economical use of orbits.

165 The ITU has three sectors, radiocommunication, standardisation and development, each with a bureau and a director. For ITU structure and more detail, see Chapter 8.

Omitting the references to radio frequencies, Art. 44.2 (196) of the ITU Constitution states that

> Member States shall bear in mind that . . . any associated orbits, including the geostationary orbit, are limited natural resources and that they are to be used rationally, efficiently and economically, in conformity with the Radio Regulations, so that countries or groups of countries may have equitable access to those orbits . . . taking into account the special needs of the developing countries and the geographical situation of particular countries.

Recognition of orbits as a limited natural resource first came in Art. 33.2 of the 1973 ITU Malaga–Torremolinos Convention.[166] Previous conventions had called only for the rational use of the radio spectrum.[167] However, in 1973, only the geostationary orbit was specified. The extension to all orbits came twenty-five years later with the Minneapolis plenipotentiary in 1998. The effect is that an orbit/resource cannot become the permanent preserve of a single state or of the users it licences.[168]

The 'rational, efficient and economic' use of orbits called for in Art 44.2 (196) is required of all states. In broad, access to an orbit operates on the basis of first come, first served[169] and subject to the non-permanency referred to above.[170] There is the limited exception of direct-broadcast satellites provided for under the WARC-ORB 1985–87 Plan (as amended). However, the last phrase of Art. 44.2 (196) is about 'taking into account the special needs of the developing countries', a phrase first introduced in the 1982 ITU Nairobi Convention.[171]

The impact of Art. 44.2 (196) is not confined to space matters, being applicable to all usage of the radio spectrum. In relation to space, however, the requirement is important in the attainment of the objectives of OST Art. I, and UNGA Res. 51/122.[172] Therefore, RR Res. 2 (Rev. WRC-03) obliges states to take all practicable measures to facilitate the use of new space systems, in particular those of developing countries.[173] In addition, by ITU Convention Art. 12.2.c (166), the Director of the Radiocommunication Bureau assists developing countries in their preparation for radiocommunication conferences.

---

166 International Telecommunication Convention, Malaga–Torremolinos, 25 October 1973, 1209 UNTS 32, 255; 1975 UKTS 104, Cmnd 6289; 28 UST 2495, TIAS 8572.

167 Cf. Art. 43 of the International Telecommunication Convention, Buenos Aires, 22 December 1952, 1958 UKTS 36, Cmnd 520; 6 UST 1213, TIAS 3266: Art. 45 of the International Telecommunication Convention, Geneva, 21 December 1959, 1961 UKTS 74, Cmnd 1484; 12 UST 1761, TIAS 4892: Art. 46 of the International Telecommunication Convention, Montreux, 12 November 1965, 1967 UKTS 41, Cmnd 3383; 18 UST 575, TIAS 6267.

168 See RR Res. 4 (Rev. WRC-03) 'Period of Validity of Frequency Assignments to Space Stations using the Geostationary-satellite and other Satellite Orbits'. See also Chapter 8, n. 153.

169 As to first-come, first-served, see Chapter 8, following nn. 131 and 144.

170 See *supra* n. 168.

171 International Telecommunication Convention, Nairobi, 1982, 1531 UNTS 1, 1985 UKTS 33, Cmnd 9557; US Tr. Doc. 99–6, Art. 12.2.c (166).

172 'Declaration on International Cooperation in the Exploration and Use of Outer Space for the Benefit and in the Interest of All States, Taking into Particular Account the Needs of Developing Countries', 4 February 1997; UNGA Res. 51/122. See CoCoSL III, 299–357.

173 'Equitable use, by all countries, with equal rights, of the geostationary-satellite and other satellite orbits and of frequency bands for space radiocommunication services', RR Res. 2 (Rev. WRC-03).

The needs of these countries are thereby more likely to be reasonable, integrated with existing rules and developments proposed by others, and cogently expressed, and therefore more likely to be met. This will be important as progress is made towards agreeing further planning of direct-broadcast services, and perhaps of telecommunications networks.[174] Even so, some countries remain concerned about the use of orbits, and particularly of the GSO.[175]

The last phrase of Art. 44.2 (196) of the ITU Constitution refers to the taking into account of 'the geographical situation of particular countries'. Like the question of the 'developing countries', this phrase was introduced by Art. 33.2 (154) of the 1982 Nairobi Convention.[176] It could have been invoked earlier had the ITU tackled the Tonga problem, but it was not.[177] The 'geographical situation of particular countries' does not give those countries preferential rights.[178]

However, there remains the unease of some that the best orbital slots in the GSO could be taken up on the first-come, first-served basis by some before others have the ability to get there. Such unease was clearly manifest in the Bogota Declaration of 1976, in which seven countries asserted rights in the GSO above their respective territories.[179] They appealed specifically to the right of a state to control its natural resources and particularly to benefit from the use of space.[180] The signatories therefore declared that since the synchronous geostationary orbit was a natural resource lying above their territories,[181] they each had sovereign rights in the portion of that orbit above their respective territories[182] and they would press for recognition of their claims in appropriate fora. They were therefore vocal at the 1979 World Administrative Radio Conference[183] and at the one held in 1985.[184]

174 See Chapter 10 as to Direct Broadcasting.
175 See COPUOS Report, 2022, UNGA A/77/20 para 180, and similar views in previous Reports. Earlier see R. Jakhu, 'Legal Issues relating to the Global Public Interest in Outer Space' (2006) 32 *J. Sp. L.* 31–110 at 72–76; R. Jakhu and K. Singh, 'Space Security and Competition for Radio Frequencies and Geostationary Slots' (2009) 58 ZLW 74–93.
176 *Supra*, n. 171.
177 As to Tonga, see Chapter 8, *c*. n. 154. Tonga's own communications needs did not require the assignments it initially notified, or all those it ended up with, and its geographical position did not justify its claims.
178 S. Gorove, The Geostationary Orbit: Issues of Law and Policy' (1979) 73 AJIL 444–461 [Gorove, 35–52]; R.S. Jakhu, 'The Legal Status of the Geostationary Orbit' (1982) 7 AASL 333–51. The developing countries had been vocal earlier in the 1979 WARC; M.L. Smith, 'Space Law/Space WARC: An Analysis of the Space Law Issues raised at the 1985 ITU World Administrative Radio Conference on the Geostationary Orbit' (1986) 8 *Houston J. Int. L.* 227–245.
179 'Declaration of the First Meeting of the Equatorial States', Bogota, 1976 (1978) 6 *J. Sp. Law* 193–196; Manual, 2: 383–387. See also Chapter 3, *c*. n. 39. Seven equatorial states, Colombia, Congo, Ecuador, Indonesia, Kenya and Zaire, participated. Brazil sent an observer. Christol, 463–533 with its notes traces the debate down to its date.
180 In particular citing 'Permanent Sovereignty over Natural Resources', UNGA Res. 2692 (XXVII) of 1970, and the 'Charter of Economic Rights and Duties of States' UNGA Res. 3281 (XXIX) of 1974 (1975) 14 ILM 251. Apart from these, the UNGA had adopted a number of Resolutions on the topic of Permanent Sovereignty – see UNGA Res. 1803 (XVII) of 1962 (1963) 57 AJIL 710, 1963 2 ILM 223; Res. 2158 (XXI) of 1966; Res. 2386 (XXIII) of 1968, Res. 2625 (XXV) of 1970; Res. 2692 (XXV) of 1970; Res. 3016 (XXVII) of 1972; Res. 3171 (XXVIII) (1974) 13 ILM 238.
181 ITU CS Art. 44.2 (196) specifies the geo-stationary orbit as one of the limited natural resources that states should use 'rationally, efficiently and economically'.
182 An application of the 'lighthouse' principle?
183 G.O. Robinson, 'Regulating the Airwaves: The 1979 WARC' (1980) 21 *Virg. J. Int. L.* 1–54.
184 The 1985 WARC decided it lacked competence to deal with the claims made in the Bogota Declaration on the ground that the claim was a question of law and not of planning. M.L. Smith, 'Space Law/Space

Now nearly fifty years on, the Bogota claims still surface in reservations made by some equatorial states to ITU Final Acts, with corresponding counter-reservations by many developed countries that use the GSO.[185] The legal status of the geostationary orbit cannot be different from that of any other part of space. Although obviously part of the continuing quest by developing countries to achieve/receive a greater degree of benefit from space,[186] the general principles of the OST do not permit such claims. The only realistic role for the equatorial states based on their location would appear not to lie in claims to the GSO but in acting as ground tethers, or bases, for the Space Elevator.[187] That said, it has been generally recognised that the efficient use of the geostationary orbit does require rules, and, to some extent, the a priori planning that has been done for direct satellite broadcasting purposes represents an advance.[188]

WARC: An Analysis of the Space Law Issues raised at the 1985 ITU World Administrative Radio Conference on the Geostationary Orbit' (1986) 8 *Houston J. Int. L.* 227–45.

185 See the Declarations made in the Final Acts of successive ITU conferences. Their repetition resembles a stately, but unimportant, minuet. See most recently the Final Acts of PP-22 where Declarations 3 and 19, were countered by Declaration 77 by 38 states, which also noted that 'the reference in Article 44 of the Constitution to the "geographical situation of particular countries" does not imply recognition of a claim to any preferential rights to the geostationary-satellite orbit.' See also G. Zhukov and Y. Kolosov (trans. B. Belitzky), *International Space Law* (New York: Praeger, 1984) 155–160; T. Gangale, *supra* n. 1, and 'Who Owns the Geostationary Orbit?' (2006) XXXI AASL 425–446; Gorove, *supra* n. 178 at 450–455.

186 Cf. OST Art. I, and UNGA Res. 51/122, 1977, the UN, 'Declaration on International Cooperation in the Exploration and Use of Outer Space for the Benefit and in the Interest of All States, Taking into Particular Account the Needs of Developing Countries'. See also CoCoSL III, 299–357. As to any reference to the 'geographical situation of particular countries', see *supra* at nn. 178 and 185.

187 Cf. A.C. Clarke, *The Fountains of Paradise* (1979). In the (2016) 69 JBIS Special Issue on the Space Elevator, see particularly P.A. Swan and D.I. Raitt, 'Space Elevator – 15 Year Update' at 202–210, and J. Knapman, 'Space Elevator Technology and Research' at 211–219. P.B. Larsen, 'Brief Statement on the Legal Regime for Space Elevators' (2009) 52 *Proc. IISL* 426–428; P. Tobias, 'Opening the Pandora's Box of Space Law' (2005) 28 *Hastings Int. Comp. L. Rev.* 299–318 at 301–305; G.H. Reynolds, 'International Space Law in Transition: Some Observations' (2005) 6 *Chic. J. Int. L.* 69–80 at 77–79. B.C. Edwards, 'The Space Elevator Development Program' (2005) IAC-04-IAA.3.8.2.01; D.V. Smitherman, 'Critical Technologies for the Development of Future Space Elevator Systems' (2005) IAC-05-D4.2.04. See also https://spaceref.com/tag/space-elevator/. Cf. 'Space Elevators: An Advanced Earth – Space Infrastructure for the New Millennium', NASA/CP-2000-210-429, 2000L: http://images.spaceref.com/docs/spaceelevator/elevator.pdf. See also the International Space Elevator Consortium: www.isec.org/.

188 L.D. Roberts, 'A Lost Connection: Geostationary Satellite Networks and the International Telecommunication Union' (2000) 15 *Berkeley Tech. L.J.* 1095–1144; M.S. Soroos, 'The Commons in the Sky: the Radio Spectrum and Geosynchronous Orbit as Issues in Global Policy' (1982) 36 *Int. Org.* 665–677; R.S. Jakhu, 'Legal Issues of Satellite Telecommunications, The Geostationary Orbit and Space Debris' (2007) 5 *Astropolitics* 173–208.

7

THE MOON, ASTEROIDS AND OTHER CELESTIAL BODIES

Introduction

Currently, most space activities use satellites in orbit near to the Earth. The exploration of space takes us further out to the planets and beyond.[1] The legal regime of the moon, asteroids and other celestial bodies is not finally settled, and will require adaption, but milestones have been passed and markers set. Commercial exploitation of the moon and of asteroids is under active discussion.

Nomenclature

Celestial bodies are a category not fully defined in law.[2] The term is used, but not defined, in several of the space treaties, and carries the implication that the body is naturally occurring. Founded in 1919, the nongovernmental International Astronomical Union (IAU) is recognised internationally as the authority responsible for the definition of such bodies and their nomenclature.[3] For instance, one might have thought that the nine-planet solar

---

1 Voyager 1, launched 5 September 1977, reached the helio-sheath at 94 AU in December 2004 and is now (November 2022) some 160 AU from Earth. Voyager 2, launched slightly earlier on 20 August 1977, is some 131 AU. See https://voyager.jpl.nasa.gov/where/. An AU (astronomical unit) is the average distance from Earth to the sun, c. 93m miles/149K km. The helio-sheath – the boundary of the solar system – is the bubble of space within which the effect of the sun is dominant. Pioneers 10 and 11 and New Horizons will also leave the solar system. All five carried out surveys of planets and moons during their time in the solar system.

2 E. Fasan, 'Asteroids and Other Celestial Bodies: Some Legal Differences' (1998) 26 *J. Sp. L.* 33–40; A.A. Cocca, 'Principles for a Declaration with Reference to the Legal Nature of the Moon' (1958) 1 *Proc. IISL* 34–37; P.B. Larsen, 'Asteroid Legal Regime: Time for a Change' (2015) 39 *J. Sp. L.* 275–326. In 'Large Space Structures and Celestial Bodies' (1984) 27 *Proc IISL* 243–246, Fasan asked whether an asteroid hollowed out to provide living quarters for astronauts should lose its status as a celestial body and become something else in law, perhaps as an 'asteroid base'? Cf. K.I. Roy et al., 'Shell Worlds: An Approach to Terraforming Moons, Small Planets and Plutoids' (2009) 62 JBIS 32–38.

3 The IAU *inter alia* defines terms and classification categories and approves names for celestial bodies, their surface features and exosolar planetary systems. It operates the Astronomical Telegram system, swiftly disseminating data on new observations and discoveries. See www.iau.org and Minor Planet Electronic Circulars, www.hohmanntransfer.com/news.htm.

DOI: 10.4324/9781003496502-7

system was unquestionable, but in 2006 the IAU General Assembly adopted a definition of planet that Pluto did not fit and re-classified it as a dwarf planet.[4] For the layman, things became more confused when it was shown in 2007 that Pluto was not even the largest of that category, Eris (discovered 2005) being about 25% larger.[5] The definition of a planet remains debated and may yet be revised. The current position is that the solar system has eight planets, not nine.

As for nomenclature, there are traditional names for the planets, for some planetary satellites[6] and for particular stars (e.g. Altair, Betelgeuse, Procyon, Rigel, Sirius and Vega). The IAU also catalogues and names other bodies – planetary satellites, astronomical objects, asteroids, comets and un-named stars.[7] It does not recognise and is strenuously opposed to the 'sale' or 'purchase' of names through the various unofficial entities that peddle such 'titles'.[8]

---

4 IAU Resolution B5 'Definition of a Planet in the Solar System', 2006: www.iau.org/static/resolutions/Resolution_GA26-5-6.pdf. IAU Res. B6 recognised Pluto as a dwarf planet, the prototype for Trans-Neptunian Objects. Named by the IAU Executive Committee in 2008 as 'plutoids', these are planet-like bodies large enough to have appreciable gravity (so far, Pluto, Eris). See L. Perek, 'The IAU Resolutions on Planet Definition' (2006) 49 *Proc. IISL* 523–525; L. Tennen, 'Legal Implications of the IAU Resolutions on Planet Definition: Some Preliminary Observations' (2006) 49 *Proc. IISL* 526–529.

  Gustav Holst (1874–1934) did not add Pluto, discovered in 1930, to his suite *The Planets* (1916). In 2000, Colin Matthews was commissioned to compose *Pluto, the Renewer*, but his addition is rarely performed as part of the suite.

5 Eris, a Trans-Neptunian and the ninth largest solar system body, orbits in the Kuiper Belt at 97 AU and has its own moon, Dysnomia. Eris, the Greek goddess of strife or rivalry, is a name not inappropriate given the circumstances. See also P.S. Lykawka and T. Ito, 'Is There an Earth-like Planet in the Distant Kuiper Belt?' (2023) 166 *Astronomical Jnl.* (2023) 118–137.

6 The principal moons of Jupiter were named by the early astronomers, but not all their suggestions survived. Discovered by Galileo Galilei (1564–1642), the Galilean moons are now known as Io, Europa, Ganymede and Callisto, names given by Galileo's rival Simon Marius (1573–1624). The major moons of Saturn are named after the Titans, on the suggestion of John, William Herschel's son. By convention, the names of moons link to their primary: Phobos ('fear') and Deimos ('dread') are suitable companions to Mars, the God of War. Pluto has three moons, Nix, Hydra and Charon. Mythology has been a useful name mine.

7 More than 165,000 celestial objects have been catalogued and given a designation number. Of these, the IAU has sanctioned the formal naming of over 14,000. Under IAU naming policy, the discoverer of an asteroid has ten years to propose a name, after which other suggestions may be made. Asteroids are not normally named for their discoverer, only comets. Names of questionable taste are not accepted, and a political or military figure will not be considered until one hundred years after death. (This seems wise: cf. the Gadarene reactions to the deaths of John Kennedy and Diana.) Some asteroids are named congruent with the general group of which they form a part; for instance, individual asteroids of the Centaurs that orbit between Saturn and Neptune are named for specific centaurs. Acceptable names include places and real and fictional persons (e.g. 5535 Annefrank and 9007 James Bond). Orbiting between Mars and Jupiter are 4659 Roddenberry named for the creator and others named for actors in the Star Trek series. Oddly, 2309 Mr Spock is not named for the Star Trek character but for the discoverer's cat. Fittingly, some asteroids are named for science fiction authors. See Wikipedia, 'List of asteroids named after people' and 'List of asteroids'.

  The IAU Working Group on Star Names is standardising the nomenclature used by the astronomical community: www.iau.org/science/scientific_bodies/working_groups/280/. For current star names, see www.pas.rochester.edu/~emamajek/WGSN/IAU-CSN.txt. For the eighty-eight constellations, see www.iau.org/public/themes/constellations/. Cf. Gazetteers of Planetary Nomenclature: https://planetarynames.wr.usgs.gov/. For names of planetary features, see www.iau.org/news/planetary_surface_features/.

8 See *infra* n. 37ff and www.iau.org/public/themes/buying_star_names/. Cf. www.nameastarlive.com/ run by Space Services Inc.

The moon is the only natural satellite of the earth.[9] Earth not only controls the lunar orbit but also significantly affects the physical features of the moon. The moon controls Earth's tides and influences some biological functions. It is important in many religions, in literature and in art. 'Lunacy' and 'lunatic' remain viable terms, though usually disparagingly. The moon is romantic and has always fascinated mankind.[10] Accounts of voyages to the moon begin in the seventeenth century,[11] and modern science fiction has made magnificent use of the moon and other celestial bodies.

No matter how scientifically accurate and well-written, stories are but stories. In fact, the moon landings were last century.[12] Now, helped by the possibility of water ice in deep craters at the poles,[13] the US has plans to return,[14] and China, India, Japan, Russia, South Korean and the European Space Agency have lunar ambitions.[15] States have legislated to allow space mining. Entrepreneurs have sought 'property rights'. There are private offers of the sale or registration of 'claims' to portions of the Moon and other celestial bodies. All such require a legal response. What is (or may be) the law?

The basic treaty *matériel* remains the 1967 Outer Space Treaty. There is also the Moon Agreement (MA) of 1979. Responsive to pressures, states are starting to legislate, affording recognition of rights that will encourage buccaneering commercial and entrepreneurial bodies.

The Outer Space Treaty, 1967

The compass of the Outer Space Treaty (OST) goes well beyond Earth-oriented matters. Its full title states that it is a 'Treaty on Principles Governing the Activities of States in the Exploration and Use of Outer Space, Including the Moon and Other Celestial Bodies'.[16] The inclusion of 'the Moon, and other celestial bodies' is repeated throughout the initial articles that lay down general principles as well as in the later articles on responsibility, liability and such-like. Italicisation brings this out.

9 In 2021, UNGA Res. 76/76 para 13 proclaimed 20 July International Moon Day to mark the anniversary of the first moon landing and 'to raise public awareness about sustainable Moon exploration and utilization'.

10 Cf. M. Lachs, 'Some Reflections on the State of the Law of Outer Space' (1981) 9 *J. Sp. L.* 3–12 at 3.

11 J. Kepler, *Somnium, seu opus posthumum De astronomia lunari* (written 1603, published 1634). M.H. Nicolson, *Voyages to the Moon* (New York: Macmillan, 1948, 1960): P.B. Gove, *The Imaginary Voyage in Prose Fiction* (New York: Columbia UP, 1941; London: The Holland Press, 1961); L.T. Sargent, *British and American Utopian Literature, 1516–1875* (Boston: G.K. Hall, 1979); B.W. Aldiss with D. Wingrove, *Trillion Year Spree: The History of Science Fiction* (London: Gollancz, 1986). Cf. B.W. Aldiss, *Billion Year Spree: The History of Science Fiction* (London: Weidenfeld and Nicolson, 1973; Corgi, 1975); J. Gunn, *The Road to Science Fiction, Vol. 1, From Gilgamesh to Wells* (New York: New American Library, Mentor Books, 1977); J. Clute and P. Nichols, eds., *The Encyclopaedia of Science Fiction* (London and New York: Orbit, 1993: now updated: http://sf-encyclopedia.com/), 'Critical and Historical Works about SF', and 'History of SF'.

12 Twelve astronauts landed on the moon during the Apollo programme.

13 F. Lyall, 'On the Moon' (1998) 28 *J. Sp. L.* 129–138; P.B. Larsen, 'Is There a Legal Path to Commercial Mining on the Moon' (2021) 83 *Univ. of Pittsburg L. Rev.* 1–49. On 23 August 2023 the Indian Chandrayaan-3 mission soft-landed the Vikram lander near the south lunar pole.

14 US Artemis Program, *infra* n. 114.

15 See CoCoSL II, 338–341.

16 Treaty on Principles Governing the Activities of States in the Exploration and Use of Outer Space, Including the Moon and Other Celestial Bodies: 610 UNTS 205; 1968 UKTS 10, Cmnd. 3519; 18 UST 2410, TIAS 6347; (1967) 6 ILM 386; [1967] 61 AJIL 644: CoCoSL I, *passim*.

Article I provides for the exploration and use of outer space, *including the moon and other celestial bodies*, to be carried out for the benefit and in the interests of all countries (Art. I.1), for outer space, *including the moon and other celestial bodies*, to be free for exploration and use by all states and for free access to *all areas of celestial bodies* (Art. I.2), and for freedom of scientific investigation in outer space, *including the Moon and other celestial bodies* (Art. I.3). Under Art. II, '[o]uter space, *including the moon and other celestial bodies*, is not subject to national appropriation by claim of sovereignty, by means of use or occupation, or by any other means'. Article III provides that states party to the Treaty are to 'carry on activities in the exploration and use of outer space, *including the moon and other celestial bodies*, in accordance with international law'.[17]

Under Art. IV, space is to be used for peaceful purposes only. Nuclear or weapons of mass destruction are not to be put into space or installed *on celestial bodies* (Art. IV.1). *The Moon and other celestial bodies* shall be used by all states party to the Treaty exclusively for peaceful purposes (Art. IV.2). In short, while it is now usual to think of the OST as laying down principles for the general exploration and use of outer space, the repetition of the phrase 'the moon and other celestial bodies' throughout its Articles should not be overlooked. The OST is concerned not only with man-made satellites in Earth orbit or beyond but also with the use of 'empty space'. It also deals with human interaction with all naturally occurring extraterrestrial physical objects. These general principles bind the OST parties, and in their generality they also constrain its signatories.[18]

Further, if, as argued in Chapter 3, the general principles enunciated in OST Articles I–IV, have passed into customary international law, they therefore bind all states. That is important because other provisions of the OST clearly bind only its parties and signatories. Particular details specifically relate to the use and exploration of the moon and celestial bodies, but the broad thrust of OST Arts I–IV are not so limited. OST Arts VI–XI and XIII, which deal with matters of concern elsewhere in this book, all contain reference to the moon and celestial bodies. Article XII specifically provides for access to 'stations, installations, equipment and space vehicles on the moon and other celestial bodies' on a reciprocal basis and subject to prior notice for reasons of safety and avoiding interference with normal activities in them.[19]

The 'moon and other celestial bodies' are therefore built into the OST. That was to be expected. One impetus for the Treaty was the space race between the US and USSR and the prospect that one would precede the other on the moon. What the moon might be used for, or whether one state might assert sovereign title to it, was of acute concern.[20]

17 OST Art. I.2 similarly provides for freedom of exploration and use of outer space 'in accordance with international law'.

18 Art. 18, Vienna Convention on the Law of Treaties, 23 May 1969, 1155 UNTS 331; (1980) UKTS 58, Cmnd. 7964; (1969) 8 ILM 679; [1969] 63 AJIL 875. Although the Vienna Convention has not been universally ratified, it is widely believed that this provision articulates customary international law.

19 On access to installations in an emergency, see Chapter 5 Long-Range Missions and *infra* n. 52.

20 Section 8 of the US statute 'Implantation of the United States Flag on the Moon or Planets' (PL. 91–119, 18 November 1969, 83 Stat. 202) provides that 'The flag of the United States, and no other flag, shall be implanted or otherwise placed on the surface of the Moon, or on the surface of any planet, by the members of the crew of any spacecraft making a lunar or planetary landing as a part of a mission under the Apollo program or as a part of a mission under any subsequent program, the funds for which are provided entirely by the Government of the United States. This act is intended as symbolic gesture of national pride in achievement and is not to be construed as a declaration of national appropriation by claim of sovereignty.' See also A.M.

Could an alternative to territorial sovereignty be found? One response was the Antarctic analogy:[21] in 1960, US President D.D. Eisenhower formally expressed the view that the Antarctica Treaty[22] should be the model for the new legal regime for outer space.[23]

The Antarctica Treaty had, according to some, declared the region to be common property (*terra communis*),[24] and the Antarctic analogy continues to be relevant for space. Certainly, in terms of OST Art. 1 the moon and all celestial bodies are 'the province of all mankind' and by Art. II 'not subject to national appropriation by claim of sovereignty'. While one should be wary of the easy use of legal (and other) analogies, there are many reflections of the Antarctic regime in our approaches to the moon.

Another aspect where the Antarctic Treaty presented a model for the OST was demilitarisation. Article IV.2 of the OST provides that the moon and other celestial bodies are to be used exclusively for peaceful purposes. Paragraph 1 had provided that no nuclear weapons or weapons of mass destruction may be stationed in space. Paragraph 2 takes that further, barring the establishment of military bases, installations or fortifications on the moon or other celestial bodies. The testing of weapons or the conduct of military manoeuvres on celestial bodies is forbidden. However, military personnel may be used in exploration, as may military equipment necessary for scientific research. The Moon Agreement Art. 3 repeats these provisions.[25]

Platoff, 'Where No Flag Has Gone Before: Political and Technical Aspects of Placing a Flag on the Moon', NASA Contractor Report 188251: https://historycollection.jsc.nasa.gov/JSCHistoryPortal/history/flag/flag.htm; A.K. Lai, *The Cold War, the Space Race and the Law of Outer Space* (Abingdon: Routledge, 2021) 30–31.

    Sec. 403 of the US Commercial Space Launch Competitiveness Act, H.R. 2262, 114th Congress (2015–2016), Public Law No: 114–90, 129 Stat. 722, 51 USC 10101, states: 'It is the sense of Congress that by the enactment of this Act, the United States does not thereby assert sovereignty or sovereign or exclusive rights or jurisdiction over, or the ownership of, any celestial body.' There was no such disclaimer in the draft text of H.R. 2617 113th Cong. Sess. 1, the proposed Apollo Lunar Landing Legacy Act, which would have added an Apollo Lunar Landing Sites National Historical Park to the responsibilities of the US National Park System. For further discussion, see *infra* at n. 71.

21 P.C. Jessup and H.J. Taubenfeld, *Controls for Outer Space and the Antarctic Analogy* (New York: Columbia UP, 1959).

22 Antarctic Treaty, 1959, 402 UNTS 71; 1961 UKTS 97, Cmnd. 1535; 12 UST 794, TIAS 4780; (1980) 19 ILM 860; [1960] 54 AJIL 477. As of 2022 the Antarctic Treaty has 55 parties: www.bas.ac.uk/about/antarctica/the-antarctic-treaty/the-antarctic-treaty-1959/. The twelve original parties together with others recognised as conducting research in Antarctica participate in the Consultative Meeting and take part in its decision-making (Art. IX.2). The remaining parties can attend Consultative Meetings but have no vote in decision-making. Such could provide a model for the operation of the Artemis Accords; see *infra* n. 114. See v A. Thorpe, 'Antarctica: the treaty system and territorial claims', House of Commons Library note SN/1A/5040, 2012,

23 See *Legal Problems of Space Exploration*, US Senate Committee on Aeronautical and Space Sciences, 87th Cong., Sen. Doc. No. 26, 1961, at 1009.

24 *Terra communis*: common territory to which sovereign title cannot be acquired. This is different from *terra nullius*, to which title may be established through the normal means. Outer space is *terra communis*. Outer space has no history of prior claims to sovereignty. Cf. Jessup and Taubenfeld, *supra* n. 21, whose statement at 181 about Antarctica is wrong. Article IV of the Antarctic Treaty freezes or suspends the then existing claims to Antarctica: they are not cancelled or renounced. Argentina, Australia, Chile, France, New Zealand, Norway and the UK have claims to Antarctic territories, those of Argentina and Chile overlapping with that of the UK. The UK has reserved its position with respect to the Continental Shelf off its territorial claim: Thorpe, *supra* n. 22, 13–15: https://researchbriefings.files.parliament.uk/documents/SN05040/SN05040.pdf.

25 For military considerations, see also Chapter 15. Note: the 1963 Nuclear Test Ban Treaty, 480 UNTS 43, applies in outer space.

Lastly, OST Art. VI requires that all nongovernmental activities have government authorisation and be subject to continuing governmental supervision. Authorisation and supervision are primary governmental duties in relation to all activities in space to ensure compliance with the Treaty. We note that it is at the stage of licensing – that is prior to the activity commencing – that governments can and must exercise the best control over nongovernmental activities in space.

The Moon Agreement, 1979

The Moon Agreement came twelve years after the OST. Following the US moon landing in 1969, public opinion expected exploration and use of the moon to increase and a definitive legal regime for the Moon and the other celestial bodies to soon emerge. Draft treaties were indeed proposed.[26] However, as described in Chapter 4, following the OST, the space-law-creating process busied itself first with the rescue and return of astronauts and space objects (1968), then liability (1972) and later the registration of space objects (1975).

In addition, during that period much effort was going into negotiating what became the 1982 UN Convention on the Law of the Sea.[27] Finally, the urgency to adopt a definitive legal regime for the moon declined when it became evident that no immediate large-scale moon exploration or exploitation was planned. The UN General Assembly adopted the Moon Agreement without vote on 5 December, and it was opened for signature on 18 December 1979.[28] Requiring only five ratifications, the Agreement came into force on 11 July 1984 (MA Art. 19.3).[29] Even though it has few ratifiers and fewer signatories, it does have useful aspects, and, if amended, may yet prove to be the Sleeping Beauty of the five UN space treaties, but will its prince arrive?[30]

The MA Preamble *inter alia* notes the achievements of states in the exploration and use of the moon and other celestial bodies and the benefits that may come from exploiting their natural resources. Article 1 then begins the operative text with two statements of great importance. First, Art. 1.1 applies the provisions of the Agreement apply to all

26 Argentina: 'Draft Agreement on the Activities in the Use of Natural Resources of the Moon and Other Celestial Bodies', A/AC.105/L. 71 and Corr. 1 (1970) (included a reference to the 'common heritage of mankind'); USSR: UN Doc. A/8391 and Corr.1.

27 UN Convention on the Law of the Sea, 1982, 1833 UNTS 3; US Tr. Doc. 103–39; (1982) 21 ILM 1261–1354; Part XI amended, 1999 UKTS 82, Cm. 4525; (1994) 33 ILM 1309–1327.

28 Agreement Governing the Activities of States on the Moon and other Celestial Bodies, UN Doc. A/34/664. New York (UN) 5 December 1979; UN Doc. A/34/20, Annex 2; UNGA Res. 34/68; 1363 UNTS 3; (1979) 18 ILM 1434. See CoCoSL II, 325–426; Cheng, 357–380, Christol 246–247 and 342–346; Tronchetti, *infra* n. 102; N.M. Matte, 'Treaty relating to the Moon', I Manual 253–282; C.Q. Christol, 'The 1979 Moon Agreement: Where Is It Today?' (1999) *J. Sp. L.* 1–33. See also 'Agreement Concerning the Activities of States on the Moon and Other Celestial Bodies', US Senate, Committee on Commerce, Science, and Transportation, Parts 1–4 (USGPO, 1980).

29 Withdrawal is contingent on one year's notice (Art. 20).

30 R. Jakhu, 'Twenty Years of the Moon Agreement: Space Law Challenges for Returning to the Moon' (2005) 54 ZLW 234–260.

As of 1 January 2023, MA members were Armenia, Australia, Austria, Belgium, Chile, Kazakhstan, Kuwait, Lebanon, Mexico, Morocco, the Netherlands, Pakistan, Peru, the Philippines, Saudi Arabia, Turkey, Uruguay and Venezuela. However, Saudi Arabia withdrew on 5 January 2024. Signatories were France, Guatemala, India and Romania. See the Annual Report of the IISL Standing Committee on the Status of International Treaties relating to Activities in Outer Space in recent *Proc. IISL*, or https://iislweb.space/2001-standing-committee-report/, or www.unoosa.org/oosa/en/ourwork/spacelaw/treaties/status/index.html.

celestial bodies within the solar system, not only our moon, except in so far as other specific legal norms may enter into force with respect to them. Second, and equally crucially, Art. 1.2 provides that references to the moon in the Agreement include orbits around it and trajectories to it. We are not dealing simply with the lunar body but also with other celestial bodies and with the 'space' they occupy.[31] So, while we speak of the Moon Agreement, we are also dealing with all celestial bodies including asteroids while they are in space. 'Extraterrestrial materials which reach the surface of the earth by natural means' (sc. meteorites) are not covered by the MA (MA Art. 1.3).

Thereafter, the MA repeats essentials of the OST as to the moon and celestial bodies but enlarges their scope. It repeats the applicability of international law (Art. 2) and that its exploration and use are to be available to, and for the benefit of, all (Art. 4). The moon is to be used exclusively for peaceful purposes (Art. 3).[32] States committed to the OST remain obliged by the principles of that treaty even should they decline to become members of the MA. However, some provisions of the MA exceed the ambit of the OST in ways that have thrown up barriers to its support. As we will see, the main area of controversy concerns the provision on the common heritage of mankind in MA Art. 11.

Sovereignty and Title to Immovables[33]

'Who owns the moon?' is a question frequently thrown at the authors when we disclose our interest in space law. In fact, whether one thinks that ultimately no one owns the moon or that we all do, the idea that there should be no state sovereignty over or on celestial bodies has long roots.[34] As far as the law is concerned, the question is cleanly answered

31 Cf. Cheng, *infra* n. 95.
32 See also *infra* Chapter 15.
33 We use the term 'immoveable' analogously to its use in terrestrial law. 'Moveable' may be different, but, although it moves in space (as do the moon and the earth), for our purposes here an asteroid is immoveable. To avoid the implications of the noun, for reasons we are coming to, we avoid the term 'immoveable property' although it appears in many relevant discussions.
34 O. Schachter, 'Who Owns the Universe?' *Colliers*, 22 March 1952, 36 and 70–1, rep. in C. Ryan, ed., *Across the Space Frontier* (London: Sidgwick and Jackson, 1952) 118 ff.; O. Schachter, 'A Preview of Space Law Problems Warning: Early Unilateral Positions', *Bar Bulletin*, NY County Lawyers Assoc, June 1958 (rep. *Legal Problems*, 345–348). In his 'Legal Aspects of Space Travel' (1952) JBIS 16–17, Schachter suggested that the moon should be put under UN jurisdiction. G. V. Leopold, 'Cosmic Surveillance by Spaceflight Momentum' (1960) 6 *Wayne L Rev.* 311–339 at 329 called for all 'non-terrestrial regions' to be claimed for the UN and put under UN administration, perhaps through modification of the trusteeship system. See also C.W. Jenks, 'International Law and Activities in Space' (1956) 5 *Int. Law Quart.* 99–114 at 99; M.S. Smirnoff, 'The Role of the IAF in the Elaboration of the Norms of Future Space Law' (1959) 2 *Proc. IISL* 147–155. Cf. UNGA Res. 1721 (XVI), 1961, Res. 1802 (XVII) 1962, and the Principles Resolution Res. 1962 (XVIII) 1963, all discussed *supra* in Chapter 2. Cf. Art. 2.1 of the David Davies Memorial Institute, 'Draft Code of Rules on the Exploration and Uses of Outer Space' (1963) 29 *J. Air L. & Comm.* 141–150. Cf. J.G. Verplaetse, *International Law in Vertical Space* (New York: Rothman, 1960) at 150 quoting a 1947 suggestion by Manuilsky, then USSR Ambassador to the UN, that space be considered an international entity. See also J.C. Cooper, 'Who Will Own the Moon? The Need for an Answer' (1966) 32 *J. Air L. & Comm.* 155–166, reprinting and updating an article from (1965) *University: A Princeton Quarterly*. For very early (historical) claims see Pop, *Unreal Estates, infra* n. 41.

Cf. US National Space Policy. The G.H.W. Bush Space Policy of 1989 stated, 'The United States rejects any claims to sovereignty by any nation over outer space, or celestial bodies or any portion thereof, . . .': https://aerospace.csis.org/wp-content/uploads/2019/02/NSPD-1-Bush-I-National-Space-Policy.pdf. This was repeated in para 3 of the Introduction to the Clinton Space Policy of 1996: https://history.

by Art. II of the OST: 'Outer space, including the moon and other celestial bodies, is not subject to national appropriation by claim of sovereignty, by means of use or occupation, or by any other means'. This is one of the provisions of the OST that we believe has passed into customary law, and that being the case, a state which is not party to, or a state that withdraws from the OST, would not have a claim recognised by other states should it assert title (whether in whole or in part) to the moon or any other celestial body. The moon and other celestial bodies are *res extra commercium*, to use the Roman law term.[35] Nor can an individual establish a right of property simply by claiming it. Only states can have sovereignty and thereby invest others with property rights. History is littered with claims by individuals and others that states have refused to recognise, and that 'recognition' by existing states is necessary for a title valid under international law.[36] None have grounded a legitimate assertion of a right of property valid against all comers to which the legal system of other states will give effect.

It follows that the various entrepreneurs who purport to sell portions of the moon, Mars, Venus or any other celestial body cannot and do not transfer any sort of legal title to 'purchasers' from them.[37] Some argue that OST Art. II prohibits only claims by states, thereby leaving open the possibility of a claim by an individual, and that such a claim creates a title which can then be passed on to a purchaser.[38] We disagree. A valid right of property to immoveable estate, or an object such as an asteroid, planet or star in space, can exist only within a legal system established by a state and in relation to property over which

---

nasa.gov/appf2.pdf *or* www.fas.org/spp/military/docops/national/nstc-8.htm, and in the 2006 G.W. Bush Space Policy Statement, Sec. 2 'Principles', bullet point 2: https://aerospace.csis.org/wp-content/uploads/2018/09/Bush-US-National-Space-Policy.pdf. The 2010 Obama Space Policy, Principles, bullet point stated, 'As established in international law, there shall be no national claims of sovereignty over outer space or any celestial bodies . . . .': https://obamawhitehouse.archives.gov/sites/default/files/national_space_policy_6-28-10.pdf. Bullet point 4 of the Trump Space Policy of 2020 also affirms that the moon and other celestial bodies are not subject to national sovereignty in that language and goes on to state an intention to 'pursue the extraction and utilization of space resources in compliance with applicable law . . .': https://trumpwhitehouse.archives.gov/wp-content/uploads/2020/12/National-Space-Policy.pdf.

35 If a right or thing cannot be owned – if it is *extra commercium* – it cannot be the subject of a right of property, nor does it devolve according to the law of succession. Justinian, *Institutes* 2.20.4; *Digest* 30.39.9 and 10 both refer to purported bequests of land that is *extra commercium*, but the principle applies also to moveables. Cf. *Digest* 31.49.2–3.

36 J.L. Erwin, 'Footnotes to History': https://footnotes.neocities.org/ for an extensive list with detail of some histories/stories. The point stands whether recognition is considered declaratory or constitutive. Whichever, 'recognition' by other states is effectively constitutive for small states or states of dubious status. See T.C. Chen, *The International Law of Recognition* (London: Stevens, 1951); G. Kreijen, ed., *State, Sovereignty and International Governance* (Oxford: Clarendon Press, 2002); H. Lauterpacht, *Recognition in International Law* (Cambridge: Cambridge UP, 1947); S. Talmon, *Recognition of Governments in International Law* (Oxford: Oxford UP, 1998); C. Warbrick, 'States and Recognition in International Law', in M.D. Evans, *International Law* (Oxford: Oxford UP, 2003) 205–266. Cf. the *Langevin* case, *infra* n. 41.

37 Cf. the Lunar Embassy: www.lunarembassy.com, or www.lunarregistry.com. The Archimedes Institute registered claims to private property rights in outer space but made it clear that registering did not confer a title or universally effective property rights: www.permanent.com/archimedes-institute.html. A 'claim' is only a claim, not a title valid against all comers. Cf. E.L. Hudgins, *Space: The Free-market Frontier* (Washington: Cato Institute, 2003) (not seen); G. Gal, 'Acquisition of Property in the Legal Regime of Celestial Bodies' (1997) 39 *Proc. IISL* 45–49; Christol 262–263. A.C. Murnane, 'The Prospector's Guide to the Galaxy' (2013) *Fordham Int. L.J.* 235–277 seems misconceived on this point. See also *infra* nn. 40 and 41.

38 Cf. the answer to Qu. 2 of the General FAQ on the Lunar Embassy website, *supra* n. 37.

that state has sovereignty.[39] Since state claims to sovereignty in space cannot exist, neither can title to immoveable property on celestial bodies in space. The US was therefore correct in refusing to give legal redress to Gregory Nemitz.[40] This matter has, of course, been discussed much over the years, and it is regrettable that it continues to generate misplaced interest. The moon and the other celestial bodies as such are not available for ownership either by private individuals or by companies.[41] The position as to materials recovered

39 That MA Art. 11.3 specifically states that the surface, subsurface or any part of the moon cannot become the property 'of any State, international governmental or non-governmental organisation, national organisation or non-governmental entity or of any natural person' is irrelevant. It does not leave a gap for an individual to claim title. Since there is no national appropriation (OST Art. II, MA Art. 11.2), no valid legal title can exist. Cf. K.A. Baca, 'Property Rights in Outer Space' (1993) 58 *J. Air L. & Comm.* 1041–1085; G.H. Reynolds, 'International Space Law: Into the Twenty-First Century (1992) 24 *Vand. J. Transnat. L.* 225–255 at 229–237.

40 Gregory Nemitz registered a claim to the Asteroid 433 Eros with the Archimedes Institute, *supra* n. 37. When in 2001 the probe NEAR Shoemaker was landed on Eros, Nemitz billed NASA US$20 for parking and storage of the probe for 100 years. NASA refused to pay. After an exchange of letters, Nemitz raised an unsuccessful court action in Nevada and appealed to the US Ninth Circuit Court of Appeals. He failed. The reasoning and argument are cluttered with technicalities of US procedural law, but the decision was in effect that Nemitz had no cognisable cause of action (i.e. no right of property) on which to base his claim because there are no property rights in space. He had argued that his claim was based on his natural right but had not asked the courts to declare he had a property right. See *Gregor William Nemitz v The United States of America et al.* No. CV-N-0300599-HDM (RAM), reported in Westlaw as 2003 WL 24268455 (D. Nev.) 6 Nov. 2003; WL 3703798 (D. Nev.) 28 Jan. 2004, WL 3703805, 11 February 2004; 2004 WL 3167042, 26 Ap. 2004; tersely affirmed by the US Court of Appeals for the Ninth Circuit, 7 February 2005, 126 Fed. Appx. 343; 2005 US App. LEXIS 2350. See R. Kelly, '*Nemitz v United States*, A Case of First Impression: Appropriation, Private Property Rights and Space Law before the Federal Courts of the United States' (2004) 30 *J. Sp. L.* 297–309, W. Whyte, 'Nemitz v US – the First Real Property Case in United States Courts' (2004) 47 *Proc. IISL* 339–351 (both written prior to the final determination of the case). K.M. Zullo, 'The Need to Clarify the Status of Property Rights in International Space Law' (2002) 90 *Geo. L.J.* 2413–2444 at 2414–2417 outlines the pre-trial correspondence; Listner, *infra* n. 53, at 64–65. See also 'The Eros Project': www.erosproject.com/.

41 In *Re Langevin*, 2012 QCCS 6132 the Quebec Superior Court rejected a claim to Earth, and separately to Mercury, Venus, Jupiter and four of its major moons, Saturn and Uranus, Neptune, and Pluto together with the space between these planets and out to the end of the galaxy. Previous claims by Langevin to the moon and Mars had been dismissed in an unreported case of 2011.

   V. Pop, *Unreal Estate: The Men Who Sold the Moon* (Exposure Publishing, 2006) considers many historic examples of such claims. See also his *Who Owns the Moon* (Springer, 2009). Cf. V. Pop, 'Appropriation in outer space: the relationship between land ownership and sovereignty on the celestial bodies' (2000) 16 *Space Policy* 275–282, and 'The Men who Sold the Moon: Science Fiction or Legal Nonsense?' (2001) 17 *Space Policy* 195–203. See also F. Lyall, 'Lunar Estates' (2008) *Scots L.T.* 271–272; F.G. von der Dunk et al. 'Surreal Estate: Addressing the Issue of "Immoveable Property Rights on the Moon"' (2004) 20 *Space Policy* 149–156; L.I. Tennen, 'Article II of the Outer Space Treaty, the Status of the Moon and Resulting Issues' (2004) 47 *Proc. IISL* 520–529; P.M. Sterns and L.I. Tennen, 'Privateering and Profiteering on the Moon and Other Celestial Bodies: Debunking the Myth of Property Rights in Space' (2002) 45 *Proc. IISL* 56–67. Cf. M.J. Listner, 'The Ownership and Exploitation of Outer Space: A Look at Foundational Law and Future Legal Challenges to Current Claims' (2003) 1 *Regent J. Int. L.* 75–94 particularly at 87–94. Listner appears to suggest that as the claims of the Lunar Embassy were intimated to the UN and Russia without response, they may have some basis. At 92 he raises the possibility of the Lunar Embassy seeking a seat at the UN as a way to 'precipitate an international controversy'. Such suggestions are not supportable.

   The IAU is trenchant: 'purchasers' should not part with monies until they have actual physical possession of any celestial 'property' that they 'buy'. See *supra* n. 8. Cf. the 2004 'Statement by the IISL Board 'Claims to Property Rights Regarding the Moon and Other Celestial Bodies': https://iislweb.space/wp-content/uploads/2020/01/IISL_Outer_Space_Treaty_Statement.pdf, and its 'Further 'Statement' of 2009: https://iislweb.space/wp-content/uploads/2020/01/Statement-BoD.pdf, and the further statement of

from the moon and celestial bodies may, however, be different, and will be different in the future.

Exploration

As a matter of law, the exploration of the moon or other celestial bodies differs from their economic exploitation. Exploration does not entail permanent appropriation of materials in situ, whereas economic exploitation may be thought necessarily to do so. The many legal problems associated with permanent or exclusive appropriation would not occur in lunar exploration.

Indeed, the OST encourages exploration, one of its purposes being 'to contribute to broad international cooperation in the scientific as well as the legal aspects of the exploration and use of outer space for peaceful purposes' (OST Preamble para 4). OST Art. I.1 provides that the exploration and use of outer space is to be 'for the benefit and in the interests of all countries, irrespective of their degree of economic or scientific development, and shall be the province of all mankind'. Free access by all states to all areas of celestial bodies and freedom of exploration and use without discrimination is accorded by OST Art. I.2, and freedom of scientific investigation is to be facilitated under Art. I.3. MA Art. 4.1 repeats the substance of OST Art. I, but adds, perhaps in clarification, that in exploring and using the moon, due regard must be paid to the interests of present and future generations and the correlative need to promote higher standards of living and conditions of economic and social progress and development in accordance with the UN Charter.[42]

The initial explorations of the moon and other celestial bodies were carried out by state agencies; in the future, private entities will engage in such activities. If so, it is imperative that in the implementation of their obligations under OST Art. VI, relevant states properly scrutinise proposals, issue appropriate licences and actively and in detail supervise the activities of their nationals because nongovernmental entities act for their states.[43]

As far as actual exploration is concerned, Art. IX of the OST calls for cooperation in the exploration and use of the moon and other celestial bodies.[44] Harmful contamination should be avoided,[45] as should any harm to the earth through the introduction to it of extraterrestrial material.[46] Harmful interference with the exploratory activity of others or their use of the moon and other celestial bodies is to be avoided and consultation engaged in if there is a known likelihood of such occurring (OST Art. IX).

2023: Statement by the IISL Board of Directors on claims to property rights regarding the Moon and other celestial bodies, 7 November 2023: https://iisl.space/index.php/2023/11/07/statement-by-the-iisl-board-of-directors-on-claims-to-property-rights-regarding-the-moon-and-other-celestial-bodies/.

42 It is difficult to see what legal point is thus made.

43 See UNOOSA compilation of national space laws: www.unoosa.org/oosa/en/ourwork/spacelaw/nationalspacelaw/index.html. Several contracting States have not yet fully implemented Art VI.

44 Cf. MA Art. 4.2.

45 This ought to veto the licensing of moon crash programmes such as Orbital Development advertised in 2004: www.orbdev.com/mooncrash.html?source=OrbDev. The crashing of the LCROSS (Lunar Crater Observation and Sensing Satellite) and part of its launch vehicle into the crater Cabeus in October 2009 was different. That was a scientific mission that successfully detected water ice. On 10 June 2009, Japan crashed the Kayuga (Selene) satellite to terminate its mission. Cf. the Ranger series of probes in the 1960s and the Lunar Prospector, 31 July 1999.

46 See Chapter 9 Contamination.

In order to achieve international cooperation, OST parties have agreed to inform the UN Secretary General as well as the international scientific community and the public 'to the greatest extent feasible and practicable' of the 'nature, conduct, location and results' of their activities (OST Art. XI).[47] The Secretary General is to disseminate such information immediately and effectively, a task fulfilled largely through UN OOSA.[48] Modelled on Art. 7 of the Antarctic Treaty,[49] OST Art. XII allows for the inspection of 'stations, installations, equipment and space vehicles on the moon and other celestial bodies' 'on the basis of reciprocity', after reasonable advance notice given for safety reasons and to avoid interfering with normal operations.[50] A similar provision is in MA Art. 15.1, but MA Art. 10.2 extends the matter of access so that 'persons in distress on the moon' are to be offered shelter in the stations, installations vehicles and other facilities' of state parties.[51]

In terms of exploration, the MA contains provisions that could usefully flesh out the skeletal provisions of the OST. One feature of the Agreement is the number of its articles that require reports to the UN Secretary General. Obviously, if complied with, their effect would be a considerable degree of transparency as to activities on the moon and other celestial bodies, but we wonder whether such obligations will survive actual practice, even if the MA or something like it comes to rule in such matters. Certainly, reporting practice will not prosper if the moon is opened to private commercial exploitation. Commercial enterprises are impatient with red tape and form-filling, let alone the potential disclosure of commercial secrets or market-sensitive information.

Under the MA, freedom of scientific investigation would include the collection and removal of samples (MA Art. 6.2)[52] as has already occurred, the silence of the OST on such matters notwithstanding.[53] The setting aside of sites of special scientific interest is contemplated in MA Art. 7.3. Such could include the projected radio-telescope

---

47 It would be interesting to compare the transparency of the reports by different agencies.
48 Electronic access to UN OOSA data has speeded such matters.
49 Antarctic Treaty, *supra* n. 22.
50 In the film *2001: A Space Odyssey* (1968), Russian access to the US site at 'Moon Base Clavius' is refused on health grounds. Cf. A.C. Clarke, *2001: A Space Odyssey* (London: Arrow, 1968).
51 The feasibility of such action was raised in Chapter 5. What if affording shelter would result in there being insufficient air to support the increased number of persons until the air supply can be augmented?
52 Cf. the first sentence of MA Art. 11.3: 'Neither the surface nor the subsurface of the moon or nor any part thereof or natural resources *in place* shall become property of any State, intergovernmental or non-intergovernmental organisation, national organisation or non-governmental entity or of any natural person' (emphasis added).
53 Samples returned to Earth have been purloined, leading to later criminal trials. The implication is that the 'non-appropriation' principle does not preclude a right of ownership of samples since one cannot steal what is not subject to a right of property. Cf. K. Martens, 'United States of America v One Lucite Ball Containing Lunar Material (One Moon Rock) and One Ten Inch by Fourteen Inch Wooden Plaque' 252 F. Supp. 2d 1367 (2003)' (2003) 13 *De Paul J. Art and Ent. L.* 465–480; M.J. Listner and J.T. Smith, 'A Litigator's Guide to the Galaxy: A Look at the Pragmatic Questions for Adjudicating Future Outer Space Disputes' (2020) 23 *Vand. J. Ent. & Tech. L.* 53–98 at 65–66. Two cases on moon dust appear to have been settled: *Carlson v. Bolden*, No. 16-CV-01367 (D. Kan. 27 June 2016) and *Cicco v. NASA* No. 18-CV-01164, 2019 WL 1670759 (D. Kan. 2019), outlined also in Listner and Smith, at 66–67. Cf. also https://query.nytimes.com/gst/fullpage.html?res=9C0DEFD91139F931A35751C1A963958260; or https://news.bbc.co.uk/1/hi/world/americas/2145915.stm; or www.usatoday.com/news/nation/2002-07-23-moon-rocks_x.htm.

facility on the lunar far side,[54] and the creation of any 'heritage site'.[55] Otherwise, lunar bases, manned and unmanned, may be established (MA Art. 9.1). These are to occupy a minimal area and be located so that free access by others to the area is not impeded (MA Arts. 9.1 and 2). Such activities create no property title to the area occupied (MA Art. 11.3).[56]

As noted, under OST Art. XII and MA Art. 15.1, moon bases and facilities are to be open to inspection by other state parties, the MA provision indicating that any inspection is to ensure that parties are complying with their obligations under the Agreement. It may be significant that MA Arts. 15.2–3 then provide for the raising of problems, making suggestions for living up to the MA requirements and for settling resultant disputes. A manned base raises questions as to the potential contamination of the surrounding area. Ideally a base would be fully secured from environmental interaction with the moon itself, but it has to be said that the state of the environment around the US Amundsen–Scott Base at the terrestrial South Pole is not reassuring.[57]

The second sentence of OST Art. IX speaks of the avoidance of 'harmful contamination' of the moon and celestial bodies.[58] MA Art. 7.1 would require its parties to take measures 'to prevent the disruption of the existing balance of' the environment of the moon or other celestial bodies,[59] 'whether by introducing adverse changes in that environment, by its harmful contamination through the introduction of extra-environmental matter or otherwise', and to inform the UN Secretary General of measures adopted for the purpose. However, this leaves open the question of precisely when contamination becomes harmful. The precautionary principle should be applied, and any error should be on the side of rigour and prevention rather than of risk.[60] While nuclear weapons are banned from space, it is obvious that nuclear reactors or radio-isotropic generators may well be used to power installations and vehicles used on the moon or elsewhere.[61] MA Art. 7.2 would therefore require the UN Secretary General to be informed of the placement and purpose of any nuclear materials on the moon.

54 F.G. von der Dunk, 'Space for Celestial Symphonies? Towards the Establishment of International Radio Quiet Zones' (2001) 17 *Space Policy* 265–274; C. Maccone, 'Lunar Farside Radio Lab' (2005) 56 *Acta Astronautica* 629–639. See also C. Maccone, ed., *Protected Antipode Circle on Lunar Farside*, IAF Cosmic Study, 1.6 (Eighth Draft, 2014): https://iaaspace.org/wp-content/uploads/iaa/Scientific%20Activity/Study%20Groups/SG%20Commission%201/sg16/sg16draftreport2.pdf with articles by C. Maccone, F. von der Dunk, L.I. Tennen, F. Lyall. See also Chapter 16, c. n. 77.

55 As to heritage sites, see *infra* following n. 62.

56 This echoes the general prohibition of claims of sovereignty by OST Art. II. See also disclaimers of such claims in US legislation, *supra* n. 20.

57 M.S. Race and R.O. Randolph, 'The Need for Operating Guidelines and a Decision Making Framework Applicable to the Discovery of Non-Intelligent Extraterrestrial Life' (2002) 50 *Adv. Space Res.* 1583–1591. Cf. Wikipedia: the 'Great Pacific Garbage Patch', a huge area of marine debris in the North Pacific gyre. In A.C. Clarke, 'Before Eden', *Tales of Ten Worlds* (1962); *Arthur C. Clarke: The Collected Stories* (London: Gollancz, 2000) 758–766, life on Venus disappears, poisoned by garbage from an Earth expedition.

58 See Chapter 9 Contamination.

59 We expand the language to take account of MA Art. 1.1.

60 P.B. Larsen, 'Application of the Precautionary Principle to the Moon' (2006) 71 *J. Air L. & Comm.* 295–306. See also L.D. Roberts, 'Ensuring the Best of All Possible Worlds: Environmental Regulation of the Solar System' (1997) 6 *N.Y.U. Env. L.J.* 126–160 at 158–160.

61 'Principles Relevant to the Use of Nuclear Power Sources in Outer Space', 1992, UNGA Res. 47/68; 1993 32 ILM 917. (1993) 32 ILM 917 at 921–926; CoCoSL III, 189–297 (discussed in Chapter 9).

Some areas of the moon should certainly be specifically protected. The creation of 'quiet zones' for radio-astronomy purposes makes sense.[62] The setting aside of particular locations for historic or heritage or other reasons was being adumbrated as we were writing the first edition of this book.[63] Action is needed.[64] Thanks to UNESCO, there is now extensive experience of the international designation and thereby the protection of a variety of scientific and 'heritage' interests.[65]

There are a number of relevant international agreements and much discussion of the idea.[66] Indeed, apart from international action, many (we guess, most) countries have rules as to the preservation of various aspects of their heritage in a variety of forms.[67] A 'heritage' regime for the moon at least, or areas of it, if not for other celestial bodies, must be established well before commercial interests intrude.[68] The success of the lobbying activities

---

62 See *supra* n. 54. See also Chapter 16.
63 Cf. 'Future Role and Activities of the Committee on the Peaceful Uses of Outer Space: Working Paper Submitted by the Chairman', 10 May 2007, A/AC.105/L. 268, Sec. F, paras 33–5, 'Protection/conservation of Designated Areas of the Moon and Other Bodies of the Solar System'.
64 L. Westwood, B.L. O'Leary, et al., *Final Mission: Preserving NASA's Apollo Sites* (Gainesville: Florida UP, 2017); B.L. O'Leary and P.J Canelotti eds., *Archaeology and Heritage of the Human Movement into Space* (Dordrecht: Springer, 2015); L. Lixinski et al., Envisioning a Legal Framework for Outer Space Cultural Heritage' (2021) 45 *J. Sp. L.* 1–45.
65 For UNESCO and World Heritage, see http://whc.unesco.org/.
66 Convention Concerning the Protection of the World Cultural and Natural Heritage, Paris, 1972, in force 17 December 1975, 1037 UNTS 152, 1985 UKTS 2, Cmnd. 9524; 1984 Misc. 6, Cmnd. 9171; 27 UST 37, TIAS 8226; (1972) 11 ILM 1358; UNESCO: 'Convention on the Protection of the Underwater Cultural Heritage', 2001 (2002) 41 ILM 40, with Introductory Note by K.R. LaMotte at 37. Cf. Agreement under the United Nations Convention on the Law of the Sea on the conservation and sustainable use of marine biological diversity of areas beyond national jurisdiction, UN Doc. A/CONF.232/2023/4, adopted 20 September 2023.
     J.A.R. Nahziger, ed., *Cultural Heritage Law* (Cheltenham: Edward Elgar, 2012); J. Blake, *International Cultural Heritage Law* (Oxford: Oxford UP. 2015); F. Francioni and A.P. Vrdoljak, eds., *The Oxford Handbook of International Cultural Heritage Law* (Oxford: Oxford UP, 2020). See also F. Francioni, 'Beyond State Sovereignty: The Protection of Cultural Heritage as a Shared Interest of Humanity' (2004) 25 *Mich. J. Int. L.* 1209–1228; and 'Thirty Years On: Is the World Heritage Convention Ready for the 21st Century' (2002) 12 Ital. YBIL 13–38; E.J. Godwin, 'The World Heritage Convention, the Environment, and Compliance' (2009) 20 *Colo. J. Int. Env. L. & Pol.* 157–198; G. Nicholson, 'The Common Heritage of Mankind and Mining: An Analysis of the Law as to the High Seas, Outer Space, the Antarctic and World Heritage' (2002) 6 *N.Z. J. Env. L.* 177–198.
     Cf. in Europe: The European Convention on the Protection of the Archaeological Heritage, 1969; CETS 066; the Convention for the Protection of the Architectural Heritage of Europe, 1985, 1496 UNTS 148; CETS 121; 1988 UKTS 46, Cm. 439; the European Convention on the Protection of the Archaeological Heritage (revised 1992), 1966 UNTS 305; CETS 143; 2002 UKTS 29, Cm. 5555, and the European Landscape Convention, 2000, 2296 UNTS 141; CETS 176; 2006 UK Misc. No. 4, Cm. 6794. There is also a strange European Convention for the Protection of the Audiovisual Heritage, 2001, CETS 183, and the Council of Europe Framework Convention on the Value of Cultural Heritage for Society, 2005, CETS 199. The tenor of these shows the reality of the impulse to protect heritage, at least in Europe.
67 Canada considers meteorites found in Canada to be part of its cultural property and controls their export: see the Canadian 'Cultural Property Export and Import Act', S.C. 1985, c.51 and the Canadian Cultural Property Export Control List, C.R.S., c. 448, Group I, sec. 2.e. The UAE has a register of meteorites. They remain the property of the emirate in which they fell, but trading them is prohibited without permission. See UAE Federal Law No. (12) of 2019 on the Regulation of the Space Sector Art. 30, *infra* n. 163.
68 F. Lyall, 'OST Art. IX Improvements: Cultural and Natural Heritage Elements' (2010) 53 *Proc. IISL* 657–665; C. Cockell and G. Horneck, 'A Planetary Park System for Mars' (2004) 20 *Sp. Pol.* 291–295; M. Rosendahl, 'Galactic Preservation and Beyond: A Framework for Protecting Cultural, Natural, and Scientific Heritage in Space' (2019) 43 *Wm. & Mary Env. L. & Pol.* 839–870; L. Lixinski et al., 'Envisioning a

of commercial interests in relation to terrestrial heritage does not reassure. The basic function of commerce is the making of profit: other considerations are taken into account, but often, we fear, for cosmetic reasons only unless imposed by law.

Setting aside lunar sites of special scientific interest is contemplated in MA Art. 7.3, which speaks of 'international scientific preserves' placed under 'special protective arrangements'. Certainly, some areas of the moon should be specifically protected. Google Earth displays of the moon and Mars signpost many sites of landings, human and rover, as well as crash sites. Some are of historic interest and should be protected.[69] In 2010, while taking account of the 'no sovereignty' provision of OST Art. II, California acted to include on its list of historic materials protected under the US Federal Historic Preservation Law various artefacts at Tranquillity Base on the Mare Tranquillitatis (lunar coordinates 00°41'15"N, 23°26'00"E).[70] Lacking territorial jurisdiction, California did not designate the area itself as a protected site. A US Congress proposal of 2013 to that effect was, however, not cogent.[71] However, in 2011, NASA itself published voluntary guidance on the protection and preservation of US artifacts on the moon, and in 2020, the US enacted the 'One Small Step to Protect Human Heritage in Space Act', Public Law 116–275, 134 Stat. 3358 (51 USC 30301), which under sec. 3 requires NASA and its contractors to protect the human artifacts at Apollo landing sites, thus incorporating the California provisions into full national law.

Again, there may be areas of lunar geology that should be protected, even if they may contain minerals that may come to be of commercial interest, and it would be better if this is done sooner than later. The problems of Antarctica should be borne in mind: the attempt to regulate the exploitation of minerals there has been abandoned *pro tempore*, but as the icefields retreat on the Graham Land Peninsula, pressure grows to allow commercial activity in Antarctica. *Mutatis mutandis* parts of the moon could be under threat. We therefore suggest, apart from invoking MA 7.3 – because the MA is so poorly accepted – that the model of the Consultative Meetings of the Antarctic system be used and that

Legal Framework for Outer Space Cultural Heritage' (2021) 45 *J. Sp. L.* 1–45; M. Hanlon, ' "Due Regard" for Commercial Space Must Start with Historic Preservation' (2021) 9 *Global Bus. L. Rev.* 130–156: A. Froehlich, ed., *Protection of Cultural Heritage Sites on the Moon* (Vienna: Springer, 2020). Section 9 of the Artemis Accords (*infra*) indicates that its signatories intend to preserve historically significant heritage: www.nasa.gov/specials/artemis-accords/img/Artemis-Accords-signed-13Oct2020.pdf. Cf. M. Dodge, 'Celestial Agriculture: Law & Policy Governing the Use of in Situ Resources for Space Settlements' (2022) 97 *N. D. L. Rev.* 161–184.

69 Cf. 'NASA's Recommendations to Space-Faring Entities: How to Protect and Preserve the Historic and Scientific Value of U.S. Government Lunar Artefacts', 2011: www.nasa.gov/directorates/heo/library/reports/lunar-artifacts.html.

70 See www.ohp.parks.ca.gov/pages/1067/files/shrc_01_29_10.pdf and related documentation at http://ohp.parks.ca.gov/pages/1067/files/tranquility%20base_draft.pdf. See also Office of Historic Preservation, California State Parks, 30 July 2010, 'Objects Associated with Apollo 11': http://ohp.parks.ca.gov/?page_id=24479. Cf. New Mexico: http://new.nmhistoricpreservation.org/assets/files/press-releases/sr-tranquility_base.pdf, and the Lunar Legacy Project: https://spacegrant.nmsu.edu/lunarlegacies/artifactlist.html.

71 H.R. 2617, 113th Cong. Sess. 1, a proposed Apollo Lunar Landing Legacy Act, would have added to the US National Park System responsibility for an Apollo Lunar Landing Sites National Historical Park. See www.congress.gov/bill/113th-congress/house-bill/2617/text. Cf. K. Ellis, 'Preserving Apollo: H.R. 2617 and the Creation of the Apollo Lunar Landing Sites National Historical Park' (2015) 26 *Fordham Env. L. Rev.* 516–558; K. Abhijeet, 'Appropriation of Space? – Apollo Lunar Landing Legacy Bill as a Trigger for Colonisation in Space?' (2015) 64 *ZLW* 653–665.

'moon-active' states agree to set aside particular sites on the moon to protect historic heritage and/or for specific scientific purposes.[72]

Apart from bases, personnel,[73] vehicles and equipment may at present be placed anywhere on a celestial body, including below the surface of the moon (MA Art. 8.2). All vehicles and equipment will remain under the jurisdiction of the relevant launching state (OST Art. VIII and MA Art. 12.1). However, MA 12.2 also deals with what might be termed 'lost property', requiring objects found in places other than their intended location to be treated in accordance with ARRA. MA Art. 13 therefore also requires a state learning of a forced or other unintended landing or the crash on the moon or elsewhere of a space object that it has not launched to inform the UN Secretary General and the relevant launching authority. Such provisions make sense, as do our suggestions as to the designation of protected areas. However, while they are clearly sensible for exploration, matters are different when questions of economic exploitation are concerned.

Exploitation

Historically, much of the exploration of Earth has been triggered by commercial considerations rather than quest for scientific knowledge, and even when the search for knowledge was a major element, a subsidiary aim was always the potential improvement of navigation so that commerce might prosper.[74] Science has led the way in the exploration of the moon and other celestial bodies, but clearly that is not going to remain the case. Now, Earth orbits are mainly used for commercial and practical reasons, and the exploitation of celestial bodies is on the horizon.[75] Resources extracted from the moon could ease the use of space, particularly if water becomes available.[76] Metals that are rare on Earth could be mined.[77] Activities farther out in space could be conveniently begun from the moon, avoiding the difficulties of getting up out of Earth's gravity well and atmosphere.[78]

For decades, there have been calls (enthusiastic but not always legally well-articulated or well-founded) for private enterprise to lead the way (or be given a wide scope) in the

---

72 See 'The Antarctic System': www.scar.org/antarctic-treaty-system, and the *Final Report of the Thirty-fifth Antarctic Treaty Consultative Meeting*, Hobart, 2012: www.ats.aq/documents/ATCM35/fr/ATCM35_fr001_e.pdf.

73 On personnel, see Chapter 5.

74 D. Sobel, *Longitude* (New York: Walker, 1995; London: Fourth Estate, 1996); J.E. Carroll, 'Of Icebergs, Oil Wells, and Treaties: Hydrocarbon Exploitation Offshore Antarctica' (1983) 36 *Stan. J. Int. L.* 207–227.

75 The last bullet point of Sec. 2 of the Bush US Space Policy of 2006 (*supra* n. 34) spoke of 'encouraging and facilitating a growing and entrepreneurial US space sector' and using 'US commercial space capabilities to the maximum practical extent', and its Sec. 7 set out 'Commercial Space Guidelines' (2007) 32 *AASL* 475–486. The 2010 US Space Policy Statement also favoured commercial uses of outer space: see *supra* n. 34. Bullet point 4 of the 2020 Trump Space Policy states an intention to 'pursue the extraction and utilization of space resources in compliance with applicable law': https://trumpwhitehouse.archives.gov/wp-content/uploads/2020/12/National-Space-Policy.pdf.

76 Cf. Lyall and Cook, both *infra* n. 81; P.B. Larsen, *supra* n. 2.

77 Helium-3 is particularly valuable and could become a significant source of energy on Earth; CoCoSL II, 339; R.B. Bilder, 'A Legal Regime for the Mining of Helium-3 on the Moon: US Policy Options' (2010) 33 *Fordham Int. L.J.* 243–299.

78 Solar power satellites in GSO might be constructed on the moon and brought back to their orbital locations. P.B. Larsen, 'Current Legal Issues Pertaining to Solar Power Systems' (2020) 16 *Space Policy* 139–144.

exploitation of the resources of the moon and other celestial bodies.[79] 'Freedom of use' (OST Art. I) has been appealed to justify minimising constraints on private activities. On the other hand, OST Art. II prohibits appropriation, and caution has been advocated. States have duties to avoid contamination and disruption of the moon or other celestial bodies by their licensing procedures.[80] That said, any economic exploitation of the moon and other celestial bodies poses legal problems, and many suggestions have been made.[81]

79 See n. 75 *supra*, together with M. Menter, 'Commercial Space Activities under the Moon Treaty' (1979–1980) 7 *Syracuse J. Int. L. and Com.* 213–238; A. Dula, 'Free Enterprise and the Proposed Moon Treaty' (1979) 2 *Houston J. Int. L.* 3–33; L.L. Risely, 'An Examination of the Need to Amend Space Law to Protect the Private Explorer in Outer Space' (1999) 26 *West. St. Univ. L. Rev.* 47–70; E. Husby, 'Sovereignty and Property Rights in Outer Space' (1994) 3 *J. Int. L. and Pract.* 359–372; C.R. Buxton, 'Property in Outer Space: The Common Heritage of Mankind Principle vs. the First in Time, First in Right Rule of Property' (2004) 69 *J. Air L. & Comm.* 689–707; L.E. Shaw, 'Asteroids, the New Western Frontier: Applying Principles of the General Mining Law of 1872 to Incentivize Asteroid Mining' (2013) 78 *J. Air L.& Comm.* 121–169. Cf. also the many contributions as to the arguable importance of property rights in outer space in successive *Procs IISL*.

80 Cf. Chapter 9 as to the application of concepts of terrestrial international environmental law to the moon. See also Larsen and Roberts, both *supra* n. 60.

81 M. Hofmann, ed., *Protecting the Environment of Celestial Bodies* (Paris: IAA Cosmic Study, 2010); E. Morozova and A. Laurenava, 'To the Moon and Back: On the Way to a Well-Balanced Liability Framework for Lunar and Cislunar Activities' (2021) 45 *J. Sp. L.* 176–200; B.R. Israel, 'Space Resources in the Evolutionary Course of Space Lawmaking' (2019) 113 *AJIL Unbound* 114–119; M. Hofmann and F. Bergamasco, 'Space Resources Activities from the Perspective of Sustainability: Legal Aspects' (2020) 3 *Global Sustainability*, e4, 1–7: https://doi.org/10.1017/sus.2019.27; Larsen, *supra* n. 2; H.A. Wassenberg, 'Speculations on the Law Governing Space Resources' (1980) 5 *AASL* 611–624; K.A. Baca, 'Property Rights in Outer Space' (1993) 58 *J. Air L. & Comm.* 1041–1085; J. Zullo, 'The Need to Clarify the Status of Property Rights in International Space Law' (2002) 90 *Geo. Int. L.J.* 2413–2444; R. Berkeley, 'Space Law versus Space Utilization: The Inhibition of Private Industry in Outer Space' (1996–7) 15 *Wisc. J. Int. L.J.* 221–243; R.P. Merges and G.H. Reynolds, 'Space Resources, Common Property and the Collective Action Problem' (1997) 6 *N.Y. U. Env. L.J.* 107–125; B.M. Hoffstadt, 'Moving the Heavens: Lunar Mining and the "Common Heritage of Mankind" in the Moon Treaty' (1994) 42 *UCLA L. Rev.* 575–621; K.V. Cook, 'The Discovery of Lunar Water: An Opportunity to Develop a Workable Moon Treaty' (1994) 11 *Geo. Int. Env. L. Rev.* 647–706; B. Jacobs, 'The Future of Energy: Lunar Resource Management and the Common Heritage of Mankind' (2012) 24 *Geo Int. Env. L. Rev.* 221–244; M.J. Listner, 'The Ownership and Exploitation of Outer Space: A Look at Foundational Law and Future Legal Challenges to Current Claims' (2003) 1 *Regent J. Int. L.* 75–94; J.R. Wilson, 'Regulation of the Outer Space Environment through International Accord: the 1979 Moon Treaty' (1991) 2 *Fordham Env. L. Rep.* 173–194; J.L. Zell, 'Putting a Mine on the Moon: Creating an International Authority to Regulate Mining Rights in Outer Space' (2006) 15 *Minn. J. Int. L.* 489–519; E.J. Reinstein, 'Owning Outer Space' (1999) 20 *Nw. J. Int. L. and Bus.* 59–98; H.H. Hertzfeld and F.G. von der Dunk, 'Bringing Space Law into the Commercial World: Property Rights Without Sovereignty' (2005) 6 *Chi. J. Int. L.* 81–99; S. Doyle, 'Using Extraterrestrial Resources under the Moon Agreement of 1979' (1998) 26 *J. Sp. L.* 111–128 [Lyall/Larsen 543–60]; F. Lyall, 'On the Moon' (1998) 28 *J. Sp. L.* 129–138; G.H. Reynolds, 'International Space Law: Into the Twenty-First Century' (1992) 24 *Vand. J. Transnat. L.* 225–255 at 229–237; A.D. Webber, 'Extraterrestrial Law on the Final Frontier: A Regime to Govern the Development of Celestial Body Resources' (1983) 71 *Geo. L.J.* 1427–1456; C.Q. Christol, 'The Moon and Mars Missions: Can International Law Meet the Challenge' (1999) 19 *J. Sp. L.* 123–136; R. Sattler, 'Transporting a Legal System for Property Rights: From the Earth to the Stars' (2005) 6 *Chic. J. Int. L.* 23–44; D. Collins, 'Efficient Allocation of Real Property Rights on the Planet Mars' (2008) 14 *B.U. J. Sci. and Tech. L.* 201–219; T.R. Irwin, 'Space Rocks: A Proposal to Govern the Development of Outer Space and Its Resources' (2015) 76 *Ohio State L.J.* 217–246; M. Powell, 'Understanding the Promises and Pitfalls of Outer Space Mining and the Need for an International Regulatory Body to Govern the Extraction of Space-Based Resources' (2018–2019) 19 *Pitt J. Tech. L. and Pol.* 1–36. A. Froehlich, ed., *Space Resource Utilization: A View from an Emerging Space Faring Nation* (Vienna: Springer, 2018). See also H. L. van Traa-Engelmann, *Commercial Utilisation of Outer Space-Legal Aspects* (Dordrecht: Nijhoff, 1993).

Some argue that concepts of sustainable development, lately a mantra in terrestrial environmental debates, should be complied with.[82] Certainly states licensing the economic exploitation of celestial bodies will need to be rigorous, requiring disruption and contamination to be avoided and policed to ensure compliance.[83] Analogues of the problems already caused by space debris, not to mention the pollution of the seas[84] and the devastation caused by some terrestrial mining,[85] must be avoided. Licences should include obligations to remove disused facilities and equipment. Suitably amended, the requirements for the removal of installations from the continental shelf could provide a model, although their various loopholes and discretions might be limited in their application in space or to celestial bodies.[86]

Unilateral acts by the commercial operators of one state may interfere with the rights of another state in outer space and could upset the balance among the states that is created by the OST. Under the Treaty, all nongovernmental acts taking place on celestial bodies

82 A.G. Apking, 'The Rush to Develop Space: The Role of Spacefaring Nations in Forging Environmental Standards for the Use of Celestial Bodies for Governmental and Private Interests' (2006) 16 *Colo. J. Int. Env. L.* 429–466; D. Tan, 'Towards a New Regime for the Protection of Outer Space as the "Province of All Mankind"' (2000) 25 *Yale J. Int. L.* 145–194.

83 L.D. Roberts, 'Ensuring the Best of All Possible Worlds: Environmental Regulation of the Solar System' (1997) 6 *N.Y. U. Env. L.J.* 126–160.

84 Cf. the International Convention for the Prevention of Pollution from Ships (MARPOL Convention) 1973 (1340 UNTS 184), and subsequent Protocols. Areas of the Pacific are covered by debris, much of it plastic. See the US National Research Council Report, *Tackling Marine Debris in the 21st Century* (National Academies Press, 2009: www.nap.edu/catalog.php?record_id=12486). See also *supra* n. 58 and Larsen, *supra* n. 13.

85 Cf. the facts behind S. Stec et al., 'Transboundary Environmental Governance and the Baia Mare Cyanide Spill' (2001) 27 *Rev. Cent. and E. Eur. Law*, 639–691; A.K.-J. Tan, 'All that Glitters: Foreign Investment Trumps the Environment in the Philippines' (2005–2006) 23 *Pace Env. L. Rev.* 183–220; R.E. Reyes, Jr., 'Nauru v Australia: The International Fiduciary Duty and the Settlement of Nauru's Claims for Rehabilitation of its Phosphate Lands' (1996) *N.Y. L. Sch. J. Int. and Comp. L.* 1–55; A. Anghie, ' "The Heart of my Home": Colonialism, Environmental Damage, and the Nauru Case' (1993) 34 *Harv. Int. L.J.* 445–508; *Certain Phosphate Lands in Nauru (Nauru v Australia) (Preliminary Objections)* 1992 ICJ 240, case instituted 1989 ICJ 1, discontinued on settlement, 1993 ICJ 322. See also UNEP Principles: 'Draft Principles on the Conduct in the Field of the Environment for the Conduct of States in the Conservation and Harmonious Utilization of Natural Resources Shared by Two or More States', UNEP Governing Council (1978) 17 *ILM* 1091–1099.

86 The second sentence of Art. 5.5 of the Geneva Convention on the Continental Shelf, 1958 (499 UNTS 311) stated, 'Any installations which are abandoned or disused must be entirely removed'. This was weakened by the parallel provision in Art. 60.3 of UNCLOS 1982 (1833 UNTS 3; (1994) 33 ILM 1309), which includes the sentence that 'Any installations or structures which are abandoned or disused shall be removed to ensure safety of navigation, taking into account any generally accepted international standards established in this regard by the competent international organization'. That allows the relevant licensing state unduly wide discretion. The 'competent international organization' for UNCLOS is the International Maritime Organisation (IMO), whose guidelines on such matters were adopted by the IMO Assembly in 1989: 'Guidelines Standards for the Removal of Offshore Installations and Structures on the Continental Shelf and in the Exclusive Economic Zone' A.672(16) 1989 (available via: www.imo.org/home.asp and the list of IMO Assembly Resolutions). These hold that the relevant state 'should ensure' the removal of abandoned or dis-used installations and structures 'as soon as reasonably practicable' and subject to some exceptions and conditions. Cf. the regional provision in Arts. 5 and 7–8 of Annex III to the Convention for the Protection of the Marine Environment of the North-East Atlantic, 1992, the 'OSPAR Convention', 2354 UNTS 67; (1993) ILM 1069, 1072. The excuse of *force majeure* in Art. 6 of its Annex III should be ignored in any analogising to space. The OSPAR Commission supervises the application of the Convention: www.ospar.org/convention. See OSPAR Commission Decision 98/3 on the 'Disposal of Disused Offshore Installations' for detailed requirements.

are the equivalent of formal government actions. By authorizing the actions of nongovernmental activities, a state takes on the full responsibility for those acts as if they were its own. In addition, however, we consider that any space activity involving the environment of the moon, or any other celestial body should as part of its licensing be made subject to an environmental impact assessment. It should be open for interested parties, not only nationals of the licensing state, to contribute to the process, and the assessment should be officially published.[87]

The scientific exploration of celestial bodies presents no legal difficulty under current international rules. The major planets have all been reached, some by way of a fly-by[88] and others now with probes in orbit around them.[89] Asteroids[90] and comets have been investigated,[91] but actual exploitation of the moon and celestial bodies other than the moon is now upon us.

'The moon' requires no definition, but the term 'celestial bodies' has not been formally defined. Two of the early UNGA Space Resolutions, Res. 1721 and 1962, referred to outer space 'and' celestial bodies.[92] In its paras 2 and 4, the latter spoke of the use of outer space in terms that imply that that use includes using celestial bodies. As part of the *travaux preparatoires* of the OST, the covering letter for the 1966 US proposal of a draft treaty referred to 'the Moon and other celestial bodies', but the annexed draft spoke only of 'celestial bodies'.[93] In contrast, Art. 1 of the USSR draft did refer to 'Outer space, including the Moon and other celestial bodies'.[94] In neither case was there an attempt to define celestial bodies.

However, OST Arts. I, II and III thereafter make it clear that the rules as to use, exploration and appropriation cover celestial bodies by specifically including them. Later treaties and UNGA Resolutions follow that practice. Notwithstanding, over the years, there has still been debate as to the exact content of the term.[95] For instance, how big must a body be to be a celestial body? That said, it is clear that asteroids and comets are included, bodies which are here of immediate interest.

---

87 Cf. F. Lyall, 'Planetary Protection from a Legal Perspective – General Issues', in M. Hofmann, *supra* n. 81, 55–62 at 62; F. Lyall, 'Protection of the Space Environment and Law' (1999) 42 *Proc. IISL* 472–482; W.R. Kramer, 'Extraterrestrial Environmental Impact Assessments – A Foreseeable Prerequisite for Wise Decisions Regarding Outer Space Exploration, Research and Development' (2014) 30 *Space Pol.* 215–222.

88 Many space probes have passed close to major planets during their manoeuvres on their way to their main objectives. See Wikipedia entry 'List of active Solar System probes'. On 14 July 2015, the New Horizons probe flew past Pluto: see Wikipedia entry 'New Horizons'.

89 Venus, Mars, Jupiter and Saturn currently have probes orbiting them, and the 'Messenger' orbited Mercury for four years (2011–2015). See Wikipedia 'List of active Solar System probes'.

90 In 2010, the Hayabusa mission brought samples from asteroid Itokawa taken in 2005: see Wikipedia entry 'Hayabusa'. See also generally Wikipedia entry 'Asteroid', sv, 'Exploration'. Many asteroids have been 'flown-by' as part of other missions. Cf. the Nemitz case, *supra* n. 40. See also data on asteroid Bennu, *infra* Chapter 9, fn. 253 para 2.

91 In 1986, ESA's Giotto spacecraft investigated Halley's comet: see Wikipedia entry 'Giotto (spacecraft)'. In 2014–2015, the Rosetta Mission orbited comet Churyumov–Gerasimenko and landed the probe Philae, and eventually the Rosetta probe itself, on it: see Wikipedia entry 'Rosetta (spacecraft)'.

92 UNGA Res. 1721 (XVI) of 1961, Part. A para 1 (a) and (b); UNGA Res. 1962 (XVIII) of 1963 paras 2 and 3.

93 See A/AC.105/C.2/L/12 and A/AC.105/32.

94 See A/AC.105/C.2/L/13.

95 E. Fasan, 'The Legal Nature of the Celestial Bodies' (1961) 4 *Proc. IISL* 267–293 and 'Asteroids and other Celestial Bodies – Some Legal Differences' (1998) 26 *J. Sp. L.* 33–40; Larsen, *supra* n. 2, at 280; B. Cheng, 'Outer Void Space: The Reason for this Neologism in Space Law' (1999) *Austl. Int. L.J.* 1–8.

Any exploitation of the resources of the moon or other celestial bodies will require those conducting it to go through a licensing process. But what should the general approach be to the opening of the new possibilities? As of 2022, apart from a general free-for-all, three approaches to an international structure for the commercial exploitation of celestial bodies have emerged: (1) common heritage, (2) the Building Blocks Proposal of 2019 and (3) the Artemis Accords of 2021. All are immediately directed to the exploitation of the moon but have wider application including to asteroids. We will consider national laws on the matter later.[96]

Common Heritage

Discussion of a legal regime for exploiting space resources has been affected by the inchoate concept of the 'common heritage of mankind'. Indeed, it is not too much to say that the common heritage concept has both enriched and trammelled discussion.[97] We therefore first briefly outline the concept in general before considering its manifestation in the MA.

The call for treating the seabed beyond national jurisdiction as part of the common heritage of mankind was made by Ambassador Pardo of Malta in 1967[98] and is generally

---

96 *Infra* at n. 134.
97 K. Baslar, *The Concept of the Common Heritage of Mankind in International Law* (The Hague: Nijhoff, 1998); cf. M.G. Schmidt, *Common Heritage or Common Burden: The United States Position on the Development of a Regime for the Deep Sea-Bed Mining in the Law of the Sea Convention* (Oxford: Clarendon Press, 1989); and S.K. Chopra, 'Antarctica as a Commons Regime' at 163 and H.J. Taubenfeld, 'The Antarctic and Outer Space' at 269, both in C.G. Joyner and S.K. Chopra, eds., *The Antarctic Legal Regime* (Dordrecht: Nijhoff, 1988); C.C. Joyner, 'Legal Implications of the Concept of the Common Heritage of Mankind' (1986) 35 ICLQ 190–199; L.F.E. Goldie, 'A Note on Some Diverse Meanings of "The Common Heritage of Mankind" ' (1983) 10 *Syracuse J. Int. L. & Com.* 69–112 and his 'Title and Use (Usufruct) – An Ancient Distinction Too Oft Forgot' (1985) 79 *AJIL* 689–714; P.D. Nesgos, 'The Proposed International Sea-Bed Authority as a Model for the Future Outer Space International Regime' (1980) 5 *AASL* 549–574; L.M. Fountain, 'Creating Momentum in Space: Ending the Paralysis Produced by the "Common Heritage of Mankind" Concept' (2003) 35 *Conn. L. Rev.* 1753–1788; J.E. Noyes, 'The Common Heritage of Mankind: Past, Present, and Future' (2012) 40 *Denv. J. Int. L. Pol.* 447–471; B.M. Hoffstadt, 'Moving the Heavens: Lunar Mining and the "Common Heritage of Mankind" in the Moon Treaty' (1994) 42 *UCLA L. Rev.* 575–621; B. Jacobs, 'The Future of Energy: Lunar Resource Management and the Common Heritage of Mankind' (2012) 24 *Geo Int. Env. L. Rev.* 221–244; M. Svec, 'Outer Space, an Area Recognised as Res Communis Omnium: Limits of National Space Mining Law' (2022) 60 *Sp. Pol.* 1–7.
Apart from in connection with Antarctica and the Deep Sea-Bed, the common heritage concept has emerged in discussions on a variety of subjects including DNA: M.L. Sturges, 'Who Should Hold Property Rights to the Human Rights Genome – An Application of the Common Heritage of Humankind' (1997) 13 *Am. U. Int. L. Rev.* 219–61; J.A. Bovenberg, 'Mining the Common Heritage of Our DNA: Lessons Learned from Grotius and Pardo' (2006) 8 *Duke Law and Tech. Rev.* no. 8, and Plant Resources: C.B. Onwuekwe, 'The Commons Concept and Intellectual Property Rights: Whither Plant Genetic Resources and Traditional Knowledge?' (2004) 2 *Pierce L. Rev.* 65–90. In substance, common heritage also appears in discussions of art, cultural objects and natural heritage: Convention on the Protection of the World Cultural and Natural Heritage (Paris: UNESCO, 1972); (1972) 11 ILM 1358–66, with Recommendations at 1367–1374: http://whc.unesco.org/archive/convention-en.pdf. G. Nicholson, 'The Common Heritage of Mankind and Mining: An Analysis of the Law as to the High Seas, Outer Space, Antarctica and World Heritage' (2002) 6 *N.Z. J. Env. L.* 177–98 at 194–6; A. Strati, 'The Implication of Common Heritage Concepts on the Quest for Cultural Objects and the Dialogue between North and South' (1995) *Proc. Am. Soc Int. L.* 439–443.
98 1515th Meeting of the First Committee, 1 November 1967. See also UNGA Res. 2749 and 2750 (XXV) both dealing with the Sea-Bed and Ocean Floor. M.W. Lodge, 'The Common Heritage of Mankind' (2012) 27 *Int. J. Marine & Coastal L.* 733–742.

accepted as the first articulation of the notion in those exact words. However, the terminology had previously been introduced by A.A. Cocca at COPUOS meetings, and indeed the idea of setting aside territory from national sovereignty has a long history.[99] The associated notion that 'all' or 'all countries' should benefit from the exploitation of the resources of a common heritage area that has been specifically set aside or that lies outwith sovereignty is more recent. Fundamentally, it is part of the drive towards a New International Economic Order (NIEO), introduced by the developing countries into international discussions and negotiations in the 1960s and 1970s.[100] That the MA and the UN Convention on the Law of the Sea (UNCLOS) use the term 'common heritage' differently is because each treaty defines its own terms.

As far as the moon is concerned, the OST has relevant provisions as to freedom of use (Art. I), the exclusion of national claims (Art. II), the rule of international law (Art. III), of affording assistance to others and reporting of dangerous phenomena (Art. V), cooperation, the avoidance of harmful contamination and of harmful interference with the activities of others (Art. IX). States licensing exploitative activities must bear these in mind.[101] That is not contentious. What is contentious is the introduction of the common heritage concept in the MA.

Article 11.1 crystallises the matter by asserting that the 'moon and its natural resources are the common heritage of mankind'.[102] The sentence continues by declaring that that common heritage 'finds its expression in the provisions of this Agreement, in particular paragraph 5 of this article', a qualifying clause intended to distinguish the common

---

99 Repeating material from Chapter 3, setting aside territory from claims of sovereignty may have begun with early twentieth-century discussions as to Spitzbergen and the Svalbard archipelago. In 1910, it was suggested that 'East and West Antarctica' (areas not claimed in 1910) should 'become the common possessions of all of the family of nations': T.W. Balch, 'Arctic and Antarctic Regions and the Law of Nations' (1910) 4 AJIL 265–275 at 274–275; cf. J.B. Scott, 'Arctic Exploration and International Law' (1909) 3 AJIL 928–941 at 941. That idea was not then carried into law, but a mutant re-emerges with the Antarctic Treaty of 1959 following the 1957 International Geophysical Year (*supra* n.22). The Svalbard Treaty of 1920 (2 LNTS 7, 2 Bevans 269 (US) 43 Stat. 18–92, TS 686) recognised Spitzbergen and the rest of the archipelago as Norwegian while providing for freedom of hunting and access to fishing grounds. See W. Østreng (R.I. Christophersen trans.) *Politics in High Altitudes: The Svalbard Archipelago* (London: Hurst, 1977).

100 See 'Declaration on the Establishment of a New International Economic Order (A/9556)' UNGA Res. 3201 (S-VI), 1974; the related 'Programme of Action' UNGA Res. 3202 (S-VI) 1974, and the 'Charter of Economic Rights and Duties of States', UNGA Res. 3281 (XXIX) 1974. M. Hudson, *Global Fracture: The New International Economic Order* (London: HarperCollins, 1977; Pluto Press, 2005); Noyes, *supra* n. 97, at 469–470. Discussion of the NIEO lies beyond the ambit of this book, but cf. Chapter 10 Direct Broadcasting as to the New International Information Order. On space and the NIEO, see S.D. Mau, 'Equity, the Third World and the Moon Treaty' (1984) 8 *Suffolk Transnat. L.J.* 221–258; Hoffstadt, *supra* n. 81, at 618–619.

101 All discussed earlier in this chapter and in Chapter 3.

102 F. Tronchetti, 'The Moon Agreement in the 21st Century: Addressing Its Potential Role in the Era of Commercial Exploitation of the Natural Resources of the Moon and Other Celestial Bodies' (2010) 36 *J. Sp. L.* 489–524; Noyes, *supra* n. 97; S.B. Rosenfeld, 'The Moon Treaty: The United States Should Not Become a Party' (1980) 74 *ASIL Proc.* 162–166; A.R. Filiato, 'The Commercial Space Launch Act: America's Response to the Moon Treaty' (1987) 10 *Fordham Intl L.J.* 763–781; C.Q. Christol, 'The Common Heritage of Mankind Provision in the 1979 Agreement Governing the Activities of States on the Moon and Other Celestial Bodies' (1980) 14 *Int. L.* 429–484; J. Frakes, 'The Common Heritage of Mankind Principle and the Deep Seabed, Outer Space, and Antarctica: Will Developed and Developing Countries Reach a Compromise?' (2003) 21 *Wisc. Int. L.J.* 409–434. See also US Senate report, *supra* n. 28.

heritage of the moon from that of the deep sea-bed beyond the limits of national jurisdiction provided by Art. 1 and Part XI (as later amended) of UNCLOS, which was being negotiated at the same time as the MA[103] and in which NIEO concepts and arguments played a role.[104] Part XI of UNCLOS and Annexes III and IV lay down detailed provisions for an International Seabed Authority to organise and license the exploitation of seabed resources beyond the limits of national jurisdiction among the UNCLOS members, and an 'Enterprise' to conduct activities and mechanisms for the transfer of technology. The common heritage provisions of the MA pale by comparison.

What the assertion in MA Art. 11.1 signifies in relation to much of the MA is obscure to the point of meaninglessness, but Arts. 11.2–8 spell out some matters more clearly. Article 11.2, prohibiting national appropriation of the moon, repeats the substance of OST Art. II. Under Art. 11.3, the moon surface, subsurface, natural resources in place, and structures on it cannot become the subject of any right of property or ownership, though this is without prejudice to any future international regime as contemplated in Art. 11.5. Article 11.4 allows parties to explore and use the moon without discrimination and on the basis of equality, in accordance with international law and the Agreement.

Those provisions would be acceptable to most in relation to exploratory activities. However, MA Art. 11.5 calls for an international governance regime to be established when exploitation of the moon's natural resources is about to become feasible.[105] Article 11.6 calls for the creation of this international regime to be facilitated by states reporting 'to the greatest extent feasible and practicable' to the UN Secretary General, to the public and to the international scientific community, of any natural resources discovered on the moon. Knowledge would apparently therefore trigger the detailed negotiation of the international regime.[106]

Article 11.7 spells out the purposes of the international regime as the orderly and safe development of the natural resources (MA Art. 11.7.a), their rational management (MA Art. 11.7.b) and the expansion of opportunities in their use (MA Art. 11.7.c). MA Art. 11.7.d then attempts a balance as it calls for an 'equitable sharing' by all state parties 'in the benefits derived from those resources, whereby the interests and needs of the developing countries, as well as the efforts of those countries which have contributed either directly or indirectly to the exploration of the moon, shall be given special consideration'. The attempt is a complete failure.

While 'equitable' is not the same as 'equal', the interests of both the space-active and the non-space-active are to be treated as 'special'. It is unsurprising therefore that no currently space-competent state (i.e. one able to get to the moon by its own efforts) has

---

103 UNCLOS, Montego Bay, 1982, 1833 UNTS 3; US Tr. Doc. 103–39; (1982) 21 ILM 1261–1354; Part XI amended, 1999 UKTS 82, Cm. 4525; (1994) 33 ILM 1309–27; UNGA Res. 48/263; L.B. Sohn et al., *Cases and Materials on the Law of the Seas*, 2nd ed. (Leiden: Nijhoff, 2014) 620–632.

104 Cf. R.L. Friedheim and W.J. Durch, 'The International Seabed Resources Agency and the New International Economic Order' (1977) 31 *Int. Org.* 343–384; G.M. Danilenko, 'The Concept of the "Common Heritage of Mankind" in International Law' (1988) 13 *AASL* 247–263; D. Yarn, 'The Transfer of Technology and UNCLOS III' (1984) 14 *Ga. J. Int. and Comp. L.* 121–154.

105 Note that the phrasing is 'is about to become feasible', not the simple 'is feasible'.

106 It has been suggested that this means that exploitation cannot start until such a regime is established. That might be true as between MA parties, but it will certainly not impede others from going ahead: cf. Rosenfeld, n. 102 *supra*. The MA does not specifically provide for a moratorium on development until the regime is agreed. Some states, e.g., the US, are of the view that no moratorium exists; others disagree.

fully committed to the MA,[107] and the history of the developing countries' argumentation makes future commitment to it by other space-faring states unlikely. In this case, therefore, the concept of common heritage coupled with international regime and benefit-sharing, hinders rather than encourages development.

The Building Blocks Proposal

After several years of discussion involving academics, industry, government and potential stakeholders in the utilisation of space resources, the Building Blocks Proposal emerged in 2019.[108] The proposal is that an international framework should provide an environment within which physical resources in space could be acquired in the interests of all. Recommendations would be made to states and international organizations as to their arrangements for such matters and best practice identified and promoted (Sec. 1). Stripped to the essentials, there would be a public register into which states authorising particular operators to engage in resource mining would enter information as to the purpose, location, orbital parameters and duration of the activity. Registration would afford priority to the registrants, to which other states would pay heed (Secs. 14 and 18).[109] Rights to resources obtained would be lawfully recognised by national law or by bi- or multilateral agreement (Sec. 8).

States would set safety, environmental and other basic operating rules (Sec. 19). International operating standards and recommended practices would be established that would include creating safety zones around extraction sites while being respectful of the OST Art I provision as to freedom of use and non-discrimination (Sec. 11).[110] As for benefit, the proposal is that states would share the benefit they secure with other states, particularly with developing countries, including information, expertise and technology, and even by joint ventures, but not by compulsory monetary benefit-sharing (Sec. 13).[111]

The Building Blocks Proposal constitutes a neutral potential method of regulating the use of celestial resources that may be accepted as COPUOS guidelines. As such, it has been

---

107 France and India have signed the MA, but France acts through ESA, which has not accepted the Agreement.

108 The Hague International Space Resources Governance Working Group: Building Blocks for the Development of an International Framework on Space Resource Activities (2019); UN OOSA Doc. A/AC.105/C.2/L.315: https://documents-dds-ny.un.org/doc/UNDOC/LTD/V20/008/95/PDF/V2000895.pdf?OpenElement; www.unoosa.org/oosa/oosadoc/data/documents/2020/aac.105c.2l/aac.105c.2l.315_0.html. 'The Hague International Space Resources Governance Working Group: Building Blocks for the Development of an International Framework' (2019) 43 *J. Sp. L.* 151–170. See also O. de O. Bittencourt Neto *et al.*, eds., *Building Blocks for the Development of an International Framework on Space Resource Activities: A Commentary* (The Hague: Eleven Publishing, 2020); P.B. Larsen, 'Is There a Legal Path to Commercial Mining on the Moon?' (2021) 83 *U. Pitt. L. Rev.* 1–50; M.J. Sundahl and J.A. Murphy, 'Set the Controls for the Heart of the Moon: Is Existing Law Sufficient to Enable Resource Extraction on the Moon?' (2020) 48 *Geo. J. Int. and Comp. L.* 683–694; F. Schilling, 'The Luxembourgish Interpretation of the Appropriation of In-Situ Resources' (2019) 68 *ZLW* 248–260.

109 It seems to be assumed that states would assign exclusive right of use of specific resources and avoid conflict with prior registrations.

110 Some feel that the Building Blocks Proposal fails to comply with the OST Art. II prohibition on appropriation of the moon or the environmental protection provisions of OST Art. 11. See Larsen, *supra* n. 13 for criticism of the Proposal. Cf. M. Stubbs, 'The Legality of Keep-Out, Operational and Safety Zones in Outer Space', in C. Steer and M. Hersch, eds., *War and Peace in Outer Space: Law, Policy and Ethics* (Oxford: OUP, 2921).

111 Contrast the benefit provisions of MA Art 11.7 *supra*.

submitted to COPUOS with the objective of its adoption.[112] Whatever happens, it will be influential.

The Artemis Program and Accords

In 2017, then US President Trump authorised the return of humans to the moon and in effect lunar exploitation.[113] The result was the Artemis program,[114] with its associated plan.[115] Cooperating with NASA in the program so far are the Canadian Space Agency, the ESA, and the Japanese Space Agency. In Artemis 1, a powerful new NASA rocket, the Space Launch System will carry an Orion spacecraft to a cislunar gateway, where a small space station will be built to support the programme.[116] From there, astronauts will land on the moon and establish a lunar site. The gateway and any lunar site will be supplied from Earth by commercial enterprises.

Associated with the program are the Artemis Accords, a development, if not a circumvention, of elements of the OST.[117] Space agencies signatory to the Accords agree

---

112 See COPUOS Report, A/77/20, sec. 11, paras 261–278 on potential legal models for activities in exploration, exploitation and utilisation of space resources and A/AC.105/1260, paras 203–230. A Working Group on Legal Aspects of Space Resource Activities has been established within the COPUOS Legal Subcommittee.

113 The Presidential Memorandum on Reinvigorating American's Human Space Program, 11 December 2017, *inter alia* called for the US to 'lead the return of humans to the Moon for long-term exploration and utilization, followed by human missions to Mars and other destinations' by 'an innovative and sustainable program of exploration with commercial and international partners': https://trumpwhitehouse.archives. gov/presidential-actions/presidential-memorandum-reinvigorating-americas-human-space-exploration-program/. The 2020 US National Space Policy set as a goal the establishment of a permanent human presence on the moon and as part of the civil space guidelines calls for the US to 'lead the return of humans to the Moon for long-term exploration and utilization, followed by human missions to Mars and other destinations': https://trumpwhitehouse.archives.gov/wp-content/uploads/2020/12/National-Space-Policy.pdf.

114 The Artemis Program: www.nasa.gov/artemisprogram (2020). Cf. NASA, 'Why How Latest': www.nasa. gov/specials/artemis/.

115 *Artemis Plan* 2020: www.nasa.gov/sites/default/files/atoms/files/artemis_plan-20200921.pdf.

116 *National Cislunar Science & Technology*, 2022: www.whitehouse.gov/wp-content/uploads/2022/11/11-2022-NSTC-National-Cislunar-ST-Strategy.pdf. For Gateway: www.nasa.gov/gateway/overview. See also the US-Japan MOU, 'Concerning Cooperation on the Civil Lunar Gateway'; TIAS 20–1231.4. Cf. M.J. Holzinger et al. *A Primer on Cislunar Space* (US AFRL, 2021): www.afrl.af.mil/Portals/90/ Documents/RV/A%20Primer%20on%20Cislunar%20Space_Dist%20A_PA2021-1271.pdf?ver= vs6e0sE4PuJ51QC-15DEfg%3D%3D.

117 The Artemis Accords: Principles for Cooperation in the Civil Exploration and Use of the Moon, Mars, Comets, and Asteroids for Peaceful Purposes: www.nasa.gov/specials/artemis-accords/img/Artemis-Accords-signed-13Oct2020.pdf: www.nasa.gov/specials/artemis-accords/index.html. B. Bartócki-Gönczi and B. Nagy, 'The Artemis Accords' (2023) 62 *ILM* 888–898; A.Y. Lee, 'The Future of the Law on the Moon' (2023) 88 *J. Air L. & Comm.* 3–103; S. Hobe, 'Commentary on the Article by Andrew Lee Entitled the Future of the Law on the Moon' (2023) 88 *J. Air L. & Comm.* 223–226; S. Hobe, 'The Artemis Accords: What They Mean for the Development of International Space Law' (2021) 70 *ZLW* 1–12; S. Mosteshar, 'Artemis: The Discordant Accords' (2020) 44 *J. Sp. L.* 591–603; Y. Osada, 'Governance of Space Resources Activities: In the Wake of the Artemis Accords' (2022) 53 *Georgetown J. Int. L.* 399–511; R. Deplano, 'The Artemis Plan: A Paradigm Shift in International Law?' (2022) 46 *J. Sp. L.* 101–133; W.A. Smith, 'Using the Artemis Accords to Build Customary International Law: Vision for US-Centric Good Governance Regime in Outer Space' (2021) 86 *J. Air L. & Comm.* 661–700; Larsen, *supra* n. 13. Cf. L. Wiser and T. Aganaba, 'An Evolving Space Government System: Balancing Interests in Five Policy Debates' (2023) 203 *Acta Astronautica* 537–543. See also *infra* n. 121.

to observe and comply with the principles and practices there set out.[118] The Accords, however, do not constitute formal, binding, legal obligations: this is not a treaty.[119] The commitment to the Accords of nongovernmental commercial entities will derive from the national regulation under which they are licensed to operate.

By entering into the Artemis Accords with NASA, parties promise to interpret the OST as set forth in the Accords. They agree to apply commercially acceptable mining practices on the moon. They agree that in accordance with OST Art. IV, commercial mining activities will be peaceful (Section 3), that national regulation will be transparent (Section 4) and that activities will be interoperable (Section 5). Parties will assist each other in accord with ARRA (Section 6). As required by the Registration Convention, parties will decide which state should register jointly owned space objects. Scientific data will be transparent, except that commercial operators will not be required to share scientific information (Section 8). Parties will preserve and protect heritage sites (Section 9).

While the parties agree to comply with the OST, they agree to interpret OST Art. II to permit the extraction of natural resources from the moon (Section 10). Parties agree to 'pay due regard to the corresponding interests of other States' and, in accordance with OST Art IX, to avoid harmful contamination and adverse changes to Earth's environment. Parties agree that commercial operations may establish reasonable safety zones around each site.[120] The purpose of the safety zones is to avoid harmful interference and to warn outsiders of possible dangers rather than to exclude them (Section 11).

Finally, parties agree to require environmental clean-up after commercial operations 'to the extent practicable' (Section 12). An informal meeting of the then twenty-one signatories to the Accords was held during the IAF Paris conference in 2022, and it is to be hoped that such meetings will become regular.[121] Best of all would be agreement on adopting a system of Consultative Meetings of parties similar to that under the Antarctic Treaty.[122]

The most controversial feature of the Artemis Accords is the agreement to exercise control over commercial mining and other business sites on the moon. OST Art. II prohibits appropriation of the moon,[123] such prohibition to be enforced by the national states authorising and supervising governmental and nongovernmental activities[124] Therefore, economic exploitation of the moon and other celestial bodies poses legal problems for Artemis non-members.[125] Might states uninvolved with the Accords argue that state agencies cannot lawfully re-interpret treaty provisions? Might the International Court of Justice be an appropriate forum? But if that argument were upheld, what then?

---

118 As of September 2023, signatories were the space agencies of Argentina, Australia, Bahrain, Brazil, Canada, Colombia, Czech Republic, Ecuador, France, Germany, India, Israel, Italy, Japan, Luxembourg, Mexico, New Zealand, Nigeria, Poland, Romania, Rwanda, Singapore, South Korea, Spain, Saudi Arabia, Singapore, Ukraine, United Arab Emirates, the UK (with the Isle of Man) and the US.

119 Cf. 'This is not a pipe' (Rene Magritte).

120 Cf. *supra* n. 110.

121 'Signatories of the U.S.-Led Artemis Accords Meet in Person for the First Time' (2023) 117 *AJIL* 133–139.

122 See *supra* n. 22.

123 OST Art. II, *supra* n. 8, see also MA Art. 11, *supra* n. 21. See Hobe, *supra* n. 117 and Larsen, *supra* n. 13 for criticism of the Artemis Accords.

124 The establishment of safety zones could raise environmental concerns; cf. Chapter 9 as to the application of concepts of terrestrial international environmental law to the moon. See also Larsen and Roberts, both *supra* n. 60.

125 See materials cited *supra* n. 81.

Again, differences in national interpretation and enforcement of the OST could result in disputes which might escalate into military conflict. The US Space Force has agreed to protect US space activities and those of its allies connected by the Artemis Accords.[126] Chinese uses of outer space may also expect the support of Chinese military authorities for their commercial activities on the moon. Despite the tenor of OST Art. 4.2, potential conflict between the US and its allies and China and its allies is not inconceivable.

Significant space powers including China and Russia do not intend to sign the Artemis Accords but will exploit the moon independently.[127] China is particularly active, with plans to establish lunar settlements. It has sent five exploratory satellites, intends commercial exploitation and will construct a lunar basis with occupation planned for 2030.[128] Another Chinese plan is to place telescopes on the moon and position satellites in lunar orbit, and it has an agreement with Russia to establish an international lunar research station.[129]

Concerns therefore arise about potential conflict between competing plans for lunar development. A lack of coordination between China and the US is particularly dangerous because of the increasing activity of national nongovernmental operators intent on profit.[130] There is also concern that the US, China and Russia are developing divergent 'rules of the road' in outer space.[131] China would prefer international rules on exploitation of outer space resources to be established by international agreement brokered through COPUOS,[132] but that seems unlikely.

126 Memorandum of Understanding between NASA and the US Space Force, 21 September 2020: www.nasa.gov/sites/default/files/atoms/files/nasa_ussf_mou_21_sep_20.pdf. The ambit of the MOU is not restricted to the Artemis Program. Cf. NASA, Release 20–091. 'US Space Force Establish Foundation for Broad Collaboration': www.nasa.gov/press-release/nasa-us-space-force-establish-foundation-for-broad-collaboration. The US Space Force was created in 2019: https://trumpwhitehouse.archives.gov/presidential-actions/text-space-policy-directive-4-establishment-united-states-space-force/. See Chapter 15.
127 Others are also active. Japan has plans to send a lander in 2023. South Korea sent a satellite to the moon and plans to send a rover in 2031.
128 Adam Mann, *China's Chang'e Program: Missions to the Moon*, SPACE.COM (Feb. 1, 2019): https://www.space.com/43199-chang-e-program.html [https://perma.cc/996C-6HPX]. M. Wall, *China's Chang'e 5 Capsule Lands on Earth with the 1st New Moon Samples in 44 Years*, SPACE.COM (16 December 2020): www.space.com/china-chang-e-5-moon-samples-capsule-landing (https://perma.cc/8UDG-SZJV).
129 *International Lunar Research Station: Guide for Partnership*, June 2021: www.cnsa.gov.cn/english/n6465652/n6465653/c6812150/content.html. China/Russia, 'Memorandum of Understanding Regarding Cooperation for the Construction of the International Lunar Research Station': www.cnsa.gov.cn/english/n6465652/n6465653/c6811380/content.html. Fengna Xu and Jun Ou, 'Promoting International Cooperation on the International Lunar Research Station: Inspiration from the ITER' (2023) 203 *Acta Astronautica* 341–350. Cf. US – China Economic and Security Commission, Report to Congress, 117 Cong. Sess. 2, November 2022, at 395: www.uscc.gov/sites/default/files/2022-11/2022_Annual_Report_to_Congress.pdf.
130 The 2011 Wolf Amendment to the US Department of Defense Appropriations restricts NASA's authority to coordinate with China: Public Law No. 112–10, para 1349, 125 Stat. 38, 123 (2011).
131 Secure World Foundation, 'Lost Without Translation, Gaps in US Perception of the Chinese Commercial Space', Section 8 (2021): https://swfound.org/media/207116/swf_caelus_lost_without_translation_identifying_gaps_in_us_perceptions_of_the_chinese_commercial_space_sector_2021.pdf. See also Elliot Ji et al. 'What Does China Think About NASA's Artemis Accords' *The Diplomat*, 2020: https://thediplomat.com/2020/09/what-does-china-think-about-nasas-artemis-accords/#!#:~:text=China%20views%20the%20U.S.%20attempt%20to%20enshrine%20new,use%20of%20outer%20space%20titled%20the%20Artemis%20Accords.
132 COPUOS Report on its Sixty-Fourth Session (2021), A/76/20 para 212. Cf. COPUOS Report on its Sixty-Fifth Session A/77/20 para 202.

China considers that the Artemis Accords unduly favour US allies and violate the OST Art II prohibition on appropriation. It is particularly concerned by the provision in the Accords that permit the establishment of safety zones around mining sites. As it is, the US and its allies, Russia and/or China and its allies may each authorise operations in overlapping 'Artemis sites' on the moon.

Finally, an interesting development is a move towards setting up a common lunar reference time for lunar systems and users. At present, each lunar effort depends on a timescale synchronised with terrestrial time. A LunaNet operating on a common reference time will allow better interaction and interoperability for individual efforts and the better operation of the gateway and other stations.[133]

Mining Celestial Bodies – National Moves[134]

There is a terrestrial market for meteorites,[135] and no one doubts the title of the American Museum of Natural History in New York to the exhibits in its Arthur Ross Hall of Meteorites, including Ahnighito, the Woman and the Dog, found by Peary in Greenland. Legal title to natural celestial bodies out in space remains impossible (OST Art. II).[136] But what of materials deliberately brought from space? The moon and asteroids will soon be mined and the product either used in space or transferred to Earth. Beyond that there is the question of Mars.[137]

Space mining has been extensively discussed.[138] There are current governmental initiatives for the exploitation of asteroids. In his 2010 Space Policy Statement, the then

---

133 See ESA Terrae Novae 2030+ Strategy: www.esa.int/Science_Exploration/Human_and_Robotic_Exploration/ Exploration/Terrae_Novae_Europe_s_exploration_vision. 'Telling time on the Moon', ESA: www.esa. int/Applications/Navigation/Telling_time_on_the_Moon. See also https://eu.usatoday.com/story/ news/nation/2023/03/01/moon-time-zone-standard-lunar-time/11373323002/, and www.space.com/ does-moon-need-its-own-time-zone. ESA also recommends a lunar GNSS using existing resources: see P. Gutierez, 'ESA Wants New Moon Missions to Use Moonlight', *Inside GNSS*, 4 October 2023: https:// insidegnss.com/esa-wants-new-moon-missions-to-use-moonlight-pnt-services.

134 Reference point *supra* n. 96.

135 Extra-terrestrial materials reaching the surface of the earth by natural means are excluded from the application of the MA (MA Art. 1.3). In 2010, the Hyabusa mission brought back samples from the asteroid Itokawa taken in 2005: see Wikipedia entry 'Hayabusa'. See also generally Wikipedia entries 'Asteroid', sv, 'Exploration' and 'Osiris Rex'. See also *supra* nn. 53 and 67.

136 See *supra* at n. 33. 'Sovereignty and Title to Immovables'.

137 T.E. Simmons, 'Deploying the Common Law to Quasi-Marxist Property on Mars' (2015) 51 *Gonz. L. Rev.* 25–78; Larsen, *supra* n. 2; C.Q. Christol, 'The Moon and Mars Missions: Can International Law Meet the Challenge' (1999) 19 *J. Sp. L.* 123–136; D. Collins, 'Efficient Allocation of Real Property Rights on the Planet Mars' (2008) 14 *B.U. J. Sci. Tech. L.* 201–219.

138 See materials cited *supra* n. 81, and IISL, Statement by the IISL Board of Directors on claims to property rights regarding the Moon and other celestial bodies, 7 November 2023: _ https://iisl.space/index. php/2023/11/07/statement-by-the-iisl-board-of-directors-on-claims-to-property-rights-regarding-the-moon-and-other-celestial-bodies/; T. Masson-Zwaan and N. Palkovitz, 'Regulation of Space Resource Rights: Meeting the Needs of States and Private Parties' (2017) 35 *QIL, Zoom-in* 5–18: www.qil-qdi. org/wp-content/uploads/2017/01/02_Space-Resources-Mining_MASSON-PALKOVITZ.pdf, or www. qil-qdi.org/regulation-space-resource-rights-meeting-needs-states-private-parties/; F. Tronchetti, 'Title IV – Space Resource Exploration and Utilization of the US Commercial Space Law Competitiveness Act: A Legal and Political Assessment' (2016) 41 *Air Sp. L.* 143–156; A. Linter, 'Extraterrestrial Extraction: The International Implications of the Space Resource Exploration and Utilization Act of 2015' (2016) 40 *Fletcher F. World Aff.* 139–158; A.C. Murnane, 'The Prospectors' Guide to the Galaxy' (2013) 37 *Fordham*

US President directed NASA to send astronauts beyond the moon by 2025,[139] and this was continued under Presidential Directive 1 of 2017.[140] NASA has therefore been developing a new launcher and crew capsule with which to capture an asteroid and move it into a lunar orbit for further examination. The experiment will also benefit potential asteroid mining enterprises,[141] and ESA has expressed interest in joining the project.[142]

Although views are divided on whether asteroid mining will be economically feasible,[143] commercial businesses to extract mineral riches from asteroids and bring them to Earth are being established. Their proponents take the view that appropriate technology now exists and that it is just a question of converting it for commercial use and obtaining financing.[144] Given that the MA has not been well ratified, and that the states most likely to be involved in the exploration and exploitation of the moon and other celestial bodies have not done so, the relevant provisions of the OST discussed remain crucial. It will be incumbent on each state that may license and supervise scientific or commercial activities in outer space fully to implement the OST. Back in Chapter 4, we expressed reservations about the potential for commercial entrepreneurs to go shopping for a state willing to take a more relaxed attitude towards its regulatory duties,[145] and here, we hope that that

---

Int. L. J. 235–277; M. Jensen, 'Asteroidae Naturae: What It Takes to Capture an Asteroid' (2016) 45 *South Western. L. Rev.* 757–778; K. MacWhorter, 'Sustainable Mining: Incentivizing Asteroid Mining in the Name of Environmentalism' (2016) 40 *Wm. & Mary Env, L. & Pol. Rev.* 645–676; L.C. Byrd, 'Soft Law in Space: A Legal Framework for Extraterrestrial Mining' (2022) 71 *Emory L. J.* 801–840; J. Su, 'Legal Status of Abiotic Resources in Outer Space: Appropriability, Ownership, and Access' (2022) 15 *Leiden J. Int. L.* 825–852; F.G. von der Dunk, 'The Moon Agreement and the Prospect of Commercial Exploitation of Lunar Resources' (2007) 32 *AASL* 91–113; A. Salmeri, 'The Integration between National and International Regulation of Space Resource Activities under Public International Law' (2019) 43 *J. Sp. L.* 60–84; T. Cheney, 'There's No Rush: Developing a Legal Framework for Space Resource Activities' (2019) 43 *J. Sp. L.* 106–150. Cf. Res. 1/2002, International Law Association, *Report of the 70th Conference, Delhi, 2002* at 13–14, and related 'Report of the Space Law Committee', 192–227 at 201–227. See links at: www.ila-hq.org/en/committees. As to methods cf. www.planetaryresources.com/#home-asteroids and https://space-agency.public.lu/en/space-resources.html.

139 National Space Policy of the United States of America, 2010, *supra* n. 34, at 11.

140 (US) Space Policy Directive 1, 'Reinvigorating America's Human Space Exploration Program (2017): https://trumpwhitehouse.archives.gov/presidential-actions/presidential-memorandum-reinvigorating-americas-human-space-exploration-program/.

141 In the NASA Redirect Mission project, robots would capture an appropriate asteroid. Subsequently astronauts would examine it and perhaps recover materials for return to Earth: www.nasa.gov/content/what-is-nasa-s-asteroid-redirect-mission.

142 See NASA's Asteroid Impact Deflection Assessment Mission: www.nasa.gov/planetarydefense/aida. Cf. ESA's Asteroid Impact Mission: www.esa.int/Our_Activities/Space_Engineering_Technology/Asteroid_Impact_Mission/Asteroid_Impact_Mission2.

143 Launching a spacecraft for space mining costs hundreds of millions of dollars, and launch costs would have to decrease drastically for the project to be profitable. No one has experience with asteroid mining, and the learning curve will be steep and expensive. Cf. G. Hasin, 'Developing Global Order for Space Resources: Regime Evolution Approach' (2020) 52 *Georgetown J. Int. L.* 77–160; Sundahl *supra* n. 108.

144 M. Jensen, 'Asteroidae Naturae: What It Takes to Capture an Asteroid' (2016) 45 *South Western. L. Rev.* 757–778; K. MacWhorter, 'Sustainable Mining: Incentivizing Asteroid Mining in the Name of Environmentalism' (2016) 40 *Wm. & Mary Env, L. & Pol. Rev.* 645–676.

145 See Chapter 4, c. n. 77.

possibility does not eventuate.[146] Further, care must be taken that mining activities do not increase the number of threatening near-earth objects.[147]

If international commerce in materials from space develops, there may be little problem in recognising a title to asteroid-derived materials in much the same way as title is recognised to fish, ownerless when in the high seas but readily sold by fishermen on shore.[148] It has therefore been intriguing to see national developments designed to legitimise and foster space mining. So far four states, none of them parties or signatories to the Moon Agreement, although all subscribers of the Artemis Accords, have introduced specific legislation on the matter. They are the US in 2015, Luxembourg in 2017, the United Arab Emirates in 2019 and Japan in 2021. In addition to these India, has stated that subject to appropriate licensing, it will permit space mining by nongovernmental entities.[149]

The US took the first steps.[150] In 2015, President Obama signed the US Commercial Space Launch Competitiveness Act.[151] Its Title IV amended USC Title 51 to introduce executive duties to facilitate commercial exploration for and commercial recovery of space resources by US citizens; to discourage government barriers to the development in the US of commercially viable, safe and stable industries needed for such activities and to promote the right of US citizens to engage in them. For the purposes of the legislation, an asteroid resource is a 'space resource found on or within a single asteroid', and a space resource is 'an anbiotic resource in outer space, including water and minerals'. A framework was to be established for the allocation of federal responsibilities under these innovations.[152] Within these bounds a new 51 USC §51303 then provides that,

> a United States citizen engaged in commercial recovery of an asteroid resource or a space resource under this chapter shall be entitled to any asteroid resource or space resource obtained, including to possess, own, transport, use, and sell the asteroid resource or space resource obtained in accordance with applicable law, including the international obligations of the United States.

---

146 All states that currently can conduct launches have ratified the OST, and ESA has accepted its obligations. Because a space launch is a necessary part of any space endeavour, as part of its compliance with the OST, every state engaged in launching should satisfy itself as to the competence of the licensees of an object to be launched if it is intended to be used to explore or exploit. Given its association with SES, Luxembourg may have such competence (s.q.). Also see *infra* n. 154.

147 Cf. Chapter 9 sv. Planetary Defence.

148 Cf. G. Gal, 'Acquisition of Property in the Legal Regime of Celestial Bodies' (1997) 39 *Proc. IISL* 45–49 at 48.

149 India Space Policy – 2023, Part 4, para 13: www.isro.gov.in/media_isro/pdf/IndianSpacePolicy2023.pdf. For India policy see also Chapter 14.

150 See also T. Conte, 'Property Rules for Martian Resources: How the Space Act of 2015 Increases the Likelihood of a Single Entity Controlling Access to Mars' (2019) 84 *J. Air L. & Comm.* 187–219.

151 US Commercial Space Launch and Competitiveness Act, Pub. L. 114–90, 2015, Title IV, §§ 401–404, 'Space Resource Exploration and Utilization', Nov. 25, 2015, 129 Stat. 721: www.congress.gov/114/plaws/publ90/PLAW-114publ90.pdf. Cf. US Federal Code, Title 51, Ch. 513, § 51303. See also US Congress, H.R. Committee on Science, Space and Technology, 'Spurring Private Aerospace Competitiveness and Entrepreneurship Act of 2015', H. Rept. 114–119. Cf. a previous attempt: H.R. 5063, 113th Congress, Sess. 2, intended to 'promote the development of a commercial asteroid resources industry for outer space in the United States and to increase the exploration and utilization of asteroid resources in outer space.' M.J. Sundahl, 'Regulating Non-Traditional Space Activities in the United States in the Wake of the Commercial Space Launch Competitiveness Act' (2017) 42 *Air and Sp. L.* 29–42.

152 Public Law 114–90, 129 Stat. 721, Sec. 40502, amending USC Title 51, Subtitle V, §§ 51301 and 51302.

The 2015 Act does acknowledge relevant US international obligations including freedom from harmful interference as is the duty of continuing supervision by the US federal government. Its Title IV concludes by declaring that 'it is the sense of Congress that by the enactment of this Act, the United States does not thereby assert sovereignty or sovereign or exclusive rights or jurisdiction over, or the ownership of, any celestial body' (Sec. 403), a genuflection to accepted international law, though under the circumstances, a miasmic one.

Luxembourg adopted specific legislation in 2017.[153] With its taxation practices and other arrangements favourable to entrepreneurs, Luxembourg has over the years made itself attractive to a variety of commercial companies.[154] *Inter alios*, in 1985 on the initiative of the Luxembourg government, the Société Européenne des Satellites (SES), now one of the largest private satellite operators, was established.[155] In the last quinquennium, Luxembourg has moved more particularly to become a base for other space activities.[156]

Through its banking institution, the Société Nationale de Crédit et d'Investissement, in 2016, the Luxembourg government entered into a cooperation and investment agreement with Planetary Resources Inc., a would-be space mining company.[157] The year 2018 saw the creation of the Luxembourg Space Agency.[158] In 2020, the Chamber of Deputies adopted a law on space activities,[159] and, as is required by the Luxembourg Constitution, approved the Registration Convention.[160] All these steps were, however, preceded by the 2017 law on space resources.[161] It has to be said that this law appears to have been crafted to encourage foreign entrepreneurs to create Luxembourg companies to engage in such activities rather than to encourage the Luxembourgeois themselves to engage in them.

Article 1 of the 'Law on the exploration and use of space resources' states baldly that 'space resources are capable of being owned',[162] although any Luxembourg body wishing to explore or use space resources (an operator) must obtain written permission from

---

153 M. Hofmann et al., *Space Legislation of Luxembourg: A Commentary* (Leiden: Kluwer Law International, 2022); F. Schilling, 'Fishing in Outer Space – The Luxembourgish Interpretation of the Appropriation of in-Situ Resources' (2019) 68 *ZLW* 248–260; J. Steele, 'Luxembourg and the Exploitation of Outer Space' (2021) 29 *Nottingham L. J.* 32–42.

154 Normally a company registering in the Grand Duchy has Luxembourg shareholders and local administration.

155 For detail, see Chapter 10, sv. SES.

156 B. Calmes et al., in J. Wheeler, ed., *The Space Law Review*, 3rd ed. 2021 (London: Law Business Research Ltd., 2021), Luxembourg: Introduction to the national legal, regulatory and policy framework: https://thelawreviews.co.uk/title/the-space-law-review/luxembourg.

157 See the Spaceresources.lu Initiative: https://space-agency.public.lu/en/space-resources/the-initiative.html. Luxembourg has also entered MOUs on such matters with Japan and the UAE, see S. Mallick and R.P. Rajagopalan, *If Space Is 'the Province of Mankind', Who Owns Its Resources? An Examination of the Potential of Space Mining and Its Legal Implications* (Observer Research Foundation, Occasional Paper 182, January 2019): www.orfonline.org/research/if-space-is-the-province-of-mankind-who-owns-its-resources-47561/.

158 Luxembourg Space Agency: https://space-agency.public.lu/en/agency/lsa.html.

159 Law on space activities: https://legilux.public.lu/eli/etat/leg/loi/2020/12/15/a1086/jo; trans: https://space-agency.public.lu/en/agency/legal-framework/Lawspaceactivities.html.

160 Law on Approval of the convention on registration of objects launched into outer space: https://legilux.public.lu/eli/etat/leg/loi/2020/12/15/a1087/jo. Luxembourg acceded to the Registration Convention in January 2021.

161 Loi du 20 juillet 2017 sur l'exploration et l'utilisation des ressources de l'espace, Luxembourg Official Journal No. 7674: https://legilux.public.lu/eli/etat/leg/loi/2017/07/20/a674/jo, trans.: https://space-agency.public.lu/en/agency/legal-framework/law_space_resources_english_translation.html.

162 The 2017 law does not apply to satellite communications, orbital positions or radio-frequency bands (Art. 2.4).

the ministers in charge of the economy and space activities (Arts. 2.1 and 6) and carry out its operations in accordance with conditions set by the permission. Activities will be supervised by the relevant ministers (Art. 15). The authorisation is personal and cannot be assigned (Art. 5), nor can what is permitted be carried out by others or intermediaries (Art. 2.2–3). As already indicated the operator must have a presence in Luxembourg (Arts. 4 and 7.1).

Articles 7–9 set out requirements as to the fitness and repute of potential operators. Under Art. 10, an application for permission must be accompanied by a risk assessment and proof that the applicant has the financial resources necessary to cover the risks, the operator being held responsible for all damage caused (Art. 16). The authorisation may contain provisions on what is done in Luxembourg, limits to the mission, how it is supervised and how compliance can be ensured (Art. 12). An authorisation can be withdrawn if its conditions are no longer met, if it is not used within three years of it being granted, if the holder relinquishes it or ceases business for six months (Art. 14. 1–2) and, of course, if it was obtained through false statements or other irregular means (Art. 14.3). Fines and imprisonment are possible (Art. 18). Lastly, a Luxembourg authorisation does not dispense with the need to obtain other approvals or authorisations (Art. 17).

United Arab Emirates Federal Law No. 12 of 2019 replaced its legislation on space activities.[163] Its Chapter 2 (Arts. 5–13) sets out the organisation of the UAE space agency and its objectives and competences (Art. 7), board of directors (Arts. 8–9), director general (Art. 10) and finances (Arts. 1113). Chapter 3 (Arts. 14–27) deals with space activities. A permit from the agency is normally required for any UAE national to own a space object or to carry out or participate in space activities (Art. 14). The rest of the chapter contains provisions on communication services (Art. 15), manned spaceflight (Art. 16), the use of nuclear power sources (Art. 17), debris mitigation (Art. 19) and liabilities and insurance (Arts. 20–27). Chapter 4 (Arts. 28–30) covers other space-related activities. Chapter 5 (Art. 31) sets up a registry of space objects, and Chapter 6 deals with other matters such as intellectual property rights (Art. 32).

'Space resources' are defined in Art. 1 as 'any non-living resources present in outer space, including minerals and water'. Apart from its other provisions, the Act expressly applies to exploration or extraction activities and the exploitation and use of space resources for scientific, commercial or other purposes (Art. 4.1(i) and (j)). Space mining is more particularly provided for in Art. 18. Permits for the exploration, exploitation and use of space resources will be decided upon by the agency's board of directors on the proposal of the director general (Art. 18.2). They will be subject to conditions and controls set by the Council of Ministers and relate to the resources 'acquisition, purchase, trade, transportation, storage' and related logistical services (Art. 18.1). While not an explicit declaration of ownership, this appears to imply proprietary rights.

In 2021, Japan became the fourth state to legislate on space mining.[164] It amended its Space Activities Act of 2016 with the Act on Promotion of Business Activities Related to

---

163 United Arab Emirates, Federal Law No. 12 of 2019 on the Regulation of the Space Sector, Federal Decree-Law No. 1/2014: www.moj.gov.ae/assets/2020/Federal%20Law%20No%2012%20of%202019%20on%20THE%20REGULATION%20OF%20THE%20SPACE%20SECTOR.pdf.aspx.

164 See H. Yotsumoto and Daika Ishikawa, 'Japan', in J. Wheeler, ed., *The Space Law Review* (London: Law Business Research Ltd., 2019) 47–56, and Hiroko Yotsumoto et al., 'Introduction to the National Legal, Regulatory and Policy Framework' *The Space Law Review: Japan*, 3rd ed. 2021: https://thelawreviews.

the Exploration and Development of Space Resources (Act No. 83 of 2021), which came into force on 23 December 2021. Under Art. 2.1 'space resources' are defined as water, minerals and other natural resources that exist in outer space, including on the moon and other celestial bodies. Any person wishing to extract space resources under the Japanese provisions must obtain a permit under Art. 3 of the Act. Applicants for such a permit must provide a business activity plan, specifying the purpose of the activity and conforming to other requirements to be specified under a Cabinet ordinance. Permits are issued by the Prime Minister after appropriate consultation. Whoever does exploit space resources in accordance with the activity plan is to be recognised as owning those resources (Art. 5).

So where have we got to? The only general international law applicable to space mining is OST Art. II, the prohibition of the 'national appropriation by claim of sovereignty, by means of use or occupation, or by any other means' of outer space, including the moon and other celestial bodies. The argument could have been made that by granting to US citizens engaged in asteroid mining entitlement to any resource so obtained, including rights of possession, ownership, transportation, use and sale, the new 51 USC §51303 is a sovereign act recognising rights of property and would therefore appear to be an act of national appropriation.[165] Other states might have refused to recognise a property title to resources brought to Earth founded only on the US legislation.

Similar argument might be levelled at the assertion in Art. 1 of the 2017 Luxembourg legislation that space resources are capable of being owned and at the implication of ownership in Art. 18 of the UAE law, as well as at the recognition of the ownership of space resources in Art. 5 of the Japanese law. In short, will states be prepared not to recognise rights of property conferred by other states in apparent contravention of the OST? Our answer is that they could, but probably will not. A modus vivendi will appear.[166] As we indicated earlier, pragmatically there may be little problem in recognising a title to asteroid- or lunar-derived materials in much the same way as title is recognised to fish, ownerless when in the high seas, but readily sold by fishermen when landed on shore.

Finally, we note that various space agencies and governments have been considering the construction of permanent dwellings on the moon.[167] Were a moon colony to be established, whether to assist in mining the moon or otherwise, that would raise questions of its government, and in due course probably, its independence. We will comment on such potential developments in Chapter 17.

co.uk/title/the-space-law-review/japan. See also the US Library of Congress (2016) *Japan: Two Outer Space-Related Laws Enacted*. [Web Page] Retrieved from the Library of Congress: www.loc.gov/item/global-legal-monitor/2016-12-19/japan-two-outer-space-related-laws-enacted/ and (2021) *Japan: Space Resources Act Enacted*: www.loc.gov/item/global-legal-monitor/2021-09-15/japan-space-resources-act-enacted/. The relevant Japanese laws are available in Japanese. 'Law Concerning the Promotion of Business Activities Related to the Exploration and Development of Space Resources', Act No. 83 of 2021: https://kanpou.npb.go.jp/old/20210623/20210623g00141/20210623g001410004f.html. Act on Launching of Spacecraft, etc. and Control of Spacecraft, Act No. 76 of 2016: https://www8.cao.go.jp/space/english/activity/documents/space_activity_act.pdf. For the law up to 2014, see S. Aoki, 'National Space Laws of Japan: Today and Tomorrow': www.unoosa.org/documents/pdf/spacelaw/activities/2014/pres10E.pdf.
165 Duck Test: 'If it looks like a duck, walks like a duck, and quacks like a duck, it is a duck'.
166 L.C. Byrd, 'Soft Law in Space: A Legal Framework for Extraterrestrial Mining' (2022) 71 *Emory L. J.* 801–840.
167 M. Dodge, 'Celestial Agriculture: Law & Policy Governing the Use of *in situ* Resources for Space Settlements' (2022) 97 *North Dakota L. Rev.* 161–184.

8

RADIO AND THE INTERNATIONAL TELECOMMUNICATION UNION

Introduction

Radio is integral to almost all uses of space.[1] It is essential for most tracking and for all telemetry, command and control.[2] All satellites depend on the ability to receive and to transmit data to Earth. The frequencies used by modern satellites are in the higher frequency ranges. Only these can penetrate the Kennelly–Heaviside layer of ionised gases above the Earth, and only they can allow the necessary precision of complex signals. Any degradation of the quality of the signal to or from a satellite at best diminishes its efficiency and at worst renders it useless. On-board computers act as programmed on input received. They do not 'know' what is 'meant' by a particular signal or the intention of its sender. A degraded signal may have no effect whatsoever or might have an unexpected result. Problems of interference are therefore significant.

Related matters have required international agreement and regulation. Common technical standards are necessary both to avoid signal interference and to ensure the compatibility of equipment. Procedures, protocols and codes for signal transmission and receipt have had to be developed. Financially, communications have to be paid for, requiring agreement on the rates charged for particular services and the settlement of accounts between international carriers. Later, it became possible to integrate the orbit of a transmitter/receiver in space with its use of the spectrum.

When the exploration and utilisation of space began, there already was an international organisation dealing with such matters at the terrestrial level. Tracing its origins back to the electric telegraph, the International Telecommunication Union (ITU) had built significant expertise in communication by telephone, telegraph and radio. It was therefore natural that Part D of Assembly Resolution 1721(XVI) of 20th December 1961, 'International Cooperation on the Peaceful Uses of Outer Space' saw a major role for the ITU.

---

1 Visual astronomy is an exception, but radio astronomy and SETI require the frequencies they 'listen to' to be secured from radio interference. See *infra* n. 149.
2 On-board computers may cope with routine operations in response to on-board sensors. Telemetry monitors the health and performance of a satellite through diagnostic information supplied by radio by the satellite itself.

DOI: 10.4324/9781003496502-8

However, in fact the ITU had taken cognisance of the radio requirements of space research as early as 1959,[3] and was already preparing a more structured approach to the needs of space which began with an Extraordinary Administrative Radio Conference in 1963.[4] In subsequent years, space has become a very important part of ITU responsibilities. Indeed the increasing requirements of space were a considerable element in the major reconstruction of the Union in 1992–1994.

History[5]

The history of the ITU has two major strands: wired services – the telegraph and the telephone – and wireless – the radio. The wired element came first.

An International Telegraph Union of nineteen European states was established in 1865 to provide uniformity in tariffs, codes, routing and operational matters through an agreed-upon regulation of international telegraphy.[6] Three years later, a permanent international bureau was added to handle the routine administrative work.[7] Paralleling technical developments, membership in the Union increased.

Telegraph conferences were held at Rome in 1871–1872[8] and at St Petersburg in 1875.[9] The 1885 Berlin Telegraph Conference brought the new-fangled telephone within the remit of the Union and made more detailed provision for the functioning of the international bureau.[10] In 1925, a Paris Conference set up International Consultative Committees for the Telephone and Telegraph to coordinate technical studies and to establish

---

3 The World Administrative Radio Conference, Geneva 1959, amended the International Radio Regulations to include definitions of a 'space station' and an 'earth station' and of a 'space service' and an 'earth/space service'. Note: in this context, 'station' refers to a transmitter station, and not to the later manned 'space stations'.

4 Partial Revision of the Radio Regulations: Final Acts of the Extraordinary Administrative Radio Conference to Allocate Frequency Bands for Space Radio Purposes, Geneva, 8 November 1963, 15 UST 887, TIAS 5603 (1964) 3 ILM 91–106.

5 F. Lyall, 1. *International Communications: The International Telecommunication Union and the Universal Postal Union* (Farnham: Ashgate, 2011); 2. *Technology, Sovereignty and International Law* (Abingdon: Routledge, 2022) 84–121. For earlier histories, see O. Mance, *International Telecommunications* (Oxford: Oxford UP, 1943); G.A. Codding, *The International Telecommunication Union: An Experiment in International Cooperation* (Leiden: Brill, 1952; rep. New York: Arno Press, 1972); J.H. Glazer, 'The Law-making Treaties of the International Telecommunication Union through Time and in Space' (1962) 60 *Mich. L. Rev.* 269–316; F. Lyall, 'The International Regulation of Telecommunications', in O. Schachter and C.C. Joyner, eds., *United Nations Legal Order* (Cambridge: Cambridge UP and ASIL, 1995) 789–823 at 801–823; F. Lyall, *Law and Space Telecommunications* (Aldershot: Dartmouth, 1989) 311–409. Cf. G.A. Codding and A.M. Rutkowski, *The International Telecommunication Union in a Changing World* (Boston: Artech House, 1982).

   Note that many materials are available via the ITU History Portal: www.itu.int/en/history/Pages/Navigation.aspx. On-line access to publicly available ITU documentation is free (Decision 12 of the ITU Plenipotentiary Conference (Rev. Busan 2014)).

6 International Telegraph Convention, Paris, 17 May 1865, 130 CTS 198: 56 BFSP 295.

7 International Telegraph Convention, Vienna, 21 July 1868, 136 CTS 292: 1868 59 BFSP 322.

8 International Telegraph Convention, Rome, 14 January 1872, 143 CTS 415; 66 BFSP 975.

9 International Telegraph Convention, with annexed regulations and schedule of rates, St Petersburg, 22 July 1875, 148 CTS 416; 66 BFSP 19; 3 Martens (2d) 614.

10 Regulations in execution of the International Telegraph Convention of 22 July 1875, Berlin, 17 September 1885, 165 CTS 212, 76 BFSP 597; 12 Martens (2d) 205.

international standards for both modalities.[11] In 1928, a Protocol to the 1875 Convention further amended the International Service Regulations of the Telegraph Union.[12] Finally, the Thirteenth International Telegraph Conference was held at Madrid in 1932, when the Telegraph Union and a radio telegraph union which had been developed along with that new technology[13] were fused to form the ITU.

Although its invention is debated, the first UK patent for wireless telegraphy stands in the name of Guglielmo Marconi in 1896. Because of the hostility of the telephone and telegraph companies, radio services initially found their main market in ship-to-shore and ship-to-ship communication. Preceded by a preliminary conference in 1903,[14] the first international agreement on radio came in Berlin in 1906.[15] One important element of that agreement was the introduction of 'universal compulsory communication' (Art. 3), according to which no ship or shore station might refuse communication from another station on the ground that it used a different system of wireless telegraphy.[16]

More important for the future were the Service Regulations annexed to the Berlin Convention since these contain provisions which are lineally and intellectually the direct ascendants of the ITU operating principles and mechanisms. These are the principles of allocation of specific wave-bands (radio frequencies) to specified services, the avoidance of harmful interference and the use of the best available technologies. Under Service Regulation II, the 300, 600 and over 1600 metre wavelengths were set aside for general public correspondence and long-distance communication. Special services were available only to coastal radio stations, and these had to be transmitted at under 300 or over 600 metres to avoid interference with the signals they carried. Regulation III allocated the 300 metre frequency to all ships carrying equipment capable of transmitting at that frequency.

Regulation V prohibited superfluous signals and allowed equipment trials only if no interference was caused to stations in normal usage. Under Regulation XXVIII, radio stations were required to exchange signal traffic with the minimum power required for effective communication. This allocation of particular frequencies for particular purposes, the provisions as to interference and the minimising of signal power remain fundamental to the operation of the ITU system today.[17] However, no radio telegraph union was established. After 1906, modifications to the arrangements were agreed on through full-scale diplomatic conferences, with implementation of their decisions administered by the International Bureau of the Telegraph Union.

11 International service regulations, annexed to the International Telegraph Convention of St Petersburg, Paris, 29 October 1925, 57 LNTS 201, 3 Hudson 1695.
12 Protocol regarding certain additions and modifications to the International Service Regulations, Brussels, 22 September 1928, 88 LNTS 347, 3 Hudson 1756.
13 The term is useful, but erroneous. See *infra* following n. 17.
14 Preliminary Conference in Berlin on Wireless Telegraphy, Process Verbaux and Final Protocol (1903) Cmnd. 1832, 120 UKSP 94. The Final Protocol is at 194 CTS 46; 97 BFSP, 467; 33 Martens (2d) 471.
15 Radio Telegraphic Convention, Final Protocol and Regulations, Berlin, 3 November 1906, 1909 UKTS 8, Cmnd. 4559; 37 Stat. 15665, TS 568; 203 CTS 101; 99 BFSP 321; [1906] 3 AJIL Supp. 330–40; 3 Martens (3d) 147; 1 Bevans 556.
16 'Intercommunication' is now required by Art. 11 (501–503) of the ITU Convention. (For abbreviate citation see *infra* n. 42). Under the Wireless Telegraphy Act 1904 the UK took powers to enforce this obligation on its shipping beyond its territorial waters (a proposal of the 1903 Berlin Conference).
17 See generally *infra* 'Radiocommunication'.

Finding 'free' spectrum in the lower ranges soon became difficult, but technical progress made a wider radio spectrum range available. As early as 1912, a wider Table of Frequency Allocations extended the number of particular identified different radio services while still limiting them to designated frequencies.[18] Then, 1927 saw major alterations.[19] The First World War had produced immense technical advances and was followed by the development of both state and commercial broadcasting and transmitting stations that than greatly increased in both number and capacity.

The 1927 documents therefore reveal a major shift from the particularity of maritime services to the general regulation of radio wherever it might occur. Frequency bands were allocated to fixed, maritime and aeronautical mobile, broadcasting, amateur and experimental services, and an international registration system for assignments to transmitting stations made by their home states was introduced. In addition, a Consultative Committee on Radio (CCIR) was established, mirroring those already existent for the wired services.

In 1932, the radio and the telegraph unions fused. They held simultaneous conferences at Madrid and agreed to establish a single telecommunications organisation, the ITU.[20],[21] Later, a conference made some changes to the international Table of Allocations for radio frequencies.[22]

The Second World War caused a further expansion in technology. A Plenipotentiary Conference was held in 1947 in Atlantic City, New Jersey, to sort out what had become a highly disorganised scene.[23] An important creation was the International Frequency Registration Board (IFRB), to which was entrusted both the bringing up to date of the registration of international frequencies and the operation of a new Master International Frequency Register on which assignments made by states in conformity with the Radio Regulations would be entered. This Register remains crucial to the operation of satellites, and in this the work of the IFRB was absolutely fundamental until its replacement in the 1992–1994 reconstruction of the Union. However, because the ITU was to join the UN family of specialised agencies, the Atlantic City Conference altered the general structure of the ITU to conform to the usual UN pattern. An Administrative Council was established to annually review the operation of the Union and a Secretary General and secretariat introduced to see to the day-to-day running of the organisation.

After 1947, the ITU structure remained more or less unaltered for some forty-five years until change was forced. In this, space was not irrelevant. The ITU had retained divisions traceable to the history of wired and wireless services.[24] Successive revisions of the ITU Convention had rendered the structure outdated, unnecessarily complex

---

18 International Radiotelegraph Convention, London, 5 July 1912, 1 LNTS 135, 216 CTS 244, 105 BFSP 219, 1913 BTS 10, Cmnd 6873; 38 Stat. 1672, TS 581, [1913] 7 AJIL Supp. 229. Compliance with the Table or its successors was not mandatory until after the Second World War.

19 Radio Telegraph Convention and General Regulations, Washington, DC, 25 November 1927; 84 LNTS 97; 126 BFSP 330; 45 Stat. 2760, TS 767; 3 Hudson 2197; 2 Bevans 683; 26 Martens (3d) 234; [1929] 23 AJIL Supp. 40 (Convention only).

20 It is curious how many still call it the International Telecommunications Union.

21 Telecommunication Convention, General Radio Regulations, Additional Radio Regulations, Additional Protocol (European), Telegraph Regulations and Telephone Regulations, Madrid, 1932; 151 LNTS 4; 49 Stat. 2391, TS 867; 6 Hudson 109; 3 Bevans 65.

22 General Radio Regulations, Cairo, 1938, 54 Stat. 1417, TS 948, 8 Hudson 41; 3 Bevans 518.

23 International Convention on Telecommunications, Atlantic City, 1947; 193 UNTS 188, 194 UNTS 3; 1950 UKTS 76, Cmnd 8124; 63 Stat. 1399, TIAS 1901; 4 Bevans 470.

24 The CCIR and CCIT fused in 1956 to form the Consultative Committee on Telegraph and Telephone (CCITT) by the Buenos Aires Plenipotentiary Conference, *infra* n. 25.

and unable to act swiftly or adequately to cope with new developments. Further, ITU membership had increased with the dissolution of the colonial empires, and the gaps between major conferences had become too long.[25] Telecommunications in general, and radio in particular, had become extremely complex. Technology was changing swiftly. The interests of both manufacturing and telecoms service providers were clamant. Simplification and efficiency became essential. And the cost of operating the Union was another element.

Dissatisfaction with the Union rose to a climax in the 1980s. In Nice in 1989, a Plenipotentiary Conference was very conscious that the ITU needed to alter its structures and procedures.[26] Globalisation, technological change, the information economy and its interactions around the world had rendered the slow mechanisms of the ITU obsolescent, if not obsolete. The Nice Conference took some steps towards revising the ITU but recognised that more radical surgery was necessary.[27] A high-level committee was set up to review the structure and functioning of the Union, and it reported in April 1991.[28] By that time, only six countries had ratified the 1989 Nice documents, so the Administrative Council decided an additional plenipotentiary conference should be held before the Nice arrangements would come into force.

The 1992 Extra-Ordinary Plenipotentiary Conference did make major structural changes to the ITU.[29] However, these were overtaken and revised by the decisions of the 1994 Kyoto Plenipotentiary Conference which came into force in 1996.[30] The previous single convention was split into a constitution and a convention. Operational responsibilities were allocated to three new sectors. A four-year cycle of plenipotentiary conferences was adopted, within which other restricted conferences are scheduled and the sectors now work.[31]

25 Cf. the dates of the International Telecommunication Convention, Buenos Aires, 22 December 1952, 1958 UKTS 36, Cmnd 520; 6 UST 1213, TIAS 3266: the International Telecommunication Convention, Geneva, 21 December 1959, 1961 UKTS 74, Cmnd 1484; 12 UST 1761, TIAS 4892: the International Telecommunication Convention, Montreux, 12 November 1965, 1967 UKTS 41, Cmnd 3383; 18 UST 575, TIAS 6267: the International Telecommunication Convention, Malaga-Torremolinos, 25 October 1973, 1209 UNTS 32, 255; 1975 UKTS 104, Cmnd 6289; 28 UST 2495, TIAS 8572: the International Telecommunication Convention, Nairobi, 6 November 1982, 1531 UNTS 1, 1985 UKTS 33, Cmnd 9557; US Tr. Doc. 99–6.
26 Significant documents include *The Missing Link* (the Maitland Commission) (Geneva: ITU, 1985) and *The Report of the Secretary General's Advisory Group on the Changing Telecommunications Environment* (the Hansen Committee) (Geneva: ITU, 1989).
27 Final Acts of the Nice Plenipotentiary Conference (Geneva: ITU, 1990), not published in an official series.
28 *Tomorrow's ITU: The Challenges of Change: the Report of the High Level Committee to Review the Structure and Functioning of the International Telecommunication Union* (Geneva: ITU, 1991).
29 Constitution and Convention of the International Telecommunication Union: Final Acts of the Additional Plenipotentiary Conference, Geneva, 22 December 1992 (ITU, 1993), 1825 UNTS 1; 1996 UKTS 24, Cmnd 3145; US Tr. Doc. 104–35. G.A. Codding, 'The International Telecommunication Union: 130 Years of Telecommunications Regulation' (1995) 23 *Denv. J. Int. L. Pol.* 501–11; F. Lyall, 'The International Telecommunication Union Reconstructed' (1993) 36 *Proc. IISL* 78–88; R. Lauria and H.L. White, 'The Impact of New Communication Technologies on International Telecommunication Law and Policy: Cyberspace and the Restructuring of the International Telecommunication Union' (1995) 32 *Cal. West. L. Rev.* 1–30; A.L. Allison, 'Meeting the Challenges of Change: Reform of the International Telecommunication Union' (1993) 45 *Fed. Comm. L.J.* 491–540.
30 Final Acts of the Plenipotentiary Conference of the International Telecommunication Union, Kyoto, 14 October 1994 (ITU, 1994); US Tr. Doc. 104–34; 1997 UKTS 65, Cm 3779.
31 Some ITU operations run to a four and some to a two-year cycle, both intercalated with the plenipotentiary conference.

The Geneva/Kyoto arrangements were further revised and amended in Minneapolis, USA, in 1998;[32] in Marrakesh, Morocco, in 2002;[33] in Antalya, Turkey, in 2006[34] and at Guadalajara, Mexico, in 2010.[35] To some extent, these implemented further reforms and make minor improvements, but they did not depart from the fundamental changes of 1992/4. Subsequent plenipotentiary conferences have been held at Busan, South Korea, in 2014,[36] Dubai in 2018[37] and Bucharest in 2022,[38] but none have amended the basic instruments of the Union, the constitution and the convention. Whether there should be simplification of the ITU was considered in 2014, but no action has been taken.[39]

The ITU Instruments

Note: In what follows, the texts of the constitution and convention are taken as of 1 January 2022,[40] and citations conform to ITU practice.[41]

The ITU Instruments are the Constitution (CS), the Convention (CV) and the Administrative Regulations (CS Art. 4.1 (29).[42] The Constitution is the basic instrument (CS Art. 4.2 (30)) and is intended to contain matters less likely to change at successive plenipotentiaries. The Convention complements the Constitution and contains other constitutional provisions (CS Art. 4.2 (30)). The Administrative Regulations, to which we will come, complement CS and CV (CS Art. 4.3 (31)).

32 Final Acts of the Plenipotentiary Conference of the International Telecommunication Union, Minneapolis, 1998 (Geneva: ITU, 1999). Instruments Amending the Constitution and Convention of the International Telecommunication (Geneva, 1992) as amended) (Minneapolis, 1998)) 2016 UKMS 2, Cm 9306.
33 Final Acts of the Plenipotentiary Conference of the International Telecommunication Union, Marrakesh, 2002 (ITU, 2003). Instruments Amending the Constitution and Convention of the International Telecommunication (Geneva, 1992) as amended) (Marrakesh, 2002)) 2016 UKMS 3, Cm 9307. The Conference considerably simplified the constitution and convention, moving many conference rules to a separate document 'General Rules of Conferences, Assemblies and Meetings of the Union', and suppressed CV Arts 26–30 (299–323). Detailed rules are for each conference concerned but within the context of the General Rules.
34 Final Acts of the Plenipotentiary Conference of the International Telecommunication Union (Antalya, Turkey, 2006) (Geneva: ITU, 2007). Instruments Amending the Constitution and Convention of the International Telecommunication (Geneva, 1992) as amended) Amendments adopted by the Conference (Antalya, 2006)) 2016 UKMS 4, Cm 9308.
35 Final Acts of the Plenipotentiary Conference, Guadalajara, Mexico 2010 (ITU, 2011). Instruments Amending the Constitution and Convention of the International Telecommunication (Geneva, 1992, as amended) Amendments adopted by the Conference (Guadalajara, 2010)) 2016 UKMS No. 5, Cm 9309.
36 Final Acts of the Plenipotentiary Conference, Busan, 2014 (Geneva: ITU, 2014).
37 Final Acts of the Plenipotentiary Conference, Dubai, 2018 (Geneva: ITU, 2018).
38 Final Acts of the Plenipotentiary Conference, Bucharest, 2022 (Geneva: ITU, 2022).
39 The 'Final Report of a Council Working Group on a Stable Constitution', which had gone to the ITU Council in 2013 (PP-14, Doc. 52), together with the Summary Record of Council discussion (PP-14, Doc. 51) went to the Busan Conference. However, the group agreed to make no changes to the 'provisions, structure of, and hierarchy between the Constitution and the Convention', and the working Group was disbanded (PP-14, Doc. 175, sec. 2.1–5).
40 A *Collection of the Basic Texts of the International Telecommunication Union Adopted by the Plenipotentiary Conference*, issued after each plenipotentiary conference, provides an informal 'clean text' of the ITU Constitution and Convention together with the Decisions, Resolutions and Recommendations that are in force.
41 'CS' denotes the Constitution and 'CV' the Convention. A number in brackets is the paragraph numbering in the document, now both customary and convenient given the complexity and the length of some articles. Suppressed articles retain their numbering, making successive versions easier to work with. ITU internal documents frequently use only such numbering.
42 See *infra* n. 44.

CS or CV can both be amended (CS Art. 55 (224–232); CS Art. 42 (519–528)).[43] CS and CV are drawn up in the six official ITU languages: Arabic, Chinese, English, French, Russian and Spanish (CS Arts. 29.1.1 (171) and 58.4 (241)), which are also the Union's working languages. In the event of a discrepancy in versions, the French text prevails (CS Art. 29.1.3 (173); CS Art. 58.5 (242)). Should there be an inconsistency between CS and CV or the Administrative Regulations, CS prevails (CS Art. 4.4 (32)). In the case of an inconsistency between CV and the Administrative Regulations, CV prevails (CS Art. 4.4 (32)).

The Administrative Regulations are the International Telecommunication Regulations and the Radio Regulations (CS Art. 4.3 (31)).[44] Both are binding international instruments and have treaty status (CS Art. 4.3 (31). They are amended by appropriate conferences.[45]

State members of the ITU must abide by the provisions of CS, CV and the Administrative Regulations. They must also require any operating agency which they authorise to observe ITU rules in all international services or activities capable of causing interference to the radio services of other countries (CS Arts 6.1–2 (37–38)). A state member is free to fix the conditions on which it, or its recognised operating agencies, exchange telecommunications with a non-member state, but any communication which it accepts must be transmitted and charged for in accordance with ITU rules (CS Art. 51 (207)).

The single exemption from the binding nature of ITU regulations and decisions is as to military radio installations (CS Art. 6.1 (37) *ad fin*).[46] These are the subject of CS Art. 48. State members retain freedom in regard to military radio installations (CS Art. 48.1 (202)). However, such installations are required as far as possible to give assistance in the case of distress and are to prevent harmful interference (CS Art. 48.2 (203)). This includes compliance with the Administrative Regulations concerning the types of emission and frequencies used according to the nature of the service the military radio installation provides (CS Art. 48.2 (203)). When a military radio installation takes part in services of public correspondence or other services governed by the Administrative Regulations (e.g. an armed forces broadcasting network), it must in general comply with the relevant ITU regulations (CS Art. 48.3 (204)).[47]

Membership

There are two different forms of ITU membership, state and sector (CS Art. 2 (20–23)). Full membership) is open only to states. As of 1 January 2022, the union had one hundred ninety-three state members, including the Vatican – virtually all countries of the world.[48]

---

43 CS Art. 54 1 and 2 (215–216), CS Art. 54 (215–223) and CV Art. 55 42 (519–528) contain detailed rules on the ratification, acceptance, etc. of amendments. Amendments usually come into force about two years after their adoption.

44 Reference point n. 42 *supra*.

45 See *infra* on the Standardisation and Radiocommunication Sectors.

46 Cf. discussion of military telecommunications in Chapter 15 *infra* c. n. 117,

47 Following concern as to the use made of Art. 48 PP-22, Bucharest adopted Resolution 216, 'Use of frequency assignments by military radio installations for National Defence Services'. It will be for WRC-23 to decide whether to implement it.

48 Palau is not a member of the ITU, which explains the 193 total for both organisations. Under Res. 99, adopted by PP-98 and revised at PP-14, the 'State of Palestine' has observer status and extensive participation

Sector membership (of which there are different forms) is membership by a state member or by a non-state entity of one or more of the sectors through which the ITU now operates.

State Membership

Under CS Art. 2 (20–23), state membership in the ITU is open to any party to any previous ITU Convention (CS Art. 2 a (21)), to any UN member acceding to the current CS and CV (CS Art. 2 b (22) with CS Art. 53 (212–4)) or to any non-member of the UN whose application for membership is approved by two thirds of the member states and which duly accedes to CS and CV ((CS Art. 2 c (23) with CS Art. 53 (212–4)). A state becomes a member of the ITU by ratification, acceptance or approval of the successive CS and CV through a single instrument deposited with the Secretary-General (CS Art. 52.1 (208)), or by appropriate accession as indicated above. Up to two years after successive versions of CS and CV come into force, states which have signed but not yet ratified have full rights within the Union (CS Art. 52.2.2 (209)) but thereafter lose the right to vote, but only the right to vote. They retain the right to participate in conferences, consultations, etc. (CS Art. 52.2.2 (210)).[49] A state member may transfer its voting powers and the right to sign Final Acts to another state member for the duration of a conference.[50]

The rights, duties, privileges and immunities of state members are set out in CV, the Administrative Regulations and the Final Acts of ITU conferences. A member is bound to implement these both within its territory and with respect to the activities of its nationals (CS Art. 6.1–2 (37–38)). Suffice it here to note that there are arguments and disputes in relation to particular territories that are claimed by different states. These points of conflict usually manifest in declarations or reservations to the Final Acts of the plenipotentiary conference or of world and regional conferences.[51]

Sector Membership

Sector membership is membership of one or more of the three Sectors established by the 1992/4 reconstruction, the Telecommunications Development Sector (ITU-D), the Telecommunications Standardisation Sector (ITU-T) and the Radiocommunication Sector

---

in ITU affairs. But cf. Bucharest Final Acts Declarations (2022), UK (No. 25), Canada (No. 30), US (No. 47), and Germany (No. 65).

49 At Bucharest, the Credentials Committee reported that the credentials of one hundred seventy-seven members were in order and that the Central African Republic, Haiti, Kiribati and Tajikistan had not deposited credentials, or ones that were not in order and so had no right to vote (PP–22 Doc, 126 Rev. 3 ss. 1–2).

50 CV Art. 31.6 (335): see transfers by the Marshall Islands to the US, Tuvalu to Australia, Costa Rica to the Dominican Republic and San Tome and Principe to Portugal (PP–22 Doc 126 Rev. 3). 'As a general rule, Member States should endeavour to send their own delegations to conferences of the Union.' (CV Art. 31.6 (336)). However, the transfer option is available when a state cannot do so for 'exceptional reasons'. Proxy voting is sufficient (CV Art. 31.7 (336)): Kiribati's mandate to New Zealand (PP-22 Doc. 113) was inactive until its original credentials were submitted and found to be in order (PP–22, Doc. 126 Rev. 3 s.3).

51 For instance, we note that in the Bucharest Final Acts (PP–22), forty-three states joined in Declaration 20 on the Russian 'annexation' of Ukraine's Donetsk, Luhansk, Zaporizhzhia and Kherson regions and in Ukraine's Declaration No. 35, which refers back to Crimea and Georgia (No. 1), both countered by Russia (Nos. 38 and 81) and Belarus (No. 80) on the politicisation of the ITU. See also Cuba (No. 1) and the US (No. 70), Argentina (No. 41) and the UK (No. 73), and Israel (No. 75) countering Nos. 10, 50, 56, 58 and 59.

(ITU-R), either as a full or an associate member.[52] Much work crucial to the modern telecommunications environment is carried out through working and study groups within these sectors. The ITU is very conscious of the need to involve persons and entities active in relevant industries, businesses and interests in its work.[53] CV Art. 19 (228–241) sets out criteria for non-state entities and organisations to participate, Art. 19.1 (228) requiring that the Secretary-General and the sector directors encourage such participation.

Sector membership consists of all state members by right[54] together with non-state entities authorised by state members.[55] Authorisation may be given in a particular case, or a state member may generally authorise entities under its jurisdiction to apply for membership direct to the Secretary-General.[56] As of 1 January 2024, there were over nine hundred sector members.[57] A category of associate member is available by permission of the sector concerned for duly authorised entities taking part in the work of only one study group within a sector.[58]

Finance

All international organisations have to pay their bills. Within the UN system, most agencies rely on mandatory contributions supplemented by voluntary contributions and on charges for services.[59] Mandatory contributions are calculated on gross national product (income) adjusted for per capita income and, on occasion, capped. The ITU, however, has never used the UN method. It uses a 'contributory unit' system: members choose the number of units they will contribute. This method, used since the earliest days of the Union, is not favoured by the developing countries.[60] They prefer the UN system, which can be more favourable to them and affords no discretion to contributors and which major countries cannot avoid without patently going into arrears of contribution. However, there is much to recommend the contributory unit concept for an organisation with limited financial requirements, namely the facilitation of international cooperation. Value for money is an important element in the efficient operation of any organisation.

---

52 See 'Comprehensive Report on the Rights, Obligations and Conditions for Participation of Sector Members, Associates and Academia', Sec. Gen. Report, PP-14, Doc. 60 and Council Working Group on Financial and Human Resources, 2015, Doc. CWG-FHR 5/18.

53 Cf. PP Res. 209 (Dubai, 2018) 'Encouraging the participation of small and medium enterprises in the work of the Union'.

54 A state member is not required to be a member of a sector.

55 Non-state sector members pay a fee and meet their own costs. One fifth of contributory units from member states is allocated to sector expenses (CV Art. 3.5 (480)).

56 CS Art. 3 (24–8C), Art. 12.3 (86–88), Art. 21.4 (134–6), Art. 17.3 (110–12); CV Art. 19.1. (228–31) and Art. 19.3–4 (234–4C).

57 Sector members are listed at www.itu.int/online/mm-new/scripts/gensel11. In 2020, five hundred forty-two sector members were distributed as follows: ITU-R = 280, ITU-T = 286, ITU-D = 307. There were also over nine hundred associate members including companies, universities, research institutes and international organisations. Information as to the exact membership of each sector is available on their websites.

58 CV Art. 19.12 (241A–241E). The fee for an associate member of a sector is less than that required of a non-state sector member (see *infra* n. 61).

59 While most UN services are free to member states, other users have to pay a charge, sometimes based on cost recovery.

60 It is also used by the Universal Postal Union (UPU): F. Lyall, *International Communications: The International Telecommunication Union and the Universal Postal Union* (Farnham: Ashgate, 2011) 213–308.

The ITU financial arrangements are provided for in CS Art. 28 (155–170) and CV Art. 33 (468–487). Under CS Art. 28.3 (160–161A) and 3ter (161H–I) and CV 33.1.1 (468–468B), both state and sector members choose a class of contribution from twenty-four classes running from 40 to 1/16;[61] from highest to lowest, this is a ratio of 640:1. Contributing more than forty units is competent (CS Art. 33.2 (469)), but no state currently does so.

It is unusual for a state or sector member to increase its contribution (CS Art. 28.5ter (165B)).[62] Unless the plenipotentiary conference so consents, a state member contributing more than three or more units may not reduce its contribution units by more than 15% from that previously selected. A state member contributing less than three units also may not reduce its contribution by more than one unit. Consent to a reduction may be given when a state shows that it cannot maintain its contribution at its previous level, for example due to natural disaster (CS Art. 28.5 (165)).[63]

A state member's unit choice lasts throughout each four-year cycle unless the Council approves a reduction on the basis of 'exceptional circumstances' (CS Art. 28.5 bis (165A)): in undefined exceptional circumstances, the Council may agree to reduce contributions for a sector member which cannot maintain its commitment (CV Art. 33.5ter (480B)). Contributions are paid annually in advance (CS Art. 28.8 (168)). A member state in arrears to the extent of its contributions or more for two years loses the right to vote until the deficit is reduced at least to that level (CS Art. 28.9 (169)).[64]

Before a plenipotentiary conference, the Council considers a draft financial plan for the ensuing quadrennium and fixes a provisional value for the contributory unit (CS Art. 28.3 bis (161B–161D)). The plenipotentiary conference sets the monetary value of the unit, but the Council may adjust it half-way through the quadrennium (CS Art. 28.4–5 (161D–E)).[65] It is disappointing, and ominous, that the choice of contributory units declined in most quadrennia after the 1992–1994 reconstruction.[66]

61 For states, the lowest two classes are available only to those the UN identifies as least developed or as allowed by the ITU Council (CV Art. 33 1.1 *bis* (468A)). Sector members may not choose anything lower than the 1/2 unit except in the case of ITU-D; its 1/16 unit class is reserved for least-developed countries as listed by the UNDP and reviewed by the ITU Council (CV Art. 33 1.1*ter* (468B)). Countries in special need are listed in the Annex to PP Res. 34 (Rev. Dubai 2018).

In 2022, the values of one contributory unit for the various grades of membership were set for the next quadrennium by PP-22, Dec. 5 and Resols. 169 (academia), 170 (developing countries) and 209 (small and medium enterprises).

62 For 2024–2027, state selections are as follows: US 35 units, an increase of 5, Brazil 11 units, an increase of 8, Equatorial Guinea 1/4, an increase of 1/8, Guinea 1, an increase of 7/8, Papua New Guinea ½, an increase of 1/4. Japan with 30 units and the US with 35 are the largest contributors. With the exceptions of those listed in the next note, all other states maintained the selection made for the preceding quadrennium. See Annex 1 to 'Member States' contributory units', PP-22 Doc. INF/3, 20 September 2022.

63 In 2022, Chile selected 1/2, a reduction of ½; Libya 1/4, a reduction of ¾; Sri Lanka 1/4, a reduction of ¼; Venezuela 1/2, a reduction of 1/2; and Yemen 1/16, a reduction of 1/16; see Annex 1, *supra* n. 62.

64 Conference can exercise discretion. At Bucharest (PP-22), five members – Antigua and Barbuda, Equatorial Guinea, Nauru, Sierra Leone and Venezuela – were two years in arrears and so had no right to vote: PP-22, Doc. 67 Rev. 8.

65 PP-22, Decision 5, 'decides 1.1' set the contributory unit for 2024–2027 at CHF 318000, unchanged from the Dubai figure.

66 F. Lyall, 'Article I of the Outer Space Treaty and the International Telecommunication Union' (2003) 46 *Proc. IISL* 96–106 at 98–99, Sec. 3.2 'Finance'; 'Re-thinking the ITU' (2000) 43 *Proc. IISL* 309–319; 'The ITU in the Modern World: Fourteen Years from the Reconstruction' (2007) 50 *Proc. IISL* 450–455.

After Minneapolis (1998), the take-up of contributory units fell from 368 3/16 units to 342 5/8 at Marrakesh (2002) and to 336 7/16 at Antalya (2006). After Guadalajara (2010), it rose to 345 1/8 units but dropped at Busan (2015) to 334 1/12.[67] However, encouragingly, at Dubai, the uptake was 343 11/16, and at Bucharest for the period 2024–2027, it is 355 7/8 units. Even so, the Council Report to the Bucharest Conference makes plain that financial concerns remain important.[68]

These figures must concern those well-disposed to the Union. Obviously, one would wish the ITU to run efficiently while expending no more than required to perform its tasks, but there is a point at which lack of finances could damage. A related problem is that there remains a colossal imbalance between contributions. As stated earlier, the range of unit classes represents a ratio of 640:1 from highest to lowest. In fact, the current active range is a ratio of approximately 220:1. A small proportion of the state membership contributes 10% of the main income.[69] For the small contributors, which include the developing countries, the ITU must be a good value and therefore to some extent can be classified as a benefit in terms of OST Art. I. They all use space telecommunications, and many gain from other space uses, all of which are dependent on the work of the ITU. But an uncharitable question may now be whether the small contributors are not to some extent freeloading.

The ITU owes its justification to the need for cooperation and agreement on the best and most efficient arrangements for telecommunications, but in its recent years there has been an increasing demand that apart from its technical duties, the Union should also serve as a channel through which technical and other assistance might flow to the developing countries: the justification of ITU-D, which only exists thanks to pressure from the developing countries. Since the ITU operates on one state, one vote, voting power within the Union is somewhat divorced from its financial implications. The developing countries benefit from the spread of technology, socially as well as otherwise. The developed countries, whose interest lies mainly in technical matters, are contributing without their financial commitment being given clear weight in decision-making.[70] This is dangerous.

Efficient financial working is increasingly relevant in modern times. Accounting procedures are obviously important. The ITU Council approved the adoption of the International Public Sector Accounting Standards by its Decision 550, and the ITU has adhered to them since 2010.[71] The Financial Regulations and Financial Rules, available from the ITU, are detailed and complex; indeed, their exploration lies beyond our scope.

PP Decision 5 contains the budget for each year of the upcoming quadrennium. Its Annex 1 currently estimates income over the period 2024–2027 as CHF651,671K. Annex

---

67 See Annex 1 to Council Doc. C15/20, *supra* n. 62.
68 'Report of the Council on the implementation of the Strategic Plan and activities of the Union', PP-22, Doc. 20, and cf. its report examining the financial position of the ITU. PP-22, Doc. 54.
69 The Bucharest selection figures, *supra* n. 62, show that in 2024–2027, state members will contribute 355 7/8 contributory units. One hundred sixty-one of the one hundred ninety-three members, 83.4%, will contribute one unit or fewer. The sixteen largest contributors (down to five units) will produce two hundred forty-five units (68.8%).
70 There is, of course, some political weight to be exerted, augmented by 'informal understandings'. A weighted decision-making process modelled on that applied in the INTELSAT Board of Governors and the INMARSAT Council before privatisation would seem a rational solution.
71 'Guide for the Application of the International Public Sector Accounting Standards (IPSAS)', Council Doc. C11/INF/9.

2 lists thirty 'options for reducing expenditure'. These include eliminating duplications, centralising finance and administration, extending the duration of vacancies, reducing paper copies for meetings, limiting the duration and number of meetings and redeploying staff. New ventures are to be scrutinised for value and for their non-duplication of existing efforts. The list ends with 'Any additional measures adopted by the Council'. As to the effectiveness of the suggestions of Annex 2, we can but wait and see. Cost recovery for some ITU products and services will remain important, including the processing of space-relevant notifications to the Radiocommunication Sector.[72] Such financial steps are desirable. It is noticeable, however, that here and there in the conference documents are occasional invitations to member states and sector members to make voluntary contributions for particular purposes. The brutal fact is that not all state members are willing to finance all that others would like to see the ITU do.

ITU Structure

From the Atlantic City Convention of 1947[73] to the Nairobi Convention of 1982,[74] the ITU consisted of seven organs in a federal structure.[75] Three met at intervals: the plenipotentiary conference, administrative conferences and the administrative council. Four permanent organs were charged with the detailed business of the Union. These were the General Secretariat, the International Frequency Registration Board, the CCIR and the International Telegraph and Telephone Consultative Committee (CCITT).[76] Under CS Art. 7 (37–46), the ITU now comprises:

- the plenipotentiary conference, which is the supreme organ of the union
- the council, which acts on behalf of the plenipotentiary conference
- world conferences on international telecommunication
- the Radiocommunication Sector, including world and regional radiocommunication conferences, radiocommunication assemblies and the Radio Regulations Board (ITU-R)
- the Telecommunications Standardisation Sector, including world telecommunication standardisation assemblies (ITU-T)
- the Telecommunications Development Sector, including world and regional telecommunication development conferences (ITU-D)
- the General Secretariat

We discuss the plenipotentiary conference, the council and the General Secretariat before turning to the sectors. Obviously the ITU is complex; it is therefore useful that a Coordination Committee – composed of the Secretary General (Chairman), the Deputy Secretary

---

72 'Cost Recovery for Some ITU Products and Services', PP Res. 91 (Rev. Guadalajara, 2010).
73 *Supra*, n. 23.
74 *Supra*, n. 25.
75 For this period, see Lyall 1, *supra* n. 5, 71–126.
76 Nairobi Convention (*supra* n. 25), Art. 5. As noted below, Art. 5 of the Nice Constitution, 1989, added a Telecommunications Development Bureau which had not properly started to function before the 1992–1994 revisions were adopted.

General and the Directors of the Bureaux of the three Sectors – acts as an internal management team (CS Art. 26 (145–6); CV Art. 6 (106–111)). The Coordination Committee endeavours to act unanimously. Should its chairman not be supported by a majority, the matter goes to the Council (CS Art. 6.2 (109)).

Plenipotentiary Conference

Before the reforms of 1992–1994, ITU plenipotentiary conferences had been held irregularly.[77] CV Art. 8.1 (47) now provides that the plenipotentiary conference 'shall be convened every four years'. This is a useful constraint and introduces a timetable for activities which, to some extent, help the ITU cope with swift technological developments.

The plenipotentiary conference is the supreme organ of the Union (CS Art. 7.a (40)), composed of delegations representing all member states (CS Art. 8.1 (47)). Its responsibilities include setting general policies, establishing the basis of the budget of the Union and related financial limits, giving general directives as to staffing and examining the Union accounts. It adopts a strategic plan for the next quadrennium.[78] It elects member states to serve on the Council (CS Art. 8.2.f (54)), the Secretary General, Deputy Secretary General, the Directors of the Sectors (CS Art. 8.2.g (55)) and the members of the Radio Regulations Board (CS Art. 8.2.h (56)). It also considers and, if appropriate, adopts proposals for amending CS and CV for submission to the plenipotentiary conference (CS Art. 8.2.i (57).

The Council

The main provisions as to the ITU Council are in CS Art. 10 (65–72)) and CV Art. 4 (50–82). Its members are elected by the plenipotentiary conference (CS Art 8.2.f (54A)) with 'due regard [for] the need for equitable distribution of the seats on the Council among all regions of the world' (CS Art. 9.1.a (61)).[79] Membership is not to exceed 25% of the total number of member states (CV Art 4.1.2 (50A)).[80] For the period 2024–2027, it consists of forty-eight member states.[81] Any member state not elected to the Council may, after prior notice to the Secretary-General, send an observer at its own expense to Council meetings, committees and working groups. An observer does not have the right to vote (CV Art. 4.9bis (60A)). Sector members may similarly be represented as observers (CV Art. 4.9ter (60B)).

---

77 See the dates of the conferences listed *supra* n. 25.
78 'Strategic Plan for the Union for 2024–2027', Res. 71 (Rev. Bucharest, 2022).
79 There are five ITU regions for this purpose: the Americas, Western Europe, Eastern Europe and Northern Asia, Africa and Asia and Australasia. See www.itu.int/online/mm/scripts/mm.world?_languageid=1. Cf. www.itu.int/en/ITU-D/Statistics/Pages/definitions/regions.aspx. These are not the regions used in the Radio Regulations, RR Arts. 5.2–5.9 (*infra* n. 150).
80 As of 1 January 2022, there were one hundred ninety-three ITU member states: 25 % = 48. Under Res. 164 (Guadalajara, 2010), the regional allocation of seats also observes the 25% rule.
81 There is no formal requirement of a rotation of membership, but under PP Rec. 6 (Marrakesh, 2002), regional and sub-regional areas should confer to facilitate rotation on a voluntary basis. This has had some (limited?) effect.

The Council meets annually in Geneva, although an extra session is possible (CV Arts 4.2.1–3 (51–3)). It elects a chairman, who serves for one year.[82] Its functions include facilitating the implementation of CS, CV and the Administrative Regulations as well as the decisions of plenipotentiary and other conferences. Through the powers delegated to it, the Council acts as the governing body of the Union (CS Art. 10.3.b (68)). Its functions are more extensively laid out in CV Art. 4 (50–82). In particular, the ITU Council supervises the management of the Union, approves staff and financial regulations (CV Art. 4.11 (62–68)), decides on the implementation of conference decisions with financial implications (CV Art. 4.11.11 (77)) and takes any action necessary for the functioning of the Union (CV Art. 4 11.12 (78)). The annual Report to Council of the Secretary General on the implementation of the PP Strategic Plan is a good source of information on what the ITU is doing (CV Art. 4.10 (61–61B)).

The Secretary-General, General Secretariat and Officials

Assisted by a single Deputy Secretary-General (CS Art. 11.1.1 (73)) and a General Secretariat, the Secretary-General coordinates the activities of the Union including implementation of the Strategic Plan and takes all actions required to ensure the economic use of Union resources (CS Art. 11.1 (73–5)). He or she is the legal representative of the Union (CS Art. 11.1 (76 bis)). The Secretary-General, Deputy Secretary-General and Sector Directors are elected by plenipotentiary conference and are required to be nationals of different countries (CS Art. 9.1.b. (62)). Under CV Art. 2.1 (13), these five top elected officials may be re-elected only once to the same post, whether or not the second election is for a term consecutive with the first.[83]

In the elections, due regard is to be given to equitable geographic distribution amongst the regions. The detailed responsibilities of the Secretary General and the General Secretariat are laid out in CS Art. 11 (CS 73–7) and CV Art. 5 (CV 83–105). We address those of the Sector Bureaux and the Radio Regulations Board later in this chapter. Under CS Art. 27, a paramount consideration in all elections and staff recruitment is 'the necessity of securing for the Union the highest standards of efficiency, competence and integrity' while bearing in mind the 'importance of recruiting the staff on as wide a geographic basis as possible' (CS Art. 27.2 (154)).[84]

The ITU Sectors

The 1992–1994 reconstruction removed three major former organs, the CCITT, the CCIR and the IFRB. In their place are now three sectors with different responsibilities from those of their fore-runners: ITU-D, ITU-T and ITU-R. Their close cooperation is called for in CS Arts 12.1.2 (79), 17.1.2 (105) and 21.1.2 (119), as well as elsewhere.

---

82 The working of the Council is facilitated by a 'Council troika', consisting of the past, present and future Chairmen of the Council: www.itu.int/en/council/Pages/troika.aspx.

83 In the interest of an efficient ITU, states should as far as possible refrain from recalling a national elected to one of the top five posts in the interval between plenipotentiary conferences (CS Art. 27.1.4 (153)).

84 Can all these requirements always be simultaneously met? This seems to be a problem common throughout the UN agencies.

Provisions Common to the Sectors

Each Sector is headed by a Director[85] elected by the plenipotentiary conference (CS Art. 8.2.g (55)) who may be re-elected once only to that post whether re-elected immediately or later (CV Art. 2.3.1 (13)). Each Sector has a Bureau and works through a variety of working groups, study groups, regional conferences (except for ITU-D), world conferences and assemblies.[86] CV Arts 19–22 (228–254)) contains provisions on participation in the work of the sectors and their abilities to refer matters to each other and to other international organisations. ITU–R AND ITU–T are also specifically required to provide technical assistance to ITU–D (CV Arts 12.4 (183), 15.4 (207)). All three are to cooperate and coordinate their activities including the distribution of work.[87]

Study groups are constrained with respect to their work and recommendations, particularly matters with regulatory and policy aspects and/or financial implications (CS Ch. IVA and CV Art. 22.5 bis.4 (246D–H)). The working methods of radiocommunication and standardisation assemblies and world development conferences that put the results of study groups into practice must be compatible with the basic instruments of the Union (CS Chapter IVA (145A)). Study groups in all three sectors conduct their business in accordance with CV Art. 20 (242–249).

The Telecommunication Development Sector (ITU-D)

'Economic and social development', words twice used in CS Preamble (1), have only relatively recently been included in the formal purposes of the Union.[88] CS Art. 1 now puts among the purposes of the Union the promotion of technical developments, including technical assistance to developing countries (CS Art. 1.1.1.b (4)), making telecommunication facilities 'so far as possible generally available to the public' (CS Art. 1.1.c (5)) and extending 'the benefits of new communications technologies to all the world's inhabitants' (CS Art. 1.1.d (6)). An interesting innovation in 1992–1994 was the inclusion of a duty 'in particular' to promote 'with international financial and development organisations . . . the establishment of preferential and favourable lines of credit to be used for the development of social projects aimed, inter alia, at extending telecommunication services to the most isolated areas in countries' (CS Art. 1.2.i (19)). This is not to say these were previously irrelevant, but now promoting cooperation and collaboration among nations particularly to benefit the less-developed remains a general undercurrent in the ITU documents.

---

85 Development, CS Art. 21.3.c (133); Standardisation, CS Art. 17.2.c (109); Radiocommunication, CS Art. 12 2.e (85).
86 Consultations may be subject to rules and time limits. Where a consultation in relation to conference or assemblies needs a majority for adoption, states which do not reply within the limits do not count in the compilation of a majority. If the number of responses is fewer than one-half of the total ITU membership, the consultation is re-run, and the result is decisive irrespective of the number of states taking part (CV Art. 3.7 (47)).
87 CS Arts 12.1.2 (79), 17.1.2 (105), 21.1.2 (119); CV Arts 11.5 (158), 11.7 (160) 14.2 (195), 14.4 (197) and 17.2 (215).
88 The language first appeared in the Preamble of the 1982 Nairobi Convention (*supra* n. 25) but not as a 'purpose' of the Union. F. Lyall, 'Space Telecommunications and the Developing Countries' (1989) 32 *Proc. IISL*, 242–247 and 'The International Telecommunication Union and Development' (1994) 22 *J. Sp. L.* 23–32; B.E. Harris, 'The New Telecommunications Development Bureau of the International Telecommunication Union' (1991) 7 *Am. U. J. Int. L. & Pol.* 83–103.

Without prejudice to CS Arts. 1.1.b (4), 1.2.d (14) and 1.2.i (19), ITU-D is the main agent through which development activities are pursued. It is based in Geneva with regional offices to help achieve its objectives. The sector operates under CS Chapter IV (CS Arts 21–24 (118–145)), CV Section 6 (CV Arts 16–18 (207A–26)) and the already noted provisions common to all sectors (CV Sec. 8, Arts 19–22 (228–54)). In fact, for some decades, the ITU ran appropriate programmes to help developing countries establish good telecommunications facilities.[89] The 1992–1994 reforms went much further. This was not welcomed by all, and the funding of the sector was under constraint, development being considered by some to depart from the original or basic technical ITU. However, increasingly, the general world interest, the spread of telecommunications through satellite coverage and the resources of the Internet have had effect.

ITU-D consists of a Director and a Bureau (CV Art. 18 (216–26)) with duties laid out in CV Art. 18 (216–226). Members of the sector and the groups it works through include states that are members by right but not by duty, together with those authorised by the appropriate procedures (CS Art. 21.4 (134–6)).[90] Groups include a Telecommunication Development Advisory Group (CV Art. 17A (215C–K)), which reviews the work of the sector, including the implementation of its operational plan, and suggests any necessary corrective measures. It also prepares reports for ITU-D conferences.

While ITU-D does much of its work through study groups (CV Art. 17 (214–15B)), courses and workshops, an important element of activity is telecommunication develop-ment conferences (CV Art. 16 (208–13A). These I, for discussion and consultation, are held within each ITU four-year cycle as are regional conferences, subject to resources and priorities (CS Art. 22.3 (141)). ITU-D conferences do not produce Final Acts (i.e. treaty-level agreements), but adopt resolutions, decisions, recommendations and reports of varying cogency. The foreseeable financial implications of any proposals must be taken into account and conferences may not adopt resolutions and decisions that might cause expenditure above limits set by the Plenipotentiary Conference (CS Art. 22.4 (142)).

World conferences establish work programmes and guidelines giving direction for ITU-D as a whole (CV Art. 16.1.1.a (209)). Regional conferences deal with matters spe-cific to that region (CV Art. 16.1.1.b (210)). Telecommunication Development Confer-ences fix objectives and strategies for a balanced, worldwide and regional development of telecommunications (CV Art. 16.1.c (211)). That paragraph goes on to indicate that the conferences should give 'particular consideration to the expansion and modernisa-tion of the networks and services of the developing countries as well as the mobilisa-tion of resources required for this purpose. They shall serve as a forum for the study of policy, organisational, operational, regulatory, technical and financial questions and related aspects, including the identification and implementation of new sources of funding' (CV Art. 16.1.c (211)). Channels of technical assistance and financial aid for developing coun-tries have been opened up and existing channels deepened ways that would have been impossible under the pre-1992/94 arrangements.[91]

---

89 Before 1992–1994, the ITU did undertake a certain amount of 'development' work in addition to facilitat-ing cooperation between ordinary commercial undertakings and developing countries. In addition, the IFRB held training courses and workshops for officials responsible for radio matters in newly emergent nations.
90 See *supra* at n. 54 and following.
91 A listing of ITU-D regional and world ITU-D conferences is at: www.itu.int/en/history/Pages/CompleteListOfTelecommunicationDevelopmentConferences.aspx.

The Sector has been significant in developing telecommunications accessibility, afford-ability and infrastructure particularly in the developing countries. Major results have been the adoption of Declarations and an Action Plan at successive World Telecommunication Development Conferences (WTDC) at Buenos Aires, 1994,[92] Valletta, 1998,[93] Istanbul, 2002,[94] Doha 2006,[95] Hyderabad, 2010,[96] Dubai, 2014,[97] and Buenos Aires in 2017.[98] The most recent WTDC was held in Kigali in October 2022.[99]

The Valletta Plan, as amended, had particular chapters on the development of a global information infrastructure and a special programme for developing countries. The Istanbul Development Plan included a special programme for least developed countries and was divided into six programmes: (i) regulatory reform, (ii) technologies and telecommunica-tion network development, (iii) e-strategies and e-services/applications, (iv) economic and finance, (v) human capacity building and (vi) a special programme for the least developed countries.[100] The Doha Declaration of 2006 indicated that most of the previous Action Plans have been implemented, but called for an increased pace in progress towards a truly global information society and further improving the position of the developing coun-tries.[101] The Doha Action Plan took these matters further. Thereafter the Hyderabad, Dubai and Buenos Aires conferences continued to develop ways the purposes of the ITU can be carried forward within the remit of ITU – D. In this recent WTDCs have been assisted by the outcomes of successive meetings of the World Summit on the Information Society, an ITU initiative when began in 2003–2005.[102]

The 'Digital Divide', economic and social inequality in access to and use of modern information and communication technologies, has been a concern both to ITU-D and the ITU in general. Countries which are analogue-based in their telecommunications may

---

92 World Telecommunication Development Conference (WTDC-94, Buenos Aires) – Final Report: https://search.itu.int/history/HistoryDigitalCollectionDocLibrary/4.144.43.en.100.pdf.

93 World Telecommunication Development Conference (WTDC-98, Valletta): https://search.itu.int/his-tory/HistoryDigitalCollectionDocLibrary/4.147.43.en.100.pdf.

94 World Telecommunication Development Conference (WTDC-02, Istanbul) – Final Report (ITU, 2002): https://search.itu.int/history/HistoryDigitalCollectionDocLibrary/4.153.43.en.100.pdf.

95 World Telecommunication Development Conference (WTDC-06-Doha) – Final Report: https://search.itu.int/history/HistoryDigitalCollectionDocLibrary/4.160.43.en.100.pdf.

96 World Telecommunication Development Conference (WTDC-10-Hyderabad, 2010) – Final Report: https://search.itu.int/history/HistoryDigitalCollectionDocLibrary/4.166.43.en.100.pdf.

97 World Telecommunication Development Conference (WTDC-14-Dubai, 2014) – Final Report: https://search.itu.int/history/HistoryDigitalCollectionDocLibrary/4.295.43.en.100.pdf.

98 World Telecommunication Development Conference (WTDC-17-Buenos Aires, 2017) – Final Report: https://search.itu.int/history/HistoryDigitalCollectionDocLibrary/4.438.43.en.100.pdf.

99 World Telecommunication Development Conference (WTDC-22-Kigali, 2022) – Final Report: www.itu.int/dms_pub/itu-d/opb/tdc/D-TDC-WTDC-2022-PDF-E.pdf.

100 See Istanbul Final Report (*supra* n. 94) at 22.

101 Doha, Final Report (*supra* n. 95) 15–18. The Doha Declaration at 19–21 took matters further.

102 WSIS Forum, 2022, 'Highlights, Announcements, and Key Outcomes': www.itu.int/net4/wsis/forum/2022/Home/Outcomes. See also WSIS Outcome Documents (ITU, 2005): www.itu.int/wsis/promotional/outcome.pdf. WSIS+10 Outcomes: Statement on the Implementation of WSIS Outcomes (Geneva: ITU, 2014): www.itu.int/net/wsis/implementation/2014/forum/inc/doc/outcome/362828V2E.pdf. See also documents at www.itu.int/net/wsis/. Cf. Res. 140 (Rev. Bucharest, 2022) on 'ITU's role in implementing the outcomes of the World Summit on the Information Society and in the overall review by United Nations General Assembly of their implementation'. See also K. Irion, 'Separated Together: The International Telecommunications Union and Civil Society' (2009) 13 *Int. J. Comm. L. & Pol.* 95–113.

lag behind those (in the main the developed countries) whose telecommunications are increasingly moving over to digitally based technologies. In 2002 the Istanbul WTDC adopted Res. 37, 'Bridging the Digital Divide' which has been successively revised by later WTDCs, most recently at Buenos Aires.[103] Such concerns have also fed through into ITU plenipotentiary conferences.[104] Standardisation within telecommunications is an important element in these efforts. While the ITU is not the sole organisation active in standard setting, its role is significant.[105]

That noted, we must also point out that there can be a digital divide within the so-called 'developed' countries because of the problems of introducing satisfactory terrestrial links for territorial and other reasons. Proposals for communications constellations in LEO and MEO may alleviate these problems.[106]

The Telecommunication Standardisation Sector (ITU-T)

The Telecommunication Standardisation Sector (ITU-T)[107] is largely provided for by CS Chapter III (CS Arts 17–20 (104–117)) and CV Section 6 (CV Arts 13–15 (184–207)), together with the provisions common to all Sectors (CV Sec. 8, Arts 19–22 (228–54)).

The ITU-T Sector is headed by a Director (CV Art. 17.2.c (109)) elected by the Plenipotentiary Conference of the Union (CS Art. 8.1.g (55)) and has a specialised Bureau. Members of the Sector include all state members of the Union as of right together with any entity or organisation authorised by the appropriate procedures to be a member of the Sector (CS Art. 21.4 (134–136)).[108] The Sector works through World Telecommunication Standardisation Assemblies (WTSA), study groups and its Bureau (CS Art. 17.2 (106–109)) and complies with the provisions common to all Sectors (CV Sec. 8, Arts 19–22 (228–254)). Its responsibility covers technical, operating and tariff questions. It adopts recommendations with a view to their standardisation on a worldwide basis (CS Art. 17.1.1 (104)).

The need for standard international procedures and practices, for compatibility between equipment, and for operating protocols gave the initial impetus for the early

---

103 See Buenos Aires Final Report (*supra* n. 98) at 377.
104 The 'digital divide' figures extensively in the ITU Strategic Plan for 2024–2027 (PP–22, Res. 71). See also Res. 64 (Rev. Bucharest, 2022) on 'Non-discriminatory access to modern telecommunication/information and communication technology facilities, services and applications, including applied research and transfer of technology, and e-meetings, on mutually agreed terms'; Res. 131 (Rev. Bucharest, 2022) on 'Measuring information and communication technologies to build an integrating and inclusive information society'; Res. 137 (Rev. Bucharest, 2022) on 'Deployment of future networks in developing countries'; Res. 139 (Rev. Bucharest, 2022) on 'Use of telecommunications/information and communication technologies to bridge the digital divide and build an inclusive information society'.
105 Cf. PP–22, Res. 123 (Rev. Bucharest, 2022) on 'Bridging the standardization gap between developing and developed countries'. See also 'Brokering standards by consensus: www.itu.int/en/mediacentre/backgrounders/Pages/standardization.aspx. Cf. R. Pritchard-Kelly, R. 'Regulatory Best Practices to Bridge the Digital Divide and Make Internet Access Available and Affordable for Everyone Using Non-Geostationary Satellite Constellations' (2018) 61 *Proc. IISL* 331–342; K.M. Dalton, 'Bridging the Digital Divide and Guiding the Millennial Generation's Research and Analysis' (2012) 18 *Barry L. Rev.* 167–190, and Shackleford *infra* n. 231; R. S. Jakhu, 'Safeguarding the Concept of Public Service and the Global Public Interest in Telecommunications' (2001) 5 *Singapore J. Int. & Comp. L.* 71–110.
106 See Chapter 10 – 'Small satellites and constellations'.
107 The designator ITU-T derives from the French text.
108 See *supra* n. 54 and following.

telecommunication agreements. Common standards were adopted so that messages could be passed across borders and from one system to the next. Fundamentally the position is no different today. Manufacturers want assurance that their products will sell. Occasionally a question of 'standard' may be left to market-place decision – the collision in video recorder standards between the Betamax and VHS system was abrupt and dispositive. However, while some matters can be left to the marketplace, other questions better settled by discussion and agreement on standards and procedures. The effect of even a substantial, let alone a consensus, view formed through an agency of the ITU should not be underestimated. Naturally in this process political and economic interests also play major and obvious roles.[109]

The CCITT and CCIR had already served as fora for discussions on standards.[110] However, their elaboration of standards had become slow and cumbersome. The separation between the CCIs, and their involvement with other aspects of ITU work, contributed to a deceleration in standard setting. There were (and are) other I through which international standards are set.[111] The risk was that the ITU would be by-passed on matters which properly ought to lie within its competence and this was part of why the High Level Review Committee was given its task.[112]

Standards adopted as part of the ITU Administrative Regulations are legal rulings. The Recommendations and Administrative Regulations established under the pre-1992/94 ITU remain in force until amended or repealed. Even so, the process could (and can) be slower than society really needs. Accordingly in 2000 a WTSA adopted an 'alternative approval' system to provide a fast-track system by which informal approval of new 'standards' can be obtained relatively quickly.[113] 'Alternative approvals' are not binding in the way that WTSA Recommendations are, but their existence has considerably increased the speed at which ITU-T reacts to swiftly developing technologies.

World Telecommunication Standardisation Assemblies (WTSA) are convened every four years, though an additional conference can be intercalated if necessary (CS Art. 18.2 (114)). Dissimilar to ITU-D or ITU-R, ITU-T does not hold regional conferences. A WTSA deals with specific matters related to telecommunications (CV Art. 13 (184–191D)). Questions to be studied and on which recommendations may be issued may be generated within the Sector or referred to it by the Plenipotentiary Conference, by other conferences, or by the Council (CV Art. 13.2 (185)). Steps are being taken to improve the role of ITU-T and its effectiveness.[114] There is also concern in the Sector as to an increasing

---

109 J.G. Savage, *The Politics of International Telecommunications Regulation* (London: Westview Press, 1989). See the journal *Telecommunications Policy*.

110 That the CCITT, not the CCIR, was the major standardisation agency within the ITU was shown by Res. PLEN/8, of the 1992 Geneva Conference by which the then CCITT Director acted as ITU – D Director until the elections of the Kyoto Plenipotentiary Conference, 1994.

111 G. Wallenstein, *Setting Global Telecommunication Standards* (Boston and London: Artech House, 1990). Cf. the European Telecommunications Standards Institute (www.etsi.org/), set up in 1988 as a joint project by the European Community and the European Postal and Telecommunication Conference (CEPT) to publish telecommunications standards for Europe. Not all standard setting institutions are intergovernmental or international.

112 See *supra* at n. 28.

113 WTSA Res. 37 (2000) 'Alternative approval process for ITU-T'. See now 'Rec. ITU – T A.8 (03.22), 'Alternative approval process for new and revised ITU – T Recommendations'.

114 PP Res. 122 (Rev. Guadalajara, 2010), 'The Evolving Role of the World Telecommunication Standardisation Assembly'.

gap between developed and developing countries in the matter of standardisation, and steps are being taken to address the problem.[115]

The 1992 Conference did not take the sword to the previous Gordian tangle of questions and responsibilities for standardisation. Duplication of effort (not to say conflict of interest) between the Study Groups of ITU-T and ITU-R had been foreseen as a potential problem. It had so been between the CCITT and the CCIR. The precise responsibilities of ITU-T and ITU-R have therefore been subject to continuing review of matters of common interest (CV Arts. 12.1.2 (79) and 17.1.2 (105)). CV Arts 11.5 (158) and 14.2 (193) therefore provide for a possible change of responsibilities between the Sectors and relevant Study Groups. In the case of failure of a timely and effective agreement, the matter is referred through the Council to the Plenipotentiary Conference.[116] Over the years this has produced some adjustment between ITU-T and ITU-R.

The International Telecommunication Regulations[117]

A separate responsibility of ITU-T is for the International Telecommunication Regulations (ITR). The ITRs are part of the Administrative Regulations, which complement CS and CV and have status as international treaties (CS Arts. 4.1 (29), 5.3 (31), 6.1–2 (37–38), 54 (215–223)). Unfortunately there are now two active sets of ITRs. The earlier was adopted by a World Administrative Telegraph and Telephone Conference at Melbourne in 1988.[118] The later was adopted at Dubai in 2012.[119] Because the Dubai text includes provisions which might affect the operation of the Internet, a significant proportion were unwilling to endorse the new text.[120] Accordingly the 1988 text remains operational for the dissentients. Both sets of ITR deal with the operation of telecommunications in general, interconnection and interoperability, routing, quality of service and the settlement of accounts for telecommunication services.[121] These are not germane to our discussion of

---

115 PP Res. 123 (Rev. Bucharest, 2022), 'Bridging the Standardisation Gap between Developing and Developed Countries'.

116 CV Art. 11.5 (158). Of all the United Nations agencies, the ITU has the best history of a pragmatic approach to problems.

117 Reference point, *infra* n. 141.

118 International Telecommunication Regulations: Final Acts of the World Administrative Telegraph and Telephone Conference, Melbourne, 1988 (ITU, 1989): www.itu.int/dms_pub/itu-t/opb/reg/T-REG-ACT-1988-PDF-E.pdf.

119 Final Acts of the World Conference on International Telecommunications (Dubai, 2012) (ITU, 2013): www.itu.int/dms_pub/itu-s/opb/conf/S-CONF-WCIT-2012-PDF-E.pdf. See also (2013) 52 ILM 846–860, with Introductory Note at 843–845.

120 New Arts. 5A and 5B introduce duties as to Internet traffic and content. 89 of the 193 ITU members signed the Final Acts, and as of 23 November 2022 91 have ratified them. Non-ratifiers include France, Germany, Italy, UK, US – cf, our discussion of direct broadcasting in Chapter 10. Cf. Cf. R. Hill, *The New International Telecommunication Regulations* (Dordrecht: Springer, 2014); S.J. Shackleford and A.N. Craig, 'Beyond the "Digital Divide": Analyzing the Evolving Role of National Governments in Internet Governance and Enhancing Cybersecurity' (2014) 50 *Stanford J. Int. L.* 120–184; Gerson and Raustalia, both *infra* n. 232.

121 The 1988 ITRs are discussed in Lyall, *supra* n. 5, 175–178, and Hill, *supra* n. 120. Under the ITR international accounts are treated as current transactions, to be dealt with either as agreed between individual Members, or if not so agreed, in accordance with the ITRs (CV Art. 38 (497–499). In the absence of bilateral agreement the monetary unit for the calculation of debits and credits is either the gold franc or the monetary unit of the International Monetary Fund (CV. Art. 38 (500)).

space, though without them modern telecommunications would not exist. We therefore limit ourselves to noting their existence as part of the overall working of the ITU. However, we would also note that the failure to come to general agreement at Dubai is worrying. It would be unfortunate were the portfolio of agreements arrived at through the ITU to splinter.[122]

The Radiocommunication Sector (ITU-R)

The major responsibilities of the Radiocommunication Sector are the formulation of the Radio Regulations and their implementation, together with aspects of standardisation in the radio sphere.[123] Structurally the Sector has two elements, its Bureau, which carries out the main responsibilities of these elements of the ITU, and the Radio Regulations Board – a creation of 1992/1994, lineally the old International Frequency Registration Board.

The Sector

The Radiocommunication Sector is dealt by CS Chapter II (CS Arts 12–16 (78–103)) CV Chapter I Section 5 (CV Arts 7–12 (112–83)) together with the common sectoral provisions (CV Sec. 8, Arts 19–22 (228–54)). The purpose of the sector is to ensure 'the rational, equitable, efficient and economical use of the radio frequency spectrum by all radiocommunication services, including those using the geostationary satellite orbit, and to carry out studies without limit of frequency range' (CS Art. 12.1.1 (78)). On the basis of its studies, the sector adopts recommendations on radiocommunication matters (CS Art. 12.1.1 (78)).

The sector works through the Radiocommunication Bureau under a director elected by the Council, World and Regional Radiocommunication Conferences, Radiocommunication Assemblies (frequently associated with world radiocommunication conferences), the Radiocommunication Advisory Group (RAG) and study groups (CS Art. 12.2 (80–85)). In addition there is a Radio Regulations Board (RRB).[124] Sector members are the ITU state members by right together with any properly authorised entity or organisation (CS Art. 12.3 (86–88)).

World radiocommunication conferences (WRCs[125]) are normally held every three to four years, although that may vary (CS Art. 13.2 (90)).[126] Their powers and duties are elaborated in CV Art. 7 (112–128). A WRC may partially or completely revise the Radio Regulations and deal with any questions of a worldwide character (CS Art. 13.1 (89); CV Art. 7.2.1 (113–117)). It may instruct the RRB or the Sector Bureau, may put matters on the agenda of future world conferences and may refer questions to the Radiocommunication Assembly (CV Art. 7.2.1.c (116)).

---

122 *Infra* at n. 225. A Working Group is working on revising the ITRs: www.itu.int/en/council/Pages/cg-itrs. aspx. See also M.A. El-Moghazi and J. Whalley, *The International Radio Regulations: The Case for Reform* (Vienna: Springer, 2021).
123 Radio communications, *infra* at n. 139.
124 See *infra* at n. 131.
125 Previously, World Administrative Radio Conferences.
126 The next WRC will be held in Dubai from 20 November to 15 December 2023.

Given the importance of the Radio Regulations, it is unsurprising that the general scope of the agenda of a world conference should be established four to six years in advance and the final agenda established by the ITU Council 'preferably' two years in advance of the conference (CV Art. 7.2.2 (118)). A WRC agenda also includes any matter the Plenipotentiary Conference directs (CV Art. 7.2.3 (19)). It can be changed on the proposal of the Council or at the request of one quarter of the member states. However, the proposed change cannot finally be adopted until a majority of states so agree.[127]

Regional radio conferences (RRCs) deal with the concerns of a particular region (CS Art. 12.2.a (81); CS Art, 13.4 (92), CS Art. 43 (194)). They are called following the decision of a plenipotentiary conference, on the recommendation of a previous world or regional radio conference if approved by the Council, at the request of at least one quarter of the state members in the region concerned or on the proposal of Council (CV Art. 3.4 (36–40)). RRCs adopt or revise provisions of the Radio Regulations, including, for example, an 'allotment plan' for a particular type of broadcasting in the region concerned.[128] An RRC can only consider matters on its agenda (CV Art. 9 (138)).

Radiocommunication assemblies are normally convened every three to four years to provide the technical basis for the work of world conferences (CS Art. 13.3 (91); CV Art 8.2.5–6 (135–136)). An RA usually acts on the basis of reports from study groups (CV Art. 8.2 (130–136)) and deals with and issues and recommendations on questions adopted by its own procedures or referred to it by a plenipotentiary conference, by any other conference, by the Council or by the RRB (CV Art. 8.1 (129) and 8.2). Particularly important is the ability to terminate study groups and to create new ones allocating the questions with which they are to deal (CV Art. 8.2.3 (133)).[129]

A RAG was added to the Sector by the 1998 Minneapolis plenipotentiary conference under CS Art. 12.2.d bis (84A) and CV Art. 11A (160A–160H). Its membership is open to all member states, representatives of sector members and the chairmen of study and other groups (CV Art. 11A.1 (160A)). Meeting annually, it advises the bureau director, reviewing the sector priorities and strategies and monitoring the progress and guiding study groups. The RAG also has a role fostering cooperation within the ITU.

Radiocommunication study groups are regulated by CV Art. 11 (148–60). Their members are appointed by an RA that also determines their remit. In terms of the CV, study groups deal with matters including the use of the radio-frequency spectrum in terrestrial and space radiocommunication and of the geostationary and other satellite orbits (CV Art. 11.2.a (151)), the characteristics and performance of radio systems (CV Art. 11.2.b (152)), the operation of radio stations (CV Art. 11.2.c (153)) and aspects of distress and safety radiocommunications (CV Art. 11.2.d (154)).[130] Studies and reports are prepared

---

127 See *supra* n. 86.
128 For regions and broadcasting areas, see *infra* n. 150. On the 'European Broadcasting Plan', Stockholm, 1961, as revised, see J.-M. Paquet, 'The Stockholm 1961 Agreement': www.itu.int/en/ITU-R/terrestrial/ broadcast/Documents/Presentations/ST61Rev2006-E.pdf. The first European Broadcasting Plan was the 'Long and Medium Frequency Plan' adopted by twenty-nine European countries in 1929. Cf. J. Doeven, 'Revision of ST61 – Lessons from History' (2002) 290 *EBU Tech. Rev.*: www.ebu.ch/en/technical/trev/ trev_290-doeven.html. The 'European Broadcasting Area' is defined in RR 5.14.
129 RA-15 was held in October 2015. WRC–15 followed in November. See Resolutions. Radiocommunication Assembly (RA–15), Geneva, 26–30 October 2015 (ITU – R, 2015).
130 Res. ITU-R 4–7 'Structure of Radiocommunication Study Groups' lists six study groups presently operating: Group 1 – Spectrum Management; Group 3 – Radiowave Propagation; Group 4 – Satellite Services;

for WRCs and RRCs (CV Art. 11.3 (156)). Study groups can take economic factors into consideration only when comparing technical or operational alternatives. They do not deal with economic considerations in general (CV Art. 11.2.3 (155)).

The Radio Regulations Board

The Radio Regulations Board (RRB) replaces the International Frequency Registration Board (IFRB).[131] Back in 1965 at the Montreux PP, there was a suggestion that the IFRB should be abolished. However, to have done away with it would have eliminated something important. The root justification of the IFRB, and now of the RRB, is instilling and maintaining confidence in the international radio regulatory system. In 1965, it was mainly the developing nations that stood out for the IFRB, perceiving it useful both as an impartial voice in arguments as to frequency allocation and as a source of disinterested advice. Even with the inception of ITU-D, these justifications continue and may have increased with the advent of satellite communications.

The composition of the RRB is not more than the greater of twelve or 6% of the total state membership of the ITU (CS Art. 14.1bis (93A)).[132] Members are elected by plenipotentiary conference (CS Art. 8.2.h (56)) but for a maximum of two terms whether or not consecutive (CV Art. 2.1 (2)). RRB members serve part-time (CS Art. 14.1 (93)), with only their travelling, subsistence and insurance expenses being met by the Union (CV Art. 10.4 (142)). In their election, regard is given to 'equitable geographic distribution' (CS Art. 9.1.c (63)). As in the previous IFRB, members serve 'not as representing their respective Member States, or a region, but as custodians of an international public trust' (CS Art. 14.3.1 (98)), a statement traceable back to the Atlantic City Convention of 1947.[133]

In 1947, there was some hope that the notion of 'public trust' would result in the election of members of the original IFRB on merit alone, but following a practice then already emergent in the UN, a regional distribution of membership was adopted. Now, under CS Art. 14.1 (93) RRB members are to be 'thoroughly qualified in the field of radiocommunications' and possess 'practical experience in the assignment and utilization of frequencies'.[134] Members must be nationals of different countries and not of the

---

Group 5 – Terrestrial Services; Group 6 – Broadcasting Services; Group 7 – Science Services. See also Res. ITU-R 5-7, 'Work Programme and Questions of Radiocommunication Study Groups'.

131 On the creation of the IFRB, see Lyall, *supra* n. 5, 101–104; G.A. Codding, *The International Telecommunication Union: An Experiment in International Cooperation* (Leiden: E.J. Brill, 1952; rep. New York: Arno Press, 1972) 241–252. On its working, see D.M. Leive, *International Telecommunications and International Law: The Regulation of the Radio Spectrum* (Leiden: Sijthoff; New York: Oceana, 1970); F. Lyall, *Law and Space Telecommunications* (Aldershot: Dartmouth, 1989); R. Lauria and H.L. White, *The Law and Regulation of International Space Communication* (Boston: Artech House, 1988). On the 1992 proposals, see F. Lyall, 'The International Frequency Registration Board' (1992) 33 *Proc. IISL* 394–399.

132 As of 1 January 2022, there are one hundred ninety-three ITU members; 6% = 11.46. The 1992–1994 Constitution provided for nine IFRB members. This was increased to twelve in 1998.

133 Atlantic City Convention (*supra* n. 23), Art. 6.5.1.

134 This statement of qualification was an innovation in 1992–1994. Members of the previous IFRB were all *technically* qualified (cf. Art. 57.1.1 of the Nairobi Convention [*supra* n. 25] and its predecessors). 'Practical experience in the assignment and utilization of frequencies' opens the door to those with only administrative experience and (or even) only of the commercial and political side of telecommunications. We reserve opinion on the desirability of this.

nationality of the ITU-R director (CS Art. 9.1.c (63)). Each is to be 'familiar with the geographic, economic and demographic conditions within a particular area of the world' (CS Art. 14.1 (93)) and to be of the highest efficiency, competence and integrity (CS Art. 27.2 (154)).

That RRB membership is part-time (CS Art. 14.1 (93)) might be thought to detract from its independence since presumably given the other requirements as to competence and that only expenses are paid to its members, they are likely to be otherwise employed, most probably in telecommunications.[135] However, a member of the Board may not intervene in decisions concerning his or her home state (CS Art. 14.3.1 (98)), and CS Art. 14.3.2 (99) prohibits the seeking or taking of instructions from anyone and from doing anything incompatible with the independence of the Board. Correlatively CS Art. 14.3.3 (100) requires state members of the union to respect the international character of the duties of the board and not to attempt to influence its members.[136] Board members take part in an advisory capacity in radiocommunication conferences. Two RRB members designated by the board advise at plenipotentiary conferences and RAs. In these instances board members are barred from membership of their national delegations (CV Arts 10.3 and 3 bis (141–141A)).

The RRB can meet up to four times a year, usually at Geneva, with at least two thirds of the membership being present (CV Art. 10.5.2).[137] However, the board also 'may carry out its duties using modern means of communication' (CV Art. 10.5.2). In general, the board seeks unanimity, but it may make a decision by voting with at least two thirds of the membership voting in favour (CV Art. 10.5.3). Proxy voting is not permitted (CV Art. 10.5.3). The RRB has a chairman and vice-chairman elected by the board from among its members to serve for one year, the vice-chairman succeeding the chairman (CV Art. 10.5.2). In the absence of both, a temporary chairman may be elected for a particular meeting (CV Art. 10.5.1).

RRB duties are wide ranging (CS Art. 14.2 (94–97); CV Art. 10.2 (140–141A)). It approves rules of procedure for the registration of frequency assignments. The rules can be commented on by union members, and in the case of a continuing dispute as to their terms, the matter is referred to a WRC (CS Art. 14.2.a (95)). The RRB also considers matters which cannot be solved through the application of the rules by the director and the bureau of the sector.

The IFRB had a major role in disputes between administrations in respect of proposed and actual assignments. This continues. Under CV Art. 10.2.1 (140), the RRB considers reports from the ITU-R director on cases of harmful interference that have been investigated on the instance of an interested administration and formulates recommendations. Further, independent of the ITU-R bureau, at the request of one or more of the interested administrations, the RRB can consider an appeal against a decision of the bureau on a frequency assignment (CV Art. 10.2.2 (140)).[138]

---

135 Cf. materials cited *supra* n. 131.

136 Again, the language of these provisions is traceable to Art. 6.5.1 of the Atlantic City Convention (*supra* n. 23).

137 Under Options 20–21 and 26 of Annex 2 to Decision 5 (Rev. Bucharest, 2022), 'Measures for reducing expenses', the RRB usually now meets only three times a year.

138 V. Veshunnov and E. Morozova, 'Establishment of a Specialised Tribunal under the International Telecommunication Union to Adjudicate Disputes as a Means to improve the Efficiency of the Management of the

The Radio Regulations

To repeat, radiocommunication is integral to most uses of space.[139] An active satellite is useless unless there is radio communication with it, and interference with the signals it uses can have deleterious or even disastrous effects.[140] As such, however, space radio is but an aspect of the international regulation of radio. That regulation depends on the implementation of a variety of rules and procedures enshrined in the ITU CV and CV and the RRs. The RRs are part of the ITU Administrative Regulations (CS Arts 4.1 (29) and 4.3 (31)) and as such have full treaty status (CS Art. 54 (215–223)). Under CS Arts 44 and 45 (195–199), member states are to ensure that radio frequencies are properly used.[141] More precisely, CS Art. 44.2 (196) states that as a limited natural resource, radio frequencies are to be used 'rationally, efficiently and economically'.[142] The international interest lies in the prevention or mitigation of 'harmful interference' (CS Art. 45 (197–9)), in using particular frequencies for identified services, in using the minimum power to provide the desired service and in using the best available technologies so that the best frequency tolerances are obtained and spectrum bandwidth is minimised.[143]

As with all regulations and procedures the possibility exists of dispute. ITU procedures call for negotiation and coordination. Apart from any separate agreement between affected states, the ITU has dispute settlement procedures including arbitration under CS Art. 56 (233–235) and CV Art. 41 (507–518) and the (never yet used) Optional Protocol on the Compulsory Settlement of Disputes.[144] However, each state is sovereign, and the ultimate sanction is the law of physics, which cannot be amended, altered or repealed by international agreement. If activities authorised by one state cause harmful interference to the activities of another, that state itself will suffer reciprocal harmful interference from the activities of the other. That fact undergirds the general success of the ITU procedures, and

Radio Frequency Spectrum' (2013) 56 *Proc. IISL* 151–156 suggest that the use of specialists could alleviate the defects of the current system.

139 Reference point, *supra* n. 123. Cf. PP Res. 186 (Bucharest, 2022) 'Strengthening the role of ITU with regard to transparency and confidence-building measures in outer space activities.'

140 The Sputniks broadcast on frequencies *inter alia* allocated to the world time standard system and also already assigned by some other national terrestrial systems: M. Aaronson, 'Space Law' (1958) *Int. Aff.* 416, rep. *Legal Problems of Space Exploration – A Symposium*, US Senate, 87th Cong. 1st Sess., S. Doc. no. 26, USGPO, 1961, 221–238 at 2289; A.J. Haley, 'Space Age Presents Immediate Legal Problems' (1958) 1 *Proc. IISL* 5–27 at 14–25 and particularly 14–16. At 16 Haley notes that at the time, because the transmitters were in space, the status of which had not been defined, the ITU regulations may not have been applicable. Now the jurisdiction of the ITU system extends to space – see *infra*.

141 See generally, H.J. Levin, *The Invisible Resource: Use and Regulation of the Radio Spectrum* (Baltimore: Johns Hopkins UP, 1971). The proper use of radio frequencies is also required by the ITRs (*supra* n. 117).

142 See RR 4. Cf. Lyall, *infra* n. 213. CS Art. 44.2 (196) also identifies orbits, including the geostationary orbit, as another limited natural resource likewise to be used 'rationally, efficiently and economically'; see Chapter 6.

143 The use of best technologies is now required by RR 3, 'Technical Characteristics of Stations' and related ITU-R Recommendations. RR 15 'Interferences' together with RR Apps. 2 and 3 deal with unnecessary transmissions, minimising of power, etc. For degrees of interference, see *infra* following n. 162. A related but different and difficult problem is illegal/unlicensed broadcasting.

144 Arbitration has occurred. D.C. Gregg, 'Capitalizing on National Self-Interest: The Management of International Telecommunication Conflict by the International Telecommunication Union' (1982) 45 *Law & Contemp. Probs* 37–52 – written prior to the 1992–1994 reforms. The Permanent Court of Arbitration has 'Optional Rules for Arbitration of Disputes relating to Outer Space Activities': see Chapter 17. Whether it would adequately cope with a dispute about radio frequencies is uncertain.

state compliance with them.[145] The Radio Regulations and related ITU-R recommendations are crucial in states' arriving at acceptable solutions to a problem, falling therefore within the concepts of permissible and accepted interference,[146]

Radio Regulations are adopted and amended at world and regional radio conferences and come into force as they may specify.[147] Portions of the usable radio spectrum are agreed to be allocated to different services on either a worldwide or regional basis. For the purpose, the radio spectrum is notionally divided into nine bands running from extremely low frequency to extremely high frequency.[148] The Table of Allocations is RR Art. 5.[149] For the purpose of the table, the world is divided into three regions within which some areas are also important.[150] The RRs also contain administrative procedures.[151]

The allocation of a frequency band to a particular service may be to one or more services (RR 1.16), and may be on a primary or a secondary basis, the primary service taking precedence should there be conflict.[152] Any exception to a particular allocation, whether for a small group of countries or even a single state, is set out in a footnote.[153] An allotment may be made to a particular region or group of states for a particular purpose (RR 1.17).[154] Very occasionally, a state may indicate by a reservation to the Final Acts its dissent from a generally agreed-on decision. These are noted and usually taken account of by other states.[155]

The assignment of a frequency to a particular radio station is the sovereign prerogative of the state having jurisdiction over the operator of the station (RR 1.18).[156] However, where use of a frequency is likely to affect other countries, RR procedures come into play

145 There can be problems. See RR 15 and RR App. 10. For examples see *infra* n. 201.
146 See text following n. 162.
147 The dates from which WRC additions and amendments to the RR and related resolutions apply are set out in RR 59.
148 The nine bands are VLF (Band 4), LF (Band 5), MF (Band 6), HF (Band 7), VHF (Band 8), UHF (Band 9), SHF (Band 10), EHF (Band 11), and an unnumbered Band 12. Frequencies run from 3 Hz to 3000 GHz (RR 2.1). Frequencies are expressed in kHz up to and including 3000 kHz, in MHz from 3 to 3000 MHz, and in GHz from 3 GHz to 3000 GHz. The Table of Allocations (RR 5) makes no allocations below 9 Hz.
149 Not all spectrum bands are set aside for transmissions. Some are protected for passive use, e.g. by radio astronomy and SETI. M.A. Stull and G. Alexander, 'Passive Use of the Radio Spectrum and the Frequency Allocation Process' (1977) 43 *J. Air L. & Comm.* 459–534, See Chapter 16.
150 Regions are mapped in RR 5.2, with lines defined in RR 5.7–5.9. Region 1 is described in RR 5.3, Region 2 in RR 5.3, and Region 3 in RR 5.4. The African Broadcasting Area is defined in RR 5.10, the European Broadcasting Area in RR 5.14, the European Maritime Area in RR 5.15 and the Tropical Zone in RR 5.16– RR 5.21, A subregion consists of two or more countries in the same region (RR 5.22).
151 K.Q. Abernathy, 'Why the World Radiocommunication Conference Continues to be Relevant Today' (2003–2004) 56 *Fed. Comm. L.J.* 287–98.
152 RR 5.23–44 set out the relative rankings of different allocations.
153 A footnote allocation (or exemption from an allocation in the main text) is as authoritative as the provision of the main text. See 'Footnotes to the Table of Frequency Allocations in Article 5 of the Radio Regulations', WRC Res. 26 (Rev. WRC-19). This may be revised at WRC-23.
154 As in the case of a regional broadcasting plan where a particular frequency or frequencies (and sometimes signal strength and/or transmitter location) are denoted for particular broadcasting stations. Cf. *supra* n. 128.
155 The major exception to our comment about 'taking account' relates to the Bogota Declaration: see Chapter 6. Signatories of the Declaration usually make a reservation as to RR provisions on use of the GSO and related frequencies and other states make counter-reservations.
156 See RR 1.18 as to an 'assignment' being an authorisation by an administration and RR Res. 1 (Rev. WRC-97) that 'unless specifically stipulated otherwise by special arrangements communicated to the Union by

in order to avoid 'harmful interference'. Procedures vary depending on the frequency and service in question.[157]

In broad summary, the telecommunications administration of the state involved notifies ITU-R of its intention to make the assignment and gives at least certain basic information.[158] The notification is published by ITU-R in the two-weekly BR International Frequency Information Service (advance publication), thus putting other states on notice.[159] ITU-R examines the notification for conformity to the Table of Allocations in RR Art. 5. It also makes calculations based on the notification and the characteristics of existing assignments to determine whether the proposed assignment would in operation cause or receive harmful interference to/from existing assignments. The result may be 'favourable' or 'unfavourable'. In the latter case the notification is returned to sender for correction.[160]

The most frequent correction required is to avoid harmful interference and will require consultation with any other affected state to coordinate assignments.[161] If the finding is favourable, the assignment is entered in the Master International Frequency Register (MIFR). Thereafter it is entitled to protection, other states being required to take it into account to avoid harmful interference when making their assignments (RR 8).

However, matters are not quite as simple as that might seem. The definition of harmful interference in the Annexes to CS and CV speaks of endangering radionavigation or other safety services or degrading, obstructing or repeatedly interrupting radiocommunication services (1003). However, the list of definitions in the Radio Regulations introduces shades of interference:[162] RR 1 defines simple 'interference' (RR 1.166), 'permissible interference' (RR 1.167), 'accepted interference' (RR 1.168) before coming to 'harmful interference' (RR 1.169). This provides some wiggle room within which affected states may attain a satisfactory solution to a problem of interference.[163] The ITU-R director assists in the resolution of cases (CV Art. 12.f (173)), and the RRB has responsibilities in making recommendations on harmful interference following the investigation of complaints (CV Art. 10.2 (140)).

The procedures outlined above apply *mutatis mutandis* to the 'planned' and 'unplanned' radio bands. They similarly apply to space. In planned bands, a WRC or RRC sets out the use of particular spectrum frequencies, allotting their use to designated states and

---

administrations, any notification of a frequency assignment to a station shall be made by the administration of the country on whose territory the station is located'.

157 RR Art. 11 sets out the requirements for the notification of an assignment and details procedures for the different possible cases. For procedures prior to the 1992–1994 reconstruction see D. Leive, 'Regulating the Use of the Radio Spectrum' (1970) 5 *Stan. J. Int., Stud.* 21–52.

158 If the notification is incomplete or too early ahead of the proposed use of the assignment, it is returned to sender. No finding is issued – see *infra*.

159 There are separate versions of the BR: IFIC, one for the Space Service and one for terrestrial services. These replace the former postal weekly circular.

160 The decision of the bureau may be reviewed (RR 14). An appeal may be made to the RRB (CV Art. 10.2.2 (140). This is separate from the normal negotiation between notifying administrations, the arbitral procedures available under CS Art. 56 (233–5) and CV Art. 41 507–18) and the Optional Protocol on the Compulsory Settlement of Disputes.

161 For example, the frequencies involved may be altered or polarised, hours of use adjusted (cf. short-wave radio services) or transmitter power varied.

162 Reference point n. 143.

163 See also M. Hofmann, ed., *Harmful Interference from a Regulatory Perspective* (Baden-Baden: Nomos, 2015).

setting out a variety of technical requirements. This can include permitting others to use the frequencies, etc. until a designated state wishes to use its allotment.[164] Such planning (sometimes known as 'engineering the spectrum') is said to be more equitable than the alternative.

In un-planned bands, the procedures mean that spectrum is taken up on a first-come, first-served basis.[165] This certainly helps comply with the duty as to 'the rational, equitable, efficient and economical use of the radio frequency spectrum by all radiocommunication services' (CS Art. 12.1.1 (78)) and that states bear in mind that frequencies are 'limited natural resources [to] be used rationally, efficiently and economically' (CS Art. 44.2 (196)). On the other hand, it does mean that late-comers may find it difficult to satisfy their requirements.

Space radio usage presents particular problems. At least one of the radio transmitters is in motion. That space would require special treatment was early realised. The World Administrative Radio Conference (WARC-59) held in Geneva in 1959 *inter alia* defined an 'earth station', a 'space station', a 'space service' and an 'earth/space service'.[166] In 1963, an Extraordinary Administrative Radio Conference was devoted entirely to space.[167]

However, although the RRs were amended by successive radio conferences, it was not until the Minneapolis Plenipotentiary Conference of 1998 that the ITU was given formal jurisdiction in relation to the GSO and other orbits (CS Art. 1.2.a and b (10–12), Art. 12.1.1 (78), Art. 44.2 (196)).[168] Now, notification to the ITU-R Bureau of a planned space station includes data as to its intended orbit.

The RRs distinguish planned and un-planned radio bands. In the planned bands, there is the allotment plan adopted by WARC-ORB 1985–8 (as amended by later WRCs) by which every state has been allocated a slot within a ten degree arc on the GSO arc together with up-link and down-link frequencies for direct broadcast purposes.[169] Until a state acts on its allotment, others may place satellites in that GSO slot. Orbits and frequencies are otherwise available on a first-come, first-served basis, provided that the frequencies concerned are lawful within the services laid down in the Table of Allocations (RR Art. 5).

---

164 Cf. the European Broadcasting Plan, *supra* n. 128; RR Apps. 25, 26 and 27 as to allotment plans for certain maritime and aeronautical mobile services.

165 In 'space', first-come, first-served has also repercussions for the use of orbits: see *infra*.

166 An earth station is located 'either on the Earth's surface or within the major portion of the Earth's atmosphere and intended for communication with one or more space stations; or with one or more stations of the same kind by means of one or more reflecting satellites or other objects in space'. (RR 1.63). (The contrast is with a terrestrial station for terrestrial services (RR 1.62)). The definitions of space station and earth/space service have now been clarified by the definitions of different satellites services in RR 1.19–1.60 on 'Radio services'.

167 Partial Revision of the Radio Regulations: Final Acts of the Extraordinary Administrative Radio Conference to Allocate Frequency Bands for Space Radio Purposes, Geneva, 1963, 15 UST 887, TIAS 5603; (1964) 3 ILM 91–106. S.D. Estep and A.L. Kearse, 'Space Communications and the Law: Adequate International Control after 1963' (1962) 60 *Mich. L. Rev.* 873–904.

168 CV Arts 11.2.a (151 and 12.2.4.a (177)) set out duties for the sector to help secure the equitable, effective and economical use of orbits.

169 See now RR Apps. 30, 30A and 30B. Procedures by which a new ITU member state can enter the allotment plan are contained in RR App. 30B, Art. 7. As to argument during the negotiations of WARC-ORB 85–88, see G.C. Staple, 'The New World Satellite Order: A Report from Geneva' (1986) 80 *AJIL* 699–720. See also E.D. DuCharme et al., 'Direct Broadcasting by Satellite – The Development of the International, Technical and Administrative Regulatory Regime' (1984) 9 *AASL* 267–287.

Space systems are expensive; satellites take time to build and launch, and once they are up are unlikely to be serviced, repaired or their characteristics altered. Accordingly, the ITU procedures for space radio services are more protracted than those for terrestrial systems.[170] The normal pattern for space assignments calls for 'advance publication' of the intention to make an assignment for a space service. Data to be given includes that of the Earth/space connections in both directions, and signal characteristics.[171] This information is made available through the ITU-R BR IFIC Space Services system, allowing other states to object, to negotiate/coordinate or to take the proposed assignment into account in their own plans.[172]

The period within which advance publication is required varies depending on the service to be provided and may be as early as nine years and not later than two years from the date the service is to be brought into operation.[173] Failure to bring the system into operation within nine years results in the cancellation of the entry in the MIFR.[174] After advance publication, the assignment passes through the normal scrutiny as to compliance with the Table of Allocations (RR 5, and the possibility of harmful interference.[175] Once that and any required coordination with other systems has been carried out satisfactorily, the assignment is entered in the MIFR, and thereafter is protected as outlined above.[176] This means that priority in registration is important.

'First-come, first served' led to the major problem of the 'paper satellite', which took time to overcome.[177] Once commercial enterprises began to use the GSO, in particular for direct broadcasting, entrepreneurs induced administrations to notify space systems that

170 The ITU-R Space Services Department deals with space systems: www.itu.int/ITU-R/go/space/en. A non-problematic terrestrial assignment can be brought into use six months from notification. Note: VHF and UHF signals are not reflected by the Heaviside Layer and travel in straight lines. Microwave signals diverge slightly and are not entirely caught by the next antenna on terrestrial systems. 'Uncaught' transmissions, therefore, can affect satellites whose orbits they intersect. Microwave systems may therefore be included in a consultation/coordination process.
171 The notification must comply with requirements of 'administrative due diligence', as to which see *infra* n. 178.
172 As to the BR IFIC see *supra* n. 159.
173 See RR Chapter III, Arts. 7–RR Art. 9, 'Procedure for effecting coordination with or obtaining agreement of other administrations'.
174 What bringing the service into operation means has been a matter of contention. In the past, occasionally a GSO orbital slot entered on the MIFR has had a satellite briefly parked there for testing before being relocated elsewhere. That was argued as 'bringing into use' the assignment for that location. However, that was abused, some operators arguing that a very short period (down to twenty-four hours) met the requirement. Now a satellite must be located and operated at an assigned slot for at least ninety continuous days for it to be considered that the service from those coordinates has met RR requirements. See RR 11.44B and 11.44C for non-geostationary systems. For actual systems, see 'Bringing into use of satellite network frequency assignments': www.itu.int/net/ITU-R/space/snl/listinuse/index.asp, and the 'Space Network List': www.itu.int/ITU-R/go/space/snl/en.
175 RR 11 provides what calculations ITU-R has to make. A constant problem is that technology can advance faster than RR revisions. Calculations required by RRs can become irrelevant and therefore require regular reconsideration.
176 RR 8, 'Status of frequency assignments recorded in the Master International Frequency Register'.
177 H. Wong, 'The "Paper Satellite" Chase: The ITU Prepares for Its Final Exam in Resolution 18' (1998) *J. Air L. & Comm.* 849–79; F. Lyall, 'Paralysis by Phantom: Problems of the ITU Filing Procedures' (1997) 39 *Proc IISL* 187–93. See also K.G. Gibbons, 'Orbital Saturation: The Necessity for International Regulation of Geosynchronous Orbits' (1979) 9 *Cal. W. Int. L.J.* 139–56; S. Cahill, 'Give Me My Space: Implications for Permitting National Appropriation of the Geostationary Orbit,' (2000) 19 *Wisc. Int. L.J.* 231–48; R. Jakhu, 'Legal Issues Relating to the Global Public Interest in Outer Space' (2006) 32 *J. Sp. L.* 31–110;

existed only as potential plans rather than actualities. The intention was to secure an entry in the MIFR, thereby achieving a protected position for the future and one which might in itself be a commercial asset. Now it is required that a notifying state exercise 'administrative due diligence' in its scrutiny of a proposed notification before submitting it to ITU-R and see that the notification includes the date of firm contracts with both the spacecraft manufacturer and the launch provider in addition to other standard data.[178] If this information is not provided timeously, the notification is cancelled.[179] Other consequences of the paper satellite phenomenon were a vastly increased work-load for the ITU-R Bureau and associated costs. The introduction of 'cost recovery' in the processing of notifications has to some extent alleviated the difficulty.[180]

'First-come, first-served' has other implications for space including the question of the frequencies to be used, and satellite orbits.[181] As far as frequencies are concerned, RR Art. 5 applies, setting aside specific bands for particular services. However, it remains the case that for various users, some designated 'space frequencies' are more suitable than others,[182] and 'first-comers' making a choice that suits them certainly get the best of the bargain. It is also coming to be recognised that the 'first' user of a particular frequency may not be the company/entity that will extract the highest value from it.[183] The same is true as to orbits.

R. Jakhu and K. Singh, 'Space Security and Competition for Radio Frequencies and Geostationary Slots' (2009) 58 *ZLW* 74–93.

178 Res. 49 (Rev. WRC–19), 'Administrative due diligence applicable to some satellite radiocommunication services', together with relevant Radio Regulations, particularly RR 4, and RR 4.2–4 and RR 8 (especially RR 8.1, RR 8.3 (international recognition of registered assignments) and RR 8.5 (duty to eliminate harmful interference caused to registered assignments). Annex 2 of RR Resols. 35 and 49 specify the data required under administrative due diligence. It includes the identity of the satellite network, the frequency bands and orbits to be used, the spacecraft manufacturer with contract date, the delivery window, the number of satellites, the launch provider with contract date, the launch or delivery in orbit window, the name of the launch vehicle and the location of the launch. Cf. also CS Art. 1.2.a (11), Art. 6 (37–8), Art. 14.2.a (95), Art. 42 (193), Art. 45 (193–7); CV Art. 12.2.2.c (172). For UK filing procedures, see *Procedures for the Management of Satellite Filings*, 14 March 2019, for the UK approach, see www.ofcom.org.uk/__data/assets/pdf_file/0022/140926/new-procedures-1.pdf; together with *Procedures for the Authorisation of Satellite Networks: A Statement on Amendments to the Procedures* (UK Ofcom, 2016): www.ofcom.org.uk/__data/assets/pdf_file/0029/58637/statement.pdf and *Procedures for the Management of Satellite Filings* (UK Ofcom, March 2016): www.ofcom.org.uk/__data/assets/pdf_file/0027/63495/new_procedures.pdf.

179 RR Res. 49 (*supra* n. 178) *resolves* 6. RR Res. 81 (Rev. WRC-2015), 'Evaluation of the Administrative Due Diligence Procedure for Satellite Networks', *noting* h) indicates that notifications for thirty-six satellite networks had been so cancelled.

180 Under n. 22 to RR 9.38.1, if the 'cost recovery payment' is not received, the Bureau will cancel publication of the notification. See also PP Res. 91 'Cost recovery for some ITU products and services' and Council Dec. 482.

181 'Equitable Use, by all Countries, with Equal Rights, of the Geostationary-satellite and other Satellite Orbits and of Frequency Bands for Space Radiocommunication Services' RR Res. 2 (Rev. WRC-03).

182 For example for cutting through tropical rainfall and storms. 'Technical cooperation with the developing countries in the study of propagation in tropical and similar areas' RR Res. 5 (Rev. WRC-15).

183 This point could interact with the 'benefit' aspects of OST Art. I and the 'Declaration on International Cooperation in the Exploration and Use of Outer Space for the Benefit and in the Interest of All States, Taking into Particular Account the Needs of Developing Countries', 13 December 1996, UNGA Res. 51/122; cf. J.N. Pelton, 'The Economic and Social Benefits of Space Communication' (1990) *Space Policy* 311–322; M.A. Rothblatt, 'Satellite Communication and Spectrum Allocation' (1982) 76 *AJIL* 56–77.

That may not be so important in relation to many orbits (space is vast), but it certainly can be so in relation to the GSO.[184] As already mentioned, some steps have been taken to 'plan' some use of the GSO,[185] but there is another problem relating to orbits – the occupation of a particular orbital slot for a prolonged period. Certainly there is no question that the continued presence of a satellite in a particular orbit involves sovereign title. Although 'title' is proscribed by OST Art. II, there has been concern that a state might in effect permanently retain the use of a particular orbit by the placement and replacement of a satellite. Most clearly the problem can occur with a GSO position. Since the 1979 WARC, RR Res. 4 has stated that the period of use of a frequency assignment is not to be considered perpetual but is taken to be that indicated in the first notification, although provision is also made for the extension of that period or the substitution of another satellite with different characteristics.[186]

'First-come, first-served' also opens the possibility that an ITU state member may seek to derive income by in effect acting as an agent for commercial interests. The first was Tonga,[187] but other states have sought such business.[188] It must be asked whether this is a good development. The function of the ITU procedures should be the satisfaction of the telecommunications needs of its members, not their setting up of a business effectively for profit. Unfortunately, because the ITU did not simply refuse to process the Tonga notification on those grounds, the pass has been sold, and it would be difficult to re-visit the question.[189] Another point, perhaps still weighty, is whether a small state has the ability properly to do due diligence in order to evaluate a request for making a filing with ITU-R or to supervise and control the activities involved as required by OST Arts VI and VIII.[190]

184 Cf. equitable access to the GSO: Chapter 6 Geostationary Orbit.
185 The WARC-ORB 1985–88 Plan, *supra* at n. 169. Plans and regional agreements for the broadcast satellite service are in contemplation: 'Establishment of Agreements and Associated Plans for the Broadcasting-satellite Service' RR Res. 507 (Rev.WRC-19).
186 'Period of validity of frequency assignments to space stations using the geostationary-satellite and other satellite orbits' RR Res. 4 (Rev.WRC-03). Obviously the orbit of major concern is the GSO, and this was the ambit of the original RR Res. 4. However, Res. 4 now applies to all space stations assignments and therefore all orbital usage. RR Res. 4 does not apply to the WARC-ORB 1985–88 Plan (*infra* n. 185).
187 D. Riddick, 'Why does Tonga own Outer Space?' (1994) 19 *Air Sp. Law* 15–29; J.C. Thompson, 'Space for Rent: The International Telecommunication Union, Space Law and Orbit/Spectrum Leasing' (1996) 62 *J. Air L. & Comm.* 279–311 [Lyall/Larsen 375–407]; Wong, *supra* n. 177 at 853–4; F. Lyall, 'The International Telecommunication Union: A World Communications Commission?' (1994) 37 *Proc. IISL* 42–7.
188 Cf. Bermuda (which is the state of registration for many space telecommunications companies), Luxembourg, Gibraltar, the Channel Islands and the Isle of Man (the last three of which interact with the ITU through UK Ofcom).
189 F.L. remains of the view that although there is no express power given in the ITU basic documents, a power to refuse to process a filing on the grounds that it does not relate to the practical and 'personal' requirements of the notifying state could have been implied. See the Advisory Opinion of the ICJ on *Reparation for Injuries Suffered in the Service of the United Nations*, 1949 ICJ Rep. 174.
190 F. Lyall, 'Small States, Entrepreneurial States and Space' (2006) 49 *Proc. IISL.* 382–390. 'Willingness and ability' to fulfil international obligations used to be a test for recognition in international law and was recently resuscitated in the break-up of Yugoslavia; 'European Community: Declaration on Yugoslavia and on the Guidelines on the Recognition of New States' (1992) 31 *ILM* 1485. On the 'willingness and ability' test cf. M.M. Whiteman, *Digest of International Law* (Washington: USGPO, 1968) Vol. 13, 206 ff; S. Talman, *Recognition of Governments in International Law* (Oxford: Oxford UP, 1998); T. Cheng, *The International Law of Recognition* (London: Stevens, 1951); H. Lauterpacht, *Recognition in International*

The world has had too many problems with the concept of the 'flag of convenience' not to want to avoid the intrusion of such into the efficient use of space.[191] Correlatively the corporate veil should be penetrated to discover who is really behind a particular filing before it is accepted.[192] On a parallel line of argument, perhaps complex satellite systems should be notified to ITU-R only by states competent to supervise such things having a real jurisdiction over the commercial interests involved and not by a minor state of limited competency. Plans for mega-constellations must worry everyone,[193] even when notified through states apparently 'benevolent' of the general world-interest. However, such a change could be accomplished only by amendment of the ITU rules so that the world interest is adequately protected and not overwhelmed by avaricious entrepreneurs.

ITU Problems and Solutions

Preparatory Meetings

The ITU remit is huge. The matériel that it encompasses is extensive. The separate interests of one hundred ninety-three members have to be balanced. Efficiency has to bow to practicability. Accommodations and compromises have to be made, always within the doctrine of state sovereignty but balanced by the laws of physics. These requirements affect the ITU decision-making processes. ITU history shows an erratic, occasionally productive, willingness to cope with the problems.[194]

Readers should not assume that the Final Acts of the various conferences sprang from negotiations always undertaken during each meeting. 'Common proposals for the work of the conference', which have been thrashed out between regional groups, sometimes, by particularly interested parties, are now usual in the initial conference documentation. These have significantly both facilitated and improved decisions, resolutions and recommendations. A full understanding of these would require their consideration and full citation, from which, fortunately, the constraints of wordage, exempt us. Suffice it to say that the preparatory conference device allows the ITU meetings to do their job in up to four intensive weeks. Other, less formal mechanisms aid these processes.

Policy Fora

Not all ITU gatherings are intended to make decisions.

An organisation such as the ITU has to be well-informed as to what is required of its organs and procedures. This cannot be entirely carried out through the formal meetings of the union or of its sectors. The ITU is very conscious that it deals with complex matters

---

Law (Cambridge: Cambridge UP, 1948) and his 'Recognition of Governments' (1946) 46 *Col. L. Rev.* 37–68 at 53–6.

191 On 'flags of convenience', see Chapter 4, *c.* n. 76 ff. Cf. Art. 91, Convention on the Law of the Sea, Montego Bay, 1984, 1833 UNTS 3; (1999) UKTS 81, Cmnd. 4524: the Final Act of the United Nations Conference on Conditions for Registration of Ships: (1987) 26 ILM 1229–1250 (1987) 26 ILM 1229–1250, Art. 19 of which requires 40 ratifications to come into force, but so far has only 15 parties).

192 *Barcelona Traction, Light and Power Co, Limited (New Application: 1962), (Belgium v. Spain)* (1962–1970) (Second Phase) 1970 ICJ 3 (1970) 9 ILM 227.

193 Marboe, *infra* n. 222, and our discussion of the matter elsewhere in this book.

194 Lyall, *supra* n. 5.

involving acute questions of policy, national and international considerations and rapidly changing technology. Information has to both come in and be disseminated. The need for a forum in which information could be exchanged, interests canvassed and strategies discussed has produced the World Telecommunication Policy Forum. Regional telecommunication policy fora may also occur.

Fora are convened irregularly and, although official, are gatherings which, though important, lie beyond the formal ITU structures of the CS and CV. They are attended by state members, international institutions, commercial enterprises and others engaged in the business of telecommunications. A world forum was first proposed by the 1992 Kyoto Plenipotentiary Conference, and world gatherings were convened in 1996, 1998, 2001, 2009 and 2013. That their content has broadened is reflected in the title of the current PP Resolution thereanent.[195]

Previous fora have ranged widely, from technical to social matters, from interconnection to the problems that have accompanied the Internet. The outcomes of the World Summit on the Information Society (WSIS) process have also had relevance.[196] In addition, the ITU has developed and continues to organise a series of telecommunications exhibitions, sometimes associated with such fora, to make countries aware of technical developments. To this end, the ITU has established 'ITU Telecom', which helps organise the forums and exhibitions.[197]

The exchange of information and views both regional and global is important. It allows the ITU more clearly to take account of emergent needs.[198] It also allows states to keep up to date in their domestic technologies and to establish where international improvement is required.[199]

The Commercialisation of Space

Commercial entities making use of space may be welcome and certainly cannot be stopped,[200] but that has its dangers. As said, the assignment of a frequency and orbit is a matter for the sovereign power of a state. In the ultimate, states could ignore RR 5, the Table of Allocations, and permit the use of a frequency allocated for another purpose or position a satellite in a location lawfully 'occupied' by another in terms of the MIFR.[201]

---

195 'World telecommunication/information and communication technology policy forum', PP Res. 2 (Rev. Dubai, 2018).

196 Cf. the WSIS Outcomes documents, *supra* n. 102.

197 'ITU Telecom events', PP Res. 11 (Rev. Dubai, 2018). Telecom events are run on a commercial basis so that the Union does not incur a loss.

198 The first forum, Geneva, 1996, proposed a Memorandum of Understanding as the way to facilitate the introduction of global mobile personal communications by satellite (GMPCS). GMPCS is now dealt with under the Arrangements of 2003, which are binding between its signatories. Systems registered with the ITU may be operated in the territories of signatories to the arrangements. ITU Doc. 11, 7 June 2003: www.itu.int/osg/gmpcs/.

199 Apart from materials to be cited *infra*, see L.D. Roberts, 'A Lost Connection: Geostationary Satellite Networks and the International Telecommunication Union' (2000) 15 *Berkeley Tech. L.J.* 1095–1144 at 1119–1134.

200 See Chapters 10 to 14.

201 Cf. the Tonga, Indonesia and China examples noted in F. Lyall, 'The International Telecommunication Union: A World Communications Commission?' (1994) 37 *Proc. IISL* 42–47. Cf. the 2008 worries over the location of Protostar-1, see E. Morozova and Y. Vasyanin, 'Dealing with Harmful Interference – the Protostar Case', in Hofmann, *supra* n. 163, 41–53.

'Harmful interference' could be caused, but a state might be willing to accept that and seek by increased power to overcome an alternative signal.

Although there are the ITU provisions for consultation and coordination, appeal to the RRB against ITU-R Bureau determinations and for the settlement of disputes, ultimately the unalterable laws of physics are the only sanction. Short of that, the functioning of the ITU depends on the practices of compromise and mutual accommodation by administrations.[202] We hope that previous practice will continue. 'Winning' is not a helpful attitude. However, looking at the current commercial environment, our fear is that commercial providers of space telecommunications and other services may press their governments to disregard the rules or to change them to satisfy their self-interest.[203]

The Berlin Space Protocol, 2012

The commercialisation of space has resulted in a development in international financing of such activities. In 2012, the private international law framework for financing mobile equipment in aviation, rail and space, established under the Cape Town Convention of 2001,[204] was extended by the adoption of the Protocol relevant to space assets.[205] Operation of the Space Protocol will require a supervisory authority and the ITU is suitable so to serve. Whether the ITU should so act was discussed in the Council, which found no objections of principle to such a step and referred the question for decision of the 2018 plenipotentiary conference.[206] However, that conference shelved the question as the Protocol was not in force, and, as of Bucharest PP–22, that remains the case.[207]

ITU Finance

The financial position of the ITU has not yet been solved and remains a matter of concern. ITU financing depends on the contributions of its members, but the take-up of unit classes did decline until recently and may do so again.[208] While that could be partially offset by setting an appropriate value for the 'unit', that remedy would not attack the fundamental problem. Within limits, ITU members select the level of their contribution.[209] Selection,

---

202 At WRC-15, some formerly 'space spectrum' was agreed to be shared with some terrestrial services. This has developed further. See WRC–19, Sharm-el-Sheikh, 2019: www.itu.int/dms_pub/itu-r/opb/act/R-ACT-WRC.14-2019-PDF-E.pdf.

203 Cf. the licensing and deploying of large constellations.

204 The Convention on International Interests in Mobile Equipment, Cape Town, 2001, 2307 UNTS 341; 2015 UKTS 31, Cm 9154; (2003) US S Doc 108–10 (in force 1 April 2004).

205 Protocol to the Convention on International Interests in Mobile Equipment and Protocol Thereto on Matters Specific to Space Assets, Berlin, 9 March 2012: www.unidroit.org/instruments/security-interests/space-protocol. The Convention and Protocol are discussed in Chapter 13.

206 Report by the Secretary-General: 'ITU's Role as Supervisory Authority of the International Registration System for Space Assets under the Space Protocol', 8 August 2914 (PP-14, Doc. 61). Chairman of Council: 'ITU's Role as Supervisory Authority of the International Registration System for Space Assets under the Space Protocol', Council, 1 June 2016, Doc. C16/DT/13. Cf. C.M. Taiatu, 'The International Telecommunication Union (ITU) as the proposed Supervisory Authority of the future International Registry for Space Assets' (2018) 23 *Uniform L. Rev.* 506–526.

207 'ITU's role as supervisory authority of the international registration system for space assets under the space protocol', Res. 210 (Dubai, 2018).

208 *Supra* n. 66.

209 A state member may not reduce its class of contribution by more than two classes from that previously selected except with the consent of the plenipotentiary conference and for cause shown (CS Art. 28.5 (165)).

however, reflects the value a member considers it gets from membership and, looking at the figures, it would seem that the developed countries have reservations.[210] Since the 1992–1994 reconstruction, development and aid to less developed countries have figured large in ITU debate and activities. The extension of ITU work into such matters may have contributed to lessening the willingness of some members to contribute to running costs.

One solution to financial problems would be to convert the financial contribution system to the UN norm, relating contribution to gross national product or other international measurement of the ability of a state to pay. However, such a step is wholly unlikely unless some weighting were given to financial contribution in decision-making. There is a major discontinuity in the ITU between voting power (one state, one vote) and financial contribution: fifty-six of the one hundred ninety-three members contribute 90% of the state contributions.[211] Unless some way is found to resolve that imbalance, perhaps by relating voting weight to financial contribution, major contributors are not likely to agree to move to another financial regime.

Other steps, however, might be more promising. Cost recovery for ITU services is now important. During preparations for the 1997 WARC, the possibility was raised of relating cost not to the actual work but to the nature of the system involved.[212] Such ideas could be broadened. It is accepted that space frequencies are a limited natural resource, so there seems little reason why those who make commercial profit from their use should not pay a fee for their use. A 'resource utilisation fee' makes sense.[213] Whether it should be an annual fee, or a one-off payment is a question, but we would decide in favour of the annual payment. Other resources are exploited on the basis of a licence coupled with a fee or an appropriate system of taxation (e.g. off-shore oil in the continental shelf).[214]

Such a line of thought can lead further. We have touched on the fear that because of the first-come, first-served system space frequencies might not be used to their full value. Many see an auction process as the way to ensure that the best use is made of resources. Market

---

210 'Article I of the Outer Space Treaty and the International Telecommunication Union' (2003) 46 *Proc. IISL* 96–106.

211 See *supra* nn. 67 ff. There has been a slight improvement; our previous edition noted that fifty-one out of one hundred ninety-one contributed that 90%.

212 'Due Diligence Considerations', UK/Luxemburg June 1996 (submitted as part of the work of RAG96 for the 1997 WARC) spoke in terms of a deposit of 2% of the cost of each satellite in the system multiplied by a charge for the amount of spectrum space sought computed in units of 1000 MHz, the deposit to be returned when the system became operational.

213 Cf. F. Lyall: 'The Rational, Efficient and Economic Use of Space: Three Suggestions', in M. Benkö and W. Kroll, eds., *Air and Space Law in the 21st Century: Liber Amicorum K-H Böcksteigel* (Cologne: Carl Heymanns Verlag, 2002) 386–95; 'The International Telecommunication Union: A World Communications Commission?' (1994) 37 *Proc. IISL* 42–7; 'Expanding Global Communications Services', in *Proceedings of the Workshop in Space Law, UNISPACE III*, July 1999 (A.CONF-184/7) 63–80; 'The Role of the World Interest in Space Telecommunication Activities' (2001) 44 *Proc. IISL* 171–180; 'The International Telecommunication Union in the Twenty-First Century', in K-H. Böcksteigel, ed., *Project 2001, Legal Framework for the Commercial Use of Space* (Cologne: Carl Heymanns Verlag, 2002) 259–281. 'The Role of the International Telecommunication Union', in *An Outlook on Outer Space Law in the Next Thirty Years*, G. Lafferranderie and D. Crowther, eds. (Amsterdam: Kluwer, 1997) 253–268; R.S. Jakhu, 'Safeguarding the Concept of Public Service and the Global Public Interest in Telecommunications' (2001) 5 *Sing. J. Int. & Comp. L.* 71.

214 J.C. Thompson, 'Space for Rent: The International Telecommunication Union, Space Law and Orbit/Spectrum Leasing' (1996) 62 *J. Air Law and Comm.* 279–311 [Lyall/Larsen, 375–407] *inter alia* discusses leasing, another way in which states can generate income from space.

forces, it is said, sort out anomalies.[215] This should be considered further for use in the assignment of space frequencies. Already a number of states have auctioned portions of the radio spectrum within their several jurisdictions.[216] This is often accompanied by spectrum trading.[217] It would be unlawful for a state to auction space frequencies with accompanying satellite orbits. That would amount to an appropriation of space contrary to OST Art. II.[218] However, the international auction of spectrum and orbits may be something to be explored for the future.[219]

215 K.W. Dam, 'Oil and Gas Licensing in the North Sea' (1965) 8 *J. L. Econ.* 51–76; 'The Pricing of North Sea Gas in Britain' (1970) 1 *J. L. Econ.* 11–44; 'The Evolution of North Sea Licensing Policy in Britain and Norway' (1974) 17 *J. L. Econ.* 213–64; R.H. Coase, 'The Auction System and North Sea Gas: A Comment' (1970) 13 *J. L. Econ.* 45–8; P. Klemperer, 'What Really Matters in Auction Design' (2002) 16 *J. Econ. Persp.* 169–189, and his *Auctions: Theory and Practice* (Princeton: Princeton UP, 2005); P. Milgrom, *Putting Auction Theory to Work* (Cambridge: CUP and Stanford UP, 2004).
  As to radio, see H.J. Levin, 'The Political Economy of Orbit Spectrum Leasing' (1984) 5 *Mich. YB L. Stud.* 41–70, and Levin *supra* n. 141; R.H. Coase, 'The Federal Communications Commission' (1959) 2 *J. L. & Econ.* 1–40; C.G. Wihlborg and P.M. Wijkman, 'Outer Space Resources in Efficient and Equitable Use: New Frontiers for Old Principles' (1981) 24 *J.L. & Econ.* 23–44; G.R. Faulhaber, 'Wireless Telecommunications: Spectrum as a Critical Resource' (2006) 79 *S. Cal. L. Rev.* 537–560; P.S. Ryan, 'Application of the Public-Trust Doctrine and Principles of Natural Resource Management to Electromagnetic Spectrum' (2004) 10 *Mich. Telecomm. & Tech. L. Rev.* 285–372 (www.mttlr.org/volten/Ryan.pdf); G.L. Rosston and J.S. Steinberg, 'Using Market-based Spectrum Policy to Promote the Public Interest' (1997) 50 *Fed. Comm. L.J.* 87–116; R.E. Hundt and G.L. Rosston, 'Communications Policy for 2006 and Beyond' (2006) *Fed. Comm. L.J.* 1–35. A. Grunwald, 'Riding the US Wave: Spectrum Auctions in the Digital Age' (2001) 25 *Telecom. Policy* 719–728; T.M. Valletti, 'Spectrum Trading' (2001) 25 *Telecom. Policy* 655–670; R. Frieden, 'Balancing Equity and Efficiency Issues in the Management of Shared Global Radiocommunication Resources' (2003) 24 *U. Pa. Int. Econ. L.* 289–327; J.C. Thompson, 'Space for Rent: The International Telecommunication Union, Space Law and Orbit/Spectrum Leasing' (1996) 62 *J. Air Law and Comm.* 279–311, at 308–309 [Lyall/Larsen, 375–407 at 404–405].
216 I. Coe, 'Legal Issues Surrounding Spectrum Auctions' (1998) 41 *Proc. IISL.* 194–204. As to the UK, see the Wireless Telegraphy Act 1998 ss. 1 and 3 permitting the use of auctions, and the related Ofcom spectrum awards home-page: www.ofcom.org.uk/radiocomms/spectrumawards/. For earlier material see the Ofcom archives: www.ofcom.org.uk/website/regulator-archives/. On the working of a UK auction, see 'The Auction of Radio Spectrum for the Third Generation of Mobile Telephones', National Audit Office, Report by the Comptroller and Auditor General, 2001–2002, HC 233, 19 October 2001. Cf. Ofcom Spectrum awards: www.ofcom.org.uk/about-ofcom/latest/features-and-news/final-spectrum-auction-results; and www.ofcom.org.uk/spectrum/spectrum-management/spectrum-awards.
  Since 1993, the US FCC can, and sometimes must, use an auction process, i.e. competitive bidding for spectrum assignments and other decisions internal to the USA (47 USC § 309(j) as amended) and has done so. For FCC data on auctions, see http://wireless.fcc.gov/auctions/default.htm?job=auctions_home. For a space example involving both spectrum and orbit, see *In the Matter of Auction of Direct Broadcast Satellite Licenses*, 19 FCC Rcd. 820; 2004 FCC LEXIS 173, Release Number FCC 04–8, January 15, 2004. The auction involved related DBS orbital positions assigned to the USA by the 1983 ITU Regional Administrative Radio Conference. However, the FCC may not use competitive bidding for the provision of international or global satellite communications services: see § 647, Open-Market Reorganisation for the Betterment of International Telecommunications Act, 2000, the 'ORBIT Act'; Pub. L. No. 106–180, 114 Stat. 48. § 647, codified at 47 USC § 765f. To auction non-DBS satellite orbits and slots would be internationally unlawful. See also text *infra* at n. 218.
217 For UK materials, see *supra* n. 216.
218 Cf. S. Mosteshar, 'Development of the Regime for the Low Earth Orbit and the Geostationary Orbit', in G. Lafferanderie and D. Crowther, eds., *Outlook on Space Law over the Next 30 Years* (The Hague: Kluwer, 1997) 81–106 at 102–103.
219 Cf. Roberts, *supra* n. 199, at 1135–1141.

Spectrum Congestion

There are at least three ways in which spectrum congestion is a growing problem. First, WRC-15 saw discussions and negotiations seeking to either detach or share frequencies between space needs and the demands of commercial enterprises for more spectrum for mobile phone services.[220] This argument continues. Second, we note that the revisions to RR Art. 5, the Table of Allocations, made by WRC-15 includes more additional allocations, alternative allocations and footnote exceptions to the general allocations. Arguably, such exceptions to the general are becoming unduly common. In some areas of the world what is agreed begins to resemble a patchwork, rather than a considered, general and rational accommodation of needs that efficiently uses valuable spectrum.[221]

Third, we observe with concern the development of cube-sats and other small satellites,[222] as well as proposals for mega-constellations of small satellites.[223] Apart from potential space debris problems, such developments will saturate some spectrum bands and could place undue stress on the existing mechanisms of the Radiocommunication Sector. The ITU will have to deal with these problems in the next few years, starting with WRC-23 in November/December 2023.[224]

The Internet

The Internet is a recent arrival and a new ITU problem.[225] For decades, in conception and operation the ITU was dedicated to technical matters. The content of what passed through the telecommunication connexions that it facilitated was not part of its remit. To an extent, that detachment is disappearing. There is much in the ITU documentation on making the Internet available as an important development from which all

---

220 Cf. UK Ofcom, 'Update on 5G Spectrum in the UK: Statement (Ofcom, 8 February 2017): www.ofcom.org.uk/__data/assets/pdf_file/0021/97023/5G-update-08022017.pdf; and 'Supporting the UK's Wireless Future: Our Spectrum Management Strategy for the 2020s': Statement (Ofcom, 19 July 2021): www.ofcom.org.uk/__data/assets/pdf_file/0017/222173/spectrum-strategy-statement.pdf.
On 30 November 2022, the FCC issued a Notice of Proposed Rulemaking on 'Expediting Initial Processing of Satellite and Earth Station Applications; Space Innovation', IB Docket Nos. 22–411, 22–271, which if adopted would permit the licensing of space frequencies for associated terrestrial use. Cf. discussion of the FCC Ligado Order of 2020 which might result in interference with the GPS network: *infra* Chapter 11, n. 126. A Report and Order on 'Revising Spectrum Sharing Rules for Non-Geostationary Orbit, Fixed-Satellite Service Systems', IB Docket No, 21–456, FCC 23–29, was issued on April 21, 2023: www.fcc.gov/document/fcc-adopts-new-rules-satellite-system-spectrum-sharing-0.
221 See *supra* nn. 153–155. Cf. the suggestion for a telecommunications regime for space mining: A.-S. Martin, 'The Relevance of ITU Rules for Regulating the Use of Radio Frequency and Associated Orbits in the Context of Space Mining Activities' (2019) 43 *J. Sp. L.* 85–105.
222 I. Marboe, ed., *Small Satellites: Regulatory Challenges and Changes* (Leiden: Brill/Nijhoff, 2016). See also Chapter 9.
223 Cf. OneWeb Satellites LLC., oneweb.world; O3b: www.o3bnetworks.com; SpaceX: www.spacex.com; Starlink: www.starlink.com/; Iridium: www.iridium.com. See also Chapter 10.
224 See Report of the CPM on technical, operational and regulatory/procedural matters to be considered by the World Radiocommunication Conference 2023: www.itu.int/dms_pub/itu-r/md/19/cpm23.2/r/R19-CPM23.2-R-0001!!PDF-E.pdf.
225 Reference point, *supra* n. 122. See the problems of the Dubai version of the ITRs, *supra* n. 121. See generally, P.D. Trooboff, 'Globalization, Globalization, Personal Jurisdiction and the Internet. Responding to the Challenge of Adapting Settled Principles and Precedents' (2021) 415 *Hague Recueil des Cours* 9–321.

countries of the world should benefit, and much has been done in the facilitation of systems.[226] However, concern has been evinced within the ITU,[227] the WSIS process[228] and elsewhere[229] as to how the Internet is governed and as to responsibility for the allocation and supervision of domain names.[230] Some states have sought to act unilaterally in such matters.[231]

We have no wish here to enter into what is obviously an area in which there is much controversy.[232] It lies outside the parameters of this book. However, we cannot but note that it is an area within which the work of the ITU in its technical aspect can be affected – arguably

226 See PP Res. 64 (Rev. Bucharest, 2022), 'Non-discriminatory access to modern telecommunication/information and communication technology facilities . . .'; PP Res. 101 (Rev. Bucharest, 2022), 'Internet Protocol-based Networks'.
227 See from the World Telecommunication Standardization Assembly: PP Resols. 47 (Rev. Dubai, 2012), 'Country code top-level domain names'; Res. 48 (Rev. Geneva, 2022), 'Internationalized (multilingual) domain names; Res. 49 (Rev. Hammamet, 2016), 'ENUM'; Res. 60 (Rev. Geneva, 2022), 'Responding to the challenges of the identification/numbering system and its convergence with IP-based systems/networks'; Res. 64 (Rev. Geneva, 2022), 'IP address allocation and facilitating the transition to and deployment of IPv6'.
228 See *supra* n. 102.
229 Cf. the UN Broadband Commission for Digital Development: www.unesco.org/new/en/communication-and-information/unesco-and-wsis/global-broadband-commission/ with which the ITU and UNESCO are involved, and the Broadband Commission for Sustainable Development: www.broadbandcommission.org/Pages/default.aspx. See also *The State of Broadband: Broadband Catalyzing Sustainable Development*, the Broadband Commission for sustainable development (ITU/UNESCO, 2016).
230 The domain name system is operated by ICANN, the Internet Corporation for Assigned Names and Numbers, a non-profit corporation originally formed by a Memorandum of Understanding between the US Department of Commerce and ICANN in 1998 and augmented by an 'Affirmation of Commitments' between the two in 2009. It has functioned independent of the US government since 1 October 2016. See www.icann.org. There are other agencies involved, including regional registries.
231 Para 1 of PP Res. 64, *supra* n. 226., invites Member States to 'to refrain from taking any unilateral and/or discriminatory actions that could impede technically another Member State from having full access to' the Internet. See also ITU PP Resols. 102 (Rev. Bucharest, 2022), 'ITU's role with regard to public policy issues pertaining to the Internet, and the management of Internet resources, including domain names and addresses' and Res. 133 (Rev. Bucharest, 2022), 'Role of administrations of Member States in the management of internationalized (multilingual) domain names'. Cf. S.J. Shackleford and A.N. Craig, 'Beyond the "Digital Divide": Analyzing the Evolving Role of National Governments in Internet Governance and Enhancing Cybersecurity' (2014) 50 *Stanford J. Int. L.* 120–184.
232 Cf. recently, J. Gerson, 'A Grand Bargain among the International Telecommunication Union's Skeptics and Proponents: Building a Third Way Toward Internet Freedom' (2017) *Georgetown J. Int. L.* 1459–1496; S.J. Shackleford and A.N. Craig, 'Beyond the "Digital Divide": Analyzing the Evolving Role of National Governments in Internet Governance and Enhancing Cybersecurity' (2014) 50 *Stanford J. Int. L.* 120–184; I. Pyetranker, 'An Umbrella in a Hurricane: Cyber Technology and the December 2013 Amendment to the Wassenaar Arrangement' (2015) 13 *Nw. J. Tech. & Intel. Prop.* 153–180; K. Raustalia, 'Governing the Internet' (2016) 110 *AJIL* 491–503; P.S. Ryan, 'The ITU and the Internet's *Titanic* Moment' (2012) *Stan. Tech. L. Rev.* 1–36. See also R.H. Weber and S. Gunnarson, 'A Constitutional Solution for Internet Governance' (2012) 14 *Col. Sci. & Tech. L. Rev.* 1–71; A. Cheung and R.H. Weber, 'Internet Governance and the Responsibility of Internet Service Providers' (2008) 28 *Wisc. Int. L. J.* 403–478; W. Kleinwächter, 'From Self-Governance to Public-Private Partnership: The Changing Role of Governments in the Management of the Internet's Core Resources' (2003) 36 *Loy. L.A.L. Rev.* 1103–1126; S.P. Crawford, 'The ICANN Experiment' (2004) 12 *Cardozo J. Int. & Comp. L.* 409–448; M. Froomkin, 'Wrong Turn in Cyberspace: Using ICANN to Route Around the APA & the Constitution' (2000) 50 *Duke L.J.* 17–186; M. Froomkin and M.A. Lemley, 'ICANN and Antitrust' (2003) *U. Ill. L. Rev.* 1–76; M.A. Froomkin, 'Almost Free: An Analysis of ICANN's Affirmation of Commitments' (2011) *J. Tel. & High Tech. L.*, 187–234. Newspaper archives have much on US congressional attempts to retain governmental control over ICANN. See also Lyall, *supra* n. 5, 188–190.

unnecessarily, and perhaps to its detriment – as attempts are made to recruit its organs to an objective irrelevant to its major functions.

As we have noted, the Final Acts of the World Conference on International Telecommunications, Dubai, 2012, have not been well-accepted. That there are now two different sets of International Telecommunications Regulations is both disappointing and arguably threatening to the integrity of the ITU system.[233] Materials adopted by a voting majority rather than by consensus have not had good results in space law.[234]

A World Communications Commission?

The Bucharest PP adopted two intriguing Resolutions that raise in our minds the following question:[235] could the ITU once more be reformed, becoming a World Communications Commission?[236] We recognise that it is unlikely that in the foreseeable future the assignment of radio frequencies and orbits would be given to any international body on a global basis.[237]

However, it is necessary that decisions as to space assignments take full account of the world public interest. At present, a state notifies an assignment based on the needs – commercial and otherwise – of its national entities or those for which it has notifying responsibilities.[238] ITU-R duly processes these assignments for conformity to the Table of Allocations (RR Art. 5), and for any question of harmful interference. We are of the view that the general world public interest should also be a factor to be considered.[239] ITU-R should be authorised to disallow a proposed assignment on the ground that the general world interest is not well served by it, to limit the duration of the assignment, or to allow its registration subject to cancellation when/if a better use is later proposed. However, and with regret, we recognise that states are unlikely in the near future so to limit their sovereign powers.

---

233 See *supra* n. 117.
234 Cf. the 'Principles Governing the Use by States of Artificial Earth Satellites for International Direct Television Broadcasting', 10 December 1982, UNGA Res. 37/92; [1983] 77 AJIL 733–736; CoCoSL III, 1–79. See discussion of the adoption and effect of these in Chapter 10 sv. Direct Satellite Broadcasting.
235 'ITU's role in the implementation of the 'Space2030' Agenda: space as a driver of sustainable development, and its follow-up and review process', Res. 218 (Bucharest, 2022), and 'Sustainability of the radio-frequency spectrum and associated satellite orbit resources used by space services', Res. 219 (Bucharest, 2022).
236 F. Lyall, 'The International Telecommunication Union: A World Communications Commission?' (1994) 37 *Proc. IISL* 42–47, and 'The Role of the International Telecommunication Union', in Lafferanderie (*supra* n. 218) 253–267 at 265–267.
237 We note that within the European Union steps have been taken which will lead to 'Europe' constraining the assignment decisions of its members: L.-J. Smith and K. Levy, 'Regulation of Access to Limited Resources in [the] Telecommunications Sector in Europe' (2005) 48 *Proc. IISL* 443–453. Cf. Final Acts of the CEPT T-DAB Planning Meeting (4) (the Maastricht 2002 Special Arrangements) (www.ero.dk/Maastricht-e) as revised at Constanza, 2007 (see revisions at: www.ero.dk/C550FB2E-CD61-46EA-87E6-9B9F2E71B538?frames=no&) (huge original in French and German) and the related (UK) Ofcom, Report by Mason Communications Ltd, 'International interference analysis for future use of 1452–1492 MHz Range' 31 January 2008: www.ofcom.org.uk/consult/condocs/1452-1492/analysis/analysis08.pdf.
238 Thus the USA notifies for INTELSAT, the UK for INMARSAT and France for EUTELSAT. See Chapter 10.
239 Cf. citations *supra* n. 213. We understand that the FCC is required to consider world interest in its decisions as to assignments, *sed quaere*.

9

ENVIRONMENTAL REGULATION

Introduction

Space presents many environmental problems to which law must respond.[1] Not all will be treated in this chapter. Radio matters are covered in particular detail in Chapter 8. The environment of the moon and other celestial bodies is largely dealt with in Chapter 7, as is the provision in the Moon Agreement as to contamination by exploration. Here we cover generalities of environmental space law before turning to the possibility of the contamination of the earth from space, the polluting results of space activities (broadly the debris problem), and new environmental issues relating to satellite observation of Earth's climate. However, we must begin with some general observations.

General

It would be wrong to consider the law of the space environment as something different, separate, and distinct from terrestrial environmental law.[2] Of its nature, space presents exceptional difficulties, but these are not sufficient to require unique concepts. Environmental space law is simply a specialised area of environmental law. Matters of law are involved. The Moon Agreement, with only eighteen ratifications as of 2022, cannot

---

1 M. Williamson, *Space: The Fragile Frontier* (Washington: AIAA, 2006) and his 'Space Ethics and the Protection of the Space Environment' (2003) 19 *Space Policy* 47–52; B.K. Schafer, 'Solid, Hazardous, and Radioactive Wastes in Outer Space: Present Controls and Suggested Changes' (1988) 19 *Cal. W. Int. L.J.* 1–46; P.B. Larsen, 'Climate Change Management in the Space Age' (2020) 45 *Wm. & Mary Env. L. & Pol. Rev.* 103–167.
2 L. Viikari, *The Environmental Element in Space Law: Assessing the Present and Charting the Future* (Leiden: Nijhoff, 2008); F. Lyall, 'Protection of the Space Environment and Law' (2000) 42 *Proc. IISL* 472–482; A.G. Apking, 'The Rush to Develop Space: The Role of Spacefaring Nations in Forging Environmental Standards for the Use of Celestial Bodies for Governmental and Private Interests' (2006) 16 *Colo. J. Int. Env. L.* 429–466; D. Tan, 'Towards a New Regime for the Protection of Outer Space as the "Province of All Mankind"' (2000) 25 *Yale J. Int. L.* 145–194.

DOI: 10.4324/9781003496502-9

pretend to affirm propositions that bind other than its parties, although many of its provisions are sensible.

The Outer Space Treaty (OST) has a better legal status with one hundred thirteen ratifications including all the space-competent states. It and the preceding UN Declaration of Legal Principles of 1963 were adopted without vote in the General Assembly.[3] As we argued in Chapter 3, the fundamental or basic principles expressed in those Principles and the OST now form part of customary international law and therefore also bind states which have neither signed nor ratified the 1967 Treaty. OST Art. III and para 2 of the 1963 Declaration state that the exploration and use of outer space is to be carried out in accordance with international law. The principles of general terrestrial environmental international law are therefore relevant for space. What are they?

A considerable body of international law now deals with environmental matters.[4] It is even arguable that its basic principles have become customary law.[5] Certainly there are many environmental treaties, declarations and similar documents,[6] and there is relevant debate in the International Law Commission (ILC). While it must be remembered that the function of the ILC is to consolidate and develop, but not to make law, its work is always of interest.[7]

One traditional starting point for discussions of state obligations in regard to the environment is the *Trail Smelter Arbitration*,[8] which articulates the duty of a state not to permit the use of its territory to the detriment of another state. Other cases have followed, for example the *Corfu Channel Case* of 1949,[9] where again a state was found liable for a use of its territory that damaged another state. The 1992 UN Framework Convention

3 Treaty on Principles Governing the Activities of States in the Exploration and Use of Outer Space Including the Moon and Other Celestial Bodies (1968) 610 UNTS 205; 1968 UKTS 10, Cmnd. 3519; 18 UST 2410, TIAS 6347; (1967) 6 ILM 386; (1967) 61 AJIL 644; 'Declaration of Legal Principles Governing the Activities of States in the Exploration and Use of Outer Space', UNGA Res. 1962 (XVIII) 1963: (1964) 3 ILM 157. Cf. Part A, para 1.b of UNGA Res. 1721 (XVI), 20 December 1961, and Preamble 'Believing' of UNGA Res. 1802 (XVII), 19 December 1962.

4 E. Techera et al., eds., *Routledge Handbook of International Environmental Law*, 2nd ed. (Milton Keynes: Routledge, 2020); P.W. Birnie, A.E. Boyle and C. Redgewell, *International Law and the Environment*, 3rd ed. (Oxford: Oxford UP, 2009); P. Sands and J. Peel et al., *Principles of International Environmental Law*, 4th ed. (Cambridge: Cambridge UP, 2018); T. Kuokkanen, *International Law and the Environment* (The Hague: Kluwer, 2002). For very early law see P.H. Sands, 'Environmental Dispute Resolution 4,500 Years Ago: The Case of *Lagash v Umma*' (2020) YB Int. Env. L. 1–6.

5 C.L. Carr and G.L. Scott, 'Multilateral Treaties and the Environment: A Case Study in the Formation of Customary International Law' (1999) 27 *Denv. J. Int. L. Pol.* 313–335.

6 P.W. Birnie and A.E. Boyle, *Basic Documents on International Law and the Environment*, 2nd ed. (Oxford: Oxford UP, 2002); P. Sands and P. Galizzi, *Documents in International Environmental Law*, 2nd ed. (Cambridge: Cambridge UP, 2004); *International Protection of the Environment: Treaties and Related Documents*, B. Ruster and B. Simma, eds., 33 vols. (New York: Oceana, 1990–).

7 The codification of International Law has been the responsibility of the International Law Commission since it was set up by UNGA Res. 174 (II) of 1947. Codification is not the same as consolidation and involves improvement as well as articulation. Over the years the Commission has produced a number of draft Codes, as well as draft treaties.

8 The *Trail Smelter Arbitration (US v Canada)* 1938/41 3 RIAA 1905; (1939) 33 AJIL 182; (1941) 35 AJIL 684. *Chorzow Factory case (Merits) (Germany v. Poland)* 1928 PCIJ 4, Ser. A, No. 13. Note the possibility of contamination of territory during a space launch, or re-entry, *infra* n. 50.

9 The *Corfu Channel Case (UK v Albania)* 1949 *ICJ Rep.* 1.

on Climate Change states the same principle.[10] However, environmental damage can be caused without involving the territory, property or personnel of another state. Damage can be done to environmental objects or areas not owned by and beyond jurisdiction of any state. Terrestrial rules are therefore of interest, for space is beyond the limits of national jurisdiction: '[O]uter space, including the Moon and other celestial bodies, is not subject to national appropriation by claim of sovereignty, by means of use or occupation, or by any other means' (OST Art. II).

That states have a responsibility to ensure activities within their 'control do not cause damage to the environment of areas . . . beyond the limits of national jurisdiction' is a major part of Principle 21 of the Stockholm Declaration of 1972.[11] Principle 22 then requires that states cooperate in developing further international law as to liability and compensation for damage caused 'by activities within the jurisdiction or control of such states to areas beyond their jurisdiction.' Similar language is found in a number of later agreements and declarations.[12] To these one must add the work of the United Nations Environmental Programme (UNEP),[13] the UN Conference on Environment and Development (UNCED), Rio de Janeiro, 1992,[14] with Agenda 21, the action programme it adopted for a variety of environmental matters[15] and, of course, the currently active procedures of the Paris Agreement implementing the UN Framework Convention on Climate Change.[16] Improvements in Earth observation satellite technology have significantly increased our knowledge of the environmental problems these are intended to combat.

10 UN Framework Convention on Climate Change, 1992, UN Doc. FCCC/INFORMAL/84; 1771 UNTS 165; 1995 UKTS 28, Cm 2833; 1992 31 ILM 851–873: https://unfccc.int/resource/docs/convkp/conveng.pdf. See also http://unfccc.int/2860.php. The Preamble to the Convention *inter alia* recognises that States are responsible 'to ensure that activities within their jurisdiction or control do not cause damage to the environment of other States or of areas beyond the limits of national jurisdiction.' The UN Framework Convention is being implemented through the process established by the 2015 Paris Agreement on Climate Change (a.k.a. the Paris Climate Accords) http://unfccc.int/paris_agreement/items/9485.php; https://unfccc.int/files/essential_background/convention/application/pdf/english_paris_agreement.pdf; https://unfccc.int/process/the-paris-agreement/status-of-ratification. See also Larsen *supra* n. 1, and *infra* at n. 33.
11 Report of the United Nations Conference on the Human Environment, Stockholm, 1972, A/CONF.48/14/Rev.1: https://documents-dds-ny.un.org/doc/UNDOC/GEN/NL7/300/05/IMG/NL730005.pdf?OpenElement; 'The Declaration of the UN Conference on the Human Environment', Stockholm, 1972; (1972) 11 ILM 1416.
12 Cf. the World Charter for Nature of 1982, UNGA Res. 37/7; (1983) 22 ILM 455 (111 states voted in favour, the US against, and eighteen abstained on the grounds that their sovereignty over their natural resources might be impaired). Cf. N.B. Robertson et al., eds., *Agenda 21 and the UNCED Proceedings*, 6 vols (New York: Oceana, 1992–3); F. Lyall, 'Protection of the Space Environment and Law' (2000) 42 *Proc. IISL* 472–82. Cf. also Part XII (Arts 192–237) on the protection of the marine environment of the UN Convention on the Law of the Sea, 1982, 1833 UNTS 3; 1999 BTS 82, Cm. 4524; (1982) 21 ILM 1261; US Tr. Doc. 103–39. See also materials cited *supra* n. 6.
13 UNEP was established following the 1972 Stockholm Conference on the Human Environment. It encourages and coordinates actions on environmental matters by national and regional nongovernmental bodies. See www.unep.org/.
14 Report of the UN Conference on Environment and Development, Rio de Janeiro, 1992: https://documents-dds-ny.un.org.doc/UNDOC/GEN/N92/836/55/PDF/N9283655/pdf?OpenElement; the 'Rio Declaration on Environment and Development' (A/CONF.151/26): www.cbd.int/doc/ref/rio-declaration.shtml.
15 Agenda 21 (Report, *supra* n. 14) is directed particularly to sustainable development and the proper use and management of environmental resources. See *Agenda 21 and the UNCED Proceedings*, 6 vols, N.B. Robertson et al., eds. (New York: Oceana, 1992–1993).
16 *Supra* n. 10.

Such declarations and statements are largely chronicles of aspirations and intentions. They are non-binding, although they are often complied with. Matters might have been taken further had the ILC persevered on the lines it considered during the long process that resulted in its Articles on 'State Responsibility' of 2001, but these do not figure in the final text.[17] In 1996 the then Draft Articles did indicate state responsibility could exist in respect of areas not under national jurisdiction.[18] It was suggested that an 'international crime' would be committed by the breach of any obligation recognised by the international community as 'essential for the protection of the fundamental interests of the international community' (Draft Art. 19.2), including obligations 'such as those prohibiting massive pollution of the atmosphere or of the seas' (Draft Art. 19.3). Draft Art. 19.4 then provided that an internationally wrongful act short of an international crime was an international delict.[19]

However, the ILC was divided, and departed from the concept of international crime, partly because of the way the concept of 'crime' was being developed within other international jurisprudence, including through the creation of the International Criminal Court and the work of the tribunals for Yugoslavia and Rwanda. Notwithstanding, the ILC discussion of Draft Article 19 demonstrates a willingness to consider damage to environments that lie beyond national jurisdiction as being of major importance. Indeed, the Commentary to ILC Draft Art. 51 of the 1996 version of the Draft Articles indicates that the introduction of a category of international crime was intended to set apart or denote 'a category of wrongful acts to which, because of their seriousness, special consequences should apply'. Later ILC discussion used the term 'exceptionally serious wrongful acts'.[20] However, it is doubtful whether 'damage' to the space environment or to a celestial body is indeed so 'essential for the protection of the fundamental interests of the international community' that it should be categorised as a crime. It remains arguable that in appropriate circumstances, it should be considered whether such damage should be classed as an international delict or should as an 'exceptionally serious wrongful act'.[21]

Another interesting line of investigation is to be found in the ILC work on 'International Liability for Injurious Consequences Arising from Acts Not Prohibited by International Law'. This discussion also might have produced ideas relevant for space. However, while still centring on questions of prevention, in order to achieve consensus within the Commission, the ambit of those Draft Articles was restricted to the 'Prevention of

---

17 'Responsibility of States for Internationally Wrongful Acts' (International Law Commission, 2001). See 2001 YBILC II(2), 26–143; A/56/10; UNGA Res. 56/83. See J. Crawford, *The International Law Commission's Articles on State Responsibility* (Cambridge: Cambridge UP, 2002); S. Rosenne, *The International Law Commission's Draft Articles on State Responsibility* (Dordrecht: Martinus Nijhoff, 1991).

18 Draft Articles on State Responsibility, 1996 YBILC II(2) 57–73; A/51/10: http://legal.un.org/docs/?path=../ilc/publications/yearbooks/english/ilc_1996_v2_p2.pdf&lang=EFSRAC

19 L. Berat, 'Defending the Right to a Healthy Environment: Toward a Crime of Genocide in International Law' (1993) *Boston U. Int. L.J.* 327–348. In Scots and other Roman based legal systems, a 'delict' is a wrongful act.

20 1998 YBILC II(2), paras 241–331, at the end of which it was agreed to put Draft Art. 19 aside 'for the time being'.

21 The Chinese destruction of its weather satellite in 2007, the Indian destruction of its defunct satellite in 2019, and the Russian destruction of its satellite in 2021 come to mind. See Chapter 6 at c. nn. 37 and 54. The intentional destruction of an inhabited celestial body could be classified similarly.

Transboundary Damage from Hazardous Activities' of 2001[22] and the 'Draft Principles on the Allocation of Loss in the Case of Transboundary Harm Arising from Hazardous Activities' of 2006.[23] Both clearly refer to environmental harm done to the territory of another state or areas under its jurisdiction, not to areas beyond national jurisdiction.

Finally, at one stage in the ILC consideration of 'War Crimes', Art. 22 of the 'Draft Code of Crimes against the Peace and Security of Mankind' included as one of the 'exceptionally serious war crimes' 'employing methods or means of warfare which are intended or may be expected to cause widespread, long-term and severe damage to the natural environment' (Draft Art. 22.2.d).[24] Further, Draft Art. 26 included the wilful causing of such damage as a crime in war or in peace for which an individual could be held guilty. However, again in order to achieve consensus within the Commission, such matters did not persist into the final form of the Draft Code.[25]

The timidity or diffidence of the ILC notwithstanding, a general international duty towards the preservation and conservation of the environment, both within and outside areas of national jurisdiction, is developing. In the Advisory Opinion of 1996 on the *Legality of the Use by a State of Nuclear Weapons in Armed Conflict*, the ICJ stated,

> the Court recognises that the environment is under daily threat and that the use of nuclear weapons could constitute a catastrophe for the environment. The Court also recognises that the environment is not an abstraction but represents the living space, the quality of life and the very health of human beings, including generations unborn. The existence of the general obligation of States to ensure that activities within their jurisdiction and control respect the environment of other States or of areas beyond national control is now part of the corpus of International Law relating to the environment.[26]

One year later, in the contentious case as to the use of the Danube River, the Court quoted its statement in the *Nuclear Weapons* case, noting that it had 'recently occasion to stress . . . the great significance that it attaches to respect for the environment, not only for States but also for the whole of mankind'.[27]

22 'Prevention of Transboundary Harm from Hazardous Activities'(A/56/10),2001YBILC(II)144–170:http://legal.un.org/docs/?path=../ilc/publications/yearbooks/english/ilc_2001_v2_p2.pdf&lang=EFSRAC.
23 Draft Principles on the Allocation of Loss in the Case of Transboundary Harm Arising from Hazardous Activities', A/61/10; 2006 YBILC II.2, 56–90: http://legal.un.org/docs/?path=../ilc/publications/yearbooks/english/ilc_2006_v2_p2.pdf&lang=EFSRA.
24 'Draft Code of Crimes against the Peace and Security of Mankind' (1995) Report of the Special Rapporteur (A/CN.4/466). See 1991 YBILC 223–228 for discussion of a draft Art. 22. Cf. UNGA Res. 47/37, 1992, on 'Protection of the Environment in Times of Armed Conflict', which remains on the ILC agenda: see ILC 68th Session, 2016: http://legal.un.org/ilc/sessions/68/index.shtml#a6. Cf. also H.A. Almond, Jr., 'War, Weapons and the Environment' (1988) 1 *Geo. Int. Env. L. Rev.* 167–197, and 'War, Weapons and the Environment' (1990) 3 *Geo. Int. Env. L. Rev.* 117–182.
25 'Draft Code of Crimes against the Peace and Security of Mankind' (1996) YBILC II(2), 17–56: http://legal.un.org/docs/?path=../ilc/publications/yearbooks/english/ilc_1996_v2_p2.pdf&lang=EFSRAC.
26 *Legality of the Use by a State of Nuclear Weapons in Armed Conflict*, Advisory Opinion, 8 July 1996, 1996 ICJ Rep. 226, para 29 (240); (1996) 35 ILM 809. At para 31 the Court also cites para 64 of its Order of 22 September 1995 in the *Request for an Examination of the Situation in Accordance with Paragraph 63 of the Court's Judgement of 20 December 1974 in the Nuclear Tests Case (New Zealand v France) Case*, 1995 ICJ Rep. 288. Para 64, dismissing that *Request*, expressly states that it is made 'without prejudice to the obligations of States to respect and protect the natural environment' (1996 ICJ 226 at 306).
27 *Case Concerning the Gabčíkovo – Nagymaros Project (Hungary/Slovakia)*, 1997 ICJ Rep. 7 at 41 (para 53) (1998) 37 ILM 168–242.

The developing international law on the environment is not confined to *post hoc* action. The 'Precautionary Principle' argues in favour of giving a hard content to international environmental duties to avoid or prevent problems. In such matters, it is better to be safe than sorry. It is better to take precautions which may not be needed than to fail to take them and risk unfortunate consequences. The Precautionary Principle originates in municipal environmental law, but it is making its way into international law.[28] It also has its echoes in relation to space.

Lastly we note the concept of the Global Commons – the idea that there are portions or aspects of the Earth not subject to state sovereignty either at all (e.g. the oceans beyond territorial limits) or not so subject in the normal way (e.g. the atmosphere, notwithstanding that some of the atmosphere necessarily lies within the air space of states).[29] Increasingly, it is suggested that Global Commons are held in some sort of trust for the whole of mankind and are to be managed as such.[30] Space, being set aside from national sovereignty, would seem to be another obvious example.[31] If, in the future, the concept of Global Commons stands, a duty to respect and manage the environment of a Global Commons in space could be inferred from terrestrial international environmental law, even in the absence of a clear universal multilateral treaty to that effect.[32] Of course, the concept of 'Global Commons' links to that of the 'common heritage of mankind' which we discussed in Chapter 7, but it is a different thing.

The idea of a general duty as to the terrestrial environment that is not limited to the avoidance of direct harm to other states is therefore coming to be accepted. There is a common interest in the avoidance of harm to the planet on which we live. Some global environmental harm can only be remedied through a global approach.[33] The same logic applies to outer space, outer space debris and contamination of celestial bodies being cases in point.

---

28 H. Hohmann, *Precautionary Legal Duties and Principles of Modern International Environmental Law* (London: Graham and Trotman; Dordrecht: Martinus Nijhoff, 1994); A. Trouwborst, *Precautionary Rights and Duties of States* (Leiden: Martinus Nijhoff, 2006); P.B. Larsen, 'Application of the Precautionary Principle to the Moon' (2006) 71 *J. Air L. and Comm.* 295–306; L.D. Roberts, 'Ensuring the Best of All Possible Worlds: Environmental Regulation of the Solar System' (1997) 6 *N.Y.U. Env. L.J.* 126–160.

29 We use the term in its technical legal sense. 'Global Commons' is also used freely (and sloppily) by some as a label for any global opportunity which they consider should be subject to little or no constraint. See P.B. Larsen, 'Outer Space: How shall the World's Governments Establish Order Among Competing Interests' (2019) 29 *Wash. Int. L. J.* 1–60 at 22–26.

30 *Our Common Future: The Report of the World Commission on Environment and Development*, G.H. Brundtland, Chairman (The 'Brundtland Commission') 1987, UN Doc. A/42/427 (Oxford and New York: Oxford UP 1987); S.J. Buck, *The Global Commons: An Introduction*, 2nd ed. (Washington: Island Press, 1998); J. Vogler, *The Global Commons: Environmental and Technological Governance*, 2nd ed. (London: John Wiley, 2000); K. Bosselmann, *Earth Governance: Trusteeship of the Global Commons* (Cheltenham: Edward Elgar, 2015) cf. L.F.E. Goldie, 'Title and Use (Usufruct) – An Ancient Distinction too oft Forgot' (1985) 79 AJIL 689–714.

31 OST Art. II; cf. V. Kopal, 'Outer Space as Global Commons' (1997) 40 *Proc. IISL* 108–116; L.D. Roberts, 'The Law of the Commons: A Framework for the Efficient and Equitable Use of the Lagrange Points' (1990) 6 *Conn. J. Int. L.* 151–172.

32 Cf. K. Gorove, 'Protection of the Global Commons: New Customary Law?' (1998) 26 *J. Sp. L.* 208–13; V. Kopal, *supra* n. 31.

33 Cf. the mounting international concern as to global warming and the efforts to mitigate the human contribution to this problem. See *supra* n. 10.

Much of the current phraseology is anthropocentric, but we need not be so confined. Harm done to 'generations unborn', as the ICJ has put it,[34] could well include the degradation of the space environment, both near and far. The point is that terrestrial environmental law is applicable to the global environment as a whole, not just to those parts that lie within the jurisdiction of particular states. Environmental rights and duties go beyond that constraint and constitute obligations *erga omnes* (owed to everyone), although the idea of an international *actio popularis* (an action brought by one to enforce a duty owed to many or to the population as a whole) has not yet gained full acceptance in international law.[35] Notwithstanding, states should exercise 'due diligence' in framing and enforcing their laws and regulations so as to secure the environment.[36]

How does all this apply to space?

Environmental Law and Space

Questions of the space environment arise in a variety of ways. When C.W. Jenks included a chapter on these sorts of problems in his *Space Law*, he perceptively entitled it 'Space Cluttering and Contamination'. We here deal with several different matters: astronomy, contamination, the near-Earth environment, space objects in orbit, space traffic management, space debris and climate change, and finish with planetary defence – cluttering indeed. Arguably the use of radio frequencies also has an environmental aspect, but this is minimal within the parameters of this chapter, and although we mention it here in relation to astronomy and orbital questions, we cover radio more extensively in Chapter 8.[37]

Astronomy

The interests of optical and radio astronomy are often overlooked in discussions of space activities and space law. Astronomy is a valid use of space.[38] Radio astronomy is a 'service'

---

34 *Supra*, n. 26. Note also the reference in MA Art. 4.1 to the interest of 'present and future generations' in the exploration and use of the moon.

35 See Sands and Peel, *supra* n. 4, at 144–158, 'International Enforcement: Damage to the Environment in Areas Beyond National Jurisdiction'; A. de Hoogh, *Obligations Erga Omnes and International Crimes* (The Hague: Kluwer, 1996); M. Ragazzi, *The Concept of International Obligations Erga Omnes*, new ed. (Oxford: OUP, 2000); C.J. Tams, *Enforcing Obligations Erga Omnes in International Law* (Cambridge: CUP, 2005).
    Which state might be willing to bring court action to enforce such an *erga omnes* obligation is uncertain. Again, it is certain that some countries would not be prepared to be sued on an *erga omnes* basis: analogously cf. the US reaction to the Nicaragua Case of 1986 as manifested in various articles in (1987) 81 AJIL. Effective international judicial proceedings depend on the consent of parties. That said, although they did not proceed to a judgement, the nuclear tests cases of 1974 may be considered as having an *erga omnes* element, contamination of the high seas being an element of the complaints. See the *Nuclear Tests Case (New Zealand v France)* 1974 ICJ Rep. 157 and the *Nuclear Tests Case (Australia v France)*, 1974 ICJ Rep. 253.

36 'Due diligence' has been a matter of discussion. Cf. Draft Art. 3 of the ILC 1998 Annual Report, A/53/10, or 1998 YBILC II(2), Chapter IV, on 'International Liability for Injurious Consequences arising out of Acts not Prohibited by International Law (Prevention of Transborder Damage from Hazardous Activities)', 'Prevention' and Commentary, both at 27–28. Cf. also Birnie and Boyle, *supra* n. 4 at 128–137, 214–236.

37 C.W. Jenks, *Space Law* (London: Stevens, 1965) 280–282. For a list of national research on space debris, nuclear power sources and related subjects as of 2015 see A/AC.105/C.1/109: www.unoosa.org/oosa/oosadoc/data/documents/2015/aac.105c.1/aac.105c.1109_0.html. See also Larsen, *supra* n. 1.

38 In 2007, UNGA Res. 62/200 declared 2009 the International Year of Astronomy in recognition of astronomy as one of the oldest basic sciences which still contributes to the evolution of other sciences and applications in many fields.

for which provision is made in the Table of Allocations in the ITU Radio Regulations. Even so, radio astronomy continues to be subjected to interference from terrestrial sources.[39] The institution of nationally and internationally protected radio 'quiet zones' would ameliorate some of these difficulties.[40]

Optical astronomy encounters two major problems, light pollution from the ground and interference caused by the albedo of space objects and other debris.[41] Satellite constellations operated by SpaceLink, One Web, SES and others threaten astronomers' views of the universe, but the increasing number of small specialised micro-satellites in LEO are also a factor.[42] Problems caused by orbiting objects and space debris will be discussed below.[43] Light pollution from terrestrial sources is a handicap for astronomers although most major observatories are now placed well away from light sources. The International Astronomical Union (IAU) has an obvious interest in these matters.[44] The International Dark-Sky Association (www.darksky.org) seeks the reduction of light pollution for a variety of environmental reasons, including the needs of astronomers, professional and amateur. In 2005, the Fifth European Symposium for the Protection of the Night Sky adopted the Declaration of Genk, calling for further action, including by the European Union.[45] The

39 We consider this particularly in Chapter 8 on radio and the ITU, and in Chapter 16 on SETI. For radio interference from satellite stations, see *infra* at n. 132.

40 F.G. von der Dunk, 'Space for Celestial Symphonies? Towards the Establishment of International Radio Quiet Zones' (2001) 17 *Space Policy* 265–274. Cf. Chapter 7 *c.* n. 58, and Chapter 16, *c.* n. 77 on the proposal for a protected site on the far side of the moon for radio astronomy purposes.

41 'Albedo' is the reflectivity of a body.

42 M. Kalouskaya, 'Large Satellite Constellations: Legal Challenges in Addressing Space Sustainability and Astronomical Observations' (2021) 70 ZLW 571–585; R. Morelle, 'Satellite Constellations: Astronomers Warn of Threat to View of Universe': www.bbc.com/news/science-environment-50870117. Cf. G. Lafferranderie, 'Space Law Relevant to Astronomy', *Seminars of the UN Programme on Space Applications*, Vol. 8, 1997, 75–79, available at A/AC.105/650: www.unoosa.org/pdf/reports/ac105/AC105_650E.pdf or (article only) at http://adsabs.harvard.edu/full/1997UNPSA . . . 8 . . . 75L.

43 *Infra* following n. 154.

44 *Keeping the Night Sky Clear: IISL Working Group on Light Pollution of the Night Sky from a Space Law Perspective. Final Report* (IISL, 2023; https://iisl.space/index.php/2023/07/05/iisl-publishes-report-of-iisl-light-pollution-wg/); *Dark and Quiet Skies for Science and Society: Report and Recommendations* (IAU and UNOOSA, 2020); www.iau.org/static/publications/dqskies-book-29-12-20.pdf. Down to 2015 IAU Commission 50 dealt with the 'Protection of Existing and Potential Observatory Sites', for both radio and optical observatories: www.iau.org/science/scientific_bodies/past_commissions/50/. See now the *IAU Strategic Plan 2020–2030*, 19–21: www.iau.org/static/administration/about/strategic_plan/strategicplan-2020-2030.pdf. G. Rotola and A. Williams, 'Regulatory Context of Conflicting Uses of Outer Space: Astronomy and Satellite Constellations' (2021) 46 *Air and Sp. L.* 545–568. See also F. Falchi et al., 'A call for scientists to halt spoiling of the night sky with artificial light and satellites' (2023) 7 *Nature Astronomy* 237–239: www.nature.com/articles/s41550-022-01864-z; P. Cinzano et al., 'The first world atlas of the artificial night sky brightness' (2001) 328 *Mon. Not. Roy. Astron. Soc.* 689: https://arxiv.org/abs/astro-ph/0108052. Cf. F. Falchi et al., *The World Atlas of Light Pollution* (CreateSpace, 2016); F. Falchi et al, 'The new world atlas of the artificial night sky brightness' (2016) 2 *Science Advances*: www.science.org/doi/epdf/10.1126/sciadv.1600377. Non-traditional astronomers also have an interest: C. Finnegan, 'Indigenous Interests in Outer Space: Addressing the Conflict of Increasing Satellite Numbers with Indigenous Astronomy Practices (2022) 11 *Laws* 1–19 at 8–19. Cf. the 2022 IAU protest of the 64 square metre antennae on Blue Walker 3: www.iau.org/news/pressreleases/detail/iau2211/.

45 The 'Declaration of Genk': www.home.uni-osnabrueck.de/ahaenel/darksky/declarationgenk.pdf. The International Dark – Sky Association has held successive symposia: see www.darksky.org/our-work/conservation/idsp/become-a-dark-sky-place/idsp-annual-reports/. The British Astronomical Association has established a UK 'Commission for Dark Skies: www.britastro.org/dark-skies/.

responsibility for such matters is, of course, that of municipal law and is perhaps best tackled at any planning stage.[46]

In the case of interference to astronomical observations by the passage of space objects in their orbits is concerned, that must be a matter for those who build such objects and those who license their use. Licensing authorities could require that the albedo of such objects is minimised.[47] Perhaps such a step could be encouraged by appropriate recommendations from COPUOS.

Contamination of the Earth from Outer Space

Before we turn to the contamination of space itself, we note that contamination of the surface and atmosphere of the Earth can occur during, or as a result of a launch, or particularly of a failed launch.[48] Some launches occur through areas of the high seas. Resultant pollution should come under the head of damage caused to areas beyond national jurisdiction, but unfortunately the ILC has not proceeded with that topic.[49]

Where a state launches its own satellites from its own territory, any pollution of that territory will be its own concern. However, we note that subsequent to Kazakhstan independence, during the continued Russian use of the Baikonour Cosmodrome, the Kazakh steppes were polluted by rocket fuel, resulting in a dispute.[50] This is a matter which non-territorial launching states, launch providers using foreign launch sites and commercial purchasers of foreign launches have to consider. We assume (but do not know) that relevant launch contracts either provide for compensation for any damage to launch-site territories or exclude liability. By contrast, where contamination is caused to the territory of a non-launching state (to invent a label) liability will be incurred either under the

---

46 Cf. 'Light Pollution and Astronomy' (UK) House of Commons, Committee on Science and Technology, Seventh Report (2002–3), HC 747-I, Evidence at HC 747-II: www.publications.parliament.uk/pa/cm200203/cmselect/cmsctech/747/74710.htm. The Committee recommended a variety of measures to reduce light pollution in the interests of professional and amateur astronomers. The Clean Neighbourhoods and Environment Act 2005 (c. 16) ss. 102–103, and s. 100 of the Public Health (Scotland) Act 2008 (asp. 5), amended s. 79 of the Environmental Protection Act 1990 (c. 43) to make artificial light nuisance a statutory nuisance in both jurisdictions, but the exemptions are such that astronomy is not helped. Para 90 of the Guidance Note, 'Statutory Nuisance from Insects and Artificial Light' issued by the then Department for Environment, Food and Rural Affairs indicates that light pollution is not necessarily a statutory nuisance and that the new offence is not a remedy for light pollution *per se*. Paras 6.2–14 of the Scottish Guidance Note is in slightly broader terms, allowing 'best practicable means' to avoid nuisance in appropriate instances. This might apply to a garden observatory. Para 6.13 suggests that after 23.00 lights should be further reduced.

   US law on light pollution is sporadic and patchy and is a matter for each state. See A.L. Johnson, 'Blinded by the Light: Addressing the Growing Light Pollution Problem' (2015) 2 *Texas A&M J. Prop. L.* 451–480; K.M. Ploetz, 'Light Pollution in the United States: An Overview of the Inadequacies of the Common Law and State and Local Regulation' (2002) 36 *New Eng. L. Rev.* 985–1039. Cf. the website of the American Astronomical Society (www.aas.org) (search 'light pollution'). The Declaration of Genk (*supra* n. 45) indicates that some European states have adopted a variety of measures, but these also are patchy and not always effective.

47 See further *infra* at n. 124 and text thereafter.

48 Cf. the major 'Space Rocket Launch Sites around the World': www.spacetoday.org/Rockets/Spaceports/LaunchSites.html. But this is not up to date thanks to the development of a number of small sites round the world.

49 See *supra* n. 18.

50 M. Hošková, 'The 1994 Baikonour Agreements in Operation' (1999) 42 *Proc. IISL* 263–272. Kazakhstan suspended Russian use of the site until compensation was agreed. M. Bjornerud, 'Baikonour Continues: The New Lease Agreement between Russia and Kazakhstan' (2004) 30 *J. Sp. L.* 13–36.

Liability Convention, or, where material of a hazardous nature is incurred, in terms of ARRA Art. 5.4.[51]

Looking outward from the Earth, space and celestial objects are contaminated, and contamination of the Earth from increasing number of returning space objects might also occur. Discussions on the contamination of and from space have their own jargon. 'Forward contamination' is contamination of space or celestial bodies by Earth through our space activities. 'Back contamination' is the contamination of Earth from space by the return of astronauts or space objects that potentially might carry viruses or bacteria into the Earth environment. There is also the contamination of Earth orbit, but we come to that in the next section.

Caution, not to say fear, as to the possibility of contamination arose early in the history of space. Indeed, the International Astronautical Federation discussed contamination at its Seventh Congress, Rome, 1956 – a year before Sputnik I. In 1958, having previously set up an *ad hoc* Committee on Contamination by Extraterrestrial Exploration, the International Council of Scientific Unions (ICSU)[52] formed the international Committee on Space Research (COSPAR)[53] in part to coordinate anti-contamination action.[54] At first, forward contamination was the major concern, especially given the early probes that were targeted to impact the moon, and emergent plans for similar encounters with Venus and Mars, but when astronauts began to return from space, back contamination rose in prominence.

The international law on these matters is sparse, national regulation being in practice crucial through its rôle in crystallising and implementing the law's generalities. The second sentence of OST Art. IX provides that

> States Parties to the Treaty shall pursue studies of outer space, including the moon and other celestial bodies, and conduct exploration of them so as to avoid their harmful contamination and also adverse changes in the environment of the Earth resulting from the introduction of extraterrestrial matter, and, where necessary, shall adopt appropriate measures for this purpose.

In that statement there is a curious tension between the duty to 'avoid . . . harmful contamination and . . . adverse changes', but only to adopt appropriate measures 'where necessary'. Further, it is noticeable that contamination *per se* is not excluded – only 'harmful contamination' – and what constitutes that 'harmful' element of the contamination is

51 See Chapter 4 The Return of Space Objects, Liability and Practice. The ARRA liability laid on a launching state to eliminate a danger of harm from hazardous materials is under the direction and control of the state that has found the relevant space object, but only if it so requires. This duty applies not only to national territory but also if a contracting state finds a space object elsewhere than somewhere under its jurisdiction.
52 The ICSU is now the International Science Council: https://council.science/.
53 COSPAR: http://cosparhq.cnes.fr/. The COSPAR Charter is at https://cosparhq.cnes.fr/about/charter.
54 'Contamination by Extra-terrestrial Exploration' (1959) *Nature* 925–928; C.R. Phillips, *The Planetary Quarantine Program: Origins and Achievements, 1956–1973* (SP-4902: NASA History Office, 1974): http://history.nasa.gov/SP-4902/sp4902.htm; G.S. Robinson, 'Interplanetary Contamination: The Ultimate Challenge for Environmental and Constitutional Challenge?' (2005) 31 *J. Sp. L.* 117–163 at 121 ff; L.I. Tennen, 'Evolution of the Planetary Protection Policy: Conflict of Science and Jurisprudence?' (2004) 34 *Adv. in Sp. Research* 2354–2362; R. Amos, 'Exploiting the Final Frontier – Some Initial Thoughts on Regulating Humanity's Relationships with Non-Terrestrial Life Forms' (2021) 45 *J. Sp. L.* 111–141.

not defined. States are therefore left rather free in their implementation of the duty, albeit that duty is one with which Art. VI requires them to ensure that their national activities comply with.

Precise implementation can be awkward, particularly where the OST is considered by a state to be non-self-executing and statutory authority is required.[55] That said, it is clear that the commercial exploitation of outer space resources will result in harmful contamination. OST Art. VI requires states to regulate and continuously supervise national and private commercial operators to assure compliance with the terms of the OST. OST Art. IX requires contracting states to conduct their activities in outer space 'with due regard' for the interests of all other states. International standards and regulation will be necessary.[56]

Contamination is also covered in the Moon Agreement of 1979. We considered the Agreement more fully in Chapter 7 but note here that its Art. 7.1 provides the following:

> In exploring and using the moon, States Parties shall take measures to prevent the disruption of its environment, whether by introducing adverse changes in its environment, by its harmful contamination through the introduction of extra-environmental matter or otherwise. States Parties shall also take measures to avoid harmfully affecting the environment of the earth through introduction of extraterrestrial matter or otherwise.

Although the Moon Agreement is relatively ineffective through its failure to gain general acceptance, it was adopted by the UN General Assembly (UNGA Res. 34/68), which makes it at least indicative of a generality of opinion as to the contamination of space.[57]

In their implementation of their non-contamination duties, states have the benefit of the COSPAR Planetary Protection Policy, which has been refined over many years. Its flaw is that it is recommendatory only, not binding.[58] Further, given recent developments, it does not specifically contemplate commercial exploitation or the mining of celestial bodies. The policy covers questions of biological contamination and deals with them in five categories of combinations of target body and space missions. An important factor in

---

55 Thus, for the US see Robinson, *supra* n. 54; G.S. Robinson, 'Forward Contamination of Interstitial Space and Celestial Bodies: Risk Reduction, Cultural Objectives and the Law' (2006) 55 ZLW 380–399; P.M. Sterns and L.I. Tennen. 'Current United States Attitude Concerning Protection of the Outer Space Environment' (1984) 27 *Proc. IISL* 398. See also L.D. Roberts, 'Ensuring the Best of All Possible Worlds: Environmental Regulation of the Solar System' (1997) 6 *N.Y.U. Env. L.J.* 126–160 at 157–160; D.A. Cypser, 'International Law and Policy of Extraterrestrial Planetary Protection' (1993) 33 *Jurimetrics* 315–339.

56 See Chapter 7 at nn. 100 and 101 ff. For a comprehensive survey of proposals down to its date see L.I. Tennen, 'Towards a New Regime for Exploitation of Outer Space Mineral Resources' (2009–2010) 88 *Neb. L. Rev.* 794–831.

57 Interring a dead astronaut would breach MA Art. 17.1. See the COSPAR rules in next para and cf. Chapter 5, n. 72. See also M.S. Race and R.O. Randolph, 'The Need for Operating Guidelines and a Decision Making Framework Applicable to the Discovery of Non-Intelligent Extraterrestrial Life' (2002) 50 *Adv. Sp. Res.* 1583–1591. Contamination was a matter of which COPUOS was seised but ineffectively preferred to refer to the non-binding recommendations of COSPAR, to which we are coming: Cypser, *supra* n. 55, at 317–231.

58 COSPAR Planetary Protection Policy (as of 2022): https://cosparhq.cnes.fr/cospar-policy-on-planetary-protection/. Cf. P.M. Sterns and L. Tennen, 'The Future of Planetary Protection: Is there Reason for Optimism' (2006) 49 *Proc. IISL* 391–400. For a practical example see the environmental assessment for the New Horizons mission of 2006, *infra* at n. 69. See discussion of asteroid and Moon mining in Chapter 7, The Moon, asteroids and other celestial bodies.

classification of forward contamination is whether the body may be of interest for understanding the process of chemical evolution or the origin of life.

In Category I, there is no such direct interest, protection of the target body is unwarranted and the policy imposes no protection requirements. In Category II, there is significant interest in the target for such understanding, but the chance that contamination carried by a spacecraft could jeopardise future exploration is remote. Only simple documentation of the activity is needed. Category III missions are fly-by or orbital missions where the likelihood of an impact on the target body is small but there is either a 'chemical evolution and/or origin of life' interest or scientific opinion thinks there is a significant chance of contamination that could jeopardise a future biological experiment. Here, documentation is to be more thorough, and 'clean room' and sterilisation procedures should be used in construction of the probe. Category IV missions involve planned landings. Documentation is to be more detailed, and the intended lander sterile.[59]

The big change of attitude in the policy rules comes in Category V with regard to any mission involving a return to Earth. In order to preserve the Earth–Moon environment, Category V missions comprise all Earth-return missions. Documentation requirements are considerable as are the requirements as to the sterility, etc. of hardware and matériel. However, where a solar system body has no indigenous life forms, the requirements are modified.

For these 'unrestricted Earth-return' projects, only the outbound Category I and II requirements are imposed. All other cases are classed as 'restricted Earth-return'. In these, any destructive impact of a probe upon its return to Earth is absolutely prohibited so as to prevent the escape of material.[60] All returned hardware which has directly contacted the target body together with any unsterilised material or samples from the target body is to be contained, such containment persisting through post-mission analysis.

Perhaps ominously, '[i]f any sign of the existence of a non-terrestrial replicating entity is found, the returned sample must remain contained unless treated by an effective sterilizing procedure'. Of course, this last is a staple of science fiction. Terrestrial bacteria may have killed H.G. Wells' Martians in *The War of the Worlds* (1898): incoming biological material might reverse that outcome. Protection against contamination is essential, and as a matter of general environmental law is, of course, dictated by the Precautionary Principle.[61]

59 Category Specific Planetary Protection Requirements are set out for solar system target bodies. Sec. 1 is on the use of clean-room technology for outer-planet missions. Secs. 2–5 are science specific. Sec. 6 gives guidelines for Category V missions. Sec. 7 is a Category-specific listing of target body/mission types. Sec. 8 sets Category II requirements for Moon missions. Sec. 9 deals with Category III, IV and V requirements for Mars, Sec. 9.3 listing 'Principles and Guidelines for Human Missions to Mars'. Sec. 10 sets out Category III, IV and V requirements for missions to Europa and Enceladus. Sec. 11 deals with small solar bodies.

60 Cf. the crash of the returning element of the Genesis probe in September 2004: http://news.bbc.co.uk/1/hi/sci/tech/3638926.stm; http://solarsystem.nasa.gov/missions/genesis. The 'Stardust' spacecraft successfully parachuted a capsule to Utah in January 2006 with material taken from comet Wild II. The spacecraft itself was sent into sun orbit: http://stardust.jpl.nasa.gov/mission/details.html. See also B.C. Clark, 'Martian Meteorites do not Eliminate the Need for Back Contamination Precautions on Sample Return Missions' (2002) 30 *Adv. Space Res.* 1593–1600; A. Debus, 'Planetary Protection Requirements for Orbiter and Netlander Elements of the CNES/NASA Mars Sample Return Mission' (2002) 30 *Adv. Space Res.* 1607–1616; *Planetary Protection Classification of Sample Return Missions from the Martian Moons* (National Academies Press, 2019): http://nap.edu/25357.

61 P.B. Larsen, 'Application of the Precautionary Principle to the Moon' (2006) 71 *J. Air L. & Comm.* 296–306; A-S. Martin and S. Freeland, 'Back to the Moon and beyond: Strengthening the Legal Framework for

Nuclear Power

Nuclear contamination of the earth could happen through the crashing of a satellite that has a nuclear power source.[62] Indeed, we already have the example of COSMOS 954, which came to Earth in Canada in January 1978.[63] In addition, the world has been alarmed by the 1986 Chernobyl nuclear accident[64] and by memories of the bombing of Hiroshima and Nagasaki at the end of the Second World War. The possibility of a major disaster involving contamination by plutonium caused the Florida Coalition, a group of environmentalists, to try to stop the launch of the Galileo spacecraft in 1989[65] and the Ulysses Project spacecraft in 1990.[66] In both cases, the spacecraft were to pass close to Earth while building up the velocities necessary for their missions.[67] However, in both cases, the Coalition was unsuccessful. In 1997, a similar result attended an attempt to

Protection of the Space Environment' (2021) 46 *Air and Sp. L.* 415–446; Amos, *supra* n. 54, at 114–125, 'III. Regulating the Risks of Bringing Alien Life Forms to Earth'. For the US rules see NASA Policy Directive NPD 8020.7G on 'Biological Contamination Control for Outbound and Inbound Planetary Spacecraft' assigning responsibilities for administering NASA's planetary protection policy. NPI 8020.7 NPD 8020.7G: nodis3.gsfc.nasa.gov/OPD docs/NPI_8020_7_.pdf. The Directive refers to OST Art. IX and stresses the importance of compliance so that contamination in both directions is avoided. See also NASA Policy Directive NPD 7100.10E on 'Curation of Extraterrestrial Materials'. For NASA NPDs and NPRs see http://nodis3.gsfc.nasa.gov. How the Memorial Spaceflights offered by Space Services Inc. (www.memorialspaceflights.com/services.asp) are regulated is unknown to us.

62 Nuclear material should be sent into space only to serve as fuel. See *infra* n. 100. Using space for the disposal of terrestrial nuclear waste would be dangerous and unrealistic: R. Dusek, 'Lost in Space: The Legal Feasibility of Nuclear Waste Disposal in Outer Space' (1998) 22 *Will. & Mary L. and Pol. Rev.* 181–281.

63 'Canada – Union of Soviet Socialist Republics: Claim for damage caused by Cosmos 954' (1979) 18 ILM 899–930; Protocol and Settlement, Moscow, 2 April 1981 (1981) 20 ILM 689. Other nuclear batteries have ended up in the Pacific from the returning Russian unmanned resupply 'Progress' spacecraft that serviced Mir and now the ISS. The Cosmos 954 incident is outlined in Chapter 4 in relation to questions of liability.

64 The Chernobyl incident was followed by action through the International Atomic Energy Agency. See Convention on Early Notification of a Nuclear Accident, 1986, 1439 UNTS 276; 1998 UKTS 1, Cm 3838; (1986) 25 ILM 1370–1376 (there are also a number of bilateral agreements on 'early notification'): the Convention on Assistance in the Event of a Nuclear Accident or Radiological Emergency, 1986, 1457 UNTS 134; 1998 UKTS 2, Cm 3839; (1986) 25 ILM 1377–1386, together with the Documents of the related IAEA Special Session (1986) 25 ILM 1387–1407, including reservations and application to incidents not covered by these agreements. See also the Tokyo Economic Summit, 'Statement on the Implications of the Chernobyl Nuclear Accident (1986) 25 ILM 1005–10006; International Atomic Energy Agency, 'Statement Summarizing Decisions Taken at the Special Session of the Board of Governors Concerning the Chernobyl Nuclear Accident' (1986) 25 ILM 1009. D. Goren, 'Nuclear Accidents in Space and on Earth: An Analysis of International Law Governing the Cosmos-954 and Chernobyl Accidents' (1993) 5 *Geo. Int. Env. L. Rev.* 855–895; M.S. Straubel, 'Space Borne Nuclear Sources – the Status of their Regulation' (1986) 20 *Valparaiso U.L. Rev.* 187–218.

65 *Florida Coalition for Peace and Justice v George Herbert Walker Bush, et al.*, Civil Action No. 89–2682-OG, US District Court for the District of Columbia, 10 October 1989; 1989 US Dist. LEXIS 12003; 1989 WL 451627. S. Gorove, 'Recent Litigation Involving the Launch of Spacecraft with NPS on Board' (1993) 36 *Proc. IISL* 298–303.

66 *Florida Coalition for Peace and Justice v George Herbert Walker Bush, et al.*, Civil Action No. 89–2682-OG, US District Court for the District of Columbia, 5 December 1990; 1990 US Dist. LEXIS 13345. S. Gorove, *supra* n. 65.

67 Many deep space missions use the fly-by technique to pick up speed. Sometime the Earth is used. New Horizons (*infra* n. 69) used Jupiter. The Messenger mission to Mercury used the Earth in July 2007, and Venus several times before arriving at Mercury in 2011. 'Deep Impact' passed some 10,000 miles above Australia on 31 December 2007 on its way to its next mission. The current Parker Solar Probe uses fly-bys of Venus to maintain its velocity in solar approach: www.nasa.gov/content/goddard/parker-solar-probe.

halt the Cassini mission.[68] More recently, it is instructive to peruse the Draft and the Final Environmental Impact Statement for the New Horizons Mission published in 2005, the initial parts of which assess the potential dangers of an accident during the New Horizons launch.[69]

The possibility of nuclear contamination from a crashing satellite certainly exists and should be planned for by national authorities.[70] International provision comes in UNGA Res. 47/68 of 14 December 1992 on 'Principles Relevant to the Use of Nuclear Power Sources in Outer Space' (NPS).[71] The application of these Principles is limited to nuclear power sources 'devoted to the generation of electric power . . . for non-propulsive purposes', generally similar to those in use at the time of the adoption of the Principles (Preamble, 'Affirming'). They do not apply to NPS used for propulsion, only to those for the on-board functioning of the satellite.[72] While Pr. 11 makes room for the revision of the Principles, that has not yet happened, but we would hope that their general tenor would be complied with in the case of a crash with a more recently developed nuclear source on-board.

Genuflecting to OST Art. III, Pr. 1 of the Nuclear Power Principles provides that the use of NPS is governed by existing international law.[73] They lay much responsibility

68 *Hawaii County Green Party, Florida Coalition for Peace and Justice, Plaintiffs v William Jefferson Clinton, President of the United States, in His Official Capacity, et al.*; 11 October 1997; US District Court for the District of Hawaii; 980 F. Supp. 1160; 1997 US Dist. LEXIS 16196. The US notified the UN of the related environmental safety: A/AC.105/677–2 June 1997.

69 NASA, *Final Environmental Impact Statement for the New Horizons Mission*, July 2005: http://pluto. jhuapl.edu/Mission/Spacecraft/docs/NH-FEIS-Vol1.pdf, with Appendices at: http://pluto.jhuapl.edu/ Mission/Spacecraft/docs/NH-FEIS_Vol2.pdf. Draft at: http://pluto.jhuapl.edu/Mission/Spacecraft/ docs/NH_DEIS_Full.pdf. See also links at: http://pluto.jhuapl.edu/Mission/Spacecraft/deis.php. The Statement was compiled under the US National Environmental Policy Act (NEPA) (42 USC 4321 ff.) to assist in the decision-making process for the project. Launched in January 2006, New Horizons explored Pluto and the Kuiper Belt, arriving in 2015. Cf. the US notification to OOSA: A/AC.105/864. Environmental assessments for other NASA launches are in the US Federal Register of Environmental Documents at: www.epa.gov/fedrgstr/EPA-IMPACT.

70 Cf. US Space Policy Directive – 6 on 'National Strategy for Space Nuclear Power and Propulsion', 2020: https://trumpwhitehouse.archives.gov/presidential-actions/memorandum-national-strategy-space-nuclear-power-propulsion-space-policy-directive-6/. Cf also special provision for licensing nuclear power in Art. 17 of the UAE space legislation in Chapter 7.

71 'Principles Relevant to the Use of Nuclear Power Sources in Outer Space', 14 December 1992, UNGA Res. 47/68; (1993) 32 ILM 917 at 921–926. See CoCoSL III, 189–266, and the 'Safety Framework for Nuclear Power Applications in Outer Space': www.unoosa.org/pdf/publications/iaea-nps-sfrmwrkE.pdf, A/AC.105/934, analysed CoCoSL III, 267–297 and outlined *infra* at n. 113. N. Jasentuliyana – 1, 'Multilateral Negotiations on the Use of NPS in Outer Space' (1989) 24 AASL 297–337; – 2, 'An Assessment of the United Nations Principles on the Use of Nuclear Power Sources in Outer Space' (1993) 36 *Proc. IISL* 312–21; V. Kopal, 'The Use of Nuclear Power in Space: A New Set of United Nations Principles?' (1991) 19 *J. Sp. L.* 103–122. See further *infra* at n. 99 ff.

72 For detail as to NPS systems see *infra* n. 102 ff.

73 Besides the material cited *supra* n. 64, relevant agreements include the Convention on Civil Liability for Nuclear Damage, 1963, 1063 UNTS 266; UKT Misc. No 9, Cmnd. 2333; (1963) ILM 727–745(amended for some parties by Protocols, 1672 UNTS 302 and 2241 UNTS 270, and the Convention on Supplementary Compensation for Nuclear Damage, 1997 36 ILM 1458–1494: the Convention on Physical Protection of Nuclear Materials, 1980, 1456 UNTS 125, 1995 UKTS 61, Cm 2945; (1969) 18 ILM 1419–1433: the Convention on Nuclear Safety, 1994, 1963 UNTS 317, 1999 UKTS 49, Cm 4422; (1994) 33 ILM 1518–1525; the Joint Convention on the Safety of Spent Fuel Management and with the Safety of Radioactive Waste Management, 1997, 2153 UNTS 357; 2012 UKTS 24, Cm 8321; (1997) 36 ILM 1436–1453.

on the 'launching state' or the 'state launching' the space object using NPS, the definition of such being limited to the state exercising jurisdiction and control (presumably in terms of Art. VIII of the OST) over the space object at the relevant time,[74] except for purposes of liability, where Pr. 9 defines the launching state broadly as in Art. VII of the OST and the Liability Convention (Pr. 2.1). When a space object has a nuclear power source on board and there is a malfunction and a risk of the re-entry of radioactive materials,[75] 'as soon as the malfunction has become known' (Pr. 5.2) its launching state (i.e. the one controlling it) is to inform the UN Secretary General and any states that might be affected (Pr. 5.1).[76] The information required comprises the system parameters (roughly those required by the Registration Convention) but particularly includes 'information required for the best prediction of orbital lifetime, trajectory and impact region' (Pr. 5.1(a)(iv)).

Principle 5.1(b) then requires information to be supplied as to the type of the nuclear power source on-board (whether it is a radio-isotopic generator or a nuclear reactor) (Pr. 5.1(b)(i)) and as to the 'probable physical form and general radiological characteristics of the fuel and any contaminated and/or activated components likely to reach the ground. The term 'fuel' refers to the nuclear materials used as the source of heat or power' (Pr. 5.1(b)(ii)). Information is to be updated as frequently as practicable and with increasing frequency as the anticipated 're-entry into the dense layers of the atmosphere approaches' 'so that the international community will be informed . . . and will have sufficient time to plan for any national response activities deemed necessary' (Pr. 5.2).[77] Principle 6 goes on to require the launching state to respond quickly to requests for further information or consultations.

Other states are also to be involved. When under the Principles the launching state notifies the possible re-entry of a nuclear power source, all states having monitoring and tracking facilities are expected to take action. They are to keep the UN Secretary General and other states informed of any information they may have so as to allow potentially affected states 'to assess the situation and take any precautionary measures deemed necessary' (Pr. 7.1). Once the re-entry has occurred, the launching state is to offer assistance in identifying the location of the impact, the detection of materials and their retrieval or clean-up (Pr. 7.2(a)).[78]

As indicated in our discussion of the Liability Convention and the NPS Principles in Chapter 4, the acceptance of an offer of help is at the discretion of the affected state (Pr. 7.2(a)). However, in contra-distinction, if the launching state is requested to help, it is to provide it (Pr. 7.2(a)). Other states and relevant international organisations with appropriate capabilities are also to offer their help (Pr. 7.2(b)). However, it is again for an affected state to accept or decline an offer.

---

74 Interestingly this formulation takes account of the transfer of responsibilities for a satellite. See *infra* n. 79 and discussion of such a transfer in Chapter 4.
75 The term used is 'risk', not 'significant risk' or 'minimal risk' or other adjectival modification of its level.
76 M. Hošková, 'The Notification Principle in the 1992 NPS Principles' (1993) 36 *Proc. IISL* 304–11.
77 The UN Secretary General is similarly to be kept informed (Pr. 5.3). An example of the Principles in action is the Russian notification of the launch of the Mars-96 probe on 15 November 1996 (A/AC.105/647) and its re-entry east of Australia on 16 November 1996 following a launch failure (A/AC.105/648).
78 Principle 3 calls for nuclear sources to be placed in non-frangible containers, but it is realistic to have provision as to a clean-up were such to fail. See also ARRA Art. 5 regarding the clean-up of hazardous and deleterious materials.

Of course, the possible crash of a nuclear power source in its territory is an emergency for which governments should have plans and procedures. There will be short- and long-term risks to the population as well as potentially significant damage to property. Less-developed countries are less likely to have such procedures. Accordingly, the last unnumbered paragraph of Pr. 7 states that in the implementation of Pr. 7.2(a) and (b) when states are helping each other, 'the special needs of developing countries shall be taken into account'. Principle 10 indicates that any dispute as to the application of the Principles is to be resolved through negotiation or any other established procedures for the settlement of disputes in accordance with the UN Charter. There have been none as yet.

Penultimately, there are, of course the questions of responsibility, liability and compensation. These are covered in Prs. 8 and 9, which we dealt with back in Chapter 4. However, we would here again note that for the purpose of liability, the term 'launching state' is defined in P. 9 as it is in OST Art. VII and the Liability Convention, while for the other Principles, that term is restricted to the state exercising jurisdiction and control (presumably in terms of OST Art. VIII) over the space object at the relevant time (Pr. 2.1).[79] Finally, Pr. 11 provides that the Principles were to be reopened for revision by COPUOS no later than two years from their adoption (in 1992). Revision has not formally occurred, though some progress has been made through the COPUOS Scientific and Technical Subcommittee.[80]

The Near-Earth Environment

Most current space activities take place in Earth orbit. That environment may be potentially affected by geoengineering, by other forms of contamination, and certainly is being affected by space debris. We will take these in that order.

Geoengineering from/in Space

Proposals have been made for the use of space-based geoengineering to mitigate or prevent terrestrial climate change.[81] Here we are mainly concerned with actions in space, particularly the placing in space of sun-shields or similar devices, commonly known as solar radiation management techniques.[82] Interference with radio or optical astronomy by materials introduced into the upper atmosphere or low orbits would clearly require international consultations. Such shields would also present problems for satellite launches and recovery. Further, any effects on the existing uses of radio would require careful study and might well require the modification of the ITU Radio Regulations.[83]

---

79 Cf. Note Verbale of 29 July 2003 from The Netherlands: A/AC105.806 as to satellites 2002–019A and 2002–057A, and its Note Verbale of 18 February 2004: A/AC.105/824 as to the removal of 1988–040A from geostationary orbit.

80 A.D. Terekhov, 'Review and Revision of the Principles relevant to the Use of Nuclear Power Sources in Outer Space' (1993) 36 *Proc. IISL* 336–48. But see also *infra* at n. 111.

81 Monitoring alterations in climate is a major function of much remote sensing. See Chapter 13.

82 See *The Regulation of Geoengineering*, UK House of Commons Committee on Science and Technology, Fifth Report, Sess. 2009–10, HC 221, 18 March 2010. In late November 2010 it was announced that the UN would research geoengineering, with 'space mirrors' being an option.

83 See Chapter 8.

Solar management techniques divide into those envisaging a shield placed far out in space and those where the shield is in orbit closer to Earth. Thus one proposal is that a number of reflectors, or even a cloud of small reflectors be positioned at Lagrange Point 1, some 1.5 million km. distant between the Earth and the Sun.[84] An alternative proposal would insert shielding materials into low earth orbit so as to create a reflective band round the earth.[85] The hope would be that the atmosphere would be cooled through regular passes into and out of the shielded area, although this might possibly disrupt weather patterns. In effect a LEO shield would constitute another variety of space debris, which it would not be possible easily to remove should its effects prove undesirable.

The treaty most clearly relevant to environmental modification activities in or from space is ENMOD, the 1976 Convention on the Prohibition of Military or any other Hostile Use of Environmental Modification Techniques.[86] Article II.1 defines 'environmental modification techniques' as 'any technique for changing-through the deliberate manipulation of natural processes-the dynamics, composition or structure of the Earth, including its biota, lithosphere, hydrosphere and atmosphere, or of outer space'. Article I prohibits the use or the encouragement of such techniques for hostile purposes. However, Art. III.1 states that the Convention 'shall not hinder the use of environmental modification techniques for peaceful purposes and shall be without prejudice to the generally recognised principles and applicable rules of international law concerning such use'. Geoengineering in space for peaceful purposes therefore appears to be lawful under ENMOD.

The provisions of the OST are not adequate to deal with the legalities of climate change techniques in or from space. Under Art. I.1, the benefit and interests of all countries should motivate the use of outer space. Article III speaks of maintaining international peace and security. The mitigation of climate change may meet these criteria in terms of intention. However, space-based mitigation action may also present difficulties since geoengineering in the interest of one group of states might not suit the interests of others. Weather patterns could be disrupted or intensified.

Of course the normal duties and responsibilities of OST Arts. VI, VII and IX would also be relevant for geoengineering activities in space. Dealing with liability Art. VII provides

---

84 Lagrange Point 1 (L1) lies between the earth and the sun and is the point at which the gravities of these two objects are in balance. A small object placed there remains relatively stationary with respect to both. All L1 orbits are dynamically unstable, and objects placed in them require station-keeping manoeuvres. An L1 positioning would be expensive to achieve and difficult to maintain and would interfere with the operation of SOHO, the Solar and Heliospheric Observatory already in Halo orbit at L1 and with the Advanced Composition Explorer, which is in a Lissajous orbit also at L1. Both are dedicated to solar science programmes and are also important in the detection of solar flares, allowing satellite operators and those involved in terrestrial microwave communications and power grids to take avoidance measures. NASA's WIND satellite is also at L1, gathering data on the solar wind and our magnetosphere.

  For proposals, see R. Angel, 'Feasibility of cooling the Earth with a cloud of small spacecraft near the inner Lagrange point (L1)' (2006) 103 *Proc, National Academy of Science, USA*, 17184; J.T. Early, 'Space Based Solar Shield to Offset Greenhouse Effect' (1989) 42 JBIS 567; C.R. McInnes, 'Minimum Mass Solar Shield for Terrestrial Climate Control' (2002) 55 JBIS 307. Cf. A.C. Clarke and S. Baxter, *Sunstorm* (London: Gollancz 2005), a science fiction novel where the plot involves a sun shield.

85 J. Pearson et al., 'Earth Rings for Planetary Environment Control' (2006) 58 *Acta Astronautica* 44–57; T. Kosuge, 'Role of sunshades in space as a climate control option' (2010) 67 *Acta Astronautica* 241–253.

86 Convention on the Prohibition of Military or any other Hostile Use of Environmental Modification Techniques (ENMOD), New York, 10 December 1976; 1108 UNTS 151; 31 UST 333, TIAS 9614; 1979 UKTS 24, Cmnd. 7469; (1977) 16 ILM 88.

that a state party is liable for damage to another OST party caused by an object for which it has launch responsibility, including for damage caused on the earth. It would, however, be difficult under this provision to bring a claim arising from tempest, floods or drought caused by an alteration to climate patterns induced by a 'space shield'. Article VII speaks of damage caused by the space object or its component parts – a reference to collision rather than the causing of temperature fluctuations.[87] Finally, Art. IX requires parties to the treaty to consult before undertaking activities that may cause 'potentially harmful interference' with the space activities of other parties.[88]

Many current uses of space would be affected by proposed space-based climate geo-engineering. For example, the establishment of a shield system at L1 would require the consultation and agreement of the states and agencies presently using that location. LEO geoengineering measures would affect many space services such as telecommunications and, indeed environmental monitoring. Securing agreement among states as to a particular programme would be very difficult. Perhaps the 2015 Paris Agreement on Climate Change, provides opportunities for States to consult and take decisions.[89]

Contamination

The contamination of orbital space, as opposed to the presence of debris, is possible. Regrettably, in the early years of space both the US and USSR deliberately detonated nuclear devices in orbit.[90] Apparently this affected the Van Allen radiation belts before their pristine condition could be examined. The position as to nuclear explosions is regulated for its parties by the Nuclear Test-Ban Treaty of 1963, Art. I of which prohibits nuclear tests *inter alia* in space.[91] The absence of France from the Nuclear Test Ban Treaty has provoked questions whether this prohibition has passed into customary international

---

87 The same consideration applies in respect to those provisions of the 1972 Liability Convention that fill out and to an extent alter Article VII of the OST. Convention on International Liability for Damage Caused by Space Objects, 29 March 1972, 961 UNTS 187 (1971) 10 ILM 965. See our discussion of the Liability Convention in Chapter 4.

88 Article IX was adopted by the OST diplomatic conference in reaction to the US insertion of 480,000 copper needles into medium Earth orbit in 1961 and 1963 (Project Ford)). The project raised international objections: https://weathermodificationhistory.com/project-west-ford-space-needles/. The requirement of Art. IX is only to consult. It does not bar continuing with such an activity following upon ineffective consultation. See also Larsen, *supra* n. 1.

89 Paris Agreement on Climate Change, *supra* n. 10. The point is recognised in much of the evidence given to the UK House of Commons Science and Technology Committee, *supra* n. 82.

90 Note also the 2019 destruction of an Indian satellite by India (Mission Shakti) (www.bbc.co.uk/news/world-asia-india-47729568; www.space.com/india-anti-satellite-test-significance.html) and the 2021 destruction of a Russian satellite by Russia. The three US Operation Argus explosions were conducted over the South Atlantic between August and September 1958, with 'Starfish' occurring in 1962. Three USSR tests over Siberia occurred in October/November 1962. Radiation from 'Starfish' destroyed three satellites: D.P. Stern, 'Birth of a Radiation Belt' http://istp.gsfc.nasa.gov/Education/wbirthrb.html. See also M.W. Mouton, 'Artificial Radiation: the Starfish Experiment', in M.W. Mouton, 'The Impact of Science on International Law' 119 *Hague Recueil* 1966-III, 183–260 at 236–238; A.G. Haley, *Space Law and Government* (New York: Appleton-Century-Crofts, 1963) at 11–12, 267–271 and 326.

91 Treaty Banning Nuclear Weapon Tests in the Atmosphere, in Outer Space or Under Water, Moscow, 5 August 1963, 480 UNTS 43; 14 UST 1313, TIAS 5433; 1964 UKTS 3, Cmnd. 2245; (1963) 57 AJIL 1026; (1963) 2 ILM 883. M.W. Mouton, 'Nuclear Bomb Tests', in M.W. Mouton, 'The Impact of Science on International Law' 119 *Hague Recueil* 1966-III, 183–260 at 242–249; 'X', 'Nuclear Test Ban Treaties' (1963) 39 BYIL 449–456; E. Schwelb, 'The Nuclear Test Ban Treaty and International Law' (1964) 58

law,[92] but, that notwithstanding, we would hope that non-parties to the Treaty would refrain from such actions. The UN General Assembly has unanimously called on states to refrain from placing in orbit around the Earth any objects carrying nuclear weapons or any other kinds of weapons of mass destruction and from installing such weapons on celestial bodies.[93] OST Art. IV makes similar provision.

Unfortunately, the UN Comprehensive Nuclear Test Ban Treaty of 1996 has not yet been brought into force and is unlikely ever to be.[94] By its Art. 1.1, states undertake not to carry out nuclear weapon tests or any other nuclear explosion and to prohibit and prevent any such explosions at any place under their jurisdiction or control. Such language would encompass nuclear explosions in space, on the moon or on any other celestial bodies.[95] It would also create difficulties for the use of nuclear propulsion systems for spacecraft as these develop. The treaty would also set up monitoring stations and an organisation to implement its provisions, including the verification of compliance, an obvious stumbling block.

While most satellites are powered by solar cells and batteries, some use nuclear power sources.[96] These are either nuclear reactors (usually used for long-range missions) or radioisotope thermoelectric generators producing heat, which is converted to electricity – in effect nuclear batteries. The objective of the Nuclear Power Principles is 'to ensure with high reliability that radioactive material does not cause a significant contamination of outer space.' (Pr. 3, preamble). As we will see, for the further protection of the earth, the

---

AJIL 642–670. Cf. the *Nuclear Tests Case (New Zealand v France)* 1974 ICJ Rep. 157 and the *Nuclear Tests Case (Australia v France)* 1974 ICJ Rep. 253, and next note.

92 Cf. Paras 105.2.A and B of the Decision, and the Opinion (particularly paras 27–9), the Separate Opinions, Declarations and Dissenting Opinions in the *Legality of the Threat or Use by a State of Nuclear Weapons in Armed Conflict*, Advisory Opinion, 8 July 1996, 1996 ICJ Rep. 226; (1996) 35 ILM 809.

93 Question of General and Complete Disarmament' UNGA Res. 1984 (XVIII), 17 October 1963. Cf. the series of Resolutions on the 'Prevention of an Arms Race in Outer Space', e.g., UNGA 61/58, 6 December 2006 and UNGA 62/20, 5 December 2007.

94 UN Comprehensive Test Ban Treaty, 1996, 1997 UKT Misc. 7, Cm 3665; (1996) 35 ILM 1439–78, US Senate Doc 105–28: www.ctbto.org/sites/default/files/Documents/CTBT_English_withCover.pdf. The Treaty does not permit reservations (Art. XV). As of mid-2022, of the one hundred ninety-three UN members, one hundred eighty-three had signed the treaty. Non-signatories were Bhutan, North Korea, India, Mauritius, Pakistan, Saudi Arabia, Somalia, South Sudan, Syria and Tonga. It had one hundred seventy-six ratifiers. However, its coming into force requires ratification by forty-four states listed in Annex 2, states possessing nuclear power or nuclear reactors (Art. XIV). Of these North Korea, India and Pakistan are non-signatories, and China, Egypt, Israel and the US are non-ratifiers. See www.ctbto.org/the-treaty/status-of-signature-and-ratification/. See the Preparatory Commission for the Comprehensive Test Ban Treaty Organisation (CTBTO) (www.ctbto.org/), and 1999 UKTS 46, Cm 4399.
   See D.A. Koplow, 'Nuclear Arms Control by a Pen: Effectuating the Comprehensive Nuclear Test Ban Treaty without Ratification' (2015) 46 *Geo. J. Int. L.*, 475–518; A. Aust, 'The Comprehensive Nuclear Test Ban Treaty – The Problem of Entry into Force', 2009 52 Jap. YBIL 1–34; D.S. Jonas, 'The Comprehensive Nuclear Test Ban Treaty: Current Legal Status in the United States and the Implications of a Nuclear Test Explosion,' (2007) 39 *N.Y.U. J. Int. L. and Pol.* 1007–1046.

95 See *infra* as to the use of a nuclear device to alter the trajectory of an asteroid on a collision course with Earth.

96 I. Bouvet, 'Use of Nuclear Power Sources in Outer Space: Key Technology Legal challenges' (2004) *J. Sp. L.* 203–226; S.A. Mirmina and D.J. Den Herder, 'Nuclear Power Sources and Future Space Exploration' (2005) 6 *Chic. J. Int. L.* 149–176; J.J. MacAvoy, 'Nuclear Space and the Earth Environment: the Benefits, Dangers, and Legality of Nuclear Power and Propulsion in Outer Space' (2004) 29 *Will. and Mary Env. L. and Pol. Rev.* 191–233.

Principles also require that after use, Earth-orbiting satellites with nuclear power sources are to be stored in high orbits (Prs. 3.2(a)(iii) with 3.2(b) and Pr. 3.3(a)).[97]

A previous section of this chapter considered the potential contamination of the earth as the result of the crash of a nuclear-powered satellite. Any explosion on a nuclear-powered satellite in orbit may result in nuclear debris in space. Here, therefore, we consider the 1992 Nuclear Power Principles in relation to nuclear power in outer space.[98]

Recognising that nuclear power sources are 'particularly suited or even essential' to some space missions, NPS Principles set goals and guidelines in an attempt generally to secure the safety of nuclear power sources.[99] As noted earlier, the Preamble states that the Principles apply only to non-propulsive nuclear power sources for the generation of electricity, leaving open the interesting possibilities of propulsion by ramjet, fission, fusion, gas, electric, photon and other methods involving nuclear materials (Preamble, 'Affirming'). It also recognises that the proper use of nuclear power sources in space requires a thorough analysis of risks to safety and appropriate assessments (Preamble, 'Recognising further'). The Principles were intended to deal with systems comparable to those in use at the time of their adoption (Preamble, 'Affirming') and therefore the need to revise and update them is also recognised (Preamble, 'Recognising') but, although Pr. 11 called for COPUOS to re-examine the Principles two years after their adoption, as noted this has not so far happened.[100]

Principle 1 restates the generality that nuclear power sources in outer space are to be used in accordance with International Law including the UN Charter and the OST. Principle 2 then sets the meaning of various terms as they are used in the text. As we have seen a distinction is made between the 'launching state' for the purpose of liability in terms of Pr. 9 and its use elsewhere in the Principles.

For liability, the term is defined broadly as in Art. VII of the OST and in the Liability Convention (Pr. 2.2). Otherwise the launching state is defined as the state having jurisdiction and control over the space object at the relevant time (Pr. 2.1). Principle 2.3 then deals with other terms and phrases used in the Principles. The modifiers 'foreseeable' and 'all possible' are not absolute but are restricted to a probability of occurrence which is credibly possible for the purpose of safety analysis.[101] Redundant safety systems for each component in order to achieve 'defence in depth' are not necessarily required. Defence in depth against a malfunction does, however, require the design of equipment and its operation so as to prevent or mitigate the effect of a malfunction. Finally, making a nuclear reactor go 'critical' does not include zero-power testing.

Principle 3 is the major core of UNGA Res. 47/68.[102] Radioactive materials in space are to be limited, and when used, severely controlled. Its introductory paragraph specifically states that 'in order to minimise the quantity of radioactive materials in space, and the risks

---

97 See *infra* n. 106.
98 For the NPS Principles and their relevance for terrestrial occurrences see *supra* at n. 71 and ff.
99 'Principles Relevant to the Use of Nuclear Power Sources in Outer Space', 14 December 1992, UNGA Res. 47/68; (1993) 32 ILM 917 at 921–926. See Jasentuliyana, Kopal, both *supra* n. 71, Hošková, *supra* n. 76, and Terekhov, *supra* n. 80.
100 See text *infra* following n. 111.
101 Both terms would be a factor in determining liability under the Liability Convention.
102 Reference point *supra* n. 72 and *infra* n. 118.

involved' the use of nuclear power sources in outer space is to be limited 'to those space missions which cannot be operated by non-nuclear energy sources in a reasonable way'.[103] Principle 3 then sets out general goals for safety and protection from radiation together with measures as to nuclear reactors and radioisotope generators.

Under Pr. 3.1, the highest standards of design and manufacture are usually to be adopted for space objects with nuclear power sources on-board. These should meet the standards set by the International Commission on Radiological Protection.[104] A distinction is made between low-probability accidents and others as to levels of radiation exposure, but these levels are under constant review (Pr. 3.1). The general concept of defence in depth is to be applied including the possibility of correction of malfunctions (Pr. 3.1(d)) and the reliability of safety systems through redundancy,[105] physical separation, functional isolation and adequate independence of components.

Nuclear reactors are the subject of Principle 3.2. Only enriched U235 is to be used on space missions (Pr. 3.2(c)). Devices using U235 may be operated on interplanetary missions, or in what is defined as 'sufficiently high' orbits around the earth, or in low Earth orbit provided that the devices are stored in a sufficiently high orbit at the end of the mission (Pr. 3.2(a)). All satellites with nuclear reactors are to have means to ensure that they can be safely disposed of into a sufficiently high orbit, colloquially a graveyard, junk or disposal orbit (Pr. 3.2(f)).[106] 'Sufficiently high' is defined as an orbit so high that the orbital lifetime will outlast the decay of the fission products on-board the satellite to approximately the activity of the actinides. Such an orbit would be well beyond the geostationary orbit.[107] In the calculation of the relevant altitude, the period for the radioactivity of the reactor itself to reduce to acceptable levels before re-entry is also to be considered (Pr. 3.2(b)). Apart from zero-power testing (Pr. 2.3), a reactor must not be made critical before reaching either the operating orbit of the spacecraft or an interplanetary trajectory (Pr. 3.2(c)) and the design and construction of the reactor should be such that it cannot become earlier critical under any circumstances including explosion, re-entry, impact or the incursion of water (Pr.3.2(d)).

Radioisotope thermoelectric generators (RTGs) are treated similarly. They may be used on interplanetary missions 'and other missions leaving the gravity field of the Earth' (which presumably means to the moon, or extra-solar missions). Earth orbital missions are also

---

103 Global positioning satellites run on nuclear batteries. Deep space probes usually now use a nuclear furnace.
104 Based in Stockholm, and a registered charity in the UK, the International Commission on Radiological Protection is an independent nongovernmental advisory body: www.icrp.org/.
105 Although, as per Pr. 2.3, not necessarily for all components.
106 M. Meija-Kaiser, *The Geostationary Ring: Practice and Law* (Leiden: Brill, 2020) 197–274. See also *infra* n. 175. In the current IADC Guidelines on Debris Mitigation (*infra* n. 191) to protect the GSO Guideline 5.3.1.1 recommends the use of graveyard orbits beyond the GSO for spent GSO satellites. See also Guideline 5.3.2–3 on Post-Mission Disposal for all orbits. Eutelsat 5 West A. decommissioned in January 2023, was re-orbited to more than 450km above GSO: www.satellitetoday.com/broadcasting/2023/01/19/eutelsat-retires-eutelsat-5-west-a-satellite/; www.businesswire.com/news/home/20230119005688/en/Eutelsat-Successfully-Decommissions-EUTELSAT-5-West-A-Satellite. Some Russian satellites have at end of mission been boosted out of orbit on trajectories that end in the Sun. See also the ITU recommendation, *infra* n. 119. The US FCC has fined an operator for its failure to relocate its defunct satellite to at least 300km above the GSO as was provided for by its license. The operator has complied with its requirements. See In the Matter of DISH Operating L.L.C., FCC DA 23–888: https://docs.fcc.gov/public/attachments/DOC-397412A1.pdf.
107 See also *infra* at nn. 118 and 119.

competent provided that at the end of the mission the satellite is placed in a 'sufficiently high orbit'. Ultimate disposal will be necessary (Pr. 3.3(a)). As with reactors, an RTG container is to be such that it can withstand atmospheric re-entry and will not fracture on impact with the ground so that the impact area can be completely cleared of radioactivity by a recovery operation (Pr. 3.3.(b)).[108]

Obviously, such provisions make for the safety of use of nuclear power sources. This is augmented by the specific requirement that, prior to a mission, a launching state must carry out a thorough safety assessment of design and construction as well as of the operational systems,[109] which procedure is to involve designers, manufacturers and contractors as well as any state which would be a 'launching state' as defined in the Liability Convention (Pr. 4.1 and 2). In accordance with OST Art. XI the result of the assessment and 'to the extent feasible', the time of the intended launch are to be made publicly available, and the UN Secretary General is to be informed of how states may obtain the results of the assessment (Pr. 4.3).[110]

Such was the 1992 provision made for the use of NPS in space.[111] While, as indicated, they were directed towards NPS used for generating electricity – which in 2022 might be thought to be an unfortunate restriction – it is possible to overlook the fact that a major element was concern over the potential threat of unguided re-entrant satellites. Principles 5 through 7 are designed to deal with re-entry, and the earlier Principles as to the design, construction and use of the NPS systems regularly refer to 're-entry' as a consideration in their planning.

That said, the intention that the quantity of nuclear materials in space should be minimised (Pr. 3, preamble), and the prescriptions as to the NPS and as to disposal in outer space are welcome. However, they remain somewhat nebulous and, thirty years on, are becoming out-dated. Principle 11 did, and does, provide for the revision of the Principles, but as stated earlier, such revision has not formally occurred.[112] However, the COPUOS Scientific and Technical Subcommittee has provided some guidance in the operation of the NPS Principles. In 2009 it adopted a 'Safety Framework for Nuclear Power Source Applications in Outer Space' that had been developed through discussion along with the International Atomic Energy Agency.[113] Later in 2009 the Safety Framework was endorsed by COPUOS main committee (A/64/20, para 138) and welcomed 'with satisfaction' by the UNGA (UNGA Res. 64/86, para 11b).[114]

---

108 The phrasing may reflect the fact that the RTG on COSMOS 954 did fracture. Specific mention is made of the possibility of a crash on return from a highly elliptical orbit where the re-entry velocity would be very great (Pr. 3.1(b)).

109 The state having control and jurisdiction over the space object will perform the safety assessment. Principle 4 allows that state considerable discretion in conducting the safety assessment. However, the atomic energy safety standards established by the International Atomic Energy Agency (IAEA) will also be relevant, see www.iaee.org. The IAEA and the COPUOS Scientific and Technical Subcommittee jointly prepared the 'Safety Framework for Nuclear Power Source Application in Outer Space', A/AC/105/934 of 19 May 2009, CoCoSL III, 267–297. See *infra* n. 113.

110 Thus, the US notification to the UN in terms of Pr. 4 for the 'New Horizons' mission is at A/AC.105/864. As to the Mission see n. 69 *supra*.

111 Reference point, *supra* n. 100.

112 Pr. 3 *ad med* does call for future modifications to the guidelines of Pr. 3 to be applied as soon as possible.

113 'Safety Framework for Nuclear Power Source Applications in Outer Space' A/AC.105/934; CoCoSL III 267–297. See *supra* n. 71, and www.unoosa.org/pdf/publications/iaea-nps-sfrmwrkE.pdf.

114 Although it lacks the fuller endorsement of a UNGA Resolution, which the NPS Principles do have, the Framework is another example of the way in which 'soft law' can develop practice in space law, this time

Drawing on the work of the International Atomic Agency, the Framework is concerned with the safe use of NPS. The fundamental objective is the protection of people and the environment of the biosphere from potential hazards associated with the launch, operation and end of service phases of NPS applications. To that end, the Framework is intended to provide a model within which NPS systems and devices may continue to be developed with due regard to safety. Its Chapter 3 provides guidance for governments as to safety policies, requirements and processes, as to launch authorisation and as to emergency preparedness and response. Chapter 4 deals with the responsibility of management for safety, and Chapter 5 gives technical guidance on nuclear safety, safety in design and development, risk assessment and the mitigation of the consequences of an accident. We hope that the objectives of the Framework are being achieved, but to be realistic, 'accidents will happen'. In that event, the NPS Principles, particularly Prs. 4–7, remain valuable.

Space Objects in Orbit

The major use of near-Earth space is the orbiting of satellites.[115] When their function is at an end satellites effectively become debris, which we will consider separately below.

Various orbital configurations are in regular use. To repeat data from Chapter 6, most satellites are in low Earth orbit (LEO) (*c.* 100–500 km/65–310 miles), taking some ninety minutes for each orbit. Orbits vary from the equatorial plane to the polar. Such orbits are roughly circular, their low and high points (perigee and apogee) being similar and are below the Van Allen radiation belts. A highly elliptical Earth orbit (HEO) has a wide variation between perigee and apogee. In their apogee phase satellites in such an orbit remain visible from a point on Earth for up to twelve hours and are used *inter alia* by communications satellites (e.g. the Russian Moliyna series). A medium Earth orbit (MEO) or intermediate circular orbit (ICO) is between 2,000 km and 35,000 km (1,240–21,750 miles) and satellites in MEO take anything from two to twelve hours to complete an orbit.

MEOs are used mainly for global positioning satellite configurations, though they are now also used for some communications satellites.[116] A geosynchronous orbit is one in which a satellite returns to the same position each day. Of these the most well-known is the geostationary orbit (GSO), an eastwards circular orbit some 35,786 km/22,236 miles above the equator. It is used by satellites providing communications and remote sensing (mainly meteorological) services.[117] A 'parking orbit' may be in LEO or MEO and is

---

through expatiating on aspects of the soft law characteristics already inherent in the Principles. See the discussion of soft law in Chapter 2.

115 About 5,500 active satellites are in orbit now, and it is estimated that additionally 58,000 will be in orbit by2030. See IADC Statement on Large Constellations of Satellites in Low Earth Orbit (Rev. 11), 2021, IADC-15-03: www.iadc-home.org/documents_public/view/id/174#u, US Government Accountability Office Report *Large Constellations of Satellites: Mitigating Environmental and Other Effects*, September 2022]: www.gao.gov/assets/gao-22-105166.pdf. Cf. 8th European Conference on Space Debris, 2021 (ESA): https://conference.sdo.esoc.esa.int/proceedings/packages: and ESA's Annual Space Environment Report, 2022; ww.esa.int/Space_Safety/Space_Debris/ESA_s_Space_Environment_Report_2022; text at www.sdo.esoc.esa.int/environment_report/Space_Environment_Report_latest.pdf. For satellite data see 'Orbiting Now': https://orbit.ing-now.com/.

116 A satellite in a suitable MEO will provide communications facilities for the North and South Polar areas. Satellites in LEO or GSO will not. See also Chapter 10 on various communications enterprises.

117 See Chapters 8, 11, 12 and 13.

used temporarily before a satellite or space probe is put on its final trajectory. Finally, a graveyard, disposal or junkyard orbit for the GSO is normally at least 300 km/250 miles higher than the geostationary. These are used for satellites that have reached the end of their useful life, and which it would be too expensive or difficult to deorbit to Earth. Defunct satellites having radioactive power sources on-board are to be placed in an orbit 'sufficiently high' to remove them from causing problems in the immediate future.[118] The ITU Radiocommunication Sector recommends that at the end of their useful life geostationary satellites are relocated to a 'supersynchronous graveyard orbit' at least 200 km higher than the GSO and that will not intersect with the GSO.[119]

Satellites come in two main forms, passive and active. Considered simply as objects active satellites have the same potential as passive satellites to interfere with other uses of space, but we first deal more particularly with passive satellites as such. Passive satellites do not possess radio facilities except perhaps for the reception of signals for their initial deployment. They are deliberately placed in LEO for a variety of purposes. Project West Ford (1961–1963) involved the insertion of small dipoles (2 cm long copper needles) with the intention of their being used to reflect radio transmissions. Some clusters of Project West Ford needles are still in orbit and may still cause problems.[120]

Other launches were of balloons. Echo 1 (1960) (diameter 30 metres) and Echo 2 (1964) (diameter 41 metres) were large, metallised polymer balloons inflated in orbit to act as passive radio reflectors and for geodetic purposes in the measurement of the earth.[121] The Echo balloons re-entered the atmosphere respectively in 1968 and 1969. PAGEOS I, in orbit from 1966 to 1975, was another geodetic project.[122] In the NASA Explorer series, Explorers 9 (1961–1964), 19 (1963–1981), 24 (1964–1968) and 39 (1968–1981)[123]

---

118 NPS Pr. 3.2(a)–(b), *supra* n. 102. See also *supra* n. 106.

119 Recommendation S.1003–2 (12/2010), 'Environmental Protection of the geostationary-satellite orbit': www.itu.int/dms_pubrec/itu-r/rec/s/R-REC-S.1003-2-201012-I!!PDF-E.pdf. First adopted in 1993 a 2004 revision incorporated IADC originating protocols for the calculation of the new orbit. Cf. www.itu.int/dms_pubrec/itu-r/rec/s/R-REC-S.1003-0-199304-S!!PDF-E.pdf and www.itu.int/dms . . . /R-REC-S.1003-1-200401-S!!MSW-E.doc. See also Regulation of Global Broadband Satellite Communications (ITU: ITU-D, 2012): www.itu.int/ITU-D/treg/broadband/ITU-BB-Reports_RegulationBroadbandSatellite.pdf.

   L. Perek, 'Planetary Protection: Lessons Learned' (2002) 45 *Proc. IISL* 462–465 at 464 noted that only two out of fourteen GSO satellites at the end of their life in 2001 had been so relocated. In 1996–2001 some fifty spent satellites had been left in GSO. We are unaware of the current figures for GSO, but data on graveyard orbits for Highly Earth Orbits (HEO) is at https://orbit.ing-now.com/high-earth-graveyard-orbit/. Data is derived from US tracking; see Wikipedia, 'Two-line element set'.

120 J.C. Mandeville and J-M. Perrin, 'Interaction between Electromagnetic Radiations and West Ford Needle Clusters: Models and Application' (2006) 58 *Acta Astronautica* 587–604; R.M. Goldstein et al., 'Radar Observations of Space Debris' (1998) 46 *Planetary and Sp. Sc.* 1007–13; M.W. Mouton, 'Project West Ford', in M.W. Mouton, 'The Impact of Science on International Law' 119 *Hague Recueil* 1966-III, 183–260 at 238–242; A.G. Haley, *supra* n. 73, at 268–269.

121 D.C. Elder, *Out from Behind the Eight-Ball: A History of Project Echo* (Washington: American Irish Historical Society, 1995) (not seen). A 'reflecting satellite' is 'a satellite intended to reflect radiocommunication signals' (ITU RR 1.181).

122 Geos I and II (1965–75) (Explorer series nos. 29 and 36) and some other early experiments allowed triangulation of a flashing or strobing beacon carried by the satellite. Technical advance, particularly through GPS programmes, has rendered such procedures obsolete. Geos I and II should not be confused with later GEOS programmes which provide Earth observation from geostationary orbit.

123 Dates are of launch and decay.

were launched to measure atmospheric density, as was another Mylar balloon launched by the US Department of Defense (1971–1991).

China has launched two balloons, also to measure atmospheric density (both 1990–1991), while a Russian balloon apparently remains in orbit (1991–). Passive satellites have been suggested for other physically larger projects and not always for scientific purposes. In the 1990s Russia considered orbiting large reflectors in low Earth orbit to illuminate portions of the northern hemisphere in winter. The possibility also exists of passive satellites being used for advertising.[124] In the remote past, it was suggested that vapour released from a pod in a crater of the moon could with appropriate masking be made to configure in space an advertisement for a well-known (US) soft drink. That was perhaps extreme, but the fact is that advertising in space has potential.

An IAU background paper submitted to COPUOS in 2001 noted proposals to put materials in orbit for advertising (or celebration) purposes including a 'Ring of Light' to celebrate the bicentennial of the French Revolution and the centennial of the Eiffel Tower in 1997, a 'Star of Tolerance' to consist of two large tethered balloons in LEO to celebrate the fiftieth anniversary of UNESCO also in 1999, the 'Space Billboard', a one square kilometre reflector to be in low Earth orbit and a similar project to advertise the Olympic Games in Atlanta in 1996.[125] As early as 1961, the International Astronomical Union (IAU) was concerned about the effect on its members' activities of all space objects whether active or passive.[126] An IAU paper of 2001 noted that some space activities necessarily affect the work of astronomers but their 'benefit to national or international interests' may be 'perceived to outweigh their adverse effects'. Nonetheless, obtrusive space advertising should be controlled, and preferably proscribed.[127] Obtrusive space advertising would

---

124 D.E Tomlinson and R.L. Wiley, 'People Do Read Large Ads: The Law of Advertising from Outer Space' (1995) 2 *Global Leg. Stud.* 2, or (1995) 47 *Fed. Comm. L.J.* 535; F.J. Balsamello, 'When You Wish upon a Falling Billboard: Advertising in an Age of Space Tourism' (2010) 98 *Geo. L.J.* 1769–1822 at 1791–1800. Russia has displayed an identifiable soft drink container in space, and for $5m has displayed an advert for a pizza product on the side of a Proton launcher.

125 See 'Obtrusive Space Advertising and Astronomical Research: Background Paper by the International Astronomical Union', COPUOS, A/AC.105/777, 18 December 2001, and discussion of the topic by COPUOS Legal Subcommittee A/AC.105/786, paras 135–42. At para 138, the Sub-Committee 'noted with appreciation' that in 2000 the US banned the commercial launch of material for use in obtrusive space advertising. See (US) Pub. L. 106–391, title III, Sec. 322(b), 30 October 2000, 114 Stat. 1598. See now 51 USC 50902 and 50911. Obtrusive space advertising is defined as 'advertising in outer space that is capable of being recognised by a human being on the surface of the earth without the aid of a telescope or other technological device' (51 USC 50902 (12)). We hope that a 2021 proposal by a Canadian company, Geometric Energy Company, to launch a billboard with SpaceX will not be licensed: www.inverse.com/innovation/spacex-ad-in-space.

126 The Echo balloons were of magnitude 1, while PAGEOS was magnitude 2. Their progress across the sky affected some astronomical observations.

127 IAU, *supra* n. 125, at paras 22 and 33–35. Tomlinson (*supra* n. 124) was of the view that all space advertising should be banned, while his co-author, Wiley, although permitting it, would favour its regulation: see D.E. Tomlinson, 'The Better Means of Preserving Free Expression: Thoughts on Vigilance, Responsibility, Stewardship, Journalism Education, and the Demise of Value Systems' (2000) 23 *U. Ark. Little Rock L. Rev.* 81 at 110. Cf. IAU 'Resolution on the Protection of the Night Sky', IAU Gen. Ass. XXIII, 1997: '*Considering that* Proposals have been made repeatedly to place luminous objects in orbit round the Earth to carry messages of various kinds and that the implementation of such proposals would have a deleterious effect on astronomical observations, *and that* the night sky is the heritage of all humanity, which should therefore be preserved untouched, *Requests the* President to take steps with the appropriate authorities to ensure that the night sky receive no less protection than has been given to the world heritage sites on earth'. J.H. Huebert

not include the display of advertising on the side of a launch vehicle, as has been done by Pepsi on the Russian Proton launches.

Both passive and active satellites can affect visual astronomical observations, as can larger pieces of space debris. A sun-illuminated object or a strobing beacon passing across the field of an image can ruin an observation. The object need not be that large; what is important is its albedo.[128] The satellites of the Iridium constellation are themselves small, but 'Iridium flares' are visible to the human eye.[129] However, it is clear that the large constellations already under construction as well as others proposed will have deleterious effects on both forms of astronomy.[130] Again, any development of an orbiting solar power array system would necessarily affect visual astronomy, and radio astronomy might also be affected by the microwave down-links from the satellites. Any 'catcher' of solar radiation is bound to be large, so interference with astronomy is unavoidable.[131]

Apart from their mere existence in orbit, satellite radio emissions may affect the use of space.[132] Active satellites are 'active' because they require radio for their tracking, telemetry and tele-command as well as for the data and other communications that they receive and transmit. An active satellite is defined in the ITU Radio Regulations as 'a station located on an object which is beyond, is intended to go beyond, or has been beyond, the major portion of the Earth's atmosphere' (RR 1.64). More particularly, it is 'a satellite carrying a station intended to transmit or retransmit radiocommunication signals' (RR 1.180). Radio frequencies are a limited natural resource to be used 'rationally, efficiently and economically'.[133] It is therefore important that, when the satellite has served its function, it is possible to terminate its radio emissions.[134]

Whether passive or active satellites are concerned, their impact or effect on the environment of space is a matter clearly within the responsibility and competence of states that license space activities (OST Art. VI). In the consideration of whether to issue a licence, 'due regard to the corresponding interest of other states' should figure (OST Art. IX). So should any potentially harmful interference to the interests of other states, although that particular factor triggers only consultations with affected states and does not operate as a bar (also OST Art. IX).[135] Both active and passive satellites should go through the

---

and G. Block, 'In Defence of Advertising in Space' (2006) 49 *Proc. IISL* 479–489, argued in favour of no regulation, basing their view on concepts of property and free speech that are derived mainly from the US. For the US rules see supra n. 125, but note that these only apply to US-licensed launches.

128 Cf. *supra* n. 126. Albedo is the reflectivity of a body.

129 P.D. Maley and J.C. Pizzicaroli, 'The Visual Appearance of the Iridium Satellites' (2003) 52 *Acta Astronautica* 629–639. The website 'Heavens Above': https://heavens-above.com, provides data on expected Iridium flares.

130 See materials cited *supra* n. 42, the *Dark and Quiet Skies* Report, *supra* n. 44, and *Impact of Satellite Constellations on Optical Astronomy and Recommendations Toward Mitigations*, Workshop Report, American Astronomical Society, 2020: https://aas.org/sites/default/files/2020-08/SATCON1-Report.pdf.

131 See Chapter 17.

132 Reference point, *supra* n. 39.

133 ITU Constitution, Arts 44.1 and 2. See Chapter 8.

134 Originally, termination might occur through telecommand, short battery life or a timing device. Now, telecommand is required by the ITU Radio Regulations: 'Space stations shall be fitted with devices to ensure immediate cessation of their radio emissions by telecommand, whenever such cessation is required under the provisions of these Regulations' (RR 22.1.1). Some early US satellites could not be switched off and continued to broadcast on space-ideal frequencies long after their experiments had been hopelessly corrupted by solar and other radiation, thus rendering those frequencies unusable for many years.

135 See Chapter 3.

procedures for national and international registration outlined in Chapter 4. Active satellites should be licensed nationally and conform to the ITU requirements and procedures
outlined in Chapter 8.

While the procedures just referred to appear to work reasonably satisfactorily, recent
developments in smaller satellites, particularly cubesats, have placed strains on these systems.[136] Modern technology has produced micro-satellites (100–500 kg), nano-satellites
(1–10 kg), pico-satellites (0.1–1 kg) and even femto-satellites (less than 0.1 kg). Obviously cubesats are small, usually up to 10 cm. in all three dimensions, though some may
be up to one metre cubed. Some are used for weather-watching and other remote sensing
purposes. Constellations of cubesats provide telecommunication services.[137] Most cubesats
go into LEO and are intended to have a short life – down to days in some cases – and will
re-enter the atmosphere and burn up.[138] Coping with the regulatory duties of the licensing
states presents difficulties, and the ITU Radiocommunication Sector are under pressure
to cope with the notifications of spectrum assignment, and of orbits.[139] The other major
environmental point is, of course, that the presence of small satellites, particularly if in
large constellations, will affect launchings both into LEO and beyond. Collisions are likely
with debris resultant.

Space Traffic Management

Two events in 2021 demonstrate the need for a system traffic management in outer
space analogous to terrestrial air traffic control.[140] On 1 July and 21 October 2021, the

136 ITU-R, Hand Book on Small Satellites, 2023: www.itu.int/hub/publication/r-hdb-65-2023/?utm_source=
Publications&utm_campaign=56541b9c2d-EMAIL_CAMPAIGN_2023_10_02_01_14&utm_medium=
email&utm_term=0_-56541b9c2d-%5BLIST_EMAIL_ID%5D&ct=t(EMAIL_CAMPAIGN_smallsat_
handbook); I. Marboe, ed., *Small Satellites: Regulatory Challenges and Chances* (Leiden: Brill/Nijhoff,
2016); N. Palkovitz, *Regulating a Revolution: Small Satellites and the Law of Outer Space* (Leiden: Wolters
Kluwer, 2019); A. Froehlich, ed., *Legal Aspects Around Satellite Constellations* (Springer, 2021); P.B. Larsen,
'Small Satellite Legal Issues' (2017) 82 *J. Air Law & Comm.* 275–310; D.M. Bielicki, 'Legal Aspects of Satellite Constellations' (2020) 45 *Air and Sp. L.* 245–264; H.A. Simpson, 'Regulating Science Fiction: The
Regulatory Deficiencies in a Rapidly Growing Commercial Space Industry' (2022) 87 *J. Air L. & Comm.*
759–797. See also www.nasa.gov/mission_pages/cubesats/index.html.
137 See GAO Report *supra* n. 115. The US FCC Second Report and Order (IB Docket Nos. 22–271 and
18–313) 'In the Matter of Space Innovation; Mitigation of Orbital Debris in the New Space Age', adopted
6 October 2022, will *require* the deorbiting of satellites from LEO (at or below 2000km) by no later than
5 years from the end of mission. The Order does not apply to satellites already in orbit. The previous Order
recommended deorbiting within 25 years. (emphases added). The new Order will come into effect in 2024.
   In 2020 the FCC conditionally licensed Kuiper Systems LLC, to establish a non-geostationary constellation
system subject to later approval of debris mitigation measures to be adopted: Kuiper Systems LLC, Application
for Authority to Deploy and Operate a Ka-band Non-Geostationary Satellite Orbit System, Order and Authorization, 35 FCC Rcd 8324 (2020). In February 2023, being satisfied with suitable proposals, it approved the
modification of that authorization: In the Matter of Kuiper Systems LLC Request for Modification of the
Authorization for the Kuiper NGSO Satellite System, DA 23–114 (2023) FCC Rcd (not yet available).
138 An accompanying cubesat monitored the impact in the DART project, *infra* n. 253.
139 See WRC-15 Res. 659, on 'Studies to accommodate requirements in the space operation service for non-
geostationary satellites with short duration missions', and the Radiocommunication Sector Report ITU –
R SA.2312–0 (09/2014), 'Characteristics, definitions and spectrum requirements of nanosatellites and
picosatellites, as well as systems composed of such satellites' of 2014: www.itu.int/pub/R-REP-SA.2312, or
www.itu.int/dms_pub/itu-r/opb/rep/R-REP-SA.2312-2014-PDF-E.pdf. Cf. *supra* n. 136.
140 P.J. Blount, 'Space Traffic Management: Standardizing on-Orbit Behavior' (2019) 113 AJIL Unbound
120–124.

Chinese space station took evasive action because of close encounters with Starlink-1095 and Starlink-2305 and raised the matter through UN OOSA.[141] In its response, the US outlined the measures it has made publicly available to avoid such problems.[142] While these are directed to the safety of human space flight, their general use would seem a good development. Any lack of communication between different national outer space activities creates uncertainties and endangers space traffic in increasingly congested outer space.[143]

A proper system of space traffic management would have many aspects.[144] As discussed in Chapter 6 on the boundary question, the transit of spacecraft through state air space on launch or re-entry requires coordination with relevant air traffic control. These controlled air space measures are required to ensure the safe launch and re-entry through areas used by LEO satellite systems such as Iridium, Starlink and others, as well as the new constellations of cubesats.[145] In space itself there is the question of the use of orbits. Various orbits are better suited for certain purposes than others: polar and near-polar orbits are ideal for certain types of remote sensing; the geostationary orbit is excellent for telecommunications and direct broadcasting.

It would make sense to rationalise the use made of these orbits so that the best can be got from space. The sensible step would be to go to a world regulatory organisation, but the surrender by states of even some control to an international regime or body seems unlikely.[146] That said the 2018 US Presidential Directive on National Space Traffic Management Policy, SPD-3, is to be welcomed.[147] More launch licensing states need to adopt similar measures.

141 Note verbale, A/AC.105/1262.

142 Note verbale, A/AC.105/1265. The US facility is available through www. spacetrack.org. China does not make use of it, probably for political reasons.

143 T. Masson-Zwaan and Yun Zhao, 'Towards an International Regime for Space Traffic Management' (2023) 48 *Air and Sp. L.* 75–92; P.B. Larsen, 'Space Traffic Management Standards' (2018) 83 *J. Air L. & Comm.* 359–387; P.B. Larsen, 'Minimum International Norms for Managing Space Traffic, Space Debris and Near Earth Object Impacts' (2018) 83 *J. Air L. & Comm.* 739–785; P.B. Larsen, 'Small Satellite Legal Issues' (2017) 82 *J. Air L. & Comm.* 275–310. See also early suggestions: C. Contant-Jorgenson, P. Lala and K-U. Schrögl, eds., *Space Traffic Management*, IAF Cosmic Study (Paris: IAA, 2006); www.iaaweb.org/iaa/Studies/spacetraffic.pdf; C. Contant-Jorgenson et al., 'The IAA Cosmic Study on Space Traffic Management' (2006) 22 *Space Policy* 283–288; L. Perek, 'Traffic Rules for Outer Space' (1982) 25 *Proc. IISL* 37; P.B. Larsen, 'Outer Space Traffic Management: Space Situational Awareness Requires Transparency' (2008) 51 *Proc. IISL* 338–350; P. van Fenema, 'Suborbital Flights and ICAO' (2005) 30 *Air and Sp. Law* 396–411; K-U. Schrögl, 'Space Traffic Management' ESPI Flash Report #3, October 2007: www.espi.or.at/images/stories/dokumente/flash_reports/stmflashrep3f2.pdf. See also Chapter 6 *ad. fin*. Space Traffic Management.

Iridium Satellite LLC (www.iridium.com/) provides worldwide voice and data communications using a system of sixty-six (as of 2023) satellites in six orbital planes in low earth polar orbit. Cf. Maley, *supra* n. 129. See also Chapter 10.

144 Cf. US Space Policy Directive – 3, National Space Traffic Management Policy, 2018: https://trumpwhitehouse.archives.gov/presidential-actions/space-policy-directive-3-national-space-traffic-management-policy/.

145 Marboe and Froehlich, both *supra* n. 136. Iridium Satellite LLC, *supra* n. 143. (www.iridium.com/) provides worldwide services. Starlink: www.starlink.com/satellites. Starlink provides services through a LEO constellation. See discussions of these in Chapter 11. See also *supra* at n. 136 ff re cubesats. Cf. Maley, *supra* n. 129.

146 B. McClintock et al., *International Space Traffic Management: Charting a Course for Long-Term Sustainability* (2023) Rand Corp. Research Report: www.rand.org/pubs/research_reports/RRA1949-1.html. See also The Cluttered Neighbourhood in Chapter 17.

147 Presidential Directive on National Space Traffic Management Policy, SPD-3, 2018: https://trumpwhitehouse.archives.gov/presidential-actions/space-policy-directive-3-national-space-traffic-management-policy/.

Knowledge is important. Awareness of the location and orbital details of space objects and debris is necessary. Space objects under active control such as the International Space Station (ISS) can be moved to avoid potential problems.[148] There are a number of methods for attaining what is occasionally, if inelegantly, categorised as 'space situational awareness'.[149] The OOSA registry mandated by the UN Registration Convention provides useful information about the whereabouts of space objects and whether they are active or passive. The ITU Master International Frequency Register (MIFR) is also a valuable source of information on both location and the nature of space objects registered with the ITU.[150] Furthermore, the United States, Russia and ESA have established surveillance networks to identify both civilian and military space objects. Military space objects are often clouded in secrecy and tracking may be the only way to know their location and movements.[151]

Direct space traffic control is exercised through individual states imposing operating conditions when they authorise outer space activities. Launching states in particular have to take into consideration where the payload is destined for, and any potential impediments on the route. A proposed European Code of Conduct[152] was essentially a movement for greater situational awareness in outer space operations. Adoption of the Code, the provisions of which lie well within the framework of the OST, could provide greater certainty, predictability and safety of space flight.

Individual states are coming to realise that unilateral monitoring and oversight is insufficient for assurance of safety. Some international coordination is necessary, and coordination could eventually widen and evolve into international standards. The draft Code of 2014 has been swept into more general discussions on disarmament and is stalemated. However, the EU and ESA are moving towards a separate STM system.[153]

Space Debris

Over the years much has been discussed and more written about space debris. Technical reports have been compiled and guidelines elaborated. Suggestions and views have been

---

148 The ISS orbit is regularly adjusted to avoid potential collision with debris and other space objects.
149 S. Hobe, 'Space traffic management: some conceptual ideas' (2016) 65 ZLW 3–21; B.D. Green, 'Space Situational Awareness Data Sharing: Safety Tool or Security Threat' (2016) 37 *A.F.L. Rev.* 39–134; S. Mosteshar. 'Space Situational Awareness: Need, Solutions and Some Consequences' (2013) 62 ZLW 719–727. See also the US 'spacetrack' service, *supra* n. 142. Cf. the IAA, IAF and IISL Memorandum of Understanding on a 'Cooperative initiative to develop comprehensive approaches and proposals for Space Traffic Management (STM)' (2022): https://iisl.space/iisl-iaa-and-iaf-conclude-major-report-on-stm/.
150 Cf. P. De Man, 'The relevance of ITU regulations for clarifying the space debris and strengthening guidelines on the removal of satellites at the end of their functional life' (2013) AASL 203–236.
151 Editorial, 'Russia's Orbital Provocations', *Space News,* 7 November 2015, at 14. In 2015, Intelsat civilian satellites experienced uncomfortably close encounters with Russian military satellites. The Russian satellite involved was intentionally located between two Intelsat satellites that were practically co-located. Apparently, the Russian satellite was only some 5 kilometres from one Intelsat satellite.
152 See Draft International Code of Conduct for Outer Space Activities, 2014: www.eeas.europa.eu/archives/docs/non-proliferation-and-disarmament/pdf/space_code_conduct_draft_vers_31-march-2014_en.pdf. An earlier draft is at http://:eeas.europa.eu/non-proliferation-and-disarmament/pdf/space_code_conduct_draft_vers_16_sept_2013_en.pdf. See also M.J. Listner, 'The International Code of Conduct: Comments on changes in the latest draft and post-mortem thoughts', *The Space Review,* 26 October 2015: www.thespacereview.com/article/2851/1.
153 'An EU Approach for Space Traffic Management', ESA/EU Joint Communication to the European Parliament and the Council: JOIN(2022) 4 final, 15.2.2022. See STM in Chapter 17.

diverse.[154] However, it remains a fact that for the present, the mitigation of space debris is a matter of voluntary action, not of clear legal duty, although individual space agencies do seek to conform to the Space Debris Mitigation Guidelines.[155] It remains another fact that precise measures for the mitigation of space debris will remain a subject of discussion for years to come.

In the early days of space, various launch elements – spent boosters, cones, explosive bolts – were simply abandoned to go where they might.[156] Some material has been deliberately jettisoned in space.[157] Yet other material has been lofted briefly into space for memorial purposes.[158] Other materials have simply been lost, including a glove, a camera, a tool bag[159] and even a golf ball.[160]

Now we have major problems to confront. Space debris is largely the result of the break-up of satellites, whether through collision or deliberate destruction,[161] and by the

154 P.B. Larsen, 'Solving the Space Debris Crisis' (2018) 83 *J. Air Law & Comm.* 475–520; H. Alshamsi et al., 'As the Grapefruit Turns Sixty, It's Time to Get Serious about Clean up in Outer Space' (2018) 83 *J. Air Law & Comm.* 45–66. For early materials see H.A. Baker, *Space Debris: Legal and Policy Implications* (Dordrecht: Nijhoff, 1989) and his 'Liability for Damage Caused by Space Debris' (1988) XII AASL 183–225; IAA Cosmic Study, 'Orbital Debris' (1993) 31 *Acta Astronautica* 168–191; Schafer, *supra* n. 1; COPUOS Scientific and Technical Subcommittee, 'Technical Report on Space Debris' A/AC.105/720, 1999. See also *infra* n. 171.

155 IADC Guidelines, *infra* n. 191. For US measures see 'Process for Limiting Orbital Debris', NASA – ATD– 8719.14C: www.nasa.gov/sites/default/files/atoms/files/process_for_limiting_orbital_debris.pdf. The 77-page document goes into useful detail while justifying its requirements. It makes plain that debris can be a problem in many areas and at a variety of altitudes. All missions where NASA has an involvement are to be planned so as to comply with the requirements of the Standard (paras 1.2 and 4.6.1.f). See also Space Policy Directive 3 (2018) www.federalregister.gov/documents/2018/06/21/2018-13521/national-space-traffic-management-policy.

156 See the Leolabs visual representation of the problem: https://platform.leolabs.space/visualizations/leo#view=objectType.

157 Garbage and urine have been jettisoned from various space vehicles. The piano-sized Early Ammonia Servicer was dumped from the ISS in summer 2007 in accordance with the ISS Jettison Policy of 2006. It re-entered the atmosphere on 2 November 2008 over Alabama with unconsumed debris falling between Australia and New Zealand: www.spaceflightnow.com/news/n0811/03eas/; www.msnbc.msn.com/id/27479972/; www.msnbc.msn.com/id/2747997. Cf. N.L. Johnson, 'The New Jettison Policy for the International Space Station' (2006) 38 *Adv. Sp. Research* 2077–2083. For predictions of re-entries see links at www.aerospace.org/cords/. Normally ISS garbage is packed into an unmanned re-supply Russian 'Progress' vehicle and is destroyed along with it on its atmospheric re-entry, usually over the Pacific.

158 Celestial Memorial Spaceflights has sent the ashes of various persons into space, including those of Timothy Leary ('druggies' guru of the 1980s), Gene Roddenberry (Star Trek) and James Doohan ('Scotty', Star Trek). Destinations offered include a brief entry to space, Earth orbit, lunar orbit or surface and deep space: www.celestis.com/. Unrelatedly, a small phial of the ashes of C.W. Tombaugh, discoverer of Pluto, was carried on the New Horizons mission which passed Pluto in 2015.

159 White lost a glove on the first space-walk, Collins a camera from Gemini-10. Stefanyshyn-Piper lost her tool bag on a Shuttle spacewalk on 18 October 2008.

160 In November 2006, a Russian, Mikhail Tyurin, hit a golf-ball from the ISS, the event being videoed and used as publicity for Element 21, a Toronto manufacturer of golf equipment. The ball was likely to remain orbit for only some three days.

161 In 2009, Cosmos 2251, an inactive Russian satellite, collided with Iridium 33, an active satellite, over Siberia. The collision could have been avoided. The US has altered its tracking/prediction practices in the hope that there will be no similar occurrence. See Secure World Foundation, '2009 Iridium – Cosmos Collision Fact Sheet', 2010, updated 2012: https://swfound.org/media/6575/swf_iridium_cosmos_collision_fact_sheet_updated_2012.pdf. In January 2007 China destroyed its Fengyun-IC weather satellite at an altitude of some 575 miles/925 km, resulting in a debris field. The US destroyed its malfunctioning and uncontrollable US-193 on 30 January 2008 at a height of some 130 miles/247 km to prevent possible

collision of existing debris including spent launcher vehicles and their parts. The fear is that orbital debris may accrue even to the preclusion of access to outer space unless new debris is curtailed, and existing debris fields diminished if not wholly removed.[162] Even if some debris does not persist in orbit, while there, it is a danger. Materials in lower orbits travel at least at 7 km per second so the kinetic energy of a collision can be considerable.[163] There is also the Kessler syndrome,[164] the risk that one collision will produce many fragments that then trigger others in a domino or cascade effect with each collision causing fragmentation into yet smaller fragments, resulting in an ever-increasing number of collisions and yet further debris. Eventually a belt of debris would be created in a particular orbit, which could imperil any space object passing through it.[165]

An intriguing question is whether pieces of space debris may be considered to be space objects for the purposes of the space law treaties. Debris is not specifically dealt with in the OST because its importance was not recognised at the time the Treaty was negotiated.[166] However, terrestrial international environmental law and the ruminations of the ILC could be built on conceptually.[167] The duty to protect the environment of areas beyond the jurisdiction of states should extend to Earth orbit.[168]

---

surface damage were it to re-enter the atmosphere intact. See G.T. Lyons III, 'New Habits and Hard Law: Putting Old Soft Law "Sanctions" and the Space Debris Epidemic out to Pasture' (2014) *J. Sp. L.* 453–479 at 457–462; CoCoSL I, 85–86, para 65.

162 UNGA Res. 76/76 (2021) para 16 '*Considers* that it is essential that Member States pay more attention to the gradually increasing probability of collisions of space objects, especially those with nuclear power sources, with space debris, and other aspects of space debris . . .' Cf. Sec. 1, para 1 *ad fin* of the Space Debris Mitigation Guidelines, cited *infra* n. 188: 'The prompt implementation of appropriate debris mitigation measures in therefore considered a prudent and necessary step towards preserving the outer space environment for future generations.'

163 Before starting a return to Earth, the Shuttle heat shield was always inspected to see that it had developed no holes through collision with debris. The 14th ISS mission in May–June 2007 installed a variety of shields intended to protect vulnerable parts of the ISS from damage through collision with space debris. Cf. *Final Report of the International Space Station Independent Safety Task Force*, February 2007: www.nasa.gov/pdf/170368main_IIST_%20Final%20Report.pdf; and *Protecting the Space Shuttle from Meteoroids and Orbital Debris* (Washington: National Academies Press, 1997): http://books.nap.edu/catalog.php?record_id=5958.

164 D.J. Kessler and B.G. Cour-Palais, 'Collision Frequency of Artificial Satellites: The Creation of a Debris Belt (1978) 83 *J. Geophysical Research*, 2637–2646 at 2644–2645: http://webpages.charter.net/dkessler/files/Collision%20Frequency.pdf. See also Leolabs, 'Today's Conjunctions': https://platform.leolabs.space/visualizations/conjunctions/today; and *infra* n. 165.

165 A number of articles cited in this chapter outline cascade problems. China's destruction of its weather satellite in 2007 (*supra* n. 161) produced a debris-ridden LEO belt; see also www.space.com/news/070202_china_spacedebris.html and www.technovelgy.com/ct/Science-Fiction-News.asp?NewsNum=931. On 19 February 2007 the Breeze M upper stage of a Russian Proton launcher exploded, its propellant not having been fully exhausted: http://news.bbc.co.uk/go/pr/fr/-/1/hi/sci/tech/6398513.stm. US 193 destroyed on 21 February 2008 as it was about to enter denser atmosphere appears not to have caused major debris problems (see Wikipedia, 'USA 193'). F. Walsh, 'Forging a Diplomatic Shield for American Satellites: The Case for Re-evaluating the 2006 National Space Policy in Light of a Chinese Satellite System' (2007) 72 *J. Air L. Com.* 759–99. CoCoSL I, 85–86, para 65.

166 M. Lachs, 'The Treaty on Principles of the Law of Outer Space, 1961–1992' (1992) 39 *Neth. Int. L. Rev.* 291–302 at 298. Thus M.S. McDougal, H.D. Lasswell and I.A. Vlasic, *Law and Public Order in Space* (New Haven and London: Yale UP, 1963) 533–534, 620–625, and 733–734, write of the legal effects of collisions between spacecraft, but not about debris (which is not indexed in the book).

167 See text *supra* at n. 17 ff.

168 Cf. Resolution 5 of the Sixty-Sixth ILA Conference, Buenos Aires, 1994, which annexes an 'International Instrument on the Protection of the Environment from Damage Caused by Space Debris', *International*

A harbinger of such a duty can be seen in the relocation of some spent satellites to orbits remoter than the geostationary. It is good practice to push older defunct geostationary satellites into graveyard orbits if not to send them on a sunwards course, thus making available their former geostationary slots.[169] The 1992 UNGA 'Principles Relevant to the Use of Nuclear Power Sources in Outer Space' dealt with above shed further light.[170] Principles 3.2 (a)(ii), 3.2.(b) and 3.3 speak of 'high' orbits into which a satellite carrying a nuclear power source should be placed at the end of its mission, there to stay until the nuclear fuel and its containment chamber have decayed to safe radiation levels.

Again, various space debris mitigation guidelines indicate that other satellites and launch vehicles should be deorbited once their operational phase is complete or else their orbits relocated so as to avoid the LEO region. However, such satellites and objects are not themselves debris, even though collisions with them may produce it. They remain identifiable space objects that are the responsibility of (as well as being under the jurisdiction) of their state of registry (OST, Arts VI and VIII) and they should remain controlled at least until parked.

However, the point about much space debris is that it is not always readily identifiable, and certainly is not really under the control of whichever state was responsible for the initial launch that produced it. There can be exceptions. Spent boosters, spent manoeuvring stages, launcher cones and shrouds, for example, appear in some entries in the UN 'Register of Objects Launched into Space' (ST/SG/Ser.) and are identifiable, but lacking propulsion or tele-command facilities, they are no longer controllable. Nor are the many fragments that are in orbit.[171]

If pieces of debris are in fact identifiable, they may come within the scope of the Liability Convention, Art. I.d of which specifically includes as a space object 'component parts of a space object as well as its launch vehicle and parts thereof'. Thus, perhaps contingent on precisely what is a 'part', and perhaps also contingent on size, particular pieces of space debris might be subject to the provisions of the Convention, provided that their origin can be identified.[172] Any prospect of liability should have a deterrent effect on the avoidable production of space debris.

The threat to spacecraft and to astronauts from space debris is very real. Space debris is monitored by the radar facilities of a number of states, and their results are coordinated through the US Space Force Command. Satellites and the ISS have altered orbit to avoid

---

Law Association, Report of the Sixth-Sixth Conference (London: International Law Association, 1995) 7–15, with Report and Final Text of the Space Law Committee of the ILA, M. Williams, ed., at 304–325.

169 See *supra* n. 119 and *infra* text at n. 192.

170 See *supra* at nn. 71 and 99.

171 See the early pages of J.P. Lampertius, 'The Need for an Effective Liability Regime for Damage Caused by Debris in Outer Space' (1992) 13 *Mich. J. Int. L.* 447–468; C.D. Williams, 'Space: The Cluttered Frontier' (1995) *J. Air L. & Comm.* 1139–1189; J.M. Seymour, 'Containing the Cosmic Crisis: A Proposal for Curbing the Perils of Space Debris' (1998) *Geo. Int. Env. L. Rev.* 891–914. Cf. T. Beer, 'The Specific Risks Associated with Collisions in Outer Space and the Return to Earth of Space Objects – the Legal Perspective' (2000) 25 *Air Sp. L.* 42–50; J.-C. Liou, 'Collision Activities in the Future Orbital Debris Environment' (2006) 38 *Adv. in Sp. Res.* 2102–2106; J. Bendisch et al., 'The MASTER-2001 Model' (2004) 34 *Adv. in Sp. Res.* 959–968; C.S.L. Keay, 'Pollution Potentials in Interplanetary Space' (1998) 21 *Adv. in Sp. Res.* 1603–1606; R. Walker and C.E. Martin, 'Cost-effective and Robust Mitigation of Space Debris in Low Earth Orbit' (2004) 34 *Adv. in Sp. Res.* 1233–1240.

172 CoCoSL III, 618–619, paras 15–17.

debris, but collisions have occurred.[173] Science acknowledges that more will occur.[174] The debris field around the Earth continues to grow, worryingly for telecommunications since the geostationary orbit is a 'debris cluster area' which gravity will not cleanse within any foreseeable period.[175] The issue therefore arises as to the steps to be taken to limit the problem.

Obviously other steps have to be taken, but for lawyers, the question is whether binding legal obligation is the best route. There is the Liability Convention,[176] but its Art. 3 makes proof of fault necessary to constitute liability for damage caused by a space object elsewhere than on the surface of the Earth or to aircraft in flight. There certainly is a case for a mutual insurance fund to meet damages claims caused by orbital debris to be contributed to by the space active.[177] There may also be a case for encouraging dedicated salvage firms to recover spent satellites through subsidies from a consortium of space agencies and commercial space users, but in the interim, basically the creation of space debris has to be lessened.

Ex facie, the best way in which to achieve international law in precision would be through the articulation of the required rules in a formal treaty, accepted by as many states as possible, and certainly in this case including all states which are space-competent.[178] We

---

173 A number of satellites have unexpectedly ceased functioning. It has occasionally been assumed that this has been because of a collision with debris or a meteorite. Thus in March 2006 the Russian Express-AM11 satellite failed on being hit by another object: http://news.skymania.com/2006/04/collision-knocks-out-satellite.html. Although the data was only published in 2008, the first known instance of a collision between identified objects is that a Russian non-functional navigation satellite, Cosmos 1934 (1988–023A, US Satellite Number 18985) and debris from Cosmos 926 in December 1991: www.spaceref.com/news/viewsr.html?pid=16201. On 16 July 1996 the UK Cerise satellite was hit by a fragment of Ariane V-16. Its stabilisation boom was halved by the impact, but the satellite continued to function: www.satobs.org/seesat/Aug-1996/0110.html; www.tbs-satellite.com/tse/online/sat_cerise.html. Cf. M.N. Sweeting et al., 'CERISE Microsatellite Recovery from First Detected Collision in Low Earth Orbit' (2004) 55 *Acta Astronautica* 139–147. In January 2005 the US rocket body (1974-015B, US Sat. no. 07219) collided with a fragment (1999-057CV, US Sat. no. 26207) from the third stage of a Chinese CZ-4 launch vehicle, which had exploded in March 2000: www.spaceref.com/news/viewsr.html?pid=16201. That report includes the statement that 'Currently, hundreds of close approaches (i.e. passes within less than one kilometre) between catalogued objects occur on a daily basis'. The orbit of the ISS is altered as necessary to avoid passing debris.

174 See ESA conference proceedings on NEOs and Debris: https://conference.sdo.esoc.esa.int/proceedings/packages.
   Cf. IAA, 'Position Paper on Space Debris Mitigation, Implementing Zero Debris Creation Zones' 15 October 2005: www.iaaweb.org/iaa/Studies/spacedebrismitigation.pdf. Cf. R.E. Glickman, 'Estimating Collision Probability for Coincident Satellite Constellations' AIAA-96-3635-CP: http://pdf.aiaa.org/preview/1996/PV1996_3635.pdf; S. Alfano, 'Satellite Collision Probability Enhancements' (2006) 29 *J. Guidance, Control and Dynamics* 588-92: www.centerforspace.com/downloads/files/pubs/JGCD.V29.N03.pdf, and their citations; T. Yasaka, 'Space Debris Protection: A Standard Procedure in Future' (2003) 53 *Acta Astronautica* 527–531.

175 M. Meija-Kaiser, 'Out into the Dark: Removing Space Debris from the Geostationary Orbit' (2019) 62 *Proc. IISL* 513–526; R.S. Jakhu, 'Legal Issues of Satellite Telecommunications, The Geostationary Orbit and Space Debris' (2007) 5 *Astropolitics*, 173–208. See also n. 119.

176 Convention on the Registration of Objects Launched into Outer Space, 14 January 1975; 1023 UNTS 15; (1978) UKTS 70, Cmnd. 7271; TIAS 8480; (1975) 14 ILM 43. See *supra* Chapter 4.

177 M.J. Sundahl, 'Unidentified Orbital Debris: The Case for a Market-Share Liability Regime' (2000) 24 *Hastings Int. Comp. L. Rev.* 125–154; Larsen, *supra* n. 151.

178 Cf. K-H. Böcksteigel, 'ILA Draft Convention on Space Debris' (1995) 44 ZLW 28–34. Schafer, *supra* n. 1, at 31–9, suggested a UN Office of Outer Space Environmental Protection.

will suggest in our final chapter that a legally binding instrument dealing with space debris would be a welcome development, while recognising that another space treaty may be unlikely. Short of that the next best is a set of principles elaborated through the Committee on the Peaceful Uses of Outer Space and then adopted, preferably without vote, by the General Assembly of the United Nations.[179]

However, a legal duty to use space for the benefit of all is already enshrined in OST Art. I, and having regard to the 'interests of other states' and the avoidance of 'harmful interference' with the activities of others is already incorporated in OST Art. IX. There have been calls for these rather vague statements to be supplemented or crystallised so that they may be used to lessen the problem of space debris,[180] but apart from the difficulty of getting a comprehensive agreement on a treaty text,[181] a major problem would be one of enforcement. While such would constrain a responsible launch authority, and might constrain an irresponsible launch authority a little, how could one attach either a civil or criminal penalty to conduct which does not mitigate space debris? A decision, whether advisory or in a contentious proceeding, of the International Court would not seem either appropriate or effective. Meantime, the self-interest of space agencies and authorities is not without effect, and efforts to diminish space debris remain recommendations and non-binding practices as applied in national licensing requirements.[182]

The major international mitigation protagonist has been the now thirteen-member Inter-Agency Space Debris Coordination Committee (IADC).[183] As ESA is a member, it is not surprising that European launching states have adopted a similar set of guidelines and procedures.[184] Continuing the policy of its predecessors,[185] the US has an extensive set

179 See previous note.
180 J.S. Goehring, 'Can We Address Orbital Debris with the International Law We Already Have? An Examination of Treaty Interpretation and the Due Regard Principle' (2020) 85 *J. Air L. & Comm.* 309–340; N.D. Welly, 'Enlightened State Interest – A Legal Framework for Protecting the "Common Interest of All Mankind" from Hardinian Tragedy' (2010) 36 *J. Sp. L.* 273–313; See also *supra* n. 168. Cf. V. Kopal, 'Present International Law Principles Applicable to Space Debris and the Need for their Supplement', in *Proc. Second European Conference on Space Debris*, Darmstadt, 1997 [ESA SP-393] (Noordwijk: ESA, 1997) at 739–747, and M. Benkö and K-U. Schrögl, 'Space Debris in the United Nations: Aspects of Law and Policy', at 749–757. Cf. *Proceedings of the First Conference on Space Debris*, Darmstadt Germany, 1993 (ESA SD-01) – Legal aspects at 673–707; *Proceedings of the Second Conference on Space Debris*, Darmstadt, Germany 1997, ESA SP-393 (SD-02) – Legal Aspects at 739–62; *Proceedings of the Third Conference on Space Debris*, Darmstadt, Germany, 2001. 2 vols (ESA SP-473) – Legal Aspects at vol. 2, 853–881.
181 Mirmina, *infra* n. 64, at 652–654.
182 P.B. Larsen, 'Profit or Safety: Where is Outer Space Headed?' (2021) 86 *J. Air Law & Comm.* 531–591; S. Mirmina, 'Reducing the Proliferation of Orbital Debris: Alternatives to a Legally Binding Instrument' (2005) AJIL 649–662.
183 Current IADC members are Canada, China, France, Germany, India, Italy, Japan, South Korea, Russia, UK, Ukraine, US, and ESA: www.iadc-home.org/.
184 The European, 'Code of Conduct for Space Debris Mitigation, 2004': ESA/IRC(2004)20, Appendix A: cf. www.esa.int/SPECIALS/ESOC/SEMZPBW797E_0.html.
185 US Space Policy, 2006 (G.W. Bush) para 11 (2007) XXXII AASL 475–486: www.ostp.gov/html/US%20National%20Space%20Policy.pdf. Cf. para (7) of the section on 'Intersector Guidelines' of the US Space Policy, 1996 (Clinton) www.fas.org/spp/military/docops/national/nstc-8.htm. The 1988 US National Space Policy 1988 was the first to include a provision as to debris: 'Presidential Directive on National Space Policy 1988, *Space Law: Selected Basic Documents* (2nd ed.), Committee on Commerce, Science, and Transportation; US Senate, 95th Cong. 2nd Sess., December 1978 (USGPO), 449–468.

of rules, regulations and procedures.[186] India has also implemented measures in its space programme.[187]

The Space Debris Mitigation Guidelines[188]

The formal definition of space debris has been elusive. Even so, major progress was made in 2007 when the UN General Assembly approved COPUOS' endorsement of a set of voluntary guidelines for space debris mitigation (SDM).[189] These, the Space Debris Mitigation Guidelines, state the following: 'For the purpose of this document, space debris is defined as man-made objects, including fragments and elements thereof, in Earth orbit or re-entering the atmosphere, that are non-functional.' However, the Guidelines do not form a binding legal document. Observance is voluntary.

While COPUOS was discussing the endorsement of the Guidelines some delegations were of the view that since the Guidelines were voluntary and legally non-binding, they were insufficient and to the disadvantage of the developing countries. They therefore argued that the Legal Subcommittee should rather develop a legally binding framework (para 123). Others thought the guidelines should be presented to the Assembly simply as a draft resolution to stress their importance, as well as draw attention to the effectiveness of COPUOS in space matters (para 125).[190] Yet others thought the guidelines would need to be reviewed, as they did not cover all debris-producing situations (para 128).

The SDM Guidelines, based on similar guidelines prepared by the IADC, were remarkably successful.[191] Commending them UNGA Resolution 62/217 recognised that the

---

186 For the 2018 US policy see Space Policy Directive-3 (2018) www.federalregister.gov/documents/2018/06/21/2018-13521/national-space-traffic-management-policy. See the National Orbital Debris Implementation Plan, July 2022: www.whitehouse.gov/wp-content/uploads/2022/07/07-2022-NATIONAL-ORBITAL-DEBRIS-IMPLEMENTATION-PLAN.pdf. The NASA Orbital Debris Program Office plays a major role: https://orbitaldebris.jsc.nasa.gov/. Technical standards are at https://standards.nasa.gov/nasa-technical-standards, with directives available through the NASA Online Directives Information System: https://nodis3.gsfc.nasa.gov/main_lib.cfm. See also the NASA Office of Safety and Assurance: https://sma.nasa.gov/home. Cf. on constellations *supra* n. 115, and the 2022 FCC Order, *supra* n. 137. In early 2023, the FAA proposed fining SpaceX for not disclosing its pre-launch data: www.faa.gov/newsroom/faa-proposes-175000-fine-against-spacex-not-submitting-required-pre-launch-data: www.satellitetoday.com/launch/2023/02/17/faa-seeks-175000-fine-against-spacex-for-not-submitting-data-before-a-starlink-launch/?oly_enc_id=8020G6675790B5S.
187 V. Adimurthy and A.S. Ganeshan, 'Space Debris Mitigation in India' (2005) 58 *Acta Astronautica* 168–174.
188 The SDM Guidelines: www.unoosa.org/documents/pdf/spacelaw/sd/COPUOS-GuidelinesE.pdf, the 2007 COPUOS Report (A/62/20) paras 116–128, and Annex; and CoCoSL III, 625–629, with analysis 630–642. Cf. the Report of the Scientific and Technical Subcommittee, 44th Sess. 12–23 February 2007, A/AC.105/890, and earlier reports. See also S. Hobe and J.H. Mey, 'UN Space Debris Mitigation Guidelines' (2009) 58 ZLW 388–403; P.B. Larsen, 'Solving the Space Debris Crisis' (2018) 83 *J. Air. L. & Comm.* 475–519.
189 'International cooperation in the peaceful uses of outer space', UNGA Res. 62/217, para 26, part of the Resolution adopted without vote. Six states voted against para 42, an endorsement of the work plan for the UN SPIDER programme: see Annex III to www.un.org/press/en/2007/ga10684.doc.htm. L. Perek, 'Space Debris at the United Nations' (2002) 2 *Space Debris* 123–136 narrates proceedings within the UN to its date. See also CoCoSL III, 611–616; Larsen, *supra* n. 182.
190 See Chapter 2 as to the effectiveness of a UNGA Resolution. The 'advertising' value of the proposal is uncertain.
191 For IADC membership, see *supra* n. 183. For the current IADC Guidelines, IADC-02-01 Revision 3 (3rd ed. 2020) see www.iadc-home.org/documents_public/view/id/172#u; or https://iadc-home.

2007 Guidelines reflected then current state practice. Although voluntary, they have been adopted by states and implemented in national regulations as de facto international standards.[192] While their observance does not end the long debate over space debris, it will probably result in a moratorium on the discussion about whether space debris should be controlled as a matter of law or rely on voluntary practice.[193] Voluntary practice rather than legal duty seems likely to remain the *modus operandi*, unless an argument prevails that the creation of space debris is potentially harmful interference with the activities of other states contrary to OST Art. IX.

The following are the Guidelines:

1. Limit debris released during normal operations.[194]

In short, space systems should be engineered so to minimise, if not eliminate, debris. The guideline does not define 'space systems', but likely they would include both the satellite and its launch vehicle. Should total elimination not be possible, space systems should minimise debris during both the launch and the entire lifetime of the space object. Permitted space debris would include materials related to that launch, including sensor covers and mechanisms for separation and deployment. It is also in the interest of the launch facility that launch vehicles be designed to drop initial debris close to the launch location because the launch facilities are usually constructed with a proximate safety zone.[195]

2. Minimize the potential for break-ups during operational phases.[196]

---

org/documents_public/view/search_field/eNortjI2tlJy1CsuTcpKTS7RdtTLS8xNBVIlielAMjk_ryQ1r-6RYyRpcMAypDUU~/search_keyword/eNortjI0sFJKL81MSc3JzEstVrIGXDA2ZQXx/page/1/id/82#u.

192 As of 2023, it is not clear to us whether agencies tend to comply with the COPUOS or the current IADC Guidelines or both. See also 'International Standards', *infra* n. 212. UN OOSA maintains a 'Compendium of space debris mitigation standards adopted by States and International Organizations': www.unoosa.org/oosa/en/ourwork/topics/space-debris/compendium.html; Larsen, *supra* n. 188. Cf. the 2022 FCC rule to require the de-orbit of defunct satellites within five years of end of life, *supra* n. 137.

The ITU Radiocommunication Assembly has adopted Recommendation ITU – R S.1003–2 'Environmental protection of the geostationary – satellite orbit' (Geneva: ITU, 2011): www.itu.int/dms_pubrec/itu-r/rec/s/R-REC-S.1003-2-201012-I!!PDF-E.pdf, which contains provisions as to debris as well as to other matters. See also *supra* n. 119.

193 But see CoCoSL III, 648–651 (paras 85–91) for suggestions by V. Kopal as to further normative development, and a Czech proposal of 2011 for another UNGA Resolution, A/AC.105/C.2/L.283, CoCoSL III, 653–657.

194 COPUOS comment: 'Space systems should be designed not to release debris during normal operations. If this is not feasible, the effect of any release of debris on the outer space environment should be minimized. During the early decades of the space age, launch vehicle and spacecraft designers permitted the intentional release of numerous mission-related objects into Earth orbit, including, among other things, sensor covers, separation mechanisms and deployment articles. Dedicated design efforts, prompted by the recognition of the threat posed by such objects, have proved effective in reducing this source of space debris.'

195 CoCoSL III, 629–630. Launch fragments would include attachments to the launch vehicle, bolts, clamps, covers, fasteners, lines etc.

196 CoCoSL III, 631. COPUOS comment: 'Spacecraft and launch vehicle orbital stages should be designed to avoid failure modes that may lead to accidental break-ups. In cases where a condition leading to such a failure is detected, disposal and passivation measures should be planned and executed to avoid break-ups. Historically, some break-ups have been caused by space system malfunctions, such as catastrophic failures of propulsion and power systems. By incorporating potential break-up scenarios in failure mode analysis, the probability of these catastrophic events can be reduced.'

Space objects should be designed to avoid break-up and produce minimal debris if break-up occurs. Questions may be raised about responsibility for the design of space systems that become non-operational. If the object was previously operational, then one may assume that it was designed to avoid break-up. The guidelines assume that the space object can be passivated or otherwise controlled. However, it may not be capable of manipulation, so that break-up or collision becomes unavoidable.

3. Limit the probability of accidental collision in space.[197]

After launch, the operator must keep close track of adjoining space objects as well as its own space objects in order to navigate around dangerous situations, as with the ISS.[198] Only a few states, such as the US, Russia, China and ESA, can afford very sophisticated tracking of debris.[199] Other states are dependent on the existing tracking systems, which they do not control. Transparency and a great deal of data sharing among individual commercial operators as well as governments go on.[200]

Space situational awareness needs to be heightened.[201] We note that the use of small satellites increases the number of objects in space and thus the danger of accidental collision. Until recently, small satellites, like existing debris fragments, are mostly non-manoeuvrable. To limit congestion in LEO, small satellites should now be required to be manoeuvrable to aid in their disposal.[202] However, micro-satellites are too small to carry suitable propellant. Operators should design space systems to fragment into as few pieces as possible and time launches to not encounter other space objects on the way to orbit.

4. Avoid intentional destruction and other harmful activities.[203]

January 2007 saw China destroy its Fengyun-1C satellite. A year later saw the intentional US destruction of the USA 193 satellite. India intentionally destroyed one of its satellites in 2019, and Russia destroyed one of its satellites in 2021.[204] Debris mitigation must apply equally to civilian and military activities. This guideline seeks to make room for policies affecting debris caused by military activities. Only when absolutely necessary should

---

197 CoCoSL III, 632–633.

198 Cf. *supra* n. 161. The orbit of the International Space Station (ISS) is occasionally altered so as to avoid space debris. The collision of the inactive Cosmos 2251 with the active Iridium 33 in 2009 was a failure to divert.

199 The US facility is available through www. spacetrack.org.

200 Major satellite communication companies, led by Intelsat, have formed a voluntary data bank into which they all contribute and share information. The Space Data Association also collects data and distribute data to its members.

201 See *supra* nn. 143 and 149.

202 Cf. the FCC reports on debris mitigation and on the Kuiper system, *supra* n. 137.

203 CoCoSL III, 634. COPUOS comment: 'Recognizing that an increased risk of collision could pose a threat to space operations, the intentional destruction of any on-orbit spacecraft and launch vehicle orbital stages or other harmful activities that generate long-lived debris should be avoided. When intentional break-ups are necessary, they should be conducted at sufficiently low altitudes to limit the orbital lifetime of resulting fragments.'

204 The debris field left by Fengyun 1-C, destroyed some 575 miles/925 km up, has spread throughout its orbit. USA 193 was in such a low orbit (130 miles/247 km) that virtually all its debris has now de-orbited. On both see *supra* nn. 161 and 165. In 2021 Russia destroyed its defunct Kosmos-1408 satellite; D. Kastinen et al, 'Radar Observations of the Kosmos-1408 Fragmentation Event' (2023) 202 *Acta Astronautica* 341–359. Cf. J. Oppenheim, 'Danger at 700,000 Feet: Why the United States Needs to Develop a Kinetic Anti-Satellite Missile Technology Test-Ban Treaty' (2013) 38 *Brook. J. Int. L.* 716–795.

space systems be destroyed intentionally, and then preferably in very low orbit where the debris quickly deorbits and falls to Earth. Some debris will have to be removed to improve safety and therefore must be permitted. The ultimate solution to the space debris problem is the removal of the debris. Whether intentional removal of debris from outer space may be considered equivalent to intentional destruction is an open question.[205]

5. Minimize potential for post-mission break-ups resulting from stored energy.[206]

On-board fuel may explode and cause fragmentation. Energy stored in fluid or solid fuel form can cause considerable damage to other space objects. Operators should use up existing fuel by expending it to deorbit the object, by changing orbit or by otherwise disposing of stored energy before ending the functional life or a satellite. Finally, remaining fluid fuel should be vented and electrical batteries discharged before a satellite becomes inactive.

6. Limit the long-term presence of spacecraft and launch vehicle orbital stages in the LEO region after the end of their mission.[207]

LEO is particularly congested. Satellites intended for higher orbits must transit it, and astronauts access the ISS in LEO. It has therefore been suggested that the LEO region be made into a zone specially protected for space flight.[208]

Total removal of space debris from orbit is the most efficient disposal of space debris. Defunct space objects, including launch vehicles, can be deorbited from LEO. If an inactive object cannot be deorbited directly, then it should be brought into as low an orbit as possible so that gravity and atmospheric drag will result in deorbiting as soon as possible. The Guideline notes that space objects de-orbiting from LEO represent a danger to people and property which operators must take into consideration in planning when and where

---

205 A.G. Mudge, 'Incentivizing "Active Debris Removal" Following the Failure of Mitigation Measures to Solve the Space Debris Problem: Current Challenges and Future Strategies' (2022) 82 *Air Force Law Rev.* 88–178. CoCoSL III at 634 contemplates debris removal as being the same as destruction. Cf. J.H. Mey, 'Space Debris Remediation: Some Aspects of International Law Relating to the Removal of Junk from Earth Orbit' (2012) 61 ZLW 251–272. In 2022 the FCC adopted a rule requiring the deorbiting of defunct satellites launched after its date within five years of end of life, *supra* n. 137.

206 CoCoSL III, 635. COPUOS comment: 'In order to limit the risk to other spacecraft and launch vehicle orbital stages from accidental break-ups, all on-board sources of stored energy should be depleted or made safe when they are no longer required for mission operations or post-mission disposal. By far the largest percentage of the catalogued space debris population originated from the fragmentation of spacecraft and launch vehicle orbital stages. Most of those break-ups were unintentional, many arising from the abandonment of spacecraft and launch vehicle orbital stages with significant amounts of stored energy. The most effective mitigation measures have been the passivation of spacecraft and launch vehicle orbital stages at the end of their mission. Passivation requires the removal of all forms of stored energy, including residual propellants and compressed fluids and the discharge of electrical storage devices.'

207 CoCoSL III, 636–638. COPUOS commented: 'Spacecraft and launch vehicle orbital stages that have terminated their operational phases in orbits that pass through the LEO region should be removed from orbit in a controlled fashion. If this is not possible, they should be disposed of in orbits that avoid their long-term presence in the LEO region. When making determinations regarding potential solutions for removing objects from LEO, due consideration should be given to ensuring that debris that survives to reach the surface of the Earth does not pose an undue risk to people or property, including through environmental pollution caused by hazardous objects from LEO, due consideration should be given to ensuring that debris that survives to reach the surface of the Earth does not pose an undue risk to people or property, including through environmental pollution caused by hazardous substances.' Cf. the FCC Order of 2022 on deorbiting defunct satellites launched after its date within five years of their end of life, *supra* n. 137.

208 CoCoSL III at 636, para 56.

to de-orbit space debris. Deorbiting space debris may also be hazardous to the Earth environment.

7. Limit the long-term interference of spacecraft and launch vehicle orbital stages with the GEO region after the end of their mission.[209]

The GSO is becoming crowded, especially in particular positions.[210] Debris must be removed. It is not feasible to deorbit expended satellites from an altitude of 35,700 km by bringing them back to Earth. The solution is for the operator to leave sufficient fuel on board the spacecraft to remove space debris into a so-called graveyard orbit, sufficiently above the GSO to eliminate the danger of interference with active satellites in that orbit.[211] Compliance would also have the possible advantage of returning satellites back into the GSO if scheduled replacements did not arrive in time.

International Technical Standards[212]

The intervention of technical experts in the matter of debris through the International Organisation for Standardisation (ISO) is to be welcomed. Based in Geneva with a General Assembly and a Council, the ISO is a nongovernmental independent organisation with a membership of some 160 national standards bodies.[213] In the field of space and debris mitigation, it has adopted a variety of standards to inform practical engineering practice. These are directed at ensuring that spacecraft and launch vehicle orbital stages are designed, operated and disposed of without generating debris during their orbital lifetime.[214]

Given their technical nature consideration of their detail lies beyond the scope of this book. Suffice it to say that they take account of the SDM Guidelines outlined above. We hope that national compliance with them will help reduce the problem of space debris. That said, once more we have to note that compliance with the ISO Standards is voluntary, not mandatory.

Finally, we consider that large constellations of small satellites in LEO constitute an urgent safety threat to traffic in outer space. They raise the spectre of the Kessler

---

209 CoCoSL III, 639–642. COPUOS comment: 'Spacecraft and launch vehicle orbital stages that have terminated their operational phases in orbits that pass through the GEO region should be left in orbits that avoid their long-term interference with the GEO region. For space objects in or near the GEO region, the potential for future collisions can be reduced by leaving objects at the end of their mission in an orbit above the GEO region such that they will not interfere with, or return to, the GEO region.'

210 See Chapter 6 for discussion of the GSO. All orbits, including the GSO, form a scarce resource: ITU Constitution, Art 44.2 (196).

211 See *supra* nn. 106, 169 and 192. Some expended satellites were left in GSO before the new space debris regime was adopted. Depleted, they cannot be controlled, and drifting, they pose constant dangers to other satellites. Cf supra n. 119. The hope is that in the future, their removal will be possible.

212 Reference point, *supra* n. 192.

213 International Organisation for Standardisation: www.iso.org/iso/home/about/about_governance.htm. F. Lyall, *Technology, Sovereignty and International Law* (Abingdon: Routledge, 2022) 166–168.

214 Cf. ISO 24113:2010, replaced by ISO 24113:2011 (currently under review) on mitigation requirements for unmanned systems launched into or passing through near-Earth space; ISO 16164:2015 on the post-mission disposal of satellites operating in or crossing LEO. See also F.A. Slane, 'ISO Space Standards': www.unoosa.org/pdf/pres/stsc2013/2013lts-02E.pdf. Compliance with a variety of ISO standards, including ISO 24113, is a condition of obtaining a UK orbital operator licence. See 'Guidance for Orbital Operator licence applicants and Orbital Operator Licensees' CAA, 20 July 2021, CAP 2021, Annex A.

syndrome threatening access to outer space through the accumulation of debris.[215] As noted, ESA, the US and other space-faring countries now mandate the 2007 Space Debris Mitigation Guidelines. Nevertheless the existing SDM rules are insufficient. Less than 60% of satellites that should be removed at the end of their useful lives are actually removed. Action and further restrictions are necessary.

Military Space Debris

Debris resulting from military action in space is a special issue. We discuss the military use of space more fully in Chapter 15. Here we simply observe that by OST Art. III and international custom, the UN Charter and international law apply in space. Chapter VII of the UN Charter, 'Action with Respect to Threats to the Peace, Breaches of the Peace and Acts of Aggression', generally prohibits the use of force, although Art. 51 preserves the 'inherent right of self-defence' subject to conditions. Exactly what 'self-defence' means – its application and constraints in the modern world – remains a matter of contention.

Of course were all-out war to happen, rules would be ignored. However, a more limited conflict could be subject to environmental considerations. In that connection, we note that OST Art. III may imply that military uses of space that do not promote 'international peace and security' are prohibited.[216] Even so, space debris would be created, for example by the use of anti-satellite measures to defend a satellite system. We would hope that as far as possible, debris would be avoided bearing in mind the duty under OST Art. IX to have 'due regard to the . . . interests of all other States Parties to the Treaty'.[217]

More particularly, Art. 35.3 of the Additional Protocol I to the Geneva Conventions of 1949 prohibits 'widespread long term and severe damage' to the natural environment.[218] The Convention on the Prohibition of Military and Any Other Hostile Use of Environmental Modification Techniques would also have a role.[219] Of course the question would be how breach of such obligations might be prosecuted. One avenue might be through the Liability Convention, absolute liability being normally involved by its Art. II for damage caused to the surface of the earth and aircraft in flight and liability based on fault for damage elsewhere by Art. III. Space debris resulting from hostilities in space causing damage to a neutral state in space would be subject to the second of these as the deliberate action would establish fault (*dolus*).[220] Convention Art. VI.1 and 2 would deal with any

---

215 *Supra* nn. 164–165.

216 S. Mirmina, 'International Law Implications of the Ballistic Missile Defense System and its Effects on the Outer Space Environment' (2005) 31 *J. Sp. L.* 287–313.

217 Cf. *supra* n. 180.

218 'Protocol Additional to the Geneva Conventions of 12 August 1949, and relating to the Protection of Victims of International Armed Conflicts (Protocol I)', 8 June 1977; 1125 UNTS 4; UN Doc. A/34/144; 1999 UKTS 29, Cm 4338; (1977) 16 ILM 1391–441: www.icrc.org/ihl.nsf/FULL/470?OpenDocument.

219 Convention on the Prohibition of Military and Any Other Hostile Use of Environmental Modification Techniques (ENMOD), 18 May 1977; 1108 UNTS 151; 31 UST 333, TIAS 9614; 1979 UKTS 24, Cmnd. 7469; UNGA Res. 31/72; (1977) 16 ILM 88–94. See M. Bourbonnière, 'A Legal Regime for Keeping Outer Space Free of Armaments' (2002) XXVII AASL 109 at 128–21.

220 In its Advisory Opinion on *Legality of the Threat or Use of Nuclear Weapons*, 1996 ICJ Rep. 226 at 261 (para 89) the ICJ held that 'international law leaves no doubt that the principle of neutrality, whatever its content, . . . is applicable . . . to all international armed conflict, whatever types of weapons may be used'.

question of exoneration and could apply as between states taking mutual hostile action, though not eliding their liabilities towards non-combatants.

Reducing Space Threats

The UN interest in outer space matters is not confined to the work of COPUOS and OOSA. It also manifests in the area of disarmament. In 2013, building on previous work, it adopted UNGA Res. 68/50 on 'Transparency and confidence-building measures in outer space activities'. Building on that and UNGA Res. 74/32 of 2019 on 'Prevention of an arms race in outer space' a year later, it adopted UNGA Res. 75/36 on 'Reducing space threats through norms, rules and principles of responsible behaviours' calling states to consider how space threats could be reduced.[221] In fact, the work of a Working Group arising from that call sheds light on both questions of military activity, a good deal of the contributions ranging well beyond that into the matters we have been considering in the previous sections of this chapter. It is interesting to see calls for compliance with suitable practices and even calls for treaty action in some areas.[222]

Planetary Defence

Planetary defence is an important aspect of our environment in space.[223] Concern about a near-earth object (NEO) colliding with Earth has been increasing.[224] Every day, small meteorites enter our atmosphere and burn up.[225] Occasionally one reaches the surface, infrequently causing minor damage. Less frequently, an object explodes at height.[226] In

---

221 Voting was 164 in favour, 12 against, 6 abstentions, 11 not voting.

222 See Report of the Secretary General, 'Reducing space threats through norms, rules and principles of responsible behaviours' A/76/77, and the 'Open-Ended Working Group on Reducing Space Threats': https://meetings.unoda.org/open-ended-working-group-reducing-space-threats-2022. See generally, Statements: https://meetings.unoda.org/meeting/57866/statements.

223 See exhaustively, I. Marboe, ed., *Legal Aspects of Planetary Defence* (Leiden: Brill, 2021); P.B. Larsen, 'International Regulation of Near Earth Objects (NEOs)' (2018) 67 ZLW 104–136.

224 NEOs are solar system bodies with a closest approach to the sun of less than 1.3 AU. A collision is possible if a NEO orbit intersects that of the earth. As of mid-June 2023, 32,218 such asteroids were known, 852 being 1 km and above, 10,492 over 140 metres: https://neo.jpl.nasa.gov/ca/. The mid-August Perseid meteors come in at about 60 km/37m a second – some 133,300 mph. See also http://lifeboat.com/ex/asteroid.shield.

An 'Astronomical Unit' (AU) is the mean earth/sun distance, c. 93 m/149.6 km. The distance from Earth to the Moon is 0.0026 AU, 241000 miles/387,000 km.

225 Meteor showers occur throughout the year: https://lifeboat.com/ex/asteroid.shield, and www.hohmanntransfer.com/news.htm. P. Jenniskens, *Meteor Showers and Their Parent Comets* (Cambridge: Cambridge UP, 2006); J.S. Lewis, *Rain of Iron and Ice: the Very Real Threat of Comet and Asteroid Bombardment* (Reading: Helix Books, 1995). For law articles see *infra* n. 255.

226 E.g. the NEO explosion over Chelyabinsk, Russia, on February 15, 2013: www.nasa.gov/feature/five-years-after-the-chelyabinsk-meteor-nasa-leads-efforts-in-planetary-defense. Given the rotation of the Earth, had the Tunguska event of 1908 happened five hours later it probably would have destroyed much of St Petersburg: W.K. Hartman, '1908 Siberian Explosion': www.psi.edu/projects/siberia/siberia.html; C. Chyba et al., 'The 1908 Tunguska Explosion: Atmospheric Disruption of a Stony Asteroid' (1993) 361 *Nature* 40–44. See also fireballs and bolides: https://cneos.jpl.nasa.gov/fireballs/. Cf. the 'facts' in the hypothetical case for the Planetary Defense Conference Exercise – 2023: https://cneos.jpl.nasa.gov/pd/cs/pdc23/. For conference papers for the ESA Second Neo and Debris Conference, 2023, see https://conference.sdo.esoc.esa.int/

the future, asteroid mining might result in debris reaching Earth, or worse, the orbit of an asteroid might be uncontrolledly disturbed, leading to its impacting Earth.[227]

Moon and Mars craters show that meteor and asteroid impacts occur. Earth too has a history. Meteor Crater in Arizona was caused by an asteroid or meteor.[228] Theories as to the demise of the dinosaurs now involve similar impacts.[229] These were boosted by the discovery of the Chicxulub Crater, which centres on the Yucatán Peninsula and extends into the Gulf of Mexico.[230] Other craters have has been identified elsewhere.[231] Fragments of comet Shoemaker-Levy-9 hitting Jupiter in 1994 aroused much interest, not to say excitement, and apprehension has been fanned by films such as *Meteor* (1979), *Asteroid* (1997), *Armageddon* and *Deep Impact* (both 1998) and *Asteroid: Final Impact* (TV 2015).[232]

Threats from asteroids and comets colliding with the earth are graded on the Torino Scale.[233] At present, however, there is no formal international legal obligation either to investigate or take steps to deal with them. The duty under OST Art. V.3 to inform the UN Secretary General of space phenomena that might be dangerous to life or health of astronauts cannot be stretched to include danger from NEOs to Earth itself. Without specificity, MA Art. 5.3 refers to danger to human life or health, but could that include NEOs?

---

227 L.I. Tennen, 'Towards a New Regime for Exploitation of Outer Space Mineral Resources' (2009–2010) 88 *Neb. L. Rev.* 794–831; G.M. Goh, 'Pella Vilya: Near Earth Objects – Planetary Defence through the Regulation of Resource Utilisation' (2008) 51 *Proc. IISL* 304–314.

228 Until recently it was known as the Barringer Crater and is still owned by the Barringer family. D.M. Barringer bought it in 1903 and hoped to mine the asteroid remains but without results.

229 The Cretaceous – Tertiary extinction (the K – T event) was some 65.5m years ago. M.W. DeLaubenfels, 'Dinosaur Extinctions: One More Hypothesis' (1956) 30 *J. of Palaeontology*, 207–218, first suggested asteroid impact as a possible cause. L. and W. Alvarez, F. Asaro and H. Michels, argued that a worldwide layer of iridium, inexplicable other than the result of an asteroid impact, meant that such might have caused the K – T event: (1980) 208 *Science* 1095–1108.

230 'The Chicxulub Debate': www.geolsoc.org.uk/chicxulub.

231 K. Amor, S.P. Hesselbo et al., 'A Precambrian proximal ejecta blanket from Scotland' (2008) 36 *Geology* 303–306. Cf. the Earth Impact Database of the University of New Brunswick, Canada: www.passc.net/EarthImpactDatabase/New%20website_05-2018/Index.html.

232 Cf. L. Niven and J. Pournelle, *Lucifer's Hammer* (1977); A.C. Clarke, *The Hammer of God* (1993). On 18 April 2017, asteroid 2014 JO25, equivalent in size to the Rock of Gibraltar, came within 4.6 LD (LD = the Lunar Distance 384,000 km.). Potentially Hazardous Objects (PHOs) may come within 0.05 AU (459,000 miles). Asteroid 99942 Apophis, c. 1000 feet/325 metres in diameter, continues to cause concern for April 2036: https://ssd.jpl.nasa.gov/tools/sbdb_lookup.html#/?sstr=apophis, or https://iawn.net/obscamp/Apophis/.

For current data, see NASA Centre for Near Earth Object Studies: https://cneos.jpl.nasa.gov/. In late 2022 it noted 1744 NEO threats to Earth. See also the International Asteroid Warning Network (IAWN): http://iawn.net. Occasionally detection is late. Historically, Asteroid 2002 MN (diameter 80 metres/260 feet) was spotted on 17 July 2002, having passed us two days earlier. Asteroid 2007 TU24, detected on 11 October 2007, passed on 29 January 2008. Asteroid 2008 BC15, discovered 30 January 2008, passed by one day later. Cf. the Chelyabinsk and Tunguska events, *supra* n. 226. Asteroid 2023 DW detected on 26 February 2023 has a 1 in 560 to 625 chance of Earth impact on 14 February 2046. It is on ESA's Risk List: https://neo.ssa.esa.int/risk-list; https://neo.ssa.esa.int/search-for-asteroids?tab=possimp&des=2023DW; https://neo.ssa.esa.int/search-for-asteroids?tab=possimp&des=2023DW. It's current Torino Scale is 1: no other asteroid is listed above 0; see next note.

233 https://cneos.jpl.nasa.gov/sentry/torino_scale.html. The scale runs: 0 (white) – no hazard; 1 (green) – normal (a pass near the Earth, but with no danger); 2–4 (yellow) – meriting attention by astronomers; 5–7 (orange) – threatening; 8–10 (red) – certain collision, 8 causing localised damage, 9 causing unprecedented regional damage and 10 causing global climatic catastrophe threatening the future of civilisation.

Avoiding causing harmful contamination in outer space, or 'adverse changes in the environment of the Earth resulting from the introduction of extraterrestrial matter', could cover debris from asteroid mining (OST Art. VIII) but injury by impact is not contamination. Harmful interference to the activities of others arguably could mean failing to alter an asteroid orbit by mining in such a way that it could collide with a satellite or the earth itself (OST Art. IX). Such an occurrence could be caused by negligence, but the Liability Convention deals only with damage by Earth-launched space objects. Unless 'caused by' were elastically interpreted, the result of uses of a space object do not appear to come within the terms of that Convention.

Notwithstanding the lack of formal international obligation, various states and organisations taken steps at least to assess and evaluate the potential dangers of NEOs.[234] Initial efforts were varied, inadequately financed and often amateur. Such as the several 'Spaceguard' projects.[235] Some observatories began to catalogue NEOs, particularly those which might cause trouble.[236] There has also been formal governmental action, including surveys by government-funded observatories.[237] In 2000, a task force set up by the then British National Space Centre noted the inadequacy of current knowledge, the problems of disaster management (if needed), and questions of possible mitigation or avoidance, as requiring governmental discussion and action.[238]

Internationally, Near Earth Objects (NEOs) came on the UN scene when it convened a major conference in 1995.[239] The COPUOS Scientific and Technical Sub-Committee first discussed the topic in 2006[240] and has done so annually since.[241] In 2013, COPUOS recommended establishing a NEO International Asteroid Warning Network (IAWN) and a Space Mission Planning Advisory Group (SMPAG), which was approved by UNGA Res. 68/75. The network and group are independent voluntary bodies which cooperate but receive no UN funding other than secretarial functions from OOSA.

Through IAWN, organisations and experts studying NEOs keep each other and COPUOS informed.[242] It operates on the assumption that the fundamental responsibility for managing the NEO threat lies with states. Members have developed appropriate

---

234 Cf. *Report of the Task Force on Potentially Hazardous Near Earth Objects* (London: BNSC, 2000): https:// spaceguardcentre.com/wp-content/uploads/2014/04/full_report.pdf.

235 Spaceguard may take its name from the Project Spaceguard that detects the incoming object Kali in A.C. Clarke's *Rendezvous with Rama* (1972).

236 E.g. the Arizona-based Spacewatch Foundation: http://spacewatch.lpl.arizona.edu/. See also the Association of Space Explorers: www.space-explorers.org/neo.

237 Cf. the (UK) Near Earth Objects Information Centre: https://spaceguardcentre.com.

238 *Report of the Task Force on Potentially Hazardous Near Earth Objects* (London: BNSC, 2000): https:// spaceguardcentre.com/wp-content/uploads/2014/04/full_report.pdf. Cf. the (UK) Near Earth Objects Information Centre: https://spaceguardcentre.com/.

239 J.L. Remo, ed., *Near-Earth Objects: The United Nations International Conference, 1995*, 822 *Annals N. Y. Acad. Sc.* (New York, 1997); J.L. Remo, 'Policy Perspectives from the UN Conference on near-Earth Objects' (1996) 12 *Space Policy* 13–17.

240 Report of the Scientific and Technical Subcommittee on its Forty-third Session, 2006, A/AC.105/869.

241 Report of the Scientific and Technical Subcommittee on its Forty-third Session, 2022, A/AC.105/1258. A Planetary Defence Conference meets regularly, the next in 2023 will tackle a hypothetical exercise: https://cneos.jpl.nasa.gov/pd/cs/pdc23/.

242 See https://iawn.net. 'Statement of Intent for Participation in the International Asteroid Warning Network': https://iawn.net/documents/iawn_statement_of_intent.pdf. For membership, see https://iawn. net/about/members.shtml.

communication systems and protocols, together with plans for the mitigation of damage by NEOs.[243] Data is regularly published.[244]

Major space agencies are voluntary members of SMPAG, a framework for executive decisions about NEOs.[245] Planning involves interacting with national civil defence groups about the management and relief of NEO disasters. SMPAG recommends criteria and thresholds for action, identifies possible NEO impacts, develops plans for joint action in the event that a credible NEO threat is identified and provides guidelines for communication of such and for future planetary defence actions and timelines for decisions on identified NEO trajectories and potential Earth impactors. It evaluates different technologies and methods for deflecting NEOs and otherwise mitigating their impact before they reach Earth and sets criteria for targeting deflections, including minimum distances, the possible use of nuclear power sources for a deflection and the essential tools for an appropriate payload.[246]

In Europe, a Planetary Defence Office is part of ESA's safety and security activities. Within the office, a Near-Earth Objects Coordination Centre (http://neo.ssa.esa.int), *inter alia* publishes a risk list (https://neo.ssa.esa.int/risk-list). Surveys are conducted through a variety of telescopes, not necessarily owned by the agency, data is assessed, mitigation measures are discussed and ESA members and the media are kept up to date.[247]

Much has been done in the US since our previous editions, notably the National Preparedness Strategy and Action Plan for Near-Earth Object Hazards and Planetary Defense, which replaces a plan of 2019.[248] NASA plays a major role in planetary defence. Its efforts are spread throughout many NASA groups but are coordinated.[249] In particular, NASA's Near Earth Object Program conducts surveys to identify and track at least 90% of asteroids larger than 140 metres by 2020. The Jet Propulsion Laboratory Center for Near Earth Object Studies (CNEOS) computes NEO trajectories and the likelihood of impact.[250] Its Sentry List tabulates NEOs of current interest.[251]

---

243 IAWN functions include providing data on tracking and identifying existing NEOs, acting as a clearing house for validated NEO information, providing access to information, planning and coordinating joint NEO observations, preparing policies for warning of impending NEO threats, establishing an information system about potential consequences of NEO impacts, analysing the results of NEO threats and helping governments understand NEO consequences and prepare plans for their mitigation.

244 See https://iawn.net/close-approaches/ca-table_multi-opp.shtml. Cf. https://minorplanetcenter.net/db_search/show_object?object_id=K22S55X.

245 Space Mission Planning Advisory Group: www.cosmos.esa.int/web/smpag

246 Cf. the 2019 SPMAG Work Plan: www.cosmos.esa.int/documents/336356/336472/SMPAG-PL-002_2_0_Workplan_2019_09-01+(3).pdf/a117c9aa-27c1-788c-7d30-513fb7c06367?t=1590414041069.

247 ESA Planetary Defence Office: www.esa.int/Space_Safety/About_asteroids_and_Planetary_Defence.

248 National Preparedness Strategy & Action Plane for Near Earth Object Hazards and Planetary Defense, April 2023: www.whitehouse.gov/wp-content/uploads/2023/04/2023-NSTC-National-Preparedness-Strategy-and-Action-Plan-for-Near-Earth-Object-Hazards-and-Planetary-Defense.pdf and NASA Planetary Defense Strategy and Action Plan, 2023: www.nasa.gov/sites/default/files/atoms/files/nasa_-_planetary_defense_strategy_-_final-508.pdf. Cf. the Plan of 2019: https://trumpwhitehouse.archives.gov/wp-content/uploads/2018/06/National-Near-Earth-Object-Preparedness-Strategy-and-Action-Plan-23-pages-1MB.pdf.

249 NASA Planetary Defense Coordination Office: www.nasa.gov/planetarydefense.

250 CNEOS: https://cneos.jpl.nasa.gov/. Cf. IAWN reports *supra* n. 244.

251 Sentry: Earth Impact Monitoring: https://cneos.jpl.nasa.gov/sentry/.

There are many proposals for dealing with a detected incoming NEO while it is a distance from Earth.[252] Despite filmic dramas, these concentrate on deflection rather than the destruction that might convert a single object into a disastrous conglomeration without removing the threat. Deflection suggestions include towing, heating one side of the object, exploding an atomic bomb close to it and by direct impact. Recently, the Double Asteroid Redirection Test project altered the orbit of the moonlet Dimorphos around the asteroid Didymus but has also resulted in new trajectories for some thirty-seven boulders of up to 22 feet.[253]

Notwithstanding all such activities, how to cope with perceived danger remains obscure.[254] What sort of practical international procedures might be adopted to cope with an asteroid impact?[255] Measures are already being developed to cope with terrestrially originating disasters, but these are not appropriate to fully cope with threats from space.[256]

First, a formal international programme should be established for the detection of incoming threats. It is not sensible to rely only on existing national programmes, or even

252 But note para 2 of n. 232 *supra*.
253 www.nasa.gov/specials/pdco/index.html#dart, and www.nasa.gov/planetarydefense/dart/dart-news. See also Project HERA: www.esa.int/Space_Safety/Hera. D.A. Koplow, 'Exoatmospheric plowshares: using nuclear explosive device for planetary defense against an incoming asteroid' (2019) 23 *UCLA J. Int. Law and For. Aff.* 76–158; P.B. Larsen, 'Minimum international norms for managing space traffic, space debris, and near earth object impacts' (2018) 83 *J. Air L. & Comm.* 739–786; J.A. Green, 'Planetary Defense: Near-Earth Objects, Nuclear Weapons, and International Law' (2019) 42 *Hastings Int. Comp. L. Rev.* 1–72; B.G. Poole, 'Against the Nuclear Option: Planetary Defence under International Space Law' (2020) 45 *Air and Sp. L.* 55–80. Cf. *Origins, Worlds, and Life: A Decadal Strategy for Planetary Science and Astrobiology 2023–2032* (Washington: National Academies Press) Ch. 18.
    Asteroid 101955 Bennu (diameter 490m) passes the Earth every six years, and there are possibilities of impact on 24 September 2182 or by 2300. See CNEOS Sentry list, *supra* n. 251. NASA is making plans to alter Bennus's orbit. The NASA OSIRIS-REx programme returned a sample from Bennu to Earth on 24 September 2023. China may conduct an experiment similar to DART involving Bennu: https://spacenews. com/china-to-conduct-asteroid-deflection-test-around-2025/; www.livescience.com/china-rocket-fleet-divert-asteroid-bennu.html.
254 Cf. C. Maccone – 1, 'Planetary Defense from the Nearest 4 LaGrange Points plus RFI-free Radioastronomy from the Far Side of the Moon: A Unified Vision' (2002) 50 *Acta Astronautica* 185–199; – 2, 'Planetary Defense From Space: Part 1 Keplerian theory' (2004) 55 *Acta Astronautica* 991–1006; S. Konyukhov and N. Slyunyayev, 'Conception of the Creation of Space Rocket Complex as Necessary Link for Anti-Asteroid Protection of the Earth' (2002) 50 *Acta Astronautica* 629–632.
255 M.B. Gerrard and A.W. Barber, 'Asteroids and Comets: U.S. and International Law and the Lowest-Probability, Highest Consequence Risk' (1997) 6 *N.Y.U. Env. L.J.* 4–49; L.I. Covert, 'Before Celestial Bodies Collide – Enhanced Dialogue and Coordination: Precursors to a Treaty for Effective New Earth Object (NEO) Response' (2003) 46 *Proc. IISL* 276–286; E.R. Seamone – 1, 'When Wishing on a Star Just Won't Do: The Legal Basis for International Cooperation in the Mitigation of Asteroid Impacts and Similar Transboundary Disasters' (2002) *Iowa L. Rev.* 1091–1139; – 2 'The Duty to "Expect the Unexpected": Mitigating Extreme Natural Threats to the Global Commons Such as Asteroid and Comet Impacts with the Earth' (2003) 41 *Colum. J. Transnat'l L.* 735–794; – 3, 'The Precautionary Principle as the Law of Planetary Defense: Achieving the Mandate to Defend the Earth against Asteroid and Comet Impacts While There is Still Time' (2004) 17 *Geo. Int. Env. L. Rev.* 1–23; J.L. Koplow, 'Assessing The Creation Of A Duty Under International Customary Law Whereby The United States of America Would Be Obligated to Defend A Foreign State against the Catastrophic but Localized Damage of an Asteroid Impact' (2004–2005) 17 *Geo. Int. Env. L. Rev.* 273–306; J.C. Kunich, 'Planetary Defense: The Legality of Global Survival' (1997) 41 *Air Force L. Rev.* 119–162.
256 The Disasters Charter system might be able to help once a disaster has occurred: 'Charter on Cooperation to Achieve the Coordinated Use of Space Facilities in the Event of Natural or Technological Disasters' (2000): www.disasterscharter.org/main_e.html. See the discussion of the Charter in Chapter 12.

on international programmes such as that of ESA. The NASA survey is unduly dependent on funding decisions of the US Congress, which may be erratic. The same applies to ESA. A small international organisation would be a better solution, with funding either from its members or from the United Nations itself. The UN funds peace-keeping forces. Running a NEO survey and monitoring agency would cost much less, particularly were its operation to be contracted out to an existing agency or entity.[257]

Second, preparing means of diverting an asteroid, meteor or cometary threat should not be delayed until an actual detection. Time might be too short adequately to deal with the crisis; missile or other technology has to be prepared.[258] Certainly as can be seen from material already cited, thought has been given to what might be done. A formal organisation (not necessarily one separate from the survey organisation) should be established to bring into being several of the potential methods of diverting an incoming threat or mitigating its result.[259]

Again, elements of this undertaking could be contracted out, but the cost of diverting an incoming asteroid or comet would be much greater than that of simply looking for them. A central organisation should be established both to provide a channel for appropriate funding and to determine when appropriate measures are activated.[260] Since all are under threat, all should bear a portion of the cost of nullifying it. Funding should come from the UN, the World Bank and the International Monetary Fund, as well as from non-donors to these. Attention will also need to be given to questions of liability. If an incoming object is diverted but nonetheless hits the Earth, or if the object is fragmented and bits cause damage, where might liability (if any) lie?[261] Concepts of terrestrial international environmental law may have an unusual role to play!

---

257 Koplow, *supra* n. 255, at 301–306. Cf. the tracking of the incoming starship by Project Spaceguard, in A.C. Clarke, ed., *Rendezvous with Rama* (1972). Cf. the Spaceguard Foundation, *supra* n. 235.
258 The media may report more near misses as a result of improved technology.
259 A cometary 'snowball' could (might?) be broken into inoffensive parts by a kinetic impact.
260 Koplow, *supra* n. 255, discusses whether the US might act alone, and whether there is an international duty to act. Cf. J.C. Kunich, 'Planetary Defense: The Legality of Global Survival' (1997) 41 *Air Force L. Rev.* 119–162.
261 Cf. R.L. Schweikart, 'The Near-Earth Object (NEO) Protocol' (2006) 49 *Proc. IISL* 574–579 at 578.

10

SATELLITE COMMUNICATIONS

Telecommunications and Direct Broadcasting

The last seventy years have seen the development of telecommunication by satellite relay and direct broadcasting from satellites. Space telecommunications began with hybrid international organisations creating global systems in the public interest though many have now become private companies. Direct satellite broadcasting has a different history, being brought about largely by commercial companies. That said, private commercial interests now greatly influence both services, but space law remains the context within which they operate. Finally, space telecommunications, like all telecommunications, are dual use, available for civil or military purposes.[1] This chapter is concerned with their civilian use.

Telecommunications

Satellite telecommunications meet the requirement of Art. I of the 1967 OST that outer space be used for the benefit of all. The new facility has had immense effect upon modern societies. Satellite relays solve many problems inherent in terrestrial communication. Cables have to be laid sometimes over difficult terrain and provide point-to-point links, have limited capacity and carry for only short distances before the signal degrades. The higher frequencies of radio required for the sophisticated signals of TV and error-free data traffic propagate in line of sight and are not reflected around the curvature of the earth by the Heaviside Layer.[2]

---

1 See Chapter 15. Cf. C.M. Petras, 'The Use of Force in Response to Cyber-Attack on Commercial Space Systems – Re-examining "Self-Defense" in Outer Space in Light of the Convergence of US Military and Commercial Space Activities' (2002) 67 *J. Air L. and Comm.* 1213–1268; R.A. Morgan, 'Military Use of Commercial Communications Satellites: A Fresh Look at the Outer Space Treaty and "Peaceful Purposes"' (1994) 60 *J. Air L. & Comm.* 237–325; D.A. Koplow, 'An Inference about Interference: A Surprising Application of Existing International Law to Inhibit Anti-Satellite Weapons' (2014) 35 *U. Pa. J. Int. L.* 737–827; S.M. Mountin, 'Intentional Interference with Commercial Communication Satellite Signals' (2014) 90 *Int. L. Stud.* 101–197.

2 VHF are metric waves in the range 30 to 300 MHz; UHF are decimetric waves in the range 300 to 3000 MHz. For ITU purposes the Radio Regulations divides the spectrum into nine frequency bands (RR Art. 2.1).

DOI: 10.4324/9781003496502-10

A space-located relay station avoids many of these problems and makes available signifi-cant signal capacity and band-width. These advantages, not to be had in the days before fibre optic cables, were attractive,[3] as was the use of the geostationary orbit. Satellites in geostationary orbit do not require tracking and for telecommunication services link to terrestrial networks through large terrestrial antennae. However, in recent years, flexible access to low earth orbit (LEO) constellations of small satellites also provide service direct to customers.[4]

Satellite telecommunications have one further benefit that deserves to be specially noted. Although fibre optic cables provide satisfactory services and are serious competitors in the telecommunication market, the existing satellite facilities have sufficient capacity to provide back-up service in the event of terrestrial cabling being damaged, whether by accident or intention. On the other hand, satellite signals can be jammed.

In the 1940s, Arthur C. Clarke foresaw telecommunication by satellite.[5] Just over ten years later, the launch of Sputnik 1 during the International Geophysical Year, 1957, showed it might be achievable. Although the exploration of space had its prestige aspects and scientific reasons, most taxpayers want to see more immediate and direct benefit from their taxes. Improving telecommunications met the bill, as well as having a tacit military aspect. Presidents Eisenhower and Kennedy both supported the cause.[6]

The international community also saw the benefits of telecommunications routed through satellites. In December 1961, the UN General Assembly took the view that 'com-munication by means of satellites should be available to the nations of the world as soon as practicable on a global and non-discriminatory basis'.[7] A year later, the Assembly empha-sised 'the importance of international cooperation to achieve effective satellite communi-cations which will be available on a worldwide basis'.[8] Given the then state of international communications facilities, the prospect was attractive. History was to produce a num-ber of international organisations, the most important being INTELSAT, INMARSAT,

---

3 Telstar I was launched on 10 July 1962.
4 Signals from GSO can be directed to all but the polar regions. Signals from an appropriate LEO are available worldwide. Cf. UK Ofcom, 'Non-geostationary Satellite Systems: Licensing Updates', 10 December 2021: www.ofcom.org.uk/__data/assets/pdf_file/0018/229311/statement-ngso-licensing.pdf. See also I. Marboe, ed. *Small Satellites: Regulatory Challenges and Changes* (Leiden: Brill, 2016); A. Froehlich, ed., *Legal Aspects Around Satellite Constellations* (Springer, 2021).
5 A.C. Clarke, 'Extra-terrestrial Relays: Can Rocket Stations Give World-Wide Radio Coverage?' *Wireless World* (October 1945), 303–308. Clarke, writing prior to the transistor, envisaged a manned relay station and the use of vacuum valves. In *The Problem of Space Travel: The Rocket Motor* (1928), Herman Potočnik discussed the establishment of a GSO space station for Earth observation but did not consider its use for telecommunica-tions; see Chapter 1, n. 21.
6 Statement on Communication Satellites by President Eisenhower, *Department of State Bulletin*, 16 Janu-ary 1961; *Documents on International Aspects of the Exploration and Use of Outer Space, 1954–1962*, Staff Report, Committee on Aeronautical and Space Sciences, US Senate, 1963, 88th Cong., 1st Sess. Doc. No. 18, at 186. President Kennedy's *Special Message to Congress on Urgent National Needs*, 25 May 1961, set the objective of putting a man on the Moon, but also asked for funding to speed 'the use of space satellites for world-wide communications': *Public Papers of the President: John F. Kennedy* (US GPO, 1961) 403–5, or the just cited *Documents . . . Outer Space 1954–1962*, 202–204.
7 Part D, 'International Cooperation in the Peaceful Uses of Outer Space', UNGA Res. 1721(XVI) (1961). The US Communication Satellite Act, *infra* n. 12, required that attention be paid to the needs of developing countries.
8 Part E.3, 'International Cooperation in the Peaceful Uses of Outer Space', UNGA Res. 1802 (XVII)(1962).

EUTELSAT, INTERSPUTNIK and ARABSAT. The first three have been privatised and will not be discussed in detail.[9] Now other private commercial companies have joined the market. Of these, we select from those providing global coverage. Last, we note that whenever private companies provide domestic or international satellite services their licensing and supervision is the duty of their home states (OST Arts. III and VIII), together with compliance with the procedures and regulations of the ITU.[10]

COMSAT

In the 1960s, telecommunications facilities in most countries were provided by the state. The US was the major exception, and with its tradition of enterprise, it was unsurprising that it took the initial steps towards establishing a global satellite telecommunication system but through a commercial company.[11] The US Communications Satellite Act of 1962[12] provided for the creation of 'a commercial communications satellite system' as part of an improved global communications network 'responsive to public needs and national objectives, which will serve the communications needs of the United States and other countries, and which will contribute to world peace and understanding'. Accordingly the Communications Satellite Corporation (COMSAT) was incorporated in 1963.[13]

Stock in the new company went on public offer in 1964 on a prospectus[14] characterised by *Newsweek* as 'a litany of caveats'.[15] However, although some limited foreign ownership of COMSAT stock was permitted it was clear that the system was to be a US-owned commercial system with others permitted to buy service from it.[16] This proved internationally unacceptable. Other states wished to share in the development and procurement of the relevant technologies and to protect their own industries.

A rival global system might have been set up by European states in association with Australia, and the US system would have been unable to provide trans-Atlantic traffic in the absence of gateways to European terrestrial networks.[17] The result was INTELSAT, in

---

9   For detail see the earlier editions of this Treatise. See also J. Hills, *Deregulating Telecoms: Competition and Control in the United States, Japan and Britain* (London: Pinter, 1986); G.A. Codding Jr., *The Future of Satellite Communications* (Boulder CO: Westview, 1990); F. von der Dunk, 'Crossing a Rubycon? The International Legal Framework for ISOs – Before and After Privatization', in McCormick and Mechanick, eds., *infra* n. 23, 223–280: https://digitalcommons.unl.edu/spacelaw/97.

10 See Chapter 8.

11 J.T. Kildow, *INTELSAT: Policy-Maker's Dilemma* (Lexington: D.C. Heath, 1973).

12 The Communications Satellite Act 1962, Public Law No. 624, 76th Cong., 2d Sess., 76 Stat. 419; 37 USC § 701; (1962) 1 ILM 331. The Act was amended during the life of COMSAT.

13 'Articles of Incorporation' (initial form) (1963) 2 ILM, 395–416; *Nomination of Incorporators*, Hearing before the Committee on Aeronautical and Space Sciences, US Senate, 19 March 1963, 88th Cong. 1st Sess., 43–51, Bye-laws at 51–63, with annotated 'legislative history' and final version of the 'Articles of Incorporation' at 112–23.

14 For the preliminary COMSAT Prospectus, see (1964) 3 ILM, 571–605. For the final version, see *Satellite Communications – 1964, Part 1*, Hearings before a Subcommittee of the Committee on Government Operations, US House of Representatives, 1964, 88th Cong. 2d Sess., 597–657.

15 *Newsweek*, 18 May 1964, 87.

16 For COMSAT to 1989, see F. Lyall, *Law and Space Telecommunications* (Aldershot: Dartmouth; Brookfield: Gower, 1989), 30–73.

17 Transatlantic telecommunications traffic was essential for the financial viability of COMSAT, a private company. In other countries, telecommunication services were provided by the state and hence not so subject to pressure from investors.

which at first, COMSAT played a major management rôle. Later, however, as INTELSAT prospered and developed its own mechanisms COMSAT declined, in due course was broken up and now no longer exists.

INTELSAT

INTELSAT began as an association of joint venturers of telecommunication providers[18] and later became a hybrid international organisation.[19] This functioned through an Assembly of Parties,[20] a Meeting of Signatories,[21] a Board of Governors and an Executive Organ.[22] Each signatory had an investment share (the 'quota') reflecting its use of the system and consequent share in investment, and, as a result, voting weight within the Board of Governors. The Board might have up to twenty-seven members, the bulk of whom represented contributory shares but included a small number of additional members not based on quota to ensure global representation.[23] INTELSAT prospered but under pressure from US commercial interests was privatised in accordance with the US ORBIT Act of 2000,[24] leaving a residual supervisory organisation (the International Satellite Organisation [ITSO]) to supervise compliance with some limited continuing public service obligations.[25] Since then it has experienced the rough waters of commerciality in full measure.[26]

18 Agreement Establishing Interim Arrangements for a Global Commercial Communications Satellite System, and Relative Special Agreement, 1964, 514 UNTS 25; 1966 UKTS 12, Cmnd. 2436 and 2940; 15 UST 1705, TIAS 5646; (1964) 3 ILM 805–14.
19 In 2005, the US Court of Appeals for the District of Columbia Circuit referred to 'INTELSAT, the US-based, 143-nation, international satellite consortium created by the Communications Satellite Act of 1962': *Northpoint Technology, Ltd v. FCC*, 367 US App. D.C. 170; 414 F. 3d 61 at 72. That assertion is at variance with the facts. Again, it is noticeable that in its chronicles of its 'Milestones' ITSO indicates that the original INTELSAT 'resulted from the willingness of nations to join the United States in 1964 to establish a commercial communications satellite system' – another misleading view of the process (see link at www.itso.int)
20 Initially members were individual states.
21 The signatories were telecommunication operators designated by each member state, one per state.
22 Agreement relating to the International Telecommunications Satellite Organisation (INTELSAT), Washington, DC, 1971, 1220 UNTS 21; 23 UST 3813, TIAS 7532; 1973 UKTS 80, Cmnd. 5610; 1973 ATS 6; (1971) 10 ILM 909. Operating Agreement relating to the International Telecommunications Satellite Organisation (INTELSAT), 1220 UNTS 149; 23 UST 4091, TIAS 7532; 1973 UKTS 80, Cmnd. 5461; (1971) 10 ILM 946. Minor amendments were made at Copenhagen in 1995 (1996 ATS 14).
23 For *INTELSAT* down to 1989 see F. Lyall, *supra* n. 16, 85–122. Cf. R.R. Colino, *The INTELSAT Definitive Arrangements: Ushering in a New Era in Satellite Telecommunications* (Geneva: EBU, 1973); M. Snow, *The International Telecommunications Satellite Organisation (INTELSAT* (Baden-Baden: Nomos Verlag, 1987). For its privatisation see P.K. McCormick, 'Intelsat: Pre and Post-Private Equity Ownership', in P.K. McCormick and M.J. Mechanick, eds., *The Transformation of Intergovernmental Satellite Organisations* (Leiden: Brill, 2013), 81–117.
24 Open-market Reorganisation for the Betterment of International Telecommunications Act, 2000, Public Law No. 106–80, 114 Stat. 48 (2000) [codified at 47 USC § 765ff.] (the ORBIT Act).
25 International Telecommunications Satellite Organization (https://itso.int); see M.J. Mechanick, 'The Role and Function of Residual International Intergovernmental Organisations Following Privatisation', in P.K. McCormick and M.J. Mechanick, *supra* n. 23, 175–221.
26 See www.satellitetoday.com/business/2022/02/24/intelsat-emerges-from-bankruptcy-as-a-private-company/

INMARSAT

As its acronym implies, the International Maritime Satellite Organization (INMARSAT) has provided services for ships since 1979.[27] INTELSAT could have provided a maritime service, but at that time, the USSR and the Eastern bloc were not INTELSAT members. However, their vast shipping and fishing fleets meant that the Eastern bloc had a significant interest in such a system.[28] More broadly, a service common to all shipping was both logical and prudent.

Although initially only a maritime service was contemplated air[29] and land–mobile[30] communications services were subsequently added. Accordingly, in 1994, the name of the organization was changed to the International Mobile Telecommunications Satellite Organisation.[31] However, to maintain business recognition, the acronym INMARSAT was retained.[32]

INMARSAT was smaller and simpler than INTELSAT. It consisted of an Assembly of Parties, a Council and a Directorate. There was no Meeting of Signatories, or Board of Governors. Investment share (the quota) played a role in its decision-making. In due course, INMARSAT was privatised in accordance with the US ORBIT Act of 2000.[33] The then member states became owners of shares in the new company in proportion to their then quotas, and most thereafter disposed of their shares. Although INMARSAT is now subject to normal commercial pressures and dealings, the UK government retains a 'golden share' allowing it some degree of control. Until recently, owned by a private equity firm it was purchased in May 2023 by VIASAT after the sale had been approved by the relevant US, UK and EU authorities.[34]

A residual organisation, the International Mobile Satellite Organisation (IMSO) (https://imso.org/) remains to supervise INMARSAT compliance with its public service and other obligations in relation to safety of life at sea. IMSO operates under the INMARSAT arrangements as amended on privatisation.[35] Its function was to supervise

27 Convention on the International Maritime Satellite Organization (INMARSAT), 3 September 1976, 1143 UNTS 105, 1979 UKTS 94, 31 UST 1, TIAS 9605 (1976) 15 ILM 1051; Operating Agreement on the International Maritime Satellite Organization (INMARSAT), 1220 UNTS 149 (1976) 15 ILM 233.

28 INTERSPUTNIK, the USSR response to INTELSAT, could have provided a maritime service, but one which the West was unlikely to join it. A new single global maritime service made better sense.

29 INMARSAT Assembly, Fourth Session, October 1985, in force 13 October 1989; (1988) 27 ILM 691–694.

30 INMARSAT Assembly, Sixth (Extraordinary) Session, January 1989. *International Maritime Satellite Organization: Amendments to the Convention and Operating Agreement*, 1991 UKTS 27, in force February 1997.

31 INMARSAT Assembly, Tenth (Extraordinary) Session, 5–9 December 1994.

32 INMARSAT is discussed more fully in previous editions of this Treatise and, down to 1989 in Lyall, *supra* n. 16, 209–243.

33 *Supra* n. 24. For INMARSAT privatisation see D. Sagar and P.K. McCormick, 'Inmarsat: In the Forefront of Mobile Satellite Communications', in McCormick and Mechanick, eds., *supra* n. 23, 35–79.

34 The UK Competition and Markets Authority gave approval in March 2023: https://assets.publishing. service.gov.uk/media/645a044cc6e8970012a0fac9/Viasat_Inmasat_Summary_.pdf; www.satellitetoday. com/government-military/2023/05/09/uk-regulatory-authority-approves-viasat-inmarsat-merger-citing-starlink-ifc-competition/. For EU concern see https://ec.europa.eu/commission/presscorner/detail/en/ip_23_768 and https://spacenews.com/europe-opens-full-scale-investigation-into-viasats-inmarsat-acquisition/. FCC approval came in an Order of May 2023, IB Docket No, 22–153: https://docs.fcc.gov/public/attachments/DA-23-427A1.pdf.

35 Text at https://imso.org/wp-content/uploads/2019/08/E.IMSO-CONVENTION.pdf. Cf. Mechanick, *supra* n. 25.

INMARSAT's continuing compliance with the public service obligations it had entered into in relation to safety of life at sea, notably the Global Maritime Distress and Rescue System (GMDSS) operated under the IMO SOLAS provisions.[36] Subsequently, the IMSO remit was extended to include supervision of the system for the Long Range Identification and Tracking of Ships (LRIT), another IMO system.[37] Further, IMSO is available to provide oversight for any public service organisation that enters into appropriate agreements with it.[38]

EUTELSAT

The European Telecommunications Satellite Organisation (EUTELSAT) was a European effort to develop and maintain a space industry east of the Atlantic. Like others, EUTEL-SAT began in an interim form in 1977 as an association of joint venturers,[39] becoming an international organisation in 1986.[40] Its original structure comprised an Assembly of Parties, a Board of Signatories and an Executive Organ. Over time its portfolio of services for television and entertainment became the major contributors to its revenues, and that remains the case. Privatised in 2001, its assets, commercial liabilities and operational activities were transferred to EUTELSAT S.A., a French société anonyme (a limited liability company).[41] An intergovernmental organisation, EUTELSAT IGO (www.eutelsatigo.int), remains to see that EUTELSAT respects basic principles of pan-European coverage, universal service, non-discriminatory access and fair competition.

INTERSPUTNIK

INTERSPUTNIK has not been privatised but has mutated. When INTELSAT was coming into being, the USSR (and hence the Communist bloc) declined to join for a variety of reasons.[42] Under the nascent INTELSAT arrangements, it would not have been entitled to a significant role in the new association. However, it was keen to develop a telecommunications satellite system to serve its vast land area[43] and to keep up with the West in invention, technology, manufacturing and operational skills. The result was an 'Agreement on the Establishment of the "INTERSPUTNIK" International System and Organisation of Space Communications'.[44] INTERSPUTNIK then consisted of a board of all members,

---

36 See F. Lyall, *Technology, Sovereignty and International Law* (Abingdon: Routledge, 2022) 55–56.

37 Lyall, *supra* n. 36, 56–57.

38 IMSO is discussed in greater detail in the second edition of this Treatise, at 296–305.

39 'Agreement on the Constitution of a Provisional European Telecommunications Satellite Organisation, "Interim EUTELSAT"', Paris, 1977.

40 Convention and Operating Agreement of the European Telecommunications Satellite Organisation (EUTELSAT), Paris, 1982, 1983 UKTS, Misc. 25, Cmnd. 9069.

41 For EUTELSAT privation see C. Roisse, 'The Evolution of INMARSAT: A Challenge successfully Met', in McCormick and Mechanick, eds., *supra* n. 23, 119–173.

42 N.M. Matte, *Aerospace Law* (Toronto: Carswell; London: Sweet and Maxwell, 1969) 197. Cf. D. McDaniel and L.A. Day, 'INTELSAT and Communist Nations Policy on Communications Satellites' (1973–1974) 18 *J. Broadcasting*, 311–321.

43 The land mass of the then USSR encompassed ten time zones with difficult terrain.

44 Agreement on the Establishment of the "INTERSPUTNIK" International System and Organisation of Space Communications, 1971; 862 UNTS 3; 2 Manual, 159: *Space Law: Selected Basic Documents* (2nd ed.), US Senate, 1978, 385–398; (2003) 29 *J. Sp. L.* 131–146. There were nine initial members. That

each with one vote, and an executive body, the Directorate. In 2003, the organisation was revised and restructured by an Amending Protocol.[45]

Now under an Establishment Agreement (Estab. Ag.)[46] and an Operating Agreement (Op. Ag.),[47] INTERSPUTNIK consists of state members,[48] and signatories.[49] It operates through a Board consisting of all members, an Operations Committee, a Directorate and an Auditing Committee (Estab. Ag., Art. 11.1). The Board contains one representative from each Member (Estab. Ag., Art. 12.1), each having one vote (Estab. Ag., Art. 12.2). Chairmanship rotates for each session on the basis of the Russian alphabet (Estab. Ag., Art. 12.5).

The Board meets annually or extraordinarily at the request of any member, or the Operations Committee, or the Director General, if one third of the members agree (Estab. Ag., Art. 12.3). The Board endeavours to act unanimously, failing which decisions are taken by a two-thirds majority of those present and voting (Art. 12.7). Decisions bind all members except a member that as a direct consequence withdraws from the organisation (Estab. Ag., Art. 12. 7). Any change in the structure of INTERSPUTNIK or in its major goals must be approved by the common consent of its members (Estab. Ag., Art. 12.7).

By Estab. Ag. Art. 12.6, the functions of the Board include setting general policy and long-term objectives (Estab. Ag., Art. 12.6.1); ensuring that the organisation conforms to the UN Charter, the ITU and other international agreements (Estab. Ag., Art. 12.6.3);[50] and supervising of the activities of the organisation (Estab. Ag., Art. 12.6.5) and of the Directorate (Estab. Ag., Art. 12.6.6). It makes decisions on recommendations of the Operations Committee (Estab. Ag., Art. 12.6.4), on official relations (Estab. Ag., Art. 12.6.9) and on any amendments to the either Agreement (Estab. Ag., Art. 12.6.10).

The Board adopts its own rules of procedure (Estab. Ag., Art. 12.6.7) and can establish further subsidiary bodies to help it perform its tasks (Estab. Ag., Art. 11.4). Importantly, the Board determines geographic regions so as to provide fair geographic representation in the Operations Committee and elects the members of that committee (Estab. Ag., Art. 12.6.8; Op. Ag., Art. 3.4). Finally, jointly with the Operations Committee it elects the Director General (Estab. Ag., Art. 13.5). The Operations Committee is the major structural innovation in the current INTERSPUTNIK and has taken over many functions that were formerly those of the Board, in addition to

INTERSPUTNIK is discussed more fully in G. Zhukov and Y. Kolosov (B. Belitzky trans.), *International Space Law* (New York: Praeger, 1984) 109–120; Y.M. Kolosov, 'International System and Organisation of Space Communications (INTERSPUTNIK)', I Manual, 401–414, and Lyall, *supra* n. 16, 296–303.

45 Protocol on Amendments to the Agreement on the Establishment of the Intersputnik International System and Organization of Space Communications, 4 November 2002: (2003) 29 *J. Sp. L.* 147–181.

46 See https://intersputnik.int/upload/en/Establishment_Agreement.pdf.

47 See https://intersputnik.int/upload/en/Operating_Agreement.pdf.

48 As of 2022, INTERSPUTNIK had twenty-six members: Afghanistan, Azerbaijan, Belarus, Bulgaria, Cuba, Czech Republic, Georgia, Germany, Hungary, India, Kazakhstan, Kyrgyzstan, Laos, Mongolia, Nicaragua, North Korea, Poland, Romania, Russian Federation, Somalia, Syria, Tajikistan, Turkmenistan, Ukraine, Vietnam and Yemen. Cuba, Nicaragua and Yemen excepted, members are located proximately. See http://intersputnik.int/about/countries/.

49 As of 2023, twenty-five signatories had been designated by members. Turkmenistan has not designated a signatory. See https://intersputnik.int/about/participants/.

50 Cf. V.S. Veshchunov, 'The Procedure of Filing and International Legal Protection of the INTERSPUTNIK'S Planned Satellite Networks' (2001) 44 *Proc. IISL* 220–222.

supervising the working of the new 'share' system. It decides INTERSPUTNIK activities (Estab. Ag., Art. 12*bis* 1) in accordance with its own rules of procedure (Estab. Ag., Art. 12bis 2.21).

All signatories are members of the Operations Committee (Op. Ag., Art. 3.1). Each appoints a representative and a deputy (Op. Ag., Art. 3.2–3). The Committee meets at least twice a year (Op. Ag. Art. 3.6). Extraordinary meetings are convened at the request of a member or the Director General if at least four committee members so agree (Op. Ag., Art. 3.7). Observers from any entity affected by a matter under discussion may attend (Op. Ag., Art. 3.4). The chairman serves a three-year term but may be re-elected without limit (Op. Ag., Art. 3.5). In deliberations each member has one vote (Op. Ag., Art. 3.13). The Committee endeavours to act by consensus (Op. Ag., Art. 3.12).

Matters of substance require a qualified majority of two thirds of the members attending and voting (Op. Ag., Art. 3.12.1). Other matters are settled by a simple majority vote of those present and voting provided that at least half of those present vote (Op. Ag., Arts 3.12.2). In exceptional circumstances the Committee may take decisions without meeting in formal session (Op. Ag. Art. 3.10).

The Committee approves the construction, procurement, including leasing, and operation of the INTERSPUTNIK system (Estab. Ag., Art. 12*bis* 2.1–2). It defines the specifications for the satellite system and Earth stations (Estab. Ag., Art. 12*bis* 2.3–7). It approves an action plan on an annual basis (Estab. Ag., Art. 12*bis* 2.10). Bridging technical and financial matters, the committee proposes the intellectual property policy for the organisation (Estab. Ag., Art. 12*bis* 19, Op. Ag., Art. 3.11.8).

The Operations Committee determines the size of the INTERSPUTNIK share capital (Estab. Ag., Art. 12*bis* 12, Op. Ag., Art. 3.11.2).[51] It decides on investment shares and their redistribution (Estab. Ag., Art. 12*bis* 2.11; Op. Ag., Art. 6). No transfer or reduction of investment share can affect the minimum investment share to be held (Op. Ag., Art. 8.3).[52] It adopts a financial policy (Estab. Ag., Art. 12*bis* 2.11; Op. Ag., Art. 3.11.1–2). It decides on all financing arrangements including those with commercial sources (Estab. Ag., Art. 12*bis* 2.13; Op. Ag., Art. 12). The Committee authorises Earth stations and sets the criteria to be met (Op. Ag., Art. 3.11.2). Finally, it fixes the system usage charges (Estab. Ag., Art.12*bis* 2.11).

The Operations Committee approves the action plan for the next year (Estab. Ag., Art. 12*bis* 2.10), approves the reports of the Director General (Estab. Ag., Art. 12*bis* 2.14) and the staffing structure of the Directorate (Estab. Ag., Art. 12*bis* 2.9), elects the Chairman and members of the Auditing Commission and approves its procedures and reports (Estab. Ag., Art. 12*bis* 2.15). Should INTERSPUTNIK be involved in an arbitration, it appoints an arbitrator (Estab. Ag., Art. 12*bis* 2.18).

The day-to-day functioning of INTERSPUTNIK is in the hands of the permanent Directorate led by a Director General (Estab. Ag., Arts 11.1 and 13.1). The bulk of the staff are nationals of member states, appointed with due regard to their professional qualifications and an equitable geographic distribution, though now it is competent to employ non-member nationals (Estab. Ag., Art. 13.6). The Director General is elected jointly by the board and the Operations Committee and may be recalled by them (Estab. Ag., Art.

---

51 For the share capital, see *infra* at n. 54.
52 The current minimum share is 1% (Op. Ag. Art. 6.2).

13.5). He and his deputy have to be nationals of INTERSPUTIK Members but from different countries (Estab. Ag., Art. 13.5).

The Director General is the chief executive of INTERSPUTNIK and represents it in all matters (Estab. Ag., Art. 13.2), including the conclusion of international and other agreements (Estab. Ag., Art. 13.4.4). He is responsible to the board and the Operations Committee, and he is guided by and implements their decisions (Estab. Ag., Art. 13.3 and 13.4.1). The Directorate reports to both bodies for their approval (Estab. Ag., Arts 12 6.6; 12*bis* 2.14 and 20; Op. Ag., Art. 3.9).

The Director General negotiates the design of the INTERSPUTNIK system, the manufacture of its space segment and its delivery (Estab. Ag., Art. 13.4.2–3). With the approval of the Operations Committee he drafts the budget, and reports to the Board on its execution (Estab. Ag., Art. 13.5). All financial matters dealt with by the Directorate are open to the scrutiny of the Auditing Commission (Estab. Ag., Art. 14.2).

The Auditing Commission consists of three persons, including a chairman, all nationals of the member states, none of whom may hold any other office in INTERSPUTNIK (Estab. Ag., Art. 14.1).[53] They are elected for three years by the Operations Committee (Estab. Ag., Art. 12*bis* 2.15). The commission supervises financial activities (Estab. Ag., Art. 11.3), has access to all necessary information (Estab. Ag., Art. 14.2) and reports to the Operations Committee (Estab. Ag., Art. 14.3). The accounting standards of INTERSPUTNIK are those approved by the International Accounting Standards Committee of London (Op. Ag., Art. 7.6).

In the redesigned INTERSPUTNIK, a fundamental change was the introduction of 'share capital'. Its size is fixed by the Operations Committee and may be increased taking into account the plans of the organisation and the ratio of debt to capital (Estab. Ag., Art. 12*bis* 2.12; Op. Ag., Art. 4.1–2).[54] The share capital is derived from investment shares contributed by the signatories (Op. Ag., Art. 4). Shares are of four types, a mandatory minimum, a mandatory investment share proportionate to system use, an additional investment share and a voluntary investment share (Op. Ag., Arts. 4 and 5.1). It is possible for services and other resources contributed by a signatory to be quantified for share purposes (Op. Ag., Art. 5.5).

The other source of funding is the revenue from system use. How that is dealt with is specified in Op. Ag. Art. 7. Tariffs for system usage are set to cover costs and make a profit (Op. Ag., Art. 7.2). Revenue pays for leasing, operational and maintenance charges and other necessary operations (Op. Ag. Art. 7.2). Thereafter a guaranteed dividend is paid to signatories in proportion to their contribution to share capital.[55] Any remaining profit may be distributed as an additional dividend. (Op. Ag., Art. 7.3.1). Alternatively, it may be added to share capital or other funds or held for additional capital investment (Op. Ag. 7.3.3.2–4). Should revenue not meet running costs, any deficit is met from reserves or equity (Op. Ag., Art. 7.5).

---

53 Is there a distinction between 'holding office' and being an employee?
54 The arrangements in the current operating agreement are much less specific than those originally adopted. The earlier arrangements referred to freely convertible currency (Art. 9.1). That has disappeared in the current version.
55 The guaranteed dividend is defined in Op. Ag. Art. 1 and the right to receive in Arts. 2.3.2 and 7.2.1.

The areas to which INTERSPUTNIK provides service are largely territorially confined so arguably the 'global' aspect of INTERSPUTNIK remains tenuous.[56] INTERSPUTNIK presently operates twelve geostationary satellites and can also use INTELSAT and EUTELSAT transponders. Some global services are provided through commercial links with other satellite networks and service providers, links now coordinated through a wholly owned subsidiary Intersputnik Holding Ltd. established in 2005. INTERSPUTNIK seems unlikely to privatise on the Western model in the near future.

ARABSAT[57]

The Agreement of the Arab Corporation for Space Communications (ARABSAT) entered into force in February 1977.[58] Members of the corporation are states that are members of the Arab League (Art. 23) and contribute to the capital requirements of the organisation (Art. 4(2) and 20).

ARABSAT functions through a General Assembly that consists of the Ministers of Communications of all member states, a Board of Directors and an Executive Organ led by a Director-General.[59] The General Assembly, which can be attended by external observers as of right or by permission (Art. 10(7)),[60] deals with general policy, planning, rate setting for the space segment, general specification for Earth stations, financial allocations and adjustments, and the suspension and withdrawal of members, investment shares, budgets and amendments to the Agreement (Art. 11). The real power lies with the Board of Directors. This consists of nine members from different member states, five having the largest financial share in the undertaking, two elected from among the members with the highest capacity usage and two from the oldest membership (Art. 12). The Board implements the policies set by the assembly and provides and maintains the space segment of the ARABSAT system (Art. 13). It appoints the Director General to head the Executive Organ, which implements the decisions of the Board (Art. 14). First funded by capital levy ARABSAT is now financed through share-based system usage that is reassessed as needed or on the accession or withdrawal of a member (Art. 6). Currently (2022) ARABSAT operates seven satellites in GSO providing telecommunication and direct broadcast services to the Arab world and Europe.

Other Service Providers

As can be seen from the original history of INTELSAT, it is necessary for companies seeking to provide telecommunication services beyond their state of nationality to secure landing

---

56 Satellite coverage runs from 14°W to 183°E. Access to INTERSPUTNIK services is outlined at www.intersputnik.int/services/.

57 ARABSAT: www.arabsat.com. Lyall, *supra* n. 16, 304–310.

58 1185 *Official Gazette of the State of Bahrain*, 22 July 1976 (Amiri Decree No. 25/1976), Gulf Public Relations Translation Service trans.; *Space Law: Selected Basic Documents*, *supra* n, 44, 449–468; II Manual, 345–360; (1977) 5 *J. Sp. L.* 157–173 (text only).

59 We use terms used by ARABSAT. Some translations speak of a General Body, an Executive Body or Department, and a General Manager.

60 Observers entitled to attend are the Arab League, the Arab States Broadcasting Union, the Arab League Telecommunications Union and the Arab League Educational, Scientific and Cultural Organisation (Art. 10(7)).

or gateway rights in other states.[61] This requirement can affect the service provided. Here we discuss the private commercial companies providing the most global services.

Iridium

Iridium Communications Inc., a commercial company (www.iridium.com/), operates a sixty-six-satellite network in six orbital planes in low earth polar orbit.[62] The system provides worldwide broadband coverage including of the polar regions. Iridium has been recognised by the International Maritime Organisation as a competent provider for the maritime safety system and as such is supervised by IMSO.[63] Iridium safely deorbits its spent satellites, thus mitigating space debris.[64]

SES

Originally the Société Européenne des Satellites, SES-Global S.A. is a private company based in Luxemburg.[65] It is one of the dominant providers of fixed satellite services,[66] its purpose being to 'take generally any interest whatsoever in electronic media and to be active, more particularly, in the communications area via satellite'.[67] SES provides broadcast services and dedicated (i.e. not public access) communications. The shareholder/investors are diverse.[68] In 2016, SES acquired O3b Networks, which operates satellites in equatorial MEO.[69] As a result, SES is the only service provider with satellites in both GSO and MEO (www.ses.com/).

SpaceX/Starlink

The commercial satellite launching company SpaceX (www.spacex.com/) is developing a LEO communication network through Starlink which operates a large constellation of

---

61 Cf. the UK licensing for Starlink services, *infra* n. 70.
62 Iridium Communications Inc.: www.iridium/com/. J. Bloom, *Eccentric Orbits: The Iridium Story* (New York: Grove Atlantic, 2016).
63 IMSO supervision, *supra* at n. 36.
64 In 2009 the Iridium-33 satellite was in collision with the derelict Russian Cosmos 2251. H.H. Hertzfeld and B. Basely-Walker, 'Legal Note on Space Accidents' (2010) 59 ZLW 230–240; O.A. Volynskaya, 'Landmark Space-Related Accidents and the Progress of Space Law' (2013) 62 ZLW 220–236; F.G. von der Dunk, 'A Sleeping Beauty Awakens: The 1968 Rescue Agreement after Forty Years' (2008) 34 *J. Sp. L.* 411–34; and his 'Too-Close Encounters of the Third-Party Kind: Will the Liability Convention Stand the Test of the Cosmos 2251-Iridium 33 Collision' (2009) 52 *Proc. IISL* 199–209; F.G. von der Dunk and M. Meija-Kaiser, 'Collision Course: 2009 Iridium-Cosmos Crash' (2009) 52 *Proc. IISL* 274–284.
65 For SES documentation, see www.ses.com/about-us/environmental-social-and-governance/governance/documents.
66 See paras 37 and 116 of the Third Report and Analysis of Competitive Market Conditions with Respect to Domestic and International Satellite Communications Services, IB Docket No. 09–16, and IB Docket No. 10–99, released 13 December 2011: https://apps.fcc.gov/edocs_public/attachmatch/FCC-11-183A1.pdf.
67 SES Articles of Incorporation: www.ses.com/21120637/Articles_of_Incorporation.pdf.
68 SES Art. 5 restricts the percentage of A shares that may be held directly or indirectly by a shareholder. These restrictions may be breached only if the Luxembourg government does not object on grounds of the general public interest and an extraordinary meeting of the company approves by a two-thirds majority vote. This seems to ensure that SES-Global is unlikely to fall into single or consortium ownership.
69 O3b Networks: www.o3bnetworks.com/

small satellites.[70] It has to be said that this particular network does make difficulties for other users of space to a greater extent than other networks, raising questions as to its conformity with the provisions of OST Art. IX on causing interference to others.[71]

Regional Systems

A number of countries that are not themselves launch capable have arranged for the construction and launch of one or more communications satellites for their own purposes.[72] Occasionally they contract out operational responsibilities. Sometimes telecommunication is combined with other functions such as Earth observation. In addition various international 'tele-communities' also exist.[73] All these lie beyond the ambit of this book.

A question remains. Have the hopes of UNGA Res. 1721 of 1961 and UNGA Res. 1802 (XVII)(1962) been met?[74] The answer must remain uncertain. Satellite telecommunications are generally available, in the main without discrimination. Thanks to their multiplicity and interconnectivity, the networks make global access possible. However, the initial intergovernmental arrangements were established to provide a public service in the world public interest. They were self-financing and to an extent non-profit-making. That has changed with the major privatisations and the introduction of other private service providers. What was a public service is now largely a service provided for profit to the public. We will return to the question of the general world public interest in Chapter 17.

70 Starlink: www.starlink.com/satellites. In 2022, the UK licensed the establishment of six ground stations for the Starlink constellation. See 'Starlink Internet Services Limited: Decision on applications for six non-geostationary earth station gateway licences', Ofcom, 10 November 2022: www.ofcom.org.uk/consultations-and-statements/category-3/starlink-gateway-licence-applications?utm_medium=email&utm_campaign=Supporting%20innovation%20and%20the%20space%20sector&utm_content=Supporting%20wireless%20innovation%20and%20the%20space%20sector+CID_0c2b4d648d9aec901437da57fef33045&utm_source=updates&utm_term=granting%20licences. During the confrontation with Russia Starlink provided satellite communication services to the Ukraine.
71 Starlink is licensed by the US. When complete, it may operate through more than 40,000 satellites. Defunct satellites will continue in orbit. Regularly, a proportion will decay from orbit, but as the satellites have no propellant, deorbiting is not controlled, and potential collision and debris are unavoidable. (Cf. China's complaint to COPUOS (A/AC.105/1262) and the US response (A/AC.105/1265)). The effect on astronomy is already considerable, and launches into LEO and beyond may be affected. The effect on other radio links is uncertain and the system's requirement for bandwidth will be great.
Other constellations are planned. Cf. the UK licensing of Telesat ground stations, 'Telesat LEO Inc: Decision on application for non-geostationary Earth Station Network licence' Ofcom 10 November 2022: www.ofcom.org.uk/consultations-and-statements/category-3/telesat-network-licence-application?utm_medium=email&utm_campaign=Supporting%20wireless%20innovation%20and%20the%20space%20sector&utm_content=Supporting%20wireless%20innovation%20and%20the%20space%20sector+CID_0c2b4d648d9aec901437da57fef33045&utm_source=updates&utm_term=approved%20an%20application.
72 See for example Hispasat (www.hispasat.com) serving Iberia and Latin America in Spanish and Portuguese; Thaicom (www.thaicom.net/) providing services for Asia, Africa and Oceania; Asiasat (www.asiasat.com/) in Asia and Oceania; Es'hailsat (www.eshailsat.qa/) operating from Qatar and serving the Middle East and North Africa; Ktsat (www.ktsat.com) serving Korea and the Far East. Most of these are allied or work in cooperation with other service providers.
73 R.C. Harding, *Space Policy in Developing Countries: The Search for Security and Development on the Final Frontier* (Abingdon: Routledge, 2013). See the Asia Pacific Telecommunity (www.apt.int) 1129 UNTS 3), the African Telecommunications Union (www.atu-ust.org), the Inter-American Telecommunication Commission (www.citel.oas.org), and the European Broadcasting Union (www.ebu.ch).
74 See *supra* nn. 7 and 8.

Direct Satellite Broadcasting

Direct broadcasting by satellite (DBS) has had a major impact all over the world, but its problems were foreseen.[75] It has made TV programming accessible by individual households using an appropriate dish aerial and, where necessary, decoders. Most satellite providers carry TV channels from a number of sources.[76] Radio broadcasting by satellite is also increasing. In short, the availability of information and entertainment by satellite has vastly increased.

Direct broadcasting presents two sets of problems. One is the use of orbital positions and appropriate radio frequencies. These are ordinarily available under the first-come, first-served basis discussed in Chapter 8.[77] However, pressure from countries apprehensive of the dominance of the space-competent states led to some planning of the direct-satellite broadcasting system.

The matter was first raised in the 1970s and eventuated in the ITU WARC-ORB 1985–88, which adopted a Plan, now RR Appendix 30B, allotting to each state for DBS purposes a location within a series of 10° GSO slots together with uplink and downlink frequencies.[78] The plan has been revised, most recently at the ITU WRC-19 in 2019. The plan also allows for the inclusion of new ITU members.[79] It may be that in the future, these arrangements will be supplemented by regional arrangements.[80]

The other problem relates to the content of DBS.[81] We note that a parallel debate as to control of content on the Internet has subsequently emerged and may be taking more attention as we write.[82] Even so the debates as to DBS provide a telling comparison.

---

75 A. Chayes and L. Chazen, 'Policy Problems in Direct Broadcasting from Satellites' (1970) 5 *Stan. J. Int. Stud.* 4–20; B.A. Hurwitz, 'The Labyrinth of International Telecommunications Law: Direct Broadcast Satellites' (1988) 35 *Neth. Int. L. Rev.* 145–180; G. Zhukov and Y. Kolosov (B. Belitzky trans.), *International Space Law* (New York: Praeger, 1984), 127–136; A.S. Piradov, *International Space Law* (Moscow: Progress, 1976) 182–196. See also Georgetown Space Law Group, 'DBS under FCC and International Regulation' (1984) 37 *Vand. L. Rev.* 67–144; P.B. Larsen et al., 'Direct Broadcast Satellites: National and International Regulation' (2004) 8 *Modern Legal Systems Cyclopedia*.

76 The ITU Radiocommunication Bureau maintains a Space Network List (SNL) (www.itu.int/ITU-R/go/space/snl/en). Cf. the channels carried by SES-Global, Astra and associated SES companies: www.ses.com/our-coverage#/ and by EUTELSAT (a 135 page list): www.eutelsat.com/products/pdf/tvlineup.pdf. The website www.satsig.net/ lists satellite frequencies including those of direct broadcast services.

77 See Chapter XX following nn. 131 and 144.

78 RR App. 30B. A List is kept of states having an allotment under the Plan. App. 30B Art. 6 (Rev. 2019) deals with the conversion of an allotment to an assignment. R.S. Jakhu, 'The Evolution of the ITU's Regulatory Regime Governing Space Radiocommunication Services and the Geostationary Satellite Orbit' (1983) VIII AASL 381–4–7; R.S. Jakhu, J.L. Magdelénat and H. Rousselle, 'The ITU Regulatory Framework for Satellite Communications: and Analysis of Space WARC 1985' (1987) *Int. J.* 276–88; M.L. Smith, 'Space Law/Space WARC: An Analysis of the Space Law Issues raised at the 1985 ITU World Administrative Radio Conference on the Geostationary Orbit' (1986) 8 *Houston J. Int. L.* 227–245 at 230–368.

79 Procedures by which a new ITU member state can enter the allotment plan are in RR App. 30B, Art. 7. See also Chapter XX, *c*. n. 135.

80 Plans and regional agreements for DBS are in contemplation: see 'Establishment of Agreements and Associated Plans for the Broadcasting-satellite Service', RR Res. 507 (Rev. WRC–19) together with Resolutions 33 (Rev. WRC–15) and 34 (Rev. WRC-19), and Chapter 8, *c*. n. 135.

81 Cf. A.C. Clarke, 'I Remember Babylon' (1960), *Arthur C. Clarke: The Collected Stories* (London: Gollancz, 2000) 702–710, where the possibility of the moral fibre of a nation being sapped by pornography from DBS is outlined. Cf., similarly, the element that gives K. MacLeod, *The Execution Channel* (London: Orbit, 2007) its title. See also D. Webster, 'Direct Broadcast Satellites: Proximity, Sovereignty and National Identity' (1984) 62 *Foreign Affairs* 1161–74; J.W. Penney, 'The Cycles of Global Telecommunication Censorship and Surveillance' (2015) 36 *U. Pa. J. Int. L.* 693–753.

82 See *infra* n. 131ff.

Balancing control of content of the media with freedom of expression has produced domestic legislation in most countries,[83] as well as regional agreements in various areas of the world.[84] However, DBS cannot be made subject to control as easily as terrestrial broadcast may.[85] In terms of general space law, though, we do have the Direct Broadcasting Principles of 1982. Adopted by majority vote both in COPUOS and in the General Assembly not by acclamation, the DBS Principles are, however, of flawed significance.[86]

The debate that led to the Direct Broadcast Principles must be seen in the context of its time and the technicalities of such broadcasts. As to the technicalities, DBS signals cannot be simply focussed on a particular state. The 'footprint' maps shown on the satellite broadcasters' websites demonstrate that it is not possible to match the area of broadcast to the boundaries of a specific state. There will always be a 'spill-over' to adjacent states caused by the angle at which the downlink beam meets the curvature of the earth.[87] That also assumes that the broadcaster is not deliberately targeting a state which does not want those broadcasts to be seen or heard in its territory. Such technical constraints aggravated the political argument.[88]

In the later 1960s and early 1970s, new states came into being through the dissolution of the old colonial empires. This brought stresses and strains. Many were dissatisfied by finding that they had limited or no control over their natural resources thanks to contracts

---

83 In the UK, questions of content initially lie the Office of Communications (Ofcom) under the Communication Acts 2003 c. 31, and the Broadcasting Acts 1990 c. 42 and 1996 c. 55, as amended. Questions of content could raise argument as to freedom of speech under the UK Human Rights Act, 1998 c.42. In 2012, Ofcom revoked the UK licences of the Iranian Press TV: www.ofcom.org.uk/__data/assets/pdf_file/0031/67198/press-tv-revocation.pdf. In the light of events in the Ukraine and failures in impartiality, in March 2022, Ofcom revoked the licences of Russia's RT service and an associated broadcaster to broadcast to or in the UK: www.ofcom.org.uk/__data/assets/pdf_file/0014/234023/revocation-notice-ano-tv-novosti.pdf;www.ofcom.org.uk/__data/assets/pdf_file/0019/241723/RT-News-RT-various-dates-and-times.pdf: www.ofcom.org.uk/__data/assets/pdf_file/0014/234023/revocation-notice-ano-tv-novosti.pdf.

In the US, the FCC has powers under the Communications Act (1934), Public Law 416, 48 Stat. 1064, 47 USC § 151, Sec. 303 (47 USC 303). T. Dermott, 'In the EYE of the Beholder: A Comparative Study of Public Morality and Free Speech across the Pacific' (2013) 26 *Colum. J. Asian L.* 105–138; M. Konar-Steenberg, 'The Needle and the Damage Done: The Pervasive Presence of Obsolete Mass Media Audience Models in First Amendment Doctrine' (2005) 8 *Vand. J. Ent. & Tech. L.* 45–70; J.C. Quale and M.J. Tuesley, 'Space, the Final Frontier – Expanding FCC Regulation of Indecent Content onto Direct Broadcast Satellite (2007) 60 *Fed. Comm. L. J.* 37–66; J.R. Paul, 'Images from Abroad: Making Direct Broadcasting by Satellites Safe for Sovereignty' (1986) 9 *Hastings Int. and Comp. L. Rev.* 329–376. For China see Yun Zhao, *National Space Law in China* (Leiden: Brill, 2015) 141–142, 146–149.

See also the 1989 EU Directive on 'Television without Frontiers', Council Directive 89/552/EEC, as amended: http://eur-lex.europa.eu/legal-content/EN/TXT/HTML/?uri=URISERV:l24101&from=EN.

84 See the 1989 Directive, *supra* n. 83, and the 'European Convention on Transfrontier Television', 1989, ETS 132; 1993 UKTS 22, Cmnd 2178; (1989) 28 ILM 859–69, as amended by Protocol of 1998, CETS No. 171, and the European Council Directive Concerning the Pursuit of Television Broadcasting Activities, 1989, EC OJ No. L 298, October 17, 1989, 23–30 (1989) 28 ILM 1492–1499.

85 The UK licensing powers were used to stop satellite broadcasts to the UK by Press TV in 2013, and to suspend the RT licence in 2022. See *supra* n. 83.

86 'Principles Governing the Use by States of Artificial Earth Satellites for International Direct Television Broadcasting', 10 December 1982, UNGA Res. 37/92; [1983] 77 AJIL 733–736; CoCoSL III, 1–79. Most DBS-competent states either voted against or abstained. See *infra* n. 106ff.

87 The more vertical the beam, the smaller the spill-over.

88 G.L. Thomas, 'Approaches to Controlling Propaganda and Spillover from Direct Broadcast Satellites' (1970) 5 *Stan. J. In. Stud.*, 167–198.

and concessions granted by their former rulers. This was rectified through negotiation or expropriation. In part to justify what was done, the UN General Assembly adopted various resolutions usually by majority vote.[89] A further dissatisfaction related to information and the media, the balance between the media of the developed countries and those of the new states.[90]

While that had some justification, it has to be said that some new governments as well as some older governments (largely within the then Communist bloc) were anxious for political reasons to control the media within their territories and therefore also to control what came in to their states. At the same time the development of telecommunications had made news-gathering and dissemination much easier and swifter. DBS therefore came onto the international agenda.

Radio transmissions received within a country whose government found its content unacceptable had been a matter of contention for decades. Propaganda, or what is considered to be propaganda, whether political or otherwise has always caused difficulties.[91] The OST Preamble contains a reference to UNGA Res. 110 (II) of 1947, which condemns propaganda likely to cause a threat to peace and states expressly that that it applies to space.[92] The field was therefore open for action.

In 1967, the General Assembly asked COPUOS 'to study the technical feasibility of communications by direct broadcasts by/from satellites (DBS) and the current and foreseeable developments in this field as well as the implications of such developments'.[93] A working group therefore worked over the next five years.[94] On the basis of COPUOS

---

89 'Permanent Sovereignty over Natural Resources', UNGA Res. 1803 (XVII) 1962; [1963] 57 AJIL 710; (1963) 2 ILM 223; 'Charter of Economic Rights and Duties of States', UNGA Res. 3281 (XXIX) 1974; (1975) 14 ILM 251. Cf. the New International Economic Order resolutions: 'Declaration on the Establishment of a New International Economic Order' (A/9556) UNGA Res. 3201 (S-VI), 1974, and the related 'Programme of Action' UNGA Res. 3202 (S-VI) 1974.

90 J.W. Penney, 'The Cycles of Global Telecommunications Censorship and Surveillance' (2014–2015) *U. Pa. J. Int. L.* 639–753. Cf. 'Symposium: International Satellite Communications and the New International Information Order' (1980–1981) 8 *Syracuse J. Int. L. & Comm.*, particularly M. Masmoudi, 'The New World Information Order and Direct Broadcasting Satellites' at 322–341, C.Q. Christol, 'Telecommunications, Outer Space and the New International Information Order (NIIO)' at 343–364; S.E. Doyle, 'International Satellite Communications and the New International Information Order: Distressing Broadcasting Satellites' at 365–374, and R.S. Jakhu, 'Direct Broadcasting via Satellite and a New Information Order' at 375–390.

91 See H. Lauterpacht, 'Revolutionary Propaganda by Governments' (1927) 17 *Trans. Grot. Soc.* 143–164; V. Van Dyke, 'The Responsibility of States for International Propaganda' [1940] 34 AJIL 58–73; E.A. Downey, 'A Historical Survey of the International Regulation of Propaganda' (1984) 5 *Mich. Y.B. Int. Leg. Stud.* 341–360; J.T. Powell, 'Towards a Negotiable Definition of Propaganda for International Agreements Related to Direct Broadcast Satellites' (1982) 45 *Law and Contemp. Probs* 3–35; P. Achilleas, 'Propaganda via Satellite' (2002) 45 *Proc. IISL* 258–262. Cf. J.R. Paul, 'Images from Abroad: Making Direct Broadcasting by Satellites Safe for Sovereignty' (1985–86) 9 *Hastings Int. Comp. L. Rev.* 329–375; Larsen, *supra* n. 75.

92 'Measures to be Taken Against Propaganda and the Inciters of a New War', UNGA Res. 110 (II), 3 November 1947.

93 'Report of the Committee on the Peaceful Uses of Outer Space' para 13, UNGA Res. 2260 (XXII) 3 November 1967.

94 The COPUOS Working Group on DBS reports that cover legal questions are A/AC.105/117 (1973) and A.AC.105/127 (1974). Christol, 605–719, covers the history down to 1981. Cf. A.E. Gotlieb and C.M. Dalfen, 'Direct Satellite Broadcasting: A Case Study in the Development of the Law of Space

reports in 1972, the UNGA thought that principles governing DBS should be elaborated with the eventual aim of an international agreement. However, this was incorporated in two separate and very different Assembly Resolutions adopted on the same day in 1972, UNGA Res. 2916 (XXVII)[95] and UNGA Res. 2917 (XXVII).[96] In addition, the USSR submitted a draft DBS convention to the Assembly, parts of which were very much in favour of control and would have imposed international duties as to content.[97] Divergent views had emerged over the freedom of the press *vis-à-vis* governmental control of media on a broad front, not just DBS.

The UN agency concerned with the media and its content is the United Nations Educational, Scientific and Cultural Organisation, UNESCO.[98] It had also been discussing satellite broadcasting and adopted in 1972 a 'Declaration of Guiding Principles on the Use of Satellite Broadcasting for the Free Flow of Information, the Spread of Information and Greater Cultural Exchange'.[99] This did affirm the importance of freedom of information and the value of direct broadcasting for education and other benefits.

However, its Art. IX implied a power vested in receiving countries to object to the content of DBS transmissions, Art. IX.1 stating it being 'necessary that states . . . reach or promote prior agreements concerning direct satellite broadcasting to the population of countries other than the country of origin of the transmission' and Article IX.2 that advertising content in such broadcasts had to be subject to prior

---

Communications' (1969) 7 Can. YBIL 33–60; C. Verdon and C.M. Dalfen, 'La coopération régionale: Nouvelle voie ou impasse dans le développement du droit des satellites de radiodiffusion directe?' (1970) 8 Can YBIL 19–60; C.M. Dalfen, – 1 'Direct Satellite Broadcasting Towards International Arrangements to Transcend and Marshal the Political Realities' (1970) 20 *U. Tor. L.J.* 366–374; – 2 'The International Legislative Process: Direct Broadcasting and Remote Earth Sensing by Satellite Compared' (1972) 10 Can. YBIL 186–211; J.J. Gehrig, 'Broadcast Satellites – Prospects and Problems' (1975) 3 *J. Sp. L.* 25–38; Jakhu *supra* n. 90. See also the *Symposium on Direct Broadcast Satellites and Space Law* (1975) 3 *J. Sp. L.* 3–98. For later see S.L. Fjordbak, 'The International Direct Broadcast Satellite Controversy' (1990) 55 *J. Air L. & Comm.* 903–938 at 907–911; V. Kopal, 'The Role of United Nations Declarations of Principles in the Progressive Development of Space Law' (1988) 16 *J. Sp. L.* 5–20, at 10–14.

95 'Preparation of an International Convention on Principles Governing the use by States of Artificial Earth Satellites for Direct Television Broadcasting', UNGA Res. 2916 (XXVII), 9 November 1972 (1972) 11 ILM 1470.

96 'Preparation of an International Convention on Principles Governing the use by States of Artificial Earth Satellites for Direct Television Broadcasting', UNGA Res. 2917 (XXVII), 9 November 1972, notes that deliberations on the 'draft Convention on Freedom of Information' by the UNGA 'may be useful in the discussion and elaboration of international instruments or United Nations arrangements relative to direct television broadcasting'.

97 USSR Draft Convention on Principles Governing the Use by States of Artificial Earth Satellites for Direct Television Broadcasting, 1972: UN Doc. A/8771; Annex III to A/AC.105/117 (1973); (1972) 11 ILM 1375–1381.

98 Constitution of the United Nations Educational Scientific and Cultural Organisation, London 16 November 1945; 4 UNTS 275; 1946 UKTS 50, Cmnd 6963; 61 Stat. 2495, TIAS 1580; 9 Hudson 786; 3 Bevans 1311; [1947] AJIL Supp. 1. The current text is at http://unesdoc.unesco.org/images/0013/001337/133729e.pdf#page=7.

99 UNESCO General Conference, Records of the 17th Sess. Res. 4.11 (1972) Vol. 1, 67–68: http://unesdoc.unesco.org/images/0000/000021/002136eb.pdf; (1973) A/AC.105/109; (1972) 11 ILM 1475–9; (1973) 1 *J. Sp. L.* 161–165. Masmoudi *supra* n. 90, at 324–32; Paul, *supra* n. 91, at 359–362.

agreement. Underlying was the belief that state control was necessary both as a recognition of its sovereignty and for the preservation of its political, economic and cultural identity.[100]

In the later 1970s in pursuit of such ideas, a majority of UNESCO members supported the establishment of a Commission to study communications problems, particularly those relating to the mass media and the dissemination of news. In what is now known as the 'MacBride Report', that commission called for the establishment of a 'New International Communication Order',[101] the 'democratisation' of communications, the strengthening of national media and the lessening of dependence on external news sources.[102] Implicit was the idea that governments should have the right to control news and other media not only within but also entering and leaving their territories. This was attractive to many of the then members of the Non-Aligned Movement, but not to the USA or the UK, which, after major disputes about the implementation of the MacBride Report, withdrew from UNESCO, protesting that such control was incompatible with the freedom of information and of the press.[103]

A significant step was taken in 1974 when a Convention Relating to the Distribution of Programme-carrying Signals Transmitted by Satellite was agreed at Brussels.[104] Its purposes were to prevent the re-transmission of DBS by distributors who were not intended recipients, and to protect copyright (Art. 2). The Convention does not apply to the direct reception of DBS intended for reception by the public (Art. 3). However, as the Brussels

---

100 Certainly, fifty-plus years on, it is very evident that cultural identity can be eroded or altered by broadcasts (particularly television) that conform to the norms of other cultures. Cultural identity remains of concern and may be explored particularly in the work of UNESCO. M. Petit, *The International Convention on Cultural Diversity (UNESCO). Context, Evolution and Perspectives.* www.cac.cat/pfw_files/cma/recerca/quaderns_cac/Q18petit_EN.pdf.

101 Sometimes also called the New Information Order, the New World Information Order or the New World Information and Communication Order.

102 S. MacBride, *Many Voices, One World: Towards a New, More Just, and More Efficient World Information and Communication Order* (UNESCO and Other Publishers, 1980). Cf. A.N. Delzeit and R.M. Wahl, 'Redefining Freedom of Speech under International Space Law; The Need for Bilateral Communication Alliances to Resolve the Debate between the "Free Flow of Information and the Prior Consent" Schools of Thought' (1995–1996) 2 *ILSA J. Int. & Comp. L.* 287–282. See also O. Batura, 'Harmful Interference and Human Rights', in M. Hoffman, ed., *Harmful Interference from a Regulatory Perspective* (Baden-Baden: Nomos, 2015) 215–230.

103 The UK left UNESCO in 1985 and rejoined in 1997. The USA left in 1984 and rejoined in 2005. In 2011, it suspended contributing over the admission of Palestine and fully withdrew in 2017. It rejoined in July 2023: www.unesco.org/en/articles/united-states-america-announces-its-intention-rejoin-unesco-july?hub=701. Letters as to the 1984 US withdrawal are at (1984) 23 ILM 220–230 and (1985) 24 ILM 489. 'United States' Return to UNESCO', Contemporary Practice of the United States' [2003] 97 AJIL 977–979; M.J. Farley, 'Conflicts over Government Control of Information – the United States and UNESCO' (1985) 59 *Tulane L. Rev.* 1071–1088; P.A. Hoffer, 'Upheaval in the United Nations System – United States' Withdrawal from UNESCO' (1986) 12 *Brook. J. Int. L.* 161–207; C.C. Joyner and S.A. Lawson, 'The United States and UNESCO: Rethinking the Decision to Withdraw' (1985–1986) 41 *Int. J.* 37–71.

104 Convention Relating to the Distribution of Programme-carrying Signals Transmitted by Satellite, 1974, 1144 UNTS 3; US Tr. Doc. 98–31, TIAS 11078; (1974) 13 ILM 1444. As of 2023, the Convention has ten signatories and thirty-eight ratifications. C.Q. Christol, 'The 1974 Brussels Convention relating to the Distribution of Program-carrying Signals Transmitted by Satellite: An Aspect of Human Rights' (1978) 6 *J. Sp. L.* 19–35.

Conference proceeded, the USSR and others sought the amendment of the draft to include controls as to content. This was resisted but the attempt demonstrated the interest in such questions.[105]

In the meantime, COPUOS had been at work. Its discussions reflected the division between the proponents of freedom of information and of the press, and those who considered state sovereignty and the preservation of political, economic and cultural identity as of overriding importance.[106] Suffice it here to say that the new states and the then Communist bloc commanded a majority within COPUOS. It may also be that some new states mistakenly thought that in the development of international rules, a voting majority meant more than in fact it did or does.

In any event, the 'Principles Governing the Use by States of Artificial Earth Satellites for International Direct Television Broadcasting' was clearly the mind of the majority within COPUOS. But, lacking consensus, COPUOS itself could not present the Principles as part of its Report, and they were presented to the General Assembly by a group of non-aligned states,[107] which, by a vote of one hundred seven, with thirteen voting against[108] and thirteen abstentions[109] on 10 December 1982 adopted UNGA Res. 37/92 with the Principles annexed thereto.[110] The negative votes and abstentions are important since they included all the states, other than the USSR, which were then able or likely in the nearer future to be able to launch and operate direct broadcast satellites. The authority of the DBS Principles compared with the other UN Space Principles is thereby diminished.[111] Like the other UN Principles, the Direct Broadcasting Principles have not subsequently been revised.[112]

The Direct Broadcasting Principles themselves are not as extreme or mandatory as some states would have wished, and occasionally are so even-handed that in certain areas the rights and obligations in effect cancel out. It is unexceptionable that DBS should be carried out in accordance with relevant international law (Pr. 4), that all states may engage in DBS (Pr. 5), that states bear international responsibility for DBS activities they license (Pr. 8), that disputes arising from DBS should be settled by peaceful means agreed between the parties in accordance with the UN Charter (Pr. 7), that in order to promote international cooperation the UN Secretary General should be informed of DBS activities

---

105 See previous note. The proposed additional article was transmitted to the UN Secretary General for forwarding to COPUOS as being relevant to its work on DBS: see (1974) 13 ILM 1444 at 1466.

106 See Masmoudi and Jakhu, both *supra* n. 90; Webster, *supra* n. 81.

107 Not including the USSR, as some assert.

108 Belgium, Denmark, Germany, Iceland, Israel, Italy, Japan, Luxembourg, Netherlands, Norway, Spain, UK and US.

109 Australia, Austria, Canada, Finland, France, Greece, Ireland, Lebanon, Malawi, Morocco, New Zealand, Portugal, Sweden.

110 See CoCoSL III, 1–79. F. Koppensteiner, 'The 1982 UN Principles Governing the Use by States of Artificial Earth Satellites for International Direct Television Broadcasting', Marboe, 161–181.

111 C.Q. Christol, 'Prospects for an International Legal Regime for Direct Television Broadcasting' (1985) 34 ICLQ 142–58; S. Gorove, 'International Direct Television Broadcasting by Satellite: "Prior Consent" Revisited' (1985–86) 24 *Col. J. Transnat. L.* 1–11 [Gorove, 65–75].

112 In 2006, Greece proposed the review of the DBS Principles with a view to transforming its text into a treaty. This was not debated but may yet be reintroduced. See COPUOS Report of the Legal SubCommittee on its 45th Sess., 3–13 April 2006, A/AC.105/871, para 154 (e).

and that he should publicise that information (Pr. 12), and that copyright should be protected (Pr. 11).

Yet in other ways, the Principles represent or mirror divergent attitudes. The protection of copyright is shaded by reference to the interest of developing states in the use of DBS to further their development (Pr. 11).[113] The affirmation of the right to engage in DBS is followed by the entitlement of all to enjoy its benefits and then by the statement that access to the needed technology should be without discrimination albeit on mutually agreed terms (Pr. 5).

DBS activities should allow people to seek and receive information[114] but 'in a manner compatible with the sovereign rights of States, including the principle of non-intervention' (Pr. 1). DBS should promote the free exchange of knowledge and assist in educational, social and economic development particularly in the developing countries and provide recreation 'with due respect to the political and cultural integrity of States' (Pr. 2). To accelerate their national development, the needs of developing countries should be given special consideration (Pr. 6). All such additions to or restrictions on the freedom of DBS emasculate the principles to which they are attached.

The content of DBS is the crux. While unavoidable overspill is considered a separate matter (Pr. 15, *infra*), under the Principles, deliberate DBS to another state is effectively subject to its prior consent should that state so insist. That troubled the states that abstained or voted against the Principles both in COPUOS and the General Assembly. The interaction of 'freedom' in DBS with 'non-intervention' and the 'political and cultural integrity' of states is not likely to be easy.

By Pr. 6, international cooperation 'should be' the basis of DBS activities and be implemented 'through appropriate arrangements'. States operating a DBS system should consult with any other state that so requests (Pr. 10). Any state commencing a DBS service is without delay to notify any other state that will receive the service and consult with it should it so require (Pr. 13). It should not establish the service without complying with Pr. 13 and in accordance with any arrangement entered into with the consultees and with the DBS Principles (Pr. 14). Disputes are to be settled by the normal means (Pr. 7).

The implementation of Prs. 13 and 14 would mean that a state receiving deliberate DBS programming would be able to block the establishment of a DBS services to its territories without its prior consent. The only exception is if the service was not actually aimed at the state's territory but was received by way of overspill. As far as overspill is concerned, the normal rules of the ITU are 'exclusively applicable' and therefore are the only relevant controls (Pr. 15). These would include ITU rules as to harmful interference, minimal power and appropriate targeting of intended recipients.[115]

As a matter of fact, although some still refer to the DBS Principles, in practice, commercial pressures have become important as to whether a particular DBS channel is

---

113 See CoCoSL III, 66–70. This is akin to current debate on patent protection for medicinal drugs in the developing world.

114 Cf. Art. 19, 'Universal Declaration of Human Rights', UNGA Res. 217 (III), 8 December 1948 H. Lauterpacht, 'The Universal Declaration of Human Rights' (1948) 25 BYIL 354–381 at 378–381.

115 See Chapter 8. J.F. Metzl, 'Rwandan Genocide and the International Law of Radio Jamming' [1997] 91 AJIL 628–651.

available within a country.[116] Such instances raise questions as to the propriety of allowing particular interests to use DBS. Religious and nationalist groups may transgress boundaries in the eyes of DBS recipient states. All that we can say is that disputes do arise. The cancellation of DBS contracts and commercial pressures appear on occasion to have an effect on the satellite operators and licensing authorities. Whether complaints are justified is a matter for case-by-case consideration by the service providers, by politicians and licensing authorities.

A further DBS problem occurs if a satellite transponder is overridden by ground transmissions and programming unacceptable to a receiving state is transmitted. This is a use of radio frequencies forbidden in the relevant ITU rules and is a matter for the state of origin of the intruding signal to deal with.[117] On occasion it may be that the satellite operator will take appropriate steps, sometimes in compliance with the views of its supervisory government.

A different problem is the deliberate use of DBS. While the Internet is now facilitating the spread of material 'obnoxious' to some governments, direct broadcast by satellite, and in particular of TV, remains powerful.[118] Our first edition suggested that problems might emerge in the future were small states to abuse their sovereign rights by seeking to generate revenue through licensing DBS services that would be unacceptable to recipient states, for example through the criticism of regimes and the encouragement of dissidence. We considered that under those circumstances, other sanctions would be required. In the penultimate the satellite service could be jammed.[119]

That problem has indeed emerged, but not as we envisaged in 2008. Programming has been carried on major networks to the annoyance of a number. Jamming had already been resorted to as indicated in our previous editions, and it appears to be a measure increasingly adopted by a variety of entities.[120] As a result, a number of systems are including anti-

---

116 Cf. the Indian 'Policy for Uplinking and Downlinking of Television Channels' Order, Ministry of Information and Broadcasting, New Delhi, 2022: https://mib.gov.in/sites/default/files/Guidelines%20 for%20Uplinking%20and%20Downhinking%20of%20Satellite%20Television%20Channels%20in%20 India%2C%202022.pdf.

117 Geo-location devices can pinpoint the source of jamming so that the relevant state may be contacted, and unauthorised jamming stopped.

118 J.J. Wolff, 'Interrupted Broadcasts? The Law of Neutrality and Communications Satellites' (2021) 45 *J. Sp. L.* 239–275; J.W. Penney, 'The Cycles of Global Telecommunications Censorship and Surveillance' (2014–2015) *U. Pa. J. Int. L.* 639–753; C.M. Schenone, 'Jamming the Stations: Is there an International Free Flow of Information?' (1984) 14 *Cal. W. Int. L. J.* 501–529.

119 Jamming is different from interference. Jamming is the deliberate disruption of a radio signal. Service by broadband provider Viasat was jammed as the Russian special military operation in the Ukraine began in February 2022: www.cnbc.com/2022/02/28/ukraine-updates-viasat-says-cyber-event-disrupting-satellite-internet-service.html; www.broadbandworldnews.com/document.asp?doc_id=775858: https://breakingdefense.com/2022/03/ satellite-jamming-normal-by-militaries-during-conflict-not-peacetime-state-dept-official/.

120 J.J. Wolff, 'Interrupted Broadcasts? The Law of Neutrality and Communications. Satellites' (2021) 45 *J. Sp. L.* 239–275; S.M. Mountin, 'Intentional Interference with Commercial Communication Satellite Signals' (2014) 90 *Int. L. Stud.* 101–197; D.A. Koplow, 'An Inference about Interference: A Surprising Application of Existing International Law to Inhibit Anti-Satellite Weapons' (2014) 35 *U. Pa. J. Int. L.* 737–827; C.M. Petras, 'The Use of Force in Response to Cyber-Attack on Commercial Space Systems – Re-examining "Self-Defense" in Outer Space in Light of the Convergence of U.S. Military and Commercial Space Activities' (2002) 67 *J. Air L. & Comm.* 1213–1268; M.J. Sundahl, 'Information Warfare: The Legal Aspects of Using Satellites and Jamming Technologies in Propaganda Battles' (2006) 49 *Proc. IISL* 354–365; C.M. Schenone, 'Jamming the Stations: Is there an International Free Flow of Information?' (1984) 14 *Cal. W. Int. L.J.* 501–529; A.C. Dale, 'Countering Hate Messages that Lead to

jamming technology in satellites being brought into service.121 That avoids rather than solves the underlying problem of objection to content. Jamming has evoked concern within the ITU because of its impact on health.[122] We can only conclude that a space-competent state could destroy a broadcast satellite whose transmissions it finds wholly unacceptable.[123]

Short of such drama, international law and some UN Resolutions may apply to particular broadcasts.[124] The International Convention on the Use of Broadcasting in the Cause of Peace of 1936 obliges its members to use their broadcasting services in accordance with its title.[125] In addition a series of UN Resolutions contain measures and recommendations. The 1947 UN Res. 110 (II) on 'Measures to be taken against propaganda and the inciters of a new War' condemns all forms of propaganda that might incite threats to the peace or acts of aggression, but only requests states to 'promote by all means and propaganda' in favour of peace and friendly relations among states.

In 1950, UNGA Res. 454 (V), 'Freedom of Information: Interference with Radio Signals', condemns jamming as contrary to freedom of information but merely invites governments to 'refrain from radio broadcasts that would mean unfair attacks or slanders against other peoples anywhere' and to 'conform to an ethical conduct in the interest of world peace by reporting facts truly and objectively'. Other UN Resolutions regarding friendly relations among states, non-intervention and the duty to respect each other's integrity are also relevant,[126] including the 1970 Declaration on 'Principles of International Law concerning Friendly Relations and Cooperation among States in accordance with the Charter of the United Nations'.[127] Article 20 of the International Covenant on Civil and Political Rights prohibits propaganda for war or the advocacy of national, racial or religious hatred that constitutes incitement to discrimination, hostility or violence.[128]

Violence: The United Nations' Chapter VI Authority to Use Radio Jamming to Halt Incendiary Broadcasts' (2001) 11 *Duke J. Comp. & Int. L.J.* 109–131; R.B. Price, 'Jamming and the Law of International Communications' (1984) 5 *Mich. Y.B. Int. Leg. Stud.* 391–403; Hurwitz, *supra* n. 75 at 176–178. Cf. M. Price, 'Public Diplomacy and the Transformation of International Broadcasting' (2003) 21 *Cardozo Arts and Ent. L.J.* 51–85.

121 Anti-jamming technology is of interest to military authorities. D. Housen-Couriel, 'Disruption of Satellite Transmission AD BELLUM and IN BELLO: Launching a New Paradigm of Convergence' (2012) 45 *Israel L. Rev.* 431–458. Cf. Penney, *supra* n. 118 at 721–730; Walsh *infra* n. 123; Mountin *supra* n. 120. Google 'Jamming' or 'satellite jamming' for recent examples.

122 'Measurement and assessment concerns related to human exposure to electromagnetic fields', ITU PP Res. 176 (Rev. Bucharest, 2022). Annual reports go to ITU Council.

123 China, India, Russia and the US have destroyed satellites in orbit, but so far only their own. F. Walsh, 'Forging a Diplomatic Shield for American Satellites: The Case for Re-evaluating the 2006 National Space Policy in Light of a Chinese Satellite System' (2007) 72 *J. Air L. Com.* 759–799.

124 Penney, *supra* n.118, and Mountin, *supra* n. 120.

125 International Convention on the Use of Broadcasting in the Cause of Peace, 1936, 186 LNTS 301; 1938 UKTS 29, Cmnd 1714; 36 Martens (3d) 744; 7 Hudson 409; [1938] AJIL Supp. 113.

126 UNGA Res. 1236/XII (9157); Res. 1301/XIII (1958); Res. 1815/XVII (1962), Res. 1966 (XVIII) (1963), Res. 2103 (XX) (1965), Res. 2181 (XXI) (1966), Res. 2327 (XXII) (1967), Res. 2463 (XXIII) (1968) and Res. 2533 (XXIV) (1969). M.S. Dauses, 'Direct Broadcast Satellites and Freedom of Information' (1975) 3 *J. Sp. L.* 59–72 at 72.

127 'Declaration on Principles of International Law concerning Friendly Relations and Cooperation among States in accordance with the Charter of the United Nations', UNGA Res. 2625 (XXV) (1970).

128 'International Covenant on Civil and Political Rights', UNGA Res. 2200A (XXI), 1966.

UNESCO has also contributed. In 2001 it adopted a 'Universal Declaration on Cultural Diversity',[129] which has some relevance for the impact of 'foreign' programming. How valuable these old affirmations are may be a question: too much depends on the state of world politics rather than on the avowal of such 'duties'.[130] Finally, we again note that satellite direct broadcasting is now only one of the arenas in which control of the media and of information has become a very live topic, not to say problem.[131]

The social and political contexts of the 1982 Direct Broadcasting Principles antedate the Internet. Current disputes as to control of content in international communications concentrate on new technologies. Thus, within the ITU there are now two sets of International Telecommunication Regulations (ITRs) those of Melbourne (1989) and Dubai (2012).[132] New Arts. 5A and 5B in the Dubai text introduce duties as to Internet traffic and control of content. This was unacceptable to many ITU members and as a result only 89 of the 193 ITU members signed the Final Acts, and fewer have ratified them.[133] Discussions as to the Internet continue.[134]

So where does this leave us? Have the hopes of UNGA Res. 1721 of 1961 been met? The answer must remain uncertain. Satellite telecommunications are generally available, in the main without discrimination. Thanks to multiplicity and interconnectivity the networks make global access possible. However, the initial arrangements were established to provide a public service in the world public interest. They were self-financing and to an extent non-profit-making. That has changed with the major privatisations and the introduction of other private service providers.

These are difficult matters. Some argue for allowing commerce to be ruled by market forces as the best way to organise. However, we note that in much private law the operation of an enterprise purely in the interest of its shareholders is being departed from. It is becoming more common to consider that a commercial enterprise has 'stakeholders'. Stakeholders are those affected directly or indirectly by the actions of the enterprise. While including the shareholders, stakeholders can also include employees, pensioners and those for whom the enterprise provides a service.[135] The concept can also be applied in interna-

---

129 Universal Declaration on Cultural Diversity, UNESCO General Conference, Records of the 31st Session, Res. 25 (2001), Vol. I, 61–64; (2002) 41 ILM 57–62.

130 Cf. *supra* n. 100.

131 Reference point, *supra* n. 82. S.J. Shackleford and A.N. Craig, 'Beyond the "Digital Divide": Analyzing the Evolving Role of National Governments in Internet Governance and Enhancing Cybersecurity' (2014) 50 *Stanford J. Int. L.* 120–184.

132 International Telecommunication Regulations: Final Acts of the World Administrative Telegraph and Telephone Conference, Melbourne, 1988 (ITU, 1989); Final Acts of the World Conference on International Telecommunications, Dubai, 2012 (ITU, 2013); (2013) 52 ILM 846–860, with Introductory Note at 843–845. See Chapter 8 at n. 117.

133 R. Hill, *The New International Telecommunication Regulations* (Dordrecht: Springer, 2014).

134 *Internet Futures, Spotlight on the Technologies Which May Shape the Internet of the Future* (UK Office of Communications, 2021); P.D. Trooboff, 'Globalization, Personal Jurisdiction and the Internet: Responding to the Challenge of Adapting Settled Principles and Precedents' (2021) 415 *Hague Receuil* 9–321.

135 The stakeholder interests field is developing. R.E. Freeman, *Strategic Management: A Stakeholder Approach* (London: Pitman, 1983); R.E. Freeman et al., *Stakeholder Theory: The State of the Art* (Cambridge: Cambridge UP, 2010); A. Friedman and S. Miles, *Stakeholders: Theory and Practice* (Oxford: OUP, 2006). Cf., 'Stakeholder Theory and the Logic of Value Concepts: Challenges for Contemporary International Law' (2010) 7 *Int. Stud. J.* 19–80; A. and B. Matwijkiw, 'Stakeholder Theory and Justice Issues: The Leap from Business Management to Contemporary International Law' (2010) 10 *Int. Crim. L. Rev.* 143–180; S. Greathead, 'The Multinational and the "New Stakeholder": Examining the Business Case for Human

tional environmental law.[136] Notions of the 'stakeholder' as all those affected could usefully inform discussion and decisions as to the activities of international telecommunication entities and the operation of monitoring organisations such as the International Satellite Organisation Agreement and IMSO. We also note that many countries curb the 'free market' through regulators with powers to ensure fair competition, and to prevent the abuse of a dominant position. There may be a case for an international telecommunications regulator acting in the world public interest and supervising the international public trust. The ideal that 'communication by means of satellites should be available to the nations of the world . . . on a global and non-discriminatory basis' requires better to be secured.[137] The role of IMSO as to the compliance of international service providers with public service obligations might provide an avenue through which international telecommunication providers could be obliged by inter-state agreement to assume and discharge such obligations. Only the ITU could provide such regulation. We return to these questions in Chapter 17.

Rights' (2002) 35 *Vand. J. Transnat. L.* 719–728; M.J. Lowenstein, 'Stakeholder Protection in Germany and Japan' (2002) 76 *Tul. L. Rev.* 1673–1690, part of a Symposium on 'Socio-Economics and Corporate Law: The New Corporate Social Responsibility' (2002) 76 *Tul. L. Rev.* 1187–1748.

Under s. 172.1 of the (UK) Companies Act 2006 in performing his duty to promote the success of the company a company director: 'must act in the way he considers, in good faith, would be most likely to promote the success of the company for the benefit of its members as a whole, and in doing so have regard (amongst other matters) to (a) the likely consequences of any decision in the long term, (b) the interests of the company's employees, (c) the need to foster the company's business relationships with suppliers, customers and others, (d) the impact of the company's operations on the community and the environment, (e) the desirability of the company maintaining a reputation for high standards of business conduct, and (f) the need to act fairly as between members of the company.' While these requirements are indefinite, they do indicate a set of considerations wider than serving the interests of shareholders only.

136 The use of many international rivers is governed by agreements between their co-riparians: cf. the Convention on the Law of the Non-Navigational Uses of International Watercourses, 21 May 1997, UNGA Res. 51/229; A/51/49 (not yet in UNTS); 2015 UKTS 5, Cm 9004; (1997) 36 ILM 700–20, and the ILC discussions thereanent. A.S. Rieu-Clarke, 'Overview of Stakeholder Participation – What Current Practice and Future Challenges – Case Study of the Danube Basin' (2007) 18 *Colo. J. Int. Env. & Pol.* 611–632; J.L. Huffman, 'Comprehensive River Basin Management: The Limits of Collaborative, Stakeholder-Based, Water Governance' (2009) 49 *Nat. Res. J.* 117–150; A. Andrew and I. Steyl, 'Encouraging Stakeholder Participation in River Basin Management: A Case Study from the Nura River in Kazakhstan' (2008) 12 *U. Denv. Water L. Rev.* 209–240.

137 See the UNGA resolutions, *supra* nn. 7 and 8. F. Lyall, 'The Protection of the Public Interest in the Light of the Commercialisation and Privatisation of the Providers of International Satellite Telecommunications' (2004) 47 *Proc. IISL* 441–451.

11

GLOBAL NAVIGATION SATELLITE SYSTEMS

Introduction

The modern world is dependent upon the operation of the global navigation satellite systems (GNSS) to a degree of which most people are ignorant. Universal Time (UTC) signals from GNSS allow the coordination of critical infrastructures round the world. They also give a high degree of precision as to the timing of the conclusion of major financial and other transactions through time-stamping. More well-known is the ability to identify location and movement to a previously unparalled degree, a tool with many applications. GNSS is therefore almost as important as the Internet. However, an increasing problem is that systems may be interfered with, deliberately or otherwise, and international tensions are exacerbating the situation.

The creation of a global navigation satellite system (GNSS) was early identified as a potential benefit of space.[1] Precise knowledge as to the location and velocity of spacecraft is essential for space activities. The spin-off is that satellites can reciprocally provide accurate data as to time and location for terrestrial purposes.[2] There have been many refinements.[3]

---

1 J.T. Hayward, 'Space Technology for World Navigation', in S. Ramo, ed. *Peacetime Uses of Outer Space* (New York: McGraw-Hill, 1961) 55–84; C.W. Jenks, *Space Law* (London: Stevens, and New York: Praeger, 1965) 268–269.

2 Coordinated Universal Time (UTC), based on the Greenwich meridian, is the successor of Greenwich Mean Time: F. Lyall, *Technology, Sovereignty and International Law* (Abingdon: Routledge, 2022) 185–188. One of the first problems caused by space technology was the interference of Sputnik I signals with the time broadcasts. Radiolocation remains important, particularly for aviation. Specific spectrum bands are allocated within the ITU Radio Regulations for radiolocation and radio determination services.

3 P.J.G. Teunissen and O. Montentbruck, eds., *Springer Handbook of Global Navigation Satellite Systems* (Vienna: Springer, 2021); B. Bhatta, *Global Navigation Satellite Systems: New Technologies and Applications*, 2nd ed. (Abingdon: CRC Press, 2021); A.A.L. Andrade, *The Global Navigation Satellite System* (Farnham: Ashgate, 2016); E.D. Kaplan and C. Hegarty, *Understanding GPS: Principles and Applications*, 2nd ed. (Boston: Artech House, 2005); *Report of the Action Team: Follow-Up to the Third United Nations Conference on the Exploration and Peaceful Uses of Space (UNISPACE III)* (UN: ST/SPACE/24, 2004) ('UN Report, 2004'). Cf. the International GNSS Service: https://igs.org/. See also US Presidential Memorandum on Space Policy Directive 7, January 2021: https://trumpwhitehouse.archives.gov/presidential-actions/memorandum-space-policy-directive-7/.

DOI: 10.4324/9781003496502-11

Global navigation satellite systems are space-based positioning, navigation and timing (PNT) systems designed to provide worldwide, all weather, three-dimensional position, velocity and timing data. Originally designed for military purposes, they are now also used for many civilian uses, providing precise, consistent and accurate information for many critical national infrastructures.[4] Navigation and positioning for many mobile services including by airplanes,[5] ships,[6] trains, cars and trucks,[7] is available. Fishermen, farmers, surveyors and hikers use the systems.[8] GNSS can be used to track individuals,[9] including children and Alzheimer sufferers,[10] as well as criminal offenders.[11] Human rights and privacy questions can therefore arise.[12] Through monitoring relatively small changes in altitude they

---

4 Possible applications are listed for the Galileo system at: www.euspa.europa.eu/galileo and for GPS at: www. gps.gov/applications/.

5 See *infra* following n. 130.

6 See *infra* following n. 136.

7 'SatNav' systems are fitted to most modern vehicles.

8 See applications *supra* n. 4. J.M. Epstein, 'The Role of the Global Positioning System in the Environment' (1997) 6 *N.Y.U. Env. L. J.* 72–92; R. Puterski, 'The Global Positioning System – Just Another Tool?' (1997) *N.Y.U. Env. L. J.* 93–106; J.C. Kluge, 'Farming by the Foot: How Site-Specific Agriculture Can Reduce Non-point Source Water Pollution' (1998) 23 *Colum. J. Env. L.* 89–135; P.B. Larsen, 'Use of Global Navigation Satellite System (GNSS) Evidence for Land Surveys: Legal Acceptability' (1995) 38 *Proc. IISL* 285–293; C. Davies et al., 'Moving Pictures: How Satellites, the Internet and International Environmental Law Can Help Promote Sustainable Development' (1999) 28 *Stetson L.R.* 1091–1151; FindMySheep www.findmysheep. com/hjem.

9 K.E. Edmundson, 'Global Positioning System Implants: Must Consumer Privacy be Lost in Order for People to Be Found?' (2005) 38 *Ind. L. Rev.* 207–238.

10 Children may be located, and Alzheimer's sufferers can, if fitted with tracers, be found if they wander from their accommodation.

11 Some US states (e.g. Florida, Missouri, Ohio, Oklahoma, South Carolina and Wisconsin) require sex and other offenders to be tracked after liberation. See also *Mickelson v US*, 433 F.3d 1050; 2006 US App. LEXIS 256, where the Court of Appeals for the Eighth Circuit permitted GPS tracking as a condition of release of a convicted person.

12 *US v Garcia* (2007) 434 F.3d 994, cert. denied, US Sup. Ct. 1 Oct 2007, held the use of a GPS tracking device attached to the defendant's car did not violate the Fourth Amendment of the US Constitution which prohibits unreasonable searches and seizures. *Garcia* distinguished *Kyllo* v *US* (2001) 533 U.S. 27; 121 S. Ct. 2038; 150 L. Ed. 2d 94; 2001 US LEXIS 4487, where the Fourth Amendment was held breached by the use of a thermal-imaging device on a house where marijuana growing was suspected. See Case Note: (2006–2007) 120 *Harv. L. Rev.* 2230–2237. See also *Hinkley* v *Roadway Express Inc*, 2007 US App. LEXIS 21938 (case no. 06–3097) 249 Fed. Appx. 13 (10th Circ. Sept. 13, 2007) on the use of GPS data for disciplinary purposes. Cf. 'On Your Tracks: GPS Tracking in the Workplace' (US) National WorkRights Institute: www.epic.org/privacy/workplace/gps-traking.pdf. In *US* v *Jones*, 615 F 3d 544; 132 S. Ct. 954, 565 US (2012) No. 10–1259, the US Supreme Court held that the warrantless installation of GPS and subsequent police surveillance was a search and thus a violation of the Fourth Amendment. Consequently the tainted evidence was excluded from trial. See also G.M. Dery III and R. Evaro, 'The Court Loses its Way with the Global Positioning System: *United States v. Jones* Retreats to the "Classic Trespassory Search"' (2013) 19 *Mich. J. Race & Law* 113–152; T. Strake, 'It's Like Tailing Your Vehicle for a Month: An Analysis for the Warrantless Use of a Global Positioning System in United States v. Maynard, 615 F.3d (D.C. Cir. 2010)' (2011) 36 *South. Ill. Univ. L. J.*, 205–222.

In the UK, *R. (on the Application of Gulliver) v. Parole Board* [2006] EWHC 2976 (Admin), appeal dismissed in *Regina (Gulliver) v. Parole Board*, [2007] EWCA Civ. 1386, [2008] 1 WLR 1116, and *Hoekstra v. HM Advocate (No. 7)*, 2002 SLT. 599, 2002 SCCR. 135, show the use of GPS tracking in criminal cases. Cf. A. Vettorei, 'Global Positioning System Evidence in Court Proceedings: The Case of Italy' (2017) 42 *Air and Sp. L.* 295–312.

can be used to monitor volcanic areas, and even to predict eruptions.[13] The technology is also used to synchronise telecommunications, power grids and similar systems.[14] GNSS can also be used to time-stamp contractual agreements, which can be crucial, for example, in currency and other financial transactions where split-seconds may be important.[15] In short, much of the working of the modern world is dependent on GNSS signals.

The service offered by GNSS can be viewed as being similar to the Internet. Both are global, easily accessible with appropriate technology, and, for many purposes, free. The use of GNSS has spread almost as quickly and as widely as that of the Internet and the technology is developing rapidly. Both GNSS and the Internet are dual use; that is both have military and civilian uses, and the military had a significant role in their creation. Their universal adoption and acceptance have not been without legal controversy but that has not stopped their progress. Both have developed with considerable speed, and in fact, the two are increasingly integrated.[16] Like the Internet, GNSS offers immediate economic benefits that will further develop. The question therefore arises whether those reliant directly or indirectly on GNSS signals have any remedy if there is a fault in the system.

Of the GNSS systems to which we will come, only the European Galileo system is willing under certain circumstances to meet a claim for damages incurred by signal error. For the rest the service is there and may be used, but that is on a user's-risk basis. The possibility that a ship may collide with a jetty, that an aeroplane may land heavily, or that the time-stamp on a currency contract for millions may be wrong, remains. Therefore, apart from any argument as to the liability of the service provider, it should be noted that in contracts for activities and commercial dealings reliant on GNSS services must take account of such possibilities.[17] Perhaps insurance cover and/or a liability fund might make sense.

---

13 Cf. Mt St Helens, 1980. The Campi Flegrei caldera west of Naples, which has been rising since 2005, is constantly monitored by 15 GPS stations. Cf. P. De Martino et al., 'GPS time series at Campi Flegrei caldera (2000–2013)' (2014) 57 *Ann. Geophys.* S0213; G. Chiodini et al, 'Magma near the critical degassing pressure drive volcanic unrest towards a critical state' (2016) 7 *Nature Communications*, Art. No. 13712: www.nature.com/articles/ncomms13712. See Wikipedia sv. Phlegraean Fields.

14 See the US government information website for the GPS system: www.gps.gov and www.gps.gov/applications/timing/.

15 Timing can be crucial in commercial transactions. Transactions can be stamped by GPS-precise time down to fractions of a second. See the GPS sites *supra* n. 14.

16 Most mobile phones and other devices are able to access several GNSS providers.

17 P.B. Larsen, 'International Regulation of Global Navigation Satellite Systems' (2015) 80 *J. Air L. and Comm.* 365–422; D. Zannoni, 'International Law Issues concerning the Interruption and the Degradation of the Radio-Navigation Signal' (2015) 64 ZLW 489–510; H.-G. Bollweg, 'GNSS Liability by International or European Union Law?' (2010) 59 *ZLW* 551–559; A.L. Loukakis, 'Product Liability Ramification for Erroneous GNSS Signals: Is an Alternative Approach Possible?' (2013) 56 *Proc. IISL* 305–326; and his 'The New HPCA's Optional Rules for Arbitration and Their Relevance to Disputes Arising from Erroneous Navigational Signals' (2014) 57 *Proc. IISL* 53–73; S. Spassova and A.L. Loukakis, 'The Legal Implications of Erroneous GNSS Signal Resulting from Harmful Interference' (2015) 58 *Proc. IISL* 79–84; D. Kong, 'Civil Liability for Damage Caused by Global Navigation Satellite Systems: A Conceptual Analysis' (2016) 41 AASL 313–338. Cf. L.J. Smith, 'The Current Challenges of Liability for Loss of Satellite-Based Services' (2013) 56 *Proc. IISL* 291–303.

UNIDROIT has begun to consider such matters. See *infra* n. 122, and U. Magnus, 'Civil Liability for Satellite-based Services' (2008) 13 *Unif. L. Rev.* 935–969; S.M. Carbone and M.E. De Maestri, 'The Rationale for an International Convention on Third Party Liability for Satellite Navigation Signals' (2009) 14 *Unif. L. Rev.* 35–55; L Peters, 'A Regime of Third-Party Liability for Global Navigation Satellite System (GNSS) Services: Recent Developments at UNIDROIT' (2012) XXXVII 465–482.

GNSS operations have three major essentials: the space segment, its control and its service users. Precise timing is the basic component of satellite navigation. Atomic clocks on the satellites keep nearly perfect time within nanoseconds. Timing is monitored by a ground control segment that corrects as required. GNSS may be active or passive. In an active system (the Chinese Beidou) the ground receiver interrogates a satellite, and its position is then determined by an interactive process. In passive systems (GPS, GLONASS and Galileo) each satellite in the system continuously broadcasts signals that are intercepted by receivers operated by users of the system. Depending on the precise location of each satellite, its signal reaches an individual receiver at a time marginally different from that from another satellite. The receivers are pre-programmed to compare the signals and, by integrating the precise times of their reception, to establish where in three dimensions the receiver is located.[18] That data is then mapped onto normal terrestrial cartographic coordinates.[19]

Harmful Interference

All parties involved in GNSS are extremely concerned about harmful interference and the continued viability of GNSS. The availability of four individual global systems provides some service alternatives. However, while use and importance of GNSS continues to grow, its operation is increasingly disrupted for both civilian and military GNSS. Military GNSS services are increasingly jammed or spoofed by false data fed into the systems. Thus during the combat in the Ukraine military-level GNSS has been subject to frequent interference all along the Russian borders from the Black to the Arctic Seas despite encryption, and the free civilian GNSS signals in the area are also not reliable.[20] Further, and as a result, the free civilian service signals are moving towards encryption in the interests of safety of life.[21] In the ultimate interference may also force positioning, navigation and timing services to fall back on technology that pre-existed GNSS.[22]

More generally radio, particularly when broadcast, can cause problems for GNSS. Frequencies are a scarce resource, subject to demand and fierce competition. Individual broadcast operators are seeking to move closer to the preferred GNSS bands, which may interfere with GNSS. Correlatively GNSS operators can have difficulty in obtaining access to interference-free spectrum for their services.[23]

18 Ground terminal receiving equipment is most accurate when receiving signals from at least three satellites.
19 Problems can occur if the terrestrial receiver applies the coordinates to an obsolete mapping system. Trucks have driven onto closed bridges. Hikers have wandered off and, following inaccurate tracks, died in deserts. Media reports are frequent. Not all users know how to update the mapping applications on their devices.
20 European Aviation Safety Agency March 17, 2022: www.aeronewsjournal.com/2022/03/easa-warns-of-intensifying-gps-jamming.html.
21 P.B. Larsen, 'Will Harmful Interference Bring GPS Down?' (2021) 86 *J. Air. L & Comm.* 3–66. Cf. E.S. Waldrop, 'Integration of Military and Civilian Space Assets: Legal and National Security Implications' (2004) 55 *Air Force L. Rev.* 157–231 at 207–208.
22 The GPS system is occasionally unavailable to civilian users when being tested or under other circumstances, and notice is provided to users in advance. See www.gps.gov/support/user/. Cf. D. Zannoni,' International Law Issues concerning the Interruption and the Degradation of the Radio-Navigation Signal' (2015) 64 *ZLW* 489–510; A. Masutti, 'Legal Problems Arising from the Installation of the Galileo and EGNOS Ground Stations in Non-EU Countries' (2012) 37 *Air and Space Law* 65–80.
23 Cf. the US 'Ligado' case, *infra* at n. 126.

The GNSS World

The Global Navigation Satellite Systems (GNSS) are one of the major technological developments of our time. Military GNSS, the original policy reason for the existence of GNSS, remains significant. It is more accurate than that available to civilians,[24] can guide missiles and is important in the deployment of soldiers, ships and warplanes. In the United States, Russia, and China GNSS therefore remains dominated by military authorities.[25] GNSS forms an essential part of military policy and military strategy. Thus, the US Congress continues to fund military GPS technology in both development and operation, a generosity that does not extend to civilian GPS. However, it remains that although military authorities continue to maintain significant control of GNSS, civilian users account for the bulk of its use. While there is some relevant national law, little international law specifically regulates GNSS.[26]

The Global Positioning System (GPS)

The Global Positioning System (GPS) is a US system operated under US Space Policy Statements and related directives.[27] As of July 2023 the US National Space Policy is that of 2020.[28]

The US Global Positioning System (GPS) began with the orbiting of eleven satellites in 1978–1985. Security considerations were the major emphasis in its development. From 1989 to 1994 the system was expanded to its present configuration, with later satellites being orbited to replace failing ones. Operationally the system now comprises a minimum of twenty-four satellites in six orbital planes, each with a period of twelve hours in circular medium earth orbit (MEO) at 20200 km/10900 nautical miles inclined at 55°. At any one time at least four GPS satellites are visible to terrestrial receivers.[29] Additional satellites provide an increased accuracy and they, together with three to five decommissioned

---

24 See GPS Accuracy: www.gps.gov/systems/gps/performance/accuracy/.

25 The Galileo system is civilian.

26 The US Policy Statement of 2004 on GNSS (www.gps.gov/policy/docs/2004/), Sec. III para 1 listed the provision of 'civil services that exceed or are competitive with' foreign GNSSs (no. (4)) as one of the goals of US GPS policy. Under Sec. III bullet point 6, while encouraging the foreign development of GNSS services based on GPS, the USA also seeks to ensure that foreign GNSSs will be interoperable with US civil GPS. Cf. next note. See also the work of the International Committee on GNSS (ICG), *infra* n. 141.

27 See 'Global Positioning System' 10 USC §2281. It is intended to serve US interests and provide an acceptable international standard: 51 USC §50112. Previous US National Space Policy statements are: 1996: https://clintonwhitehouse4.archives.gov/WH/EOP/OSTP/html/gps-factsheet.html; 2004; www.gps. gov/policy/docs/2004/; 2010: www.gps.gov/policy/docs/2010/. See P.B. Larsen, *supra* n. 17, and 'Regulation of Global Navigation and Positioning Services in the United States', in R. Jakhu, *National Regulation of Space Activities* (Springer 2010) 459–466.

28 On current GPS policy see Sec. 4 (e) of the 2020 National Space Policy: www.federalregister.gov/documents/2020/12/16/2020-27892/the-national-space-policy#p-56, and the 2021 Memorandum on Space Policy Directive 7: www.gps.gov/policy/docs/2021/. Cf. B.M. Orschel, 'Assessing a GPS-based Global Navigation Satellite System within the Context of the 2004 US Space-based Positioning, Navigation and Timing Policy' (2005) 70 *J. Air L. & Comm.* 609–635; J.M. Epstein, 'Global Positioning System (GPS): Defining the Legal Issues of its Expanding Civil Use' (1995) 61 *J. Air L. & Comm.* 243–285.

29 2021 Memorandum on Space Policy, Directive 7, *supra* n. 28. See also the US Federal Radionavigation Plan 2020 (2019).

satellites, can readily be deployed whenever a satellite fails. A number of ground stations round the world monitor the system. A master control station at Colorado Springs checks the satellite clocks and orbits and updates the navigation message of each satellite and transmits updates by signal from the monitoring stations.[30]

GPS provides two services, the Standard Positioning Service (SPS) and the Precise Positioning Service (PPS). The Standard Positioning Service is available to all users without restriction,[31] whereas the encrypted PPS is available only to the US military services, for other US government use and for authorized foreign governments and military forces. The PPS service uses a special and encrypted code (the P-code), which is more difficult to jam than the civilian code (the C/A code – sc. the 'coarse acquisition' code). Each GPS satellite transmits signals on two L-band radio frequencies, L.1 in the 1559–1620 MHz band and L.2 in the 1215–1260 MHz band. A third civil signal, L-5, is scheduled to transmit at 1176.45 MHz in the 1164–1215 MHz band. GPS provides global coverage, which, for civilian use, is accurate to 7.8 metres with a reliability of 99.94%.[32]

GPS is constantly upgraded. The GPS Block IIR-M satellite of 2005 had two civilian signals effectively separating future military and civilian GPS services. Now in its third phase of development, GPS III satellites have greater capability than their predecessors and are more resistant to jamming than the earlier satellites. GPS III which carries signals for civilian and military use and for safety of life will be further developed.[33]

GPS is the most widely used GNSS. Operated by the US Department of Defense, it is compatible with almost all GNSS receivers now in operation.[34] Users are accustomed to the reliability and availability of GPS and the service continues to be updated and improved. GPS provides both a standard positioning service open to all users and a precise positioning service open to US military, government agencies and to allied governments. US policy assures continuous availability of global GPS service, interoperability and compatibility with international GNSS services, no civil user fees, and free civilian access.[35]

Military uses of GPS are extensive, but many remain secret.[36] Soldiers use GPS for personal location on the ground. Military airplanes navigate by GPS. Bombs and cruise missiles may be guided by GPS. Volumetrically civilian use of GPS now surpasses the military use. The duality of the civilian and military uses of GPS is an advantage to civilians because GPS is funded by the military and might well not exist but for the military connection.

---

30 The orbit of each satellite, and therefore the accuracy of signals received on Earth, can be affected by gravitational anomalies, solar wind pressure and other factors. Though the orbit may be minimally affected, uncorrected signals, travelling at the speed of light, will misinform a receiver. See also *infra* n. 32.

31 For the specific capabilities of this service see 'Global Positioning System Standard Positioning Service Performance Standard' (2020): www.gps.gov/technical/ps/2020-SPS-performance-standard.pdf. See also www.gps.gov/technical/ps/.

32 See www.gps.gov/systems/gps/performance/accuracy/ and SPS Standard (*supra* n. 31). Cf. M. Bourbonniere, 'Law of Armed Conflict (LOAC) and the Neutralisation of Satellites or *IUS in Bello Satellitis*' (2004) 9 *J. of Conflict & Security L.* 43–69 [Lyall/Larsen 515–541].

33 See Wikipedia sv. 'GPS Block III' and 'GPS Block IIIF'.

34 P.B. Larsen, *supra* n. 17; D. Turner, 'GNSS Interoperability through International Cooperation': www.gps.gov/multimedia/presentations/2011/05/CSNC/turner2.pdf. See also 'Global Positioning System', 10 USC §2281 with §2279d.

35 US Memorandum on Space Policy Directive 7, 25 January 2021: www.gps.gov/policy/docs/2021/. See also *infra* n. 38. Cf. S.A. Kaiser, 'Satellite Navigation Systems: The Impact of Interoperability' (2012) XXXVII AASL 369–397.

36 See discussion of military uses of outer space in Chapter 16.

However, the military connection can disadvantage civilians through the withdrawal of service when there is testing or re-calibration of the system, or, more seriously through the military pre-emption of GPS or the degrading or withdrawal of the civilian service.[37] That said, civilian GPS is free and the US Government does not plan to impose user charges for the system.[38] The US military GPS provider is of the view that, as the GPS service is free for all users civilian users have no legal basis for complaint if the service is faulty. The US provider has no appetite for negligence claims from civilian users.[39]

Within the USA the GPS system is the responsibility of a number of US agencies, with the Department of Defense as lead, as is clear from the Federal Radionavigation Plan,[40] although that Plan is the responsibility of three Departments, Defense, Transportation and Homeland Security. A National Space Based Positioning Navigation and Timing Committee (the National PNT EXXCOM) established in terms of the 2004 Space Policy Statement and chaired by the Deputy Secretaries of Defense and Transportation, makes recommendations to the various agencies involved.[41] The Federal Communications Commission also has a role in the licensing and assignment of radio frequencies.

International coordination and the interoperability of GPS is arranged through the International Civil Aviation Organization (ICAO), the International Maritime Organization (IMO), the International Telecommunication Union (ITU), and the COPUOS International Committee on GNSS (ICG),[42] and by bilateral arrangements with the EU, Russia, China, India and Japan.

US law and policy now favours the adoption of international standards for GNSS.[43] This shift towards international cooperation was marked by the 2010 US National Policy Statement to '[e]ngage with foreign GNSS providers to encourage compatibility and interoperability, promote transparency in civil service provision, and enable market access for US industry'.[44] The Statement seeks to avoid provocative unilateral activities in outer space and directed the US Government to enter into new areas of international cooperation

---

37 P.B. Larsen, *supra* n. 21. GPS signals can be interfered with even by small portable equipment: Google 'GPS jamming'. Cf. E.S. Waldrop, 'Integration of Military and Civilian Space Assets: Legal and National Security Implications' (2004) 55 *Air F.L. Rev.* 157–231 at 207–208.

    For 5–16 October 2015 GPS coverage in the west of Scotland was blocked during a NATO exercise in the North Atlantic. Civilian users, particularly ramblers and hill-walkers were warned. See www.scotsman. com/news/scotland/top-stories/gps-blackout-fears-over-nato-drill-off-scottish-coast-1-3905921 or www. bbc.co.uk/news/uk-scotland-highlands-islands-34413696.

38 2021 Memorandum on Space Policy Directive7: www.gps.gov/policy/docs/2021.

39 J. Huang, 'Development of the Long-term Legal Framework for the Global Navigation Satellite System' (1997) XXII-I AASL 585–600; B.E. Ehrhart, 'A Technological Turned Legal Nightmare: Potential Nightmare Liability of the United States Under the Federal Torts Claims Act for Operating the Global Positioning Service' (2000) 33 *Vand. J. Transnat. L.* 371–425; E.S. Waldrop, *supra* n. 37, at 213–215.

40 See the Federal Radionavigation Plan, 2019: https://rosap.ntl.bts.gov/view/dot/43623, and Department of Transportation, Radionavigation Systems Planning; www.transportation.gov/pnt/radionavigation-systems-planning.

41 See US Space Policy Statement, *supra* n. 35. EXXCOM members include the Departments of Commerce, Defense, Homeland Security, State and Transportation, together with the Joint Chiefs of Staff and NASA: see http://pnt.gov/site.shtml.

42 See *infra* n. 141. The International Committee on Global Navigation Satellite Systems (ICG): www.unoosa. org/oosa/en/ourwork/icg/icg.html.

43 49 USC 101, 10 USC 2281, 51 USC §50112. P.B. Larsen, *supra* n. 17.

44 See US Memorandum *supra* n. 35. Cf. P.B. Larsen, 'Issues Relating to Civilian and Military Dual Uses of GNSS' (2001) 17 *Space Policy* 111–119.

on GNSS issues. As a consequence, the US is increasingly active in relevant activities in organisations such as the ITU, ICAO and the IMO, as well as in various United Nations fora including the International Committee on GNSS (ICG).[45]

GPS suffers more jamming and spoofing than other GNSS services because its signals are most widely used around the world, and because it is controlled by the US military authorities. Thus both military and civilian GPS are jammed and spoofed by warring parties in the Ukraine to the extent that they are almost non-operational in those areas. GPS is also subject to interference by governments and by criminals in other parts of the world.[46]

GLONASS

GLONASS is the Russian counterpart to GPS and like it is of military origin.[47] The system was begun in 1976 by the former USSR but suffered during Russia's economic difficulties of the 1990s.[48] It was designed to be a global system and its satellites orbit in three planes separated by 120° in MEO at *c.* 19100 km, with a period of eleven hours fifteen minutes, at an inclination of 68.4°. The system uses twenty-four operational satellites, with twenty-seven in the constellation including 1 in-orbit spare. GLONASS was transferred to Russian civilian ROSCOSMOS but remains under military control.[49] When the system is being upgraded or coping with problems notice is given through NAGU.[50]

Now fully reconstituted and operational, GLONASS is available world-wide, providing a range of services. The system was made freely available to civilian use when the US GPS was so opened. It provides a standard precision navigation signal for civilians and a high-precision navigation signal access to which is restricted and has military relevance. The accuracy of the civilian signal is said to be 4.5–7.4 metres horizontal and 2–8.75 metres vertical with a service performance of 95%.[51] The system transmits signals in the L-1, L-2, L-3 frequency bands, and also carries COSPAS-SARSAT support of the international search and rescue system.[52] Performance is monitored and corrected mainly through ground stations in Russia and Brazil, with a central control station in the Moscow region. GLONASS has also created a global system of differential correction and

---

45 For the ICG see *infra* n. 141. P.B. Larsen, *supra* n. 17.
46 P.B. Larsen, *supra*, n. 21. A. Joerger, C. Fan and S. Jada, 'The Unsolved Mystery of the 2022 Texas Interference', Inside GNSS, 7 September 2023: https://insidegnss.com/the-unsolved-mystery-of-the-2022-texas-interference/; Z. Clements, T.E. Humphreys and P.B. Ellis, 'Pinpointing GNSS Interference from Low Earth Orbit' Inside GNSS, 10 September 2023: https://insidegnss.com/pinpointing-gnss-interference-from-low-earth-orbit/.
47 The acronym GLONASS derives from the Russian 'GLObal NAvigation Sputnik System'. See ABOUT GLONASS: www.glonass-iac.ru/en/about_glonass/ (2021); UN Report, 2004, *supra* n. 3, at 19–25, paras 72–114.
48 UN Report, 2004, *supra* n. 3, 21, para 86. For a time a more elliptical configuration of orbits was adopted so as to provide service to the USSR successor states, but operational life was short. See our first edition at 394. The system was returned to its original configuration in December 2015.
49 ABOUT GLONASS, *supra* n. 47.
50 See Notice Advisory to GLONASS Users (NAGU): https://veripos.com/support/faqs/glossary/notice-advisory-to-glonass-users-nagu.
51 Our source is Wikipedia. These figures are a considerable improvement on the 25 metres horizontal and 60 metres vertical indicated in the UN Report, 2004, *supra* n. 3, 22–23, para 99. See also www.insidegnss.com/glonass.
52 See https://insidegnss.com/category/a-system-categories/glonass/.

monitoring intended to establish integrity data and local correction data in order to increase accuracy.[53]

The current policy of Russia is to cooperate actively in the International Committee on GNSS.[54] Russia also cooperates with the European Galileo system, with the US GPS administration and with the Chinese Beidou with the goal of establishing compatibility and interoperability of the four services, and to obtain assistance in establishing monitoring and reference facilities around the globe necessary for ensuring the accuracy of the GLONASS system.[55] Use of Russian GLONASS by belligerent parties and by civilian users are subject to interference wherever GLONASS is deployed.

Galileo

Galileo is a joint undertaking by the European Union (EU) and the European Space Agency (ESA), the EU being its major funding source.[56] At first not all favoured the project,[57] the US considering a second 'western' system unnecessary.[58] A variety of reasons of varied weight led Europe on.[59] These included that both GPS and GLONASS were military/governmental controlled, uncertainty whether their 'free to user' policies would continue, the possibility that access to either might be restricted or even interdicted,[60] the political and financial problems then confronting Russia,[61] the unlikelihood that the US would share control of GPS to allow Europe control of its own service, the experience of the EGNOS augmentation to GPS which had shown the advantages of a positioning more accurate than that then available from civilian GPS,[62] the stimulus that

---

53 A. Arena and I. Bauman, 'GNSS and World Trade Law: Playing by the Rules', *InsideGNSS*, July/August 2015: www.insidegnss.com/node/4547. GLONASS provoked the adverse US legislative reaction described by Eric Schmitt and Michael Schmitt, 'New Law all but Bars Russian GPS Sites in the US', New York Times, Dec. 29, 2013, at 11. P.B. Larsen, 'International Regulation of Global Navigation Satellite Systems' (2015) 80 *J. Air L. & Comm.* 365–422 at 394.

54 The International Committee on GNSS (ICG): see *infra* n. 141.

55 GLONASS *supra* n. 53. P.B. Larsen, *supra* n. 53. UNOOSA, 'Current and Planned Global and Regional Navigation Satellite Systems and Satellite – based Augmentation Systems' (New York 2010). It is notable that Russian GLONASS uses the voluntary International GNSS Service (IGS) system. See discussion *infra* at n. 151.

56 On Galileo history and a comparison with GPS see S.W.D. Han, 'Global Administrative Law: Global Governance of the Global Positioning System and Galileo' (2008) 14 *ILSA J. Int. & Comp. L.* 572–593. F. von der Dunk, *infra* n. 119; '12 Things You Never Knew about Galileo Satellites': https://tinyurl.com/2p85xjcu. See also https://insidegnss.com/category/a-system-categories/galileo/.

57 The (UK) House of Commons Transport Committee was not in favour. See Galileo: Recent Developments, HC 53, Sess. 2006–2007, 12 November 2007: www.publications.parliament.uk/pa/cm200708/cmselect/cmtran/53/53.pdf.

58 J. Beclard, 'With the Head in the Air and the Feet on the Ground: The EU's Actorness in International Space Governance' (2013) 19 *Global Governance* 463–480, at 471–473. The US Memorandum of 2021, *supra* n. 28, indicated that the USA intends GPS to remain dominant.

59 'EU Galileo Task Force Report to Commissioner Neil Kinnock', 4 June 1999. Cf. 'Involving Europe in a New Generation of Satellite Navigation Systems', EU Commission 1999 (54 Final); *Project 2001: Workshop on Legal Framework for Privatising Space Activities*, Vienna, 1999 (Cologne: IASL, 2000) 210–248.

60 See *supra* n. 37. A local jamming device could selectively deny service to civil users within a specific area.

61 EU Task Force, *supra* n. 59, at para 3.2.

62 EGNOS: see 'Augmentation', *infra*. An extremely accurate service is needed for aviation, navigation and various safety services. Because the UK has withdrawn from the EU UK access to EGNOS may be barred: https://rin.org.uk/news/572850/Withdrawal-of-EGNOS-for-UK-users.htm.

the construction and operation of a European GNSS system would give to European space industries and services, and, last, questions as to potential liabilities arising from reliance on a malfunctioning system.

Galileo began as part of a programme to improve European transportation systems and the mobility of people and goods.[63] Because the private sector proved reluctant to invest in the venture it was decided that the EU itself would mainly fund the project, with the aid of ESA.[64] EU Council Regulation (EC) 1321/2004 established a Galileo Supervisory Authority to own the system.[65] Subsequently this arrangement was revised, and the Authority has been transmuted into an agency of the EU, the European Global Navigation Satellite Systems Agency,[66] with ownership of the system passing to the European Commission. ESA acts in the deployment of the system and in the design and development of the new generation of systems that has now come on stream, as well as infrastructure development. It also deals with procurement for the system, based on relevant EU rules.[67] Cooperation agreements with various entities exist. In May 2007 the then Authority signed a cooperation agreement with ESA, clarifying their relationship and this has been replaced by an agreement with the Commission. Since 2005 China had been associated with Galileo in research and development through an EU – China agreement on industrial and technical cooperation, but at present China is not represented in the official structure. The US and the Galileo states entered into a cooperation agreement in June 2004.[68] In addition cooperation agreements have been negotiated with a number of potential users other than the EU members.[69]

63 European Parliament and Council: Decision no. 1692/96/EC, 23 July 1996; OJ L, 228, 9.9.96. See also Commission Doc. COM (1999) – 54 Final, 10 February 1999, 'Involving Europe in a New Generations of Satellite Navigation Services', *Project 2001: Workshop on Legal Framework for Privatising Space Activities*, Vienna, 1999 (Cologne: Institute of Air and Space Law, 2000), 210–248; S. Andries, 'The European Initiative Galileo: a European contribution to the Global Navigation Satellite System (GNSS)' (2000) 25 AASL 43–65. A major step was the approval of the Commission Communication on Galileo of 22 November 2000, which rehearses the history in its Introduction: COM 2000, 750 Final: http://ec.europa.eu/dgs/energy_transport/galileo/doc/gal_com_2000_750_en.pdf.
64 'Progressing Galileo: Re-profiling the European GNSS Programmes', Commission Communication, COM(2007) 534, 19 July 2007; related Staff Working Document (SEC(2007) 1210); 'Council Conclusions on the European Galileo and EGNOS Satellite-navigation Programmes', 2821st Transport, Telecommunications and Energy Council Meeting, Luxembourg, 1–2 October 2007: http://ec.europa.eu/dgs/energy_transport/galileo/documents/doc/council_conclusions_021007.pdf.
65 The Regulation also provided for the participation of non-EU states that are members of ESA.
66 See Regulation (EU) No. 912/2010, as amended by Regulation (EU) No. 512/2014. The European GNSS Agency website at www.gsa.europa.eu/gsa/about-gsa provides a full listing of the relevant legislation. See also http://galileognss.eu/ and www.euspa.europa.eu/about/what-we-do/european-gnss-service-centre.
67 See www.gsa.europa.eu/about/how-we-work/procurement
68 'Agreement on the Promotion, Provision and Use of Galileo and GPS Satellite Based Navigation Systems and Related Applications', 2008 UKTS European Communities No. 2, Cm. 7384; www.gps.gov/policy/cooperation/europe/2004/gps-galileo-agreement.pdf. Cf. M Dodge, 'The GPS-Galileo Agreement and Treaty Law' (2012) 3 *J. Sp. L.* 227–288.
69 Cf. the Cooperation Agreements on a Civil Global Navigation Satellite System (GNSS) between the European Community, its Member States and (1) The Ukraine (Kiev, 1 December 2005), 2007 UKTS, European Communities No. 11, Cm. 7199; (2) Israel (Brussels, 13 July 2004), 2007 UKTS, European Communities No. 10, Cm. 7200; (3) Morocco (Brussels, 12 December 2006), 2007 UKTS European Communities No. 9, Cm. 7201; (4) China (Beijing 30 October 2003), 2007 UKTS European Communities No. 7, Cm. 7202; (5) The Republic of Korea (Helsinki, 9 September 2006, 2007 UKTS European Communities No. 8, Cm. 7203.

After an initial test phase, launch of the Galileo constellation began in 2011, became functional on 15 December 2016, and was completed by 2020. The Galileo system is now global. It consists of twenty-four satellites plus spares orbiting approximately every fourteen hours at some 23222 km with always at least four satellites visible to any user. A NAGU (Notice Advisory to Galileo Users) service provides data on the system including launches, satellite status and health, manoeuvres and decommissioning as well as outages or other difficulties.[70] Several kinds of GNSS service are offered providing different levels of accuracy: an open access service (corresponding to the GPS Standard Positioning Service), a safety of life service, an encrypted high accuracy commercial service for which Galileo will charge fees, and an encrypted Public Regulated Service (PRS) for use by government agencies.[71] Galileo guarantees the quality of the high-end service. It will therefore accept liability for defective high quality service, a liability that other GNSS services will not contemplate. Galileo expects that its guarantee of high-end services will attract users and will motivate high-end users to pay its charges. The European EGNOS augmentation system is integrated with it, and Galileo and EGNOS have established coordination with GPS and WAAS. Galileo coordinates with other GNSS providers and users in the United Nations International Committee on GNSS (ICG),[72] as well as bilaterally with other providers in order to provide seamless global services.[73] Concerned about increasing harmful interference, Galileo decided in 2022 to authenticate its open service navigation signals.[74]

In common with other GNSSs Galileo may suffer both deliberate and accidental interference. Like GPS it is subject to interference in the contested areas of the Ukraine where Galileo signals are increasingly employed by the Ukrainian forces. Galileo therefore can no longer be considered a purely civilian system.

UK SBAS

When the UK withdrew from the EU it lost access to Galileo and the EGNOS and related services. However, it is proposed that, in a new arrangement between One-Web and INMARSAT, a separate PNT system including a Satellite-based Augmentation System (SBAS) will be made available to interact with GPS. The new arrangements are currently in their test phase.[75] Eventually full global GNSS services may be provided. That said, in 2023 negotiations for the UK to re-join the EU Horizon programme were undertaken,

70 See NAGUs (Notice Advisory to Galileo Users): www.gsc-europa.eu/system-service-status/nagu-information; www.gsc-europa.eu/system-service-status/constellation-information.

71 See European GNSS Galileo Open Service Definition Document, Issue 1.2: www.gsc-europa.eu/sites/default/files/sites/all/files/Galileo-OS-SDD_v1.2.pdf; Galileo User Segment: https://gssc.esa.int/navipedia/index.php/Galileo_User_Segment. Cf. the terms of the Cooperation Agreements, *supra* n. 69. Galileo is now dual use, civilian and military. Note the 2022 statement by Internal Market Commissioner Tierry Breton "Space is a contested domain. We should develop new infrastructures as dual use by design integrating the defence needs from the outset', *Inside GNSS*, May/June 2022, at 49.

72 The International Committee on GNSS (ICG): see *infra* n. 141.

73 See 'The future of Positioning, Navigation and Timing': www.esa.int/esaNA.

74 Galileo Open Service Navigation Message Authentication: https://gssc.esa.int/navipedia/index.php/Galileo_Open_Service_Navigation_Message_Authentication.

75 See 'UK's SBAS signal repurposed for sovereign UK PNT capability': www.gpsworld.com/uks-sbas-signal-repurposed-for-sovereign-uk-pnt-capability/. Cf. https://rin.org.uk/news/572850/Withdrawal-of-EGNOS-for-UK-users.htm, and https://ukdefencejournal.org.uk/first-british-gps-style-satellite-to-transmit-test-signal/. See also: www.uksbas.org/.

which may include renewed access to technical contracting for developing Galileo and related services, and might allow access to the systems themselves/

Beidou

The Beidou Navigation Satellite System is Chinese.[76] Of military origin it is now administered by the Chinese National Space Agency but remains under Chinese military supervision. The system was completed in 2020.[77] It consists of a space segment of five geostationary satellites and thirty non-geostationary satellites (twenty-one in medium earth orbit, and seven in geosynchronous orbit), and a ground segment including control and monitoring stations.[78] Users must have receivers that are compatible with other GNSS systems.

BeiDou provides positioning, navigation and timing as well as a search and rescue service and is supported by satellite and ground-based augmentation. Unlike other systems it allows text messaging between its users. Its positioning, navigation and timing services are available in two service modes. The open service is free of charge and provides a location or positioning accuracy of 10 metres, a velocity accuracy of 0.2 metres per second and a timing accuracy of 10 nanoseconds. Domestic smart-phones are programmed to use Beidou.[79] The authorized service, available to government and the military, is encrypted. The system is compatible with other GNSS, and the standards set respectively by ICAO and IMO for navigation.[80] Beidou is an active participant in the International Navigation Committee.[81] In common with other GNSS services and affecting its reliability Beidou may be subject to interference by governments and by criminals.

NAVIC: The Indian Regional Navigation Satellite System (IRNSS)

The Indian system, known operationally as NAVIC, provides an independent satellite navigation service tailored to India's regional strategic needs. India has no wish to have to rely on service from external GNSS providers, particularly in hostile times. Through three geostationary and four geosynchronous satellites its service area extends some hundreds of miles beyond India's boundaries.[82] A civilian standard positioning service is free to users, while an encrypted service is restricted to authorised users, including India's military.[83]

76 BeiDou: http://en.beidou.gov.cn/. 'Military and Security Developments Involving the People's Republic of China 2022: Annual Report to Congress' US Defense Department, at 91: https://media.defense.gov/2022/Nov/29/2003122279/-1/-1/1/2022-MILITARY-AND-SECURITY-DEVELOPMENTS-INVOLVING-THE-PEOPLES-REPUBLIC-OF-CHINA.PDF.
77 See https://insidegnss.com/category/a-system-categories/compass-beidou/ and https://en.beidou.gov.cn/WHATSNEWS/202008/t20200803_21013.html.
78 See BeiDou Open Service Standard (*infra* n. 79) at para 4.1.
79 BeiDou Navigation Satellite System Open Service Performance Standard (Version 2.0) (China Satellite Navigation Office, 2018): http://en.beidou.gov.cn/SYSTEMS/Officialdocument/201812/P020181227424526837905.pdf. See also: https://gssc.esa.int/navipedia/index.php/BeiDou_Performances#:~:text=The%20BeiDou%20System%20has%20been%20designed%20to%20reach,BeiDou%20Performances%201.1%20BeiDou%20Navigation%20Test%20System%20%28BeiDou-1%29.
80 See ICAO, *infra* n. 130, and IMO, *infra* n. 136.
81 The International Committee on GNSS (ICG), *infra* n. 141. See also P.B. Larsen, *supra* n. 117.
82 See www.isro.gov.in/irnss-programme.
83 In Hindi NAVIC (*NAVi*gation with *I*ndian *C*onstellation) means sailor or navigator. G. Singj, 'How India Built NAVIC, the Country's own GPS Network': www.planetary.org/articles/how-india-built-navic. See also

The Quazi – Zenith Satellite System (QZSS)

The Japanese Quasi – Zenith Satellite System (QZSS) was introduced in 2018 with four of a seven planned satellites in geo-synchronous orbit.[84] Coverage runs from Japan south to central Australia. As such it provides a more stable service than that provided by GPS for part of the Asia-Pacific region but can be used in an integrated way with it.

Iridium

Iridium Communications Inc. is a commercial provider of satellite communications and operates a constellation of 66 satellites in low earth orbit.[85] Such a system is difficult to jam or spoof. Iridium services are available to both stationary and mobile users, and its portfolio now includes the provision of 'Satellite Time and Location' (STL) services usable for a variety of purposes.[86] It has been approved by the International Maritime Satellite Organisation and participates in the Global Maritime Distress and Safety System (GMDSS) organised by the International Maritime Organisation.[87]

Augmentation

GNSS antennae and receivers continue to improve, leaving less need for augmentation. Nonetheless, for many purposes, the accuracy of existing GNSS systems remains insufficient. Aircraft landing systems, ship-movement in confined waters and similar tasks require a precision beyond that currently offered direct from space. However, it is possible to 'augment' accuracy through sophisticated triangulation and the introduction of a third navigational and positioning reference point which may come from another satellite or may be provided by ground-based beacons.[88] Various systems presently exist.

In the US and Canada GPS accuracy is improved by the Wide Area Augmentation Service (WAAS).[89] The system was developed for aviation purposes by the US Federal Aviation Administration (FAA) to interact with the World Meteorological Organisation (WMO) Global Observing System (GOS),[90] but it can be used with any suitably adapted

---

'India Regional Navigation Satellite System: Signal in Space ICD for Standard Positioning Service' (Version 1.1, 2017): www.isro.gov.in/sites/default/files/irnss_sps_icd_version1.1-2017.pdf.

84 QZSS: https://qzss.go.jp/en/index.html.

85 Iridium: www.iridium.com; www.iridium.com/network/.

86 See www.iridium.com/blog/2017/04/04/inspiring-innovation-spotlight-orolia-adopts-satellite-time-and-location-stl/.

87 F. Lyall, *Technology, Sovereignty and International Law* (Abingdon: Routledge, 2022) 55–56. See Chapter 10 Iridium and IMSO.

88 See 'Augmentation Systems': www.gps.gov/systems/augmentations/. US Memorandum on Space Policy Directive 7, 2021, Sec. I, defines GNSS augmentation as: 'any system that provides users of PNT signals with additional information that enables users to obtain enhanced performance when compared to the augmented signals from a primary PNT service. 'Improvements can include better accuracy, availability, integrity, and reliability, with independent integrity monitoring and alerting capabilities for critical applications'. For the TerraStar system see www.gpsworld.com/how-terrastar-is-meeting-the-growing-demand-for-correction-services/?utm_source=Navigate%21+Weekly+GNSS+News&utm_medium=Newsletter&utm_campaign=NCMCD220629002&oly_enc_id=6466E5046834B1Z.

89 See the (US) Federal Aviation Agency at www.nstb.tc.faa.gov/.

90 See 'Augmentation Systems': www.gps.gov/systems/augmentations/.

GPS receiver.[91] WAAS allows accurate vertical and lateral separation of airplanes for all phases of flight, except Category II and Category III flights – these involve landing at particular major US city airports. In the future a Local Area Augmentation System (LAAS) will allow accurate GNSS augmentation landing at suitably equipped airports.[92]

Maritime navigation using GNSS usually also requires augmentation of the service, particularly in ports and narrow navigation channels. The maritime differential service augments the accuracy of GNSS by use of land-based reference beacons, which transmit correction messages to maritime users. The US maritime differential GPS Service provides better than 1 metre accuracy and is available for all US coastal areas and US navigable rivers. Thus augmented, GPS is also used for safety management of trains and for many emergency purposes, for example to provide location services for ambulances and fire engines.

The European Geostationary Navigation Overlay Service (EGNOS), which is financed by the EU and developed by ESA,[93] is an all-purpose augmentation system for all kinds of users.[94] Its aviation application was developed tested and is certified by Eurocontrol.[95] The system has a ground segment for monitoring, a support system, a space system of three geostationary satellites, which broadcast corrections to the overlay service signals, and a user segment.[96] Three services are offered, an Open Service, a Data Access Service and a Safety of Life Service for critical transport applications, including civil aviation.[97] Users require EGNOS compatible receivers. Thanks to its having left the EU the system is not presently available to UK users, but a UK alternative is being developed.

Other countries are also establishing systems to augment GPS and other GNSS systems.[98] The Japanese Multi-functional Transport Satellite-based Augmentation System (MTSAS) augments GPS accuracy in the Asian and Pacific Ocean regions.[99] The Indian GAGAN system augments GPS accuracy in the Indian region,[100] and the South Korean KASS augmentation system has operated since 2022.[101]

---

91 UN Report 2004, *supra* n. 3, paras 176–81. For the WMO GOS system see www.wmo.int/pages/prog/www/OSY/GOS.html.
92 US Federal Radionavigation Plan (2005), *supra* n. 40, Chapter 3.
93 See 'What Is EGNOS?': www.gsa.europa.eu/egnos/what-egnos.
94 See www.esa.int/esaNA/egnos.html; www.Galileoju.com; UN Report 2004, *supra* n. 3, paras 169–175.
95 Eurocontrol deals with the safety of air navigation within Europe: www.esa.int/esaNA/egnos.html.
96 See EGNOS System: www.gsa.europa.eu/european-gnss/egnos/egnos-system.
97 See EGNOS Services: www.gsa.europa.eu/egnos/services.
98 UN Report 2004, *supra* n. 3, paras 162–203. F. Lyall, 'Legal Issues of Expanding Global Satellite Communications Services and Global Navigation Satellite Services' (2001) 5 *Sing. J. Int. & Comp. L.* 227–245 at 230–233.
99 MTSAS augments GPS and other GNSS services. Augmentation service is available in Japan and proximate ocean areas. The basic interoperable service is free. See 'Japan's GPS Augmentation Systems Gets MTSAT-2', *Inside GNSS*, March 2006: www.insidegnss.com/node/107. Japan launched its fourth satellite in the augmentation system on 31 May 2017: https://phys.org/news/2017-06-japan-satellite-super-accurate-gps.html.
100 India's Geo-Augmented Navigation System (GAGAN) improves the accuracy of GNSS in Indian airspace: https://gssc.esa.int/navipedia/index.php/GAGAN. See also 'GAGAN – India's SBAS', *Inside GNSS*, January 2016: https://insidegnss.com/gagan-indias-sbas/.
101 See www.gpsworld.com/south-korea-launches-kass-satellite-to-augment-gps/?utm_source=Navigate%21+Weekly+GNSS+News&utm_medium=Newsletter&utm_campaign=NCMCD220622002&oly_enc_id=8808G7421578G6C.

International GNSS Law

UN COPUOS continues to discuss GNSS and has encouraged its development.[102] All states currently providing GNSS services are parties to the Outer Space Treaty, ARRA, the Liability Convention and the Registration Convention. Effectively therefore GNSS is subject to the normal rules as to the use of outer space.

As space objects GNSS satellites are subject to the rules and requirements discussed in Chapter 4. The financing of a GNSS satellite system remains subject to national law of its state of registry.[103] The Space Protocol to the 2001 Convention on International Interest in Mobile Equipment (the Cape Town Convention) is not yet in force, but were it in force for a party, it would apply to financial securities constituted over the satellite if appropriately registered.[104] A GNSS satellite found outside the state of registry, must, under OST Art VIII, be returned to that state after proper identification. However, should ARRA apply, a state finding a satellite is to make it available to its launching state, subject to the expenses incurred being borne by the launching authority.[105] GNSS satellites are more likely to be found and retrieved on Earth following an unsuccessful launch rather than while in orbit.[106]

Under OST Art. VI states are responsible for national activities in outer space and ensuring that they conform with the Treaty. States are to conduct their space activities in accordance with international law, including the UN Charter (OST Art. III). This might be thought to impose some restrictions on GNSSs. The GPS, GLONASS and BeiDou systems basically provide a military service although civilian use is permitted. It follows that all the UN Charter provisions as to the maintenance of international peace and security (Art. 1), non-intervention (Art. 2), the settlement of disputes (Art. 2) and non-aggression (Arts 39–51) are relevant. Using GNSS as part of self-defence would be permitted (Art. 51).[107] Parties may 'not place in orbit around the Earth any object carrying nuclear weapons or any other kinds of weapon of mass destruction' (OST Art. IV). In that some GNSS systems are available for both military and civilian purposes they can be used to guide weapons of mass destruction. It does not seem to be argued, however, that they therefore are part of these weapons and prohibited by OST Art. IV.

OST Art. 1 provides that the use of outer space 'shall be carried out for the benefit and in the interest of all countries, irrespective of their degree of economic or scientific development'. Further, 'outer space . . . shall be free for exploration and use by all States without

---

102 See the COPUOS Report, UN GAOR, A/76/20, paras 101–104. Cf. UNGA Res. 2223 (XXI), 19 December 1966, para 4, and the International Committee on GNSS (ICG), *infra* n. 141.

103 OST Art. VIII: Convention on the Registration of Objects Launched into Outer Space, 14 January 1975; 1023 UNTS 15; (1978) UKTS 70, Cmnd. 7271; TIAS 8480; (1975) 14 ILM 43.

104 Convention on International Interests in Mobile Equipment, 2001, 2307 UNTS 285. The Space Assets Protocol at www.unidroit.org/instruments/security-interests/space-protocol, or www.itu.int/en/ITU-R/space/spaceAssetsProtocol/potocolSpaceAssets09032012-EN.pdf. For the Cape Town system and the Space Protocol see *infra*, Chapter 13.

105 Agreement on the Rescue of Astronauts, the Return of Astronauts and the Return of Objects Launched into Outer Space, 1968; 672 UNTS 119, Art. 5. See *supra* Chapter 4.

106 Palapa B-2 and Westar VI were refurbished and sold after recovery by the Shuttle in November 1984 in operations paid for by insurers. D.F.S. Portree and R.C. Treviño, *Walking to Olympus: An EVA Chronology*, 57–58: https://historycollection.jsc.nasa.gov/JSCHistoryPortal/history/walking/EVAChron.pdf.

107 See Chapter 15 on military uses of outer space.

discrimination of any kind, on a basis of equality and in accordance with international law'. Clearly, while GNSS access remains available and free for civilian use a potential benefit for all is provided.[108] However, the article does not specifically require that all countries or users shall have access to particular space benefits. Denial of access to GNSS services would be possible under various circumstances. One would be were the UN Security Council acting under Chapter 7 of the UN Charter, to adopt a resolution authorising GNSS disruption as a sanction against a state breaching the peace. Alternatively a state might decide to shut down its GNSS for reasons of national security.[109] Again a GNSS operator may remove civilian access to its system, or introduce charging for what was previously a service free to users all without breaching OST Art. I. That said, we note that other international legislation may be relevant in that case.[110] In aviation, for example, the 1998 ICAO 'Charter on Rights and Obligations of States Relating to GNSS Services' provides that states and aircraft 'shall have access on a non-discriminatory basis under uniform conditions, to the use of GNSS services' and all current GNSS providers are ICAO members.[111] However, although GNSS is significantly provided for in Annex 10 to the ICAO Convention,[112] the ICAO Charter remains only a resolution, not formal binding law. ICAO has not managed to construct a generally acceptable agreement that would hold providers liable for faulty GNSS within its sectoral interest.

By OST Art. IX, state parties must conduct their activities in outer space 'with due regard to the corresponding interests of all other States Parties to the Treaty'.[113] Consultation may be requested if a state suspects interference with its space activities from those of another party. The coordination between GNSS providers indicated elsewhere in this chapter appears to meet this requirement.[114]

Under OST Art. VII a state may be liable for damage caused by its space object. Liability is, of course, also the matériel of the Liability Convention, which all GNSS provider states have ratified.[115] What we may call 'normal liability' is not in question for GNSS – a crashing GNSS satellite will be dealt with under OST Art. VII (113 parties), or the Liability Convention (98 parties), failing either of which the traditional rules as to inter-state damage could apply.

---

108 Cf. 'Declaration on International Cooperation in the Exploration and Use of Outer Space for the Benefit and in the Interest of All States, Taking into Particular Account the Needs of Developing Countries', UNGA Res. 51/122, 1997. See CoCoSL III, 299–362.

109 Waldrop, *supra* n. 37.

110 See *infra* sv. 'Other International Law: ITU Constitution, ICAO and IMO'.

111 ICAO, 'Charter on the Rights and Obligations of States Relating to GNSS Services', ICAO Res. A32–19, 1998, in 'Assembly Resolutions in Force (as of 8 October 2004)' ICAO Doc. 9848, Sec. V, 'Legal Matters'.

112 Use of GNSS is covered in Aeronautical Telecommunications, Annex 10 to the ICAO Convention, Vol. V, 'Surveillance and Collision Avoidance Systems'. The individual state membership of ESA results in the inclusion of Galileo.

113 Compare *UK v. Iceland*, 1974 ICJ 3 where the Court held that, on the high seas, states have 'the obligation to pay due regard to the interests of other States in the conservation and equitable exploitation of these resources'. This principle of customary law is articulated in Arts. 56–59 of UNCLOS, 1984: UN Convention on the Law of the Sea, Montego Bay, 1984, 1833 UNTS 3; (1999) UKTS 81, Cm. 4524; (1982) 21 ILM 1261.

114 Cf. the International Committee on GNSS (ICG), *infra* n. 141.

115 Convention on International Liability for Damage Caused by Space Objects, 29 March 1972; 961 UNTS 187. See *supra*, Chapter 4.

More interesting is whether a GNSS provider has any liability if its system fails or delivers inaccurate signals, with resultant damage to a user reliant on it.[116] Presumably system failure or corruption due to natural events such as a solar flare or meteor collision would exempt from liability, but what might be the case were the provider negligent? The answer might be important.

Discussion of GNSS tends to concentrate on the positioning or locating services. However, among the list of services with which our chapter began is that of time certification. That can be overlooked in discussions of the law. Time-certification has become essential in modern electronic commerce. Major international financial transactions, and others, are dated by reference to GNSS signals with a precision down to fractions of seconds as to time. Computer systems, financial and otherwise, can talk to each other but their interaction might well be blocked were one system to be unable to connect to another because of a defect or error in the GNSS system on which it relies for calibration. As a result of GNSS error many modern functions on which we rely could be paralysed, affecting banking, telecommunications, electricity and gas supplies, aviation and train services and so on. And, apart from all that, the familiar positioning and location services may be degraded or halted.

Under the Liability Convention a launching state is liable absolutely to pay compensation for damage caused by its space object for damage caused on the surface of the Earth (Art. II), but for damage elsewhere to a space object of another launching State or to persons or property on-board such an object only if the damage is its fault or the fault of persons for whom it is responsible (Art. III). Were an aircraft, reliant on a faulty GNSS, to crash or collide with another aircraft – is absolute liability to be invoked? What if a space-launch reliant on the GNSS of another state goes amiss through its defective signals? At first sight the language of Arts. II and III might appear to apply to damage caused by reliance on faulty GNSS. However, the Liability Convention has been interpreted by some to apply only to direct damage attributable to a crashing space object or a collision between space objects in outer space. On this view the Liability Convention would not apply to damage caused indirectly through an orbiting GNSS space object transmitting faulty navigation and positioning data.[117] On the other hand the language does not specifically dictate such a narrow interpretation. Some are of the view that the Liability Convention applies to both direct and indirect damages caused by space objects.[118]

Apart from the Liability Convention. some states not party to it are parties to the OST. By its Art. VII, launching states are liable for damage caused on Earth, in air space and outer space. Neither Art. VII, nor its origin, para 5 of the UNGA 'Declaration of Legal Principles Governing the Activities of States in the Exploration and Use of Outer Space', UNGA Res. 1962 (XVIII), 1963, specify the narrow view of liability that is applied by some major space powers. It therefore remains a question whether compensation could be recovered from a state operating or licensing a faulty GNSS system either because of the fault itself (OST Art. VII), or because the fault indicates its failure properly to supervise and control its own space activities or those of its nationals (OST Art. VI).

---

116 Reference point, *supra* n. 17. See also materials there cited.
117 This is the US interpretation expressed at the Senate Hearings on the ratification of the Liability Convention.
118 Several parties to the Convention have not expressed their views.

Another question may be whether the national law of a GNSS provider could be brought into play. That is a matter for the several legal systems that might become involved. Some would probably refuse an action through the doctrine of 'sovereign immunity'.[119] Other states might apply a doctrine of 'injurious reliance' and allow an action. Again, direct action against the manufacturer of a defective satellite might be contemplated. The solution may be the drawing up of an international agreement on GNSS liability, akin to the Warsaw Convention, 1929, as amended,[120] setting maximum recovery limits, or the Convention on Third Party Liability in the Field of Nuclear Energy.[121] At the urging of some European states, UNIDROIT has done preparatory work on a treaty that would allow users to present claims for defective GNSS service.[122] However, the UNIDROIT third party liability project would seem applicable only to Galileo and not to all GNSS providers.

Other International Law: ITU Constitution, ICAO and IMO

Radio is fundamental to all GNSS and their augmentations. The navigation and positioning satellites cannot function without clear radio signals. Harmful interference with GNSS radio frequencies creates safety hazards for navigation of airplanes, ships and trains, and its avoidance or elimination is therefore particularly important. GNSS radio signals are weak and as it happens the radio frequencies used by its service providers are all close to each other, increasing the potential of harmful radio interference between the GNSS providers themselves entirely apart from other terrestrial interference.

The international use of radio is a matter for the ITU, discussed in Chapter 8. Briefly, since radio is a limited natural resource, ITU members are to limit their use of the radio spectrum to the absolute minimum necessary for the services intended.[123] Frequencies are

---

119 Under the US Foreign Sovereign Immunities Act, 28 USC §§ 1604 et seq., foreign governments enjoy immunity from suit in US courts. GPS has US governmental immunity under the US Federal Tort Claims Act (FTCA), 28 USC §§ 1346, 1402, 2402–5, 2671–80. The FTCA permits the US government to be held liable for its negligent acts if those acts are not 'discretionary acts' – a term which is not defined in the statute, but cf. *Dalehite v. United States*, 346 US 15 (1954); *United States v. Union Trust*, 350 US 907 (1955). GLONASS and BeiDou are also governmental activities. Galileo may claim sovereign immunity even though it will charge for high-end use: F.G. von der Dunk, 'Liability for Global Navigation Satellite Services: A Comparative Analysis of GPS and Galileo' (2004) 30 *J. Sp. L.* 129–167 [Lyall/Larsen 429–67] at 153–7 (written before the collapse of the projected public/private joint-undertaking arrangement for Galileo).
120 Convention for the Unification of Certain Rules Relating to International Transportation by Air, Warsaw, 1929; 137 LNTS 11; 49 Stat 3000; (1934) TS 876; 1933 UKTS 11, Cmd. 4284; [1934] 28 AJIL Supp. 84.
121 Convention on Third Party Liability in the Field of Nuclear Energy, Paris, 29 July 1960, 956 UNTS 251; 1969 UKTS 69, Cmnd. 3755; [1971] 55 AJIL 1082. We believe that Supplementary Conventions of 1963 (1963) 2 ILM 685) and 1997 (1997) 36 ILM 1473) are not yet in force.
122 'Third Party Liability for Global Navigation Satellite (GNSS) Services'. See Unidroit 2010, Study LXXXIX – Preliminary Study, and subsequent discussions available through links at www.unidroit.org. See also H.G. Bollweg, 'Initial Considerations regarding the Feasibility of an International UNIDROIT Instrument to Cover Liability for Damage Caused by Malfunctions in Global (Navigation) Satellite Systems' (2008) 13 *Unif. L. Rev.* 917–934; U. Magnus, 'Civil Liability for Satellite-based Services' (2008) 13 *Unif. L. Rev.* 935–969; S.M. Carbone and M.E. De Maestri, 'The Rationale for an International Convention on Third Party Liability for Satellite Navigation Signals' (2009) 14 *Unif. L. Rev.* 35–55. J.E. Woodward, 'Oops, My GPS made me do it!: GPS Manufacturer Liability under a Strict Products Liability Paradigm when GPS Fails to Give Accurate Directions to GPS End-Users' (2009) 34 *U. Dayton L. Rev.* 429–466.
123 ITU Constitution Arts. 44.2 (196) and 44.1 (195). The ITU RR allocate a number of frequencies to be used for radionavigation purposes, and their use by RR Arts. 35–45.

to be used rationally, efficiently and economically, and in conformity with the provisions of the Radio Regulations so that all may have equitable access to the resource.[124] Article 45 of the ITU Constitution prohibits the causing of harmful interference to other users of the radio spectrum. The Annex to the ITU Constitution defines harmful interference as 'interference which endangers the functioning of a radio navigation service or of other safety services or seriously degrades, obstructs or repeatedly interrupts a radiocommunication service operating in accordance with the Radio Regulations'.[125] Clearly this applies to interference to GNSS services.

In the US radiofrequencies are licensed by the Federal Communication Commission (FCC), which is not part of the Executive Branch. Unfortunately, frequencies most useful for GNSS purposes are also ideal for mobile satellite and mobile phone services, so the providers of these also seek allocations within the same spectrum bands. In the US the LightSquared Communication Network proposed to build a network using radiofrequencies close to those used by GPS. The US Departments of Defense and Transportation through the US National Telecommunication and Information Administration, joined by the GPS Industry Council, objected. Tests indicated potential interference with GPS signals, and the FCC withdrew its grant of licence. Subsequently LightSquared's assets were transferred to Ligado, which renewed efforts to obtain FCC permission to operate on frequencies close to those used by GPS. In 2020 the FCC issued a licence to Ligado conditional on the elimination of several possible sources of harmful interference to spectrum used by aviation navigating by GPS. Aviation requires complete safety. Landing at airports requires a higher safety standard for interference than that applied by existing FCC broadcast licensing standards.[126] The interference issues remain unresolved. The 2021 National Defense Authorization Act required the Department of Defense to establish a review committee to evaluate the objections to the FCC 2020 Ligado Order and to make recommendations to Congress. The review committee is still at work.[127] The Ligado case not only illustrates the fierce competition for radio frequencies but also underscores that GNSS has major safety of life, emergency and guidance purposes which should be given priority within the allocation and assignment processes. It's other importance is that whatever the US FCC decides will have spill-over effects throughout the Americas.

Proposed assignments in the space frequency bands are given advance publicity through the ITU, with data as to frequencies and satellite orbits made known. Before a firm assignment is notified to the ITU Radiocommunication Bureau an assigning state should try to ensure that no interference will be caused to another user, entering into appropriate

124 ITU Constitution Art. 44.2 (196).
125 Annex to the ITU Constitution (1003). Gradations of interference are set out in ITU RR 1.167–169.
126 FCC Order Regarding Possible Interference with GPS Frequencies by Ligado (2020) (Order 20–48). In the Matter of LightSquared Tech. Working Group Report 35 FCC Rcd. 3772 (2020). P.B. Larsen, *supra* n. 21, at sec. III. See also G. Warwick, 'LightSquared Plans Reignite GPS Interference Issue', *Av. & Sp. Tech.*, July 28, 2015. See also T.W. Hazlett and B. Skorup, 'Tragedy of the Regulatory Commons: Lightsquared and the Missing Spectrum Rights' (2014–2015) 13 *Duke L. & Tech. Rev.* 1–35; M. Hersh, 'A Study on the Role of Spectrum Usage Rights within Disputes' (2014) 12 *Col. Tech. L.J.* 455–478.
127 See Sec. 1663, 'Independent Technical Review of Federal Communications Commission Order 20–48', National Defense Authorization Act for Fiscal Year 2021, Public Law 116–283, 134 Stat. 4075. D.M.K. Zoldi, 'Déjà Vu All Over Again: Ligado's 5G Network Collision Course with GPS', *Inside GNSS*, May/June 2022, at 22. Strong representations have been made that the FCC Order be reversed: GPS World Staff, 26 April 2023: www.gpsworld.com/vast-coalition-seeks-reversal-of-ligado-order/.

negotiations if needed. An assignment is processed by the Radiocommunication Bureau, and, if all is well, is entered on the Master International Frequency Register. Thereafter a registered assignment is entitled to protection from interference by later-comers.[128]

Two major international organisations play an important role as to GNSS, the International Civil Aviation Organisation (ICAO) and the International Maritime Organisation (IMO), both having treaty-based requirements as to GNSS.

ICAO regulates world-wide civil aviation in considerable detail.[129] As part of that function ICAO deals with air safety at the international level. Members of ICAO include all the states that provide or license GNSS services.[130] Article 28 of the Chicago Convention requires ICAO parties to provide in their territories air navigation facilities that comply with the international standards and practices that ICAO adopts under powers conferred by Art. 37. In 1998 the ICAO Assembly instructed the ICAO Council and the Secretariat 'to consider the elaboration of an appropriate long term framework to govern the operation of GNSS systems, including consideration of an international convention for this purpose'.[131] In the meantime Annex 10 to the Convention sets navigation standards for both GNSS and for augmented GNSS. However, also in 1998 the ICAO Assembly adopted a 'Charter on Rights and Obligations of States Relating to GNSS Services'.[132] The Charter is not legally binding and is not part of Annex 10.[133] However, as the resolution of an Assembly with worldwide competence within its field, it must be considered significant. Its major elements are:

1. States recognize that 'the safety of international civil aviation shall be the paramount principle' in providing and using GNSS.
2. States and aircraft 'shall have access, on a non-discriminatory basis under uniform conditions, to the use of GNSS services'.
3. (a) States possess sovereignty over their own air space and the right to control aircraft operation in their sovereign air space and (b) GNSS providers shall not restrict states' control over their sovereign air space.
4. GNSS providers 'shall ensure the continuity, availability, integrity, accuracy and reliability of such services, including effective arrangements to minimize the operational impact of system malfunctions or failure, and to achieve expeditious service recovery. Such State shall ensure that the services are in accordance with ICAO standards.'
5. States shall 'cooperate to secure the highest practicable degree of uniformity of GNSS services' including regional and sub-regional services.

128 See Chapter 8 re Interference.
129 See ICAO '2016–2030 Global Air Navigation Plan', 5th ed. 2016, ICAO Doc. 9750: www.icao.int/publications/Documents/9750_5ed_en.pdf, and '2014-2016 Global Aviation Safety Plan', ICAO Doc. 10004: www.icao.int/publications/Documents/10004_cons_en.pdf.
130 Convention on International Civil Aviation, Chicago, 7 December 1944 (1944) (Chicago Convention) 15 UNTS 295; 61 Stat. 1180, TIAS 1591; (1953) UKTS 8, Cmd. 8742; 9 Hudson 168; 3 Bevans 944; [1945] 39 AJIL Supp. 111; ICAO Doc. 7300/9. Lyall, *supra* n. 2, 62–83.
131 ICAO Assembly Res. A32–20, 'Development and Elaboration of an Appropriate Long-term Legal Framework to Govern the Implementation of GNSS': Assembly Resolutions in Force (as of 4 October 2013), ICAO Doc. 10022. Cf. *Global Navigation Satellite Systems*, 2nd ed. (ICAO, 2013).
132 ICAO Assembly Res. A32–19, 'Charter on Rights and Obligations of States Relating to GNSS Services', Assembly Resolutions, *supra* n. 131.
133 Note: It is a 'Charter on', not a 'Charter of'.

6. GNSS charges are to comply with Art. 15 of the Chicago Convention.
7. In planning and providing GNSS services, states are to be 'guided by the principle of cooperation and mutual assistance'.
8. In providing GNSS, states are to have due regard to the interests of other states.
9. States may provide GNSS services jointly with other states.

Much of this is unexceptionable. However, the suggestion in 1 that safety is the paramount principle in the provision and use of GNSS is wrong. Other uses have an equal claim to importance.

That said, the ICAO Communication, Navigation and Surveillance/Air Traffic Management system (CNS/ATM) relies on GNSSs.[134] ICAO therefore continues to play an important role in their development and use.[135] Under Assembly Resolution A32–20 ICAO has been working on a broader legal framework additional to the GNSS Charter, which might include issues such as air navigation, regulation of GNSS providers, and related issues. However, first, as noted, ICAO interests cannot take precedence over those of non-aviation users. Second, any generalisation of liability may well not figure in ICAO proposals because ICAO interest is limited to aviation, while GNSS has a plethora of users represented by many agencies both national and international. Third, relevant GNSS providers might claim state immunity and be unlikely to accede to any treaty-based variation of their rights.

The International Maritime Organisation (IMO) is the maritime counterpart to ICAO and there is a considerable overlap in their membership.[136] Article 16 of the IMO Convention authorizes the IMO to regulate international maritime safety. IMO establishes standards and practices for maritime transportation. Universality and uniformity of GNSS navigation standards for maritime transportation are as important for maritime navigation as are the ICAO standards for air navigation. IMO actively adopts and reviews maritime navigation rules and procedures for navigation by GNSS. GNSS search and rescue functions are also particularly important for maritime activities. In 1997 IMO established a maritime policy for all future GNSS systems,[137] and since 2000 has required GNSS receivers to be carried on all ships engaged in international carriage.[138] The commercial company INMARSAT provides and supports global, regional and domestic satellite services,

134 CNS/ATM has been a major development in aviation. Cf. ICAO Assembly Res. A29–11 on 'Use of space technology in air navigation', Assembly Resolutions, *supra* n. 131.
135 B.D.K. Henaku, *The Law on Global Air Navigation by Satellite* (Leiden: AST, 1998); J. Huang, 'Sharing Benefits of the Global Navigation Satellite System within the Framework of ICAO' (1996) 39 *Proc. IISL* at 128–131.
136 Convention on the International Maritime Consultative Organization, Geneva, 6 March 1948; 289 UNTS 48; 1958 UKTS 54, Cmnd. 589; 9 UST, TIAS 4044. Its name was changed to the International Maritime Organisation in 1975. Lyall, *supra* n. 2, 33–61.
137 'Maritime Policy and Requirements for a Future Global Navigation Satellite System (GNSS)', IMO Res. A.860(20), revoked by A.915(22). See next note.
138 'Revised Maritime Policy and Requirements for a Future Global Navigation Satellite System (GNSS)', IMO Res. A.915(22), 29 November 2001: https://wwwcdn.imo.org/localresources/en/KnowledgeCentre/IndexofIMOResolutions/AssemblyDocuments/A.915(22).pdf. By IMO Res. A.915(22), all ships engaged in international service must carry GNSS receivers. Location coordinates are currently taken from GPS, GLONASS, Galileo or Beidou GNSS services. Cf. P.B. Larsen, 'Expanding Global Navigation Services', Proceedings of the Workshop on Space Law in the Twenty-first Century, UNISPACE III, July 1999 (UN: ST/SPACE/24, 2004) 155.

including radio determination and radio navigation, with maritime navigation and safety functions as well as its augmentation support of GNSS through EGNOS.[139]

Other Arrangements

Apart from the formalities of ICAO and the IMO other arrangements that fall within the category of soft law now affect the GNSS world. Participants in these tend to be represented by technical experts rather than by lawyers. This may be a good thing since technical experts are motivated towards the solving of practical problems rather than linguistic niceties. In particular we note the International Committee on GNSS (ICG), the GNSS Providers Forum and the International GNSS Service (IGS).[140]

The International Committee on GNSS (ICG)[141]

The 1999 UNISPACE III Resolution 54/68 recommended the international coordination of GNSS.[142] In 2004 UN COPUOS proposed an Action Plan for the implementation of the recommendations of UNISPACE III, and this was agreed by the UN General Assembly (UNGA Res. 59/2). The Plan included setting up an International Committee on GNSS (ICG) to promote international GNSS coordination and to act as an international forum for discussion of GNSS issues.[143] Accordingly in 2005 the ICG was established on a voluntary basis as an informal forum for the purposes of promoting international GNSS cooperation, coordination and interoperability.[144] It reports annually to the COPUOS Scientific and Technical Subcommittee. The ICG is serviced by UN OOSA, which also acts as a point of information about ICG activities and informs other international conferences about ICG activities. UNOOSA also provides GNSS education.[145]

The ICG divides its work programme among working groups. These were systems, signals and services; enhancement of GNSS performance; new services and capabilities; information dissemination and capacity building; reference frames, timing and applications.[146] Much has been achieved. An ICG Interoperability Working Group reported to the 2013 ICG regarding protection of the spectrum against radio signal interference, open service

139 For INMARSAT, see Chapter 10.
140 See P.B. Larsen, 'International Regulation of Global Navigation Satellite Systems' (2015) 80 *J. Air L. & Comm.* 365–422 at 395–407. For the UN background see *10 Years of Achievement of the United Nations on Global Navigation Satellite Systems* (UN OOSA, 2011): www.unoosa.org/pdf/icg/2011/11-85461_ICG-ST-55_eBook.pdf, and The *Interoperable Global Navigation Satellite Systems Space Service Volume* (2nd ed.), UN OOSA 2021): www.unoosa.org/res/oosadoc/data/documents/2021/stspace/stspace75rev_1_0_html/st_space_75rev01E.pdf.
141 Reference point nn. 34, 45, 54, 72 and 81.
142 See P.B. Larsen. 'Expanding Global Navigation Services', Proceedings of the Workshop on Space Law in the Twenty-first Century, UNISPACE III, July 1999, UN Doc. St/SPACE/24, 2004, at 155.
143 See A59/174: 'Review of the implementation of the recommendations of the Third United Nations Conference on the Exploration and Peaceful Uses of Outer Space'.
144 The ICG Terms of Reference are now contained in ICG/TOR/2014: www.unoosa.org/pdf/icg/2014/icg-9/ICG_ToR2014amended.pdf.
145 The UNOOSA Education Curriculum on Space Law (2014) includes a special module on GNSS: www.unoosa.org/res/oosadoc/data/documents/2014/stspace/stspace64_0_html/st_space_064E.pdf.
146 See 'Fifteenth Meeting of the International Committee on Global Satellite Systems', 1 December 2016, A/AC.105/1251.

performance and monitoring the open services. Recommendations were also made to improve interoperability.[147] In 2014 it discussed coordination of satellite based augmentation systems with the aim to establish standardized augmentation to serve all four GNSS systems. The plan is to propose interoperable, standardized augmentation systems to the ICAO Radio Technical Commission for Aeronautics for approval. Ideally all the GNSS receivers should be able to receive signals from all the providers. However, for cost reasons some GNSS equipment manufacturers are reluctant to build receivers with access to all four GNSS services. They may plan only two options. The EU has therefore required that GALILEO be made one of the two available GNSS options within the EU.[148] Such a regulation may require extensive international consultations because that would be contrary to the ICG recommendation for augmentation serving all the GNSS systems.[149]

The GNSS Providers Forum

In 2007 the ICG established a separate voluntary GNSS Providers Forum, delegating to it those issues on which the ICG considers it needs detailed GNSS information.[150] The Forum reports annually to the ICG. All four major GNSS Providers as well as the augmentation services are active participants. The objective is to promote compatibility and interoperability among present and future GNSS providers. The Providers Forum was not intended to be a policymaking group. It is a venue for the exchange of information about operative systems so as to avoid conflicts and to make them interoperable, as well as to discuss and coordinate guidelines for the open GNSS services. The ICG and the GNSS Providers have much in common and can help remedy weaknesses in their global systems.

Serviced by UN OOSA the Forum meets at least once a year, can meet more often should the need arise, and on occasion meets simultaneously with the ICG. Although the Providers Forum is consultative only, GNSS industry participants are rather freewheeling and stray easily into formulation of voluntary guidance principles amounting to soft law. In 2008 the GNSS and augmentation providers agreed in the Forum that all GNSS signals and services should be mutually compatible. They agreed further that all the open GNSS

---

147 UN Doc. A/AC.105/1059, at 7.

148 European Union, Regulation (EU) 2015/758 of the European Parliament and of the Council of 29 April 2015 Concerning Type-Approval Requirements for the Development of the eCall In-Vehicle to System, Based on the 112 Service and Amending Directive 207/46/EC OJ.L.123/77 of 19.5.2014.

　The EU initiative may be contrary to World Trade Organization (WTO) policy on provision of services, and may violate the basic principles on national treatment, most favoured nation treatment, and the rules on domestic regulation. See A. Arena and I. Bauman, GNSS and World Trade Law, Playing by the Rules, *supra* n. 53.

149 The equipment manufacturers' plans and the EU reaction would also both be contrary to current plans in the Providers' Forum to establish complete transparency and to require that GNSS receivers do not prefer one GNSS provider over another. In 2015 the ICG Working Group agreed that all GNSS providers, including the various augmentation systems, would all use common channels for GNSS augmentation around the globe. The IWG agreed that all GNSS augmentation signals for the planned second generation satellite-based augmentation systems (SBAS) would be standardised, utilising dual frequency multi-constellation signals. The new interoperable standard particularly benefits international aviation www.spacenewsfeed.com/index.php/news/3679-global-satnav-augmentation-systems-settle-on-common-channels-post-2020.

150 See Terms of Reference of the Providers' Forum, UN Doc. ICG/PF/TOR/2016: www.unoosa.org/pdf/icg/2016/pf-16/PF_ToR2016amended.pdf. The original members were China, India, Japan, Russia, the United States and the European Union but other states have subsequently joined.

signal and systems should be interoperable so as to provide the best possible service to all GNSS users. Since the Forum is primarily concerned with improving their open services they coordinate in compatibility and interoperability of their services, transparency, non-discrimination of equipment by manufacturers, performance monitoring and spectrum protection.

The International GNSS Service (IGS)

Originally created by the International Association of Geodesy in 1993 to track and monitor the US GPS service, the International GNSS Service (IGS) was brought under the auspices of UNOOSA and the ICG in 2005.[151] Its goal is to provide a non-profit source of high quality GNSS data products standards and expertise. Now composed of more than 350 governmental and private institutional bodies, its participants have established a global voluntary monitoring and tracking scheme for all the GNSS systems. IGS participants maintain coordinating reference points and monitoring stations, including an archive, which track GNSS activities all over the world. Headquartered at NASA's Jet Propulsion Laboratory in California the IGS network currently includes 512 stations around the globe, tracking the services of the GNSS providers and checking the quality of GNSS receivers and other GNSS products.[152]

The Future

GNSS is important. The services that it provides through positioning and time-stamping are now essential in modern life. The four current systems, GPS, GLONASS GALOEO and Beidou are interoperable and operate globally. All operate in Mid – Earth Orbits. Because their signals are weak they are easy to jam and or spoof. Both civilian and military GNSS become immobilised in combat situations like the Ukraine war. Criminal elements have also jammed or spoofed GNSS services. Return to old PNT technology is possible but transition from free civilian GNSS signals to encrypted signals would be difficult. States cooperate actively in COPUOS. Cooperation will also have to extend to action within the ITU to set aside appropriate frequencies, and states will have to ensure that, as the ITU Constitution requires, the best use is made of these resources by the systems. There remains the worrying fact that GNSS is dual-use, and the requirements of the military forces of the major providers will remain a fundamental and overriding element. Such considerations can take us into rather different territory, as to which see Chapter 15 on the military uses of space. In the meantime we hope that the various GNSS systems will continue to provide their variety of useful services while cooperating with each other.[153]

---

151 International GNSS Service (IGS): www.igs.org/about. Cf. the Global Differential GPS System: www.gdgps.net/.
152 See the IGS at http://mgex.igs.org/.
153 The over-all adverse effect on accuracy and consistency of global GNSS is evident. Both monitoring services report to the IGS, which has to some extent ameliorated the situation, but that arrangement is not as satisfactory as fuller cooperation would be. Cf. *supra* n. 53.

12

REMOTE SENSING

Introduction

Sensing from space provides invaluable data.[1] It is used for many purposes ranging from archaeology,[2] to mapping earthquakes and geology,[3] to meteorology[4] (*infra*), to disaster management (*infra*), wild-fire detection,[5] environmental[6] and other monitoring, to the

1 A. Ito, *Legal Aspects of Satellite Remote Sensing* (Leiden: Nijhoff, 2011); C. Brünner et al eds., *Satellite-based Earth Observation: Trends and Challenges for Economy and Society* (Springer, 2018); R. Purdy and D. Leung, eds., *Evidence from Earth Observation Satellites: Emerging Legal Issues* (Leiden: Nijhoff, 2013); *Peoples and Pixels: Linking Remote Sensing and Social Science* (US National Academies Press, 1998: www.nap.edu/catalog.php?record_id=5963; *Global Integrated Intelligence, Surveillance, & Reconnaissance Operations: Air Force Doctrine Document 2–0* (USAF and USDOD, 2012); R.R. Rowberg, *Commercial Remote Sensing by Satellite: Status and Issues* (UN Cong. Research Services: 2002 (RL31218): www.licensing.noaa.gov/RL31218-RemoteSensing.pdf; E.C. Barrett and L.F. Curtis, *Introduction to Environmental Remote Sensing*, 4th ed. (Milton Keynes: Routledge, 1999). See also materials archived at https://earthobservatory.nasa.gov/features/RemoteSensing/remote_10.php.
2 S.H. Parcak, *Satellite Remote Sensing for Archaeology* (London: Routledge, 2009); R. Lasaponara and N. Masini eds., *Satellite Remote Sensing: A New Tool for Archaeology* (Vienna: Springer, 2012); W.S. Hanson and I.A. Oltean eds., *Archaeology from Historical Aerial and Satellite Archives* (Vienna: Springer, 2013). Cf. K.A. Bard, *An Introduction to the Archaeology of Ancient Egypt* (New York: Wiley, 2015). See also: https://weather.ndc.nasa.gov/archeology.
3 See results from ESA's Sentinel series: www.sentinel-hub.com/. For the 2016 earthquakes in Italy see www.esa.int/spaceinimages/Images/2016/11/Mapping_Italy_s_30_October_2016_earthquake, and www.esa.int/Our_Activities/Observing_the_Earth/Copernicus/Sentinel-1/Sentinel_satellites_reveal_east_west_shift_in_Italian_quake. For the 2016 Kaikōura, New Zealand event see I.J. Hamling et al., 'Complex multifault rupture during the 2016 Mw7.8 Kaikōura earthquake, New Zealand' 355 *Science*, 6331, 23 March 2017 and ESA, March 2017: www.esa.int/Our_Activities/Observing_the_Earth/Copernicus/Sentinel-1/Satellites_shed_new_light_on_earthquakes. Cf. Everest, 2015: www.esa.int/Our_Activities/Observing_the_Earth/Copernicus/Sentinel-1/Nepal_earthquake_on_the_radar, and www.independent.co.uk/news/world/asia/mount-everest-has-moved-an-inch-and-changed-direction-because-of-the-nepal-earthquake-10323617.html.
4 The US TIROS-I, launched in 1960 as the first Earth observation satellite, gathered meteorological data.
5 Cf. www.asc-csa.gc.ca/eng/satellites/wildfiresat/; www.satellitetoday.com/imagery-and-sensing/2023/05/09/canadian-space-agency-awards-spire-and-ororatech-wildfire-detection-contract/?oly_enc_id=8020G6675790B5S.
6 Again see the data available from the Sentinel Hub, *supra* n. 3. See also C. Davies et al, 'Moving Pictures: How Satellites, the Internet and International Environmental Law Can Help Promote Sustainable Development'

DOI: 10.4324/9781003496502-12

policing of agreements,[7] cartography and the delimitation of international boundaries. The ICJ has been referred to and accepted aerial photography and satellite imagery as evidential.[8] It has also been used in international criminal trials.[9] Sensing for military purposes, whether reconnaissance, compliance with arms control agreements or 'confidence building', is highly important.[10] The use of sensing-acquired data in municipal courts has

---

(1999) 28 *Stetson L. Rev.* 1091–1153; J.M. Epstein, 'The Role of the Global Positioning System in the Environment' (1997) 6 *N.Y.U. Env. L. J.* 72–92; R. Puterski, 'The Global Positioning System – Just Another Tool?' (1997) 6 *N.Y.U. Env. L.J.* 93–106; C. Crandall, 'Why Aren't We Using that Intel Stuff – Using Satellite Imagery in Domestic Disaster Prevention and Response' (2010) *BYU L. Rev.* 1831–1868; C. Pittman, 'A modest proposal: using remote sensing to monitor and promote waste anni-hilating molten salt reactors and nuclear waste recycling' (2018) 42 *J. Sp. L.* 135–170; Larsen 'The OSO Landslide', *infra* n. 94; Ginzky, *infra* n. 11. Cf. www.esa.int/spaceinvideos/Videos/2017/02/Sentinel_services_for_agriculture2.

7 M. Onoda, 'Satellite Earth Observation and "Systematic Observation" in Multilateral Environmental Trea-ties' (2005) 31 *J. Sp. L.* 339–411; J.K. Hettling, 'The use of remote sensing satellites for verification in international law' (2003) 19 *Space Policy* 33–39; N. Peter, 'The Use of Remote Sensing to Support the Application of Multilateral Environmental Agreements' (2004) 20 *Space Policy* 189–195.

8 Cf. Ito, *supra* n. 1, 135–143; M. Williams, 'Satellite Evidence in International Institutions', in Purdy *supra* n. 1, 195–216. The ICJ used satellite obtained data in the joined cases *Certain Activities carried out by Nicaragua in the Border Area (Costa Rica v Nicaragua and Construction of a Road in Costa Rica along the San Juan River (Nicaragua v Costa Rica)*, 2015 ICJ 1, paras 79–81, 202 and 206, though remarking that in some instances the imagery was insufficiently clear.

In the *Case Concerning the Frontier Dispute, Benin v. Nigeria*, 2005 ICJ 90, both Benin and the Chamber referred to satellite data obtained from aerial photographs (para 41) and SPOT imagery (para 116). In the *Case Concerning the Territorial and Maritime Dispute between Nicaragua and Honduras in the Caribbean Sea (Nicaragua v. Honduras)*, 2007 ICJ 1, Honduras apparently introduced a satellite photograph as part of its argument (see para 276). See also the *Case Concerning Kasikili/Sedudu Island (Botswana v. Namibia)* 1999 ICJ 1045 at paras 31, 33–36, and *Land and Maritime Boundary between Cameroon and Nigeria (Cameroon v. Nigeria: Equatorial Guinea intervening)* 2002 ICJ 303 at paras 88, 90, 93 and 95.

In *The South China Sea Arbitration Award*, 12 July 2016, Philippines v China, PCA Case No. 2013–19, satellite imagery is treated with caution as to the determination of actual low tide elevations in the past (para 326), but extensive use is made of it as to China's construction activities in building up and adapting what were small atolls in the South China Sea.

There seems no good reason to separate aerial from satellite imagery. Cf. the ICJ Chamber on the proba-tive value of maps: *Case Concerning the Frontier Dispute (Burkina Faso v. Republic of Mali)* 1986 ICJ 554 at paras 54–56. Satellite photography has increased the reliability of maps (para 55) but the weight to be put on maps depends on whether and how they express the will of states (paras 54–56). Photography and imagery from whatever sources can illustrate the changing course of a river, but the effect of that evidence will depend on other factors. Here the approach of municipal courts may be valuable. See *infra* n. 11.

9 J. Sandalinas, 'Satellite Imagery and its Use as Evidence in the Proceedings of the International Criminal Court' (2015) 64 ZLW 666–675; A. Froelich, 'Space related data: from justice to development' (2011) 54 *Proc. IISL* 221–227, and her 'The Impact of Satellite Data used by High International Courts like the ICJ (International Court of Justice) and ITLOS (International Tribunal for the Law of the Sea' (2012) 55 *Proc. IISL* 471–483; E.D. Macauley 'The Use of EO Technologies in Court by the Office of the Prosecutor of the International Criminal Court', in Purdy, *supra* n. 1, 217–240.

10 Here we simply cite without comment: 1) Anonymous, 'Note: Legal Aspects of Reconnaissance in Airspace and Outer Space' (1961) 61 *Col. L. Rev.* 1074–1102; 2) C.M. Petras, ' "Eyes" on Freedom – A View of the Law Governing Military Use of Satellite Reconnaissance in US Homeland Defense' (2005) 31 *J. Sp. L.* 81–115; 3) D.A. Koplow, 'Back to the Future and Up to the Sky: Legal Implications of Open Skies Inspec-tion for Arms Control' (1991) 79 *Cal. L. Rev.* 421–496; 4) A. Deeks, 'An International Framework for Surveillance' (2015) 55 *Va. J. Int. L.* 291–368; 5) J. Gutzman, 'State Responsibility for Non-State Actors in Times of War: Article VI of the Outer Space Treaty and the Law of Neutrality' (2019) 80 *Air Force Law Rev.* 87–148.

increased, although it has been the subject of argument.[11] The market for satellite Earth observation (EO) is developing rapidly. It is estimated to grow to $ 4.5 billion annually by 2025. The highest resolution images are most valuable and are in particular demand. Governments are the largest customers for commercial EO images, but private demands are increasing rapidly.[12] Technical progress has been massive since the early days of remote sensing, but lawyers were early interested in the regulation of the new facility.[13] However, when remote sensing from space came on the scene its legal problems were not novel.

The Technology

Remote sensing is the gathering of data from a distance by a variety of means.[14] Although the development of space systems has greatly increased remote sensing activity, its roots and legal regulation go far back. Relevant rules are to be found in municipal legal systems as well as in both terrestrial and international space law. Simple ocular observation is a form of remote sensing,[15] but it is commonly accepted that the remote sensing we discuss here involves the use of a mechanical recording medium. The invention of photography in the mid-nineteenth century was significant. Camera technology has since been consistently improved. Flight, whether by free balloon, dirigible balloon, or by airplane afforded a platform from which camera observations could be made. Remote sensing from space at first depended on the use of orthodox film, canisters of film being ejected from satellites

---

11 The admissibility of remote sensing data is subject to the requirements of a national court as to scientific data, including its reliability, the chain of custody and data security. Different courts may apply different and different levels of requirements: cf. the US Supreme Court's reasoning in *Daubert v. Merrill Dow Pharmaceuticals Inc.* (1993) 509 US 579; 113 S. Ct. 2786; 125 L. Ed. 2d 469, 1993 US LEXIS 4408, and cases cited in its considering and departing from *Frye v. United States* (1923) 54 App DC 46, 293 F 1013, 34 ALR 145 (*Daubert*, cert. denied, 516 US 869; 116 S Ct. 189; 133 L. Ed. 2d 126).

See H.A. Latin, G.W. Tennehill and R.E. White, 'Remote Sensing Evidence and Environmental Law' (1976) 64 *Cal. L. Rev.* 1300–1446; L.J. Steele, 'The View from on High: Satellite Remote Sensing Data and the Fourth Amendment' (1992) 6 *High Tech. L.J.* 317–34; C. Artz, 'Use of Satellite Imagery in Legal Proceedings' (1999) 24 *Air & Sp. L.* 195–203; H. Ginzky, 'Satellite Images in Legal Proceedings relating to the Environment – a US Perspective' (2000) 25 *Air & Sp. L.* 114–128; S. Moens 'The Use of Data from Earth Observation Satellites in Criminal Proceedings: Case Study of Illegal Oil Discharges at Sea' ((2012) 55 *Proc. IISL* 451–461; A. Dos Santos 'The Use of Satellites for Prosecuting Persons and Companies that have Caused Deforestation in the Amazon Region' (2012) 55 *Proc. IISL* 462–470; R. Abeyratne, 'The Use of Satellite Imagery as Evidence in Pre-Trial and Trial Hearings' (2003) 52 ZLW 221–36; S.H. Hodge, 'Satellite Data and Environmental Law: Technology Ripe for Litigation Application' (1997) 14 *Pace Env. L. Rev.* 691–732; R. Purdy, 'Legal and Privacy Implications of "Spy in the Sky" Satellites' (1999) 3 *Mountbatten J. Leg. Stud.* 63–79; R. Purdy and R. Mcrory, 'The Use of Satellite Images as Evidence in Environmental Actions in Great Britain' (2001) 51 *Droit Et Ville*, 70–78, and their 'Satellite Photographs – 21st Century Evidence?' (2003) 153 *New L.J.* (UK) 337–8; M. Wright, 'The Use of Remote Sensing Imagery at Trial in the United States' – One State Court Judge's Observations', in Purdy, *supra* n. 1, 313–320; C.M. Billiet, 'Satellite Images as Evidence for Environmental Crime in Europe A Judge's Perspective', in Purdy, *supra* n. 1, 321–355.

12 See Larsen 'The OSO Landslide', *infra* n. 94.

13 N. Mateesco-Matte and H. De Saussure, *Legal Implications of Remote Sensing from Outer Space* (Leiden: Sijthoff, 1976).

14 P.J. Gibson, *Introductory Remote Sensing: Principles and Concepts* (London: Routledge, 2000).

15 During the US Civil War gunnery officers were posted by US General Grant in the gondolas of tethered balloons to observe and calibrate the shelling of the Confederate trenches at Petersburg: 'Balloons in the Civil War' (2021): www.battlefields.org/learn/head-tilting-history/balloons-civil-war.

and recovered for processing. Now digital technology permits the easy transmission of data from satellites to ground stations for later analysis and interpretation. In all cases the acquisition of varieties of electromagnetic data is the material of the observation. That data may be emitted by an object as infra-red, 'normal' to human vision, or ultra-violet radiation, or it may be diffracted or refracted by an object illuminated either by natural light or by artificial radiation being reflected by it.

Traditional 'film' systems involve the capture of data by the alteration of chemical layers on the film. Digital systems capture the wavelengths of radiation reaching the individual pixels of a sensor array with the advantage that that data can be processed by appropriate computer programmes.[16] Sensors used by satellites are either panchromatic (PAN) or multispectral (MS). Panchromatic sensors produce data in black and white, while multispectral sensors produce data in a variety of wavelengths, which can be manipulated to provide images, 'coloured' to assist their interpretation. The 'resolution' that a particular remote sensing system provides has four aspects. 'Spatial resolution' depends on the relation between an individual pixel and the object it represents.[17] It is the smallest dimensions that an object can have and still be distinguishable from another object beside it. Thus 'one metre resolution' means that one square metre is recorded by each pixel, and 'ten metre resolution' that ten square metres are so recorded.[18] Present commercial space remote sensing systems provide a resolution of down to two-thirds of a metre (2 feet) at a distance of two to three hundred miles. Half-metre (c. 19.5 inches) resolution and better is now commercially available. 'Temporal resolution' or 're-visit time' is the frequency at which data of the target may be acquired. This depends on the orbit, the sensing capacity and the periodicity of the remote satellite. 'Spectral resolution' is the narrowness of the frequency band that is employed for scanning. 'Radiometric resolution' measures the number of levels of grey that can be determined on a black and white image.

Sensing may be active or passive. Active sensing requires the sensing device to illuminate electromagnetically the target being sensed (usually by radar) and capturing the reflection by its sensors. In passive sensing, the sensing device simply collects electromagnetic or other radiation emanating from the target whether that is reflected radiation (e.g. sunlight) or originates in the target itself (e.g. heat, visible in the infra-red wave bands).

There are two major manifestations of remote sensing. The first lies in the gathering of information by observation from aeroplanes. Indeed, remote sensing from aeroplanes remains a valuable data source.[19] However, the second manifestation, remote sensing by satellites, has captured public attention, particularly through the availability of Google Earth to anyone with internet access. Satellite sensing has developed from being the exclusive preserve of states to that of a mixed economy. States and intergovernmental organisations still run very active satellite systems and programmes, but commercial companies are increasingly active. Some of these handle data provided by the state systems. Yet others launch their own satellites and contract with states and other commercial entities to provide remote sensing services.[20]

---

16 A 'pixel' is a single unit of data which contributes to an array of pixels, which if properly processed eventually produces an 'image' which human perception can interpret.
17 As to a 'pixel' see *supra* n. 16.
18 The difference between resolutions is apparent in some of the images available through Google Earth (www.google.earth.com).
19 See next section, and cf. Hanson and Oltean *supra* n. 2.
20 J.I. Gabrynowicz, 'The Perils of Landsat from Grassroots to Globalisation: A Comprehensive Review of US Remote Sensing Law with a Few Thoughts for the Future' (2005) 6 *Chi. J. Int. L.* 45–67; E. Ambrosetti,

Aerial Remote Sensing

Remote sensing from the air is a matter for both international law and the rules of the relevant municipal legal system. International law has been concerned with such questions for over one-hundred years.

As indicated in Chapter 6, balloon flights crossing international boundaries provoked the 1890s and 1900s discussion of the rights of states in and to the air space above their territories.[21] This was triggered in part by reasons of state security. The Paris Conference on Aerial Navigation of 1910 spent much time discussing what rules should apply to the new activities and produced a variety of sensible suggestions. However there was no final agreement on the text of a Convention.[22] The major failure to agree was on the nature of access of foreign aircraft to the air space of a state: should access be permitted as a 'right of innocent passage', or should it be subject to the specific permission of the over-flown state because of its absolute rights in respect its air space.[23] That military officers had been found to be carrying cameras aboard 'foreign' dirigible balloons which just happened to over-fly military fortifications was but a strand in the 1910 argument. The development of aviation spurred by the exigencies of combat in the First World War and the potential threat that that posed swept aside vacillation. The 'complete and exclusive' right of sovereignty of a state over its air space was easily agreed and appears as Art. 1 of the Paris Convention on the Regulation of Aerial Navigation, 1919.[24] However, it is noteworthy that in Art. 1 the High Contracting Parties *recognised* the complete and exclusive sovereignty of '*every Power*'. The language of Art. 1 therefore purported to articulate customary law as to the 'complete and exclusive sovereignty' of all states, not just as between the parties to the Convention. While that notion may have been an overstatement at the precise time of its promulgation, it was swiftly accepted as being indeed a principle of customary law.

As a matter of law therefore, since Paris 1919 all states have had 'complete and exclusive sovereignty' over their own air space, a sovereignty that has over the years been enforced, sometimes with disastrous results for intruders.[25] However, Art. 2 of the Paris Convention

---

'Relevance of Remote Sensing to Third-World Economic Development: Some Legal and Political Aspects' (1980) 12 *N.Y.U. J. Int. L. & Pol.* 569–598; and 'Remote Sensing from Outer Space: Its Significance and Problems from a Third World Perspective' (1984) 17 *N.Y.U. J. Int. L. & Pol.* 1–34. See also the other notes to this chapter, and the utility of remote sensing in Chapter 9.

21 The first photography from a balloon was in 1858 by G-F. Tournachon, who used the pseudonym 'Nadar'. See F. Nadar (trans. E. Cadava and L. Theodoratou) *When I Was a Photographer* (Boston: MIT Press, 2015) 57–73, 'The First Attempt at Aerostatic Photography'. Nadar was a friend of Baudelaire.

22 Draft International Convention on Aerial Navigation, Paris 1910. See Appendix to Reports of the Civil Aerial Transport Committee, 1918, UKSP Reports, Vol. V, 17, Cd. 9218. See further *supra* Chapter 6 text at n. 22 and following.

23 While the UK negotiators were persuaded of the desirability of relative freedom of access, considerations of military security and sensitivity to fears of invasion from the Continent overruled. See the Reports of the Civil Aerial Transport Committee, 1918, *supra* n. 22.

24 Convention on the Regulation of Aerial Navigation, Paris, 1919, 11 LNTS 173; 1922 UKTS 2, Cmd. 1609; 1 Hudson 359; 13 Martens (3d) 61; [1923] 17 AJIL Supp. 195.

25 See the facts behind *Aerial Incident of July 27, 1955 (Preliminary Objections) Israel v. Bulgaria*, 1959 ICJ Rep 127, and *Aerial Incident (Pakistan v. India)* Application, 10 August 1999, and Judgement, 2000 ICJ Rep. 12 (case dismissed for lack of jurisdiction). See also: 'Documents concerning the Korean Air Lines Incident' (1983) 22 ILM 1109; O.J. Lissitsyn, 1) 'The Treatment of Aerial Intruders in Recent Practice and International Law' [1953] 47 AJIL 559–589; 2) 'Some Legal Aspects of the U-2 and RB-47 Incidents' [1962] 58 AJIL 135–142; F. Hassan, 'A Legal Analysis of the Shooting Down of Korean Airlines Flight 007 by the Soviet Union' (1984) 49 *J. Air L. & Comm.* 555–590; M. Kido, 'The Korean Airlines Incident on September 1 1983 and Some Measures Following It' (1997) 62 *J. Air L. & Comm.* 1049–1070. Cf. Chapter 6, n. 28.

also provided as between its parties for the freedom of innocent passage of civil aircraft subject to compliance with various conditions. These included controls on what we would now call remote sensing. During the First World War aerial reconnaissance had been highly important and included the photographing of enemy trench emplacements and mustering areas. It was therefore not surprising that Art. 27 of the 1919 Convention permitted parties to regulate or forbid not only the use, but even the carriage, of photographic apparatus over their territory. More broadly, Art. 3 permitted states for military or public safety reasons to establish zones through which aircraft were not to fly, and Art. 15 required over-flying foreign aircraft to follow prescribed routes. Under Art. 32 foreign military aircraft required specific permission for entry to or transit of a state. Remote sensing by camera from the air could therefore be considerably constrained.

Similar provision is made in the now ruling Convention on Civil Aviation, Chicago, 1944.[26] Its Art. 1 repeats the 1919 general recognition of the complete and exclusive sovereignty of subjacent states over the air space above their territory. Article 3.c requires over-flight by foreign state aircraft to be authorised.[27] Article 9 allows states to create prohibited areas, and by Art. 36, a state may regulate or prohibit the use of photographic apparatus in aircraft over its territory.[28]

An addition to the 1919 provisions is that by Chicago Art. 8, no pilotless aircraft may be flown over the territory of a state without special authorisation. Aerial surveillance by foreign aircraft therefore depends on the consent of the over-flown state. Consent may be for a particular flight or flights or be more open-ended.[29] Thus the Open Skies Treaty of 1992 provides for its parties to overfly the territories of other parties to carry out military inspections.[30]

26 Convention on International Civil Aviation, Chicago, 7 December 1944 (1944) 15 UNTS 295; 9 Hudson 168; 61 Stat. 1180, TIAS 1591; 3 Bevans 944; (1953) UKTS 8, Cmd. 8742; [1945] 39 AJIL Supp. 111; current version ICAO Doc. 7300/9: www.icao.int/publications/Documents/7300_cons.pdf.

27 'State aircraft' are defined as aircraft used in military, customs and police services: Chicago Convention, Art. 3.b.

28 The French text speaks of photographic apparatus 'á bord' an aircraft, which is clearer for our purpose than the 'in' of the English, Spanish and (?) Russian texts.

29 On the U-2 and the RB-47 incidents see Lissitzyn *supra* n. 25; Cheng, 103–119.

30 Treaty on Open Skies, Helsinki, 24 March 1992, in force 1 January 2002; 2002 UKTS 27, Cm. 5539; US TS 102–37: www.oscc.org/files/f/documents/1/5/14127.pdf: https://2009-2017.state.gov/t/avc/trty/102337.htm.

Implementation of the treaty is supervised by an Open Skies Consultative Commission composed of representatives of all member states: www.osce.org/oscc. At the option of the state to be over-flown one of its national planes may have to be used for such inspection. As to what may be seen, cf. on Google Earth (www.google.earth.com) the aircraft graveyard southeast of Tucson, AZ, at roughly 30°N by 110°W. Of course in some countries there may be constitutional obstacles to be overcome:

The US withdrew from the Treaty in November 2020 (www.armscontrol.org/act/2020-12/news/us-completes-open-skies-treaty-withdrawal: www.defense.gov/News/Releases/Release/Article/2195239/dod-statement-on-open-skies-treaty-withdrawal/) and so did Russia in December 2021 (www.armscontrol.org/act/2021-07/news/russia-officially-leaves-open-skies-treaty). The thirty-two states party to the Open Skies Treaty as at mid-2023 were: Belarus, Belgium, Bosnia, Bulgaria, Canada, Croatia, Czech Republic, Denmark, Estonia, Finland, France, Georgia, Germany, Greece, Hungary, Iceland, Italy, Latvia, Lithuania, Luxembourg, Netherlands, Norway, Poland, Portugal, Romania, Slovak Republic, Slovenia, Spain, Sweden, Turkey, Ukraine and the UK. Kyrgyzstan has signed but not yet ratified. J. Boulden, 'Open Skies: the 1955 Proposal and its Current Revival' (1990) 13 *Dalhousie L.J.* 611–649; D.A. Koplow, 1) 'Arms Control Inspection: Constitutional Restrictions on Treaty Verification in the United States' (1988) 63 *N.Y.U.L. Rev.* 229–359, and 2) 'Back to the Future and Up to the Sky: Legal Implications of Open Skies Inspection for

Such an agreement had been first proposed to Soviet Premier Khrushchev by President Eisenhower in July 1955.[31] These things take time.

The laws of various countries have dealt with aerial remote sensing, or on occasion ignore it. Of course the balance between privacy and the requirement for information is a matter of concern.[32] In the UK, some local authorities use cameras mounted on drones or model aircraft to identify unlicensed building and other activity. The legal basis for this is unknown.[33]

However, surveillance by state agencies for environmental purposes is possible. Overflight is permitted by the UK Civil Aviation Acts, and in *Bernstein v. Skyviews* [1977] All ER 902, interdict against the over-flight of a property for the purpose of taking photographs later to be offered for sale to the owner or others was refused.[34] In the US such questions involve consideration of the Constitution. Over-flight by aircraft above safety height is permitted,[35] as is over-flight for the purpose of surveillance by official agencies.[36]

Remote Sensing from Space

Sensing from space has many advantages over aircraft-based sensing. Once a satellite is in an appropriate orbit it is easily controlled and can regularly re-visit sites of interest. Subject to the arguments indicated *infra*, it requires no permission for over-flight of territory and raises no questions of sovereignty. Depending on its equipment it can image a large area or provide significant detail for a smaller target. Nowadays, in that the satellite imagery is in digital form, it readily allows processing by computer to provide a vast quantity of data.

Given the unwillingness to permit unregulated aerial surveillance by foreign aircraft, the emergence of remote sensing by satellite was guaranteed to produce argument. However, that argument came late. The basic principles of space law had been formulated before the matter was directly addressed. As discussed in Chapter 3, the Outer Space Treaty

Arms Control' (1991) 79 *Cal. L. Rev.* 421–496. But see H. Spitzer, 'Open Skies in Turbulence. A Well Functioning Treaty is Endangered by Outside Developments' (2011) 22 *Sec. & H. Rts.* 373–382.

31 D.D. Eisenhower, 'Statement on Disarmament Presented at the Geneva Conference, July 21, 1955', Public Papers of the Presidents of the United States, Eisenhower 1955, doc. 165, 713–716, at 715–716 (U Michigan Digital Library: http://quod.lib.umich.edu/p/ppotpus/). See also R. Cargill Hall, 'The Origins of US Space Policy: Eisenhower, Open Skies and Freedom of Space', in J.M. Logsdon et al., eds., *Exploring the Unknown: Selected Documents in the History of the US Civil Space Program* (NASA SP-4407, 1995) 213–29; J. Boulden, 'Open Skies: the 1955 Proposal and its Current Revival' (1990) 13 *Dalhousie L.J.* 611–649; D.R. Terrill, Jr, *The Air Force Role in Developing International Outer Space Law* (Maxwell AFB, AL: Air UP, 1999; UP of the Pacific, 2004) (http://aupress.maxwell.af.mil/Books/Terrill/terrill.pdf) at 6–9.

32 A.M. Froomkin, 'The Death of Privacy' (2000) 52 *Stan. L. Rev.* 1461–1543; Davies, *supra* n. 6 at 1141–1144; famously, S.D. Warren and L.D. Brandeis, 'The Right to Privacy' (1890) 4 *Harv. L. Rev.* 193–220, and much subsequent discussion.

33 Entry into the air space of a UK curtilage without authority or permission is unlawful: Cf. F. Lyall, 'The Maxim "Cuius Est Solum" in Scots Law' 1978 *Jur. Rev.* 147–169. However, the amateur use of drones has become popular.

34 *Bernstein* was a single-judge case, an unsatisfactory basis for an important legal principle. Perhaps a different result may be obtained were the later (UK) Human Rights Act, 1998, to be invoked. A number of UK private companies offer aerial photographs of houses and estates.

35 *US v. Causby* (1946) 328 US 256.

36 *California v. Ciraolo* (1986) 476 US 207; 106 S. Ct. 1809; 90 L. Ed. 2d 210; *Dow Chemical v. US*, 476 US 227; 106 S. Ct. 1819; 90 L. Ed. 2d 226. The use of such evidence is subject to the restrictions of the Fourth Amendment to the US Constitution as to unreasonable search and seizure.

1967 provides that outer space and celestial bodies are free for use by all states without discrimination of any kind, on a basis of equality (OST Art. I para. 2) and that there is freedom of scientific investigation in space (OST Art. I para. 3).[37] These principles, which have passed into customary international law, were clear sufficiently early to ensure that there was no obstacle to the inception of remote sensing programmes by the states which had the ability to engage in them, and in due course the activities became subject to the requirements of the treaties on Rescue and Return, Liability and Registration insofar as these were relevant.[38] The rules of the International Telecommunication Union as to the use of radio frequencies were also developed and are complied with.[39] However, the actual lawfulness of what might be done by remote sensing was not raised until long after its practice was established. Space law permitted the passage of a satellite over any territory without permission, no state having formally protested over-flight by a satellite. Passage is one thing. What the satellite might be doing could be another.

As with direct broadcasting,[40] the early arguments over remote sensing fall to be seen as part of the effort of the developing countries in the 1960s and 1970s to gain control over their own affairs and their own resources. Many had come into being and then found that by reason of contracts and concessions entered into by their former colonial masters they did not have the freedom to control and dispose of their natural resources that they wished. Sometimes the matter was resolved by negotiation: on other occasions recourse was had to nationalisation/expropriation. The United Nations was perceived as a major forum in which to affirm the lawfulness of such efforts.[41] Amid all this an obvious question was whether information about natural resources formed part of those resources. Through information derived from satellite remote sensing systems a speculator might gain at the expense of a crop-grower in a developing country.[42] Another element was of general concern: military security. Not all states thought that allowing others to 'see' their military installations might contribute to peace rather than affording an enemy free access to useful information.

Article I para. 1 of the 1967 OST provides that the use of outer space should (must?) be for the benefit of all states, without any kind of discrimination, based on equality of all

---

37 Treaty on Principles Governing the Activities of States in the Exploration and Use of Outer Space Including the Moon and Other Celestial Bodies, London, Moscow and Washington, 27 January 1967 (1968) 610 UNTS 205; (1968) UKTS 10, Cmnd. 3519; 18 UST 2410, TIAS 6347; (1967) 6 ILM 386; [1967] 61 AJIL 644.

38 As to which see Chapter 4.

39 See Chapter 8 and Larsen 'The OSO Landslide', *infra* n. 94, at 351.

40 See Chapter 10 Direct Satellite Broadcasting.

41 'Permanent Sovereignty over Natural Resources', UNGA Res. 1803 (XVII) 1962; [1963] 57 AJIL 710; Charter of Economic Rights and Duties of States, UNGA Res. 3281 (XXIX) 1974; (1975) 14 ILM 251. Cf. the New International Economic Order resolutions: the 'Declaration on the Establishment of a New International Economic Order' (A/9556) UNGA Res. 3201 (S-VI), 1974, and the related 'Programme of Action' UNGA Res. 3202 (S-VI), 1974. See also Christol, 'Mexican Contributions' *infra* n. 45 at 5–6.

42 It is possible from satellite imagery to identify disease starting in, say, a coffee crop before that is noticeable on the ground. A speculator with that knowledge might enter into a fixed price contract with a coffee producer in a commercial 'futures' market, and then profit considerably when the crop fails, and market prices inevitably rise. He has the right to buy from his supplier at the fixed price, and then to sell on the product at whatever the market price might then be. In the worst case the supplier would have to buy at the higher price in order to fulfil the fixed price contract. R. Harris, CoCoSL III, 187 para 277, notes complaints that sensing states may know more about a sensed state than that state does.

states, and must be in accordance with international law. How might that be reflected in the regulation of remote sensing?

The first point to note is that no international treaty directly governs remote sensing in general. In 1968, one year after the OST, UNISPACE I indicated that remote sensing was a topic requiring consideration, and the matter was put in the agenda of UN COPUOS. In 1978 the USSR sponsored a treaty that would have given much of what the developing countries wanted,[43] but it attracted only eight parties, and the law generally has gone on a different track.

'Principles Relating to the Remote Sensing of the Earth from Outer Space' were drafted in COPUOS. Discussions began in 1968, but the process took time. Formal proposals were made in 1974 and, after prodding by the General Assembly, the Principles were finally adopted as a General Assembly Resolution in 1986.[44]

From the very beginning of the discussions in COPUOS its members disagreed.[45] At one extreme some states, particularly developing countries, were of the view that their property ownership in their natural resources included information as to those resources, and that other states should not sense their resources without permission. They were also concerned about military security. The argument was founded on the basic concept of state sovereignty. Thus they argued *inter alia* that remote sensing should not occur without the prior consent of the sensed state. Modifications of the argument were that a sensed state should have priority rights to satellite-acquired data of its territory and/or that data as to one state should not be transferred or made available to others without its consent. At the other extreme the argument ran that under OST Arts I and II, outer space was free for all users and those uses included remote sensing. Prior consent, with the implicit correlative right to forbid sensing, was not consistent with that freedom. Further, priority rights for sensed states or rights to embargo the dissemination of data would also restrict the free use of outer space guaranteed by the OST. Another strand of debate centred on technology. Sensed states wanted to acquire relevant technologies together with the establishment of their own ground stations and processing facilities. Sensing states wished to

---

43 Convention on the Transfer and Use of Data of the Remote Sensing of the Earth from Outer Space, Moscow, 19 May 1978; UN Doc. A/33/162; (2005) XXX AASL Part II, 141–145; *Space Law: Selected Basic Documents*, 2nd ed., US Senate, Committee on Commerce, Science and Transportation, 95th Cong. 2d Sess., 480–496: www.jaxa.jp/library/space_law/chapter_2/2-2-2-19_e.html; http://ops-alaska.com/IOSL/ V1P4/1978_RemoteSensingConvention_EN.pdf. Cf. G. Zhukov and Y. Kolosov (trans. B. Belitzky), *International Space Law* (New York: Praeger, 1984) 141–151; A.S. Piradov, *International Space Law* (Moscow: Progress, 1976) 214–221.

44 'Principles Relating to the Remote Sensing of the Earth from Outer Space', 3 December 1986; UNGA Res. 41/65. cf. (1986) 25 ILM 1334–6 with note at 1331–1333. The Principles are extensively analysed in CoCoSL III, 81–88. See also Cheng, 572–597; Christol, 720–764, and his 'Remote Sensing and International Space Law' (1988) 16 *J. Sp. L.* 21–44, rep. C.Q. Christol, *Space Law: Past, Present and Future* (Deventer: Kluwer, 1991) 73–95; C.M. Haywood, 'Remote Sensing: Terrestrial Laws for Celestial Activities' (1990) 8 *Bost. Univ. Int. L.J.* 157–185.

45 Cheng 572–97; Christol 720–810; H. DeSaussure, 'Remote Sensing Satellite Regulation by National and International Law' (1989) 15 *Rutgers Computer & Tech. L.J.* 351–381; C.M. Dalfen, 'The International Legislative Process: Direct Broadcasting and Remote Earth Sensing by Satellite Compared' (1972) 10 Can. YBIL 186–211; S. Mossinghoff and L.D. Fuqua, 'United Nations Principles on Remote Sensing': Report on Developments, 1970–1980' (1980) 8 *J. Sp. L.* 103–153; D.A. Greenburg, 'Third Party Access to Data Obtained via Remote Sensing: International Legal Theory versus Economic Reality' (1983) 15 *Case W. Int. L. Rev.* 361–395; C.Q. Christol, 'Mexican Contributions to the Development of Principles Relating to Remote Sensing of the Earth, its Natural Resources and its Environment' (1984) 14 *Cal. W. Int. L.J.* 1–21.

preserve their industries and intellectual property in the technology. Tenuous consensus in COPUOS was finally reached in 1985.[46] The original objective had been a treaty on remote sensing,[47] however the COPUOS delegates scaled back and settled for a UN General Assembly Resolution declaring international policy on remote sensing.[48]

The 'Principles Relating to the Remote Sensing of the Earth from Outer Space' are fifteen in number. Principle I begins by restricting their application. For the purpose of the Principles remote sensing is the sensing of the Earth from space, making use of the properties of electromagnetic radiation emitted, refracted or diffracted by the sensed objects 'for the purpose of improving natural resources management, land use, and the protection of the environment' (Pr. I (a)). Aerial remote sensing is therefore excluded, as are military and other applications of the technology. Natural resources management, land use and the protection of the environment cover much but are not exhaustive of the potentialities of the techniques. Not all commentators on the Principles, or those who appeal to them as constitutive of rights and duties regarding remote sensing data, appreciate this. In short the Principles do not cover all remote sensing.

Within these constraints the 'remote sensing activities' dealt with by the Principles comprise 'the operation of remote sensing satellite systems, primary data collection and storage stations, and activities in processing, interpreting and disseminating the processed data' (Pr. I (e)) – a very wide definition.

Principle I divides remote sensing data into three categories, the duties as to which may diverge. Raw, unenhanced 'primary data' are data acquired by the remote sensing satellite and transmitted or delivered to the ground by telemetry as electromagnetic signals, photographic film, magnetic tape or any other means (Pr. I (b)). 'Processed data' results 'from the processing of the primary data, needed to make such data usable' (Pr. I (c)). 'Analyzed data' is information resulting from 'the interpretation of processed data, inputs of data and knowledge from other sources' (Pr. I (d)). All three categories of remote sensing data, including their dissemination, constitute the 'remote sensing activities' for which the Principles have relevance.

Principle II begins by in effect quoting OST Art. I, requiring remote sensing to be carried out for the benefit and in the interest of all countries irrespective of their degree of economic, social or scientific or technological development. However, it also makes the specific point that the needs of the developing countries should be given particular consideration. Principle III restates OST Art. III, that remote sensing shall be conducted in accordance with the UN Charter and other international instruments. Principle IV bundles together a number of ideas, not all of which are easily integrated into mutual coherence. The legitimate rights of all states under OST Art. I are recognised, including the freedom of exploration and use of outer space on a basis of equality subject to the 'benefit'

46 L.J. Smith and Reynders, 'Historical Background and Context', CoCoSL III, 86–87. C.Q. Christol, 'Remote Sensing and International Space Law' (1988) 16 *J. Sp. L.* 21–44, rep. in his *Space Law: Past, Present and Future* (Deventer: Kluwer, 1991) 73–95; S.M. Jackson, 'Cultural Lag and the International Law of Remote Sensing' (1998) 23 *Brook. J. Int. Law* 853–885 [Lyall/Larsen 69–502]; G. Catalano Sgrosso, 'International Legal Framework for Remote Sensing' Workshop on Legal Remote Sensing Issues, Project 2001, University of Cologne Institute of Air and Space Law (Cologne, 1999) 5–23; R. Jakhu, 'International Law Governing the Acquisition and Dissemination of Satellite Imagery' (2003) 29 *J. Sp. L.* 65–91.

47 Cf. H. DeSaussure, 'Remote Sensing by Satellite: What Future for an International Regime' [1977] 71 AJIL 707–724.

48 As to the legal significance and weight of a General Assembly Resolution, see Chapter 2.

concept already quoted in Pr. II. However Pr. IV goes on to provide that remote sensing activities 'shall be conducted on the basis of respect for the principle of full and permanent sovereignty of all States and peoples over their own wealth and natural resources, with due regard to the rights and interests, in accordance with international law, of other States and entities under their jurisdiction' – statements acceptable to both sides of the COPUOS debate, but which may cancel each other out. Then, as if to avoid that potential elision and to underline the point that was a major concern of the developing countries, Pr. IV ends: '[s]uch activities shall not be conducted in a manner detrimental to the legitimate rights and interests of the sensed State'. The true interpretation of Principle IV is therefore unclear: it speaks from both sides of its mouth.

Principles V and following move to other concerns including cooperation and technology transfer.[49] States engaged in remote sensing 'shall make available to other States opportunities for participation therein. Such participation shall be based in each case on equitable and mutually acceptable terms' (Pr. V). To maximise the availability of the benefits of remote sensing states are encouraged to establish centres for data collection, storage stations and processing and interpretation facilities. Such could be regional facilities 'wherever feasible' (Pr. VI). On 'mutually agreed terms' sensing states are to make technical assistance available to other interested states (Pr. VII).

Principles VIII and IX give a role to the UN, Pr. VIII assigning it the international role of coordinating and promoting remote sensing, a task now undertaken by UNOOSA. Principle IX requires states to keep the UN Secretary General informed about their remote sensing programmes. Sensing states are also 'to the greatest extent feasible and practicable' to keep other states informed about relevant sensed data, upon the request of the sensed state and particularly to any developing country that is affected by a sensing programme. However, Pr. IX does not define exactly what information a sensing state shall provide to a sensed state.

Principle X recognises the importance of remote sensing for the protection of the natural environment. Sensing states discovering data capable of averting harm to the environment are therefore required promptly to make it known to endangered states. Principle X does not distinguish between the different categories of data. Unenhanced as well as enhanced data should therefore be supplied to endangered states although knowing when 'endangerment' is present is obviously impossible to establish at least in advance of an occurrence. Principle XI is more specific requiring sensing states to transmit processed and analysed data concerning natural disasters, actual and potential, to states that may be affected by them. In that connection practice has shown that remote sensing is increasingly important, for example, to allow authorities to monitor potential flooding and mitigate its effects.[50]

Principle XII is a fundamental. It reflects an expectation that remote sensing data shall be openly available. By implication it expresses the right of states to sense other states by providing for the access to information about it in the possession of a sensing state. The sought-for requirement of prior consent by the sensed state is absent. Neither is the sensed

---

49 But on the problems of such provisions cf. D. Yarn, 'The Transfer of Technology and UNCLOS III' (1984) 14 *Ga. J. Int. & Comp. L.* 121–154.

50 On the duty in Prs. X and XI to inform others of actual and potential disasters see Larsen, *infra* n. 94. Cf. *infra*, Disasters, and nn. 113 and 114.

information to be provided free of cost. However, 'the sensed state shall have access to [primary and processed data] on a non-discriminatory basis and on reasonable cost terms'. Likewise, the sensed state is to have access to analysed data concerning its territory in the possession of a sensing state on the same basis and terms, the needs and interests of the developing countries being taken particularly into account. While this language appears to guarantee all states access to data acquired by the remote sensing of their territory, as we will see, in practice sensing states withhold remote sensing data on national security and other grounds. Of course the data may simply not be available because some other organisation has bought it up.[51] And what does 'reasonable cost terms' mean? This is a question to which we will return. Another question implicit in Pr. XII is whether an endangered state can be refused remote sensing data regarding its own territory simply because it cannot pay for its cost.[52] There is also the problem of mutually hostile adjacent states, one of which initiates a programme which, coincidentally, remotely senses the border or a disputed region. Has the other state a right to access the imagery?[53]

Under Principle XIII sensed states have the right at their request to be consulted by a sensing state in order to aid cooperation 'especially with regard to the needs of developing countries'. Certainly one result might be the modification of a sensing programme to include the capture of data of interest to the sensed state and to which it would have access under Pr. XII. As practice has developed, however, it seems little consultation goes on. Because of the magnitude, variety and scope of remote sensing the needs of most states are already coped with. *Per contra* the exclusion of data is difficult to arrange and is better tackled at the post-sensing stage when analysis and interpretation is taking place. As we will see, 'shutter control' and national and military security are difficult matters.

Principle XIV is redundant as a matter of law, but politically usefully repeats the legal position that sensing states have international responsibility for the compliance of their remote sensing programmes with international law. Additionally compliance with the Principles is also insisted on. That said, Pr. XIV is to be 'without prejudice to the applicability of the norms of international law of State responsibility for remote sensing activities'.

Finally, Principle XV requires states to resolve their disputes about the application of the Principles through the established procedures for the peaceful settlement of disputes.[54]

So?

First it has to be said that evaluations of the Principles diverge. Some hold that the Principles have 'no significant limiting effect on remote sensing activities'.[55] Others consider that the Principles 'have already served to guide important remote sensing nations in many of their practices' and that the Principles are legally binding on nations because they have been negotiated, adopted, referenced and practised for twenty-five years.[56] It still seems too premature to suggest that *in toto* the UN Remote Sensing Principles constitute

---

51 J.I. Gabrynowicz, Discussion paper, 'Expanding Global Remote Sensing Services', UNISPACE III, Proceedings of the Workshop, July 1999, at 97. Cf. R. Harris and R. Browning, *Global Monitoring: The Challenges of Access to Data* (London: Cavendish, 2005).

52 DeSaussure, *supra* n. 45, at 362.

53 India/Pakistan and Kashmir, and Israel and Syria are among the examples that come to mind.

54 To 2023 no dispute has been dealt with under Pr. XIV: CoCoSL 186, para 274.

55 Jackson, *supra* n. 46, at 872. H. Feder, 'The Sky's the Limit. Evaluating the International Law of Remote Sensing' (1991) 23 *Int. L. & Pol.* 599–669.

56 Gabrynowicz, *supra* n. 51, at 103.

customary international law.[57] They may be 'soft law',[58] and it is true that states which have not adopted national legislation have only the UN Principles and general international space law as their guide.[59] A number of states have indeed adopted national laws and regulations on satellite remote sensing. While such national laws and regulations are broadly consonant with the UN Principles, many have deviated significantly from the Principles particularly to protect national security and political interests. One explanation is that the UN Principles were adopted when the available pixel resolution was coarse compared with that now possible. Now, the data that can be acquired from satellite sensing has been considerably increased in recent decades as processing has become more sophisticated and computer applications developed. Again, security is a much more sensitive consideration if a potential enemy or a terrorist has access to resolutions of 1 metre or even less compared with the 30+ metre resolution of the 1980s.[60]

The UN Principles relating to remote sensing are important. Although they apply to remote sensing for only a limited range of purposes – improving natural resources management, land use and the protection of the environment – the fact is that a satellite simply scans and reports what is there. It cannot be instructed not to see military installations or other sensitive areas. Obscuring such can only be done at a later different stage of it being processed.[61] The Principles are therefore more properly to be appreciated as setting out general policy with which states ought to comply and, in appropriate instances, incorporate into national regulation.

Circumstances have changed since 1986. Back then, apparently, when the non-COPUOS developing countries first had sight of the Principles that were being proposed they demanded that the matter be reconsidered and revised because they considered their interests were not sufficiently well-protected in them. That demand was faced down. The US and others, which had reluctantly acceded to the wording as drafted, stated that that was as far as they were willing to go. The matter would not be re-opened, and if that which had been drafted was unacceptable to the developing countries, the draft Principles would fall and the current sensing states would continue to sense, using their legal right under the OST. Given their voting majority the developing countries might have forced an alternative set of Principles by the UNGA, but the experience of the Direct Broadcasting Principles of 1982 had shown that course to be self-defeating.[62] Accordingly the COPUOS

---

57 It has been suggested that 'most of' the Principles 'reflect customary law': *International Law Association, Space Law Committee*, Berlin 2004, 'Report on the Legal Aspects of the Privatisation and Commercialisation of Space Activities: Remote Sensing and National Space Legislation' at 4, and the subsequent *Report*, Toronto 2006 at 699 where it was noted that 'a majority' considered the UN Principles as 'declarative of customary international law' but others had some doubts as to certain of the Principles; in 'Some Legal Aspects of Remote Sensing', in A.P. Cracknell, ed., *Remote Sensing in Meteorology, Oceanography and Hydrology* (Chichester: Ellis Horwood; New York: John Wiley, 1981) at 205 FL was then of the view that there was no customary law as to remote sensing, but now considers that practice is constituting custom at least in some areas.

58 J. I. Gabrynowicz, 'The UN Principles Relating to Remote Sensing of the Earth from Outer Space and Soft Law', in Marboe 183–93.

59 As the ILA, *supra* n. 57, notes, the UN Principles do clarify relevant ideas found in the OST.

60 For many areas two-thirds of a metre pixel resolution is available. See Google Earth. Apparently commercial imagery is being used in the Ukraine conflict.

61 Google Earth imagery does have fuzzy areas.

62 'Principles Governing the Use by States of Artificial Earth Satellites for International Direct Television Broadcasting', UNGA Res. 37/92, 10 December 1982; (1983) 22 ILM 451; [1983] 77 AJIL 733–736. Cf. Chapter 10 Direct Satellite Broadcasting.

draft was presented to the General Assembly and duly adopted without vote on 3 December 1986 as UNGA Res. 41/65. Some states and commentators consider that the Remote Sensing Principles are still open for renegotiation, but we consider this unlikely.[63] In their present form they seem to be working adequately.

The Sensing Principles seem to be working, but much of that is because circumstances have changed. Going through the Principles it is striking how many of the obligations indicated for the sensing state to provide data and opportunities to a sensed state are subject to qualification. What is 'practicable' or 'feasible' and its extent is a subjective decision for the sensing state to make. Similarly 'reasonable cost terms' and 'mutual agreement' are slippery notions. In the 1980s this terminology provided loopholes and escape hatches for the sensing states. However, as said, circumstances have changed. Developing countries have come together to establish their own remote sensing programmes.[64] Yet the most effective catalyst for change has been the privatisation of remote sensing. Now sensed states can use the levers of market competition to obtain the concessions they require, or even to commission and contract for their own remote sensing surveys.[65] As part of this they may insist on technical training in data handling, on the siting of ground stations within a commissioning state, on technology transfer and on training being provided by the remote sensing corporation.[66]

The same may apply to the question of costs for the provision of remote sensing data. Competition will drive down prices. The general tendency is toward the reduction or even total elimination of charges for certain remote sensing data down to a particular level of resolution. Originally the USA provided Landsat data free on application, although now there is a low charge. Google Earth images are free to users. Australia also provides much sensed data free on the Internet. The policy of Japan is to charge very little. Thailand provides free data for educational purposes and for disaster monitoring.[67] ESA policy is the similar.[68] Brazil is a major provider of free remote sensing imagery for environmental purposes.[69] In most cases, however, more specialised data is to be paid for and, of course, the providers of commercial remote sensing data charge for their services. A question may therefore arise as to price differential as between different users. All that Principle XII

---

63 Cf. V.S. Mani, 'The Emerging Legal Regime of Remote Sensing: A General Survey', in V.S. Mani, S. Bhatt and V.B. Reddy, eds., *Recent Trends in International Space Policy* (New Delhi: Lancers Books, 1997) 235–254.

64 Thus Vietnam and Brazil are cooperating in a remote-sensing programme, as are various African states.

65 Cf. Art. 56.e of the Treaty Establishing the African Economic Community, 1991 (1991) 30 ILM 1241, text at 1245–82; Art. 31.2.h of the Revised Treaty of the Economic Community of West African States, 1993 (1996) 35 ILM 660, text at 663–697.

66 Of course some of this may be subject to control or direction by the national state of a commercial contractor.

67 See NOAA Survey, *supra* n. 38, at 17–18.

68 ESA divides its users into two categories, Category 1 being (roughly) scientific and technical users, and Category 2 operational and commercial. Cf. 'ESA Data Policy for ERS, Envisat and Earth Explorer missions' 2012: https://earth.esa.int/eogateway/documents/20142/1564626/ESA-Data-Policy-ESA-PB-EO-2010-54.pdf#:~:text=The%20ESA%20Data%20Policy%20is%20applicable%20to%20the,according%20to%20the%20UN%20terminology%20%28UN%20resolution%20A%2FRES%2F41%2F65%29. Data policy is set by the ESA Earth Observation Programme Board – see http://eopi.esa.int/esa/esa?filename=esaDataPolicy&cmd=staticfile. Cf. also the draft 'Principles of the Provision of ERS Data to Users', Workshop on Legal Remote Sensing Issues, Project 2001 (Cologne IASL 1999) 169–168. On data policy for the Copernicus project, *infra* n. 82, see *infra* nn. 85 and 86. M. Ferrazzani, 'ESA Rules and Practices' Workshop (*supra*) 43–52.

69 J. Monserrat, Filho, 'Fifty Years of Earth Observation from Space and Space Law' (2008) 51 *Proc. IISL* 401–409.

indicates is that access by a sensed state to primary, processed, and analysed remote sensing data shall be 'on a non-discriminatory basis and on reasonable cost terms'. Whether in this phrase 'and' is conjunctive or disjunctive is not immediately apparent. However, Principle XII ends that access is to take 'particularly into account the needs and interests of the developing countries'. In practice a differentiation is made between different users: discrimination in price and in access does occur.[70] As to the matter of price 'reasonable cost terms' does not imply that price must be uniform for all purchasers: it means a 'market price', which does allow for variation. Thus, when exigible ESA prices are lower for ESA members and their nationals than for non-ESA entities.[71] The justification is that ESA members have already contributed to the cost of acquiring the remote sensing data through their participation in the relevant ESA programmes. EUMETSAT (*infra*) is even more discriminating, pricing its product dependent on such factors as membership of the organisation, ability to pay, the purpose for which the data is requested (commercial or scientific) and intended distribution of the eventual product, but is also willing to waive charges for purposes such as disaster relief.

One area of controversy is the denial of access to remote sensing data that a sensing state may impose on grounds of its national security or at the request of an ally. Different countries act differently, and given the normalities of international relations, what they may do is in practice not susceptible to effective international objection.[72] Total denial of access can occur but given the commercialisation of remote sensing and the Internet, that is not as effective as it used to be.[73] Another strategy is the localised degrading of satellite imagery. States do not view with equanimity the availability of imagery of sites in their territories that might be subject to attack. Thus following negotiation, Google Earth has degraded images of sensitive sites in India and elsewhere.[74] US systems are forbidden to provide detail on the Israel/Syria border,[75] and it does seem silly for publicly available imagery to provide clear detail of sites of interest to terrorists or other unwelcome visitors.[76] By analogy we return to these matters when dealing with the US law.[77]

---

70 Gabrynowicz, *supra* n. 51, at 109–110.

71 See ESA policies *supra* n. 68.

72 J.I. Gabrynowicz, 'Land Remote Sensing Laws and Policies of the National Government, a Global Survey for the National Oceanic and Atmospheric Administration (NOAA) by the Univ. of Mississippi National Center for Remote Sensing, Air, and Space Law' (2007), at 11–12 indicated that as of January 2007 the USA, Canada, India, France, Italy and Israel had adopted formal regulation regarding denial of data. The Survey is in the 'online resources' at www.spacelaw.olemiss.edu. See also *International Law Association: Report of the Space Law Committee*, Toronto 2006, 693–729.

73 The US and EUMETSAT have agreed that when in time of emergency the US restricts access to weather data, a list of public duty users in the USA and EUMETSAT member states will continue to have real-time access to data from US instruments. EUMETSAT may be asked by NOAA to deny others access to direct read-out NOAA data or other global or regional products from US instruments on the MetOp satellites (polar orbiters). Authorised users may not further distribute data to unauthorised third-parties. Cf. the EUMETSAT Data Denial Guide: www.eumetsat.int/media/44847. For EUMETSAT see *infra* at n.103.

74 See BBC Report: http://news.bbc.co.uk/go/pr/fr/-/1/hi/technology/6331033.stm.

75 C. Hanley, 'Regulating Commercial Remote Sensing Satellites over Israel: A Black Hole in the Open Skies Doctrine' (2000) 52 *Admin. L. Rev.* 423–442; R. Prober, 'Shutter Control: Confronting Tomorrow's Technology with Yesterday's Regulations' (2003) 19 *J. L. & Pol.* 203–252.

76 The Google Street View service covering US locations has degraded material relating to the housing of senior politicians. The Pentagon has similarly banned views of military bases. Such 'exclusions' are understandable.

77 Text *infra* at n. 129.

The protection of remote sensing data remains another area of debate. Within Europe the rules of copyright are used to protect the interests of the relevant actors. It is normal for data to be supplied to users with a prohibition on resale or further dissemination. Technically the data is not 'sold' until it has been transformed or (more properly) transmuted into a form from which the original data is not recoverable – an intriguing application of the old Roman doctrine of *specificatio*, the making of a new thing (*nova species*) from (or including) the property of another.[78] Within the USA copyright is used as a protective device, as are patents, trademarks and the concept of 'trade secret'.[79]

The question remains open whether the 1986 Principles should be revised, or even replaced by an international treaty. Certainly the developing countries would like to see more specific obligations made binding upon sensing states and what they perceive as defects in the Principles repaired.[80] Whether such developments are practicable is obscure. The detail now available through remote sensing makes the attainment of a common mind difficult. Sensing states are more likely to wish to preserve their freedom of action. Domestic rules are more likely to produce development than is international action, but that also means that individual national commercial and security policies will be major determinant factors in the future of remote sensing law.[81]

International Efforts

Copernicus (Formerly GMES)[82]

Copernicus is a European system for monitoring the Earth and currently is the largest single earth observation programme. It began as a 1998 initiative of ESA and the Commission of the then European Communities as the programme GMES (Global Monitoring for Environment and Security) which used Envisat (2002–2012) as its space component.[83] What has become Copernicus was instituted in 2008 and became fully operational in 2014, the name of the programme being formally changed in December 2014.[84] The programme is intended to bring together earth monitoring data from all sources, making

---

78 The intellectual justification of 'specification' (to use the modern term) is controverted. See W.W. Buckland, *A Textbook of Roman Law*, 3rd ed. rev. P. Stein (Cambridge: Cambridge UP, 1976) 215–221; R.W. Lee *The Elements of Roman Law*, 4th ed. (London: Sweet & Maxwell, 1956) 134–135; B. Nicholas, *An Introduction to Roman Law* (Oxford: Oxford UP, 1962) 136–138. Cf. D. Carey Miller, *Corporeal Moveables in Scots Law* (Edinburgh: W. Green, 1991), 'Specification' at 64–70.

79 S. Pace et al., *Data Policy Issues and Barriers to Using Commercial Resources for Mission to Planet Earth* (Santa Monica: Rand, 1999): www.rand.org/pubs/documented_briefings/2007/DB247.pdf; P.A. Salin, 'Proprietary Aspects of Commercial Remote-Sensing Imagery' (1992) 13 *Nw. J. Int. L. & Bus.* 349–373.

80 See e.g. J. Monserrat, Filho, ILA Report (*supra* n. 57) at 8–10 and comments by other members of the ILA Space Law Committee.

81 Cf. M. Williams, 'Comments and Conclusions from the Committee Chair', ILA Report 2004 (*supra* n. 57) 14; *International Law Association: Report of the Space Law Committee*, Toronto 2006, 693–729 at 699 – amendment of the Principles or their incorporation in treaty form is held unlikely in the absence of new or unexpected factors.

82 Reference point, *supra* n. 68.

83 Envisat became non-operational in 2012, but remains in Sun-synchronous polar orbit at 490 miles/790 km.

84 Documentation of the various changes through the EU structure may be found at www.copernicus.eu/library, with policy noted at www.copernicus.eu/en/documentation/copernicus-policy/copernicus-policy. See also Larsen, 'The OSO Landslide', *infra* n. 94, at 344.

them available to government, other institutions and those who can use that data to their benefit.

Copernicus gathers its data through a space segment, the Sentinel series currently being launched, together with terrestrial-based sensors, ground stations and air and sea-borne sensors. The services provided are grouped into six thematic areas, land, marine, atmosphere, climate change, emergency management and security, which are capable of many applications.[85] Some services are free while others are paid for by users.[86] The programme is managed by the European Commission with the space segment being handled by ESA. There is also a supervisory Copernicus Committee and a User Forum. Copernicus is the European participant in the Global Earth Observation System of System (GEOSS).

The Global Earth Observation System of Systems (GEOSS)

The Global Earth Observation System of Systems (GEOSS) is the creation of the Group on Earth Observations (GEO).[87] A problem of current earth observation systems is that they acquire, disseminate and store data in different forms or architectures. GEOSS endeavours to agree common architectures and technical standards to ease access to data.[88] GEO works through regional caucuses, an annual Plenary Meeting at which all members and participating organisations are represented,[89] and a 16-member Executive Committee.[90] There is also a Director, a Secretariat and a Programme Board.[91]

Specialised Sensing: Meteorology and Disasters

OST Art. I requires space to be used for the benefit of all. The UN General Assembly underlined the point by its 1997 Res. 51/122.[92] Remote sensing clearly can provide benefit,

---

85 For Copernicus applications see www.copernicus.eu. For an outré example see the 2019 Report 'Copernicus services in support to Cultural Heritage': www.copernicus.eu/sites/default/files/2019-06/Copernicus_services_in_support_to_Cultural_heritage.pdf.

86 Subject to any security implications data from the Sentinel series of satellites will be free to users. See www.copernicus.eu/main/faqs.

87 The Group on Earth Observations: www.earthobservations.org/index.php. Membership is open to all UN members and organisations which have accepted its Strategic Plan. As of 2023 GEO had 114 members and 144 participating organisations. Larsen, *infra* n. 94, at 366–369; M. Borghi, 'Towards full and open access: challenges and opportunities for the legal interoperability of earth observation data' (2021) 45 *J. Sp. L.* 142–175.

88 See the Global Earth Observation System of systems (GEOSS) 10–Year Implementation Plan, February 2005: https://earthobservations.org/documents/10-Year%20Implementation%20Plan.pdf. GEOSS is now implementing its 'GEO Strategic Plan 2016–2025: Implementing GEOSS': www.earthobservations.org/documents/GEO_Strategic_Plan_2016_2025_Implementing_GEOSS.pdf, with Reference Document: www.earthobservations.org/documents/GEO_Strategic_Plan_2016_2025_Implementing_GEOSS_Reference_Document.pdf.

89 Cf. the GEO, 'Canberra Declaration' 2019: www.earthobservations.org/canberra_declaration.php.

90 See the GEO Rules of Procedure: www.earthobservations.org/documents/GEO_Rules_of_Procedure.pdf.

91 The Programme Board has between 16 and 32 members, at least 40% from members and at least 40% from participating organisations (Rule 5.3). Members of the Board serve three year terms but may be reappointed. We note that the both the Executive Committee (Rule 4.7) and the Board (Rule 5.6) decide 'by consensus' and recall our discussion of 'consensus' in Chapter 1, *c.* n. 102.

92 'Declaration on International Cooperation in the Exploration and Use of Outer Space for the Benefit and in the Interest of All States, Taking into Particular Account the Needs of Developing Countries': UNGA Res. 51/122, 4 February 1997. CoCoSL III, 299–362.

and among others both UN OOSA and ESA have conducted training programmes and spread knowledge of the technology. In two major related areas international institutions have been established to provide general benefit: meteorology and disaster management. Storms and tempests, earthquakes and other natural occurrences can be observed, and appropriate action taken with the aid of remote sensing. So can be environmental change and the threats caused by human activity, of which the Chernobyl incident of 1986 is a worrying example.[93] The UN Remote Sensing Principles cover such matters. Principle X deals with the protection of the natural environment and Pr. XI with the protection of mankind from natural disasters. In both instances states in possession of relevant data are to transmit relevant information to any affected state as quickly as possible.[94] Whether this amounts to a legal duty to warn of approaching disasters may be a question, and whether there might be liability for failure to inform or failure to detect such occurrences if imminent is unclear. Another question is whether such circumstances should constitute a special waiver for the provision of data 'on reasonable cost terms' (Pr. XII). Finally we would ask whether humanitarian assistance may be developing as a norm of customary law. The broad area of humanitarian relief is of course of major interest to the UN as a whole as well as to other international organisations. The ILC has had the protection of persons in the event of disasters on its agenda for some years.[95] Within the UN the Department of Humanitarian Affairs operates a website, Reliefweb, as 'the global hub for time-critical humanitarian information on Complex Emergencies and Natural Disasters'.[96] Certainly it is a good source of information. However, there are other international arrangements that make clearer use of space facilities in warning, mitigation and coping with such matters.

93 'Disaster' tends to be understood as a sudden occurrence. The slower degradation of the environment is also a set of disasters that remote sensing can observe and monitor. See Ito, *supra* n. 1, 99–148.

94 D. Zannoni, *Disaster Management and International Space Law* (Leiden: Brill, 2019). Cf. P.B. Larsen, 'The Oso Landslide: Disaster Management Law in the Space Age' (2016) 40 *Will. & Mary Env. L. & Pol. Rev.* 335–386; P.B. Larsen, 'Disaster Management Law in the Space Age' (2015) 58 *Proc. IISL* 865–876. Cf. the NASA Earth Observing System Data and Information System (EOSDIS): https://earthdata.nasa.gov/, and the Land Processes Distributed Active Archive Center (LP DAAC): https://lpdaac.usgs.gov/.

   A continuing defect of remote sensing is that much remotely sensed data has not been reviewed. In the early 1990s when writing of the law as to dams and raised reservoirs in Scotland for the *Stair Memorial Encyclopedia of the Laws of Scotland*, FL read somewhere that subsequent to the 1980s failure of two dams in Northern Italy with considerable loss of life, later scrutiny of remotely sensed imagery had shown evidence that the dams were failing.

95 Cf. Report of the International Law Commission, 66th Session, 2014, A/69/10, Chapter V, 'Protection of persons in the event of disasters', at 84–138; Report of the International Law Commission, 66th Session, 2014, A/71/10, Chapter IV, 'Protection of persons in the event of disasters', at 12–73. Cf. T. O'Donnell and C. Allan, 'Identifying Solidarity: The ILC Project on the Protection of Persons in Disasters and Human Rights' (2016) *Geo. Wash. Int. L. Rev.* 53–96.

   S. Sivakumaran, 'Arbitrary Withholding of Consent to Humanitarian Assistance in Situations of Disaster' (2015) 64 ICLQ 501–532; M. Eburn, 'International Law and Disaster Response' (2010) 36 *Monash Univ. L. Rev.* 162–189; D.P. Fidler, 'Disaster Relief and Governance after the Indian Ocean Tsunami: What Role for International Law?' (2005) 6 *Melb. J. Int. L.* 458–473; T.R. Sacchao, 'Natural Disasters and the Duty to Protect: From Chaos to Clarity' (2007) 32 *Brook. J. Int. L.*, 663–707; A. de Urioste, 'When Will Help Be on the Way? The Status of International Disaster Response Law' (2006) 15 *Tulane J. Int. & Comp. L.* 182–206; P. Macalister-Smith, *International Humanitarian Assistance: Disaster Relief Operations in International Law and Organisation* (Dordrecht: Nijhoff, 1986).

96 Reliefweb: www.reliefweb.int/. See also such series as 'Strengthening of the Coordination of Emergency Humanitarian Assistance of the United Nations', UNGA Res. 46/182, 1991; UNGA Res. 51/194, 1997; UNGA Res. 75/127, 2020; UNGA Res. 77/28, 2022.

Meteorology

Initially most meteorological satellites and weather services were operated by governments because of its importance. Indeed Sec. 602 of the US Land Remote Sensing Act of 1992 prohibits 'any efforts to lease, sell, or transfer to the private sector, or commercialise, any portion of the weather satellite systems operated by the Department of Commerce or any successor agency'.[97] Other countries have moved to a wholly or partially privatised weather satellite service. For example the German Meteorological Services, apart from its official functions, sells weather information commercially but remains under the administration of the German Ministry of Transport. The Ministry supervises the weather service staff, the organisation, budget, the development of tasks, represents Germany in principal international negotiations, and takes the final decision on issues of principle. However it is for the Service to employ staff and has its own separate budget together with limited authority to enter into private contracts.[98]

Meteorological satellites sense the Earth's atmosphere and are crucial in modern weather forecasting. Advance warning of hurricanes, snow, storms, drought, temperature fluctuations and so on can be provided, sometimes by reliance on the satellite data alone, and in other instances by the concurrent use of land-based sensors and data collection. Meteorological history also contributes to the analysis. And, of course, the study of climate change has been facilitated.

The World Meteorological Organization

The World Meteorological Organization (WMO) was established in 1947 as a UN specialised agency to coordinate, standardise and improve world meteorology and related activities.[99] As such it took over from the International Meteorological Organisation of 1879, itself a product of a previous Permanent Committee established 1873 to coordinate the work of the then European meteorological services.[100]

As of 2023 WMO had one-hundred and eighty-seven members together with six associated territories (Art. 4). Its supreme body, the World Meteorological Congress, which meets every four years, is responsible for general policy (Arts 7–10).[101] A thirty-seven member Executive Council is composed of twenty-seven elected by WMO Congress, a

---

97 Formerly HR 6133, Public Law 102–555; 15 USC Chap. 82, Sec. 5671. See now 51 USC § 60161–60162. The National Oceanic and Atmospheric Administration (NOAA) is the major US weather agency: www. noaa.gov/. See also Larsen, *supra* n. 94, at 342.

98 M. Koester, 'Legal Framework Regarding the Commercialization of the German Meteorological Service', Workshop on Legal Remote Sensing Issues, Project 2001, University of Cologne Institute of Air and Space Law (Cologne, 1999) 53–79.

99 Convention of the World Meteorological Organisation, Washington, DC, 11 October 1947. 77 UNTS 142; 1 UST 281, TIAS 2052; 1950 UKTS 30, Cmnd. 7989; 4 Bevans 638. The Convention has been amended several times. The current clean text is in *WMO Basic Documents No. 1*, 2021 edition: https:// library.wmo.int/index.php?lvl=notice_display&id=14206#.Y7RU4OLP2Eu.

100 D.D. Smith, 'The Conclusion of International Agreements by International Organisations: A Functional Analysis Applied to the Agreements of the World Meteorological Organisation' (1971) 2 *Loyola U. L.J.* 27–68 at 35–6.

101 See the 'Abridged Final Report of the Extraordinary Session, Virtual Session, 11–21 October 2021': https://library.wmo.int/doc_num.php?explnum_id=11113. See also Larsen, 'The OSO Landslide', *supra* n. 94, at 343.

President and three Vice-Presidents also elected by Congress, and the presidents elected by each of the six regional associations into which WMO divides the world (Art. 13). It implements programmes agreed by the Congress and supervises the activities of the organisation (Art. 14). A Secretary-General and a Secretariat carry out the day-to-day functions of the Organisation (Arts 20–22). Much of the work of WMO is done through a variety of Technical Commissions which study and make recommendations to the Congress on any subject within the purposes of the organisation (Art. 19). The WMO coordinates the environmental satellites services employed in WMO programmes and those of its members, providing international guidance on their use. It seeks to improve and integrate the collection of data and the use of satellites for the operation of the Global Observing System (GOS).[102] For the purpose WMO consolidates satellite observations, develops space-based elements of the GOS, improves access to satellite weather data and to satellite services and enhances user ability to apply the products of weather satellite systems.

EUMETSAT

The European Organisation for the Exploitation of Meteorological Satellites (EUMETSAT), established in 1983, started functioning in 1986.[103] It has an avowedly commercial aspect. European interest in such matters had begun with the inception of the European Space Research Organisation (ESRO) Meteosat programme in 1976.[104] This was taken over by the incipient European Space Agency (ESA).[105] Discussions as to the creation of a separate organisation to handle such matters began in 1981. The purposes of the EUMETSAT organisation are to provide Europe with a comprehensive satellite weather service and to cooperate to establish services that its members could not afford individually. Operational European meteorological satellites are established and maintained, contributing *inter alia* to climate monitoring and the detection of global climate changes (Art. 2.1). In this advantage is taken of European technologies (Art. 2.3(a)) and as far as possible the recommendations of the WMO are taken into account (Art. 2.1). The organs of EUMETSAT are its Council and a Director General who is assisted by a specialised staff (Art. 1.4). The Council is composed of not more than two representatives of each member, one of whom should be the head of each national meteorological service (Art. 4.1). Council meets at least once a year (Art. 4.3). Membership of EUMETSAT consists of the states participant in its preparatory conference and those later acceding to the Convention with the consent of the Council. The Organisation operates through mandatory and optional programmes (Arts. 2.6–8 and 3), the financing of the organisation reflecting this

---

102 See the 'Manual on the WMO Integrated Global Observing System (WMO-No. 1160), 2021: https://library.wmo.int/index.php?lvl=notice_display&id=19223.

103 Convention for the Establishment of a European Organisation for the Exploitation of Meteorological Satellites (EUMETSAT), 1983; 1434 UNTS 3; 1990 UKTS 32, Cm. 1067; The amended Convention of 1991 (amendments at 1991 UKSP Misc. 16) and other documents are in *EUMETSAT Basic Documents*. www.eumetsat.int/search?text=basic%20documents&context=1&f%5B0%5D=categories%3A10; including www.eumetsat.int/media/44253; www.eumetsat.int/media/15805 and www.eumetsat.int/media/40625.

104 On ESRO see Chapter 1, n. 133.

105 On ESA see Chapter 1 at n. 123.

division.[106] As the provider of meteorological data to Europe and elsewhere EUMETSAT is an important contributor to our understanding of the world eco-system. That said, we note that, as in so many circumstances, the possession of information is important. The NOAA-EUMETSAT agreement on the Data Denial Implementation Plan is understandable, however much the need for it is to be regretted.[107]

Disasters

We now turn to international arrangements that are based on a marriage of remote sensing and telecommunications and are directed more particularly to disaster and its avoidance.[108] International systems and organisations have been established for the special management, mitigation and avoidance of disasters both natural and man-made. These find their roots in general humanitarian principles, but, for example, more directly reflect Prs. X and XI of the UN Remote Sensing Principles as well as such as Pr. 18 of the Stockholm Declaration of 1972[109] and Prs. 18 and 19 of the Rio Declaration of 1992.[110] States ought to warn each other of impending disasters both natural and man-made, as well as assisting states that have been harmed. Meteorology may, of course, provide warning of imminent disaster sufficient to allow some avoidance measures to be implemented.[111] In other instances what is required is assistance after an occurrence.[112] In all cases two essentials are information and a swift and accurate communications system.[113]

---

106 EUMETSAT Data Policy as of 2022 is available at www.eumetsat.int/data-policy/eumetsat-data-policy. pdf. See also www.eumetsat.int/legal-framework/data-policy, and www.eumetsat.int/eumetsat-data-licensing#:~:text=The%20EUMETSAT%20Data%20Policy%20distinguishes%20between%20%27 Essential%27%20and,are%20subject%20to%20specific%20licensing%20terms%20and%20conditions.

107 See *supra* at n. 72. Larsen, *supra* n. 94, at 343.

108 Ito, *supra* n. 1, 149–195. Larsen, *supra* n. 94, at 335.

109 'The Declaration of the UN Conference on the Human Environment', Stockholm, 1972; (1972) 11 ILM 1416: https://vdocuments.site/stockholm-declaration-1972.html; or www.un-documents.net/ unchedec.htm.

110 Report of the UN Conference on Environment and Development, 1992 (The Rio Declaration) UN Doc. A/CONF.151/26; www.un.org/documents/ga/conf151/aconf15126-1annex1.htm; www.unep.org/ Documents.Multilingual/Default.Print.asp?DocumentID=78&ArticleID=1163 (1983) 22 ILM 455. Cf. N.B. Robertson et al., eds., *Agenda 21 and the UNCED Proceedings*, 6 vols (New York: Oceana, 1992–1993); F. Lyall, 'Protection of the Space Environment and Law' (2000) 42 *Proc. IISL* 472–82.

111 Many lives were saved in Bangladesh when, before the arrival of Cyclone Sidr on 15 November 2007, cyclists with megaphones were sent out to warn the population to seek safety on higher ground. Contrast the inaction of the Burmese authorities when warned of Cyclone Nargis in May 2008.

112 Article XXI of the Liability Convention (as to which see *supra* Chapter 4) makes special provision were a space object to cause damage presenting a 'large scale danger to human life' or 'seriously interfering with the living conditions of the population or the functioning of vital centres'. In such a case on its request all states party to the Convention (and in particular launching states) are to examine the possibility of rendering appropriate and rapid assistance to a state which has suffered whether that state is a party to the convention or not. Principles 5 and 7 of UNGA Res. UNGA Res. 47/68 of 14 December 1992 on 'Principles Relevant to the Use of Nuclear Power Sources in Outer Space' deal with the notification of the re-entry of a satellite with a nuclear source on-board, and assistance to affected states. See Chapter 9, n. 60ff.

113 When the December 2004 Indian Ocean tsunami was happening the USA detected what was occurring but was unable to identify who or which agency to contact in the countries likely to be affected by the tidal wave.

The Disasters Charter

The International Charter on Space and Major Disasters is one result of UNISPACE III.[114] An inter-agency agreement, the 'Disasters Charter', became operational in 2000. The organisation functions through a Board on which all parties are represented, and a Secretariat (Art. III.3). Its members are national space agencies with responsibility for remote sensing and national or international space system operators who can usefully contribute to the purposes of the Charter.[115] Participation in the Charter is voluntary, and no funds are exchanged between the parties (Art. III.1). Each makes available information about their space systems, and in case of crisis makes the systems themselves available (Art. IV). In the case of a natural or technological disaster the aim is to provide to authorised users (our term) a unified system of space data acquisition and delivery so as to allow the anticipation and management of potential crises, and reconstruction and subsequent operations.[116] The organisation also analyses recent crises to see what contribution space facilities could have or did provide, and what improvements could be made (Art. IV.2).[117] Authorised users are parties to the Charter and 'associated bodies'. These latter are institutions or services responsible for rescue and civil protection, defence and security under the authority of a state having jurisdiction over a party, a member of ESA, or any other international organisation that is a party (Art. V). When a party and a relevant associated body identify a crisis a request for aid goes to other parties, to cooperating bodies and/or to the Secretariat (Art. III.4–5). In effect, through the Secretariat one single communication will bring the resources of the parties to bear in the matter. An authorised user therefore need only make one contact in order to receive both space- and ground-based information from the entire battery of member agencies. The duration of the coordinated emergency response

---

114 'The Charter on Cooperation to Achieve the Coordinated Use of Space Facilities in the Event of Natural or Technological Disasters', 2000: www.disasterscharter.org/charter_e/html. As of 2023 its mechanisms had access to more than 270 satellites. See also 'International Charter: Space and Major Disasters' Annual Report 2021: https://disasterscharter.org/documents/10180/66908/21st-annual-report/f94f48e7-edee-4fcd-8401–989b4aede12b. See also *International Charter "Space and Major Disasters". A Journey of 15 Years: 2000–2015*: www.disasterscharter.org/documents/10180/66908/15-Years-of-The-International-Charter.pdf, and articles connected with its 20th anniversary: https://disasterscharter.org/web/guest/20th-anniversary. A.A. Severance, 'The Duty to Render Assistance in the Satellite Age' (2006) 36 *Cal. West. Int. L.J.* 377–400. Cf. ILC Reports 2014 and 2016, *supra* n. 95. See also Larsen, *supra* n. 94, 360–362.

115 As of 2022, intergovernmental agency members were ESA and EUMETSAT, together with the space agencies of fifteen governments: Argentina (CONAE), Brazil (INPE), Canada (CSA), China (CNSA), Germany (DLR), India (ISRO), Japan (JAXA), Korea (KARI), Russia (ROSCOSMOS), the UAE (UAESA/MBRSC), the UK (UKSA/DCMII), the US Geological Survey (USGS) and the US National Oceanic Research Administration (NOAA), Venezuela (ABAE). As well as governmental agencies other space system operators may become signatories on the recommendation of the Board and with the unanimous consent of existing parties (Art. VI). For a full membership list see www.disasterscharter.org/web/guest/charter-members.

116 'The term "natural or technological disaster" means a situation of great distress involving loss of human life or large-scale damage to property, caused by a natural phenomenon, such as a cyclone, tornado, earthquake, volcanic eruption, flood or forest fire, or by a technological accident, such as pollution by hydrocarbons, toxic or radioactive substances' (Art. I – Definitions). Cf. ILC Reports 2014 and 2016, *supra* n. 95, in which 'Disaster' is defined in Draft Art. 3 on the protection of persons in the event of disasters as 'a calamitous event or series of events resulting in widespread loss of life, great human suffering and distress, or large-scale material or environmental damage, thereby seriously disrupting the functioning of society.'

117 The Secretariat designs and proposes to the Board 'scenarios' for each type of crisis (Art. IV.2).

to the crisis includes the time period immediately before and after the emergency (Art. I – Definitions). The definition of the 'crisis' period normally does not include the period of reconstruction after an emergency.[118] However, under no circumstances do the Charter arrangements prevent parties from intervening in a crisis on their own initiative (Art. III.4 fin). The Disasters Charter has no provision as to the settlement of any dispute nor as to the effect of any failure of its systems.

The duration of the Disasters Charter was five years in the first instance (i.e. from 2000), with automatic renewal for similar periods thereafter (Art. VII.2). It may be terminated at any time by consent of the parties, but until termination occurs the withdrawal of a party is competent on one-hundred and eighty days' notice (Art. VII.1). That said, the Disaster Charter system seems to be working, as is apparent from the information on its recent activations that is available from its website.[119]

The Tampere Convention

The Tampere Convention on the Provision of Telecommunication Resources for Disaster Mitigation and Relief Operations was adopted in 1998 on the initiative of Finland, the ITU and the UN Office for the Coordination of Humanitarian Affairs (OCHA). The Convention came into force in 2005.[120] Its root is Art. 46 (200) of the ITU Constitution which places a duty on states to receive and communicate distress messages and take necessary actions. The purpose of the Tampere Convention is to improve and coordinate communications services in the mitigation and relief of disasters. While recognising the sovereignty of states as to their control over telecommunications in their several territories, and therefore their right to control any relief activities conducted in their territories, the Convention seeks in time of emergency relief to reduce the regulatory and other barriers which may apply at other times. However it is noticeable that throughout the Convention the obligations and rights with which it deals remain ultimately at the option and control of the states concerned, and any party may terminate assistance granted under the Convention at any time (Art. 6).

The Tampere Convention establishes the UN Emergency Relief Coordinator as its international coordinator (Art. 2). Participating states undertake to make telecommunication resources available for disaster prediction, mitigation and relief (Art. 3), a provision which expressly includes satellite telecommunications. Article 4 deals with the organisation of the provision of telecommunication assistance from the time of request (whether made directly or through the coordinator) to its delivery. Privileges and immunities are to be given to incoming personnel providing assistance, to the extent that national law

---

118 J. Ito, 'Indian Ocean Tsunami: Highlighting Issues Relating to the Use of Space Technology for Disaster Management', *Proceedings of the ISRO-IISL Space Law Conference 2005*, at 3/9.

119 For recent activations see https://disasterscharter.org/web/guest/home;jsessionid=6AE586B2CE7F017 DCA09E9C86FCC641F.APP1. Cf. N.E. Clark, 'Gauging the Effectiveness of Soft Law in Theory and Practice: A Case Study of the International Charter on Space and Major Disasters' (2018) 43 *Air & Sp. L.* 77–112.

120 Tampere Convention on the Provision of Telecommunication Resources for Disaster Mitigation and Relief Operations, 18 June 1998, 2296 UNTS 44; 2005 UKTS 21, Cm 6573: www.ifrc.org/Docs/idrl/I271EN. pdf. Y. Zhao, 'Disaster Management and the Tampere Convention' (2008) 1 *J. East Asia and Int. L.* 141–152; A. Rahrig, 'Love Thy Neighbour: The Tampere Convention as Global Legislation' (2010) 17 *Ind. J. Global Legal Stud.* 273–288; Larsen, *supra* n. 94, 362–366.

permits (Art. 5). Article 7 provides that the cost, if any, of the telecommunication services provided in accordance with equitable principles is to take into consideration the nature of the disaster, its location and the area affected, the capacity of the state involved and the special needs of developing countries. The Convention seeks the reduction or waiver of regulatory barriers to the export or import of telecommunications equipment, its use for disaster mitigation and relief, to the movement of foreign personnel in connection with its use, and the elimination of delay in any of these objectives (Art 9). At present, however, the Convention has a disappointing insufficiency of parties. Its success will depend upon it becoming more widely accepted, and compliance with it becoming no longer voluntary.[121]

UN – SPIDER

The United Nations Platform for Space-based Information for Disaster Management and Emergency Response (UN-SPIDER), established pursuant to UNGA Res. 61/110 of 14 December 2006, implements one of the recommendations of UNISPACE III.[122] UN-SPIDER provides an integrated space-based global information system for the prevention of natural disasters, the mitigation of natural disasters and for disaster relief.[123] Remote sensing and telecommunications are involved in a structure of international cooperation. UN-SPIDER offers technical support, training and technical advice on managing the response to disaster.[124] It has offices in Vienna, Bonn and Beijing and works through a network of international, regional and national partners, some of which second experts to it.

The Sendai Framework

Spurred by the 2004 Indian Ocean tsunami the UN adopted a Framework to implement a strategy for the reduction of risks of disaster in 2005.[125] This has been replaced by the 'Sendai Framework for Disaster Risk Reduction 2015–2030'.[126] In both the role of

---

121 Fidler, *supra* n. 95, at 471–472 and n. 74; Sachaeo *supra* n. 95, at 671 n. 51. The Convention required thirty ratifications to come into force, which it did in 2005. As of 2022 it had 49 parties, and a further 31 signatories. See www.itu.int/en/ITU-D/Emergency-Telecommunications/Pages/TampereConvention.aspx, and https://treaties.un.org/pages/ViewDetails.aspx?src=TREATY&mtdsg_no=XXV-4&chapter=25&clang=_en.
122 Resolution adopted by the Third United Nations Conference on the Exploration and the Peaceful Uses of Outer Space: The Space Millennium: Vienna Declaration on Space and Human Development, Vienna 30 July 1999: www.unoosa.org/pdf/reports/unispace/viennadeclE.pdf. See also Larsen, *supra* n. 94, 357–360.
123 See www.unoosa.org/oosa/en/ourwork/un-spider/index.html.
124 Annual reports are submitted via COPUOS to the UNGA. See UN OOSA Annual Report, 2021, 'Leveraging Space for Disaster Risk Reduction and Management' 38–47. 'Report on activities carried out in 2021 in the framework of the United Nations Platform for Space-based Information for Disaster Management and Emergency Response', 1 December 2021, A/AC.105/1250, and the reports to which it refers.
125 Larsen, *supra* n. 94, 353–357. See the 'World Conference on Disaster Reduction, Kobe, Hyogo', January 2005, A/CONF.206/6, and the 'Hyogo Declaration', Res. 1 adopted by the Conference: see www.unisdr.org/2005/wcdr/intergover/official-doc/L-docs/Final-report-conference.pdf and www.unisdr.org/2005/wcdr/intergover/official-doc/L-docs/Hyogo-declaration-english.pdf. The Declaration was approved by the UNGA in 2006 by Res. 60/195, 'International Strategy for Disaster Reduction'.
126 Sendai Framework for Disaster Risk Reduction 2015–2030, A/CONF.224.CRP1: www.preventionweb.net/files/43291_sendaiframeworkfordrren.pdf; http://reliefweb.int/sites/reliefweb.int/files/resources/Sendai_Framework_for_Disaster_Risk_Reduction_2015-2030.pdf, together with the related Declaration, A/CONF.224/CRP2: http://reliefweb.int/sites/reliefweb.int/files/resources/Political_Declaration_

remote sensing is important. UN-SPIDER was and is involved in developing compliance with the Frameworks.[127] However, we note that compliance with the Frameworks is voluntary – soft law rather than treaty law.[128]

US Regulation of Remote Sensing

States which have adopted national remote sensing regimes take authority to control what is done by use of the technology.[129] This implements their duty under OST Art. VI to authorise and supervise space activities over which they have jurisdiction. Of these regimes the US has enacted the most detailed national regulation and it is instructive to consider it. The US system is a compromise between a governmental need for remote sensing for national purposes (including national security) and a wish to promote commercial remote sensing by US enterprises.[130] In 2003 the US President announced a new US commercial remote sensing policy favouring the private sector.[131] The US Government, 'to the maximum extent possible, will rely on US commercial remote sensing space capabilities for filling imagery and geospatial needs for military, intelligence, foreign policy, homeland security, and civil users'.[132] The US Government operates remote sensing only when commercial remote sensing is not available. The US National Geospatial Intelligence Agency (NGA) buys commercially generated remote sensing data from both subsidised and unsubsidised commercial satellite imaging companies.[133] The NGA also uses reconnaissance satellites operated by the US National Reconnaissance Office (NRA). NGA policy is to use a variety of remote sensing providers (both US and non-US providers, mainly US allies) in order to assure future supply. The National Oceanic and Atmospheric Administration (NOAA), part of the US Department of Commerce, also makes extensive use of satellite imagery from a number of sources, commercial and otherwise.[134]

WCDRR.pdf. The Declaration was approved by the UNGA in 2015 by Res. 70/204, 'International Strategy for Disaster Reduction'. See also 'International cooperation on humanitarian assistance in the field of natural disasters, from relief to development', UNGA 77/29, 2022.

127 See 'Space-based information and the Sendai Framework for Disaster Risk Reduction' 10 June 2015, A/AC.105/2015/CRP.16: www.unoosa.org/res/oosadoc/data/documents/2015/aac_1052015crp/aac_1052015crp_16_0_html/AC105_2015_CRP16E.pdf. See also M. Wahlström, 'New Sendai Framework Strengthens Focus on Reducing Disaster Risk' (2015) 6 *Int. J. Disaster Risk Sci.* 200–201: https://doi.org/10.1007/s13753-015-0057-2.

128 See Larsen, *supra* n. 94, at 354–357. Cf. the US Tsunami Warning System: www.tsunami.gov/, and the Pacific Tsunami Warning Center: www.weather.gov/prh/aboutPTWC.

129 Gabrynowicz, NOAA Survey, *supra* n. 72.

130 M.R. Hoversten, 'US National Security and Government Regulation of Commercial Remote Sensing from Outer Space' (2001) 50 *Air Force L. Rev.* 253–280.

131 US Commercial Remote Sensing Policy, April 25, 2003: www.fas.org/irp/offdocs/nspd/remsens.html. R.A. Williamson and J.C. Baker, 'Current US Remote Sensing Policies: Opportunities and Challenges' (2004) 20 *Space Policy* 109–116.

132 US Commercial Remote Sensing Policy, April 25, 2003 (*supra* n. 131), Sec. II, 'Background': 'Vital national security, foreign policy, economic, and civil interests depend on the United States ability to remotely sense Earth from space. Toward these ends, the United States Government develops and operates highly capable remote sensing space systems for national security purposes, to satisfy civil mission needs, and to provide important public services. United States national security systems are valuable assets because of their high quality data collection, timeliness, volume, and coverage that provide a near real-time capability for regularly monitoring events around the world.'

133 The US National Geospatial-Intelligence Agency is part of the Department of Defense: www.nga.mil.

134 The National Oceanic and Atmospheric Administration (NOAA): www.noaa.gov/.

In its current incarnation the US regime is the product of the history of the involvement of the USA in remote sensing.[135] As far as legislation is concerned most of the relevant US statutory provision was consolidated and codified in 2010 by Public Law 111–314, 18 December 2010, 124 Stat. 3328, and transferred to Title 51 of the United States Code (USC), 'National and Commercial Space Progams'. Earth observation is dealt with in Subtitle VI.

US national regulation makes a greater distinction between enhanced and unenhanced data than do the UN Principles. Originally adopted pursuant to the US Land Remote Sensing Policy Act of 1992, the US regulations define unenhanced data as 'remote sensing signals or imagery products that are unprocessed or subject only to data pre-processing'. Data pre-processing may include rectification of systems and sensor distortions in the data as it is received directly from the satellite, registration of such data with respect to features of the Earth, and calibration of the data spectral response. However, conclusions, manipulations or calculations derived from remote sensing data do not qualify as un-enhanced data.[136]

The US began remote sensing with the government built and operated Landsat series of satellites. Data was provided free to users. Then, in a change of policy the marketing of US remote sensing data was turned over to private commercial companies under the Land Remote Sensing Commercialization Act of 1984.[137] This attempt to commercialise remote sensing, however, proved to be a handicap to rather than a promotion of US remote sensing, as residual governmental concern over national security interests proved to be a barrier to international trade in the data.[138] Elsewhere the French commercial remote sensing company, Spot Image, and other commercial operators, swiftly developed and prospered because they operated with greater freedom. Consequently, the US Congress enacted the 1992 Land Remote Sensing Policy Act in order to give the US remote sensing industry a similar freedom.[139]

All US private operators are now required to obtain a licence in accordance with the US regulations before engaging in remote sensing.[140] The licence is subject to a number of conditions and restrictions, one of which will require the provision of material for the US National Satellite Land Remote Sensing Data Archive.[141] The application for a licence

---

135 See materials, *supra* n. 46; C.C. Joyner and D.R. Miller, 'Selling Satellites: The Commercialisation of LANDSAT' (1985) 25 *Harv. Int. L.J.* 63–102; M.A. Roberts, 'US Remote Sensing Data from Earth Observation – Law, Policy and Practice' (1997) *Air & Sp. L.* 30–49.

136 See National and Commercial Space Programs, Subtitle VI – Earth Observation, 51 USC Sec. 60, Ch. 601, with definitions at §60101.

137 The Land Remote Sensing Commercialization Act, 1984, 98 Stat. 451. Now 51 USC §§ 601–605. Landsat 9 was launched in September 2021.

138 Jackson, *supra* n. 46, at 861; Joyner, *supra* n. 135.

139 The Land Remote Sensing Policy Act, 1992, now 51 USC 601–603. Jackson, *supra* n. 46, at 865. Note: US space weather satellites can not be privatised (51 USC §§ 60101, 60161–2).

140 15 CFR §§ 960.1–15, 'Licensing of Private Remote Sensing Systems'. See also: www.nesdis.noaa.gov/commercial-space/regulatory-affairs/licensing. Cf. Gabrynowicz, NOAA Survey (*supra* n. 72), Williamson (*supra* n. 131) and Chapter 15.

141 51 USC § 60142. The US Secretary of Interior maintains a long-term archive of basic global land remote sensing data for 'historical, scientific and technical purposes, including long-term global environmental monitoring'. The Department of Interior consults with users of remote sensing data to obtain their advice and guidance about their future data needs. The Archive of Remote Sensing Data contains Landsat data

must contain a detailed description of the applicant's planned remote sensing business. The government annually audits the licence to assure the operator's compliance with all government rules, regulations, conditions and restrictions. Non-compliance may result in termination of the operating licence.

Licensing is dealt with by the Department of Commerce, through the Administrator of National Oceanic and Atmospheric Administration (NOAA).[142] The Commerce Department is, however, required to consult and coordinate its actions with other relevant agencies, a class that includes the Department of Defense and the State Department.[143] These last are very concerned to ensure that US national defence and its international relations are not endangered by the licensing of remote sensing providers, a concern that continues even after a licence is issued.[144]

A licensee is required to apply for an amended licence if a foreign purchaser acquires an interest in it in excess of 10%. An amended licence is also required should a foreigner acquire assets of a US remote sensing company on default of a security interest or as a precondition for obtaining a loan.[145] In either case NOAA will prescribe appropriate conditions to protect US national security interests.[146] Furthermore, a licensee is to inform NOAA if the licensee intends to conclude an agreement with a foreigner. In such cases, NOAA consults with the Departments of State and of Defense in order to provide appropriate restrictions on foreign control of remote sensing data to ensure the licensee's continuing obligation to submit data to the National Satellite Land Remote Sensing Data Archive and to comply with requirements as to reporting and the keeping of records.

A remote-sensing licence is normally valid until the end of the licensed operation, until the licensee violates its terms or until US national security interests requires its termination. A licensee must inform the US Department of Commerce of its insolvency, or of the dissolution or discontinuance of its business, in which case the licence will be terminated. Notwithstanding termination of a licence, the licensee remains obliged to provide existing

---

as well as data collected by foreign remote sensing systems. After the expiration of any exclusive rights, the data enters the public domain and is accessible subject to cost recovery. Unenhanced data in the archive may be distributed by any licensee on the condition that the data not be reproduced or sold by the purchaser. Japan intends to establish a national archive of remote sensing data to facilitate user access and to improve its circulation: Gabrynowicz, NOAA Survey, *supra* n. 72 at 31.

142 See 'Commercial Remote Sensing Regulatory Affairs': www.nesdis.noaa.gov/CRSRA/licenseHome.html.

143 51 USC §60121.a.1. Also see 5 USC §552 on the withholding of land remote sensing data. A Memorandum of Understanding between the Departments of Commerce, Defense, State, Interior, and the US Intelligence Communities of 25 April 2006 is at 71 Fed. Reg. 24490.

144 The US Commercial Remote Sensing Policy, April 25, 2003 (*supra* n. 131) states that 'because of the potential value of its products to an adversary the operation of a US commercial remote sensing space system requires appropriate security measures to address US national security and foreign policy concerns'. See also 'Licensing of Private Land Remote-Sensing Space System: Final Rule', 15 CFR 960.1. The NOAA, 'General Conditions for Private Remote Sensing Space System Licenses' in the 'Reference Materials' (*supra* n. 142) state that the Licensee must use a data downlink from its satellites that will allow the USA to access and use data 'during periods when national security or international obligations and/or foreign policies may be compromised'. Cf. the 2006 US National Space Policy statement Secs 5–7: (2007) XXXII AASL 475–86, and Presidential Decision Directive 23 (1994), and the 2020 US National Space Policy statement: https://trumpwhitehouse.archives.gov/wp-content/uploads/2020/12/National-Space-Policy.pdf.

145 Cf. Chapter 14.

146 15 CFR § 960.7. See also Chapter 14 regarding US controls on non-US participants in remote sensing systems.

data to the US Land Remote Sensing Data Archive, and to make data available to a sensed state, subject to any existing data distribution conditions.[147]

The 2003 US Commercial Remote Sensing Policy statement further provides: 'The United States Government may condition the operation of US commercial remote sensing space systems to ensure that appropriate measures are implemented to protect US national security and foreign policy interests'.[148] The approach has been to issue licences allowing a system to gather data anywhere, imposing temporal and geographic limits only when necessary. National security institutions are less comfortable with this approach for commercial systems using newer technologies, like hyper-spectral and radar instruments, and have begun to apply new ones. The new approaches attempt to control individual products more than remote sensing operations. Remote sensing technology is developing rapidly, and the US shutter control policy has developed along with the technology. This pertains in particularly to the higher resolutions that are now available and those that will become available. The US now usually imposes a twenty-four hour delay on the distribution of high-resolution images in order to give the Executive time to decide whether to permit that distribution.[149] However in the case of disaster the USA will make space-based capabilities immediately available for disaster warning, monitoring and response activities and facilitates 'open access to government environmental date on equitable terms'. Thus the US Government waived its normal twenty-four hour waiting period for access to remote sensing data during the Indian Ocean tsunami of 2004.[150]

The US has specific law allowing shutter control. Section 1044 of the 1997 National Defense Appropriation Act[151] (the Kyl – Bingaman Act) prohibits a US Government agency from issuing of any licence permitting a private operator to collect or disseminate satellite images of Israel, unless the resolution of such images is less that the resolution of images regularly available for sale in the commercial market.[152] This restriction places

---

147 See *supra* n. 141, and *infra* as to access to data.
148 Sec. IV, 'Licensing and Operational Guidelines for Private Remote Sensing Space Systems', US Commercial Remote Sensing Policy, 25 April 2003 (*supra* n. 131).
149 71 Fed. Reg. at 24475 (2006). Shutter control reduces the private remote sensing operator's market for data services and the operator may be denied access to certain markets. US law allows US licensed private operators to recover for lost market opportunities: 51 USC § 60147(d): 'If, as a result of technical modifications imposed on a licensee . . . on the basis of national security concerns, the Secretary [of Commerce] in consultation with the Secretary of Defense or with other Federal agencies, determines that additional cost will be incurred by the licensee, the Secretary may require the agency or agencies requesting such technical modifications to reimburse the licensee for such costs, but not for anticipated profits'.
150 See US Tsunami Warning Centers, *supra* n. 128. Cf. US Space Policy Statement, 2003, *supra* n. 144, Sec. 6, 'Civil Space Guidelines' *ad fin.*: 'The United States will utilize government and commercial space-based and related capabilities wherever feasible to enhance disaster warning, monitoring, and response activities; and take a leadership role in international fora to establish a long-term plan for coordination of an integrated global Earth observation system and promote the adoption of policies internationally that facilitate full and open access to government environmental data on equitable terms'. The US National Geospatial-Intelligence Agency (NGA) assumed responsibility for providing remote sensing information for natural disasters such as the Hurricane Katrina disaster in New Orleans.
151 Now included in 51 USC §60121.
152 The applicant for a licence is required to submit a plan showing that the applicant can control collection and distribution of imagery in order to satisfy the Kyl – Bingaman Act. The Act requires the Department of Commerce to make a finding regarding the level of detail or precision of images of Israel available on the commercial market. To determine commercial availability the Department of Commerce uses foreign availability for export control purposes as the model. Based on this test the Department of Commerce determines whether an item is comparable in quality to an item subject to US national security export controls

statutory limits on non-discriminatory access to remote sensing and in turn on the business opportunities of US private operators. Operators and providers are disadvantaged *vis-à-vis* foreign competitors who can freely produce high-resolution images of Israel for the international market. The statute clearly establishes a precedent for discriminatory access to remote sensing data.[153] It also permits the US President to prohibit remote sensing of other designated areas and localities. Such provision conflicts with Principle XII of the UN Principles Remote Sensing which provides for non-discriminatory access to all remote sensing data at reasonable cost.

While the US exercises shutter control over US private remote sensing operators for national security purposes, it does not have a similar control over foreign operators. Thus US national control over its domestic operators and providers may be undercut by foreign operators and providers who can supply the world market (including the US market) with high-resolution data as well as with data from geographical areas prohibited by US laws, such as Israel.[154] International controls or standards regulating remote sensing of sensitive areas would necessitate the negotiation of a new international agreement. Further technological and political developments would dictate the nature of such agreement and should include effective international enforcement. However, a binding international agreement as to the sensing of sensitive areas seems less likely than some provision modelled on the familiar voluntary agreements on weapons control.

---

and available in sufficient quantities to make US export control ineffective. The applicant for a licence can free itself of this restriction on its commercial enterprise by proving that the remote sensing data in question are commercially available from foreign remote sensing operators. See 15 CFR 768; 71 Fed. Reg. 24479 (2006).

153 Gabrynowicz, *supra* n. 51, at 109–110.
154 Cf. text and note *supra* n. 152.

13

FINANCE AND INTERNATIONAL TRADE LAW

Introduction

In the immediate post-Sputnik era space commerce was both conducted and regulated by governments. Except in science fiction there were no private activities in outer space. In the 1980s space industries changed thanks to technological advance and developments in the regulatory environment, commercial strategies and consumer demand. In parallel private space commerce developed. Government deregulation and agreement in the World Trade Organisation (WTO) on basic telecommunications boosted private enterprise in that sector of space commerce.[1] Increasing launch capability, growth in the size and capacity of satellites including the number of transponders per satellite, and decreasing costs of manufacturing, launching and operating satellites stimulated space industries.[2] Demand for space services grew as they became robust and more reliable. Private and public satellite infrastructure and satellite service companies increased. But how are these to be financed? Occasionally a lender will want some security interest to guarantee repayment of sums provided. How is that achieved?

Privately owned satellite networks normally use existing national contract laws, including 'choice of law' clauses when different national systems may be relevant.[3] The products of the UN Commission on International Trade Law can be helpful, its model laws having

1 World Trade Organisation: Agreement on Telecommunications Services (Fourth Protocol to General Agreement on Trade in Services), Geneva, 15 February 1997 (1997) 36 ILM 354; www.wto.org/english/tratop_c/serv_e/4prote_e.htm. Y. Zhao, 'The Commercial Use of Telecommunications under the Framework of GATS' (1999) 24 *Air and Sp. Law*, 303–328.
2 J.L. Reed, 'The Commercial Space Launch Market and Bilateral Trade Agreements in Space Launch Services' (1997) 13 *Am. U. Int. L. Rev.* 157–218; H.P. van Fenema, *The International Trade in Launch Services: the Effect of U.S. Laws, Policies and Practices on Its Development* (Leiden, 1999).
3 Examples of 'choice of law' treaties are the Convention on the International Recognition of Rights in Aircraft, 1948, 310 UNTS 152, 1948 UK Misc. Ser. 7, Cmd. 7510, 4 UST 1830, TIAS 2847, and the UNIDROIT Convention on International Financial Leasing, Ottawa, 1988, 2321 UNTS 197: www.unidroit.org/instruments/leasing/convention/. The latter entered into force on 1 May 1995. As of November 2022 it had ten ratifications and ten other signatories.

DOI: 10.4324/9781003496502-13

been adopted by many countries.[4] However, a distinction must be drawn between the law relating to the facilitation of international trade and the controls that may be relevant for military and political reasons. We will therefore discuss civil questions before turning to controls on trade exercised for other reasons. Ironically, both have to do with 'security' of one kind or another. Finally, some controls on international trade in space assets are based on non-military considerations.

Civil Law Securities

Many contracts for the construction of satellites, launches and services are entered into in the US or in Europe, although India, Japan, and China are increasing their share of these markets. US and 'Ariane' (ESA) launches are subject to US or national European laws either because of a 'choice of law' clause in the contract, or the applicability of US or a national European law governing questions of private international law (sc. In older terminology 'conflict of laws').

The US national law relevant for commercial space contracts is almost entirely contained in the US Uniform Commercial Code (UCC).[5] The UCC is not US federal law. Technically an unofficial instrument in that it is not created by a legislature, the UCC has been incorporated into the individual law of most US states thereby establishing a virtual uniformity of law on commercial matters throughout the US. As a result US space equipment sales are usually subject to the UCC. It is only natural that US manufacturers, financiers and borrowers located in the US where a satellite 'property' (the 'res') is also located, feel most comfortable in being subject to familiar US law. Even non-US parties may feel secure in choosing US law to govern their contracts (assuming they understand the vagaries of US state law). Thus the UCC has come to govern many international contracts for space equipment through a particular US state law being the selection made by a 'choice of law' provision in the contract.[6]

Where applicable, US laws may govern not only the contract to purchase or operate space assets but also the financing of that contract/endeavour, since space assets may be purchased or operated subject to secured interests in them.[7] The UCC therefore applies to

---

4 UN Commission on International Trade Law (UNCITRAL): https://uncitral.un.org/. UNCITRAL seeks the modernisation and harmonisation of international business. See *The UNCITRAL Guide: Basic Facts about the United Nations Commission on International Trade Law* (Vienna: UN, 2007): https://uncitral.un.org/sites/uncitral.un.org/files/media-documents/uncitral/en/12-57491-guide-to-uncitral-e.pdf.

5 J.J. White and R.S. Summers, *Uniform Commercial Code* (West Publishing, 1989); *The Portable Universal Commercial Code,* 2nd ed. (American Bar Association, 1997).

   The Uniform Commercial Code, adopted by the American Law Institute and the US National Conference of Commissioners on Uniform Laws, attempts to bring uniformity as to certain commercial matters in the laws of the US states notwithstanding that under the US Constitution they are free to make their own arrangements. The Code is subject to occasional editorial alteration in the light of case law. Forty-eight US states, the District of Columbia, Puerto Rica, Guam and the US Virgin Islands have adopted it without variation. Louisiana has adopted it with minor variation based on its separate roots in the Civil Law tradition that stems from continental European and ultimately Roman law. California has adopted it with minor variations, which stem from historic Spanish influences. See also Larsen and Heilbock, *infra* n. 27, at 716–729.

6 Cf. F. Lyall, 'Space Law: What Law or Which Law?' (1992) 34 *Proc. IISL* 240–243.

7 Space equipment is 'mobile equipment' under the provisions of the UCC. See also Chapters 13 and 14 for US licensing controls on technology.

most US-constituted agreements on security interests in space assets. UCC Sec. 9–103(3) provides:

> The law (including the conflict of laws rules) of the jurisdiction in which the debtor is located governs the perfection and the effect of perfection or non-perfection of the security interest. If, however, the debtor is located in a jurisdiction which is not a part of the US, and which does not provide for perfection of the security interest by filing or recording in that jurisdiction, the law of the jurisdiction in the US in which the debtor has its major executive office governs the perfection and the effect of perfection or non-perfection of the security interests through filing.

UCC Sec. 9–203, identifies three situations in which a security interest may attach to space equipment: (1) when the debtor enters into a security agreement with the creditor and the agreement describes the collateral; (2) when the loan has been issued for value; and (3) when the debtor has rights in the collateral. The holder of the security interest may then register the security interest in a state registry in order to obtain the protection added by such filing. The major premise of the registry system is 'that a good faith effort at filing would be successful and that a good faith search would reveal the presence of the secured creditor's claim'.[8] Under UCC Sec. 9-312(5) the claims of secured creditors to priority in access to collateral are based on the time/date of filing. Priority is accorded to the first filing.

Most European law as to security interests and other code-based systems modelled on the French, Spanish or German Civil Codes, originate in concepts of Roman law. Under Roman law a creditor had title to the chattel over which the security is constituted until the debt was paid in full. Not having title the debtor could not transfer ownership of the chattel to a third party until the debt was discharged. Continental European laws respect legal rights derived from the law of the original *situs* (location) of mobile property if those legal rights can be accommodated within the municipal law of the new *situs*. If legal rights can not be accommodated under the municipal law of the new *situs*, the European approach may result in a failure to recognise legal rights in space equipment, thus potentially causing financial loss to putative financiers. Any uncertainty as to the legal rights of the financier of the secured interest impedes both the creation of, and trade in space assets.[9] To create certainty, therefore, the parties to a financing contract that has a security element may (should) include a choice of law clause in the security contract. That choice may well be for a US national state law should that result in greater certainty for the parties as to their rights and obligations.

Negotiation of finance is a normal part of any modern commercial activity. One method of obtaining finance is 'asset-based financing'. In this the security for a loan is constituted over some (or all) of the assets of the enterprise. The process is simple when the asset involved is fixed, for example a building. However, difficulties can emerge when major assets of the enterprise are mobile. Such assets may traverse the jurisdictions of a number of legal systems, which may not be uniform in the securities law which they enforce. An airplane may spend considerable time over the high seas where there is no sovereignty and

---

8 White and Summers, *supra* n. 5, at 797.
9 Larsen and Heilbock, *infra* n. 27, at 716–729.

then land in a country different from that of its registration. At least in such cases there is the possibility of the security-holder gaining physical control of the asset in case of default. The position as to a security over a satellite in orbit in outer space is a step further, for there is no real prospect of possession of the asset. A company seeking financing may offer rights over the satellite or satellites in the system it operates or intends to create as security for the loan. It may even borrow on the basis that it will effect a security over space assets following the take-over of another company for which purpose the finance is required.[10] The sums involved are considerable. Accordingly the sources of the finance will require clarity and effective security arrangements. Some steps have already been taken.

The Cape Town Convention

The Cape Town Convention on International Interests in Mobile Equipment, 2001,[11] is the product of UNIDROIT, the International Institute for the Unification of Private Law.[12] The Convention is designed to regulate and facilitate the international movement and financing of mobile property, as distinguished from real property. It provides a method through which securities constituted over mobile objects can be recognised and internationally enforced. Currently, rights in mobile equipment and their enforcement may be governed by different national laws as just described.

The Cape Town Convention is an umbrella or framework convention. The Convention has little significance of itself because it applies only as specified by one of four separate protocols. An Aviation Protocol was adopted along with the Cape Town Convention on 16 November 2001. Now in force it is successful and has provided a model for the later protocols.[13] A Rail Protocol, adopted in 2007, is not yet in force,[14] neither is a Mining, Agricultural and Construction Equipment Protocol (MAC protocol), adopted in 2019.[15] The Space Protocol of 2012 is discussed separately below.

The Cape Town convention creates an optional private international law regime for the subjects of its protocols which facilitate the financing of mobile equipment by qualifying the equipment as an international interest subject to the regulation and protection of the Convention, and by establishing remedies for creditors. Each regime creates an international registry of international interests that is transparent and easy to access by electronic means, that meets the needs of the relevant industry, and thereby fosters the confidence

---

10 Cf. the history of INTELSAT, INMARSAT and EUTELSAT.

11 Convention on International Interests in Mobile Equipment, Cape Town, 2001, 2307 UNTS 341; 2015 UKTS 31, Cm 9154; (2003) US S Doc 108–10.

12 The International Institute for the Unification of Private Law (UNIDROIT), Rome: www.unidroit.org.

13 Protocol to the Convention on International Interests in Mobile Equipment on matters specific to Aircraft Equipment (with annex), Cape Town, 16 November 2001, 2367 UNTS 517 (Eng. at 556), 2015 UKTS 32, Cm 9155: www.unidroit.org/instruments/security-interests/aircraft-protocol/. See R. Goode, *Cape Town Convention and Aircraft Protocol Official Commentary*, 5th ed. (Rome: UNIDROIT, 2023).

14 Protocol to the Convention on International Interests in Mobile Equipment on matters specific to Railway Rolling Stock, Luxembourg, 2007; (2007) 46 ILM 662–676: https://www.unidroit.org./instruments/security-interests/rail-protocol. See R. Goode, *Cape Town Convention and Luxembourg Protocol, Official Commentary*, 2nd ed. (UNIDROIT, 2014).

15 Protocol to the Convention on International Interests in Mobile Equipment on matters specific to Mining, Agricultural and Construction Equipment: www.unidroit.org/instruments/security-interests/mac-protocol/.

of potential investors. It is hoped that such measures will lower the financing costs in the separate areas covered by the protocols.[16]

The Cape Town Convention comes into force for a specific category of mobile equipment when a protocol for that category has been adopted and comes into force (Art. 49).[17] To become subject to the Convention and a specific protocol a state adopts the particular protocol for transactions within its jurisdiction (Arts. 49.1–2). For the application of the system the debtor must be situated in a contracting state at the time when the agreement creating or providing for the international interest concerned is entered into (Art. 3.1). To be so situated the debtor may be incorporated or formed in that contracting state, have a registered office or statutory seat in it, or have its centre of administration or place of business there (Art 4.1). Should the debtor have more than one place of business its principal place of business or its habitual residence are looked to (Art. 4.2). The location of the creditor is irrelevant (Art. 3.2).

Protection under the Convention regime is only granted to international interests in particular mobile equipment.[18] Article 7 requires such interests to be constituted in writing, to relate to an object of which the chargor, conditional seller or lessor has power to dispose, and which allows the object to be identified in conformity with the relevant protocol (Art. 7.a – c). In a security agreement it must be possible to determine the secured obligations, but without necessarily specifying a sum or maximum sum secured (Art. 7.d).

The Convention regime allows these international interests to be registered. For Sir Roy Goode, one of the architects of the scheme, registration 'is at the heart of the Convention's system of priorities'. In his view: 'Registration gives public notice of an international interest or a prospective international interest and enables the creditor to preserve priority and the effectiveness of the international interest in insolvency proceedings against the debtor.'[19]

The structure of the system established under the Cape Town Convention rests on two pillars, the supervisory authority and the international registry for each of the three protocols.

A supervisory authority is established under the relevant protocol. It is designated at, or pursuant to a resolution of the diplomatic conference at which the protocol is adopted, provided that the supervisory authority is able and willing to act in that capacity. It is for the supervisory authority to appoint a registrar and oversee the operations and administration of the international registry (Art. 17). The authority also arranges the proper transfer of the registry should that be needed. The authority prescribes regulations and administrative procedures for the operation of the registry, and regularly reviews the fee structure for the registry services. Finally the authority regularly reports to the contracting states on the operation of the registry (Art. 17.2.a – j). The supervisory authority owns all proprietary rights in the databases and archives of the international registry (Art. 17.4) and its assets,

---

16 Cf. Goode, *infra* n. 28, at 2.6. H-G. Bollweg and S. Schultheiss, 'Das Berliner Weltraumprotocoll' (2012) ZLW 389–425 at 390, indicates that there has been a cost-saving of up to 30% in aviation financing.
17 The categories are airframes, aircraft engines and helicopters; railway rolling stock; and space assets (Art. 2.3), corresponding to the three areas covered by the separate protocols.
18 See *supra*, n. 17.
19 Goode, *infra* n. 28, at 2.117

documents, databases and archives are inviolable (Art. 27.4).[20] It has international legal personality (Art. 27.1) and it, and its employees have such immunity from legal or administrative process as may be specified in the relevant protocol (Art. 27.2). It may be exempt from taxes and have other privileges as agreed with its host state (Art. 27.3).

Three international registries are contemplated: one for each Protocol.[21] Their function is to maintain a record of international interests in the mobile equipment dealt with under its ruling protocol. These interests consist of existing and prospective international interests and registrable non-consensual rights and interests, assignments and prospective assignments of international interests, acquisitions of international interests by legal or contractual subrogations under the applicable law, notices of national interests, and subordination of any of these interests (Art. 16). Registration of an interest requires the consent of all the parties to the relevant security agreement (Art. 20). The records are not arranged by identification of debtors but by identification of the assets registered.[22] Each international registry can be accessed through electronic means and any person may search it. The registrar issues a search certificate stating the information on file, if any. The registrar may be held liable for errors and omissions that result in damages. Therefore the registrar may purchase insurance to cover potential liability (Art. 28). Under the Convention, the courts at the Registrar's place of business have exclusive jurisdiction to issue orders and to award damages for errors and omissions by the Registrar.

The Cape Town Convention adopts the priority principle by which whoever files first in time prevails. 'A registered interest has priority over any other interest subsequently registered and over an unregistered interest' (Art. 29). The first to file thus has priority even over known but unfiled prior interests. Furthermore, subsequent filings are subject to prior filed interests. However, priorities may be varied by the parties to the security agreements (Art. 29).[23] Sometimes new equipment may be added to existing equipment, for example as replacement for equipment that has failed. Such equipment may already have been purchased under a separate security agreement prior to installation, and/or be subject to existing national law. Priority for such equipment is not affected by the priority principle of first in time filing (Art. 29.7).

In the event of default, sellers under a conditional sales contract and lessors having title to the assets, may terminate the security agreement and assume possession or control of the asset (Art. 10).[24] The chargor/holder of a secured obligation may take possession and control of the asset or begin to collect income from managing the asset.[25] A court

---

20 The authority may waive this immunity (Art. 27.6). Claimants against the registrar have any access necessary if pursuing a claim (Art. 27.5).

21 For the aviation and rail protocols see *supra* nn. 13 and 14. The aviation registry is based in Dublin: www.internationalregistry.aero/ir-web/. It may be that local registries will serve the purposes of the Rail Rolling Stock Protocol; M. Fleetwood and P. Bloch, 'The Cape Town International Rail Registry and the Development of State Registries' (2014) 3 *Cape Town Conv. J.* 95–107. Art. 16.2 does contemplate the establishing of different registries for categories of objects and associated rights.

22 Goode, *infra* n. 28, at 2.118.

23 R. Goode, 'The priority rules under the Cape Town Convention and Protocols' (2012) 1 *Cape Town Conv. J.* 95–108.

24 Convention Chapter III (Arts. 8–15) deals with remedies.

25 The terms charge and chargor are defined as: 'creditor' means a chargee under a security agreement, a conditional seller under a title reservation agreement or a lessor under a leasing agreement (Art. 1.(i)); 'debtor' means a chargor under a security agreement, a conditional buyer under a title reservation agreement, a lessee

order may be required to retrieve title to the assets should title have passed to the debtor, the chargor. A chargee may also obtain a court order to enforce default remedies (Arts. 8–9).[26]

The Space Protocol, 2012

The Space Protocol is the first multilateral private international law treaty relating to outer space activities.[27] Agreed at Berlin on 9 March 2012,[28] it will require ten ratifications to enter into force.[29] Its purpose is to provide a means to cope with security interests in space assets. These otherwise could be difficult to assert. Prior to launch the physical assets are accessible. They either exist or are planned. But after launch they will be in outer space, which is not subject to the sovereignty of any state and is not ordinarily accessible to bailiffs or other official enforcers. Also, unlike other movable assets such as ships and airplanes, spacecraft do not have nationality as such.[30]

Previously, the regulation of private commercial activities in outer space was left almost entirely to public international law treaties and national law. Now, a significant number of largely international nongovernmental commercial companies are active in space. Their enterprises require financing from ordinary commercial sources. Other parties also seeking financing are the equipment manufacturers, operators and launch companies. Financial and insurance companies seek security in the arrangements they enter into with entrepreneurs.

---

under a leasing agreement or a person whose interest in an object is burdened by a registrable non-consensual right or interest (Art. 1(j)).

26 Sundahl (2013), *infra* n. 28, at 80. See also D. Weber-Steinhaus and D.N. Chearbhaill, 'Security Rights over Satellites: An Overview of the Proposed Protocol to the Convention on International Interests in Mobile Equipment on Matter Specific to Space Assets', in L-J. Smith and I. Bauman, *Contracting for Space* (Farnham: Ashgate 2011), 221–231 at 226–227.

27 P.B. Larsen and J.A. Heilbock, 'UNIDROIT Project on Security Interest: How the Project Affects Space Objects' (2002) 64 *J. Air L. Com.* 703–770; O. Heinrich and E. Pelletier, 'International Registry for Space Assets: Report on the Work of the Preparatory Commission' (2014) 63 *ZLW* 287–293; Sundahl (2013), *infra* n. 28, discusses the relationship between the Space Protocol and the US UCC.

28 Protocol to the Convention on International Interests in Mobile Equipment and Protocol Thereto on Matters Specific to Space Assets, Berlin, 2012: www.unidroit.org/instruments/security-interests/space-protocol/. It is also annexed to Stanford, *infra*, at 169–184.

R. Goode, *Convention on International Interests in Mobile Equipment and Protocol Thereto on Matters Specific to Space Assets, Official Commentary* (UNIDROIT, 2013); M. Sundahl, *The Cape Town Convention, Its Application to Space Assets and Relation to the Law of Outer Space* (Leiden: Nijhoff, 2013). See also M.J. Stanford, 'The UNIDROIT Protocol to the Cape Town Convention on Matters Specific to Space Assets' (2012) 55 *Proc. IISL* 153–184; M. Sundahl, 'The Cape Town Convention and the Law of Outer Space: Five Scenarios' (2014) 3 *Cape Town Conv. J.*, 109–121; P.B. Larsen, 'The Berlin Space Protocol: Update' (2015) 64 ZLW 361–395.

29 Cape Town Convention, *supra* n. 11, Art. 49.2; Protocol, Art XXXVIII. States favouring the Protocol advocated a low number while less supportive s proposed a high number. Ten is a high for a specialised treaty such as the Space Protocol. As of 2022 the Protocol has no ratifications but four states, Burkina Faso, Germany, Saudi Arabia and Zimbabwe, are signatories. For comparison the Rail Protocol will enter into force after four ratifications and the Aviation Protocol entered into force after eight. The high requirement for the Space Protocol reflects the efforts of the large space operators to delay the Protocol coming into force.

30 Bin Cheng, *Studies in International Law* (Oxford: Clarendon Press) Chapter 17, 'Nationality for Spacecraft', at 491: 'Nationality for spacecraft would sweep away much of the confusion which now prevails regarding jurisdiction over space objects, confusion inherent in the various space treaties in outer space which has been made more confounded by *inter alia* Article II of the Registration Convention.'

However, compared with maritime or aviation, the financial underpinnings of outer space commerce are at an early stage of development.[31]

The Space Protocol is intended to reduce the risks of space asset financing, and to provide default remedies in the area, thus facilitating and encouraging investment in space activities through security arrangements constituted over the assets. Space asset financing should not only become more transparent, but financiers would be enabled to enforce the security expeditiously in case of default. Further, reduction of the risks attendant on financing space assets should lower the cost of finance.[32] Entry into space business is difficult and risky and requires a large infusion of capital. For finance most new entrants have to resort to traditional banks and financiers. But start-up companies do not have the easy entry into the capital markets possessed by the established operators. The Space Protocol should help.

Established space operators have not welcomed the innovation. Originally the draft Space Protocol was sponsored and prepared by a space industry working group,[33] but was transferred to UNIDROIT for final processing as a treaty.[34] A change in satellite industry attitude towards the Space Protocol emerged gradually in the early part of the century as the private space business matured and became less risky and as operators began to discover alternative ways to finance their ventures. Satellite operators became less dependent on banks and specific financiers for finance. Instead they found it to their advantage to enter the capital market directly.

Because additional sources and methods of financing were emerging, some large satellite companies ceased to support the draft Protocol and tried to stall its finalisation. UNIDROIT invited them to engage with it to resolve their concerns. Changes were made and UNIDROIT finalised the draft Protocol. Germany offered to host the diplomatic conference in 2012. However, just before the conference, eighty-nine major satellite companies issued a joint letter opposing the Space Protocol. Opposition was founded on a belief that banks and special investors did not value security interests in space assets adequately by considering the satellite operators' business plans, projected revenue flows, insurance and licenses and other assets. They considered that the capital markets presented a better source of financing, making the Space Protocol unnecessary.[35] It must therefore be noted

---

31 In space project financing the lenders usually receive debt repayments from the income generated by the project. The lender receives a security interest (collateral) in the satellite as protection against default: see Sundahl (2013), *supra* n. 28, at 4. Apart from basic financing security a need remains for some protection for an endeavour. Some licensing authorities protect from total catastrophe by limiting the liability of a licensee. P.B. Larsen, 'Liability Limitation under National Law and the Liability Convention' (2010) 53 *Proc. IISL* 416–423. See Chapter 4, sv. 'Compensation for Damage, Liability Caps and Insurance'.

32 See Bollweg, *supra* n. 16.

33 P.B. Larsen, 'Future Protocol on Security Interests in Space Assets' (2002) 67 *J. Air L. and Com.* 1071–1106. P.B. Larsen participated in the space industry working group that began drafting the Protocol in late 1997. A number of observations in the following pages are based on that involvement.

34 M. Stanford, 'The Availability of a New Form of Financing for Commercial Space Activities: The Extension of the Cape Town Convention to Space Assets' (2012) 1 *Cape Town Conv. J,* 109–123.

35 Cf. Report by the UNDROIT Secretariat: 'Intersessional Consultations with Representatives of the International Commercial Space and Financial Communities', Rome, 18 October 2010, UNIDROIT 2010, C.G.E./Space Pr./5/W.P. 4: www.unidroit.org/english/documents/2010/study72j/cge-session5/cge-5-wp04-e.pdf. Cf. Panel discussion 'Reimaging the Space Protocol' 2021: www.unidroit.org/space-protocol-panel-discussion-organised-in-collaboration-with-the-space-court-foundation/. See materials at www.unidroit.org/work-in-progress-studies/studies/security-interests/1374-study-lxxii-j-protocol-to-the-convention-

that the parties to a security agreement over space assets are not required to use the Space Protocol. They can choose whether to register their interests in accordance with the Space Protocol, or to leave the security agreement subject to the relevant national law under which it is constituted.

The Space Protocol remains aimed at securing finance for space activities from banks and private investors and in protecting those investments. Were it shunned by the major operators, who needs it? Many will. First, capital markets are fickle and may change as they did during the recent recession, and the established operators may again have to resort to traditional ways of financing. Second, many small space operators, though unable to obtain financing from capital markets, still obtain funding from banks and private financiers. Third, some countries, such as Germany, China, and Russia, with attitudes about financing different from the large satellite companies, continue to be interested in the Protocol. Fourth, developing countries are increasingly seeking satellite services, either their own or from commercial providers. Their financial needs and resources differ from those of the major countries. They may need to borrow, so financial arrangements adequately meeting the interests of both borrowers and lenders are needed. In short, there continues to be a need and a place for the Space Protocol.

The Protocol must be read in conjunction with the Cape Town Convention. Of the two and as between parties to a security agreement, the Protocol is the governing treaty instrument. It varies the terms of the Convention but only as to matters that fall within the scope of the Space Protocol. A user therefore needs to know the terms of the Cape Town Convention in order to identify and apply those provisions as changed by the Protocol, as well as its additional provisions.

The Cape Town Convention, Chapter XIV, provides multiple opportunities for the state parties to design their own treaty. They have options to opt in or out of treaty provisions. That may facilitate the individual needs of states and of parties to security agreements. The Space Protocol, Chapter VI, likewise provides extensive options for its parties. For example, the Parties may decide whether to apply the stricter or the more liberal protective clause of the Article XXI remedies on insolvency. Individual State choices may increase flexibility and choice, but they undermine the general uniformity of the Space Protocol, affecting its predictability.

The Supervisory Authority

The Authority that will supervise the registry was to be designated at or pursuant to the resolution of the diplomatic conference which adopted the draft protocol.[36] In fact the Berlin diplomatic conference made no appointment. Instead it established a preparatory commission to act as a temporary supervisory authority, and discussions began to identify an appropriate permanent supervisor.[37] During the negotiation of the Protocol the ITU had indicated interest and, given the ITU's involvement with space, and particularly its maintenance of the International Master Frequency Register, that made sense. It was

---

on-international-interests-in-mobile-equipment-on-matters-specific-to-space-assets. See also Larsen, *supra* n. 28, at 355.

36 Space Protocol, Art. XXVIII. Cf. Cape Town Convention, Art. 17.1.

37 Final Acts of the Berlin conference, Res. 1: www.itu.int/en/ITU-R/space/spaceAssets/DCME-SP-Doc43-resolution1-EN.pdf. Cf. the Report of the Preparatory Commission, Rome, 2013: www.unidroit.org/english/documents/2013/depositary/ctc-sp/pcs-01-06rev-e.pdf. For its composition see para 4 of its Report.

followed up.[38] In 2014 the ITU plenipotentiary conference referred the matter for fuller consideration by the ITU Council.[39] In 2016, having found no objections in principle to such a step, the Council passed the question for decision by the next plenipotentiary conference,[40] which decided no action needed to be taken until the Protocol comes into force.[41] The question was therefore not revisited at the 2022 ITU plenipotentiary conference.

When established the Supervisory Authority will have the same immunity from legal and administrative process as an international organization. The Authority will appoint a commission of experts to assist it (Art. XXVIII). It will appoint the International Registry, establish international regulations for the conduct of the registry and supervise the registry and make regular reports on the operation of the Registry to the contracting states. (Convention Art. 17). The regulations will enter into force when the Protocol enters into force (Art. XXIX).

The International Registry

The International Registry will function partially under the Cape Town Convention outlined above, and partially under the Space Protocol.

There are, of course, other registries that deal with space. States responsible for the launch of objects into space should have their own registers and notify specified data to the international registry maintained by UNOOSA.[42] The ITU Radiocommunication Sector maintains the International Master Frequency Register, which contains data on orbits and the use of radio frequencies. Those registries serve purposes different from that of the Space Protocol. The UN system serves a safety purpose. The ITU facilitates the practical use of space. The Space Protocol serves a financial objective. National registries and that of the UN deal with space objects. The Space Protocol registry registers space assets, including financial interests, which, by definition, are not space objects. The Space Protocol is in a sense voluntary in that it requires registration for its users to receive its benefits. Further, its users will be private parties to security agreements. The UN and ITU systems require action by states and affect public law. While the Cape Town Convention as implemented by the Space Protocol is also treaty-based, the system is concerned to regulate matters of private international law and is voluntary on the part of those who wish to make use of it.[43]

---

38 Final Acts of the Berlin conference, Res. 2: www.itu.int/en/ITU-R/space/spaceAssets/DCME-SP-Doc43-resolution2-EN.pdf.

39 Report by the Secretary-General: 'ITU's Role as Supervisory Authority of the International Registration System for Space Assets under the Space Protocol', 2014 (PP-14, Doc. 61).

40 See Chairman of Council: 'ITU's Role as Supervisory Authority of the International Registration System for Space Assets under the Space Protocol', 1 June 2016, Doc. C16/DT/13. See generally ITU-R, 'Supervisory Authority of the future international registration system for Space Assets': www.itu.int/en/ITU-R/space/Pages/spaceAssets.aspx. C.M. Taiatu, 'The international Telecommunication Union (ITU) as the Proposed Supervisory Authority of the Future International Registry for Space Assets' (2016) 21 *Unif. L. Rev.* 508–527.

41 'ITU's role as supervisory authority of the international registration system for space assets under the space protocol', Res. 210 (Dubai, 2018).

42 See OST Art. VIII, and Arts. II – IV of the Registration Convention, discussed in Chapter 4. Larsen, *supra* n. 28, at 378.

43 A hypothetical example of events where the Protocol would protect the holder of an interest secured over a space object is the following. A satellite operator borrows money from a financier on the basis of a security agreement, enters into contract with Boeing to build a satellite, contracts with Arianespace to launch from

Transparency is a major benefit of the Space Protocol. The International Registry gives notice to the world of the existence of the international interests registered with it. Creditors are thereby able to preserve and protect the priority of their registered interests. Subsequent investors are made aware of interests that already hold a priority, and consequently are not misled about the inferior security of any later security interests they may possess. In addition the owners of registered interests are themselves protected against unregistered interests. The registration of an international interest will last until the interest expires or for the time period stated in the record. The registration of the international interest is not affected by the destruction of the space asset (Convention, Art. 21).

The International Registry will hold a record of international interests, rights assignments and reassignments, notices of public service, and other registrable information. The register is not arranged by the names of individual owners of the assets registered but on the international interests being filed.[44] Held electronically its data will be accessible twenty-four hours a day. A new registration or the termination of an existing registration requires the consent of the beneficiary of the registration.[45] The written consent of the parties to the security agreement to register an international interest must be submitted, and, because the specific space assets registered must be uniquely identified in the registry (Art. VII), that identification must be supplied.[46] The Registrar will charge fees to cover the cost of registration, of maintaining the register and of insurance to cover any potential liability the Registrar may incur (Art. XXXII).

Application

The Space Protocol specifically provides that the Cape Town Convention applies to 'space assets, rights assignments and rights reassignments' only 'as provided by the terms of this Protocol'.[47] Because space assets pass through air space in order to reach outer space, the Space Protocol is explicitly distinguished from the scope of the Aviation Protocol.[48] Further, the Space Protocol does not apply to aircraft objects that may temporarily enter outer space.[49,50] Last, the Protocol supersedes the UNIDROIT Convention on International

French Guyana, and finally engages in the business of remote sensing from outer space. Subsequently the operator becomes insolvent and may default on the security agreement by failure to make payments to the financier, or the satellite may be sold to another operator of a different nationality in violation of the security agreement. A rogue satellite operator might also seek surreptitiously to use that satellite as security for other loans, thus raising the issue of priorities of security interests. It is these kinds of international movements of mobile equipment and of creditors' security interests that the Space Protocol is intended to chronicle and regulate.

44 Goode, Commentary, *supra* n. 28, at 2.118.
45 Cape Town Convention, *supra* n. 11, Arts. 20. 1 and 3. Goode, Commentary, *supra* n. 28, at 2.121.
46 Cape Town Convention, *supra* n. 11, Arts. 18–20, Protocol, Art XXX.
47 Protocol, Art. II.1.
48 Protocol Art. II. 3. 'The Protocol does not apply to objects falling within the definition of "aircraft objects" under the Protocol to the Convention on International Interests in Mobile Equipment on Matters specific to Aircraft Equipment except where such objects are primarily designed for use in space, in which case the Protocol applies even while such objects are not in space.' For the Aviation Protocol see *supra* n. 13.
49 Protocol, Art. II.4. 'This Protocol does not apply to an aircraft object merely because it is designed to be temporarily in space.' The Protocol therefore will not apply to suborbital traffic when that business develops.
50 Protocol, Art. I.2.j, defines 'space' as 'outer space, including the Moon and other celestial bodies'.

Financial Leasing of 1988 as between those States that are parties to both that treaty and the Protocol.[51]

The Space Protocol will apply to three categories of interests.[52] First, the security interests created by agreement creating an encumbrance on a title to space assets in the form of a lien or mortgage. In case of default the creditor may sell the space assets to recover monies lent.[53] Second are conditional sales agreements under which title remains with the seller until the final payment. On default the seller may retake possession of the space asset.[54] Third are leasing agreements under which possession of a space asset is obtained by payment or a periodic fee or rental. Here title remains with the lessor.[55]

The Space Protocol applies only to space assets that can be identified as international interests in accordance with the Cape Town Convention.[56] To qualify as a space asset it must first be man-made. Second, it must be uniquely identifiable. Under Protocol, Art. VII, a description of a space asset is satisfactory for that purpose if it describes by item, by type and by a statement that the agreement covers all present and future space assets except for specified items or types. Third, the space asset must be designed and intended to be launched into outer space. Fourth, the space asset must be a spacecraft such as 'a satellite, space station, space module, space capsule, space vehicle or reusable launch vehicle' or a payload that can be individually registered, or a part thereof such as a transponder that can be separately registered, 'including all accessories, parts and equipment and all data, manuals and records relating thereto.'[57]

The ownership of rights or interests in a space asset is not affected by the docking of the asset with another space asset in space, by its installation on or removal from another space asset, or the return of space asset from outer space (Art. III). The Protocol extends the

---

51 Protocol, Art. XXVI. The Convention deals with the leasing of equipment. See the UNIDROIT Convention on International Financial Leasing, Ottawa, 1988, 2321 UNTS 197; (1988) 27 ILM 931; www.unidroit. org/instruments/leasing/convention/.

52 For a good discussion of the scope of the Protocol, see Sundahl (2013) *supra* n. 28, at 30–33.

53 See definitions of security agreement and of security interest in the Cape Town Convention, *supra* n. 11: Art. 1(ii): 'security agreement' means an agreement by which a chargor grants or agrees to grant to a chargee an interest (including an ownership interest) in or over an object to secure the performance of any existing or future obligation of the chargor or a third person. Art. 1 (jj) 'security interest' means an interest created by a security agreement.

54 Cape Town Convention, *supra* n. 11, Art. 1(ll): 'title reservation agreement' means an agreement for the sale of an object on terms that ownership does not pass until fulfilment of the condition or conditions stated in the agreement.

55 Protocol, Art I. 1: 'In this Protocol except where the context otherwise requires, terms used in it have the meanings set out in the Convention.' Cape Town Convention, *supra* n. 11, Art. 1(q): 'leasing agreement' means an agreement by which one person (the lessor) grants a right to possession or control of an object (with or without an option to purchase) to another person (the lessee) in return for a rental or other payment.'

56 Convention, Arts. 1 and 2; Protocol, Arts. I and II.

57 More fully Protocol Art. I.2(k) defines the term thus: 'space asset' means a man-made uniquely identifiable asset in space or designed to be launched into space and comprising (i) a spacecraft, such as a satellite, space station, space module, space capsule, space vehicle or reusable launch vehicle, whether or not including a space asset falling within (ii) or (iii) below. (ii) a payload (whether telecommunications, navigation observation, scientific or otherwise or otherwise) in respect of which a separate registration may be effected in accordance with the regulations, or (iii) a part of a spacecraft or payload such as a transponder, in respect of which a separate regulation may be effected in accordance with the regulations, together with all installed, incorporated or attached accessories, parts and equipment and all data manuals and records relating thereto.' See also Sundahl (2013) *supra* n. 28, at 46–48.

Cape Town Convention to include sales of space assets. Convention Article 1(gg) defines a sale as 'a transfer of ownership of an object pursuant to a contract of sale.' Accordingly under Protocol Art. IV, the buyer of a space asset may protect the purchaser's title to the space asset simply by registering it as an international interest.[58]

The contract of sale of a space asset must comply with particular formalities for it to be Eligible to be classed an international interest (Protocol Art. V). The agreement must be in writing, must concern a space asset that the seller has authority to sell, and the space asset must be identifiable in accordance with the Protocol. It must transfer the seller's interests to the buyer, and the registration of the sale must be without a time limit. International interests in space assets and asset rights under the Convention and the Protocol may be registered by any person having that interest, or through an agent or trustee or other representatives (Art. VI).

Under Convention Arts. 2. 2 and 7(c) each Protocol may set the requirements for the registration of assets in its registry. For the Space Protocol a description is satisfactory if it describes the space asset by item, contains a description of the space asset by type, and that the agreement covers all present and future space assets except for specified items or types (Art. VII.1). Future space assets can be similarly identified, and an international interest constituted as soon as the chargor, conditional seller or lessor acquires the power to dispose of the space asset, without the need for any new act of transfer (Art. VII.2).[59]

Protocol Art. VIII provides choice of law rules for specific situations unless a contracting state expressly exempts itself from the choice of law provisions.[60] Except when the parties to a relevant contract agree on different choice of law, the law applicable will be the domestic law of the state designated by the parties (Art. VIII.2–3). However interpretation must take the international character of the Convention into consideration. Disputes arising under the Convention and the Protocol must be settled 'in conformity with the general principles on which it is based or in the absence of such principles, in conformity with the applicable law'. That law is the domestic rule of law based on the choice of law rules of the forum state.[61] The courts will apply the national choice of law rules in situations not otherwise provided. As Sundahl indicates, the issue of the validity of the security agreement itself would be governed by local law.[62] In the case of a state consisting of several territorial units, such as the United States, Canada or Australia, where the relevant individual law of the units may differ, the choice of law will be in accordance with the laws of the unit that is the forum territory (Conv. Art. 5.4; Protocol Art. VIII.3).[63]

The Protocol visualises a lively trade in international interests because banks and other financiers frequently trade loans and assign rights to payments under those loans. Thus the purchaser steps into the shoes of the seller and acquires the seller's rights to payments as well as rights of recourse in the event of the debtor's failure to make payment. Chapter IX of the Convention (Arts. 31–38) provides for assignment of associated rights, defined

---

58 See Sundahl, *supra* n. 28, at 78.
59 See Sundahl, *supra* n. 28, at 46–48.
60 Pursuant to Art. XLI.2(a) of the Protocol. Cf. Y. Zhao, 'Legal Issues in China's Future Participation in the Space Protocol to the Cape Town Convention', in P.M. Sterns and L.I. Tennen, eds., *Private Law, Public Law, Metalaw and Public Policy in Space* (Vienna: Springer, 2016).
61 Cape Town Convention, Art 5.1–3.
62 Sundahl, *supra* n. 28, at 116.
63 Sundahl, *supra* n. 28, at 117.

in Art. 1(c) as 'rights of payments or other performance by a debtor under an agreement which are secured by or associated with the object.'[64]

Article I.2(h) of the Protocol defines 'rights assignment' as: 'a contract by which the debtor confers on the creditor an interest (including an ownership interest) in or over the whole, or part of existing or future debtor's rights to secure the performance of, or in reduction or discharge of, any existing or future obligation of the debtor to the creditor which under the agreement creating or providing for the international interest is secured by or associated with the space asset to which the agreement relates'. By Art. I.2(i), a 'rights reassignment' is where the creditor transfers to an assignee, or an assignee transfers to a subsequent assignee the whole or part or rights of interest under a rights assignment, or a debtors rights otherwise transferred under the Protocol.[65]

A rights assignment also applies to the transfer to the buyer of a space asset 'rights to payment or other performance due or to become due to the debtor by any person with respect to a space asset' (Art. IV.2). An enforceable assignment of a debtor's right requires the assignment to be in writing. The assignment must clearly identify the debtor's rights that are the subject of the assignment, the space asset concerned, and 'in the case of a rights assignment by way of security, the obligations secured by the agreement', but the amount of money secured need not be stated (Art. IX). In consequence of a rights assignment, the debtor transfers to the creditor 'the subject of the rights assignment to the extent permitted by the applicable law'. Defences and set-off rights of the obligor against the creditor are determined by the applicable law; and the obligor may waive those defences and rights of set-off, except for 'defences arising from fraudulent acts on the part of the creditor' (Art. X) Assignment of future rights takes effect without new and additional acts of transfer at such time in the future when those rights mature (Art. XI).

The current holder of assigned rights may register them by identifying them. Thus a search certificate issued by the registrar will disclose those rights and their current holder. Ultimate discharge of the registration of the international interest will include the registration of the assigned rights (Art. XI). The recording of the assignment of rights results in transfer of rights of priority over any other transfer of the debtor's rights. The recording or attempted recording of a space asset that does not qualify as an international interest does not become effective unless and until it matures into an international interest. However, when that happens the record becomes effective as of the time when recorded (Art. XIII). To the extent they have been assigned to a creditor under a rights assignment, rights of the debtor must be paid to the creditor, but only if the creditor duly notifies the debtor in writing of the assignment and identifies the rights assigned (Art. XIV).[66]

Assigned rights in international interests may be reassigned.[67] Reassigned rights may be registered in the registry 'only as part of the registration of the assignment of the

---

64 Under Convention Art. 35. 1 and 36 assignees of associated rights are only given priority over other space assets to the extent that they relate to sums lent for purchase of a space object, sums used for purchase of another space object in which the assignor holds another duly registered international interest, or monies used for purchase, rental or other obligation relating to the space object.

65 By Convention Arts. 31–32 rights of a debtor may be transferred to a creditor. Under Protocol Art. XII.4(a) such transfer operates as an assignment.

66 Protocol, Art. XIV.1–2. Broadly a debtor may assign any income stream related to a space asset that is due to the debtor. This could include the assignment of accounts receivable and other obligations of performance. See Sundahl, *supra* n. 28, at 72–73.

67 *Supra* n. 65. Sundahl, *supra* n. 28, at 74–75.

international interest to the person to whom the rights reassignment was made' (Art. XV). Finally the parties may by special written agreement agree to derogate from or vary the Protocol provisions regarding rights assignments, with the exception of Art. XVII.1–2, which relate to remedies in case of default (Art. XVI).

The possibility that a debtor might fail to meet the conditions of the security agreement renders essential the default remedies and enforcement procedures that are available to creditors.[68] Convention Art. 8.1 lists the remedies available to a creditor in the case of default. These are to take possession of the object, to sell or lease the asset, or to obtain the income or profits from the use of the asset.[69] Protocol Art. XVII modifies these by creating two alternative default remedies. Under Alternative A, the debtor will be obligated to give possession or control of the defaulted space asset to the creditor within a specific time period. The creditor may retain possession or control until the debtor has remedied the default. The creditor is free to pursue other remedies. This alternative is most favourable to the creditor.[70] Under Alternative B the debtor may either cure the default and recommence performance of the contract or give possession or control of the space asset to the creditor in accordance with applicable law. If the debtor fails to do either of these, a court, in accordance with applicable law, may make decisions regarding the debt and the international interest.[71] The insertion of the state court having the primary insolvency jurisdiction into the remedial process is the main difference between the alternatives.[72]

At ratification a Protocol contracting state may choose to apply one of the two alternatives, however, the two alternatives only become relevant if the state decides to adopt one of the two,[73] otherwise Protocol Art. XXI, does not become applicable. Alternatives A and B are not mandatory for the parties to a security agreement, because Protocol Art. XVI specifically provides that: 'The parties may by agreement in writing, exclude the application of Article XXI of this Protocol and, in their relations with each other, derogate from or vary the effect of any of the provisions of this Protocol except Article XVII.2.'[74] Assuming that the creditor obtains possession and control of the defaulted space assets, then the income stream from the space asset must be applied to satisfy the creditors' claims and the costs of processing them (Convention Art. 8).

The enforcement of default remedies is facilitated if the parties agree in the security agreement as a condition of financing to place the command code of the space asset, and related data, in escrow with a third person in order to facilitate the creditor's repossession and control of the asset as is allowed by Art. XIX.

---

68 P.B. Larsen, 'Creditors' Secured Interests in Satellites' (1991) 34 *Proc. IISL* 233–239 at 233.
69 There are actually three possibilities because the parties to the security agreement may themselves decide to apply neither Alternative A nor Alternative B, in which case local law applies. See Goode Commentary, *supra* n. 8, on likely enforcement approaches., on likely enforcements approaches.
70 Protocol, Art. XXI, Alternative A. This alternative is more advantageous to the creditor.
71 Protocol Art. XXI, Alternative B. This alternative is more advantageous to the debtor.
72 See Protocol Art. I(4) as to the contracting state in which a space object or space asset is considered to be located for the purpose of the court proceeding.
73 Protocol Art. XLI.1–4. The courts of contracting states are to apply Art. XXI in accordance with the declaration of the contracting state that has the primary insolvency jurisdiction: Art. XLI.5. Art. XLI. 4 allows a state that consists of several legal units to apply Art. XXI as it sees fit.
74 Protocol Art. XVII.2 requires at least 14 calendar days' notice of the sale of an international interests in a space asset.

Describing how default remedies under the Space Protocol differ significantly from remedies under the Aviation Protocol Goode states: 'Physical repossession is likely to be impracticable; in the ordinary way the only types of action capable of affecting the availability of the space asset or physically linked space asset are electronic interference and constructive repossession in the shape of the assumption of control through such measures as the taking over of command codes.'[75] Consequently creditor remedies under the Protocol are more likely to consist of negotiated settlements with the debtors and access to the stream of income from the space assets in outer space, rather than physical repossession.

The default remedies available to creditors are, however, limited by public laws affecting the national interests of the contracting states. Under OST Art. VI states must authorise and supervise the activities of their private and public entities for compliance with international space law. The default remedies under the Protocol are subject to the authority of a contracting state to authorize service. Furthermore, the default remedies under the Space Protocol are subject to state regulations on export of controlled goods and national security (Art. XXVI).

Default remedies must also to a limited extent respect the public service needs of the contracting states.[76] Protocol Art. XXVII provides that the contracting state and the parties may file a Public Service Notice with the registrar to inform the public of the state's interest in maintaining the service provided by the space asset. Such a notice may limit or delay the creditor exercising any of the previously described default remedies to the extent that they would affect public services. The public service notice must specify the duration of the delay, which may not be longer than six months. Both the debtor and the state must be notified specially. The delay will not prevent the creditor from continuing to provide the service in question. Furthermore, after the delay time expires the creditor is able to exercise the delayed default remedies.

In sum, enforcement of default remedies will be limited. Repossession and the exercise of control over space assets in orbit are likely to be limited. The debtor's cooperation will be necessary for an orderly transfer of control to the creditor. However, cooperation by a debtor may be handicapped because the debtor may be in liquidation and unable to control the assets in question.[77]

Salvage

Salvage of space assets is common in the space insurance industry. In case of failure of the space assets, the insurers are required to pay the value of the space assets. An insurer receives salvage rights to the space assets, that is, the legal or contractual right to their remaining value after the insurer's payment of the loss.[78] During the Space Protocol negotiations insurers elected to forgo registration of salvage rights as international interests. Consequently, the Protocol leaves salvage rights to space assets wholly outside its scope, and these remain subject to national laws.[79] Protocol Art. IV provides that nothing

---

75 Goode *Commentary*, *supra* n. 28, at 3.82.
76 See Sundahl, *supra* n. 28, at 104 and Weber-Steinhaus, *supra* n. 26.
77 See Weber-Steinhaus, *supra* n. 26, at 222.
78 Protocol, Art. IV.3.
79 Cf. personal report by P.B. Larsen at www.iislweb.org/docs/2012_unidroit.pdf.

in the treaty 'affects any legal or contractual rights of an insurer to salvage recognized by applicable law.'[80]

The Space Protocol, the UN Space Treaties and the ITU

Protocol Art. XXX simply provides that: 'The [Cape Town] Convention as applied to space assets shall not affect State Party rights and obligations under the existing United Nations outer space treaties or instruments of the International Telecommunication Union'.[81] Nonetheless, because the new private law treaty cuts across these public law treaties it is necessary to consider its relationship with them. To an extent the public law treaties delimit the scope and operation of the Space Protocol. Indeed, from the first discussions that initiated the Protocol it was assumed that public law would prevail over private law. That was almost so fundamental that it did not need to be stated *in haec verba*.[82] As OST Art. III affirms, activities in outer space are subject to international law and the Charter of the United Nations. Licensing decisions authorised under space law must happen for there to be an enterprise to which the mechanisms of the Convention and Protocol may become associated. Various considerations may intrude.

There is a difference in scope between the Protocol and the existing space law treaties. The space law treaties apply only to space objects but none of them fully define the term, whereas the Protocol applies to space assets and defines the term.[83] An 'international interest' as defined in Convention Art. 1(r) and Art. 2 can be registered under the Protocol. Again, for the purposes of the Protocol Article I.3 classifies as an 'internal transaction' falling within the terms of the Convention a transaction taking place within the state of registry of the relevant object if the transaction takes place when the space asset is located in outer space.[84] If the object is not in space when the transaction takes place Art. I.4 adds the contracting state that has licensed the operation of the space object and the contracting state where the mission control centre for its operation is located. It would seem that if a security interest is constituted while a space object is in space, in the absence of registration of the space object with an appropriate state the Protocol is irrelevant. However, as we have noted elsewhere there may be a divergence of view as to where a space object should be registered.[85]

80 Protocol, Art. IV.3. See Sundahl, *supra* n. 28, at 111.
81 Although it can be overridden by specific provision in the later treaty, the general rule is that a treaty later in time prevails over previous treaty: Art. 30, Vienna Convention on Law of Treaties, 1969, 1155 UNTS 332. Most of the Convention, including Art. 30, is accepted as a statement or codification of customary law.
82 P.B. Larsen's personal recollection as a member of the original space industry working group, *supra* n. 33. Larsen, *supra* n. 28, at 378.
83 Protocol Art. I.2(k) enumerates the 'space assets' to which an 'international interest' and therefore the Protocol may apply. Clearly in terms of the UN treaties they are 'space objects'. See *supra* n. 57. Liability Convention Art. I(b) says that for it the term 'space object' includes 'component parts'.
84 Registration must be under the OST, the Registration Convention or UNGA Res. 1721: Protocol Art. I.3(a)–(c).
85 Art. II.1 of the Registration Convention requires the launching state to register the launch in a domestic registry and by Art. IV to inform the UN Secretary General of particular data as to the space object. Art. I.(a) (i)–(ii) identifies for the purpose four possible 'launching states' – the State which launches the object, the State which procures the launch, the state from whose territory a space object is launched, and a state from whose facility an object is launched. Where there are multiple contenders they must agree among themselves

The need for the registration of a space object in the state registry system may have other effects that could constrain the operation of the Cape Town regime. Parties to the OST are required to authorise and supervise the activities of their nongovernmental entities and bear international responsibility for those activities as well as their own (Art. VI).[86] Such state authority involves a licensing process during which the licensing authority, among other concerns, may be concerned about the arrangements for the financing of the enterprise, including concluded or potential asset-based financing.[87]

By OST Art. VII, launching states, whether or not they are the state of registry, are internationally liable for damage caused to states and to individuals whether on Earth, or in outer space or on a celestial body. Thus states are fully liable for damages caused by both governmental and the nongovernmental entities which they may license to conduct space activities. In addition, as discussed in Chapter 4, any liability for damage is further refined by the Liability Convention, when it is applicable. States licensing space activities might be particularly concerned about the possible consequences of participating in a launch. A few states are parties to the OST but are not parties to the Registration Convention, which might affect their licensing decisions.[88]

By OST Art. VIII, the state of registry of a space object launched into outer space 'shall retain jurisdiction and control over such object and over any personnel thereof, while in outer space or on a celestial body', which would include the jurisdiction of its national courts.[89] Therefore the increasing practice of transferring space objects to non-launching states presents a problem.[90] In the case of a default under a security, only the courts of the state of registry have jurisdictional power to order default remedies, determine priorities and enforce assignments. That would be particularly important for an investor who seeks to recover title to, or control of space assets designated as security of a loan. The retention

---

which is to act as the state of registry (Art. II.2). For discussion see Chapter 4. As of 1 January 2023 75 states had ratified the Registration Convention.

An estimated 7% of space objects remain unregistered. See S. Di Pippo, 'Registration of Space Objects with the Secretary-General': www.unoosa.org/documents/pdf/copuos/lsc/2016/symp-03.pdf. See also S. Di Pippo, 'Registration of Space Objects with the United Nations Secretary-General' (2016) 63 ZLW 364–374 and discussion in Chapter 4, c. n. 51ff.

86 'The activities of nongovernmental entities in outer space as commercial space activities described in Article VI (Outer Space Treaty 1967) owe their existence and legitimacy to public international law', per L.J. Smith in *Contracting for Space, supra* n. 26, at 45.

87 Peripherally we note that states may also be concerned about national security.

88 As of 1 January 2023 113 states were parties to the OST. The Registration Convention definition of space object includes component parts as well as launch vehicles and parts thereof (Art. I(b)): cf. the definition of space assets under Art. I.2(k) of the Protocol, detailed *supra* n. 57.

89 P.B. Larsen, 'The Space Protocol to the Cape Town Convention and the Space Law Treaties' (2012) 55 *Proc. IISL* 195–207; S. Aoki, 'In Search of the Current Legal Status of Registration of Space Objects' (2010) 53 *Proc. IISL*, 245–255. See also CoCoSL I, at 156. However, Art. II.2 of the Registration Convention does contemplate that states may agree that aspects of jurisdiction and control of an object be exercised by different states. Cf. Cheng, *supra* n. 30, at 484, on the legal uncertainties regarding jurisdiction created by the Registration Convention. See also UNGA Res. 62/101, 'Recommendations on Enhancing the Practice of States and International Intergovernmental Organizations in Registering Space Objects' (2007); CoCoSL III, 401–481 and discussion in Chapter 4.

90 K-U. Horl and J. Hermida, 'Change of Ownership, Change of Registry? Which Objects to Register. What Data to Be Furnished. When, and Until When?' (2003) 48 *Proc. IISL* 454–463. See also Chatzipanagiotis, *infra* n. 94. Note also the (US) Commercial Space Launch Competitiveness Act, H.R. 2262, 114th Congress (2014–2016) purporting to give the US Federal Courts exclusive jurisdiction over all claims to asteroid resources made by US nationals. See discussion in Chapter 7.

of jurisdiction and control by the state of registry clearly reflects the thinking and technology of 1967. That may not fit the present needs of the nongovernmental entities which readily transfer space assets to purchasers in other states. Creditors may need to enforce default remedies in other jurisdictions.[91]

Last, we note that OST Art. IX, adds the avoidance of 'harmful contamination and also adverse changes' to the Earth's environment to the requirements of state control over nongovernmental activities in their space activities.

Because all the currently space competent states are parties to the OST all security agreements may be affected by these public space law restrictions because the OST requires that space activities be licensed and supervised. The ability of nongovernmental entities to enter into security agreements that in any way limit the prerogatives of the responsible state is constrained. While this may be a restriction on doing business, it is not new. It is a restriction that has existed since nongovernmental activities were given access to outer space on the OST terms.

That said, some consider that OST Art. VIII does not confer exclusive jurisdiction and control to the state of registry. Weber-Steinhaus is of the view that the jurisdictional provisions of Art. VIII were not intended to apply to private law.[92] Sundahl argues that such an interpretation would be absurd because the Protocol would be severely limited if creditors could not take enforcement action in a state which controls a space asset,[93] and refers to authors who argue that jurisdiction under the Outer Space Treaty Art. VIII is not exclusive.[94] Nevertheless, the issue cannot be avoided because of the specificity of the language of the Outer Space Treaty. In the event of default in a relevant security agreement, those space objects may come to be owned and managed by creditors in other states over which the launching state has little control. Irresponsible management of those space objects may result in substantial liability for the launching state.

OST Art. VII, provides that 'each State Party from whose territory or facility an object is launched, is internationally liable for damage to another State Party to the Treaty or to its natural or juridical person by such object or its component parts on the Earth, in air space or in outer space, including the Moon and other celestial bodies.' This sweeping unlimited liability of the launching, procuring, territorial and facilitating states could result in extensive liability of those states for damages caused by its own financed space objects and for financed space objects that it authorises to be launched. Potential liability may result in state intervention affecting financing contracts in order to ascertain that licensees have adequate resources to meet compensation for damages caused, thus freeing the launching state from secondary liability under Article VII.

There may be particular concern about the liability consequences of transfers of jurisdiction and control to non-launching states. Such transfers could happen when creditors from non-launching states gain control through default in compliance with securities granted by operators in launching states.[95] The continuing liability of states for damage caused by the

---

91 Sundahl, *supra* n. 28, at 175–176.
92 Weber-Steinhaus, *supra* n. 26, at 222.
93 Sundahl, *supra* n. 28, at 271.
94 M. Chatzipanagiotis, 'Registration of Space Objects and Transfer of Ownership in Outer Space' (2007) 56 ZLW 229–238.
95 CoCoSL I at 156–158. See also Weber-Steinhaus, *supra* n. 26, at 223, stating that transfer of control from the jurisdiction of a launching state leaves that state in an undesirable and risky situation because it cannot control the space object for which it is liable.

space activities of nongovernmental entities is a burden because of the increasing volume of trade in space assets by which states transfer control over space objects for which they nevertheless remain liable. Repossession and control by creditors in default situations will further aggravate this strain.[96]

Finally we would underline that the Protocol, as delimited by the OST, can function within the limits of that Treaty, just as financing arrangements not falling within the scope of the Protocol presently function within its constraints and those of the other space treaties.

Trade Restrictions Based on National Security

Throughout the world agreements between private individuals are subject to public policy and national public laws. Public policy also affects the willingness of states to enter into agreements with other states under which technology is transferred physically or in the form of intellectual property. Considerations of national security impinge on the sale, transfer or lease of space assets, their technology and their financing. Virtually any space asset may serve both military and civilian purposes either directly or through the possibility of it being adapted or the technology analysed, copied and perhaps used for nefarious purposes.[97] One example we consider in Chapter 11 is the Global Navigation Satellite System (GNSS). Again some technology supplied for one purpose, might could be analysed and copied to the benefit of a foreign manufacturer.[98] As a result many states restrict the export of space equipment or related intellectual property so that other states may not gain military or other advantage from knowledge of that technology. The degree of concern over such matters does vary between states, but at bedrock security is always a major concern.[99] Broadly the multilateral international agreements on trade would need to be greatly strengthened in order to satisfy the concerns of security-conscious states before they would replace the stricter unilateral restrictions that can be imposed by individual countries. As it is, however, some international agreements are important. Within Europe, for example, there is an agreement between ESA state members and ESA as an agency as to the protection and exchange of classified information.[100] For the West, however, the unilateral US trade restrictions often remain the most relevant.[101]

The first major attempt at establishing multilateral arrangements as to the transfer and export of militarily sensitive materials was COCOM, the Coordinating Committee for Multilateral Export Controls, established in 1949 as an informal and unofficial

---

96 Sundahl, *supra* n. 28, at 153; Larsen, *supra* n. 28, at 385.

97 Cf. the Wassenaar Dual-Use list, *infra* n. 103.

98 Cf. the restrictions and freedoms in the 'original' INTELSAT arrangements as to the use of patents and other technology invented for INTELSAT purposes: F. Lyall, *Law and Space Telecommunications* (Aldershot: Dartmouth; Brookfield: Gower, 1989) 129–141.

99 Cf. National Space Policy of the United States of America, 6 December 2020: https://trumpwhitehouse. archives.gov/wp-content/uploads/2020/12/National-Space-Policy.pdf and the US National Defense Space Strategy June 2020: https://media.defense.gov/2020/Jun/17/2002317391/-1/-1/1/2020. See also Unilateral Trade Restrictions Based on National Security, and Chapter 15 *infra*.

100 Agreement between [the ESA states and ESA] for the Protection and Exchange of Classified Information, Paris, 19 August 2002, UKTS Misc. No. 14 (2003), Cm. 5936. The UK has not yet ratified this Agreement. The UK has concluded a number of bilateral agreements with ESA members and others that cover such matters. We have not explored what other states have done in this regard,

101 Cf. the effect of US requirements on Galileo, Chapter 11 *supra*. See *infra* as to 'Unilateral Arms Controls'. Cf. J.L. Spencer, 'State Supervision of Space Activity' (2009) 63 *A.F.L. Rev.* 75–128.

system based in the US Embassy in Paris.[102] Under it three control lists of munitions, nuclear related material and high-technology industrial items, were agreed. Applications by members to export such had to have the unanimous approval of the other members, the intention being to supervise and on occasion block trade in them. COCOM was dissolved in 1994 since it proved unable to cope with the change in the then international situation.

The Wassenaar Arrangement, the largest of the current multilateral arms control agreements, has been operational since 1996.[103] A voluntary international agreement between some forty very diverse states scattered around the globe. Its Secretariat is in Vienna. Interestingly, and in contrast to COCOM, Russia and other former members of the Communist bloc are members.104 In terms of its 'Initial Elements' participation in the Arrangement is open on a global and non-discriminatory basis to states that comply with certain agreed criteria, but entry to membership is subject to the consensus of existing participants.[105] Criteria include whether a potential member state is a manufacturer or an exporter of arms or industrial equipment, whether it has taken the Wassenaar lists as a referent in its export controls, whether its export controls and its non-proliferation policies are fully effective. Operating through an annual plenary meeting and often on the basis of the recommendations of subsidiary bodies, decisions are taken by consensus, and the deliberations of the participating states are confidential. The Arrangement requires export control to be exercised in relation to both conventional arms and dual-use goods and technologies. Participants must inform other members when conventional arms or dual use equipment are transferred from one country to another. The intentions are to promote transparency, to increase responsibility; and to establish reporting requirements. However, one criticism is that the Arrangement does not have an effective enforcement mechanism, being

---

102 K.A. Dursht, 'From Containment to Cooperation: Collective Action and the Wassenaar Arrangement' (1997) 19 *Cardozo L. Rev.* 1079–1124 at 1098–1106.

103 Wassenaar Arrangement on Export Controls for Conventional Arms and Dual-Use Goods and Technologies: www.wassenaar.org/. See the *Founding Documents*: www.wassenaar.org/app/uploads/2021/12/Public-Docs-Vol-I-Founding-Documents.pdf, and the compilation Public Documents, Vol. IV: www.wassenaar. org/app/uploads/2022/12/Public-Docs-Vol-IV-Background-Docs-and-Plenary-related-and-other-Statements-Dec.-2022.pdf. Public Documents, Vol. II is the 'List of Dual-Use Goods and Technologies and Munitions List: www.wassenaar.org/app/uploads/2022/12/List-of-Dual-Use-Goods-and-Technologies-Munitions-List-Dec-2022.pdf.

   P. van Fenema, 'Export Controls and Satellite Launches: What's New?' (2003) 46 *Proc. IISL* 239–245; L. Crapart, 'The Implementation of Export Controls in the European Community – Making Balance Between Security and Commercial Considerations' (2003) 46 *Proc. IISL* 246–249.

   Cf. I. Pyetranker, 'An Umbrella in a Hurricane: Cyber Technology and the December 2013 Amendment to the Wassenaar Arrangement' (2015) 13 *Nw. J. Tech. & Intel. Prop.* 153–180; Cf. materials cited *infra* n. 120.

104 The 42 current (2023) members are: Argentina, Australia, Austria, Belgium, Bulgaria, Canada, Croatia, Czech Republic, Denmark, Estonia, Finland, France, Germany, Greece, Hungary, India, Ireland, Italy, Japan, Latvia, Lithuania, Luxembourg, Malta, Mexico, The Netherlands, New Zealand, Norway, Poland, Portugal, Republic of Korea, Romania, the Russian Federation, Slovakia, Slovenia, South Africa, Spain, Sweden, Switzerland, Turkey, Ukraine, UK and US – a fascinating collection.

105 See the compilation of Best Practice Documents, December 2022: www.wassenaar.org/app/uploads/2022/12/Public-Docs-Vol-III-Comp.-of-Best-Practice-Documents-Dec.-2022.pdf, and www. wassenaar.org/best-practices/. Cf. R. Jakhu and J. Wilson, 'The New United States Export Control Regime: Its Impact on the Communications Satellite Industry' (2000) 25 AASL 157; Dursht, *supra* n. 102, and Shehadeh, *infra* n. 106.

dependent on compliance and self-enforcement by its members. Another is that it does not necessarily achieve its aims.[106] It remains, however, significant.[107]

The Missile Technology Control Regime (MTCR)[108] is another voluntary inter-state arrangement, originally established in 1987, between Canada, France, Germany, Italy, Japan, the UK and the US.[109] Admission to membership of the MTCR depends upon the consensus of existing members. Examined is whether a prospective member would strengthen the regime, whether it is committed to the aims of the MTCR, whether it has a strong export control system that would implement the regime, and whether it enforces these controls.

MTCR works through annual plenary meetings, with intercalated informal meetings and discussions to restrict the proliferation of missiles, complete rocket systems and unmanned air vehicles as well as of related technologies that might carry a 500 kg payload at least 300 km (186 miles). It also covers systems intended for the delivery of weapons of mass destruction. MTCR issues 'Guidelines for Sensitive Missile-Relevant Transfers'[110] which are augmented by an Annex on 'Equipment, Software and Technology'.[111]

The Annex distinguishes between Category I items and Category II items and covers a variety of space-related items.[112] Category I items include equipment, materials, relevant software and technology. If any of these are included in a system, the system is also classified as Category I unless it can be separated or otherwise duplicated. Category I items are subject to presumption of denial of permission to export. Category II covers a wide area of parts, components such as propellants, structural materials, test equipment and flight instruments. These may be exported on a case-by-case basis. As under the Wassenaar Arrangement, the MTCR depends on self-enforcement by its members. There is no mechanism other than the political to deal with a 'breach' of its terms.

106 K.K. Shehadeh, 'The Wassenaar Arrangement and Encryption Controls: An Ineffective Export Control Regime that Compromises United States' Economic Interests' (1999) 15 *Am. U. Int. L. Rev.* 271–320; R.J. Seivert, 'Urgent Message to Congress – Nuclear Triggers to Libya, Missile Guidance to China, Air Defense to Iraq, Arms Supplier to the World: Has the Time Finally Arrived to Overhaul the U.S. Export Control Regime – The Case for Immediate Reform of Our Outdated, Ineffective, and Self-Defeating Export Control System' (2002) 37 *Tex. Int. L.J.* 89–110.

107 E.S. Waldrop, 'Integration of Military and Civilian Space Assets: Legal and National Security Implications' (2004) 55 *Air Force L. Rev.* 157–231 at 190–192; J. Jafer, 'Strengthening the Wassenaar Export Control Regime' (2002) 3 *Chi. J. Int. L.* 519–526.

108 The Missile Technology Control Regime: https://mtcr.info/.

109 Missile Technology Control Regime: http://mtcr.info/partners. Membership as of 2023 is thirty-five: Argentina, Australia, Austria, Belgium, Bulgaria, Brazil, Canada, Czech Republic, Denmark, Finland, France, Germany, Greece, Hungary, Iceland, India, Ireland, Italy, Japan, Luxembourg, The Netherlands, New Zealand, Norway, Poland, Portugal, Republic of Korea, the Russian Federation, South Africa, Spain, Sweden, Switzerland, Turkey, Ukraine, UK and US. Adherents are Estonia, Kazakhstan and Latvia. The dates of joining and absences are instructive.

110 MTCR Guidelines for Sensitive Missile-Relevant Transfers: https://mtcr.info/guidelines-for-sensitive-missile-relevant-transfers/.

111 MTCR Annex: https://mtcr.info/wordpress/wp-content/uploads/2022/10/MTCR-TEM-Technical_Annex_2022-10-21-Final.pdf.

112 Annex Part 2 'Definitions' include ballistic missiles, space launch vehicles, unmanned air vehicles and cruise missiles. GPS/GNSS satellites are included in the Regime as Category II Item 11 'Avionics' materials since they may be used to guide cruise missiles.

The Hague International Code of Conduct against Ballistic Missile Cooperation, 2002 (HCOC),[113] supplements the Missile Technology Control Regime (MTCR). Any state may subscribe to the Code.[114] Annual and other meetings are held (Art. 5.a) but decisions are only by consensus (Art. 5.b). Under the Code members agree to restrain the proliferation of missiles. The Code applies to space vehicles because space vehicle programmes may be used to conceal ballistic missile programmes or the proliferation of such technologies (Art. 2.f and g).[115] Transparency in order to increase mutual confidence is the major aim of the Code (Art. 4.a). Members annually declare their ballistic missile and space vehicle programmes (Art. 4.i – ii), the latter to the extent consistent with principles of commercial and economic requirements (Art. 4.a.ii). They also notify each other in advance of launches into outer space or test flights giving details of the planned launch notification window, the launch area and the planned direction of launch (Art. 4.a.iii).[116] Detail is also annually reported as to what has been done in the previous year (Art. 4.a.i – ii). Subscribers to the Code are resolved to exercise vigilance in assisting the space vehicle programmes of other countries so as to prevent contributing to delivery systems for weapons of mass destruction (Art. 3.d), to exercise the maximum restraint in their own ballistic missile programmes including if possible the reduction of national missile holdings (Art. 3.c), and not to contribute to or support a foreign ballistic missile programme that contravenes the obligations of that country under international disarmament and non-proliferation treaties (Art. 3.e). All of which looks very well, but the HCOC has no enforcement mechanism. All that exists is the voluntary resolution of questions that may be raised, particularly from the various declarations (Art. 5.c bullet point 2). That said, the HCOC aims could usefully inform the decisions of states as to their own export control rules and procedures.

Unilateral Trade Restrictions Based on National Security

When states consider multilateral trade controls weak, they adopt unilateral controls. One example is the US Export Control legislation of 1999, the result of US congressional concern over the export of satellites to China.[117] It establishes national security as of primary importance as against the interests of business, and significantly restricts the US export of advanced satellite technology. It also restricts the onward export by other countries of

---

113 'International Code of Conduct against Ballistic Missile Proliferation', The Hague, 26 November 2002: www.hcoc.at/background-documents/text-of-the-hcoc.html. For the organisation see www.hcoc.at/. Its original title was the 'International Code of Conduct against Ballistic Missile Cooperation' (ICOC); Van Fenema, *supra* n. 103.

114 As of January 2023 143 states had subscribed the Code: www.hcoc.at/subscribing-states/list-of-hcoc-subscribing-states.html.

115 Interestingly, under HCOC Art. 3.a subscribers to the Code resolve to 'ratify, accede to or otherwise abide by' the OST and the Liability and Registration Conventions.

116 Cf. S.C. Larrimore, 'International Space Launch Notifications and Data Exchange' (2007) 23 *Space Policy* 172–179. See also Chapter 4.

117 US Public Law 105–261, 1999. See Waldrop, *supra* n. 107, at 191–195. Luo, *infra* n. 129, at 448–472 details history of US controls and summarises some cases. See also B.R. Reed, 'The United Kingdom's New Export Control Act of 2002 and its Possible Impact on United Kingdom Universities and Academic Freedom: A Comparison of Export Control in the United States and the United Kingdom' (2003) 8 *UCLA J. Int. L. and For. Aff.* 193–237 at 198–215.

any restricted technology that originates in the US. The process includes the following elements:

1. Export licence plans must first be approved by the US Department of Defense (DOD).
2. A Crash Investigation licence is required for US participants in a foreign accident investigation. The DOD monitors such investigations. This requirement does not apply to members of NATO.
3. An annual report is made to US Congress on export of US satellites for launch by China.
4. Registration and licensing requirements include all articles whether of US or foreign manufacture. Nothing may be exported or imported without a licence. Violation is a criminal offence.
5. Munitions transactions with countries that support terrorism is prohibited.
6. A Presidential power of waiver of trade restrictions exists if essential for US national security.

US arms control is administered by the US Department of State (DOS) under the International Traffic in Arms Regulations (ITAR)[118] and by the US Department of Commerce (DOC) under the Export Administration Regulations (EARS).[119] A stricter US export control of space technology was established by the 1999 legislation when the US Congress transferred responsibility for satellite export control from the Department of Commerce (DOC) to the Department of State (DOS). Satellites were placed in the same export category as military weapons systems. DOS regulation has proved to be more extensive, restrictive and time-consuming than DOC regulation. Added regulation has resulted in added cost. Most of the consequential impact has been felt on the US satellite manufacturing business and its share of that world market has fallen. It is commonly considered that these export and import controls are also having adverse effects on the US launch vehicle market.[120] The 2010 US National Space Policy Statement[121] did adopt a more favourable export policy seeking 'to enhance the competitiveness of US space industrial base'.

---

118 International Traffic in Arms Regulations (ITAR): (US) 22 CFR Parts 120–130: www.pmddtc.state. gov/?id=ddtc_kb_article_page&sys_id=24d528fddbfc930044f9ff621f961987, and www.ecfr.gov/current/ title-22/.
119 Export Administration Regulations (EARS), 15 CFR Parts 730–730: www.ecfr.gov/current/title-15/ subtitle-B/chapter-VII/subchapter-C.
120 M.C. Mineiro, *Space Technology Export Controls and International Cooperation in Outer Space* (Dordrecht: Spring, 2014); P.J. Blount, 'The ITAR Treaty and its Implications for US Space Exploration Policy and the Commercial Space Industry' ((2008) 73 *J. Air L. & Comm.* 705–722; J.A. Crook, 'National Insecurity: Iftar and the Technological Impairment of US National Space Policy' (2009) 74 *J. Air L. & Comm.* 525–526; M.D. Burns, 'Tilting at Windmills – The Counterpoising Interests Driving the US Commercial Satellite Export Control Reforms Debate' (2010) 66 *A.F.L. Rev.* 255–330; R.L. Spencer, 'State Supervision of Space Activity' (2009) 63 *A.F.L. Rev.* 75–128; A. Bini, 'Export Controls of Space Items: Preserving Europe's Advantage' (2007) 23 *Space Policy* 70–72; R.C. Clifton and H. Stanislawski, 'Aerospace and Defense Industries' (2007) 41 *Int. Law.* 483–490; L.M. Weinberg and L. Van Buren, 'Impact of U.S. Export Controls and Sanctions on Employment' (2006) 35 *Public Contract L.J.* 537–62; R. Zelnio, 'A Short History of Export Control Policy' *The Space Review*, 9 January 2006: www.thespacereview.com/ article/528/1, and 'The Effect of Export Controls on the Space Industry', *The Space Review*, 16 January 2006: www.thespacereview.com/article/533/1. See also Chapter 15 *infra*.
121 Space Policy Statement, 2010 White House: https://obamawhitehouse.archives.gov/sites/default/files/ national_space_policy_6-28-10.pdf; modified by 2020 US National Defense Policy Statement, *supra* n. 99.

Accordingly more space-related products have been transferred from the DOS export controls to the more liberal Department of Commerce (DOC) export controls.[122]

The Russian seizure of the Crimean Peninsula in 2014 caused the United States to implement a series of sanctions based on national security, placing restrictions on Russia and on Russian individuals.[123] In 2017 US Congress adopted the Countering America's Adversaries Through Sanctions Act, Public Law 115–44, imposing further sanctions on Russia for actions threatening the peace in the Ukraine and in the Middle East. The renewal in 2022 of the Russia/Ukraine conflict resulted in additional export controls, visa restrictions, asset freezes, including sanctions on individual Russians together with restrictions on US citizens' investing in Russian commercial companies.[124] These were augmented by similar sanctions by European members of the North Atlantic Treaty Organization (NATO). In retaliation Russia reduced and/or terminated the flow of gas and oil through several pipelines to European countries resulting in shortages of energy.

China has also been of increasing concern to western nations, resulting it the imposition of some trade and other restrictions. A protectionist policy in the US continues to prevail. US unilateral trade restrictions on China are best illustrated by the so-called Wolf Amendment of 2013. The Wolf Amendment expresses US concerns to protect its space technology from being appropriated by China.[125] Another general example of trade restriction is the US Export Control legislation of 1999.[126] In 2022 the United States adopted further export controls on the availability of high technology of semiconductor computer chips.[127] China's reaction has been to urge bilateral and multilateral negotiations to resolve trade disputes with the US.[128]

---

122 For details of regulations issued by the State Department and the Commerce Department see links at 'Satellite Export Control Regulations' compiled by the Office of Space Commerce: www.space.commerce.gov/regulations/satellite-export-control-regulations/.

123 Executive Orders 13660, 13661, 13685, 13694, 13757.

124 See www.state.gov/ukraine-and-russia-sanctions/. See also Congressional Research Service, Russia's 2022 Invasions of Ukraine: Overview of US Sanctions and Other Responses: https://crsreports.congress.gov/product/pdf/IN/IN11869

125 The Wolf Amendment restricts NASA's ability to engage with China regarding space exploration.

    (a) None of the funds made available by this division may be used for the National Aeronautics and Space Administration or the Office of Science and Technology Policy to develop, design, plan, promulgate, implement, or execute a bilateral policy, program, order, or contract of any kind to participate, collaborate, or coordinate bilaterally in any way with China or any Chinese owned company unless such activities are specifically authorized by a law enacted after the date of enactment of this division.

    (b) The limitation in subsection (a) shall also apply to any funds used to effectuate the hosting of official Chinese visitors at facilities belonging to or utilized by the National Aeronautics and Space Administration.Department of Defense and Full-Year Continuing Appropriations Act, Pub. L. No. 112–10, §1340, 125 Stat. 38, 123 (2011).

126 US Public Law 105–261, *supra* n. 117. See Waldrop, *supra* n. 107, at 191–195. Luo, *infra* n. 129, at 448–72 details history of US controls and summarises some cases. See also B.R. Reed, 'The United Kingdom's New Export Control Act of 2002 and its Possible Impact on United Kingdom Universities and Academic Freedom: A Comparison of Export Control in the United States and the United Kingdom' (2003) 8 *UCLA J. Int. L. and For. Aff.* 193–237 at 198–215.

127 'Biden administration imposes sweeping tech restrictions on China', Guardian 7 Oct. 2022 www.theguardian.com/us-news/2022/oct/07/biden-administration-tech-restrictions-china.

128 Huan Zhu, China's Reaction to Recent Statements by U.S. Officials on U.S.-China Trade Relations, China Trade Monitor Oct 11, 2021

Ultimately, US regulation of international trade in space products reflects US government policy.[129] The 2010 US National Space Policy statement remains important.[130] Subsequently the US Government decided to move space technology from the Restricted Munitions list and make most space technology subject to the less restrictive Commerce Export Administration Regulations. However, trade restrictions on Russia and China remain.

Many national and international laws prohibit unfair trade practices and restrictions of competition. The US Trade Act of 1974 Sec. 301[131] prohibits unreasonable burdens and restrictions on US commerce.[132] We note that this was effectively an attempt by a US company to restrict the activities of a foreign international organisation. The impact on trade in space assets by general competition laws is also significant.[133]

Last, there is the area of trade in the ownership and provision of services. Here telecommunication is of major importance and encompasses a variety of considerations.[134] Many states now do not permit monopolies in radio communication.[135] In the US the FCC has the task of enforcement in the area of satellite communication.[136] Furthermore, the US Department of Justice and the US Federal Trade Commission may regulate monopolies and mergers under US antitrust laws. Many states regulate transfer of radio frequencies

---

129 C.P. Bown, 'Export Controls: America's Other National Security Threat' (2020) 30 *Duke J. Comp. & Int. Law* 283–308. For a survey including historical review see W. Luo, 'Research Guide to Export Control and WMD Non-Proliferation Law' (2007) 35 *Int. J. Leg. Inf.* 447–449.

130 US National Space Policy, *supra* n. 121.

131 19 USC §2411(a). The Agency of the US Trade Representative supervises international trade issues.

132 One example of a §301 action, now superseded by the WTO Agreements, is the Transpace case. In 1984 a US company, Transpace Carriers, an entrant into the launch market, filed a petition under § 301 with the US Trade Representative alleging unfair competition through the European Space Agency (ESA) subsidising the launch operator Arianespace. There were four grounds of complaint: (1) that Arianespace applied a two tier pricing policy – a lower price (perhaps below cost) for ESA members and a higher price for others; (2) that France subsidised the launch range facilities; (3) that France provided free technical expertise; and (4) that France provided free insurance. Transspace lost the case indicating that the §301 procedure may not be an effective tool for the US regulation of unfair practices in the trade of space assets: see Determination (1985) 50 Federal Register, no. 140, at 29631–29632. In his decision the US Trade Representative compared ESA and US practices, finding ESA practice to be not so sufficiently different from US practices as to be considered unreasonable. Cf. T.A. Brooks, 'Regulating International Trade in Launch Services' (1991) 6 *High Tech. L.J.* 59–109 at 93–94.

133 EU Council Regulation No. 139/2004, Art. 2 authorises the EU Commission to review concentrations of ownership to determine whether or not they are compatible with the Common Market. Cf. the relevance of the WTO, *infra* n. 134.

134 World Trade Organisation: Agreement on Telecommunications Services (Fourth Protocol to General Agreement on Trade in Services), Geneva, 15 February 1997 (1997) 36 ILM 354; www.wto.org/english/tratop_e/serv_e/4prote_e.htm. Cf. Y. Zhao, 'The Commercial Use of Telecommunications under the Framework of GATS' (1999) 24 *Air and Space Law*, 303–328.

135 See Chapter 10.

136 The FCC is an independent government agency authorised by the (US) Federal Communications Act as amended, 47 USC Sec. 314. Through its communications responsibilities *inter alia* it regulates many new space age activities: e.g. it recently required new satellites in LEO to deorbit within five years (see Chapter 9 n. 135). In 2023, the FCC opened a special Space Bureau for satellite business activities: www.fcc.gov/document/fcc-space-bureau-office-international-affairs-launches-april-11.

In Europe, the News Corporation control of the European DBS operator BSkyB caused the EU Commission to examine whether the corporation transgressed its rules as to dominance and thus EU competition rules. The EU Commission concluded that the rules on ompetition had not been breached; P.B. Larsen et al., 'Direct Broadcast Satellites: National and International Regulation,' 8 *Modern Legal Systems Cyclopedia*, William S. Hein, Publ. 1985, Rev. 2004.

and orbital slots for reasons of public policy. For example, under the 1934 Communications Act as amended FCC permission is required for the transfer of the use of radio frequencies and orbital slots under FCC jurisdiction.[137] The US legislation limits foreign ownership of certain US radio licences, restricting ownership by foreign governments, corporations and individuals. Section 310(4) of the Act is of particular significance because it requires the FCC to address indirect ownership greater than 25% in broadcast common carrier licences. In reviewing proposed foreign investment pursuant to § 310, the FCC relies on principles set forth in its 1997 Foreign Participation Order (as amended), which includes a rebuttable presumption that foreign investment from WTO member countries is consistent with the public interest.[138]

In the UK under the Communications Act, 2003, c. 21, the Office for Communications (Ofcom), established by the Office of Communications Act, 2002, c. 11, exercises functions similar to that of the US FCC. UK restrictions on the ownership of broadcasting and other media as well as telecommunications carriers are not as stringent as those of the US, and now do not take foreign nationality into consideration.[139] Other countries take a variety of positions on such matters.

---

137 49 USC 309. In ascertaining the US public interest the FCC must evaluate many elements, including technical, competitive, financial, legal factors, foreign ownership, utilisation of the radio spectrum, national security, law enforcement, considerations of foreign policy and trade implications.

138 See *Amendment of the Commission's Regulatory Policies to Allow Non-US Licensed Satellites Providing Domestic and International Service in the United States*, Report and Order, IB Doc. No. 96–111, adopted 25 November 1997, 26 November 1997 Released; (1997) 12 FCC Rcd 24094; 1997 FCC LEXIS 6743; 10 Comm. Reg. (P & F) 587; *Rules and Policies on Foreign Participation in the US Telecommunications Market, Report and Order and Order on Reconsideration*, IB Doc Nos. 97–142 and 95–22, adopted 25 November 1997, released 26 November 1997 (1997) 12 FCC Rcd 23891; 1997 FCC LEXIS 6601; 10 Comm. Reg. (P & F) 750; *In the Matter of Rules and Policies on Foreign Participation in the U.S Telecommunications Market*, Order on Reconsideration (2000), IB Doc. No. 97–142, adopted 12 September 2000, released 19 September 2000. 15 FCC Rcd 18158; 2000 FCC LEXIS 4936; 22 Comm. Reg. (P & F) 867; Larsen, 'Future Protocol', *supra* n. 18, at 1099.

139 Nationality controls on ownership of UK broadcast media were abolished the amendment of the relevant parts of the Broadcasting Act 1990, c. 42, by s. 348 of the Communications Act 2003, c. 21.

14

COMMERCIAL ACTIVITIES AND THE IMPLEMENTATION OF SPACE LAW

Introduction

Space activities take place within a framework of international law that includes multilateral and bilateral treaties and customary international law.[1] All the space-competent and space-faring states are party to the Outer Space Treaty,[2] and most are also party to ARRA,[3] the Liability Convention[4] and the Registration Convention.[5] All are members of the ITU.[6] There is therefore broad-based multilateral agreement as to the international law of space.[7] Apart from these instruments, sixteen states are parties to the Moon Agreement.[8] None have yet ratified the 2012 Space Protocol to the Cape Town Convention.[9] In addition, a

1 For the multilateral treaties see the Annual Report of the IISL Standing Committee on the Status of International Treaties relating to Activities in Outer Space: in *Proc IISL* or https://iislweb.space/2001-standing-committee-report/, or www.unoosa.org/oosa/en/ourwork/spacelaw/treaties/status/index.html.
2 Treaty on Principles Governing the Activities of States in the Exploration and Use of Outer Space Including the Moon and Other Celestial Bodies (1968) 610 UNTS 205; (1968) UKTS 10, Cmnd. 3519; 18 UST 2410, TIAS 6347; (1967) 6 ILM 386; (1967) 61 AJIL 644. See Chapter 3. As of 1 January 2023, the OST had 113 ratifications.
3 Agreement on the Rescue of Astronauts, the Return of Astronauts and the Return of Objects Launched into Outer Space, 22 April 1968; 672 UNTS 119; 1969 UKTS 56, Cmnd. 3997; 19 UST 7570, TIAS 6559; (1968) 7 ILM 151; (1969) 63 AJIL 382. 99 ratifications as of 1 January 2023.
4 Convention on International Liability for Damage Caused by Space Objects, 29 March 1972; 961 UNTS 187; (1974) UKTS 16, Cmnd. 5551; 24 UST 2389, TIAS 7762; (1971) 10 ILM 965; (1971) 66 AJIL 702. 98 ratifications as of 1 January 2023.
5 Convention on the Registration of Objects Launched into Outer Space, 14 January 1975; 1023 UNTS 15; (1978) UKTS 70, Cmnd. 7271; TIAS 8480; (1975) 14 ILM 43. See Chapter 4. 75 ratifications as of 1 January 2023.
6 For the ITU see Chapter 8.
7 Intriguingly, North Korea ratified the OST and the Registration Convention in 2008 and ARRA and the Liability Convention in 2015.
8 Agreement Governing the Activities of States on the Moon and Other Celestial Bodies, 5 December 1979; 1363 UNTS 3; (1979) 18 ILM 1434. 18 ratifications as of 1 January 2023, but Saudi Arabia withdrew as of 5 January 2024. See Chapter 7.
9 Protocol to the Convention on International Interests in Mobile Equipment on Matters Specific to Space Assets: www.unidroit.org/instruments/security-interests/space-protocol; (2012) 17 *Uniform L. Rev.* 756–806. See Chapter 13.

DOI: 10.4324/9781003496502-14

complex bundle of bilateral agreements, formal and informal, may be relevant in any given instance.

After the basic space treaties, it proved difficult to establish further broadly accepted multilateral treaties to regulate what happens in space.[10] Stalemated, COPUOS has had recourse to statements of 'Principle' which have been approved by the UN General Assembly, but that is different from formal law. It is a variety of the 'soft law' that includes UN Resolutions, inter-state and inter-agency agreements, memoranda of understanding,[11] and codes of practice, which are increasingly complied with albeit they lack enforcement mechanisms.[12] How and how well space-competent and space-faring states exercise their rights and implement their international obligations and unofficial practices as to space within their national legislation is therefore important.

Many new issues can usefully be regulated by national legislation; some implementing such international codes of practice, while others may reflect a view on important unsolved issues as they crystallise.[13] Licensing often has an important role to play. Commercial use of space requires regulation that is consistent with international law. Requirements range from launch permits, debris mitigation and the assignment of radio frequencies to the restrictions a state may impose for reasons of national security.[14] In addition, private commercial users enter into a variety of contracts, for example as to the construction and launch of satellites, constituting securities over space assets, and for the resolution of disputes. Commercial operators are therefore regulated by private as well as public law. States that do not have specialised national space legislation are coming to realise that countries that have such do exert greater influence in and over the various space markets. OOSA and COPUOS therefore arrange workshops to educate and encourage the adoption of national space legislation.[15]

Obviously, we cannot here discuss the whole gamut of 'domestic' space law. But it is interesting to see how, within the constraints of their several constitutions, some space-competent states have arranged such matters. The US and Australia have very well-developed national legislation. New Zealand and the UK have laws that meet their domestic needs. Russia, China and India are moving from state space economies to include private enterprise and are designing national legislation to regulate private space activities. Many other countries are adopting their own national legislation.[16]

---

10 S. Hobe, 'Future Perspectives', CoCoSL I, 14–17.

11 See 'Soft Law' in Chapter 2. Cf. also the Memoranda of Understanding that undergird the construction and operation of the International Space Station considered in Chapter 4 Space Stations.

12 E.g. the debris mitigation guidelines; see Chapter 9 sv. Space Debris.

13 E.g. Denmark and Australia have set 100 km as the height above which activities require licensing. The UAE has gone for 80 km. See Chapter 6 at n. 81ff and *infra* n. 49. Notwithstanding, where space begins is not settled in international law.

14 See Chapters 6 and 15.

15 The 2012 Space Protocol, designed to facilitate asset-based space financing, has been slow to appeal to national systems. See *supra* n. 9 and P.B. Larsen, 'The Berlin Space Protocol: Update' (2015) 64 ZLW 361–395.

16 See *infra* n. 41. S. Aoki, 'Japanese Space Activities Act in the Making' (2012) 61 ZLW 111–128; I. Marboe, 'The New Austrian Outer Space Act' (2012) 61 ZLW 26–61; L.J. Smith, 'Legislating for Outer Space: The Example of Germany: Considerations on a National Space Law' (2012) 61 ZLW 62–78; P. Martinez, 'The Development of Space Law in South Africa' (2015) 64 ZLW 353–360.

The Major Obligations

Space activities are conducted by governments, intergovernmental organisations, and private civil entities.[17] Early expectations were different. At the start of the space age many thought that only states would be active in space and the notion of private entrepreneurs in space was limited to science fiction. Even so, the negotiators of the 1967 OST were farsighted. Its terms left open the possibility of private enterprise in outer space, and that has developed in the subsequent decades. Now many different uses of space range from the purely scientific to the frankly commercial. However, undergirding all is the responsibility of individual states, which is set out in the OST.

OST Art. VI provides that

> States Parties to the Treaty shall bear international responsibility for national activities in outer space, including the Moon and other celestial bodies, whether such activities are carried on by governmental agencies or by nongovernmental entities, and for assuring that national activities are carried out in conformity with the provisions set forth in the present Treaty. The activities of nongovernmental entities in outer space, including the Moon and other celestial bodies, shall require authorization and continuing supervision by the appropriate State Party to the Treaty'.[18]

Of course, as we saw in Chapter 3, OST Art. VI does not define which is the 'appropriate' state.[19] Its language simply rephrases para 5 of the 1963 UN Declaration of Principles, which speaks of the 'State concerned'. No matter how one may interpret 'appropriate' or 'concerned' it is clear that the language is in the singular: the drafters intended only one state to authorise and supervise and therefore be responsible for a particular private space activity.

Correlatively, by OST Art. VII a state that launches. or procures the launching of a space object, or whose territory or facility is used for a launch, is liable internationally to another state party to the OST for damages the object may cause. The obligation, further developed in the Liability Convention, is an obligation which the (as of 2022) 112 parties to the 1967 Treaty must take into account in their domestic arrangements.

OST Art. VIII provides that a state party retains jurisdiction and control over a space object and its personnel (if any) which has been entered on its registry while the object is in outer space, which ownership is not affected by the object being in space, on a celestial body, or by its return to Earth. Such objects and personnel are to be returned to the state of registry if found elsewhere.[20]

---

17 Cf. F.G. von der Dunk, 'Sovereignty versus Space – Public Law and Private Launch in the Asian Context' (2001) 5 *Sing. J. Int. and Comp. L.* 22–47.

18 Art. VI goes on to provide for shared responsibilities between international organisations and their members.

19 '[T]he appropriate state' has been substituted for the 'State concerned' which appears in para 5 of the 1963 'Declaration of Legal Principles Governing the Activities of States in the Exploration and Use of Outer Space', UNGA Res. 1962/1963 (XVIII); (1964) 3 ILM 157.

20 These provisions have, of course, been expanded for the parties to ARRA and the Registration Convention but the basic thrust of obligation is contained in the 1967 treaty.

OST Arts. VI and VII and particularly Art. VIII, make the transfer of space objects between private parties difficult because the authors of these articles did not envision such transfers. The Treaty was written with state-owned space objects in mind.[21]

It follows from the OST 'Principles' that space-competent and space active state parties to that Treaty, are responsible in law for their own acts. They are also responsible for the space activities of their national private commercial entrepreneurs and operators, and therefore in their own self-interest should make proper provision for licensing and supervision. States have also to implement in national law the obligations they may have assumed under the other space agreements such as ARRA and the Liability and Registration Conventions and may also introduce rules and regulations incorporating any other requirements that they determine desirable. These may include compliance with all or part of UN Resolutions relevant to what is being dealt with, and with the various unofficial codes that are being developed, for example as to the mitigation of space debris.[22]

The rights and obligations under the OST and the other space treaties are those of states. Under international law access to space is therefore controlled by states, but the commercial use of space is increasing, as is the demand for commercial launches.[23] OST Art. I para 2 provides for the freedom of space 'for exploration and use by all states without discrimination of any kind on a basis of equality and in accordance with international law'. Given that a state governs the activities of persons and entities under its jurisdiction, it has power to allow access to space to its nationals, subject to the OST regime. OST Art. II excludes any national appropriation of outer space whether 'by claim of sovereignty, by means of use or occupation, or any other means.' Thus states cannot authorize nongovernmental entities to appropriate outer space celestial bodies. They cannot grant any rights which they themselves do not possess.[24]

OST Art. XI requires that users of space shall be careful and protective of the interests of other users. Further as Art. 44.2 (196) of the ITU Constitution recognises, 'radio frequencies and any associated orbits, including the geostationary-satellite orbit are limited natural resources and they must be used rationally, efficiently and economically'.[25] When a state permits private users to have access to outer space that access will therefore be restricted in a variety of respects. This will include control through licensing of the launch provider, the date, time and location of a launch, the orbit and radiofrequencies to be used and the function and functioning of the particular satellite(s) to be deployed. Individual states may add their own additional requirements. In its decision as to the licensing of a space activity a state will balance the national interest with the international. States may confer rights of access to space on individual commercial operators on a case-by-case basis and may proceed on a more general basis through national implementing legislation that sets appropriate procedures and requirements for licensing. Whether states adopt

---

21 Cf. the provisions of the Registration Convention discussed in Chapter 4, and the effect of transfer in the operation of the Space Protocol, *supra* n. 9, and its discussion in Chapter 13. See also Larsen, *supra* n. 15.

22 See Chapter 9 sv. 'Space Debris'.

23 E.J. Reinstein, 'Owning Outer Space' (1999) 20 *Nw. J. Int. L. and Bus.* 59–88.

24 This accords with the legal maxim *nihil dat qui non habet* (he gives nothing who has nothing: you cannot pass on a title that you do not possess). But note the developments as to space mining considered in Chapter 7.

25 Cf. F. Lyall, 'The Rational, Efficient and Economic Use of Space: Three Suggestions', M. Benkö, ed., *Air and Space Law in the 21st Century: Liber Amicorum K-H. Böckstiegel* (Cologne: Carl Heymanns Verlag, 2002) 386–395.

implementing legislation is often determined by the volume of private space commerce for which they are responsible. Thus Australia, the UK and the US have adopted legislation conferring rights of access to qualified private commercial launch operators. On the other hand India and many others have not yet adopted general national legislation but issue individual launch permits based directly on the rights of the state under the space treaties and international law.[26]

It has to be said that a state would have more effective and uniform oversight of commercial space launches and outer space activities by adopting its own general national legislation. A state that does not have general national legislation may well find that its nationals have engaged in unreasonably risky activities, and thereby subjected it to an unexpected liability for damage they cause. Further, commercial operators will usually prefer to bring themselves under the jurisdiction of a particular licensing state where they know in advance the likely terms of the licence, including whether their liability is capped or has to be met by appropriate insurance.[27] Investors want to be able to quantify the risks, particularly because of the large sums required by space activities. However, arguably capping of liability operates as a subsidy to launch and other entrepreneurs active in the space market.[28] More generally, commercial operators may wish to place themselves under the jurisdiction of a government that will exercise lenient oversight over their activities.[29]

The drafters of the existing space law treaties did not foresee changes in the private ownership of satellites in orbit.[30] This can cause problems if a privately owned satellite is transferred to a new owner located in a state different from the launching state. In such a case, the registration and oversight responsibilities as well as the potential liability for damage of the original launching state or states under the OST or the other space treaties continue even though the original launching state is no longer the state appropriate to supervise the satellite.[31]

One instance is the New Skies NV saga. During the progress of INTELSAT towards privatisation, New Skies NV was created in The Netherlands and received ownership of several satellites formerly owned by INTELSAT. The Netherlands refused to register these satellites under the Registration Convention because of the possible liability and oversight implications of registration.[32] An alternative scenario could emerge under the Space Protocol to the Cape Town Convention should an element of the 'security' over a satellite involve the transfer of its ownership in the event of a default.[33]

It does seem obvious that the state 'appropriate' to authorise and exercise the continuing supervision of the activities of a private operator required by OST Art. VI ought to be the state with the best connections to it.[34] However, we also note that the space treaty arrangements as to rights and duties are framed in terms of the single integral ownership of a satellite. In modern commercial arrangements that situation will not necessarily apply.

---

26 As to India see *infra* n. 126 ff.
27 For example the United States Commercial Space Launch Act, 51 USC 50914.
28 See Chapter 4 – 'Compensation for Damage, Liability Caps and Insurance.'
29 This is similar to the 'flag of convenience' in the maritime industry. See comment in Chapter 4 at n. 73 ff.
30 Larsen, *supra* n. 15, at 383.
31 Cf. *supra* n. 21.
32 Cf. Note Verbale of 18 February 2004 from The Netherlands, UN Doc. A/AC.105/824. See Chapter 4, at nn. 112 and 121.
33 See *supra* n. 9, Larsen, *supra* n. 15, and discussion of the Protocol in Chapter 13.
34 Cf. our reference to the *Barcelona Traction* case in Chapter 4, n. 74.

Multiple ownerships (e.g. of different transponders – separate transponder leases are common) or joint ownership of a satellite, including where the 'owners' are of different nationalities, are conceivable. The relevant treaties therefore require amendment to provide for multi-ownership and for changes in the ownership of satellites in orbit. An alternative is the use of bilateral agreements under which a state assumes the OST Art. VI responsibilities of the appropriate state, together with other emergent liabilities.[35] The corollary is that a state could refuse to license the 'new' activity until such matters are satisfactorily arranged. The basic position is that a state will not permit unlooked for duties and potentially major liabilities to be imposed upon it merely by the will of commercial entities or entrepreneurs.

Satellites have to be launched. Although governments are not immune to such considerations, launch costs particularly affects commercial users of space. Fortunately, the development of small launchers has brought down the cost of sending small satellites into LEO, but the large launch vehicles needed for access to higher orbits remain expensive. In 2008, it cost US$10,000–20,000 per kg to launch objects into outer space. Launch cost has been reduced greatly. Now one launch may deploy the satellites of several customers thus reducing the cost to each. Again cost varies depending on whether a US, French, Russian, or Chinese launch operator is used because launch operators have different mixes of direct and indirect subsidies to launch operators. However, competition among launch operators has recently changed. A new US space launch operator, Space-X, has emerged among the providers of large launchers. It has been able substantially to reduce its costs and therefore the price of launch by simplifying and rationalizing the entire launch process. Its launcher, the Falcon 9, is reusable and has proved reliable. As a consequence its launch insurance has become significantly cheaper, further reducing launch costs. Space-X now delivers cargo and astronauts to the International Space Station and will send a satellite to the planet Mars to recover mineral samples. It also delivers nongovernmental communication satellites into geostationary orbit and is launching the Spacelink constellation. However, it may be difficult to quantify or compare SpaceX and the exact costs of other launch operators. This is because of the development of small launchers by such as RocketLab and their use of small and simpler launch sites.[36]

Governments have different mixes of direct and indirect subsidies to their launch operators because they wish to maintain a national launch service thus assure themselves of access to outer space for national security reasons.[37] While the cost of launches has declined significantly, launch services remain expensive, making many potential commercial enterprises difficult to finance. One time launches of communication and earth observation satellites have been profitable, but such as space mining activities which would require repeated launches and return deliveries to Earth will probably require significantly greater reduction in the cost of launch services than is currently available.[38] Nevertheless, launching satellites is a significant commercial activity. Whether the purpose is public or private all satellites have to be launched, and launch is part of the cost of doing space business. States

---

35 R.J. Lee, *The Australian Legal and Regulatory Framework for Space Launches, Guide for the Space Industry*, at 28–33.

36 On RocketLab and New Zealand see *infra* n. 159. On the development of small sites cf. the development of UK domestic launch sites *infra*, particularly at nn. 182 and 198.

37 Many European states, members of the European Space Agency (ESA), use the European launch service 'Arianespace' though others do so also.

38 On space mining see Chapter 7.

have been very active in regulation of commercial launches. The following discussion will therefore focus mostly on this area of national regulation. Internal laws governing commerce within a state are a matter for individual states to determine and police.

Particular States

The number of states involved in outer space commerce is increasing rapidly.[39] Virtually all depend on satellites for communication, navigation and earth observation. How and how well particular states implement their obligations is important. Some are major players involved either directly or through their national entities in launch activities and/or in the construction and operation of appropriate satellites. Other states are active through purchasing services and technologies provided by others. Some states allow non-national operators to use their launch sites.[40] Here, we confine ourselves to outlining the steps taken by only a few space-active states.[41] International Launch Services,[42] SpaceX, Arianespace, Orbital Sciences and others are in the market to provide commercial launches. Various of the source materials cited hereafter contain information about the attitudes of states other than those indicated in their titles.[43] We would also caution readers that what follows is of civilian relevance. Where appropriate it should be balanced by pertinent data from the discussion of the military use of space in Chapter 15.

Australia

Australia, lying near to the Equator, is well suited for space launches having wide-open spaces removed from dense urban centres.[44] The Australian Space Agency (ASA) was

---

39 R.S. Jakhu, ed., *National Regulation of Space Activities* (Dordrecht: Springer 2010); P.S. Dempsey, 'National Legislation Governing Space Activities': www.unoosa.org/documents/pdf/spacelaw/activities/2014/pres06E.pdf.
40 A number of small states have contemplated the building of a space-port on their territories. Commercial spaceports for orbital and suborbital launches are licensed or planned in Canada, the US (Alaska, California, Florida, New Mexico, Oklahoma, Texas, Virginia), the United Arab Emirates and Singapore. US investors have also considered constructing a space-port in the Virgin Islands or Venezuela. See *infra* for Australia, New Zealand and the UK.
41 UN OOSA maintains a collection of national space legislation at www.unoosa.org/oosa/en/ourwork/spacelaw/nationalspacelaw/index.html. For other OOSA data on national implementation of space law see www.unoosa.org/oosa/en/ourwork/spacelaw/nationalspacelaw.html. For comparison with data down to 2000: 'Review of Existing National Space Legislation Illustrating how States are Implementing, as Appropriate, their Responsibilities to Authorize and Provide Continuing Supervision of Non-governmental Entities in Outer Space: Note by COPUOS Secretariat', A/AC.105/C.2/L.224: www.unoosa.org/pdf/limited/c2/AC105_C2_L224E.pdf.
42 International Launch Services began as a US/Russian collaboration. It is now a US company largely owned by Krunichev, the designer and builder of the Proton system: www.ilslaunch.com/about-us/.
43 For data down to its date, see J.A. Manner, 'President Bush's 1990 Policy on the Commercial Space Launch Industry: A Thorn in Economic and Political Reform in the Former Soviet Union: A Proposal for Change' (1993) 58 *J. Air L. & Comm.* 981–1040 (data on China, Australia, the US and Russia); J.L. Reed, 'The Commercial Space Launch Market and Bilateral Agreements in Space Launch Services' (1997) 13 *Am. U. Int. L. Rev.* 157–218 (data down to its date on US bilateral arrangements with China, Russia and the Ukraine).
44 T. Jones et al., "Australia' in (2023) 4 *The Space Law Review*: https://thelawreviews.co.uk/title/the-space-law-review/australia; N. Siemon and S. Freeland, 'Regulation of Space Activities in Australia' in Jakhu, ed., *supra* n. 39, 37–60; S. Freeland, 'The Final Piece of the Puzzle? The Launch of Australia's Satellite Utilisation

established in 2018 as a non-statutory body within the Department of Industry, Innovation and Science to oversee the development of space industry.[45] Australia's emphasis is on development of commercial operations.[46] The Australian Space Industry Centre of Commerce is active in support of the development of an Australian space industry, as is the Australian Commonwealth Scientific and Industrial Research Organisation.[47]

The Australian space legislation was recently reviewed.[48] As a result, in 2018, the Australian Space Activities Act, passed in 1998 and amended in 2002 was replaced by the Space (Launches and Returns) Act 2018.[49] The purposes of the legislation are to implement Australian obligations under the space treaties; to attract investors in outer space; to offset the liability of the Australian Government under the Liability Convention by transferring much of it to private launch operators, and to create a safe environment for launches. The Act specifically applies to launches or attempted launches to an altitude of at least 100 km above mean sea level.[50] It provides for the authorisation and supervision of private space activities through the issue of licences, permits and exemptions. It also provides for the limitation of the liability of a licensed launch operator. Launches are registered in accordance with the Registration Convention. Australia has entered into a number of bilateral cooperation agreements which are also implemented by the Act. Violation of the Act may result in penalties. Launch accidents will be investigated. An applicant for a space launch licence must also comply with a number of other legislative provisions,[51] including the Australian Radiocommunications Act of 1992 to obtain authorisation of the necessary radio frequencies, the Civil Aviation Safety Regulations of 1998 for access to cleared air space for the launch or re-entry route, the Customs Regulations of 1998 to comply with export controls on national security assets, the Customs Tariff Amendment Act of 2001, the Transport Safety Investigations of 2002 regarding the investigation of accidents, and the special regulations regarding the Christmas Island Launch Centre.[52]

Policy 2013' (2013) 62 ZLW 429–452. For a map of potential spaceports see https://spaceanddefense.io/australias-old-and-new-potential-spaceports/

45 Australian Space Agency: www.industry.gov.au/australian-space-agency.

46 Cf. T. Jones and T. Macken, 'Australia' in J. Wheeler, ed., *The Space Law Review*, 3rd ed. 2021, and T. Jones et al, 'Australia', in J. Wheeler, ed., *The Space Law Review*, 4th ed. 2023.

47 Australian Space Industry Centre of Commerce: www.asicc.com.au/: Australian Commonwealth Scientific and Industrial Research Organisation (CSIRO): www.csiro.au/. See also the Interim Report of the Senate Inquiry into 'The Current State of Australia's Space Science and Industry Sector', June 2008.

48 In 2016, S. Freeland, a member of the IISL Board of Directors was appointed advisor to a major review of the Australian legislation. For the review see https://industry.gov.au/industry/IndustrySectors/space/Pages/Review-of-the-Space-Activities-Act-1998.aspx#header.

49 Space (Launches and Returns) Act of 2018: www.legislation.gov.au/Details/C2021C00394. The previous legislation, the Space Activities Act, 1998 (No, 123, 1998), is amended. See its text in *Project 2001 Workshop on Legal Framework for Commercial Launch and Associated Services* (Cologne: Institute of Air and Space Law, 2001) 259–303. or *Project 2001 Legal Framework for Privatising Space Activities*, 340. R.J. Lee, *The Australian Legal and Regulatory Framework for Space Launches, Guide for the Space Industry* (published before the 2018 amending legislation). See also Hunt and Hunt, *Regulatory Handbook for Australian Launch Operators*.

50 By Sec. 8, 'Definitions', to 'launch a space object' means to 'launch the whole or a part of the object into an area beyond the distance of 100 km above mean sea level or attempt to do so'.

51 For the Commonwealth of Australia Consolidated Acts see www.austlii.edu.au/au/legis/cth/consol_act/. Secondary legislation is available from the Australian Legal Information Institute: www.austlii.edu.au/.

52 A space-port, for use by an Asia-Pacific Space Centre, was developed on Christmas Island, in the Indian Ocean some 2,600 km/1,800 miles north-west of Australia.

The Space (Launches and Returns) Act regulates commercial launches by Australian nationals both in Australia and abroad and launches from Australian territory by non-Australian entities.[53] The Act governs both launches to and re-entry from outer space, and it requires an overseas launch certificate for a launch outside of Australia by an Australian national. Special authorisation is required for the return to Australia of a space object launched overseas. Finally, a launch operator may obtain an exemption certificate for emergency launch(es).

Whereas in some states (e.g. the US) commercial launches frequently use a government operated launch facility, the Australian Act assumes launches will be from private facilities where the launch site is duly authorised.[54] The Act, therefore, places special emphasis on the licensing of private launch facilities in Australian territory and the issue of a launch permit. To obtain a licence the launch facility operator must show: competence to operate the launch facility; compliance with Australian environmental laws; assurance that the public health and safety risks of the launch are reasonable; that the planned flight will be safe; and that the launch facility and the launches from it will be safe. The launch must not endanger Australian national security.[55]

The launch licence provides for a particular kind of launch craft, whether by direct insertion or air launch, being launched in a specific direction. Any change in launch craft and launch direction requires a variance or a new licence. In special cases the Australian Government may recognise a foreign government certification of the engineering of the technical details of a launch facility and of the launch operation itself. The operator must file an application for such recognition along with the launch application.[56]

An application for a launch facility licence must be accompanied by: (1) a management plan explaining how the entire launch facility will be managed; (2) an environmental protection plan demonstrating ability to monitor environmental effects to comply with Australian environmental laws and a compliance statement from an independent environmental expert; (3) an emergency plan indicating how the operator will meet any emergencies; (4) a technology security plan assuring compliance with Australian obligations under arms control agreements including the prevention of unauthorised access to sensitive information; (5) a risk hazard analysis plan showing how the operator will comply with Risk Hazard Analysis Methodology of the relevant Flight Safety Code; (6) a flight test plan regarding the launch of new technology vehicles describing the reason for the flight, the configuration of the craft, the vehicle tracking system, launch and launch termination procedures, and reporting the flight test to the Australian Government.[57]

To obtain a permit for a launch in Australia the private commercial operator of the launch vehicle must show evidence of: (1) a programme management plan showing

53 The Act does not apply to intergovernmental organisations wholly or mainly active in space of which Australia is a member (s. 17).
54 Space (Launches and Returns) Act, ss. 18–27. Also see the Australian Space Licensing and Safety Office at www.industry.gov.au. See map, *supra* n. 44.
55 E.g. Space (Launches and Returns) Act, ss. 26(1)(b), 28(3)(e).
56 Lee, *supra* n. 49, at 10. The recognition of a foreign government certification encourages foreigners to launch in Australia as does the efficiency obtained through avoiding unnecessary duplication of certification requirements.
57 Lee, *supra* n. 49, at 10.

planned management of ground operations, the adequacy of flight safety and of launch procedures, employee awareness of their duties and ability to meet emergencies and relevant communication arrangements; (2) a technology security plan indicating procedures for prevention of unauthorised access to technology information as well as compliance with national security restrictions; (3) a flight safety plan indicating compliance with the Australian Flight Safety Code, data supporting risk analysis and a report to the government on compliance with and independent assessment of compliance with the Flight Safety Code; (4) an insurance plan giving the name of the insurer, risks covered and insurer's certification of sufficient financial means; (5) an environmental plan showing preparations for monitoring and mitigating environmental hazards, and the means of carrying out such plans.[58]

The applicant for an Australian launch permit is required to obtain insurance coverage against possible third party liability as well as insurance against possible liability for damage caused to the Australian government during launch operations. Alternatively, the applicant may self-insure by proving possession of assets sufficient to cover potential liabilities. The required insurance is for either 750 million Australian dollars or maximum probable loss (MPL) as determined by a formula that takes into consideration probability of casualty loss, third-party property loss, environmental damage and economic loss, and the cost of accident investigation in the case of a failed launch.[59] An applicant for a launch permit is required to mitigate the formation of debris. The applicant must present a plan to prevent impact of debris on designated areas – primarily densely populated areas and valuable facilities such as oil wells and factories.[60] Australia further requires an environmental plan showing preparations for monitoring and mitigating environmental hazards and means of carrying out such plans.[61]

On occasion Australia may license a launch by an Australian entity that is to be carried outside Australian territorial jurisdiction. In that connection it may enter into intergovernmental agreements with foreign governments allowing them to supervise launches overseas by Australians.[62] Thus, if an Australian citizen launches in the US, Australia may refer oversight responsibility to the US Government (similar to US deference to Australia if a US citizen is to launch in Australia). In the absence of a relevant intergovernmental agreement, the Australian applicant must (1) meet the Australian insurance requirements, (2) show that threats to public safety and health are low, (3) that the application does not prejudice Australian national security interests, and (4) provide evidence of the insurance coverage required for domestic launches.[63]

Part 5 (Secs 76–79) of the Australian Act creates a Register of Space Objects. This records the information prescribed by Art. IV of the Registration Convention but may

---

58 Australian Space (Launches and Returns) Act, s. 28. See Lee, *supra* n. 49, at 23–37. The Australian Space Licensing and Safety Office is at www.industry gov.au. See also the Australian Space Agency publications on the definition of the space sector (www.industry.gov.au/publications/definition-australian-space-sector), the Flight Safety Code (www.industry.gov.au/publications/flight-safety-code) and on Maximum Probable Loss Methodology (www.industry.gov.au/publications/maximum-probable-loss-methodology).
59 See also *supra* text at n. 54.
60 Lee, *supra* n. 49, at 29–33.
61 Lee, *supra* n. 49, at 10 at 25–29.
62 Cf. the US legislation to which we are coming.
63 Space (Launches and Returns) Act, s. 12; Lee, *supra* n. 49, at 47–44.

contain additional information. It is held on computer and is available for public inspection. Australia has been diligent in registering the required information with the United Nations in accordance with the Convention.[64]

Part 4 of the Australian Act deals with liability for damage by space objects.[65] Aside from the liability of Australia itself for damages under international law, damages are recoverable by third parties from the party responsible for an Australian authorised launch provided that the damage occurs during a 'liability period'. This is a fixed period of thirty days after a launch, or from the initiation of re-entry movement to the landing on the surface of the Earth.[66] The liability of the responsible party is capped to the 'maximum probable loss' discussed above if the terms of the relevant permits and licences have been complied with by the responsible party.[67] Part 4 otherwise imposes time-limits from the bringing of an action that repeat those of the Liability Convention. Liability under the Act implements the Liability Convention in that the responsible party is absolutely liable for loss and damage to the surface and in the air. Damage to objects in outer space will result in liability only if the claimant can prove that the damage was caused by the fault of the responsible party. However, extraterritorial liability under the Australian Act is questionable. An Australian launch operator might be sued elsewhere than in Australia thereby avoiding the Australian Act limitation of liability. An injured foreign party might be motivated to bring a large claim abroad should it or a relevant state not proceed under the Liability Convention.[68] In the event of a successful international claim against the Commonwealth of Australia under the Liability Convention, the responsible party has to repay the Commonwealth of Australia the lesser of the compensation payable by Australia or the insured 'maximum possible loss' provided that the terms of relevant licences and permits have been complied with.

The Australian Space Activities Act 1998 as amended must be read in the context of other Australian legislation and procedures relating to outer space, for example the radio-communication laws, the assignment and registration of orbital slots and military considerations. R.J. Lee draws attention to several problems of the Australian launch licence. For example, the launch permit covers both the launch and re-entry of the launch vehicle but does not clearly regulate the re-entry of any space object that may be launched by the launch vehicle. Lee suggests that the government should specifically include the return of the satellite or object from outer space in an 'Authorisation of Return'.[69] It would be in the interest of a launch applicant to request authorisation of the space object both while in outer space and during re-entry in order to bring the existence of the object properly under Australian supervision and as a result obtaining limited liability protection while in outer space and during re-entry.

64 Lee, *supra* n. 49, at 50–51.
65 Siemon and Freeland, *supra* n. 44. Compare with the US legislation, *infra* at n. 148.
66 Australian Space Activities Act, ss. 63.1.b and 63.2.b, the 'liability period' being defined in s. 8.
67 Lee, *supra* n. 49, at 10 at 51–67. Australian Space Licensing and Safety Office, at www.industry gov.au.
68 Lee, *supra* n. 49 at 59–63. Not all states are members of the Liability Convention and so in a particular incident the option of proceeding under the Convention might not be open.
69 Lee, *supra* n. 49 at 23.

China

The Chinese space programme is dominated by the Government.[70] It is administered through the China National Space Administration.[71] It has also provided launch services at favourable prices to foreign operators from its launch site at Xichang. China has ratified the four basic international space law treaties but not the 1979 Moon Agreement nor the Space Protocol. China relies on the international treaties for its regulation of commercial space activities and has not yet adopted national legislation of the nature of the Australian and US laws.[72] China does have national legislation of limited application and is considering more comprehensive space measures.[73] A White Paper on its space activities, issued in 2000 and revised in 2003, stated the Chinese primary focus on space policy as:

> Adhering to the principle of long-term, stable and sustainable development and catering to the development of space activities and serving the State's comprehensive development strategy; upholding the principles of independence and self-renovation and actively promoting international exchanges, self-reliance and self-renovation and actively promoting international exchanges and cooperation; selecting a limited number of targets and making breakthroughs in key areas according to China's national situation and strength; enhancing the social and economic returns of space activities and paying attention to the motivation of technological progress; sticking to integrated planning, combination of long-term and short-term development, combination of spacecraft and ground equipment, and coordinated development.[74]

This has been supplemented by a further White Paper issued by the State Council Information Office in January 2022.[75]

OST Art. VI, obliges China, when the 'appropriate state', to 'require authorisation and continuing supervision' of the activities of nongovernmental entities in outer space. This

---

70 We note, but have not seen, Xiaodan Wu, *China's Ambition in Space: Program, Policy and Law* (The Hague: Eleven International Publishing, 2022).

71 China National Space Administration: www.cnsa.gov.cn/n6443408/index.html.

72 Yun Zhao, 1: *National Space Law in China* (Leiden: Brill, 2015). See also: 2. his 'Liberalization of Launch Services within a Plurilateral Regime, with Reference to China's Commercial Launch Services' (2006) 7 *J. World Trade and Invest.*, 433–441 (our pagination is from the original paper at the Bangalore Space Law Conference 2005, 1–49); 3. his 'National Space Legislation, with Reference to China's Practice' (2007) XXXII AASL 131–146; 4. 'National Space Legislation in Mainland China' (2007) 33 *J. Sp. L.* 427–36, with legislation at 437–56; 5. 'Regulation of Space Activities in the People's Republic of China', in Jakhu, ed., *supra* n. 39, 247–266. See also M. Xiaofeng, 'National Liability for Damage Outside Territory Caused by Space Objects and Suggestion for China's Legislation' (2003) 46 *Proc IISL* 202–209.
    Based on prior UK legislation the Hong Kong Special Administrative Region has separate rules on commercial activities. See *The Outer Space Ordinance*, Chapter 523, 1999, Gazette no. 55 of 1999. This includes the requirement of a licence for space activities (ss. 4–7), the operation of a register of space objects (s. 9), an obligation on licensees to indemnify against damages claims (s. 12) and criminal offences (s. 14).

73 The State Council Information Office, China's Space Activities in 2016: www.cnsa.gov.cn/n6443408/n6465652/n6465653/c6768527/content.html. See also the report for 2006 at www.cnsa.gov.cn/n6443408/n6465645/n6465648/c6477657/content.html. Other materials are available via www.cnsa.gov.cn/n6443408/index.html.See also China legislation (2007) 33 *J. Sp. L.* 437–456.

74 We quote from the first edition of this book but cannot trace a current URL for this material.

75 'China's Space Program: A 2021 Perspective': www.cnsa.gov.cn/english/n6465645/n6465648/c6813088/content.html. Cf. US – China Economic and Security Commission, Report to Congress, 117 Cong. Sess. 2, November 2022: www.uscc.gov/sites/default/files/2022-11/2022_Annual_Report_to_Congress.pdf.

can involve licensing of launches, which is done in two ways. China has designated the China Great Wall Industry Corporation to administer the launch of foreign owned space objects. Launches of Chinese owned space objects are administered by the China Satellite Launch and Tracking Control General of the State Administration for Science, Technology and Industry for National Defence. Different contracts are concluded depending on whether the applicant is foreign or domestic. Both kinds will be subject to Chinese law if they are to be performed in China.[76] Activities under both contracts are also subject to Chinese law of Torts for loss and damages caused during their performance, as well as to existing Chinese treaty obligations.

Chinese launch licensing regulations[77] were adopted in 2002 incidental to a new space object registration requirement in 2001.[78] Both licensing regulations provide instructions about how to launch in China. The regulations apply to civilian launches, not to military launches. All civilian launches require government launch permits. Although many space objects are of dual military and civilian uses, launch applications by nongovernmental entities are inherently considered to be civilian applications and thus subject to the civilian launch license requirements. Applications for launches must be directed to the Commission of Science, Technology and Industry for National Defense. An application for a civilian launch licence and the launch permit itself must describe the space project, the time and place for the launch, the duration for which the permit is required, and must indicate the office issuing the permit. The application must contain information about the qualifications of the applicant, technical information about the launch vehicle, the intended orbit as well as assurance that the project does not conflict with national rules and regulations. A launch in China must include information about the radio frequencies to be used to control the space object. Thus the launch applicant must have a communication licence from the Information Industry Ministry. The Applicant must also provide information about having adequate preventive measures to minimize space debris and emissions. Finally the regulatory agency must be assured of the safety of the launch project.[79] The Administration for Science, Technology and Industry for National Defense will decide on an application within 30 days. A foreign launch application will be referred to a Chinese foreign trade company for evaluation.[80]

As party to the Registration Convention, China has promulgated national procedures for the registration of space objects. The registration office is maintained by the Chinese Administration for Science, Technology and Industry for National Defense, which in turn passes the registration information on to the Ministry of Foreign Affairs for registration with the UN, as required by the Convention.[81] The Administration has also issued regulations under which it issues licences for non-military launches and for the re-entry of space objects.[82] The Chinese definition of space objects that are subject to registration is broader than that of the Registration Convention Art 1. It's definition includes 'artificial

---

76 Yun Zhao 1, *supra* n. 72, at 53.
77 Yun Zhao 1, *supra* n. 72, Order No. 12.
78 Yun Zhao 1, *supra* n. 72, Order No 6.
79 Yun Zhao 1, *supra* n. 72, at 59.
80 Yun Zhao 1, *supra* n. 72. Arts, 7 and 9 of the Licensing Regulations.
81 Yun Zhao 2, *supra* n. 72, at 15. Registration regulation *supra* n. 78.
82 Ministry of Foreign Affairs, Commission of Science, Technology and Industry for National Defense, Interim Measures, 2002, Art. 4. Yun Zhao 2, *supra* n. 72, at 15.

satellites, crewed spacecraft, space probes, space stations, launch vehicles and parts thereof, and other human made objects launched into outer space.' This leaves open the possibility that human-made space debris may be included within the definition of space object. The definition, however, excludes from the definition ballistic missiles temporarily passing through outer space.[83] The Administration for Science, Technology and Industry for National Defense was reorganized in 2000, and the Chinese national registry was relocated to the China National Space Administration.[84]

A significant number of foreign satellites are launched in China. Current Chinese registration rules require those space objects to be registered in their own national state. China will assist the foreign operator in making its national registration.[85] The implication is that the national state will see to the registration in the UN register. It is interesting that China requires registration to be made within 60 days, an improvement of the Registration Convention's requirement that space objects be registered 'as soon as practicable'.[86]

The licensee must also obtain third-party liability insurance coverage for when the launch vehicle arrives at the location of the intended launch and extending for one year after the launch.[87] It is important for the Government to regulate insurance risk because China is a party to the Liability Convention which provides that China may be liable for third party loss and damage caused by the non-government entities that it launches.

Due to early Chinese launch failures foreign space insurers have been reluctant to enter the Chinese space insurance market. Therefore the Chinese Government initially has had to arrange availability of governmental insurance. A sufficiently large Chinese space insurance pool is gradually being accumulated. But international reinsurance is still necessary.[88] Insurance is presently obtainable from private companies in China, They in turn arrange for reinsurance,[89] which must be obtained in accordance with the government reinsurance provisions[90] When China became a member of the World Trade Organization in 2001, it committed to liberalise insurance regulations in conformity with international practices.[91]

A licensee planning to launch a space object manufactured in China must first obtain a permit for the space object to leave the point of manufacture. The permit must be obtained six months before the planned launch. The Science, Technology and Industry Administration's regulations are linked to possible civil and criminal penalties for fraud, for unauthorised launches, and for abuses leading to liability of and damage to the state.[92]

Because space objects may have military significance, the Chinese regulations also trigger national security regulations. Launches may not endanger Chinese national security. Thus the military authorities have a role in decisions on launch applications.[93] Export

83 Yun Zhao 1, *supra* n. 72, Registration Regulation, Art 2, *supra* n. 78.
84 Yun Zhao 1, *supra* n. 72, at 64.
85 Yun Zhao 1, *supra* n. 72, at 64.
86 Yun Zhao 1, *supra* n. 72, at 64. Chinese Registration Regulation, Art. 9(2).
87 Yun Zhao 1, *supra* n. 72, at 80.
88 Yun Zhao 1, *supra* n. 72, at 77.
89 Yun Zhao 1, *supra* n. 72, 82. The Chinese government's development plan for reinsurance issued in 2007 accepts the need for Chinese reinsurance.
90 Yun Zhao 1, *supra* n. 72, at 82. Reinsurance Provisions, Art 23.
91 Yun Zhao 1, *supra* n. 72, at 78.
92 Yun Zhao 1, *supra* n. 72, at 78.
93 Yun Zhao 1, *supra* n. 72, at 59; Art. 5.2 of the Chinese Licensing Regulations.

of objects with a military value is controlled by the Chinese Government and satellites, launchers and missiles are included on the Chinese Military Products Export Control List.[94]

Presently the Chinese Government experiments with piecemeal regulation and intends to study the results of short-term measures. Based on its experience China may then proceed to adopt comprehensive legislation on the licensing of commercial enterprises, liability, insurance, financing, international cooperation and coordination. This will implement China's obligations and duties under the space law treaties. Finally China is instituting a space debris monitoring and mitigation programme. The plan is not only to track debris in space in order to avoid collisions, but also to mitigate the generation of new debris.[95]

Another area of Chinese commercial space activity is the increasingly important Earth observation. This involves remote sensing, weather and global navigation satellite systems (GNSS) and to some extent communication satellites for reporting earth observations. China is involved in all four areas internationally and domestically. Furthermore, China has to deal with foreign commercial activities in these areas because they operate in non-sovereign outer space over China. China actively protects its national security interests in all these areas.[96]

The Chinese Commission of Science, Technology and Industry for National Defence has issued guidance for some remote sensing activities; in particular the China-Brazil Earth Resources Satellite (CBERS) arrangement has resulted in regulatory activity by the Chinese Centre for Resources Satellite Data and Application (CRESDA). China has created a nationwide Brazilian data bank of remote sensing data for users such as farmers, foresters, and water and land resource managers.[97] The Chinese government has agreed with Brazil that these data are cost-free for the users of the two countries and is also free for the developing countries. CRESDA freely processes, archives and distributes all data above 5 meter resolution. Outside of China and Brazil the data are available on the basis of a fee. However in 2010 the two countries decided to make the data freely available to developing countries.[98]

Chinese and foreign commercial entities may obtain permission to use remote sensing for land surveying and mapping and for business. They may protect their work by filing for copyright protection. In examining surveys the Government will determine whether the work product is affected by the State Secrets Law, and this will involve the military authorities. Survey data that concern important geographical landmarks is restricted.[99]

---

94 Yun Zhao 1, *supra* n. 72, at 78. Regulations on Export Control of Missiles and Missile-related Items and Technologies, at 165.

95 Yun Zhao 1, *supra* n. 72, Chapter 8 and Yun Zhao 2, *supra* n. 72, at 15–18; Xiaofeng, *supra* n. 72. Regulations on Control of Military Products Export. However, we note China's destruction of its own 1999 Feng Yun 1-C polar orbit weather satellite on 11 January 2007 – see Chapter 9.

96 Yun Zhao 1, *supra* n. 72 at 89, lists the following civilian areas: ocean and weather observation, agriculture and forestry, disaster prevention and management, water resource management, resource mapping and surveying, environmental monitoring, climate monitoring and forecasting. To this must be added monitoring and enforcement of obligations assumed under the 2015 Paris Climate Agreement. See also the National Security Law, 2015: www.chinalawtranslate.com/en/2015nsl/.

97 Yun Zhao 1, *supra* n. 72, at 92–96; see the administrative rules on distribution of CBERS domestic data.

98 Yun Zhao 1, *supra* n. 72, at 93.

99 Yun Zhao 1, *supra* n. 72, at 96–99.

Sensing of geological data is regulated by the Chinese Administrative Regulation on Geological Data. Business entities must obtain a permit from the government departments of land and resources either at the State Council level or at the level of the pertinent province depending on whether the sensing is comprehensive and includes large Chinese territory or whether it pertains to specific, local geological resources.[100] An application by the US company Google in 2006 illustrates that commercial entry into the Chinese remote sensing market may be difficult. Google's application pended for four years. In making its application Google agreed to abide by Chinese national security oversight. The matter was not resolved until 2010 when Google decided to withdraw it application and instead to centre its Chinese activities in Hong Kong. In doing so Google declared that it would no longer submit to Chinese national security oversight. Google may now be able to operate freely in Hong Kong, but it will be subject to strict government controls in doing business with the mainland. Thus it may indeed be concluded that the Chinese government strictly controls the distribution and use of remote sensing data.[101]

Europe and the European Union

The European Union originated in 1958 as the European Economic Community, established by the Treaty of Rome of 1957.[102] Its purpose was the creation of a common market.[103] Unsurprisingly, at the time questions of space did not come within its purview. As a result space was left to the initiative of individual states, resulting in the European Space Agency (ESA). ESA is very space active, involved both in research and providing space services.[104]

The idea that a general European space policy was desirable did start to circulate in the 1980s, but it was not until 2003 that a formal White Paper on European Space Policy was published.[105] This reviewed the developing importance of space and indicated that the Community intended to be more active in the area. A Framework Agreement between the Community and ESA followed.[106] This, entering into force in 2004 as the first step toward a formal EU stance as to space, saw the creation of a 'Space Council' to coordinate and

---

100 Yun Zhao 1, *supra* n. 72, at 100.
101 Yun Zhao 1, *supra* n. 72, at 102.
102 TRAITE instituant la Communauté Économique Européenne, Rome 1957, 294 UNTS 23: https://eur-lex.europa.eu/legal-content/FR/TXT/PDF/?uri=CELEX:11957E/TXT. The original parties were Belgium, France, Germany, Italy, Luxembourg and the Netherlands.
103 Case 26162, *Van Gend en Loos*, 1963 [1963] ECR 1; ECLI:EU:C:1963:1, is often cited as a basic statement of the point.
104 For the European Space Agency see Chapter 1.
105 'Space: a new European Frontier for an Expanding Union: An Action Plan for Implementing the European Space Policy', European Commission COM (2003) 673; cf. European Commission, Green Paper, 'European Space Policy', COM (2003) 17: http://esamultimedia.esa.int/docs/space-green-paper_en.pdf. By then the European Commission was the executive of what had by then become the European Community. See R-E. Papadopoulou, 'The European Union and Space: A "Star Wars" Saga?' (2019) 21 *Eur. J. L. Reform* 505–525 at 514 ff. Cf. 'Europe's Access to Space Secured' ESA Bulletin 114, May 2003: www.esa.int/esapub/bulletin/bullet114/chapter1_bul114.pdf.
106 Framework Agreement between the European Community and the European Space Agency, 6.8.2004, OJ EU, L 261/64–L 261/64. Cf. Consultation on 'Common Guidelines' for the signing of the Framework Agreement between the EC and ESA, EU Council, RECH 152, 12858/03.

facilitate cooperative activities.[107] In 2005 a European Space Policy Institute (ESPI) was established in Vienna in 2005 by decision of the ESA Council, to conduct studies and provides reports on mid- to long-term issues of space policy in order to assist relevant decision-makers.[108] A Community Council Resolution on space policy of 2007 aimed at the further coordination of space activities between ESA, the EU and their member states.[109] The process continued through the amendment of the EU basic documents by the Lisbon Treaty of 2009, which, *inter alia*, by Art. 4(3) brought in space competence as an EU function with Art. 189 providing a specific legal basis for developing a European space policy.[110] However, neither of these provisions give the EU power to require harmonisation on its members: space remains a 'parallel competence'.[111] For that and other reasons ESA is not likely to become part of the EU. Not all EU members are members of ESA, and it has too many links with other space active states and agencies, including the post-Brexit UK, to sit as part of the EU.

2016 saw two major developments. First, on 16 June 2016 the UK voted to withdraw from the EU.[112] It continues as a member of ESA. However, 'Brexit' remains a factor in EU space developments. The loss of UK contributions to the EU budget may affect what the EU can afford to spend on space activities. That said, UK companies may have difficulty in attracting procurement contracts for ESA programmes where EU contracting requirements are relevant.

Second, October 2016 saw the adoption of a new space policy for Europe, Europe not just the EU.[113] It pointed out that much had been achieved within Europe, including by ESA, EUMETSAT[114] and by other European states. The EU had invested in such as Copernicus,[115] Egnos and Galileo,[116] had eighteen satellites in orbit with more than thirty planned and was the largest institutional customer for launch services in Europe. Space

---

107 Framework Agreement, *supra* n. 106, Art. 8. The Space Council members comprise all EU and ESA Member and Cooperating States.

108 ESPI: www.espi.or.at/. ESPI reports may be downloaded from the ESPI website.

109 N. Peter, 'The EU's Emergent Space Diplomacy' (2007) 23 *Space Policy* 97–107. For archived data to Feb. 2015 see http://ec.europa.eu/enterprise/space/index_en.html.

110 Treaty of Lisbon amending [the EU Treaties], 2702 UNTS 3; 2010 UKTS 7, Cm 7901; 2007 EC Ser. 13, Cm 7294. Cf. *Consolidated Texts of the EU Treaties as Amended by the Treaty of Lisbon*, UKSP Cm 7310: www.gov.uk/government/uploads/system/uploads/attachment_data/file/228848/7310.pdf and *A Comparative Table of the Current EC and EU Treaties as Amended by the Treaty of Lisbon*, Cm 7311: www.gov.uk/government/uploads/system/uploads/attachment_data/file/228835/7311.pdf. F. Mazurelle, J. Wouters and W. Thiebaut, 'The Evolution of European Space Governance: Policy, Legal and Institutional Implications' (2009) 6 *Int. Org. L. Rev.* 155–189; F.G. von der Dunk, 'The EU Space Competence as per the Treaty of Lisbon: Sea Change or Empty Shell?' (2011) 54 *Proc. IISL* 382-392.
   Cf. I. Marboe, 'European Union as a new actor in outer space' CoCoSL III 601–602.

111 M. Hofmann, 'EU Integrative Approach to Space and Telecommunications Areas' (2020) 63 *Proc. IISL* 493–506 at 495/

112 Technically the withdrawal date was 31 January 2020 following protracted negotiations as to UK/EU future relationships.

113 'Space Strategy for Europe', Communication from the Commission: https://eur-lex.europa.eu/legal-content/EN/TXT/PDF/?uri=CELEX:52016DC0705&from=EN. See also 'A new Space Strategy for Europe': https://ec.europa.eu/commission/presscorner/detail/en/AC_16_3888.

114 The European Organisation for the Exploitation of Meteorological Satellites (EUMETSAT): www.eumetsat.int/. EUMETSAT is discussed in Chapter 12.

115 See Chapter 12.

116 See Chapter 11.

services had become extremely important, and the EU in particular would seek to foster a globally competitive innovative European space sector.

In 2021, the UN General Assembly adopted UNGA Res. 76/3 on 'The "Space2030" Agenda: space as a driver of sustainable development'. Reflecting this and other concerns the ESA Director-General set up a High Level Advisory Group on Accelerating the Use of Space in Europe, which reported in October 2021.[117] The result was an ESA Council Resolution in November 202, the 'Matosinhos Manifesto'.[118] This, once more recognising the importance of space and the space of change, will see particular attention paid to three 'Accelerators', a Green Future Accelerator, a Rapid and Resilient Crisis Response Accelerator, and a Protection of Space Assets Accelerator. The intention is to expand European activities in a competitive and thriving space sector. Accordingly, an informal European Space Summit was held in 2022 to take matters further.[119] Progress continues.

Separately, but not unconnectedly in later 2021 the EU brought forward a proposal to develop an EU strategy on space traffic management to assure the safe and sustainable use of space while maintaining the competitiveness of the EU space industry.[120] There is concern that the US strategy on space traffic management[121] may give a competitive advantage to US commercial interests.[122] After consultations the European Commission sent a lengthy communication to the EU Parliament and Council.[123] This pointed out that there was no globally accepted method of space traffic management particularly for objects in low earth orbit, and the need to preserve EU interests in the matter. Space traffic management was defined as the means and rules to access, conduct activities in and return from outer space safely, sustainably and securely, involving situational awareness, debris mitigation and remediation, the management of orbits and radio spectrum, the life cycle of an operation and re-entry.[124] European practice required systematisation.[125]

Further European developments both within Europe generally and the EU in particular are awaited.

---

117 High Level Advisory Group on Accelerating the Use of Space in Europe: Final Report, October 2021: https://esamultimedia.esa.int/docs/corporate/Accelerating_the_use_of_space_in_Europe.pdf.

118 ESA/C(2021)176 On 'Accelerating the Use of Space in Europe': https://esamultimedia.esa.int/docs/corporate/ESA_C_2021_176_EN.pdf.

119 ESA. 'Decisions from the 2022 Space Summit': www.esa.int/Newsroom/Press_Releases/Decisions_from_the_2022_Space_Summit.

120 ''Space traffic management': https://ec.europa.eu/info/law/better-regulation/have-your-say/initiatives/13163-Space-traffic-management-development-of-an-EU-strategy-for-safe-and-sustainable-use-of-space_en.

121 (US) Space Policy Directive – 3, National Space Traffic Management Policy, 2018: https://trumpwhitehouse.archives.gov/presidential-actions/space-policy-directive-3-national-space-traffic-management-policy/.

122 Cf. Annex 2 to the Eurospace Space Traffic Management Position Paper: https://eurospace.org/wp-content/uploads/2021/03/eurospace-pp_space-traffic-management_opportunity-for-europe_final_february-2021.pdf.

123 High Representative of the Union for Foreign Affairs and Security Policy: Joint Communication to the European Parliament and the Council on 'An EU Approach for Space Traffic Management' and 'An EU contribution addressing a global challenge': https://data.consilium.europa.eu/doc/document/ST-6321-2022-INIT/en/pdfCite. file:///Users/Francis/Downloads/090166c5c9bb138d-1.pdf.

124 Joint Communication, *supra* n. 123, Ch. 2.1. M. Barbano, 'Space Traffic Management and Space Situational Awareness: The EU Perspective' (2022) 47 *Air and Sp. L.* 451–466.

125 For further EU STM developments see Chapter 17, Our Cluttered Neighbourhood.

India

As we write commercial space activities in India are controlled by the Indian Government,[126] but, as outlined below, change is pending.[127] An Indian Space Commission and a Department of Space (DOS) were first set up in 1972, and later the Indian Space Programme was administered directly by the Office of the Prime Minister.[128] Within this framework, the Indian Space Commission established a national space policy implemented by the Department of Space through four agencies: the Indian Space Research Organization (ISRO),[129] the National Remote Sensing Agency (NRSA),[130] the Physical Research Laboratory (PRL) and the National Mesosphere – Stratosphere – Troposphere Radar Facility (NMRF). The Antrix Corporation was created in 1992 to facilitate commercialisation of space activities and develop space launch services.[131] Private operators were encouraged to engage in space activities,[132] and commercial uses of outer space were developed.[133] However, comprehensive legislation specifically on outer space was not adopted.[134] Notwithstanding, India complied with the four basic space treaties,[135] and other obligations.[136]

India is intensely concerned about national and international security and arms control. Indian law requires a licence for export of all dual-use space materials and discourages investments from 'unfriendly countries'.[137] Foreign high technology companies doing business in India must not endanger India's national security.[138] In 2020 the Indian government established IN-SPACE (the Indian National Space and Promotion and Authorization Centre) further to promote Indian private commercial communication space enterprises It arranges for commercial operators' satellite radio frequencies and related orbital slots somewhat similar to US Federal Communication Commission assignment of radio frequencies.

126 See R. Kaul and R.S. Jahku, 'Regulation of Space Activities in India', in Jakhu, ed., *National Regulation of Space Activities* (Dordrecht: Springer 2010) 153–198.

127 See *infra* n. 139.

128 R. Kaul, 'National Space Legislation: A Blueprint for India', Proceedings of the ISRO – IISL Space Law Conference 'Bringing Space Benefits to the Asian Region', Bangalore, India, 2005 at 2–3; K.S.R. Murthi et al., 'Legal Environment for Space Activities' (2007) 19 *Current Science* 1823–1827.

129 See www.isro.gov.in/ and www.isro.gov.in/profile.html.

130 The National Remote Sensing Agency: www.nrsc.gov.in/.

131 Antrix Corporation Ltd: www.antrix.gov.in/.

132 Kaul, *supra* n. 128 at 2–20.

133 Kaul, *supra* n. 128 at 2–19.

134 N. Sarin and V. Longani, 'India', in J. Wheeler, ed., *The Space Law Review*, 3rd ed: 2021.

135 Were the India government to incur a financial liability under the Liability Convention, legislation would be required to authorise the necessary funds. This may alter when the 2023 Space Policy is implemented, *infra* n.139.

136 Thus the Weapons of Mass Destruction and their Delivery Systems (Prohibition of Unlawful Activities) Act 2005 implements UN Security Council Res. 1540 (2004) on the 'Non-proliferation of Weapons of Mass Destruction'.

137 An application by a Chinese company for a trading licence was rejected because the Indian Government considered that the company had unduly close links to Chinese military forces: Kaul and Jakhu, *supra* n. 126, at 168.

138 S. Rai, 'As Foreign Investment Rises, India Addresses Security Concerns', NY Times, 24 August 2006 at C-4; M. Pracha, 'Commentary Paper on National Space Legislation', ISRO-IISL Space Law Conference, Bangalore, 2005, at 2–59.

In 2023 a new formal comprehensive space policy was announced, with an Indian Department of Space as its administrator.[139] A main objective is to enable nongovernmental commercial operators to engage in all kinds of space activities, ranging from what may be termed the traditional to the extraction of resources from outer space, including moon mining.[140]

Section 5 of the policy statement sees the establishment of a new Indian National Space Promotion and Authorization Centre (IN-SPACe) as a regulatory agency supervising nongovernmental actors operating space objects, launching vehicles into outer space, establishing and operating private launch sites, managing the re-entries, tracking operating facilities from Earth, engaging in remote sensing, selling space objects, and providing for other unspecified space activities.[141]

The policy authorises IN-SPACe (1) to establish operating standards either by itself or by joining international standards and to enforce them; (2) to facilitate nongovernmental operators' 'acquisition' of radio frequencies and orbits; (3) to arrange the transfer of new ISRO space technology to nongovernmental operators; (4) to facilitate nongovernmental operators' launch of governmental cargoes; (5) to establish guidelines to avoid liability for damage; (6) to arrange registration of space objects; (7) to arrange dissemination of ow resolution remote sensing; and (8) to enforce the security regulation of high resolution remote sensing data.

The new space policy represents a significant shift of responsibility from the Indian Space Research Organization (ISRO) to the private sector. ISRO will continue to perform basic research and develop new technologies, while transferring its technology to commercial operators. It will also study extraterrestrial habitability and prepare for human life on the moon.[142]

Russia[143]

Russia's commercial space program is currently disrupted by the war with the Ukraine. As the main successor to the former Soviet Union, Russia inherited much of the USSR space

---

139 Indian Space Policy – 2023: www.isro.gov.in/media_isro/pdf/IndianSpacePolicy2023.pdf. For criticism see S. Bhat, 'Outlining Inconsistencies in the Indian Space Policy 2023' (2023) 3 *Lex ad Coelum*, Issue I: https://caslnujs.in/2023/05/01/outlining-inconsistencies-in-the-indian-space-policy-2023/.

140 It seems Indian oversight of exploitative activities will be similar to that of Luxembourg described in Chapter 7. In August 2023 India soft-landed a probe and a rover at the south lunar pole, making India the fourth country to soft-land on the Moon.

141 As of April 2023, India had launched 424 satellites for 34 countries, including Israel, the United Arab Emirates, Kazakhstan, the Netherlands, Belgium and Germany.

142 Space policy, *supra* n. 139, sec. 6. In September 2023 India launched Aditya-L1 to Lagrange point 1 to observe the sun.

143 Russia adopted a 10-year plan for outer space in 2016. (1) Russia wanted not only legal access to outer space but intended to have the necessary technology. Russia would develop a new generation of heavy lift launch rockets. (2) Russia wanted to maintain and to further develop its satellite communication network. (3) Russia planned to maintain and increase its satellite observation capability. (4) Russia planned to continue its partnership with the European Space Agency in the ExoMars science program. (5) In 2016 Russia planned to continue its cooperation in the International Space Station program. Russia's total budget for the 10-year period was planned to be $20.5 billion. The size of this budget was dictated by its economic situation caused by low oil prices and the sanctions related to the conflict with the Ukraine. Russia hoped to earn extra-budget funds from launches of foreign commercial space objects and carriage of foreign astronauts.

launch capability.[144] While Russia suffered economically after the dissolution of the USSR, it also enjoyed an economic advantage through having an excess of space launch capability that could be and was offered at attractive prices to Western commercial operators. Consequently, Russia became a major commercial launch operator aggressively marketing private launches while the excess supply lasted.[145] Furthermore, after the US space shuttle ceased to operate in 2011, Russia became the sole carrier of astronauts to the International Space Station. Thereafter NASA and other non-Russian entities became dependent on the Russian Soyuz space vehicles until 2020 when the US commercial operator Space-X began to transport astronauts to the ISS with its Dragon system.

The Russian Law on Space Activity entered into force in 1993.[146] Its primary purpose is to implement and enforce the international space treaties to which Russia is party (Art. 4). Other purposes include the development of 'entrepreneurial activity', the maintenance of safety, environmental protection, the protection of intellectual property and the promotion of science and national security (Art. 4). The Russian law differs significantly from the Australian and US commercial space laws as to the licensing of private operators. The focus of the Russian law is rather on giving legislative authority to state agencies to engage in state activities and to control participation by non-Russians.

Under Russian law the Russian Space Agency (Roscosmos) is responsible for space activities. In conjunction with the Russian Ministry of Defence the Agency allocates all budgetary resources for use in outer space activities. The Agency has authority to license outer space activities, to supervise safety, and to interact with international organisations on space activities (Art. 6). The Ministry of Defence is responsible for military uses of outer space and, in cooperation with Roscosmos, establishes and implements the Russian Space Programmes (Art. 7).

The Russian Space Agency supervises the space activities of Russian citizens as well as those of foreigners while under Russian jurisdiction, if their activities include 'tests, manufacture, storage, preparation for launching and launching of space objects, as well a

---

See A. Switak and M. Pyadushkin, 'Russia Rethink, Low Oil Prices and Sanctions Leave Little Money for Space Over Next Decade', *Aviation Week and Space Technology*, March 28–April 10, 2016, at 22.

144 National Law Governing Space Activities: Russian Federation, available from OOSA: www.unoosa.org/oosa/en/ourwork/spacelaw/nationalspacelaw/index.html. See S. Malkov and C. Doldrina, 'Regulation of Space Activities in the Russian Federation', in Jakhu, ed., *supra* n. 39, 315–334; S.F. Teselkin, 'Legal Regulation of Space Activities in Russia', in K.-H. Böckstiegel, ed., *'Project 2001: – Legal Framework for the Commercial Use of Outer Space* (Cologne: Carl Heymanns Verlag, 2002) at 511–9; C. Mathieu, *Assessing Russia's Cooperation with China and India: Opportunities and Challenges for Europe*, ESPI Report 12 (Vienna: ESPI, 2008), 'The Russian Federation', 52–79: www.espi.or.at/images/stories/dokumente/studies/espi%20final%20report%20ric.pdf. Cf. J.A. Manner, 'President Bush's 1990 Policy on the Commercial Space Launch Industry: A Thorn in Economic and Political Reform in the Former Soviet Union: A Proposal for Change' (1993) 58 *J. Air L. & Comm.* 981–1040. The Ukraine inherited many ballistic missiles. Baikonour Cosmodrome is in Kazakhstan.

145 V. Gubarev, A. Lavrov and S. Teselkin, 'Commercial Space: Major Direction of Activities, Legal Framework and General Privatization Policy in Russia', *Project 2001 Workshop on Legal Framework for Privatising Space Activities*, Vienna, 1999 (Cologne: Institute of Air and Space Law, 1999) 108–17 at 108 and 113.

146 Russian Federation Law on Space Activity 1993, *supra* n. 144. The following discussion refers to Articles of this law.

See also Malkov and Doldrina and Teselkin, both *supra* n. 144. Russian Federation Law on Space Activity (translated) in *Project 2001: Workshop on Legal Framework for Privatising Space Activities*, Vienna, 1999 (Cologne: IASL, 2000) 249–260; *Project 2001 Workshop on Legal Framework for Commercial Launch and Associated Services*, Bremen, 2000 (Cologne: IASL, 2001) 313–324, *supra* nn. 144 and 145.

control over space flights'. The Act further provides that the 'types, forms, and terms of licences, the conditions and procedures for their issue, withholding, suspension or termination thereof, as well as other questions of licensing [are] regulated by the Russian legislature' (Art. 9).

The Russian space programme includes the construction of space hardware performed by contractors. Preference is given to Russian participants (Art. 16). While collaboration with foreign entities is allowed in the construction of space hardware, foreign participation in Russian companies may not exceed 49% (Art. 14). Article 17 requires registration of Russian space objects, and these must display Russian national markings.[147]

Control of flight in outer space is exercised by Russian Flight Control, which may permit foreign spacecraft to enter or use Russian air space as necessary for the launch of a foreign space object on a Russian launcher or its re-entry.[148] Flight Control coordinates as necessary with local authorities as well as with foreign countries and international organisations (Art. 19). Manned Russian spacecraft must be under the command of Russian cosmonauts. The commander is fully responsible for the flight, the safety of the crew and any other participants and the preservation of the spacecraft. Foreigners may be carried on Russian spacecraft, but they must be trained in Russia, be under the command of the Russian commander and are subject to Russian law while in the spacecraft (Art. 20).

The Russian Space Agency and the Ministry of Defence are jointly responsible for the safety of space objects. Space objects must function and operate in accordance with state safety regulations (Art. 22). Accidents are required to be investigated and any conclusions may be appealed to the Russian courts of justice (Art. 23). The Russian government conducts search and rescue operations for lost space objects and cosmonauts and cleans up after accidents, costs being met by the Federal Russian Government (Art. 24).[149]

Foreign operators doing business in Russia have the same legal rights as domestic operators. Foreign companies receive full protection for patents and the copyright and other intellectual property rights enjoyed by Russian companies on a reciprocal basis (Art. 27). Any legal dispute involving a foreign company functioning in Russia is subject to Russian law, unless otherwise arranged by international agreement (Art. 28).

Liability is extensively regulated under Russian law. Compulsory insurance is required for space activities in order to cover possible liability to third persons and private parties. Operators of space objects must therefore obtain liability insurance in the amounts required by the Russian Government. The proceeds of insurance policies will be applied to

147 Under Arts. 4.1(b) and 5 of the Registration Convention states may designate their space objects with markings analogous to the registration markings of airplanes required under Art. 20 of the Convention on International Civil Aviation, Chicago 1944, 15 UNTS 295.
148 'The space object of a foreign state can execute a single innocent flight through the air space of the Russian Federation with the purpose to insert such an object into an orbit around the Earth or further in outer space, as well as with the purpose to return it to the Earth under the condition of advance notice of appropriate services of the Russian Federation about time, place, trajectory and other conditions of such flight' (Art. 19.4).
149 Russia and Kazakhstan argued over pollution caused by launches from the Baikonour launch site in Kazakhstan, Kazakhstan suspending Russian use of the site until compensation was agreed: M. Hošková, 'The 1994 Baikonour Agreements in Operation' (1999) 42 *Proc. IISL* 263–272. Cf. M. Bjornerud, 'Baikonour Continues: The New Lease Agreement between Russia and Kazakhstan' (2004) 30 *J. Sp. L.* 13–36. See also www.msnbc.msn.com/id/14346394/. Russia is now building a new spaceport in its Eastern Amur region which will be able to launch cosmonauts, See Svitak and Pyadushkin, *supra* n. 143, at 22.

compensate personal injury losses and damages sustained by cosmonauts and other personnel (Art. 25). The Russian Government guarantees full compensation for direct damage resulting from outer space activities. Full compensation must be paid by the responsible commercial companies and individuals. Liability is based on proof of fault and is limited by the amount of insurance obtained (Arts. 29 and 30). According to Russian space legal experts: '[I]f a foreign customer of a space launch is not a government juridical person, Russia is, actually, the only launching country. In our opinion, on the basis of Article VII of the 1972 Convention, the conclusion may be drawn that in these cases the provisions of the 1972 Convention will not be applied to the Russian Federation. Russia will only be liable to its citizens and/or juridical persons on the basis of civil liability in conformity with national legislation of the Russian Federation.[150] Under Russian law juridical persons are required fully to indemnify loss and damages they cause. As space activities are considered to be ultra-hazardous perpetrators of damage are fully liable to third parties.[151] However, in conformity with the Liability Convention, Art. 30 of the Russian Act provides for Russian Government liability for loss and damages caused by a Russian state-owned spacecraft. This is absolute for damage caused on the surface of the earth or in air space, and for loss and damage caused in outer space on proof of fault. In the latter case if a number of entities are involved in liability any compensation exigible is either proportionate to the fault of each, or if that cannot be established, equally.

Russian commercial launch contracts always contain clauses requiring insurance covering possible loss and damage to launch facilities together with coverage for civil liability to third parties. The purpose of this compulsory insurance requirement is to cover Russia's potential liability as the launching state under the contracts to launch foreign space objects.[152]

Disruption to the Russian commercial space program began in 2020 as Russian cosmonauts began to travel to the ISS on US commercial spacecraft, the space budget proving inadequate. Then from 2022 Russia started to divert its resources to its war effort and the European Union and other Western operators withdrew from joint space activities with Russia. In addition US support of the Ukraine led to the US Government to restrict Russian access to US technology, including amending the US Export Administration Regulations (15 CFR, Part 746) further to restrict space technology exports to Russia. In 2022 Russia announced it planned to end its ISS partnership with NASA in 2024 but later revised that date to 2028.[153] Instead it will join China in building a lunar research station on the Moon in the 2030s.[154] NASA however intends to continue the ISS at least until 2030. There may therefore be a problem as ISS propulsion is located on the Russian segment of the ISS and a different propulsion agent will be needed to raise the orbit of the ISS.[155]

150 V. Gubarev, A. Lavrov and S. Teselkin, 'Civil Liability to Third Parties in the Course of Russia's International Cooperation in Outer Space: Legal Regulation Issues', in Böckstiegel. *Project 2001, supra* n. 145, 159–166, at 162.

151 Gubarev et al., *supra* n. 145.

152 Gubarev et al., *supra* n. 150, at 166.

153 The ISS partners are Russia, US, Canada, ESA, and Japan; see further re the ISS in Chapter 4.

154 See Chapter 7 c. n. 128 ff.

155 U. Pavlova and K. Fisher, 'Russia says it will quit the International Space Station after 2024', CNN July 26, 2022: www.cnn.com/2022/07/26/world/russia-quit-iss-scn. M. Koren, 'The Russian Space Program is

New Zealand

New Zealand is a recent entry to adventurous space activities. By way of preparation a New Zealand Space Agency was set up in 2016 as the lead agency for NZ space policy, regulation and development of the space sector.[156] In 2017 the Outer Space and High-altitude Activities Act, 2017 was passed to facilitate the development of a NZ space industry, to ensure its safe and secure operation and to comply with relevant international obligations (s. 3).[157] While it had ratified the OST, ARRA and the Liability Convention New Zealand only adhered to the Registration Convention in 2018 when it entered the launch market.[158] Not unconnectedly, the US company Rocket Lab,[159] had identified the Mahia peninsula on the NZ North Island east coast at c. 39°S as a potential spaceport, from which an associated NZ company, Rocket Lab NZ, now operates.[160]

The 2017 Act applies to space activities carried out from New Zealand territory, and to NZ nationals and entities conducting space operations overseas (ss. 23 and 31). The legislation sets up a system of licences and permits. A licence is required to launch a launch vehicle from the land territory of New Zealand (ss. 7–14), to launch a launch vehicle overseas (ss. 23–30), to operate a launch facility in New Zealand (ss. 38–44), or to launch a high-altitude vehicle from New Zealand, or from a vehicle in the air that was launched from New Zealand (ss. 45–49). A payload permit is required for the launch of a payload from New Zealand (ss. 15–22), and for the launch of a payload overseas (ss. 31–37).

Licences and permits are issued by the Minister of the Crown (a senior government minister) responsible for the Administration of the Act (s. 4).[161] The Minister must take into consideration a variety of matters including the fitness and propriety of the applicant (s. 52), the technical capability of the applicant, public safety, the national interest, consistency with international obligations, and other requirements deemed relevant.[162] For a launch licence the Minister must be satisfied as to the 'orbital debris mitigation plan' for the launch (s. 9.1.c), and consult the security Ministers and follow their advice (s. 55). The Minister may take into account authorisations issued by another country, provided he is satisfied that its considerations and requirements meet those that New Zealand itself would have applied (s. 51). Licences and permits may require the holder to indemnify the Crown in whole or in part for any liability arising from New Zealand international obligations including the Outer Space Treaty and the Liability Convention (ss. 14.3 and 18.2).[163]

A separate section of the Act deals with 'high-altitude' activities and in effect regulates air launches (ss. 45–49). For the Act 'high altitude' is defined as being above the higher of flight level 600 and the highest upper limit of NZ controlled airspace as defined by the Civil Aviation

---

Falling Back to Earth', *The Atlantic*, 14 October 2022: www.theatlantic.com/science/archive/2022/10/us-russia-space-programs-spacex-collaboration-ukraine/671740/

156 NZ National Space Policy 2023: www.mbie.govt.nz/dmsdocument/26656-national-space-policy. NZSA website://www.mbie.govt.nz/science-and-technology/space/.

157 New Zealand legislation is available at www.legislation.govt.nz/.

158 New Zealand has not signed the Moon Agreement of 1979.

159 Rocket Lab constructs and launches small lightweight rockets: www.rocketlabusa.com/.

160 M. De Zwart and D. Stephens, 'The Space (Innovation) Race: The Inevitable Relationship between Military Technology and Innovation' (2019) 20 *Melb. J. Int. L.* 1–28 at 8–10.

161 Outer Space and High-altitude Activities (Licences and Permits) Regulations 2017 (2017/250).

162 For reasons of wordage, we do not cite all the provisions for the different forms of licence and permit.

163 This will permit the introduction of a liability cap in the licence or permit. We do not know whether any have been applied.

Act 1990 (s. 4).[164] A high altitude vehicle is defined as an aircraft or other vehicle that travels or is capable or intended to travel at high altitudes. However, certain kinds of high altitude balloons and model rockets are excluded from regulation under the Act.[165] Licensing and payload permits are required. Suffice it to say that the requirements for these mirror the licence and permit provisions that have just been summarised. There are, of course, criminal sanctions for unlicensed activities, or for failing to provide accurate necessary information and so on.

Part 3, Subpart 2 deals with the 'protection of sensitive space technology'. This involves the setting aside of areas of land. For the purpose of the US-NZ Technology Safeguards Agreement (defined in s. 63(9)),[166] s. 63 gives power to the Minister to declare an area as segregated (s. 63(1)(a)), or as an area specially set aside for work with US launch vehicles and US spacecraft, or related equipment (s. 63(1)(b)). An area is declared as segregated or set aside by appropriate perimeter signage or other appropriate notification (s. 63(1)). It may consist of private property, but only with the consent of the owner or occupier of the land concerned (s. 63(2)). Entry to a segregated or set aside area is limited. Persons that may enter if authorised by the US participants, are an enforcement officer on official duties; a person wearing an official identity card, or a person accompanied by someone wearing such a card (s. 63(3)(a)). In addition a police constable, a person exercising a statutory function or fire, or ambulance services may enter (s. 63(3)(b)). Persons in a relevant area must be able to identify themselves, justify their presence, and leave the area if ordered by an enforcement officer or other person in control of the area (ss. 63(4)–(8)). Refusal to comply is an offence (ss. 63(7) and 73)).

Apart from the matters covered in s. 63, which clearly relate to the spaceport and are applicable to the Mahia Spaceport and area, s. 64 provides for the declaration of a debris protection area. This clearly will relate to an accident or unscheduled incident. Interestingly, the unauthorised taking of photographs etc., and removal of debris or samples is specifically prohibited in the statute (s. 64(3)).

United Kingdom[167]

The UK was swift to ratify the four basic space law treaties.[168] However, it was slow to adopt domestic legislation to regulate its own space activities.[169] The Outer Space Act, c. 38 of 1986, which did not come into force until 1989 remained unchanged for thirty years until the government took the decision further to encourage the UK space industries, and, in the light of technological developments, to permit launches to space from mainland UK.[170] Now two separate but inter-related sets of provisions deal specifically with space, the Outer

---

164 Roughly speaking, flight level 600 is 60000 feet above sea level (c. 18200 metres).

165 Outer Space and High-altitude Activities (Definition of High-altitude Vehicle) Regulations, 2017 (2017/251).

166 The NZ-US Agreement on Technology Safeguards Associated with United States Participation in Space Launches from New Zealand is available from the NZSA website.

167 An earlier version of the following is 'United Kingdom Space Law' (2022) 71 ZLW 216–223. See also J. Wheeler, 'United Kingdom' in J. Wheeler, ed., *The Space Law Review*, 3rd ed: 2021.

168 The UK has not signed the Moon Agreement.

169 Scuttlebutt has it that the UK had not noticed the obligations that it had undertaken until the Japan Government, intending to implement its own obligations under the OST, inquired what the UK had done.

170 *National Space Strategy* (HM Government, 2021); *A Strategy for Space in Scotland* (Scottish Government, 2021). See also National Space Strategy in Action (HM Government, 2023): www.gov.uk/government/publications/national-space-strategy-in-action/national-space-strategy-in-action.

Space Act, 1986 as amended now dealing with space activities outside the UK, and the Space Industries Act, 2018, which regulates activities within the UK. Apart from this legislation all UK space activities remain subject to relevant international agreements including as to telecommunications,[171] and to normal civil obligations such as arise from contract and intellectual property rights. We do not here cover matters military,[172] or the UK participation in scientific and commercial space projects.[173]

The Outer Space Act, c. 38, as amended, is concerned with UK space activities taking place anywhere except in the UK. Duties and powers are assigned to the Secretary of State (s. 4),[174] which, since 2010, have been administered by the UK Space Agency (UKSA) as overseer of the UK civil space programme.[175] The UK register of all UK space objects wherever launched (s. 7(1)–(2)), is open to public inspection free of charge (s. 7(3)).[176]

As amended the Act applies to launching or procuring the launch of a space object, operating a space object, and 'any activity in outer space' (s. 1(1)(b)),[177] but does not apply to activities on mainland UK, or to activities that require authorisation under the 2018 Space Industry Act (s. 1(2)). UK nationals and British subjects, Scottish firms,[178] and bodies incorporated under UK law that intend to launch, procure a launch or operate a space object are required to obtain a licence from the Secretary of State (ss. 2–3). However, an activity may be exempted from UK licensing requirements where the UK government has an arrangement with another state under which the UK obligations under the space treaties are fulfilled (ss. 3(2)(b) and 3(3)).

Licences are granted at the discretion of the licensing authority (s. 4(1)) and may be time-limited and subject to conditions (s. 5). A licence may be issued provided that public health and the safety of persons and property are adequately protected, that the activities are consistent with UK international obligations, and that UK national security is not impaired (Art. 4(2)).[179] The Secretary issues regulations implementing the Act (Art. 4(3)) and in practice the UKSA sets the form and content of the application for a licence, the procedures for its processing, time limits, and licence fees (ss. 4 and 4A). Data to be supplied

---

171   The Office of Communications (Ofcom), operating under the Office of Communications Act 2002, c. 11, and the Communications Act 2003, c. 21, is the UK telecommunications supervisory agency and deals *inter alia* with UK frequency assignments.

172   A UK Space Command, staffed by personnel from the Royal Navy, the British Army, the Royal Air Force and the Civil Service and operating as a Joint Command, was formed on 1 April 2021.

173   At the time of writing UK participation in various European scientific and commercial after its withdrawal from the European Union is still under discussion, not to say negotiation. The UK remains a member of the European Space Agency (ESA).

174   By UK practice any Secretary of State, a senior government minister in charge of one or more departments, may exercise the functions of 'the' Secretary of State.

175   The UKSA was established on 1 April 2010. Its website is www.gov.uk/government/organisations/uk-space-agency.

176   UK Registry of Outer Space Objects (UKSA, 2010): www.gov.uk/government/publications/uk-registry-outer-space-objects.

177   'Outer space includes the moon and other celestial bodies' (s. 13(1)(b)). There is no indication that altitude or any other objective factor is to be considered in defining where outer space 'is'. However, see *infra* at n. 187 for the application of the 2018 Space Industries Act.

178   A 'Scottish firm' has a legal personality separate from that of its members, although it is not a registered company: Partnership Act, 1890, c. 39, s. 4(2).

179   An example of a UK licence is at https://assets.publishing.service.gov.uk/government/uploads/system/uploads/attachment_data/file/744342/Example_of_an_Outer_Space_Act_License_Updated_September_2018__002_.pdf.

in the application includes the date and location of the launch and the basic parameters of the intended orbit for the space object. There must be no interference with the activities of others, nor any breach of UK international obligations, and UK national security must be secured (s. 5(2)(a)–(e)). Finally, the licensee must comply with any requirements regarding disposal of the payload in outer space once the licensed activity has ceased, including in an appropriate case a 'graveyard' disposal (s. 5(2)(g)).

A licensee is liable to indemnify the UK government against any claims that arise from the activities defined in s. 1 and incur UK state liability under the Liability Convention (s. 10). A licensee must therefore obtain insurance from the public insurance market (s. 5(2)(f)). However, it is possible for the licensee to be exempted from the requirements of s. 10 (s. 3(3A)). In addition, the licence may set a limit to the liability of the licensee (s.10(1A)), in which case the UK government will meet any excess above that limit.[180]

A licence may be revoked or suspended if its conditions no longer exist, if its termination or suspension is required for reasons of public health, national security, or to comply with UK obligations under the space treaties (s. 6). An appeal against revocation or suspension is possible under procedures contained in the 2018 Space Industries Act (s. 6A).[181] The Secretary may enforce the terms of a licence (ss. 8–9). Violation of the licence or any other defect (e.g. false statements, obstruction of government inspectors, failure to comply with the requirements of a licence) may result in fines and other penalties (s. 12(1)). Offences are treated as committed in the UK no matter where they occur and are subject to enforcement under UK law (s. 12(4)). Due diligence and the taking of all reasonable precautions to avoid the commission of the offence are defences to a criminal charge (s. 12(5)).

The Space Industry Act 2018, c. 5, is intended generally to encourage the domestic UK space sector.[182] Previously all UK satellites were launched from foreign launch sites, but the recent development of smaller rockets and micro-satellites have made it feasible to launch objects from the UK itself at least into low earth orbit. In addition limited space tourism may be practicable.

Many of the provisions of the 2018 Act involve UK domestic law, for example as to local planning law and the purchase of land for launch facilities, so we omit consideration of these as not directly concerning space law as such. These elements apart, the new legislation permits the launch of small satellites, scientific experiments and orbital and suborbital spaceflights from the UK mainland and islands. Direct, and indirect launches by carrier aircraft, are envisaged. Spaceports will operate, and the law governing the use of UK airspace and related matters has been amended to take account of such developments (s. 67 and Schedule 12).[183]

---

180 'Guidance: Commercial spaceflight: launch liabilities and insurance' (Department of Transport, 2021). Currently for standard operations a cap of £60m is set, but other considerations may alter the requirement in a particular case.

181 The Space Industry (Appeals) Regulations 2021, 2021 SI 816.

182 See LaunchUK: www.gov.uk/guidance/how-we-are-promoting-and-regulating-spaceflight-from-the-uk. The Act was brought into force from 21 July 2021 by the Space Industry Act 2018 (Commencement No. 1), 2018, 2018 SI 1224, the Space Industry Act 2018 (Commencement No. 2, Transitional and Savings Provisions) Regulations, 2021, 2021 SI 817, and the Space Industry Act 2018 (Commencement No. 2, Transitional and Savings Provisions) (Amendment) Regulations, 2021, 2021 SI 874. See also 'Launch UK: The UK's Spaceflight Programme' (UKSA, 2019).

183 The Airports Act, 1986, c. 31, Civil Aviation Act 1982, c. 16, Aviation Security Act, 1982, c. 36, Aviation and Maritime Security Act, 1990, c. 31, Transport Act, 2000, c. 38, and various statutes relating to policing and criminal justice are amended.

While UK space activities carried out elsewhere than in the UK remain governed by the 1986 Act, the 2018 Act regulates space activities, suborbital activities and associated activities carried out in or from the UK (s. 1(1)). By ss. 16(1) and (3), the Secretary of State[184] may appoint one or more regulators to administer and supervise the operation of the Act.[185]

Unlike the 1986 Act, the application of the 2018 Act is not limited by UK national connection. It applies to anyone carrying out or continuing space activities in the UK (s. 1(2)). 'Space activities' are defined as launching or procuring the launch or the return to earth of a space object, operating a space object, or any activity in outer space (s. 1(4)(a)–(c)). Unhelpfully, s. 69(1) provides that 'outer space has the same meaning as in the Outer Space Act 1986'.[186] 'Suborbital activities' do not include any space activity, and consist of the launching or procuring the launch or the return to earth of an aircraft carrying a rocket or other craft capable of operating above the stratosphere, or a crewed or passenger carrying balloon that is capable of reaching the stratosphere (ss. 1(4) and 1(5)), but the term 'stratosphere' is not defined in the statute.[187] Spacecraft or objects going beyond the stratosphere are to be entered on the UK Register (ss. 61(1)–(2)). Space activities and suborbital activities are collectively referred to as 'spaceflight activities' (s. 1(6)).

The Civil Aviation Authority (CAA) has been appointed to regulate spaceflight activities that are subject to the 2018 Act,[188] and a complex set of regulations has been issued.[189] Spaceflight activities must be licensed (s. 3(1)). Unlicensed activities are criminal (s. 3(7)) and penalised by a fine and/or up to two years imprisonment (s. 53). A long list of considerations is relevant in the grant of a licence. Public safety is paramount (s. 2(1)), but many other interests are taken into account, including national security, the environment,[190] and UK international obligations (s. 2(2)). Conditions in each licence will include the mitigation of space debris and the disposal of payloads (s. 13(1) and Sched. 1).

A spaceport is a site from which spacecraft or carrier aircraft are launched or landed (s. 3(2)) but is not a sea-borne installation that is moveable without major dismantling or modification (s. 3(3)).[191] Spaceports within the UK must be licensed (ss. 3(1)(b) and 3(2)). The regulator must consider the risks involved and be satisfied that these have

---

184 See *supra* n. 174.
185 See *infra* n. 188.
186 See *supra* n. 177.
187 The stratosphere can lie anywhere between 10 and 40/50 km above sea level depending on air density and temperature. However, Sec. 1.13 of the Guidance on Applying for a Licence issued by the UK regulator, the CAA, states: 'By way of clarification, the regulator proposes to use the International Standard Atmosphere (47km) as the stratopause (i.e. the upper limit of the stratosphere) for the purposes of determining whether an activity is "sub-orbital"': https://assets.publishing.service.gov.uk/government/uploads/system/uploads/attachment_data/file/904285/guidance-on-applying-for-a-licence.pdf.
188 The Space Industry Act 2018 (s. 16; s. 69(1)) together with Reg. 3 of the Space Industry Regulations, 2021, 2021 SI 792. The CAA website is www.caa.co.uk/.
189 The Space Industry Regulations, 2021, 2021 SI 792; the Space Industry (Appeals) Regulations, 2021, 2021 SI 816. Cf. 'Unlocking Commercial Spaceflight for the UK. Space Industry Regulations Consultation: summary of views received and the Government's response' (UKSA, March 2021) and the House of Commons Science and Technology Committee, 'The Draft Spaceflight Bill', Fourteenth Report of Session 2016–17, HC 1070.
190 Section 2.2(e) together with 'Guidance to the regulator on environmental objectives relating to the exercise of its functions under the Space Industry Act 2018' (Department of Transport, 2021).
191 This provision takes account of any possible revivification of sea-launches.

been minimised so far as practicable (s. 9). A spaceport licence will not be issued unless the regulator is satisfied that all reasonable steps have been taken to ensure that risks to public safety are as low as reasonably practicable, and any prescribed criteria or requirements have been met (s. 10). Proximate to and including the spaceport a 'range' or zone of airspace, land or sea, is designated, within which controls or restrictions necessary for the spaceport to operate are applied (s. 5). The acquisition and the restriction of other uses within the range or zone are provided for (ss. 39–50). 'Range control' powers, exercised by a licensed range controller, will define the zone, set appropriate requirements, and monitor actual activities and their conformity with requirements (ss. 6–7, and 11 with Sched. 1).

An 'operator licence' is required to carry out space activities in the UK from a spaceport (ss. 3(1)(b) and 3(2)). As with the issuance of the spaceport licence the regulator will consider the risks involved, and have to be satisfied that, so far as practicable, these have been minimised (s. 9).[192]

In the case of manned flight the operator must obtain the informed consent of individual participants (s. 17). Training will be required, as will appropriate qualifications and medical fitness, though presumably the eventual requirements will be adapted dependent on the role the individual is to play; a tourist is unlikely to be required to undergo the training programme required of operational crew (ss. 17, 18 and Schedule 2).[193]

Licensed spaceflight activities will not result in action for nuisance or trespass, but licensees will be liable for personal injury, death or physical damage that they may cause.[194] Section 34 dealing with such matters loosely reflects the provisions of the Liability Convention and includes absolute liability. A licensee will be required to indemnify the UK against claims (s. 36), but the licence may set a cap on the sum required, the UK meeting any liability above that limit (ss. 12(2) and 34(6)).[195]

The new launch facilities will not be used by UK firms and businesses only. Foreign spacecraft will be launched from the UK. In addition what is done may well involve foreign technologies. Certainly the UK expects that US technology will have a role to play and a US – UK Technology Safeguards Agreement was signed on 16 June 2020.[196] The Space Industry Regulations therefore include provision for the observance of the terms of any relevant agreement that may be entered into, particularly with the US.[197]

---

192 Space Industry Regulations, 2021, 2021 SI 792, Part 4, Regulations 25–30, 'Grant of a spaceflight operator's licence: risk'.
193 Detailed 'Informed consent' procedures and requirements are set out in the Space Industry Regulations, 2021, 2021 SI 792, Part 12, Regulations 203–217.
194 The Spaceflight Activities (Investigation of Spaceflight Accidents) Regulations, 2021, 2021 SI 793.
195 It is possible that a statutory cap will be set, but at present the matter will be covered in each case by the individual licence.
196 UK-US: Agreement in the form of an Exchange of Notes between the United Kingdom and the United States of America on Technology Safeguards associated with United States Participation in Space Launches from the United Kingdom [CS USA No.1/2020], CP 307. The US firm Lockheed Martin is involved in the Shetland programme: Press release 16 July 2018: www.gov.uk/government/news/lockheed-martin-and-orbex-to-launch-uk-into-new-space-age.
197 Space Industry Regulations, 2021, 2021 SI 792, Part 10, 'Spaceport Safety', Regulations 151–167; Part 11, 'Security', Regulations 168–202. Matters dealt with include the appointment of security site managers, access to imported US technology, the screening of personnel, site access and security, and other physical and cyber-security considerations.

Given the location of the UK proximate to Europe, a launch to orbit in any direction will have to be carried out with care.[198] Over-flight of the European mainland on the way to orbit is unlikely in the foreseeable future. However, a northern launch trajectory over the eastern North Atlantic is entirely feasible. To that end appropriate Memoranda of Understanding have been entered into with Iceland and the Faroe Islands.[199] Another factor to be considered will be the numbers of trans-Atlantic flights that transit the UK. Space tourism from UK spaceports will have to penetrate that flow on the way up and on the way down.[200] In short, accommodating all the interests affected by the UK developments will require skill. It is a pity that the opportunity to define where 'space' begins for the UK was not taken,[201] but that apart we await further UK developments with interest.

United States

The US emphasis is on promotion of commercial space activities.[202] Two strands of regulation deal with space. One strand governs the governmental agency, the National Aeronautics and Space Administration (NASA), established under the National Aeronautics and Space Act of 1958.[203] NASA deals with the authorisation and supervision of US governmental space activities. NASA does, however, promote a number of private activities in outer space where these are of governmental interest. For example transportation to the International Space Station may be provided within NASA's legislative authority and oversight.[204]

---

198 Sites for direct launches to space include Lamda Ness, Unst, in the Shetland Isles (c. 60° N), and the A' Mhòine peninsula in Sutherland (c. 58° N). Air-launch from sites further south is also feasible including from Prestwick and in Moray. A licence has been issued for flights from Spaceport Cornwall, based at Newquay Airport.

199 Iceland: https://assets.publishing.service.gov.uk/government/uploads/system/uploads/attachment_data/file/1010867/UKSA_Iceland_MOU.pdf; Faroe Islands: https://assets.publishing.service.gov.uk/government/uploads/system/uploads/attachment_data/file/914515/Faroe_Islands_Memoranda_of_understanding.pdf.

200 Cf. the English Channel ferries that pass through the shipping flowing between the Atlantic and the North Sea, or familiar computer games such as 'the hedgehog crossing the road'.

201 New Zealand has adopted the higher of Flight Level 600 and the highest upper limit of NZ controlled airspace as defined by its Civil Aviation Act, 1990, as the point at which a licence is required for launches from its territories: Outer Space and High-altitude Activities Act, 2017, No. 29, ss. 45–49. Australia requires a licence for launches intended to reach more than 100km above sea level: Space (Launches and Returns) Act 2018, No, 123, 1998, Compilation No. 10, s. 8, Definitions: 'launch'.

202 Cf. M. Smith, USA' in J. Wheeler, ed., *The Space Law Review*, 3rd ed: 2021. But see also 'United States' in Chapter 15 *infra*.

203 National Aeronautics and Space Act, 1958, 72 Stat. 426: http://uscode.house.gov/download/annualhistoricalarchives/pdf/2010/2010usc51.pdf. J.C. Cooper, 'Memorandum on the "National Aeronautics and Space Act of 1958"' (1958) 25 *J. Air L. & Comm.* 247–52 (text of Act at 253–64); S.N. Hosenball, 'NASA and the Practice of Space Law' (1985) 13 *J. Sp. L.* 1–7. The original Act and its current incarnation are respectively available at http://history.nasa.gov/spaceact.html and www.nasa.gov/offices/ogc/about/space_act1.html. Cf. *Legislative Origins of the National Aeronautics and Space Act of 1958*, NASA History Series, No. 8, 1998: http://history.nasa.gov/45thann/images/legorgns.pdf. See National and Commercial Space programs, 51 USC 101

204 Berger, 'NASA Places $500 Million Bet on Two Very Different Firms', *Space News*, 28 August 2006 at 6.

The other strand of US regulation deals with civilian use of space. The US actively pro-motes private space commerce,[205] and has licensed many private commercial launches.[206] The Commercial Space Launch Act regulates only launches and re-entry. It does not man-date US government 'authorization and continuing supervision' of US nongovernmental activities in outer space.[207]

The US Commercial Space Launch Act, as amended,[208] requires the Secretary of Trans-portation not only to regulate commercial launches and re-entries, but also to promote the commercial launch industry. Parallel duties as to safety regulation and promotion of the launch industry could place the Secretary in the uncomfortable position of hav-ing to choose between safety and industry promotion. Analogously, the Secretary was until recently in a similar dilemma with regard to air commerce because the US Federal Aviation Act similarly mandated the Secretary to regulate air safety and to promote the aviation industry. The US Congress finally decided that aircraft flight safety would be enhanced if the Department of Transportation concentrated on air safety and so it elimi-nated the mandate for the promotion of the industry. The dilemma facing the Secretary's potentially conflicting duties as to the space launch industry has not yet risen to congres-sional attention.

The statutory functions of the Secretary of Transportation under the Commercial Space Launch Act have been delegated to the Federal Aviation Administration Office of Commercial Space Transportation (FAA AST). The FAA is the largest Administration within the Department of Transportation (DOT). The Commercial Space Launch Office is administered by the Associate Administrator in charge of the Office of Commercial Space Transportation.[209] This Office administers the commercial space launch laws and the regulations adopted pursuant to the Commercial Space Launch Act. The FAA licenses only private commercial launches. It has no legal authority to authorise US Government launches which are a matter for NASA.

---

205 Cf. 'A Strategic Framework for Space Diplomacy' US State Department, May 2023: www.state.gov/wp-content/uploads/2023/05/Space-Framework-Clean-2-May-2023-Final-Updated-Accessible-5.25.2023.pdf.

206 US Code, Title 51 – Commercial Space Launch Activities – 51 USC 50901–50923. See S. Mirmina and C. Schenewerk, *International Space Law and Space Laws of the United States*, 'Federal Aviation Administration Office of Commercial Space Transportation (FAA AST)' 128–152 (Cheltenham: Edward Edgar Publishing, 2022).

207 OST Art VI requires governmental authorization and continuing oversight of nongovernmental activities in outer space.

208 51 USC §50901(b). US Commercial Space Launch Act, *supra* n. 206. Cf. Mirmina and Schenewerk, *supra* n. 206; M.S. Straubel, 'The Commercial Space Launch Act: The Regulation of Private Space Transporta-tion' (1987) 52 *J. Air L. & Comm.* 941–972; A.R. Filiato, 'The Commercial Space Launch Act: America's Response to the Moon Treaty' (1987) 10 *Fordham Int. L.J.* 763–81; J.L. Reed, 'The Commercial Space Launch Market and Bilateral Agreements in Space Launch Services' (1997) 13 *Am. U. Int. L. Rev.* 157–218; K.M. Costello, 'The Commercial Space Launch Act Amendments of 1988 and Launch Industry Insur-ance Reform' (1991) 14 *Suffolk Transnat. L.J.* 492–522; J.A. Manner, 'President Bush's 1990 Policy on the Commercial Space Launch Industry: A Thorn in Economic and Political Reform in the Former Soviet Union: A Proposal for Change' (1993) 58 *J. Air L. & Comm.* 981–1040; T.R. Hughes and E. Rosenberg, 'Space Travel Law (and Politics): The Evolution of the Commercial Space Launch Amendments Act of 2004' (2005) 31 *J. Sp. L.* 1–79. P.A. Vorwig, Regulation of Private Launch Services in the United States, in Jakhu, ed., *supra* n. 39, 405–420 (Springer, 2010).

209 Details at http://ast.faa.gov. Mirmina and Schenewerk, *supra* n. 206, 128–152.

The Commercial Space Launch Act requires private operators to be licensed to operate a launch site in the US or to launch in the US. A permit is also required for the re-entry of space objects. A US citizen must obtain a FAA launch licence for a launch outside of the US unless a foreign government having jurisdiction over the launch agrees to authorise and supervise the launch.[210] For a launch licence to be issued, the payload must comply with US requirements.[211]

The FAA may transfer a licence to another licensee after it has been satisfied that the transferee will comply with the requirements of the Commercial Space Launch Act. The FAA prescribes safety regulations for launch vehicles, re-entry vehicles and for persons involved in launch and re-entry. In order to ensure compliance with the laws and regulations the FAA is permitted (but not required) to have a federal employee observe the launch and the launch operator must coordinate the launch with the FAA representative if one is present.[212] The FAA may modify a launch licence and the operator must comply with any such modification. The FAA may also suspend a licence should the operator fail to conform to the licence as issued. The FAA may revoke a licence for reasons of public health, safety, national security or foreign relations. Revocation, and any modification of a licence, takes effect immediately, unless this is differently stated in the relevant notice.[213]

In addition to licensing a launch, the FAA also approves the safety of launch and re-entry vehicles, their safety systems, processes and services and of persons employed in launch activities.[214] FAA safety approval is voluntary on the part of the operator, but safety approval will facilitate the issuance of the launch licence, a powerful incentive to request the process. Separate FAA safety approval is persuasive in convincing customers that a launch vehicle is safe and dependable. FAA safety approval is also of value in the launch operator's negotiations for the use of government launch ranges since the FAA will coordinate the safety approval request with the safety officials attached to government owned launch ranges. For the safety approval the FAA examines activities that may endanger public health and safety including a review of the licence applicant's safety organisation, the design of the launch vehicle, and its operation. Much of the safety examination is of the kind that a launch range would require in any case.

The procedure established by the FAA Commercial Space Launch Office for the issue of a licence for launch into outer space, including the possible re-entry of a reusable launch vehicle, involves several steps. The FAA consults with the applicant in order to guide the preparation of the application. Policy is reviewed to ascertain whether the application will affect US national interests in national security, public health and safety. The applicant's capability of launching from the designated launch facility, including the object's re-entering at designated re-entry point, is considered. The FAA reviews the applicant's organisational safety plan, estimates the risks of the mission, examines safety process, mission

---

210 Cf. the Australian legislation, *supra* n. 41.
211 50 USC §50904.
212 51 USC §50907.
213 51 USC §50901.
214 51 USC §750905. The 2015 US Commercial Space Launch Competitiveness Act, H.R. 2262, 114th Congress (2014–2016), s. 111, authorised the Secretary of Transportation to facilitate the development of voluntary industry consensus standards based on recommended best practices to improve the safety of crew, government astronauts and space flight participants. Text at www.congress.gov/114/plaws/publ90/PLAW-114publ90.pdf.

readiness and the rules, plans and checklists for the mission, and studies the plans for communication, operations and accident investigation, and emergencies. FAA launch and re-entry licensing examines whether the launch of the payload and its re-entry will cause any special safety or policy problems. The FAA reviews the environmental consequences in accordance with the National Environmental Policy Act.[215]

The potential US governmental unlimited absolute liability under the Liability Convention for damage caused by private commercial activities is a major factor in the licensing process. Launch operators want their potential liability limited. The government wishes to control its liability and to keep its risks as low as possible.

Potential private operators claimed that they could not engage in private space business activities unless a ceiling for their liability was established by national legislation.[216] Their argument was in particular that unlimited absolute liability would either crush them or would prevent them from starting up a business unless there was a ceiling on their possible exposure to catastrophic risk. Without a limitation of their liability the US would be deprived of the benefits of their initiative, their ingenuity, and in particular their inventiveness directed towards the bringing down of launch costs. On the other side non-US launch providers might argue that the mitigation of risk exposure for US nationals is a subsidy, conceals the true price of a launch into outer space, and distorts equitable competition.

Balancing these considerations the Commercial Space Launch Act provides for a distribution of liability and costs.[217] In order to obtain a launch licence various requirements must be met. (1) The operator is required to obtain third-party liability launch insurance of US$500 million or as much liability insurance as is available at reasonable cost.[218] (2) The operator must obtain liability launch insurance of US$100 million, or as much insurance as is available at reasonable cost on the insurance market, in order to cover the operator's possible liability to the US Government.[219] The amount of the insurance policy thus becomes the operator's *de facto* liability limit. (3) The operator must also agree to enter into reciprocal waivers of claims with its contractor, subcontractors, owners of payloads and the contractors and subcontractors of the owners of the payload and flight participants. In the cross-waivers the parties agree to assume responsibility for property damage or loss as well as for personal injury or death of employees resulting from the launch.[220] The purpose of the cross-waivers is to spread the risk of loss as widely as possible and yet limit it to the input of each party to the enterprise. The result is that each contractor or sub-contractor can calculate what it needs to sustain a loss of a launch or payload without losing all available assets through liability to other sub-contractors involved in the enterprise. Possible losses will be smaller. Each separate contractor and sub-contractor will be able to purchase

---

215 42 USC §§4321 *et seq.*
216 G.H. Reynolds and R.P. Merges, 'Toward an Industrial Policy for Outer Space: Problems and Prospects of the Commercial Launch Industry' (1988) *Jurimetrics* 7–42; G.H. Reynolds, 'The Omnibus Space Commercialization Act of 1993' (1994) 20 *Rutgers Comp. and Tech. L.J.* 581–605 (the bill was not enacted). The ceiling on liability exposure is temporary, but it has been renewed repeatedly.
217 51 USC §50914. Mirmina and Schenewerk, *supra* n. 206, 128–152.
218 The FAA required Bert Rutan to obtain third-party insurance in the amount of only $3.1 million for his X Prize effort. See Hughes and Rosenberg *supra* n. 178, at 37.
219 Hughes and Rosenberg *supra* n. 178, at 56. So far, the amount of available insurance has always been less than the statutory liability limits.
220 P.B. Larsen, 'Cross-Waivers of Liability' (1992) 35 *Proc. IISL* 91–96. For private actions cf. S. Eigenbrodt, 'Out to Launch: Private Remedies for Outer Space Claims' (1989) 55 *J. Air L. & Comm.* 185–222.

affordable insurance because its risk exposure is smaller and does not involve liability to other contractors should a launch failure be attributable to it. (4) The operator is also required to enter into a cross-waiver with the Secretary of Transportation. While the statute requires a cross-waiver of claims, courts will not read a cross-waiver into the contract between the parties should they neglect to include one.[221] In the case that a state party to the Liability Convention brings a claim against the US that exceeds the statutory liability limits, the Act holds the US Government liable for damages in excess of the liability limits up to US$2 billion. Should the exigible compensation exceed that amount it is assumed that special congressional legislation would be passed to meet that liability.[222]

While the licensing of private launch operators has the benefit of limiting their liability, insurance may be expensive. The cost of insurance becomes part of the expense a private launch operator incurs in doing business and therefore increases the market price of a launch. A government launch operator is not required to obtain launch insurance. It may be argued that the government operator therefore has a competitive advantage over the private operator.[223] Another view is that the Government self-insures.

The FAA requires that an applicant for a launch licence make efforts to mitigate the formation of space debris in accordance with the international space debris guidelines. The applicant must plan to prevent collisions between the components of the launch vehicle and the satellite being launched.[224] Reusable launch vehicles must also avoid endangering human presence in outer space.[225] Other US government agencies such as the Federal Communications Commission (FCC) and the National Oceanic and Atmospheric Administration (NOAA) also require debris mitigation by applicants for their permits. These national debris mitigation regulatory requirements are in conformity with the international voluntary debris mitigation rules adopted by the Inter-Agency Space Debris Coordination Committee (IADC) and endorsed by both COPUOS and the UN General Assembly in 2007.[226] An environmental review in accordance with the criteria of the National Environmental Policy Act (NEPA) is also carried out to insure that the launch does not have a significant impact on the human environment.[227] In addition other US national legislation establishes procedures and clearances for radiofrequencies and orbital slots, remote sensing[228] and the registration of satellites.

---

221 The issue arose in the case of *Martin Marietta v INTELSAT* (1991) 763 F. Supp. 1327; (1993) 991 F.2d. 94. The court held that it would not enforce a cross-waiver if it was not formally included by the parties in their contract. In the case the reason for the omission of cross-waivers was that the contract was negotiated prior to the entry into force of the Commercial Space Launch Act, but the relevant launch took place after the Act had entered into force. K.B. Watson, 'Have the Courts Grounded the Space Law Industry? Reciprocal Waivers and the Commercial Space Launch Act' (1998) 39 *Jurimetrics* 45–58.

222 50 USC §50915.

223 R.J. Lee, 'Legal and Policy Aspects of Launch Services Provided by Governmental and Private Providers', Bangalore, India, IISL Conference 'Bringing Space Benefits to the Asian Region', 26–29 June 2005.

224 Mirmina and Schenewerk, *supra* n. 206, 128–152.

225 Id.

226 For the IADC Guidelines see https://iadc-home.org/; www.iadc-home.org/documents_public/view/id/172#u; or https://iadc-home.org/documents_public/view/search_field/eNortjI2tlJy1CsuTcpK TS7RdtTLS8xNBVIliclAMjk_ryQ1r6RYyRpcMAypDUU~/search_keyword/eNortjI0sFJKL81MSc3Jz-EstVrIGXDA2ZQXx/page/1/id/82#u; or UN Doc. A/62/20, Annex; UNGA 62/217; CoCoSL III, 605–657. For a more extensive consideration of space debris, see Chapter 9 Space Debris.

227 Mirmina and Schenewerk, *supra* n. 206, 128–152.

228 See Chapter 12.

In 2004 the US Commercial Space Launch Act was amended to give the FAA authority to issue a private commercial launch licence for a space vehicle to carry human beings for compensation in order to encourage and promote the safety of commercial vehicles designed to carry human beings.[229] The purpose is to foster and promote private commercial launch initiatives in human space flight.[230] Under it the FAA sets standards for the design and operation of launch vehicles to protect the health and safety of the crew and the flight participants. Prior to executing any contract or other arrangement to employ a prospective crew member, the holder of a RLV licence or permit must notify the crew members and flight participants that the US Government has not certified the launch vehicle as safe.[231] The law does not require crew members to waive the potential liability of the licensee or permit holder. Space flight participants must provide written 'informed consent' to participate in the flight thus transferring the risks of the flight to the space flight participants themselves. The flight operator can thus escape liability, and the participants do not have benefit of coverage under the liability insurance policy for the launch.[232] Because adequate consent is such an important element of human space flight, the FAA has issued guidance about what constitutes informed consent. The adequacy of informed consent will depend on the kind of spacecraft used for human (touristic) space flight. This is an important issue relevant to viability of the 'informed consent'. If disclosure is insufficient, then the statutory requirement will not have been met.[233]

Flight crew and flight participants on US licensed launches must comply with US laws regarding the launch.[234] Space flight participants (e.g. tourists on-board) are defined as anyone who is not a member of the flight crew.[235] Under this distinction between crew and participants, it would appear that crew members would be entitled to assistance under ARRA, but arguably flight participants would not be so entitled in law.[236] The holder of the launch licence or permit may not launch into outer space or re-enter to land on Earth unless the flight crew has been adequately trained and meets FAA medical standards. The pilot of a US reusable launch vehicle (RLV) in US air space must hold an FAA pilot certificate and

229 Public Law 108–492, 118 Stat. 3974–83, now incorporated into 50 USC § 50905; Hughes and Rosenberg, *supra* n. 178. See also Chapter 5.
230 Cf. R. Sattler, 'Transporting a Legal System for Property Rights: From the Earth to the Stars' (2005) 6 *Chic. J. Int. L.* 23–44 at 23–7. Investment in space was sought to be encouraged by the proposed Invest in Space Now Act 2003 (HR 2358, 108th Cong.) and the Zero Gravity, Zero Tax Act 2003 (HR 1024, 108th Cong.) (Sattler at n. 17), but neither was enacted.
231 Hughes and Rosenberg, *supra* n. 178, at 51–60. The FAA wants to ensure that crews and flight participants clearly to know that the launch vehicle does not meet FAA certification standards.
232 Mirmina and Schenewerk, *supra* n. 206, 128–152.
233 Hughes and Rosenberg, *supra* n. 178, at 55, 59; C.M. Hearsay, 'The Foreign Space Flight Participant Problem: Can a Space Flight Operator Balance Satisfaction of FSS Informed Consent Information Requirements with ITAR?', [2012–2013] 6 *Phoenix L. Rev.* 303–358; S.A. Langston, 'Suborbital Flights: A Comparative Analysis of National and International Law' (2011) 37 *J. Sp. L.* 299–329 at 389–391; S. Hobe, G.M. Goh and J. Neumann, 'Space Tourism Activities – Emerging Challenges to Air and Space Law' (2007) 33 *J. Sp. L.* 359–374; T. Knutson, 'What is "Informed Consent" for Space-flight Participants in the Soon-to-Launch Space Tourism Industry?' (2007) 33 *J. Sp. L.* 105–22; S.H. Bromberg, 'Public Space Travel – 2005: A Legal Odyssey into the Current Regulatory Environment for United States Adventurers Pioneering the Space Frontier' (2005) 70 *J. Air L. & Comm.* 639–71.
234 Mirmina and Schenewerk, *supra* n. 206, 128–152.
235 Cf. discussion of 'informed consent' in Chapter 5.
236 It is difficult to envisage rescuers insisting on the strict letter of the law. Cf. discussion in Chapter 5.

the flight crew must have FAA Second Class medical certificates.[237] Flight participants must also be medically fit. The crew must be trained in air as well as space flight. For safety reasons the Department of Transport (DOT) requires the members of the flight crew to be carefully trained to perform their crew functions. Furthermore, the flight participants must refrain from any interference with the flight crew operating the space vehicle.

Flight crew and flight participants require dependable life support within the RLV. The RLV operator must provide a controlled environment.[238] Flight crew must be able to suppress fire on-board the space vehicle and prevent the crew from being incapacitated.[239] Most accidents involve human factors. The space vehicle must be designed to prevent the possibility of human error.[240] Flight crew could lose consciousness if subjected to uncontrolled extreme acceleration, noise or vibration. RLVs must therefore be designed and operated so that the crew can tolerate these factors. Launches are to be monitored by the US Government. The DOT may suspend a licence when a life support on-board the space or re-entry vehicle fails and results in serious accident. The suspension will terminate when DOT ascertains that the licence holder has taken steps to remedy the cause of the accident. DOT can also modify the licence to remove the likelihood of accidents.[241]

We note that the US Commercial Space Launch Act only regulates the launch and de-orbiting of space objects. It does not regulate operations while the object is in outer space. In the absence of a clear causal connection to a licensed launch or re-entry, operations or occurrences in orbit would not be part of the FAA statutory responsibility.[242]

In 2015 at the urging of prospective private mining companies the US adopted the Commercial Space Launch Competitiveness Act,[243] which interprets the OST as permitting individual national states to authorize commercial exploitation (mining) of celestial bodies. That brings into play OST Art. I, which states that celestial bodies may be freely used 'for the benefit and in the common interests of all countries.' Art. I is subject to OST Art. II that: 'Outer Space, including the Moon and other celestial bodies, is not subject to national appropriation by claim of sovereignty, by means of use or occupation, or by any other means.'[244] The question posed by the US Act is therefore whether authorisation of private commercial mining operators constitutes a national appropriation of celestial

---

237 The FAA requires Second Class medical certificates for commercial non-airline-flight functions. Pilots of scheduled air service must have the more stringent First-Class medical certificates.

238 This includes air supply, atmospheric pressure, air circulation, reserve oxygen, controlled humidity, controlled concentrations of gas and particulates that may be inhaled, storage to avoid interference with the flight, and plans to mitigate decompression. Mirmina and Schenewerk, *supra* n. 206, 128–152.

239 Id.

240 'Human factors engineering' includes elements of psychology, physiology, engineering, ergonomics and medicine.

241 51 USC §50908.

242 Hughes and Rosenberg, *supra* n.178, at 21. Cf. the Australian position, *supra*. The 2015 US Commercial Space Launch Competitiveness Act, *supra* n.184, requested the US Government to prepare an approach that would prioritize safety, utilize existing authorities, minimize burdens on industry and meet US international obligations.

243 *Supra* n.184.

244 See discussion in Chapter 7, c. n. 116 ff. P.B. Larsen, 'Asteroid Legal Regime, Time for a Change?' (2014) 39 *J. Sp. L.* 275–326. P.B. Larsen, 'Is There a Legal Path to Commercial Mining on the Moon' (2021) 83 *Univ. of Pittsb. L. Rev.* 1–49.

bodies. That section provides that it is specifically made subject to existing international law, so the 2015 legislation is indeed circumscribed by the Outer Space Treaty.

The US initiative has activated discussion of its compliance with the OST. The US, supported by some countries, has argued that its legislation does comply with the OST.[245] Other countries have questioned how celestial resources can or will be distributed 'for the benefit and in the interest of all countries', and they have stated the need for countries to agree on the sharing of celestial resources. That lack of consensus could prevent the US interpretation from becoming 'evidence of a general practice accepted as law'. Formal agreement will be needed.

Last, the US Federal Communications Commission is involved in the rules for the use of radio frequencies and licensing assignments to operators and supervising various matters.[246] In view of increasing demands for regulation and decisions on such matters a specialised space bureau within the FCC has been established.[247]

Conclusion

States and their nongovernmental entities benefit from adopting national space legislation regulating access to and use of outer space. The US, UK, Australia, New Zealand and Russia are examples of states that have such. Other countries having significant space commerce, for example, China, India, Indonesia and Thailand, are considering the development of comprehensive national legislation for commercial space activities. Ultimately, whether to adopt national space legislation depends on national interests, the stage of economic and social development, constitutional structure and the nature of the private space activities a state will allow.[248]

OST Art. VI requires its parties to exercise 'continuing supervision' over the activities of their nationals engaging in commercial parties in outer space. The national legislations of some states limit their application to the launch phase. The Australian legislation can also be made applicable to the de-orbit phase. The US legislation has also been amended to include the de-orbiting of satellites and reusable launch vehicles. However, the commercial space laws of these two countries do not yet regulate space objects while in space, thus leaving a possible vacuum in their national oversight. This is a serious omission because Art. VI specifically requires continuing oversight. Increasingly, commercial operators have continuous activities in outer space. Commercial activities in outer space, in particular any involving human beings in outer space and national appropriation 'by any means', require extensive national supervision; they could involve emergencies requiring rescue of space participants.[249] In view of the very specific language of OST Art. VI we suggest that national space legislation should include supervision of commercial activities while in outer space. Of course other national laws govern the use of space objects while they are in outer space. For example, national communications laws implementing the rules agreed through

---

245 The Act states that it is made subject to existing international law (§ 51303).
246 See *inter alia* FCC action on the deorbiting of LEO satellites (Chapter 9 at n. 136) and the sharing of space and terrestrial frequencies (Chapter xxx at n.)
247 See https://docs.fcc.gov/public/attachments/DOC-390599A1.pdf and https://docs.fcc.gov/public/attachments/DOC-392418A1.pdf.
248 Yun Zhao 2, *supra* n. 72, at 9.
249 See Chapter 5 Astronauts

the International Telecommunication Union regulate the use of space frequencies and the occupation of orbital slots.[250]

The 'boundary question' remains. COPUOS has not arrived at a consensus on the matter. Knowing exactly where space legislation applies would add a useful legal certainty and predictability for commercial space activities. The OST applies to space objects in orbit. Minimum orbital altitude is about 100 kilometres (62 miles) but states in general do not recognise minimum orbital altitude as the boundary of outer space. The Bogota Declaration asserted that the geostationary orbit (GSO) at *c.* 22,500 miles above the respective territories of its signatories is the national territory of each.[251] The Australian legislation specifically refers to an altitude of 100 km above the surface of the Earth, making that in effect the boundary of outer space for the purpose of its legislation. The US national legislation does not state a specific boundary between outer space and air space.[252] In the absence of international agreement, an increasing delimitation by national regulation would benefit space commerce provided that states adopt the same limits.[253]

We suggest that steps should be taken to cope adequately with the transfer between states of the OST Art. VI supervisory duties and authority on changes to the ownership of a space object in space. Preferably this should be done on a universal basis by a multilateral agreement to secure international consistency. It would benefit launching states seeking to terminate potential liability after transfer of space object ownership to persons in non-launching states. That would also benefit and make certain security transfers of security interests in space objects.[254]

Lastly, the new space age has arrived. The number of commercial satellites in non-sovereign outer space has greatly multiplied in recent times and continues to multiply. Entire constellations such as Starlink are profitable. Earth observation satellites have also significantly increased in number. This growth in commercial satellites causes their states of registry to become interested in protecting nationally registered satellites from interference by other states, which has caused states to declare outer space to be military domain. They acquire means to assert military power to protect commercial activities from interference both in outer space itself and on celestial objects such as the moon. The current confrontation in outer space between the United States and China is an example not only of confrontation between space powers, but also of the need for the space powers to recognize the scarcity of space resources. As indicated by the meeting of US President Biden with Chinese President Xi in 2022 the space powers are beginning to recognise that they have to respect each other as they resolve conflicts.[255]

---

250 See Chapter 8 Radio and the International Telecommunication Union.
251 The Declaration of the First Meeting of the Equatorial States, Bogota, 1976 (1978) 6 *J. Sp. L.* 193–6; Manual 2: 383. See Chapter 6.
252 Cf. the (US) New Mexico 'Gross Receipts and Compensating Tax Act, 2007' where, in dealing with deductibles from taxable receipts from space and space port activities, 'space' is defined by Sec. 7-9-54-2.(3) as meaning 'any location beyond altitudes of sixty thousand feet above the earth's mean sea level': http://nxt.ella.net/NXT/gateway.dll?f=templates$fn=default.htm$vid=nm:all. See also Chapter 6.
253 We would wish not to see a diversity in limits. The precedent of the very varied territorial sea claims made by states prior to the 1982 UN Convention on the Law of the Sea should be taken as a warning.
254 See Larsen, *supra* n. 15, at 380, and discussion of the Space Protocol in Chapter 13.
255 'Beb Adler, Biden and Xi agree to resume cooperation on fighting climate change', 14 November 2022, *Yahoo News*: www.aol.com/news/biden-xi-agree-resume-cooperation-1811806847.hrml

15

THE MILITARY USE OF OUTER SPACE

Introduction

Some two and a half thousand years ago Sun Tzu wrote *The Art of War*.[1] Dealing with 'Terrain' in his Tenth Chapter Sun Tzu recommended that if possible one should occupy the high ground. Space provides a new aspect to that principle. Unimpeded access to outer space and unrestricted freedom to use outer space and celestial bodies provide a tempting opportunity for a technologically advanced country to seize control of outer space and deny freedom of use to other countries that stand in its way. A country in possession of unique advanced space technology and with the will and means to use it for military purposes might achieve dominance over non-space-faring countries and otherwise to impose its will.[2] For that reason it is both concerning and reassuring to see the topic being analysed, and, we hope, defused.[3] That said, commercial space operators and other civilian users also have interests in the space domain. Issues of incompatibility among claims to the

---

1 Sun Tzu, *The Art of War* (various editions).
2 R.A. Ramey, 'Armed Conflict on the Final Frontier: The Law of War in Space' (2000) 48 *A. F. L. Rev.* 1–158. At 4 Ramey asserted that US practice in outer space was so far advanced that it would 'dominate' the practices of other states.
3 Manual on International Law Applicable to Military Uses of Outer Space, Vol. 1, Rules: www.mcgill.ca/milamos/. See also J. Grunert, *The United States Space Force and the Future of American Space Policy: Legal and Policy Implications* (Leiden: Brill, 2022); A.K. Lai, *The Cold War the Space Race, and the Law of Outer Space* (Abingdon: Routledge, 2021); J.J. Klein, *Understanding Space Strategy: The Art of War in Space* (Abingdon: Routledge, 2020); B.E. Bowen, *War in Space: Strategy, Spacepower, Geopolitics* (Edinburgh: Edinburgh UP, 2020); L. Dawson, *War in Space: The Science and Technology Behind Our Next Theater of Conflict* (Vienna: Springer, 2018); J. Johnston – Freese, *Space Warfare in the 21st Century: Arming the Heavens* (Abingdon: Routledge, 2017); *Preventing the Weaponization of Space*, Science for Peace, 2003: https://scienceforpeace.ca/preventing – the – weaponization – of – space/.

   Needless to say the UNGA and UN Office for Disarmament Affairs (UNODA): www.un.org/disarmament/) have been active. There is an annual Conference on Disarmament (www.un.org/disarmament/conference – on – disarmament/). See its 2022 Report to the General Assembly, GAOR A/77/27. For UNGA resolutions see most recently UNGA Res. 77/40 'Prevention of an arms race in outer space' (2022) and UNGA Res. 77/250 (2022) 'Further practical measures for the prevention of an arms race in outer space', and other materials cited *infra*.

DOI: 10.4324/9781003496502-15

domain may therefore arise. But how far might this go? As an extreme example perhaps space mining or lunar bases might result in future conflict were the military be called in to defend national interest.[4]

This chapter considers whether and to what extent military control of outer space is lawful under the peacekeeping legal regime of the United Nations, as well as under the space law treaties and general international law.[5] We are aware of the parallel doctrinal debate as to the 'Just War' but will not pursue that topic.[6] We are also aware of the existence of the cyber sphere of conflict, potential and actual, but lack the data to do other than to note it briefly.[7] Again the military aspects of outer space interact with matters considered in other chapters of this book. In particular the closely related area of controls applied to international trade in military and dual-use technologies by national and international rules and procedures is outlined in Chapter 13.

One simple question is 'where is space'? We have discussed the 'boundary question' in Chapter 6. Here we simply observe that it is all very well to agree that space should be used only for peaceful purposes, to prohibit the orbital stationing of nuclear weapons or weapons of mass destruction in space, or to attempt to regulate the use in space of weaponry normally used in air space, but, unless it is known where 'space' 'is', the ambit of such duties is unclear.

---

4 P.B. Larsen, 'Outer Space: How shall the World's Governments Establish Order Among Competing Interests' (2019) 29 *Wash. Int. L.J.* 1–60. S. Isakowitz, 'Toward a Better Space Industry' *Av. Wk. & Sp, Tech,* May 30–July 21, 2022.

5 F.G. von der Dunk, 'Armed Conflicts in Outer Space: Which Law Applies?' (2021) 97 *Int. L. Stud.* Ser., US Naval War College, 188–231; M. De Zwart and D, Stephens' The Space (Innovation) Race: The Inevitable Relationship between Military Technology and Innovation' (2019) 20 *Melb. J. Int. L.* 1–28; J. Gutzman, 'State Responsibility for Non – State Actors in Times of War: Article VI of the Outer Space Treaty and the Law of Neutrality' (2019) *Air Force L. Rev.* 87–148; I.M. Vasilogeorgi, 'Military Uses of Outer Space: Legal Limitations, Contemporary Perspectives' (2014) 39 *J. Sp. L.* 379–451; R.A. Morgan, 'Military Use of Commercial Communications Satellites: A Fresh Look at the Outer Space Treaty and "Peaceful Purposes" ' (1994) 60 *J. Air L. & Comm.* 237–325; M. Bourbonniere, 'Legal Regime for Keeping Outer Space Free of Armaments' (2002) 27 AASL 109 (Bourbonniere I); his, 'Law of Armed Conflict (LOAC) and the Neutralization of Satellites or *Jus in Bello Satellitis*' (2004) 9 *J. Conflict and Security L.* 43 (Bourbonniere II) [Lyall/Larsen, 515–541]; his 'National – Security Law in Outer Space: The Interface of Exploration and Security' (2005) 70 *J. Air L. & Comm.* 3–62 (Bourbonniere III); and his 'The Ambit of the Law of Neutrality and Space Security' (2007) 36 *Israel Y.B.H.Rts.* 205–29; A. Rosas. 'The Militarization of Space and International Law' (1983) 20 *J. Peace Research* 357–364; L. Tate, 'The Status of the Outer Space Treaty during "War" and "Those Measures Short of War" ' (2006) 32 *J. Sp. L.* 177–202; W. von Kreis, 'Military Space Activities – Legally Unconstrained?' A. Kerrest, ed., *L'Adaption du Droit de l'Espace ses Nouveau Défis – Liber Amicorum, Mélanges en l'honneur de Simone Courtieux* (Paris: Editions Pedone, 2007) 105–118; G.B. Fernandez, 'Where No War Has Gone Before: Outer Space and the Adequacy of the Current Law of Armed Conflict' (2019) 43 *J. Sp. L.* 245–279. See also successive 'Space Security' reports from 'Project Ploughshares' of the Secure World Foundation: www.swfound.org and spacesecurity.org. See also US Air Force and T. Hagmaier, *Air Force Operations and the Law: A Guide for Air, Space and Cyber Forces,* 2nd ed. (USAF: CreateSpace IPP, 2014); *Space Operations,* Air Force Doctrine Document 3–14 (USAF, 2011).

6 M.T. Karoubi, *Just or Unjust* War?: *International Law and Unilateral Use of Armed Force by States at the Turn of the 20th Century* (Aldershot: Ashgate, 2004); O. O'Donovan, *The Just War Revisited* (Cambridge: Cambridge UP, 2003); M. Walzer, *Just and Unjust Wars: A Moral Argument with Historical Illustrations,* 3rd ed. (New York: Basic Books, 2000); J.T. Johnson, *Just War Tradition and the Restraint of War: a Moral and Historical Inquiry* (Princeton: Princeton UP, 1981).

7 US arrangements, *infra* n. 212; the UK, *infra* n. 227. See also P.D. Trooboff, 'Globalization, Globalization, Personal Jurisdiction and the Internet. Responding to the Challenge of adapting settled Principles and Precedents' (2021) 415 *Hague Recueil des Cours,* 9–321.

Military control of outer space or its militarisation has two main aspects. One is straightforward – the stationing and potential use of clearly military equipment in space. The other (and more difficult) is that almost all space activities can have a military aspect.[8] Basic technologies such as launch vehicles, their guidance systems and operation are dual use, carrying the potential for civil or military use. Satellite technologies are the same. Remote sensing is usable for intelligence gathering and the acquisition of relevant meteorological data. GNSS systems have been used in conflict.[9] Telecommunication satellites transmit civilian and military messages. Other satellites may serve to monitor and intercept telecommunications traffic whether carried on terrestrial radio systems or passing through satellite transponders. An unstated fact is that states find possession of space technologies an advantage in their relationships with other states.[10]

The danger of the military use of outer space is increasing as states continue to develop technology capable of operating in outer space and therefore available for military purposes.[11] Law must respond.[12] On occasion it will seek to regulate technology when there is the political will to comply, but the political will must be there.[13] The law of outer space is not a wholly coherent set of rules and practices. Its provisions reflect its evolution through the Cold War, the accommodations between the parties involved, and current and future expectations. We accept that it is by no means clear how the corpus of space law would operate in time of war: there is the old maxim, *inter arma leges silentia sunt* (in time of war the laws are silent).[14] Certainly space technology is regularly used short of physical conflict as well as in modern hostilities. However, the very existence of space law may constrain the military use of space and hopefully (Sun Tzu notwithstanding) avert devastating possibilities.[15]

---

8 F. Tronchetti, 'The Right of Self – Defence in Outer Space: An Appraisal' (2014) 63 *ZLW* 92–120; J.D. Rendleman, 'Brave New World of Hosted Payloads' (2013) 39 *J. Sp. L.* 129–180. The point was early recognised, e.g. H.J. Taubenfeld, 'A Regime for Outer Space' (1961) 56 *Nw. U. L. Rev.* 129–167 at 156–159; J.C. Cooper, 'Self – Defense in Outer Space and the United Nations' (1962) 5 *Air Force and Space Digest* 51–60 (rep. I.A. Vlasic, ed., *Explorations in Aerospace Law: Selected Essays by John Cobb Cooper* (Montreal: McGill UP, 1968)) 415–422; D.G. Brennan, 'Arms and Arms Control in Outer Space', in L.P. Bloomfield, ed., *Outer Space: Prospects for Man and Society* (Englewood Cliffs: Prentice – Hall, 1962) 123–149; H. DeSaussure et al., 'Self – Defense – A Right in Outer Space' (1965) 7 *Air Force L. Rev.* 38–45. See also E.S. Waldrop, 'Integration of Military and Civilian Space Assets: Legal and National Security Implications' (2004) 55 *Air Force L. Rev.* 157–231 at 168–74.

9 Waldrop, *supra* n. 8 at 173–174; P.B. Larsen, 'Issues Relating to the Civilian and Military Uses of GNSS' (2001) 17 *Space Policy* 111–119. Note: the US GPS, Russian GLONASS and Chinese Beidou are military systems.

10 Cf. D. Paikowski, 'Israel's Space Program as a National Asset' (2007) 23 *Space Policy* 90–96.

11 I.M. Vassilgeorgi. 'Military Uses of Outer Space; Legal Limitations and Contemporary Perspectives' (2001) XXVI AASL 379–453. Cf. E.S. Waldron, 'Weaponisation of Outer Space: US National Policy' (2004) XXIX AASL 329–355; I. Sourbes – Verger, 'La Militarisation de L'Espace; Perspective Européenne' (2004) XXIX AASL 357–375; R. Lee and S.L. Steele, 'Military Use of Satellite Communications, Remote Sensing and Global Positioning Systems in the War on Terror' (2014) 79 *J. Air L. & Comm.* 69–112.

12 Bourbonniere III, *supra* n. 5. Cf. material on law and technology, Chapter 1 at nn. 8 and 9, and Chapter 2 at n. 32.

13 US/USSR: Treaty on the Limitation of Antiballistic Missile Systems, Moscow, 1972, 23 UST 3435, TIAS 7545; (1972) 11 ILM 784. The US denounced the treaty as of 2002. See *infra* nn. 115 and 116.

14 M.T. Cicero, in his undelivered defence of Titus Annius Milo, *Pro Milone*.

15 Cf. P.C. Jessup, 'The Reality of International Law' (1939–1940) 18 *For. Aff.* 244–253. See also '"Peaceful" and Military Uses of Outer Space – Law and Policy', Report from the Center for Research on Air and Space Law, McGill University, R. Jakhu, Principal Investigator (2005) XXX – II AASL 511–530.

Context

It would be wrong to treat the law on the military use of outer space as entirely separate and distinct from other international law on military matters. OST Art. III provides that 'States Parties . . . shall carry on activities in the exploration and use of outer space . . . in accordance with international law, including the Charter of the United Nations, in the interest of maintaining international peace and security and promoting international cooperation and understanding'. OST Art. IV para 1 prohibits various military uses of space, including the stationing of nuclear or other weapons of mass destruction in space or on celestial bodies. Celestial bodies are to be used 'for peaceful purposes only' (OST Art. IV para 2).[16] Space cannot therefore be treated in isolation. Its military potential is part of the general law as to war.

The law of war has two aspects, the *ius ad bellum* – the circumstances under which it is lawful to go to war – and the *ius in bello* – the law as to how war is conducted.[17] In the past such as the Kellogg – Briand Pact of 1928 sought to outlaw war,[18] and conspiracy to wage aggressive war and waging aggressive war were Counts One and Two in the Charges at the Trial of the Major War Criminals at the Nuremburg Tribunal.[19] The Hague Conventions of 1899 and 1907 together with their Regulations and the 1949 Geneva Conventions remain directed to the conduct of war.[20]

16 S. Hobe, 'The Meaning of "Peaceful Purposes" in Article IV of the Outer Space Treaty' (2015) XL *AASL* 9–24.

17 Y. Dinstein. (1) *War, Aggression and Self – Defence*, 4th ed. (Cambridge: Cambridge UP, 2005); (2) The *Conduct of Hostilities under the International Law of Armed Conflict* (Cambridge: Cambridge UP, 2004); T.M. Franck, *Recourse to Force, State Action against Threats and Armed Attack* (Cambridge: Cambridge UP, 2002); C. von Clausewitz, *On War* (many eds); M. Bourbonniere and L. Haeck, 'Jus in Bello Spatiale' (2000) 25 *Air and Sp. L.* 2–11. Cf. J. Stone, *Aggression and World Order* (London: Stevens, 1958); L.B. Sohn, 'The Definition of Aggression' (1959) 45 *Va. L. Rev.* 697–701; I. Brownlie, *International Law and the Use of Force by States* (Oxford: Oxford UP, 1963). 'Aggression' was defined by UNGA Res. 3314 (XXIX) 1974. The first use of armed force is *prima facie* evidence of aggression though in a given instance the Security Council may decide otherwise (Art. 2). Cf. *infra* on self – defence and Art. 51, nn. 24 and 27 ff.

18 General Treaty providing for the Renunciation of War as an Instrument of National Policy (the Kellogg – Briand Pact, aka. the Pact of Paris), Paris, 1928, 94 LNTS 57; 46 Stat. 2343, TS 796; 3 Bevans 732.

19 *Trial of the Major War Criminals at the Nüremberg Tribunal* (Nüremberg, 1946–9) Vol. 1. Cf. Charter of the International Military Tribunal, Nüremberg, 1945: www.law.umkc.edu/faculty/projects/ftrials/nuremberg/NurembergIndictments.html.

20 The four Geneva Conventions include an original Convention of 1864 (the 'First Geneva Convention'), revised in 1949 at the conference which adopted the Second, Third and Fourth Conventions. In addition there are three Protocols (two in 1977 and one in 2005). Levels of signature and ratification vary. For the Conventions, Protocols and Regulations see A. Roberts and R. Guelff, *Documents on the Laws of War*, 3rd ed. rep. (Oxford: Oxford UP, 2002). The International Committee of the Red Cross (an independent neutral organisation) maintains an electronic database of the Geneva Conventions and Protocols, with commentaries: www.icrc.org/ihl.nsf/CONVPRES?OpenView.

The Hague Conventions and Regulations are now part of customary international law: 'Judgement of the International Military Tribunal of Nüremberg', 1946, *Trial of German Major War Criminals: Proceedings of the International Military Tribunal Sitting at Nüremberg, Germany* (London: HMSO, 1946–50) vol. 1, 254; *Legality of the Threat or Use of Nuclear Weapons*, Advisory Opinion, 1996 ICJ Rep. 226 at 256–7 (paras 75–80) (1996) 35 ILM 869 and 1343; *Legal Consequences of the Construction of a Wall in the Occupied Palestinian Territory*, Advisory Opinion, 2004 ICJ Rep. 136 at 172 (para 89). See also UNGA Res. 95 (I), 1946, 'Affirmation of the Principles of International Law recognized by the Charter of the Nüremberg Tribunal'. The ICJ appears now to consider The Hague and Geneva Conventions, Protocols and Regulations as aspects of 'international humanitarian law'.

The Preamble to the UN Charter states *inter alia* that the 'People of the United Nations' are determined to 'save succeeding generations from the scourge of war'.[21] To that end they have agreed to unite their strength 'to maintain international peace and security, and, to ensure, by the acceptance of these principles and the institution of methods, that armed force shall not be used, save in the common interest'. In Art. 1.1 the first listed Purpose of the UN is therefore '[t]o maintain international peace and security, and to that end: to take effective collective measures for the prevention and removal of threats to the peace, and for the suppression of acts of aggression or other breaches of the peace, and to bring about by peaceful means, and in conformity with the principles of justice and international law, adjustment or settlement of international disputes or situations which might lead to a breach of the peace'.[22] By Art. 2.4, 'All Members shall refrain in their international relations from the threat or use of force against the territorial integrity or political independence of any state, or in any other manner inconsistent with the Purposes of the United Nations'.[23] Such provisions form part of the over-arching context within which space law in its military aspect is placed. Of course the UN Charter does contemplate the use of force. Chapter VII deals with 'Action with respect to Threats to the Peace, Breaches of the Peace and Acts of Aggression'. Article 39 gives the Security Council the duties of determining the existence of any threat to the peace, breach of the peace or act of aggression, and of making recommendations or of taking action under Arts. 41 (non-military measures) and 42 (military measures). Thereafter Arts. 42 *ad fin*–50 deal with the technicalities. The history of the effectiveness of these provisions is mixed, and perhaps in recognition that this might be the case, those provisions are followed by Art. 51:

> Nothing in the present Charter shall impair the inherent right of individual or collective self-defence if an armed attack occurs against a Member of the United Nations, until the Security Council has taken measures necessary to maintain international peace and security. Measures taken by Members in the exercise of this right of self-defence shall be immediately reported to the Security Council and shall not in any way affect the authority and responsibility of the Security Council under the present Charter to take at any time such action as it deems necessary in order to maintain or restore international peace and security.[24]

Before discussing Art. 51 an important point must be made. By Art. 103 of the Charter:

> In the event of any conflict between the obligations of the members of the United Nations under the present Charter and their obligations under any other international obligation, their obligations under the present Charter shall prevail.

---

21 Charter of the United Nations, 59 Stat, 1031, TS 993; (1946) UKTS 67, Cmnd. 7015; 9 Hudson Int. Leg. 327; 3 Bevans 1153; [1945] 39 AJIL Supp. 190.
22 See *supra* n. 17.
23 The UN Charter system may require amendment or reinterpretation under modern conditions. Cf. Agora: 'Future Implications of the Iraq Conflict' [2003] 97 AJIL 553–642, inc. R.N. Gardner, 'Neither Bush nor the Jurisprudes' [2003] 97 AJIL 585–590; R.A. Falk, 'What Future for the UN Charter System of War Prevention' [2003] 97 AJIL 590–598.
24 Reference point, *infra* n. 159.

As the Vienna Convention on the Law of Treaties states, the general rule in the application of successive treaties that deal with the same subject matter is that obligations under a later treaty supersede those under an earlier one.[25] However, Art. 30.1 of the Convention specifically provides that that general rule is subject to UN Charter Art. 103. For our purposes therefore Art. 51 and the other Charter provisions as to the use of force remain, later treaties or agreements notwithstanding.[26]

The 'inherent right of individual or collective self-defence' of Art. 51 is the major justification for the maintenance of armed forces by states throughout the world.[27] It is the concomitant qualification 'if an armed attack occurs' that can cause logicians trouble: what of anticipatory self-defence or pre-emptive self-defence?

Anticipatory self-defence does not require an actual 'armed attack'. It is a response to the expectation of being attacked. It requires belief that an attack is imminent. The anticipation is argued to trigger 'the inherent right of individual or collective self-defence' of Art. 51.[28] Key to understanding anticipatory self-defence is the customary international law founded on the 1842 *Caroline* incident at Buffalo and the Niagara River involving the UK and the US. In that instance the US Secretary of State agreed that legal unilateral self-defensive action requires that 'the necessity of that self-defence is instant, overwhelming, and leaving no choice of means, and no moment of deliberation'. Such anticipatory self-defence was declared by the parties to be legal under international law.[29] Anticipatory self-defence must be in 'response to an imminent threat of armed attack'.[30] Furthermore, the response must be proportionate to the threat.[31] However, while it is easy to write these

25 Art. 30. 2–5, Vienna Convention on the Law of Treaties, 1969, 1155 UNTS 331; (1980) BTS 58, Cmnd. 7964; 8 ILM 679; [1969] 63 AJIL 875: http://untreaty.un.org/ilc/texts/instruments/english/conventions/1_1_1969.pdf. The Convention is generally taken to articulate customary international law.

26 S. Rosenne, 'The Temporal Application of the Vienna Convention on the Law of Treaties,' (1970) 4 *Cornell Int. L.J.* 1–24; H.W. Briggs, 'Procedures for Establishing the Invalidity or Termination of Treaties under the International Law Commission's 1966 Draft Articles on the Law of Treaties' [1967] 61 AJIL 976–989; S. Ford, 'Legal Processes of Change: Article 2(4) and the Vienna Convention on the Law of Treaties' (1999) 4 *J. Armed Conflict L.* 75–116; R.J. Lee, 'The Jus ad Bellum in Outer Space: The Interrelationship Between Article 103 of the Charter of the United Nations and Article IV of the Outer Space Treaty' (2002) 45 *Proc. IISL* 139–148. See also 1963 I YBILC (Meetings 685, 687 and 703), and the Third Report of H. Waldock, Special Rapporteur, 1964 II YBILC 34–35: http://untreaty.un.org/ilc/documentation/english/a_cn4_167.pdf (on Draft Art. 65, later to become Art. 30) and ILC discussions at 1963 I YBILC just cited.

27 Reference point *infra* n. 214.

28 See T.M. Franck, 'The Power of Legitimacy and the Legitimacy of Power: International Law in an Age of Power Disequilibrium' [2006] 100 AJIL 88–106 at 101–6; cf. his 'Legitimacy in the International System' [1988] 82 AJIL 705–759; J. Rohlik, 'Some Remarks on Self – Defense and Intervention: A Reaction to Reading *Law and Civil War in the Modern World*' (1976) 6 *Ga. J. Int. and Comp. L.* 395–435 at 415–430; and materials *supra* n. 17.

29 Memorandum by US Secretary of State Daniel Webster to H. Fox, UK Minister in Washington: J.B. Moore, *A Digest of International Law*, vol. 2, 409–414 (1906); R.Y. Jennings, 'The *Caroline* and McLeod Cases' [1938] 32 AJIL 82–99 (*Caroline* facts at 82–84). See also R.Y. Jennings and A. Watts, eds., *Oppenheim's International Law*, 9th ed. Vol. I, 'Peace' (London: Longman, 1996) 420–427.

30 *Case Concerning Military and Para – Military Activities in and against Nicaragua (Nicaragua v United States) (Merits)*, Judgement, 1986 ICJ Rep, 14 at 102–104 (paras 193–195); (1986) 25 ILM 1023.

31 *Nicaragua v United States, supra* n. 30, at 94 (para 176); *Nuclear Weapons*, Advisory Opinion, *supra* n. 20, at 245 (para 41); *Case Concerning Armed Activities on the Territory of the Congo (Democratic Republic of the Congo v Uganda)* 2005 ICJ Rep, 1 at 53 (para 147); (2006) 45 ILM 271–395, where the Court, indicating that it did not find self – defence present and had therefore no need to inquire whether the response was 'proportionate' also commented that action far from the Congo/Uganda border did not appear proportionate to a series of trans – border attacks. In *Nicaragua v US, supra* n. 30, the ICJ required that the US response,

words, the actual determination whether the required conditions are met remains in the purview of the individual state.[32] That is the problem of anticipatory self-defence, rendering it controversial in practice or if adumbrated during a developing situation.

Pre-emptive self-defence is even more controversial.[33] It differs from anticipatory self-defence in that it is triggered not by a specific event, but from the apprehension of being attacked. It could be labelled as preventative or prophylactic self-defence. The triggering situation is a hostility between states. However, it is difficult to see its application as was argued in relation to the 'War on Terror' where some of those alleged to be involved were not states and the invasion of Iraq was not authorised by the Security Council.[34] When military action is predicated on a claim to act pre-emptively the circumstances require close examination.[35] Because it is likely to be claimed as justification for unilateral preventative military use of outer space, it is a matter of grave concern for space lawyers.

Article 51 indicates that self-defence, whether individual or collective, has a boundary. Its relevance exists 'until the Security Council has taken measures necessary to maintain international peace and security'. States are immediately to report acts taken in self-defence to the Security Council, and that body then has 'the authority and responsibility . . . to take at any time such action as it deems necessary in order to maintain or restore international peace and security'. What the Council does is not affected or constrained by what states may already have done. The UN 'High-level Panel on Threats, Challenges and Change' considered that anticipatory or pre-emptive self-defence should be taken only after proper authorisation by the UN Security Council, on the ground that '[a]llowing one to so act

---

if based on self – defence, should approximate to the Nicaraguan offense. Cf. Bourbonniere I, and Bourbonniere II at 49–50 (both *supra* n. 5).

32 O. Schachter, 'International Law: The Right of States to Use Armed Force' (1983–1984) 82 *Mich. L. Rev.* 1620–1646; Franck, *supra* n. 28, at 101.

33 C.D. Gray, *International Law and the Use of Force*, 2nd ed. (Oxford: Oxford UP 2004); O. Schachter, 'Self – Defense and the Rule of Law' [1989] 83 AJIL 259–277; A. Garwood – Gowers, 'Pre – Emptive Self – Defense: A Necessary Development or the Road to International Anarchy' (2004) 23 Aust. YBIL 5–72; W.M. Reisman and A. Armstrong, 'The Past and Future of the Claim of Preemptive Self – Defense' [2006] 100 AJIL 525–550; D.W. Bowett, *Self – Defence in International Law* (Manchester: Manchester UP, 1958; Law Book Exchange 2014) and his '*International Law and the Use of Force by States* Revisited' (2000) 21 Aust. YBIL 21–37; (2002) 1 *Chinese J. Int. L.* 1–19.

34 C. Gray, 'The Bush Doctrine Revisited: The 2006 National Security Strategy of the USA' (2006) 5 *Chinese J. Int. L.* 555–578 at 556; A. Garwood – Gowers, 'Self – Defence against Terrorism in the Post–9/11 World' (2004) 4 *Queensland U. Tech. L. and Just. J.* 1–18; D. Hovell, 'Chinks in the Armour: International Law, Terrorism and the Use of Force' (2004) 27 *Univ. N.S.W. L.J.* 398–427; W.M. Reisman, 'International Legal Responses to Terrorism' (1999) 22 *Houst. J. Int. L.* 3–62; Maggs *infra* n. 35. Cf. R. Lee and S.L. Steele, 'Military Use of Satellite Communications, Remote Sensing and Global Positioning Systems in the War on Terror' (2014) 79 *J. Air L. & Comm.* 69–112.

35 The ICJ construes Art. 51 relatively strictly. See *Nicaragua v. United States, supra* n. 30, at 94–104 (paras 176–195); *Case concerning Oil Platforms (Iran v. United States)* Judgement, 2003 ICJ Rep. 161 at 178–199 (paras 31–78); *Legal Consequences of the Construction of a Wall in the Occupied Palestinian Territory*, Advisory Opinion, 2004 ICJ Rep. 136 at 171–177 (paras 86–100); (2004) 43 ILM 1009–97; *Congo v Uganda*, 2005 ICJ Rep (*supra* n. 31) 1 at 52–57 (paras 143–165). Cf. C.J. Tams, 'Note Analytique – Swimming with the Tide or Seeking to Stem It – Recent ICJ Rulings on the Law of Self – Defence' (2005) 18 *Rev. quebecoise de droit int'l* 275–290. See also R.C. Hendrickson, 'Article 51 and the Clinton Presidency: Military Strikes and the UN Charter' (2001) 19 *B.U. Int. L.J.* 207–230; G.E. Maggs, 'How the United States Might Justify a Preemptive Strike on a Rogue Nation's Nuclear Weapon Development Facilities under the UN Charter' (2007) 57 *Syracuse L. Rev.* 465–496; G. Simpson, 'The War in Iraq and International Law' (2005) 5 *Melb. J. Int. L.* 167–188 (at 173, Simpson notes the Soviet invasions of Hungary, Czechoslovakia and Afghanistan as actions that had been claimed to be preventive); Agora, *supra* n. 23.

is to allow all'.[36] That may be a counsel of perfection, and unlikely always to prevail. However, it raises two possibilities for space. One is that a space-competent state may decide to act in the belief that its national interests are under threat. The other is intriguing possibility that the Security Council might take or authorise the taking of action unlawful under space law.[37] So, for us the question remains what may states lawfully do militarily either through the direct use of space assets or capabilities or through using space simply as a medium for indirect action.

Excessive use of retaliatory force is unlawful. The exercise of force is limited by the need for its exercise. States may be held responsible for disproportionate use of force.[38] Inherent in self-defence, anticipatory self-defence and pre-emptive self-defence is the requirement that a state must have the military capabilities needed for the purpose. Possession of or investment in appropriate technologies may, of course, be constrained by treaty. In relation to space there are treaty obligations that proscribe space activities which may be lawful if conducted elsewhere. Notwithstanding, it is now clear that some state are seeking a military preparedness to use space even in the face of those proscriptions.

History

Even before Sputnik I reached outer space in 1957, there was debate whether military activities should be permitted in outer space and whether aggressive military uses should be prohibited.[39] In the wake of the German development of the V-1 and V-2 rockets during the Second World War, it is not surprising that in 1952 Professor Alex Meyer, then Director of the Institute of Air and Space Law at the University of Cologne, expressed the view that 'the States should make an agreement in which they declare to abstain from using outer space for war-purposes'.[40]

Sputnik caused a crisis in Western military thinking.[41] The possibility of a surprise attack from outer space had emerged. Equally apparent was the advantage of reconnaissance from outer space.[42] The law was unsettled. In 1958 the USSR proposed a ban on 'the use of cosmic space for military purposes' to go along with states undertaking to launch rockets into space only as part of an 'agreed international programme'. The proposal was, however, allied with the elimination of foreign military bases on the territories of other states, the establishment of that international programme and the creation of a UN agency

---

36 'A more secure world: our shared responsibility; Report of the High – level Panel on Threats Challenges and Change', UN Doc. A/59/565, 2 December 2004, paras 188–197, 191 *ad fin*: https://documents – dds – ny.un.org/doc/UNDOC/GEN/N04/602/31/PDF/N0460231.pdf?OpenElement; www.securitycouncilreport.org/atf/cf/%7B65BFCF9B–6D27–4E9C–8CD3–CF6E4FF96FF9%7D/CPR%20A%2059%20565.pdf.
37 Bourbonniere III (*supra* n. 5) at 7–10; R.J. Lee, 'The *Jus ad Bellum* in Spatialis: The Exact Content and Practical Implications of the Law on the Use of Force in Outer Space' (2003) 29 *J. Sp. L.* 93–119.
38 Vasilogeorgi, *supra* n. 5, at 416.
39 D.R. Terrill, Jr, *The Air Force Role in Developing International Outer Space Law* (Maxwell AFB, AL: Air UP, 1999; UP of the Pacific, 2004): http://aupress.maxwell.af.mil/Books/Terrill/terrill.pdf.
40 A. Meyer, 'Legal Problems of Flight into the Outer Space', *Legal Problems* 8–19 at 18.
41 Terrill, *supra* n. 39.
42 Cf. G. Zhukov, 'Space Espionage Plans and International Law' (1960) *Int. Aff.* (Moscow) 53–7, rep. *Legal Problems* 1095–1101.

to coordinate and supervise what was done.[43] This was all too complex for the time, but it showed a possible way forward.[44] Military and political opinion in the US varied. The US Air Force and some writers were inclined to consider that the USSR had violated US sovereign space by the Sputnik overflight.[45] However, US President Eisenhower, a former military man and mindful of the surprise attack on Pearl Harbour in 1941, opted for freedom of reconnaissance and 'open skies'.[46] Outer space should not be subjected to claims of sovereignty; it should be free. Accordingly he delivered a major speech in the 1960 UN General Assembly regarding military satellites in space. Calling in aid the 1959 Antarctic Treaty during the negotiations of which the US had agreed to the demilitarisation of Antarctica,[47] Eisenhower asked[48]:

Will outer space be preserved for peaceful use and developed for the benefit of all mankind? Or will it become another focus for the arms race – and thus an area of dangerous and sterile competition? The choice is urgent. And it is ours to make.

He went on:

The nations of the world have recently united in declaring the continent of Antarctica 'off limits' to military preparations. We could extend this principle to an even more important sphere. National vested interests have not yet developed in space or in celestial bodies. Barriers to agreement are now lower than they will ever be again.

He therefore proposed that outer space, like Antarctica, should not be used for 'warlike activities'.[49] Thereafter the analogy of the Antarctica Treaty became part of the COPUOS discussions that were to result in the UN Resolutions of 1961, 1962 and 1963, all leading to the 1967 Outer Space Treaty in which the peaceful use of outer space is a major principle.[50] The USSR and the US positions as to the (non-)military use of space were apparently converging.

---

43 *Documents on Disarmament*, 1945–1959 (Vienna: World Council on Peace, 1956) II, 976–977, extracted *Legal Problems* 994–995.
44 Cf. E. Korovin, 'International Status of Cosmic Space' (1959) *Int. Aff.* (Moscow) 53–9, rep. *Legal Problems* 1062–1071.
45 See authors cited by Korovin, *supra* n. 44. See also Terrill, *supra* n. 39, 41–57.
46 For earlier discussions and proposals of aerial 'open skies' see J. Boulden, 'Open Skies: the 1955 Proposal and its Current Revival' (1990) 13 *Dalhousie L.J.* 611–649. See also *supra* Chapter 13, n. 32.
47 The Antarctic Treaty 1959, 402 UNTS 71; 12 UST 795, TIAS 4780; (1960) UKTS 71, Cmnd. 1535; (1980) 19 ILM 860; [1960] 54 AJIL 477.
48 D.D. Eisenhower, 'Address before the Fifteenth General Assembly of the United Nations, 22 September 1960', 1960 US Cong. 1st Sess., S. Doc. no. 26, at 1006; *Public Papers of the Presidents of the United States*, Eisenhower 1960–I, Doc. 302, 707–720, § v at 714 (U. Michigan Digital Library: https://quod.lib.umich.edu/p/ppotpus/). See Art. 32 of the Vienna Convention, *supra* n. 25, on the relevance of preparatory work on treaties.
49 Cf. Antarctic Treaty, *supra* n. 47, Art. 1.
50 Treaty on Principles Governing the Activities of States in the Exploration and Use of Outer Space Including the Moon and Other Celestial Bodies, London, Moscow and Washington, 27 January 1967 (1968) 610 UNTS 205; (1968) UKTS 10, Cmnd. 3519; 18 UST 2410, TIAS 6347; (1967) 6 ILM 386; [1967] 61 AJIL 644. See *supra* Chapter 3; CoCoSL I.

Launch expertise had been accelerated by the Second World War, and a major advocate and exponent of the technology, Wernher von Braun, was to continue his post-War career with at least half an eye on its military application.[51] Notwithstanding, public attention to the potentialities of the military use of space diminished at the end of the 1960s with the onset of other uses of space and of human space flight, a high point being the race to the moon. However, attention has returned to questions of the military uses of space, triggered in part by the emergence of China as a major space power.[52] Since 2000, the US Congress has required reports on China's military power to be submitted to it annually,[53] and space has formed an important part of each report.[54] During the Reagan Presidency, similar reports were prepared from 1981 as to Soviet military power.[55] The National Security Strategy of the United States reports now serve a similar function.[56]

Space-Specific International Law

The USA and USSR, then the sole space-competent powers, were the major players in the negotiation of the Outer Space Treaty. Both were keenly interested in keeping their adversary from occupying the higher ground.[57] Thus US President Lyndon Johnson characterised the OST as 'the most important arms control development since the Limited Test Ban Treaty of 1963'.[58]

The OST requires that outer space activities 'be carried out for the benefit and in the interest of all countries, irrespective of their degree of economic and scientific development . . .' and later there is the obligation to explore and use outer space 'in the interest of

51 M. Neufeld, *Von Braun: Dreamer of Space, Engineer of War* (New York: Clarkson Potter/Knopf, 2007) and his ' "Space Superiority" – Wernher von Braun's Campaign for a Nuclear – armed Space Station, 1946–1956' (2006) 22 *Space Policy* 52–62; R. Ward, *From Nazis to NASA: The Life of Wernher von Braun* (Stroud: History Press, 2006) and *Dr. Space: The Life of Werner von Braun* (US: Naval Institute Press, 2009); W. Biddle, *Dark Side of the Moon: Wernher Von Braun. The Third Reich, and the Space Race* (New York: Norton, 2009). Cf. P.M. Sterns and L.I. Tennen, 'Ethics and the Conquest of Space: From Peenemunde to Mars and Beyond' (2007) 50 *Proc. IISL* 456–467 at 464–467.
52 S-H. Liao, 'Will China Become a Military Space Superpower?' (2005) 21 *Space Policy* 205–212.
53 See the US National Defense Authorization Act for Fiscal Year 2000, § 1202.
54 US Department of Defense, 'Military and Security Developments Involving the People's Republic of China 2022: Annual Report to Congress': https://media.defense.gov/2022/Nov/29/2003122279/–1/–1/1/2022–MILITARY – AND – SECURITY – DEVELOPMENTS – INVOLVING – THE – PEOPLES – REPUBLIC – OF – CHINA.PDF. The 2021 Report is at https://media.defense.gov/2021/Nov/03/2002885874/–1/–1/0/2021–CMPR – FINAL.PDF. Cf. M.A. Stokes, 'China's Strategic Modernisation: Implications for the United States', Report to the US Strategic Studies Institute, September 1999: www.fas.org/nuke/guide/china/doctrine/chinamod.pdf.
55 Cf. the US Defense Intelligence Agency, 'Soviet Military Power': www.fas.org/irp/dia/product/smp_index.htm. See also earlier, *Soviet Space Programs: Organization, Plans, Goals, and International Implications*, Staff Report, Committee on Aeronautical and Space Sciences, US Senate, 87th Cong. 2d Sess, May 31 1962, and *Soviet Space Programs, 1962–1965: Organization, Plans, Goals, and International Implications*, Staff Report, Committee on Aeronautical and Space Sciences, US Senate, 89th Cong. 2d Sess, 30 December 1966; M. Russell, 'Military Activities in Outer Space: Soviet Legal Views' (1984) 25 *Harv. Int. L.J.* 153–194.
56 National Security Strategy of the United States: https://history.defense.gov/Historical – Sources/National – Security – Strategy/. The unclassified 2022 National Security Strategy is at https://media.defense.gov/2022/Oct/27/2003103845/–1/–1/1/2022–NATIONAL – DEFENSE – STRATEGY – NPR – MDR.PDF.
57 See again Sun Tzu, *The Art of War*, *supra* n. 1.
58 Statement by President Johnson, *infra* n. 78.

maintaining international peace and security and promoting international cooperation and understanding' (Art. III). It would be difficult to conduct military activities in outer space in compliance with those obligations.[59]

Our quotation above of the Art. III obligation is incomplete. The excerpt is preceded by the requirement that space activities be carried on 'in accordance with international law, including the Charter of the United Nations'. As a matter of treaty-law the UN Charter and international law are reaffirmed as applying in outer space by OST Art. III. We therefore note that pursuant to UN Charter Art. 4, para 4, states may not threaten other states or use force against them in any manner that contravenes the Charter and the objectives of the UN.[60] Parties to the OST are bound by UN Charter Chapter VI on the pacific settlement of disputes, Chapter VII on actions with respect to threats to the peace, breaches of the peace and acts of aggression, as well as the rights of individual and collective self-defence in the event of armed attacks under Art. 51 of the Charter. States are likewise subject to the authority of the UN General Assembly regarding 'maintenance of international peace and security.' As we have seen, these obligations cannot be eroded by provisions of later treaties.[61]

At an early stage some might have considered the effect of the UN Space Resolutions of 1961, 1962 and 1963 would be that space could not lawfully be used for any military purpose. The titles of the first two Resolutions speak of the 'peaceful uses of outer space' while their texts indicate how these purposes could be furthered.[62] The 1963 'Declaration of Principles' governing the activities of states in space is different, although its text also deals with the peaceful use of space.[63] Military uses are not mentioned. A 'non-peaceful use' is implicitly disapproved by being ignored. However the *argumentum ex silentio* is always fragile. The great fear of the time was of nuclear weapons, and that was dealt with effectively, not primarily in the negotiations as to space, but in the debates on disarmament. In August 1963 some four and a half months ahead of the 'Space Principles' resolution, what is now known as the Partial or the Limited Test Ban Treaty emerged from the Disarmament negotiations.[64] As its long title indicates, the ban imposed on its parties by Art. 1 of the Test Ban Treaty includes nuclear explosions in space. Two months later in UNGA Res. 1884 (XVIII) of October 1963 the Assembly welcomed statements by the USSR and the US of their separate intention not to put nuclear weapons or weapons of mass destruction in space and called on all states to resolve similarly.[65]

---

59 Bourbonniere and Lee. *infra* n. 95, at 885
60 See the decision in the *Case concerning Military and Paramilitary Activities in and against Nicaragua (Merits)* 1986 ICJ Rep. 14, *supra* n. 30.
61 See discussion surrounding n. 25 *supra*.
62 'International Co – operation in the Peaceful Uses of Outer Space', UNGA Res. 1721 (XVI) 1961; UNGA Res. 1802 (XVII) 1962.
63 'Declaration of Legal Principles Governing the Activities of States in the Exploration and Use of Outer Space', UNGA Res. 1962 (XVIII), 13 December 1963.
64 Treaty Banning Nuclear Weapon Tests in the Atmosphere, in Outer Space and Under Water, Moscow, 1963; 480 UNTS 43; 14 UST 1313, TIAS 5433; (1964) UKTS 3, Cmnd. 2245; (1963) 2 ILM 883; [1963] 57 AJIL 1026. Cf. the UN Comprehensive Test Ban Treaty, 1996, UNGA Res. 50/245, 1996; (1996) 35 ILM 1439, which many states have signed but few have ratified. D.S. Jonas, 'The Comprehensive Nuclear Test Ban Treaty: Current Legal Status in the United States and the Implications of a Nuclear Test Explosion' (2007) *39 N.Y.U. J. Int. L. and Pol.* 1007–1046.
65 'Questions of General and Complete Disarmament', UNGA Res. 1884 (XVIII), 1963. As early as 1957 the Assembly had urged the 'joint study of an inspection system designed to ensure that the sending of objects

438   The Military Use of Outer Space

The negotiation of the OST brought such matters together. Discussions took place in the newly formed UN Committee for the Peaceful Uses of Outer Space (COPUOS). Of course military matters were only a part of the concerns of the negotiators; however, we consider it important that military matters were on the table. COPUOS may still have a role to play. We have discussed the other elements of those negotiations in Chapter 3. Here we are concerned with the military side of things.

After 1963 and the OST, the arms race between the US and the USSR had continued, as had the race to be first to reach the moon and to achieve pre-eminence in outer space. However, stemming from the disarmament negotiations and their related UN resolutions, demilitarisation of outer space was on the delegates' minds since the military potential of outer space was well understood.[66] The negotiators had 'a particular desire to limit the use of celestial bodies, if not outer space as well, for military purposes'.[67] The demilitarisation of Antarctica by the Antarctic Treaty was an important precedent and model, as, in a different connection, was its setting aside of Antarctica from claims of sovereignty at least for the duration of the treaty.[68] Military questions were not, however, the preoccupation of only the space-faring states. Other states had hopes and expectations for their future and wanted their interests secured.[69] The proponents of the OST sought the adoption of a text by the greatest possible number of states in order to maximise its authority. Because the then non-space-competent states were the overwhelming voting majority in the General Assembly the interests of the non-space-farers had to be clearly secured to achieve that general acceptance. Thus, in the OST Preamble the paragraph '*Believing*' states 'that exploration and use of outer space *should* be carried on for the benefit of all peoples irrespective of the degree of their economic or scientific development'. That principle is then incorporated as Art. I para 1 of the operative text, with the addition that outer space '*shall* be the province of all mankind'.[70] Article I para 2 provides that outer space is 'free for exploration and use by all states without discrimination of any kind, on a basis of equality and in accordance with international law, and there [is] free access to all areas of celestial bodies'. Freedom of space was therefore not confined to the space-competent of 1967 by the OST but extends to all states. Those that lacked space competence in the 1960s now have that capability and many states one way or another now assert user rights in outer space.

However, freedom is never absolute or unfettered. We have seen in Chapter 3 various limitations that the OST places on the use of space. We will come to the question of 'peaceful uses' in due course, but here we note other elements. For example, by OST Art.

---

through outer space shall be exclusively for peaceful and scientific purposes': UNGA Res. 1148 (XII) 1957 'Regulation, Limitation and Balanced Reduction of All Armed Forces . . .', para 1.f. (Paras 1.a – c dealt with nuclear weapons and fissionable materials}. Cf. the USA/USSR Draft Treaty on the Non – Proliferation of Nuclear Weapons submitted to the 18–Nation Committee on Disarmament, 1968 (1968) 7 ILM 155.

66   P.G. Dembling and D.M. Arons, 'The Evolution of the Outer Space Treaty' (1967) 33 *J. Air L. & Comm.* 432–456 at 429–435 [Lyall/Larsen 151–188] ('Evolution'). See also P.G. Dembling and D.M. Arons, 'The United Nations Celestial Bodies Convention' (1966) 32 *J. Air L & Comm.* 525–50 ('Celestial Bodies').

67   Dembling and Arons, *supra* n. 66, 'Evolution,' at 427.

68   See *supra* n. 66.

69   N. Jasentuliyana, 'Article 1 of the Outer Space Treaty' (1989) 17 *J. Sp. L.* 129–144.

70   Emphases added. Note that this language is repeated in the 1979 Moon Agreement, Art. 4. See Chapter 7. Cf. E. Fasan, 'The Meaning of "Mankind" in Space Legal Language' (1974) 2 *J. Sp. L.* 125–131.

IX states using space have to have 'due regard' to the interests of other users.[71] While the general 'civilian' application of the obligation is clear, whether or how this would operate to prevent hostile military action is obscure. There are also the constraints that emerge from obligations to secure the space environment.[72] While these have civil application, they may also have a role as to the effects of conflict in space.[73] The major legal constraint as to military use at present is, however, OST Art. IV.

It may be asked whether it would not have been better simply to bar all military uses of or access to space.[74] That would have been quite unrealistic. At the time of negotiation, both the USSR and US already had military satellites in orbit. Intent that the legality of their actions should not be impugned, they were not willing to open up any diminution of their use of satellites for military purposes.[75]

OST Art. IV provides that:

States Parties to the Treaty undertake not to place in orbit around the Earth any objects carrying nuclear weapons or any other kinds of weapons of mass destruction, install such weapons on celestial bodies, or station such weapons in outer space in any other manner.

The moon and other celestial bodies shall be used by all States Parties to the Treaty exclusively for peaceful purposes. The establishment of military bases, installations and fortifications, the testing of any type of weapons and the conduct of military manoeuvres on celestial bodies shall be forbidden. The use of military personnel for scientific research or for any other peaceful purposes shall not be prohibited. The use of any equipment or facility necessary for peaceful exploration of the moon and other celestial bodies shall also not be prohibited.

At the time of the OST negotiations the world was preoccupied with the dangers of radioactive fallout from nuclear tests and behind that the threat of nuclear weapons.[76] Article IV was a step towards nuclear military containment that goes farther than the 1963 Nuclear Test Ban Treaty.[77] When US President Johnson characterised the OST as 'the most important arms control development since the Limited Test Ban Treaty of 1963', he went on to note that '[i]t puts in treaty form the "no bombs in orbit" resolution of the UN. It guarantees access to all areas and installations of celestial bodies. This openness

71 For 'due regard' for the interests of others see the *Fisheries Jurisdiction Case (UK v Iceland) Merits*, 1974 ICJ Rep. 3 and the *Fisheries Jurisdiction Case (Germany v Iceland) Merits*, 1974 ICJ Rep. 175. Cf. the 'reasonable regard' in exercising the freedoms of Art. 2 of the Convention on the High Seas, Geneva, 1958, 450 UNTS 82; 13 UST 2312, TIAS 5200; 1963 UKTS 5, Cmnd. 1929; [1958] 52 AJIL 842, and Art. 87.2 of the UN Convention on the Law of the Sea, Montego Bay, 1984, 1833 UNTS 3; (1999) UKTS 81, Cm. 4524; (1982) 21 ILM 1261.
72 See Chapter 9.
73 See *infra* 'Military Action in Space'.
74 Cf. the very early Statement on 'Outer Space' adopted by the US National Association of Women Lawyers, 'A. Basic Declaration of Principles', para 4: 'Flight instrumentalities shall not be used in any part of Outer Space for military purposes' (1958) 44 *Women Lawyers J.* 8.
75 Dembling and Arons, 'Evolution', *supra* n. 66, at 433.
76 Cf. H. Kahn and E. Jones, *On Thermonuclear War* (Princeton NJ: Princeton UP, 1960; new ed. with introduction by E. Jones (Transaction Publication, 2007); cf. also the later *The Effects of Nuclear War* (US Congress; Office of Technology Assessment June 1979, OTA – NS–89).
77 Nuclear Test Ban Treaty, *supra* n. 64.

taken with other provisions of the treaty should prevent warlike preparations on the Moon and other celestial bodies'.[78] While this may be thought to understate the value of the other elements of the OST, it does indicate the general understanding and importance of Art. IV at the time of its negotiation.

Article IV does not specifically ban conventional arms from outer space nor the military from outer space, but to a degree it restricts military activities. There is a 'common interest of all mankind in the progress of the exploration and use of space for peaceful purposes',[79] but how does that interest interact with military concerns? 'Military use' has a variety of aspects: the employment of military personnel and equipment; the passive or non-aggressive use of space; the use of civilian space systems for military purposes; the use of weapons in space; the incursion into space of military weapons; the interference with space-located equipment from space; the interference with space-located equipment from Earth. We begin with military personnel and equipment.

Military Personnel and Equipment

OST Art. IV para 2, deals with the larger concept of the peaceful use of the moon and celestial bodies. It does not exclude military personnel and their equipment from outer space. Its third and fourth sentences specifically provide that employing military personnel for scientific research and other peaceful purposes, and the use of military equipment for those purposes, are not prohibited.[80] In retrospect, this was inevitable. To have excluded either military persons or machines would have been neither reasonable nor effective. The most that could have been expected was what was agreed and provided by Art. IV para 2. The basic operational technologies are rooted in military research and requirements. Military personnel were already engaged in space activities – indeed without such the exploration of space would not have been taking place. But what of weapons?

Weapons

Weapons and the weaponisation of space are matters of difficulty both in law and as to practice because military security means that not all the data necessary to come to a clear view are generally available.

In fact, some particular weaponry is specifically dealt with. By OST Art. IV para 1, parties have undertaken to ban all nuclear and weapons of mass destruction (WMD) from outer space. They have undertaken 'not to place in orbit around the Earth any objects carrying nuclear weapons or any other kinds of weapons of mass destruction, install such weapons on celestial bodies, or station these weapons in outer space in any

78 L.B. Johnson, 'Statement by the President Announcing the Reaching of Agreement on an Outer Space Treaty, 8 December 1966', *Public Papers of the Presidents of the United States*, Johnson 1966–II, Doc. 643, 1441 (Univ. of Michigan Digital Library: http://quod.lib.umich.edu/p/ppotpus/): *NY Times*, 9 December 1966 at 1 col. 8.

79 OST, Preambular para 'Recognising'. Art. IV is analysed in CoCoSL I, 70–93. For a discussion of 'peaceful purposes' see Hobe, *supra* n. 16.

80 Dembling and Arons, 'Evolution' *supra* n. 66, at 433. The 'shall not be prohibited' formulation of Art. IV.2 lacks elegance.

manner'.[81] The use of the phase 'in orbit' is significant because it is the only clue to defining the scope of the OST. Space objects in orbit and in partial orbit are subject to the Treaty. Minimum unassisted orbital height is approximately at 100 kilometres or 60 miles above the surface of the Earth.[82] Specifically the OST restrictions on military uses begin to apply when minimum orbital height is reached, and all orbits above minimum orbital height are restricted by Art. IV. Again the prohibition on the stationing of nuclear weaponry or WMD in space ends with the curious syntax 'in space or any other manner' (Art. IV para 1) This may be clarified by reference to the later MA Art. 3.3, which prohibits the placing of nuclear or WMD weapons into moon orbit, on any trajectory to or around the moon or placing or using such weapons on or in the moon. If both the OST and MA apply, such weapons are forbidden anywhere in space or on celestial bodies.

Nuclear weaponry is known technology. In the 1963 Nuclear Test Ban Treaty the parties agreed 'to prohibit, to prevent, and not to carry out any nuclear weapons test explosion' in outer space.[83] The ICJ Advisory Opinion on the *Legality of the Threat or Use of Nuclear Weapons* is also helpful.[84] However the term 'weapons of mass destruction' (WMD) is not defined in the OST, leaving leeway for a narrow or a wide interpretation.[85] Aids towards its

81 'Placing in orbit' might be taken to imply that the weapon vehicle makes a complete orbit. However, a weapon placed in orbit to complete only part thereof before it is diverted to a target would also be considered to be in orbit and its use restricted. Thus fractional orbital bombardment systems are considered to be limited by Art IV. See CoCoSL I at 79, para 30. Cf. V. Vereschetin, 'Limiting and Banning Military Use of Outer Space: Issues of International Law', in J. Makarczyk, ed., *Essays in Honour of Judge Manfred Lachs* (The Hague: Nijhoff, 1984) 671.
    Ballistic missiles where trajectories are suborbital are not covered by the OST Art. IV prohibition. However they may be subject to OST Art. VII, the Liability Convention and to other international space law: CoCoSL I, 86–87. See D.R. Reinhardt, 'The Vertical Limit of State Sovereignty' (2007) 72 *J. Air L. & Comm.* 65–140.
82 See discussion of orbital heights in Chapter 6 Of Boundaries and Orbits.
83 Nuclear Test Ban Treaty, *supra* n. 64
84 *Legality of the Threat or Use of Nuclear Weapons*, Advisory Opinion, 1996 ICJ Rep. 226.
85 C – G. Hasselmann, 'Weapons of Mass Destruction' (1982) 25 *Proc. IISL* 99 at 102; W. Luo, 'Research Guide to Export Control and WMD Non – Proliferation Law' (2007) 35 *Int. J. Leg. Inf.* 447–498. The term WMD (Weapons of Mass Destruction) has been variously traced to the 1937 saturation bombing of Guernica during the Spanish Civil War, of Dresden in February 1945, and to the use of nuclear weapons six months later in Japan. Nowadays it would include radiological, biological and chemical weapons: see *infra* nn. 87 and 88. Its precise legal content remains uncertain. The basic element of the concept appears to be that a weapon of mass destruction indiscriminately kills a large number. Whether that is a large number of innocent persons or a large number of persons *simpliciter* (i.e. including military personnel) remains obscure, but in the *Nuclear Weapons* Advisory Opinion (*supra* n. 84) the ICJ stated that 'methods and means of warfare, which would preclude any distinction between civilian and military targets, or which would result in unnecessary suffering to combatants, are prohibited'; 1996 ICJ Rep. 226 at 262–263, para 95. S. Gorove, 'Arms Control Provisions in the Outer Space Treaty: a Scrutinising Reappraisal' (1973) 3 *Ga. J. Int. and Comp. L.*, 114–123 at 115–6 considered 20–30 persons as constituting a 'mass' and even fewer in the case of bacteriological or chemical attack. Article 35.2 of the Additional Protocol I to the 1949 Geneva Conventions prohibits 'weapons, projectiles and material and methods of warfare of a nature to cause superfluous injury or unnecessary suffering' – Protocol Additional to the Geneva Conventions of 12 August 1949, and relating to the Protection of Victims of International Armed Conflicts (Protocol I), 8 June 1977; 1125 UNTS 4; UN Doc. A/34/144 (1977) 16 ILM 1391–1441: https://ihl – databases.icrc.org/en/ihl – treaties/api–1977?activeTab=1949GCs – APs–and–commentaries. Cf. generally: International Humanitarian Law Databases: https://ihl–databases. icrc.org/en/ihl – treaties.

definition in international law come in UN Security Council Res. 1540 of 14 April 2004 on 'Non-proliferation of Weapons of Mass Destruction' as well as in the context of the discussions of the UN Disarmament Commission,[86] and in such treaties as the Biological Weapons Convention of 1972[87] and the Chemical Weapons Convention of 1992.[88]

As far as the testing of weapons is concerned, OST Art. IV, para 2 prohibits the testing of any type of weapon on celestial bodies, while MA Art. 3.3 repeats that prohibition. However, as far as 'nuclear' in space is concerned, the prohibition is of 'nuclear weapons'. The use of nuclear power in space is unaffected by these provisions, and nuclear power sources are frequently used by the US, Russia and others to power their space objects.[89]

An interesting question has arisen as to the potential use of a nuclear bomb to deflect a near Earth asteroid threatening to collide with the Earth.[90] That might contravene the Nuclear Test Ban Treaty and possibly the self-defence provision contained in UN Charter Art. 51. Would such be the unlawful use of a 'nuclear weapon' or would the circumstances exclude it from the category 'weapon'? The drafters of the OST may not have contemplated such a scenario, and the prohibitions of Art. 4 are directed to arms control not to questions of the environment or the physical protection of the Earth. Schrögl and Neumann conclude that a nuclear bomb is a weapon whether it is used against an enemy or to cope with a dangerous near earth object.[91] That would be consonant with the Nuclear Test Ban Treaty, which prohibits all nuclear explosions in outer space.[92] However, Art IV para 1 prohibitions pertain only to the placing or stationing of nuclear weapons in outer space in any manner.[93] Would the use of nuclear bomb be permissible if the bomb is not placed in full or even partial orbit but directly targeted from launch? Arguably that would be a form of global 'self-defence'. Whatever, we think it unlikely that in the case of a major threat from an incoming asteroid many would invoke the nuclear treaties and prohibitions.[94]

---

86 The UN Disarmament Commission (UNODA) was created in 1952 by UNGA Res. 502 (VI) 'Regulation, Limitation and Balanced Reduction of all Armed Forces and all Armaments: International Control of Nuclear Energy': www.un.org/disarmament/institutions/disarmament – commission/. See also second para *supra* n. 3 As to WMD see the website of the Weapons of Mass Destruction Branch of the UN Office for Disarmament Affairs: http://disarmament.un.org/wmd/.

87 Convention on the Prohibition of the Development, Production and Stockpiling of Bacteriological (Biological) and Toxin Weapons and their Destruction, 1971, UNGA Res. 2826 (XVI) 1972; 1015 UNTS 164; (1975) UKTS 11, Cmd. 6397; (1972) 11 ILM 309–315. Cf. the Protocol on the Prohibition of the Use in War of Asphyxiating, Poisonous or Other Gases, and of Bacteriological Methods of Warfare [the 1925 Geneva Chemical Weapons Protocol], Geneva, 1925 (1929) 94 LNTS 65; (1975) 14 ILM 49–50. US ratification procedures lapsed in 1926, but President Nixon revived them in 1974. As of 2022 it has 38 signatories and 65 ratifications. J.N. Moore, 'Ratification of the Geneva Protocol on Gas and Bacteriological Warfare: A Legal and Political Analysis' (1972) 58 *Va. L. Rev.* 419–509.

88 Convention on the Prohibition of the Development, Production and Stockpiling and use of Chemical Weapons and their Destruction, Paris, 1993, 1997 UNTS 317; (1993) 32 ILM 800 with text at 804–73. See also the Chemical Weapons Protocol, Geneva, 1925, *supra* n. 87.

89 See Chapter 9, its discussion of UN Nuclear Power Principles, and UNGA Res. 47/68 'Principles Relevant to the Use of Nuclear Power Sources in Outer Space, 14 December 1992' (1993) 32 ILM 917 at 921–926.

90 CoCoSL I, 76–77, para 23. See Chapter 9 sv. Planetary Defence, and the DART project.

91 CoCoSL I, 76–77, para 23, *ad fin*.

92 Nuclear Test Ban Treaty, *supra* n. 64.

93 CoCoSL I, 78. See also P.B. Larsen, 'Asteroid Legal Regime: Time for a Change?' (2015) 39 *J. Sp. L.* 275–326 at 311.

94 Cf. the Torino Scale of threats, in Chapter 9 at n. 228.

Non-nuclear weaponry is permissible in space.[95] Military satellites are permitted, and in practice some of these may be 'active' weapons incorporating the kinetic,[96] laser and radio possibilities that might be used in anti-satellite measures (ASATs).[97] OST Art. IV para 2 specifically prohibits the testing of any type of weapons on celestial bodies but that prohibition would appear not to apply to tests in space itself.[98] The weaponisation of space is an ever-present worry in the UN.[99]

Bases

As we have seen, during the OST negotiations the demilitarisation of outer space was on the minds of delegates, the drafters having 'a particular desire to limit the use of celestial bodies, if not outer space as well, for military purposes' before the planned manned landings occurred and while the celestial bodies were 'as yet practically untouched by man'.[100] The then USSR wanted an air-tight (?) exclusion of military bases from the moon and celestial bodies. It insisted that the description of prohibited facilities should include military 'installations'. This was accepted. The establishment of military bases, installations and fortifications on celestial bodies is prohibited by OST Art. IV para 2, as are military manoeuvres on celestial bodies.[101]

OST Article IV para 2 emphasises that the moon and other celestial bodies 'shall be used exclusively for peaceful purposes.' It has been noted that this limitation does not prohibit the development of military – relevant technologies.[102] In addition, or correlatively, as we saw above the last two sentences of para 2 leave the door open for military personnel to engage in activities of a peaceful nature including scientific research and to use military equipment for the peaceful exploration of the moon and other celestial bodies.[103] Indeed, subject to the prohibition of the military use of the moon, the establishment of 'peaceful' bases is allowed.

OST Art IX requires a state to conduct its activities in space, on the Moon and other celestial bodies 'with due regard' for the interests of other states.[104] This requirement

---

95 CoCoSL I, 80–81, para 39. M. Bourbonniere and R.J. Lee, 'Legality of the Deployment of Conventional Weapons in Earth Orbit: Balancing Space Law and the Law of Armed Conflict' (2007) 18 *Eur. J. Int. L.* 873–901; N. Jasentuliyana, *International Space Law and the United Nations* (The Hague: Kluwer, 1999) 104–105.

96 A development as to kinetic weapons is the agreement of all the space – faring nations to the IADC Guidelines on debris. Kinetic ASATs cause debris: their use is therefore inhibited by the Guidelines. See Chapter 9 sv. Military Space Debris and nn. 179 and 200. The intentional destruction of satellites for reasons other than safety is worrying.

97 As to which see *infra* at n. 153.

98 Nuclear weapons would fall under the prohibitions of the Nuclear Test Ban Treaty, *supra* n. 64. But cf. now the possible use of nuclear or other weaponry as part of planetary defence, *supra* n. 90 and Chapter 9 – 'Planetary Defence.'

99 See discussion *infra* 'Military Action in Space'.

100 Dembling and Arons, 'Evolution' *supra* n. 66 at 427. Cf. R.D. Crane, 'Soviet Attitudes Toward International Space Law' [1962] 56 AJIL 685–723, and his 'Basic Principles in Soviet Space Law: Peaceful Coexistence, Peaceful Cooperation, and Disarmament' (1964) 29 *Law and Contemp. Probs.* 943–955; M. Russell, 'Military activities in Outer Space: Soviet Legal Views' (1984) 25 *Harv. Int. L.J.* 153–194.

101 See Chapter 7.

102 CoCoSL I, 82–83. Bourbonniere III, *supra* n. 5, at 11.

103 Dembling and Arons, 'Evolution,' *supra* n. 66, at 432–435.

104 As to the meaning of 'due regard' and similar expressions see the Cases and Conventions cited *supra* n. 71.

further restricts the military activities of states in outer space. China's 2007 destruction of its own satellite with much consequent space debris to the detriment of many other states is an example of failure to pay due regard to the interests of other states.[105]

In a direct borrow from Art. VII. 2 and 3 of the Antarctic Treaty, by OST Art. XII all bases, equipment and vehicles are to be open to inspection by other state parties, provided that reasonable advance notice is given,[106] and on the basis of reciprocity. Whether reciprocity will be forthcoming remains to be seen. These provisions, and the possibility under OST Art. X, for observation of the flight of space objects by OST parties other than the launching state are, of course, intended to be reassuring.

The UN Registration Convention of 1976 has relevance for the military use of outer space.[107] Its Art. II requires a launching state to record in its registry each space object, regardless of whether it is civilian or military. Four different states may possibly qualify as launching states, so they are required to agree among themselves which one will register the space object in its domestic registry. Pursuant to Art, IV that state then furnishes specified information to the UN Secretary-General which is entered on the public register maintained by UN OOSA.

In this way, the state identity of a military space object becomes known. Thus, if a military satellite experiences an accident, the satellite and any astronauts on board will be returned to the state of registry. Furthermore, a combatant satellite operating in outer space against enemy satellites would have to be clearly marked with national military identification as required by the laws of war.[108] Finally, Art IV requires each state of registry to provide the UN information whether a registered military space object is no longer in outer space.

The Agreement on the Rescue of Astronauts, the Return of Astronauts and the Return of Objects Launched into Outer Space (ARRA) of 1968 is also relevant to the military uses of outer space.[109] The Agreement applies to military astronauts and to military space objects in the same way as to civilian astronauts and space objects. If 'personnel of a spacecraft' land in the territory of another state, that state must rescue them, assist them as necessary, and must 'promptly return' them to the launching state. Interestingly the requirement to return is compulsory, unconditional and without exception. The foreign astronaut is not permitted to stay, nor to be sent to a third country of his or her choice. The treaty does not directly regulate interrogation of military personnel of military space objects, but we wonder whether interrogation might interfere with 'prompt' return (Arts 1–4).

Any foreign military space object that lands in a foreign country by accident, distress, or emergency must also be returned to its launching state. No distinction is made between

105 CoCoSL I, 85–86, para 65. In January 2007 China destroyed its Fengyun – IC weather satellite; in 2008 the US destroyed its malfunctioning US–193; in 2019 India destroyed a satellite; in 2021 Russia destroyed its Kosmos–1408 satellite: D. Kastinen et al, 'Radar Observations of the Kosmos–1406 Fragmentation Event' (2023) 202 *Acta Astronautica* 341–359. Again see Chapter 9, nn. 88 and 200 and references.

106 Antarctic Treaty, *supra* n. 47, Art. VII paras 2 and 3 do not require notice of a visit. However, it is reasonable that notice should be given for visits on celestial bodies, if only to ensure that there is an adequate air supply for all present. As noted in Chapter 7, in the film *2001: A Space Odyssey* (1968), and the related novel by Arthur C. Clarke, Russian access to the US 'Moon Base Clavius' is refused on health grounds.

107 See the fuller treatment of the Convention in Chapter 4.

108 1907 Hague Convention IV Re-enacting the Laws and Customs of War on Land, 36 Stat. 2277, TS 539, 1 Bevans 631. See para 2 of n. 20 *supra*; Bourbonniere and Lee, *supra* n. 95, at 894.

109 See the fuller treatment of ARRA in Chapter 4.

military and non-military space objects. A military space object may contain secret and valuable equipment of interest to the foreign state that finds it. Examination to acquire military secrets is also not mentioned in the treaty. Supposedly the obligation of 'prompt' return would mean that the object must be returned quickly before examination of secrets, but that may not in practice be enforceable. Military space objects may contain toxic and hazardous materials such as fuel for propulsion or nuclear batteries for power. ARRA Art 5 provides that the receiving state may request assistance and or reimbursement of clean-up expenses from the launching states in removing such materials.[110]

Albeit that it is relatively ineffective the Moon Agreement of 1979 (MA) also has relevance in military matters.[111] For its parties the MA applies to all celestial bodies within the solar system not just the moon, and to orbits around or trajectories to it except where other 'specific legal norms' have been established for such a body (MA Art. 1.1–2). It also sometimes augments previous OST provisions.[112] Deriving from OST Art. IV para 2, MA Art. 3.1 reiterates the 'peaceful purposes' requirement and Art. 3.4 repeats OST Art. IV para 2 on military bases etc. and the use of military personnel and equipment. But MA Art. 3.3 clarifies the prohibition on nuclear or WMD weaponry in space. OST Art. IV para 1 had dealt with Earth orbiting or the stationing of 'such weapons in outer space in any other manner'. MA Art. 3.3. prohibits putting such weapons in moon orbit or into a trajectory to or around the moon or on the moon itself. However, the major military innovation is Art. 3.2:

> Any threat or use of force or any other hostile act or threat of hostile act on the Moon is prohibited. It is likewise prohibited to use the Moon in order to commit any such act or to engage in any such threat in relation to the Earth, the Moon, spacecraft, the personnel of spacecraft or man-made space objects.

The specific prohibition of threat is an innovation in explicit space law albeit it is to be found in the UN Charter (Art. 2.4) part of space law by OST Art. III. How the terms of Art, 3.2 interact with those of MA Art. 3.1 as to 'exclusively . . . peaceful purposes' is an intriguing conundrum.[113] MA Art. 3 does not clarify what a 'peaceful purpose' may be, but it does, perhaps, indicate some content for the contrary.

Finally, MA Art. 15.1 provides for the inspection of bases, equipment etc. subject to reasonable notice, but, unlike OST Art. XI, without a condition of reciprocity. The MA may therefore contain a stronger legal deterrent to military use of outer space than the OST. Ratification of the MA could therefore appeal to states that oppose military uses of outer space as well as to those who accept the common heritage principle enshrined in MA Art. 11.

Ballistic and anti-ballistic missiles are a potential military use of space.[114] Attempts to reduce this threat produced the 1972 US – USSR ABM Treaty, with related agreements

---

110 Cf. the COSMOS 954 crash in Northern Canada discussed in Chapter 4.

111 As of 1 January 2023, the MA had 18 ratifications and four signatories though one member, Saudi Arabia, is to withdraw as from 5 January 2024. See the fuller treatment of the Agreement in Chapter 7.

112 R.J. Zedalis, 'Will Article III of the Moon Agreement Improve Existing Law? A Textual Analysis' (1980) 5 *Suffolk Transnat. L.J.* 53–71.

113 Zedalis, *supra* n. 112, at 65–9.

114 *Commission to Assess the Ballistic Missile Threat to the United States,* 2001: https://irp.fas.org/threat/missile/rumsfeld/toc.htm. F. Walsh, 'Forging a Diplomatic Shield for American Satellites: The Case for Re –

with the UK and Canada.[115] However, the US – USSR treaty was abrogated by the US in 2001.[116] The trajectory of a ballistic missile may take it into space, depending on where 'space' is. Ballistic missiles are not vehicles in Earth or other orbit although they may briefly intrude into space. This means *inter alia* that ballistic missiles with nuclear or WMD warheads, whether in orbit or not, are not covered by the prohibition on the stationing of such weapons in space under OST Art. IV, albeit that other treaties may apply.[117]

Actual Use

We turn now to the actual uses of space, acknowledging that 'dual-use' makes it increasingly difficult to distinguish between military and non-military usage of space. GNSS systems are usable for both civilian and military purposes. Ironically in view of the topic of this chapter, three of the present operational systems, US GPS, Russian GLONASS and Chinese Beidou are systems designed, operated and owned by the military to which civilians have been granted access. Only the European Galileo system is civilian, and it permits military use of its restricted service.[118] Again while operational the Shuttle could have been used for military purposes so, presumably, later similar craft might.[119]

The military interest in telecommunications is obvious. Indeed, until the doctrines of privatisation began to spread, with the only clear exception of the US, military considerations played an important role in state control of modern telecommunications facilities.[120] As outlined in Chapter 8, internationally telecommunications are normally subject to the rules and procedures of the International Telecommunication Union (ITU).[121] Two points are important for this chapter. First, because they operate digitally interference-free signalling is necessary for satellite operating and messaging.[122] Second, radio frequencies

---

evaluating the 2006 National Space Policy in Light of a Chinese Satellite System' (2007) 72 *J. Air L. & Com.* 759–799.

115 Treaty on the Limitation of Anti – Ballistic Missile Systems, Moscow, 26 May 1972, 944 UNTS 14; 24 UST 1439. See also US/UK 371 UNTS 46 and 307 UNTS 208; US/Canada 353 UNTS 239. Cf. 'ABM Treaty Interpretation Dispute', Hearing before the Subcommittee on Arms Control, International Security and Science of the Committee on Foreign Affairs, US House of Representatives, 99th Cong. 1st Sess., 22 October 1985 (USGPO, 1986).

116 E.K. Penney, 'Is that Legal? The US Withdrawal from the Anti – Ballistic Missile Treaty' (2002) 51 *Cath. Univ. L. Rev.* 1287–1322; R. Mullerson, 'The ABM Treaty, Changed Circumstances, Supreme Interests and International Law' (2001) 50 ICLQ 509–539; J.B. Rhinelander, 'The ABM Treaty: Past Present and Future (Part 1)' (2001) *J. Conflict and Sec. L.* 91–114, and '(Part 2)' at 225–244. North Korea, party to the OST and the Registration Convention, has been sanctioned by the UN Security Council for developing and using ballistic missiles (see most recently S/RES/2397 (2017) and citations therein). However, it has also been accused of using the development of a launcher for access to space to mask testing ballistic missile technology.

117 See Reinhardt *supra* n. 81. W.D. Reed and R.W. Norris, 'Military Use of the Space Shuttle' (1980) 13 *Akron L. Rev.* 665–688. Cf. also n. 85 *supra* on the application of OST Art. IV to weapons in partial orbits.

118 See Chapter 12, sv. Galileo, n. 56.

119 Reed and Norris, *supra* n. 117.

120 Cf. F. Lyall, *International Communications: The International Telecommunication Union and the Universal Postal Union* (Farnham: Ashgate, 2011).

121 Constitution and Convention of the International Telecommunication Union: Final Acts of the Additional Plenipotentiary Conference, Geneva, 22 December 1992 (Geneva: ITU, 1993), 1825 UNTS 1; 1996 UKTS 24, Cm. 3145; US Tr. Doc. 104–35. The informal *Collection of the Basic Texts of the International Telecommunication Union Adopted by the Plenipotentiary Conference* is published by the ITU after each plenipotentiary Conference. The ITU is more fully discussed in Chapter 8 *supra*.

122 Satellites are controlled by on – board computers: a garbled signal will not be recognised.

are limited natural resources that should be used rationally, efficiently and economically through states complying with the ITU Radio Regulations.[123] States are required to limit the spectrum used to the minimum essential to provide satisfactory services,[124] and must avoid harmful interference with the frequencies used by others.[125] However, by Art. 6.1 (37) *ad fin* and Art. 48.1 (202) of the Constitution members of the ITU retain entire freedom as to military radio installations, language that includes military satellites.[126] That noted, Art. 48.2 (203) goes on to require that military services should comply with duties as to assistance in case of distress, to the avoidance of harmful interference and to having regard to the types of emissions and frequencies used. Article 48.3 (204) requires military installations providing public correspondence and other services governed by the ITU Administrative Regulations (sc. a broadcasting or public telecommunications service) in general to comply with the appropriate ITU regulatory provisions.[127] Such provisions do not appear as a matter of law to encompass the frequencies and orbits for military satellites. Nonetheless it is understood that many satellites with military applications pass through the notification procedures and are registered on the ITU International Master Frequency Register.[128] Such as GNSS and remote sensing satellites remain dual use, and as such come into the ordinarily registrable category. On occasion this may result in compromises and mutual accommodation. For example the US and Europe negotiated to obviate a possible encroachment by the then projected Galileo system on a radio frequency used by the GPS thus enabling the US to register an unhampered radiofrequency under the ITU procedures.[129] Some satellite systems are registered with the ITU and the UN under the Registration Convention of 1975, with their use or purpose being undesignated.[130] It seems to be that there are in addition a number of satellites whose existence is confidential or undisclosed.[131] We do not know whether these include any wholly dedicated military satellite systems.[132]

---

123 ITU Constitution, CS Art. 44.2 (196).
124 ITU Constitution, CS Art. 44.1 (195).
125 ITU Constitution, CS Art. 45 (197–9). Satellites are in orbit and therefore potentially affect and are affected by the radio transmissions of many states.
126 The terms of Art. 48 go far back into ITU history and have not been altered by ITU plenipotentiary conferences held since 1992: see Lyall, *supra* n. 120. There seems to be a discontinuity between it and Art. 45.1 (197) on the avoidance of harmful interference which applies to 'All stations, *whatever their purpose*' (emphasis added).
127 Following concern about the operation of Art. 48 PP–22 (Bucharest) adopted Resolution 216, 'Use of frequency assignments by military radio installations for National Defence Services'. The Resolution may or may not be implemented by WRC–23.
128 For these procedures, see Chapter 8.
129 US – EU Agreement on GPS – Galileo Cooperation, 26 June 2004: https://georgewbush – whitehouse. archives.gov/news/releases/2004/06/20040626-8.html. The Agreement ensures that Galileo's signals 'will not harm the navigation of warfare capabilities of the US and NATO military forces and ensures that the US and the European Union can address individual and mutual security concerns'.
130 Military satellites usually operate on ITU registered frequencies but have the option of altering frequencies should circumstances so require but see next note.
131 Cf. Chapter 4 on the operation of the Registration Convention, and S. Di Pippo, 'Registration of Space Objects with the Secretary – General': www.unoosa.org/documents/pdf/copuos/lsc/2016/symp–03.pdf. See also S. Di Pippo, 'Registration of Space Objects with the United Nations Secretary – General' (2016) 63 ZLW 364–374. Such satellites may include remote sensing and signal traffic monitoring satellites. It remains possible that not all military satellites have been registered.
132 It is known that some military operations in Syria, Iraq, Afghanistan, Pakistan and Yemen involved unmanned Predator and Reaper drones controlled via satellite links by operators in the US.

Military services have their own communication satellites but may also use civilian commercial satellite systems. For example, when the Iridium satellite system neared bankruptcy some years ago, the US Defense Department employed it for some purposes, and we believe continues to do so.[133] Other military establishments use civilian telecommunication systems as needed.[134] In a sense this is to be welcomed as cost-effective, and clear example of practical 'dual-use'.

Finally, despite all that has been said, it has to be recognised that in military conflict states may seek to disrupt the telecommunications of their opponents. 'Harmful interference' can be caused deliberately.[135]

Remote sensing systems are another category of dual-use space technology. We discussed these more fully in Chapter 12 where to an extent their military aspect was implicitly included. Reconnaissance and surveillance are always militarily important. Sensing by satellite is more flexible, controllable, secure and frequent method of data gathering than aerial sensing, and has to an extent replaced the latter.[136] There is an argument that the acquisition of such data is an infringement of the privacy of a state.[137] A more cogent contrary argument is that monitoring and therefore awareness of what is actually going on is a better guarantee of prolonging peace than assumptions made in the absence of data.[138] Remote sensing may also serve in the military sphere to monitor compliance with arms control agreements.[139] There are, of course, the UN Remote Sensing Principles of 1986,[140] but they apply only to the activities denominated by its Pr. I – the improvement 'of natural resources management, land use and the protection of the environment'. It strains credulity to interpret this as including military sensing on the ground that natural resources, land use and the environment might be indirectly affected by military data or operations. Military sensing does, however, throw up three problematic areas. The first is that sensing satellites do not discriminate. They see whatever is there. Civilian sensing carried out for the purposes covered by the 1986 Principles may acquire data of military significance: can

---

133 Iridium Satellite LLC: www.iridium.com/about/about.php. The system operates a constellation of sixty – six satellites in low Earth orbit, providing complete global coverage, including the polar areas. See Chapter 10.

134 Waldrop, *supra* n. 8, at 164. Cf. the report of the *Commission, 2001, supra* n. 114. The Starlink system was and may still be used in the Ukraine conflict: 'The satellites that saved Ukraine', *Economist* 7 January 2023, 13–15.

135 See the discussion of harmful interference in Chapter 8, *circa* n. 144 and ff. Cf. D. Zannoni, 'International Law Issues Concerning the Interruption and Degradation of the Radio Navigation Signal' (2015) 64 ZLW 487–510; S.M. Mountin, 'Intentional Interference with Commercial Communication Satellite Signals' (2014) 90 *Int. L. Stud.* 101–197; Tronchetti *supra* n. 8.

136 C.M. Petras, '"Eyes" on Freedom – A View of the Law Governing Military Use of Satellite Reconnaissance in US Homeland Defense' (2005) 31 *J. Sp. L.* 81–115. Cf. Anonymous, 'Note: Legal Aspects of Reconnaissance in Airspace and Outer Space' (1961) 61 *Col. L. Rev.* 1074–1012; D.A. Koplow, 'Back to the Future and Up to the Sky: Legal Implications of Open Skies Inspection for Arms Control' (1991) 79 *Cal. L. Rev.* 421–496; Lee and Steele. *supra* n. 11.

137 Is it helpful to introduce the private law concept of privacy into international law?

138 See *infra* 'Military Action in Space'. Cf. G. Catalano Sgrosso, 'International Legal Framework for Remote Sensing', Workshop on Legal Remote Sensing Issues, Project 2001, University of Cologne Institute of Air and Space Law (Cologne, 1999) 5–23 at 16–20.

139 N. Jasentuliyana, *International Space Law and the United Nations* (The Hague: Kluwer, 1999) 319–20.

140 'Principles Relating to the Remote Sensing of the Earth from Outer Space', 3 December 1986; UNGA Res. 41/65; (1986) 25 ILM 1334–6 with note at 1331–1333. See discussion in Chapter 12 and CoCoSL III, 81–188.

teleology solely determine whether the Principles apply? Second, under Pr. XI a sensed state is supposed to have access to data: but the data thus accessed may be of military use to the sensed state, which the sensing state may not wish to disclose. Under what circumstances may access to that data be refused on the basis of military considerations?[141] Third, there is the whole question of the general availability of remote sensing data whether on a commercial or other basis. Certainly some states exercise 'shutter control' for military or other security reasons and may make imagery available only in a degraded form.[142]

Peaceful Purposes

Underlying these elements is the concept of the use of space for 'peaceful purposes' which we must now properly consider. We have deferred this because it can be properly appreciated only in the context of the technologies and actual use of space.[143] International agreement has prevented (sometimes only slowed) the proliferation of particular weaponries and on occasion secured the reduction of armaments. We would hope that international agreement would affect the development of certain technologies. However, such steps are dependent upon that agreement, and compliance with it. It is useless merely to 'prohibit' – no matter how vociferously.[144] In a sense the concept of a 'peaceful purpose' falls to be considered as aspirational as well as prescriptive.

At the end of the fifth negotiation session of the OST the USSR representative indicated that '[a] number of questions would, of course, remain to be dealt with after the elaboration of the Treaty particularly the use of outer space for exclusively peaceful purposes'.[145] Writing of the negotiations before the sixth and final session, Dembling, who was the US representative, commented that until the completion of the OST text, 'any military use of outer space must be restricted to non-aggressive purposes in view of Article III which makes applicable international law including the Charter of the United Nations'.[146] That remains true now as a matter of customary international law even after the completion of the OST. Yet what are 'peaceful purposes'?

'Peaceful' is the adjective used in the title and text of the pre-OST UNGA space resolutions, and in several articles of the OST itself often to modify the noun 'purpose' or

141 US, Canada, India, France, Italy and Israel have all adopted formal regulations regarding denial of data: see J.I. Gabrynowicz, 'Land Remote Sensing Laws and Policies of the National Government, a Global Survey for the National Oceanic and Atmospheric Administration (NOAA) by the Univ. of Mississippi National Center for Remote Sensing, Air, and Space Law' (2007), at 'online resources' at: www.spacelaw.olemiss.edu.
142 C. Hanley, 'Regulating Commercial Remote Sensing Satellites over Israel: A Black Hole in the Open Skies Doctrine' (2000) 52 *Admin. L. Rev.* 423–442; R. Prober, 'Shutter Control: Confronting Tomorrow's Technology with Yesterday's Regulations' (2003) 19 *J. L. and Pol.* 203–52; R. Jakhu, 'International Law Governing the Acquisition and Dissemination of Satellite Imagery' (2003) 29 *J. Sp. L.* 65–91. See also discussion of 'shutter control' and access to data in Chapter 12.
143 See *supra* at n. 12.
144 Cf. the *Nuclear Weapons*, Advisory Opinion, 1996 ICJ Rep. 226. By the casting vote of the President the Opinion does not rule out the use of such weapons by a state in circumstances when its survival is at stake or as part of a policy of deterrence: see Opinion at 262–263, paras 95–96 and at 266 'Dispositive 2. E'. Cf. Declaration of Judge Vereshchetin at 279–281 and Dissenting Opinion of Judge Higgins at 583–593.
145 UN Doc. A/AC,105/C2/SR.62m, at 6, quoted by Dembling and Arons 'Evolution' (*supra* n. 66) at 434.
146 By the time of the 1966 negotiations the text of Art. III had been agreed: Dembling and Arons, 'Evolution', *supra* n. 66, at 434.

'purposes'.[147] On occasion 'peaceful' is further modified by the adverb 'exclusively'.[148] The UN Committee that deals with space matters is the Committee on the *Peaceful* Uses of Outer Space (COPUOS). The concept may well be referred back to uses of the term in the UN Charter. Its Arts. 1 and 2 require states to settle their disputes by peaceful means and in particular by Art. 2(3) that states settle their disputes 'in such a manner that international peace, and security, and justice, are not endangered'.[149] The OST drafters did not clearly define the term as used in Art. IV, nor the 'peaceful uses' of outer space that are allowed. Does 'peaceful' mean 'non-military' or does it mean 'non-aggressive'? The US and other Western states take the latter view.[150] That is in line with the UN Charter division of disputes into pacific disputes to be settled under its Chapter IV, and actions with respect to threats to the peace, breaches of the peace and acts of aggression which come under Chapter VII. Others would adopt (or would have adopted) a broader definition of 'peace' so as to outlaw all military uses of space.[151] The issue remains important because weapons technology continues to develop, and some national policies have become increasingly explicit about planning for military uses of outer space.[152]

Questions may also arise as to the use of the International Space Station (ISS), a development which we outlined in Chapter 4. The intergovernmental agreements and memoranda of understanding governing the use of the ISS indicate that it is to be used for peaceful purposes, but exactly what this might mean in a particular instance remains unclear. Beyond that what of other space stations established or planned?

Military Action in Space

May states protect their investment in military satellites, or defend any satellites they may have? This takes us into the area of anti-satellite technologies.[153] Anti-satellite technology

---

147 I.A. Vlasic, 'Disarmament Decade, Outer Space and International Law' (1981) 26 *McGill L.J.* 135–206; and his 'The Legal Aspects of Peaceful and Non – Peaceful Uses of Outer Space', in B. Jasani ed. *Peaceful and Non – Peaceful Uses of Space* (New York: Taylor and Francis, 1991) at 37–55; A. Meyer, 'Interpretation of the Term "Peaceful" in the light of the Space Treaty' (1968) 11 *Proc. IISL* 24–29; G.P. Zhukov, 'On the Question of Interpretation of the Term "Peaceful Use of Space" in the Space Treaty' (1968) 11 *Proc. IISL* 36–39; Hobe, *supra* n. 16. Cf. B. Jasani, ed., *Space Weapons and International Security* (Oxford: OUP, 1987).
    There is an argument that the space treaties are too unspecific to be of much use were actual conflict to occur: S. Freeland and R.S Jakhu, 'The Application of the United Nations Space Treaties during Armed Conflict' (2015) 58 *Proc. IISL* 157–173.
148 OST Art. IV para 2 stipulates that states use the Moon and celestial bodies 'exclusively for peaceful purposes'. Cf. MA Art. 3.1, *supra* at n. 112 and ff.
149 UN Charter, *supra* n. 21. Cf. the statement in Art. 6 of the Antarctic Treaty, *supra* n. 47, that 'Antarctica shall be used for peaceful purposes only'.
150 Dembling and Arons, 'Evolution', *supra* n. 66, at 434; Reed and Norris, *supra* n. 117, at 677–679. The US National Aeronautics and Space Act of 1958 clearly required and still requires that US space activities be for 'peaceful purposes' while also contributing to national defence: 42 USC §§ 2451 *et seq.*
151 Cf. R.D. Crane, 'Soviet Attitudes Toward International Space Law' [1962] 56 AJIL 685–723 at 700–704, and his 'Basic Principles in Soviet Space Law: Peaceful Coexistence, Peaceful Cooperation, and Disarmament' (1964) 29 *Law and Contemp. Probs.* 943–955 at 949–955. Cf. the 1952 proposal of Professor Alex Meyer, *supra* n. 40, that war – like activities in outer space be prohibited: Cheng, 523–538.
152 See *infra* 'Military Practices and Developing Attitudes'.
153 D.A Koplow, 'ASAT – ISFACTION: Customary International Law and Regulation of Anti – Satellite Weapons' (2009) 30 *Mich. J. Int. L.* 1187–1272; and 'An Inference about Interference: A Surprising Application of Existing International Law to Inhibit Anti – Satellite Weapons' (2014) 35 *U. Pa. J. Int. L.* 737–827; S.M. Mountin, 'Intentional Interference with Commercial Communication Satellite Signals' (2014) 90 *Int. L. Stud.* 101–197; S. Kuan, 'Legality of the Deployment of Anti – Satellite Weapons in Earth Orbit:

has four basic modes. A kinetic weapon will destroy or cripple a satellite by collision either by a single missile, or a number of small objects – the buckshot technique.[154] Launched from the Earth or from a space platform, a kinetic weapon would have the disadvantage of producing a cloud of debris, with all its potential consequences.[155] An alternative is the laser, which could be used to knock out a satellite, again either from Earth or from space.[156] A different possibility is the use of radio jamming either to overwhelm a satellite itself, or to prevent its signals being used.157 Last, in a modern age dependent on electronics and the Internet, a less obvious but real possibility is a terrestrial cyber-attack on a perceived enemy, part of which could involve interference with command, control and use of satellite systems.[158]

Present and Future' ((2010) 36 *J. Sp. L.* 207–230; Bourbonniere I and III, *supra* n. 5, and Bourbonniere and Haeck, *supra* n. 17; C.M. Petras, ' "Space Force Alpha": Military Use of the International Space Station and the Concept of Peaceful Purposes' (2002) *A.F.L. Rev.* 135–182 at 172–180; S. Mirmina, 'The Ballistic Missile Defense System and its Effects on the Outer Space Environment' (2005) 31 *J. Sp. L.* 287–313; J.A. Jiru, 'Star Wars and Space Malls: When the Paint Chips Off a Treaty's Golden Handcuffs' (2000) 42 *S. Tex. L. Rev.* 155–182.

Cf. earlier H. DeSaussure, 'Prospects for the Demilitarization of the Manned Space Station' (1984) 18 *Akron L. Rev.* 183–191, and his 'The Impact of Manned Space Stations On the Law of Outer Space' (1984) 21 *San Diego L. Rev.* 985–1014 at 1009–1013; A.J. Young, *Law and Policy in the Space Stations Era* (Dordrecht: Nijhoff, 1989) 201–239; *Arms Control in Space: Workshop Proceedings* (US Cong. Office of Technology Assessment OTA – BP – ISC–28, 1984): http://govinfo.library.unt.edu/ota/Ota_4/DATA/1984/8404.PDF; *Commission, 2001, supra* n. 114.

154 Koplow (2009) *supra* n. 153, at 1201. An example is the 'Brilliant Pebbles' system conceived in the US in the 1980s as part of the then 'Strategic Defence Initiative' but not persisted with. See E. Reiss, *The Strategic Defence Initiative* (Cambridge: Cambridge UP, 2008); E. Reiss et al., *The Strategic Defence Initiative: The Development of an Armaments Programme* (Cambridge: Cambridge UP, 1992); F. Walsh, 'Forging a Diplomatic Shield for American Satellites: The Case for Re – evaluating the 2006 National Space Policy in Light of a Chinese Satellite System' (2007) 72 *J. Air L. & Comm.* 759–799; R.J. Zedalis and C.L. Wade, 'Anti – Satellite Weapons and the Outer Space Treaty of 1967' (1978) 8 *Cal. W. Int. L J.* 454–482; R.J. Zedalis, 'On the Lawfulness of Forceful Remedies for Violations of Arms Control Agreements: Star Wars and Other Glimpses at the Future' (1985) 18 *N.Y.U.J. Int. L. and Pol.* 73–168; J.N. Halpern, 'Antisatellite Weaponry: The High Road to Destruction' (1985) 3 *Boston U. Int. L.J.* 167–208. Cf. M. Krepon, 'Lost in Space: The Misguided Drive towards Antisatellite Weapons' (2001) 80 *For. Aff.* 2–7; S.M. Meyer, 'Anti – Satellite Weapons and Arms Control: Incentives and Disincentives from the Soviet and American Perspectives' (1980–1981) 36 *Int. J.* 460–484; A.D. Burton, 'Daggers in the Air: Anti – Satellite Weapons and International Law' (1988) 12 *Fletcher Forum* 143–162.

155 F.M. Walsh, 'Forging a Diplomatic Shield for American Satellites: The Case for Re – evaluating the 2006 National Space Policy in Light of a Chinese Satellite System' (2007) 72 *J. Air L.& Comm.* 759–799; E.F. Hennessey, 'Liability for Damage Caused by the Accidental Operation of a Strategic Defense Initiative System' (1988) 22 *Cornell Int. L.J.* 317–337; Mirmina, *supra* n. 153. See also *supra* Chapter 9 Environmental Regulation sv. Debris.

156 More than 30 States have ASAT laser technology: Koplow (2009) *supra* n. 153, at 1213. It is said that a Chinese laser has on occasion 'painted' a US satellite in space: www.globalsecurity.org/space/world/china/asat.htm. For an early speculation see I.E. Sänger, 'The Future of Spaceflight', *Universitas*, trans. in *The Next Ten Years in Space, 1959–1969*, Staff Report, House Sel. Ctee on Astronautics and Space Exploration, H. Doc. 115, 86th Cong. 1st Sess. (USGPO, 1959) 158–172 at 164 as to 'the development of stationary ultra – violet searchlights, exerting a radiation pressure of many tons, which by means of their high energy beam, are capable of destroying flying objects up to a distance of several hundred miles in a fraction of a second'.

157 See on jamming Chapter 10, Satellite Telecommunications and Chapter 11, Global Navigation Satellite Systems. In hostilities jamming communications is normal. J.J. Wolff, 'Interrupted Broadcasts? The Law of Neutrality and Communications Satellites' (2021) 45 *J. Sp. L.* 239–275. Electronic jamming of GNSS is a known strategic option.

158 C.M. Petras, 'The Use of Force in Response to Cyber – Attack on Commercial Space Systems – Re – examining "Self – Defense" in Outer Space in Light of the Convergence of US Military and Commercial Space

The short answer as to the lawfulness of ASATs is that under international law it is permitted to defend personnel and technologies within the legal framework of the 'inherent right of self-defence' provided that defence is proportionate.[159] As far as space is concerned there are, of course, particular considerations to be borne in mind. Precision weapons should be used properly,[160] 'harmful interference' with the activities of others should be avoided as far as possible,[161] and the creation of debris should in the general interest be minimised.[162] ASAT tests in outer space, such as the Chinese destruction of its defunct satellite, are rare and there have been suggestions that there may be a gradual development of customary international law restricting deployment of ASATs. An international soft law regime appears to be developing for deployment of non-WMD space weaponry.[163]

For the future we first note Art. 36 of the Additional Protocol I to the Geneva Conventions states that: 'In the study, development, acquisition or adoption of a new weapon, means or method of warfare, a High Contracting Party is under an obligation to determine whether its employment would, in some or all circumstances, be prohibited by this Protocol or by any other rule of international law applicable to the High Contracting Party'.[164]

Second, there remains the difficulty of integrating the speed and density of modern communications with the traditional concept of 'inherent self-defence' recognised by Art. 51 of the UN Charter and the ICJ.[165] Copious conflicting data may arrive simultaneously, and a swift military response to a rapidly unfolding situation may be deemed necessary. Modern weaponry can be devastating. The ability by unilateral determination to exercise the option of 'self-defence' is dangerous. It is therefore important that states err on the side of caution and be reluctant to engage in pre-emptive self-defence. As the UN Panel stated: the alternative of leaving decisions on 'self-defence' to states rather than channelling them through the Security Council would mean that '[a]llowing one to so act is to allow all'.[166] Further, even a stated willingness to engage in pre-emptive self-defence may begin a process of escalation, responsive, or matching action by other states resulting in the undermining of international security.[167] Arguably ASAT testing is such undermining.[168]

Third, a correlative and equally urgent problem is the emergent militarisation of outer space. The US seems to consider militarisation necessary,[169] and has exercised a solitary

---

Activities' (2002) 67 *J. Air L. & Comm.* 1213–1268. For US response see *infra* n. 212, and for the UK *infra* n. 227.

159 See discussion of UN Charter Art. 51, *supra* at n. 24. But cf. C.S. Thompson, 'Avoiding Pyrrhic Victories in Orbit: A Need for Kinetic Anti-Satellite Arms Control in the Twenty-First Century' (2020) 85 *J. Air Law & Comm.* 105–166.

160 Koplow (2009) *supra* n. 153, at 1198. D.S. Rudesill, 'Precision War and Responsibility: Transformational Military Technology and the Duty of Care under the Laws of War' (2007) 32 *Yale J. Int. L.* 517–545. See also E.F. Hennessey, 'Liability for Damage Caused by Accidental Operation of a Strategic Defense Initiative System' (1998) 22 *Cornell Int. L. J.* 317–337.

161 OST Art. IX; Bourbonniere III, *supra* n. 5, at 13.

162 Mirmina, *supra* n. 153, at 304–308 indicates relevant US environmental practice. See Chapter 9 Environmental Regulation.

163 CoCoSL I, at 85–86, para 65.

164 Additional Protocol I, *supra* n. 85.

165 See ICJ cases *supra* nn. 30, 31 and 84.

166 See *supra* n. 36.

167 Reisman and Armstrong, *supra* n. 33, at 548–549.

168 See *supra* n. 105.

169 See discussion of US at n. 176 *infra*. P.B. Larsen, 'Outer Space Arms Control: Can the US, Russia and China Make This Happen?' (2017) 22 *J. Conf. & Sec. Law* 137–159.

vote against successive UN General Assembly Resolutions on the matter.[170] Sadly the UN has had to persist with consideration of these matters for many years.[171]

Fourth, either formal or informal international agreements or understandings would be an obvious means to de-escalate tensions. A number of arms control proposals are currently being considered in disarmament negotiations. In particular the establishment of the Open-Ended Working Group on Reducing Space Threats (OEWG) by UNGA Res. 75/36 was welcome.[172] However Russia did vote against it, and, preferring that discussions be carried on as to a treaty rather than 'norms', has, with a few others, been hampering progress.[173]

Military Practices and Developing Attitudes[174]

The United States, Russia and China possess significant military space technology which they continue to develop. They have ratified the four basic space law treaties. Nevertheless each have adopted separate policies for the military use of outer space while expressing the wish to avoid conflict. Unfortunately for this treatise, security limits the availability of data. The US appears to be ahead in preparing for defensive and offensive war in outer space. Russia and China are catching up.[175]

United States

The US military world has been organised and re-organised ever since the early days of space exploration, but for wordage reasons we will not go into that detail. US national space policy has grown layer upon layer, greatly influenced by the different views of successive presidents, with the Department of Defense and other agencies acting as appropriate.[176] The main legal sources are the statements of policy to which we will come, and

---

170 UNGA Res. 77/40 'Prevention of an arms race in outer space' (2022), and 77/250 (2022) 'Further practical measures for the prevention of an arms race in outer space' are the latest on this matter.

171 The process was initiated by the UNGA Tenth Special Session, 23 May–30 June 1978, a Session devoted to disarmament. UNGA Res. S–10/2 para 80 calls for international negotiations to prevent an arms race in outer space. See also the sequence that led to UNGA Res. 77/42 (2022) 'No first placement of weapons in outer space'.

172 See Report of the Secretary General, 'Reducing space threats through norms, rules and principles of responsible behaviours' A/76/77, and the 'Open – Ended Working Group on Reducing Space Threats': https://meetings.unoda.org/open – ended – working – group – reducing – space – threats–2022. A.A. Ortega and H.L. Koller, 'The Open – Ended Working Group on Reducing Space Threats Through Norms, Rules and Principles of Responsible Behaviours: The Journey so Far, and the Road Ahead' (2023) 48 *Air and Sp. L.* 19–40. See also *supra* Chapter 9 sv. Reducing space threats.

173 The Seventy-Eighth Session of the UN General Assembly may vote to set up separate groups to work respectively on norms and on a draft treaty. See UN press release: https://press.un.org/en/2023/gadis3730.doc.htm.

174 Consideration of subsequent practice in the application of a treaty can establish 'the agreement of the parties regarding its interpretation': Art. 31 3(b), Vienna Convention, *supra* n. 25.

175 Cf. Ramey, *supra* n. 2. Now see following text and Larsen, *supra* n. 4.

176 S. Mirmina and C. Schenewerk, *International Space Law and Space Laws of the United States* (Cheltenham: Edward Elgar Publishing, 2022). Cf. 'Space Operations', US Joint Chiefs of Staff, Joint – Publication 3–14, 26 October 2020: www.jcs.mil/Portals/36/Documents/Doctrine/pubs/jp3_14ch1.pdf?ver=qmkgYPyK BvsIZyrnswSMCg%3d%3d. This ante – dates the Trump Space Policy of December 2020. See also other military joint publications: www.jcs.mil/Doctrine/Joint – Doctrine – Pubs/.

the series of presidential Space Policy Directives (SPDS).[177] In addition, though ranging beyond space, the reports on US National Security are not irrelevant.[178] We also note that the various presidents have issued other important general statements about space, but we confine our attention to military matters.

President Carter issued two statements specifically on space policy that are now only available in summary form,[179] so we begin with the National Space Policy of President Reagan of 1988. This stressed the importance of a coherent approach to space and included military elements and the potentialities of space for deterrence.[180]

The 1989 National Space Policy of President G.H.W. Bush committed the US to the peaceful use of outer space.[181] Under the sub-heading 'National Security Space Policy' it spoke of deterring or defending against enemy attack, ensuring that hostile nationals could not prevent US use of space and if necessary 'negating' hostile space systems. Similar sentiments are in the policy statement of President Clinton.[182] President G.W. Bush published a fresh National Security statement in 2002,[183] followed by a space policy in 2006.[184] The National Security section of the space policy emphasised the critical importance of developing space capabilities including that of denying freedom of action to adversaries. Its Principles section bullet point 6 stated that the US would 'oppose the development of new legal regimes or other restrictions that seek to prohibit or limit US access to or use of space. Proposed arms control agreements or restrictions must not impair the rights of the United States to conduct research, development, testing, and operations or other activities in space for US national interests'.[185] Paragraphs 8–11 of the policy contain further provisions on international cooperation, nuclear power, orbital management, radio frequency spectrum and interference protection, and orbital debris, all matters of special interest to the military.

---

177 For current Directives etc see the Space Briefing Book (Space Foundation): www.spacefoundation.org/ space_brief/space – policy – directives/.

178 Available from the Historical Office of the Department of Defense: https://history.defense.gov/Historical – Sources/National – Security – Strategy/.

179 Directive NSC–37, 11 May 1978, and Directive NSC–42, 10 October 1978: https://spp.fas.org/military/ docops/national/nsc–42.htm. W.D. Reed and R.W. Norris, 'Military Use of the Space Shuttle' (1980) 13 *Akron L. Rev.* 665–88 at 673–674.

180 Presidential Directive on National Space Policy, 11 February 1988: https://spp.fas.org/military/docops/ national/policy88.htm. The Policy is summarised in National Security Strategy of the United States of America, January 1988 at 22–23: https://history.defense.gov/Portals/70/Documents/nss/nss1988. pdf?ver=uXpmo – mT0TKzq2Ut6PmfjA%3d%3d. Cf. D.A. Koplow, 'Deterrence as the MacGuffin: The Case for Arms Control in Outer Space' (2019) 10 *J. Nat. Sec. L. and Pol.* 293–350.

181 National Space Policy, 16 November 1989: https://aerospace.csis.org/wp – content/uploads/2019/02/ NSPD–1–Bush – I – National – Space – Policy.pdf.

182 National Space Policy, 19 September 1996: www.fas.org/spp/military/docops/national/nstc-8.htm; http://history.nasa.gov/appf2.pdf; https://spp.fas.org/military/docops/national/nstc–8.htm. See also National Security Strategy statements 1995–2000, available via https://history.defense.gov/Historical – Sources/National – Security – Strategy/.

183 National Security Strategy, September 2002: https://georgewbush – whitehouse.archives.gov/nsc/ nss/2002/; https://georgewbush – whitehouse.archives.gov/nsc/nss/2002/print/index.html.

184 US National Space Policy, 30 August 2006: https://obamawhitehouse.archives.gov/sites/default/ files/microsites/ostp/national – space – policy–2006.pdf; https://aerospace.csis.org/wp – content/ uploads/2018/09/Bush – US – National – Space – Policy.pdf.

185 The US continues to vote against the UN Resolutions on preventing an arms race in outer space, *supra* n. 170.

President Obama published his National Security Strategy in May 2010,[186] followed by a National Space Policy in June.[187] The latter was wide-ranging. It reiterated ideals accepted by many and affirmed compliance with the basic space treaties and practices. The US would 'help assure the use of space for all responsible parties, and, consistent with the inherent right of self-defence, deter others from interference and attack, defend our space systems and contribute to the defence of allied space systems, and, if deterrence fails, defeat efforts to attack them'. Goals and inter-sectoral guidelines were set for space in general, though again some elements have military aspects. The Policy's treatment of national security is extensive and includes duties for the Department of Defence and the Director of National Intelligence. Like the earlier policy statements there is a brief paragraph on developing capabilities, plans and options to deter, defend and if necessary to defeat efforts to interfere with or attack US space or allied systems.

Thus far, however, the military aspect of US space policy was muted, inherent rather than explicit. That changed with the Trump presidency which saw many developments.[188] In December 2017 President Trump published his National Security Strategy.[189] Like its predecessors this covered the entire field of relevant national security concerns, this time classified under four Pillars. In Pillar III, 'Preserve Peace through Strength' a section 'Space' affirms the importance of space to the US followed by a set of priority actions including the re-establishment of a National Space Council to review long-range goals and strategy.[190] In the following years February 2019 saw the creation of the US Space Force,[191] and a Defence Space Strategy Summary was published in June 2020.[192]

At forty pages the US National Space Policy of 9 December 2020,[193] is twice the length of that of 2010 and, covering many matters, has not so far been replaced.[194] The Principles set out in its initial pages are extensive and expressly conform to the rules of space law of the four basic treaties and the ITU. However, in relation to the military use of space the

---

186 National Security Strategy, May 2010: https://history.defense.gov/Portals/70/Documents/nss/NSS2010.pdf?ver=Zt7IeSPX2uNQt00_7wq6Hg%3d%3d.

187 National Space Policy of the United States of America, 20 June 2010: https://obamawhitehouse.archives.gov/sites/default/files/national_space_policy_6-28-10.pdf. G.S. Robinson, 'The 2010 United States National Space Policy' (2010) 59 ZLW 534–550; T. Barnett, 'United States National Space Policy: 2006 & 2010', [2011] 23 *Fla. J. Int. L.* 277–291.

188 All Presidential Space Policy Directives were revised during the Trump presidency. See www.spacefoundation.org/space_brief/space – policy – directives/.

189 National Security Strategy of the United States of America, December 2017: https://history.defense.gov/Portals/70/Documents/nss/NSS2017.pdf?ver=CnFwURrw09pJ0q5EogFpwg%3d%3d.

190 National Security Strategy, *supra* n. 189, 31.

191 Space Policy Directive–4: Establishment of the United States Space Force: https://trumpwhitehouse.archives.gov/presidential – actions/text – space – policy – directive-4–establishment – united – states – space – force/. Its functions include organising, training and equipping military forces to defend US national interests, and asserting US freedom of operations in, from and to the military space domain. *Spaceforce: Doctrine for Space Forces*: www.spaceforce.mil/Portals/1/Space%20Capstone%20Publication_10%20Aug%202020.pdf; J. Grunert, *The United States Space Force and the Future of American Space Policy: Legal and Policy Implications* (Leiden: Brill, 2022) 128–164.

192 Defense Space Strategy Summary: https://media.defense.gov/2020/Jun/17/2002317391/–1/–1/1/2020_DEFENSE_SPACE_STRATEGY_SUMMARY.PDF.

193 National Space Policy of the United States of America, 6 December 2020: https://trumpwhitehouse.archives.gov/wp – content/uploads/2020/12/National – Space – Policy.pdf.

194 Apart from other matters the Policy provides for the return to the moon and the extraction and utilisation of space resources 'in accordance with applicable law'. On the Artemis programme and space mining see Chapter 7.

initial paragraph of the National Security section is blunt. The US 'seeks a secure, stable, and accessible space domain, which has become a *warfighting* domain as a result of competitors seeking to challenge United States and allied interests in space'.[195] While this echoes previous presidential policy statements as to defending national interests, the clarity is striking, albeit it had been anticipated in the Defense Space Strategy Summary of the previous June.[196] There, however, the transformation into space as a warfighting domain had been blamed on others. Its section on the 'Central Problem' stated that the 'actions, intentions, and military strategies of potential adversaries have transformed space into a warfighting domain.'

The second paragraph of the Policy's National Security Space Guidelines set out a series of measures necessary because: 'Strength and security in space contribute to United States and international security and stability. It is imperative that the United States adapt its national security organizations, policies, strategies, doctrine, security classification frameworks, and capabilities to deter hostilities, demonstrate responsible behaviours, and, if necessary, defeat aggression and protect United States interests in space'. Particularly as to military preparedness the US Space Force is to 'deliver combat and combat support capabilities necessary to enable prompt and sustained offensive and defensive space operations'.[197]

So far President Biden has not replaced the 2020 Space Policy statement. In December 2021, however, he issued a Space Priorities Framework,[198] This concentrates on the general importance of all sorts of space activity and is generally eirenic. However, it does acknowledge that military interests may be involved. 'The military doctrines of competitor nations identify space as critical to modern warfare and view the use of counterspace capabilities as a means both to reduce US military effectiveness and to win future wars. Confrontation or conflict, however, is not inevitable.' However, to deter aggression against US, allied, and partner interests the US would 'accelerate its transition to a more resilient national security space posture and strengthen its ability to detect and attribute hostile acts in space' and take steps to protect its military forces from space-enabled threats.'[199] The Biden Interim National Security Strategic Guidance of March 2021 sets out how the US will engage with the world in order that departments and agencies can align their actions as work is done on a National Security Strategy.[200] While this does speak of defending the interests of the US and its allies, of continuing 'to defend access to the global commons, including freedom of navigation and overflight rights, under international law' . . . and of positioning 'ourselves, diplomatically and militarily, to defend

---

195 Emphasis added, but see *infra* n. 201.
196 Space Policy Directive–4 and *Spaceforce*, both *supra* n. 192.
197 National Security Space Guidelines, Policy *supra* n. 193, final para at 27–28. See 'Commercial Space Protection Tri-Seal Strategic Framework' (August 2023): www.nga.mil/assets/files/Tri-Seal_Exec_Summ_Releasable.pdf and 'NGA, NRO, USSPACECOM plan for threats to commercial satellites': www.nga.mil/news/NGA_NRO_USSPACECOM_plan_for_threats_to_commercial.html.
198 United States Space Priority Framework, December 2021: www.whitehouse.gov/wp – content/uploads/2021/12/united – states – space – priorities – framework–_–december–1–2021.pdf. See also the 'A Strategic Framework for Space Diplomacy' US State Department, May 2023: www.state.gov/wp – content/uploads/2023/05/Space – Framework – Clean–2–May–2023–Final – Updated – Accessible–5.25.2023.pdf.
199 Priority Framework, *supra* n. 198, 6.
200 Interim National Security Strategic Guidance, 3 March 2021: www.whitehouse.gov/wp – content/uploads/2021/03/NSC–1v2.pdf; with Introduction at www.whitehouse.gov/briefing – room/statements–releases/2021/03/03/interim – national – security – strategic – guidance/.

our allies', it does not speak of space as a military or a warfighting domain.[201] Avoidance of conflict through diplomacy is preferred.[202] Suitable US behaviour in space is to be pursued.[203] However, the prior presidential statement of 2020 has not been abrogated, the various presidential directives subsist,[204] and the recent financing for the Department of Defence and the Space Force make allocations for warfighting in space.[205] As the 2020 Space Policy states, it is US policy for its advanced technology to flow only to its allies.[206] As a result there are such things as the International Traffic in Arms Regulations (ITAR), and the Export Administration Regulations (EARS),[207] together with specific controls for particular cases.[208]

The so-called Wolf Amendment characterizes the US-China relationship regarding flow of space technology.[209] It is US policy to maintain 'practical, result-oriented diplomacy with Beijing and work to reduce the risk of misperception and miscalculations',[210] Nevertheless, there is decreasing coordination on space between the two governments. The failure of the two countries to coordinate their lunar activities is a potential cause of conflict; a lack of coordination of governmental and nongovernmental traffic in congested orbits or locations are potential crisis points that might even lead to military confrontation.[211]

Finally we note that the US taken measures for its cybersecurity.[212]

---

201 Reference point, *supra* n. 195. But cf. S.M. McCall, 'Space as a Warfighting Domain: Issues for Congress', Cong. Res. Service, 10 August 2021.

202 Cf. 'Our National Security Priorities', Policy *supra* n. 193 at 9 ff.

203 'Tenets of Responsible Behavior in Space', Secretary of Defense, Memorandum for Secretaries of the Military Departments, 7 July 2021: https://media.defense.gov/2021/Jul/23/2002809598/–1/–1/0/ TENETS – OF – RESPONSIBLE – BEHAVIOR – IN – SPACE.PDF.

204 Space Policy Directives, *supra* n. 177.

205 See US Department of Defense Fiscal Year 2024 Budget Request: https://comptroller.defense.gov/ Portals/45/Documents/defbudget/FY2024/FY2024_Budget_Request.pdf, and the relevant materials: https://comptroller.defense.gov/Budget – Materials/Budget2024/. 'Space warfighting capabilities' are listed in the funding request for the Space Force, Request *supra*, 11, sv. Campaigning Readiness.

206 Cf. the last para of 'Goals', 2020 National Space Policy Statement, *supra* n. 193, at 5.

207 International Traffic in Arms Regulations (ITAR) CFR Title 22. Parts 120–130: www.pmddtc.state. gov/?id=ddtc_kb_article_page&sys_id=24d528fddbfc930044f9ff621f961987, and www.ecfr.gov/current/ title–22/. Export Administration Regulations (EARS), 15 CFR Parts 730–730: www.ecfr.gov/current/ title–15/subtitle – B/chapter – VII/subchapter – C. For discussion of these see Chapter 13 *supra*, Finance and International Trade Law, sv. Unilateral Trade Restrictions Based on National Security.

208 Cf. the Technology Safeguard Agreements with New Zealand and the UK noted in Chapter 15, Commercial Activities.

209 The Wolf Amendment restricts NASA's ability to engage with China regarding space exploration.

   (a) None of the funds made available by this division may be used for the National Aeronautics and Space Administration or the Office of Science and Technology Policy to develop, design, plan, promulgate, implement, or execute a bilateral policy, program, order, or contract of any kind to participate, collaborate, or coordinate bilaterally in any way with China or any Chinese – owned company unless such activities are specifically authorized by a law enacted after the date of enactment of this division.

   (b) The limitation in subsection (a) shall also apply to any funds used to effectuate the hosting of official Chinese visitors at facilities belonging to or utilized by the National Aeronautics and Space Administration.Department of Defense and Full – Year Continuing Appropriations Act, Pub. L. No. 112–10, §1340, 125 Stat. 38, 123 (2011) [Wolf Amendment].

210 See Interim National Security Guidance, 2021, *supra* n. 200, at 21.

211 J. Perlez suggested that the US and China adopt a code for unplanned encounters of its agents in order to reduce potential military confrontation: 'Frost Thickens as U.S Faces Rising China', NY Times, 15 August 2022 at A1.

212 US: National Cybersecurity Strategy, March 2023: www.whitehouse.gov/wp – content/uploads/2023/03/ National – Cybersecurity – Strategy–2023.pdf; www.whitehouse.gov/briefing – room/statements –

North Atlantic Treaty Organisation (NATO)

The North Atlantic Treaty Organisation was established by the North Atlantic Treaty of 1949.[213] Unlike its members it conducts no space activities itself but relies on theirs. However, it is relevant to the military use of space. By its Art. 5, its parties have agreed that an attack on any of them will be responded to by the exercise of the right of self-defence recognised by Art. 51 of the UN Charter.[214]

Unsurprisingly NATO has kept an eye on space as a matter of security.[215] This has recently become explicit. In para 6 of the London Declaration of 4 December 2019, looking to the security needs of the future the members of the NATO Council 'declared space an operational domain' important 'in keeping us safe and tackling security challenges . . ..'[216] What this involved was amplified in January 2022 when NATO issued its overarching Space Policy.[217] Subsequently NATO, reflecting its function as a defensive organisation, has continued in its measured approach to space. It has adapted its Allied Command system,[218] developed its satellite communications systems,[219] and extended its surveillance programme.[220]

United Kingdom

Although aware of the need for space security,[221] for many years the UK was content to contribute to the work of others rather than taking its own initiatives. Thus in December 2015 an encouraging National Space Policy was published.[222] However, March 2021 saw a major governmental review of security, defence, development and foreign policy,[223] soon followed

---

releases/2023/03/02/fact – sheet – biden – harris – administration – announces – national – cybersecurity – strategy/. See also the Cybersecurity and Infrastructure Agency (CISA) whose role includes coping with such problems in many fields: www.cisa.gov/.

213 North Atlantic Treaty, 1949, 34 UNTS 243; 1949 UKTS 45, Cmd. 7789; 63 Stat 2241; TIAS 1964; [1949] 43 AJIL Supp. 159; 4 Bevans 828: www.nato.int/cps/en/natohq/official_texts_17120.htm. As of March 2024 NATO has thirty-two members.

214 For Article 51 see *supra* n. 27.

215 See the Fact Sheet, 'NATO's Approach to Space': www.act.nato.int/space; updated by www.nato.int/cps/en/natohq/topics_175419.htm. A previous example of NATO consideration of space is in 'Active Engagement, Modern Defence' NATO Council, Lisbon, November 2010: www.nato.int/cps/en/natohq/official_texts_68580.htm?selectedLocale=en.

216 London Declaration (NATO, 4 December 2019): www.nato.int/cps/en/natohq/official_texts_171584.htm?selectedLocale=en.

217 'Space Policy': www.nato.int/cps/en/natohq/official_texts_190862.htm.

218 See 'NATO's New Space Policy Launches Activity of Allied Command Transformation': www.act.nato.int/articles/nato – space – policy – launches – activity – act.

219 'Satellite Communications': www.nato.int/cps/en/natohq/topics_183281.htm. See also the NATO Communications and Information Agency: www.nato.int/cps/en/natohq/topics_69332.htm.

220 Factsheet, February 2023, 'Alliance Persistent Surveillance from Space (APSS)': www.nato.int/nato_static_fl2014/assets/pdf/2023/2/pdf/230215–factsheet – apss.pdf.

221 National Space Security Policy, April 2014 (UK Gov., 2014): www.ukspace.org/wp – content/uploads/2019/05/National – Space – Security – Policy–1.pdf.

222 National Space Policy (UK Gov, 2015): https://assets.publishing.service.gov.uk/government/uploads/system/uploads/attachment_data/file/484865/NSP_–_Final.pdf.

223 Global Britain in a competitive age: The Integrated Review of Security, Defence, Development and Foreign Policy, March 2021, CP 403: https://assets.publishing.service.gov.uk/government/uploads/system/uploads/attachment_data/file/975077/Global_Britain_in_a_Competitive_Age–_the_Integrated_Review_of_Security__Defence__Development_and_Foreign_Policy.pdf.

by publication of a general 'National Space Strategy'.[224] In its Part One this reviewed the state of affairs then existing, established particular goals for the UK in Part Two and in Part Three set out pillars through which these would be attained. Part Four considered how these objectives could or should be approached. Among the matters catalogued Part Two Goal Four was the protection and defence of UK national interests in space and Part Three Pillar Four was the development of resilient national space capabilities and services.

On 1 April 2021 the UK established the UK Space Command, a Joint Command staffed from the Royal Navy, British Army, Royal Air Force and Civil Service.[225] February 2022 saw the publication of the UK 'Defence Space Strategy: Operationalising the Space Domain'.[226] Its Chapter 1 identifies space as an 'operational domain', presenting its own threats and hazards. Strategic intent is the subject of Chapter 2, with protection and defence covered in Chapter 3, the necessity of continued collaboration with allies being expressly noted. The UK is taking space seriously, including its military aspects. It is also aware of the problems of cyber-security and takes appropriate measures.[227]

Russia

Russia possesses both space technology and significant military capability.[228] It is party to the four basic space law treaties (but not the Moon Agreement) and other treaties that have a bearing on military space activities.[229] It is a member of the ITU. It is active in COPUOS and the Conference on Disarmament.[230] Its launch of Sputnik I in 1957 ushered in the potentialities of space. During the Cold War Russia developed a Fractional Orbital Bombardment Systems (FOBS), an Intercontinental Ballistic Missile System (ICBM). An active military space programme was maintained until 1972 when it entered into an interim agreement with the US on the limitation of strategic offensive arms and the Anti-Ballistic Missiles Treaty.[231] Russia then adopted a policy of disarmament in outer space

---

224 National Space Strategy, September 2021 (UK Gov., 2021): https://assets.publishing.service.gov.uk/government/uploads/system/uploads/attachment_data/file/1034313/national – space – strategy.pdf.

225 UK Space Command: www.gov.uk/guidance/uk – space – command. As the UK Space Agency was established on 1 April 2010, do the dates of establishment reveal a sense of humour?

226 Defence Space Strategy: Operationalising the Space Domain, February 2021 (UK Gov., 2022): https://assets.publishing.service.gov.uk/government/uploads/system/uploads/attachment_data/file/1051456/20220120–UK_Defence_Space_Strategy_Feb_22.pdf.

227 A UK National Cyber Force was established in 2020. See Government Cyber Security Strategy: Building a cyber resilient public sector, 2022–2030: https://assets.publishing.service.gov.uk/government/uploads/system/uploads/attachment_data/file/1049825/government – cyber – security – strategy.pdf; The National Cyber Force: Responsible Cyber Power in Practice, March 2023: www.gov.uk/government/news/national – cyber – force – reveals – how – daily – cyber – operations – protect – the – uk.

228 S. Bendett et al, 'Advanced military technology in Russia: Capabilities and implications', Research Paper, Chatham House, September 2021: www.chathamhouse.org/sites/default/files/2021–09/2021–09–23–advanced – military – technology – in – russia – bendett – et – al.pdf.

229 E.g. the Treaty Banning Nuclear Weapon Tests in the Atmosphere, in Outer Space and Under Water, Moscow, 5 August 1963 (in force 10 October 1963); 480 UNTS 43; 14 UST 1313, TIAS 5433; (1964) UKTS 3, Cmnd. 2245; (1963) 2 ILM 883; [1963] 57 AJIL 1026.

230 UN Conference on Disarmament: www.un.org/disarmament/.

231 Interim Agreement between the US and the USSR on certain measures with respect to the limitation of strategic offensive Arms, 1989, 944 UNTS 3; Treaty on the limitation of anti – ballistic missile systems, Moscow 1972, 944 UNTS 13. See also the US/USSR Memorandum of Understanding on consultations as to arms limitation, Geneva 1972, 944 UNTS 27.

and engaged with the US in the 1972–1979 SALT II discussions as to the prohibition of putting nuclear weapons or weapons of mass destruction into orbit.[232] However, in 2001 the US denounced the ABM Treaty and Russia began to rebuild its military capability, including in space, re-establishing a separate military space branch called the Russian Space Forces.

Notwithstanding, Russia's stated aim is to demilitarise outer space and turn it into a weapons-free zone. It would prefer a treaty instrument banning the weaponisation of outer space. In 2004 it unilaterally declared that it would not be the first to introduce weapons into outer space, and in 2008 joined China in submitting a draft Treaty on Prevention of the Placement of Weapons in Outer Space and of the Threat or Use of Force against Outer Space Objects (PAROS) to the Conference on Disarmament.[233] In civilian activities Russia cooperated in operating the International Space Station and, for a period after the US Shuttle was retired, its Soyuz vehicles provided the only transportation to the ISS. In 2022, perhaps in consequence of the Ukraine imbroglio, it announced that it would cease participation in the ISS in 2024, but more recently extended that to 2028. Russia may construct its own space station, purpose unknown.[234]

Russia has been a major supporter of the UNGA Resolutions on 'Prevention of an Arms Race in Outer Space' and on 'No First Placement of Weapons in Outer Space'.[235] These proposals would not replace existing limitations but be in addition to the existing limitations on military activities in outer space. Both resolutions passed the UN General Assembly with overwhelming majorities but have been regularly opposed by the US. On the other hand, Russia did not support the European proposed Code of Conduct for Outer Space,[236] which was supported by the United States. Russia's preferred strategy is to discuss all issues relating to the weaponisation of outer space in the Conference on Disarmament (CD) in Geneva.[237] By contrast, other states view the Conference on Disarmament as a dead-end for arms control in outer space and have favoured shifting all or part of the arms control discussions to COPUOS. Russia participates in discussions of the UN Open-Ended Group on Reducing Space Threats,[238] but does not support US proposals to ban the testing of ASATs in outer space.[239]

---

232 SALT II did not result in a formal treaty, though the parties did respect its principles and those of the Interim Agreement *supra* n. 231.

233 Conference *supra* n. 230. For 2014 text of the draft PAROS treaty see https://reachingcriticalwill.org/images/documents/Disarmament – fora/cd/2014/documents/PPWT2014.pdf. The United States opposed PAROS because compliance would not be adequately verifiable and because it would not include ground – based space weapons.

234 The ISS is discussed in Chapter 4.

235 See *supra* nn. 170, 171.

236 The Code is discussed in Larsen, *supra* n. 4, at 150–153.

237 Amb. Alexander Yakovenko, 2013, 15 statements: 'Why Russia is Against Weapons in Space: www.rt.com/op – edge/weapons – russia – space – destruction–282/ Also www.rt.com/nes/239533–russia – treaty – weapons – space, and https://www,rt.com/op – edge/weapons – outer – space – russia. A. Kapustin, 'Prospects for the Demilitarization of Outer Space: From "Soft Regulation" to "Hard" Treaty Mechanisms?' (2020) 44 *J. Sp. L.* 433–449; Larsen, *supra* n. 4. See also Wikipedia, Militarization of Space.

238 See *supra* n. 172, but note n. 173.

239 Statement by Head of Russian Delegation to First Session in Statements: https://meetings.unoda.org/meeting/57866/statements.

Despite Russia's stated aim of the demilitarisation of outer space it is preparing for and engaging in military uses of outer space. It has an extensive space surveillance network.[240] Militarily it has deployed an increasing number of cruise and ballistic missiles. In the Ukraine it has used jamming and other radio interference measures together with electronic warfare. Its destruction of its defunct Cosmos-1408 satellite in LEO by a direct-ascent ASAT in 2021 resulted in orbital debris multiplying close to the ISS which on occasion has caused personnel in the ISS to take shelter.[241] Other countries protested, arguing that destroying Cosmos-1408 was a blow to the long term sustainability of outer space. In response Russia noted that its ASATs could destroy the US Global Navigation Satellite System (GPS).[242] Last we note that US and Western support of Ukraine has led to sanctions and an end to much coordination with Russia in space and in other matters.[243]

China

China is a member of the ITU, is party to the four basic outer space treaties (not the Moon Agreement) and other treaties that relate to military activities in space. It participates actively in COPUOS and the Conference on Disarmament including the work of the Open-ended Working Group.[244] Its space programme is self-reliant and largely independent. Thus it has not joined the Artemis Accords but has plans with Russia for the construction of a lunar base.[245] As indicated in Chapter 13 its space activities are carried out for civil and military purposes.[246] Much of the Chinese activity in space is conducted by the People's Liberation Army but is directed by central government.

Like the US and Russia the implementation of Chinese military space policy is in tension with its treaty obligations and its general space programme.[247] In contrast to the US, China's launch activities have no reliance on commercial space operators. It conducts launches for its own purposes but also provides launch services for others at commercial

---

240 NASASPACEFLIGHT: Russia's space surveillance network: https://forum.nasaspaceflight.com/index. php?topic=55993.0.

241 D. Kastinen et al, 'Radar Observations of the Kosmos–1408 Fragmentation Event' (2023) 202 *Acta Astronautica* 341–359. See also Wikipedia, Kosmos–1408. On the risk of a cascading chain activity of space debris (the Kessler Syndrome) see Chapter 9. As to the law applicable to ASATs see *supra* n. 159.

242 D. Messner, Russia Threatens to Destroy US GPS Satellite Constellation, Aug 1, 2121: https://parabolicarc.com/2021/12/01/russia – threatens – to – destroy – u–s – gps – satellite – constellation/.

243 Cf. trade sanctions on Russia outlined in Chapter 13.

244 See China: Statement to Third Session: https://docs – library.unoda.org/Open – Ended_Working_Group_on_Reducing_Space_Threats_(2022)/202301~1.PDF. However, China has shared Russia's position within these discussions (*supra* n. 173).

245 See Chapter 7 *supra*.

246 See China National Space Administration: www.cnsa.gov.cn/english/index.html. See also Chapter 7 as to its lunar activities.

247 See also China in Chapter 14 *supra*. Yun Zhao *National Space Law in China* (Leiden: Brill, 2015); Y. Zhao, 'Regulation of Space Activities in the People's Republic of China', in R.S. Jakhu, ed. *National Regulation of Space Activities* (Vienna: Springer, 2010) 247–266; P.B. Larsen, 'Outer Space Arms Control: Can the US, Russia and China Make This Happen?' (2017) 22 *J. Conf. & Sec. Law* 137–159 at 148–150; 'Military and Security Developments Involving the People's Republic of China 2022: Annual Report to Congress' US Defense Department, at 91: https://media.defense.gov/2022/Nov/29/2003122279/–1/–1/1/2022–MILITARY – AND – SECURITY – DEVELOPMENTS – INVOLVING – THE – PEOPLES – REPUBLIC – OF – CHINA.PDF. The 2021 Report is at https://media.defense.gov/2021/Nov/03/2002885874/–1/–1/0/2021–CMPR – FINAL.PDF.

rates.[248] China supports Russian efforts to keep discussion of military space in the Conference on Disarmament rather than in COPUOS. It prefers the treaty approach to preventing an arms race in outer space and argues for the peaceful use of space and against its weaponisation. Accordingly it votes for the UNGA Resolutions on 'Prevention of an Arms Race in Outer Space' and on 'No First Placement of Weapons in Outer Space',[249] and associated with Russia in the PAROS proposal.[250] Notwithstanding, like the US and Russia it is developing its space and counter-space capabilities.[251] It has an extensive intelligence, surveillance and reconnaissance programme that includes a satellite network,[252] together with communications systems that *inter alia* use the Beidou constellation. It has demonstrated an ASAT capability by its destruction of its own 1999 Fengyun 1-C weather satellite in 2007.[253]

The US has been wary of the increasing Chinese space activity and competence, notably barring NASA cooperation with China.[254] Future conflict in space might result from Chinese projected lunar activities in that, unlike many others intending such endeavours, it has not approved the Artemis Accords.[255]

North Korea

Finally, we note the position of the People's Democratic Republic of North Korea (DPRK), which is party to the four basic space treaties,[256] and member of the ITU since 1975.[257] Its National Aerospace Development Administration (NADA) is very active. Ballistic missile and other tests are frequent.[258] The Kwangmyŏngsŏng (Bright Star) satellite programme has been running since the 1980s. The UN was notified of successful launches in 2013 and 2016,[259] and a military satellite is intended for launch in Spring 2023. As a result of its nuclear programme, other actions and bellicose statements North Korea has been subject to international sanctions for many years.[260] However, for the present it persists on its

---

248 There has been concern as to whether foreign satellites sent to China for launch are inspected by the local authorities.
249 See *supra* nn.168, 169.
250 For the PAROS proposal see *supra* n. 233.
251 See particularly 2022 Report to Congress, *supra* n. 247, 87–94.
252 We note China also uses controllable high altitude reconnaissance balloons, as seen in February 2023.
253 See: www.space.com/3415-china – anti – satellite – test – worrisome – debris – cloud – circles – earth.html.
254 See *supra* n. 209 and Chapter 13.
255 See Chapter 7.
256 North Korea acceded to the OST and the Registration Convention in 2009, and ARRA and the Liability Convention in 2016. It established its Registry in 2015: UNOOSA ST/SG/SER.E/INF/31 www.unoosa.org/pdf/reports/regdocs/SERE_INF_031E.pdf.
257 P.B. Larsen, 'Outer Space Arms Control: Can the US, Russia and China Make This Happen?' (2017) 22 *J. Conf. & Sec. Law* 137–159 at 153–154.
258 At least eight missile tests have used inter – continental rockets, five in 2022: C. Zwirke, 6 March 2023: www.nknews.org/2023/03/north – korea – touts – brisk – space – program – work – ahead – of – military – satellite – launch/.
259 2013, UNOOSA ST/SG/SER.E/662: www.unoosa.org/documents/pdf/ser662E.pdf, and 2016, UNOOSA ST/SG/SER.E/662 www.unoosa.org/documents/pdf/ser662E.pdf
260 UN Charter Art. 41. To 2022 there have been nine Security Council Resolutions on North Korea, Resolutions 1718 (2006), 1874 (2009), 2087(2013), 2270 (12016), 2321 (2018), 2371 (2017), 2375 (2017) 2379 (2017). For application cf. currently, US: US 83 Federal Register 9187; 31 CFR, Part 510, North

course. Certainly its conduct raises the question of 'self-defence' discussed earlier in this chapter, but we hope that UN Charter Art. 42 does not become involved.

Conclusion

Military uses of outer space must be viewed within the context of, and the limitations established by, existing international law a considerable portion of which is relevant to military uses of outer space. The legal framework consists not only of the UN Charter and special international laws on military activities in outer space. It also includes existing space law treaties and agreements. All states want to preserve the existing legal framework of the space law treaties, the UN Charter, the ITU legal treaties and other widely adopted international law. Many states would like to go further and ban all weapons from outer space. Others contemplate developing deterrent remedies.[261] In the absence of consensus in COPUOS and OEWG, the status quo therefore continues.

Civilian activities in outer space have increased significantly since the space treaties were negotiated in the 1960s and 1970s. Commercial space activities would be severely affected, some possibly terminated, by military action in outer space. Modern telecommunications would be crippled by the loss of satellite systems. Remote sensing and global positioning systems would be impaired. Scientific endeavours such as the space telescopes and other scientific probes would suffer and possibly be destroyed. Many interests of space commerce and space science run contrary to military activities in outer space and constitute a counterbalance to the greater military use of space. That may have been recognised, resulting in the encouragement of private commerce by the 2020 US Space Policy statement and the maximum use of US commercial space products in outer space. including by its military.[262] Civilian activities in outer space have developed international cooperative projects such as the ISS. Collaboration is needed for future developments such as the exploration and economic use of the moon, asteroids and eventually Mars. Such cooperation must be in harmony with the existing legal regimes for outer space. *Per contra*, domination by one major space power over its partners would endanger cooperation.[263]

Unilateral military action in outer space would move the world towards chaos. Once one state begins to assert unilateral authority to weaponise outer space, with the implicit threat of the use of those weapons, other states will copy that precedent and assert their own unilateral authority. The result could be the disintegration of the existing and legal framework of the peaceful uses of outer space. We therefore view with unease the decreasing trust and harmony between the major space powers.

Korea Sanctions Regulations; UK: Sanctions and Anti – Money Laundering Act 2018, c. 13; Democratic People's Republic of Korea (Sanctions) (EU Exit) Regulations 2019, 2019 SI 411.

261 Cf. P.H. Henry et al., 'The militarization and weaponization of space: Towards a European space deterrent" (2008) 24 *Space Policy* 61–66; Larsen, *supra* n. 169.

262 US National Space Policy (2020), *supra* n. 2. Cf. G.H. Reynolds and R.P. Merges, 'The Role of Commercial Development in Preventing War in Outer Space' (1985) 30 *Jurimetrics* 130–46; G.H. Reynolds, 'Space Law in Transformation: Some Observations' (2005) 6 *Chic. J. Int. L.* 69–80, at 71–76.

263 Editorial, 'Jingoism Will Get Us Nowhere in Global Space Affairs', *Aviation Week and Space Technology*, 30 October 2006, at 58; Larsen, 'Outer Space Arms Control: Can the US, Russia and China make this Happen?' *supra* n.3.

16

THE SEARCH FOR EXTRATERRESTRIAL INTELLIGENCE

Introduction

Some may consider this chapter an unnecessary waste of space. We think not. The modern Search for Extra-Terrestrial Intelligence (SETI) dates from the 1960s.[1] For some spending time and effort on SETI is proof of lunacy.[2] Others accept it as tolerable as a harmless if puzzling hobby. Many consider that public funds should not be used for the endeavour.[3] However, interest has renewed, and efforts continue.[4] For example the US Congress and the Department of Defence have recently been considering unexplained phenomena.[5]

---

1 P. Morrison, J. Billingham and J. Wolfe, eds., *The Search for Extraterrestrial Intelligence* (NASA SP–419, 1977). Cf. S.J. Dick, 'Back to the Future: SETI Before the Space Age', IAC Graz, 1993, IAA.9.2-93-790.
2 Notwithstanding the film *E.T. the Extraterrestrial* (1982), it is customary to refer to Extra-Terrestrial Intelligence (ETI), making the acronym for the Search, SETI. CETI, 'Communication with ETI', dropped out of use as too optimistic. SATI, the 'Search for Alien Intelligence', is not favoured since 'Alien' might imply hostility and/or arouse xenophobia.
3 In 1979 US Senator William Proxmire awarded SETI a 'Golden Fleece' for wasteful federal expense, and in 1982 got its funding cut off. Carl Sagan later persuaded him otherwise. S.J. Garber, 'A Political History of NASA's SETI Program', in Vakoch, *infra* n. 6, 23–48, F. Drake and D. Sobel, *Is Anyone Out There?* (New York: Delacorte Press, 1992) 191–196; L. Billings, 'From the Observatory to Capitol Hill', in B. Bova and B. Preiss, eds., *First Contact: The Search for Extra-terrestrial Intelligence* (New York: New American Library 1990) 279–304.
4 R.B. Bilder, 'On the Search for Extraterrestrial Intelligence (SETI)' (2020) 114 AJIL 87–95, 88 at nn. 3 and 4; L.M. Gindilis and L.I. Gurvits, 'SETI in Russia, USSR and the Post-Soviet Space: A Century of Research' (2019) 162 *Acta Astronautica* 1–13; S.J. Dick, *Space, Time and Aliens: Collected Works on Cosmos and Culture* (Vienna: Springer, 2020) (not seen). The IAA has a permanent SETI study group, website: https://iaaseti.org/.
5 Cf. 'Preliminary Assessment: Unidentified Aerial Phenomena', Office of the Director of National Intelligence, 21 June 2021: www.dni.gov/files/ODNI/documents/assessments/Prelimary-Assessment-UAP-20210625.pdf. In 2022 the US Department of Defense set up an All-Domain Anomaly Resolution Office (AARO) which *inter alia* investigates unexplained phenomena: www.aaro.mil/. See 'The US Defense Department & the UAP Mission': www.aaro.mil/Portals/136/PDFs/AARO%20Mission%20Brief_DOPSR%20Reviewed%20July%20 2023.pdf. A website accessed via the main site will carry current reports. For aerial sightings and shapes of UAVs see AARO Office, 'UAP Reporting Trends 1996–2023': www.aaro.mil/Portals/136/PDFs/Latest_UAP_Reporting_Trends.pdf. So far credible evidence of extraterrestrial activity or of off-world technology

DOI: 10.4324/9781003496502-16

Finding ETI would have significant intellectual and social effects. SETI must therefore be considered in any exposition of general space law.[6] Extra-legal Protocols do exist that set out mechanisms for the announcement of the electronic detection of ETI, and the framing of a possible reply to any message, should such be appropriate.[7]

Speculation as to whether there is intelligent life elsewhere in the universe began many years ago,[8] and searches began as telescopes improved.[9] Recently intense media interest has been triggered by the regular discoveries of new exoplanets,[10] not to mention the 2017 appearance of the interstellar Asteroid 1I/2017, Oumuamua,[11] and speculation as to what the James Webb telescope may disclose.

Before going on to SETI we note that the detection of any form of extraterrestrial life short of intelligence may occur as we explore our near neighbours.[12] That is why there are

---

has not been found: www.defense.gov/News/News-Stories/Article/Article/3368109/dod-working-to-better-understand-resolve-anomalous-phenomena/. But see also NASA Unidentified Anomalous Phenomena: Independent Study Team Report, September 2023: https://science.nasa.gov/science-pink/s3fs-public/atoms/files/UAP%20Independent%20Study%20Team%20-%20Final%20Report_0.pdf. Cf. the activities of the Mutual UFO Network: https://mufon.com/.

6 R.B. Bilder, *supra* n. 4; H.P. Shuch, ed., *Searching for Extraterrestrial Intelligence: SETI Past, Present, and Future* (Berlin: Springer, 2011); D.A. Vakoch, ed., *Communication with Extraterrestrial Intelligence* (Albany: State U of NY Press, 2011); L. Billings, *Five Billion Years of Solitude: The Search for Life among the Stars* (New York: Current, 2013); D.A. Vakoch, ed., *Archaeology, Anthropology and Interstellar Communication* (Washington: NASA, 2014) (NASA History Series, NASA SP-2013-443); M. Lupisella, *Cosmological Theories of Value* (Dordrecht: Springer, 2020). See also *infra* n. 14.

7 Sciences such as 'Astrobiology' and 'Astrobotany' are developing: D.A. Vakoch, ed., *Astrobiology, History and Society: Life Beyond Earth and the Impact of Discovery* (Dordrecht: Springer, 2013); M. Ashkenazi, *What We Know About Extraterrestrial Intelligence: Foundations of Xenology* (Vienna: Springer, 2017); *Origins, Worlds, and Life: A Decadal Strategy for Planetary Science and Astrobiology 2023–2032* (Washington: National Academies Press, 2022). See also *infra* n. 99.

8 See *infra* n. 14.

9 C.L. Devito, *Space, Life, Science and Stories: Our Recurring Interest in the Possibility of Cosmic Visitors* (Cambridge: Cambridge Scholars Publishing Ltd, 2016). Cf. the 'canals on Mars': G. Schiaparelli (*La Vita sul Planeta Marta*, 1877); P. Lowell (*Mars and Its Canals*, 1894) (both Project Gutenberg). See NASA Note, 'The "Canali" and the First Martians': www.nasa.gov/audience/forstudents/postsecondary/features/F_Canali_and_First_Martians.html.

10 Cf. Wikipedia s.v. 'Exoplanet'. By 2009 300, and by 2018 3500 extra-solar planets had been discovered. 2022 saw 5059 confirmed discoveries and over 2000 potentials. See now: NASA Exoplanet Archive: https://exoplanetarchive.ipac.caltech.edu/index.html. The US search for exoplanets is sanctioned by s. 312 of the 2014 NASA Authorization Act, 2015, H.R. 810, and financed for 2016–2027 by sec. 312 of the NASA Authorization Act 2015, H.R. 2039, and 2016–2027 and sec. 508 of the NASA Transition Authorization Act, 2017, 131 Stat. 50, Public Law 115–10.

11 A. Loeb, *Extraterrestrial: The First Sign of Intelligent Life Beyond Earth* (London: John Murray, 2021). One factor in the discussion was that Oumuamua appeared to accelerate, which could indicate purposeful intent. However, in 'Acceleration of 1I/'Oumuamua from radiolytically produced H2 in H2O ice' (2023) 615 *Nature* 610–615, J.B. Bergner and D.Z. Seligman have provided an explanation for the acceleration. Separately, in 'Physical Constraints on Unidentified Aerial Phenomena' A. Loeb and S.M. Kirkpatrick raise the possibility that UAPs may have been left by extra-solar visitors to monitor life on Earth: https://lweb.cfa.harvard.edu/~loeb/LK1.pdf. It has also been suggested that recently detected 'fast radio bursts' may be from an alien communications system.

12 The programmes of many space agencies may turn up proof of life. The rover 'Perseverance' is on Mars seeking any trace of life. ETI is not expected. Cf. *Planetary Protection Considerations for Missions to Small Bodies in the Solar System* (Washington: National Academies Press, 2022). Again, the Webb telescope may detect changes in the atmosphere of remote planets that are explicable only by the presence of life. It has detected water, methane, carbon dioxide and possibly dimethyl sulphide (which on Earth is only produced by phytoplankton life) in the atmosphere of K2–18b, which is in the 'goldilocks zone' around its sun some 124 light

international legal obligations to avoid the harmful contamination of the earth, moon and other celestial bodies (Art. IX, OST).[13] There is also a duty under Art. 5.3 of the Moon Agreement to report the finding of any evidence of organic life, an obligation that we hope would be complied with even were the state making the discovery not party to the Agreement.

Extra-Terrestrial Intelligence

Whether this world may be the only location of intelligence in the universe has long been debated.[14] The question has arisen among philosophers as well as among cosmologists and shows no signs of exhaustion.[15] Lawyers have also been active. The books

---

years away in the Leo constellation. See NASA Press Release re K2–18b: www.nasa.gov/goddard/2023/webb-discovers-methane-carbon-dioxide-in-atmosphere-of-k2-18b and accompanying material.

13 See Chapters 7 and 9 s.v. Contamination.

14 Assuming it is intelligence that we can recognise. S.J. Dick, *Plurality of Worlds: The Origins of the Extra-Terrestrial Life Debate from Democritus to Kant* (Cambridge: Cambridge UP, 1982); M.J. Crowe, *The Extra-Terrestrial Life Debate, 1750–1900: The Idea of a Plurality of Worlds from Kant to Lowell* (Cambridge: Cambridge UP, 1986). See also M.J. Crowe and M.F. Dowd, 'The Extraterrestrial Life Debate from Antiquity to 1900', in Vakoch, *supra* n. 7, 3–56; K.S. Guthke, *The Last Frontier: Imagining Other Worlds from the Copernican Revolution to Modern Science Fiction* (Ithaca: Cornell UP, 1990); A. Koestler, *The Sleepwalkers, A History of Man's Changing Vision of the Universe* (London: Hutchinson, 1959; Pelican Books, 1968). An early book was W. Whewell, *Of the Plurality of Worlds, an Essay* (London: Parker, 1853) republished, M. Ruse, ed. (Chicago University Press, 2001), and E. Hitchcock, ed. (Michigan: Scholarly Publishing, 2006). Cf. T. Chalmers, *Discourses on the Christian Revelation Viewed in Connection with the Modern Astronomy* (Edinburgh: Constable, 1854). Fasan, *infra* n. 17, and Sullivan, *infra* n. 15, note earlier writers. Bishop John Wilkins (Chester, England) wrote several works including *A Discovery of a World in the Moone* (1638) (New York, Olms, 1981). See also G. McColley: (1) 'The Doctrine of the Plurality of Worlds as a Factor in Milton's Attitude toward the Copernican Hypothesis' (1932) 47 *Mod. Lang. Notes.* 319–325; (2) 'The Seventeenth-Century Doctrine of a Plurality of Worlds' (1936) 1 *Ann. Sci.* 385–430; (3) 'The Universe of De Revolutionibus' (1939) 30 *Isis* 452–472; (4) with H.W. Miller. 'Saint Bonaventure, Francis Mayron, William Vorlong and the Doctrine of a Plurality of Worlds' (1937) 12 *Speculum* 386–389. Cf. M. Livio, 'Winston Churchill's Essay on Alien Life Found' (2017) 542 *Nature* 289–291: www.nature.com/news/winston-churchill-s-essay-on-alien-life-found-1.21467. See also Wikipedia, 'Cosmic Pluralism'.

Note: this is not the 'plurality of worlds' found in discussions of 'modal realism' in philosophy: cf. D. Lewis, *On the Plurality of Worlds* (Oxford: Blackwell, 1986, 2001); J. Divers, *Possible Worlds* (London: Routledge, 2002).

15 Cf. S. Dumas, *Catalogue of SETI Publications.* http://alpha.sinp.msu.ru/~panov/Lib/Papers/SETI/Catalogue-Duma.pdf (2015). See also *supra* n. 6. Earlier see R.D. Ekers et al., *SETI 2020: A Roadmap for the Search for Extraterrestrial Intelligence* (Mountain View: SETI Press, 2002); M.A.G. Michaud, *Contact with Alien Civilizations* (New York: Copernicus, 2007). Cf. F. Drake and D. Sobel, *Is There Anyone Out There?* (New York: Delacorte Press, 1992); W. Sullivan, *We Are Not Alone: The Search for Intelligent Life on Other Worlds* (London: Pelican Books, 1964, rev. ed. 1970); B. Bova and B. Preiss, *supra* n. 3; J. Heidmann, *Extra-terrestrial Intelligence* (Cambridge: Cambridge UP, 1995); P. Davies, *Are We Alone? Implications of the Discovery of Extraterrestrial Life* (London: Penguin, 1995); A.A. Harrison, *After Contact: The Human Response to Extraterrestrial Life* (New York: Plenum, 1997); S. Dick, ed., *Many Worlds: The New Universe, Extraterrestrial Life and the Theological Implications* (Philadelphia: Templeton Foundation Press, 2000); E. Regis Jr., ed., *Extraterrestrials: Science and Alien Intelligence* (Cambridge: Cambridge UP, 1985); B. Zuckerman and M.H. Hart, *Extraterrestrials: Where Are They?* 2nd ed. (Cambridge: Cambridge UP, 1995); P. Schenkel, *ETI: A Challenge for Change* (New York: Vantage Press, 1988); J. Billingham, ed., *Life in the Universe* (NASA: 1971 CP-2156: https://history.nasa.gov/CP-2156/cp2156.htm); M.A.G. Michaud, *Contact with Alien Civilizations* (New York: Copernicus, 2007). Special issues of *Acta Astronautica* have been devoted to SETI: Vols. 21, 1990; 26, 1992; 42, 1998. Cf. *The Limits of Organic Life in Planetary Systems* (Washington: National Academy Press, 2007). See also P. Davies, *The Goldilocks Enigma: Why Is the Universe Just Right for*

of Haley,[16] Fasan,[17] Robinson and White,[18] and McDougal, Lasswell and Vlasic[19] contain important discussions of the field, as do papers by Lasswell,[20] Fasan,[21] Cocca,[22] Goodman,[23] Kopal,[24] Reijnen,[25] Sterns,[26] and Sterns and Tennen.[27] This chapter draws on all these materials and on papers by one of the authors.[28] 'SETI and Society' was the topic of the Seventeenth IAF/IISL Roundtable in 1997.[29] SETI remains one of the subjects of IAA Commission 6, and an annual a two-session symposium on SETI is part of the IAC proceedings.

As far as this book is concerned two preliminary aspects must be considered: the probability or otherwise of the existence of ETI, and whether we may encounter it. These are not the same. The probability of its existence comes first.

The question of the existence of ETI was transformed by the development of radio-astronomy and the formulation of the Drake Equation. We will deal with radio-astronomy later while discussing SETI programmes.[30]

Life? (London: Allen Lane, 2006) and his *The Eerie Silence: Are We Alone in the Universe?* (London: Allen Lane, 2010).

16 A.G. Haley, *Space Law and Government* (New York: Appleton Century Crofts, 1963; IISL website, 2023) 394–421.

17 E. Fasan, *Relations with Alien Intelligences* (Berlin: Berlin Verlag, 1970), reprinted in P.M. Sterns and L.I. Tennen, eds., *Private Law, Public Law, Metalaw and Public Policy in Space: A Liber Amicorum in Honor of Ernst Fasan* (Vienna: Springer, 2016) 181–246.

18 G.S. Robinson and H.M. White Jr., *Envoys of Mankind* (Washington: Smithsonian Institution, 1986).

19 M. McDougal, H.D. Lasswell and I.A. Vlasic, *Law and Public Order in Space* (New Haven: Yale UP, 1963), 974–1021.

20 H.D. Lasswell, 'Anticipating Remote Contingencies: Encounters with Living Forms' (1960) 4 *Proc. IISL* 89–104.

21 E. Fasan, 'Discovery of ETI: Terrestrial and Extraterrestrial Legal Implications' (1990) 21 *Acta Astronautica* 131–135.

22 A.A. Cocca, 'XII Tables for Researchers on Extraterrestrial Intelligence' (1990) 21 *Acta Astronautica* 127–130.

23 A.E. Goodman, 'Diplomatic and Political Problems Affecting the Formulation and Implementation of an International Protocol for Activities Following the Detection of a Signal from Extraterrestrial Intelligence' (1990) 21 *Acta Astronautica* 103–108; and his 'Diplomacy and the Search for Extraterrestrial Intelligence (SETI)' (1990) 21 *Acta Astronautica* 137–141.

24 V. Kopal, 'International Law Implications of the Detection of Extraterrestrial Intelligent Signals' (1990) 21 *Acta Astronautica* 123–126.

25 G.C.M. Reijnen, 'Basic Elements of an International Terrestrial Reply Following upon the Detection of a Signal from Extraterrestrial Intelligence' (1990) 21 *Acta Astronautica* 143–148.

26 P.M. Sterns, 'SETI and Space Law: Jurisprudential and Philosophical Considerations for Humankind in Relation to Extraterrestrial Life' (2000) 46 *Acta Astronautica* 759–763; and her 'Metalaw and Relations with Intelligent Beings Revisited' (2004) 20 *Space Policy* 123–130 [Lyall/Larsen 561–568].

27 P.M. Sterns and L.I. Tennen, 'Exobiology and the Outer Space Treaty: From Planetary Protection to the Search for Extraterrestrial Life' (1997) 40 *Proc. IISL* 141–149; and their 'SETI, Metalaw and Social Media', in Sterns and Tennen, *supra* n. 17, 159–179.

28 F. Lyall, 'Legal Aspects of SETI – Present and Future Arrangements' 1993 IAA.9.2–93–788; rev. (1998) 42 *Acta Astronautica* 661–665; 'Communications with Extra-Terrestrial Intelligence: A New Dimension of Space Law' 1996 IAA-96-IAA.9.2.04; 'SETI and the Law: What if the Search Succeeds?' (1998) 14 *Space Policy* 75–77; 'SETI and International Law' (1999) 41 *Proc. IISL* 334–344; 'SETI and International Radio Law', in Vakoch, ed., *Communication, supra* n. 6, 333–340; 'Daedelus and Radio', in C. Maccone, ed., *Protected Antipode Circle on Lunar Farside*, IAF Cosmic Study, 1.6: http://iaaweb.org/iaa/Scientific%20 Activity/Study%20Groups/SG%20Commission%201/sg16/sg16draftreport2.pdf. See also Chapter 7.

29 Seventeenth IAA/IISL Scientific/Legal Roundtable on SETI and Society (1998) 41 *Proc. IISL* 303–346.

30 SETI Programmes, *infra* n. 53.

The fundamental question for SETI is whether there are any civilisations elsewhere in the galaxy capable of communicating with those of other solar systems.[31] We may be unique, or but one of very few.[32] A probability tool, the Drake Equation, allows some assessment of that question.[33] It sets out particular objective factors relevant in considering whether extra-terrestrial intelligences may exist. Probability can then be assessed according as different weight is assigned to each factor. The Equation can also inform the discussion of a subsidiary question, whether an ETI society can be contacted.

The Drake Equation was first articulated at an informal conference held in 1961 at Green Bank Observatory, West Virginia, US, to discuss the possibility of communicating with other worlds.[34] Frank Drake, the progenitor of Project Ozma,[35] presented the focus of the conference in the form of the equation:

$$N = R^* \cdot f^p \cdot n^e \cdot f^l \cdot f^i \cdot f^c \cdot L$$

Non-mathematical minds (such as those of the authors) tend to boggle when confronted by such formulae, but the Drake Equation is useful.[36] The elements or factors now commonly considered as appropriate are:

N: (replaced in some formulations of the Equation by the less useful P (= probability)) denotes the number of ETI civilisations and is the result of the interaction of the factors to the right of the equation.

R^*: the rate at which stars were being formed in the Galaxy when our solar system was coming into being. The inference is that solar systems of a similar age may exhibit similar propensities to support life, and (importantly) that that life may have reached a maturity roughly simultaneously with our own. Younger sun systems will not yet have life trying to communicate. In older systems life may have died out.

f^p: the fraction of stars round which a solar system comes into being.

n^e: the number of habitable planets per solar system which have an environment suitable for life.

f^l: the fraction of those suitable planets on which life actually does appear. In the belief that if life is possible it will occur, this factor is usually taken as '1'.

f^i: the fraction of life-bearing planets on which at least some of that life develops intelligence.

f^c: the fraction of those intelligent species that develop a society both capable and willing to attempt communication with other worlds.[37]

---

31 M. Lachs did not rule out the possibility of life 'beyond our planet': *The Law of Outer Space: An Experience in Contemporary Law-Making* (Leiden: Sijthoff, 1972; reissued Leiden: Nijhoff, 2010) 21.

32 P.D. Ward and D. Brownlee, *Rare Earth: Why Complex Life Is Uncommon in the Universe* (New York: Copernicus, 2000). Cf. *infra* at n. 41.

33 D.A. Vakoch and M. F. Dowd, eds., *The Drake Equation: Estimating the Prevalence of Extraterrestrial Life Through the Ages* (Cambridge: Cambridge UP, 2015).

34 Drake and Sobel, *supra* n. 15, 45–64. See also 'Is There Intelligent Life on Earth', in W. Sullivan, *supra* n. 15, 268–289.

35 See *infra* at n. 67.

36 F.D. Drake, 'The Drake Equation: A Reappraisal', in Bova and Preiss, *supra* n. 3, 150–153. See also J.D. Barrow and F.J. Tipler, *The Anthropic Cosmological Principle* (Oxford: Clarendon Press, 1986) particularly at 576–612; P. Davies, *The Goldilocks Enigma: Why is the Universe Just Right for Life?* (London: Allen Lane, 2006); C. Sagan, *Cosmos: The Story of Cosmic Evolution, Science and Civilisation* (London: MacDonald, 1981) 328–332.

37 Strictly, capability and willingness should be separated, but to estimate willingness is impossible.

L: the length of time during which a space-communications-capable society may continue to exist, before, for one reason or another, it loses that capability (the longevity factor). Our own world society has been thus 'capable' for about a hundred years.

Such is the Drake Equation as originally formulated. Modifications have been suggested, but these need not detain us.[38] Variant results can be obtained by assigning different values to its factors. From their own particular areas of study, astronomers and cosmologists, physicists, chemists, biologists, historians and sociologists have provided their guesses for these values. Some are pro-ETI, others are against. Viewing the argumentation from another discipline, we cannot but occasionally feel that 'result-oriented jurisprudence' is taking place – that is that a line of argument is presented in order that a particular conclusion (for or against ETI) is arrived at, rather than that the result is derived from the argument. This seems to be a natural phenomenon of most disciplines. Suffice it therefore to say that solutions to the Drake Equation can be arrived at which 'prove' that the probability of ETI is nil, while others indicate that we should be at least prepared for detection and/or contact.

Other aspects of ETI and the Drake Equation are sometimes invoked. One relates to the physical nature of the Universe and indicates that, even were the Equation to indicate a definite probability that ETI exists, the laws of physics mean that we can never know of its existence. To an extent this is covered in factors f^c and L, but in brief the argument is that interstellar distances are such that, absent science fiction's various law-bending inventions, travel between the stars is impossible and communication virtually so. It is therefore said that time, distance, the absolute of the speed of light and the implications of Einstein's Theory of General Relativity, rule out interaction with any ETI.[39]

Another possibility relates to the 'R^*' factor in the Equation; that in older systems life may have died out. Worryingly we note the possibility that technological civilisations tend to wipe themselves out, so there may now be no ETI extant out there. Humanity may need to take steps to avoid the 'Great Filter' which has the potential to eradicate life.[40]

Some arguments arise from the fact that (so far as we know) we have not yet had contact with an ETI. One possibility is that they are yet to come into being. If their solar system is young within our galaxy, it may be that we are the older and ETI has yet to develop.[41] This is not, however, the premise on which most SETI discussion has proceeded. A more usual

---

38 Some formulations of the Drake Equation omit factors R^* and L as unnecessary for the purpose of the Equation. The main essential of factor R^* is comprised within the remaining factors, and L can be subsumed within factor f^c as an element of the likelihood of an ETI communicating. Thus the simplified Drake Equation used in Barrow and Tipler, *supra* n. 36, at 586 is: $p = f^p n^e f^l f^i f^c$, where p = probability. Heidmann, *supra* n. 15, 117–119 presents another simplified version. I.S. Shklovskii and C. Sagan (P. Fern, trans.), *Intelligent Life in the Universe* (San Francisco: Holden Day, 1966), report another variant form of the Equation suggested by Sebastian von Hoerner. See also Vakoch and Dowd, *supra* n. 33; Michaud, *supra* n. 15, 53–57 and *SETI 2020*, *supra* n. 15, at xxxv.

39 The implication of $E = mc^2$ is that the closer the velocity of an object approaches that of light, the closer its mass approaches infinity. Travel beyond the solar system to likely planet-bearing solar systems will therefore take centuries since speed will always be less than light-speed and distances are immense.

40 R. Hanson, 'The Great Filter – Are We Almost Past It?', 1998: http://mason.gmu.edu/~rhanson/greatfilter.html; J.H. Jiang et al., 'Avoiding the "Great Filter": Extraterrestrial Life and Humanity's Future in the Universe': *Popular Physics*, 2022: https://arxiv.org/abs/2210.10582v2 (awaiting peer review).

41 P. Behroozi and M.S. Peeples, 'On the History and Future of Cosmic Planet Formation' (2015) 454 *Mon Not R Astron Soc* 1811–1817.

approach is that if intelligent ETs did exist, we should already be aware of them. So, as Enrico Fermi asked in 1950: 'Where are they?'[42] Our solar system is relatively young compared to the age of the universe and any older Beings would have had time both to evolve and to conquer the other constraints on interaction between their solar systems and ours. The argument then runs that since evidently the aliens are not in contact with us,[43] they do not exist.[44] Three responses can be made. First, the 'Fermi paradox' (otherwise known as the 'Great Silence') provides no evidence for or against the existence of ETI. It can stand only as an interesting comment. Second, perhaps the ETs are here already, incognito. They may be hiding,[45] and/or the solar system may be under some sort of quarantine.[46] In that case it would be prudent to plan for the day when they shrug off their previous constraint or diffidence. Third, even if they have not yet arrived, ETs may be on their way, in which case we should be thinking about how to meet them. When the aliens appear there may be little we can do. Some science fiction visitors, particularly in films, are less than benign but we may hope that well-developed intelligence blunts aggression.[47]

42 There is much written on the Paradox. P. Horowitz, 'The Fermi Paradox', App. J to R.D. Ekers et al., eds., *SETI 2010: A Roadmap for the Search for Extraterrestrial Intelligence* (Mountain View: SETI Press, 2002) 373–374; Drake and Sobel, *supra* nn. 3 and 15, 130–131, 203; Baum, *infra* n. 46, at Part 2.1. Cf. R.A. Freitas, 'There Is No Fermi Paradox' (1985) 62 *Icarus* 518–520; J.R. Lindsey, 'SETI From the Perspective of Intercivilizational Politics' (2022) 60 *Space Policy* 101490: https://doi.org/10.1016/j.spacepol.2022.101490.

43 This assumes 'conspiracy' theorists, who think that governments are already in touch with ET or have ET artefacts stored in secret, are wrong. Cf. *supra* n. 5, and Wikipedia on UFO conspiracy theory.

44 Barrow and Tipler, *supra* n. 36, at 586, quote the aphorism of M. Rees: 'Absence of evidence is not evidence of absence'.

45 Caio Yu and Jiajan Liu suggest ETI may be concealing themselves to avoid unknown risks: 'The Dark Forest Rule: One Solution to the Fermi Paradox' (2015) 68 JBIS 142–144. Perhaps we should do so also, though we have been broadcasting our presence for well over a century. Another suggestion is that ETI civilisations may be deliberately aestivating, awaiting future eras: A. Sandberg, S. Armstrong and M. Ćirković, 'That Is Not Dead Which can Eternal Lie: The Aestivation Hypothesis for Resolving Fermi's Paradox' (2016) 69 JBIS 406–415.

46 This is the 'Zoo hypothesis'. J.A. Ball, 'The Zoo Hypothesis' (1973) 19 *Icarus* 347–349; S.D. Baum et al., 'Would Contact with Extraterrestrials Benefit or Harm Humanity? A Scenario Analysis' (2011) 68 *Acta Astronautica* 2114–2129 at Part 4.1.
    Numerous science fiction tales envisage the infant Humanity as under quarantine, surveillance or tutelage, e.g. C.S. Lewis's trilogy *Out of the Silent Planet* (1938), *Voyage to Venus* (a.k.a. *Perelandra*) (1943), *That Hideous Strength* (1945); A.C. Clarke, *Childhood's End* (1954) or *2001* (1968). Such ideas are a staple of the UFO-Hunters: cf. www.mufon.com/. That said the UK Government found no evidence of ET visitors in its analysis of Unidentified Aerial Phenomena released in May 2006 under the (UK) Freedom of Information Act: http://minotb52ufo.com/pdf/Condign-Report-Executive-Summary.pdf; http://disclosureproject. org/docs/pdf/uap_exec_summary_dec00.pdf. For the UK UFO reports released down to 2013 see www. nationalarchives.gov.uk/ufos/existing-files.htm. The UK Ministry of Defence UFO Desk was closed in 2009: www.nationalarchives.gov.uk/ufos/. CNES has made available French UFO reports: www.ufoevidence.org/ topics/Gepan-Sepra.htm; www.psychedelicadventure.net/2008/09/france-opens-secret-ufo-files-to-public. html. For the US see *supra* n. 5.
    Cf. *The Roswell Report: Facts vs Fiction in the New Mexico Desert* (USGPO: Headquarters US Air Force, 1995) and *The Roswell Report: Case Closed* (USGPO: Headquarters US Air Force, 1997). See generally the Wikipedia entry for Unidentified Flying Objects.

47 Cf. *supra* n. 45. H.G. Wells, *The War of the Worlds* (1898); B. de Las Casas, *A Short Account of the Destruction of the Indies* (N. Griffen trans.) (London: Penguin, 1992); N. Watson and H. Douglas, *Indigenous Legal Judgements: Bringing Indigenous Voices into Judicial Decision Making* (Milton Keys: Routledge, 2021): contrast A.C. Clarke, *Childhood's End* (1953). Cf. the films *Independence Day* and *Mars Attack* (both 1996) and contrast *Arrival* (2016). See also the (2006) 443 *Nature*, 606, editorial which, commenting on a meeting of the IAF SETI study group, said: 'It is not obvious that all extraterrestrial civilizations will be benign, or that contact with even a benign one would not have serious repercussions'. Cf. D. Raybeck, 'Predator – Prey

There is another possibility short of physical contact, which is that we will discover evidence as to the existence of ETI, but in a form such that no interaction is required of us. Numerous science fiction stories narrate the exploration of deserted ruins on the moon, Mars or further away.[48] The ruins of ET civilisations remain a staple of the science fiction genre. Alternatively, given that the US Pioneer 10 and 11 and Voyager I and II probes have now left the solar system, perhaps one day an incoming probe or a derelict will provide evidence of ETI.[49]

Even if we are not likely to encounter ETs, we might detect them. The emergence of radio has at least increased the possibility that evidence will be forthcoming for the existence of ETI, even if interaction with it proves problematic. This could occur either through overhearing their chatter (cf. our radio and TV broadcasting) or by their deliberate transmission of a definite signal.[50] In 1974, the Arecibo radio-telescope was reversed to send a signal rather than receive,[51] and others have more recently done likewise.[52] If we have done so, why might not ETI? So the detection of ETs may be possible whether or not they arrive, will arrive, have arrived or have gone away onwards past Sol III. Various SETI programmes have therefore been undertaken.

SETI Programmes[53]

There are two forms of SETI, active and passive. Active SETI involves attempts to contact ETI with the hope of a reaction. Passive SETI endeavours to detect evidence of ET. Most developments have been in the latter form.

Models and Contact Considerations', in D.A. Vakoch, ed., *Extraterrestrial Altruism: Evolution and Ethics in the Cosmos* (Dordrecht: Springer, 2014) 49–64, and H.A. Geller, 'Harmful ETI Hypothesis Denied: Visiting ETIs Likely Altruists', ibid. at 65–78; D. Brin, *Shouting at the Cosmos . . . Or How SETI Has Taken a Worrisome Turn into Dangerous Territory*. Lifeboat Foundation Special Report, 2006: https://lifeboat.com/ex/shouting.at.the.cosmos.

48 A.C. Clarke, *The City and the Stars* (1956) latterly takes its hero on a Grand Tour of deserted planets.

49 Cf. Loeb, *supra* n. 11. A.C. Clarke, *Rendezvous with Rama* (1972) begins with the detection of an incoming space-ship by a system for detecting asteroids on a collision course with Earth. In his *Passer-by* (1957) an astronaut in Earth orbit glimpses what may be the passing hulk of an alien spaceship.

50 P. Musso, 'The Problem of Active SETI: An Overview' (2012) 78 *Acta Astronautica* 43–54; J. Haqq-Misra et al., 'The Benefits and Harm of Transmitting into Space' (2013) 29 *Space Policy* 40–48; I.K. Romanovskaya, 'Migrating Extraterrestrial Civilisations and Interstellar Colonization: Implications for SETI and SETA' (2022) *Int. J. Astrobiology* 1–25.

51 F. Drake and D. Sobel, *Is There Anyone Out There?* (New York: Delacorte Press, 1992) 174–180, 180–185; C. Sagan, L.S. Sagan and F. Drake, 'A Message from Earth' (1972) 175 *Science* 881–884; 'The Arecibo Message of November 1974'. (1975) 26 *Icarus* 462–466. According to a SETI Institute FAQ, the Arecibo message was 'a simple picture describing our solar system, the compounds important for life, the structure of the DNA molecule, and the form of a human being. The message was transmitted in the direction of the globular star cluster M13, about 25,000 light years away.'

52 Cf. *supra* nn. 50 and 51. On 9 October 2008 a message, transmitted towards Gliese 581c, 20 light years away, should get there in 2029. See Wikipedia 'A Message from Earth'. On 5 February 2008 the Beatles' song 'Across the Universe' was transmitted by the NASA Deep Space Network towards Polaris (the 'North Star'), some 431 light years away: www.nasa.gov/topics/universe/features/across_universe.html; www.newscientist. com/article/dn13273. Z. Merali, 'Stepping up the Search for ET', 2642 *New Scientist*, 9 February 2008: www.newscientist.com/article/mg19726424.300-stepping-up-the-search-for-et.html. Not all were happy about this. Should a Polaris ET reply immediately we hope there will be someone around to receive its message, and that Earth residents of 2870 will have no problems in identifying the referent.

53 M. Huston and J. Wright, 'SETI in 2021' (2022) 199 *Acta Astronautica* 166–173; R.D. Ekers et al., *SETI 2020: A Roadmap for the Search for Extraterrestrial Intelligence* (Mountain View: SETI Press, 2002). Down

Active SETI

Active SETI (also known as METI – 'Messaging Extraterrestrial Intelligence') is the intentional attempt to communicate with ETI.[54] This requires the transmission of radio signals.[55] That brings the Radio Regulations and the procedures of the ITU into play.[56] No radio frequencies have been allocated for Active SETI in the 'Table of Allocations' set out in ITU RR Art. 5. That does not mean that it is unlawful under international law to send a SETI radio message, although it may be prohibited by national law. However, there is a general obligation under the ITU Constitution to avoid causing harmful interference to other radio users.[57] An active SETI signal is likely to be powerful and will punch through the orbital location of many satellites. A transmitted signal that affects a satellite service either directly by use of an assigned, registered and operational satellite frequency, or indirectly through generating spurious emissions, distorting polarisation, or in any other way, would be unlawful. Were a satellite to be affected, disabled or killed by an active SETI signal a civil or international claim might be brought against either the generator of the signal or the relevant licensing state or both. An unlicensed transmission would (?should?) be unlawful and potentially criminal under national laws.

A separate question arises were the active signal to have discernible content. We consider this separately below, while dealing with the question of any 'reply' to a proven detected ETI signal.[58] Suffice it here to note that there is a degree of disquiet among the SETI community as to active SETI, with or without content.[59] Some sort of societal approval should be sought.[60]

Passive SETI

Optical SETI

One form of passive SETI uses optical means and has the advantage of not being subject to interference by terrestrially generated radio signals. This method for the detection of ETI

---

to its date see its Archive of SETI Searches, Apps. L to R, 381–425. Cf. also C. Sagan, ed., *Communication with Extraterrestrial Intelligence (CETI)* (Cambridge: MIT Press, 1973).

54 Cf. the non-profit corporation METI International: www.meti.org.

55 See *supra* n. 50, 51 and 52. The use of light frequencies is also possible.

56 As to the ITU, see Chapter 8.

57 ITU Constitution, Arts. 6.2 (38); 45.1–3 (197–199).

58 *Infra*, text following n. 121.

59 A message was sent to Trappist-1 in 2022: www.newscientist.com/article/2315676-group-that-wants-to-contact-aliens-will-transmit-to-trappist-1-system/, but subsequently the Webb telescope showed that its planet 1b has no atmosphere: www.scientificamerican.com/article/jwst-sees-no-atmosphere-on-earthlike-trappist-1-exoplanet/. Cf. discussion in (2014) 67 JBIS: J. Benford. 'Introduction to the METI issues' at 5–7; D. Brin, 'The Search for Extraterrestrial Intelligence (SETI) and Whether to Send "Messages" (METI): A Case for Conversation, Patience and Due Diligence' at 8–16; J. Billingham, 'Costs and Difficulties of Interstellar "Messaging" and the Need for International Debate on Potential Risks' at 17–23; M. Michaud, 'Seeking Contact: Issues to Consider' at 244–226; S. Shostak, 'Sending Signals into Space: Is It Really a Bad Idea' at 27–29; A. Zaitsev, 'Calling ET or Not Even Answering the Phone?' at 30–32; S. Dumas, 'The Fear of Contact' at 33–37; and D. Brin, 'METI: Rebuttals' at 38–43. J. Gertz, 'Post-Detection Protocols & METI: The Time Has Come to Regulate Them Both' (2016) 69 JBIS 263–270; S. Ashworth, 'Quantifying the Assumptions behind the METI Debate' (2016) 69 JBIS 419–428. See also I. Almár and H.P. Shuch, 'The San Marino Scale: A New Analytical Tool for Assessing Transmission Risk' (2007) 60 *Acta Astronautica* 57–59; Hatfield *infra* n. 122: https://setiathome.berkeley.edu/meti_statement_0.html, and comments in https://meti.org/. Cf. *supra* n. 50.

60 Cf. Hatfield and Trueblood, *infra* n. 122.

was first proposed in 1961.[61] However, it was not really taken up until the mid-1990s when sporadic observations were made. In April 2006 a dedicated project funded by the (US) Planetary Society, began to examine the light from stars in the hope that ETI would use lasers to signal presence, if not actually to communicate.[62] Other observatories have been similarly engaged.[63] Optical SETI may be assisted by the implementation of appropriate controls on nearby land development and utilisation including street and other lighting.[64]

Radio SETI

The basic premise of most SETI detection programmes is that electromagnetic radiation in the form of radio waves can be detected across interstellar distances. The artificial generation of radio waves and the modulation of their frequency or amplitude is a major telecommunications medium on Earth. An ET society may use similar modalities, and the artificiality of such signals would allow their detection as non-natural occurrences. Radio has been in use on Earth for about a century. The earliest signals would now be detectable from one hundred light years away. In the correlative belief that the inadvertent signals of a society elsewhere may be detectable, various programmes have 'listened to the stars' for artificial radio emissions, so far without result. If Beings on a remote planet have recognised the artificiality of signals emanating from Earth and responded immediately, a reply could arrive at least double the time from their emission – assuming that we recognise there has been a reply: as to which, see below. But interstellar conversations would be difficult, if not unlikely, if a reply takes many years to arrive.[65]

Radio astronomy, a discipline accidental in its birth, is the basis of the radio SETI effort. Radio astronomy began in 1931when Karl G. Jansky, working for Bell Telephone Laboratories, tried to find the source of various high frequency interferences with radio signals. Lightning storms adequately explained much of the interference, but, using a steerable antenna, Jansky detected a constant source at 20,000 k/cs that appeared to rotate with the Earth. Over time he established that its origin lay in the direction of the constellation

---

61 See www.coseti.org/. R.N. Schwartz and C.H. Townes, 'Interstellar and Interplanetary Communications by Optical Masers' (1961) 190 *Nature* 205–208; G.V. Leopold, 'Cosmic Surveillance by Spaceflight Momentum' (1960) 6 *Wayne L Rev*. 311–339 at 312 n. 3 prints data on early investigation of lasers, and refers to I.E. Sänger, 'The Future of Spaceflight', in *The Next Ten Years in Space, 1959–1969*, Staff Report, House Select Committee on Astronautics and Space Exploration, H. Doc. 115, 86th Cong. 1st Sess. (USGPO, 1959) 158–172. At 164 Sänger wrote of 'the development of stationary ultra-violet searchlights, exerting a radiation pressure of many tons'. See also S.A. Kingsley, Columbus Optical SETI Observatory: www.coseti. org/introcoseti.htm.

62 The Allen telescope sited at the Harvard University Oak Ridge Observatory outside Boston (not the same as the Allen Telescope Array, *infra* n. 72) is used. See also 'LaserSETI', the SETI Institute: www.seti.org/laserseti.

63 Columbus, Ohio: www.coseti.org/; Bournemouth, UK: www.coseti.org/www.boseti.org/; Berkeley, California: https://seti.ssl.berkeley.edu/opticalseti/ Harvard: https://seti.harvard.edu/oseti/. See also www.seti.org/seti-institute/project/optical-seti. See also https://meti.org/optical-seti.

64 *Dark and Quiet Skies for Science and Society: Report and Recommendations* (UN OOSA, 2022). Cf, the International Dark-Sky Association (IDA): http://darksky.org/; Cf. www.darkskydiscovery.org.uk/. For England and Wales, the Clean Neighbourhoods and Environment Act 2005, c. 16, s.102; for Scotland, the Environmental Protection Act 1990, c. 43, s. 79, inserted by s. 110 of the Public Health etc (Scotland) Act, 2008, 2008 asp. 5. A.L. Johnson. 'Blinded by the Light: Addressing the Growing Light Pollution Problem' (2015) 2 *Tex. A&M J. Prop. L*. 461–480; R. Mizon, *Light Pollution: Responses and Remedies* (London: Springer, 2002). See also the discussion of dark skies in Chapter 9.

65 Thus, any response to the message to Gliese, *supra* n. 52, might arrive c. 2040.

Sagittarius, and probably in the centre of our galaxy. Others took matters further and, particularly after the Second World War using the more sophisticated equipment made possible by war-time invention, developed radio astronomy as a science.

In the late 1950s Giuseppe Cocconi and Philip Morrison of Cornell University realised that, given the sensitivity of the then available equipment, natural radiation was not the only signal from the stars that could be intercepted. Artificial radiation might also be present. Our nearest star (other than the Sun) is Alpha Centauri, two light years away and some one hundred stars similar to our own Sun lie within fifteen light years' distance. They therefore suggested a search programme should be begun to 'listen' for artificial signals from certain of these stars, and that at a frequency of 1420 m/cs (21 cm).[66]

Even as Cocconi and Morrison were formulating their suggestion, Project Ozma, the first SETI project, established and masterminded by Frank D. Drake, the later progenitor of the Drake Equation, was using the 85-foot radio-telescope at Green Bank Observatory, West Virginia. For some two hundred hours during April through July 1960, Tau Ceti and Epsilon Eridani were targeted. At first a positive result was obtained, but further analysis established that the cause was terrestrial – nearby military aviation radar experiments.[67]

Thereafter many attempts have been made to 'hear' ETI transmissions, whether deliberate broadcast to space or the leakage of communications traffic. Some projects have been official, and government financed. Others, established by universities and similar establishments, have come and occasionally gone. Until 1997 Ohio State University ran the now defunct 'Big Ear' radio-telescope, which 'heard' the so-far unrepeated 'Wow' signal referred to in most journalistic writing on SETI.[68] Project Serendib was run by the University of California, Berkeley.[69] Southern Serendib and SETI Australia are run by the University of Western Sydney (https://seti.uws.edu.au/). SETI Italia is the major European centre (www.setileague.org/photos/italia.htm). In the UK a SETI Research Network has been established.[70] A major participant in the Search is the SETI Institute, a non-profit California corporation founded in 1984. The SETI Institute, initially partially financed by the US Government, now largely depends on private donations and grants from philanthropic foundations. Apart from the Search itself the Institute designs hardware and invents algorithms for the analysis of signals.[71]

A major SETI effort was the NASA High Resolution Microwave Project (the NASA SETI Program), begun in October 1992. Using the radio-telescope at Arecibo in Puerto

66 G. Cocconi and P. Morrison, 'Searching for Interstellar Communications', *Nature*, 19 September 1959. See also P. Morrison, J. Billingham and J. Wolfe, eds., *The Search for Extraterrestrial Intelligence: SETI*, 1977, NASA SP-419. As to the development of radio astronomy and the Cocconi – Morrison material see Sullivan, *supra* n. 34, 196–217; Drake and Sobel, *supra* n. 15, 31–43 and index sv. 'Hydrogen line'. Twenty-one centimetres is the radio emission frequency of hydrogen, a frequency to which our atmosphere is transparent and, of course, hydrogen is a constituent of water (H_2O), on which our own life forms depend.

67 Drake, *supra* n. 15, 21–43; and 'Project Ozma', Sullivan, *supra* n. 34, Ch. 14, 218–228, and index.

68 The 'Wow signal', 15 August 1977, was a strong narrowband signal lasting some 77 seconds. J.R. Ehman, who noticed the signal, circled the record and wrote 'wow' beside it. It has never been seen since: G.R. Harp et al., 'An ATA Search for a Repetition of the Wow Signal' (2020) 160 *Astronomical J.* 162. For the Big Ear radio-telescope see www.bigear.org/. Cf. M. Keech, 'Strong Signals from Space: What Does It Mean for International Law?' (2016) 1 *Geo. L. Tech. Rev.* 188–191.

69 See https://seti.berkeley.edu/serendip. Berkeley also ran the now hibernating SETI@Home project using unused processing capacity of personal computers to analyse signals: https://setiathome.ssl.berkeley.edu/.

70 For the activities of the UK SETI Research Network see www.seti.ac.uk/.

71 SETI Institute: www.seti.org.

Rica, and the Goldstone radio-telescope in the Mojave Desert in California, the program was scheduled to run for ten years at a cost of some US$100 million. The first stage was targeted at around one thousand stars within one hundred light years and known to be similar in both age and size to our Sun since the Drake Equation indicates that a similarity of star would probably result in similar development of planets, life and intelligence. Government funding was withdrawn in 1994 but the SETI Institute continued the search as 'Project Phoenix' using telescopes situated round the world. Over ten years some eight hundred stars out to two-hundred and forty light years were observed, but no artificial signals were detected. In 2001 in collaboration with the University of California (Berkeley) development began of an array of radio telescopes to serve both radio astronomy and SETI. The One Hectare Telescope was renamed the Allen Telescope Array (ATA) in recognition of the major contribution made by the Paul Allen Foundation to its costs.[72] In addition space and terrestrial telescopes have been detecting exoplanets, of which some, lying in the 'habitable zone' of their suns (the 'Goldilocks' zone – neither too hot, nor too cold) may be potential life-bearing Earth-sized planets.[73] Other radio-telescopes are planned or been built, and ETI searches may be conducted using their facilities.[74] The 'Search' continues.

Radio SETI operates in the microwave spectrum bands. In particular the microwave window between 1000 and 10,000 MHz suffers least from terrestrial atmospheric and galactic background noise. Signals of a highly technological civilization in the far distance may thus be there more easily detected. It even might be that a rational ETI astronomer has established a 'lighthouse' somewhere in these high spectrum bands.[75] One waveband of particular interest, known as the 'waterhole', is that around 1420 MHz, the 'hydrogen line' in the electromagnetic spectrum. Hydrogen is a component of water, essential for life on Earth and is prevalent in the Universe.[76] Beings similar to us might see the connection and therefore transmit on or near that frequency to show their presence, just as animals come to a waterhole in desert areas.

SETI and the Law

'SETI and the Law' has both national and international aspects. Under the general concept of state sovereignty it is for a state to determine the lawfulness of SETI activity within

---

72   The Allen Telescope Array is at the Hat Creek Radio Observatory some 300 miles northeast of San Francisco: www.seti.org/seti-allen-telescope-array-ata. It will consist of three-hundred and fifty 6m antennae, of which forty-two antennae were active by 2022.

73   Cf. P. Davies, *The Goldilocks Enigma: Why Is the Universe Just Right for Life* (London: Allen Lane, 2006).

74   For example the Square Kilometre Array (www.skatelescope.org/) or (www.skao.int/en/news/403/welcome-our-new-website), will operate through sites in Australia and South Africa where it will include the MeerKat radio telescope (www.ska.ac.za/gallery/meerkat/). The Five hundred metre Aperture Spherical Telescope (FAST), located in Guizhou Province, Southwest China, became operational in September 2016: https://fast.bao.ac.cn/.

75   Cf. the Arecibo message of 1974, *supra* n. 51. Of course the 'lighthouse' might be using optical frequencies, as to the search for which see *supra* at n. 61.

76   Water has been detected in the atmosphere of a planet orbiting HD209458b, some one-hundred and fifty light years away from Earth: https://exoplanets.nasa.gov/resources/80/water-water-everywhere-on-an-extrasolar-planet/. See also WASP-39b: www.nasa.gov/feature/goddard/2018/nasa-finds-a-large-amount-of-water-in-an-exoplanets-atmosphere.

its jurisdiction, and should it so wish, to regulate what is done.[77] The simple reception and analysis of signals, whether radio or optical, lies wholly within the jurisdiction of a state. International rules impose relevant duties on a state particularly as to radio. Thus questions of the protection of 'water-hole' and other radio frequencies are matters to be tackled domestically in implementation of international rules as to the use of radio spectrum.[78]

As far as international law is concerned, SETI is a lawful activity: what is not prohibited is permitted.[79] As Art. I of the Outer Space Treaty 1967 states, the exploration and use of outer space are free for all and there is freedom of scientific investigation. Article I also states the duty to carry out space exploration in the general benefit and interest of all countries, and the importance of cooperation. Duties of cooperation, mutual assistance, and regard for the interests of others are contained also in OST Art. IX and by Art. XI the states agree to inform the public, the scientific community and the UN Secretary General of activities and any results, albeit only 'to the greatest extent feasible and practicable'.[80] However, ETI could change things, presenting potential danger. We will come to such matters later.[81]

The body of international law relevant to most SETI inquiry is that securing the allocation and use of the radio spectrum through the mechanisms of the International Telecommunication Union (the ITU). To summarise what is more fully covered in Chapter 8, the ITU basic agreements are linked international treaties, the Radio Regulations (RR) being

77 M.A. Stull and G. Alexander, 'Passive Use of the Radio Spectrum for Scientific Purposes and the Frequency Allocation Process' (1977) 43 *J. Air Law & Comm.* 459–534.

78 For US protection of SETI and radio astronomy sites see Stull, *supra* n. 77: cf. (1) *In the Matter of the 4.9 GHz Band Transferred from Federal Government Use*; WT Docket no. 00–32; 2002 17 FCC Rcd 3955; 2002 FCC LEXIS 1007; 26 Comm. Reg. (P & F) 50, February 27, 2002 released; adopted February 14, 2002 (sites included Goldstone and the Allen Telescope Array). This proceeding resulted in *In the Matter of The 4.9 GHz Band Transferred from Federal Government Use*, WT Docket no. 00–32, 2003 18 FCC Rcd 9152; 2003 FCC LEXIS 2492, released May 2, 2003, adopted April 23, 2003. (2) *In the Matter of Amendment of the Commission's Rules to Establish a Radio Astronomy Coordination Zone in Puerto Rico*; ET Docket no. 96–2; RM-816511 FCC Rcd 1716; 1996 FCC LEXIS 629; Rel. no. FCC 96–12 February 1996 released; adopted January 18, 1996 (Arecibo). (3). *In the Matter of Amendment of the General Mobile Radio Service (Part 95) and Amateur Radio Service (Part 97) Rules to Establish Procedures to Minimize Potential Interference to Radio Astronomy Operations.* 1981 85 FCC 2d 738. In the UK five radio telescopes are each surrounded by an exclusion zone within which radio usage is forbidden: Wireless Telegraphy Licence Exemption (Ofcom, 2007) Annex 3. See Reg. 4(7) of the Wireless Telegraphy (Automotive Short Range Radar) (Exemption) (No. 2) (Amendment) Regulations 2005 (2005 SI 1534) as amended by Reg. 2(4) of the Wireless Telegraphy (Automotive Short Range Radar) (Exemption) (No. 2) (Amendment) Regulations 2008 (2008 SI 237). See also Statement 'Protecting passive services at 23.6–24 GHz from future 26 GHz uses' (Ofcom, 2022): www.ofcom.org.uk/consultations-and-statements/category-2/protecting-passive-services-at-23.6-24-ghz-from-future-26-ghz-uses, 'Consultation on Satellite Earth Station Network licences: Proposals to enable NGSO maritime services and adopt new conditions on coexistence' (Ofcom, May 2023): www.ofcom.org.uk/__data/assets/pdf_file/0024/261267/esn-licence-condoc.pdf, and Satellite Earth Station Network licences: enabling NGSO maritime services and introducing new conditions of coexistence' (Ofcom, September 2023): www.ofcom.org.uk/__data/assets/pdf_file/0025/268108/satellite-earth-station-network-licences-statement.pdf.

79 *The SS Lotus (France v Turkey)* 1927 PCIJ 3, Ser. A, No. 10; (1935) 2 *Hudson World Court Reports* 20. Doubt was cast on this simple formulation of the rule in the Advisory Opinion of the International Court of Justice on the 'Legality of the Threat or Use of Nuclear Weapons', 1996 ICJ 226.

80 As noted *infra*, the requirement to notify the UN Secretary General of 'results' is incorporated in para. 3 of the 'Declaration of Principles Concerning Activities Following the Detection of Extraterrestrial Intelligence', *infra* n, 115.

81 See text following n. 108.

one part of the arrangements.[82] The Table of Frequency Allocations contained in RR Art. 5 allocates particular frequency bands to identified services on a worldwide or regional basis. In descending order of protection these allocations may be primary, primary but shared with another service, or secondary. In addition a footnote may provide for particular use other than the normal by a state or limit a freedom to allocate. The assignment of a frequency for use is a matter for the state having jurisdiction over a transmitting station. An (or sometimes a proposed) assignment is notified to the ITU Radiocommunication Bureau, which circulates the notification to other states and itself checks that the assignment is (a) in conformity with the RR allocations and (b) does not conflict or cause interference to another assignment already notified. Subject to these conditions lawful assignments are entered in the Master International Frequency Register (MIFR). Where there is potential interference to an existing lawful assignment steps are taken to settle matters by agreement. In many bands assignments are first coordinated with other states whose stations might be interfered with. Technically, priority of notification will normally secure protection from interference by a later notified assignment, although in the last analysis a state may persist with an irregular assignment. Apart from such procedural safeguards, the ITU documents also include duties to use minimum necessary output in transmissions, to fine-tune equipment and to make speedy use of the latest technical advances.[83] Such rules operate to the benefit of SETI by reducing interference.[84]

That said, SETI is not well-protected by the Radio Regulations (RR).[85] SETI and radio astronomy receivers do not (usually) transmit and hence may be invisible to the MIFR. Its protection depends on others complying with the Table of Allocations. Although the RR makes some allocations and other special provision for it, radio astronomy is sheltered rather than absolutely protected.[86] Without going into fuller detail, we note that under RR 11.12, it is competent for an administration to notify a frequency or frequencies that are to be used by a particular radio astronomy station, and that information will be included in the MIFR, presumably in the hope that another administration will take this into account in making its own frequency assignments. In addition, RRs 5.149 and 5.208A, 5.379A, 5.402. 5.458A list frequencies which Administrations are urged to take 'all practicable steps' to protect for radio astronomy purposes.[87] RRs 5.372, 5.376A, 5.504B prohibit harmful interference to radio astronomy in specified wave-bands. Under RR 5.556 radio astronomy observations in the bands 51.4–54.25, 58.2–59, 64–65, 72.77–72.91 and 93.07–93.27 GHz may be carried out under national arrangements, but this affords no

---

82 T.A.Th. Spoelstra, 'Radio Astronomy in Telecommunication Land: The ITU and Radio Astronomy' (1997) 22 *Air and Sp. Law* 326–333. Cf. Stull, *supra* n. 77, at 491–501, on the 1977 situation.

83 RR 5 and related Annexes and Appendices deal with technical characteristics. In the ITU Constitution CS Arts 6.1 (37) and 2 (38) impose duties on member states themselves to abide by the rules as to inference, and to see that operating agencies they authorise also do so. Military radio installations are exempt except insofar as they operate services for public correspondence or similar (CS Art. 48 (202–204)). See Chapter 8.

84 Article 4 of the Radio Regulations contains 'General Rules for the Assignment and Use of Frequencies'. Specific provisions of the ITU Constitution and Convention impose duties to implement the ITU arrangements (CS Art. 6.2 (38)), see n. 83 *supra* and generally Chapter 8.

85 Note: changes may be made by WRC-23. See particularly Chapter 3 of the Report of the CPM on technical, operational and regulatory/procedural matters to be considered by the World Radiocommunication Conference 2023: www.itu.int/dms_pub/itu-r/md/19/cpm23.2/r/R19-CPM23.2-R-0001!!PDF-E.pdf.

86 RR 1.13 defines radio astronomy as 'Astronomy based on the reception of radio waves of cosmic origin'. See also Chapter 9 sv. Astronomy.

87 'Practicable' is not an absolute term.

protection at the level of international law. While radio astronomy therefore does receive some limited degree of consideration, it also appears that the frequencies protected are not always those most appropriate for the science.

Given that radio astronomy is not well protected it is not surprising that SETI is barely mentioned and as such gets no particular protection in the ITU Radio Regulations.[88] RR 5 sets aside a number of wave-bands for passive activity including in Earth Exploration-Satellite, Radio Astronomy and Space Research. RR 5 340 prohibits all emissions in a variety of bands including these, but again with limited exception.[89] Under RR 5.340.1 the 'allocation to the earth exploration-satellite service (passive) and the space research service (passive) in the band 50.2–50.4 GHz should not impose undue constraints on the use of the adjacent bands by the primary allocated services in those bands'. RR 5.341 does state: 'In the bands 1400–1727 MHz, 101–120 GHz and 197–220 GHz, passive research is being conducted by some countries in a programme for the search for intentional emissions of extraterrestrial origin'.[90] The bands noted in RRS5.341 as of interest to SETI are also allocated to fixed and mobile services, to space operations, maritime and aeronautical mobile satellite, meteorological satellite, and to radiolocation services. Other portions of Art. 5 also protect passive services. Bands 1660.5–1668.4 MHz are allocated to Radio Astronomy, passive Space Research and on a secondary basis to mobile services, excepting aeronautical mobile. Secondary allocations are given for Radio Astronomy and passive Space Research in bands 2.6550–2.670 and 2.670–2.690 MHz and for passive Space Research in bands 4990–5000 MHz. In the higher frequencies the bands 4990–5000 GHz are allocated *inter alia* to radio astronomy and to passive space research on a primary basis, but these bands are also shared with Earth Exploration-Satellite (passive) Fixed and Mobile Services except aeronautical mobile, together with radiolocation on a secondary basis. Bands 10.68–10.7 and 15.35–15.4 GHz and 23.6–24, 31.3–31.5, 36–37 GHz are allocated similarly though without the Fixed and Mobile Services allocations. In the 18.6–22.21 and 31.5–31.8 GHz bands different provision is made for these services in ITU Regions 1–3, while 22.21–22.5 GHz allocates for Radio Astronomy and passive Space Research on a primary basis, but these bands are also shared with Earth Exploration-Satellite (passive) Fixed and Mobile Services. Bands 50.2–50.4 and 52.6–54.25 GHz are allocated on a primary basis to Earth Exploration (passive) and Space Research (passive), with bands 54.25–55.78 GHz including these as well as Inter-Satellite Services. Further similar provision for exploration and research is made in the allocations for the 55.78–66, 86–119.98, 119.98–158, 158–202, 02–400 GHz wave-bands. Apart from these, by RR 5.565, the 'frequency band 275–1000 GHz may be used by administrations for experimentation with, and development of, various active and passive services. In this band a need has been identified for the following spectral line measurements for passive services: radio astronomy service, 275–323, 327–371, 388–424, 426–442, 453–510, 623–711, 795–909 and 926–945 GHz; and Earth exploration-satellite service (passive) and space research service (passive): 275–277, 294–306, 316–334, 342–349, 363–365, 371–389, 416–434, 442–444, 496–506, 546–568, 624–629, 634–654, 659–661,

---

88 H.C. Kahlmann, 'SETI and the Radio Spectrum' (1992) 26 *Acta Astronautica* 213–217 refers to the equivalent provision in previous versions of the Radio Regulations.

89 The 'hydrogen line', the 'water-hole', is 1.420 MHz.

90 V. Kopal, 'International Law Implications of the Detection of Extraterrestrial Intelligent Signals,' (1990) 21 *Acta Astronautica* 123–126 at 124 quotes the equivalent provision in the previous Radio Regulations. Cf. para. 170 of the FCC inquiry *Preparation for the 1979 ITU World Administrative Radio Conference* (1978) 70 FCC 2d 1193.

684–692, 730–732, 851–853 and 951–956 GHz. Footnote RR 5.565 as amended continues: 'Future research in this largely unexplored spectral region may yield additional spectral lines and continuum bands of interest to the passive services. Administrations are urged to take all practicable steps to protect these passive services from harmful interference until the date when the allocation Table is established in the abovementioned frequency band'.

Although such provisions may help radio SETI by giving some protection to frequencies intended for radio astronomy, the position of terrestrial SETI remains weak. Various papers and comments draw attention to problems of interference with SETI observations. Thus the Quarterly Update to June 1993 on the NASA High Resolution Microwave Survey then in progress reported interference problems, and that all fifteen interfering signals that were investigated proved to be terrestrial.[91] Other reports of similar problems have been published.[92]

The Radio Regulations remain the source of protection for SETI and for Radio Astronomy at an international level.[93] More could be done by national administrations to comply with their duties to secure that interference to passive use of the spectrum is minimal. There is a community of interests between the radio astronomers and the SETI specialists. They should tackle such matters jointly, both through lobbying national administrations, and through the appropriate mechanisms of the ITU, including the working groups of the Radiocommunication Sector. Perhaps it is unrealistic to expect further radio channels to be freed from other use, but that is an option which should be preserved.

Finally as to the protection of SETI activities, as part of the projected return to the moon, NASA has started to discuss the construction of a radio telescope facility in a lunar far-side crater.[94] The idea, which is not new,[95] is a potential use of the moon contemplated

91 The Quarterly Reports were available electronically on NASA Space link. Similar data is now to be found on the NASA website, using a search for 'radio frequency interference' or 'extraterrestrial radio waves'.

92 M.K. Klein and others, 'An Assessment of the Impact of Radiofrequency Interference on Microwave SETI Searches' (IAA-87-593) (1992) 26 *Acta Astronautica* 227–232; J. Tarter, 'Summary of Interference Measurements at Selected Radio Observatories' (IAA-90-580) (1992) 26 *Acta Astronautica* 233–238; J. Tarter, 'Radio Frequency Interference at Jodrell Bank Observatory within the Protected 21cm Band' (IAA-86-425) (1989) 19 *Acta Astronautica* 907–912; W.J. Welch, 'A Strategy for SETI Observations at Arecibo Observatory' (IAA-88-540) (1992) 26 *Acta Astronautica* 219–221 at 220; G.K. Hovde, 'Frequency Management and SETI: Threats to SETI Observations in the 1–3 GHZ Band' (2000) 46 *Acta Astronautica* 677–682; J. Tarter et al., 'Studies of Radio Frequency Interference at Parkes Observatory' (2000) 46 *Acta Astronautica* 683–691.

93 For the ITU Radio Regulations, see Chapter 8.

94 Cf. C. Maccone, ed., *Protected Antipode Circle on Lunar Farside*, IAF Cosmic Study, 1.6 (Eighth Draft, 2014): https://iaaweb.org/iaa/Scientific%20Activity/Study%20Groups/SG%20Commission%201/sg16/sg16draftreport2.pdf. The UK may participate in such an endeavour: *The Times*, London, 1 December 2006. This project is additional to the possible establishment of a Moon base at one or other of the lunar poles.

95 J. Heidmann (1) 'Saha Crater: A Candidate for a SETI Lunar Base' (1994) 32 *Acta Astronautica* 471–472; (2) 'What Legal Questions are Raised by the Establishment of a Dedicated Lunar Farside Specific Crater for High Sensitivity Radioastronomy?' (1994) 37 *Proc. IISL* 255; (3) 'Recent Progress in the Lunar Farside Crater SAHA Proposal', 1997 IAA-97-IAA.9.1.05; A.A. Cocca, 'Reservation of a Lunar Zone for SETI Purposes' (1995) 38 *Proc. IISL* 270–273; F.G. von der Dunk, 'Space for Celestial Symphonies: towards the establishment of radio quiet zones' (2001) 17 *Space Policy* 265–274; F. Lyall, 'On the Moon' (1998) 28 *J. Sp. L.* 129–138. It was subsequently determined that the crater Daedelus was more suitable for the purpose, and it has replaced Saha in the discussions. See F. Lyall, 'Daedelus and Radio', in C. Maccone, ed., *supra* n. 94, *Protected Antipode Circle on Lunar Farside*, IAA Cosmic Study 1.6 (forthcoming). Cf. 'Lunar Farside Radio Lab: A Study by IAA', C. Maccone, coordinator: www.setileague.org/iaaseti/lunar02.pdf, and C. Maccone (1) 'Planetary Defense from the Nearest 4 LaGrange Points plus RFI-free Radioastronomy from the Farside of the Moon: A Unified Vision' (2002) 50 *Acta Astronautica* 185–199; (2) 'The Quiet Cone above the Farside of the Moon' (2003) 53 *Acta Astronautica* 65–70; (3) 'Lunar Farside Radio Lab' (2005) 56 *Acta Astronautica* 629–639.

under Art. 7.3 of the Moon Agreement, which foreshadows the setting aside of lunar areas of special scientific interest. Should it be proceeded with, SETI observations from a radio telescope on the lunar far-side would be protected by the mass of the moon itself from man-made interference as well as naturally occurring terrestrial phenomena such as lightning. In that regard Sec. V of Art. 22 of the ITU Radio Regulations (RR 22.22–25) prohibits radio emissions causing harmful interference in the 'shielded zone' of the Moon.[96] When such a radio-telescope is established we would expect that the astronomers would allow SETI investigators access to the facility.[97]

First Evidence: First Contact[98]

The social and societal implications of the detection of ETI would be considerable.[99] The excitement that accompanied the 1996 announcement that a meteorite from Mars (ALH 84001) might contain fossilised primitive extraterrestrial life was considerable.[100] In the intervening years the media has eagerly reported the discovery of exo-planets,[101] and on the attempts to detect microbial life on Mars. How much more so were intelligence to be detected. How should such a development be coped with? The SETI Institute produced a report connected with the 1992 High Resolution Microwave Survey suggesting various methods by which information as to SETI could be disseminated through the media, which to some extent might help prepare society for any development.[102]

96 The shielded zone is defined as 'the area of the Moon's surface and an adjacent volume of space which are shielded from emissions originating within a distance of 100,000 km from the centre of the Earth' (RR 22.22.1, fn. 31). Emissions causing harmful interference to radio astronomy observations and 'to other users of passive services' within the zone are, with exceptions, 'prohibited in the entire frequency spectrum' (RR 22.22.1). The level at which harmful interference occurs is to be 'determined by agreement between the administrations concerned, with the guidance of the relevant ITU-R Recommendations' (RR 22.22.2, fn. 32). Exceptions to the blanket prohibition of RR 22.22.1 are frequency bands allocated to space research using active sensors (RR 22.23), and bands allocated to the space operation service, Earth-exploration using active sensors, radiolocation using space-borne platforms, required for the support of space research, as well as for radiocommunication and space research transmissions within the lunar shielded zone (RR 22.24).
97 Cf. L. David, 'How Robots Could Build a Radio Telescope of Far Side of the Moon', Space.com, 29 July 2015: www.space.com/30084-moon-far-side-rovers-radio-telescope.html.
98 Cf. J Billingham, ed., *Social Implications of the Detection of an Extraterrestrial Civilization* (Mountain View: SETI Press 1999); A.A, Harrison, *After Contact: The Human Response to Extraterrestrial Life* (New York: Plenum, 1997); M. Michaud, *Contact with Alien Civilizations: Our Hopes and Fears About Encountering Extraterrestrials* (New York: Springer, 2006). Cf. *Workshop on the Societal Implications of Astrobiology, Final Report*, Ames Research Center, 1999, NASA, 2000: https://astrobiology.arc.nasa.gov/workshops/societal/societal_report.pdf; B. Finney, 'The Impact of Contact' (1990) 21 *Acta Astronautica* 118–122.
   For fictional treatment see *inter alia*: I. Asimov, M.H. Greenberg and C. Waugh, *Encounters* (London: Headline Books, 1988): C. Sagan, *Contact* (New York: Simon and Schuster, 1985; London: Century, 1986); various entries (including Communications) in J. Clute and P. Nicholls, eds., *The Encyclopaedia of Science Fiction* (London: Orbit; New York: Little, Brown, 1993) (with updates: www.dcs.gla.ac.uk/SF-Archives/Misc/sfec.html).
99 NASA Technical Memorandum, *Workshop on the Societal Implications of Astrobiology: Final Report, 1999*: www.astrosociology.org/Library/PDF/NASA-Workshop-Report-Societal-Implications-of-Astrobiology.pdf. NASA runs an Astrobiology Program, encouraging multidisciplinary astrobiology research: (https:/astrobiology.nasa.gov/), a replacement for its Astrobiology Institute which ran for twenty years,
100 'On the Question of the Mars Meteorite': www.lpi.usra.edu/lpi/meteorites/mars_meteorite.html and www.lpi.usra.edu/lpi/meteorites/The_Meteorite.html.
101 See *supra* n. 10
102 'Social Aspects of SETI': www.seti.org/seti-institute/project/details/social-impact-eti-detection-workshop-findings.

The interaction of humanity with newly discovered ETI is a staple of science fiction. Broadly the tales exhibit two opposite reactions. Sometimes the knowledge that there is intelligent alien life is simply absorbed and makes little impact on life in general. Other works acknowledge that proof of ETI could have a significant effect. One area would be in religion. Thus in both *Childhood's End* (1953) and *The Fountains of Paradise* (1979) Arthur C. Clarke suggests that only a mutant Buddhism would survive the knowledge of ETI, the more structured religions such as Christianity, Judaism and Islam being unable to adapt to the new information and therefore dying out. However, others have taken a different view and there have been fascinating stories exploring religion.[103]

In SETI-related discussion of such matters opinions have varied. R.R. Malina has indicated that ecclesiastical opposition was one reason why the NASA terminated funding for its SETI projects.[104] In 1992 M. Ashkenazi was of the view that both Judaism and Islam would have no fundamental problem with ETI since neither clearly holds to a uniqueness of Man, and both lay stress on the power of God to act as He will. However in his view Christianity, and particularly orthodox (small 'o') Protestant Christianity, would encounter more problems with any proven ETI because of its stress on the human form as created in the image of God, and through the questions that ETI might pose as to the uniqueness of redemption through the Crucifixion.[105] Nonetheless, on the basis of unselective interviews with theologians, Ashkenazi's general view was that ETI would not profoundly affect religion, even were a non-religious ETI to be encountered. P. Musso's paper of 2004 pointed out that the Roman Catholic Church has not committed itself on the matter, and that the few theologians that have published on the topic have tended to adopt a 'wait and see' attitude.[106] Some have not.[107]

103 Many science fiction stories explore religious questions. Cf. the collection, P. Warrick and M.H. Greenberg, eds., *The New Awareness: Religion Through Science Fiction* (New York: Delacorte Press, 1975); and notably J. Blish, *A Case of Conscience* (1958).

104 R. Malina, 'Search Strategies: SETI Activity and Society' (1998) 41 *Proc. IISL* 304–308, at 306 and response to a question by S.E. Doyle during the discussion session (ibid. at 345).

105 M. Ashkenazi, 'Not the Sons of Adam: Religious Responses to ETI' (1992) 8 *Space Policy* 341–349. Cf. T. Peters, 'Would the Discovery of ETI provoke a Religious Crisis?', in Vakoch, ed., *supra* n. 7, 341–355, and T. Peters and J. Froelich, 'The Peters ETI Religious Crisis Survey' (2013): (https://counterbalance. org/etsurv/PetersETISurveyRep.pdf; T.M. Hesburgh, President, University of Notre Dame, Foreword to NASA SP-419, *supra* n. 1.

106 P. Musso, 'Philosophical and Religious Implications of Extraterrestrial Intelligent Life', 2004 IAC.04.1.1.2.11. In *Religions and Extraterrestrial Life: How Will We Deal with It?* (Leiden: Springer, 2014) D.A. Weintraub surveys how the major religions may react. See also material cited *supra* n. 15. See also D.A. Vakoch, 'Roman Catholic Views of Extraterrestrial Intelligence: Anticipating the Future by Examining the Past', in Tough, *infra* n. 107, 165–174, and the material he cites.

107 Discussions include G. Consolmagno, SJ, and P. Mueller SJ, *Would You Baptise an Extraterrestrial?: . . . and Other Questions from the Astronomers' in-Box at the Vatican Observatory* (New York: Image, 2014) 249–286; P. O'Meara, *Extraterrestrials and Christian Revelation* (Collegeville: Liturgical Press, 2012); P. Wilkinson *Science, Religion and the Search for Extraterrestrial Life* (Oxford: Oxford UP, 2013), and his *Christian Eschatology and the Physical Universe* (London: T&T Clark, 2010). C. Weidemann, 'Christian Soteriology and Extraterrestrial Intelligence' (2014) 67 JBIS 418–425, considers the traditional Christian theology of salvation incompatible with belief in numerous ET civilisations.

    For older material see 'Discourse V' of Chalmers, *supra* n. 14; J. Baillie, *The Place of Christ in Modern Christianity* (Edinburgh: T&T Clark, 1929) 202–212; M. Thomson, 'Extraterrestrial Life and the Cosmic Christ as Prototype' (2000) 18 *Scot. Bull. Ev. Theol.* 160–178; J.J. Davis, 'Search for Extraterrestrial Intelligence and the Christian Doctrine of Redemption' (1997) 9 *Science and Christian Belief*, 21–34; G. McColley *supra* n. 14. Cf. C.L. Fisher and D. Fergusson, 'Karl Rahner and the Extra-Terrestrial Intelligence Question' (2006) 47 *Heythrop J.* 275–290; D.A. Vakoch, 'Roman Catholic Views of Extraterrestrial Intelligence: Anticipating the Future by Examining the Past', in A. Tough, ed., *When SETI Succeeds: The Impact of High-Information*

There is little law on such matters. As already noted, SETI activities are lawful under international law,[108] and appear to be so under national legal systems. To repeat: SETI activities may be subject to the requirement of Art. XI of the OST as to a state's duty to inform the public, the scientific community and the Secretary General of the United Nations of activities and any results, albeit only 'to the greatest extent feasible and practicable'.[109] Yet what about the matter of potential danger? There are the indications of action to be taken to report and avoid a variety of dangers in OST Arts V and IX of the OST, and MA Art. 5.3.[110] The obvious meaning of these provisions relates to physical phenomena: OST Art. V is concerned with dangers to astronauts and Art. IX deals with contamination of the Earth or of celestial bodies. The fact is that ETI was not in the minds of those drafting, signing or ratifying these agreements. The only clear reference to life in outer space is in MA Art. 5.3, and that is to organic life – a far remove from Extraterrestrial Intelligence. However, detection of or contact with ETI could be covered under a broader interpretation of 'dangerous phenomena', 'dangerous' at least *in potentia*. It is therefore useful that some have been thinking of such matters.[111]

The SETI Protocols

Given the potential impact of a proven detection of ETI it is good that steps have been taken to organise procedures through which such a detection might be announced, and, in an appropriate case, a signal responded to.[112] Of course it might be that the detector of a signal might remain quiet or might be ignorant of any SETI Protocols, but we cannot here take account of these possibilities.[113]

We consider the original detection protocol of 1989, the draft Reply Protocol of 1995 and the Search principles of 2010.[114]

Contact (Foundation for the Future, 2004) 165–174; M.A.G. Michaud, *Contact, supra* n. 15, 202–206. See also data in Dick and in Crowe, both *supra* n. 14. as to theological discussions in the periods they cover.

108 See text *supra* following n. 79.

109 As noted *infra* following n. 119, the requirement to notify the UN Secretary General of 'results' is incorporated in Pr. 3 of the 'Declaration of Principles Concerning Activities Following the Detection of Extraterrestrial Intelligence'.

110 The Moon Agreement, discussed *supra* Chapter 7, has not been widely accepted. As of 2023 it had garnered only 18 ratifiers (one of which will be withdraw in 2024) and 4 signatory states. Some would argue that reliance on its terms as law is not justified except as between its members. However, it may have a use in spelling out in more detail the content of duties as to dangers in space law.

111 See following text, and G.H. Reynolds, 'International Space Law: Into the Twenty-First Century' (1992) 25 *Vand. J. Transnat. L.* 225–255 at 246–255. Gertz, *supra* n. 59, suggests that OST Art. IX proscribes METI as potentially endangering Earth, but this is overstated. However, perhaps Art. IX could be invoked to request international consultations on proposed METI activities.

112 Cf. J. Billingham, 'Pesek Lecture: SETI and Society – Decision Trees' (2002) 51 *Acta Astronautica* 667–672. See also G.H. Reynolds, 'International Space Law: Into the Twenty-First Century (1992) 24 *Vand. J. Transnat. L.* 225–255 at 246–255. The involvement of the IAA can only be described as sporadic: C. Maccone, 'SETI and the IAA Permanent Committee: Past, Present and Potential Future', in P.M. Sterns and L.I. Tennen, eds., *Private Law, Public Law, Metalaw and Public Policy in Space, A Liber Amicorum in Honor of Ernst Fasan* (Vienna: Springer, 2016) 145–158.

113 A. Tough, 'A Critical Examination of Factors that Might Encourage Secrecy' (1990) 21 *Acta Astronautica* 99–104.

114 Sterns and Tennen, *supra* n. 112, 164–174.

The Post-Detection Protocol 1989[115]

The 'Declaration of Principles Concerning Activities Following the Detection of Extraterrestrial Intelligence', the Post-detection Protocol, outlines principles, which, it suggests, should be followed following the detection of extraterrestrial intelligence. The Protocol was approved in 1989 by a number of relevant bodies including the IAA and the IISL. Aware of the potential impact of a disclosure it provides that there should be no public announcement of the detection of ETI until its credibility has been thoroughly tested and evaluated.[116] To ensure any announcement is well-grounded a set of consecutive steps is indicated. A signal or other evidence should be verified by its detector as most plausibly coming from an ET source. Of course here the meaning of 'plausibility' is fundamental. To help its definition I. Almar and J. Tarter suggested what is now known as the 'Rio Scale' as a suitable tool for assessing plausibility.[117] Amended the following year, this scale now appears to have been accepted as normative.[118] The possibility of hoax has also to be guarded against, and there have been examples of such.[119] Under the Protocol if a detection cannot plausibly be verified as a true detection of ETI it should be reported as an unknown phenomenon (Pr. 1). Before any public announcement of the detection of ETI other signatories to the Declaration should be notified so that they can run their own checks and the relevant national authorities should be informed (Pr. 2). Then the rest of the astronomical scientific community, the ITU and, in compliance with OST Art. XI, the UN Secretary General should be informed, those with expertise being given 'all pertinent data and recorded information' (Pr. 3). Information as to a confirmed detection should be disseminated promptly, openly and widely – the discoverer having the privilege of the first public announcement (Pr. 4). All relevant data should be made widely available (Pr. 5). The discovery should be properly recorded and monitored (Pr. 6). Should the detection rely on electromagnetic signals, their frequencies should be protected through the mechanisms of the ITU (Pr. 7). Importantly, no response should be made or sent until the matter has been the subject of international consultations held under procedures that are to be agreed (Pr. 8). Finally the Protocol indicates that there should be a continuing review of procedures for the detection of ETI and the handling of data. For this purpose an international committee has been established representing relevant major organisations and interested individuals.[120]

115 The 'Declaration of Principles Concerning Activities Following the Detection of Extraterrestrial Intelligence': www.seti.org/protocols-eti-signal-detection; https://resources.iaaseti.org/protocols_rev2010.pdf. For the original text see https://iaaseti.org/en/protocols/; www.setileague.org/general/protocol.htm; Sterns and Tennen, *supra* n. 112, 174–176; (1990) 21 *Acta Astronautica* 153–154; Appendix 1 to M. Michaud, 'An International Agreement Concerning the Detection of Extraterrestrial Intelligence' (1992) 26 *Acta Astronautica* 291–294 at 293, and his 'A Unique Moment in Human History', in B. Bova and B. Preiss, *supra* n. 3, 325–328. See also M. Michaud, *Contact*, *supra* n. 15, 358–375.
116 Cf. S. Harris, 'The First Amendment and the End of the World' (2007) 68 *U. Pitt. L. Rev.* 785–833. Also note the effect of the announcement regarding the Mars meteorite of 1996, *supra* n. 100, and the persistent media interest in new exoplanets.
117 I. Almár and J. Tarter, J., 'The Discovery of ETI as a High-Consequence, Low-Probability Event,' (2011) 68 *Acta Astronautica* 358–361. See now the IAA SETI Permanent Committee: 'The Rio Scale': https://iaaseti.org/en/rio-scale/. It was approved by the IAA SETI Permanent Study Group in 2002 though revision will continue: see https://iaaseti.org/. See also S. Shostak and I. Almár, 'The Rio Scale Applied to Fictional SETI Detections', IAA-02-IAA.9.1.06.
118 I. Almár 'How the Rio Scale Should be Improved', IAA-01-IAA.9.2.03, and 'The SETI and the London Scale' (2011) 69 *Acta Astronautica* 899–904.
119 H.P. Shuch, 'SETI Sneak Attack: Lessons Learned from the Pearl Harbor Hoax', IAF Bremen, 2003, IAC-03-IAA.9.2.03; www.setileague.org/articles/iaa2003.htm; H.P. Shuch, 'Anatomy of a SETI Hoax' (1999) www.setileague.org/articles/setihoax.htm.
120 IAA SETI Permanent Study Group: https://iaaseti.org/.

The Reply-Communication Draft Declaration 1995[121]

Principle 8 of the Post-detection Protocol suggested that no response should be made to a signal or other evidence of ETI until international consultations have taken place. In fact there has been considerable discussion of mechanisms through which a reply on behalf of the Earth to a detected ETI signal might be formulated.[122] In 1995 the IAA SETI Committee brought forward a draft Reply-communication Declaration.[123] This is a corollary to the Post-detection Protocol, but unlike it, has not been adopted by all relevant bodies. Unlike the Post-detection Protocol it was aimed at eventual treaty status as an agreement between states rather than just between SETI practitioners. However, that proved over-ambitious.

The draft Reply Communications Protocol provided a framework within which the question of whether to reply, and an outline of the content of any reply, could be considered. Previous discussions had ranged over questions of content as well as procedure, and the separation of these matters is to be welcomed. Now the only indication as to possible content is that the procedure should reflect 'a careful concern for the broad interests and well-being of Humanity' (Pr. 6). Consultations on the question of sending communications should be begun (Pr. 1). Whether a message should be sent should be discussed within UN COPUOS and other governmental and nongovernmental organisations including participation by qualified interested groups (Pr. 2). Interested states should take part and the discussions should result in recommendations arrived at through consensus (Pr. 3). On the basis of a recommendation from COPUOS and the other participants in the discussions the UN General Assembly should consider whether to send a message, and its content if any. Any message should be from Humankind, not from any particular state (Pr. 5). As noted, its content should 'reflect concern for the broad interests and well-being of humanity' (Pr. 6). Principle 6 also suggests that the content of the message should be publicised before being sent, though it is not clear what possibility there might be for objections to be raised or amendments agreed. Since any exchange of messages is likely to take years, a long-term institutional framework for conducting such an exchange should be considered (Pr. 7). Perhaps indicating that the drafters were conscious that not everyone may pay heed to the Reply-communication Declaration, Pr. 8 states that states should not send a message prior to international consultation, nor cooperate with any attempts to

121 'Draft Declaration Concerning Sending Communications with Extraterrestrial Intelligence': https:// iaaseti.org/en/seti-reply-protocols/; Sterns and Tennen, *supra* n. 112, 177; IAA Position Paper, at the North American Astrophysical Laboratory Post-detection SETI Protocol website Part III and Annex 2: www.naapo.org/SETIprotocol.htm#annex2. See also J. Billlingham at https://iaaseti.org/en/decision-process-examining-possibility-sending-communications-ex/; M. Michaud, 'An International Agreement Concerning the Detection of Extraterrestrial Intelligence' (1992) 26 *Acta Astronautica* 291–294 at 294, and 'A Unique Moment in Human History', in B. Bova and B. Preiss, *supra* n. 3, 328–329.

122 P. Hatfield and L. Trueblood, 'SETI and democracy' (2021) 180 *Acta Astronautica* 596–603; A.E. Goodman, 'Diplomacy and the Search for Extraterrestrial Intelligence' (1990) 21 *Acta Astronautica* 137–142; D. Goldsmith, 'Who Will Speak for Earth? Possible Structures for Shaping a Response to a Signal Detected from an Extraterrestrial Civilization' (1990) 21 *Acta Astronautica* 149–151; M. Michaud, J. Billingham and J. Tarter, 'A Reply from Earth?' (1992) 26 *Acta Astronautica* 295–297: www.setv.org/online_mss/reply92. pdf; R.P. Norris, 'How to Respond to a SETI Detection', *Bioastronomy 2002: Life Among the Stars* (2004) IAU Symposium, Vol. 213, 1–6; www.atnf.csiro.au/people/rnorris/papers/n188.pdf; M. Michaud, *Contact, supra* n. 15, 358–375; Reijnen, *supra* n. 25.

123 *Supra* n. 121. In 1997 the SETI League endorsed and commended the draft Reply Protocol: 'SETI Reply Protocols': www.setileague.org/general/reply.htm.

do so.[124] In their deliberations states should draw on the services of experts (Pr. 9), and if the decision is indeed to communicate, encoding and transmitting the message should be entrusted to scientists and engineers specialising in the technologies involved (Pr. 10).

The Search Principles Declaration 2010

The two documents just outlined were published respectively in 1989 and 1995. In 2010 a further 'Declaration of Principles Concerning the Conduct of the Search for Extraterrestrial Intelligence' was issued by the IAA SETI Committee.[125] This is an attempt to bring the major elements of its predecessors into a single document.[126]

Under the Principles of 2010 SETI experiments are to be conducted transparently, participants in the Search being free to inform the public of their activities and results (Pr. 1). If/when evidence of ETI is suspected it should be verified. There should be collaboration with other investigators, whether or not signatories to the Declaration. There is no obligation to disclose that verification efforts are under way, and there should be no premature disclosure. While verification efforts are in progress inquiries from the media should be responded to promptly and honestly (Pr. 2).[127] Information should be treated as any scientist would treat provisional laboratory results, and the Rio Scale used as a guide for the benefit of non-specialist audiences (Pr. 2).[128] A detection deemed to be of a credible degree of certainty, and with the consensus of any other investigators involved, should be reported 'in a full and complete open manner' to the public, to the scientific community, to the UN Secretary General, and to the International Astronomical Union. The report would include basic data, the process and results of verification, conclusions and interpretations, and any detected information content. (Pr. 3). Subsequently all necessary data would be widely circulated to the international scientific community (Pr. 4). The discovery would be monitored, and data recorded and stored to the greatest extent practicable and made available to others (Pr. 5). If the evidence is of an electromagnetic signal, international agreement should be sought to protect the relevant frequencies through ITU procedures (Pr. 6).[129] A Post-Detection Task Group has been established the IAA SETI Permanent

124 This is weak. There have already been speculative transmissions to space, *supra* nn. 51, 52, but a 'reply' to a detected signal would be of a different order. Should we consider that as part of its OST Art. VI obligations to supervise space activities engaged in by those under its jurisdiction, a state should prevent or punish unauthorised signalling to suspected ETIs? Could licensing be used? In the UK s. 7 of the Telecommunications Act 1984, c. 12 requires a licence to use the radio spectrum for transmissions and s. 3 of the Outer Space Act 1986 c. 38 and s. 3 of the Space Industry Act 2018 c. 5 require a licence to engage in space activities. Such requirements might, however, bring into question issues regarding which individual states may have pre-existing laws (e.g. the First Amendment to the US Constitution (freedom of speech)).
125 The 'Declaration of Principles Concerning the Conduct of the Search for Extraterrestrial Intelligence': www.avsport.org/IAA/protocols_rev2010.pdf; Sterns and Tennen, *supra* n. 112, 178–179.
126 The 2010 Declaration adopted unanimously by the IAA SETI Permanent Study Group on 30 September 2010, was intended formally to replace the 1989 Protocol. The draft 1995 Reply Protocol did not require that formal step.
127 Responding thus to the media and the previous comment as to non-disclosure do not fit together. On 'Disclosure' and a potential premature leak see Sterns and Tennen, *supra* n. 112, 165–169.
128 For the Rio Scale, see *supra* at nn. 117 and 118.
129 For the relevant ITU procedures, see Chapter 8. The text of para 6 refers to the 'World Administrative Radio Council' of the ITU. Such does not exist. Perhaps the ITU World Radiocommunication Conference was intended, but it meets only every four years. A faster procedure is needed!

Study Group to assist and support analysis, giving guidance, interpretation and discussion of the wider implications of any detection (Pr. 7). Finally, Pr. 8 contains the promise that signatories to the Principles Declaration will not respond to the detection of a confirmed ET signal 'without first seeking [the] guidance and consent of a broadly representative international body, such as the United Nations' (Pr. 8).[130]

Binding Protocols?

Detection of ETI would be significant. Communication with ETI even more so. Influential bodies and individuals active in SETI have indicated they will abide by the principles and procedures set out in the three documents just considered. But what is their practical weight? Compliance is voluntary. The Post-detection Protocol has been approved by relevant bodies. Indeed, given the involvement of major players in the field it might be thought to have a weight similar to that of a UNGA Resolution, and perhaps in practice within its area an even greater weight. This is better than nothing, but it is less than formal obligation. The IAA Permanent SETI Committee proposals of the Reply Protocol and the Search Principles Declaration share a lesser status.

The problem comes if people do not comply. There is no remedy for non-compliance. Should the principles therefore be given binding legal status? Individual states could choose to legislate. Conversion into treaty form is another possibility.[131] However, more obviously pressing concerns are taking the attention of our lawmakers, national and international. And even if there were a legal obligation, what sanctions could usefully be imposed? Were SETI to succeed many things would be more important than penalising a premature announcement. On the other hand, given the projected social effects of an announcement, it might be wise to put legal discouragements in the way of excitable discoverers. To be effective a treaty on the post-detection principles would need to require ratifying states to incorporate them into national law. Legal force for the principles should not provide an excuse for bureaucrats to issue more blue forms, or to secure that breach of a licence is punished. It is suggested in the belief that, while most scientists are law-abiding, ones on the margin might comply with a formal legal requirement but might ignore what amounts to a private agreement among their colleagues.

'Reply' is separately important. Interaction with ETI could massively affect humankind. Any treaty on SETI should bind states not to allow unlicensed practitioners or private groups to respond to ETI.[132] International agreement is needed. A formal procedure should be established ahead of requirement to discuss whether a reply should be made, and to establish any content. Some have thought that the appropriate mechanism for creating such an obligation should be the UN process, starting off with UN COPUOS,[133] but the COPUOS agenda is already well occupied. An *ad hoc* body might be more suitable.

---

130 We understand that the IAA holds a list of signatories. Cf. comment *supra* n. 124.
131 Gertz, *supra* n. 59. Cf. from forty years ago, P. Ney, 'An Extraterrestrial Contact Treaty?' (1985) 36 JBIS 521–522.
132 Cf. 'Post-detection Responses', Sterns and Tennen, *supra* n. 112, 169–173. Pr. V of a proposed revision to the 1996 Protocol, also circulated in 1996, suggested that states should not cooperate with private attempts to communicate with ETI since such efforts did not conform to the Principles. See also comment *supra* n. 124.
133 V. Kopal, *supra* n. 24 at 124–125.

Yet, as a famous American judge, Oliver Wendell Holmes, said: 'The life of the law has not been logic: it has been experience'.[134] All these considerations do not displace the point that at present too much else is taking the attention of the state departments of the nations. It may also be doubted whether states would be willing so to confine their freedom of action. In short formal legal status for the SETI Principles seems unlikely. SETI enthusiasts should therefore not over-welcome the preceding paragraphs.

Communication Content

As indicated above, apart from the question of how the decision whether to reply or not is taken, there has been much discussion as to the content of any reply. Suggestions vary.[135] Fasan puts the matter cogently,[136] but this takes us through to questions of Metalaw.

Metalaw

If we encounter ETI the question of mutual relationships will arise.[137] At one level the matter might be simple – we are conquered, or placed in quarantine, or excluded from further intercourse with space.[138] However, short of that, successful relationships run on rules, express or unacknowledged. Consideration must be given to the possibility of encounter or contact with cultures of superior, equal or lesser science and technology.[139] Of course 'first contact' stories are a staple of science fiction, but legal discussion has been sparser. In modern times A.G. Haley was one of the first to raise such matters.[140] In his view if extrater-

---

134 O. Wendell Holmes, *The Common Law* (1881) (Boston: Little, Brown, 1948) 1.

135 See materials, *supra* n. 15, together with citations in Fasan, *supra* n. 21; Reijnen, *supra* n. 25; Michaud, Billingham and Tarter, *supra* n. 106. Cf. J. Heidmann, 'A Reply from Earth: Just Send Them the Encyclopedia' (1993) 29 *Acta Astronautica* 233–235.

136 Fasan, *supra* n. 21, at 134 lists possible significant elements of a reply as including; we will not harm you or permit you to harm us, we will restore unwitting harm done to ET, we respect mutual equality, mutual promise-keeping, the will of both sides to live, the need for living-space but without invasion of the other's space, and the intention to help each other, if possible. See also his *Relations with Alien Intelligences, infra* n. 143, at 82–83, or 246 in Sterns and Tennen, *supra* n. 112.

137 See generally A.A. Harrison, *supra* n. 15. For an early IISL consideration see H.D. Lasswell, 'Anticipating Remote Contingencies: Encounters with Living Forms' (1960) 4 *Proc. IISL* 89–104.

138 Or eaten: an apocryphal suggestion attributed to an eminent astronomer is that to 'reply' to a detection of ETI is to put up a sign saying, 'Protein Here'. We note that an early commentator discussing how space law should develop suggested that manned spacecraft might permissibly carry 'the most powerful atomic and ultra-sonic rays devices in order to protect the astronauts against attack from unknown evil races'. J.E. Faria, 'Draft to an International Covenant for Outer Space – The Treaty of Antarctica as a Prototype' (1960) 3 *Proc. IISL* 122–127 at 124 (quotation from Art. 1.3 of the Draft). Otherwise, on relationships with a superior civilisation see McDougal et al., *supra* n. 19, at 1006–1021.

139 McDougal et al., *supra* n. 19, 980–1005; M. Bohlander, 'Joining the "Galactic Club": What Price Admission? ((2021) *Futures* 102801.

140 A.G. Haley, *Space Law and Government* (Appleton Century Crofts, 1963) 394–421, which brings together (and bibliographs) many of his papers. On Haley see S.E. Doyle, 'Andrew G. Haley', in S. Hobe, ed., *Pioneers of Space Law* (Leiden: Nijhoff, 2013) 71–96.

See also S. Freeland, 'A Natural System of Law – Andrew Haley and the International Regulation of Outer Space' (2013) 39 *J. Sp. L.* 77–98; A. Korbitz, 'Altruism, Metalaw, and Celegistics: An Extraterrestrial Perspective on Universal Law-Making', in Vakoch, ed., *supra* n. 47, 231–250; R. Amos, 'Exploiting the Final Frontier – Some Initial Thoughts on Regulating Humanity's Relationships with Non-Terrestrial Life Forms.' (2021) 45 *J. Sp. L.* 111–141, 'Alien Rights?' at 133–140.

restrials were contacted or encountered it was necessary to press through from the variety of anthropocentric laws to a generality of principle avoiding anthropocentricity that could inform the new relationships. This Haley dubbed 'Metalaw'. Although his view depends on concepts of 'good' and 'bad' which some consider inadequate, and of which other criticisms have been made,[141] others have found helpful Haley's articulation of a general natural principle common to all life as 'do unto others as they would have you do unto them'.[142] Ernst Fasan suggests that Metalaw is 'a rule of conduct for intelligent beings', and that therefore 'the Categorical Imperative will apply'.[143] On that basis, and after reviewing a variety of ancient and modern texts, Fasan elaborates eleven fundamental 'Rules of Metalaw', and discusses the ground for arriving at each.[144] Then, acknowledging that not all of these Rules are of equal validity and strength, he re-orders them on the grounds that '[n]orms based on the concept of life itself are stronger than rules based on the concept of intelligence' and that rules likely 'to check and fight entropy will have preference over rules that are less anti-entropical'. The revised Fasan listing is therefore[145]:

1. No partner of Metalaw may demand an impossibility.
2. No rule of Metalaw must be complied with when compliance would result in the practical suicide of the obligated Beings.
3. All intelligent Beings of the universe have in principle equal rights and values.
4. Every partner of metalaw has the right of self-determination.
5. Any act which causes harm to another race of Beings must be avoided.
6. Every race of Beings is entitled to its own living space.
7. Every race of Beings has the right to defend itself against any harmful act performed by another race.
8. The principle of preserving one race of Beings has priority over the development of another race of Beings.

---

141 G.H. Reynolds and R.P. Merges, *Outer Space: Problems of Law and Policy* (Boulder: Westview Press, 1989) 408; P. Magno, 'Possibility of Existence of Extraterrestrial Beings' (1963) 6 *Proc. IISL* 40, and his 'Prematurity and Anthropocentricity in Legal Regulation of Space?' (1964) 7 *Proc. IISL* 46; G.S. Robinson, '"Metalaw" – Prolegomena to Quantification of Jus Naturale' (1971–1972) 40 *Geo. Wash. L. Rev.* 709–725, where Robinson considers unhelpful the reliance of McDougal et al., *supra* n. 19, on technology as a means of classification for these purposes; G.S. Robinson, 'The Biochemical Foundations of Evolving Metalaw: Moving at a Glance to the Biological Basis of Sentient Essence' (2013) 39 *J. Sp. L.* 181–216.
142 A.G. Haley, 'Space Law and Metalaw, a Synoptic View' (1956) 23 *Harv. Univ. Law Rec.* or (1956) 4 *Proc. IISL* at 25. This attitude is the inverse of Charles Kingsley's Mrs Doasyouwouldbedoneby in *The Water Babies* (1863), whose alternative is Mrs Bedonebyasyoudid. (Did Haley know this book?) Cf. Confucius, *Analects* XV.24. One might also have looked for fuller consideration of the Universal Declaration of Human Rights, UNGA Res. 217 (III), 8 December 1948.
143 E. Fasan. (1) *Relations with Alien Intelligences* (Berlin: Berlin Verlag, 1970) 9; (2) reprinted in P.M. Sterns and L.I Tennen eds., *Private Law, Public Law, Metalaw and Public Policy in Space: A Liber Amicorum in Honor of Ernst Fasan* (Vienna: Springer, 2016) 181–246; (3) 'Legal consequences of a SETI detection' (1998) 42 *Acta Astronautica* 677–679. Haley also made use of the Categorical Imperative (as to which see I. Kant, *Groundwork of the Metaphysics of Morals* (1785) (many translations and eds), or more easily as it is outlined or summarised by many commentators.
144 Fasan, *supra* n. 143, (1) 58–70; (2) 230–236. This is the order in which they are taken in P.M. Sterns, 'Metalaw and Relations with Intelligent Beings Revisited' (2004) 20 *Space Policy* 123–130 [Lyall/Larsen 561–568].
145 Fasan, n. 143, (1) 71–72; (2) 237–238. With permission of Dr Fasan we slightly re-phrase the list.

9. In case of damage, the causer of the damage must restore the integrity of the damaged party.
10. Metalegal agreements and treaties must be kept.
11. To help other Beings by one's own activities is not a legal but a basic ethical principle.

Of course it may be long before such questions require answers, but it is well that some is given thought to them. The writings of Haley and others often contain an initial passage that mentions or cites ancient philosophers (e.g. Lucretius), theologians (e.g. Bruno, Aquinas) and lawyers (e.g. Vittoria, Suarez).[146] However, that history of thought does not seem greatly to have affected or restrained the spread of regional cultures into other parts of the world. The interaction of various imperial authorities with indigenous peoples is not reassuring.[147] However, the discussion and musing as to ETI and law seems to have been undertaken largely by those whose real knowledge of that history or of basic philosophy is uncertain – picking up an idea from a secondary source and throwing it in to flavour or bolster an argument or viewpoint already decided upon. Jurisprudents and philosophers still need to work on this area properly to build on that of Haley and Fasan. That said, it has also to be said that the alternative view of Jenks has its attractions. Commenting on 'Haley's Rule of Metalaw' Jenks saw it as 'the keynote of a moral approach to policy rather than a principle susceptible of expression in legal terms; as such it is of fundamental importance'.[148] But Law and Morals must always interact for Law and Society to be healthy.

---

146 Fasan, *supra* n. 143, (1) 42–51; (2) 215–222, gives a brief survey of early literature.
147 The point is also made in S.S. Lall, 'Space Exploration – Some Legal and Political Aspects' (1959) 2 *Proc. IISL* 75–110 at 79–81 and R.K. Woetzel, 'Sovereignty and National Rights in Outer Space and on Celestial Bodies' (1962) 5 *Proc. IISL* 20. Cf. de Las Casas, *supra* n. 47; F. Jennings, *The Invasion of America: Indians, Colonialism and the Cant of Conquest* (New York: Norton, 1976) and *The Ambiguous Iroquois Empire: The Covenant Chain Confederation of Indian Tribes with English Colonies* (New York: Norton, 1984). Cf. cases on 'native rights' in Australia, Canada, New Zealand and the US. See also Indigenous Law Resources: www.austlii.edu.au/au/other/IndigLRes/. Cf. the much discussed 'United Nations Declaration on the Rights of Indigenous Peoples' (UNDRIP), UNGA Res. 61/295, 1970: 143 in favour, 11 abstentions, the 4 against – Australia, Canada, New Zealand and the US, have case law on the matter. Canada subsequently withdrew its objection and the others have modified their stance.
148 C.W. Jenks, *Space Law* (London: Stevens, 1965) at 114. Cf. M. Bohlander, 'Metalaw – what is it good for?' (2021) 188 *Acta Astronautica* 400–404.

17

THE FUTURE

Modern society has become dependent on space and takes its benefits for granted. Satellite telecommunications are part of life, and news and entertainment are easily available by direct broadcast from space. Global positioning means that many drivers no longer use maps. Remote sensing allows such as land management, environmental monitoring and increasingly accurate weather forecasts. All this and more happens within constraints set by the complexities of space law.

Since our last edition the privatisation of space activities has accelerated and entrepreneurial start-ups offering new and improved services have proliferated. The cost of getting into space has dropped significantly. Launch-sharing to cut the expense for individual projects even has brokers offering their services. Low earth orbit is proving ideal for many specialist satellites, particularly cubesats. New launchers can easily insert such into orbit from sites much smaller than the traditional. Last, many states now want to have their own sovereign systems and see merit and prestige in having their own programmes. They are willing to obtain technology and expertise from private enterprise, and tumbling costs encourage their ambitions.

This chapter will not rehearse the detail of material presented in the prior chapters, but, looking to the future, identify a selection, some areas to note and others as causing concern.

Bifurcation: Public and Private International Space Law

Our previous editions noted that space law was bifurcating. Public international space law and private international space law are separate areas of expertise. Just as we have the Law of the Sea and Maritime Law, so there is a body of space law that regulates inter-state relationships, and an increasing mass of law that regulates the commercial activities that use space. The process continues. Amid all the activity is a danger that those operating in the private international law of space will perhaps through ignorance, disregard or worse even seek to subvert basic principles and rules. Public international law is the context

DOI: 10.4324/9781003496502-17

within which all space activities take place. Commercial space law is the creation of national legal systems. Such as launch contracts, insurance, copyright and intellectual property, are matters for national legislatures and courts.[1] However, it is possible to identify areas that require or would benefit from international development and agreement. The temptation, to which lawyers can occasionally succumb, is to have recourse to analogy. Confronted by new problems lawyers have an ingrained tendency to analogise from the known to the unknown. For the future of space that tendency must be curbed. Seminal though the exercise can be, it can be unwise to innovate in law by such means.[2]

Apart from being careful as to innovation, we must also ensure that international space law does not become detached from general international law. Were it so to do it would become encysted and sterile. Of course there is an argument that space law is a lex specialis, and to some extent some of its provisions are indeed such. However, those who too easily argue for space law as lex specialis may in fact be thereby intentionally, or through ignorance of their own limitations, concealing their ignorance of general international law. That must be resisted. Law is law. In space, as elsewhere, we should seek the 'rule of law', not a 'rule by law' where rules are adhered to when convenient to the powerful, but to be altered at their behest. A different but substantial peril is that resistance to what is labelled 'the dominance of Western powers' will impede or block the development of useful general rules and coordinated practices.

The Governance of Outer Space

Governance of the use of outer space through law is necessary.[3] Some early proposals for the development of space law were intriguingly visionary, but for political reasons were often impractical, particularly the idea of a World Space Authority. It was never likely that the US and the USSR, then the only two space-competent powers, would consent to the transfer of their authority, let alone their technologies, to the control of an 'International Space Agency'. Nonetheless, echoing the background of many 'Golden Age' science fiction

---

1 F.G. von der Dunk, ed., *National Space Legislation in Europe* (Leiden: Nijhoff, 2011); L.J. Smith and I. Baumann, eds., *Contracting for Space: Contract Practice in the European Space Sector* (Farnham: Ashgate, 2011). See also Chapter 14. Cf. K.-H. Böckstiegel, ed., *"Project 2001" – Legal Framework for the Commercial Use of Outer Space* (Cologne: Carl Heymanns Verlag, 2002); K.-H. Böckstiegel, 'Commercial Space Activities: Their Growing Influence on the Law' (1987) *XII AASL* 175; P.D. Nesgos: (1) 'Commercial Space Transportation: A New Industry Emerges' (1991) *XVI AASL* 193; (2) 'The Practice of Commercial Space Law' (1992) *XVII-I AASL* 177; (1997) *XXII AASL* 43; (3) 'New Developments in Space Law Concerning Risk Management' (2002) *XXVII AASL* 477; Bin Cheng, 'The Commercial Development of Space: The Need for New Treaties' (1991) 19 *J. Sp. L.* 17–44; R. Berkley, 'Space Law versus Space Utilization: The Inhibition of Private Industry in Outer Space' (1996–1997) 15 *Wis. J. Int. L.J.* 421–443; V. Kayser, *Launching Space Objects: Issues of Liability and Future Prospects* (Dordrecht: Kluwer, 2001).

2 'One of the most treacherous tendencies in legal reasoning is the transfer of generalisations developed for one set of situations to seemingly analogous, yet essentially very different, situations'. Frankfurter J. dissenting, in *Braniff Airways, Inc.* v. *Nebraska State Board of Equalization & Assessment* (1953) 347 US 590 at 603, 74 S. Ct. 757; 98 L. Ed. 967, quoted by H.J. Taubenfeld, 'A Regime for Outer Space' (1961) 56 *Nw. U. L. Rev.* 129–167 at 160 n. 162, and by D.B. Craig, 'National Sovereignty at High Altitudes' (1957) 24 *J. Air L. & Comm.* 384–397 at 395. This wisdom may be balanced for our purposes by: 'Logic Is a Wonderful Thing But Doesn't Always Beat Actual Thought', T. Pratchett, *The Last Continent* (1998).

3 P.B. Larsen, 'Outer Space: How Shall the World's Governments Establish Order among Competing Interests' (2019) *Wash. Int. L.J.* 1–60.

novels, proposals were made.[4] Indeed the suggestion still occasionally appears.[5] However, it remains clear that in the foreseeable future neither a global international operational space agency nor an authoritative supervisory body will be created. Instead we have what we have. Certainly there is room for discussing the improvement of current structures, but it is always dangerous to seek to dismantle a system that is working satisfactorily.[6] Instead some areas, identifiable by the technologies and the problems they involve, are already being dealt with by mechanisms that range from treaty-based procedures to legally informal but effective consultation.[7] Our preceding pages shows a wide spectrum between

4 R.H. Mankiewicz, 'The Regulation of Activities in Extra-Aeronautical Space, and Some Related Problems' (1961–2) 8 *McGill L.J.* 193–211 at 199–205; G.V. Leopold and A.L. Scafuri, 'Orbital and Super-Orbital Space Flight Trajectories – Jurisdictional Touchstones for a United Nations Space Authority' (1959) 36 *U. Det. L.J.* 515–534 (rep. *Legal Problems* 520–539) after arguing for a International Space Authority suggest at 528–534 the UNGA take over the question and create a Space Authority under the procedures of the 'Uniting for Peace Resolution' (UNGA Res. 377 (V), 3 November 1950); A.S. Primadov, *International Space Law* (Moscow: Progress Publishers, 1976) 258 (though the international agency would coordinate but not replace national activities). See also G.V. Leopold, 'Cosmic Surveillance by Spaceflight Momentum' (1960) 6 *Wayne L Rev.* 311–339 proposing at 320 ff. an International Cosmic Surveillance Authority within or outside the UN to supervise all activities in space; C.G. Wihlborg and P.M. Wijkman, 'Outer Space Resources in Efficient and Equitable Use: New Frontiers for Old Principles' (1981) 24 *J.L. & Econ.* 23–44 arguing for space to be considered as held in common and for an international orbit and frequency condominium to auction user rights and distribute the revenues equitably among the nations; G.P. Sloup, 'Peaceful Resolution of Outer Space Conflicts Through the International Court of Justice: The Line of Least Resistance' (1971) 20 *DePaul L. Rev.* 618–698 at 691–692; E. Kamenetskaya, 'Establishment of a World Space Organisation: Some Considerations and Remarks' (1989) 32 *Proc. IISL* 358–360 re the 1988 USSR proposal, Annex II to COPUOS Annual Report 1988, GAOR A/43/20; C.Q. Christol, 'Alternative Models for a Future International Space Organisation' (1981) 24 *Proc. IISL* 173 (rep. C.Q. Christol, *Space Law, Past, Present and Future* (Deventer: Kluwer, 1991) 427–442). Cf. many suggestions in the earlier annual *Proc. IISL* (many cited in the Christol article just cited) including M. Smirnoff, 'The Future International Agency for the Administration of Cosmos – The ICAO's Candidature' (1965) 8 *Proc. IISL* 409; H. DeSaussure, 'Evolution Toward an International Space Agency' (1976) 13 *Proc. IISL* 32–40, and (1978) 27 *ZLW* 86–96. Cf. the visionary G. Clark and L.B. Sohn, *World Peace Through World Law: Two Alternative Plans*, 3rd ed. (Cambridge: Harvard UP, 1966) 'A United Nations Space Agency' at 296–302, and the USSR proposal UN A/SPC/40/3 of 14 November 1985, quoted by A.J. Young, *Law and Policy in the Space Stations' Era* (Dordrecht: Nijhoff, 1989) (UNGA Res. 40/162, *UN Yearbook, 1985*, 108; International Cooperation in the Peaceful Uses of Outer Space: Report of the Special Political Committee, A/40/1023, 1985) but contrast G. Zhukov and Y. Kolosov (trans. B. Belitzky), *International Space Law* (New York: Praeger, 1984) 187.
5 L.L. Manzione, 'Multinational Investment in the Space Station: An Outer Space Model for International Cooperation' (2002) 18 *Am. U. Int. L. Rev.* 507–536 at 532–534; D. Tan, 'Towards a New Regime for the Protection of Outer Space as the "Province of All Mankind"' (2000) 25 *Yale J. Int. L.* 145–194 at 190–193; S. Courteix, 'Towards a World Space Organisation?', in G. Lafferranderie, ed., *Outlook on Space Law Over the Next Thirty Years* (The Hague: Kluwer, 1997) 423–427, and her 'Is It Necessary to Establish a World Space Organisation?' (1993) 36 *Proc. IISL* 20–30; J.M. Faramñián Gilbert and C. Zhangi, L'Organisation Mondiale de l'Espace: Un Défi Oublie?', in A. Kerrest, ed., *L'Adaption du Droit de l'Espace ses Nouveau Défis – Liber Amicorum, Mélanges en l'honneur de Simone Courteix* (Paris: Editions Pedone, 2007) 161–175; J.B. Ashe III, 'Space Station Alpha: International Shining Star or Legal Black Hole?' (1995) 9 *Temp. Int. & Comp. L.J.* 333–363 at 358–363; R.J. Lee, 'Reconciling International Space Law with the Commercial Realities of the Twenty-First Century' (2000) 4 *Sing. J. Int. & Comp. L.* 194–251; P.D. Nesgos, 'The Proposed International Sea-Bed Authority as a Model for the Future Outer Space International Regime' (1980) 5 *AASL* 549–574.
6 Cf. A. Froehlich, ed., *A Fresh View on the Outer Space Treaty* (ESPI, Springer, 2018); G.D. Kyriakopoulos and M. Manoli, eds., *The Space Treaties at Crossroads: Considerations de Lege Ferenda* (Springer, 2019); R.S. Jakhu and S. Freeland, 'Vital Artery or Stent Needing Replacement: Global Space Governance System without the Outer Space Treaty' (2018) 61 *Proc. IISL* 505–520.
7 E. Tepper, 'The Big Bang of Space Governance: Towards Polycentric Governance of Space Activities' (2022) *N.Y.U. J. Int. L. and Politics* 485–558. Cf. N. Tannenwald, 'Law versus Power on the High Frontier: The Case for a Rule-Based Regime for Outer Space' (2004) 29 *Yale J. Int. L.* 363–422.

such as the International Telecommunication Union of Chapter 8 and the Interagency Space Debris Committee of Chapter 9. Other areas need to be brought into at least some similar degree of cooperation and/or control. One avenue to progress will certainly be the use of non-legally binding UN resolutions, with COPUOS as their major origin.[8] In the meantime we endorse the aspirations for space expressed by the UN.[9]

The World Public Interest

As we survey developments in space and the relevant law points of concern emerge.

First, space is to be used 'for the benefit and in the interests of all countries' (OST Art. I, para 1) 'in the interest of maintaining international peace and security and promoting international cooperation and understanding' (OST Art. III). However, a service for the public is not the same as a service provided to the public. Certainly space services deliver many benefits, but privatisation can affect their provision. It is frequently claimed that privatisation improves a service, and that may often be technically true. But it is also true that privatised services are normally provided to make profit for their providers, the level of profit being set by competition if that exists. Profit is maximised to benefit investors, whether commercial companies or hedge funds. Further, the location of potential markets can result in the selective provision and availability of a service. The ideal of a public service being provided at cost for the benefit of the public has been obscured, if not in some cases lost.[10]

Second, nothing in public international space law sets out a hierarchy of the uses which may be made of the new domain. There is the requirement that space be used exclusively for peaceful purposes in OST Art. IV, and there is the 'due regard' and 'harmful interference' elements of Art. IX. But, other than that there is no guidance as to priority where uses conflict. Public benefit should be a strong factor in such decisions. Some uses are of obvious public benefit and should have precedence. But there must be balance. One use should not eliminate or unacceptably degrade the utility of another. For example, in the abstract telecommunication services qualify, but questions arise when one particular use, LEO constellations, may affect launch trajectories, radio frequencies, or other legitimate uses such as optical astronomy.[11]

Orbital Congestion

Space proximate to the Earth is increasingly congested. Satellite numbers increase. The controlled deorbiting of satellites is rare. Defunct space objects and unidentifiable space debris grow in numbers. The efficient use of space requires knowing what is already in

---

8 Cf. the *General exchange of information on non-legally binding UN instruments on outer space*, Draft report COPUOS Legal Subcommittee, March 2023: A/AC.105/C.2/L.324/Add.10.

9 'The "Space2030" Agenda: space as a driver of sustainable development' UNGA Res. 76/3, 21 October 2021. Our Common Agenda Policy Brief 5: For All Humanity – the Future of Outer Space Governance, May 2023: www.unoosa.org/res/oosadoc/data/documents/2023/a77/a77crp_1add_6_0_html/our-common-agenda-policy-brief-outer-space-en.pdf.

10 In the operation of the Global Maritime Distress and Safety Service (GDMSS) only the initial messages are cost free. See also Chapter 10 on the public interest in telecommunications and stakeholders and F. Lyall, *Technology, Sovereignty and International Law* (Abingdon: Routledge, 2022) 55–56.

11 G. Rotola and A. Williams, 'Regulatory Context of Conflicting Uses of Outer Space: Astronomy and Satellite Constellations' (2021) 46 *Air and Sp. L.* 545–568.

orbit, the management of space traffic, and the mitigation of debris through less being generated and more removed one way or another from orbit. We have considered these elements in both Chapters 4 and 9, but they are closely intertwined and cannot be contained or considered as wholly separate matters.[12]

Space situational awareness involves radar scanning and data processing so as to track as far as possible what is in orbit, allowing the future trajectories and configuration of space objects to be predicted. Potential future problems can thereby be identified and avoided.[13] Of the few states that have the necessary abilities the US, and in particular its Department of Defense, is the best known, in part because it publicises its major findings and permits access to relevant data.[14] Other states tend to make their predictions of the behaviour of their space objects known only where there is reason for concern, e.g. when a re-entrant object may not be wholly destroyed high in the atmosphere. However, it is regrettable that, despite one possible interpretation of the 'benefit and interests' terms of OST Art. 1.1, states do not consider there is any legal duty to make such data available, and there is no likelihood of a universal central source for such situational awareness information. Nonetheless, data on what is already up there is an essential part of decisions on the launch of new satellites into particular orbits – in short, space traffic management.

Space traffic management (STM) is necessarily conducted by the states that license launches. While the detail of national traffic management systems lie outwith the ambit of this book, we have outlined its requirements in Chapter 9. Suggestions have been made that an international management service be established to cope with what is essentially a matter of governance rather than of technicalities, but security considerations and international tensions have discouraged general action. In the ultimate a single global agency or authority would be ideal, but that seems unlikely in the near future.[15] Launcher states may participate in the US system should they so wish, but US STM is thought by some to favour US space operators over non-US operators, reservations shared by China and Russia for that and other reasons. The projected European STM system is yet another step towards multiplicity.[16] But an undue diversity of STM systems is perilous.[17] International guidelines for space traffic safety to which individual systems could conform would constrain the possibility of divergence between the systems of major actors. COPUOS may have set out on that path.[18] A standing COPUOS working group on international STM coordination similar to the International Committee on GNSS might help reduce

---

12 P.B. Larsen, 'Profit or Safety: Where Is Outer Space Headed?' (2021) 86 *J. Air Law & Comm*. 531–584.

13 Space weather is also monitored which is important as solar flares can affect satellites. Cf. www.spaceweather.com/.

14 See the US Note Verbale, A/AC.105/1265, 28 January 2022, secs. 2 and 3. US Space Command is now involved.

15 B. McClintock et al., *International Space Traffic Management: Charting a Course for Long-Term Sustainability* (2023) Rand Corp. Research Report: www.rand.org/pubs/research_reports/RRA1949-1.html.

16 'An EU Approach for Space Traffic Management', ESA/EU Joint Communication to the European Parliament and the Council: JOIN(2022) 4 final, 15.2.2022, and the EU Space Surveillance and Tracking (EU SST) Partnership Agreement, November 2022: www.eusst.eu/newsroom/new-eu-sst-partnership-signed-2/. Tracking by the EU Agency for the Space Programme began on 1 July 2023 – a precursor to EU STM. M. Barbano, 'Space Traffic Management and Space Situational Awareness: The EU Perspective' (2022) 47 *Air and Sp. L*. 451–466. See also Chapter 14 sv. Europe and the European Union.

17 T. Masson-Zwaan and Yun Zhao, 'Towards an International Regime for Space Traffic Management' (2023) 48 *Air and Sp. L*. 75–92.

18 COPUOS Annual Report, 2022, A/77/20, Sec. 8, paras 245–252.

uncertainties.[19] Space traffic experts would meet to exchange views on space traffic safety without being subject to East/West political overtones. But, while one may respect the desire of experts to produce the best possible workable system, other considerations may over-ride objective practicability.

Space debris looms over us all, both figuratively and actually. At worst the Kessler prospect of a cascade of inter-debris collisions and clouds of fragments travelling at orbital velocities could deny all access to outer space.[20] Licensing states must be diligent to secure that as little debris as possible is caused by or through the activities of their licensees. Last, in the general interest more must be done on the removal of debris from orbit. Reliance on gravity is not enough.[21]

Exploitation of Celestial Bodies

The moon and asteroids are now of major practical and legal interest as lunar and other resources are becoming accessible. The successful delivery of the Vikran lunar lander and Pragyan rover to a location near the south pole of the moon by the Indian Chandradrayaan-3 in August 2023 was significant. More will follow, and activities will increase. Law and practice must be developed harmoniously. Commercial interests have tilted the balance between the 'benefit and interest of all' and freedom of scientific investigation and the use of space provided for in OST Art. I and a strict interpretation of the Art. II ban on national appropriation. Matters are moving. As outlined in Chapter 7 several states have already legislated to accommodate the activities of space mining enterprises. Others may follow. The US-inspired Artemis Accords, also discussed in Chapter 7, are a major innovation, the parties as it were agreeing to performing an end-run round the disallowance of state sovereignty in space in any form that OST Art. II presents. As exploitation of space resources begins discussion of the Accords will continue that may clarify some of their elements.[22] But the Accords are not the final word.

Not all space agencies have joined with the Accords, and some with proven lunar and similar ambitions will not do so. The unilateral 'recognition' of the 'rights' of an entrepreneurial entity may prejudice international discussions, and in any event misunderstands the term 'recognition' as known in international law.[23] Ideally some process to permit the

19 Cf. P.B. Larsen, 'International Regulation of Global Navigation Satellite Systems, Section IV, GNSS Regulation Within the Scope of the UN International Committee on GNSS' (2015) 80 *J. Air L. & Comm.* 365–422 at 392–401.

20 D.J. Kessler and B.G. Cour-Palais, 'Collision Frequency of Artificial Satellites: The Creation of a Debris Belt (1978). 83 *J. Geophysical Research*, 2637–2646 at 2644–2645: http://webpages.charter.net/dkessler/files/Collision%20Frequency.pdf.

21 COPUOS Legal Committee, Draft Report, 'General exchange of information and views on legal mechanisms relating to space debris mitigation and remediation measures, taking into account the work of the Scientific and Technical Subcommittee', A/AC.105/C.2/L.314/Add. 5, 8 June 2021. Cf. Draft Report, *supra* n. 8, paras 8–9.

22 A.Y. Lee, 'The Future of the Law on the Moon' (2023) 88 *J. Air L. & Comm.* 3–103; S. Hobe, 'Commentary for the Journal of Air Law and Commerce on the Article by Andrew Lee Entitled the Future of the Law on the Moon' (2023) 88 *J. Air L. & Comm.* 223–226. Cf. S. Bhat, 'Chandraan-3: An Opportunity to Set Right the Mistake of Artemis Accords' (2023) 3 *Lex ad Coelum*, Issue II: https://caslnujs.in/category/volume-3-issue-ii/.

23 A. Wasser and D. Jobes, 'Space Settlements, Property Rights and International Law: Could a Lunar Settlement Claim the Lunar Real Estate It Needs to Survive?' (2008) 73 *J. Air L. & Comm.* 37–78. Although

general acknowledgement of, and therefore a degree of protection, for a particular exploitative activity on celestial bodies would be welcome, but seems unlikely under present conditions.[24] Instead the potential of confrontation appears inherent in current developments, particularly if the Accords are seen as a means of further extending US influence in such matters.[25] Notwithstanding, it is also clear that as the exploitation of lunar and other celestial resources increases accommodations other than the Accords will have to be agreed if difficulties and confrontations are to be avoided. In arriving at such the 'Building Blocks' also discussed in Chapter 7 could be very helpful.[26]

Looking further ahead the question of moon bases and their interaction (if any) will have to be dealt with. Presumably jurisdiction within a base established by a single state will be run in accordance with the law of that state and may include the national forms of governance and authority within it. Collaborative bases are likely to operate analogous to the arrangements for the International Space Station. The independence of a lunar or Mars base is sufficiently in the future to excuse our not pursuing it in these pages.[27]

Satellites and the Use of the Radio Spectrum

Satellite telecommunications and direct broadcasting by satellite are important uses of space that have world-wide effects. Both continue mainly as services provided by commercial companies subject to national controls and the exigencies of market forces. State provided services have different rules.

The problems inherent in three matters that bridge Chapters 8, 9 and 10 will continue into the future. First, the ITU remains resilient as such a basic pillar of international law and relations should. It continues to develop. The reconstruction of the 1990s saw development grafted on to its technical responsibilities. As a result the ITU has become activist particularly on behalf of the newer states that now form the major portion of ITU membership. Through the ITU-D sector and by such as the WSIS processes, the ITU has helped states cope with the digital divide. These efforts and new problems are putting the ITU under strain. The radio spectrum is a finite resource and frequencies, particularly

---

some passing reference is made to other legal traditions, the major thrust of this article is grounded in the parochial insularities of Nineteenth Century US law and practice. This is an instance where analogy misleads.

24 A register of active operations could be constituted within the framework of the Artemis Accords, but it might create a list of phantom claims seeking on the basis of priority of registration as 'first registrant' to stockpile potentially valuable sites. Non-signatories of the Accords are not likely either to heed such or themselves to use the register. See also Building Blocks *infra* n. 26, Sec. 14 on registers. Cf. C.Q. Christol, 'The Moon and Mars Missions: Can International Law Meet the Challenge?' (1999) 19 *J. Sp. L.* 123–136; D. Collins, 'Efficient Allocation of Real Property Rights on the Planet Mars' (2008) 14 *B.U. J. Sci. & Tech. L.* 201–219. A. Froelich, ed., *Assessing a Mars Agreement Including Human Settlements* (Vienna: Springer, 2021); T. Masson-Zwaan, 'New States in Space' (2019) 113 *AJIL Unbound* 98–102.

25 Cf. W.A. Smith, 'Using the Artemis Accords to Build Customary International Law: A Vision for a US – Centric Good Governance Regime in Outer Space' (2021) 86 *J. Air L. & Comm.* 661–700, and materials cited *supra* n. 22–23.

26 Building Blocks for the Development of an International Framework of an International Framework on Space Resource Activities: The Hague International Space Resources Working Group: A/AC.105.C.2/L.315: www.unoosa.org/oosa/oosadoc/data/documents/2020/aac.105c.2l/aac.105c.2l.315_0.html. 'The Hague International Space Resources Governance Working Group: Building Blocks for the Development of an International Framework' (2019) 43 *J. Sp. L.* 151–170. See also A-S. Martin, 'The Relevance of ITU Rules for Regulating the Use of Radio Frequency and Associated Orbits in the Context of Space Mining Activities' (2019) *J. Sp. L.* 85–105.

27 A. Froehlich, ed., *Assessing a Mars Agreement Including Human Settlements* (Vienna: Springer, 2021).

those most usable for space, are under high demand. The Radio Regulations continue to differentiate particular uses, but pressures are increasing as more and more satellites are launched.[28] Spectrum sharing between space and terrestrial services is increasingly sought for commercial rather than technical reasons and representatives of commercial interests are vocal. However, progress has been made in ITU decision-making through the introduction of 'common proposals' agreed by interested parties prior to radio conferences. Second, the increased deployment of constellations of communication satellites, apart from adding to the congestion problems of the low earth orbit, will further intensify pressure on the ITU Radiocommunication Sector.

Third, some states continue to seek to monitor or control the content of electronic communication in any form. International communications by satellite is now largely the province of commercial enterprise rendering them subject to the rigours of the international business world. Terrestrial broadcasting is fragmented in the degree to which it is state controlled, but direct broadcasting from space or otherwise is less easily supervised by receiving states.[29] Agreed regional plans can help, but interference extending to jamming occurs where there are inter-state tensions. This is not a problem solvable only by law.

Militarisation of Outer Space

Our previous edition expressed concern as to unrestrained military uses of outer space. Our concern has grown in the intervening years. Chapter 15 shows how outer space is now being seen and prepared for as a war-fighting domain. The deteriorating relationships of China, Russia and, led by the US, the West, is worrying. Little progress has been made towards the reduction of weaponry in space or elsewhere. Instead the 'dual-use' capabilities of GNSS, remote sensing and telecommunication has been demonstrated in the Ukraine conflict. The disabling of such services on a broad basis in the event of wider active hostilities would have major effects world-wide and would be most certainly not be in the world public interest. Climate change and economics are very important, but the militarisation of space and its new acknowledged status as a warfighting domain are a departure from the 'peaceful' principles of the OST. The bellicose nature of current public pronouncements by some leaders increases our anxiety. So many of the benefits of space could be imperilled. So much progress could be lost.

Dispute Settlement

Disputes arising from space law or space activities may arise between states, between commercial entities or between a state and a commercial entity.

The space treaties contain little provision as to the resolution of inter-state disputes,[30] and of course the normal rules of international law require recourse to a variety of

---

28 Footnote exemptions to allocations in the ITU Radio Regulations have proliferated. It is to be hoped that WRC-23 will not follow precedent. Revision of 'Footnotes in the Table of Frequency Allocations in Article 5 of the Radio Regulations' WRC Res. 26 (Rev. WRC-19) is on the agenda.
29 There is a difference between direct broadcasting from a fixed and from a non-GSO satellite. Cf. UK Ofcom, 'Non-Geostationary Satellite Earth Stations: Licensing Guidance', 10 December 2021.
30 OST Art. XIII as to the activities of international organisations, Liability Convention Arts. XIV – XX, MA Art. 15. See also Chapter 8 for the ITU procedures.

methods of dispute settlement.[31] In the ultimate an inter-state dispute on a space matter could end up at the International Court of Justice,[32] although we may hope that matters will usually be settled before that. The International Law Association has adopted a relevant draft Convention, but whether there should be a separate general dispute settlement mechanism or procedure dedicated only to space law has remained open for discussion for many years.[33] That gap may have been met by the 2011 adoption by the Permanent Court of Arbitration of optional rules for the arbitration of space-related disputes.[34] There is also an 'International Court of Aviation and Space Arbitration' based in Paris.[35] Such may be suitable for some specialised matters. However, the 2006 Report of the International Law Commission Study Group on 'Fragmentation of International Law: Difficulties arising from the Diversification and Expansion of International Law' might indicate a general 'space court' is undesirable.[36] It is sometimes said that space law as a lex specialis, that is a law particularised for space, displaces a rule of general law which might otherwise have application. Too easy a recourse to such argument for space law could be pernicious. As we have said, so far as possible space law should be integrated with general international law, and perhaps especially in relation to its environmental rules.

31 J. Collier and V. Lowe, *Settlement of Disputes in International Law: Principles and Procedures* (Oxford: OUP, 1999); J.G. Merrills and E. De Brabanere, *Merrills' International Dispute Settlement*, 7th ed. (Cambridge: Cambridge UP, 2022); G.M. Goh, *Dispute Settlement in International Space Law: A Multi-Door Courthouse for Outer Space* (Leiden: Nijhoff, 2007); L. Viikari, *The Environmental Element in Space Law: Assessing the Present and Charting the Future* (Leiden: Nijhoff, 2008) 287–316; *Dispute Resolution in the Telecommunications Sector: Current Practices and Future Directions* (Geneva: ITU, 2004).

32 V.S. Vereshchetin, 'International Court of Justice as a Potential Forum for the Resolution of Space Law Disputes', in M. Benkö and W. Kroll, eds., *Air and Space Law in the 21st Century: Liber Amicorum K.-H. Böcksteigel* (Cologne: Carl Heymanns Verlag, 2002) 476–483.

33 See for example, K.-H. Böcksteigel, 'Proposed Draft Convention on the Settlement of Space Law Disputes' (1985) 12 *J. Sp. L.* 136–140; and his 'The Settlement of Disputes Regarding Space Activities after 30 Years of the Outer Space Treaty', in G. Lafferranderie, ed., *Outlook on Space Law over the Next Thirty Years* (The Hague: Kluwer, 1997) 237–249; I.H.P. Diederich-Verschoor, 'The Settlements of Disputes in Space: New Developments' (1998) 26 *J. Sp. L.* 41–49; *International Law Association: Report of the Space Law Committee* (Helsinki Conference, 1996) M. Williams, Rapporteur, 457–476 and *International Law Association: Report of the Space Law Committee* (Taipei Conference, 1998), M. Williams, Rapporteur, 239–272 with text of a 'Convention on the Settlement of Disputes Related to Space Activities' at 249–267; D.H. Kim, 'Proposal for Establishing an International Court of Air and Space Law' (2010) 59 ZLW 362–371. See generally Goh, *supra* n. 31.

34 Permanent Court of Arbitration, *Optional Rules for Arbitration of Disputes Relating to Outer Space Activities*, 2011: https://pca-cpa.org/wp-content/uploads/sites/175/2016/01/Permanent-Court-of-Arbitration-Optional-Rules-for-Arbitration-of-Disputes-Relating-to-Outer-Space-Activities.pdf. The PCA will assemble a panel of arbitrators and experts to act under the Rules. F. Pocar, 'An Introduction to the PCA's Optional Rules for the Arbitration of Disputes Relating to Outer Space Activities' (2012) 38 *J. Sp. L.* 171–185, with the Rules at 187–210; S. Hobe, 'The Permanent Court of Arbitration Adopts Optional Rules for the Arbitration of Disputes Relating to Outer Space Activities' (2012) 61 *ZLW* 1–25; C. Arbaugh, 'Gravitating Toward Sensible Resolutions: The PCA Optional Rules for the Arbitration of Disputes Relating to Outer Space Activity' (2014) 42 *Ga. J. Int. & Comp. L.* 825–850; D.M. Rojas Garcia, 'Out-of-State Solutions for Outer Space Disputes: Delocalizing the Troubles of the Province of Mankind' (2019) *Air and Sp. L.* 393–407.

35 'International Court of Aviation and Space Arbitration: By-Laws and Rules' (1995) 193 *Rev. Fr. de Droit Aérien et Spatial* 1–136 (five languages) (Paris: Pedone, 1995).

36 See 'Fragmentation of International Law: Difficulties arising from the Diversification and Expansion of International Law' 2006 II YBILC Part Two, Chapter XII, 175–184.
  Cf. E.B. Weiss, 'The Rise or the Fall of International Law?' (2000–2001) 69 *Fordham L. Rev.* 346–372.

As far as space-related disputes between commercial entities are concerned proposals have been made,[37] and the International Law Association draft Convention is appropriate for private enterprises.[38] However, already the normal business procedures of compromise and arbitration have swung into play.[39] As we have pointed out in Chapter 2, commercial secrecy leads to it being unusual for settlements arrived at through those mechanisms to be made public (let alone the argumentation and the reasoning justifying an award).[40] This leaves commentators unable to see how fundamental concepts are being developed. There is a greater transparency where matters end up in national courts through a 'choice of law' clause, but that may create other problems. As indicated in the second section of this chapter, in giving advice advisers ought to know the relevant international law. They also need both to know and to understand (not always the same thing) the intricacies of the concepts and procedures of divergent legal systems and be alive to the possibility that the same term may differ in meaning in different jurisdictions before they can be confident in advising acceptance of a particular contract or a 'choice of law' clause.

SETI

Assuming that interaction is not already happening, the possibility remains that the search for extraterrestrial intelligence (SETI) discussed in Chapter 16 may succeed. Absent actual physical interaction with ET short-circuiting them, the procedures of the 'Detection Protocol' exist, but recent media interest in ET makes us wonder whether they would be complied with. In any event the draft 'Reply Protocol' and the 'Search Principles' issued by the IAA SETI Committee in 2010 could do with being adopted. In the meantime let the Search continue.

And Finally

So, we conclude as we did our previous editions. SETI raises the correlative question whether there is intelligent life on Earth. With due regard to the inherent problems of academe,[41] we hope the previous pages help answer that conundrum.

---

37 See materials *supra* n. 33, and Goh, *supra* n. 31.
38 'Convention on the Settlement of Disputes Related to Space Activities', *International Law Association: Report of the Sixty-Eighth Conference*, Taipei, Taiwan, 1998, 249–267.
39 M. Hunter and A. Redfern, *The Law and Practice of International Commercial Arbitration*, 4th ed. rev. (London: Sweet & Maxwell, 2004); M.L. Moses, *The Principles and Practice of International Commercial Arbitration*, 3rd ed. (Cambridge: Cambridge UP, 2017); J.D.M. Lew, L.A. Mistelis and S. Kroll, *Comparative International Commercial Arbitration* (The Hague: Kluwer, 2003). Cf. the work on dispute settlement of the UN Commission on International Trade Law (UNCITRAL): www.uncitral.org/uncitral/en/index.html and the World Trade Organisation (WTO): www.wto.org/.
40 'Absolute secrecy' on the part of all involved is provided for by Art. 3 of the Rules of Arbitration of the specialised Paris Court, *supra* n. 35.
41 W.L. Prosser, 'Lighthouse No Good' (1948–1949) 1 *J. Legal Educ.* 257–267.

INDEX

Note: Index entry page numbers with an "n" refer to notes.

Made in the USA
Coppell, TX
08 January 2025

44133040R00293